W9-BRY-860

FRONT PAGE

Major Events of the 20th Century Selected by the Associated Press

GALLERY BOOKS
An imprint of W.H. Smith Publishers Inc.
112 Madison Avenue
New York, New York 10016

ISBN 0-8317-3633-X
E173.F86 1985 973 85-10852

Project Director: Dan Perkes
Compiled and Written by Norm Goldstein
Designed by CBG Graphics

Special thanks to AP member newspapers and AP bureaus worldwide.

Printed in Hong Kong

Prepared and produced by Wieser & Wieser, Inc., 80 Madison Avenue, Penthouse B, New York, New York 10016.

Published by Gallery Books, An imprint of W. H. Smith Publishers Inc., 112 Madison Avenue, New York, New York 10016.

Introduction

Maybe you can't tell a book by its cover, but the front page can tell you a lot about a newspaper.

The front page always has reflected the newspaper's personality. But it reflects more than that.

The front page offers a diary of our dreams and disasters, a reflection of fleeting fame mixed with events that make history.

The front page has changed, as we have changed.

When the U.S. Constitution was signed in 1787, the front page of the *Pennsylvania Gazette* consisted mostly of advertising notices, as was the wont of newspapers of the time. The text of the Constitution, with the headline "Plan of the new Foederal Government," was on pages 2 and 3 of the four-page weekly. And, of course, there were no photographs.

But it wasn't long before the front page did become the storefront display for the inside wares.

Some front pages shout, others speak in more moderate tones.

In their own way, they all try to capture one instant in time, a moment assembled for us by reporters, writers, editors, photographers, makeup men, headline writers—the largely unseen army of the journalism profession.

This sampling of front pages over the years provides a picture of our past from the perspective of the present.

Louis D. Boccardi
President and General Manager
The Associated Press

1787

The *Pennsylvania Gazette* was a four-page weekly in 1787, the year that the U.S. Constitution was written.

It had been known as *The Universal Instructor in All Arts and Sciences and Pennsylvania Gazette* when it first started publication in 1727, but its name—and reading popularity—was changed when Benjamin Franklin took over the Philadelphia newspaper in 1729, and guided it until 1766.

In 1787, Franklin was eighty-one years old and a delegate to the convention that wrote the Constitution. The delegates met in closed sessions in the State House of Pennsylvania, keeping doors and windows shut to ensure secrecy, despite the heat and humidity of that important summer. They started at the end of May and argued and debated until they finally signed the Constitution on September 19.

The *Pennsylvania Gazette* reprinted the text of the proposed laws of the land in this September 19 issue, but on pages 2 and 3 under the heading "Plan of the New Foederal Government."

It was customary for newspapers of the time to use the front page for public notices and advertisements.

SEPTEMBER, 1787. THE NUMB. 2990.

PENNSYLVANIA GAZETTE.

WEDNESDAY, SEPTEMBER 19, 1787.

STERLING & NORCROSS,

MERCHANTS, IN BURLINGTON,

Having this day, by mutual consent, dissolved their Partnership in Trade,

REQUEST all persons indebted to them, especially those of a long standing, on bond, bill, note or book account, to call and settle their respective ballances, to prevent trouble. And every person having any just demands against them, are desired to bring in their accounts for liquidation and payment, to

Sept. 4, 1787. 54w JAMES STERLING.

Fayette county taxes for the year 1787.

A TRANSCRIPT of the returns and assessment of the lands of non-residents in the county of Fayette, agreeably to an act of Assembly, passed the 11th day of September, 1786, is now published in No. 334 of the Freeman's Journal, printed by Mr. Bailey, Sept. 12. All persons concerned are hereby required to pay the taxes for the present year on their land in said county, into the State Treasury, before the 12th day of November next, when the names of the delinquents will be transmitted to the Commissioners of the county, that they may proceed to enforce payment as the laws direct.

Sept. 12, 1787. DAVID RITTENHOUSE, State Treasr.

One Hundred Dollars Reward.

WAS broke open last night, the house of Peter Knight, and robbed of the sundry articles underneath mentioned:

1 Bag containing about 90 French Crowns.

1 Ditto ditto 90 Spanish milled Dollars.

1 China faced silver watch, with a steel chain, and a silver seal representing Noah's ark, with a dove holding an olive branch in its mouth.

A large double fold sattin pocket book, in which were a large number of funded and unfunded certificates, &c. viz.

The following NEW LOAN CERTIFICATES, two years interest paid on each,

No.	Name	£	s.	d.
No. 11271	Sheets,	£ 69	5	0
10717	Reed and Forde, for	176	7	6
10384	Ditto,	157	3	4
10634	Abraham Sheridan,	81	15	1
10551	Isaac Melcher, Esquire,	82	4	2
9695	Samuel Hays,	116	5	0
266	James M'Crea,	338	13	0
265	Ditto,	63	15	0
262	Ditto,	283	2	6
336	Peter Knight,	26	5	0
335	Ditto,	417	9	2
334	Ditto,	375	0	0
333	Ditto,	150	0	0
332	Ditto,	112	10	0
30	Ditto,	150	0	0
20	Ditto,	187	10	0
27	Ditto,	225	0	0
1485	Ditto,	1208	5	4
5486	Ditto,	24	10	0
9542	Nicholas Knight,	30	16	8
331	Peter Knight,	1500	0	0
		£ 5375	6	7

2 Funded Jersey certificates, one endorsed with interest paid for two years, the other one year, about 1468 Dollars.

1 Of Nourse's unfunded certificates to Peter Knight, 1468 Dollars. 1 Ditto, about 800 Dollars.

Facilities to the amount of about 280 Dollars.

A red Morocco calendar (Gaine's) for 1775.

A mortgage and judgment bond from Richard Mason to Peter Knight, dated 1784, for 5500 Pounds.

A number of valuable papers, in which were a state of transactions between George Ingraham and Peter Knight.

A number of loose papers taken out of the pidgeon holes of the desk, in which were blank checks, &c.

A black sattin cloak lined with black tammy, supposed to be taken to wrap the papers in.

A reward of Fifty Dollars will be paid for the cash, and Fifty Dollars for the papers, or in proportion for the property recovered, and no questions asked.

Philad. Sept. 6, 1787. PETER KNIGHT.

TO BE SOLD,

By the subscribers, executors of the last will and testament of David Schaffer, senior, deceased,

A Certain Plantation and tract of land in Bensalem township, Bucks county, bordering on the river Delaware, about 14 miles from the city of Philadelphia, containing 160 acres of land, late the property of Joseph Galloway, and now in the tenure of David Germon. There is a good Frame Dwelling-house erected on the premises, with a well of water near the door. About 40 or 50 acres are already cleared and in good fence, a considerable proportion whereof is meadow ground, and more may be made at a moderate expence, so as to render it convenient for a grazier. The remainder is woodland, a part of which has excellent timber. There is also a valuable fishery belonging to the same. For further particulars apply to David Germon, on the premises, to the Widow Schaffer, or John Schaffer, in the city of Philadelphia. An indisputable title will be given, and the terms made easy by the subscribers,

CATHARINE SCHAFFER, Executrix,
CHRISTOPHER KUCHER,)
3m FREDERICK A. MUHLENBERG,) Executors.

TO BE LET,

THAT neat Stone HOUSE, situate on the west-side of Schuylkill, adjoining the Middle-ferry; 9 acres of upland belongs to the house, of which one acre is an excellent garden, well fenced in and stocked with a variety of fruit trees, strawberries and other valuable plants; there are about seven acres of marsh between the upland and Schuylkill, that affords good pasture. The house is a Licensed Tavern, with a well of excellent water near the door, and a stable that will hold several horses. The situation is convenient for a tavern or store, and suitable for both businesses. For terms, apply to WILLIAM BISPHAM, on the premises. Sept. 11, 1787.

CAME to the plantation of John Hannis, deceased, in Passyunk township, on the banks of Schuylkill, on the 25th of August, a small red COW, with a piece off one of her ears. The owner is desired to come, prove property, pay charges, and take her away. 5

H A G U E, July 18.

THE Marquis de Verac, the French Ambassador, has sent to the President of their High Mightinesses a note the tenor of which is as follows:

" *High and Mighty Lords!*

" The King has been informed that the states of the province of Holland have proposed on the 7th of this month to your High Mightinesses to recur to his mediation for the reconciliation of the differences which divide the Republic; his Majesty is highly sensible of this mark of confidence, and he has commanded the underwritten, his Ambassador, to declare to your High Mightinesses, that he is not only disposed to correspond with their wishes, but that he will also anxiously concur in every thing that depends on him for the restoration of tranquility between the different members of the union. The King anxiously seizes this opportunity of expressing to your High Mightinesses the real concern which the troubles give him, by which the United Provinces are torn. And he recommends to them to consider the disasters which must be the consequence of them, if not speedily terminated.

" His Majesty thinks, that in order to attain this salutary end, it is incumbent on their High Mightinesses, to adopt the readiest and most effectual measures for discontinuing, from hence forward, the hostile steps which some of the provinces have taken. Thus, your High Mightinesses will prevent a civil war, and facilitate the success of that reconciliation which it is so desirable to effect: This admonition on the part of the King is dictated by the friendship which he bears the Republic, and by the concern he has for its preservation and prosperity, as well as by the particular affection he possesses for each of the members of which it is composed."

July 20. In a district called Oud-Byerland, one side of Dordrecht, enormous ravages were caused by the seditious, when a detachment of the three armed corps of the city of Dordrecht came to stop the fury of the incendiaries: these outrageous persons attempting to make resistance, were immediately dispersed in consequence of a discharge from two field pieces, by which four fell on the spot, and others were wounded; fifteen have been taken prisoners, who were committed to the prison of Dordrecht, where they will meet solid and speedy justice.

The Pensionary Counsellor has laid before the states of Holland, a letter from the Baron de Rheede, our Envoy at the Court of Berlin. His Excellency informs the states, that it is absolutely false, *that the King of Prussia has given the smallest orders to march towards the territory of Cleves, or elsewhere.*

From Cleves they write, that his Prussian Majesty, having ordered the march of 40 battalions and 30 squadrons of the hussars of Zheiten and dragoons, making together an army of from 50 to 60,000 men, the Regency and Council of War had an extraordinary meeting on the arrival of this intelligence, to consider of the proper places for stationing the above troops, which were hourly expected to arrive, and had issued orders for the supply of horses to draw the artillery which is to accompany them.

The general complexion of the letters received from France by the last mail, confirm the news of the Marquis de Verac's recal from the Hague, who is to be succeeded by another nobleman fully empowered to offer the mediation of his most Christian Majesty in the present troubles in Holland. Which office the Holland mail of yesterday mention his most Christian Majesty to have accepted.

The Court of France entered into a treaty of alliance, offensive and defensive, with the States General last year. This treaty consisted of seventeen articles, exclusive of four private articles; the exact tenor of which are, indeed, only guessed at; and this treaty the French Minister at the Hague has officially declared his master will faithfully abide by.

No man has therefore occasion to doubt of the decisive measure his most Christian Majesty will adopt, as soon as their High Mightinesses have publicly declared themselves.

From the complexion of the affairs of all Holland, a civil war appears to be inevitable; and the activity of the French Naval equipment seems to indicate the certainty of such an event. It is evident that nothing less than the total revocation of all the powers vested in the Stadtholder can satisfy so strong a party as the republicans. All Europe waits in patient expectation for the first stroke, likely to come from the great powers most interested in the fate of Holland: nor can it be supposed that England, France and Prussia stand less anxious about the conduct which may be adopted by each other, in consequence of further violence in the provinces.

The states of Holland have forbidden the admiralty to obey any orders from the Captain General, nor to equip any vessel for sea, except for the protection of their external commerce: they have also ordered that every cutter that can be employed, shall be commissioned to cruise on the coasts of Overyssel and Gueldres, in the Zuyder-Zee.

L O N D O N.

U T R E C H T N E W S.

Notwithstanding what may be asserted to the contrary, this city has more reason to apprehend an attack from the Stadtholder's army, than the province of Holland, in the present conjuncture of affairs. The rival States of Amersfoort and our patriotic regency disputing the Sovereignty of the province, invites the ambition of the Orange party to subjugate the whole to the self-created regency of the former; to this may be added the decisive measures of the States General, which give every countenance to the partisans of the Stadtholder's faction. All these apprehensions, which seem well founded to us, do not in the least abate the ardour of our brave armed fellow citizens, who seem to gain new courage from the impending menaces. The zeal of our co-patriots of Amsterdam has abundantly supplied us with auxiliaries in men and money. We are determined to brave the worst, against an army, whose want and licentiousness must render us a prey to pillage and slaughter, if once they get us in their power.

The amity that subsists between the Prince Bishop of Liege, and the patriotic States of this Republic, will facilitate the arrival of these succours, which our emergencies may require from France. The troops destined for the camp formed at Givet, will have but a small distance to march to our relief, when occasion may require them. We have a farther advantage; our allies can approach to our assistance unopposed, whilst the abetters of the Orange party, who are said to be forming an encampment at Cleves, will have an opposition to contend against, in a country overrun with water.

Extract of a letter from Helvoetsluys, July 18.

" The fleet, which has been fitting out here for some time, has just sailed from this port for the West-Indies, and for the coast of Africa, under the convoy of the Rupert and the Vanstadt frigates of 30 guns each. The fleet consists of 32 sail, laden with military, naval, and other stores, for the different settlements. Twenty are destined to the coast, and the remainder, with the frigates, for St. Eustatius. In this fleet a number of engineers and other military artificers were embarked, for the erection and repairs of forts in different places."

July 7. Both the encrease of the national wealth, and the support of our naval power, depend on the extension of foreign trade. It must, therefore, afford no small satisfaction, to such as wish to see the people independent and secure, to observe, that our foreign commerce receives every day fresh augmentations. Indeed, it is matter of surprise, to those who know at what a low ebb our exports and imports were when the coalition was dismissed from office, to remark their present flourishing condition. Nothing but the closest attention to the support of public credit on the par of Government; and the most active industry on the part of the people could have brought about so happy a revolution.

There is no truth in the assertion, that many of our naval officers and seamen have been obliged to go into foreign service through bad treatment or necessity. It is true, every officer who wanted to be promoted has not been promoted; but it is equally true, that all who had a just title to promotion have been rewarded. As to seamen—our foreign trade at this moment employs more shipping than it ever did in any period during peace: it, therefore, is seamen's own fault if they are employed by British masters. In fact they are so employed—almost to a man.

The invention of the stock-jobbers seems to be exhausted. Why don't they massacre the Princess of Orange; or engage the French and Russian armies? It would be easy enough to do so; and as such events are amusing, it is a pitty John Bull should not be indulged.

Wednesday Messrs. Tenon and Colomb, accompanied by the Marquis d'Herbouville, deputed by the Royal Academy of Sciences of France, and at the expence of the French Government, to view the prisons and hospitals of this country, visited Worcester Infirmary and prison, attended by Dr. Johnstone. The French Government have in view, by this survey, an object of great consequence to humanity, the rendering prisons less injurious to health and morals, and hospitals as conducive as possible to the welfare of mankind.

July 10. The public not being disposed to be any longer deceived by the fictions of the malecontents of the day, soon shewed their disapprobation and detestation of the rumours circulated, respecting the acts of injustice said to be practised by the French Consuls and Farmers General. They will soon have equal reason to smile at the fabrications which regard the French armaments at Brest.—The French as well as the English generally review their shipping once a year; And they will doubtless do so in 1787. However, many surmises the Patriots of England may raise respecting their intentions. The Dutch, one should think, are as much concerned in the decision of the affairs of Holland, as the English and French:—How comes it then that they fit out no men of war? Perhaps their fleets are to join the neutral powers.

July 13. Let the republican spirits of Great-Britain look to the intestine feuds, and we may say domestic broils of the Hollanders; let them look to the happy tranquility and settle moderation of the government here, and then praise republicanism if they can.

The same correspondent adds, that the King of Great-Britain governs freemen by their own election and laws, whilst their High Mightinesses, as they are styled, rule slaves by arbitrary force and violence. From such a government the Dutch may justly say, " Good Lord deliver us."

The last letters from Elsinore, dated the 4th instant, mention that two East-Indiamen bound to Copenhagen, passed the Sound from China, under jury masts, the 2d; and that 50 sail of merchant ships were then at anchor in the Sound, wind bound.

July 16. It is said in a private letter, that the army committed great excesses on their entry into Wyk. Immediately on the confirmation, that a French army was advancing towards Holland; an augmentation to the amount of 30,000 men in the whole, was made in the Prussian army in the Duchy of Cleves, and those letters say, on the arrival of the mutual guarantee from England, they will be in action. A small river only parts the Duchy of Cleves from Holland.

July 17. From Utrecht we learn, that in the night between Saturday and Sunday Se'nnight, a body of one thousand men, in two divisions; one commanded by the Rhinegrave of Salem, and the other by Lieutenant General Vander Boch, marched from hence to attack the out-post of the Stadtholder's camp. A smart skirmish ensued, in which they killed several horsemen of Vander Hoop's regiment. They returned back to Utrecht on the 8th instant. Two hundred of the Stadtholders troops have deserted, and come into Utrecht.

July 21. Yesterday goods to the amount of 10,000l. were entered at the Custom-House for France, the principle part was earthen ware, that article being very scarce in that country.

July 24. The mischief of our finances is, that our mode of taxation is without determined principles, without any rule but the immediate want of money, and the possibility of procuring it; taxing lands, employments, money, industry, or whatever occurs to a hurried imagination.

July 26. An unhappy contest is likely to take place between the King of Sardinia and the Republic of Genoa. His Majesty thinking himself insulted by the hardships which the Piedmontese shepherds are subjected to by the Genoese, when they are driving their cattle through the Republic, has forcibly taken four fourths and the town of Savona, and now keeps possession of them. As soon as the news of this invasion was brought to Genoa, the Senate dispatched three Couriers, one to Paris, the other to Vienna, to implore the protection and mediation of these Courts, and the third to Swisserland, to obtain of the Helvetian Cantons a body of six thousand men, to defend the Republic against this unforeseen attack of the King of Sardinia.

1865

Lawrence A. Gobright of The Associated Press was working late in his Washington office on the evening of April 14, 1865.

He had already sent out reports about President Abraham Lincoln's theater party, with the news that General Ulysses S. Grant had changed his mind about seeing the play *Our American Cousin* in order to go to New Jersey with Mrs. Grant.

Then, the door burst open and an excited friend rushed in with the news of the tragedy at Ford's Theater.

Gobright quickly wrote out a dispatch before going to work on a more detailed account of developments:

WASHINGTON, FRIDAY, APRIL 14, 1865—THE PRESIDENT WAS SHOT IN A THEATRE TONIGHT AND PERHAPS MORTALLY WOUNDED.

The President, shot by actor John Wilkes Booth, died the next morning.

Booth escaped in the confusion of the assassination, but was found by Union soldiers twelve days later, hiding in a barn in Virginia. The barn was set afire and Booth found dead.

THE NEW YORK HERALD.

WHOLE NO. 10,456. NEW YORK, SATURDAY, APRIL 15, 1865. PRICE FOUR CENTS.

IMPORTANT.

ASSASSINATION OF PRESIDENT LINCOLN.

The President Shot at the Theatre Last Evening.

SECRETARY SEWARD DAGGERED IN HIS BED, BUT NOT MORTALLY WOUNDED.

Clarence and Frederick Seward Badly Hurt.

ESCAPE OF THE ASSASSINS.

Intense Excitement in Washington.

Scene at the Deathbed of Mr. Lincoln.

J. Wilkes Booth, the Actor, the Alleged Assassin of the President, &c., &c., &c.

THE OFFICIAL DESPATCH.

WAR DEPARTMENT,
WASHINGTON, April 15—1:30 A. M.

Major General DIX, New York:—

This evening at about 9:30 P. M., at Ford's Theatre, the President, while sitting in his private box with Mrs. Lincoln, Mrs. Harris and Major Rathburn, was shot by an assassin, who suddenly entered the box and approached behind the President.

The assassin then leaped upon the stage, brandishing a large dagger or knife, and made his escape in the rear of the theatre.

The pistol ball entered the back of the President's head and penetrated nearly through the head. The wound is mortal.

The President has been insensible ever since it was inflicted, and is now dying.

About the same hour an assassin, whether the same or not, entered Mr. Seward's apartments, and under pretence of having a prescription was shown to the Secretary's sick chamber. The assassin immediately rushed to the bed and inflicted two or three stabs on the throat and two on the face.

It is hoped the wounds may not be mortal. My apprehension is that they will prove fatal.

The nurse alarmed Mr. Frederick Seward, who was in an adjoining room, and he hastened to the door of his father's room, when he met the assassin, who inflicted upon him one or more dangerous wounds. The recovery of Frederick Seward is doubtful.

It is not probable that the President will live through the night.

General Grant and wife were advertised to be at the theatre this evening, but he started to Burlington at six o'clock this evening.

At a Cabinet meeting, at which General Grant was present, the subject of the state of the country and the prospect of a speedy peace were discussed. The President was very cheerful and hopeful, and spoke very kindly of General Lee and others of the confederacy, and of the establishment of government in Virginia.

All the members of the Cabinet except Mr. Seward are now in attendance upon the President.

I have seen Mr. Seward, but he and Frederick were both unconscious.

EDWIN M. STANTON,
Secretary of War.

THE HERALD DESPATCHES.

WASHINGTON, April 14, 1865.

Assassination has been inaugurated in Washington. The bowie knife and pistol have been applied to President Lincoln and Secretary Seward. The former was shot in the throat, while at Ford's theatre to-night. Mr. Seward was badly cut about the neck, while in his bed at his residence.

SECOND DESPATCH.

WASHINGTON, April 14, 1865.

An attempt was made about ten o'clock this evening to assassinate the President and Secretary Seward. The President was shot at Ford's Theatre. Result not yet known. Mr. Seward's throat was cut, and his son badly wounded.

There is intense excitement here.

Details of the Assassination.

WASHINGTON, April 14, 1865.

Washington was thrown into an intense excitement a few minutes before eleven o'clock this evening, by the announcement that the President and Secretary Seward had been assassinated and were dead.

The wildest excitement prevailed in all parts of the city. Men, women and children, old and young, rushed to and fro, and the rumors were magnified until we had nearly every member of the Cabinet killed. Some time elapsed before authentic data could be ascertained in regard to the affair.

The President and Mrs. Lincoln were at Ford's theatre, listening to the performance of the American Cousin, occupying a box in the second tier. At the close of the third act a person entered the box occupied by the President, and shot Mr. Lincoln in the head. The shot entered the back of his head, and came out above the temple.

The assassin then jumped from the box upon the stage and ran across to the other side, exhibiting a dagger in his hand, flourishing it in a tragical manner, shouting the same words repeated by the desperado at Mr. Seward's house, adding to it, "The South is avenged," and then escaped from the back entrance to the stage, but in his passage dropped his pistol and his hat.

Mr. Lincoln fell forward from his seat, and Mrs. Lincoln fainted.

The moment the astonished audience could realize what had happened, the President was taken and carried to Mr. Peterson's house, in Tenth street, opposite to the theatre. Medical aid was immediately sent for, and the wound was at first supposed to be fatal, and it was announced that he could not live; but at half-past twelve he is still alive, though in a precarious condition.

As the assassin ran across the stage, Colonel J. B. Stewart, of this city, who was occupying one of the front seats in the orchestra, on the same side of the house as the box occupied by Mr. Lincoln, sprang to the stage and followed him; but he was obstructed in his passage across the stage by the fright of the actors, and reached the back door about three seconds after the assassin had passed out. Colonel Stewart got to the street just in time to see him mount his horse and ride away.

This operation shows that the whole thing was a preconcerted plan. The person who fired the pistol was a man about thirty years of age, about five feet nine, spare built, fair skin, dark hair, apparently bushy, with a large mustache. Laura Keene and the leader of the orchestra declare that they recognized him as J. Wilkes Booth the actor, and a rabid secessionist. Whoever he was, it is plainly evident that he thoroughly understood the theatre and all the approaches and modes of escape to the stage. A person not familiar with the theatre could not have possibly made his escape so well and quickly.

The alarm was sounded in every quarter. Mr. Stanton was notified, and immediately left his house.

All the other members of the Cabinet escaped attack.

Cavalrymen were sent out in all directions, and despatches sent to all the fortifications, and it is thought they will be captured.

About half-past ten o'clock this evening a tall, well dressed man made his appearance at Secretary Seward's residence, and applied for admission. He was refused admission by the servant, when the desperado stated that he had a prescription from the Surgeon General, and that he was ordered to deliver it in person. He was still refused, except upon the written order of the physician. This he pretended to show, and pushed by the servant and rushed up stairs to Mr. Seward's room. He was met at the door by Mr. Fred Seward, who notified him that he was master of the house, and would take charge of the medicine. After a few words had passed between them he dodged by Fred Seward and rushed to the Secretary's bed, and struck him in the neck with a dagger, and also in the breast.

It was supposed at first that Mr. Seward was killed instantly, but it was found afterwards that the wound was not mortal.

Major Wm. H. Seward, Jr., paymaster, was in the room, and rushed to the defence of his father, and was badly cut in the *melee* with the assassin, but not fatally.

The desperado managed to escape from the house, and was prepared for escape by having a horse at the door. He immediately mounted his horse, and sung out the motto of the State of Virginia, "*Sic Semper Tyrannis!*" and rode off.

Surgeon General Barnes was immediately sent for, and he *examined Mr. Seward and pronounced him safe*. His wounds were not fatal. The jugular vein was not cut, nor the wound in the breast deep enough to be fatal.

WASHINGTON, April 15—1 A. M.

The streets in the vicinity of Ford's Theatre are densely crowded by an anxious and excited crowd. A guard has been placed across Tenth street and F and E streets, and only official persons and particular friends of the President are allowed to pass.

The popular heart is deeply stirred, and the deepest indignation against leading rebels is freely expressed.

The scene at the house where the President lies *in extremis* is very affecting. Even Secretary Stanton is affected to tears.

When the news spread through the city that the President had been shot, the people, with pale faces and compressed lips, crowded every place where there was the slightest chance of obtaining information in regard to the affair.

After the President was shot, Lieutenant Rathbun, caught the assassin by the arm, who immediately struck him with a knife, and jumped from the box, as before stated.

The popular affection for Mr. Lincoln has been shown by this diabolical assassination, which will bring eternal infamy, not only upon its authors, but upon the hellish cause which they desire to avenge.

Vice President Johnson arrived at the White House, where the President lies, about one o'clock, and will remain with him to the last.

The President's family are in attendance upon him also.

As soon as intelligence could be got to the War Department, the electric telegraph and the Signal corps were put in requisition to endeavor to prevent the escape of the assassins, and all the troops around Washington are under arms.

Popular report points to a somewhat celebrated actor of known secession proclivities as the assassin; but it would be unjust to name him until some further evidence of his guilt is obtained. It is rumored that the person alluded to is in custody.

The latest advices from Secretary Seward reveals more desperate work there than at first supposed. Seward's wounds are not in themselves fatal; but, in connection with his recent injuries, and the great loss of blood he has sustained, his recovery is questionable.

It was Clarence A. Seward, instead of Wm. H. Seward, Jr., who was wounded. Fred. Seward was also in attendance upon the Secretary, showing the desperate struggle took place there. The wounds of the whole party were deemed ...

ONE O'CLOCK A. M.

The President is perfectly senseless, and there is not the slightest hope of his surviving. Physicians believe that he will die before morning. All of his Cabinet, except Secretary Seward, are with him. Speaker Colfax, Senator Farwell, of Maine, and many other gentlemen, are also at the house awaiting the termination.

The scene at the President's bedside is described by one who witnessed it as most affecting. It was surrounded by his Cabinet ministers, all of whom were bathed in tears, not even excepting Mr. Stanton, who, when informed by Surgeon General Barnes, that the President could not live until morning, exclaimed: "Oh, no, General; no—no;" and with an impulse, natural as it was unaffected, immediately sat down on a chair near his bedside and wept like a child.

Senator Sumner was seated on the right of the President's couch, near the head, holding the right hand of the President in his own. He was sobbing like a woman, with his head bowed down almost on the pillow of the bed on which the President was lying.

TWO O'CLOCK A. M.

The President is still alive, but there is no improvement in his condition.

THE PRESS DESPATCHES.

WASHINGTON, April 14—12:30 A. M.

The President was shot in a theatre to-night, and is perhaps mortally wounded.

SECOND DESPATCH.

WASHINGTON, April 15—1 A. M.

The President is not expected to live through the night. He was shot at a theatre.

Secretary Seward was also assassinated. No arteries were cut.

Additional Details of the Assassination.

WASHINGTON, April 15—1:30 A. M.

President Lincoln and wife, with other friends, this evening visited Ford's theatre, for the purpose of witnessing the performance of the American Cousin.

It was announced in the papers that General Grant would also be present; but that gentleman took the late train of cars for New Jersey.

The theatre was densely crowded, and all seemed delighted with the scene before them. During the third act, and while there was a temporary pause for one of the actors to enter, a sharp report of a pistol was heard, which merely attracted attention, but suggested nothing serious, until a man rushed to the front of the President's box, waving a long dagger in his right hand, and exclaiming "*Sic semper tyrannis*" and immediately leaped from the box, which was in the second tier, to the stage beneath, and ran across to the opposite side, making his escape, amid the bewilderment of the audience, from the rear of the theatre, and mounting a horse, fled.

The screams of Mrs. Lincoln first disclosed the fact to the audience that the President had been shot, when all present rose to their feet, rushing towards the stage, many exclaiming "Hang him! Hang him!"

The excitement was of the wildest possible description, and of course there was an abrupt termination of the theatrical performance.

There was a rush toward the President's box, when cries were heard:—"Stand back and give him air." "Has any one stimulants?"

On a hasty examination it was found that the President had been shot through the head, above and back of the temporal bone, and that some of the brain was oozing out.

He was removed to a private house opposite to the theatre, and the Surgeon General of the army and other surgeons sent for to attend to his condition.

On an examination of the private box blood was discovered on the back of the cushioned rocking chair on which the President had been sitting, also on the partition and on the floor. A common single barrelled pocket pistol was found on the carpet.

A military guard was placed in front of the private residence to which the President had been conveyed. An immense crowd was in front of it, all deeply anxious to learn the condition of the President. It had been previously announced that the wound was mortal, but all hoped otherwise. The shock to the community was terrible.

At midnight the Cabinet, with Messrs. Sumner, Colfax and Farnsworth, Judge Curtis, Governor Oglesby, General Meigs, Colonel Hay, and a few personal friends, with Surgeon General Barnes and his immediate assistants, were around his bedside.

The President was in a state of syncope, totally insensible, and breathing slowly. The blood oozed from the wound at the back of his head.

The surgeons exhausted every possible effort of medical skill; but all hope was gone.

The parting of his family with the dying President is too sad for description.

The President and Mrs. Lincoln did not start for the theatre until fifteen minutes after eight o'clock. Speaker Colfax was at the White House at the time, and the President stated to him that he was going. Mrs. Lincoln had not been well, because the papers had announced that General Grant and they were to be present, and, as General Grant had gone North, he did not wish the audience to be disappointed.

He went with apparent reluctance, and urged Mr. Colfax to go with him; but that gentleman had made other engagements, and, with Mr. Ashmun, of Massachusetts, bid him goodby.

When the excitement at the theatre was at its wildest height reports were circulated that Secretary Seward had also been assassinated.

On reaching this gentleman's residence a crowd and a military guard were found at the door, and on entering it was ascertained that the reports were based on truth.

Everybody there was so excited that scarcely an intelligible word could be gathered. But the facts are substantially as follows:—

About ten o'clock a man rang the bell, and the call having been answered by a colored servant, he said he had come from Dr. Verdi, Secretary Seward's family physician, with a prescription, at the same time holding in his hand a small piece of folded paper, and saying, in answer to a refusal, that he must see the Secretary, as he was entrusted with particular directions concerning the medicine.

He still insisted on going up, although repeatedly informed that no one could enter the chamber. The man pushed the servant aside, and walked hastily towards the Secretary's room, and was then met by Mr. Frederick Seward, of whom he demanded to see the Secretary, making the same representation which he did to the servant.

What further passed in the way of colloquy is not known; but the man struck him on the head with a billy, severely injuring the skull and felling him almost senseless.

The assassin then rushed into the chamber and attacked Major Seward, Paymaster United States Army, and Mr. Hansell, a messenger of the State Department, and two male nurses, disabling them all.

He then rushed upon the Secretary, who was lying in bed in the same room, and inflicted three stabs in the neck, but severing, it is thought and hoped, no arteries, though he bled profusely.

The assassin then rushed down stairs, mounted his horse at the door, and rode off before an alarm could be sounded, and in the same manner as the assassin of the President.

It is believed that the injuries of the Secretary are not fatal nor those of either of the others, although both the Secretary and the Assistant Secretary are very seriously injured.

Secretaries Stanton and Welles, and other prominent officers of the Government, called at Secretary Seward's house to inquire into his condition, and there heard of the assassination of the President.

They then proceeded to the house where he was lying, exhibiting of course intense anxiety and solicitude.

An immense crowd was gathered in front of the President's house, and a strong guard was also stationed there. Many persons evidently supposing he would be brought to his home.

The entire city to-night presents a scene of wild excitement, accompanied by violent expression of indignation and the profoundest sorrow; many shed tears.

The military authorities have despatched mounted patrols in every direction, in order, if possible, to arrest the assassins. The whole metropolitan police are likewise vigilant for the same purpose.

The attacks, both at the theatre and at Secretary Seward's house, took place at about the same hour—ten o'clock—thus showing a preconcerted plan to assassinate those gentlemen. Some evidences of the guilt of the party who attacked the President are in the possession of the police.

Vice President Johnson is in the city, and his headquarters are guarded by troops.

THE STATE CAPITAL.

Rejection of the New York Fire Commissioners—Passage of the Central Railroad Fare Bill—Great Excitement Over the Health Bill, &c.

ALBANY, April 14—11:40 P. M.

Legislation each day is now so rapid here that a detail or analysis of its progress is out of the question. To-day the long pending Central Railroad bill passed the Senate, and is virtually a law if the Governor does not veto it. But the result may be foreshadowed in the veto sent in to-day of the Dry Dock and Battery Railroad.

The Health bill, which two days since was bound by caucus rules to have a sure passage, was to-night defeated by republican votes. The Collector of the port of New York, who has had an elaborate organization up for his retention in the office of Commissioner of Charities, was thrown overboard and the power of all his patronage disregarded in the strife to secure this position, which has been his pet desire and speciality for many years. All these occurrences have a political significancy which it would take too much time and space to develop. The excitement of the day has been the Health bill, and that excitement has been so incoherent as to be indescribable. The attempt made last night to kill off the bill was renewed to-day at an early hour. It was then lost for want of a sufficient vote, and laid on the table for reconsideration. A motion was made to call it up for a final vote, a short time after the reading of the journal, by its opponents. The tactics against the measure were led by Weed, of Clinton, in whose fresh abilities the democrats have gained their ablest accession in the Legislature. He moved to take from the table, and upon that the previous question. The vote of fifty-three to sixty-one disclosed the fact that the friends of the bill were in the minority, and a panic at once was created among them. An adroit suggestion was sent to the Speaker understood—to be from Henry J. Raymond, who was on the floor—to rule that the vote did not carry the bill, and another must be taken. ... the third reading of the bill. Here ... Wood, of New York, moved to adjourn ... the Speaker ... and the greatest uproar. Weed and others insisting that such action was out of order.

While the vote was being taken a few more republicans were drummed up, and the motion carried by one or two votes. Hereupon the wildest scenes of confusion took place, all the members gathered in a crowd before the Speaker's desk in the most excited condition, shouting, disputing and threatening each other and the Speaker. One member from New York got upon a desk, and in the midst of a clamor for bets, offered at a thousand dollars, shouted and taunted the republicans, daring any man to bet. He shook his two fists with handsful of greenbacks. Others clamored in like manner, and the scene resembled the most exciting days at the gold room in New York. In the midst of all this were heard the clapping of hands and the triumphant imitations of the mock chanticleer of the republicans, while the democrats uttered the most violent denunciations of the Speaker to his face for his rulings.

This scene was disposed of only to be reproduced for the evening session. Mr. Weed renewed his assaults upon the bill to bring it to a final vote, while its diminished friends sought to postpone this action. Messrs. Van Buren, Stuart, Reed, Brandreth, Wood and Parker sought alternately to postpone or to kill time by filibustering, after prolonged, excited and most disorderly proceedings.

A final vote was forced upon the friends of the bill at a late hour. Sixty-one voted for the bill and fifty-one against it. Sixty-five votes being necessary to its passage, it was lost. Mr. Salmon, of New York, who had made himself obnoxious by the vehemency of his opposition to the bill, was sought to be involved in proceedings before the bar of the House; but the Speaker was evidently discouraged from any such attempts. The management for the bill on the floor of the House was understood to be in the hands of the radicals, under the lead of Fields. Boole was in the lobby in person. Mayor Gunther, Carr and others of his opponents were here yesterday to urge on the passage of the bill. It is alleged that the republican interest was sold out by the radicals.

The Fire Commissioners encountered a decided capsize in executive session. The defeat of the Health bill was pending on their consideration, and the Assembly had adjourned in the extraordinary manner of the morning. The names were at first confirmed. Senator Laimbier, who had made the chief opposition, moving the confirmation. This action was, however, reconsidered on motion of Senator Andrews, on the ground of the promises made in the Assembly to the democrats, who passed it, that the board would comprise two democrats. The names were accordingly sent back to the Governor.

The continuation of Boole in office by the defeat of the Health bill is accompanied by the passage of a resolution continuing the Senate investigating committee, to sit during the summer and examine the other departments. The feeling here is that Boole was treated as an invidious exception, and the thing will be made even all round.

The action determined on in caucus yesterday in regard to Draper and the Board of Charities, was decked by resolution to-day, and is coupled with the defeat of Rufus F. Andrews as candidate for United States District Attorney at New York, as a satisfactory manifestation of Thurlow Weed's power.

The passage of the Central Railroad Fare bill was conducted through the form of third reading with no excitement, and with the limit of seven per cent dividends. The increase of half a cent per mile for three years is thought only reasonable.

IMPORTANT FROM SOUTH AMERICA.

Surrender of Montevideo to Gen. Flores—Brazil in Possession of the City, &c.

The Brazilian mail arrived at Lisbon April 2, bringing the following advices:—

Montevideo has surrendered to General Flores.

The Brazilians now (March 11) occupy the city.

RIO JANEIRO, March 11, 1865.

Exchange 25⅛ a 26¼.

Coffee—Sales of good firsts at 65.66. Shipments, 100,000 bags. Stock, 100,000 bags. Freights, 50 a 52¼.

BAHIA, March 11, 1865.

Exchange 26¼. Cotton nominal.

PERNAMBUCO, March 11, 1865.

Exchange 26¼ a 27.

News from San Francisco.

SAN FRANCISCO, April 13, 1865.

The exports of treasure for the quarter just ended show a falling off of about six and a half millions as compared with the same period last year.

SAN FRANCISCO, April 14, 1865.

The Pacific mail steamship Sacramento sailed to-day, with a large number of passengers, for New York, and $2,153,006 in treasure, of which nearly $700,000 go to New York.

The steamship Moses Taylor sailed for San Juan del Sur, with numerous passengers.

The market continues variable and unsettled, and traders pursue a continuous policy. Prices of Eastern goods are slowly falling.

Sailed, ship Flying Eagle, for Boston.

New Orleans Markets.

NEW ORLEANS, April 8,
VIA CAIRO, April 14, 1865.

The New Orleans markets are at a stand still. Low middling cotton is quoted at 42c per pound, and good superfine flour at 60 per barrel.

THE REBELS.

JEFF. DAVIS AT DANVILLE.

His Latest Appeal to His Deluded Followers.

He Thinks the Fall of Richmond a Blessing in Disguise, as it Leaves the Rebel Armies Free to Move from Point to Point.

He Vainly Promises to Hold Virginia at All Hazards.

Lee and His Army Supposed to be Safe.

Breckinridge and the Rest of Davis' Cabinet Reach Danville Safely.

The Organ of Governor Vance, of North Carolina, Advises the Submission of the Rebels to President Lincoln's Terms, &c., &c., &c.

Jeff. Davis' Last Proclamation.

VIRGINIA TO BE HELD BY THE REBELS AT ALL HAZARDS.

DANVILLE, Va., April 5, 1865.

The General-in-Chief found it necessary to make such movements of his troops as to uncover the capital. It would be unwise to conceal the *moral and material injury to our cause resulting from the occupation of our capital* by the enemy. It is equally unwise and unworthy of us to allow our own energies to falter and our efforts to become relaxed under adverses, however calamitous they may be. For many months the *largest and finest army* of the confederacy, under command of a leader whose presence inspires equal confidence in the troops and the people, has been greatly trammelled by the necessity of keeping constant watch over the approaches to the capital, and has thus been forced to forego more than one opportunity for promising enterprise. It is for us, my countrymen, to show by our bearing under reverses how wretched has been the self-deception of those who have believed us less able to endure misfortune with fortitude than to encounter dangers with courage.

We have now entered upon a new phase of the struggle. Relieved from the necessity of guarding particular points, *our army will be free to move from point to point* to strike the enemy in detail far from his base. *Let us but will it and we are free.*

Animated by that confidence in spirit and fortitude which never yet failed me, I announce to you, fellow countrymen, that it is my purpose to maintain your cause with my whole heart and soul; that I will never consent to abandon to the enemy one foot of the soil of any one of the States of the confederacy. That Virginia—noble State—whose ancient renown has been eclipsed by her still more glorious recent history; whose bosom has been bared to receive the main shock of this war; whose sons and daughters have exhibited heroism so sublime as to render her illustrious in all time to come—that Virginia, with the help of the people and by the blessing of Providence, *shall be held and defended*, and no peace ever be made with the infamous invaders of her territory.

If by the stress of numbers we should ever be compelled to a temporary withdrawal from her limits, or those of any other border State, again and again will we return, until the baffled and exhausted enemy shall abandon in despair his endless and impossible task of making slaves of a people resolved to be free.

Let us, then, not despond, my countrymen: but, relying on God, meet the foe with fresh defiance and with unconquered and unconquerable hearts.

JEFFERSON DAVIS.

The Evacuation of the Rebel Capital.

THE FIRST REBEL ACCOUNT OF HOW THE CITY WAS ABANDONED.

[From the Danville (Va.) Register, April 5.]

Persons who left the capital Sunday night and Monday morning represent that the scene which followed the evacuation of the city by our troops beggars description. To preserve order and protect the property of the citizens who unavoidably remained there, as far as could be done, the Nineteenth Virginia militia, under Colonel Evans, was placed on police duty in the city, to await the coming of the enemy; but accounts state that they failed to render any aid or protection to the people whatever. On Sunday night a mob of the lower classes of the city, composed, it is said, mostly of the foreign element, visited a number of the largest storehouses of the city and robbed them of their contents. It is affirmed that Main street was pillaged, and then burned, and that some of the milling establishments were also committed to the flames. We have no doubt that a considerable portion of that brave city has been laid in ashes, and a number of its people insulted, outraged, robbed and massacred. How painful the thought that the place should be given over to rapine and plunder even before the public enemy entered its limits. But the fact only proves that the people of Richmond have had secret enemies in their own midst scarcely less savage and even more treacherous and vindictive than the open foe.

We are told that the people banded together during the violent proceeding of the mob and resisted them with force, a street fight ensuing, in which several persons were killed.

No intelligence has reached us of the enemy's troops occupying the city. The last trains on the Danville railroad which came out of the place left Monday morning, and passengers upon them had heard nothing from the enemy. The greater portion of Grant's army was transferred to the south side of James river some days ago, only the command of General Ord, which is composed mostly, if not entirely, of negro troops, being left on the north side. This command will enter and occupy the city. Some of our people who are acquainted with the character of General Ord think they have reason to hope that his treatment of the unfortunate people of Richmond will not be so hard, and cruel and inhuman as that which has fallen upon the heads of our fellow citizens in some other captured cities.

The newspapers of Richmond, we suppose, all fell into the hands of the enemy. The evacuation of the city was so sudden and unexpected—scarcely any one being prepared for it—that no time was left for the removal of so cumbrous an establishment as a city newspaper office. In a few days we may expect to hear that the *Enquirer* or the *Whig* or the *Examiner* is issued as a Yankee paper.

All the rolling stock of the Richmond and Danville Railroad in running order was saved on the retreat from Richmond. A few old cars, not in a movable condition, were left at Manchester. No train was captured by the enemy near the junction, as was at one time reported; and, indeed, we do not believe that any body of Yankees had struck the road at any point up to yesterday evening.

The Secretary of War, the Quartermaster General, Commissary General and a number of other officers of the government, left Richmond on horseback, and will probably arrive at this place to-morrow.

Should General Lee establish his lines east of the junction, we suppose the State Legislature will be convened at Lynchburg.

All the specie and other valuables belonging to the banks in Richmond were removed from the city on Sunday, and have been carried to places of safety.

A considerable amount of goods purchased by the State for distribution to the people, we regret to learn, had to be left behind. Also the State archives remained in the city; but we perceive no motive the enemy can have in destroying them, as they will, no doubt, endeavor to occupy the city permanently, and establish a State government at Richmond under the federal Union.

Lee's Army Supposed to be in a Safe Position.

[From the Raleigh Confederate, April 7.]

This is the time for rumor manufacturers who are engaged in a wholesale business. Sometimes they have it that whole brigades deserted in the last great battle; among others, Cook's brigade is selected as the bearer of this stigma. We are assured that such a statement has no foundation whatever; that no treachery induced the disaster at Petersburg; that our forces fought splendidly, and the enemy only succeeded by overwhelming numbers. We are convinced, too, from facts which we cannot mention, that *Lee's army is in a safe position, and that his future movements will be directed with the skill and energy which distinguish this great captain.*

Having anticipated the probable loss of Richmond, and fully recognizing the importance of the disaster, we are, nevertheless, not of the number of those who give up the cause. In the Southern confederacy this day there is military strength of men, material and supplies to make independence certain. It is with the *people themselves* whether they secure or lose their liberties.

Rebel Particulars of the Battle at Petersburg.

[From the Raleigh Confederate, April 7.]

An officer who left Richmond at nine o'clock on Monday morning last informs us that at the time he left the city was in flames from Cary to Canal streets. The Shockoe warehouse and other entrepots of supplies were burning. The bridges also had been fired.

No mob or violence of any kind had occurred up to the period when he left, so that the reports of a destructive mob on Sunday night are untrue. The enemy's cavalry entered the city as the train moved off that he came out in. The story of the mob, therefore, we hope, is entirely erroneous.

This officer describes the fighting on Saturday as terrific beyond description. The enemy forced column after column on our works, lapping our lines on the extreme right. They came nine columns deep. Eight lines faltered and were broken by the obstinacy of our defences; but the ninth broke over our forces like a whirlwind. He says the destruction of the enemy was immense. Our loss, we think, consisted mainly in the prisoners taken by the enemy. All the prisoners whom we captured were drunk, having been prepared according to Yankee tactics for this dreadful ordeal. Lieutenant General A. P. Hill was certainly killed. General Fitz. Lee was not killed, as reported, nor General W. H. F. Lee. No general officer from North Carolina was killed, as far as he heard. On Monday Sheridan attacked Fitz. Lee and was handsomely repulsed.

The Organ of Governor Vance, of North Carolina, Advising General Lee to Submit on Mr. Lincoln's Terms.

[From the Raleigh Confederate, April 7.]

The *Conservative* occasionally seems to fall into very mysterious hands, and to come under the control of an incomprehensible influence. On the day before yesterday that paper availed itself of a period of extreme reverse and disaster to renew the attempt to cast odium on a portion of our own citizens, which has been a favorite policy with its political leaders ever since the reverses began, and after it was no longer politic to claim that they "made the revolution." Yesterday it sends to the public a leader of still more extraordinary import. From what we comprehend of it, it seems to be a *distinct proposition to submit and surrender upon the terms proposed by Lincoln.* This has never yet, that we recollect of, been more distinctly proposed, even by journals whose loyalty has been called in question. The *Conservative* again ... to propose to treat with the North ... the concession that the confederacy is a government," and hence, says the *Conservative*, "if our authorities are determined to force this condition upon the North as a basis of negotiation, then the North will never negotiate." What is this but surrender? Not only surrender, but an assertion to the world that the defence of the last four years has been of a position which is one of sheer nonsense—one which the North "never could admit!" We have not seen in this controversy so bold and unconditional a justification of the Northern invasion; for, if we sought to force a claim inconsistent with reason, and to demand an "admission" which "is an absurdity in anything like government," and the North only resisted such claim and refused such admission, then we are in the wrong and the Yankee government is right, and the writer of the article to which we are replying does well when he advises *General Lee not to "block up his way, at the threshold, by presenting a basis to which he knows the enemy will not yield,"* but "to meet him on his own ground," as "the only way to open the negotiation." When we remember what "his own ground" is, upon which the *Conservative* proposes to meet the enemy, we may readily understand how much it is prepared to concede. "His own ground" measured the length of three propositions; submission to the laws and constitution of the United States, the laying down of our arms, and acquiescence in Lincoln's proclamations. This is the ground on which the author of the editorial desires General Lee to meet Lincoln and "secure a talk about peace." We have no idea that Governor Vance will support this idea; but it is very unfortunate that now, at the very moment when everything should be said to uphold the hopes and confidence of the army and people, such sentiments should obtain publication in the organ of the Governor.

High Prices in an Overstocked Market.

[From the Raleigh Confederate, April 7.]

Our market, on the arrival of the Weldon train, on yesterday, *became overstocked* with shad; *they went off slowly at $50 per pair.*

Exchange of the Rebel General Vance.

[From the Ashville (N. C.) News.]

The exchange of prisoners seems to go steadily on. We have seen a large number of our mountain boys, who have reached home after a protracted imprisonment. Among others we were gratified to meet Brigadier General R. B. Vance, who reached home some days since. He looks rather worsted by his long confinement, but, as usual with him, is full of life, cheerful and buoyant. The General is a great favorite of the people of this section, and everybody was glad to see him.

City Intelligence.

EASTER SUNDAY AT ST. ANN'S CHURCH.—The admirers of sacred music, made truly effective by a well trained choir, have an opportunity of indulging their taste by repairing to St. Ann's church on Easter Sunday evening, the doors opening at seven, the concert beginning at eight. Three of the pieces are from Gordigiani, three from Rossini and one from each of the composers Verdi, Donizetti, Verrimst, Dachauer and Gounod. We need only mention the names of Signor Remi and Messrs. Schmitz, Schubert and Dachauer to insure confidence in the vocal results. The ladies are quite distinguished for contralto and soprano execution, and no exertion will be spared to make the musical feast worthy of the day.

A NEW CHURCH.—An advertisement among our religious notices announces the opening of the new Church of the Holy Trinity, Madison avenue, corner of Forty-second street, on Sunday. Sermons will be preached at the three sessions by Rev. Dr. Tyng, of St. George's; Rev. Dr. Dyer, and the Rev. Stephen H. Tyng, Jr., the pastor of the church. It promises to be an occasion of great interest to residents on Murray Hill.

CROTON AQUEDUCT CONTRACTS.—The following contracts have been issued by this department:—Laying crosswalks from southeast corner of Fifty-ninth street and Broadway to the junction of Broadway and Eighth avenue, Matthew Murray, $625. Cobble stone pavement in Hammond street, west of Thirteenth avenue, Christy Dowd, $1,896 50. Sewer in Forty-third street, from Lexington avenue to Fourth avenue, John Duffy, Jr., $1,913 50. Sewer in Forty-sixth street, from Eleventh avenue to seventy-five feet west of Tenth avenue, John Rourke, $5,228 50. Fifty-second street, sewer from Sixth to Seventh avenues, Joseph Moore, $4,880. Sewer in 128th street, from Fifth avenue through Manhattan street to Tenth avenue, James Cunningham, $22,941 27.

MRS. EMMA HARDINGE delivers her able lecture on "Politics in the Pulpit" this evening, at Dodworth Hall. To test the lady's ability, any questions the audience desire to ask will be answered.

MAN DROWNED.—On the morning of the 13th instant a journeyman housepainter, whose name is believed to be Barnard Burns, was accidentally drowned at Gunther-ville, Long Island. His body has not yet been found ... by his friends. Mr. J. B. Acker, of No. 9 Macdougal street, will give facilities to any one who can identify the corpse.

1871

Chicago had become a city built of wood by 1871. Even the sidewalks were of pine.

A dry season during the summer had made the city a virtual tinderbox by October 8, when fire devastated an area three and a half miles square. It killed some 300 people, left almost 100,000 people homeless, and consumed more than 17,000 buildings. Property damage was estimated at $200 million.

How it all started has never really been determined, although tradition has it that Mrs. O'Leary's cow knocked over a lamp. There's no evidence to support the theory, but it was determined that the fire started in the barn of Patrick O'Leary.

The year 1871 was also the year that the Suez Canal opened. Verdi composed the opera *Aida* to celebrate the event.

And President Ulysses S. Grant appointed the first Civil Service Commission.

THE CHICAGO TRIBUNE.

VOLUME 25. WEDNESDAY, OCTOBER 11, 1871. NUMBER 66.

FIRE!

Destruction of Chicago!

2,600 Acres of Buildings Destroyed.

Eighty Thousand People Burned Out.

All the Hotels, Banks, Public Buildings, Newspaper Offices and Great Business Blocks Swept Away.

Over a Hundred Dead Bodies Recovered from the Debris.

Tens of Thousands of Citizens Without Home, Food, Fuel or Clothing.

Eighteen Thousand Buildings Destroyed.

Incendiaries and Ruffians Shot and Hanged by Citizens.

Fatalities by Fire, Suffocation, and Crushed by Falling Walls.

Relief Arriving from Other Cities Hourly.

Organization of a Local Relief Committee.

List of Names of Over Two Hundred Missing Men, Women, and Children.

The City Without Light or Water.

Crosby's and Hooley's Opera Houses, McVicker's and the Dearborn Theatres, Wood's Museum, and all the Art Galleries in Ashes.

During Sunday night, Monday, and Tuesday, this city has been swept by a conflagration which has no parallel in the annals of history, for the quantity of property destroyed, and the utter and almost irremediable ruin which it wrought. A fire in a barn on the West Side was the insignificant cause of a conflagration which has swept out of existence hundreds of millions of property, has reduced to poverty thousands who, the day before, were in a state of opulence, has covered the prairies, now swept by the cold southwest wind, with thousands of homeless unfortunates, which has stripped 2,600 acres of buildings, which has destroyed public improvements that it has taken years of patient labor to build up, and which has set back for years the progress of the city, diminished her population, and crushed her resources. But to a blow, no matter how terrible, Chicago will not succumb. Late as it is in the season, general as the ruin is, the spirit of her citizens has not given way, and before the smoke has cleared away, and the ruins are cold, they are beginning to plan for the future. Though so many have been deprived of homes and sustenance, aid in money and provisions is flowing in from all quarters, and much of the present distress will be alleviated before another day has gone by.

It is at this moment impossible to give a full account of the losses by the fire, or to state the number of fatal accidents which have occurred. So much confusion prevails, and people are so widely scattered, that we are unable for a day to give absolutely accurate information concerning them. We have, however, given a full account of the fire, from the time of its beginning, reserving for a future day a detailed statement of losses. We would be exceedingly obliged if all persons having any knowledge of accidents, or the names of persons who died during the fire, would report them at this office. We also hope that all will leave with, or at No. 15 South Canal street, a memorandum of their losses and their insurance, giving the names of the companies.

THE WEST SIDE.

At 9:30 a small cow-barn attached to a house on the corner of DeKoven and Jefferson streets, one block north of Twelfth street, emitted a bright light, followed by a blaze, and in a moment the building was hopelessly on fire. Before any aid could be extended the fire had communicated to a number of adjoining sheds, barns and dwellings, and was rapidly carried north and east, despite the efforts of the firemen. The fire seemed to leap over the engines, and commenced far beyond them, and, working to the east and west, either surrounded the apparatus or compelled it to move away. In less than ten minutes the fire embraced the area between Jefferson and Clinton for two blocks north, and rapidly pushed eastward to Canal street.

When the fire first engulphed the two blocks, and the efforts of the undaunted engineers became palpably abortive to quench a single building, an effort was made to head it off from the north, but so great was the area that it already covered at 10:30 o'clock, and so rapidly did it march forward, that by the time the engines were at work the flames were ahead of them, and again they moved on north. From the west side of Jefferson street, as far as the eye could reach, in an easterly direction—and that space was bounded by the river—a perfect sea of leaping flames covered the ground. The wind increased in fierceness as the flames rose, and the flames wailed more hungrily for their prey as the angry gusts impelled them onward. Successively the wooden buildings on Taylor, Forquer, Ewing, and Polk streets became the northern boundary, and then fell back to the second place. Meanwhile, the people in the more southern localities bent all their energies to the recovery of such property as they could. With ample time to move all that was movable, and with a foreboding of what was coming, in their neighborhood, at least, they were out and in safety long before the flames reached their dwellings. They were nearly all poor people, the savings of whose lifetime were represented in the little mass of furniture which blocked the streets, and impeded the firemen. They were principally laborers, most of them Germans or Scandinavians. Though the gaunt phantom of starvation and homelessness, for the night, at least, passed over them, it was singular to observe the cheerfulness, not to say merriment, that prevailed. Though mothers hugged their little ones to their breasts and shivered with alarm, yet, strange to say, they talked freely and laughed as if realizing the utter uselessness of expressing more dolefully their consciousness of ruin. There were many owners of the buildings who gave themselves up to the consolation of insurance. But even that appeared to weaken as the flames spread, and they gave themselves up to their fate. Many of the victims were stowed away in the houses on the west [illegible]

THE FIRE AS SEEN FROM THE WINDWARD.

[illegible]

THE GREAT CONFLAGRATION.

THE SOUTH SIDE—THE BEGINNING.

[illegible]

RIGHT AND LEFT

[illegible]

ACROSS WELLS STREET.

[illegible]

NORTHWARD AND EASTWARD

[illegible]

LEAPED THE RIVER.

[illegible]

FASTER THAN IT COULD BE TRACED.

[illegible]

A PERFECT WHIRLPOOL.

[illegible]

WABASH AVENUE AND STATE STREET.

[illegible]

THE HOPE OF THE FIREMEN.

[illegible]

SOUTH SIDE STRUCTURES.

[illegible]

FROM THE TRIBUNE BUILDING.

[illegible]

GREAT LOSS OF LIFE—HORRIBLE OCCURRENCE.

[illegible]

AT CHICAGO AVENUE.

[illegible]

SURROUNDED BY THE FLAMES AND STIFLED BY THE SMOKE.

[illegible]

FIFTEEN MEN WERE LOST

[illegible]

SCENES ON WABASH AVENUE.

[illegible]

ESCAPE OF PEOPLE INTO THE WEST DIVISION.

[illegible]

THE ROADS WERE FILLED WITH PEOPLE.

[illegible]

NORTH DIVISION.

[illegible]

LATE ON MONDAY EVENING

[illegible]

BETWEEN TWO DEATHS.

[illegible]

THE FIRE REACHED THE WATER WORKS

[illegible]

TILL IT REACHED WRIGHT'S GROVE.

[illegible]

WHAT REMAINS.

[illegible]

WHAT WAS DESTROYED.

[illegible]

WHAT IS LEFT.

[illegible]

IN THE NORTH DIVISION

[illegible]

ON THE WEST SIDE.

[illegible]

INCENDIARIES KILLED.

[illegible]

FATAL INCIDENTS.

DEARBORN STREET.

[illegible]

SIX MEN LOST.

[illegible]

FIVE MEN CRUSHED.

[illegible]

A WOMAN PERISHES.

[illegible]

BODY FOUND.

[illegible]

LIST OF MISSING.

[illegible]

ITEMS IN GENERAL.

[illegible]

1881

President Garfield, who had been inaugurated on March 4, was shot on July 2 while he was waiting for a train in Washington, D.C., on his way to Williams College in Massachusetts.

Garfield held on through the summer, but died on September 19, 1881.

Chester A. Arthur became President.

The assassin, Charles J. Guiteau, who was caught on the spot, was tried and hanged in 1882. It was said that he blamed Garfield for his not getting a job with the new administration.

The Indianapolis News.

VOL. XII—NO. 179. WHOLE NO. 3,600.

INDIANAPOLIS, SATURDAY EVENING, JULY 2, 1881.

{PRICE, TWO CENTS. SIX DOLLARS PER YEAR.

The Assassination.

Since the killing of Lincoln nothing has so convulsed the nation as the announcement that President Garfield had been shot. Horror was dumb. There arose to every lip expressions of blind and bitter fury against every element that had antagonised this man who was the people's choice, and the nation's head. Under the terrible strain of a realization of the awful deed, immediate motive was less reckoned than ultimate consequences.

Either is far ahead of the needs of the hour. For the present there is the awful fact of this splendid man, in the high-noon of life, equipped by natural gifts and attainments as few who preceded him have been; the honored occupant of the highest earthly station; one moment in the fullness of his powers, the next in the throes and agonies of death, it may be. The mind flashes back to the martyred president. He had cast aside the cares of state, and for the moment in the mimic show of the stage had immunity from the burden he bore. Then from behind crept the assassin and in a flash Lincoln had left all earthly concern.

Garfield too had left behind him the burden of his great office. He was just setting forth to the scenes of his young manhood, where he had toiled and striven to become what he was. Pleasant farewells were upon his lips and in his heart. Then came the assassin from behind, and this noble manhood is a writhing form in the dust!

Alas for the aged mother! Alas for the stricken wife! Alas for this nation!

What does it mean? What is the assassin's awful boast? He puts in words the cruel comment that sprang to thousands of lips. He gives to his awful crime not the vulgar tint that colors so many attempts at the life of a nation's chief—the crazy freak of lunacy, the outgiving of bitter personal disappointment—but the triumph of a hostile force in the administration of affairs. Mexicanisation! "I am a Stalwart and Arthur is president now." These are the lying words of a dastardly villian. So far as they are calculated to have any further significance they should be stamped out; and the same thought spoken should be recalled, and the unspoken thought given no tongue. The deadly hate of this assassin's personal disappointments and revenge would naturally find refuge in the antagonism that has met the president, and seek to have its bloody stain there.

There is no time now for a nation to sit in judgment on this crime; but only time for prayer that an all-wise God may give back to this people that life which trembles in the balance.

"God Reigns."

LONG BRANCH, July 2.—So far the only particulars of the shooting of the president received here are from the following dispatch:

EXECUTIVE MANSION, WASHINGTON, D. C., July 2.

General Swaim, Elberon, N. J.:

We have the president safely and quietly settled in his room at executive mansion and his strong and [illegible]. So far as I can determine from what the surgeons say and from general condition I feel very hopeful. Come as soon as you can get a special. Advise of the movement of your train when you can be expected. As the [illegible] said on a similar occasion sixteen years ago, "God reigns and the government at Washington still lives."

[Signed.] A. F. ROCKWELL.

An Official Account.

WASHINGTON, July 2.—The following has been forwarded by cable:

DEPARTMENT OF STATE, Washington, July 2.

James Russell Lowell, Minister, etc., London:

The president of the United States was shot this morning by an assassin named Charles Guiteau. The weapon was a large sized revolver. The president had just reached the Baltimore and Potomac station at about 20 minutes past nine, intending, with a portion of his cabinet, to leave on the limited express for New York. I rode in the carriage with him from the executive mansion, and was walking by his side when he was shot. The assassin was immediately arrested, and the president was conveyed to a private room in the station building, and surgical aid at once summoned. He has now, at about 10 minutes past 10, been removed to executive mansion. The surgeons in consultation regard his wound, very serious, though not necessarily fatal. His vigorous health gives strong hopes of his recovery. He has not lost consciousness for a moment. Inform our ministers in Europe.

[Signed.] JAMES G. BLAINE, Sec'y of State.

The Medical Bulletin.

The following latest official bulletin with regard to the condition of the president, has just been issued:

Executive Mansion, 12:25 p. m.: The reaction from the shock of the injury has been very gradual. He is suffering some pain, but it is thought best not to disturb him by making any exploration for the ball until after a [illegible] at 3 [illegible]. D. W. BLISS, M. D.

THE DOCTORS.

The following physicians are in consultation at the executive mansion: Drs. Bliss, Ford, Huntingdon, Woodward, U. S. A., Townsend, Lincoln, Reyburn, Norris, Purvis, Patterson, Surgeon General Barnes, and Surgeon General Wales.

The Stock Market Reacts.

NEW YORK, July 2.—The news down town was received with consternation and caused much excitement on Wall street. Brokers and bankers forgot their business, in eagerness to get further particulars. They besieged Kiernan's news agency on Broad street where dispatches from Washington were constantly arriving and being distributed. Groups were seen in the streets anxiously discussing the subject and news boys did a heavy business in extras. At the opening of the stock exchange the news depressed the market, but further dispatches announcing the wounded president was in a fair way to recover and was not so dangerously wounded as first reported, caused a reaction.

News by Telegraph.

12:15 P. M.

MURDER MOST FOUL.

Attempted Assassination of President Garfield, this Morning.

As He was About to Start to Long Branch.

The Assassin Gives His Name as Charles Guitteau, of Chicago.

And Said: "I am a Stalwart, Arthur is Now President."

The President was Removed to the White House Immediately.

First Dispatch.

WASHINGTON, July 2.—President Garfield was shot in the depot, while on his way to Long Branch, this morning.

Second Dispatch.

WASHINGTON, July 2.—It is reported that President Garfield is dead, but the excitement is so intense that it is impossible to find out anything definite at present. The man who shot him has been arrested. Full particulars will be sent shortly.

Third Dispatch.

WASHINGTON, July 2.—President Garfield was shot this morning, at the depot; said to be killed; probably true. Particulars as soon as we can get them. Dr. Bliss says the president's wound is not a mortal one.

Fourth Dispatch.

WASHINGTON, July 2.—President Garfield is now lying in a private room in the officers quarters of the Baltimore and Potomac depot. Doctor Bliss, Surgeon-general Barnes and Dr. Purvis (colored) are in attendance. The shooting was done by a slender man about 5 feet 7 inches in height. He refused to give his name, but it is said by persons who profess to know him that his name is Doty. The prisoner was arrested immediately after the firing by officers in the depot. He was first taken to the police headquarters and subsequently removed to the district jail.

The shooting occurred in the ladies' room of the depot, immediately after the president had entered walking arm in arm with Secretary Blaine, on their way to the limited express train, which was about ready to leave. Secretary Blaine, on hearing the pistol shots, two in number, rushed in the direction from which they came with a view of arresting the would be assassin. Before reaching the man however, the secretary returned to the president and found him prostrated. Both shots took effect, the first in the right arm, and the second just above the right hip and near the kidney The physicians have probed for the ball unsuccessfully.

10:20 a. m.—The president is now being conveyed to the executive mansion under a strong escort of metropolitan police. Two companies of regulars from the Washington barracks have been ordered out to preserve quiet. Great excitement prevails, and the streets are thronged with anxious inquirers eager to learn the condition of the president. The shooting occurred in the presence of some fifty or sixty ladies. There is a rumor now that the shooting was done by the ex-consul to Marseilles, Gatto, who was removed from office. The pistol with which the firing was done is a California weapon, with an extremely heavy calibre, better known as a "bull dozer."

Fifth Dispatch.

WASHINGTON, July 2.—The president has been made as comfortable as possible in his chamber at the White house, and all persons are excluded from the grounds surrounding the mansion. Immense crowds surround the grounds. The physicians attending the president are now holding a consultation. Various rumors are afloat; one is that the president is dangerously, and another that he has been mortally wounded.

Sixth Dispatch.

"I AM A STALWART."

WASHINGTON, July 2.—At 9:30 o'clock this morning, when the president was at the Baltimore and Potomac depot with his party, waiting to take the train, he was shot twice by a man standing within two feet of him. The president's friends rushed to him as he fell, and Blaine called for Colonel Rockwell. Station Agent Carney arrested the assassin, who said, "I did it. I am a stalwart, and Arthur is now president. Take a letter I have here to General Sherman, and he will tell you all about it." The president's wounds are now said to not be mortal.

Seventh Dispatch.

VERY LITTLE HOPE FELT.

WASHINGTON, July 2.—The president was shot twice, one ball entered from the rear to one side and is believed to have passed through the kidneys. The doctors hold out some hope of possible recovery, but its plain that they feel but little if any hope. One shot went through the arm. The president talked to a newspaper man, said he felt pretty strong, considering his wounds, but complained of a tingling sensation in his feet, as annoying him more than anything else. The man who shot him wrote his name on a card as Charles Gitteau, attorney at law of Chicago.

Washington is wild with excitement and the whole populace is gathered about the Baltimore and Potomac depot. The man evidently had deliberately planned the assassination with the idea, so far as can now be ascertained of making Arthur president.

Eighth Dispatch.

THE PRESIDENT CONSCIOUS.

WASHINGTON, July 2, 11:05 a. m.—President Garfield is conscious and does not complain of great suffering. He has just dictated a telegram to his wife. It is impossible to say as yet, what the result will be, but the surgeons are of the opinion that the wounds are not necessarily fatal. The following telegram has been sent:

Mrs. Garfield, Elberon, Long Branch:

The president wishes me to say to you, from him, that he has been seriously hurt. How seriously he can not yet say. He is himself and hopes you will come to him soon. He sends his love to you.

[Signed] A. F. ROCKWELL.

Ninth Dispatch.

WASHINGTON, July 2.—The name of the assassin, as written by himself, is Charles Gitteau, and he says that he is an attorney at law in Chicago. The Star says in an extra, just issued, that when the assassin was arrested he said, "I did it and want to be arrested. I am a stalwart and Arthur is president now. I have a letter here that I want you to give to General Sherman. It will explain everything. Take me to the police station."

Tenth Dispatch.

WASHINGTON, July 2.—It is utterly impossible to gain access to the White House, the police and soldiers being all around it, and they will not let any one but cabinet officers in. There is communication by telegraph which is the only way to reach them.

Eleventh Dispatch.

WASHINGTON, July 2.—Dr. Bliss, in attendance upon the president, says his wounds are probably not fatal.

Twelfth Dispatch.

HIS CONDITION IMPROVING.

WASHINGTON, 11:30.—The condition of the president is very much improved. Immediately after the shooting his pulse went down to 58 and his face, as he was removed to the White House, was of an ashen hue. His pulse has now recovered to 68, and the color is returning somewhat to his face. His general symptoms moreover denote a very considerable improvement. It is not thought wise to make any further attempts at present to withdraw the bullet, and it is difficult to determine until a thorough examination is made how serious the internal injuries may be. Surface indications however give good ground for hoping that the president will rally.

Thirteenth Dispatch.

WHO THE ASSASSIN IS.

Charles Gitteau, the would-be assassin, is a foreigner by birth, has been a very persistent applicant for a consular position. He has haunted the executive mansion for several weeks, and his disappointment in not getting what he wanted led to a temporary aberration of mind.

Fourteenth Dispatch.

WASHINGTON, 11:35.—President Garfield's strength is increasing every minute, and he is quite cheerful. The physicians announce that as soon as his pulse reaches 70 another attempt will be made to probe for the ball.

Fifteenth Dispatch.

President Garfield continues to improve.

THE RECEPTION OF THE NEWS.

Intense Excitement Aroused All Over the Country.

Excitement in the City.

It took, apparently, but an instant for the news to get about the city. The first report was scarcely credited, but the speedy confirmation caused the greatest excitement. Large crowds quickly packed around bulletin boards of the newspaper and telegraph offices. Wherever any intelligence was displayed the sidewalks were impassable, and masses surged out into the streets. As in all events of similar import the telegraph could not bring the news fast enough. In the beginning, speculations as to the motive of the then unknown assassin were rife. "Must have been a star route man," "Wonder if it was a stalwart?" "Of course he was insane," "Nihilist scheme," and a thousand expressions of this sort could be heard on every hand, showing the readiness of the general mind to put things together. The opinion seemed to rapidly crystallize that the assassin was certainly insane for no reasonable motive could be assigned, and when the bulletin came that such was the case it was received as though it was a matter of course. When the further news floated over the wires that the man had been caught, it was unanimously declared on all sides that he should have been lynched on the spot. "There is only one remedy for president-killing," said one man, "and that is to torture the murderers to death." The most temperate expression was in favor of instant hanging to the nearest lamp post. The excitement was intense all the while, but for the most part subdued, the feeling of vengeance being subordinated to the general anxiety for the president's life. The bulletins which reported the wounds as not necessarily fatal did nothing to allay apprehension. Occasionally in the crowds some thing could be heard as to the president's accession and the effect upon the Albany dead-lock. During the entire morning from the first intelligence as to the shooting, business was suspended almost entirely. A rush was made upon Benj'n Harrison, Postmaster Wildman, Congressman Peelle and others for news, it being thought they might have received private telegrams. The court house was almost instantly deserted. Merchants, lawyers, clerks, ladies, children and people of every grade and condition blocked the news centers and hung about the bulletin boards, oblivious of everything, except the impending calamity. Democrats republicans and members of all parties joined in denunciation of the assassin, and the vengeful sentiments of the one were not more emphatic than those of the others.

The Stock Market.

NEW YORK, July 2, 11 A. M.—Stocks opened generally firm, but a free selling movement was soon inaugurated, and the entire list broke rapidly, the decline ranging from 1 to 5½ per cent. The sudden decline was due to the announcement of the shooting of the president, and when the excitement had subsided somewhat there was a rally of ½ to 2½ per cent,

SECOND EDITION.

2:00 P. M.

BUSINESS ALMOST SUSPENDED.

Mrs. Garfield Almost Frantic—Her Return to Washington.

BULLETIN, 1:20 p. m.—Executive mansion. The president is somewhat restless but is suffering less pain, pulse 112, some nausea and vomiting has recently occurred, considerable hemorrhage has taken place from the wound. D. W. BLISS, M. D.

Gen. Grant Sympathetic.

LONG BRANCH, July 2.—General Grant has just arrived and expressed deep regret at the attempted assassination of the president.

GOD HELP HER.

Mrs. Garfield is almost frantic over the news. Her physicians allow her to see none of the serious dispatches, but dictate hopeful ones to her.

A dispatch to General Grant has relieved Mrs. Garfield's anxiety. It says, "The president's wounds not mortal. Shot in arm and hip." Mrs. Garfield will depart on the special train for Washington, at 1 o'clock. She is now much composed. Dr. Bliss has just telegraphed that the wounds are not necessarily mortal.

THE ASSASSIN SECURELY HELD.

WASHINGTON, June 2.—The district jail at the eastern extremity of the city was visited by an associated press reporter after eleven o'clock, for the purpose of obtaining an interview with Charles Guitteau, the would-be assassin of President Garfield. The officers refused admittance to the building, stating as a reason therefor that they were acting under instructions received from the attorney general, the purport of which were that no one should be allowed to see the president. At first, indeed, the officers emphatically denied that the man had been conveyed to the jail, fearing, it appears, that should the fact be made known that he was there, the building would be attacked by a mob. Information had reached them that such a movement was contemplated. A large guard, composed of regulars from the barracks and metropolitan police force, are momentarily expected to arrive at the jail to be in readiness to repel any attack. The statement that the assassin is Guitteau, was verified by the officer in charge of the jail. The prisoner arrived and was placed in a cell about 10:30 o'clock, just one hour after the shooting occurred. He gave his name is Charles Guitteau, of Chicago, Ills. In appearance he is a man about thirty years of age and is supposed to be of French descent. His height is about five feet five inches.

Guitteau's Antecedents.

CHICAGO, July 2.—Charles Guitteau, the man who attempted the assassination of the president, has been more or less known in Chicago for the past ten years. He was a disreputable lawyer, and has generally been considered half insane. He went to New York seven or eight years ago, and upon his return in 1876 professed to have been converted, and delivered several lectures under the auspices of the Y. M. C. A. He next appeared at the head of a scheme to buy the Chicago Inter-Ocean, and run it on the plan of the New York Herald, but as he had neither capital nor backing, the scheme was soon dropped by him. He left for Washington several months ago.

He has a sandy complexion, is slight, weighing not over 125 pounds. He wears mustache and slight chin whiskers, and his sunken cheeks and eyes far apart from each other give him a sullen, or as an official describes it, a "looney" appearance. The officer in question gave it as his opinion that Guitteau is a Chicago communist, and states that he has noticed it to be a peculiarity of all murderers that their eyes are set far apart and Guitteau has, he said, proved no exception to the rule. When the prisoner arrived at the jail he was attired in a suit of blue and wore a drab hat pulled down over his eyes, which gave him the appearance of an ugly character. It may be worthy of note to state that some two or three weeks ago Guitteau went to the jail for the purpose of visiting it but was refused admittance on the ground that it was not visitors day. He at that time mentioned his name as Guitteau and said he came from Chicago. When brought to the jail to-day he was admitted by the officer who had previously refused to allow him to enter, and mutual recognition took place, Guitteau saying, "You are the man who would not let me go through the jail some time ago." The only other remark he made before being placed in his cell was that General Sherman would arrive at the jail soon. The two jailors who are now guarding his cell state they have seen him around the jail several times recently, and that on one occasion he appeared to be under the influence of liquor. On one of his visits, subsequent to the first one mentioned, these officers say that Guitteau succeeded in reaching the rotunda of the building, when he was noticed examining the scaffold from which the Hirth murderers were hanged. Pursuant to his orders from the attorney general the officer in charge of the jail declined to give any further information nor would he state in what cell the prisoner was confined. This officer was an attendant at the old city jail at the time of the assassination of President Lincoln.

Arthur Informed.

NEW YORK, July 2.—Vice President Arthur and Mr. Conkling arrived from Albany this morning. The boat was late, not arriving until about 10 o'clock. As soon as she touched the wharf a telegram was handed Mr. Arthur. Upon reading it he dropped back in his chair greatly shocked. It is presumed the telegram announced the shooting of President Garfield.

THIRD EDITION.

3:30 P. M.

A Detailed Account of the Assassination.

The Assassin Prepared Both to Escape and to Get Protection from the Mob.

The Character and Severity of the Wound to be Found by Probing.

Little Hope of His Recovery.

BULLETIN.

WASHINGTON, July 2, 2:20 p. m.—The president's symptoms at this time are more unfavorable. It is thought there is an internal hemorrhage.

2:30 p. m.—The president's symptoms continue to grow more unfavorable.

No Hope of Recovery.

WASHINGTON, July 2, 2:40 p. m.—Dr. Beckwith, an old physician of the president says President Garfield has but few chances of recovery and that he may not live twelve hours. The general expression at the executive mansion is that the president is sinking.

2:45 p. m.—No official bulletin has been furnished by Dr. Bliss since 1 o'clock. The condition of the president has been growing more unfavorable since that time. Internal hemorrhage is taking place, and the gravest fears are felt as to the result.

Death Very Near.

WASHINGTON, July 2, 3 p. m.—Hon. Samuel Shellabarger, who has just left the bedside of the president, says that there seems to be absolutely no hope of his rallying. His symptoms are growing more and more alarming, and his death is thought to be very near.

Another Detailed Account.

WASHINGTON, D. C., July 2.—The president had alighted from his carriage, and was passing through the ladies' rooms to the cars. When five feet inside of the room the assassin, who was within three feet of him, fired one shot. The president was dazed, and made no attempt toward self protection. As the assassin turned towards one door [illegible] a second shot. In the seconds the president fell, and Mrs. White, who attends the ladies' waiting room, rushed to him and raised up his head. Mr. Blaine also rushed to the assistance of the president.

The assassin passed out towards B street but Captain Parke, ticket agent, jumped through the window and caught the assassin, who made no resistance. Officer Carney, a depot policeman, rushed up and took hold of the assassin, and immediately after Officer Scott also took hold of him. Parke let the officers have him, and turned his attention to the president. Help came, and the president was taken upstairs. He said not a word until he was laid down when he asked that his wife be taken off, saying he felt pain in his feet. As soon as his shoes were removed he said to Secretary Windom: "Go, right now, and send a telegram to Mrs. Garfield, saying, 'I feel considerably better, and if she feels well enough, tell her to come to Washington immediately.'"

The dispatch was sent and a special train was at once sent to Long Branch for Mrs. Garfield. Secretary Blaine was not going with the party, but went down to bid the president good bye. He said: "The president and I were walking arm in arm toward the train. I heard two shots and saw a man run. I started after him, but seeing that he was grabbed just after he got out of the room, I came to the president and found him lying on the floor. The floor was covered with the president's blood. A number of people, who were around shortly afterwards, have some of that blood on their person. I think I know the man. I think his name is Ditton."

The assassin is about five feet seven inches in height, of strong, though not stout build. The weapon he used was a revolver about seven inches long; it had an ivory handle. The calibre was very large. It is what is known as a California pistol; it made a very loud report. Parke says both shots were fired while the assassin was behind the president. When officers Scott and Carney got hold of the assassin, and were taking him to police headquarters, he said voluntarily to them, "I did it and will go to jail for it—I am a stalwart, and Arthur will be president."

He had a letter in his hand and wanted the officers to take it to General Sherman, saying it would be all right. The prisoner made no resistance saying he had contemplated the killing of the president and it was for the good of the country. About nine o'clock the assassin went to a hack-stand adjoining the depot and engaged a hack from Barton, a colored hackman. He said he wanted to go to Glenwood cemetery in a short time, and wanted the hackman to drive very fast when he should get in the hack. He agreed to pay two dollars for the hack on condition that the hackman would drive fast. When stopped, the assassin was going toward the hack he had engaged, and he insisted it was important for him to go and deliver a message to General Sherman. When the officers refused to let him go, he begged them to take the letter he had to General Sherman.

Dr. Townshend, health officer, was the first to reach the president. The president was shot from the right, as he entered the ladies' reception room of the depot with Secretary Blaine. The ball entered above the third rib, but whether it has taken its course toward the spine has not yet been ascertained. The wound was probed by Dr. Bliss, who reports that, in inserting the probe, the course of the ball did not extend toward the spine, still it is not certain that it did not. It was the unanimous opinion of the physicians that what was needed for the president was not the probing of the wound but rest. The extent of danger from the wound is not yet known, and more can be told when urine passes, as the kidneys are injured.

The Assassin's Letter.

The following letter was taken from the assassin's pocket at police headquarters:

JULY 2, 1881.

To the White House—The president's tragic death was a sad necessity, but it will unite the republican party and save the republic. Life is a flimsy dream, and it matters little when one goes it up. A human life is small value. During the war thousands of brave boys went down without a tear. I presume the president was a Christian, and that he will be happier in paradise than here. It will be no worse for Mrs. Garfield, dear soul, to part with her husband this way than by natural death. He is liable to go any time any way. I had no ill will toward the president. His death was a political necessity. I am a lawyer, a theologian and a politician, and I am a stalwart of the stalwarts. I was with Gen. Grant and the rest of our men in New York during the canvass. I have some papers for the which I shall leave with Byron Andrews and his co-journalists at 1420 New York avenue where all the reporters can see them. I am going to the jail.

CHARLES GUITTEAU.

The papers referred to above have not yet been given out for publication. Byron Andrews who is the Washington correspondent of the Chicago Inter-Ocean says that while it is true a package of papers are in the hands of the police accompanied by a note addressed to himself (Andrews), he has no personal acquaintance with Guitteau, and never heard of his existence until this morning.

The Letter to Sherman.

The following letter was found on the street shortly after Guitteau's arrest with the envelope unsealed and addressed: "Please deliver at once to General Sherman or his first assistant in charge of the war department."

"To General Sherman, I have just shot the president. I shot him several times as I wished him to go as easily as possible. His death was a political necessity. I am a lawyer, theologian and politician. I am a stalwart of the stalwarts. I was with General Grant and the rest of our men in New York during the canvass. I am going to jail, please order out your troops and take possession of the jail at once.

[Signed] Very respectfully

CHARLES GUITTEAU.

On receiving the above, General Sherman gave it the following indorsement:

"Headquarters of the army, Washington, July 2, 1881, 11:35 a. m.—This letter was handed me this minute by Major Wm. J. Twining, U. S. engineers the commissioners of the District of Columbia, and Major Wm. G. Brock, chief of police. I don't know the writer, never heard of or saw him to my knowledge, and hereby return it to the keeping of the above named parties as testimony in the case.

W. T. SHERMAN, General.

FOURTH EDITION.

4.45 P. M.

The President Sinking Rapidly.

All Accounts of His Condition Unfavorable.

Some Further Particulars About Guitteau.

Four O'clock Bulletin.

EXECUTIVE MANSION, 4 p. m.—The following official bulletin has just been issued:

4 p. m.—The president's condition is somewhat less favorable, evidences of internal hemorrhage being distinctly recognised. Pulse, 130; temperature 96. That is a little below the normal state. He suffers a little more pain, but his mind is perfectly clear. D. W. BLISS, M. D.

Guitteau at Chicago.

CHICAGO, July 2.—There are many recollections of Charles J. Guitteau, which is his right name, who lived here several years, and acquired an unenviable reputation. He was at one time on the point of marriage with an estimable young lady on the south side, but his character became known just in time to prevent such a calamity to the lady and her family. Guitteau left town immediately after this for some months.

One gentleman remarked, "I remember Charles Guitteau well; he was here two or three years ago and seemed to have no visible means of support. He preached or lectured on religious and social subjects, upon which he was an enthusiast. He started in here as a lawyer, but failed utterly, and then tried to lift himself into notoriety by lecturing on religion one evening in each week. His card in the newspapers is produced to-day and is a literary curiosity. He bored the newspapers by trying to get his manuscript printed. He failed also as a lecturer and then began life as a tramp of the more respectable order. He was branded by the hotel keepers' association as a "dead beat." In appearance he is an American of French extraction, 35 to 40 years old, of medium hight, slender build, fair complexioned, brown hair, French shaped moustache and beard, tinged with gray. His whole appearance was that of a dandified man of small mental caliber. He was unusually fond of notoriety and would go to almost any length to get his name in a paper. He was arrested here once for embezzlement. He got the idea in his head that he was fit for an official position, and has been trying with all his power to get a consulate at Marseilles.

At Milwaukee.

MILWAUKEE, WIS., July 2.—The assassin of Garfield was a former resident of this city, where he practiced law. His name, as inscribed upon his old sign, is Charles J. Guiteau. He had an office at 295 Broadway, and claimed ten years' practice in New York and Chicago. Interviews with Judge Mallory and Harold Emmonds, Esq., both of whom knew Guitteau well, established the fact that he was generally considered by the few who formed his acquaintance as either a vicious person, or else one who was insane. He was very erratic in his business, talk and general relations. Among other things, he wrote a book upon "Morals." The excitement here is simply awful, exceeding anything since the death of Lincoln. The entire populace is absolutely wild. Thoughtless persons charge the crime to political jealousy, etc., and loudly denounce Conkling and Arthur while discussing the sad event.

Mrs. Garfield Knows All.

LONG BRANCH, July 2.—Gen. Swaim, Mrs. Garfield, Mrs. Rockwell and Miss Mollie Garfield left here on a special car at 12:47 p. m. Mrs. Garfield knows all and is standing it bravely.

Conkling Utters a Prayer.

NEW YORK, July 2.—A reporter called at the Fifth avenue hotel this morning, about an hour after the receipt of the dispatch, and sent his card to the rooms of Vice-President Arthur and ex-Senator Conkling. Word was immediately returned that the president's assassination was too serious to be talked of on the moment and neither would be seen under any circumstances. The reporter saw Conkling in the hall way near his room a few minutes after, and when asked his opinion of the shooting begged to be excused: "The news has found me so unprepared and overwhelmed with personal cares that it almost staggers me. May God grant it may not be true. It is the most terrible incident in our history since the death of Lincoln. If it is true then may heaven help us." Mr. Conkling turned away and went to his room.

One Surgeon's Report.

WASHINGTON, July 2.—Dr. Townshend, health officer of the district, in a conversation this afternoon said: "I found the president, when I arrived at the Baltimore and Potomac depot about five minutes after the shooting occurred, in a vomiting and fainting condition. I had his head lowered, which had been elevated by an attendant, and administered aromatic spirits of ammonia and brandy to revive him. This had the desired effect, and the president regaining consciousness, was asked where he felt most pain. He replied, in the right leg and foot. The doctor then examined the wound. Introduced his fingers, which caused a slight hemorrhage, I then decided to have him moved up-stairs from the crowd. After getting him there Drs. Smith and Purvis arrived, and upon consultation with them it was decided to remove him to the White house. Dr. Smith and myself accompanied the president, in the ambulance, to the White house, where another examination was made, and stimulants again administered. An ineffectual attempt was made to trace the course of the wound, and at 12:30, the president suffering much pain, a hypodermic injection of morphia was administered.

Dr. Townshend left the president shortly afterward somewhat revived. The doctor said at two p. m. that he could not give an intelligent opinion as yet, but pronounces the wound as dangerous.

Blaine to Arthur.

WASHINGTON, July 2.—The following dispatch has just telegraphed:

WASHINGTON, July 2.

"Hon. C. A. Arthur, vice president, New York: At this hour (1 p. m.) the president's symptoms are not regarded as unfavorable, but no definite assurance can be given until after the probing of the wound at 3 o'clock. There are strong grounds for hope, and at the same time gravest anxiety as to the final result.

[Signed.] JAMES G. BLAINE, Secretary of State.

Second Dispatch.

WASHINGTON, July 2.—The following telegram has just been sent from the executive mansion:

HON. CHESTER A. ARTHUR, Vice President, New York City:

At this hour (3:30) the symptoms of the president are not favorable. Anxiety deeper.

JAMES G. BLAINE, Secretary of State.

Mrs. Garfield's Arrival.

PHILADELPHIA, July 2.—Mrs. Garfield left Long Branch at 1:24 in a special train. She will arrive at Washington about 7 p. m.

A Private Dispatch.

WASHINGTON, July 2.—The president is seriously wounded; is now sleeping from the effects of opiates. Further probing for the ball this afternoon.

H. C. CORBIN, Ass't Adj't. General.

Public Sentiment.

From every section of the country came reports of the almost total cessation of business, the universal sorrow, the outspoken horror and the fierce threats of vengeance with which the assassination of the president has been received. In many cities, especially cities throughout the south, the mayor has called for meetings of citizens to action.

Mrs. Garfield's Movements.

PHILADELPHIA, July 3.—The Pennsylvania railroad has ordered a locomotive and car, at Jersey City, to carry Mrs. Garfield to Washington. She had arranged to meet her husband at Jersey City to-day, and left Long Branch this morning on the Central road for Jersey City. The message informing her of the attempted assassination is awaiting her arrival at the latter place. There is much excitement here.

Uncertainty About the Wound.

WASHINGTON, July 2.—An effort has been made to probe for the ball, but without reaching it. Another attempt will be made, and until the direction taken by the ball is known the extent of the injuries and immediate danger can not at present be known. There are no signs of serious internal hemorrhage and very little external bleeding. A consultation of the most eminent surgeons of the city will be called at 3 p. m. The doctors at this hour hope for the best.

FIFTH EDITION.

6.00 P. M.

No Great Change Noticeable.

The Doctors Have but Faint Hopes.

His Mind is Unclouded and He Talks Freely.

5 O'clock Bulletin.

WASHINGTON, July 2—5 P. M.—The president is a little easier and says he suffers rather less pain just now. His mind continues unclouded and he converses freely with those around his bedside.

The Latest.

WASHINGTON, EXECUTIVE MANSION, July 5:20 p. m.—Dr. Bliss says the president is resting more comfortably, but his condition is very critical. Mrs. Garfield is expected to arrive about 5:45 p. m.

WASHINGTON, EXECUTIVE MANSION, July 2, 5:45 p. m.—President is now sleeping quietly. He dropped asleep about 15 minutes ago. A telegram was just received at the executive mansion from the superintendent of the B. & P. railway, stating that a special train, with Mrs. Garfield on board, left Baltimore at 5:23 and will arrive here about 6:10 p. m. A gentleman from the sick room, said the president's son James was crying, and that when the president noticed it he said: "Jimmie, don't cry; the head is still all right but the trouble is elsewhere."

Not Much Hope Felt.

WASHINGTON, July 2.—While the doctors hold out hopes of his recovery the truth is they feel very doubtful, and the candid opinion of most of them is that the chances are against the president. The best they say is that it is possible for the ball to have entered where it did and to have missed all vital organs.

Another Medical Guess.

WASHINGTON, July 2.—Dr. Lincoln denies the report telegraphed from here, that he said the president would not live two hours. Dr. Lincoln said just now that the surgeons could not yet tell whether the wound is fatal or not. He said the ball was a very large one, that it entered about three inches from the spinal column and at the lower edge of the ribs, that it may have struck vital organs and may have entered the cavity of the abdomen. He is afraid it entered the cavity, but says the ball may have taken such a course as not to injure any vital organ.

Might Have Shot Blaine.

WASHINGTON, July 2.—Benson, ex-chief of the secret service, who happened to be standing near, heard the shots and rushed to the assassin, and just as he was about to raise his pistol with three chambers still loaded, to shoot Secretary Blaine it is thought, throttled him and threw him to the ground.

Guitteau's Life in Washington.

WASHINGTON, July 2.—Charles Guitteau, the assassin of the president, is a Canadian-Frenchman by birth, and hails from Chicago. He came here in the month of February, with recommendations from various parties in Illinois, to secure the United States consulship to Marseilles, France. He went in March to the well known boarding house of Mrs. Lockwood, formerly Mrs. Rines, 810 Twelfth street, and tried to secure board. Mrs. Lockwood didn't like his appearance, and gave him an out-of-the-way room in the house, in hopes of getting rid of him. He pretended to know General Logan and others then boarding there. Mrs. Lockwood states he acted strangely at times, and about the middle of the month, when she presented his bill, he could not pay it. He afterwards left the house and sent Mrs. Lockwood a note, saying he was expecting a $6,000 position and would soon pay his bill. Mrs. Lockwood showed this note to General Logan, who said the man was crazy. Three weeks ago he met Mrs. Ricksford, of Mrs. Lockwood's boarding house, on the street and requested her not to say anything about the bill he owed, as it would hurt him in his efforts to secure a position. Mrs. Lockwood says that Guitteau was a great bother to General Logan, so persistent was he in his efforts to secure that gentleman's services in his behalf. Since leaving Mrs. Lockwood's house he has been stopping at various places but never at a great length of time, for the reason that he appeared to have no funds. He told one of the boarders at Mrs. Lockwoods, that he expected to be appointed minister to France, but did not desire it to be known. Up to day before yesterday when he registered at the Riggs house, Guitteau has been stopping for the last six weeks with no baggage but a paper box at 920 Fourteenth street.

What Arthur Said.

NEW YORK, July 2.—Gen. Arthur and Senator Conkling, who arrived in town this morning from Albany, put up at the Fifth avenue hotel. The vice-president was found in the lobby of the hotel. He said he had not received any private dispatch in regard to the shooting, and knew nothing more than was announced on the bulletin boards. If it were true, he said he felt exceedingly sorry for Mrs. Garfield whose present state of health is precarious. Senator Conkling remained in his room.

A PLOT SUSPECTED.

Guitteau Not a Lunatic, But a Scheming Scoundrel.

WASHINGTON, July 2.—There is a theory which has many adherents that the attempted assassination was not the work of a lunatic, but the result of a plot much deeper and darker than has been suspected. It is cited in support of this theory, that Guitteau arranged before hand with a hackman to be in readiness to drive swiftly in the direction of the Congressional cemetary as he made his appearance on return from the depot. In the meantime he had a bundle of papers in the hands of a boy, with a view, it is maintained, to creating a belief in his insanity in case of his capture. Guitteau said on his way to jail that the president's assassination was premeditated, and he went to Long Branch with the purpose of shooting him there, and was deterred by the enfeebled and saddened condition of Mrs. Garfield, which appealed so strongly to his sense of humanity that he came back without carrying out his intention. Those by whom Guitteau has been examined since the shooting, says he shows no symptoms of insanity, and it is understood that the letter which has already been telegraphed to "The White House" is the only document in the collection which supports the theory of insanity. It is reported that Guitteau had accomplices whose descriptions are in the hands of the police and further developments are anxiously looked for.

The Feeling Here.

The apprehension of the morning had given way in a measure, owing to the more or less assuring telegrams about noon, that the president would recover, and people returned to business and their usual routine. The crowds about the bulletin boards gradually diminished, although there was no other topic than the assassination discussed in offices, stores or on the streets. At this hour, (3:30) however, the telegrams announcing the desperate condition of the president have started the excitement anew and with additional intensity, and expressions are of deeper sympathy and louder for immediate vengeance. Many can not be convinced but that the assassination is the result of a conspiracy, and the terrible calamity of the president's death, which seems to impend is bringing out feelings of the deepest grief and working the temper of every one to the highest point. There has been no organized effort to give expression to the general sentiment of distress, but the utmost anxiety prevails.

At five o'clock nothing is doing in the city. Owing to the doubt that exists as to the recovery of the president, neither the mayor or governor have sent any dispatches expressive of the sentiment of the city or state. The instant there should be a decided change for the better, or in the event of death official and immediate expression of the sentiment of the people will be given by them.

Arthur Should Resign.

To the Editor of The Indianapolis News.

The assassination of the president is the result of Grantism. The vice president is in a measure responsible, from the fact that he has so far prostituted the dignity of the office he holds by going to Albany to play the part of a pothouse politician in behalf of the avowed enemies of his superior, the president, etc. An indignation meeting should be called, and Arthur should be asked for the sake of the dignity of the nation and the honor of the republican party, to resign as vice president of the United States. O.

1892

Grover Cleveland and Adlai Stevenson were elected President and Vice-President on the Democratic ticket.

This was Cleveland's second term, having previously served from 1885 to 1889, before losing out to Benjamin Harrison, even though he won a plurality of the popular vote.

When Cleveland became the first President to take office for a second, but nonconsecutive, term, the nation faced economic disaster. The bankruptcy of overexpanded railroads combined with low farm prices and a depression in Europe that had cut the sales of American products abroad.

That same year, strikers at the Carnegie steel plant in Homestead, Pennsylvania, protesting pay cuts and demanding union recognition, killed ten Pinkerton detectives who were hired by management to break the strike. The state militia was called in to restore order.

The Morganton Herald.

VOL. VIII. MORGANTON, N. C., THURSDAY, JUNE 23, 1892. NO. 15.

CLEVELAND!

The Greatest of Democrats Again Our Leader.

Grover Cleveland Nominated on the First Ballot, Notwithstanding the Two-Thirds Rule.

At 4.40 o'clock this [Thursday] morning the Democratic Convention at Chicago, after an exciting all night session, nominated Grover Cleveland for the Presidency on the first ballot.

GROVER CLEVELAND, OUR NEXT PRESIDENT.

There were 910 votes in the convention, and the two-thirds rule prevailing, 608 were necessary to a choice.

The result of the first and only ballot was:

CLEVELAND	616½,
HILL	112,
BOIES	103,
GORMAN	36½.

The remainder of the votes were scattered among six or eight different candidates.

Everything points to the nomination of Governor Gray, of Indiana, for the Vice-Presidency this afternoon, although A. E. Stephenson. Governor Horace Boies and others have been prominently mentioned in connection with the nomination.

Full telegraphic reports of the convention appear in to-day's HERALD.

CHICAGO CONVENTION.

Summary of the Press Bulletins from the Democratic Wigwam.

CHICAGO, June 21.

Early papers nearly all agree and the impression prevails among delegates that Cleveland will be nominated without serious opposition.

WILLIAM C. WHITNEY, Leader of the Cleveland Forces at Chicago.

It is now thought that Gray, of Indiana, will be chosen Vice-President. Convention will probably conclude its labors to-morrow, or Thursday at latest.

CHICAGO, 10.20 a. m.

Report current that both Gray and Gorman have withdrawn, and Cleveland's nomination on first ballot is assured.

CONVENTION HALL, 12.30 p. m.

The delegates are slowly assembling. A heavy rain storm has started. The wigwam leaks, and the people in the galleries have to raise umbrellas. Prominent Democrats are being cheered as they enter the hall. It is remarked at this hour that the opponents of Cleveland are trying to form a combination on Gorman and Boies, but so far without success.

12.46 p. m.—The storm is over.

CONVENTION HALL, 12.19 p. m.

The convention has been called to order by National Chairman, Senator Calvin S. Brice, who is now reading call for convention and announcing names of temporary officers. Owens, of Kentucky,

CALVIN S. BRICE, Chairman National Democratic Committee.

Henry Watterson's candidate, is announced as temporary chairman.

CHICAGO, June 21, 1.15 p. m.

It is understood that Wilson, of West Virginia, will be permanent chairman. Governor Abbett, of New Jersey, will present Cleveland's name. Cochran or Fellows will probably present Hill's name. Breckenridge, of Kentucky, will

DON DICKINSON.

probably present the name of Senator Carlisle, but if Carlisle's name should not be presented he will second the nomination of Cleveland. The platform is practically agreed on now. The Syracuse or "anti-snap" delegates, will not contest for seats in the convention, feeling assured of Cleveland's nomination. It is

GOVERNOR GRAY. Who may be Vice-President.

claimed that they have made this decision at the solicitation of Whitney, Don Dickinson, Ex-Secretary Bayard and Mr. Vilas. They will issue a formal statement saying that they have waived their claims in the interest of Democratic harmony.

CONVENTION HALL, 12:56 p. m.

Temporary chairman Owens has been well received. He says in his speech that unity and harmony are the only things neccesary for success. Rule six, governing last convention, has been adopted.

1.09 p. m.—The roll of States is being called for members of the various committees.

1:53 p. m.—Resolutions extending sympathy to James G. Blaine were greeted with great cheering and passed unanimously.

1:56 p. m.—The convention adjourned until 11 o'clock to-morow.

Wednesday's Bulletins.

CHICAGO, June 22, 11:40 a. m.

Cleveland men are confident this morning of 626 votes on first ballot, and will push for ballot today, leaving nomination of vice-president for to-morrow. It is said that Adlai E. Stephenson, of

DAVID B. HILL.

Illinois, is likely to be chosen Vice-President instead of Gray, of Indiana. A Chicago morning paper says a combination has been formed to beat Cleveland.

11.42 a. m.—Banners emblazoned with portraits of leading Democrats just brought in. Cheering all over the hall. Report of committee on credentials called for, and committee of two appointed to wait on committee and find out when it will be ready to report. There are continued calls for Senator Mills, of Texas, from all over the Hall, delegates on their feet cheering. A committee escorts Mills to the platform, but he is too ill to address the convention, and is compelled to leave the hall and return to his hotel. The delegates and the galleries are determined to have a speech, and there are loud calls for Palmer, of Illinois. A motion requesting him to address the convention is carried, and Palmar takes the platform. There is general cheering. Palmer makes a strong appeal for party harmony, which he declares is essential to success. He is frequently interrupted by applause. He says the Democracy has good

HORACE BOIES.

men to choose from. There are loud cries for Hill, mingled with hisses. Palmer predicts a great Democratic victory this fall on both Presidential and State tickets. He concludes his remarks amid great cheering.

12:09 p. m. There are calls for District Attorney Fellows, of New York, but he replies that he is a delegate, and that the time has not yet arrived when in would be proper to address the convention. The committee on credentials makes its report, which is unanimously adopted, and the report of the committee on permanent organization is called for: The report is read, making Hon. W. L. Wilson, of West Va., permanent chairman. A heavy rain storm comes on, and bands play while it clears up, as hall is dark. There is great cheering when the band plays "Dixie."

12:16 p. m. The report of the committee on permanent organization is adopted, and a committee of five is appointed to notify Wilson of his selection as permanent chairman.

12:25 p. m.—Committee escorting Hon. W. L. Wilson, permanent chairman, to the platform amidst the greatest cheering. Wilson takes the platform. Great demonstrations in galleries and among the delegates.

WILSON'S ELOQUENT SPEECH.

12.32 p. m.—Wilson says: "Much as we owe to the Democratic party, we owe more to this grand country of ours. Democrats should see to it that legislation is not in the interest of any class or section, but for the good of the whole people" He bitterly denounced the McKinley tariff bill and the force bill which the Republicans are endeavoring to incorporate into the legislation of the country. Most important of all measures demanding the attention of the people, he says, is taxation and tariff reform, and the record showed that the regulation of these matters could be safely entrusted to the Democratic party. He declares that the McKinley bill and the reciprocity scheme were two of the greatest absurdities of the age. He makes an eloquent appeal for harmony in the convention and in the party, no matter who shall be chosen by this convention to lead the Democracy in the ensuing campaign. His speech is concluded amidst the geatest cheering.

UNIT RULE ADOPTED.

12.47 p. m.—The New York delegation has just announced that they have determined not to op-

RICHARD CROKER, Chieftain of Tammany Hall

pose unit rule, and will therefore not present minority report of committee on rules opposing it. The report of the committee on rules is adopted making unit rule prevail in the convention.

12.59 p. m.—Roll of States is ordered called for naming members of national committee and committee to notify candidates. Convention decides to dispense with call of roll of states, but states are requested to send up names to Secretary. The convention is waiting for report of committee on platform.

CALLING FOR FAVORITES.

1.08 p. m.—There are loud calls for Carlisle to address the convention, but he does not seem to be in the hall. A committee appointed to look for him reports that he is not in the hall. There are calls for Senator Voorhees, but no response.

1.15 p. m.—Convention still waits for report of committee on platform. Governor Campbell, of Ohio, is requested to address the convention. The band plays "The Campbell's are Coming," while the delegates cheer.

1:18 p. m. Governor Campbell takes the platform and returns thanks to the convention for the compliment of asking him to make a speech. He asks Democrats to keep their eyes on Ohio next November. Upon the conclusion of Governor Campbell's remarks there are calls for Hensel, of Pennsylvania, Governor Bob Taylor, of Tennessee, editor Watterson, of Kentucky, and Bourke Cochran, of New York. Cochran is asked to address the convention amidst great cheering. He declines to take the platform but remarks that he expects to have business with it later on.

1:45 p. m. Convention takes recess until five o'clock to give committee on platform time to report.

EVENING SESSION.

CONVENTOIN HALL, 5.35 p. m.

Delegates coming in slowly Anti-Cleveland men claim 330 votes, and say they will concentrate on a candidate after first ballot. There is great cheering as Boies banner is brought in. Many delegates are on their feet. Convention has been called to order, and while waiting for report of committee on platform time is filled in with music.

5:56 p. m. Motion to adjourn until to-morrow lost. At this New York delegation rise and cheer. An Ohio man says that it is probable that State will vote solidly for Brice on first ballot Cleveland men in Ohio delegation refuse to join in Brice movement. Brice says if the vote is cast for an Ohio man it must go to Gov Campbell.

PLATFORM.

6.18 p. m.—Chairman Jones, of platform committee, takes stand to read report, and asks Senator Vilas to read resolutions. Patterson, of Colorado, announces that there will be a minority report on silver plank. This occasions great excitement. Minority report demands free silver.

CHEERS FOR CLEVELAND.

6.30 p. m.—Vilas mentions Cleveland. This calls forth great demonstrations. Many delegations on their feet, cheering, waving

GOVERNOR CAMPBELL.

hats, handkerchiefs and banners. A picture of Cleveland is carried around hall, and there is tremendous cheering. Iowa men bring in Boies banner and place it beside Cleveland's. Cheering for Cleveland breaks out afresh, and continues unabated for nineteen minutes. The demonstration equals any ever seen in a national convention.

6.58 p. m.—Order restored and Vilas continues reading platform. Platform denounces force bill and pledges the party to defeat it, to keep down government expenses and to reduce taxation. Endorses the action of the present congress in attempting to modify most objectional features of McKinley bill, and declares that since the adoption of that measure there have been ten reductions of wages to one advance. It declares reciprocity a sham. It asks for coinage of both gold and silver without discrimination; and that both gold and silver coin shall be equal, in value in payment of debts.

MINORITY TARIFF REPORT ADOPTED.

7.22—Col. Jones moved adoption of platform as read. Neal of Ohio objects, and asks for substitution of a tariff plank practically that of 1876 for majority report on tariff. His substitute declares that the government has no power to collect taxes except for purposes of revenue only, and demands that taxation be limited to the actual necessities of the government. The minority report is warmly advocated by Neal of Ohio. Watterson of Kentucky takes platform and pleads eloquently for minority report Vilas speaks for majority report. There is great confusion and much cheering and hissing, but upon a call of the States minority report is adopted by a vote of 564 to 342.

9:15 p. m. Patterson, of Colorado, takes platform to move the adoption of minority report on silver platform. The substitute advocates free coinage of both gold and silver, the unit to be of equal intrinsic and exchangable value. Speaker is frequently interrupted. Patterson's motion lost, and platform with amended tariff plank adopted.

Nominations Begin.

9:20 p. m. Roll of States called for presentation of candidates. It is now thought ballot will be reached to-night. Gov. Abbet, of New Jersey, takes platform to present Cleveland's name. At the mention of Cleveland's name there is great cheering throughout the hall. Half the delegates are on their feet. Michigan banner, with Cleveland's portrait carried

GOVERNOR ABBETT.

to New York delegation and is angrily pushed aside by delegates. Much confusion, cheering and demonstration for Cleveland still continues.

Abbett says Cleveland will receive support of every democrat in the land [cries of "no" and hisses.] I repeat, of every Democrat, says Abbett," and in addition thousands of independent voters." Abbett is making a strong appeal and is being listened to with marked attention. Mention of Pattison and Boies creates cheering. When Hill's name is mentioned there is great applause. New York and other delegates on their feet cheering and waving hats and handkerchiefs. Demonstration has now been kept up for fifteen minutes, and seems as strong as ever. Portraits of Hill are being carried around the hall, and part of the galleries join in demonstration. Abbett resumes his speech after an interruption lasting 20 minutes.

THE THUNDERSTORM.

10.21 p. m.—A heavy thunderstorm is raging, and the wigwam is leaking badly. Speaker has had to leave his desk which is drenched with water. Delegates and spectators drenched with rain. The call of states proceeds amidst the greatest confusion.

10.42 p. m.—Dewitt, of New York, takes platform to nominate Hill. Motion that galleries be cleared if confusion is continued carried. Rain still falling in torrents in many parts of hall. Fellows of New York seconds Hills nomination after applause subsides.

11:37 p. m. Green, of Illinois and English, of Indiana, second nomination of Cleveland.

11:45 p. m. Duncomb, of Iowa, takes platform to nominate Boies. There are great demonstrations all over hall at mention of Boies' name, New York delegation taking prominent part. Fulton, of Kansas, seconds Boies, as does also Watterson of Kentucky. Stephenson, of Kentucky, seconds Cleveland, and keeps convention in a roar of laughter. Hensel, of Pennsylvania, seconds Cleveland, Senator Daniels, of Virginia, seconds Hill. Motion to adjourn lost. Goode, of Virginia, seconds Cleveland. Bourke Cochran, of New York, seconds Hill and denounces mugwumps. He said Cleveland was a popular man every day in the year except on election day. Cochran made a powerful speech and was greeted with prolonged cheers.

Thursday, June 23.

2 46 a. m.—Roll of states called for first baliot amidst the greatest excitement. Motion to adjourn voted down. Great cheering throughout the hall.

The following is the result of the first ballot, which was concluded at 3.37 a. m. [4.37 a. m. by Morganton time.

THE BALLOT.

	Votes.	Cleveland.	Hill.	Boies.	Gorman.	Stephenson.
Alabama,	22	14	2	1		
Arkansas,	16	16				
California,	18	18				
Colorado,	8		3	5		
Connecticut,	12	12				
Delaware,	6	6				
Florida,	8	5				
Georgia,	26	17	5		4	
Idaho,	6			6		
Illinois,	48	48				
Indiana,	30	30				
Iowa,	26			26		
Kansas,	20	20				
Kentucky,	26	18		2		
Louisiana,	16	3	1	11	1	
Maine,	12	9	1		1	
Maryland,	16	16				
Massachusetts,	30	24	4	1		
Michigan,	28	28				
Minnesota,	18	18				
Mississippi,	18	8	3	3	4	
Missouri,	34	34				
Montana,	6			6		
Nebraska,	16	15			1	
Nevada,	6			4	2	
New Hampshire,	8	8				
New Jersey,	20	20				
New York,	72		72			
North Carolina,	22	3½		2		16
North Dakota,	6	6				
Ohio,	46	14	6	16	5	
Oregon,	8	2		6		
Pennsylvania,	64	64				
Rhode Island,	8	8				
South Carolina,	18	8			10	
South Dakota,	8	8				
Tennessee,	24	24				
Texas,	30	30				
Vermont,	8	8				
Virginia,	24	12	11		1	
Washington,	8	8				
West Virginia,	12	11	1			
Wisconsin,	24	24				
Wyoming,	6	3			3	
Arizona,	6	5				
New Mexico,	6	4		2		
Oklahoma,	2	2				
Utah,	2	2				
Dist. of Columbia,	2	2				
Alaska,	2	2				
Indian Territory,	2	2				
Totals,	910	616½	112	103	36½	16

Necessary to a choice, 608

Scattering—Secretary Morrison 5, Carlisle 15, Campbell 2, Pattison 1, Whitney 1, Russell 1.

3.44 a. m —There is great confusion and cheering in hall over result. Ohio moves to suspend the rules and make the nomination of Cleveland unanimous. Daneil, of Virginia and Flower, of New York, second the motion which is carried unanimously.

3 48 a. m. Thursday June 23. The convention adjourns until 2 o'clock p. m.

NORTH CAROLINA'S VOTE.

Most of Her Delegates for Adlai E. Stephenson.

Special to The Morganton Herald.

CHICAGO, June 22, 5.10 p. m.

Convention organized with Hon. W. L. Wilson, of West Virginia chairman. We are now awaiting report of committee on platform. It looks like Cleveland and Gray on first ballot. It is the field organized against Cleveland. The only chance for the opposition to succeed is to get as many complimentary votes as possible on first ballot for "favorite sons" so as to prevent Cleveland from getting the necessary two-thirds on the first roll-call. North Carolina will vote on first ballot 3½ for Cleveland, 1 for Hill, 1 for Morrison, and 16½ for ex-Assistant Postmaster General Adlai E. Stephenson. W. W. SCOTT.

TAMMANY SUBMITS.

The Editor of the Lenoir Topic Gives the Herald the News.

Special to Morganton Herald.

CHICAGO, ILL., June 23, 9 a. m.

Cleveland was nominated at 4.30 this morning. He had 615 votes on first ballot, and before the result was announced the rules were suspended and the nomination made by acclamation. Tammany cowed submissively. SCOTT.

The Herald.

Successor to "The Morganton Star."

HERALD PUBLISHING CO., Publishers.

W. C. ERVIN, - - EDITOR.

SUBSCRIPTION PRICE, - - $1.00

THURSDAY, JUNE 23, 1892.

DEMOCRATIC NATIONAL CONVENTIONS.

Since the memorable Democratic Convention in Charleston in 1860, which resulted in a party split, and that small gathering of the Northern Democrats in Chicago in 1864, which nominated McClellan and Pendleton and declare the war a failure, six conventions of the party have been held, exclusive of the one now in session at Chicago. Of these one met in New York City, one in Baltimore, two in St. Louis, one in Cincinnati and one in Chicago.

In the convention of 1868, which was held in New York City, delegates from the Southern States were admitted for the first time since 1860. The Western Democrats, under the leadership of the brilliant editor McLean, wanted George H. Pendleton, and the Eastern men, under the guidance of Samuel J. Tilman scattered their votes between Andrew Johnson, Sanford E. Church and General Hancock, the Tilden wing, it is alleged, intending at the proper time to spring the name of Chief Justice Chase on the convention and secure his nomination. The fight between the Tilden and McLean forces was one of the most skillful ever exhibited in a national convention. After many ballots the Ohio delegation, at McLean's suggestion, sprung the name of Horatio Seymour of New York on the convention, and stampeded it into nominating him. Frank P. Blair, of Missouri, was named for Vice-President. The Republicans nominated Grant and Colfax, who in the succeeding election received 214 electoral votes to 80 for Seymour and Blair.

In 1872 a split in the Republican party led to the call for a convention at Cincinnati of what was called a convention of "Liberal Republicans." In this convention that brilliant journalist, Carl Schurz, and the then young ambitious Hungarian, Joseph Pultizer, who has since made the New York *World* the greatest of newspapers, were prominent figures. David Dudley Field, Col. McClure, of the Philadelphia *Times*, David A. Wells, the great apostle of free trade, Theodore Tilton, Edward Atkinson, Stanley Mathews, and many other brilliant men, took part in that strange gathering of discordant elements. Horace Greeley was named by this convention for President and Gratz Brown for Vice-President. The regular Democratic convention which met in Baltimore two months later formally nominated the same ticket named at Cincinnati in May and inconsistently adopted the platform which that body had promulgated. As might have been expected, the opposition ticket carried almost every State, Grant receiving 296 electoral votes out of a total of 356.

In 1876 the Democratic National Convention assembled in St. Louis on June 28th. Samuel J. Tilden, the man who had overthrown the rule of the old Tammany chieftain, Tweed, and with "reform" as his platform had been elected Governor of New York, was nominated for the Presidency with only one formal ballot, and the great Western leader, Thomas A. Hendricks, of Indiana, was named for Vice-President. How this splendid ticket swept the country, and how by the fraudulent and extra constitutional "Electoral Commission" the will of the people was defied and Hayes and Wheeler placed in the seats to which Tilden and Hendricks had been elected are matters of history.

When on June 22nd, 1880, the Democratic convention met in Cincinnati it was conceded that the only thing for the convention to do was to renominate Tilden, and appeal to the country to right the wrong and shame of 1876. Unfortunately for the party, Tilden, who had not entered politics until more than sixty years of age, had written a letter declining, on account of ill health, to accept a renomination. This letter was entrusted to the keeping of William C. Whitney, subsequently secretary of the Navy under Mr. Cleveland's administration, and this week the leader of the Cleveland forces at Chicago. Notwithstanding the letter of declination there was a strong feeling that Tilden should be nominated anyway, and subsequent events proved that this would have been the course of wisdom. The outcome of the convention was the nomination of General W. S. Hancock for President and W. H. English for Vice-President. The election resulted in 214 electoral votes being cast for Garfield and Arthur to 155 for Hancock and English. New York, in this as in many other elections the pivotal state, was carried for Garfield by a very narrow margin.

In 1884 the Democrats, with the lesson of 1880 fresh in their minds, went to the convention, which assembled in Chicago on the 23rd of June, with the determination to nominate a candidate who could assuredly carry New York. Two years before Grover Cleveland, whose record as mayor of Buffalo, had been endeared him to all who knew him, had been nominated for the Governorship of New York, and had gone in on the tidal wave of 190,000 majority. Democrats all over the country had turned their attention to the popular New Yorker as the man to lead the party to victory. At Chicago, however, the enthusiastic Westerners, who were urging the nomination of Thomas A. Hendricks, crowded the galleries of the convention hall with Hendricks shouters, and when the voting commenced it looked like there would be a stampede to Indiana's "favorite son." The Cleveland forces were badly rattled, and had it not been for the coolness of their leader, Daniel Manning, one of Mr. Tilden's most apt pupils in political science, it is likely that the Hendricks men would have carried the day with a storm. When New York was called, Mr. Manning who headed that delegation, cool and unperturbed rose in his seat and said: "Mr. Chairman, the New York delegation instructs me to cast its united vote for Grover Cleveland." This calm, measured utterance, with the significance of the united vote of the great pivotal state which it expressed, hushed the Hendricks enthusiasts and turned the tide to Mr. Cleveland, who, with Hendricks as his running mate, carried New York and secured 219 electoral votes to 182 cast for Blaine and Logan.

The Democratic Convention which met in St. Louis on June 20, 1888, renominated Mr. Cleveland by acclamation and gave the Vice-Presidential nomination to Judge Allen G. Thurman, of Ohio, in place of the lamented Hendricks, who had died within a year after his election. The vote of New York again decided the contest, and being recorded against the Democrats, they were defeated by Harrison and Morton.

ON the application of certain capitalists owning the bulk of Richmond & Danville securities, that big corporation was put into the hands of receivers last week by Judge Bond, of the U. S. District Court. It is needless to say that the appointment of receivers for this great corporation, so intimately connected with the material interests of the South, created a considerable sensation all over the magnificent territory pierced by its lines. But to those who have been watching the condition of that road and its various leased and controlled lines the receivership occasioned no surprise. For the good of the South it is to be hoped that the road will be speedily reorganized and placed on a sound financial footing. Heavy investments in non paying branch roads has been one fruitful cause of the bad financial condition of the system, so it is said.

EX-SECRETARY James G. Blaine has been tried hurt of late. Following close upon the death of his daughter, Mrs. Coppinger and his son Walker and the matrimonial troubles of his son James G. Blaine, Jr., came the ruin of his political fortunes at Minneapolis. Now, when he has barely had time to realize how great was his overthrow by the Republican party, comes the sudden death of his favorite son, Emmons Blaine, which occurred at Chicago last Saturday. The Democratic convention at Chicago did a graceful thing in tendering to the stricken statesman the sympathy of the party.

THE HERALD again rises to remark that it does not get left on the news. We venture to predict that no weekly paper and very few of the daily papers in the South will give the news of the Chicago convention to their readers sooner than THE HERALD.

GROVER, Frances and little Ruth form a combination that will win.

1898

The U.S. battleship *Maine* had been sent to Cuba by President McKinley to protect American lives and property after a series of anti-U.S. riots in that Spanish-held island.

On the night of February 15, 1898, two explosions ripped the ship apart as she rode at anchor in Havana harbor. She went to the bottom with 266 men aboard.

Although no one satisfactorily established the cause of the explosion, some American newspapers—like the New York *Journal*—made it appear that the Spanish government was indirectly responsible. The *World* was somewhat more cautious.

Large headlines and dramatic illustrations such as this front page of the *World* on February 17 became common in some big-city newspapers. The *World* devoted its first three pages daily to the story.

Whether it was the rebels, or the Spanish, or a spontaneous explosion that sank the *Maine*, President McKinley asked Congress on April 11 for "forcible intervention," and two weeks later the Spanish-American War began.

$50,000 REWARD.—WHO DESTROYED THE MAINE?—$50,000 REWARD.

The Journal will give $50,000 for information, furnished to it exclusively, that will convict the person or persons who sank the Maine.

NEW YORK JOURNAL

AND ADVERTISER. FIRST EDITION.

The Journal will give $50,000 for information, furnished to it exclusively, that will convict the person or persons who sank the Maine.

NO. 5,572. Copyright 1898 by W. R. Hearst.—NEW YORK, THURSDAY, FEBRUARY 17, 1898.—16 PAGES. PRICE ONE CENT

DESTRUCTION OF THE WAR SHIP MAINE WAS THE WORK OF AN ENEMY

$50,000!

$50,000 REWARD! For the Detection of the Perpetrator of the Maine Outrage!

The New York Journal hereby offers a reward of $50,000 CASH for information FURNISHED TO IT EXCLUSIVELY, [illegible]

The $50,000 CASH [illegible]

[illegible] FOR THE PERPETRATOR OF THIS OUTRAGE HAD ACCOMPLICES.

W. R. HEARST.

Assistant Secretary Roosevelt Convinced the Explosion of the War Ship Was Not an Accident.

The Journal Offers $50,000 Reward for the Conviction of the Criminals Who Sent 258 American Sailors to Their Death. Naval Officers Unanimous That the Ship Was Destroyed on Purpose.

$50,000!

$50,000 REWARD! For the Detection of the Perpetrator of the Maine Outrage!

The New York Journal hereby offers a reward of $50,000 CASH for information FURNISHED TO IT EXCLUSIVELY, which shall lead to the detection and conviction of the person, persons or government criminally responsible for the explosion which resulted in the destruction at Havana of the United States war ship Maine and the loss of 258 lives of American sailors.

The $50,000 CASH offered for the above information is on deposit with Wells Fargo & Co. and will be paid upon the production of the convicting evidence.

[illegible]

This offer has been cabled to Europe and will be made public in every capital of the Continent and in London this morning.

The Journal believes that any man who can be bought to murder can also be bought to betray his comrades. FOR THE PERPETRATOR OF THIS OUTRAGE HAD ACCOMPLICES.

W. R. HEARST.

NAVAL OFFICERS THINK THE MAINE WAS DESTROYED BY A SPANISH MINE.

George Eugene Bryson, the Journal's special correspondent at Havana, cables that it is the secret opinion of many Spaniards in the Cuban capital that the Maine was destroyed and 258 of her men killed by means of a submarine mine, or fixed torpedo. This is the opinion of several American naval authorities. The Spaniards, it is believed, arranged to have the Maine anchored over one of the harbor mines. Wires connected the mine with a powder magazine, and it is thought the explosion was caused by sending an electric current through the wire. If this can be proven, the brutal nature of the Spaniards will be shown by the fact that they waited to spring the mine until after all the men had retired for the night. The Maltese cross in the picture shows where the mine may have been fired.

Hidden Mine or a Sunken Torpedo Believed to Have Been the Weapon Used Against the American Man-of-War---Officers and Men Tell Thrilling Stories of Being Blown Into the Air Amid a Mass of Shattered Steel and Exploding Shells---Survivors Brought to Key West Scout the Idea of Accident---Spanish Officials Protest Too Much---Our Cabinet Orders a Searching Inquiry---Journal Sends Divers to Havana to Report Upon the Condition of the Wreck. Was the Vessel Anchored Over a Mine?

Assistant Secretary of the Navy Theodore Roosevelt says he is convinced that the destruction of the Maine in Havana Harbor was not an accident.

The Journal offers a reward of $50,000 for exclusive evidence that will convict the person, persons or Government criminally responsible for the destruction of the American battleship and the death of 258 of its crew.

The suspicion that the Maine was deliberately blown up grows stronger every hour. Not a single fact to the contrary has been produced.

Captain Sigsbee, of the Maine, and Consul-General Lee both urge that public opinion be suspended until they have completed their investigation. They are taking the course of tactful men who are convinced that there has been treachery.

Spanish Government officials are pressing forward all sorts of explanations of how it could have been an accident. The facts show that there was a report before the ship exploded, and that, had her magazine exploded, she would have sunk immediately.

Every naval expert in Washington says that if the Maine's magazine had exploded the whole vessel would have been blown to atoms.

1900

It was a new century.

President McKinley was reelected; Theodore Roosevelt was his Vice-President.

U.S. forces helped relieve Peking during the Boxer Rebellion.

Hawaii was made a territory of the United States.

Carrie Nation, a temperance advocate, denounced liquor and supported prohibition laws.

A cyclone with winds up to 120 mph drove the waters of the Gulf of Mexico over the land, killing some six thousand people at Galveston, Texas. Property damage was later estimated at $20 million.

The lure of gold brought prospectors to Alaska and the Yukon.

MAILABLE EDITION. TWELVE PAGES.

HOUSTON DAILY POST.

XVITH YEAR—NO. 161. HOUSTON, TEXAS, WEDNESDAY, SEPTEMBER 12, 1900. PRICE: 5 CENTS

5000 IS NOW ESTIMATED

Mayor Jones Issues a Statement to the People of the United States.

SETS FORTH IN FEW WORDS THE AWFUL CONDITIONS EXISTING AT GALVESTON.

Many Bodies Are Still In the Ruins of the Brick Buildings; Others Have Been Burned, and Still Others Buried at Sea---Twenty-Five Men Were Shot By Soldiers Last Monday Night.

To the People of the United States.

Galveston, Texas, September 11.—It is my opinion, based on personal information, that 5000 people have lost their lives here. Approximately one-third of the residence portion of the city has been swept away. There are several thousand people who are homeless and destitute; how many, there is no way of finding out. Arrangements are now being made to have the women and children sent to Houston and other places, but the means of transportation are limited. Thousands are still to be cared for here. We appeal to you for immediate aid.

WALTER C. JONES, Mayor.

Galveston, Texas, September 11.—(Noon, via La Porte, by Long Distance 'Phone.)--Mayor Walter C. Jones estimates the number of dead at 5000, and he is conservative. Hundreds are yet to be taken from the ruins; these bodies are all badly decomposed now, and they are being buried in trenches where they are found. Others are being burned in the debris where this can be done safely. Others are in the mass of wreckage and are taken to sea on the barges. There is little attempt at identification, and it is safe to say that there will never be a complete list of the dead, or of the living, for there are many missing, some of whom are dead and some alive.

Chief of Police Ed Ketchum is in charge of the work of burying the dead. There are large bodies of men engaged in this work. They are tearing the ruins up and getting out the dead.

Some of those whose bodies are being taken out were probably only injured when they were first struck down, but there was no way of getting relief to them and they perished miserably.

Mayor Jones is in supreme control here now. The correspondent asked him for a statement, which is given elsewhere.

The remnant of the force of regular soldiers who were stationed here—and it is a small remnant—have joined the police in patrolling the city. Several persons have already been shot, it is reported. A soldier of Captain Rafferty's battery while patrolling the beach this morning ordered a man to desist from looting; the fellow drew a weapon and was shot dead. The soldier was attacked by four other men and he killed all of them. He had five cartridges in his rifle and each of them found a billet.

Other men have also been shot but the details are not known, nor can the exact number be ascertained, probably twenty-five. Some of these were shot for failing to halt when ordered to do so; others for vandalism.

The ruins of the heavier brick buildings have not yet been searched for the dead and there are a large number there. In the mass of rubbish which marks the site of the Lucus Terrace boarding house forty to fifty people were killed outright, and their bodies are still in the ruins.

The orphan home on the beach is totally demolished; ninety-two children and eleven nuns were killed there; it is rumored that one sister escaped, but if she did no trace can be found of her.

Of the regular soldiers few remain. Twenty-three were drowned at the barracks at Camp Hawley and seven at Bolivar. One man drifted in the bay until Monday morning and was taken out alive. There are many narrow escapes told of, but this was probably the closest call.

The correspondent stood at the foot of Tremont street and counted nine floating bodies without moving, and this is only an instance. It is not known whether these were water front victims or whether they are the dead being cast up by the repellant sea. A lot of rubbish was being loaded on barges and this stuff had many bodies in it.

C. ARTHUR WILLIAMS.

A GENERAL REVIEW OF THE CALAMITY AND ITS RESULTS.

General McKibbin, commander of the department of Texas, came over from San Antonio and passed through Houston yesterday morning on his way to Galveston, accompanied by his aide, Lieutenant Perry. He was joined by Adjutant General Scurry, who had ordered out the Houston troops, as the situation in Galveston had become critical and it was necessary that while the civil authorities attended to one part of the business a strong military arm was needed to hold in check the lawless element.

General McKibbin was requested to take control of the Galveston, Houston and Henderson road and prevent any persons going down to Galveston—pass or no pass—but declined to do so, and then the Galveston, Houston and Henderson refused to run any more trains to Galveston.

On one of the relief trains a number of volunteers went down, but when the train reached it destination they refused to assist in either burying the dead, caring for the injured, handling provisions or moving skiffs. This is what led the Galveston, Houston and Henderson management to request the government to take charge of the road and allow no person to go down to Galveston.

General Manager Hill of the Galveston, Houston and Northern says it would be a crime to allow outsiders to go down to Galveston just now. The people there are in distress. They need, more than anything else, ice, then pure water, then food and raiment and disinfectants would be acceptable, and would undoubtedly save a good deal of sickness.

Why were troops necessary in Galveston?

Because human vultures, like the buzzards and the carrion crows, were holding an orgie over the dead. The majority of these human hyenas were negroes; but there were also whites who took part in the desecration of the dead. Some of them were home vultures and some had been allowed to go over from the main land under the guise of "relief" work. They did "relief" work by relieving the dead of the jewelry or valuables on their persons and by looting premises.

It seems horrible to contemplate; to think that human beings can be so debased as to rob the dead, and not only that, but that they should mutilate bodies in order to secure their ghoulish booty.

A party of negroes were returning from a looting expedition. They had stripped corpses of all valuables, and the pockets of some of the looters were fairly bulging out with fingers of the dead which had been cut off because they were so swollen the rings could not be removed.

Incensed at this desecration and mutilation of the dead, the looters were promptly shot down, and it was determined that all found in the act of robbing the dead shall be summarily shot.

During the robbing of the dead, not only were fingers cut off, but ears were stripped from the head in order to secure jewels of value. The few government troops who survived have been assisting in patrolling the city. Private citizens have also endeavored to prevent the robbing of the dead and on several occasions have killed the offenders. It is said that at one time eight were killed and at another time four. Singly and in twos and threes the vultures were thus shot down until the total of those thus executed amounts to fully fifty.

When the troops get the situation under control the robbing of the dead will be stopped and some more systematic method of searching for, handling and identifying the dead will be adopted than now prevails.

In twos, in threes, and in groups, sometimes of a score, men can be seen in Houston discussing the one topic—the Galveston disaster. Except such business as must be attended to nothing is being done. The city is shocked and stunned. It is in deep sympathy with the stricken sister town and can think of naught else but the awful calamity. Each new piece of information is eagerly looked for. Newspaper men are besieged with the same question which is put to them every few moments: "What's the latest from Galveston?"

News comes in from neighboring towns and communities which have been almost completely obliterated. Under ordinary circumstances these disasters would have caused a shudder to come over the people and relief parties would have ere this been aiding these afflicted neighbors who have lost their all and are homeless and hungry. But the Galveston disaster is so overwhelming the small communities are overlooked. In fact, the loss by the

1901

President McKinley was attending the Pan-American Exposition at Buffalo, New York, on September 6, 1901, when he was shot in the chest and stomach.

His assassin was identified as Leon Czolgosz, an anarchist who had a small pistol hidden in his hand, concealed by a scarf.

McKinley died eight days later.

Theodore Roosevelt became President.

In the same year, Dr. Walter Reed discovered that yellow fever was caused by a virus and spread by mosquitoes.

And oil was discovered in Texas.

BUFFALO EVENING NEWS.

TEN PAGES EIGHTY COLUMNS.

VOL. XLII—NO. 126. BUFFALO, N. Y., FRIDAY, SEPTEMBER 6, 1901. PRICE ONE CENT.

EXTRA! EXTRA! EXTRA! EXTRA!

PRESIDENT M'KINLEY SHOT!

Two Bullets Sent Into His Body By a Stranger at the Pan-American.

He Sank Down and Was at Once Taken to the Exposition Hospital.

Pan-American Grounds—4:15 P. M.—Bulletin—President McKinley has been shot at the Temple of Music.

He was taken to the hospital on the Exposition grounds.

It is feared the President is fatally shot.

One bullet took effect in his right breast and another in his abdomen.

The name of his assailant not yet known.

The villain shot the President as he was shaking hands with people at the public reception in the Temple of Music.

Officers Foster and Ireland of the U. S. Secret Service were stationed at the time on the lookout. Mr. Cortelyou was at the left of the President, while Mr. Milburn was on the right.

They saw a man with a black mustache approach the President from the left. He had a handkerchief on his left hand. They supposed the man's hand was injured, but kept an eye on him.

He walked as if to shake the President's hand when suddenly he fired two shots in rapid succession from a revolver concealed beneath the handkerchief. Detectives Foster and Ireland sprang upon him, disarmed and arrested him. He was taken at once to No. 13 Police station.

The assassin wore a student's cap.

One bullet lodged against breast bone. This has been taken out. The other perforated the walls of the abdomen and must be extracted by a surgeon. President McKinley is conscious and resting easily.

William McKinley was born in Niles, O., on January 29, 1843. He was educated in public schools in Polon College and Allegany College. He taught in the public school and in 1861 enlisted as a private in the 23rd Ohio Vol. Inf. Promoted to Commissary Sergeant in 1862; second lieutenant a few months later; first lieutenant in 1863, captain in 1864. Served on staffs of Generals R. B. Hayes, George Crook and Winfield S. Hancock; breveted Major U. S. Vol. by President Lincoln for gallantry in battle March 13, 1865. Detailed as acting assistant adjutant general first division, first army corps until mustered out July 26, 1865. Studied law in Mahoning county, O., took a course at Albany, N. Y., law school 1867, admitted to Ohio bar 1867, and settled at Canton, Ohio, which has since been his home.

Prosecuting attorney of Stark county O., 1869; Member of Congress 1876-1891 and as chairman of the Committee on Ways and Means, reported the Tariff Bill of 1890 known as "The McKinley Bill"; he was especially known in Congress as an advocate of high protective tariff.

His districts having been changed by a Democratic legislature, he was defeated for Congress at the November election in 1890.

He was elected Governor of Ohio in 1891 and re-elected in 1893. He was a delegate-at-large to the National Republican convention and a member of the Committee on Resolutions in 1884, and supported James G. Blaine. Holding the same position in the Convention of 1888 he supported John Sherman.

He was a delegate-at-large to Convention in 1892 and was made chairman. At this convention he received 182 votes for President but refused to allow his name to be considered, supporting the re-nomination of Benjamin Harrison.

He was nominated for President at the National Republican convention at St. Louis June 18, 1896, receiving 661 out of a total of 906 votes. He was elected in November, 1896, by the popular plurality of 600,000 votes and received 271 Electoral votes as against 176 for William J. Bryan.

His unanimous re-nomination by the Republican National Convention of 1900 and his triumphal election last November will be remembered by all.

WANTS TO GO TO BUFFALO.

SPRINGFIELD, Ill., Sept. 6.—Col. J. [illegible] Sanborn of Chicago, commanding the [illegible] regiment, has asked permission from Adjt.-Gen. J. N. Reece to leave the state with his regiment to attend the Pan-American Exposition with Gov. Yates on Sept. 16. Permission will probably be given.

The Weather.

Fair weather tonight and Saturday, moderate temperature, light to fresh variable winds.

Conditions point to fair weather Sunday.

EXCITING RACE BETWEEN TWO FAST TRAINS.

Speedy Special Chasing Lake Shore Flyer With Important Mail for England.

(By Associated Press.)

CHICAGO, Sept. 6.—A special train of one car bearing important letters from Australia to Joseph Chamberlain and other high officers of the British government arrived over the Chicago, Burlington & Quincy railway at 9:10 A. M. in order to catch the Southampton steamer, which leaves New York tomorrow, an effort is being made to break all records to catch the Lake Shore "Flyer," which leaves here at 8:30 A. M.

The mail was transferred here to another special train and pulled by an engine with a record of 100 miles an hour, and in charge of officials of the Lake Shore & Michigan Southern railway, left at [illegible] o'clock in hot pursuit of the flyer.

WOULDN'T TAKE M'KINLEY'S DOLLAR.

Programme Boy Made Himself Happy by Giving President a Present.

The proudest programme boy on the Exposition grounds is named Kloenhammer. He is stationed at the Lincoln Parkway gate and has a voice like a fog horn. He rose to the occasion this morning, however, and now is a hero among his fellows.

It was when the President's carriage drove into the grounds, at an early hour, before the crowds were there, that Kloenhammer distinguished himself. The prancing horses were pulled up for an instant to allow the President to admire the beautiful scene that bursts to the view, just before the Lion bridge is reached.

"Here's a programme for you, Mr. President," said the boy, eluding the police escort and stepping close to the carriage. He handed Mr. McKinley three.

The President took them, smiled, reached into his pocket and handed the boy a dollar.

Kloenhammer put his hand behind him and took a backward step. "No, sir, that's a present," he said determinedly.

The President smiled again, returned the coin to his pocket, nodded a thanks and was whisked away. Kloenhammer stood in the middle of the roadway and watched the carriage until it was out of sight.

ADJUDGED IN CONTEMPT AND FINED $6000.

Heavy Punishment Meted Out to John F. Moffett by Justice Lambert.

"Moffee adjudged guilty of contempt and fined $6000. J. S. Lambert."

This notation was made on a legal document by Justice Lambert this morning, and is the official record of the heavy punishment meted out to John F. Moffett of Watertown, N. Y., for having put in a fictitious surety several years ago and for having committed perjury as an incident thereto, as was alleged before Justice Lambert when arguments were submitted to him several days ago, as told exclusively in the NEWS at the time.

Moffet is receiver of the Medina Gas and Electric Light Company and the title of the action in the course of which the contempt was committed is the Buffalo Loan, Trust and Safe Deposit Company against the Medina Gas and Electric Light Company and the Holland Trust Company. The plaintiff since has assigned its claim in this suit, which was a foreclosure action, to Cornelius Fitzgerald of New York City, who is now prosecuting Moffett.

The papers submitted to the court assert that several years ago Moffett swore that he was worth $10,000 above all debts and liabilities, and, on this statement, his bond was accepted and he was able to stave off the litigation in question. The fine imposed, it is understood, represents the value of the deficiency judgment reported in the foreclosure proceedings. It is said to be the heaviest fine ever imposed for contempt of court in Erie county.

THE SHERIFF O' LONDON TOWN.

An Exalted Official of the English Metropolis and M. P. Visits the Pan.

Joseph Lawrence, member of the English House of Commons for Monmouth, made famous in Shakespeare's Henry V., and sheriff of the city of London, is in Buffalo.

When asked what district he represented in parliament Mr. Lawrence answered in the poet's words: "There is a gallant town called Monmouth,'" said he. I represent Monmouth Burroughs which embrace five towns. Fluellen, one of the poet's characters has immortalized it in these words: 'There is a river in Monmouth and a river in Macedon.'"

Mr. Lawrence is a man of most pronounced American appearance, ideas and speech. He is clean-cut, dresses in better taste than one Englishman in a thousand, is alert-minded and says exactly what he wants to say with lightning rapidity. He is a man who "eats up work," the kind of man who is characterized in "Fire Alarm" Foraker's description of Roosevelt—"a steam engine in trousers."

HIS ACQUAINTANCE WAS A SHARPER.

William Jeffries of Louisville Separated From His Wallet and $40.

William Jeffries of Louisville, Ky., is mourning the loss of $40, which a sharper relieved him of yesterday. Jeffries went to the Falls and met a stranger, with whom he struck up an acquaintance. The two roamed around the Falls, then came to Buffalo. On the way up Jeffries was robbed of his wallet. He complained to the police, giving a description of the alleged thief.

WHOLE COMMANDO CAPTURED.

MIDDLEBURG, Cape Colony, Sept. 6.—Lotter's entire commando has been taken by Maj. Scobell south of Petersburg. One hundred and three prisoners were captured, 12 Boers were killed and 46 wounded. Two hundred horses also were captured.

PERSONAL AND PROFESSIONAL.

Regular morning services will be resumed next Sunday at Zion's Second Evangelist Lutheran Church.

The supporters of Dr. Bonnar for Mayor will hold a meeting tomorrow night at Union Bank Hall, 7 West Mohawk street.

A. Nicol Simpson with a party of twelve from Scotland, are at Mrs. Agnes Jackson's house, 1606 West avenue, attending the Exposition.

Mr. Henry D. Fitzgerald will speak at the public meeting of the Theosophical Society on Sunday evening, at 8 o'clock. The lecture is free.

"Followed President Package in Hand. Detectives Four Times Pushed Away a Young Man Who Might Have Had an Infernal Machine." These were headlines from a morning paper. That young man may have been a book agent. Think of the horrible possibilities.

Rev. Jasper N. Field and children of Fargo avenue leave town today for Ft. Wayne, Ind., where the family will move the last of the month. Miss Ethel and Mr. Ernest Field, after a week's visit in Ft. Wayne, will return to their studies in Denison University at Granville, Ohio.

The Ancient Order of Foresters in convention at Troy yesterday broke a record, as announced in our telegram, they elected Everand A. Hayes of this city, High Chief Ranger of the Order. This is the first re-election of a High Chief Ranger in the history of the Foresters. A magnificent basket of flowers was presented to Mr. Hayes and there was great enthusiasm in the convention. Mr. Hayes was tendered an ovation.

DIED.

THOMPSON—Sept. 5th, 1901, John Russell infant son of John L. and Grace Hurdley Thompson, aged 6 months. The funeral will take place from the family residence, No. 12 Woodlawn avenue, Saturday afternoon at 4 o'clock.

HAMMEL—September 5, 1901, Henry, husband of Emily Hammel, and father of John, Peter, August, Charles, Emily, Josephine and Clara Hammel and Mrs. Frank Demlar, Mrs. Joseph Day and Mrs. John F. Vanhoff. Funeral Saturday from the residence of his daughter, Mrs. Frank Demlar, No. 16 Garner avenue, at 8:30 A. M., and from the Church of the Annunciation at 9 o'clock.

TOEPEL—Died at Prairie Du Chien, Wis., Julia Toepel, sister of Mrs. C. W. Bingemann, 160 High street, aged 21 years. Batavia papers please copy.

WATERBURY—Thursday, Sept. 5, 1901, Sarah A., widow of Francis N. Waterbury, mother of Frank and Harry Waterbury. Funeral services from the residence of her son, No. 471 West Ferry street, Saturday, Sept. 7th, at 3:30 P. M. Interment at Noroton, Conn.

RUTH—In this city, Sept. 4, 1901, Henry Ruth, aged 64 years, 10 months, 7 days. Funeral from the family residence, 65 Camp street, Saturday afternoon at 2 o'clock, from St. Jacob's Church, Jefferson, near High, at 2:30. Friends are invited to attend.

SCOTT—In this city, Sept. 5, 1901, Charlotte D., mother of Robert S. Scott, in her 83d year. Funeral from the family residence, No. 306 Fulton street, Saturday afternoon, at 2:30 o'clock. Friends are invited to attend. Burial at convenience of the family.

STEEL MEN'S LAST OFFER IS REJECTED.

(By Associated Press)

PITTSBURG, Sept. 6.—In steel corporation circles in Pittsburg today it was positively announced that the last offer made by the big steel combination had been rejected by the Amalgamated board and that all negotiations were ended.

It is strongly intimated that a number of men had agreed to return to work in the event of a failure to settle through the peace committee of the National Civic Federation.

The local officers of the steel corporation were unusually busy this afternoon. All who were seen declined to discuss the plans except to say that all the works are to be put in operation at once and that no further propositions are to be made by the United States Steel Corporation.

PITTSBURG, Pa., Sept. 6.—A conference of the members of the executive committee of the Amalgamated Association to consider what is believed to be the final proposition of the United States Steel Corporation, will be held here today.

President Shaffer was early at the headquarters, and at 10 o'clock seven of his assistants had reported. The conference will begin as soon as the other members of the board arrive.

TEXT OF THE TERMS TO BE CONSIDERED.

These are the terms for a settlement of the great steel strike agreed upon by President Charles M. Schwab of the Steel Trust and the Board of Conciliation of the National Civic Federation of Labor, but which President Shaffer of the Amalgamated Association refused to accept:

That the striking employes of all the [illegible] be ordered back to work at 6:30 o'clock Wednesday night.

That all union mills which the trust has not succeeded in operating since the strike be reopened as union mills and recognized as such by the Steel Corporation.

That all union mills which the trust has succeeded in operating since the strike be reopened as non-union mills and recognized as such by the Amalgamated Association.

The number of these non-union mills are to be determined after an examination has been made of the number of men employed since the strike, the tonnage manufactured by non-union help, etc.

The acceptance of these terms would, it is said, reduce the strength of the Amalgamated Association by more than 50 per cent.

ADVISORY BOARD ARRIVES IN PITTSBURG.

The advisory board or general executive committee of the Amalgamated Association has been ordered to this city, it is said, to consider what is believed to be the practical ultimatum of the United States Steel Corporation. At 11 o'clock nine of the out of town members had arrived, as follows:

W. C. Davis of Chicago; C. H. Davis of Newport, Ky.; Walter Larkins of Martin's Ferry, O.; John Morgan, Cambridge, O.; John F. Ward, Youngstown, O.; Clem Javis, Anderson, Ind.; Elias Jenkins, Youngstown, O.; David Rees, Pittsburg; John Chappelle, New Castle, Pa., and F. J. Williams, Birmingham, Ala.

President Shaffer was early at the Amalgamated rooms, but he refused to give any information or admit that a conference had been called. The others were equally reticent. Among the rumors current was one to the effect that the board would go to New York tonight.

Another report was that a plan for the settlement of the strike would be decided upon that would be acceptable to the steel officials.

STEEL MANAGER ATTACKED BY STRIKERS.

A Canal Dover, O., dispatch says General Manager Cline of the American Sheet Steel Company's plant was assaulted by a striker this morning and carried to his carriage unconscious. It is not known how seriously he was injured. Two sheet mills are going this morning and preparations are being made to start several more.

At 11:10 o'clock President Shaffer called a conference together. The board, as far as could be learned, was complete, with the exception of two vice-presidents.

STEEL CORPORATION TO PAY NO FURTHER ATTENTION TO STRIKERS

NEW YORK, Sept. 6.—It is understood here that it is highly improbable that the United States Steel Corporation will take any cognizance of the Amalgamated Association executive board at Pittsburg today, whatever the conclusion may be.

It was learned today from an authoritative source that the time named in the tentative agreement reached by the conference here on Wednesday had expired, that the Steel Corporation had decided to participate in no further peace discussions, and that there would be an immediate move for the general resumption of work with non-union men and such strikers as were willing to return to their places.

DEMMLER TIN PLATE WORKS RESUME.

PITTSBURG, Sept. 6.—The Demmler Tin Plate Works at McKeesport resumed operations at 8 o'clock this morning. Six mills out of fifteen were started with nearly 100 men, many of them old employes.

There was no disorder. The deputy sheriffs were on duty, but there was nothing for them to do, as only a few strikers were about the premises. Thirty-six men were taken into the works by boat from Duquesne and 38 went through the gates. On account of the heavy fog the strikers' pickets, who lined the river banks, were unable to see the boat until the men had been landed. Manager Lauck stated that he had 54 men in the hot mill department, and by night he expected to have 100 men working, every one of them old employes. Two more mills, he said, would be started this afternoon.

NOTICE POSTED AT THE DEMMLER PLANT.

At noon a notice was posted at the Demmler works calling the attention of the old employes to the fact that the plant had resumed and requesting all who wished to return to work to report for duty not later than next Monday morning or their places would be filled by other workmen. The notice was signed by the American Tin Plate Company. Manager Lauck stated at that time that he had seven mills running and had enough men to operate them fully.

Later advices from McKeesport indicated that the statement this morning that 1000 men were at work at the National [illegible] was exaggerated. It was said in McKeesport [illegible] the strikers seemed to feel that their fight was lost, though they would continue their picket duty and endeavor to induce the men not to return to the mill.

At the Painter Works in this city the management announced today that it had enough men to run double turn and five mills would be put on at night next week.

Rumors were current on the South Side today that the Monongahela Tin Plate Works would be started in a few days. A wagon load of cots was said to have been taken into the works last night, and sleeping and eating quarters were being erected in the mill for the use of the imported men to be brought here to break the strike.

MORE MEN WORKING IN NATIONAL TUBE.

Five hundred more men were at work at the National Tube Company's plant at McKeesport this morning, making 1000 men now in the plant. A large number of others applied for work, but they were turned back because the mill was not in shape to take any more men on. There was no attempt made by the strikers to stop the men as they went in, and the management say by next week, the entire establishment will be in operation, and the strike a thing of the past.

The situation at the plants in Pittsburg was not greatly changed today. Twenty more men returned to the Pennsylvania Tube Works today and over 300 men are now at work. A meeting of the former employes who are still out has been arranged for tomorrow afternoon at Moorhead's Hall when Manager Latshaw will have a conference with the men.

At the Star Tin Plate Works it is said there are now more men than are needed and arrangements are being made to send 100 to other plants.

(Continued on Page Seven.)

FAST MAIL WRECKED.

SIOUX CITY, Iowa, Sept. 6.—It is reported that the Chicago & Northwestern fast mail has been wrecked near Carroll, Iowa. No details have been received.

TOO LATE TO CLASSIFY.

BIG SHAKE-UP OF POLICE OFFICERS.

Capt. Michael Regan Transferred to No. 1 Station and Capt. John Taylor to No. 3.

CAPT. FRANK KILLEEN SENT TO NO. 13 AT BLACK ROCK.

Capt. Burfeind Transferred to No. 4—Inspectors Martin and Donovan Change Places—Two Precinct Detectives Shifted.

The biggest shake-up that has occurred in the Police Department since Supt. Bull has been at the head of the police force occurred this afternoon. Mayor Diehl and Police Commissioners Rupp and Cooper got together, ordered the two department inspectors to change places, shifted six captains and ordered two precinct detectives to go to new houses. The shake-up was the talk of the entire department this afternoon and bids fair to be the chief topic of conversation among captains and men for several days.

Mayor Diehl appeared at Police Headquarters shortly after noon today and went at once into a conference with [illegible]. The three were closeted together for more than an hour. Supt. Bull was not invited to the conference. Neither was Clerk James A. Taggert present.

At 1:15 the Commissioners threw open the door of their office and sent for Supt. Bull. Commissioner Rupp then told him that a few "little changes" had been decided on and gave them to Supt. Bull.

SUPT. BULL ASTONISHED.

The latter's eyes opened wide with astonishment when he read the list. This is the way it read:

Inspector John Martin has been transferred from the first to the second district. Inspector Michael Donovan has been transferred from the second to the first district. Capt. Michael Regan has been transferred from the Fourth Precinct to the old First Precinct, which he commanded up to the time of the election scandals in 1898. Capt. John H. Taylor, who has been in charge of the First Precinct since Regan's removal in 1898, has been sent to the Third Precinct, known as the red light district.

Capt. Burfeind, who has commanded the Thirteenth Precinct since he was made a captain, has been sent to take Capt. Regan's place in the Fourth. Capt. Frank Killeen of the Third has been transferred to the Thirteenth. Capt. Notter, who has been assisting Capt. Burfeind in the Thirteenth since the Pan-American Exposition opened, has been ordered back to the Ninth. Acting Capt. Girven of the Ninth has been ordered back to the Third to do duty as a sergeant.

Precinct Detective Caney of the Thirteenth has been ordered to change places with Precinct Detective Cornish of the Tenth.

GO INTO EFFECT TONIGHT.

The changes all go into effect at 6 o'clock tonight.

Supt. Bull gave out the news of the changes at 2 o'clock. A NEWS man asked him the cause of the changes.

"I don't know anything about them," said the superintendent. "I was called in by the commissioners just before the meeting adjourned and they gave me the list. I did not know they [illegible] to make."

The changes will be pleasing to several of the captains. Capt. Regan has been trying to get out of the Fourth for some months. He has been working to get into the Third, and is greatly surprised at being sent back to his old command. Capt. Killeen probably won't be pleased. The Third is considered the most important in the city. He will be nearer home, however, as he lives in the Thirteenth. Capt. Taylor likes the First Precinct, but as he has been sent to an important precinct, the change will not be displeasing. Capt. Burfeind would rather be in any precinct in Buffalo than the Fourth, it is said.

NO POLITICS, SAYS MAYOR.

Mayor Diehl, when seen at his home by a NEWS man, said that the transfers were not influenced by politics.

"I attended the meeting for a short while this morning, but did not take any part in making the transfers," said he. "The other Commissioners told me that they expected to make some. I told them to go ahead and make them, but took no part myself.

"There is no political significance to the changes. The Police Department is out of politics as far as I am concerned and as it should be. In talking with the other Commissioners they said the changes were to be made for 'the good of the department.' That is all I am looking for, so I was satisfied that they should go ahead without me."

Today at the Exposition.

MAYFLOWER DAY.
MUNICIPAL ELECTRICIANS' DAY.
ROYAL ARCANUM DAY.

Gates open from 8 A. M. to 11 P. M.

Exhibit buildings open from 8:30 A. M. to 10 P. M.

Fine Arts building open from 8:30 A. M. to 6:30 P. M.

U. S. Government building open from 9 A. M. to 6 P. M.

Elevator in Electric Tower runs from 9 A. M. to 10 P. M.

Electric Fountain, North Bay, Park Lake, 8:15 to 9:30 P. M.

Illumination Electric Tower and grounds at 7:30 P. M.

Band concerts, 10 A. M., 2, 7:30 and 8 P. M.

Orchestra concerts, Temple of Music, 11 A. M. and 3 P. M.

Organ recital, Temple of Music, 4 P. M.

Drills by the U. S. Hospital Corps, 10:15 A. M. and 3:30 P. M.

Drill by U. S. Seacoast Artillery, 10:15 A. M. and 3 P. M.

Drills by U. S. Marines, 7:15 P. M.

U. S. Life-saving Service Exhibition, 2:30 P. M.

Signaling by the use of the Heliograph, 3:30 P. M.

Wireless Telegraph Demonstration, 11 A. M. and 2 P. M.

Tiffany Fountain, 8:15 P. M.

U. S. School Exhibits, 10:30 A. M. to 5 P. M.

5 O'CLOCK BULLETINS.

NEWARK, N. Y., Sept. 6.—The death list of the wreck of the Northern Central Accommodation train which occurred last Thursday at Fairville was increased.

NEW YORK, Sept. 6.—The Shamrock did not go out for a spin this forenoon owing to fog and light winds. Sir Thomas Lipton said at noon that she might get out later.

NEW YORK, Sept. 6.—A coroner's warrant was issued at Yonkers today for the arrest of Frederick Imhoff on suspicion of having killed John Durn, the Mt. Vernon saloonkeeper, whose body was found near Yonkers last Tuesday morning.

CLEVELAND, O., Sept. 6.—Ninety people who ate clams at a lunch incident to the opening of a new public building a few days ago have been ill since, suffering, it is alleged, from ptomaine poisoning. No person has died, but many are still in bed.

NEW YORK, Sept. 6.—Secretary J. V. S. Oddie of the New York Yacht Club said today that no letter protesting against the right of the club to exclude the Lawson boat, Independence, from the trial races for the selection of the defender of the America cup had yet been received.

MATTERS OF MOMENT.

John McConnell, a liquor dealer of this city, has filed a petition in voluntary bankruptcy, which shows liabilities of $2,682.[illegible] with no assets.

TOO LATE TO CLASSIFY.

1903

The United States was beginning to stretch its transportation ingenuity and provide glimpses of the nation it was to become.

At Kitty Hawk, North Carolina, brothers Orville and Wilbur Wright, Ohio bicycle makers, launched the first successful manned flight in a motorized airplane. The flight covered 852 feet and lasted 59 seconds.

An experimental electric trolley was installed in Scranton, Pennsylvania.

A Packard automobile arrived in New York fifty-two days after leaving San Francisco. It was the first cross-country auto trip.

12 Pages
In Two Parts

Virginian-Pilot.

True to the Democratic ...Party In Victory or Defeat

VOL. XIX. NO. 68. NORFOLK, VA., FRIDAY DECEMBER 18, 1903. TWELVE PAGES. THREE CENTS PER COPY.

'LYING MACHINE SOARS 3 MILES IN TEETH OF HIGH WIND OVER SAND HILLS AND WAVES AT KITTY HAWK ON CAROLINA COAST

LLY SHEETS WILL DECIDE CONTEST

rman Forced to Re- Richmond to Get .ets For Committee

HY FACTION HAS ADVANTAGE THUS FAR

roxles Ruled Out of Meet- g by Decisive Vote Be- fore Fight Began

H SIDES TO ABIDE BY FINAL DECISION

Special to Virginian-Pilot.)
RICHMOND, VA., Dec. 17.

all indications pointing to vic- or the Treby faction, the state ratic committee, after spending hearing the Norfolk election con- djourned just before midnight 0 o'clock tomorrow morning, after session, in which some radical was taken. Meanwhile Captain Dey, under instructions from the ttee, left for Norfolk, accompa- his two deputies and by Police sioner Reid. They are expected rn here in the morning and pro- he books and tally sheets of the of October 13, which Dey has in his safe in the seaside city. from this, the important feature day was the passage of a resolu- oing away with proxies for good . The committee will probably a decision by tomorrow night.

committee met at Murphy's hotel re Chairman Ellyson, who pre- ced the call for the meeting, and . Button called the roll of mem- owing the following present at ne or later during the meeting, a number of persons holding of absentees:

District—Lloyd T. Smith, Clag- Jones, J. Boyd eSars, R. L. All- and H. H. Wallace.

d District—W. W. Dey, George es, J. N. Curtis.

District—John C. Easley, P. V. John J. Lynch, John S. Har- nd B. L. Winston.

h District—T. E. Clarke, A. D. s, Robert Gilliam, J. W. .

District—R. A. James, T. G. and George M. Helms.

District—D. Q. Eggleston, W. P. ale, H. O. Humphreys and A. P. k.

th District—John S Patton, E. man.

h District—C. P. Janney, Gren- lres, Gardner L. Boothe.

District—Thomas A. Lynch, M. and P. F. St. Clair.

District—Joseph Button, J. P. ead and Edward Echols.

s these thirty-five members of mmittee present in person, the g had sent proxies: George W. Sidney Sheltman, E. W. Carpen- L. Gordon, G. S. P. Triplett and Hubbard.

ES RULED OUT.

on as the meeting was open for . Mr. Whitehead, of Amherst, ognized and took the floor in op- to the participation in the of proxies. He declared that not fair to those members who the meetings at great cost and to have others send their prox- ocal partisans and allow these to dominate the meetings of the ee and decide the destinies of y in the state. He therefore of- resolution as follows:

ed, That it is the sense of this ee that proxies be not allowed cipate in the deliberations of the ntral democratic committee at ubsequent meetings.

Whitehead briefly advocated the of the resolution, and George , of Norfolk county, stated that red the principle of the resolu- thought that on the eve of a so radical a change should not ed at this meeting.

uestion was put on the White- solution refusing proxies the participate in the meeting and lared adopted, 23 to 9, as fol-

Messrs. Smith, Jones, Allworth, Cogbill, Winston, Clarke, Wat- liam, Folkes, Eggleston, Hum- Barksdale, Craddock, Gaines, St. Clair, Button, Whitehead, James, Burch and Helms—23. Messrs. Janney, Lynch, Clarke, urtis, Easley, Harwood, Patton rman—9.

SIDE DECISION.

seph T. Lawless, of counsel for faction, the petitioners in the ted that it went without say- he and his principals would missively to the decision of mittee. They were not the kind rats who after submitting a to decision refused to abide ion.

orge C. Cabell, Jr., of counsel testees or respondents, stated le he recognized the commit- on as to proxies was an over- of long established precedent, uthorized to say that the par- ties he represented will abide the de- cision of the committee and always sub- mit to lawful authority. With some spirit he repudiated any implication that he and his clients were of the class who ever refused to abide the decision of the duly constituted party authority.

Mr. Lawless, of counsel for petition- ers, referred to the clause in the peti- tion asking the chairman to request the production of the tally sheets used in the election.

DISCREPANCY ON NOTICES.

Chairman Ellyson stated that he had written two letters, naming the dates, to Mr. Dey, requesting the production of the tally sheets.

Mr. Cabell thereupon stated that nei- ther of the two letters had ever been received, and that no legal notice of contest had ever been served on the contestees. He had never heard the pe- tion read until it was read by the chairman a few minutes before. He thereupon read a brief notice served upon him by the contestants' counsel.

"While we recognize that this is not a legal tribunal," he said, "it is never- theless customary to serve upon the contestees in all such cases notice of the contest with specifications. In this case no bill of particulars has been filed."

The notice was read which had been served by the counsel for the petition- ers. It was dated November 25, where- as the election was held October 13, a month and twelve days before.

The statement that his two letters asking for the books and tally sheets had never been received was accepted by Chairman Ellyson, but he read a memorandum showing that one letter had been mailed December 7 and the other December 13.

CABELL IN THE DARK.

Mr. Echols asked if the election held in the city of Norfolk was legalized.

Col. Cabell replied in the negative.

Mr. Jeffries, of counsel for petition- ers, then presented communications bearing on the request for books and tally sheets. He said that the petition had been printed in the Norfolk Land- mark. Captain Dey could not plead that he was not familiar with the mat- ter. The request for an inspection of the books had brought the information that any voter could examine the books as to his own name, but none other.

Colonel Gaines moved the naming of a committee to go to Norfolk, hear the evidence and make a report, no mem- ber of the committee to come from the Second or any contiguous district.

Colonel Cabell said that he was not prepared to go on with the hearing, not having seen the charges or heard them until they were read at the secre- tary's desk.

Mr. Jeffries said he did not ask for a continuance. He had come full- handed and ready to go on. Every means had been exhausted in an effort to examine the books and tally sheets, but without success.

Mr. Pebrell, associate of Colonel Cabell, replied. He said that one of the reasons why the tally sheets were not shown was that it was desired to protect voters.

Mr. Allworth got tired of the argu- ment of the lawyers and he moved that the committee take up the mat- ter.

Colonel Cabell said he desired that the hearing go on. The committee had come a long distance, and he would waive all technicalities and let the matter proceed. Replying to a question, he said he would accept the publication of the petition in the news- papers.

"The newspapers have been teeming with reports of fraud, and he was not willing to rest under the imputation," exclaimed Colonel Cabell, "and we will meet the charges as best we can."

Colonel Cabell then asked that a spe- cific charge be filed, saying what voters were challenged.

Mr. Jeffries said that he had replied as far as possible, but until he was able to get the tally sheets he could not specify a voter.

(Continued on Page 6.)

U. S. LANDING PARTY FINDS STRONG CAMP OF COLOMBIAN TROOPS

Natives Order American Flag Hauled Down on Cutter But it Stays Put

(By Cable to Virginian-Pilot.)
COLON, DEC. 17.

The United States cruiser Atlanta, Commander William H. Turner, re- turned here last night from the Gulf of Darien. She discovered December 15 a detachment of Colombian troops, numbering visually about 500 men, but, according to their statements, totaling 1,500 to 2,000 men, at Titumati, on the western side of the gulf, just north of the mouth of the Atrato river. The commander of the Atlanta sent ashore an officer, who conversed with the Co- lombian commander. The latter pro- tested energetically against the pres- ence of an American warship in Co- lombian waters, in so much as war be- tween Colombia and the United States had not been declared, and politely re- quested the Atlanta to leave the gulf, because it belonged to Colombia. Com- mander Turner ignored the request, and the Atlanta returned to Colon to report to Rear Admiral Coghlan. The Colombians are clearly busy with pro- tective and strengthening measures. Although they treated the Americans courteously they decidedly resented the presence of the Atlanta's landing party. The Colombian force was composed of the men landed recently at the Atrato river by the Colombian cruisers Car- tagena and General Pinson.

Early in the morning of December 15 the Atlanta sighted a small schooner in the center of the Gulf of Darien and followed her to the western shore, where the schooner attempted to hide behind an islet. Lieutenant Harlan P. Perrill, of the Atlanta, was ordered to board her and thereupon a whaleboat was lowered and pulled towards the schooner.

It was found that the schooner had on board a hundred Colombian soldiers, commanded by General Rafael Novo, who said General Daniel Ortis, com- mander-in-chief of the Colombian forces of the Atlantic and the Pacific, had a large camp, a mile away, on the mainland. General Novo requested Lieutenant Perry to land and confer with General Ortis. After temporarily returning to the Atlanta, Lieutenant Perrill went back to the schooner, which in the meantime had taken up a position off a beach within a small bay. Great excitement prevailed among the Colombians on the whaleboat's ap- proach. There were repeated cries of "Viva Colombia," and there was a sud- den concentration of about 150 Colom- bian soldiers on the beach. For some moments the situation appeared dan- gerous and had the appearance of am- buscade. General Ortis appeared on the beach when Lieutenant Perrill went ashore, the whaleboat in the meantime lying close to the beach. General Ortis insisted that Lieutenant Perrill should fly the Colombian flag at the bow of the whaleboat, or lower the American flag at her stern, because she was in Colom- bian waters.

Lieutenant Perrill replied that he did not have a Colombian flag and refused to lower the stars and stripes. eGenral Ortis did not insist upon his so doing, but he protested in writing against the presence of the Americans in Colom- bian waters. Lieutenant Perrill accept- ed the protest and conveyed it to Com- mander Turner ,who handed it to Rear Admiral Coghlan on his arival here.

General Ortis and others freely ex- pressed the determination of Colombia to fight to the bitter end in case Gen- eral Reyes' visit to Washington is not succeccsful and Panama is not returned to Colombia.

COTTON TRADE TO DEFEAT COTTON GAMBLING

English Spinners to Meet in Manchester to Discuss Cur- tailing the Production—Inter- national Movement Possible

(By Telegraph to Virginian-Pilot.)
CHARLOTTE, N. C., Dec. 17.

Following the example of the south- ern manufacturers who met in Char- lotte on the 8th instant, the spinners of England have called a meeting to be held in Manchester, England, on Decem- ber 29 to discuss the matter.

C. B. Bryant, of this city, secretary of the American Cotton Manufacturers' association, received the following ca- blegram today:

"Manchester, England, Dec. 17, 1903.

"Bryant, American Cotton Manufac- turers' Association, Charlotte, N. C.:

"Lancashire suggesting short time in cotton trade to defeat cotton gambling. Will you call meeting to see if your as- sociation is prepared to join interna- tional movement? Trade meeting called here for the 29th. Reply.

(Signed)
"MASTER SPINNERS'
"FEDERATION."

The following telegram was forwarded in reply:

"Charlotte, N. C., Dec. 17, 1903.

"Master Spinners' Federation, Manches- ter, England:

"Committee of American Cotton Man- ufacturers now endeavoring to solve short crop cotton situation.

(Signed)
"AMERICAN
"COTTON MANUFACTURERS'
"ASSOCIATION."

The committee to which reference was made in the cablegram sent in reply is the committee appointed at the inde- pendent meeting of the mill men held in Charlotte on the 8th instant. This committee will act in entire indepen- dence of the Cotton Manufacturers' as- sociation."

Mill men here agree that if such a thing were possible national curtailment would result in raising the price of cot- ton goods.

TO MARK GRAVES OF CONFEDERATE DEAD

(Telegraph to Virginian-Pilot.)

Washington, Dec. 17.—Favorable reports were ordered by the senate committee on military affairs today on the bill pro- viding for the appropriate marking of graves of soldiers and sailors of the Con- federate army and navy; also one appro- priating $32,000 to complete the construc- tion of the road to the national cemetery near Pensacola, Fla.

JAPANESE TROOPS TO COREA.

(By Cable to Virginian-Pilot.)

London, Dec. 17.—A cablegram from Tokio says the dispatch of troops to Co- rea is imminent and that the elder statesmen have been summoned to meet the emperor today.

WOOD TRIAL POSTPONED.

(By Telegraph to Virginian-Pilot.)

Washington, Dec. 17.—The senate committee on military affairs met today and decided to postpone action on the case of Gen. Leonard Wood until Janu- ary 4.

TO DEEPEN THE HARBOR AT NORFOLK

Secretary of War to Report Plan to Congress For Making Ship Channel Here 35 Feet Deep to Float Big Warships

SENATOR MARTIN INTRODUCED MEASUER

(Special to Virginian-Pilot.)

Washington, Dec. 17.—Senator Martin introduced and had passed today a res- olution directing the secretary of war to have made a survey of Norfolk har- bor and to report to congress a plan, to- gether with an estimate of the cost, by which there may be obtained a channel of 35 feet from deep water to the navy yard, and also the cost of a channel 30 feet deep. The channel is in places only 28 feet deep, and the department com- plains that there is always some fear that a warship will strike one of these shallows when coming into the navy yard.

All of the Atlantic ports are now clamoring to have the depth of waters in their harbors increased, so as to ac- commodate the increased size of modern ships. The need in Norfolk and of the Norfolk navy yard in this respect are as important as those of any other Atlan- tic port. Looking at the matter from a naval standpoint, the commandant of the Norfolk navy yard has for some time been taking a deep interest in this matter. Last spring Senator Martin, Admiral Harrington and others were invited by the commercial bodies of the city of Norfolk to make a personal in- spection of the harbor and the channel to it from deep water, with a view to considering what could be done to se- cure for this harbor the same advan- tages which were being clamored for by almost all other Atlantic ports.

Senator Martin, at the time of that visit, stated that he would take the matter up when the next congress con- vened and would endeavor to secure in the next river and harbor bill a provi- sion for the widening, straightening and deepening of this channel.

SCARE OF SHORTS ADVANCES COTTON

(By Telegraph to Virginian-Pilot.)
NEW YORK, DEC. 17.

Liverpool cables were up today owing to a scare of shorts and aggressive bull tactics, and this caused the New York cotton market to shake off the lethargy recently noted. First prices were at an advance of 17 to 27 points. January sold at 12.40, March 12.70; May, 12.80, and July, 12.77, these being new high records for the two last positions and net gains on the active months of 21 to 29 points. Liverpool houses bought here as well as in their home market and commission houses, though in many cases selling for profits, also had orders on the buying side. Of course, the gains, particularly in reference to the later positions, which had passed all previous records, brought out heavy realizing, and shortly after the call these months reacted from the highest, but generally speaking the market ruled very strong.

All day the market continued very strong. There was more or less irreg- ularity, and trading was not so active as has frequently been the case. The market was flooded with bullish news from the south. The highest point was reached in the afternoon, when January sold at 12.59, March 12.80, May 12.90 and July 12.93, these being net gains of 35 to 42 points. The market closed firm, net 32 to 41 points higher, with sales estimated at 1,000,000 bales.

REWARD FOR CAPTURE OF HARVEY LOGAN

(By Telegraph to Virginian-Pilot.)

Knoxville, Tenn., Dec. 17.—The Great Northern Express company today de- posited with the Knox county chancery court $2,116.64, out of which amount the company asks the chancery court to adjudicate and pay the various claims for rewards for the capture of Harvey Logan near here December 15, 1901.

CUBAN BILL IS NOW A LAW.

(Telegraph to Virginian-Pilot.)

Washington, Dec. 17.—The president signed the Cuban reciprocity bill a few minutes before 1 o'clock this afternoon. The president then issued a proclamation reciting the passage of the Cuban recip- rocity bill and declaring the Cuban re- ciprocity treaty to be effective ten days from today.

TO CONVOY FLOTILLA.

(By Telegraph to Virginian-Pilot.)

New York, Dec. 17.—The United States cruiser Buffalo sailed today for Key West and San Juan, from which port she will proceed as a convoy to the torpedo boat flotilla ordered to the Phil- ippines.

"WANTS CANAL BUILT WITHOUT SUSPICION OF NATIONAL DISHONOR"

Senator Hoar and Gorman in Fiery Debate on Floor of the Senate

(By Telegraph to Virginian-Pilot.)
WASHINGTON, DEC. 17.

The senate today was the scene of a most important debate on the isthmian canal question as affected by the presi- dent's recognition of the independence of the republic of Panama. The dis- cussion began with a speech by Mr. Hoar on his resolution of inquiry and lasted several hours. In addition to Mr. Hoar's address there were speeches by Mr. Gorman and Mr. Foraker. All three were notable utterances and of historical interest.

Mr. Hoar confined his remarks to his resolution, and they were carefully written out and read from manuscript. He held that this country has not yet received full official information con- cerning the isthmian revolution, and criticised in sharp terms the conduct of this country as shown by what has been given out.

There was no reservation in Mr. Gor- man's utterances. He practically al- leged that the situation in Panama had been created to make a campaign issue, and said that unless further light was thrown on the subject he would oppose the Panama treaty.

Mr. Foraker took Mr. Hoar to task severely for his remarks reflecting on the administration. He defended the administration for its attitude toward the Panama revolt. A heated colloquy took place between Mr. Foraker and Mr. Hoar during an effort of the Mas- sachusetts senator to explain more fully his position in the matter.

Mr. Hoar said he was in favor of the isthmian canal, but was anxious that the canal should be built "without taint or suspicion of national dishonor."

"What we want to know is," he said, "did this givernment, knowing that a revolution was about to take place, so arrange matters that the revolution, whether peaceable or otherwise, should be permitted to go on without interrup- tion, and whether our national authori- ties took measures to prevent Colombia from stopping it."

Mr. Hoar quoted the correspondence bearing upon the revolution, and asked: "Why this great anxiety before any disturbance had occurred?" It was, he said, clear that if the correspondence so far printed included all the informa- tion possible to give on the subject, that from twenty-four to forty-eight hours before the revolution broke out this gov- ernment had instructed a man-of-war to prevent Colombia from doing any- thing to prevent it. "I want to know, and the American people want to know and have a right to know, whether this mighty policeman on the isthmus, see- ing a man about to attack another, is justified, before the blow is struck, in manacling the assailed party, and whether, after the assault has been made, the policeman is justified in claiming the pocketbook which has been taken from the victim by the assailant should be turned over to him (the po- liceman) on the ground that he was the rightful owner?"

Mr Gorman took the floor as soon as Mr. Hoar had concluded, and there was from the start evident interest in what he might say. He began with reference to Mr. Hoar's speech and compliment- ed that senator highly on his attitude and alluded to the democratic attitude on the canal question. On the latter point he said that democratic senators generally are as favorable to the con- struction of the canal as are republi- cans. Mr. Gorman said the facts were all that were desired, and he proceeded to refer to the extension of the execu- tive influence, saying that that influence had been extended from time to time until "the senate had become practi- cally the agent of the executive."

The affair in Panama, he declared, "was the most flagrant act of trans- gression that has ever taken place in theh istory of thec ountry, and it should be resisted without regard to party."

Mr. Gorman criticised Mr. Loomis for his discussion of the Panama situation at a New York banquet before injunc- tion of secrecy had been removed by the senate. Mr. Gorman said Mr. Loomis had discussed the Panama situation at a banquet at which perhaps many were excited by wine, and had "given infor- mation which the senate had not had from the administration or from any source. He did not," Mr. Gorman con- tinued, "tell the country all the facts, but he made the broad assertion that the president was a bold and great man, who had had the courage and the pa- triotism to land marines and seize a part of the teritory of the repblic of Colombia, which we were under con- tract to guarantee to that country. This is," he added, "in the light of the facts before us, nothing less than usurpa- tion."

Mr. Gorman then discussed the pres- ident as a "second Napoleon," which title had, he said, "been assigned to him by some." "A second Napoleon, indeed," he exclaimed. Had it come to this that the United States must have a Napoleon to shape its destinies and to distort the presidential office from its proper functions?

Here Mr. Aldrich interrupted Mr Gor- man with a question as to whether it

(Continued on Page 9.)

THIRTY MILLION FOR RUNNING RISK

(By Telegraph to Virginian-Pilot.)
NEW YORK, Dec. 17.

The hearing on the application to make permanent the receivership of the United States Shipbuilding company was resumed here today, Charles Steele, a member of the firm of J. P. Morgan & Co., being on the witness stand for a short examination as to the connection of that firm with the promotion of the shipbuilding company and the sale to it of the Bethlehem steel plant.

Mr. Untermeyer asked what reason there was that Mr. Schwab, owning no Bethlehem stock at the time, should re- ceive $30,000,000 in shipbuilding bonds and stock at the time of its sale, to which Mr. Steele replied that it was in consideration for the risk Mr. Schwab assumed in making the contract for the pudchase of Bethlehem stock, which was immediately assigned to Morgan & Co. Mr. Schwab had not told him that these securities would give him a control of the shipbuilding company.

SENSATIONAL INCIDENT IN THE OYSTER FIGHT

(Special to Virginian-Pilot.)
RICHMOND, VA., DEC. 17.

After a brief, but somewhat sensa- tional incident, the senate today post- poned further consideration of the bill to break the Baylor oyster survey until tomorrow.

Mr. Sears had begun a speech in op- position to the bill, when Mr. Keezell, of Rockingham, interrupted him, say- ing that he desired to offer certain amendments, which were being type- written.

"I only desire to give fair notice of this," he concluded.

"If that is what the senator calls fair notice," rejoined Mr. Sears in cutting tones, "I shall have to accept the state- ment, but I must say that I was edu- cated in a different school."

Mr. Sears thereupon took his seat, de- clining to debate the matter further until he had read the amendments, which were, he said, offered after a long debate and almost as the roll was about to be called on the bill. Further consideration was thereupon postponed until tomorrow.

The senate, at the instance of Judge Mann, resolved to insist on a rule adopted at a recent caucus, that after the morning hour the affairs of the body should be in the hands of a busi- ness committee composed of the presi- dent, chairman of the finance commit- tee and three members of the revision committee, and that no measure shall be considered without their consent. It was pointed out that there is no other practical way to get through with the business before the body. The rule was enforced today with good effect.

The Bland bill amending the charter of Portsmouth so as to allow the peo- ple to choose city officials now elected by the council was passed.

The senate refused to concur in the house amendments to the bill regulat- ing social clubs. This action was com- municated to the house and a confer- ence committee asked for.

The bill was passed validating the qualifications of county officials before county courts up to this time. There have been many such, the coun- ty officials overlooking the fact that the new constitution provides that they shall qualify before circuit judges.

The senate also passed the bill extend- ing the terms of the officers of Atlantic City ward, Norfolk.

The house amendments to senate bill No. 396, relating to general and special elections, were rejected. The amend- ments made it necessary for candidates to take two aditional Barksdale law oaths, making four in all.

The senate reconsidered the vote by which it defeated the bill relieving for- eign insurance companies coming into Virginia from the payment of charter fees, and the bill was passed.

A joint resolution was adopted pro- viding for the election tomorrow of a judge of the county court of Princess Anne.

The senate at 1:30 took a recess until 3 p. m.

At the afternoon session a large num- ber of revision bills were passed, and also two amending the charters of Richmond and Hampton.

There was a great fight in the house over the Anderson bill, which has pass- ed the senate, prescribing the method to be pursued in annexing territory to towns or cities. It was defeated and the house refused to reconsider. The bill is, therefore, dead for this session.

It provided that judges from other districts than those interested shall hear evidence where a city or town desires to annex territory, and either order or refuse to order such annexation. From this decision right of appeal to the su- preme court is allowed.

The house was evidently disinclined to enact any law on the subject at pres- ent, as it refused to accept as a substi- tute the Gardner bill which allows the matter to be settled by vote of the peo- ple of the territory sought to be an- nexed.

A bill was offered by Lowry to pro- vide for the pensioning of Confederate discharged from the army be- disability.

NO BALLOON ATTACHED TO AID IT

Three Years of Hard, Secret Work by Two Ohio Brothers Crowned With Success

ACCOMPLISHED WHAT LANGLEY FAILED AT

With Man as Passenger Huge Machine Flew Like Bird Under Perfect Control

BOX KITE PRINCIPLE WITH TWO PROPELLERS

The problem of aerial navigation without the use of a balloon has been solved at last.

Over the sand hills of the North Car- olina coast yesterday, near Kitty Hawk, two Ohio men proved that they could soar through the air in a flying machine of their own construction, with the power to steer it and speed it at will.

This, too, in the face of a wind blow- ing at the registered velocity of twenty one miles an hour.

Like a monster bird the invention hovered above the breakers and circled over the rolling sand hills at the com- mand of its navigator and, after soar- ing for three miles, it gracefully de- scended to earth again and rested light- ly upon the spot selected by the man in the car as a suitable landing place.

While the United States government has been spending thousands of dollars in an effort to make practicable the ideas of Professor Langley, of the Smithsonian Institute, Wilber and Or- ville Wright, two brothers, natives of Dayton, O., have, quietly, even secretly, perfected their invention, and put it to a successful test.

They are not yet ready that the world should know the methods they have adopted in conquering the air, but the Virginian-Pilot is able to state authen- tically the nature of their invention, its principle and its chief dimensons.

HOW MACHINE IS BUILT.

The idea of the box kite has been ad- hered to strictly in the basic formation of the flying machine.

A huge framework of light timbers, 33 feet wide five feet deep and five feet across the top forms the machine pro- per.

This is covered with a tough, but light canvas.

In the center, and suspended just be- low the bottom plane is the small gaso- line engine which furnishes the motive power for the propelling and elevating wheels.

These are two six-bladed propellers one arranged just below the center of the frame, so gauged as to exert an upward force when in motion, and the other extends horizontally to the rear from the center of the car, furnishing the forward impetus.

Protruding from the center of the car is a huge fan-shaped rudder of can- vass, stretched upon a frame of wood. This rudder is controlled by the navi- gator and may be moved to each side, raised or lowered.

START WAS SUCCESS.

Wilber Wright, the chief inventor of the machine, sat in the operator's car and when all was ready his brother un- fastened the catch which held the in- vention at the top of the slope.

The big box began to move slowly at first, acquiring velocity as it went, and when half way down the hundred feet the engine was started.

The propeller in the rear immediately began to revolve at a high rate of speed, and when the end of the incline was reached the machine shot out into space without a perceptible fall.

By this time the elevating propeller was also in motion, and, keeping its altitude, the machine slowly began to go higher and higher until it finally soared sixty feet above the ground.

Maintaining this height by the action of the under wheel, the navigator in- creased the revolutions of the rear pro- peller, and the forward speed of the huge affair increased until a velocity of eight miles an hour was attained.

All this time the machine headed into a twenty-one mile wind.

COAST FOLK AMAZED.

The little crowd of fisher folk and coast guards, who have been watching the construction of the machine with unconcealed curiosity since September 1st, were amazed.

They endeavored to race over the sand and keep up with the thing of the air, but it soon distanced them and continued its flight alone, save the man in the car.

Steadily it pursued its way, first tack- ing to port, then to starboard, and then driving straight ahead.

"It is a success," declared Orville Wright to the crowd on the beach after the first mile had been covered.

But the inventor waited. Not until he had accomplished three miles, put- ting the machine through all manoeuvres en route, [illegible]

(Continued on Page [illegible])

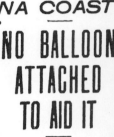

1904

Theodore Roosevelt was elected President, with Charles W. Fairbanks his Vice-President.

In what became known as the Roosevelt Corollary to the Monroe Doctrine, President Roosevelt declared the right of the United States to intervene in Latin American affairs to maintain order and to prevent European interference.

In the biggest fire since Chicago in 1871, a conflagration in Baltimore, Maryland, destroyed most of the business district. The fire burned for thirty hours and caused an estimated $80 million in damages.

Rolls-Royce was founded in England.

The first perfect major league baseball game was pitched by Cy Young of the Boston Americans. He did not allow any Philadelphia player to reach first base.

EXTRA THE

SUN EXTRA

VOLUME CXXXIV—NO. 84. BALTIMORE, MONDAY MORNING, FEBRUARY 8, 1904. PRICE ONE CENT

TWENTY-FOUR BLOCKS BURNED IN HEART OF BALTIMORE

CITY'S MOST VALUABLE BUILDINGS IN RUINS

LOSS VARIOUSLY ESTIMATED AT FROM $50,000,000 TO $80,000,000

BLAZE STILL SPREADING EASTWARD AND SOUTHWARD AT 3.30 A. M.

Starting In John E. Hurst Building The Fire Sweeps South To Lombard, East To Holliday And North To Lexington, Destroying Wholesale Business Houses, Banks, Continental, Equitable, Calvert, B. And O. Central, The Sun And Other Large Buildings.

Fire, which started at 10.50 o'clock yesterday morning, devastated practically the entire central business district of Baltimore and at midnight the flames were still raging with as much fury as at the beginning.

To all appearances Baltimore's business section is doomed. Many of the principal banking institutions, all the leading trust companies, all the largest wholesale houses, all the newspaper offices, many of the principal retail stores and thousands of smaller establishments went up in flame, and in most cases the contents were completely destroyed.

What the loss will be in dollars no man can even estimate, but the sum will be so gigantic that it is hard for the average mind to grasp its magnitude. In addition to the pecuniary loss, will be the immense amount of business lost by the necessary interruption to business while the many firms whose places are destroyed are making arrangements for resuming business.

There is little doubt that many men, formerly prosperous, will be ruined by the events of the last 24 hours. Many of them carry little or no insurance, and it is doubtful if many of the insurance companies will be able to pay their losses dollar for dollar, and those that do will probably require time in which to arrange for the payment.

APPALLED INTO SILENCE.

All day and all night throngs crowded the streets, blocking every avenue to the fire district and moving back out of danger only when forced to do so by the police on duty. Many of the spectators saw their all go up in flame before their eyes, and there were men with hopeless faces and despairing expressions seen on every hand. In fact, the throng seemed stunned with the magnitude of the disaster and scarcely seemed to realize the extent of it.

They stood around usually in dazed silence, and only occasionally would a word of despair be heard. That they were almost disheartened was apparent to the casual observer, and there is little wonder, for the crushing stroke fell with the suddenness of lightning from a cloudless sky.

STARTS IN HURST BUILDING.

At 10.50 o'clock in the morning the automatic fire-alarm box, No. 854, in the basement of the wholesale dry goods house of John E. Hurst & Co., German street and Hopkins place, sounded an alarm. Almost before the alarm had reached the various engine houses the entire building was a roaring mass of flames from top to bottom.

GASOLINE EXPLODES.

After burning fiercely for perhaps 10 minutes there was a loud explosion from the interior of the building as the gasoline tank used for the engine in the building let go. Instantly the immense structure collapsed and the flying, flaming debris caused the flames to be communicated to the adjacent buildings on all four corners.

By this time the first of the fire apparatus had reached the scene and was quickly put to work, but the fire had already gone beyond control and swept with irresistible force and incredulous swiftness on its devastating way. It was known that the conflagration would prove vastly destructive, but not one of those who witnessed it at this time imagined for an instant the terrible results that would ensue.

CHIEF HORTON DISABLED.

Chief Engineer Horton, of the Fire Department, was quickly on the ground, but scarcely had he begun to direct the force of firemen when a live trolley wire fell on him at the corner of Liberty and Baltimore streets, knocking him senseless, and he had to be carried to his home and placed in bed. By this accident the city was deprived of the services of its most experienced and trusted firefighter, and, although District Chief Emerich, who succeeded Chief Horton in command on the ground, did apparently all that was possible, those present could not but regret that Chief Horton was not there.

Mayor McLane came down and was on the ground until a late hour in the night. He walked around the burning district and conferred with various officials as to the steps necessary to be taken at various stages of the fire.

It is thought the loss will be over $50,000,000.

AID FROM WASHINGTON.

Four general alarms were speedily sent in and within half an hour after the first alarm every piece of fire apparatus in Baltimore was on the ground and at work. Realizing the gravity of the peril a telegram was sent to Washington for aid and two engines from that city were placed on a special train and hurried to the city over the Baltimore and Ohio railroad in record-breaking time. It was said that the trip was made in 37 minutes.

It was an awe-inspiring sight to witness the progress of the flames. A building eight or ten stories in height would suddenly break into flames from top to bottom almost in an instant and would burn fiercely until with a crash that could be heard for blocks the walls would collapse and the spot be marked only by a heap of blazing ruins. The crash of falling walls was almost incessant and now and then could be heard the muffled roar of an explosion as some gasoline tank or chemical substances became ignited by the heat and let go with terrific force.

MANY FIREMEN INJURED.

Every minute almost the lives of the firemen were in imminent danger from falling walls or leaping flames, and more than 50 of them were carried from the ground more or less severely burned. Undismayed by the danger or the hopelessness of the task, however, they continued the unequal struggle, and took the hose into narrow alleys, where the flames roared menacingly overhead on both sides of them, and directed streams of water where it was thought some effect could be produced.

Long ladders were placed against the walls of fiercely burning buildings and brave firemen climbed up and broke in windows and turned streams of water into the doomed buildings until the walls swayed and rocked and the crowd of onlookers shouted to them to come down, and many turned away their eyes in momentary apprehension of a fatal calamity.

Apparently every person in Baltimore was in the vicinity of the fire, and the various streets leading to the fire district were packed during the entire day. The entire police force, in charge of Marshal Farnan and Deputy Marshal Manning, was on the ground and with ropes succeeded in keeping the crowd back from the dangerous points. As the fire spread farther and farther the ropes were shifted and the crowd moved back one block at the time.

GREAT BUILDINGS GONE.

The section devastated contains the largest and most modern buildings in the city and this renders the calamity the more appalling. Immense office buildings, 10 and 12 stories high, large modern wholesale houses made of brick and steel, all disappeared as if built of the flimsiest material.

The exact origin of the fire is not known, but the explosion which started the spread of the flames to other buildings is said to have been caused by a gasoline engine in the [illegible] Building. [illegible] who was standing on the corner of Sharp and Baltimore streets when the fire first broke out, said that in less than 10 minutes the entire Hurst Building was a roaring mass of flames from top to bottom. When the explosion occurred Mr. Ball was cut on both hands and a hole was cut through his hat by flying fragments of glass.

TO LOMBARD STREET.

From German street the fire spread rapidly to Lombard street, leaping from building to building, and sometimes skipping two or three buildings, and in this way a block would become ignited in a remarkably short space of time. At Lombard street the fire paused for some time and the large building of Guggenheimer, Weil & Co. stood for a time apparently undamaged. It was evidently doomed, however, and all arrangements were made for dynamiting it in order to save the Lloyd L. Jackson building, just across Lombard street. The Guggenheimer, Weil & Co. building suddenly burst into flame and in a very short time the floors began falling in with a crash, the heavy lithographing machinery, weighing many tons, causing a detonation that made many think the place had really been dynamited. The walls quickly followed the floors and the Jackson building was saved after a hard struggle.

A number of the other buildings on the south side of Lombard street became ignited, however, and both sides of that street from Liberty to Charles were practically ruined, the houses on the north side being completely destroyed and those on the south side, with the exception of the Jackson building, badly damaged.

ACROSS SHARP STREET.

Meantime the flames had swept through the block to the east and quickly began the destruction of the buildings on the west side of Sharp street. With scarcely a pause they jumped over to the east side of Sharp and the large row of buildings on that side of the street began to crackle and burn. Hardly had a portion of the fire apparatus been shifted to meet [illegible] threatened when the [illegible] madly across to the [illegible] street, and here th[illegible]d. Almost before the [illegible] the fact the buildings [illegible] Hanover street were [illegible].

TO [illegible]RE STREET.

[illegible] scene in this portion of the [illegible] was magnificent in its [illegible] grandeur. Looking up Hanover [illegible] to Baltimore nothing but a seething, roaring mass of flames, mingled with dense smoke, could be seen. Baltimore street was itself a roaring furnace, and on every side were flying cinders. The roar of the flames was broken at frequent intervals by the crash of falling walls, and now and again the detonation of some explosion sounded above the other noises.

DYNAMITE USED.

After crossing Hanover street there was little to oppose the onrushing flames and the blaze continued its destructive course without a check to Charles street. Prior to this time there had been much talk of dynamiting the material was on the ground and Mr. Roy C. Lafferty, the Government expert, who had come from Washington especially to take charge of the work of dynamiting the buildings, was on the ground with his apparatus in readiness.

By this time it was thoroughly realized that the flames were completely beyond control and [illegible] this strait City Engineer Fendall and Mr. Lafferty laid a charge in the building adjoining Armstrong, Cator & Co.'s on the west and set it off. The building fell with a crash, but the blazing ruins ignited the Armstrong building and the situation was, if anything, made worse.

Armstrong, Cator & Co.'s building burned rapidly. A large charge of dynamite was let off in it, but the structure failed to collapse and the idea of destroying it with dynamite was abandoned.

The flames by this time were raging fiercely all along German street to Charles and it was then that Mr. Lafferty set off six charges of dynamite, each charge containing 100 pounds, in the building at the southwest corner of Charles and German streets. The tremendous force of the explosions tore out the massive granite columns that supported the building and left it with apparently almost no support, but the wals failed to collapse and stood until the flames had crossed Charles street and were eating into the block between Gharles and Light streets.

THE CARROLLTON GOES.

The fire had meantime been communicated to the row of buildings on South Charles street, between German and Lombard streets, and all those places, occupied principally by wholesale produce and grain dealers, were in flames.

Shortly before midnight the Carrollton Hotel was in flames and the fire was sweeping toward Calvert street with irresistible fury.

The firemen working on the south side had succeeded in checking the flames at Lombard street, and as the wind was blowing from the northwest there was no danger of it spreading farther in that direction. The western limit had also been reached at Howard street, and the danger was now to the east and north.

The progress of the flames toward the north had in the meantime been so rapid as to be simply appalling. From structure to structure they flew, licking up the massive buildings as if they were composed of paper. In the block between German and Baltimore streets they flew along, and almost before it could be realized the buildings along Baltimore street were blazing from roof to basement.

MULLIN'S IN RUINS.

For a time it was hoped the fire could be kept from crossing to the north side of Baltimore street and the firemen made a desperate effort to prevent it. The effort was useless, however, and soon the tall, narrow building of Mullin's Hotel began to dart out tongues of flame from several stories and in a few minutes the entire building was an immense flaming torch. At almost the same instant the remainder of the buildings between Sharp and Liberty streets were ablaze and the fire began its march to the north. The small two and three story buildings on Little Sharp street burned comparatively slowly and in this narrow space the two Washington companies fought a plucky battle with the devouring element. They were hemmed in on both sides by fire and directed the streams at the buildings from which smoke and flame were pouring, at a distance of only two or three yards.

ACROSS CHARLES STREET.

It was utterly, heartbreakingly useless. The flames darted rapidly from place to place, and soon the entire south side of Fayette street was in the grasp of the flames. Down Fayette to Charles they swept, and in a space of time that seemed incredibly short the building occupied by J. W. Putts & Co. was evidently doomed.

Seeing that nothing could save it Mr. Fendall, acting under instructions from Chief Emerich, decided to destroy the building with dynamite, in the hope of preventing the fire from crossing Charles street. The explosion was successful in accomplishing the object, and the entire corner collapsed instantly, but this had, apparently, no effect upon the progress of the fire, for almost before the sound of the falling walls had died away the building on the east side of Charles street began to blaze, and it was evident that the block between Charles and St. Paul streets was doomed.

CALVERT AND EQUITABLE GO.

In a desperate, but futile, effort to prevent the fire going further to the east, building after building was dynamited in this block, but it was all of no avail and the fire proceeded steadily onward. The Daily Record Building was soon in flames, and not many minutes later the fire had leaped over St. Paul street and the lofty, massive Calvert Building began to emit smoke and flame. The Equitable Building, just over a narrow alley, quickly followed, and these two immense buildings gave forth a glare that lighted the city for miles around.

It was thought that the fire could be prevented from crossing to the north side of Fayette street and here again a desperate stand was made by the firemen. Again it was useless, and soon the large building of Hall, Headington & Co., on the northwest corner of Charles and Fayette streets, was blazing brightly. With scarcely a pause the fire darted across to the east side of Charles street and began to lap up the handsome building of the Union Trust Company, while at the same time the large buildings to the west of Hall, Headingon & Co., occupied by Wise Brothers and Oppenheim, Oberndorf & Co., were aflame throughout.

MILLIONS IN A FEW BLOCKS

A Detailed Estimate Of Loss In The Wholesale District.

A careful and conservative estimate of the loss in the wholesale business district, in which the fire originated, places it at something over $1[illegible],000. This district is bounded by Baltimore, Liberty, Charles and Lombard streets and contained many of the largest dry goods, clothing and shoe houses in the city, besides two prominent banks—the National Exchange and Hopkins Place Savings Bank. This estimate was made for The Sun last night by Mr. George E. Taylor, of the insurance firm of Jenniss & Taylor, Holliday and Water streets. Mr. Taylor [illegible] to a reporter of The Sun until it was stated that the fire was only a few doors away, when he found it necessary to remove the valuables and papers from his office.

The estimate is for each building in this section, the loss given representing the building with its contents. According to this the heaviest losers were John E. Hurst & Co., R. M. Sutton & Co. and the Daniel Miller Company, all of which were heavily stocked with dry goods, and in each of which cases the loss in building and contents was placed at $1,500,000. The Armstrong, Cator & Co.'s loss is estimated at half a million, and the great majority were $100,000 or more apiece. This district contained about 125 buildings, among them some of the finest business structures in town, which were occupied by more than 150 firms. The list follows:

HOPKINS PLACE.

12 to 20—John E. Hurst, dry goods, $1,500,000; over $1,000,000 insurance.

22—Vacant building, $50,000.

24—William Koch Importing Company, toys, $150,000

26—Samuel D. Goldberg, pants; F. & Chas. Burger & Co., clothing; $75,000.

28 to 32—The Daniel Miller Company, dry goods; $1,500,000; carry more than $1,000,000 insurance on contents.

34—Dixon-Bartlett Company, shoes; $175,000.

36—Joyner, Witz & Co., hats and caps; $100,000.

38—Spragins, Buck & Co., shoes; $125,000.

40—Cohen-Adler Shoe Company; $125,000.

LIBERTY STREET.

35 and 37—L. S. Fiteman, ladies' wrappers; Jacob R. Seligman, paper, and Nathan Rosen, ladies' cloaks; $100,000.

39—Morton, Samuels & Co., boots and shoes, and Strauss Bros., storage; $100,000.

41—Baltimore Rubber Company, $135,000.

43—Guggenheimer, Weil & Co., lithographers and printers, $125,000.

WEST BALTIMORE STREET.

127—M. Friedman & Sons, clothing, and F. Schleunes, cloths; $150,000.

129—Schwarzkopf Toy Company, $100,000.

131—A. Federleicht & Sons, cloths, $75,000.

SOUTH LIBERTY STREET.

5—Whitaker's saloon, $15,000.

7—C. J. Stewart & Sons, hardware, $25,000.

9—O'Connell & Bannan, saloon, $25,000.

11 and 13—National Exchange Bank; building, $75,000; contents, $50,000.

AT 3.30 THIS MORNING.

At 3.30 o'clock this morning the fire had not crossed Jones falls on the east, although a number of lumber yards on the west side of the falls were ablaze. The wind was still from the north.

West of Charles and north of Lombard the fire had practically burned out. East of Charles and south of Lombard the flames are still spreading. It was expected to reach Pratt street before daylight. The fire probably will reach the water front west of Jones falls.

The Lutheran Church at Broadway and Canton avenue caught fire at 3 o'clock.

SIGNS OF ABATING.

Mayor McLane and Doctor Geer have just returned from a circuit of the fire. The Mayor said:

"I feel the conflagration shows some signs of abating. I have received a telegram from New York stating that the Fire Department of that city has sent over six engines, six hose carriages, six trucks and horses. These will probably reach Baltimore between 6 and 7 o'clock A. M."

Police Marshal Farnan said:

"I think the fire is practically under control."

HOPKINS PLACE.

21—S. Lowman & Co., clothing, $125,000.

23—John E. Hurst & Co., storage, $150,000.

25—Findlay, Roberts & Co., hardware, $75,000.

27—Lawrence & Gould Shoe Company and Bates Hat Company, $125,000.

29—S. Ginsberg & Co., clothing, $125,000.

31—Winkelmann & Brown Drug Co., $125,000.

33 and 35—R. M. Sutton & Co. dry goods, $1,500,000.

37—Chesapeake Shoe Company, $100,000.

39—S. F. and A. F. Miller, clothing manufacturers $150,000.

41—S. Halle Sons, boots and shoes, $100,000.

43 and 45—Strauss Bros., dry goods, $250,000.

Rear of 37 and 39—A. C. Meyer & Co. patent medicines, $150,000.

WEST LOMBARD STREET

108 and 110—Matthews Bros., paper-box manufacturers, $75,000.

112 and 114—Strauss, Eiseman & Co., shirt manufacturers, $150,000.

116 and 118—North Bros. & Strauss, have been moving to new building formerly occupied by Heywood Bros.-Wakefield Company, northeast corner Pratt and Greene streets; building $75,000; stock may be about $75,000.

WEST GERMAN STREET.

103—Standard Suspender Company and Daniel A. Boone & Co., liquors, $60,000.

105—Bradley, Kirkman, Reese Company, paper, $75,000.

107—George A. Eitel, neckwear manufacturer; Charles L. Linville and J. J. Murphy, sewing silks, $75,000.

109—McDonald & Fisher, wholesale paper, $100,000.

111—Wiley, Bruster & Co., dry goods, and F. W. & E. Dammann, cloth, $125,000.

113—Henry Oppenheimer & Co. clothing, and Vansant, Jacobs & Co., shirts, $175,000.

16—Joseph R. Stonebraker & Co., liquors, $75,000.

18—Lewis Lauer & Co., shirts, $100,000.

20—Champion Shoe Manufacturing Company and Diggs, Currin & Co., shoes, $100,000.

22—Mendels Bros., ladies' wrappers, $125,000.

24—Blankenberg, Gehrmann & Co., notions, $125,000.

26—Leo Keene & Co., ladies' cloaks, and Henry Pretzfelder & Co., boots and shoes, $125,000.

28—Peter Rose & Son harness manufacturers, $125,000.

30—James Robertson Manufacturing Company, plumbers' supplies, $100,000.

32—R. Jandorf & Co., boots and shoes, and James Robertson Manufacturing Company, storage, $100,000.

34—Rasch & Gaynor, window shades, $75,000.

36—Fusselbaugh-Balke Company, wall paper, $65,000.

BALTIMORE STREET.

101—Ades Bros., umbrella manufacturers, and Ferdinand Hahn & Sons, cloth, $75,000.

103—Ades Bros. and A. Hoff, clothing; $75,000.

105—Douglas, Henry & Co., hosiery and underwear, $75,000.

107—L. Greif & Bros., clothing, $150,000.

109—Maas & Kemper, embroidery and laces; $125,000.

111—Florence W. MacCarthy Company, notions and laces; $150,000.

113—Thalheimer Bros., clothing; $150,000.

115—Fisher Bros., liquors, wholesale, and Silberman and Todes, notions, dry gods, etc.; $150,000.

117—Silberman & Todes, $150,000.

119 and 121—New building, not occupied; $75,000.

123—M. Moses & Son, merchant tailors; $75,000.

125—J. Goldsmith & Son, clothing, and Sugar & Shear, clothing; $100,000.

HOPKINS PLACE.

7 and 11—Hopkins Place Savings Bank, $75,000.

13—Cohen & Samuels, hats and caps; $75,000.

15—F. Arnold & Sons, surgical instruments; $60,000.

17 and 19—Michael Ambach & Sons, clothing; $250,000.

HANOVER STREET.

2 and 4—Marburg Bros., tobacco; $100,000.

6—United Shirt and Collar Company, $50,000.

8—Mack Bros. & Mack, clothing, and John A. Griffith & Co., tailors' trimmings; $60,000.

10—Standard Cap Manufacturing Company and Elias Coplan, neckwear manufacturer, $75,000.

12—Reliable Pants Manufacturing Company, clothing, and L. M. Levering, druggists' supplies, $75,000.

14—Simon Neuberger & Bro., dry goods, $100,000.

HANOVER STREET.

1—S. M. Fleischer, ladies' and gents' furnishings, $75,000.

3—D. S. Wallerstein, millinery, $50,000.

5—The Brainerd-Armstrong Company, silks, and Carter, Webster & Co., storage of notions, $75,000.

7—Vogts, Quast & Co., tailors' trimmings, $75,000.

9 and 11—Woodward, Baldwin & Co., dry goods, $150,000.

13 and 15—Bouldin Bros., notions, $150,000.

17 and 19—Carter, Webster & Co., white goods, $150,000.

21—Edward Jenkins & Sons, coach and harness makers' supplies, $150,000.

23—Johnson, Boyd & Co., notions, $200,000.

25—Linthicum Rubber Company, boots and shoes, $125,000.

27—M. I. Blum & Bro., clothing, $100,000.

29—S. Kirson & Bro., clothing, $75,000.

31—Edward Jenkins & Sons, storage, and Lapsley & Bro. Company, storage, window shades, $75,000.

33 and 35—Philip F. Gehrman & Co., laces and embroideries, and Phillips Bros.' Company, dry goods, $200,000.

WEST GERMAN STREET.

5 and 7, Amon, Green & Co., cotton, and other offices; $75,000.

9, Sadler, Rowe & Co., books and stationery; $50,000.

11, George Mayo, manufacturer and proprietary medicines, $50,000.

13, Van Zandt, Jacobs & Co., shirts, $50,000.

15, Caplan & Greenbaum, clothing, and Crucible Steel Company, $50,000.

17, Carey, Bain & Smith, dry goods, and F. R. Kent, spool cotton and thread, $50,000.

WEST BALTIMORE STREET.

1—Oehm's Acme Hall, $150,000.

5 and 7—Consolidated Gas Company, $100,000.

9 and 11 and back to 4 and 10 West German—Armstrong, Cator & Co., notions and millinery, $500,000.

13 and 15—Wiegert & Co., shoes; Steiger Bros., trunks; Dowell, Helm & Co., storage, and M. and J. Oppenheimer & Sons, jewelry, $100,000.

17 and 19—Dowell, Helm & Co., millinery, $150,000.

THE SUN TODAY.

This edition of The Sun is printed from the presses of the Washington Star, through the courtesy of that paper. When the great fire was close to The Sun Building, in Baltimore, a force of editors, reporters, compositors and stereotypers was sent to Washington and duplicate news facilities were installed in the Star office.

SUMMARY OF THE NEWS.

Government Weather Report.

Washington, Feb. 7.—The Government Weather Bureau issued the following forecast for Monday and Tuesday:

Maryland, District of Columbia, Virginia, Delaware and Eastern Pennsylvania, fair, much colder Monday; cold wave at night; brisk to high northwest winds; Tuesday fair and cold.

West Virginia, fair Monday, except snow in the mountain districts, cold wave; Tuesday fair and cold.

North Carolina, fair and colder Monday, cold wave at night in the interior; Tuesday fair and cold; diminishing northwest winds.

Forecast For Baltimore And Vicinity.

The Government forecast for Baltimore and vicinity is for fair and much colder weather, with cold wave at night.

$20,000 IN MONEY SAVED

Officers Of Federal Savings Bank Find Vault Empty.

Early in the afternoon $20,000 in coin and bills was taken out of the vaults of the Federal Savings Bank, on the northeast corner of Hanover and Lombard streets. The money, it was said, was secured by Mr. James H. L. Foote and placed in the vault of the National Enameling and Stamping Company, two squares down Hanover street and out of the track of the fire.

Later some of the officers of the bank came around and, not knowing that the money had already been saved, with the aid of Deputy Marshal Manning, Sergeant Armiger, Sergeant Hughes and Patrolmen Scheib and Bagnell, effected an entrance into the bank and opened the safe, which they found empty.

Although for three hours nearly everything around the bank building was blazing, it did not catch fire until 7 o'clock and was only partially destroyed.

RINGS IN BANK SAFE

Treasurer Rabbe Has To Be Identified To Get Them.

While the fire was blazing a red furnace half a square away and the building of the Federal Savings Bank, at the southwest corner of Lombard and Hanover streets, was beginning to smoke, Mr. Conrad C. Rabbe, the treasurer of the bank, entered the building in company with Patrolman Scheib, of the Northwestern district, and Patrolman Johnson, of the Western, and got from the safe in the bank two handsome diamond rings belonging to him. Patrolman Scheib took possession of the [illegible] them until Mr. Rabbe had appeared before Deputy Marshal Manning and been identified.

PHONE SERVICE CRIPPLED

Trolley Cars Switched Over Different Routes.

The underground conduits proved the salvation of the telephone and telegraph systems in the heart of the city. They both worked with a reasonable degree of satisfaction until the telephone operators in the Exchange Building, on St. Paul street, and the Western Union and Postal Telegraph operators in the Equitable and Continental buildings had to abandon their posts. The telephone operators had to move about 7 o'clock, but the telegraph operators remained for a considerable time later. In the outlying districts, where the telephone service was controlled by branch exchanges there was not much trouble.

The trolley service, thanks to the system of switches and curves laid within the last few years, was in good shape in nearly all parts of the city, except where the fire was blazing. The cars were crowded all day.

STEAMERS READY TO MOVE

Vessels At Light Street Wharf On The Alert.

Along Light street wharves all the steamers had steam up and crews standing by ready to leave at any moment. The Tivoli moved from her wharf to one farther down the stream.

Captain Fowler had the steamer Anthony Groves, Jr., loaded and ready to leave for Philadelphia. The fruit steamer Salvatore di Giorgio, at Bowley's wharves, was ready to start.

The city fireboat Cataract took up a position at Pratt and Light streets at 7 o'clock P. M. and forced water through 2,000 feet of hose, which it was supposed would reach to German street. The hose was cut by wagons running over it and the attempt was abandoned.

ENGINE AND TRUCK LOST

Walls Of Hurst Building Fall On And Wreck Them.

The city Fire Department lost two fine pieces of apparatus. They were No. 15 engine and No. 2 truck. Arriving first on the scene of action, they took up their stations at Hopkins Place and German street. It was but a very short while before the heat became so intense as to drive the firemen away, and the falling walls from the Hurst Building fell on the apparatus, wrecking it. The horses, which were not far away, had their hair singed, but were not seriously burned.

CHIEF HORTON HURT

Stunned By Stepping On A Live Wire And Rendered Unconscious.

Chief Horton was badly shocked by stepping on a live wire early in the afternoon, and was taken in a patrol wagon up to his headquarters at No. 23 Engine House, Saratoga street, near Howard, where he was attended by Dr. Geer.

The Chief showed no burns, but [illegible] stunned, and was in a semi-conscious condition until late in the afternoon. He suffered acute pain in the head and was given opiates to relieve him. His driver, Clarence Kl[illegible], was given the post of nurse and Dr. Geer paid several visits during the course of the afternoon.

1906

Earthquakes can and do occur anywhere. But a good percentage of them come from a belt of land encircling the Pacific Ocean.

One of the most active zones within this belt is the San Andreas fault, a fracture in the earth's crust. It extends 650 miles from the Gulf of California to Cape Mendocino.

On April 18, 1906, a section of the San Andreas fault split and a series of shocks rocked the city of San Francisco. The quake and the fires that followed it caused the death of some seven hundred people.

The Call—Chronicle—Examiner

SAN FRANCISCO, THURSDAY, APRIL 19, 1906.

EARTHQUAKE AND FIRE: SAN FRANCISCO IN RUINS

DEATH AND DESTRUCTION HAVE BEEN THE FATE OF SAN FRANCISCO. SHAKEN BY A TEMBLOR AT 5:13 O'CLOCK YESTERDAY MORNING, THE SHOCK LASTING 48 SECONDS, AND SCOURGED BY FLAMES THAT RAGED DIAMETRICALLY IN ALL DIRECTIONS, THE CITY IS A MASS OF SMOULDERING RUINS. AT SIX O'CLOCK LAST EVENING THE FLAMES SEEMINGLY PLAYING WITH INCREASED VIGOR, THREATENED TO DESTROY SUCH SECTIONS AS THEIR FURY HAD SPARED DURING THE EARLIER PORTION OF THE DAY. BUILDING THEIR PATH IN A TRIANGUAR CIRCUIT FROM THE START IN THE EARLY MORNING, THEY JOCKEYED AS THE DAY WANED, LEFT THE BUSINESS SECTION, WHICHTHEY HAD ENTIRELY DEVASTATED, AND SKIPPED IN A DOZEN DIRECTIONS TO THE RESIDENCE PORTIONS. AS NIGHT FELL THEY HAD MADE THEIR WAY OVER INTO THE NORTH BEACH SECTION AND SPRINGING ANEW TO THE SOUTH THEY REACHED OUT ALONG THE SHIPPING SECTION DOWN THE BAY SHORE, OVER THE HILLS AND ACROSS TOWARD THIRD AND TOWNSEND STREETS. WAREHOUSES, WHOLESALE HOUSES AND MANUFACTURING CONCERNS FELL IN THEIR PATH. THIS COMPLETED THE DESTRUCTION OF THE ENTIRE DISTRICT KNOWN AS THE "SOUTH OF MARKET STREET." HOW FAR THEY ARE REACHING TO THE SOUTH ACROSS THE CHANNEL CANNOT BE TOLD AS THIS PART OF THE CITY IS SHUT OFF FROM SAN FRANCISCO PAPERS.

AFTER DARKNESS,THOUSANDS OF THE HOMELESS WERE MAKING THEIR WAY WITH THEIR BLANKETS AND SCANT PROVISIONS TO GOLDEN GATE PARK AND THE BEACH TO FIND SHELTER. THOSE IN THE HOMES ON THE HILLS JUST NORTH OF THE HAYES VALLEY WRECKED SECTION PILED THEIR BELONGINGS IN THE STREETS AND EXPRESS WAGONS AND AUTOMOBILES WERE HAULING THE THINGS AWAY TO THE SPARSELY SETTLED REGIONS. EVERYBODY IN SAN FRANCISCO IS PREPARED TO LEAVE THE CITY, FOR THE BELIEF IS FIRM THAT SAN FRANCISCO WILL BE TOTALLY DESTROYED.

DOWNTOWN EVERYTHING IS RUIN. NOT A BUSINESS HOUSE STANDS. THEATRES ARE CRUMBLED INTO HEAPS. FACTORIES AND COMMISSION HOUSES LIE SMOULDERING ON THEIR FORMER SITES. ALL OF THE NEWSPAPER PLANTS HAVE BEEN RENDERED USELESS, THE "CALL" AND THE "EXAMINER" BUILDINGS, EXCLUDING THE "CALL'S" EDITORIAL ROOMS ON STEVENSON STREET BEING ENTIRELY DESTROYED.

IT IS ESTIMATED THAT THE LOSS IN SAN FRANCISCO WILL REACH FROM $150,000,000 TO $200,000,000. THESE FIGURES ARE IN THE ROUGH AND NOTHING CAN BE TOLD UNTIL PARTIAL ACCOUNTING IS TAKEN.

ON EVERY SIDE THERE WAS DEATH AND SUFFERING YESTERDAY. HUNDREDS WERE INJURED, EITHR BURNED, CRUSHED OR STRUCK BY FALLING PIECES FROM THE BUILDINGS, AND ONE OF TEN DIED WHILE ON THE OPOPERATING TABLE AT MECHANICS' PAVILION, IMPROVISED AS A HOSPITAL FOR THE COMFORT AND CARE OF 300 OF THE INJURED. THE NUMBER OF DEAD IS NOT KNOWN BUT IT IS ESTIMATED THAT AT LEAST 500 MET THEIR DEATH IN THE HORROR.

AT NINE O'CLOCK, UNDER A SPECIAL MESSAGE FROM PRESIDENT ROOSEVELT, THE CITY WAS PLACED UNDER MARTIAL LAW. HUNDREDS OF TROOPS PATROLLED THE STREETS AND DROVE THE CROWDS BACK, WHILE HUNDREDS MORE WERE SET AT WORK ASSISTING THE FIRE AND POLICE DEPARTMENTS. THE STRICTEST ORDERS WERE ISSUED, AND IN TRUE MILITARY SPIRIT THE SOLDIERS OBEYED DURING THE AFTERNOON THREE THIEVES MET THEIR DEATH BYRIFLE BULLETS WHILE AT WORK IN THE RUINS. THE CURIOUS WERE DRIVEN BACK AT THE BREASTS OF THE HORSES THAT THE CAVALRYMEN RODE AND ALL THE CROWDS WERE FORCED FROM THE LEVEL DISTRICT TO THE HILLY SECTION BEYOND TO THE NORTH

THE WATER SUPPLY WAS ENTIRELY CUT OFF, AND MAY BE IT WAS JUST AS WELL, FOR THE LINES OF FIRE DEPARTMENT WOULD HAVE BEEN ABSOLUTELY USELESS AT ANY STAGE. ASSISTANT CHIEF DOUGHERTY SUPERVISED THE WORK OF HIS MEN AND EARLY IN THE MORNING IT WAS SEEN THAT THE ONLY POSSIBLE CHANCE TO SAVE THE CITY LAY IN EFFORT TO CHECK THE FLAMES BY THE USE OF DYNAMITE. DURING THE DAY A BLAST COULD BE HEARD IN ANY SECTION AT INTERVALS OF ONLY A FEW MINUTES, AND BUILDINGS NOT DESTROYED BY FIRE WERE BLOWN TO ATOMS. BUT THROUGH THE GAPS MADE THE FLAMES JUMPED AND ALTHOUGH THE FAILURES OF THE HEROIC EFFORTS OF THE POLICE FIREMEN AND SOLDIERS WERE AT TIMES SICKENING, THE WORK WAS CONTINUED WITH A DESPERATION THAT WILL LIVE AS ONE OF THE FEATURES OF THE TERRIBLE DISASTER. MEN WORKED LIKE FIENDS TO COMBAT THE LAUGHING, ROARING, ONRUSHING FIRE DEMON.

NO HOPE LEFT FOR SAFETY OF ANY BUILDINGS

San Francisco seems doomed to entire destruction. With lapse in the raging of the flames just before dark, the hope was raised that with the use of the tons of dynamite the course of the fire might be checked and confined to the triangular sections it had cut out for its path. But on the Barbary Coast the fire broke out anew and as night closed in the flames were eating their way into parts untouched in their ravages during the day. To the south and the north they spread; down to the docks and out into the resident section, in and to the north of Hayes Valley.. By six o'clock practically all of St. Ignatius' great buildings were no more. They had been leveled to the fiery heap that marked what was oncethe metropolis of the West.

The first of the big structures to go to ruin was the Call Building, the famous skyscraper. At eleven o'clock the big 18-story building was a furnace. Flames leaped from every window and shot skyward from thecircular windows in the dome. In less than two hours nothing remained but the tall skeleton.

By five o'clock the Palace Hotel was in ruins. The old hostelry, famous the world over, withstood the seige until the last and although dynamite was used in frequent blasts to drive

Continued on Page Two

BLOW BUILDINGS UP TO CHECK FLAMES

The dynamiting of buildings in the track of the fire, to stay the progress of the flames, was in charge of John Bermingham, Jr., superintendent of the California Powder Works. Several experienced men from the powder works, assisted by policemen and members of the fire department, did the hazardous work of blowing up the buildings. They were razed in sets of threes, but the open spaces where the shattered buildings fell were quickly turned into holocausts of flame. The work was most effective in the business blocks east of Kearny street.

WHOLE CITY IS ABLAZE

At 10 o'clock last night the Occidental Hotel was destroyed by the flames which swept unchecked across Montgomery street and attacked the block bounded by Montgomery, Sutter, Bush and Kearny. The new Merchants' Exchange building was a mass of flames from [illegible] to tower.

The Union Trust building and Crocker-Woolworth Bank were both ablaze and the Chronicle building and other buildings in that block were threatened by the flames.

Shortly after 10 o'clock the fire had eaten its way westward from Portsmouth Square to Kearny and California streets. The entire section fronting on the west side of Kearny street seemed doomed.

All the building adjoining the Hall of Justice were ablaze and the firemen were striving to save the structure by using dynamite. It is almost a certainty that every building contained in the section bounded by Clay, Kearny, Market and East streets will be consumed.

The flames had eaten their way westward in the residence section as far as Gough street. There [illegible] dynamiting blocks after blocks, the firemen [illegible] in checking the [illegible] element.

CHURCH OF SAINT IGNATIUS IS DESTROYED

The magnificent church and College of St. Ignatius, on the northwest corner of Van Ness avenue and Hayes street represents in its destruction a material loss of over $1,000,000. The actual cost of the great building was over $900,000, but during the years which have elapsed since its erection the church has been enriched by paintings and frescoes, which were priceless. Some of them were works of art which can never be replaced, however willing those interested in the church might be to meet any expense in the effort.

MAYOR CONFERS WITH MILITARY AND CITIZENS

At 1 o'clock yesterday afternoon 50 representative citizens of San Francisco met the Mayor, the Chief of Police and the United States Military authorities in the police office in the basement of the Hall of Justice. They had been summoned thither by Mayor Schmitz early in the forenoon, the fearful possibilities of the situation having forced themselves upon him immediately after the shock of earthquake in the morning, and the news which at once reached him of the completeness of the diaster. He lost no time in making out a list of citizens from whom to seek advice and assistance, and in summoning them to the conference. It was called at the Hall of Justice, as virtually the first news which reached the Mayor regarding the extent of the disaster was that of the ruin of the City Hall. He did not realize that even while the conference was to be going on cornices would be crashing down and windows falling in fragments in the Hall of Justice also, and that before sunset desperate efforts would be made to blow the structure up in the vain endeavor by this means to check the advance of the flames in the northern section of the down town district.

All, or nearly all of the citizens summoned to the conference

Continued on Page Two

1907

Marines landed in Honduras to protect Americans living there and their property, threatened by revolutionaries.

The U.S. Navy sailed to the Pacific and around the world to show off its power.

A financial panic began with the fall of the stock market. Many banks failed throughout the country.

In Monongah, West Virginia, a coal mine exploded, killing 361 miners.

The steamship *Lusitania* set a speed record of five days, fifty-four minutes, in a trip from Ireland to New York.

THE BROOKLYN DAILY EAGLE

FOUR O'CLOCK. NEW YORK CITY, THURSDAY, MARCH 14, 1907.—VOL. 68. NO. 72.—26 PAGES, INCLUDING PICTURE SECTION. THREE CENTS.

JEROME EXPERT CALLS THAW SANE

The District Attorney Puts a Voluminous Hypothetical Question.

TO RECALL EVELYN NESBIT

Delmas Will Use Her to Seal the Lips of Hummel as to Their Talk.

MANY LONG ARGUMENTS.

Goes Down to a Question of Veracity Between Hummel and Thaw's Wife.

This afternoon District Attorney Jerome put his expert alienists on the witness stand to swear that Thaw was sane when he killed Stanford White.

Only six experts were sworn for the prosecution to pass on the hypothetical question this afternoon. Directly after recess the six experts were called to the stand and sworn together. They gathered around the Bible and took the oath as one man. The experts were Dr. Allan Ross Diefendorf, of Middletown, Conn., and professor of mental disease at Yale; Dr. William D. Pritchard, of the New York Polyclinic; Dr. William Hirsch, of Cornell Medical School; Albert Warren Ferris, of the College of Physicians and Surgeons, and the other two New York experts, Drs. William Mabon and Austin Flint.

There was great curiosity as to the reason why Dr. Carlos F. McDonald was not sworn. There was a report that Dr. McDonald had disagreed with his fellow experts. Mr. Delmas was curious to know about Dr. McDonald and the other experts. He wanted to know if there were not other experts. Mr. Jerome did not satisfy his curiosity. Then Mr. Delmas said:

"Unless the very learned District Attorney will state that these are all the experts he had to be sworn I will object to any stipulation as to the arrangement of the examination."

"That is a matter of entire and complete indifference to me," said Mr. Jerome.

Dr. Allen McLane Hamilton had asked at recess that he did not want to be confused with the experts for the prosecution.

"I am here under subpena, and not as the prosecution's expert," he said.

Dr. Hamilton was formerly an expert for the Thaw defense.

Jerome Proceeds to Qualify His Experts.

Mr. Jerome called Dr. Austen Flint to the stand as his first expert. He said he would qualify each expert before having them testify.

"I intend to qualify these gentlemen as experts," Mr. Jerome said, "and then I will read to them the hypothetical question asked by the defense, and, after asking a question on that, I will read my own hypothetical question."

This made it look as though the experts would be on the stand several hours.

Dr. Flint was qualified by his own statement as to his qualifications and experience. Then Mr. Jerome read to him the same hypothetical question asked by Mr. Delmas of his experts—the identical question on which Dr. Wagner and Dr. Evans based their opinion that Thaw was insane when he killed Stanford White.

Thaw Was Sane, Says Dr. Flint.

Dr. Austin Flint's sworn opinion, based on the assumed fact contained in the hypothetical question, which Mr. Delmas asked his experts, was that Thaw was sane and rational when he killed Stanford White.

"In my opinion, he knew the nature and quality of the act he was doing and he knew it was wrong," said Dr. Flint.

Experts for the defense basing their opinions on the same set of facts had sworn that Thaw was insane. Mr. Jerome was so fatigued by reading the hypothetical question for the defense that he had his assistant, Mr. Garvan, read his own hypothetical question.

While Mr. Jerome was reading the hypothetical question of the defense, Harry Thaw amused himself with the advance proofs of a magazine article headed "Thaw's Finish: How the Thaw Trial Will Put Him on the Bum."

Assistant District Attorney Garvan read the prosecution's hypothetical question. In answer to it Dr. Flint declared that in his opinion Thaw knew the nature and quality of the act of shooting Stanford White and that the act was wrong.

Evelyn Nesbit to Be Recalled.

To close the lips of "Abe" Hummel and to [illegible] dangerous testimony the Thaw defense secured permission this afternoon to recall Evelyn Nesbit Thaw to the stand to swear that everything she told to Hummel was told as a client to her counsel, and that the matter is, therefore, [illegible].

The recalling of Mrs. Thaw was forced on the defense by Mr. Jerome's persistent efforts to get in Hummel's story of the affidavit.

The affidavit was barred out by the court, but Mr. Jerome would not confess defeat. He strove to get from Hummel the matter contained in the affidavit. The lawyer was on the witness stand all of the morning session, but he was asked only two questions. One of these was answered before he could be stopped. The answer to the other question was [illegible] by the plea of Mr. Delmas that Hummel had been Evelyn Nesbit's counsel and that his lips were sealed by law in regard to all revelations made by her [illegible].

[illegible] relations of Hummel to Miss Nesbit at the [illegible] Stanford White. Delmas said he would recall her and prove by her that she regarded Hummel as her counsel.

Hummel's Word Against Evelyn Nesbit's.

The Thaw case has now reduced itself to a question of veracity between Hummel and Evelyn Nesbit Thaw. She swore on the stand that she never told Hummel certain things. Hummel swore that she did. She swore that she told all the Stanford White story to Thaw, in Paris. Hummel swore to-day that she told him she did not tell the story to Thaw.

Mrs. Thaw, on past performances, has just a little the better of Hummel on a question of veracity, as Hummel is now under sentence for a year in Sing Sing on a charge involving perjury and has two indictments for perjury pending against him. However, Mrs. Thaw's position is hardly that of a witness whose every word compels belief.

There was a sensational clash of counsel just before adjournment this morning. As soon as Justice Fitzgerald announced that Mrs. Thaw could be recalled one of Thaw's lawyers hastened to an anteroom where Mrs. Thaw was sitting.

Delmas Hotly Resents an Insinuation by Jerome.

Mr. Delmas asked for an adjournment to give him time to go over the long hypothetical question. It was then only 15 minutes before time for adjournment, but Mr. Jerome protested against adjournment. He insinuated that Evelyn Thaw be put on the stand at once and that no time be given her counsel to coach her. This aroused the wrath of Mr. Delmas, who demanded to know if it was not legal on the Atlantic seaboard for counsel to consult with witnesses. Justice Fitzgerald squelched the District Attorney by announcing an adjournment.

Jerome's 39-Page Hypothetical Question.

Mr. Jerome's hypothetical question is an epitome of the case. Printed copies of the question were distributed to alienists and lawyers for both sides this morning. The question covered 39 printed pages.

The prominence given by the hypothetical question to the testimony of James Clinch Smith shows that Mr. Jerome relies chiefly on the story told by White's brother-in-law.

Practically the whole of Smith's story is embodied in the question.

The entire hypothetical question would fill about eight columns of the Eagle.

Delmas Argues Against the Affidavit.

A goodly part of the morning session was consumed in argument for and against the admission of the Evelyn Nesbit affidavit. Mr. Delmas, for the defense, argued that the witness "Abe" Hummel should not be permitted to testify because Hummel, though acting for Stanford White at the time the affidavit was drawn, subsequently had the relation of counsel to Evelyn Nesbit. He said the affidavit could not prove that Evelyn Nesbit did not tell the story to Harry Thaw in Paris. He said that if the District Attorney had any paper or had any evidence showing that Evelyn Nesbit had, either in writing or in oral statement, said she had never told the story to Thaw, then the evidence should be admitted. He contended, however, that the affidavit was no such thing and was not admissible as evidence.

The affidavit, Mr. Delmas said, could not be admitted as a whole under any circumstances, as it surely contained matter of an objectionable nature. He was willing that Hummel should testify as to whether or not Evelyn Nesbit had denied to him that she ever told the story to Thaw in Paris. He had no objection to questions concerning Thaw's wish to get White in the penitentiary. He showed that Evelyn Thaw herself had testified that she told Hummel that Thaw wanted to get White in the penitentiary. He said that Hummel's corroboration of her testimony in that respect could not possibly show that she had never told the story.

Willing to Admit Certain Testimony From Hummel.

Mr. Delmas said that it was perfectly natural that Thaw wanted to have papers signed involving White, and that Evelyn Nesbit's story to Thaw could not impeach her statement as to telling the story to Thaw.

"I and my associates and the defendant are willing to assume the responsibility for admitting a question as to whether or not Evelyn Nesbit told this witness that she never told Thaw in Paris these things against Stanford White," said Mr. Delmas.

He added that he was willing to do this in view of the peculiar circumstances surrounding the witness and the offer of the evidence.

Mr. Delmas made a spirited attack on the methods employed yesterday by Mr. Jerome in getting into his argument before the jury all the essential statements contained in the alleged affidavit. Mr. Delmas referred to Mr. Jerome's methods as being very objectionable.

"I could use a stronger term," he said, "but I will refrain from doing so."

Court Rules Out the Affidavit.

The argument went into the cases cited yesterday by Mr. Jerome. Mr. Delmas attacked these alleged authorities, and declared that they could not be considered as authoritative. Mr. Jerome defended his position, but not convincingly enough to persuade the court that he was right. The question of admitting the affidavit was decided against Mr. Jerome. The famous paper was excluded.

"The propositions stated are not at all authorities, and the objection must be sustained," said Justice Fitzgerald.

This was a bitter pill for Mr. Jerome. He sat for a moment without a word. After a short conference with Mr. Garvan he returned to the examination of Hummel.

Hummel's Snap Answer Enrages Delmas.

He asked this question:

"Did Evelyn Nesbit, as she then was, on her visit to your office on October 27, 1903, say to you that she never told Thaw in Paris that she had been drugged and ravished by Stanford White?"

"She certainly did," said Hummel.

The little lawyer spoke like a flash, with the evident determination to beat out an objection.

The answer was on the record before Mr. Delmas could even rise to object. The California lawyer was furious.

Continued on Page 2.

MANY HAVE PERISHED IN FLOODED STREAMS

Rivers in Pennsylvania and Ohio Made Raging Torrents by Heavy Rains.

PROPERTY LOSSES ARE HEAVY.

At Pittsburg the Flood Will Probably Be the Worst Ever Known—32 Feet Stage Reached.

Pittsburg, March 14—Pittsburg is in the throes of one of its greatest floods. The record of ten years has already been passed and the rivers are still rising. If the rise continues at the present rate the record of 1884, when the water reached the highest stage since 1835, will have been passed long before nightfall. The stage in 1884 was 33 feet 4 inches.

To-day at 10 o'clock the marks registered 32 feet, with the water creeping up at the rate of 5 inches an hour and still rising at all headwater points. Every tributary along the upper rivers is swollen and dispatches from all sections of Western Pennsylvania report the smaller streams beyond their banks and the surrounding districts submerged.

By 11 o'clock to-day the flood had reached Penn avenue and Sixth street, in this city, and all the Point district was inundated. The lowlands of Allegheny and the South Side were submerged and every mill and factory along the banks of the Monongahela and Allegheny rivers was forced to suspend operations. Traffic on all railroads entering Pittsburg has been seriously affected, but the lines are still running, although the water is rapidly encroaching on their tracks.

The residents of lower Allegheny were caught unawares by the flood. It is usual for the police to notify them of threatened high water, but no one regarded the situation as serious and no precautions were taken. During the night the water began to rise rapidly and by daylight in hundreds of houses it had reached almost to the second stories. The greatest excitement prevailed and scores of people were taken from their homes in skiffs. At 9 o'clock the street cars between Pittsburg and Allegheny were forced to stop running. Hundreds of wagons of all descriptions were pressed into service to convey the people to the bridges between the two cities.

During the morning the water reached the boilers of the pumping station of the Monongahela Water Company, on the South Side, and the pumps had to be stopped. A special warning was sent out by the company requesting the residents of the South Side to use the water as sparingly as possible.

Weather Bureau officials predict 34 feet or over, at Pittsburg.

If this stage is reached the flood will not only be the greatest in 75 years, but the most disastrous in the history of the city.

Property Loss May Be $1,000,000.

Warm, heavy rains throughout this entire section for nearly 48 hours added to by the melting snow from the hills and mountains, caused all the streams to rise with alarming rapidity. Until an early hour to-day, however, a flood of unusual proportions was not expected, and the rushing waters caught the people unprepared.

As a result of this the damage will be much heavier. It was estimated early to-day that the loss from the closing down of manufacturing plants alone would exceed a half million dollars, and the damage to property from the high water would be as much more.

Many Lives Lost Thus Far.

Nine deaths are attributed to the flood thus far. This includes the three trainmen who lost their lives by the collapse of the Harmarsville bridge yesterday, and two men drowned last night when the towboat Cruiser capsized in the Ohio River. The other fatalities reported are:

Lloyd Weyand, aged 30 years, and William Beers, 40 years old, drowned in Laurel Hill Creek, near Somerset, while trying to ford a stream; George Johnston, aged years, drowned in Girty's Run, Millvale; Annie Shutt, aged 7 years, drowned in Bluebaker Creek, near Hastings.

Three May Have Perished at Mahaffey.

Clearfield, Pa., March 14—Warm, heavy rain causing a rapid thaw of snow and ice on the mountains, has swollen the west branch of the Susquehanna River above its banks in many places in this county, and at other up-river points. It is reported that a man, woman and child were drowned at Mahaffey by the sudden rise of the water.

There is an eleven-foot flood here and reports from other points show the water to be higher than at any time since 1889. A horse and buggy which floated down the river were taken out of the water here. There is no clew to the owner of the rig.

Hoxham, Residence Section of Johnstown, Under Water.

Johnstown, Pa., March 14—The Conemaugh River and Stony Creek early this morning broke out of their banks as a result of the heavy rains of the past 24 hours. The street car service has been abandoned and a number of mills have been forced to suspend operations. Hoxham, the aristocratic residential section of the city is under varying depths of water, while a rise of 6 inches more will inundate many of the principal business streets. Residents along the river are greatly excited over the flood and many people are spending the night in anxious vigils.

Three Drowned at Zanesville, Ohio.

Zanesville, O., March 14—Three Hungarians were drowned here as a result of the flood this morning. A score or more of foreign workmen were living in a house that was surrounded by the Muskingum River overflow during the night. When they started to wade to land three were caught in the current and swept out into the river.

Flood conditions throughout Muskingum County are unprecedented for years and are growing worse every hour. Both the Muskingum and Licking rivers are out of bounds in this city, and more than a hundred homes have been invaded by the high water. It is believed that three hundred families will be homeless here by to-morrow, as the crest of the flood will not be reached before that time. With the exception of the Cincinnati and Muskingum Valley railroads connection with the Pennsylvania at Trinway, sixteen miles north, every railroad entering the city is tied up.

LOCAL WEATHER PROBABILITIES. Rain, followed by clearing and slightly colder to-night; Friday, generally fair; fresh to brisk southwest to west winds.

The high waters have crossed West Main street to a depth of four feet, and interurban traffic from Columbus and Newark has been abandoned. The Southeastern Ohio Interurban has suffered thousands of dollars loss from washouts between here and Crooksville and it will be a month before traffic will be resumed.

Conditions Bad at Findlay, Ohio.

Findlay, O., March 14—Constant rainfall for the past thirty-six hours has put the Blanchard River on a rampage. Many families in the lower sections of the city were forced to the second story of their homes last night, and the Cincinnati, Hamilton and Dayton, the Toledo, Findlay and Fostoria electric railway companies are cut off from entering the city. Hacks are being used to transport passengers to the outlying districts, where they take the trains.

Lima, O., March 14—The heavy downpour of rain in this section has raised the Ottawa River beyond its bounds, the small waterway being unable to drain the district on the crest of Ohio's watershed. Fifty families were forced to move out of their homes here last night.

Oil operators have sustained heavy losses throughout northwestern Ohio. Pipe lines have been unearthed and power plants rendered useless by the high waters. Wheat is washed out in many sections of this county and adjoining territories.

Five Marooned on Island Off Latrobe, Pa.

Latrobe, Pa., March 14—Hundreds of people are homeless as the result of the flood, which is the greatest in the history of the town. Sycamore Island is submerged and five men and a woman are marooned on the island having climbed into trees to await a boat which is being brought from Ligonier. Great alarm prevails in the villages of Baggaley and Dorothy and the residents have taken to the hills.

The bridge between Latrobe and Youngstown, on the West Pennsylvania Railroad, has been destroyed, trolleys are blocked, the Ligonier Railroad is washed out and the coal mines are flooded.

103 BODIES RECOVERED.

President Fallieres Will Attend Funeral of Victims of the Jena.

Toulon, March 14—Up to this morning 103 bodies of victims of the explosion, March 12, on board the battleship Jena had been recovered. Very few of them could be identified. The difficult task of recovering the dead from the hulk of the warship continued throughout last night, relays of survivors of the crew participating in the work. The bodies recovered were transported on gun-carriages, covered with the tri-colored flag, to the mortuary before daylight, in order to avoid harrowing spectacles and increasing the sorrow of the distracted relatives. Most of the injured are making favorable progress toward recovery.

Paris, March 14—President Fallieres has decided to attend the funeral of the victims of the battleship Jena disaster, at Toulon, which will occur March 16. The President will leave Paris Friday evening for the South. The Chamber of Deputies and the Senate adjourned to-day as a sign of mourning for the Jena victims, after the presidents of the two Houses had referred sympathetically to the disaster.

SCHOLES PROPERTY SOLD.

An Apartment House to Be Erected on Corner of Keap Street and Bedford Avenue.

The residence of H. B. Scholes, at 575 Bedford avenue, occupying a plot 50x100, with an adjoining plot of the same dimensions, embracing the corner of Keap street and Bedford avenue, which the family has maintained for many years as a garden, has been sold through Albert G. McDonald, attorney, of 215 Montague street, to a Manhattan investor, at a price approximating about $35,000. It is reported that the Scholes house is thirty years old. The property has been in the family since 1851, and in many respects has constituted an Eastern District landmark. It is said that the residence itself is not likely to be torn down for some time, at least, but that on the corner lot will shortly be erected a first-class apartment house. The property is restricted to a certain class of buildings.

POLICE KILL FIVE STRIKERS

And Wound Twenty More in Conflict at Belgrade, Servia.

Belgrade, Servia, March 14—In a conflict between police and strikers here to-day five of the latter were killed and twenty wounded, and further collisions were narrowly averted.

A strike of the men employed in the sugar and leather trades began March 9, and the employers to-day made an effort to compel the strikers to permit non-unionists to take their places. With this object in view a number of non-unionists were escorted by police into the factories, where the non-union men were attacked by the strikers. The police eventually were obliged to use their firearms, with the result that five strikers were killed and twenty were wounded. The bodies of the dead were immediately taken possession of by the strikers, who formed a procession and marched toward the cemetery.

On the way to the cemetery the procession passed by the Parliament Building and the palace occupied by King Peter, and in each case the strikers were only prevented by strong forces of police from marching into the buildings with their dead comrades.

REAR-END COLLISION ON L.

Only One Man Was Painfully Injured—Passengers Shaken Up.

As the result of the rear-end collision of a northbound elevated trains on the Canarsie line at Church avenue, Canarsie, this morning, Samuel Maimam of 317 Powell avenue, is at his home suffering from painful injuries about the head and shoulders. Immediately the cause of the smash-up, the forward L train stopped at the Canarsie station, and the engineer on the following train was unable to stop. The first train was obscured by the [illegible]. A surgeon from St. Mary's Hospital found, on his arrival, that, although all the passengers had been severely shaken up, Maimam was the only one who really needed medical attendance.

EXCHANGE IN A PANIC AS STOCKS GO WAY DOWN

Reading Loses 18 1-2; Union Pacific 20, B. R. T. Falls Off 9 Points.

BREAK ALL ALONG THE LINE.

Bear Raid Successful for the Day. Many Rumors; No Real Basis Shown for the Fall.

Another violent break occurred in the stock market to-day, the prices of several of the leading securities falling to the lowest quotations recorded this year. Early in the afternoon, following a morning of panicky fluctuations, Reading dropped 18½ points to 95⅛. A semi-panic at once swept over the Stock Exchange, and the whole list collapsed without any manifest resistance.

Union Pacific, which next to Reading ruled weakest, fell off 14 points. Delaware and Hudson went down 12¾ points, National Lead 12¼, and St. Paul, Amalgamated Copper and Smelting 8⅛ to 10 points each. There was a drop in Brooklyn Rapid Transit of 9¼, in Atchison of 7½, in Northern Pacific of 8, in Great Northern preferred of 7¼ and in Steel preferred of 4⅜. Throughout the entire list, in short, there was a sensational decline, Union Pacific finally falling off 20 points to 125¼.

As soon as the slump set in the wildest scenes enacted on the Stock Exchange this year occurred. Brokers rushed here and there in an effort to unload, and thousands of share were dumped on the market in less time than the telling of it takes. The spectators who crowded the gallery watched the excitement below with bated breath, expecting every minute to hear the gavel of the president fall and some failure announced. Up to the time the Eagle went to press, however, no failures of any consequence were recorded.

A number of alarming rumors accompanied the collapse of prices. Among them was one to the effect that the Attorney General would move for the indictment of E. H. Harriman. Another rumor had it that the administration at Washington had made it known in response to inquiries that its attitude toward the railroad corporations had not changed.

In banking quarters, however, the opinion prevailed that the sensational decline was largely due to bear raids, though further liquidation had been brought out by the slump.

There was a quick recovery from the lowest figures in some shares. Atchison rose to 86 1-8 and Reading to 99. The market continued feverish and erratic, however, U. S. Steel, preferred, falling to 95½ and St. Paul to 128⅛. Union Pacific was largely dealt in at from 132 to 122, Northern Pacific rallied 6 points to 125.

Baltimore and Ohio went up 3½ points, Reading 3¼ and Union Pacific 2⅛ from the lowest. Reading later sold at par.

The market opened active and irregular this morning. Most of the opening changes were fractional, but Reading went up 1¼, while Amalgamated Copper showed an opening decline of ¾. Soon after the opening the trend of prices turned sharply downward, some of the active issues sinking below the low point of yesterday.

Trading in the first hour amounted to 637,000 shares. Call money opened at 10 per cent, and the supply was small. All the leading commission houses had selling orders at the opening. The Western wire houses were especially prominent in the movement and offered large quantities of Amalgamated and Anaconda Copper, Smelting, Union Pacific and the Hill stocks.

London on the other hand was a reported purchaser of 50,000 shares in the first hour. There was some absorption on the downward scale elsewhere in the room by investors.

The steadiness in the market which followed the first bad break lasted until well after noon. At that time another precipitate movement developed. Amalgamated Copper sold at 91, Reading at 106, Union Pacific at 129¼ and St. Paul at 134. Following this sudden slump, Union Pacific dropped 7.. points to 138. Wholesale unloading of Amalgamated Copper and Smelting followed, the former dropping 7⅜ and the latter 4⅝. Reading was also heavily sold at a decline of 7¼, and the whole railroad list then ran off rapidly.

Delaware and Hudson lost 8⅝, Central Railroad of New Jersey 8, St. Paul 4½, Northern Pacific 3⅛, and Anaconda 4⅛.

Another period of comparative steadiness followed with an upward tendency, and then the worst break of the year developed.

As a result of the big break in stocks yesterday the members of the Stock Exchange and bankers and brokers generally awaited the Clearing House settlement this morning with considerable anxiety. Consequently an audible sigh of relief went up in the financial district when at 11 o'clock an announcement was read on the floor of the Stock Exchange that all Clearing House sheets had gone through without trouble.

Bankers received reassuring advices from London during the morning, relieving some apprehension that was felt regarding the banking situation. Banking conditions were pronounced sound and the difficulty over the scarcity of money, common to that market and to this, was believed to be in course of correction by the extensive liquidation of securities going on. The failures on the London Stock Exchange were pronounced unimportant and the principal anxiety in London was said to be over the New York situation.

The circulation of rumors of a break in relations between Kuhn, Loeb & Co. and E. H. Harriman, although denied, was an influence in the renewed weakness of the market.

James Speyer of the banking firm of Speyer & Co., who had a conference in Washington yesterday with President Roosevelt and Secretary of the Treasury Cortelyou regarding the financial and railroad situation, returned to his office this morning. Asked concerning the conference Mr. Speyer said:

"I came away realizing that the administration thoroughly understands the financial situation and also the conditions as they apply to railroads and industrial corporations."

Boston, March 14—Trading opened active on the Boston Stock Exchange to-day with prices generally lower than yesterday. North Butte opened to-day at 93, off ¾ from yesterday, but later reached 92¾. Copper Range was off ½ to 82½, and Quincy fell ½ to 120. Within ten minutes Quincy declined steadily to 118½. Old Dominion broke one point to 50 after opening unchanged at 51.

In the later dealings the break in stocks continued. There seemed to be no vigorous buying sentiment in the market and prices easily fell away. North Butte broke to 90, a loss of 1¾ from yesterday. Quincy went to 115. Tamarack tumbled 8 points to 115. Bingham eased 2⅜ to 13½, and Copper Range continuing weak, fell to 79½, off 3½.

DR. MARVIN LOSES HOPE.

Afraid That He Will Never Again See His Little Son.

Dover, Del., March 14—Worn and wearied by nearly two weeks of terrible anxiety and uncertainty over the probable fate of his missing 4-year-old son, Dr. H. N. Marvin has about abandoned hope of seeing the lad alive again.

"I have about given up hope of ever again seeing my little boy," he said. "With the full and complete investigation made at the farm, I am convinced that he has not been lost there, but has been kidnapped. If the little fellow had strayed among the briars and hedges, his woolien cap and mittens would have become entangled among the briars and bushes, but such has not been the case, or, at least, we have been unable to find any trace of that kind."

PRESIDENT CALLS GOVERNOR.

Will Hold Conference at White House With Executive of Illinois.

(Special to the Eagle.)

Washington, March 14—There will be a conference at the White House next Monday of much importance. The President has asked Governor Deneen, of Illinois, and Attorney General Stead, of that state, to come to Washington and confer with him. While the authorities will not say what subject is to be discussed, there is no doubt that the Chicago and Alton bond issues negotiated by Mr. Harriman and his associates will be the topic of conversation.

Attorney General Stead has called on the Inter-State Commerce Commission for a transcript of Harriman's testimony before the commission in New York. His object is to see whether the adissions made there warrant action by the state to secure the annulment of the famous $32,000,000 bond issue for the Chicago and Alton "Air Line." It has been contended by god authorities that the dividends on this issue were contrary to the constitution of Illinois.

FIERCE BATTLE IN NICARAGUA.

Honduras Revolutionists Win a 15 Hours Fight at Tegucigalpa—Many Killed and Wounded.

Managua, Nicaragua, March 14—The Honduran revolutionists yesterday defeated the forces of President Bonilla, of Honduras, near Tegucigalpa, after fifteen hours fighting. The revolutionists captured 70 officers and soldiers. Many were killed or wounded on both sides. The commander of the defeated Honduran troops was General Sotero Barahona, the minister of war of Honduras.

The following dispatch has been received here from President Zelaya, of Nicaragua, dated Sanchez, Honduras, March 13:

"The enemy was completely defeated at Maraita to-day after two days' fighting.

"I have confiscated at Corinto a thousand rifles destined for the Honduran Government."

THINK BUCKLEY WAS SLAIN.

Believed That He Was Shot and Body Placed on Tracks.

Evidence tending to show that Henry Buckley of Mount Kisco, was murdered on the New York Central railroad tracks between Chappaqua and Mount Kisco on Monday night was given to the coroner to-day and an investigation was undertaken. Buckley had been to this city to call upon a young woman and was on his way home when he met his death. He must have left the train at Chappaqua and started to walk to Mount Kisco early Monday evening. Two pistol shots were heard from the direction of the tracks and and soon afterward a train ran over Buckley's body.

There was a bullet wound in the side of his head and another in his body. To-day it was learned that his own revolver was found loaded in his pocket, where it is believed he could not have placed it if he had shot himself.

ADMIRAL DAVIS PRAISED.

British Foreign Secretary Speaks in High Terms of His Action at Kingston.

London, March 14—The incident involving Governor Swettenham, of Jamaica, and Rear Admiral Davis, U. S. N., at the time of the Kingston earthquake, was brought up in the House of Commons today in a hypothetical question, by Jesse Collins, Liberal Unionist, member for the Bordesley division of Birmingham, (who was in Kingston at the time of the disaster,) which brought out from Foreign Secretary Grey a generous tribute to the American admiral. Mr. Collins asked if it was in accordance with international law and international etiquette for an admiral of a foreign country to land an armed force in a British colony without the permission of the governor. The foreign secretary, in reply, said:

"No, and I may add that no such rights were claimed in the incident referred to. What I am convinced of is that while, in the presence of such a catastrophe, there naturally was a certain amount of misunderstanding the American admiral was inspired by single-minded motives and a desire to relieve suffering. Any other construction placed on his action is most unworthy and untrue."

Mr. Collins then asked if the fact did not remain that in opposition to the governor armed troops were landed when there was no cause or warrant for such action, but the foreign secretary replied:

"According to my information the question conveys a statement which is not borne out by the facts."

The foreign secretary's tribute to Rear Admiral Davis was heartily cheered by the members of the House of Commons.

CUT AT BEVERLEY ROAD.

Station Cannot Be Used for at Least Eight Days From To-morrow.

Access to the Beverly road station of the Brighton Beach road from the east will be cut off to-morrow morning, and passengers who live on the Flatbush avenue side of the cut will be compelled to use either the Avenue C or the Church avenue station. The work of digging the cut at Beverly road will then begin. It will require about eight days before the company can again make use of the Beverly road station.

It was announced at the B. R. T. office to-day that unless unforeseen complications arise, the Brighton Beach road will be completed in time for early summer business.

RECEIPTS OF CUSTOMS TO BE PLACED IN BANKS

Secretary of Treasury Cortelyou Will Try to Avert a Panic.

NOT TO AID WALL STREET.

Administration Says That Reaction Is the Result of Harriman's Juggling With Railroads.

Eagle Bureau,
608 Fourteenth street.

Washington, March 14—For the past twenty-four hours the White House and the Treasury Department have been bombarded by frantic telegraphic, telephonic and mail appeals for the government to do something to check the tumbling of stocks in Wall street and avert a threatened panic. These calls for help are being accepted at their worth and so far have not created a profound impression on any of the men whom they are intended to influence.

There is excellent authority for the statement, however, that Secretary Cortelyou will soon direct the collectors of customs in certain cities to deposit customs receipts in national banks. If this should be done, and in well-informed circles it is accepted as a fact that it will be done, the action will not be in response to the cries from Wall Street. There is not sufficient knowledge at present of the exact intentions of the administration in dealing with the money situation to state whether all the customs receipts or only a portion of them will be deposited in the banks.

There are straws that lead to the belief that only banks in the non-sub-treasury cities will be aided. The administration would be more inclined to help New York but for the suspicion that the scare in Wall Street has been manufactured by Anti-Roosevelt interests in an effort to convince the country that the President's extreme railroad legislation views are destroying public confidence in securities are ruining business. The Washington authorities have received advices from New York to this effect. It is pointed out that conditions throughout the country are in first class shape, aside from a slight tightness in money. The only evidences of alarm are among the speculators in Wall Street.

The shrinkage in railroad stock values is no surprise to administration officials. They say that just such a reaction was to be expected as soon as the investing public realized the fraudulent character of Mr. Harriman's juggling with bond issues in the Chicago and Alton deal. It is pointed out also that the stocks that are falling off are chiefly railroad issues. Therefore, the disposition here is to let Wall Street take care of itself in the belief that the ruling spirits there have brought on the slump by their own wrongful acts.

Secretary Cortelyou is in full charge of the government money situation. He is not at all alarmed at having to handle so serious a situation at the outset of his administration. The urgent and repeated calls for help from Wall Street have not stampeded him in the slightest. Many of them come to him via the White House. Mr. Cortelyou accepts them at their real value because he knows by reason of his long service in the White House, that such appeals are always made to the President every time a flurry visits Wall Street.

As before stated there is little sympathy in administration circles with the present disturbance in Wall Street. Consequently iti is believed that no action will be taken tat will furnish the basis for a charge that the Treasury Department is rushing to the aid of Wall Street gamblers. The Aldrich law was intended primarily to turn the customs receipts over to the national banks, but if the receipts are so deposited only in cities where there is no sub-treasury, it will afford only indirect relief to New York. The volume of money so deposited will also be comparatively small. Seventy per cent. of the customs receipts are taken in at New York. Last year only $24,000,000 were received in the non-sub-treasury cities.

Much of the present demand for money is from the interior cities that are levying on New York, and the deposits will bring a let up in the pressure on eastern financial centers. The Sub-Treasury cities are New York, Boston, St. Louis, Baltimore, Cincinnati, Philadelphia, New Orleans and San Francisco. While the chances favor the issuing of a statement by the President on the subject of railroad baiting, it is learned that it is not settled that such an announcement will be made. The President seriously doubts the advisability of denouncing the action of the various states that have passed anti-railroad law.

There was some criticism of his letter to Governor Gillet, of California, asking that the legislature of that State adopt no anti-Japanese laws. The President realizes that it is a most delicate matter for him to attempt to advise the states about legislation, and will consider the subject fully before deciding to do so.

RUSSIAN ROBBERS SLAY SEVEN

Bound and Decapitated Landlord, Five Laborers and a Woman.

Yelisavetgrad, Russia, March 14—An estate in this vicinity was attacked by robbers yesterday, who bound and decapitated the proprietor, five laborers and a woman. Two witnesses of the slaughter, a soldier who hid in a haystack and a child, lost their reason. The soldier subsequently died in a hospital of delirium. The booty secured by the robbers amounted to $1,000.

On the occasion of the funeral yesterday of a prominent reactionary, who was killed by Revolutionists, an attempt was made to start anti-Jewish excesses. Rioters began beating Jews in the streets and sacking the Bazaar and Jewish lodgings, but they were stopped by the prompt intervention of the troops. A number of Jyws were wounded, one of whom died in the hospital. The local rabbis have telegraphed complaints to the Lower House of Parliament and to Premier Stolypin.

HONOR FOR BROOKLYN BOY.

Edward Farrier, a Freshman at Amherst College, has won the A. Lyman Williston prize of $15 for the best lecture notes in the freshman course in hygiene. Farrier prepared for college at the Manual Training High School.

1908

In Europe, King Carlos I of Portugal was assassinated in a Lisbon public square.

President Roosevelt refused to run for a third term of office and William Howard Taft of Ohio was nominated on the Republican ticket. Taft was elected, with James Sherman his Vice-President.

"All the News That's Fit to Print."

FOURTH EDITION

The New York Times.

THE WEATHER.
Fair to-day; fair, colder to-morrow; westerly gales.
4 A. M.

VOL. LVIII...NO. 18,547. **** NEW YORK, WEDNESDAY, NOVEMBER 4, 1908.—SIXTEEN PAGES ONE CENT In Greater New York, Jersey City, and Newark | Elsewhere, TWO CENTS.

TAFT WINS

Falls Only 22 Short of Roosevelt's Electoral Vote.

GETS 187,902 IN THIS STATE

Has 314 Electoral Votes — The House Republican by Increased Majority — But Some Western States Vote for Bryan.

William H. Taft will be the twenty-seventh President of the United States, having swept the country by a vote which will give him **314** ballots in the Electoral College against Mr. Bryan's **169**, or only **22** less than Mr. Roosevelt had in 1904. His majority will be **145**. William J. Bryan yesterday suffered his third and most crushing defeat in his twelve-year run for President of the United States.

To enforce his policies President Taft will have an overwhelmingly Republican Congress, the Senate being as strongly Republican as before, and the House increasing its Republican majority from **57** to **65**.

About every so-called doubtful State went Republican, though Indiana is still in doubt. It was noticeable that the majorities in the East were greater than those in the West. In New York, for instance, Taft beat the great Roosevelt majority of 1904, getting **187,902** majority, as against Roosevelt's **175,000**.

The greatest surprise of the election was the Republican victory in New York City, where **Taft's** majority was **9,378**. Never before this has this city gone Republican in a **Presidential** election except in 1900, when it voted for McKinley as against Bryan. Chanler's plurality in the city was **56,000**.

Taft's plurality on the popular vote is estimated at **1,098,000**, as against Roosevelt's plurality of **2,543,515** over Parker.

Bryan, however, has improved on Parker's run by carrying Missouri, Nevada, and apparently his own State of Nebraska, though later returns may change the last-named State's position in the Electoral College.

In his great sweep of this State Taft carried with him Gov. Hughes, though the Governor's majority fell far below his, being only **71,189**.

Speaker Cannon will be sure to make the race to succeed himself, having downed his opponent in the Danville district by about **10,500** majority in spite of Samuel Gompers's efforts.

Morris Hillquit, the Socialist candidate for Congress in the Ninth New York District, was defeated by Republican votes which were cast for his opponent Judge Goldfogle.

A noticeable feature of the election was the increase of the Republican vote in the Southern States. In Florida, for example, it increased so much that early in the evening there was a report that the State had gone Republican. Everywhere in the Southern States along the Atlantic Coast there was this unusual Republican vote.

In Illinois, which Bryan's managers had claimed, there was a smashing vote against him. Cook County, where Roger Sullivan is supreme, went against him by **50,000**. The majority in the State is estimated at **170,000**.

Indiana is still in doubt, and it seems likely that Thomas R. Marshall, the Democratic candidate for Governor, has been elected, though the State may have cast its vote for Taft.

Maryland, which was claimed by the Democrats and almost conceded by the Republicans—actually conceded, in fact, by President Roosevelt—has gone Republican by a majority of about **5,000**. Kentucky is for Bryan by about **15,000**.

The biggest surprise was in Senator La Follette's State of Wisconsin, where cutting of the ticket was freely predicted even by Republican observers, and where nobody looked to see Taft do more than squeeze through. He has bettered Roosevelt's 1904 majority there, and the La Follette men have apparently played fair.

Michigan may have elected a Democratic Governor. That State is still in doubt on its Gubernatorial ticket, though it has voted for Taft.

Connecticut's majority is as usual, and Representative Lilley has been elected Governor by **13,000**.

Taft carried his own State, Ohio, by [illegible],000, but Harmon (Dem.) is elected Governor.

New Jersey went Republican by over [illegible],000.

The city election was full of surprises, the least being the victory here of Taft and Chanler. In Kings County McCarren made good by carrying it for Chanler by **5,241**, though it went for Taft by **22,500**. These extraordinary results led to the report that wholesale trading had been going on in the great city.

Texas is actually in doubt on the Governorship. Cecil Lyon's prediction, at which everybody laughed at Chicago in June, that a Republican might be elected Governor this year, may come true. Col. Simpson, an old Confederate [illegible], is Boss Lyon's candidate.

STATE VOTE FOR PRESIDENT.

County.	Pluralities. Taft. Rep.	Bryan. Dem.
Albany	5,500	——
Allegany	4,000	——
Broome	4,100	——
Cattaraugus	3,187	——
Cayuga	4,000	——
Chautauqua	3,230	——
Chemung	1,500	——
Chenango	2,231	——
Clinton	1,593	——
Columbia	500	——
Cortland	2,000	——
Delaware	2,522	——
Dutchess	452	——
Erie	6,870	——
Essex	2,940	——
Franklin	3,100	——
Fulton	2,000	——
Genesee	2,533	——
Greene	450	——
Hamilton	400	——
Herkimer	2,460	——
Jefferson	5,072	——
Kings	21,364	——
Lewis	1,400	——
Livingston	2,100	——
Madison	3,400	——
Monroe	10,353	——
Montgomery	2,214	——
New York	——	9,835
Nassau	4,622	——
Niagara	2,500	——
Oneida	5,000	——
Onondaga	10,370	——
Ontario	2,800	——
Orange	4,000	——
Orleans	2,274	——
Oswego	4,500	——
Otsego	1,800	——
Putnam	813	——
Queens	——	1,456
Rensselaer	4,026	——
Richmond	——	695
Rockland	700	——
St. Lawrence	8,000	——
Saratoga	1,500	——
Schenectady	2,947	——
Schoharie	——	500
Schuyler	600	——
Seneca	1,000	——
Steuben	4,084	——
Suffolk	4,500	——
Sullivan	3,048	——
Tioga	1,573	——
Tompkins	1,236	——
Ulster	1,650	——
Warren	1,800	——
Washington	4,400	——
Wayne	3,582	——
Westchester	9,000	——
Wyoming	3,200	——
Yates	1,400	——
Total	200,388	12,486
Taft's plurality		187,902

THE ELECTORAL VOTE.

TAFT.

California	10
Colorado	5
Connecticut	7
Delaware	3
Idaho	3
Illinois	27
Indiana	15
Iowa	13
Kansas	10
Maine	6
Maryland	8
Massachusetts	16
Michigan	14
Minnesota	11
Montana	3
New Hampshire	4
New Jersey	12
New York	39
North Dakota	4
Ohio	23
Oregon	4
Pennsylvania	34
Rhode Island	4
South Dakota	4
Utah	3
Vermont	4
Washington	5
West Virginia	7
Wisconsin	13
Wyoming	3
Total	314

BRYAN.

Alabama	11
Arkansas	9
Florida	5
Georgia	13
Kentucky	13
Louisiana	9
Missouri	18
Mississippi	10
North Carolina	12
Nevada	3
Nebraska	8
Oklahoma	7
South Carolina	9
Tennessee	12
Texas	18
Virginia	12
Total	169

Total number of votes in Electoral College, 483; necessary to a choice, 242.

PARIS HEARS NEWS.

Taft's Election Known to Throng of Americans in Cafes at 2 A. M.

PARIS, Nov. 4.—The cafés and restaurants, where the election returns from the United States were received, were thronged until early morning by Americans.

Definite news of Mr. Taft's election reached here about 2 o'clock and was made the occasion of great merrymaking, as the supporters of the Republican nominee were largely in the majority.

LAMB CONCEDES NOTHING.

CHICAGO, Nov. 3.—At midnight John E. Lamb, Vice Chairman of the Democratic National Committee, in charge of Western headquarters, refusing to admit defeat, issued the following statement:

"I do not care to estimate the probable final result, although we do not concede anything. It looks as though we had won Montana, Nebraska, and Colorado. We have not enough from Ohio, West Virginia, or Maryland to give any indications."

CITY VOTE

Taft Carries New York by 9,378.

CHANLER BY 56,000

Hughes Loses Kings by 5,241 and Queens by 4,635—Trading at Bryan's Expense Shown in Brooklyn.

This city contributed one of the great surprises of the election, William H. Taft carrying it by a probable plurality of **9,378**. The heaviest Taft vote was in Kings County, where the Republican plurality of about **22,500** was amply sufficient to overcome the Bryan plurality of **9,835** in Manhattan and the Bronx. This is with some ninety districts missing.

Chanler's vote in the city ran far below the expectations of every one, including the Republican leaders. He developed great strength in Kings County, and this, taken in connection with the heavy Taft vote there, was regarded as evidence of trading, the assumption being that Senator McCarren traded Bryan votes for Chanler votes very successfully.

In Manhattan and the Bronx, while Bryan ran behind Chanler, there was not so much evidence of trading. Chanler's plurality in the whole city will not be above 56,000, about half what was expected.

Gov. Hughes developed great strength in New York County especially, and Queens did not do as well by Chanler as the Democrats had hoped. Chanler's plurality in that borough will be apparently about 5,146.

There will be no change in the city's representation in Congress as a result of the election. Morris Hillquit, the Socialist, running in the Ninth District was again beaten by Goldfogle. Bennet and Olcott both hold their districts, though hard fights were made on them. In Brooklyn, Foelker, who as Senator, saved the anti-race track gambling bills, was elected to Congress from the Third District.

As far as the Assembly is concerned, the representation from this city will be about the same. The Republicans make a gain in the First and Fifteenth Districts of Kings, but two districts in New York County which were won last time by Republicans with Independence League indorsements have gone Democratic again. The State Senate remains practically as it was as far as this city's representation is concerned.

The Independence League ticket did not poll as heavy a vote as was expected. Hisgen and Shearn ran about evenly, getting approximately 28,000 votes in the whole city.

The Tammany county ticket has seemingly been elected by a reduced plurality. The general belief is that the new registration law is responsible for the reduced Tammany pluralities.

Surrogate Beckett, whose nomination was indorsed by practically the whole of the New York Bar, was defeated by John P. Cohalan, 640 districts out of 891 in Manhattan and the Bronx, giving Cohalan a lead of something like 28,000.

Mr. Beckett early this morning, however, was still hopeful that complete returns might show his election.

"I have the greatest confidence," he said, "and if this is justified my success will be due to the strenuous support given to my cause by the whole bar."

Tammany's two City Court Judges, La Fetra and Lynch, were elected by pluralities of approximately 34,000, Wasservogel and Matthewson going down to defeat.

STATE PLURALITIES.

REPUBLICAN.

California	45,000
Colorado	20,000
Connecticut	40,000
Delaware	3,500
Idaho	20,000
Illinois	175,000
Indiana	5,000
Iowa	45,000
Kansas	26,000
Maine	31,500
Maryland	5,000
Massachusetts	70,000
Michigan	100,000
Minnesota	80,000
Montana	7,000
New Hampshire	20,000
New Jersey	65,000
New York	190,000
North Dakota	10,000
Ohio	49,000
Oregon	25,000
Pennsylvania	350,000
Rhode Island	16,000
South Dakota	32,000
Utah	20,000
Vermont	28,000
Washington	40,000
West Virginia	10,000
Wisconsin	100,000
Wyoming	1,000
Total	1,629,000

DEMOCRATIC.

Alabama	45,000
Arkansas	20,000
Florida	21,000
Georgia	40,000
Kentucky	15,000
Louisiana	40,000
Mississippi	50,000
Missouri	30,000
Nevada	5,000
Nebraska	10,000
North Carolina	40,000
Oklahoma	25,000
South Carolina	40,000
Tennessee	20,000
Texas	100,000
Virginia	30,000
Total	531,000

Taft's Plurality over Bryan, 1,098,000.

TIMES'S BULLETINS IN BERLIN

American Colony Cheers Taft Victory at Hotel Adlon.

Special Cable to THE NEW YORK TIMES.

BERLIN, Nov. 4.—At 4 A. M. Wednesday Berlin's American colony, headed by Ambassador Hill, is bivouacked in the lobby of the Hotel Adlon. All through the night they have been awaiting the bulletins from THE NEW YORK TIMES.

Early indications of Taft's victory were greeted vociferously, men and women breaking out into cheers, while the orchestra struck up "Yankee Doodle."

Among those who held the long vigil were American Minister to Persia Jackson, Consul General Thackara of Berlin, Consul General Gaffney of Dresden, Secretaries Hitt, Grew, and Orr of the American Embassy; Vice Consul General Cauldwell of Berlin and President Hessenberg of the American Chamber of Commerce.

HUGHES, TOO

Runs Behind Taft, but Wins by 71,189 Plurality.

BIG CUT IN UP-STATE CITIES

Rural Districts Return Large Vote for Republican Candidate, Offsetting Democratic Gains Elsewhere.

Charles Evans Hughes was re-elected Governor of New York State yesterday by a plurality of **71,189**. His plurality two years ago when he ran against William Randolph Hearst was **57,897**. In nearly all the counties of the State Gov. Hughes ran behind the Republican candidate for President, whereas in 1906 the votes cast for Hughes exceeded by from about **60,000** to **70,000** the votes cast for his running mates on the Republican State ticket.

The early returns which came from the cities up the State showed that the Governor had been cut to the extent, in some of the larger cities, of many thousand votes. The returns from the rural districts of the up-State counties, however, saved the day for the Republican candidate for Governor, bringing him down to the Bronx with a plurality of about 127,500 over Lewis Stuyvesant Chanler, his Democratic opponent. Chanler's plurality in New York City was **56,000**, reducing Gov. Hughes's net plurality to **71,189**.

In Erie and Saratoga Counties, where the Personal Liberty League was very active, the fight against Gov. Hughes was reflected in heavy losses from the Republican vote two years ago in Buffalo and Saratoga Springs. In Buffalo, where Taft received yesterday a plurality over Bryan of over **4,000** votes, Chanler piled up a plurality against Hughes of over **5,000** votes. The Saratoga Springs vote for Chanler was offset by the returns from other districts in that county, and Saratoga County remained in the Republican column with a plurality of about **1,000** for Hughes and about **1,500** for Taft. The total vote in Erie County gave Taft a plurality of **7,000** and Chanler a plurality of about **3,000**. Two years ago Hughes had a plurality of **1,282** in Erie County.

In Onondaga County Gov. Hughes proved stronger than the rest of his ticket, running several hundred votes ahead of Horace White, candidate for Lieutenant Governor on the Republican ticket.

FORAKER EXPECTED IT, TOO.

Ohio Senator Says So—Will Not Comment Further on Result.

CINCINNATI, Nov. 3.—Senator Joseph B. Foraker, when asked for an expression on the election said:

"It is just as I expected."

He would not discuss the matter further.

STATE VOTE FOR GOVERNOR.

County	Pluralities. Hughes Rep.	Ch'nl'r Dem.
Albany	3,900	——
Allegany	3,900	——
Broome	3,300	——
Cattaraugus	3,150	——
Cayuga	2,786	——
Chautauqua	3,100	——
Chemung	1,000	——
Chenango	2,200	——
Clinton	1,134	——
Columbia	300	——
Cortland	2,425	——
Delaware	2,200	——
Dutchess	200	——
Erie	——	3,000
Essex	2,080	——
Franklin	2,761	——
Fulton	1,900	——
Genesee	2,221	——
Greene	400	——
Hamilton	100	——
Herkimer	1,050	——
Jefferson	3,765	——
Kings	——	2,152
Lewis	1,200	——
Livingston	1,900	——
Madison	2,897	——
Monroe	7,599	——
Montgomery	1,700	——
New York	——	48,035
Nassau	2,700	——
Niagara	1,000	——
Oneida	4,000	——
Onondaga	8,167	——
Ontario	2,500	——
Orange	2,700	——
Orleans	2,005	——
Oswego	3,600	——
Otsego	1,700	——
Putnam	——	——
Queens	——	5,146
Rensselaer	2,479	——
Richmond	——	1,510
Rockland	——	——
St. Lawrence	6,800	——
Saratoga	141	——
Schenectady	1,612	——
Schoharie	——	520
Schuyler	500	——
Seneca	480	——
Steuben	3,015	——
Suffolk	3,500	——
Sullivan	650	——
Tioga	1,561	——
Tompkins	1,175	——
Ulster	1,475	——
Warren	1,400	——
Washington	3,200	——
Wayne	2,426	——
Westchester	7,000	——
Wyoming	2,400	——
Yates	1,429	——
Total	131,552	60,363

Hughes's plurality, 71,189.

NEBRASKA FOR BRYAN.

His Plurality 10,000—Republican Precincts Change.

NEBRASKA—Voted for Presidential electors, Congressmen, Governor, and State officers, and a Legislature. Vote in 1904: Republican, 138,558; Democrat, 51,876.

Special to The New York Times.

LINCOLN, Neb., Nov. 4, 1 A. M.—Nebraska has gone Democratic. The State may give more than 10,000 majority for Bryan if returns now on hand hold good throughout. T. S. Allen, Chairman of the Democratic State Central Committee, claims the State by 15,000 and the Republican State Committee has no statement to make. Many Republican precincts in the State have given a strong Democratic majority.

Shallenberger, (Dem.) for Governor is also elected.

OMAHA, Neb., Nov. 5.—At midnight only 264 out of the 1,800 precincts outside of Omaha and Douglas Counties had reported. In those precincts Bryan's plurality is 1,550. At this ratio Bryan's majority in the State will not reach the figures named. Shallenberger, the Democratic candidate for Governor, is losing his heavy lead over Gov. Sheldon. However, he will carry the State by about 8,000. The entire Democratic State ticket was elected.

The Omaha Bee claims that Taft has carried Nebraska by 12,000.

Omaha complete gives Bryan, 10,732; Taft, 10,609; Shallenberger, (Dem.) for Governor, 10,913; Sheldon, (Rep.,) 9,875.

The first precinct to come in gave Taft, 205; Bryan, 405, a gain of 100 for Bryan.

Indications are that Bryan has nearly overturned a normal Republican plurality of 1,600 in the City of Lincoln. Three precincts complete give Bryan 542; Taft 493. Estimates on the remainder show that Taft will not carry the city by more than 200 plurality.

Bryan carried his precinct 106 to 52 for Taft.

Scattering returns from Nebraska indicate a heavy loss to Bryan in the country precincts, with a gain in Omaha and Lincoln. The State is claimed for Taft by Republican managers by between 7,000 and 10,000 majority.

The first country precinct reporting, Ravenna, Buffalo County, showed a gain for Taft of 54 over that for McKinley eight years ago, and a gain for Bryan of 15 over his own vote eight years ago.

Blue Springs, Gage County, showed a net gain of one vote for Taft.

Bryan is making slight gains over eight years ago at Grand Island, and Taft shows a loss compared with the vote for McKinley.

Forty-one precincts outside of Lincoln and Omaha give: Taft, 5,392; Bryan, 5,602. The same precincts in 1900 gave: McKinley, 4,778; Bryan, 4,812. Bryan probably has carried the State by from 8,000 to 14,000.

Nine precincts out of a total of twenty-one in Lincoln gave Bryan a plurality of 388 votes. The Republicans are already conceding the city and county to Bryan. Returns from thirty precincts throughout the State give Bryan a plurality of 41. With this gain it is estimated that Bryan will carry the State by about 1,000. Mr. Bryan carried his home district by 57 votes.

Map Showing How the Country Voted.

1909

The first of Robert Peary's seven expeditions to the Far North took place in 1886. He finally made it to the North Pole on April 6, 1909—the first to do so.

His claim was blighted, however, by Dr. Frederick Cook, who said he was there a year before. Cook's claim was proved false.

Peary reached the Pole with his aide, Matthew Henson, and four Eskimo.

"All the News That's Fit to Print."

The New York Times.

THE WEATHER.
Fair, warmer to-day; clouding to-morrow; light, variable winds.

VOL. LVIII...NO. 18,854. * * * NEW YORK, TUESDAY, SEPTEMBER 7, 1909.—EIGHTEEN PAGES. ONE CENT In Greater New York, Jersey City, and Newark { Elsewhere, TWO CENTS.

GAYNOR, UNPLEDGED, CONSENTS TO RUN

Writes Business Men He Will Accept Support of Any Party, but Make No Promises.

SAYS TAMMANY IS FOR HIM

Assured by Leaders of the Nomination, He Declares—Is for War on Machine Control and "City Spoliation."

Supreme Court Justice William J. Gaynor of Brooklyn has announced his willingness to become a candidate for Mayor in a letter written to a committee of influential Brooklyn citizens who urged him soon after his return from Europe to enter the fight. The long-awaited declaration of his position was made public last night together with the names of the committee of citizens and their letter to the Brooklyn jurist.

Justice Gaynor reviews the entire Mayoralty situation, assails "mere political control," which has resulted in "spoliation of the city treasury." He declares, however, that he has reason to believe that he will receive the Democratic nomination and Republican support, as well as that of the Independence League.

An interesting part of the letter is that in which Justice Gaynor refers to the printed statements that he would not receive the indorsement of the Republican organization unless he made some definite pledge of his position. While declaring that he does not believe that the majority of the organization demand any such condition of him, he emphatically states that he will pledge himself to no organization. "I shall not take a nomination from any organization to which is annexed any pledge, promise or condition whatsoever other than to be Mayor in fact, and do my duty if elected," says he.

In referring to his expectation of welcoming all voters to his standard, Justice Gaynor says: "When an organization or party vouches for one and nominates him and wants him elected I have always understood that it welcomes help from any and all quarters to elect him."

Promises from Tammany.

He goes on to make the significant declaration that he has received assurance from influential Democrats that the Tammany City Convention will give him an "unconditional nomination" and that no one can prevent the election of delegates who will nominate me." He states that he is aware that there is opposition to him in the organization, but that he does not believe "an undivided delegation can be brought into the convention opposed to my nomination."

"As to the Independence League," he continues, "inasmuch as it has always stood for the uplifting of city government, I think I may justly expect its support."

Justice Gaynor concludes with a solemn pledge to discharge his trust with fidelity and honesty, ending with the words, "No party or party machine can drag us down if we stand fast together: on the contrary, we may lift city politics up in all parties, and make the spoliation of the city's treasury, through mere machine political control, a thing impossible in the future."

Here is Justice Gaynor's answer:

Justice Gaynor's Letter.

Sept. 4, 1909.

Messrs. Abraham Abraham, James McMahon, Archibald R. Watson, Judson G. Wall, Michael H. Drummond, James Creelman, Charles M. Higgins, M. M. Belding, Jr., and Frank J. Price:

Dear Sirs—Your letter added to my very great anxiety, already caused by similar letters and requests and public discussion, but has finally helped to enable me to see my way through it. I put myself in your hands, and consent to be a candidate for nomination for Mayor. No doubt you have observed that several bodies of citizens have nominated me already. I specially note your statement, "We do not care who, or what party convention, joins in nominating and voting for you if you will give us your consent to run," etc. It requires me to say something of recent occurrences in order that there may be no misunderstanding, and that I may say it without a bit of unkindness to any one.

The Republican City Committee has met since your letter was written and apparently give out a statement that the Republican City Convention will not nominate any one who will not pledge himself in advance not to accept a nomination from the Democratic City Convention also. Although published in all of the newspapers, and in no way questioned, I have doubted whether it was in fact authorized. I know that many Republicans will not acquiesce in it. As is well enough known, I have long been of those who look upon such extreme partisanship in city or local elections as most unfortunate. Its main result is to play everything year after year into the hands of city spoilers.

In years gone by I have worked shoulder to shoulder with Republicans and Democrats alike and together in efforts to prevent official wrongdoing and lift the city Government up and make it intelligent and decent. I so worked successfully with those who prevented the fraudulent purchase of the water company, and later even worse things, still in general remembrance, and with those who moved upon and destroyed John Y. McKane and his corrupt control, results and benefits from which were accepted by leaders and the machines of both parties in turn through a series of years.

We never paused then to inquire of one another's politics, or to put any ban or bar on one another because of politics, and we shall not do the like now. Must I now in order to run for Mayor first get up and unjustly offend men who so worked with us then, and thousands of others who gave us their good-will and sympathy in such work, by saying that I shall not suffer the city convention of their party to also nominate me? If I should do so I could not expect their votes.

Far the bulk of the voters here who are Democrats in National politics are in favor of intelligent and good local government the same as the corresponding bulk of Republican voters are. How much better it would be for the city if they could work together instead of proscribing and ostracizing each other.

Base Men in the Minority.

Base men are in the minority in all parties and everywhere. There are 75,000 or more voters in this great city who now never allow National politics to influence their votes in city elections. What,

Continued on Page 7.

HARRIMAN SUFFERS RELAPSE.

Diagnosed as Acute Indigestion—His Physician Says, 'We Hope for the Best.'

Special to The New York Times.

TURNER'S, N. Y., Sept. 6.—That E. H. Harriman has had a relapse was admitted this afternoon by Dr. W. M. Gordon Lyle, his physician, at the Harriman home here. Acute indigestion is Dr. Lyle's diagnosis of his patient's trouble.

The attack came on yesterday after Mr. Harriman had appeared to be doing nicely for several days. A telephone message was sent from the Harriman home in the early hours of this morning to Miss Taylor, Superintendent of St. Luke's Hospital nurses' registry, at 214 West 108th Street, Manhattan, asking her to send her best nurse here with all speed. The nurse arrived within three hours.

According to Dr. Lyle, Mr. Harriman is resting easily to-night. He said that it was he who sent for the nurse. There is a report that there are four other nurses here, but this could not be confirmed. Certain it is that Mr. Harriman's state of health is such that both day and night nurses are required.

When Dr. Lyle was seen this afternoon he was much perturbed over the presence here again of newspaper men. It was pointed out to him, however, that they were withdrawn on the understanding that the press was to be apprised of any change in Mr. Harriman's condition through his office at 1.. Broadway. He was told that nothing could be learned from that source to-day.

"It is true," said Dr. Lyle, "that Mr. Harriman has had a relapse. Yesterday he had a sharp attack of indigestion, but he is better to-day, and is now resting comfortably. We hope for the best."

Mr. Harriman's entire family is at Tower Hill, while Judge Robert S. Lovett, general counsel to most of the important Harriman interests, was summoned to Arden and arrived last night. It is said that two of the physicians who were called into consultation with Dr. George W. Crile, the Cleveland surgeon, shortly after Mr. Harriman's return from Europe, are again at Arden. They are Dr. Walter B. James of 17 West Fifty-fourth Street and Dr. George E. Brewer of 61 West Forty-eighth Street.

Dr. Lyle gave out this bulletin at 4 P. M.: "Mr. Harriman had an attack of acute indigestion at 11 P. M. last night, having partaken of a dinner a little heartier than his strength would allow. His condition is improved to-day, although there are still slight indications of a bad stomach."

At Dr. Brewer's home last night it was said that the doctor was at Cedar Camp in the Adirondacks, so far as any of his household here knew. He may have gone to Arden from there, however. There was no response to the telephone when a TIMES reporter tried to reach Dr. James's house over the wire.

DYNAMITE HOUSE AND PLANT.

Official Who Had Discharged Men Kicks Explosive to the Ground.

Special to The New York Times.

TYRONE, Penn., Sept. 6.—The handsome residence of Thomas Calderwood, an official of the American Lime and Stone Company, and all of the buildings of the Company at the quarry near here, were completely wrecked and one unidentified fire engineer was killed by explosions of dynamite early to-day.

Calderwood some time ago discharged some foreign employes of his company, and it was the general belief here that the explosions were acts of revenge.

Mr. Calderwood arose at 3 o'clock and smelled something burning. Upon investigation he found a large bundle of dynamite securely bound with wire on his kitchen window. He immediately tore the window open, and kicked it to the ground, and shouted for his wife and daughter to run for their lives. They had barely reached the street before the explosion occurred. Every window in the house was smashed to atoms. The doors and walls were badly damaged. Windows for blocks were broken.

At the quarries a ton of dynamite had been stored. The whole amount was exploded, completely destroying the buildings about the works, and blowing a large steel car 100 feet from the tracks.

The home of Harry Houck, near the quarries, was completely destroyed. The scales used for weighing cars were wrecked, and windows were broken in the houses within a radius of five miles.

HUGHES'S DEPUTIES AT RACES

Make No Secret of Their Mission, but Find No Betting at Sheepshead Bay.

Four investigators of race-track conditions from Albany visited the Sheepshead Bay race course yesterday, as the representatives of Gov. Hughes, after presenting themselves, with credentials which were accepted, to Sheriff Hobley of Kings County.

The investigators made no secret of their mission, but made no claim to official standing of any kind, except to say that they came to observe what was going on and ascertain the conditions concerning betting at the race track for a report to the Governor.

The visitors watched the proceedings of the holiday crowd through the afternoon, and agreed that they saw nothing fitting the description of race-track betting published in an afternoon newspaper early last week, which report caused Gov. Hughes to request reports from the New York police officials and the officials of Kings County on the matter of race-track bookmaking.

MISS STEWART A PRINCESS.

Emperor Francis Joseph Confers the Rank in Her Own Right.

VIENNA, Sept. 6.—Emperor Francis Joseph has conferred upon Miss Anita Stewart, whose marriage to Prince Miguel of Braganza will take place Sept. 15, the rank of Princess in her own right.

Miss Anita Stewart is the daughter of Mrs. James Henry Smith by her first husband, William Rhinelander Stewart, whom she divorced in South Dakota to marry Mr. Smith. When Mr. Smith died in Kobe, Japan, he left his stepdaughter an income of $40,000 a year, to which her mother will add another $40,000 a year on her marriage to Prince Miguel next month in London.

In order to get the consent of his father, Dom Miguel, the Prince had to renounce all claims to the throne of Portugal in favor of his younger brother, Prince Francis Joseph.

LONDON APPLAUDS PEARY'S EXPLOIT

Instant Acceptance of His Report a Contrast to Skepticism Toward Dr. Cook.

HAD AWAITED HIS VERDICT

Admiral Nares Thinks It Peculiar That the Announcements Should Come So Close Together.

Special Cable to THE NEW YORK TIMES.

LONDON, Sept. 6.—The news that Commander Robert E. Peary had reached the north pole was made known throughout London by late editions of the evening papers, which displayed the brief announcement under headlines which suggested none of the reservations with which the reports of the discovery by Dr. Cook have been received.

In marked contrast with the skepticism with which Dr. Cook's reports were printed is the immediate and whole-hearted acceptance of Peary's dispatch. Nothing could show this better than a comparison of headlines upon the two announcements.

A Difference in Headlines.

"North pole reached by Peary. Official news that the American flag was hoisted April 6, 1909." That is the way in which Commander Peary's dispatch is presented to its readers by a London paper which headed Dr. Cook's report as follows: "The north pole reported discovered. American explorer's statement."

With the general public a similar readiness to accept Commander Peary's statement is strikingly apparent and bears out the saying frequently heard here recently to the effect that had it been Commander Peary instead of Dr. Cook who had come forward with a bare announcement of the discovery of the pole not a single voice would have been raised in question. It is a testimony to Commander Peary's high reputation as a man and an explorer that the world accepts his word without a shadow of hesitation.

Had Awaited Peary's Testimony

Mr. Peary's announcement is hailed with peculiar satisfaction, because, throughout the controversy that has been raging in the last few days, it has been stated again and again that Mr. Peary's testimony would settle the question definitely. "Peary will know the truth," it was said. Thus, Peary is the witness for whom the whole world is waiting. There was a consensus of opinion among the people with whom I talked to-night that if Commander Peary contests the claims put forward by Dr. Cook, the latter will find it an extremely difficult task to establish his pretensions to be the discoverer of the pole, even should the "proofs" which he is now withholding prove to be as good as he says they are.

Cook Expects Confirmation.

Dr. Cook, on being informed in Copenhagen to-night of the news from Mr. Peary, said:

"I hope it is true, for Peary's reports will confirm all my claims."

An arctic explorer to whom to-night I showed Mr. Peary's message to THE NEW YORK TIMES, saying, "I have the pole," made the comment that Mr. Peary, by implication, denied any other claim to the honor of discovering the pole, and that, consequently, it was to be inferred that the confirmation which Dr. Cook expects from Mr. Peary is hardly likely to be forthcoming.

Peculiar Coincidence, Says Nares.

Sir George Nares, who led the arctic expedition of 1875-6, when interviewed to-night with regard to Commander Peary's message announcing the discovery, said:

"It is difficult to avoid the conclusion that Commander Peary's Eskimos at Etah must have known that Dr. Cook had crossed Smith's Sound and passed Etah last Winter to reach Ellamere Land. Dr. Cook, then," continued the Admiral, "gets down from his Eskimo headquarters at Annotook to Upernavik by a Greenland route never before traversed, passing all the sea glaciers in Baffin Bay just in time to catch a Danish Government vessel which leaves Upernavik early in the year before the whaling vessels are due.

"My first impression was that Dr. Cook had got hold of Commander Peary's Eskimos in some way or other and ought to have communicated either with Commander Peary or with the Eskimos at Etah.

"The question now arises how it comes about that Cook and Peary announce at practically the same time the discovery of the north pole. Is it not a peculiar fact that this coincidence takes place, in view of the possibility of news having reached Etah of the success of one or the other of the men?"

Capt. Scott of the exploring ship Discovery stated to-night that Commander Peary's message put it beyond doubt that the Stars and Stripes was the first flag to fly at the north pole.

The Proper Witness Arrives.

"Just at the very moment when men were saying that only the evidence of an independent witness who had himself visited the north pole could estab-

Continued on Page 2.

In order not to miss The New York Times of to-morrow, in which will be printed exclusively Lieut. Peary's own story of his discovery of the North Pole, order a copy from your newsdealer early to-day.

COOK GLAD PEARY REACHED THE POLE

Unmoved When, Wreathed with Flowers at Banquet, He Hears the News.

HOPE NOW FOR OTHERS

Believes More Expeditions Will Reach the Pole Within the Next Ten Years.

COPENHAGEN, Sept. 6.—Copenhagen was electrified to-night by the report of Commander Peary's announcement that he had reached the north pole. Dr. Cook was immensely interested and said:

"That is good news. I hope Peary did get to the pole. His observations, and reports on that region will confirm mine."

Asked if there was any probability of Peary's having found the tube containing his records, Dr. Cook replied:

"I hope so, but that is doubtful on account of the drift. Commander Peary would have reached the pole this year, probably, while I was there last year. His route was several hundred miles east of mine. We are rivals, of course, but the pole is good enough for two.

"The fact of two men having reached the pole along different paths," continued the explorer, "should furnish large additions to scientific knowledge. Probably other parties will reach it in the next ten years, since every explorer is helped by the experience of his predecessors, just as Sverdrup's observations and reports were of immeasurable help to me.

"I can say nothing more concerning Commander Peary's success without knowing farther details, than that I am glad of it."

While Dr. Cook was conversing casually this morning with some friends, a possibility of the dénouement which electrified the world to-day was laughingly suggested. Dr. Cook remarked:

"It is quite possible that Peary will turn up now. He is about due to get back if he carries out his plans."

Those who have had the best opportunities to become acquainted with Dr. Cook here believe that he is not likely to enter into a controversy with Commander Peary.

It is doubtful if history furnishes a more dramatic episode than the breaking of the news to Dr. Cook that Peary had realized the goal of his life's ambition and repeated struggles. Dr. Cook was seated at a dinner, surrounded by explorers and correspondents, in the gilded ballroom of the Tivoli Casino. Around his neck was hung a garland of pink roses, according to the Scandinavian method of honoring heroes, which the explorer wore blushingly and with visible embarrassment. Several speeches, acclaiming him, had been given and repeated toasts to him drunk with clamorous cheers.

Amid this scene a whisper went around that Peary had planted the Stars and Stripes at the pole. Cook was perfectly cool and unmoved. He made a striking speech, in which he paid high tribute to the work of Sverdrup, who sat near, to whose discoveries he largely owed his success; to John R. Bradley, who had financed the expedition; to "the intelligence, endurance, and faithfulness" of the Eskimos who had assisted in the preparations, and those who had accompanied him. The whole story of the expedition, he said, has not come out, and will not come out for some time, nor will it come out in installments, but only when it is completed.

Dr. Cook did not permit the whispers which came to his ear of Peary's success to move him in the least, but when he had finished he was surrounded by correspondents who looked for some sign of emotion, but the explorer said smilingly: "I am glad."

Nothing but arctic exploration has been thought of here for the last few days. The people at first refused to believe that such a report as that telling of Peary's success had been received. They thought it must be a canard or a practical joke. The Danish news agency, which received the telegram from London, feared that it had been imposed upon and cabled to London for confirmation before it would circulate the report.

Minister Egan characterized it as one of the most dramatic events of history. The rumor spread that Peary was returning by way of Denmark, and this made an immense sensation. Some questioned the authority of the Peary telegram on the ground that it was improbable that a scientific man would use such dramatic language.

After the dinner to-night Dr. Cook stood about talking with Sverdrup and the other guests in a most unconcerned manner. Later, with the roses still decorating his shoulders, his hosts led him through the Casino grounds to an automobile. A crowd of several hundred, half of the number being women, surrounded and followed him, cheering, but the people were not able to get near enough to shake hands, because of a cordon of police.

PEARY DISCOVERS THE NORTH POLE AFTER EIGHT TRIALS IN 23 YEARS

Notifies The New York Times That He Reached It on April 6, 1909.

HE WIRES FROM LABRADOR

Returning on the Roosevelt, Which He Reports to Bridgman Is Safe.

IS NEARING NEWFOUNDLAND

Expects to Reach Chateau Bay To-day, When He Will Send Full Particulars.

McMILLAN SENDS WORD

Explorer's Companion Telegraphs Sister: "We Have the Pole on Board."

SEVEN VAIN EXPEDITIONS

Many Years Consumed in Learning the Feasible Route—Picked Men Were His Assistants.

Commander Robert E. Peary, U. S. N., has discovered the north pole. Following the report of Dr F. A. Cook that he had reached the top of the world comes the certain announcement from Mr. Peary, the hero of eight polar expeditions, covering a period of twenty-three years, that at last his ambition has been realized, and from all over the world comes full acknowledgment of Peary's feat and congratulations on his success.

The first announcement of Peary's exploit was received in the following message to THE NEW YORK TIMES:

> Indian Harbor, Labrador, via Cape Ray, N. F., Sept. 6.
> THE NEW YORK TIMES, New York:
> I have the pole, April sixth. Expect arrive Chateau Bay, September seventh. Secure control wire for me there and arrange expedite transmission big story. PEARY.

Following the receipt of Commander Peary's message to THE NEW YORK TIMES several other messages were received in this city from the explorer to the same effect.

Soon afterward The Associated Press received the following:

> INDIAN HARBOR, Via Cape Ray, N. F., Sept. 6.—To Associated Press, New York:
> Stars and Stripes nailed to the pole. PEARY.

To Herbert L. Bridgman, Secretary of the Peary Arctic Club, he telegraphed as follows:

> Herbert L. Bridgman, Brooklyn, N. Y.:
> Pole reached. Roosevelt safe. PEARY.

This message was received at the New York Yacht Club in West Forty-fourth Street:

> INDIAN HARBOR, Via Cape Ray, N. F., Sept. 6.—George A. Carmack, Secretary New York Yacht Club:
> Steam yacht Roosevelt, flying club burgee, has enabled me to add north pole to club's other trophies. (Signed) PEARY.

Cipher Shows Authenticity.

The telegram to Mr. Bridgman was sent in cipher. The cipher used was a private one and indicated clearly that the dispatch was undoubtedly from Commander Peary.

Commander Peary also sent a message to his wife at South Harpswell, Me., where she has been spending the Summer.

"Have made good at last," said the explorer to his wife. "I have the old pole. Am well. Love. Will wire again from Chateau."

The message was signed simply "Bert," an abbreviation of Robert, Commander Peary's first name. Mrs. Peary sent a wife's characteristic reply, with love and a blessing and a request for him to "hurry home."

By a strange coincidence, Mrs. Frederick A. Cook, too, was in South Harpswell, Me., when she received the first news from her husband.

Peary's Companion Reports.

Two messages were received in this country also from Donald B. McMillan, who accompanied Peary. Mr. McMillan was an instructor in mathematics and physical training at the academy in Worcester, Mass., until the close of school last year, when he obtained a leave of absence of two years to go on the Peary expedition.

In addition to his message to Dr. D. L. Abercrombie, Principal of the academy, Mr. McMillan sent the following to Mrs. W. C. Fogg, his sister, who is Postmistress at Freeport, Me.:

> Indian Harbor, Sept. 6, 1909.
> Mrs. W. C. Fogg, Freeport, Me.:
> Arrived safe. Pole on board. Best year of my life. BEN.

Follows Cook's Report Quickly.

These messages, flashed from the coast of Labrador to New York and thence to the four corners of the globe while Dr. Frederick A. Cook is being acclaimed by the crowned heads of Europe and the world at large as the discoverer of the north pole, added a remarkable chapter to the story of an achievement that has held the civilized world up to the highest pitch of interest since Sept. 1, when Dr. Cook's claim to having reached the "top of the world" was first telegraphed from the Shetland Islands.

The two explorers, Dr. Frederick A. Cook and Commander Robert E. Peary, both Americans, had been in the arctic seeking the goal of centuries, the impossible north pole, whose attainment has at times seemed beyond the reach of man. Both were determined and courageous, and both had started expressing the belief that their efforts would be crowned with success.

Peary the Better Known.

Peary was well known to both scientists and the general public as a persistent striver for the honor of reaching the "farthest north." Dr. Cook, on the other hand, had held the public attention to a lesser degree. He made his departure quietly and his purpose was hardly known except to those keenly interested in polar research.

Then suddenly, and with no word of warning, a steamer touched at Lerwick, in the Shetland Islands, and Dr. Cook's claim to having succeeded where expedition after expedition of the hardiest explorers of the world had failed was made known. Dr. Cook's announcement was that he had reached the pole on April 21, 1908.

Three days later Dr. Cook arrived at Copenhagen and received a welcome such as no explorer had ever received before.

Peary Announces Success.

Five days after the receipt of the Lerwick message, almost to the hour, came the sensational statement from Indian Harbor, Labrador, that Commander Peary also had been successful on his third expedition to the coveted goal, the date being April 6, 1909.

He filed his brief messages and continued on his way to the south, leaving the world to marvel at a dramatic situation such as has seldom been recorded—the double achievement of a purpose that for almost ten centuries had baffled the endeavor of man and had taken many an explorer to his death in the frozen north.

It is almost certain that Commander Peary did not know of Dr. Cook's announcement when he sent his messages from Indian Harbor.

Under ordinary circumstances Commander Peary's announcement would have evoked world-wide interest, but the existing conditions conspired to add many times to the importance of his communication.

According to Dr. Cook's account of his expedition, he buried the American flag at the pole in a metal tube; Peary's words would indicate that the Stars and Stripes were raised by him and left standing.

How the News Came.

The message from Commander Peary to THE NEW YORK TIMES was received in New York at 12:39 yesterday through the Postal Telegraph Company. It was handed in at Indian Harbor, Labrador, and was sent from there by wireless telegraph to Cape Ray, Newfoundland, and from Cape Ray to Port aux Basques by the Newfoundland Government land lines; thence to Canso, Nova Scotia, by cable, and to New York from there over the lines of the Commercial Cable Company.

PEARY REPORTS TO THE TIMES

ANNOUNCES HIS DISCOVERY OF THE POLE AND WILL SEND A FULL AND EXCLUSIVE ACCOUNT TO-DAY.

Indian Harbor, Labrador, via Cape Ray, N. F., Sept. 6.

The New York Times, New York:

I have the pole, April sixth. Expect arrive Chateau Bay September seventh. Secure control wire for me there and arrange expedite transmission big story.

PEARY.

PEARY'S MESSAGE TO HIS WIFE.

SOUTH HARPSWELL, Me., Sept. 6.—Commander Robert E. Peary announced his success in discovering the North Pole to his wife, who is summering at Eagle Island here, as follows:

INDIAN HARBOR, via Cape Ray, Sept. 6, 1909.

Mrs. R. E. Peary, South Harpswell, Me.:

Have made good at last. I have the old Pole. Am well. Love. Will wire again from Chateau.

(Signed) BERT.

In replying Mrs. Peary sent the following dispatch:

SOUTH HARPSWELL, Me., Sept. 6, 1909.

To Commander R. E. Peary, Steamer Roosevelt, Chateau Bay:

All well. Best love. God bless you. Hurry home.

(Signed) JO.

CONFIRMED BY FELLOW-VOYAGER.

INDIAN HARBOR, Labrador, Sept. 6, 1909.

Dr. D. W. Abercrombie, Worcester Academy, Worcester, Mass.:

Top of the earth reached at last. Greetings to Faculty and boys.

(Signed) D. B. McMILLAN.

DR. COOK CABLES THE TIMES.

To the Editor of The New York Times:

COPENHAGEN, Sept. 6.

Glad Peary did it. Two records are better than one, and the work over a more easterly route has added value.

COOK.

WASHINGTON CREDITS PEARY.

Believes Cook, Too, but Has Said That He Must Produce Records.

Special to The New York Times.

WASHINGTON, Sept. 6.—There was instant acceptance among the geographers in Washington of the assertion in Commander Peary's laconic cable message that he had discovered the north pole. And there was just as ready rejoicing for Peary is popular with the scientific men in the National capitol, and they are ready to take his word at its face value without examination or delay.

In the manner of their acceptance of this announcement of a second discovery of the point that has baffled discovery for so many years there is a sharp contrast to the attitude of the same men toward the announcement from Dr. Cook. Most of them, indeed, accept Cook's assertion, and announce their belief that the Brooklyn man actually did reach the north pole in April, 1908. But there

1910

There it was, just as astronomer Edmund Halley had said—in 1705.

The British astronomer had analyzed twenty-four comets for which historical sightings then existed and noticed a startling coincidence. One of the comets he had studied was one that he himself had observed in 1682. And its orbit was the same as that of comets seen in 1607 and 1531.

He concluded that this was actually a single comet that periodically returned to Earth. Then he made the prediction that earned him scientific immortality: the comet would return around 1758.

Halley wasn't alive to see it, but the comet that now bears his name appeared right on schedule—and has every seventy-five or seventy-six years since.

It was back in 1910 and the earth survived it, despite the belief of many that the earth would pass through the comet's tail and be destroyed.

And it is back again in late 1985 and early 1986.

"All the News That's Fit to Print."

The New York Times.

THE WEATHER.

Fair to-day; increasingly cloudy to-morrow; wind light, variable.

VOL. LIX...NO. 19,109. NEW YORK, FRIDAY, MAY 20, 1910.—EIGHTEEN PAGES ONE CENT, In Greater New York, Jersey City, and Newark. | Elsewhere, TWO CENTS.

NINE KINGS TO RIDE AT FUNERAL TO-DAY

Kaiser Arrives and Clasps Hands of George V. Before Edward's Bier.

50,000 TROOPS IN LONDON

Thousands of Persons Staying in the Streets All Night to Get Good Places to See the Procession.

Special Cable to THE NEW YORK TIMES.

LONDON, Friday, May 20.—King Edward will be laid to rest to-day in St. George's Chapel, Windsor, after two weeks of mourning, which have given rise to scenes unparalleled in the history of the world.

To-day's obsequies will be a magnificent tribute from the powers of the world to the memory of Edward the Peacemaker. Nine monarchs will ride behind his coffin: first his successor, King George, and then the rulers of Germany, Spain, Portugal, Denmark, Norway, Greece, Belgium, and Bulgaria. It will be the most numerous assemblage of crowned heads ever brought together in any European city, with the solitary exception of the gathering at the Diamond Jubilee of Queen Victoria. It is a notable fact that every one of these nine monarchs is a descendant of that William the Silent, who was assassinated in 1584 at the instigation of his kinsman, Philip II. of Spain.

Russia will be represented by the Grand Duke Michael, the brother of the Czar, and the Princes Fushimi and Tsai Tao will bring the sympathy of the Orient. Over a score of royal Dukes and hereditary Princes will swell the mounted cortège, behind which will come a dozen state carriages conveying Queens and Princesses, and, as notable figures as any in the procession, two plain citizens of the two great republics of the world—His Excellency the Hon. Theodore Roosevelt and His Excellency M. S. Pichon, to give them the designations adopted in the official order of the ceremonial published in the Gazette.

London's millions and great crowds of visitors from the provinces, the Continent, and America will line the route of the funeral procession through streets which to-day took on a mourning garb of crepe and royal purple.

While the body of the King is being committed to the vault at Windsor all England will, so to speak, stand still in sympathy. Factories will cease work, no trains on all the railways will be started, and the telegraph and cable wires will be idle.

Throughout to-day, as yesterday, there was a ceaseless procession of people through Westminster Hall, where King Edward's body lay in state. It is estimated that over 400,000 persons filed before the coffin since the lying in state began, although the difficulties and delays which met all those desirous of paying this tribute were enough to discourage any but the most determined.

At 4:30 o'clock this morning the streets were filled with streams of people flowing toward the line of the funeral procession. Charing Cross Station is disgorging thousands from early trains. The people are nearly all carrying wraps and parcels with food. Hawkers and scores are selling official programmes.

There has been a sharp thunderstorm, but the weather is now clear, and it is believed that it will continue fine during the day.

LONDON, May 19.—Emperor William arrived in London at noon to-day. The German imperial yacht Hohenzollern reached Sheerness last evening, but the Emperor did not land until this morning, when he proceeded to the capital. At Victoria Station the Emperor was received by King George, his majesty's eldest son, the Duke of Cornwall; the Duke of Connaught, Prince Henry of Prussia, and other royalties and diplomats.

The greeting of the monarchs was most affectionate. From his cousin the Emperor turned to the young Duke of Cornwall and kissed him on both cheeks.

As the Emperor and King George drove to Buckingham Palace great crowds in the streets exhibited lively interest in the German ruler. The men raised their hats, and the women waved their handkerchiefs as the royal carriage passed. Arriving at the palace, the Emperor was taken at once to the chamber where the Queen Mother Alexandra, where there was an affecting meeting.

This afternoon Emperor William paid tribute to the memory of his uncle, the late monarch. Accompanied by King George and their suites, he went to Westminster Hall, where thousands of persons of all classes were passing the bier. The Emperor approached the casket and remained before it for some minutes. He personally placed upon the casket a magnificent wreath. He then knelt by the catafalque and for a few moments was engaged in prayer.

Upon rising to his feet his Majesty turned to King George, who had knelt with his cousin before the bier, and clasped his hands, which the other grasped. Both monarchs were visibly affected.

For the few moments while the Emperor and the King knelt beside the coffin the thousands who were waiting in line to file past the catafalque were held in check, though those within Westminster Hall were permitted to remain. The striking scene as the two monarchs gripped hands, standing with bowed heads beside the body of King Edward, greatly moved all those who witnessed it.

Nine crowned heads of Europe and several heirs to thrones sat down in Buckingham Palace to-night at a dinner which King George gave to all his eminent guests assembled in London for the funeral of King Edward to-morrow. The guests included Mr. Roosevelt. After the

Continued on Page 2.

GIVES AWAY MILLIONS.

Pardridge, Objecting to Will Contests, Distributes His Fortune in Life.

Special to The New York Times.

CHICAGO, May 19.—Charles W. Pardridge, real estate holder and part owner of Hillman's State Street Store, believes in distributing wealth while he is alive rather than leaving it all only to be tied up pending litigation after his death. So while robust and hearty, he to-day put more than $2,000,000 worth of property into the hands of the Northern Trust Company to hold in trust for his four children.

The property is to be shared equally between the sons, Edward W. and Albert J. Pardridge, and the daughters, Evelyn, now the Princess Engalitcheff, and May, the wife of William D. Sargent of Orange, N. J. Albert J. is to be the manager of the property. Included in the assignment of realty is a deed to the land occupied by the Boston Store, estimated to be worth $1,275,000, and producing a ground rent annually of $51,000. Another deed covers the Reliance Building at State and Adams Streets, valued by the Board of Review at $925,595. The property values amount in all to $2,200,595.

"All there is in the transaction is that I decided to distribute the property to my children, and have done so," said Mr. Pardridge when asked about the move.

"Then you like to see property distributed by your own hands?" suggested the interviewer.

"Yes, that is my feeling to an extent," responded Mr. Pardridge.

Mr. Pardridge was told that the distribution had given rise to a theory that he was contemplating matrimony.

"Ridiculous," he responded, good-humoredly. "Why, I haven't the shadow of an idea of such a thing."

Mr. Pardridge is a man of quiet habits. He lives with his son, E. W. Pardridge, at 3,200 Michigan Avenue, and finds recreation in the evenings driving about.

While his face would be a strange one on the Board of Trade, it has been his fortune to make large sums of money in speculation. His first made a big mark on the blackboards in 1902, getting away with what generally is believed to have amounted in itself to a fortune. In June, 1907, he won $1,500,000 out of the wheat pit, giving his orders through brokerage firms.

Mr. Pardridge was the founder of the Boston Store. After disposing of his interest in it he became interested in Hillman's. His career on State Street has been that of a successful merchant.

Financial gossip has it that during the panic of 1907 Mr. Pardridge had enough ready money to loan to persons who needed it badly and that he relieved the pressing needs of many business men.

SENDS A BABY BY MESSENGER

But There Is No One to Receive It—Stranger Disappears.

Shortly after 5 o'clock last night a well-dressed young man of medium height, wearing a checked suit, derby hat, and tan shoes, walked into the branch office of the Western Union Telegraph Company, at Sixty-second Street and Columbus Avenue, and asked the manager, Benjamin Stumpf, if he had a colored messenger boy, who could be trusted to deliver a baby safely. Stumpf said he had, and the young man left. He returned at 5:30 o'clock with a baby carefully wrapped and a basket.

Stumpf called Max Cassmof of 47 East 112th Street, who has a number of smaller brothers and sisters, and gave him the commission on account of his presumptive experience with babies.

"Take it to 312 East 126th Street," said the young man, "and ask for Mrs. Sarah Jacobs. She is waiting there for it. Here's a quarter for you."

The young man paid 35 cents messenger charges and went out. The baby was found a bit too large for the basket, so Max started out with it on his arm. He found the address all right. It was an apartment house, but there was no one of the name of Jacobs on any of the cards at the door. Neither had the janitor heard of such a family. Max went to every apartment, and the nearest he could find to the name was a man who said his wife's cousin had married a Mr. Jacobs, but they had moved to San Francisco and he died several years ago.

Then the messenger started down the block ringing door bells. Still no result. He went across the street and tried strategy—rang the first doorbell and said: "Here's the baby you sent for."

The door was slammed in his face. Discouraged, Max took a car back to his office.

Manager Stumpf took the baby to the West Sixty-eighth Street Station, where Matron Rose Daly looked it over and reported that the only mark of identity on any of its garments was the label "Kaufmann's Big Store, Pittsburg, Penn.," inside the jacket collar. The baby was about a week old. It was later sent to Bellevue Hospital.

Y. M. C. A. GOT STOLEN MONEY.

Hall Confesses Looting of Southbridge Bank and Tells of His Benefactions.

WORCESTER, Mass., May 19.—After a plea of guilty to thirteen of the fifteen counts in an indictment charging the larceny of $106,000 from the Southbridge Savings Bank, and a subsequent recital of his disposal by gifts to charities and to relatives, and by bad investments of a sum of money which he estimated at $370,000, John A. Hall, defaulting Treasurer of the bank, was sentenced by Judge Robert T. Raymond in the Superior Court to-day to serve not less than twelve nor more than fifteen years in the State Prison at Charlestown. One day of this sentence is to be passed in solitary confinement.

Hall's peculations had their beginning about twenty years ago, he said on the stand, when he took $100 out of the cash drawer in the bank to take a flier in Atchison stock. This investment, like many others in later years, was unsuccessful.

Although he kept no record, Hall said he estimated the total amount of his stealings at about $370,000. Expert accountants who have gone over his books at the bank since the discovery of the shortage assert that about $600,000 is missing.

When asked by the court what he did with the money, Hall produced a memorandum from which he read extracts showing, among other things, a gift of $50,000 to the Southbridge Young Men's Christian Association to build a new building; $30,000 to his brother, Clare Hall, to help him establish a sheep farm in Montana; $6,500 for the education of his brother, Frederick Hall, and to start him in business; $50,000 in a stock deal; various sums to the Good Will Home and the Home for Orphans and Little Wanderers in Boston, to the Worcester Young Men's Christian Association and State Young Men's Christian Association; about $20,000 to poor people at different times, and $30,000 in unfortunate real estate deals in the Back Bay district, Boston. Hall said his living expenses had averaged $7,500 a year and that his salary as bank Treasurer was $2,500.

In imposing sentence, Judge Raymond said that Hall had shown himself to be an habitual criminal. "It is easy to be charitable when it costs nothing," Judge Raymond remarked. Hall showed no sign of emotion.

THE REAL PRESIDENT, MY WIFE, SAYS TAFT

Thus Introduces Mrs. Taft to World's Sunday School Convention After Chautauqua Salute.

GIVES PRAISE TO THE WORK

Does What Public Schools Cannot Do, He Says—Negroes Excluded from Sunday School Parade.

WASHINGTON, May 19.—Mrs. Taft made her first public appearance since she was taken ill about a year ago at to-night's session of the World's Sunday School Association, whither she accompanied the President. Mr. Taft introduced her to the immense audience as "the real President of the United States."

This happened after the President had finished his speech. The Rev. Dr. F. B. Meyer, who was in the chair, mentioned Mrs. Taft's presence, whereupon Mr. Taft took her by the hand and led her up into the speakers' stand. Loud applause greeted her appearance.

To-night's convention hall was surrounded by a crowd fully as large as the 6,000 within the big structure. Mr. Taft's entrance was greeted with the Chautauqua salute of fluttering handkerchiefs, followed by hand clapping, and in his speech his praises of the Sunday school were cheered to the echo again and again.

"It is one of the two or three great instrumentalities," he declared, "for making the world better, more moral and more religious. As the twig is bent, so the tree is inclined; and youth is the time to inculcate for results, moral and religious ideas. No matter what views are taken of general education, we all agree, Protestant, Catholic, and Jew, that Sunday school education is necessary to secure moral uplift and religious spirit."

Dr. Meyer of England, President of the association, in introducing President Taft, declared that for the past twenty years he "had prayed for the President of the United States every Sunday after prayer for the King of England." "And this," he added, "is a common custom in England."

Mr. Taft replied to this by saying that he hoped these prayers would continue.

"My experience," he said, "is that these prayers are needed."

Mr. Meyer thanked the President for the "noble cablegram which he sent when King Edward died," and Mr. Taft replied:

"The reference to the death of the late King and the feeling of mourning on both sides of the world brings to mind how much such a convention as this means in perpetuation of the peace of nations.

"Our public school education," he said, "has only secular teaching with the teaching of morality in general. But that is not enough. There are those whose opinions I respect, who feel that it is dangerous to have education at all unless it is associated with religious training. But this has not been found practical in this country. Therefore, there is need for Sunday school education."

Speaking of the rise of the Sunday School movement and of its growth in the United States he declared "a movement of such strength should be welcomed in every community for the good it is doing."

Other speakers at to-night's meeting were the Rev. Dr. Samuel H. Greene of this city, former Postmaster General John Wanamaker, the Rev. J. Monroe Gibson, England; Bishop Yoitsu, Japan, and Bishop Hartsell of Africa.

The race question has invaded the convention. Local negro Sunday School leaders are protesting because members of their race are to be barred from the men's monster Bible class parade to-morrow. In a statement issued by them to-night they declare that "it is unfortunate that any one who hears His name should at this time, when the evangelization of the world in this generation is the watchword of millions, should resort to such offensive forms of race prejudice as the local committee of Washington has done in, completely, as far as it concerned, eliminating the colored people from any part in the sixth world's Sunday School convention."

Members of the local committee say the negro Sunday schools of the District of Columbia have had plenty of opportunities to join the Sunday School Association of the District, without taking advantage thereof, and that therefore they have "no more right in the parade," as the Chairman of the Press Committee expressed it, "than if they were members of a labor union, or any other unaffiliated organization."

Where there are a number of negro delegates present at the convention from various States and Territories throughout the United States, and from some foreign countries, there are none from the District of Columbia. The local committee has entire charge of the arrangements for the convention, so that the General Committee declares itself helpless to do anything in the matter.

ERIE STRIKE AVERTED.

But Not Until After the Men Were Ready to Call It.

It looked for a while yesterday as if nothing could prevent a strike of the trainmen and conductors on the Erie Railroad from this city to Chicago, involving 6,000 men, to enforce the demand for the Baltimore & Ohio schedule. Whether or not there will be a strike depends on a final proposal from the road to be put in the hands of the heads of the men's National organizations at 10 o'clock this morning.

President Lee of the Brotherhood of Railroad Trainmen and President Garretson of the Order of Railroad Conductors had what was to have been their final conference yesterday with General Manager Stuart. The conference ended at 1 o'clock and the unions' representatives, who were more or less angry, went out to notify their Grievance Committees that there was nothing to do but to call the strike which was voted on.

Shortly afterward a telephone message came to the two organization heads from Mr. Stuart's office to the effect that he wanted to see them. Another brief conference was held at 4 P. M., at which it was stated that the final proposal of the Erie would be made. The men agreed to hold back the strike until it is received.

On behalf of the Erie Railroad a statement was then issued stating that a new wage schedule had been agreed upon and that the details of the settlement were being worked out.

"The only question to be settled," said the statement, "is when some of the rates in the New York Central award will go into effect on the Erie."

Capital of the World.

William George Jordan has written an article for next Sunday's Times on the proposed new headquarters of the Peace Movement at The Hague. The plan is a stupendous one, and this story of it is bound to attract wide attention.

Be sure to order next Sunday's Times early.

AEROPLANE CRASHES INTO MINEOLA CROWD

E. C. Baldwin Loses Control of His Machine as He Attempts to Make a Landing.

IN DANGER OF HORSES, TOO

Onlookers Flee to Escape Frightened Animals—Clifford Harmon Makes Flights at Hempstead Plains.

Special to The New York Times.

MINEOLA, L. I., May 19.—Over the heads of the big crowd which had watched him in four successful flights over the Hempstead Plains, Capt. Edward C. Baldwin manipulated a Curtiss biplane early this evening in one last skim about the mile-and-a-half course. The air craft was about sixty feet from the ground, and the crowd clapped and shouted applause as the aviator swept toward them, evidently intent on making a landing.

Every one in the throng, which included folk from the Wheatley Hills and Meadow Brook sections, expected momentarily to hear the final whirr of the Captain's engine as he shut it off to alight, but the throb of the motor did not pause, and presently, too late to get out of the way, the watchers realized that the machine was headed right for them.

As startled, frightened cry arose and men and women turned to flee. But the air craft was among them. It skimmed downward until men and women avoided its outspread wings only by throwing themselves flat on the ground. Others fled to right and left and finally the big machine came to a stumbling halt in the very midst of the frightened crowd.

Its startling approach had caused a dozen horses to dash away in a panic and men and women afoot had all they could do to avoid the flying hoofs of the runaways. Several reached the roadway and disappeared at full speed in the direction of town. They were caught afterward. No one apparently was hurt, although many were rumpled and bruised from their hurried efforts to avoid the biplane.

Though frightened as they were, every one remained to see Clifford B. Harmon try his hand at flying. He, too, used a biplane and managed to point it upward and into the air within a very few feet of the starting point. His first lap around the course was made in about two minutes and he started immediately on another circuit.

The second trip was made in as good time as the first until the navigator, in making one of the turns, came too close to the ground. The aeroplane struck and the steering gear was wrecked in such a way that it was fifteen minutes before Mr. Harmon's French mechanicians could repair it.

Then he tried another flight. He was in the air within 75 feet of his starting point, and rose to a height of about 60 feet. He made six fast circuits of the course in eleven minutes without a stop, maintaining at all times the original level. Approaching darkness compelled him to abandon the flight, and he came gracefully and easily to the ground. He was greeted by cheers and the prolonged tooting of hundreds of automobile horns.

A fire alarm in Mineola started the crowd on a run in that direction, and Mr. Harmon's French attendants, not understanding what had happened, and fearing that it was some manifestation of the comet, as they were firmly convinced, fled too. Friends of the aeroplanist chased them and finally persuaded them to come back to work.

$32,000 EXPRESS ROBBERY.

Cash and Vouchers of Pennsylvania Railway Taken from Oil City Office.

Special to The New York Times.

OIL CITY, Penn., May 19.—Detectives of the Pennsylvania Railroad from Buffalo and Pittsburg and officials of the Adams Express Company are in the city bent upon finding out what became of $12,000 in cash and vouchers representing $20,000 more, which disappeared from the express company's office at 8 o'clock this morning.

The cash and vouchers were deposited with the agent of the Adams Company at 8 o'clock Wednesday night by Pennsylvania Railroad Paymaster F. S. Montelius for shipment to the Treasurer of the railroad company at Philadelphia. The checks represented wages that had not been paid employes who were on their runs when the pay car was here Tuesday.

The office of the express company is of a temporary character, the three packages were too large to be placed in the safe and were stowed under the desk. The night agent, John Truby, and his assistant left the office shortly before 3 A. M. Thursday to load express matter on an outgoing train. A case of cigars had been overlooked, and Truby returning for it in less than three minutes from the time he had left the office found the front door ajar, and, suspecting theft, searched for the package. He found the packages gone.

Agents and detectives of the railroad and express company were notified, and Truby and his assistant, F. S. Harding, have been under a rigorous grilling all day. J. A. Murphy, General Superintendent, and H. C. Hurt, General Manager of Adams Express Company, will arrive early to-morrow morning to aid in the investigation.

No arrests have been made, but the railroad detectives are of the opinion that the theft was the work of one man, who knew that the money was in the station and who knew just where it was located.

BALL FROM THE BAT KILLS BOY PITCHER

Though Mortally Hurt, Young Becker Clung to the Ball and Put Runner Out.

THEN DIES IN THE BOX

Ball Straight from Home Plate Broke Through Becker's Hands and Hit Him in the Stomach.

Two men were out, and the umpire had just called two strikes and three balls when Capt. Andrew Towart, 14 years old, of the "Young Websters," faced Harry Becker, the fourteen-year-old pitcher of the "Young Twilights" for the decisive ball in a game of baseball in a vacant lot at 149th Street and Gerard Avenue, the Bronx, late yesterday afternoon.

Young Becker, who had been star pitcher on the Townsend Harris High School team last year until he was disabled by a batted ball, curled himself up for a fancy throw. The ball, a small leather-covered sphere of twisted rubber bands, shot toward the batter, and a moment later whizzed at comet speed from Towart's bat, directly back at the pitcher. So swift was its rebound that it shot through Becker's clenched hands and buried itself with a thud in the pit of his stomach.

The boy's face went instantly white. But the next moment he had thrown the ball with swift, accurate aim to first base, putting Towart out. Even the umpire, Robert Ragatta, 15 years old, of 277 East 148d Street could not help admiring Becker's "nerve."

"Fine work!" he shouted.

Then the boys on both teams, looking back to the pitcher, saw Becker sink to the ground. When they reached him his eyes were glazed, and he died before Policeman McCormick, whom one of the boys called from the Alexander Avenue Station, could summon an ambulance from the Lincoln Hospital.

Young Towart was detained by the policeman as a material witness until Coroner Schwanecke paroled him later in the evening. The boys of both teams carried the body of their fellow-player to his home, at 274 East 146th Street. At the sight of them the boy's mother, Mrs. Rosa Becker, fainted away. She was under a physician's care and in a serious condition last night.

TROLLEY CAR HITS AN AUTO.

Mrs. Morrell, Wife of a Long Island Police Justice, Badly Hurt.

MINEOLA, L. I., May 19.—While turning into the Jericho Turnpike this morning in an automobile, accompanied by his wife, Police Justice H. C. Morrell of Great Neck was struck by a trolley car of the New York & Long Island Traction Company, and Mrs. Morrell received injuries from which she may die.

As Mr. Morrell was well on the car track, he suddenly saw the car bearing down on him, and knew he could not cross in front, so swerved his car and ran ahead for a short distance, thinking to get a little lead on the trolley car. But the car was coming too fast to be avoided in so short a space of time, and Mr. Morrell started to turn into the road just as the trolley car struck his automobile, upsetting it and throwing both him and Mrs. Morrell to the stone road. The auto was smashed into junk.

Both Mr. and Mrs. Morrell were knocked unconscious, and Mrs. Morrell had her left hip fractured. An ambulance was called from the Nassau Hospital and both were removed to that institution. Mr. Morrell's injuries were not very serious, and he was soon able to walk about the hospital.

CUT OFF COLONEL'S BEARD.

Now They Go to Jail for Trying to Intimidate Louisiana Voters.

NEW ORLEANS, May 19.—For intimidating voters last Fall at Kenner, La., including Col. E. A. O'Sullivan, whose long, wavy beard of wide reputation was cut off, Paul Felix, formerly Mayor of Kenner, and W. W. Stiles, a Deputy Sheriff, were found guilty in the Federal Court to-day. Felix was sentenced to six months in the Parish Prison, with a fine of $1,000, while Stiles was sentenced to serve eleven months and pay the same fine.

Felix and Stiles were alleged to have been among an armed gang, including several Deputy Sheriffs, who drove from the polls voters representing an opposing faction in the politics of Jefferson Parish.

DENVER ELECTS A WOMAN.

Also Adopts Initiative, Referendum, and Recall Charter Amendments.

DENVER, May 19.—Practically complete returns from Tuesday's election show that Miss Ellis Meredith, a well-known club woman, has been chosen Election Commissioner, her total of 20,997 exceeding the combined vote of her seven men competitors. She is the first woman elected to office in the City of Denver. Miss Meredith ran on the Citizens' ticket.

The practically complete count also show that the initiative and referendum and recall charter amendments have been adopted.

CHICAGO, May 19.—Mrs. Ella Flagg Young, Superintendent of Schools, was elected to succeed herself for six months at a meeting of the Board of Education yesterday.

Yale Man to Wed Girl He Rescued.

Special to The New York Times.

NEW HAVEN, Conn., May 19.—Wedding bells will ring June 1 for Miss Enid Rice of Flatbush Avenue, Brooklyn, who was rescued from drowning by Stanton Higgins, a Yale law school senior, last year, at Woodmont-on-the-Sound. They were summering at that shore resort and Miss Rice fell out of a boat. Higgins leaped into the water after her and saved her life. They will be married in St. Paul's Episcopal Church, Brooklyn. Five hundred invitations have been issued. Higgins was graduated from the law school last year.

OUR TROOPS IN BLUEFIELDS.

One Hundred and Sixty Bluejackets Landed with Artillery.

BLUEFIELDS, Nicaragua, May 19.—The United States gunboats Dubuque and Paducah landed 160 bluejackets here to-day to protect American interests in Bluefields and to prevent fighting within the town limits.

The American force is prepared for an emergency, having taken ashore several field guns and rapid-firers.

HIT BY A TRAIN AND LIVES.

"I'm Not Badly Hurt," Says a Jerseyman as Rescuers Pick Him Up.

PASSAIC, N. J., May 19.—While crossing the tracks of the Erie Railroad at the Paterson Avenue Crossing shortly after 7 o'clock this morning, John Sigler of 85 Woodlawn Avenue, Nutley, was struck by a train. The engineer applied the brakes and brought his train to a stop.

"I'm not badly hurt," said Sigler, as the trainmen approached him.

They lifted him from the ground while a telephone call was sent to St. Mary's Hospital for an ambulance. When it arrived the physician, after an examination, said that Sigler had only a fractured rib and a bruised hip. He will recover.

MONKS BUY ECKELS ESTATE.

Country Home of Late Controller Will Be a Seminary.

OGONOMOWOC, Wis., May 19.—James H. Eckels's country home on Lake La Belle, valued at $250,000, was sold at an administrator's sale to-day to the Redemptorist Fathers of St. Louis for $33,000.

The property comprises twenty-nine acres of land and a handsome residence. It will be used for a Catholic theological seminary. Mr. Eckels, who was formerly Controller of the Currency, died several months ago.

BALLOON ON LONG FLIGHT.

Capt. Honeywell Starts from St. Louis to Win the Lahm Cup.

ST. LOUIS, May 19.—Capt. H. E. Honeywell of the Aero Club of St. Louis sailed to-night at 5:30 o'clock in the balloon Centennial in an attempt to win the Lahm Cup for a long distance flight. W. F. Assmann of St. Louis accompanied him as an aid.

The ascension was made under favorable conditions. The balloon started northeast toward the Great Lakes. Capt. Honeywell said he hoped to land somewhere in New England.

The Centennial has a capacity of 78,000 cubic feet.

CHALONER'S GUN STOPS AUTO.

Then His Horse Shied and Sent Him and Autoist Into a Ditch.

Special to The New York Times.

COBHAM, Va., May 19.—John Armstrong Chaloner, member of the Chanler family of New York, to-day held up an autoist on the road at the point of a double-barreled shotgun and forced the man to assist in leading his horse past the machine. As the autoist approached rapidly Chaloner, pointing the gun, cried: "You'll pass over my dead body before you pass this cart!"

The car stopped and the motorist alighted, but the horse shied and threw the cart and its occupant into a ditch; then shied again and sent both the autoist and Chaloner there. Neither was seriously hurt.

Chaloner has no friendly feeling for automobiles nor their drivers. He has his cart equipped with an auto horn and he uses it every time he meets a machine. He advocates the use of a gun by all farmers for stopping motorists by shooting at the tires.

PILLOWCASE A POOR BANK.

Woman Forgot She Put $2,000 in One and Shook It Out the Window.

Abner Mansfield, a liveryman of 105 Thirteenth Street, Hoboken, has come to the conclusion that a pillow case is a poor substitute for a bank. On Wednesday night Mansfield gave $2,000 in bills to his wife.

"Put this in some safe place and keep it until to-morrow," he said. Mrs. Mansfield put the roll of banknotes into a pillow case and slept on them all night. Yesterday Mr. Mansfield wanted to know if the money was safe. Mrs. Mansfield screamed and ran to the front window of their bedroom, which looks out upon the street. She grabbed a pillow which lay airing on the window sill and ran her hand inside. She shook the pillow out of the slip and peered into the case. The bills were gone.

Mr. Mansfield and his wife searched in the street. No bills were to be found. So Mr. Mansfield went to the Hoboken Police Station and told Police Chief Hayes about it. Detective Quinn was detailed to hunt for the roll of bills.

RUBBER TIRES MAY GO.

Westinghouse Believes His New Air-spring Will Make Them Unnecessary.

Special to The New York Times.

PITTSBURG, May 19.—An invention which he believes will do away with much of the cost of tires to autoists has been completed by George Westinghouse. It is known as the air spring. Mr. Westinghouse says the expense of rubber-tired vehicles will be decreased at least 60 per cent., since the rubber tire may be dispensed with.

The new air spring device is being tried out on autos with steel tires. It consists of a series of plungers working on air cushions on the same principle as an elevator plunger. The air spring is placed under each corner of the frame of an auto. Mr. Westinghouse says it takes the shock with greater ease than does the rubber tire now in use. Each spring for an automobile is a cylinder set upright, a plunger connected with the auto frame working up and down as required.

$1,000,000 Mortgage on Nassau Hotel.

MINEOLA, L. I., May 19.—A mortgage for $1,000,000 was filed here to-day by the Nassau Hotel Company of Long Beach Estates in favor of the Columbia Trust Company of Brooklyn. This sum absorbs a first mortgage of $700,000 already standing against the hotel company, and an additional $300,000 cash. The mortgage is for a period of five years and draws interest at 5 per cent.

DIDN'T GET THROUGH THE COMET'S TAIL

Observatories Confirm Times's Unexpected Discovery of It in the East Yesterday Morning.

ALL ASK: WHERE IS IT NOW?

Can It Be That Band Across the Sun the Yerkes Observatory Detected Yesterday?—Varied Views.

TIMES OBSERVATIONS CONFIRMED.

These dispatches from leading astronomers were received by THE TIMES last night confirming the unexpected discovery of the comet's tail in the east when it should have been in the west, as announced in THE TIMES yesterday morning.

SAN JOSE, Cal., May 19.

The object which you saw this morning was the brighter part of the comet's tail. Our observations agree with yours and extended the tail to the Milky Way. We have this evening observed the nucleus exactly in its predicted position. No other part of comet certainly visible in evening sky.

W. W. CAMPBELL, Director Lick Observatory.

YERKES OBSERVATORY, WILLIAMS BAY, Wis., May 19.

Your observation was of the comet's tail. I observed it here this morning. It was over 120 degrees long and about 20 degrees wide. Cloudy now.

E. E. BARNARD, of the Yerkes Observatory.

YERKES OBSERVATORY, WILLIAMS BAY, Wis., May 19.

Your observations of band of light entirely verified here. This was undoubtedly the comet's tail. The earth's entry into it was probably delayed by a pronounced curvature of the tail.

S. A. MITCHELL, Professor of Astronomy at Columbia University.

PRINCETON, N. J., May 19.

Saw just the same thing at the same time. Undoubtedly the comet's tail. For details see signed statement to Associated Press.

H. N. RUSSELL, Professor of Astronomy at Princeton University.

CAMBRIDGE, Mass., May 19.

Observation this morning at Lick Observatory renders it probable that the object you saw was Halley's comet.

E. C. PICKERING, Director of the Harvard Observatory.

AMHERST, Mass., May 19.

Nothing was seen of the tail of Halley's comet here to-night, so I infer that your observer must have seen it early this morning without a doubt, as description corresponds exactly with the position where the comet's tail should have been. Will look there again to-morrow morning if sky continues clear.

D. TODD, Professor of Astronomy at Amherst College.

The earth, apparently, did not pass through the comet's tail, as generally predicted by astronomers, between the hours of 10:50 on Wednesday night and 4:50 yesterday morning, after all. In late editions yesterday THE TIMES was able to announce that from observations taken on the tower of the Times Building between 2:30 and 3:15 A. M. the wanderer's tail was still in the eastern sky at a time when the earth should have been passing through it preparatory to its being seen last night in the west.

The announcement was made in these words:

Between 10:30 and 11:30 P. M. Miss Mary Proctor, the astronomer, and the other watchers on the top of the Times tower saw what appeared to be several flashes in the northeastern sky. Miss Proctor remained on watch all night, and at 2:30 this morning just after the moon had set, discovered a band of light 100 degrees in length stretching from the horizon at the point of sunrise up through the great square of Pegasus and Andromeda to Aquila.

At its widest part, just beneath the first magnitude star, Altair, the width of the band was about 10 degrees, and toward the length it had a brilliance equal to that of the Milky Way, near which it terminated. The path of this band of light was very nearly that along which the comet was last seen, and Miss Proctor was convinced that it was the outer boundary of the tail through which the earth was passing. The band of light was still there at 3 o'clock this morning.

Other watchers who have seen the comet and its tail repeatedly during the last two weeks confirmed Miss Proctor's view.

When this discovery was made THE TIMES immediately telegraphed to the chief observatories throughout the country asking for verification of the observation, and received the replies confirming it printed above. The views of the astronomers on this contradiction of their prediction and its possible causes are printed elsewhere.

An Apparition on the Sun.

The latest news of the comet is contained in dispatches received last night from Director Campbell of the Lick Observatory, in the dispatch printed at the head of this column, notes an observation of the nucleus last evening in its predicted position after crossing the face of the sun. From the Yerkes Observatory, at Wil-

1911

"Sweatshops," they were called, manufacturing places in which workers toiled long hours for low wages under poor conditions.

Many of the workers in the sweatshops were unskilled immigrants, exploited by employers.

The disastrous fire in the New York City loft building occupied by the Triangle-Shirtwaist Co. resulted in the death of 146 people, mostly women and girls trapped on the top three floors.

The proprietors were indicted but acquitted.

As a result of the tragedy, the International Ladies Garment Workers Union was able to gain new legislation to improve working conditions and safety for those in the trade.

THE BROOKLYN DAILY EAGLE

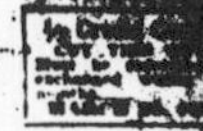

SECTIONS. ★ NEW YORK CITY, SUNDAY, MARCH 26, 1911. ★ 68 PAGES. THREE CENTS.

ER 150 PERSONS, MOST OF THEM GIRLS, DIE AS FIRE TRAPS HAPLESS FACTORY WORKERS IN MANHATTAN SKYSCRAPER

ed to Windows by Flames, Scores Jump to Death on Pavements Far Below. Many Frightfully Injured.

Scenes Follow, as Flames, Starting in Rooms of the Triangle Waist Company at 23 Washington Place, Envelope 10-Story Structure Containing 800 Employes.

FIED CROWDS LOOK ON AS DOOMED VICTIMS JUMP

ore than 150 persons, according to the estimate at an hour this morning—nine-tenths of them girls from the East were crushed to death on the pavements, smothered in , or shriveled crisp yesterday afternoon in the worst fire York has known since the steamship General Slocum was to the water's edge off North Brother's Island in 1904.

arly all, if not all, of the victims were employed by the Shirtwaist Company on the eighth, ninth and tenth floors -story loft building at 23 Washington place, on the west- ge of the downtown wholesale clothing, fur and millinery . The partners of the firm, Isaac Harris and Max Blanck, unscathed from the office on the tenth floor, carrying with over an adjoining roof Blanck's two young daughters and a ess. There was not an outside fire escape on the building.

Only Fire Escape Led Into a Pit.

he fire broke out at 4:45 P.M. Fire Chief Croker declared e mortality from the outbreak exceeded the deaths from the place disaster, the Windsor Hotel fire and the Park Avenue onflagration. In this case the fire spread with such rapidity was impossible for all of the 800 people penned in the , ninth and tenth stories of the building, which was sup- to be fireproof, to get out. The single fire escape leading he huge structure, apart from the stairways, the elevators windows, ran down to a courtyard of the sort that is in many business structures in Manhattan; a pit from which ould be no outlet in such an emergency.

he building, which is at the corner of Greene street and gton place, runs about 100 feet on each street and is used rious manufacturers. It adjoins the big University Press g, where there is a printing office, a huge bookbindery and school. There were few people in the University Press g at the time the fire started, and although there was a panic among them the young women and men, and profes- who were there got out safely, and tried to help the unfor- in the burning building. The three upper floors were oc- by the Triangle Waist Company, manufacturing shirt- and other articles of women's attire. Just what caused the not known and probably will not be discovered until the ing investigation already under way, is completed. All that n at the present time is that the flames broke out on the floor at about fifteen minutes before 5 o'clock. Although spread with great rapidity the men employed in the factory ir best to prevent a panic.

ut the young women were panicstricken. There were so of them that it was impossible for all to get away. The rear building looked out on an airshaft which backed on the walls rounding buildings. Leading to this shaft was the only fire on the building. The other exits were by the elevator, inadequate in an emergency, and by the roof.

Doomed Operatives Fight for Their Lives.

any of those on the two upper floors had sense enough to the roof, but the crowds of the panicstricken operatives great that the stairways and the scuttle leading to the roof ronged and jammed. Women and men tore at each others in their frenzy to get away.

e story of the awful panic cannot be told coolly by any of vivors. They were all suffering from the shock last night ld not give details.

they knew was that there was a wild delirium of anxiety out. The stairs leading to the street were fire-locked and in that direction was impossible.

here was flame all around the workers in a few minutes. n in charge of the elevator proved to be a hero. He is Zitto, a young Italian, who stuck to his post bravely. He is trips, carrying passengers to the limit of the car, just ly as possible. The elevator made seventeen trips to the stories and even while the heat was so intense that the of the car seemed to twist the elevator man stuck bravely work. But when he got to the eighth floor on the eighteenth found the doors to the elevator so jammed with shrieking and men that he could not open them. The people, so , with fire burning all about them, were left to their fate.

People in Street Witness Horrible Scenes.

ile all this was going on the people in the street were wit- the most horrible scenes. Women were at the windows, e glaring behind them, their clothing in some cases burn- their bodies, all imploring assistance. An alarm had out from a nearby box and the engines and hook and lad- s came tearing into the street.

crowds on the sidewalks were imploring those at the win- to jump and shouting to them to wait for the firemen. firemen were powerless to help when they came. ir ladders only reached to the seventh floor of the big sixteen feet from the victims at the windows. Before the got there women and men were jumping, shrieking and the street.

Continued on Page 6.

RUSHING TEMPORARY COFFINS FOR THE VICTIMS.

In Washington Place the Charred Dead Lay in Rows Before Being Taken to Improvised Morgue.

LIST OF DEAD AND THE INJURED

The list of identified dead is as follows:

MOSES BERNSTEIN—Address on bank book, 309 East Fifth street, Manhattan.
JANE BUELLO—23; 49 Stockholm street, Manhattan.
JULIUS ABESSTEIN—$7.71 in pocket; no address.
ROSE CREBO—25; address unknown.
A. DOHRMAN—(Man) 235 Gold street, Brooklyn.
——KLOBER—(Woman); name on time card; $27.05 in pocketbook.
FANNY LAUNSWALD—24; address unknown.
MAX LEVINE—Address unknown; identified by pay envelope.
BECKY NEIBERER—19; operator; 19 Clinton street.
MRS. ROSEN—37; identified by pay envelope, with $60 and $447 wrapped around her leg.
R. ROTHER—
TEDDIE RATHNER—$2.05 in pocket; union card of Shirt Waist Workers.
——STRINT—
M. SELTZER—
REBECCA SEIDIECH—17; 10 Attorney street.
COTETA TERRANOVA—104 President street, Brooklyn.
MRS. WITZNER—27; identified by pay envelope.
ROSIE WEYNER—

The following bodies have been identified:

Vincenzo Caputta, 17 years old, 81 De Graw street, Brooklyn. This girl identified by her father Francesco. The father [illegible] nized his daughter's face.

Nicolina Nichols, 440 East Thirteenth street, 22 years old. Identified by her uncle, D. J. Leone.

Samuel Lehrer, 144 Essex street. Identified by card and letter found on person. euuR fl. ocNineteenthl HT RA DO LIU

ANNIE ALTMAN—16, of 33 Pike street, Manhattan. Identified by brother, Morris Altman.
BEATRICE ALTRASK—of 108 Degraw street, Brooklyn.
GUSSIE BIERMAN—22, of 8 Rivington street, Manhattan.
ABRAHAM BINAWETZ—30, of 474 Powell street, Brooklyn. Identified by step-brother, Isaac Weismann.
MARY GULLO—26, of 437 East Twelfth street, Manhattan. Identified by brother, James Gullo.
ESTHER GOLDSTEIN—20, of 143 Madison street, Manhattan. Identified by brother, Isidor Goldstein.
BESSIE KOPPERMAN—16, of 191 Madison street, Manhattan. Identified by brother, James Kopperman.
FANNIE LANSNER—21, a fore-woman, of 78 Forsythe street, Manhattan. Identified by brother-in-law, Charles Preus.
LUCY MANTES—19, address not certain. Identified by brother, William Mantes.
SARAH MANTES—18 years, address uncertain. Identified by brother, William Mantes.
ANTIONETTE PTSQUALIETA—16, of 509 East Thirteenth street, Manhattan.
BEREL SKLAZER—25; of 160 Madison street, Manhattan; identified by cousin, Joel Reedsky, of 228 Clinton street, Manhattan.
ROSE WEINER—22; of 119 East Eighth street, Manhattan; identified by married sister, Mrs. Marie Rashkan, of 306 East Eighth street, Manhattan.

THE LIST OF UNIDENTIFIED DEAD

The police decided to attach tags, numbered consecutively, to the dead bodies as they were removed from the scene of the fire. All dead bodies will be indicated by numbers until they are identified. Owing to the confusion, the police were unable to keep a consecutive record.

The following are the dead at the Morgue:

No. 3. Unidentified woman, 21 years old, 5 feet 2 inches, black hair, black button shoes and black stockings, clothing burned off; gold signet ring on left hand.

No. 4. Unidentified man, 25 years, 5 feet 7 inches, smooth shaven, black hair, brown striped coat, black trousers, black patent leather shoes.

No. 11. Unidentified woman, 24 years, 5 feet 2 inches, black hair, white bead earrings, black waist and skirt, white underwear, black shoes, signet ring with the initials "T. L."

No. 13. Unidentified woman, 23 years, 5 feet 3 inches, dark complexion, long black pony coat, black skirt, black stockings, tan shoes, envelope in stocking with $11 bo[illegible] bearing [illegible] Replan.

No. 24. Woman, 25, 5 feet 3 inches, black button shoes, black stockings, [illegible] garters, most of the clothing burned off, light underwear, weighing about 120 pounds.

[illegible] metal ring on left hand set with blue stone, apparently an Italian, 27 years, 5 feet 7 inches.

No. 18. Woman, 20, 5 feet 1 inch, black hair, black skirt, white waist with black stripes, no shoes, envelope with $10.17, another with $10, another with $60, another with $17, making $97 in all; two notes from foreign (Italian) banks; on one of the envelopes a name very much blurred; looked like "Shena."

No. 150. Woman, 24 years, dark hair, red skirt, white underwear, black button shoes, black stockings.

No. 22. Girl, 15 years, all clothing burned off except black stockings and black lace shoes.

No. 20. Woman, 25 years, clothing burned off, ring on left hand, black stockings, lace shoes, white underskirt, apparently Italian.

No. 12. Woman, 25 years, 5 feet 6 inches, dark hair, pair of earrings with white stones, plain ring on left hand, gray plaid skirt, white underwear, black and gray waist.

No. 26. Girl, 16 years, black hair, 130 pounds, 5 feet 1 inch, blue skirt, brown coat, blue underskirt, black stockings and black button shoes.

No. 27. Woman, 20 years, Italian, 5 feet 8 inches, black hair, dark complexion, signet ring on left hand, with initials "G. S.," black velvet shoes.

No. 203. Woman, 35 years, 5 feet 3 inches, dark complexion and hair, black skirt, white waist, white underwear, black lace shoes, gold ring on left hand, gold ring on right hand, with a black and a white stone.

No. 212. Woman, 20 years, 5 feet 2 inches, 130 pounds, dark complexion, blue eyes, good teeth, black silk skirt, white waist, black handbag with the name Frances Denent on pay envelope in the bag, containing $10.95.

No. 213. Woman, 22 years, 5 feet 5 inches, dark hair and complexion, black skirt, white waist, white underwear, lace shoes, black stockings, postcard with the name Clotete Terrinoza, 104 President street, Brooklyn.

No. 214. Woman 25 years, 5 feet 5 inches, gold teeth, one in upper jaw and one in lower jaw, black skirt, black stockings, button shoes, ring on right hand with initials which appeared to be "A. O."

No. 216. Woman, 30 years, 5 feet 2 inches, black hair, black skirt, button shoes, white underwear, handbag containing $10.

No. [illegible]. Woman, 21 years, 5 feet, black eyes, dark complexion, black skirt, black waist, two rings, one with three small stones and another with three small white stones.

No. 217. Woman, 19 years, 115 pounds, black hair, white waist, gray skirt, black stockings, no shoes, one ring with one opal setting, one plain gold ring, small gold locket.

No. 221. Woman, 30 years, 135 pounds, 5 feet 5 inches, black hair, fur coat, black shoes with cloth uppers, gold earrings, black dress, black stockings, plain gold ring, one ring with white stone, gold upper teeth.

No. 223. Woman, 23 years, 135 pounds, 5 feet 4 inches, dark complexion, black fur coat, yellow ring with two red stones and one pearl, $9 in envelope with name Rose Weiner.

No. 229. Woman, 24 years, 5 feet 2 inches, 125 pounds, dark hair, dark clothes, black velvet shoes.

No. 228. Woman, 24 years, Italian, 125 pounds, dark hair, black waist and skirt.

No. 220. Woman, 19 years, 5 feet 9 inches, 135 pounds, black waist, gray sweater, gray striped dress, black stockings and shoes, gold ring with a greenstone.

No. 231. Woman, 19 years, Italian, most of clothes burned off; envelope with $15, with name Rose Crepo.

No. 236. Male, 21 years, bank book with name Moses Bernstein, 309 East Fifth street.

No. 235. Woman, 20 years, red hair, 125 pounds, 5 feet 3 inches, black skirt, blue waist, black jacket, velvet button shoes, turquoise earrings.

No. 234. Woman, 20 years, 150 pounds, 5 feet 6 inches, white waist, black skirt, black shoes and stockings, one opal earring, other ear burned off.

No. 238½. Woman, 19 years, 123 pounds, 5 feet 6 inches, brown eyes and black hair, white waist, black skirt, velvet slippers, black stockings, plain gold ring.

No. 246. Woman, 24 years, 125 pounds, 5 feet 4 inches, brown eyes, black hair, white waist, black skirt, black shoes and stockings.

No. 251. Man, 165 pounds, 5 feet 9 inches, 30 years, gray eyes, black hair, black trousers, time book with no name but with card bearing the inscription Mr. and Mrs. J. Klein, 1638 Washington avenue, the Bronx, gold watch with hunting case bearing the initials "A. D."

No. 258. Woman, 24 years, pay check with $14 with name Weltner and no first name, white waist, black shoes and stockings, brown hair and brown eyes.

No. 272, 271, 269, 274, 165 and 276 all burned beyond recognition.

Untagged Woman, 24 years, dark hair, red skirt, white underwear, black [illegible]

button shoes, black stockings.

No. 239. Man, who by registered letter receipts is K. Dorman, 235 Gold street, Brooklyn.

No. 249. Woman, 28 years; black waist, black skirt, 120 pounds, black shoes and stockings, plain gold wedding ring.

No. 225. Man, by letter in pocket written by H. Scott, 174 Walworth road London, England, believed to be Tedie Rothner.

No. 254. Woman, 125 pounds; $40 in purse and $10 in envelope in stockings with the name Sprunt.

No. 208. Man, 40 years; name on pay envelope Feltzer.

No. 238½. Woman, 135 pounds; 5 feet 7 inches, 30 years, brown hair, black shirt waist, black skirt, white underwear, black shoes and stockings.

No. 201. Woman, 35 years; 130 pounds, 5 feet 6 inches, brown hair, clothes burned off.

Woman with name of pay envelope Julia Aberstein, $7.50 in envelope.

No. 210. Man, 20 years; time book in pocket, was named Shear.

No. 242. Woman, 22 years; lottery ticket check with name of lottery man, I. Goldberg, Pike street.

No. 207. Man, name on time book was Max Levine.

No. 262. Woman, 20 years; 5 feet 4 inches, 130 pounds, black waist and skirt, black shoes and stockings.

No. 208½. Woman, 19 years; 112 pounds, 5 feet 7 inches, blue waist and skirt, black stockings and blue pumps, plain gold bracelet.

No. 211. Woman, brown hair, blue eyes, one gold tooth, black plush coat, red and black plaid waist, blue skirt; 125 pounds, 26 years, 5 feet 6 inches.

Man with time book with the name Klober, 27 years.

Nos. 284 and 279, burned beyond recognition.

No. 238. Woman, 27 years, 130 pounds, 5 feet 5 inches, red waist, black skirt, pay envelope with the name Mrs. Rosen, $852 tied around her ankle inside her stocking.

WOMEN BATTLE TO SEE THE DEAD

The scenes on Charities Pier, beside the morgue, at the foot of East Twenty-sixth street, where the dead bodies were laid out in a long row were like a new and vivid chapter of Dante's Inferno. Hundreds of men, women and children—but mostly men—fought, cursed, sobbed, struggled, raved and flung themselves in hysteria again and again at the policemen that held them back from the grisly line of corpses, each of which was covered with its little white sheet. They were mad with the thought that a sister or a daughter or a sweetheart, crushed or charred almost beyond recognition, might be lying there on the pier. And the policemen, even while they wrestled with them and thrust them back, sobbed and cursed in sympathy.

At 11 o'clock 136 bodies had been laid on the pier, and the writhing and moaning line of relatives reached for a full block along First avenue. Of these 136 bodies fifty-four were charred and burned beyond the possibility of recognition. The rest of the victims had met their death when they leaped to the street from the

Continued on Page 5

LOWERING A BODY AFTER THE FIRE.

About Fifty Burned Remains Were Found in the Various Floors by the Firemen and Taken to the Street by This Means.

1912

It was supposed to be not only the most luxurious but also the world's most seaworthy ship, a paragon of naval engineering.

It cost $7.5 million to build, was the largest ship of its kind at 882½ feet long, and the fastest afloat. It was considered unsinkable because of its double-bottomed, watertight hull.

But the *Titantic* hit an iceberg off Newfoundland and sank with the loss of fifteen hundred lives early on the morning of April 15, 1912.

Nearly seven hundred other passengers were rescued from the icy waters.

In the aftermath of the disaster, new regulations were passed requiring all ships to maintain twenty-four-hour radio watches and to carry enough lifeboats to accommodate all passengers and crew.

"All the News That's Fit to Print."

The New York Times.

THE WEATHER.
Unsettled Tuesday; Wednesday, fair, cooler; moderate southerly winds, becoming variable.
For full weather report see Page 23.

VOL. LXI....NO. 19,805. NEW YORK, TUESDAY, APRIL 16, 1912.—TWENTY-FOUR PAGES. ONE CENT In Greater New York, Jersey City, and Newark. | Elsewhere, TWO CENTS.

TITANIC SINKS FOUR HOURS AFTER HITTING ICEBERG; 866 RESCUED BY CARPATHIA, PROBABLY 1250 PERISH; ISMAY SAFE, MRS. ASTOR MAYBE, NOTED NAMES MISSING

ol. Astor and Bride, sidor Straus and Wife, and Maj. Butt Aboard.

RULE OF SEA" FOLLOWED

omen and Children Put Over Lifeboats and Are Supposed to be Safe on Carpathia.

CKED UP AFTER 8 HOURS

ncent Astor Calls at White Star ffice for News of His Father and Leaves Weeping.

ANKLIN HOPEFUL ALL DAY

anager of the Line Insisted itanic Was Unsinkable Even After She Had Gone Down.

AD OF THE LINE ABOARD

Bruce Ismay Making First Trip on Gigantic Ship That Was to Surpass All Others.

he admission that the Titanic, the gest steamship in the world, had n sunk by an iceberg and had gone he bottom of the Atlantic, probably rying more than 1,400 of her pasgers and crew with her, was made the White Star Line offices, 9 adway, at 8:20 o'clock last night. n P. A. S. Franklin, Vice President General Manager of the International Mercantile Marine, conceded that bably only those passengers who e picked up by the Cunarder Carnia had been saved. Advices reed early this morning tended to ease the number of survivors by

ne admission followed a day in h the White Star Line officials been optimistic in the extreme. At time was the admission made that ry one aboard the huge steamer was safe. The ship itself, it was confitly asserted, was unsinkable, and uirers were informed that she would h port, under her own steam prob, but surely with the help of the an liner Virginian, which was reted to be towing her.

s the day passed, however, with no authentic reports from the Titanic any of the ships which were known have responded to her wireless call help, it became apparent that aunic news of the disaster probably d come only from the Titanic's sisship, the Olympic. The wireless ge of the Olympic is 500 miles. That he Carpathia, the Parisian, and the ginian is much less, and as they ed the position of the Titanic they further and further out of shore ge. From the Titanic's position at time of the disaster it is doubtful ny of the ships except the Olympic d establish communication with re.

anic Sank at 2:20 A. M. Monday.

the White Star offices the hope held out all day that the Parisian the Virginian had taken off some ne Titanic's passengers, and efforts e made to get into communication these liners. Until such commution was established the White officials refused to recognize the sibility that there were none of the nic's passengers aboard them.

ut by nightfall came the message n Capt. Haddock of the Olympic to e Race, Newfoundland, telling of foundering of the Titanic and of rescue of 655 of her passengers by Cunarder Carpathia, which, the eless message said, reached the posiof the Titanic at daybreak. All found there, however, was lifes and wreckage. The biggest ship he world had sunk at 2:20 o'clock erday morning.

r. Franklin admitted late last night the Parisian and the Virginian, gh they were among the first to wer the Titanic's calls for help, d not have reached the scene before o'clock yesterday morning, seven a half hours after the big Titanic ed her nose beneath the waves and hed downward out of sight. The pathia, so the wireless dispatch Capt. Haddock to Cape Race aneed, reached the scene of the Tic's foundering at daybreak, several hours before the expected arrival of the Virginian and the Parisian.

1,465 Lives Lost First Report.

It is unbelievable, so White Star Line officials were compelled to concede finally, that the Carpathia should have failed to pick up every lifeboat which still floated on the waves. If they failed to pick up more than 655 passengers, it was because the others of the ship's complement had gone with her to the bottom.

But it was not until nearly nightfall that the extent of the disaster was realized. Before that the reassuring nature of the bulletins issued by the White Star line was sufficient to quiet the fears of those who had relatives or friends aboard the unfortunate ship and to prevent widespread belief in a serious disaster.

Capt. Haddock's message from the Olympic, which is printed in another column of THE TIMES, strongly indicated that none but the 655 taken from life boats by the Carpathia had been saved. This message was relayed immediately to the White Star offices, but Mr. Franklin positively declined to make the text of the message public. He offered still the hope that passengers were aboard the Parisian and the Virginian, and even when the admission was wrung from him that there seemed little hope of the saving of any others than the 655 aboard the Carpathia, he clung to the hope that in some unexplained way there were other passengers abroad the two Allan liners.

First Reported Titanic in Tow.

Throughout the day there had been reassurances that the Titanic was being towed to port by the Virginian, and when Capt. Haddock's message proved this to be untrue only the admission was made at the White Star offices that the Titanic had sunk. Mr. Franklin said that Capt. Haddock's message was brief and "neglected to say that all the crew had been saved." But the inference was not that all the passengers had been saved. Rather it was that many of them had died, and presently Mr. Franklin admitted the fear that there had been a terrible loss of life on the Titanic.

This version of Capt. Haddock's wireless had been given at the White Star offices:

Capt. Haddock of the Olympic sends a wireless message to the White Star offices here that the steamer Titanic sank at 2:20 A. M., after all the passengers and crew had been lowered to life boats and transferred to the Virginian. The steamship Carpathia, with several hundred passengers of the Titanic, is now en route to New York.

At 9 o'clock, however, he modified this statement, declaring:

As far as we know the situation, there have been rumors from Halifax that three steamers were at the scene of the Titanic's sinking, namely, the Virginian, the Parisian, and the Carpathia. We have heard from Capt. Haddock of the Olympic, who says that the Titanic sank at 2:20 o'clock this morning. Haddock also informs us that the Carpathia has 675 survivors on board. It is very difficult to say whether the Virginian and the Parisian have any survivors on board until we can get a report from those vessels.

Fears Serious Loss of Life.

We have asked for that report from Capt. Haddock, and we are expecting a reply at any time. The Carpathia is proceeding to New York direct. We very much fear that there has been serious loss of life, but it is impossible for us to say definitely concerning this sad part of the situation until we are able to reassure ourselves whether or not any of the Titanic's passengers are aboard the Allan liners.

We are hopeful that the rumors which have reached us by telegraph from Halifax that there are passengers aboard the Virginian and the Parisian will prove to be true, and that these vessels will turn up with some of the passengers. It is the loss of life that makes this thing so awful. We can replace the money loss, but not the lives of those who went down.

Another version of the message from the Olympic was current last night and included the sentence: "Loss likely total 1,800 souls." This sentence was not in the message received by THE TIMES from Cape Race nor in that sent to the White Star line offices.

Continued on Page 2.

The Lost Titanic Being Towed Out of Belfast Harbor.

CAPT. E. J. SMITH,
Commander of the Titanic.

THE PROBABLE LOSS.

Number Aboard.	
First cabin	325
Second cabin	285
Steerage	710
Crew, (estimated)	800
Total	2,120
Saved.	
By the Carpathia	866
Probably drowned	1,254

PARTIAL LIST OF THE SAVED.

Includes Bruce Ismay, Mrs. Widener, Mrs. H. B. Harris, and an incomplete name, suggesting Mrs. Astor's.

Special to The New York Times.

CAPE RACE, N. F., Tuesday, April 16.—Following is a partial list of survivors among the first-class passengers of the Titanic, received by the Marconi wireless station this morning from the Carpathia, via the steapship Olympic:

Mrs. JACOB P. ——— and maid.
Mr. HARRY ANDERSON.
Mrs. ED. W. APPLETON.
Mrs. ROSE ABBOTT.
Miss G. M. BURNS.
Miss D. D. CASSEBERE.
Mrs. WM. M. CLARKE.
Mrs. B. CHIBINACE.
Miss E. G. CROSSBIE.
Miss H. ROSEBIE.
Miss JEAN HIPACK.
Mrs. HY. B. HARRIS.
Mrs. ALEX. HALVERSON.
Miss MARGARET BAYS.
Mr. BRUCE ISMAY.
Mr. and Mrs. ED. KIMBERLEY.
Mr. F. A. KENNYMAN.
Miss EMILE KENCHEN.
Miss G. F. LONGLEY.
Mrs. A. F. LEADER.
Miss BERTHA LAVORY.
Mrs. ERNEST LIVES.
Miss MARY CLINES.
Mrs. SINGRID LINDSTROM.
Mr. GUSTAVE J. LESNEUR.
Miss GIORGETTA A. MADILL.
Mme. MELICARD.
Mrs. TUCKER and maid.
Mrs. J. B. THAYER.
Mr. J. B. THAYER, Jr.
Mr. HENRY WOOLMER.
Miss ANNA WARD.
Mr. RICHARD M. WILLIAMS.
Mrs. F. M. WARNER.
Miss HELEN A. WILSON.
Miss WILLARD.
Miss MARY WICKS.
Mrs. GEO. D. WIDENER and maid.
Mrs. J. STEWART WHITE.
Miss MARIE YOUNG.
Mrs. THOMAS POTTER, Jr.
Mrs. EDNA S. ROBERTS.
Countess of ROTHES.
Mr. C. ROLMANE.
Mrs. SUSAN P. ROGERSON. (Probably Ryerson).
Miss EMILY B. ROGERSON.
Mrs. ARTHUR ROGERSON.
Master ALLISON and nurse.
Miss K. T. ANDREWS.
Miss NINETTE PANHART.
Miss E. W. ALLEN.
Mr. and Mrs. D. BISHOP.
Mr. H. BLANK.
Miss A. BASSINA.
Mrs. JAMES BAXTER.
Mr. GEORGE A. BAYTON
Miss C. BONNELL.
Mrs. J. M. BROWN.
Miss G. C. BOWEN.
Mr. and Mrs. R. L. BECKWITH.
Miss RUTH TAUSSIG.
Miss ELLA THOR.
Mr. and Mrs. E. Z. TAYLOR.
GILBERT M. TUCKER.
Mr. J. B. THAYER.
Mr. JOHN B. ROGERSON.
Mrs. M. ROTHSCHILD.
Miss MADELEINE NEWELL.
Mrs. MARJORIE NEWELL.
HELEN W. NEWSOM.
Mr. FIENNAD OMOND.
Mr. E. C. OSTBY.
Miss HELEN R. OSTBY.
Mrs. MAMAM J. RENAGO.
Mlle. OLIVIA.
Mrs. D. W. MERVIN.
Mr. PHILIP EMOCK.
Mr. JAMES GOOGHT.
Miss RUBERTA MAIMY.
Mr. PIERRE MARECHAL.
Mrs. W. E. MINEHAN.
Miss APPIE RANELT.
Major ARTUR PEUCHEN.
Mrs. KARL H. BEHR.
Miss DESSETTE.
Mrs. WILLIAM BUCKNELL.
Mrs. O. H. BARKWORTH.
Mrs. H. B. STEFFASON.
Mrs. ELSIE BOWERMAN.

The Marconi station reports that it missed the word after "Mrs. Jacob P." In a list received by the Associated Press this morning this name appeared well down, but in THE TIMES list it is first, suggesting that the name of Mrs. John Jacob Astor is intended. This supposition is strengthened by the fact that, except for Mrs. H. J. Allison, Mrs. Astor is the only lady in the "A" column of the ship's pasenger list attended by a maid.

NAMES PICKED UP AT BOSTON.

BOSTON, April 15.—Among the names of survivors of the Titanic picked up by wireless from the steamer Carpathia here to-night were the following:

Mr. and Mrs. L. HENRY.
Mrs. W. A. HOOPER.
Mr. MILE.
Mr. J. FLYNN.
Miss ALICE FORTUNE.
Mrs. ROBERT DOUGLAS.
Miss HILDA SLAYTER.
Mrs. P. SMITH.
Mrs. BRAHAM.
Miss LUCILLE CARTER.
Mr. WILLIAM CARTER.
Miss CUMMINGS.
Mrs. FLORENCE MARE.
Miss ALICE PHILLIPS.
Mrs. PAULA MUNGE.
Mrs. JANE ———
Miss PHYLLIS O. ———
HOWARD B. CASE.
Miss MINEHAN.
Miss BERTHA ———

Biggest Liner Plunges to the Bottom at 2:20 A. M.

RESCUERS THERE TOO LATE

Except to Pick Up the Few Hundreds Who Took to the Lifeboats.

WOMEN AND CHILDREN FIRST

Cunarder Carpathia Rushing to New York with the Survivors.

SEA SEARCH FOR OTHERS

The California Stands By on Chance of Picking Up Other Boats or Rafts.

OLYMPIC SENDS THE NEWS

Only Ship to Flash Wireless Messages to Shore After the Disaster.

LATER REPORT SAVES 866.

BOSTON, April 15.—A wireless message picked up late to-night, relayed from the Olympic, says that the Carpathia is on her way to New York with 866 passengers from the steamer Titanic aboard. They are mostly women and children, the message said, and it concluded: "Grave fears are felt for the safety of the balance of the passengers and crew."

Special to The New York Times.

CAPE RACE, N. F., April 15.—The White Star liner Olympic reports by wireless this evening that the Cunarder Carpathia reached, at daybreak this morning, the position from which wireless calls for help were sent out last night by the Titanic after her collision with an iceberg. The Carpathia found only the lifeboats and the wreckage of what had been the biggest steamship afloat.

The Titanic had foundered at about 2:20 A. M., in latitude 41:46 north and longitude 50:14 west. This is about 30 minutes of latitude, or about 34 miles, due south of the position at which she struck the iceberg. All her boats are accounted for and about 655 souls have been saved of the crew and passengers, most of the latter presumably women and children.

There were about 2,100 persons aboard the Titanic.

The Leyland liner California is remaining and searching the position of the disaster, while the Carpathia is returning to New York with the survivors.

It can be positively stated that up to 11 o'clock to-night nothing whatever had been received at or heard by the Marconi station here to the effect that the Parisian, Virginian or any other ships had picked up any survivors, other than those picked up by the Carpathia.

First News of the Disaster.

The first news of the disaster to the Titanic was received by the Marconi wireless station here at 10:25 o'clock last night [as told in yesterday's New York Times.] The Titanic was first heard giving the distress signal "C. Q. D.," which was answered by a number of ships, including the Carpathia,

Virginian-Pilot.

AND THE NORFOLK LANDMARK.

14 PAGES.

VOL. XLIII. NO. 17. NORFOLK, VA., WEDNESDAY, APRIL 17, 1912. FOURTEEN PAGES. THREE CENTS PER COPY.

Carpathia Rescues 868 Titanic Survivors; 1302 Passengers And Crew Still Missing

Story Of Disaster By An Eye Witness Remains Untold

Sinking By Head, Have Cleared Boats And Filled Them With Women And Children, Last Message

HEROISM OF CREW AND MEN PASSENGERS BEYOND QUESTION

All Hope Abandoned Last Night That Any Of Survivors Were Rescued By Virginian Or Parisian--Negative Reports Received

Appalling Figures Tell The Story

New York, April 16.—Approximate statement of Titanic disaster: First cabin passengers, 325; second cabin passengers, 285; third cabin passengers, 710. Total number of passengers, 1,320. Members of the crew, 860. Total passengers and crew, 2,180.

Number of known survivors, 868.

Number who probably perished, 1,312.

Total number of named survivors, 328.

Approximately twenty lifeboats, manned by seven members of the crew, each 140.

Estimated saved steerage passengers, 400.

Named survivors, first cabin passengers: Women, 141, men 63, children, 6. Total 210.

Second cabin passengers: Women, 92; men, 16; children, 10. Total, 118. Total number survivors saved, 328.

That the final roll of the rescued from the Titanic disaster had practically been made up was the impression that grew almost into conviction last night as the hours wore on without the revision of lists adding measurably to the total of known survivors.

Of definite news of the disaster the night added little. Down the Atlantic coast, fog enveloped in many places as the report showed, crept the Cunarder Carpathia, bearing on her the 868 lives that had been snatched from the waters when the Titanic's twenty boats, laden to their limit, one by one, made their way from the giant liner as it became known that she was soon to take her fatal plunge.

Wireless Hampered By Air Conditions

But although the rescue ship was reported within wireless range of the Sable Island station at a comparatively early hour and every wireless ear was waiting to catch the snap of a receiver which might mean that the great secret of the liner's death was about to be given up, midnight came and went and the night began to grow old—and still the word had not been spoken.

Carefully compiling the available lists, the record of the named survivors of the disaster stands significantly thus:

Men, 79; women, 233; children, 16. Total, 328.

Of the remaining 540 known survivors it is estimated that not more than 100 were seamen required to man the boats. This would leave approximately 440, and in the ordinary proportions of women and children in the steerage, where the passengers in the Titanic's care number 710, it seems probable that the greater part of these 440 were women and their little ones.

Heroism Of Men Aboard Self-Evident

Nothing could show more plainly the heroism of the crew and the men passengers who stood by the doomed ship, facing practically inevitable death, and sent the women and children away in the life boats. Some would have to be left; that was a certainty. Hundreds in fact were left. But to all appearances the men who were left stayed behind deliberately, calmly, stepping aside to let the weaker ones, those to whom they owed protection, take their way to safety.

"Sinking by the head. Have cleared boats and filled them with women and children."

This was the final message these brave men sent the world, for it was directly afterward that their wireless signals sputtered and then stopped altogether.

Masters Of Millions Among Lost

The picture that inevitably presents itself, in view of what is known, is of men like John Jacob Astor, master of scores of millions; Benjamin Guggenheim, of the famous family of bankers; Isidor Straus, a merchant prince; William T. Stead, veteran journalist; Major Archibald Butt, soldier; Washington Roebling, noted engineer—of any or all of these men stepping aside and bravely, gallantly, remaining to die that the place he otherwise might have filled, could perhaps be taken by some sabot-shod, shawl-enshrouded illiterate and penniless peasant woman of Europe.

Of the survivors, what? Their story of peril and suffering, with the revelation they will furnish of just what happened on board the stricken ocean giant—pictures which will leave the imagination nothing to draw upon—still remains to be told. How quickly they will be able to tell it and clear up all the mysteries of identity which the limited carrying capacity of the Carpathia's wireless has left the world in doubt, seemed tonight to depend largely upon atmospheric condition.

The weather was thick on the coast last night, not only interfering, it is believed with wireless communication from the liner to Sable Island, but probably with her rate of progress toward New York whither she is heading. Meanwhile, other methods of communication with her than by the land stations are being tried.

Cruisers Speeding For Carpathia

From the Virginia Capes the scout cruisers Salem and Chester, armed with powerful wireless apparatus, arespeeding toward the Carpathia and before very many hours have elapsedit is hoped they will be in close touch with her.

All hope that some of the Titanic's survivors might be on board either the steamer Parisian or the Virginian had to be abandoned late yesterday when it was definitely learned that neither steamer had picked up any one from the big liner.

Search for bodies in the vicinity of the disaster it was learned tonight will be taken up by the White Star Line from Halifax, where the cable

(Continued on Page 9.)

Prominent Americans Aboard The Titanic

Wife And Little Baby Of A Norfolk Tailor Were Aboard Titanic

S. Aks Anxiously Awaits News Of Their Safety—Not Among List Of Survivors.

Hoping against fate that his wife and seven months old baby were among those saved from the White Star Line steamer Titanic, when she went to the bottom early Monday morning after striking an iceberg, S. Aks, a tailor at 232 Chapel street, was anxiously awaiting news from her yesterday.

Mrs. Aks, accompanied by her seven months old baby, were on their way to this country to join her husband. She had never been to this country, her husband having come over ahead of her.

Mr. Aks had just received a postal from his wife stating that she would leave London, where she was visiting her parents, on the Titanic, as she had rather wait a few days and come over on a new and larger ship than the one she intended sailing on.

All reports received from the Carpathia regarding those saved fail to show the name of Mrs. Aks, and unless she did not take passage on the Titanic, she and the baby were probably lost.

Mr. Aks left London about eight months ago for this country and has been in the tailoring business in this city for about seven months.

List Of Survivors Aboard Steamer Carpathia

Steamer Carpathia, via Cape Race, April 16.—The first-class passengers on board, saved from the Titanic, follow:

Harry Anderson, Miss E. W. Allen, Mrs. E. W. Appleton, Mrs. John Jacob Astor and maid.

A. H. Barkworth, Mrs. James Baxter, George A. Brayton, Mr. and Mrs. R. T. Beckwith, Karl H. Behr, Mr. and Mrs. D. H. Bishop, Henry Blank, Miss Caroline Bonnell, Miss G. C. Bowen, Miss Elsie Bowerman, Mrs. J. M. Brown, Mrs. J. J. Brown, E. P. Calderhead.

Mrs. Churchill Cardell, Mrs. J. W. Cardoza, Thomas Cardoza, Mrs. Lucille Carter, Mrs. Wm. E. Carter, Master Wm. Carter, Howard B. Chase (probably Case), Mrs. T. W. Cavendish and maid, Mrs. H. F. Chaffee, Mr. and Mrs. M. E. Chambers, Miss Gladys Cherry, Paul Chevro, Mrs. E. G. Crosby, Miss Crosby, Mrs. Walter Clarke, Mrs. John B. Cummings.

Robert W. Daniel, Mrs. Thornton Davidson, Mrs. B. Devilliers, Mr. and Mrs. A. A. Dick, Mr. and Mrs. Washington Dodge and son, Mr. Frederick Douglas, Mrs. Walter Douglas.

J. I. Flynn, Mrs. Mark Fortune, Miss Lucille Fortune, Miss Alice Fortune, Dr. and Mrs. Henry Frauenthal, Mr. and Mrs. T. G. Frauenthal, Miss Margaret Frolicher, Mrs. Jacques Futrelle.

Mrs. Leonard Gibson, Miss Dorothy Gibson, Mrs. Samuel Goldenberg, Miss Ella Goldenberg, Sir and Lady Cosma Duff Gordon, Col. Archibald Gracie, Mr. Graham, Miss Margaret E. Graham, Mrs. Lee D. Greenfield, Mr. William H. Greenfield, Mrs. William Grahaan.

Henry Haruer, Mr. and Mrs. George A. Harder, Henry S. Harper, Henry J. Hawkesford, Mrs. Charles M. Hays and daughter, Mrs. Henry B. Harris, Miss Jean Hippach, Mrs. Ida S. Hippach, Mrs. John C. Hogeboom, Mr. and Mrs. Fred M. Hoyt.

J. Brunce Ismay.

Mrs. A. F. Leader, Mrs. Ernest Lines, Miss Mary C. Lines, Miss G. F. Longley.

Miss Georgetta A. Maddill, Pierre Marshall, Mrs. D. W. Marvine, Mrs. W. E. Minnihan, Miss Daisy Minnihan.

Miss Madeline Newell, Miss Marjorie Newell, Miss Helen Newsom.

E. C. Ostby, Miss Helen Ostby, Mr. F. Ormond.

Major Arthur Peuchen, Mrs. Thomas Potter Jr.

Mrs. George Rheims, Mr. Edward S. Robert, C. Roymano, Miss Edith Rosenbaum, Mrs. Martin Rothschild, Countess of Rothes.

Adolphe Saalfield, Abraham Saloman, Mrs. P. Schabert, Frederick Seward, Mrs. William D. Silver, Col. Alfonso Simmonius, William T. Sloper, Mr. and Mrs. John Snyder, Mrs. W. A. Spencer and maid, Dr. Max Stahelin, I. Spencer Silverthorne, Mr. and Mrs. C. E. H. Stengel, Mrs. George M. Stone, Mrs. Frederick J. Swift.

Miss Ruth Taussig, Mr. and Mrs. J. B. Taylor (X), Gilbert M. Tucker, Mr. and Mrs. J. B. Thayer.

Mrs. F. M. Warren, Mrs. J. Stuart White, Miss Mary Wick, Mrs. George D. Widener and maid, Miss Constance Willard, Hugh Woolner.

Miss Mary Young.

The second-class passengers on board, saved from the Titanic, are:

William Angie.

Hann A. Belson, Ada R. Ball, Miss Kate Biss, Edward Beane, Miss Ethel Beane, Miss Dagmar Bryhl, Mrs. Karolina Bystrom.

Mrs. Charlotte Collyer, Miss Marjorie Collyer, Mrs. Alice Christy, Mrs. Ada M. Clarke, Miss Cameron, Mrs. Stuwart Collett, Albert F. Caldwell, Mrs Sylvia Caldwell, Alden G. Caldwell, Miss Julia Christy.

Mrs. Lulu Drew, Miss Agnes Davis, John M. Davis, Florentina Durand, Ascuncion Duran, Miss Mary Davis, Mrs. Ada Doling, Miss Elise Doling.

Mrs. Lizzie Faunthorpe.

Miss Ethel Garside.

Miss Alice Herman, Miss Mary D. Hewlett, George Harris Mrs. Jane Herman, Miss Kate Herman, Miss Annie Hold, Mrs. Esther Hart, Miss Eva Hart, Miss Nina Harper.

H. Harmalaimer, W. Harmalaimer, Anie Harmalainer and son, Mrs. Elizabeth Hocking, Miss Nellie Hocking.

Mrs. Amy Jacobsohn.

Miss Nora Keane, Miss Fannie Kelly.

Miss Louisa Laroche, Miss Jessie W. Leitch, Mrs. Lamore, Mrs. Alice Louch, Miss Bertha Lehman.

Mrs. Elizabeth Mellinger and child, Mrs. A. Mallet, Master Andrero Mallet.

Mrs. Elizabeth Nye.

Miss Alice Phillips, Emilio Pallas, Julian Padro, Mrs. L. Parish, Mrs. Emilio Portaluppi

Mrs. Jane O. Quick, Miss Wennie O. Quick, Miss Phyllis O. Quick.

Mrs. Lillie Rebouf, Mrs. Lucy Ridsdale, Miss Emily Rugg, Mr. and Mrs. Emile Richard and son.

Miss Maude Sincock, Mrs. Marion Smith.

Miss Edna S. Trout.

Mrs. Matilda Weisz, Miss Susan Webber, Miss Marion Wright, Miss Marion Wright, Miss Bessie Watt, Miss Bertha Watt, Mrs. West and two children, Mrs. Addie Wells, Miss J. Wells, Ralph Wells, Charles Williams.

Mrs. Allen Becker, daughters Ruth and Mary and son Richard, Miss Mary Davidson.

In the following list the names as received by wireless are given their probable interpretation:

SECOND CABIN.

"Juliet, Mr. Laroche" (probably Mrs. Joseph Laroche).

"Mr. Laroche Simone" (probably Simon Laroche).

Linkkanea, Miss Anna (probably Mrs. William Lahtigen).

Marshall, Miss Kate (probably Mrs. Marshall).

Marge, Mrs. Paula (probably Mrs. William Angle.)

Mallcroft, Miss Millie (probably Miss Nellie Walcroft).

Mellors, J. N. (probably William Mellers).

Naseraell, Mrs. Adela (probably Mrs. Nicholas Nasser).

Oxenham, Percy J. (probably Thomas Oxenham).

Rogers, Miss Eliza (probably Selina Rogers).

Anxious Relatives and Friends Besiege Offices Of White Star Line Clamoring For News Of Survivors

DEEPER DEPRESSION PREVAILS AS BAD NEWS IS BULLETINED

Serious Charge Against Company

Chicago, April 16.—That Captain Edward J. Smith of the Titanic, believed that the steamer was not properly equipped with lifeboats and other life saving apparatus, and that he protested, without success, against lack of precaution, was the statement made by Glenn Marston, a friend of the captain, here tonight.

Marston said that while returning from Europe on the Olympic in company with Captain Smith he remarked on the small number of lifeboats carried by such a large passenger steamer. It was then, according to Marston, that Captain Smith spoke of the life preserving equipment of the Titanic, then in course of construction.

New York, April 16. "We are waiting for a complete list of the names of the survivors and until this is received we can give no definite information."

This was the only answer that could be given today at the White Star Line offices here to the thousands of anxious persons who gathered there seeking information regarding relatives and friends who are among the victims of Titanic disaster. From early morning until late tonight pathetic scenes were witnessed in lower Broadway and in Bowling Green Park, opposite the steamship offices. Hundreds of anxious inquiries were received also by long distance telephone.

Multitudes remained in the vicinity of Bowling Green throughout the day, hoping against hope that their loved ones were included among the survivors on board the Carpathia, which is now speeding to New York with the passengers who were rescued from the life boats after the Titanic sank.

Anxious Relatives Seek Information

Clerks in the White Star offices were kept busy informing those seeking news that no information had been received from either the Carpathia or the Olympic. The complete list of survivors was posted at the entrance of the White Star offices. Those who failed to find the names of their kin or friends, in this list could only hope that when the complete roster of the rescued was received it would bring welcome news.

When word reached the scores of men and women crowded into the narrow corridors of the offices that Vice-President Franklin of the International Marine Company, had announced that he was confident that the Virginian and the Parisian of the Allan Line had none of the Titanic's passengers on board an atmosphere of deep depression prevailed.

Newspaper men were besieged by the anxious inquirers who could not believe that the White Star officials were giving out all news of the disaster.

Mrs. Guggenheim Becomes Hysterical

Vice-President Franklin was locked in his private office throughout the day and few persons were permitted to see him.

Mrs. Benj. Guggenheim, wife of the smelter millionaire, was one of the first visitors in the forenoon. When informed that no word had been received of her husband she became hysterical.

"Isn't there something that can be done?" she pleaded.

"Can't you send steamships out to search for life boats which may be afloat?"

She was told that every steamship within the zone of wireless had been requested to give assistance. After she had been assured that she would be notified by telephone as soon as any word came from the Carpathia or Olympic Mrs. Guggenheim was assisted to her automobile and returned to her home.

There was a constant procession of automobiles and taxicabs and women from Fifth avenue and the Bowery mingled together in the foyer of the building, while they scanned the bulletins giving the latest news of the tragedy. Many pleaded with the clerks not to withhold information from them.

BEGS FOR TRUTH ABOUT HER BROTHER, ON TITANIC

"If you have definite news that my brother has lost his life," said one woman, "do relieve this terrible suspense by telling me the truth."

Scores of boys were calling out extra newspapers announcing that more than two-thirds of the Titanic's passengers had lost their lives, and so anxious were waiting crowds for every bit of news bearing on the disaster that they bought the newspapers and scanned the list, hoping that the one in whom they were interested might be found among those who had been rescued.

After having waited in Bowling Green Park for more than 15 hours Mrs. W. A. Wheelock of this city was summoned when the first list of names of the survivors came by wireless. She was told that her niece, Mrs. D. W. Marvin, who with her husband was returning from her honeymoon, had been saved, but that no word had been received as to the fate of Mr. Marvin. Later in the day Mr. Marvin's mother and father called in quest of some news of their son.

Telegrams of inquiry were received from President Taft and from scores of other public officials in Washington and other cities. Many cable messages came from London and Paris.

Insistent Clamor For News

In uptown New York wherever means of information were available the clamor for news was no less insistent. The streets in front of bulletin boards were thronged with crowds eager to get the latest news and watching intently for the appearance of names of relatives or friends for whose fate [is] feared.

Similar conditions prevailed in the lobbies of the more prominent hotels where lists of passengers reported saved from the Titanic were posted.

Memorial services for those who have lost their lives in the sinking of the Titanic will be held next Sunday morning at the Cathedral of St. John the Divine. Bishop Greer will make an address and there will be special music.

Mr. Franklin's Explanation

Vice President Franklin was criticized today for his definite reassuring declarations of yesterday which tended, as alleged, to mislead the public. Mr. Franklin this afternoon gave the public the full text of the wireless message received from Captain Haddock of the Olympic yesterday.

"The reason I did not give it out last night," Mr. Franklin said, "was because it was so discouraging that I felt that it would not be right to alarm the public unnecessarily. Now that the worst is known I am willing to give it out. Here it is:

"'Carpathia reached Titanic's position at daybreak. Found boats and wreckage only. Titanic had foundered about 2:20 a. m. in 41.16 N., 50.14 W. All boats accounted for. About 675 souls saved, crew and passengers. Latter nearly all women and children. Leyland Liner Steamship Californian remaining and searching for exact position of disaster. Carpathia returning to New York with survivors. Please inform Cunard. Haddock.'"

Silwana, Miss Synly (probably Lillie Sylven).

Karl Barrett, Miss Lillian Bentham, Miss Bessette, Mrs. William Bucknell, Mr. W. E. Carter, H. Heron Daniel, Miss Sarah Dodge, Mrs. Henry S. Harper, Olivia Middle (d), Mrs. Washington Newell, Mrs. Ostby, Miss H. Rosibee, Robert Douglas Sheddell, Mrs. P. Stephenson, Mrs. Walter Stephenson, Emil Taussig, Mr. and Mrs. E. Z. Taylor, Miss Helen A. Wilson.

In the following list the names as received by wireless are given their probable interpretation:

First cabin list:

Abbott, Mrs. Rose (probable Mrs. Aubert).

Andrews, Miss K. T. (probably Cornelia I.)

Chibinace, Mrs. (probablye Mrs. B. Chibnall).

Douglas, Robert (probablye Mr. Mrs. W. Douglass, or Mrs. F. Douglass).

Ellis, Miss (may be Miss [illegible]

Kenchen, Miss Emile ([illegible] F. R. Kenyon).

Kimberley, Mr. and [illegible]

(Continued [illegible])

THE WEATHER
Arizona — Fair Tuesday and Wednesday; Not Much Change in Temperature.

THE ARIZONA REPUBLICAN

THE REPUBLICAN — Fair, Candid, Straightforward—A newspaper for all the people.

TWENTY-SECOND YEAR — 12 PAGES — PHOENIX, ARIZONA, WEDNESDAY MORNING, FEBRUARY 14, 1912. — 12 PAGES — VOL. XXII. NO. 269.

The Forty-eighth State Steps Into the Union Today

PORTALS SWING WIDE TO ADMIT THE NEW STATE

President Will Sign Proclamation and Arizona Will Step Into Union at Eight O'clock Today Mountain Time.

PLANS COMPLETE FOR BIG EVENT

Inaugural Ceremonies Will be of the Simplest Character But the After Exercises Will be Most Hilarious.

When the clocks of Phoenix indicate the eighth hour this morning, William Howard Taft, president of the United States, will seat himself in his office chair, dip his pen in ink and affix his signature to the proclamation which will make Arizona a state in the Union.

That will be 10 o'clock, in Washington, of course. By that time of day in Phoenix thousands of citizens of the new state will be celebrating the first Admission day. Railroads will run special trains and the number of visitors who were in town last night will be increased many times.

The weather man forecasts a fair day. He says that there will be lots of sunshine to fall on the new flag with its forty-eight stars and make the colors shimmer as the bunting floats in the warm breeze. Lots of flags out, too, awaiting this breeze. Washington street for six blocks in the heart of the city is decorated. Business houses did a little decking out yesterday and more will display the national colors today.

The first event on the program will be the inauguration of George Washington Peter Hunt, the first governor of the state of Arizona. Although the ceremonies are to be simple, it is probable that a big crowd will flock to the capitol grounds.

At 1:30 in the afternoon the parade will form, the first division resting in the rear of city hall. At 2 o'clock the first gun of the forty-eight-gun salute will be fired and, while each star is being hailed by an explosion of powder, the parade will start moving.

Every organization of note in the city will be represented in the line of march. The militia, fraternal orders, labor organizations, fire department, school children, three bands, automobiles, horsemen, Spanish war veterans, Grand Army men and a long list of other orders will parade before the reviewing stand in front of the court house from which the dignitaries will watch.

At ? o'clock the governor will hold

(Continued on Page 5).

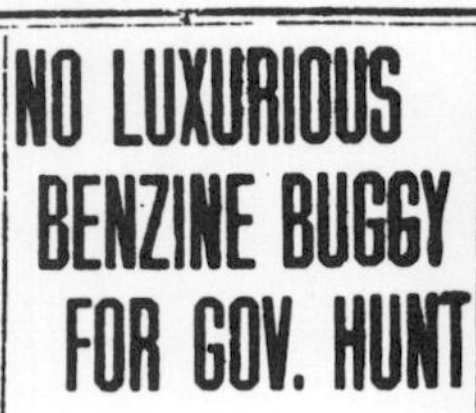

NO LUXURIOUS BENZINE BUGGY FOR GOV. HUNT

Will Walk to the Capitol and Thus Set an Example of Thrift for Everybody.

SAYS HE COULD AFFORD TO RIDE

But Mr. Hunt Fears if He Did So He Might Lead Some of the Rest of us Astray.

Governor-elect G. W. P. Hunt is here, and with his ear to the ground. He has had a premonition that President Taft will say something of special interest today that will necessitate his visiting the capitol, and he was never a man to run away from duty.

When the time comes he will go to the capitol.

What's more, he'll walk.

This is no figure of speech but a statement of fact.

Mr. Hunt said last night that his previously announced intention of walking to the capitol on inauguration day was made seriously and he intends to stick to it.

He has his reasons but did not care to discuss them except to say he believed it fitting that one in his position should set an example of economy and simplicity. He intimated that he could well afford to ride on the street car or possibly an automobile, but he says that isn't the point. As a private individual he may do what he likes, but as governor of the great state of Arizona, he should not set an example of extravagance, even though he is subjected to the charge of affectation.

So much for the governor.

He walks.

The oath of office will probably be administered by Chief Justice Alfred Franklin who will have subscribed his own oath earlier in the day and be ready to pass it along to the executive. Present on the portico with the chief justice and governor-elect will be a numerous company. Who will comprise it cannot be told at this time, but probably the retiring territorial officials, at least a part of them, will be in the party, and among the notables will be William Jennings Bryan and Governor Thomas R. Marshall, of Indiana, who arrived here yesterday. Mr. Bryan was in Tucson yesterday and was seen by Governor Hunt as he passed through that city. He said he would arrive from the Pima capital on this morning's train.

Mr. Hunt reached here last night at 10:45, accompanied by Mrs. Hunt

(Continued on Page 5).

¶ Hon. George W. P. Hunt, who today becomes first governor of the state of Arizona. Mr. Hunt is a business man of Globe, where he is heavily interested in a mercantile enterprise. He was also president of the constitutional convention and is an advocate of insurgent doctrines

ARIZONA WILL DON THE GARB OF STATEHOOD

Glorious Climax of Long Fight Will Come With Signing of Proclamation Today.

HISTORY IS A SPLENDID ONE

Population is Small But it Possesses the Spirit That Has Made the West.

Arizona slept last night as a territory. After her long struggle against adverse circumstances, her repeated trials to emerge from the lower condition and take her place in the ranks of the commonwealths which combine to make up the union, after conquering her warring Indians and reclaiming her waste places, Arizona watchd the dawn of this morning as the dawn of her statehood.

For over twenty years a systematic struggle for statehood has been going on. For over thirty years the pioneers of this corner of the world have dreamed of that day when they would no longer rightfully say, "back in the states" when referring to the domain which lies to the east. Now it is an accomplished fact.

The enabling act was passed September 2, 1910, and on October 10th of that year the constitutional convention met. For sixty days the delegates wrestled with knotty constitutional problems, fought their bitter little fights—the bitterness of which has now been forgotten—and framed the constitution which was submitted to the people. The vote, of course, was overwhelmingly in favor of the document and, as soon as the official canvass could be made the returns were sent on to Washington with the proposed constitution. The returns arrived March 3, 1911, one day before the sixty-first session of congress adjourned. A fillibustering sally and both houses adjourned without giving the boon of statehood to Arizona and her people.

Then, at the next session, came the debates, the hopes and fears of various factions. The constitution was finally approved August 20, 1911, and the election of the first state officers was held December 12. Today those officers will take their oaths.

Arizona became a territory February 24, 1863, when President Abraham Lincoln signed the following act of congress:

An act to provide a temporary government for the territory of Arizona, and for other purposes.

Be it enacted by the senate and house of representatives of the Unit-

(Continued on Page 5).

LOOKS FORWARD TO BECOMING A STYLISH ANGEL

Hill Files Plans and Specifications for His Choice in Matter of Feathers.

RED AND WHITE WILL SUIT HIM

Some Rather Picturesque Testimony is Given by Him Before House Committee.

[Associated Press Dispatch]

WASHINGTON, Feb. 13.—James J. Hill told the Stanley steel investigating committee he would be a "first class angel with red and white wings" before he would go into the steel business and he predicted competition would be the rule long after the present laws are wiped off the statute books. Hill's last day of testimony was replete with sage utterances. He said the stockholders of the Great Northern were not "wearing any crepe" because United States Steel "in its fright" had cancelled the Great Northern's ore lease. Stanley suggested that Hill be in a comfortable position whether or not the lease is cancelled as he could start a steel company of his own with four hundred million tons of ore in the ground. "I'll be a first class angel with red and white feathers in my wings long before I ever consider going into the steel business," replied Hill. "I'll be 74 my next birthday, don't mind telling you that I have done about all the hard work I intend to do in this life."

Just before he was excused Representative Beall of Texas called his attention to assertions of E. H. Gary and others to the effect the day of competition is past and the time come for the government to regulate prices on commodities. "I think you'll have to tame human nature to eliminate all selfish motives that rule human beings and every other form of life before you'll eliminate competition," Hill remarked. "There will be competition just as long as the doctrine of the survival of the fittest lasts and that will be operating long after all present statutes are wiped off the books."

He declared it the federal government assumed control of business, it would be no federal government but would be a monarchy. Asked if he believed the United States should undertake to regulate business replied, "I would lay down a law to right the wrong. I would limit the power of corporations. I would see that every corporation that started business put all the money in, and I wouldn't be jealous on account of

(Continued on Page 5).

PLOTTERS ARE GIVEN SINGLE DAY OF GRACE

Arrest of Men Charged With Dynamiting Has Been Delayed for Unknown Reason.

ATTORNEY SAYS ALL IS READY

[Associated Press Dispatch]

INDIANAPOLIS, Ind., Feb. 13.—United States District Attorney Miller said tonight the arrests of fifty-four men indicted for the dynamite conspiracy is set for tomorrow.

"The reason why they didn't take place today," Miller said, "can't be revealed. The arrest of one man at Rochester today was probably due to a local condition unknown to me."

Before night tomorrow the defendants apprehended are expected to be of sufficient number to reveal the extent of the plots the government charges have been carried on for six years against iron and steel contractors who maintained "open shops," in which the confessed dynamiters, the McNamaras and Ortie McManigal, acted as accomplices of others.

Among the cities not before mentioned where arrests are expected are Syracuse, Scranton, Springfield, Ill., Grand Rapids, Omaha and Peoria.

Clarence E. Dowd, business agent of the machinists' union at Rochester, arrested today, was formerly national organizer for the International Association of Machinists, with headquarters in Detroit, which was one of the fields of operation of the dynamiters. There McManigal was induced to become a member of the "dynamiting crew" directed by J. J. McNamara, according to the former's confession. There, also, McManigal and J. B. McNamara were arrested last April at the time it is alleged they were preparing with the assistance of local men to cause explosions under five bridges and other structures erected by employers of non-union labor.

ROCHESTER, N. Y., Feb. 13.—Clarence E. Dowd, business manager of the machinists' local No. 93, was arrested today by federal marshals on a warrant charging him with illegal transportation of dynamite from one state to another. Dowd made no comment when arrested. He was lodged in the county jail. The warrant was based on an indictment returned by the federal grand jury at Indianapolis. Dowd is 35 years old.

MOVING PICTURES.

WASHINGTON, Feb. 13.—For the first time in the history of the White House, moving pictures of an event of national importance will be taken tomorrow when President Taft signs the proclamation admitting Arizona to statehood. The pictures will be taken by an employe of the treasury department and will be presented to the president. Another set may be made part of the official record.

NOBODY KNOWS.

Seem to Have No Idea Who New Justice Will Be.

[Associated Press Dispatch]

WASHINGTON, Feb. 13.—President Taft spent much time today in considering the appointment to the supreme bench. Kansas men who are interested in Judge Hook saw the president, and a delegation of Pennsylvania lawyers pressed their claims for Judge Buffington of Pittsburg. Friends of Nagel would not admit tonight that the president has eliminated him from consideration.

WOOL IS ACTIVE.

Boston Market Shows a Strong Demand For Domestic Product.

[Associated Press Dispatch]

BOSTON, Feb. 13.—Activity in domestic wool keeps pace with the demand for the foreign product and holders report a firm market. Finer grades at a slight higher price is the tendency. Interest seems turning to the west, where bidding for the new clip continues with 1; offered for Utah and Nevada. Good sales are reported in that territory.

THIRTY WERE HURT IN RAILWAY WRECK

Broken Rail Causes a Great Northern Train to Leave The Tracks Near Dakota Town.

[Associated Press Dispatch]

DOYON, N. D., Feb. 13.—Thirty are said to have been injured, some seriously, in a wreck on the Oriental Limited of the Great Northern two miles east at 9:25 tonight. Every car of the train, the engine and tender turned over going down a thirty foot embankment. A broken rail was the cause.

A special relief train has started from Devil's Lake for the scene of the wreck. The Limited left Devil's Lake shortly after three and was due at St. Paul at 8:45 in the morning. It will be nearly morning before the relief train arrives. There is no telegraph nor telephone service at the scene of the accident.

REBELS CARRY THE WAR INTO ALL SECTIONS

Revolution Spreads and Madero's Position is Critical.

CONSULS APPEAL FOR PROTECTION

[Associated Press Dispatch]

MEXICO, Feb. 13.—The spread of the rebellion in Mexico is shown by dispatches tonight. The rebels have overrun Laguna district in Coahuila and appears in the states of Durango, Zacatecas and Guanajuato. In the south of Zapatistas continue their campaign and in Guerrero, followers of Salgado are showing remarkable activity. The government has repeatedly said the Salgado uprising is practically ended. In Chihuahua Rojas and Braulio Hernandez continue to evade the government troops. On the other hand, Orozco has persuaded the rebels at Casas Grandes to quit fighting, according to an official dispatch tonight. In Durango the rebel ranks have been filled for the most part by field hands, who have joined in looting haciendas at which they have been employed. Today consuls at the city of Durango sent messages to their diplomatic representatives here appealing to them for additional military protection. In the state of Zacatecas the rebel outbreak is characterized by looting and raiding. In many instances the mobs committing the depredations cry "Vive Zapata." The report of the quieting of Casas Grandes included a copy of a message sent Orozco by the former mutineers. It is said they had risen in the behalf that Orozco would espouse the cause of Gomez, but since that is not so they were placing themselves at his disposition. Minister of the Interior Gonzales spent the day in Chihuahua conferring with Orozco and other authorities regarding a solution of the movement.

WASHINGTON, Feb. 13.—Reports to the state department today from Mexico indicate the situation in the south is substantially unchanged, though in Vera Cruz and Oaxaca conditions are probably worse and anti-American feeling seems also to have arisen in San Luis Potosi. Foreigners at Colima reported they feared an outbreak and at Guantajuato Americans are apprehensive. Bandits are reported to have taken several small towns between Parras and Saltillo, and burned the railroad bridge. Notwithstanding signs of continued disorder, the attitude of this govern-

(Continued on Page 5.)

MICHAEL G. CUNNIFF, of Yavapai county, who is sure to be president the state senate. Cunniff is an insurgent. He was a member of the constitutional convention and took an important part in the framing of the state organic law. Because of his literary attainments he was made chairman of the revision committee and the rhetorical work in the constitution largely his. He has a forceful character, is a good parliamentarian, and certain to leave his impress on the work of the first state legislature.

HON. C. B. WOOD, of Maricopa county, state senator elect. Wood is a modified insurgent and because of his equipment and grasp of affairs will in all probability be one of the leaders of the first state legislature. He is a college graduate, a native of Missouri, and is certain to be placed on some of the most important committees of the senate. Wood has a plan for systematizing the educational work of all the schools of the state that will doubtless be worked out by the legislature.

1913

The Sixteenth Amendment—income tax—became law.

So did the Seventeenth Amendment, providing for direct election of U.S. senators by the electorate, instead of by state legislatures.

Willa Cather's *O Pioneers!* was published.

Walter Johnson pitched fifty-six consecutive shutout innings.

In the Miami Valley in Ohio, a flood killed more than four hundred people.

ONLY NEWSPAPER IN DAYTON RECEIVING DOUBLE WIRE ASSOCIATED PRESS SERVICE.

DAYTON DAILY NEWS

8 PAGES

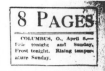

COLUMBUS, O., April 5.—Fair tonight and Sunday. Frost tonight. Rising temperature Sunday.

VOL. XXVII. No. 194. DAYTON, OHIO, SATURDAY, APRIL 5, 1913 PRICE TWO CENTS. BY CARRIER 10 CENTS A WEEK.

First Connected Account of Disaster To Be Published in a Dayton Newspaper

Main Facts are Told in Effort to Give a More Complete Idea of the Events of the Flood Period Than Has Been Obtainable From Fragamentary Accounts Made Necessary by Limited Publication Facilities—Hard to Realize the Extent of the Peril, Suffering and Loss of Property. Generosity of the People of the Country Unprecedented—Relief Comes With First Receipt of News—Extended With Liberality and Dispensed With Splendid Efficiency.

What shall follow is in no sense an attempt to tell the history of the great March flood of 1913. Rather it is merely an effort to set down the main facts of that disastrous event, and with the intent of making it of some account to the reader of The Daily News who may desire to file away a paper, with which he may refresh his memory in time to come.

The powers of public information were staggered. The newspapers, practically out of business for the time, were able to publish only scraps of newspaper, at least so it seemed to us who are charged with the dessemination of current history. All that has been published in Dayton, up to this time has been fragmentary. It is to be hoped, therefore, that this connected account—however imperfect it may be, however inadequate it may seem to those who have gone through the horror and the suffering—may be of value.

It was not an unusual rain—it has rained harder many a time. That was the solemn verdict of townsfolk who talked with one another in the first days of the high water. That was why there was so firm a contention that the reservoir at the headwaters of the Miami in Logan county had been let down upon the fair valley. But the truth is, it was an extraordinary rain. The fall for three days was five and one-half inches.

The river had not been high since January. Two weeks ago today, the gauge at the Main street bridge showed less than two feet of water. That was a beautiful day, with happy Easter crowds everywhere.

Sunday morning, Easter Sunday, broke with the clouds pouring rain. It kept it up through the forenoon. There were no Easter bonnets worn to church that morning—they have not been worn since, many never will adorn the heads for which they were intended. It continued to rain at intervals during the afternoon and night. The day was distinctly stormy. The wind was gusty, violent at times, the clouds queer looking. It was a condition which depresses those sensitive to weather conditions. There are periods when such temperaments are filled with a sense of impending trouble, a feeling vague and foreboding. Usually nothing happens, but there is a mysterious connection between mind and atmosphere. Scientists, psychologists, know about it and why. For the rest of us it is to know that there is such a connection, and that there is mischief abroad, the elements plotting carnage.

So it was that there was nothing surprising Monday morning in the news of the Omaha tornado. It had been expected that there was something afoot—or a-sky. Dayton people shuddered at the news of the western catastrophe, thanked God—it is to be hoped—that they had been spared, and went about their business as well as the rain would let them.

That Monday it seemed as if the windows of heaven had been opened. The rain descended in floods. The sky would lighten, the sun seem to be at the point of shining. Another black mass of cloud would sweep across the sky, there was lightning, and mad rain. Time and again, throughout the day, the process was repeated.

By noon the river was higher than it had been since January—perhaps higher than during the present year. The city employes were riding about, shutting off the storm water sewers, starting the big electric pumps that keep the lowlands dry when the river level is above them—on the other side of the levee.

By nightfall the waters were mounting rapidly, the gauge showing 12 feet at 5 o'clock. At the Daily News office there was discussion of "holding for an extra," but it was decided that as the danger point would not be reached before the river reached some 17 or 18 feet, there would be no need of keeping vigil during the night.

Shortly after 5 o'clock the lowlands were filled—the very lowest points, such as Lehman street at the Mathews greenhouses in Riverdale. At this time the water got too deep for the street cars. Just at that time an automobile managed to flounder through, but the cars had to back up. Through the evening they ran to this growing lake from either direction.

Warning Sounded.

Toward morning the whistles began to blow. They screeched a warning to those in the lowlands. The river was climbing, had passed the 17-foot stage—and it was still raining. It poured almost incessantly through the night. Those who remembered the two seasons of high water in the past—15 or more years ago—were uneasy, and there were many who were sleepless as the whistles continued to blow.

Those in the more dangerous places, close up to a levee where the current was strong, fled in early morning. Others mocked at the peril.

Those who went early to their work heard forebodings, and those who had to cross the river were astounded at its fury. It was running almost level with the top of the levees, ready by 7 o'clock to lap over into Riverdale, and North Dayton was already filling up.

So also was the city's business district. The rush of water, sweeping down from the north, joined by Stillwater and Mad rivers almost at the same point, strikes with terrific impact a sharp curve in the channel. If free to force its way from this point, it would plough a course through the vitals of the downtown section. It would cross the present south bank a square or two east of Main street, and sweep to the southwest till it should meet the old channel again, somewhere between Washington street and the Stewart street bridge at the N. C. R. factory.

That is why, when the water came, it ran across the city with such terrible swiftness. That is why it was not safe to venture to wade as the waters came to be knee deep. That is why swimmers remained imprisoned, and why boatmen could not bring aid to those imperiled. Most cities subject to flood are not in the path of such force. Backwater is unpleasant, very, and expensive, but it is not particularly dangerous. The trouble in this flood was with the current. The whole flooded district, with a few exceptions, was in the grasp of a torrent of rushing waters.

The water, as the river became brimful, poured into the business district. It was at a fortunate time. It came too early to catch the great mass of clerks and office people. A few early comers were on hand and, of course, those in hotels and apartment houses.

But the business section was a small part of the inundated territory. Immediately to the west of the central section is a part of the town in which families of wealth have magnificent homes. South of these are other houses, not so fine, but containing more people. All these were caught by the water, and the residents cut off from escape, had they wanted to get away.

That was not all. North Dayton was in the flood as a matter of course. Everybody expected it. Riverdale has been in the path and, in view of the tremendous rain, nobody was particularly surprised. There is a great flat district to the east and southeast of the business district. It is safe to say that probably 90 per cent of the people living here never thought of themselves as being in an area within reach of a flood—unless it should be another deluge. The question of elevation had never been raised. They knew that Dayton View, or Huffman Hill, or the Soldiers' Home, was higher, but a flood—the idea of water in their houses was preposterous. There was a tradition that the water had run into the downtown streets in 1866, but the levees had been built since that time.

So in many places in the higher parts of Riverdale, and West Dayton, and the lower ground of Dayton View. Many persons lost their goods because it was simply unbelievable that the water could come so high. After the levees were seen to have failed, that fact brought

(CONTINUED ON PAGE 2.)

Telephone Numbers. In Case of Fire.

The public is requested by Safety Director Dodds to use the telephone wherever possible in calling the fire department. The fire boxes in the section of the city which was not flooded are in working order, but to make certain, call Main 35 or Home 2133. All the firemen are again on duty and the fire apparatus is in good working order.

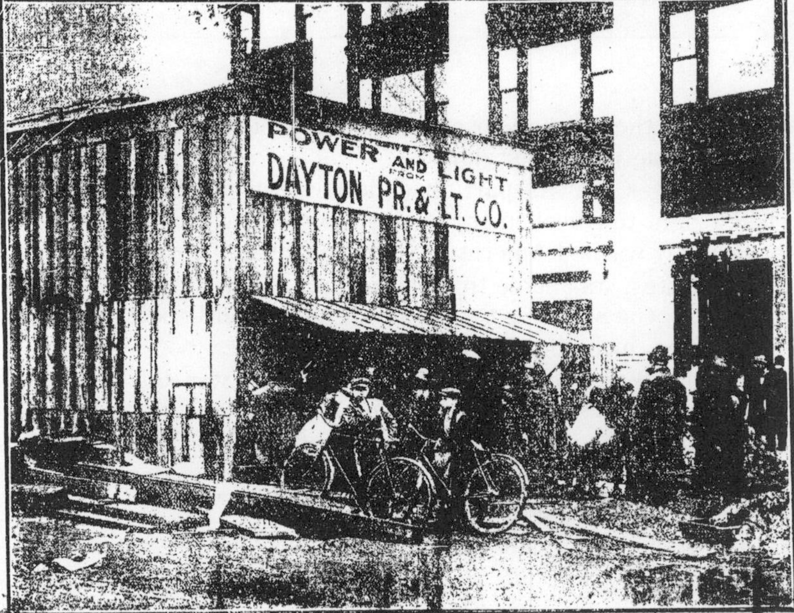

Waiting for the papers from the emergency press erected on the Fourth street side of The Daily News building. The photograph was taken just a moment before the press was started on its initial run Friday afternoon.

NO PAPER ON SUNDAY

No paper will be issued by The Daily News on Sunday. Its entire force has been incessantly at work since the receding water permitted them to get to printing a newspaper. It decided to insure the employes, so far as possible, a day of rest.

It is believed that the people do not want a continuous stream of news of the flood. Today there is presented the first connected account of the disaster that came to Dayton. It does not pretend to be complete, but it is believed the main points are touched upon.

With this, The Daily News proposes to turn its face to the future. The people have had enough of calamity. This newspaper shall see to it that there are no more reminders of the harrowing days of the flood than shall be necessary to relate.

Of the reconstruction, the building of the new Dayton, the return of prosperity, the great projects which may be the outgrowth of the disaster, there will be volumes to print. It is time to forget, to let the dead past bury its dead, to attack the task of today with new energy, to center our hopes on a new ambition.

By Monday morning The Daily News hopes to have its plant in fairly good running order.

NOTICE.

All transportation vehicles bearing the registered relief car signs are directed to report to the commanding officer of the second and third zones at Room No. 101, Algonquin hotel, before 5 o'clock p. m., Saturday, April 5th, 1913.

JOHN H. PATTERSON,
Chairman Relief Committee.

BRIGHT SUNLIGHT HAS INSPIRING EFFECT ON THE MANY WORKERS

River is Falling and Fears in This Direction are Entire Removed—Work of Cleaning Up the City and of Extending Relief to Victims Begun Saturday Morning With Renewed Energy—Hearty "Good Mornings" Exchanged By the Men Who Were Early on Their Jobs—Tens for the Homeless Erected at Fairgrounds.

With the river falling, a warm sun beaming down anw with all the dreariness of Friday forgotten, Dayton awoke Saturday morning filled with energy to take up the work of reconstruction which has progressed so rapidly within the past few days. Early the streets were filled with people rapidly uhstling to their places of work. They greeted each other with a happy word, which showed that none of the effect of a bright spring morning was lost.

It seemed as though not a moment was lost by workmen in "falling to" the tasks before them. During Friday many of the streets were cleared for many blocks by the systematic efforts of large gangs of workmen and the downtown district began to show show some of the usual "hum of business of old with the reopening of stores, restaurants, and a gradual reutrn to business.

The Miami river bell over a foot from Friday night to Saturday morning, and continued to fall Saturday. It showed a guage of 10.5 at the Main street engine house.

LEGISLATURE TO PROVIDE FOR PRESENT EMERGENCY

COLUMBUS, O., April 5.—The joint legislative committee to prepare the necessary legislaton for the flood emergency has decided to prepare a bill to take care of only the present emergency and not provide a permanent general law.

It was expressed as the sentiment of the committee that none of the restrictions as to tax levies and bond issues should be disturbed, except for the present emergency, and the special sub-committee, consisting of Senator Cunningham of Knox, and Representatives Snyder of Pickaway, and Diser of Mahoning, was instructed to prepare a bill along that line.

It will carry a provision for boards of education as well as counties and cities, whereby they may reconstruct destroyed structures. The committee will meet to consider the bill drafted by the sub-commitee at 10 a. m. next Monday.

NO BODIES ARE RECOVERED SATURDAY

No bodies were received at the morgue Saturday and the coroner is of the opinion that few bodies, if any, remain in the residence district, although there is a possibility that the river may give up a number of bodies when it recedes to its accustomed proportions.

The N. C. R. officials who have had charge of the morgue turned the charge over to Coroner McKemy and his assistants Saturday, and in the future this work will all be under the care of the county.

The health officer reports that there are no unusual diseases in the city that might not be expected at this time of the year. The N. C. R. hospital has been removed to the various city hospitals and the patients are all getting along nicely.

WEEK YET BEFORE C. H. & D. CAN RUN

That the C. H. & D. Railway company has six miles of track and roadbed washed away between this city and Tippecanoe City, and that it will be at least a week before a train can come into Dayton on the C. H. & D. from the north was the statement made Thursday by J. H. Baker, head clerk of the United States railway mail service, who has been traveling on the C. H. & D. for years.

"This is the worst demoralization and congestion of mail service that I have witnessed in the 25 years that I have been in this work," Mr. Baker said. Baker, who lives at the Bellevue apartments here, brought two carloads of mail from Toledo to Troy on Thursday, March 27, the first mail train to come through on the C. H. & D. for four days.

Daily News Doing Business at Old Stand

This newspaper, as it appears today, is entirely a Dayton product. Every process, from typesetting to printing, was carried out in its plant. The Daily News has resumed business at the old stand. In so doing difficulties have been overcome, but no greater than are being successfully met by the majority of those who have been companions in misfortune.

What the Daily News has done others are doing and will do. The effort required is tremendous, but Dayton individually and collectively has tremendous strength. The realization of this will be a precious heritage when, with wounds healed and strength increased, Dayton can close the pages of the past with the inscription: "I Have Conquered".

THE WAR YEARS, I

During World War I, the German government claimed the right to attack and sink any Allied vessel, including passenger ships.

The United States, for its part, had declared its neutrality and insisted that Americans had a right to travel on any ship without threat to their lives. Nonetheless, the Germans formally warned Americans that the British liner *Lusitania*, about to sail from the United States, was liable to be attacked.

On May 7, 1915, the ship was torpedoed by a German U-boat. It went down with the loss of 1,198 lives, including 128 Americans.

The sinking provoked many to urge a declaration of war, but the Germans apologized, promised reparations, and vowed to end unrestricted submarine warfare.

In 1916, the Germans attacked the French at Verdun. The British launched an offensive at the Battle of the Somme. Germany declared war on Portugal. Romania declared war on Austria-Hungary.

In the United States, Woodrow Wilson was reelected President. He had campaigned with the slogan, "He kept us out of war."

[*text continued*]

The Courier-Journal.

VOL. CXXI. NEW SERIES—NO. 16,616. LOUISVILLE, MONDAY MORNING, JUNE 29, 1914.—10 PAGES. PRICE { THREE CENTS. ON TRAINS FIVE CENTS.

THE WEATHER.

Kentucky—Generally fair Monday and Tuesday with nearly stationary temperature.

Tennessee—Generally fair Monday and Tuesday with nearly stationary temperature.

Indiana—Generally fair Monday and Tuesday with nearly stationary temperature.

THE LATEST.

Gen. Carranza, first chief of the Constitutionalists, has replied to the invitation of the mediators to participate with representatives of the United States and Huerta in considering plans for a provisional government in Mexico, that he desires time to consult with his Generals.

Archduke Francis Ferdinand, heir to the Austria-Hungarian throne, and the Duchess of Hohenberg, his morganatic wife, were assassinated by a student in the streets of the Bosnian capital a short time after they had escaped death from a bomb hurled at the royal automobile.

Secret peace negotiations between Carranza and Huerta have been in progress at Mexico City, according to reports circulated by an American, who stated that it was positively known that representatives of Carranza had been in the capital for several days.

The directors of the National Association Opposed to Woman Suffrage have addressed a letter to President Wilson in which it is denied that 1,000,000 members of the General Federation of Women's Clubs is in favor of the ballot for women.

Clay Arthur Pierce, son and business associate of Henry Clay Pierce, issued a statement last night emphatically denying published reports and letters purporting to show that the elder Pierce had aided the revolution in Mexico.

According to the catalogue for the Fourth annual State Fair, 50,000 copies of which have been issued for distribution, the premium lists have been greatly increased and many innovations will be seen when the fair is held in the fall.

Rear Admiral Frank Fletcher, who directed the American occupation of Vera Cruz, has arrived in Washington and it is expected that he will soon be recommended to succeed Rear Admiral Badger as commander-in-chief of the Atlantic fleet.

Two trainmen were killed, one was perhaps fatally injured and several negro passengers were hurt when Louisville & Nashville passenger train was wrecked three miles south of Trenton, Ky.

Convinced, it is said, that there is no other path to adjournment but the one which leads to trust legislation, the Senate will settle down this week to the steady grind on the Trade Commission Bill.

When Representative A. B. Rouse files in the House to-day his campaign expenses he will be the first Congressman, it is stated, to follow the letter of the new law regarding expenditures.

Bombardment of the rebel city of Puerta Plata by President Bordas, of Santo Domingo, was silenced by fire from the battery of the American gunboat Machias, it was learned last night.

A fierce storm in which rain, wind and hail were combined, threatened to destroy the Rodman Wanamaker trans-Atlantic flyer, at Hammondsport, N. Y., and prevented any attempt at flying.

Declaring that much of the plumbing in Lexington is unsanitary, the Housing Inspector, John R. Richards, will seek to have a plumbing inspector appointed for that city.

Creditors of the defunct bank of Worden D. Alexander & Co., at Paris, Ky., have appointed a committee to take such steps as may protect the interests of depositors.

Secretary Bryan says that the State Department has received no confirmation of the report that George Fred Williams, American Minister to Greece, has resigned.

The Anchor Line steamer California is reported to be on rocks off Tory Island. Passengers, it was said, were transferred from the vessel.

Judge James W. Alcorn, one of the leading lawyers of the State, died yesterday at his home at Stanford after an illness of several weeks.

Farmers of Todd county declare that they will feed their wheat to the hogs rather than accept 75 cents a bushel, the current price.

Mrs. Cyrus V. Doise, of New Orleans, upon learning that her months-old child had been killed in a wreck, died of shock.

A detachment of Federal troops sent to Santa Rosalia, Lower California, has repulsed an attack of Constitutionalists upon the town.

The cotton condition and acreage reports of the Federal Department of Agriculture are due Wednesday of this week.

A recent strike in the deep sand of Lawrence county oil field shows pumping test of thirty barrels daily.

ARCHDUKE FERDINAND AND DUCHESS KILLED IN STREET

Youthful Student Shoots Royal Pair In Bosnian Capital After They Had Escaped Death From Assassin's Bombs Hurled At Automobile.

Austrian Heir Struck Full In the Face By Missile.

His Wife Shot Through Abdomen and Throat.

Murderers Barely Escape Lynching By Populace.

CURSE FOLLOWS HAPSBURGS

Sarayevo, June 28.—Archduke Francis Ferdinand, heir to the Austro-Hungarian throne, and his morganatic wife, the Duchess of Hohenberg, were assassinated to-day while driving through the streets of Sarayevo, the Bosnian capital. A youthful Servian student fired the shots which added another to the long list of tragedies that has darkened the reign of Emperor Francis Joseph.

The Archduke and his wife were victims of the second attempt in the same day against their lives. First a bomb was thrown at the automobile in which they were driving to the town hall. Forewarned, however, of a possible attempt against his life, the Archduke was watchful and struck the missile aside with his arm. It fell under an automobile which carried members of his suite, wounding Count von Boos-Waldeck and Col. Merizzi.

On their return from the town hall the Archduke and the Duchess were driving to the hospital when the Servian, Gavrio Prinsip, darted at the car and fired a volley at the Archduke and his wife were mortally wounded. With them at the time was the Governor of the city. The Governor escaped injury. His companions stepped across him and protected him from stray bullets.

Orders Rush To Palace.

The Governor shouted to the chauffeur to rush to the palace at top speed. Physicians were in prompt attendance, but their services were useless, as the Archduke and his wife were dead before the palace was reached.

Until the Emperor's wishes are known the bodies will lie in state at the palace here. They will doubtless be interred in the Hapsburg vaults in the Capuchin church at Vienna.

In Sarayevo there is mourning everywhere, with black craped flags and streamers on all public buildings. The President has sent a message to the Emperor, expressing the grief and horror of the whole population at the ruthless crime and assuring his majesty of the people's unalterable devotion to the ruling house.

Throughout the day weeping women were seen in groups, while great crowds surrounded the spots where the bomb exploded and where the fatal shots were fired. The bomb was filled with nails and lead filings and the explosion was violent. The iron shutters on many shops were pierced by flying fragments and iron railings were shattered. About a score of persons were injured, several of them being women and children.

Culmination of Sorrows.

This final tragedy which has come to the house of Hapsburg is the culmination of the personal sorrows that have overshadowed the life of the Emperor. His reign began with sinister omens, for he faced internal dissensions and external aggressions from the moment he came to the throne. In 1853 the list of tragic incidents began with an attempt upon his own life, when a Hungarian named Lebenyi wounded him with a knife.

Fourteen years later his brother, Archduke Maximilian, Emperor of Mexico, was captured by those who rose against him, condemned to death by court-martial and executed. Then followed the burning to death of a niece in Vienna, a sister in Paris and the death by suicide in Stahrenberg Lake of a cousin.

In 1898 the Emperor's wife, who was the daughter of Maximilian Joseph, Duke of Bavaria, was stabbed to death at Geneva by a mad Italian anarchist. They had been estranged for many years, but the Emperor had never ceased to show a deep affection for her.

Less than ten years before the Emperor's only son, Crown Prince Rudolph, a man of ability and promise, upon whom the Austrians had pinned their hopes, met death in a mystery which to this day has not been cleared. On January 30, 1889, his body was found in a hunting lodge at Meyerling, not far from Vienna. Beside his body lay that of the Baroness Marie Vetsera.

Succeeds To Throne.

Archduke Charles Francis, known popularly as Karl, who becomes heir to the Austrian throne owing to the Morganatic birth of Archduke Francis Ferdinand's children, debarring their succession, has been carefully educated with a view to fitting him for the position of Emperor. He is the first member of the imperial house to have been educated in the public schools of Vienna, where he mixed with pupils representing every class of society. He associated with workingmen and trades people and joined them in their games, thus getting into closer touch with the aspirations and ideals of the people than any of the other Hapsburgs. He is a First Lieutenant in the Austrian navy.

The murders occurred with such rapidity that many persons near the scene did not even hear the shots. The street is very narrow and the assassin was able to fire at close range.

* * *

Anti-Servian Demonstration.

Anti-Servian demonstrations began to-night. The crowds knelt in the streets and sang the national anthem. The Mayor of Sarayevo issued a proclamation to the residents of the city denouncing the crime and declaring that by the conviction of the assassins it was shown beyond all doubt that the bomb thrown at the Archduke's car came from Belgrade. It is said that after the attempt with the bomb near the Girls' High School the Duchess tried to dissuade the Archduke from venturing in the motor car again. To allay her fears M. Potiorek, Governor of Bosnia, said:

"It's all over now. We have not more than one murderer in Sarayevo," whereupon the Archduke decided to go on.

At a meeting of the provincial Diet tonight the president of the chamber expressed Bosnia's profound sorrow and indignation over the outrage and paid a glowing tribute to the Archduke and the Duchess. He also declared his unshakable love and devotion to the Emperor and the ruling house.

* * *

Struck In Face.

The Archduke was struck full in the face and the Duchess was shot through the abdomen and the throat. They died a few minutes after reaching the palace, to which they were hurried with all speed.

Those responsible for the assassination took care that it should prove effective, as there were two assailants, the first armed with a bomb and the second with a revolver. The bomb was thrown at the royal automobile as it was proceeding to the town hall, where a reception was to be held. The Archduke saw the deadly missile hurtling through the air and warded it off with his arm. It fell outside the car and exploded, slightly wounding two aide-de-camps in a second car and half a dozen spectators.

* * *

Story of Murder.

It was on the return of the procession that the tragedy was added to the long list of those that have darkened the pages of the recent history of the Hapsburgs. As the royal automobile reached a prominent point in the route to the palace an eighth-grade student, Gavrio Prinsip, sprang out of the crowd and poured a deadly fusillade of bullets from an automatic pistol at the Archduke and Princess.

Prinsip and a fellow conspirator, a compositor from Trebinje named Gabrinovics, barely escaped lynching by the infuriated spectators. They finally were seized by the police, who afforded them protection. Both are natives of the annexed province of Herzegovina.

* * *

First Attempt.

The first attempt against the Archduke occurred just outside the Girls' High School. His car had received after a brief pause for an inspection of the troops, when Gabrinovics hurled the bomb. This was so successfully warded off by the Archduke that it fell directly beneath the following car, the occupants of which, Count Von Boos-Waldeck and Col. Morizzo, were struck by slivers of it.

Archduke Francis Ferdinand stopped his car and, after making inquiries as to their injuries and finding what aid he could, continued his journey to the town hall. There the Burgomaster began the customary address, but the Archduke sharply interrupted and snapped out:

"Herr Burgomaster, we have come here to pay you a visit, and bombs have been thrown at us. This is altogether an amazing indignity."

After a pause, the Archduke said:

"Now you may speak."

* * *

Archduke Leaves Hall.

On leaving the hall the Archduke and his wife announced their intention of visiting the wounded members of their suite at the hospital on their way back to the palace. They were actually bound on their mission of mercy when, at the corner of Rudolf strasse and Franz Josef strasse, Prinsip opened fire.

A bullet struck the Archduke in the face. The Princess was wounded in the abdomen and another bullet struck her in the throat, severing an artery. She fell unconscious across her husband's knee. At the same moment the Archduke sank to the floor of the car.

The assassins were interrogated by the police and both seemed to glory in their exploit. Prinsip said he had studied for a time at Belgrade. He declared he had long intended to kill some eminent personage from nationalistic motives. He was awaiting the Archduke at a point where he knew the automobile would slacken speed, turning into Franz Josef strasse. The presence of the Princess in the car caused him to hesitate, but only for a moment. Then his nerve returned and he emptied his pistol at the imperial pair. He denied that he had any accomplices.

Prinsip is 18 years of age. Nedeljo Gabrinovics is 21. He told the police he had obtained the bomb from anarchists at Belgrade, whose names he did not know. He denied, also, that he had accomplices, and treated the tragedy with cynical indifference.

After his unsuccessful attempt to blow up the imperial visitors, Gabrinovics sprang into the river Miljachka in an effort to escape, but witnesses of his crime plunged after him and seized him.

A few yards from the scene of the shooting an unexploded bomb was found which, it was suspected, was thrown away by an accomplice after he had noted the success of Prinsip's attack.

* * *

Francis Ferdinand.

Archduke Francis Ferdinand, who was heir-presumptive to the throne of Austria, was born December 18, 1863. His father, the Archduke Carl Ludwig, was a brother of Emperor Francis Joseph, and his mother was Maria Annunziata, daughter of Ferdinand II. of Naples. Francis Ferdinand was still a boy when his mother died.

In 1862 his father, then over 50, married Princess Maria Theresa Von Braganza, the 18-year-old daughter of King Miguel of Portugal.

The new stepmother established an exemplary home. Ferdinand always held her in high esteem. She and her daughter, the Archduchess Maria Annunziata, were the only ladies present as witness of Francis Ferdinand's morganatic marriage to the Bohemian Countess Zophie Chotek, who later was elevated to the rank of Duchess of Hohenberg by the Emperor.

Francis Ferdinand became the heir presumptive when the Crown Prince Rudolph, the only son of Emperor Francis Joseph, met a tragic death in what is

(Continued On Second Page.)

Late Heir Presumptive To Austrian Throne and Family

ARCHDUKE FERDINAND, late heir presumptive to the Austrian throne; the Duchess and their children. The young children of the Archduke and Duchess were with the aged Emperor Francis Joseph at Ischl, and were playing in the garden at the palace when the shock of the news of their parents' assassination was received. Nobody had the heart to inform them of their bereavement.

ADVANCE GUARD OF STATE ENCAMPMENT

QUARTERMASTER WOODYARD IS EXPECTED TO-DAY.

MILITIA AND REGULARS WILL PITCH TENTS WEDNESDAY.

MANY VISITORS EXPECTED

Lexington, Ky., June 28.—(Special.)—Maj. T. W. Woodyard, Quartermaster of the Kentucky National Guard, with a detail of assistants, will arrive to-morrow at Bluegrass Park, near this city, to put the grounds in shape for the annual encampment of the Kentucky militia and the regular soldiers from the United States army, who will take part in the school of instruction. The tents and other equipment will also arrive from Frankfort to-morrow, and before Wednesday, when the encampment officially opens, everything will be ready for the reception of the 2,500 soldiers who will take part in the encampment.

Already waterworks and light fixtures have been established on the camp grounds by the Interurban Car Company, which owns Bluegrass Park, and every arrangement will be made for the comfort of the soldiers. Telephones will be installed in the officers' tents and many other useful necessities of camp life will be placed in use. Camp Ft. Spring will be under the joint direction of Gen. Roger D. Williams, Brigadier General of the First Brigade, Kentucky National Guard, and Col. William J. Nicholson, of the Second Cavalry, United States army. The soldiers after they arrive here will be transferred to the electric car lines to be conveyed to the park grounds, which are located seven miles from Lexington on the Versailles line.

The encampment will continue to July 10, inclusive, and large crowds of visitors from all over the State are expected to attend the entertaining features which will take place every day of the encampment.

CALIFORNIA REPORTED ON ROCKS OFF TORY ISLAND

PASSENGERS TRANSFERRED AS VESSEL TAKES WATER THROUGH TWO HOLES.

London, June 28.—The Anchor line steamer California is on the rocks off Tory Island and calling for assistance. Gunboats have left Londonderry to assist the steamer.

The California's bows are badly damaged and she is taking in water through two holes. It is reported that the passengers have been transferred from the vessel and are expected to reach Londonderry at noon to-morrow.

The Anchor line steamer sailed from New York June 20 for Moville and Glasgow. On board the vessel were 121 cabin and over 300 second-class passengers.

Tory Island lies off the Northwestern coast of the county Donegal, Ireland. It is a rocky reef two and one-third miles long and half a mile wide. On the northern end of the island is a lighthouse.

The accident to the California is attributed to fog.

REAR ADMIRAL FLETCHER REACHES WASHINGTON

It Is Expected Officer Will Soon Be Given Command of Atlantic Fleet.

Washington, June 28.—After serving in Mexican waters more than a year, during which he directed the occupation of Vera Cruz, Rear Admiral Frank Fletcher reached Washington to-night aboard the dispatch boat Dolphin. A terrific rain pelted the Potomac when the Dolphin steamed to her berth at the Navy Yard, and the Rear Admiral remained aboard. Secretary Daniels has chosen Rear Admiral Fletcher to succeed Rear Admiral Badger as commander-in-chief of the Atlantic fleet, and it is expected the recommendation for the promotion will be made to the President during the officer's furlough in Washington.

EFFORT TO CHECK BUBONIC PLAGUE IN NEW ORLEANS

GOVERNOR, MAYOR AND LEGISLATIVE MEMBERS MEET.

WAR OF EXTERMINATION UPON RATS AND FLEAS.

RAISING FUNDS FOR FIGHT

New Orleans, June 28.—Following the death here to-day of Charles Lundene, whose malady yesterday was diagnosed as bubonic plague, and the discovery of a second case, Gov. Hall, of Louisiana; Mayor Behrman, of New Orleans; members of the Legislature and health authorities went into conference to determine upon methods to be employed by the city and State in stamping out the disease.

While definite announcement has not been made, it is known that a campaign for the extermination of rats and fleas is among the preventive measures to be undertaken. It was stated to-night that a bill would be introduced in the Legislature at Baton Rouge to-morrow appropriating funds with which to fight the contagion.

W. W. Wilkinson, an inmate of the Volunteers of America Home, was yesterday sent to a large local hospital supported by the municipality. This afternoon his malady was diagnosed as bubonic plague. He is 50 years old and a native of Texas, but has resided here for the past six months.

Charles Lundene, a Swede, aged 49, who died to-day, was also an inmate of the Volunteers of America Home.

The twenty-seven other members of the home this afternoon were marched through the streets to an abandoned ruin in the outskirts of the city, where they were placed in quarantine. Every article of furniture and bedding the home contained was piled on the street in front of the building and a bonfire started. A quantity of second-hand clothing was among the articles destroyed, as it was thought possible that the contagion had been communicated by the cast-off garments. As the inmates of the home marched through the streets large crowds gathered to watch the unusual procession.

It is expected that to-morrow the city and State health authorities will take vigorous steps for a general clean-up campaign.

A telegram was sent to-day to Surgeon General Rupert Blue, of the United States Public Health Service, urging him to come here on a personal trip of inspection, and to detail two experts from the Public Health Service for duty here.

TODD COUNTY DRYING UP BECAUSE OF LONG DROUTH

CROPS IN DANGER, GARDENS RUINED AND SHORTAGE OF WATER.

Trenton, Ky., June 28.—(Special.)—The six weeks of drouth in this section have resulted in a serious condition as regards water for both the home and stock. Many cisterns are dry and water is being carried for family use some distance, while only perennial ponds and wells are supplying stock water. As for corn and tobacco, a half crop now would be surprising. Gardens are dried up.

Crops Languishing.

Carlisle, Ky., June 28.—(Special.)—It is now nearly four weeks since rain has fallen in Nicholas county, and there has only been one rain since May 4. As a result drouth conditions here are becoming alarming. Many tobacco growers were unable to finish transplanting tobacco, and other crops are languishing. The potato crop is a failure and gardens are suffering greatly.

MURDER INDICTMENTS IN SIMPSON COUNTY

Franklin, Ky., June 28.—(Special.)—Judge John S. Rhea yesterday adjourned Circuit Court until Wednesday of next week, during which time the equity docket will be heard. The grand jury was dismissed after returning two indictments for murder and others for minor offenses.

MUST CONSULT HIS GENERALS

Carranza Asks For Time To Consider Proposal.

Constitutionalist Chief Promises To Avoid Delay.

Perplexing Conditions Caused By Disagreement With Villa.

REPORTS AROUSE REBELS

Washington, June 28.—Gen. Venustiano Carranza, first chief of the Mexican Constitutionalists, has replied to the invitation extended for participation by his agents in an informal conference with representatives of Gen. Huerta and the United States concerning plans for a Provisional Government in Mexico, asking that he be given time to consult his Generals.

Gen. Carranza, it was learned here to-night, informed the mediators in his latest communication that because of the plan of Guadaloupe, under which he was chosen first chief of the Constitutionalists, it would be necessary for him to confer with his associates in the movement before entering upon such important negotiations. Acceptance of any proposed Provisional Government to succeed Huerta, he said, necessarily might require some changes in the terms of the Guadaloupe plan, and this could not be done without the consent of the various military leaders in the revolutionary movement.

* * *

To Hasten Consultation.

Assurances are said to have been given the mediators by Gen. Carranza that he would hasten the proposed consultation with his chiefs in order that some definite understanding could be reached quickly as to the position to be taken with regard to the informal mediation conference. Some of the Constitutionalist representatives in Washington still insist that Gen. Carranza has been influenced to look with favor upon the proposal to confer with the United States commissioners and Huerta representatives.

Others, however, are not as certain of the outcome, and they insist that, whatever happens, the military campaign against Huerta is to be pursued with renewed vigor toward Mexico City, with Aguascalientas, San Luis Potosi and Queretaro as the next objective points of the revolutist armies.

* * *

Break With Villa.

Many perplexing elements have developed in the situation, however, among them being the apparent disagreement between Carranza's agents here over the recent break with Villa and the publication of the statement attacking Gen. Angeles, authorized by Alfredo Breceda, Gen. Carranza's personal aide, who came to Washington from Saltillo for this purpose.

In the preparation of the statement attacking Angeles and confirming the fact that the breach between Villa and Carranza had not been altogether healed, Breceda was aided by Luis Cabrera, one of Carranza's principal agents here, who is advocating participation in the informal conference. Cabrera and Rafael Zubaran, a member of Carranza's Cabinet, disagreed as to the wisdom of giving out such a statement. Zubaran late last night, several hours after Breceda's statement had been given to the press, sought to have the statement recalled. Zubaran, it has become known, wanted the statement tempered at least, if it was to be published at all.

To-day Fernando Iglesias Calderon, leader of the Mexico Liberal party, and Leopoldo Hurdiata Espinosa joined the Mexican Constitutionalists in Washington to await developments regarding the informal peace conference. Neither would discuss their plans.

* * *

Aroused By Reports.

Publication to-day of certain correspondence alleged to have passed between Gen. Carranza and Sherburne G. Hopkins, a Washington lawyer, relating to a plan for conserving properties of the National Railways of Mexico, aroused the Constitutionalist leaders. The correspondence also included alleged communications between Mr. Hopkins and H. C. Pierce, head of the Pierce Oil Corporation, and one of the heaviest owners of National Railways' stock. Statements published in this connection intimated that American financial interests were backing the revolution in Mexico. This Mr. Hopkins emphatically denied in a statement issued to-night, asserting that he had done all he could for Mr. Pierce, as his representative, to conserve the properties in Mexico.

Rafael Zubaran and Luis Cabrera issued statements, declaring that the Constitutionalists had not received financial assistance from any American interests, and specifically deny any connection with Mr. Pierce. "It is absurd to believe," said Mr. Zubaran, "that the Mexican people would be shedding their blood to free themselves from certain finanical tyrannies in order to deliver themselves into the hands of other tyrannies."

Senator William Alden Smith also made public a statement declaring that publication of the correspondence confirmed assertions he had made to the Senate. He added that the matter might be noted by the Foreign Relations Committee, and that he himself might discuss it on the floor of the Senate. Senator Shively, another member of the committee, said he did not know whether the committee would consider the subject one for official investigation.

INTERFERENCE RESENTED.

Alleged Declaration By Carranza at Banquet.

Laredo, Tex., June 28.—"Constitutionalist leaders, who have the sympathy of all the people of Mexico behind them, will not allow the dignity of the nation to be lowered by the interference of any foreign power in the internal affairs of the country."

This declaration was made by Gen. Venustiano Carranza at a banquet at Monterey Saturday night, according to travelers who arrived here to-day. Carranza, it was said, asserted that the United States was assuming a dictatorial attitude. The 400 Mexicans who attended the banquet received the declaration with cheers, it is declared.

"The Constitutionalist movement has now proceeded to such a point," the first chief is quoted as having said, "that the party has nothing to fear except from the Judases in its own ranks." He mentioned no names.

Carranza, those who reached here today declared, made no reference to mediation, but other Constitutionalist leaders who spoke at the banquet expressed the view that, by international custom, the "good offices" were strictly defined

(Continued On Second Page.)

FAIR AND WARM WEATHER

Washington, June 28.—Except for showers to-morrow in New England and the Middle Atlantic States fair and warm weather is forecast for the first half of the coming week over most of the country.

"Over the extreme Northwestern portion of the country from the Dakotas westward," said the Weather Bureau's bulletin to-night, "the weather will probably be unsettled and showery until after the middle of the week, with somewhat higher temperatures after Monday. Over the Middle and Southern districts west of the Rocky Mountains, the Central Plains States, the Southwest, the Gulf States and the Ohio Valley generally fair weather will prevail during the week, with continued high temperatures to the southward and with rising temperatures over the Central districts by the middle of the week.

"In the Missouri and Upper Mississippi valleys and the Lake region fair weather with moderate temperatures during the first half of the week will be followed during the second half by unsettled and showery weather with higher temperatures, while in the Middle Atlantic States and New England showers Monday will be followed by fair weather over both districts, and by somewhat more moderate temperatures over the Middle Atlantic States until toward the end of the week, when showers are indicated with rising temperatures.

"In the South Atlantic States high temperatures will continue with occasional relief through local thunderstorms."

JUDGE J. W. ALCORN DIES AT STANFORD

KNOWN AS ONE OF THE LEADING LAWYERS OF STATE.

DEATH OF JURIST DUE TO HEMORRHAGE OF BRAIN.

SOLDIER UNDER MORGAN

Stanford, Ky., June 28.—(Special.)—Judge James W. Alcorn, the nestor of the Lincoln county bar and one of the most prominent and ablest lawyers in this part of Kentucky, died at his home here this evening after a short illness. Judge Alcorn was in his seventy-seventh year. A fortnight ago, after an unusually heavy term of Circuit Court in which he gave his personal attention to a large number of cases, Judge Alcorn was affected by a neuralgic attack which proved a severe tax upon his tired frame. Hemorrhage of the brain developed and for almost a week he hovered on the brink of death, nothing but his sturdy constitution and remarkable vitality sustaining life. All of his large family was present when the end came.

For more than half a century Judge Alcorn has been a prominent figure in this part of Kentucky. He was a native of Lincoln county, being a son of Alfred Alcorn and Mary Walker, both of prominent families. Judge Alcorn was born on July 21, 1838. His father was a Captain of Kentucky volunteers in the War of 1812. Judge Alcorn was graduated from Centre College at Danville, and then studied law in the office of the late Col. L. P. Hill, of this city. He joined Morgan's command when the Civil War began and was a gallant soldier, following his famous leader in all the daring raids. He was captured with Morgan on the raid through Indiana and Ohio. At the close of the war he resumed the practice of law in Stanford and formed a partnership with Col. Hill. Judge Alcorn attained an eminent position at the bar and has long been recognized as one of the ablest lawyers in the State. For many years he had been one of the district attorneys for the Louisville & Nashville railroad. Judge Alcorn was a man of great energy and fine judgment. He is survived by his wife, who was Miss Sophia Kendrick, of Somerset, and five of their seven children—namely, Mrs. James N. Saunders, Misses Kate, Pattie and Sophia Alcorn and Kendrick Alcorn, who has been his father's law partner for several years. The funeral of Judge Alcorn will be from the family residence here Tuesday afternoon.

CHILD KILLED IN AUTO RIDE NEAR NEW ORLEANS

Mother, Also Passenger, Dies of Shock On Learning Fate of Her Daughter.

New Orleans, June 28.—When a rescue party of policemen and physicians reached Littlewoods, ten miles from here, to-day, in response to urgent telephone calls, they found the automobile of Yves Le Monnier, Jr., lying wrecked in a drainage canal and 3-months-old Juanita Doize dead. Other members of the party of six were thought to have escaped serious injury. On the trip to the city an automobile ambulance sent out from here was met at Press street and a transfer of the wounded was made. Mrs. Cyril V. Doize, mother of the dead girl, suddenly collapsed, and a moment later was dead from shock and grief. Her sister, Miss Amelia Bertus, also thought to be slightly injured, is now reported to be dying from shock in a local hospital.

Yves Le Monnier, Jr., sustained a broken arm when his car plunged from a bridge into the canal, while his 3-year-old daughter, Julia, was severely shocked. Cyril V. Doize, whose wife and child are dead, was badly bruised.

The Le Monnier and Doize families, neighbors, went for a spin in the Le Monnier car. Some reclamation work is being done at Littlewoods, and it is thought that Mr. Le Monnier was not familiar with recent changes in the road.

ROUSE WILL BE FIRST MEMBER TO FILE EXPENSES

Kentucky Congressman, Who Is Unopposed, Will Appear To-day and Submit Schedule.

Washington, June 28.—(Special.)—As a measure of precaution, Representative A. B. Rouse will appear before the clerk of the House to-morrow and file his campaign expenses, which amount to less than $100. He will be the first member of the House to file under the new law, requiring that members seeking renomination must file their expense accounts both before and after election.

The law states that ten days before the primaries a congressional candidate must file his expenses with the clerk of the House and then again ten days following the primaries. Representative Rouse is unopposed in the nomination, and in order to maintain the spirit of the law and also as a precautionary move, Mr. Rouse will file his expenses to-morrow.

Representative Harvey Helm is in the same position as Mr. Rouse. He is unopposed in the primaries and his nomination is conceded. It is not known just what course Mr. Helm will pursue.

SENATE TO TAKE PRIMROSE PATH

Must Pass Trust Bills Before Adjournment.

Far From Resigned To Long Summer Discussion.

Trade Commission Measure Is Unfinished Business.

CLAYTON PROBLEM UNSOLVED

Washington, June 28.—Convinced that there is no other path to adjournment but the one which begins with trust legislation, the Senate will settle down this week to the steady grind of work on the Federal Trade Commission Bill.

The Senate is far from resigned to the thought of six weeks or more of discussion of trust legislation in midsummer, but it is not probable that the spirit of open revolt will show itself on the floor, and unless Senate leaders are at fault in the predictions the three House bills, or legislation designed to cover the same ground, will be put through by the familiar process, weeks of debate, fruitless effort to amend, and then passage.

There is not doubt whatever that if the President would relent in his insistence upon the anti-trust programme Congress could and would get away from Washington in two weeks or less. The House is in such shape that it could be ready to get away in a few days, and the Senate is not far behind, as far as appropriation measures are concerned. Many of these bills are still in conference, but if there was any real chance of adjournment it would not take more than a few days to have them finally disposed of.

* * *

Trade Bill.

The Trade Commission Bill is the unfinished business of the Senate; the Clayton Anti-Trust Bill is still unfinished by the Judiciary Committee and the Railway Capitalization Bill is in about the same shape in the hands of the Interstate Commerce Committee. Just when the latter two measures will get to the Senate floor is still a problem. The Judiciary Committee has found the Clayton bill, already passed by the House, a difficult problem, and has made and remade many of its sections. This bill deals with interlocking directorates and holding companies, with price fixing, with labor union exemption from the anti-trust laws and with the question of injunctions in labor disputes.

Although many of the leading lawyers of the Senate are on this committee, they have discovered their task to be most difficult, and the trouble in committee is regarded as a prelude to the fight which will come when it reaches the floor.

* * *

Railway Securities.

An effort will be made by the Interstate Commerce Committee to get together on the Railway Securities Bill this week. Chairman Newlands will ask representatives of the railroads and of the Interstate Commerce Commission to meet with the committee to discuss a plan proposed by Louis D. Brandeis, of Boston, for the regulation of railway security issues.

The Senate Foreign Relations Committee will continue its investigation into the transactions leading up to the negotiation of the proposed treaty with Nicaragua.

The Banking and Currency Committee plans to meet Thursday to take up President Wilson's nominations for the Federal reserve board.

The House to-day devoted a brief session to eulogies of the late Representative George King, of Maryland. Tributes were paid by Representatives Coady and Linthicum, of that State.

To-morrow will be a field day for those Representatives who want to bring up bills under a suspension of the rules. The Lever Bill for regulation of cotton futures is among the bills on this suspension calendar that rests on Speaker Clark's desk.

The General Dam Bill, offered by Representative Adamson, chairman of the Interstate Commerce Committee, will be the center of interest in the week's proceedings in the House.

YOUTHFUL ELOPERS HELD AS THEY STEP FROM TRAIN

GRAYSON COUNTY COUPLE'S PLANS TO WED NIPPED BY LOUISVILLE POLICE.

Plans of Miss Grace Burns, 17 years old, and Oliver Hale, of the same age, to wed in Jeffersonville last night, following an elopement yesterday morning from their homes in Clarkson, Grayson county, were thwarted when Corp. John Sullivan, acting under directions of Night Chief of Police Ridge, stopped the runaway pair as they were entering a taxicab at the Seventh-street railroad station.

While members of her family were at church Miss Burns and Hale drove six miles to Leitchfield, where they boarded a train for Louisville, accompanied by Miss Rita Grayson.

A. O. Burns, the father, notified Maj. Ridge, night chief of police of Louisville, who sent Corp. Sullivan to the railroad station. The officer saw a couple answering the descriptions and heard the young man engage a taxicab to drive to Jeffersonville. He took them into custody.

After being questioned at Central station the two girls were taken to the Detention Home, while the young man was released. Hale is a farmer of Grayson county. After being notified his daughter was being held here Burns said he would come to Louisville this morning to take her back home.

REPORTED RESIGNATION HAS NOT BEEN CONFIRMED

Washington, June 28.—Secretary Bryan said to-night the State Department had received no confirmation of press reports that George Fred Williams, American Minister to Greece, had forwarded his resignation after issuing a statement denouncing conditions in turbulent Albania. Pending receipt of word from the Minister himself, the Secretary declined to comment.

BODY FOUND IN RIVER.

William Seaman Had Been Absent From Home Since Saturday.

Frankfort, Ky., June 28.—(Special.)—The body of William Seaman, 20 years old, the son of John Seaman, a farmer living at Woodlake, this county, was found this afternoon in the Kentucky River near the lock. The body was fully attired, and it is supposed, on this account, that the young man fell into the water. He had not been seen since yesterday afternoon when he left home. The young man worked for his father.

THE KANSAS CITY STAR.

MAIN EDITION

VOL. 34. NO. 336 KANSAS CITY, AUGUST 19, 1914.—WEDNESDAY FOURTEEN PAGES PRICE IN THE CITY, ONE CENT. OUTSIDE, TWO CENTS.

POPE PIUS IS DYING

Sudden Relapse Brought End Near This Afternoon to Roman Pontiff.

WAR CAUSED HIS ILLNESS

The Outbreak of Hostilities Was a Great Shock to Head of the Church.

Had Prayed Constantly for Peace and Exhorted All Catholics to Pray.

BELIEVED DEAD ONCE

Suffocation of the Patient Made Doctors Fear End Had Come.

(*By the Associated Press.*)

Rome, Aug. 19, 2:55 p. m., via Paris, Aug. 19, 6:55 p. m.—For a moment this afternoon the doctors thought that the Pope was dying through suffocation.

Fortunately the patient succeeded in expectorating, and now the crisis seems to be over.

Nephritis complications, however, are seriously feared.

An earlier dispatch from Rome which was printed in the first edition of The Star announced that the Pope was dead.

Rome, Aug. 19.—The doctors have administered oxygen to the pope. He was given stimulating injections and cupped when death seemed imminent.

These energetic remedies brought about an amelioration, but nobody is yet able to say whether they are only temporary or indicate that the crisis has been overcome.

Earlier bulletins today indicated that the pope was in a very bad way. The first bulletin today said that he was threatened with pneumonia.

Sisters at His Bedside.

It was stated that his sisters and a doctor were constantly at his bedside. It was later reported that Cardinal Merry Del Val had summoned back to Rome all the cardinals who recently left here.

Up until hostilities actually commenced the pope did not believe that war could come between civilized nations at this late day.

Broke Down When War Was Declared.

When he heard that Germany had declared war on Russia and realized that the conflagration actually had been kindled, he broke down. He swooned and was unconscious for several minutes. His physicians were called in and had to administer powerful restoratives.

There was a slight recovery and the pope was able to be about the Vatican. He spent most of his time in prayer and in all of his devotions impressed upon every member of his household that his entire heart was set on the restoration of peace.

Prayed for the Dying.

Finally he issued an appeal to every Catholic throughout the world to pray for peace. This appeal was distributed broadcast everywhere.

POPE PIUS X.

THE WEATHER—UNSETTLED.

7 a. m.	77	11 a. m.	82
8 a. m.	73	12 m.	85
9 a. m.	74	1 p. m.	88
10 a. m.	77	2 p. m.	*90

*Unofficial.

The Forecast—Slightly unsettled, with a chance for light local thunderstorms tonight or Thursday; slightly cooler Thursday.

Three hundredths of an inch of rain fell in Kansas City this morning. Other showers fell over Northwestern Kansas, Nebraska, Iowa and Northern Missouri.

M'REYNOLDS IS A JUSTICE.

President Appoints Attorney General to Supreme Court.

Washington, Aug. 19.—President Wilson today nominated Attorney General James C. McReynolds to the United States Supreme Court to fill the vacancy caused by the death of the late Justice Lurton, and at the same time named Thomas W. Gregory of Austin, Tex., assistant to the attorney general, to succeed McReynolds at the head of the Department of Justice.

Opposition loomed up in the Senate to the nomination of Mr. McReynolds to the supreme court vacancy caused by the death of the late Justice Horace H. Lurton. Several senators let it be known that they would vigorously oppose McReynolds. Little trouble, however, was expected by Democratic leaders in insuring his confirmation.

That McReynolds was to be chosen has been known for months. The New Haven Railroad dissolution was the only drawback. He desired to clean that matter up before retiring from the Department of Justice. With the amicable court settlement assured, McReynolds now feels free to accept the promotion to the high court.

Thomas W. Gregory of Austin, Tex., the special assistant of the Attorney General, who is slated to succeed McReynolds, now is in charge of the New Haven case. Gregory is 53 years old, a native of Mississippi, and has been actively identified with the Texas bar. He is said to have the support of Col. E. M. House of Texas, reputed "political mentor" of the President.

"FRANCE HASN'T WON YET."

Stephen Pichon Warns Against Accepting Outpost Combats as Victories.

Paris, Aug. 19.—"Outpost combats, however interesting and characteristic, do not justify us in counting upon the certainty of a prompt and definite victory," writes Former Minister of Foreign Affairs Stephen Pichon in the Petit Journal. "I find too much said about the Germans being demoralized. Their original overconfidence may have given place to doubts, but that is all. The war now beginning is a war to the death. On it hangs the existence of Germany as well as that of France. It will be waged furiously on both sides. It will probably be long and the losses enormous.

"Let us make our minds up to the fact that we have to contend with the most redoubtable army in Europe and have need for all our material and moral forces."

INTO AUSTRIA WITH 70,000.

The Russian Army Is Pushing Across by Several Routes.

St. Petersburg, Aug. 19.—The war office announces that the invasion of the Austrian provinces of Galicia and Bukovina is well in progress. It is stated that several divisions, totalling more than seventy thousand men, chiefly infantry and artillery, are moving into Austria by several routes, the location of which are withheld. The general staff announces that the capture of Czernowitz, the capital of Bukovina, may soon be looked for.

BET WAR IS OVER BEFORE 1915

Lloyds Offers Even Money on Premiums.

London, Aug. 19.—The odds are even at Lloyds that the war will be over by December 31. The underwriters have quoted a 50 per cent premium on policies to insure the payment of total loss in the event of no peace pact being signed by the last day of this year.

FROM WAR MAD EUROPE

MEMBER OF STAR STAFF, BACK TODAY, TELLS EXPERIENCES.

Berlin, Enthusiastic Before the Kaiser's War Declaration, Is Awed Now—Soldiers Go Sternly to the Front—Raced Back Home.

The following is by a member of The Star staff who returned today from a 5-months' trip in Europe.

Americans 2,500 miles from the roar of the guns at Liége, know as much about the progress of the war in Europe as does the Londoner or Parisian who gets his morning paper with full official reports every morning at breakfast.

In London, for instance, troops were moving everywhere, the artillery and wagon trains were to be seen in the Strand and the big yard at the Law Courts was filled with recruits being drilled, but no one knew where the troops were going. London knew that the British fleet was somewhere between the German fleet and the English coast, but just where it did not know and the admiralty gave out nothing upon which even to conjecture.

Waiters left their work in the middle of meal hours and taxicab drivers turned over their vehicles and left to fight, they didn't know where or whom, but they knew the struggle they had been fearing ever since they were old enough to know of war.

WAR DECLARATION AWED BERLIN.

An American friend of mine, who was in Berlin when Germany declared war on Russia, told of his experiences there. For several days and nights preceding the declaration the streets had been crowded with wildly enthusiastic crowds shouting for war, but the news of the declaration hushed the cheers. The crowds were there, but they were quiet, serious crowds and they were trying to realize what it all meant.

At all the railway stations great multitudes were trying to get upon trains, but even in the excitement the great German machine worked almost without a hitch. Passengers were treated with every courtesy possible under the circumstances, but they had to ride in cars that were jammed to capacity and in which every bit of standing room was taken.

COURTESY TO A FRENCH WOMAN.

At the Friederich Strasse station a French woman with three small children was trying to get a train to France. She could not speak German and she was crazed with worry. A German colonel, speaking excellent French, reassured her and escorted her and her children, two of them in his arms, to the train.

And there were strange leave takings at the station. German reservists, off for their mobilization stations, did not say *Aufwiedersehen*, as the German usually says when he parts from his dear ones. *Aufwiedersehen* means "Till we meet again." What the German reservists said was "Adieu." The war had come at last. Germany must crush France and turn on Russia before the great bear could get out of his lair and trample down the Teutonic race. The Germans were fighting for their nation's life and they thought not of *Aufwiedersehen*.

DEATH TO OPEN A CAR WINDOW.

The trains, carrying their anxious crowds of non-residents, mostly Americans, were often stopped and searched by the German troops, but the searchers, almost without exception, were courteous. Germany must know who every person seeking to leave Germany was, and it found out, but it found out in as easy a way as possible. Trains were stopped four and five times before the Dutch border was reached. Windows were kept rigidly closed to lessen danger of bombs being dropped upon bridges and passengers were informed that the opening of a window was an automatic order to the soldier on guard in each corridor to shoot the man who opened it.

"And the trouble was not ended when Holland was reached. Europe was at war and Holland had to protect its boundaries and so every man of Holland's two hundred thousand troops was on duty, most of them at the German frontier. The call to arms came in the midst of the harvest. The grain gathering was left to the women and the men marched away. I asked a young soldier in heavy marching order, who was waiting for a train at Amsterdam, where and whom he was going to fight.

DIKES THE DUTCH DEFENSE.

"'I'm ordered to the German frontier,' he said. 'I don't know whom we must fight, but if we have to fight I hope it will be Germany. But we won't know until we see who tries to break through Holland. We'll fight that nation and if necessary we still know how to flood our nation. No army ever will march through Holland. Our troops are especially trained in destroying bridges and dikes for just this emergency. We've known it would come.'

The Friday before the war was declared, I visited the great Edam cheese market at Alkmar where weekly some 200,000 cheeses are sold for shipment throughout the world. The 200,000 cheeses were piled in great rows in the market again, but there were few buyers and most of the cheeses had to be taken back. Dealers dared not tie up their money with the war coming on.

REFUGEES IN LONDON WORRIED.

The first Americans to arrive in London after the declaration of war were worried because they found the banks closed for the August holiday which, as an emergency measure, was extended to four days by the government to prevent a run on the supply. The travel agencies and the Great Eastern Railroad, however, cashed checks for limited amounts every day and all those who had checks, unless they were the ones issued by the German steamship companies, got money, at least enough to keep them comfortable, although many were worried.

There were great crowds at the Amer-

(*Continued on Fourth Page.*)

RAINS FALLING IN KANSAS.

South Central Counties Get About an Inch at Noon.

Wichita, Kas., Aug. 19.—Nearly an inch of rain fell in this section between 12 and 1 o'clock this noon. It will be of great benefit to the corn.

Hutchinson, Kas., Aug. 19.—Central Kansas is covered with showers today, scattering somewhat but nevertheless of much benefit. The rain started to fall here at 11 o'clock and it is great for the alfalfa and corn, and will put the wheat ground in fine condition for plowing.

Greeley, Kas., Aug. 19.—A good rain fell here this morning, breaking a prolonged drought.

Junction City, Kas., Aug. 19.—A half inch of rain fell here early this morning. It will be of great benefit to corn and pasture lands.

WHAT GERMAN MOVES MEAN.

The Plan Is to Drive Allies to Antwerp and There Bottle Them Up.

(*By J. W. T. Mason, Former European Manager of the United Press.*)

New York, Aug. 19.—The key to Germany's battle plan on the Belgian plains is evident from the seriousness of the fighting at Dinant, described as the first real battle of the war, and the general German movement toward Wavre and Gembloux.

The German objective is to get between the allied forces in Belgium and the French frontier, so that in case of defeat, the allies can be driven northward into Antwerp and locked up for the rest of the war.

The principal detail of this movement is the Dinant attack. Dinant marks the chief crossing of the Meuse between the twenty miles that separate the Belgian fortress of Namur from the French border fortress of Givet.

If the Germans can force a crossing of the Meuse at Dinant, their way will be northwest over the Sambre River. Once across the second stream, their strategy will have gained what may be a vitally important advantage. The troops at Wavre and Gembloux can then swing round parallel with the Sambre, and the enveloping movement will be complete. The strategic struggle for possession, in all probability, is what now is occurring in Belgium.

Obscurity concerning the objective of the French advance into Alsace-Lorraine is beginning to clear. It seems evident that the French general staff is attempting to drive the Germans out of the lost provinces into Strassburg and turn Strassburg into a German Sedan.

The retreat of the Germans from Saarburg (French Sarrebourg) is an important success for the French plans. It shows an enveloping movement is succeeding, advancing eastward in crescent formation from Abresweiler to Chateau Saline.

The retreat from Saarburg, the most important garrison center between Metz and Strassburg, indicates great strength on the part of the French forces. The threatening position at Metz, from which might come a flank and rear attack, also suggests the French have a very large body of troops in the district.

By co-ordinating this southeastward enveloping movement with the sweeping advance northward from Mulhausen, the French may succeed in bottling up an important part of the German army in Strassburg.

Reports of the Alsace-Lorraine movements are issued by the French war department as coming from General Joffre himself, the commander-in-chief. The fact that the eastern plan of campaign is under the direct supervision of General Joffre suggests that while the world has its attention fixed on Belgium, the first news of supreme importance may come from the lost provinces in the east.

GREAT BATTLE ON

Huge Armies Are at Death Grip in First Decisive Conflict of the War.

MOVING ON BRUSSELS

Germans Are Pressing Forward in Attempt to Break Through Defending Lines.

MAY BE SECOND WATERLOO

The Final Fighting May Center on the Historic Battlefield.

More Than 400,000 Men Are Said to Be on First Line of Invaders.

NO NEWS FROM LIEGE

But the Reports Persist That the Forts Have Been Taken or Abandoned.

Bulletin.

Rotterdam, Aug. 19.—The Cologne Gazette asserts that the advance of the German troops, while slow, has not been seriously checked anywhere.

London, Aug. 19, 2:20 p. m.—The curt announcement from Brussels of fierce fighting between Belgian and German troops along an extended front is generally accepted in London today as indicating the real beginning of the first great battle in the war.

The German attack is today again reported made on the direct orders of Emperor William.

The extent of the line of fighting has not yet been revealed, but presumably stretches in a north and south line.

Tells of Advance by Allies.

A dispatch to the Reuter Telegraph Company from Brussels says the German advance posts covering the region between Gembloux and Jodoigne, are being gradually pushed back before the advance of Belgian and French forces.

The Belgians and French are now in close junction and in contact with the advance lines of the German army.

Paris, Aug. 19 (1:09 p. m.).—Careful study of the military situation on the northern frontier leads French military observers to the conclusion that the events transpiring in Belgium today are the beginning of operations on an immense scale.

France Is Confident.

Germany, it is declared, is making a fresh and mightier effort to break into France through the comparatively open Belgium country.

Government opinion in Paris, however, is confident that the allies will be able to meet this shock successfully and reply to it crushingly.

Interest in the situation in Belgium has distracted attention from the French operations in Alsace-Lorraine. It is realized that the kaiser is staking everything on his offensive movement through Belgium. The German infantry was reported as moving steadily forward, intrenching as it came, with its chief strength directed against the center of the allied armies in an effort to divide the opposition.

Terrible Carnage at Dinant.

No word is being received direct from Brussels today, but whether this is due to the censorship or the presence of the Germans, is not known here.

Details of the fighting at Dinant between the French and German troops show that the carnage was terrible. The first French company, although decimated, held a position until another company came up with artillery, which destroyed a bridge. The French cavalry then advanced and pushed the German attackers back into the Meuse.

London, Aug. 19.—Northern and Eastern Belgium are today a solid battle line. The first real struggle for possession of the gateway through Belgium toward the French frontier is in progress.

Fighting starting at dawn yesterday continues. Despite the strictest censorship in the history of the world, it is evident that the allied armies are being hard pressed before Waterloo and Brussels.

Two Armies Have Combined.

Germany's fighting machine, its wonderfully trained infantry, is being pushed forward all along the line. The army of the Meuse and the first army of the Moselle have combined. Their lines stretch from the Dutch boundary far south into Belgian Luxembourg. One section is attacking the Namur fortifications.

The fate of Liége is unknown. It is cut off from the Belgian lines. Not a word can get through regarding the fate of the forts. The Belgian war office says they still hold out. Unconfirmed reports from Brussels and from Dutch cities say that, finding it impossible longer to hold them against the fire of the heavy siege guns, the Belgians dynamited and destroyed them.

A "Waterloo" for Germany?

That Brussels will be taken is accepted here as practically certain. In this connection the military expert of the Daily Express says today:

"Brussels is being held out to Germany as a bait. Germany may destroy Brussels, but the deeper she strikes the more surely does her head enter the lion's mouth. In front and on all sides Germany will find a hostile army. History is to repeat herself. A second emperor is to meet his Waterloo."

All of the London papers agree that it will be asking too much to expect the allied armies to keep the Germans out of Brussels. They point out that the German forces engaged total more than 400,000 and that, with reserves parked in the rear, the kaiser has a total of close to ¾ million men available for this first offensive operation. But they insist that it will be impossible for the Germans to reach the Belgian-French boundary.

THE CAMPAIGN IN BELGIUM TODAY CENTERS ABOUT BRUSSELS.

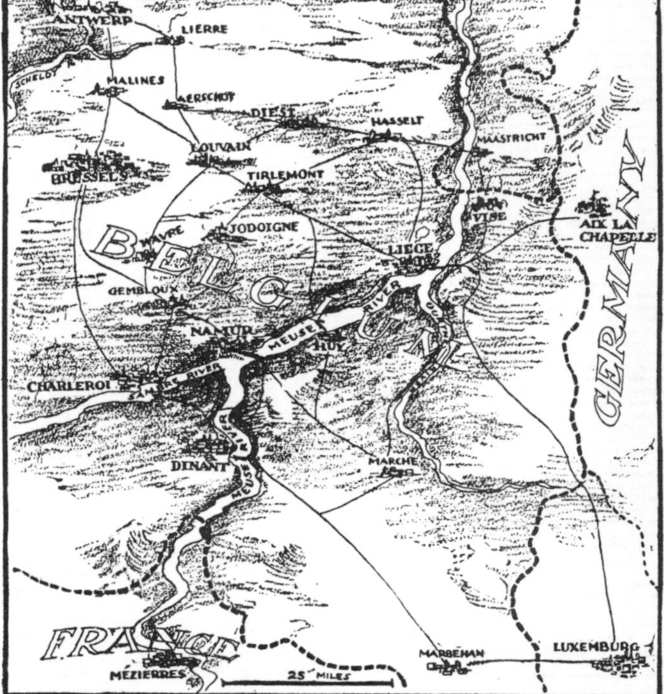

The battle field of Waterloo is on the plains south of Brussels and just west of Wavre. Near there the allied army is supposed to be centered.

The Belgian line is believed to be between Brussels and Antwerp, with headquarters at Malines.

For the impending general engagement the Northern German army that passed through Aix-la-Chapelle has been joined with the German forces that were massed in Luxemburg.

DRYS START IN THE RAIN

SIXTEEN MOTOR CARS IN THE COUNTY CAMPAIGN TRIP.

"We Have Driven Our Nails, and Now We Are Clinching Them," Said E. F. Jones, Leader in the Movement, as the Parade Started.

TODAY'S ITINERARY OF THE JACKSON COUNTY "DRY" CAMPAIGNERS.

Raytown,	Oak Grove (dinner),
Lees Summit,	Levasy,
Greenwood,	Buckner,
Lone Jack,	Independence.

A hundred crusaders bent on driving out the saloons and roadhouses of rural Jackson County ignored the rain this morning and departed from Eighth and McGee streets in sixteen motor cars for a speaking and moral suasion tour through the county.

The start was made at 9 o'clock. A light rain was falling, but the rain failed to cause any gloom. The cars had been lining up an hour before the departure and there was much visiting back and forth between the tourists. Something in the spirit of the men and women going on the trip caused them to laugh and jest.

"I'd rather drive in the rain than in the dust," one woman said, which expressed quite clearly the feeling of the corps.

CHICKEN AT OAK GROVE.

The motorists were to visit Raytown, Lees Summit, Greenwood, Lone Jack, Oak Grove, Levasy, Buckner and wind up in Independence, where the tour will disband. A chicken dinner was scheduled for Oak Grove by the temperance women of the town. Ten-minute speeches will be made in every town visited.

E. F. Jones, legislative superintendent of the Missouri Anti-Saloon League, and Ross Ream, a Mount Washington attorney, will do most of the speaking, although there will be many extemporaneous speeches. E. C. Hamilton, an Independence attorney, was to have been one of the chief speakers, but he was too ill this morning to make the trip.

"I have about ten 8 to 10-minute speeches bottled up in my system ready to turn loose," Mr. Jones said. "We're going into this tour with a lot of energy and we're going to make some votes. The rain won't hurt us a bit, but we would have had many more cars if the sky had been clear. The way I look at today's movement is—we've driven all our nails and now we're clinching them."

WHITE RIBBONS AND FLAGS.

Most of the cars were decorated with white ribbons and American flags. One of them carried the following motto, posted on the back:

> Down rum by vote; not by throat.
> Muzzle it; not guzzle it.

A list of the motorists follows:

Alfred Peterson, A. J. Ream, Ross J. Ream, Mrs. A. J. Ream and Harry Walker, owner. This was the pilot car.

E. J. Jones, Miss Nora Peterson, Mrs. E. J. Jones and G. H. Compton, owner. This car was from Independence.

J. L. Peek, owner; Mrs. Peek, Mrs. H. K. Miller, Mrs. R. C. Doake and Mrs. D. C. Ireland. This car was from Mount Washington.

Roy L. Kuhns, Mrs. R. L. Kuhns, Miss L. Anna Mallinson, Mrs. L. W. Ballinger, Mrs. Della Hollis, W. D. Buford and E. T. Morton, owner.

J. W. Rogers, owner; J. P. Spencer, Reuben Shrout, Thomas H. Shrout, George Rogers, J. W. Rogers.

C. C. Montgomery, owner; Mr. and Mrs. W. J. Gove and Mrs. J. T. Brown, Blue Springs.

J. C. Waugh and family.

Dr. E. H. Kelly, owner; Mrs. Kelly, J. G. White.

Dr. C. E. Nickson, owner; Mrs. Nickson, Mrs. C. L. Greer, Mrs. A. D. Thompson, Mrs. E. S. Stutzman, Mrs. J. N. Gillispie.

Mrs. N. S. Shannon, owner; Mr. and Mrs. George L. Waldo, Albert Smith.

A. C. Shaur, owner; Mrs. Shaur, Herbert Shaur, Buel Shaur, Miss Bessie May.

The Mount Washington band in two cars belonging to G. R. Baker and R. C. Field; Dean Fitzer, Carl Fitzer, B. L. Claridy, H. C. Claridy, Early Daily, A. D. Daily, Mrs. Roscoe Field.

Mount Washington Male Quartet in the car of Dr. W. A. Stewart, W. J. Dockum, W. F. Daut, W. M. Mundell.

C. E. Rugle, George A. Tryon, W. R. Ward, Benjamin H. West, J. T. Bainbridge and W. J. Hite, owner.

ARRIVE WITH BAND PLAYING

Twenty Cars Went Into Lees Summit at 11 o'Clock.

Lees Summit, Mo., Aug. 19.—Jackson County's dry crusaders reached here with a string of motor cars shortly before 11 o'clock this morning. The parade had some additions at Raytown which was reached at 10 o'clock, and more than twenty cars entered Lees Summit. One of them bore the legend "Better Babies."

E. F. Jones was the speaker at both towns. At each place the motorists toured the principal streets with the Mount Washington Band playing before coming to a stop. The Mount Washington Men's Quartette also took part in the program.

In his speeches Mr. Jones struck hard at the corrupting joints out in the county. He swept away the statements of the liquor men that the county will lose a good deal of revenue if it goes dry by presenting figures on the subject. Only nine out of the fifty-two places in the county that sell liquor pay county licenses and their annual amount is less than $1,200 a year, not enough to build one county bridge. The state legislature, Mr. Jones said, has a dry majority in both houses, and Jackson County has nothing to fear from adverse legislation from the dry legislators if it votes the joints out of the county.

Grain Valley, Mo., Aug. 19.—After leaving Lees Summit the party went to Blue Springs, where there was a large crowd. Ross Ream spoke there for ten minutes. The next stop was here, where Mr. Ream and Mr. Jones spoke to one of the best crowds on the trip. From Grain Valley the party proceeded to Oak Grove for the big chicken dinner.

The crowds in the towns were large and enthusiastic and everywhere the "dry" speeches were applauded enthusiastically. As the morning progressed additional motor cars from out in the county joined the procession.

One feature of the trip was the number of "dry" posters in the farmhouses. Most of the houses had large signs posted in windows with "Vote dry fo

EXTRA **THE NEWS-HERALD.** EXTRA

T. G. COBB, Editor and Owner. | The Burke County News / The Morganton Herald } Consolidated November 29, 1901. | Subscription Price $1 Per Year in Advance.

VOL. XXXII. | MORGANTON, N. C., JULY 18, 1916. | NO. 9.

Bridges and Buildings Swept Away by the Flood

Water Highest in History of County, and Reports Which Have Come from Outside Show That Even Greater Damage Has Been Done Further Down the Catawba--Railroad Bridges Gone--No Mails--No Telegraphic Connections--Situation Alarming.

In the terrific rainstorms which visited this section Friday, Saturday and Sunday and which by Sunday morning had caused the rivers and smaller streams to flood the surrounding territory as it had never been flooded before, and to sweep before their mighty current almost everything that came within their path, Burke county has experienced the greatest calamity in her history. It is impossible to estimate in dollars and cents the financial loss. So far there has been no report of loss of human life in the county, but at this writing it is impossible to get into communication with any but a small section immediately surrounding Morganton, and it is possible that there has been loss of life. Telephone connection with Hickory was never cut off but that was the only nearby town with which any communication at all could be had.

The seven steel bridges over the Catawba river in Burke county were swept away Saturday night. This isolates large portions of the county and makes it difficult to get food supplies to Morganton, the situation all the more serious because there are no trains running.

Late Saturday afternoon it was seen that the loss of the bridges was inevitable, as the waters were rising very rapidly. Watchers say that the two near Morganton, known as the upper and lower bridges, went very early Sunday morning, the latter going first. It is said that the creaking and groaning of the steel as it broke from the supports sounded almost like some animal in great despair.

When these bridges were built after the freshet of 1901 they were placed over 10 feet above what was then thought to be the record breaking water mark. Judging from high water we have had in the past, it was thought to be improbable that these splendid steel structures would ever be swept away.

The railroad bridge over the Catawba near Catawba station suffered the same fate as other bridges and this cuts off the whole western section of the State from railway connection with the outside world. It is not known when it will be possible for trains to run. Guesses vary from four or five days to a month or six weeks, the first based upon the belief that the Southern will probably arrange for a transfer by boat or ferry of at least of mail and passengers. Likely it will be more than a month before shipments of freight can reach us.

SEVENTEEN FEET HIGHER THAN IN 1901.

Mr. W. E. Walton made measurements yesterday afternoon of the height reached by the water at the Upper bridge and found it to have been 41 feet above normal, this 17 feet higher than the highest water mark that had been reached previous to this flood—in 1901 the water was 24 feet above normal at this point. At the Lower bridge the measurement showed 44 feet above normal.

DARING RESCUE FROM TOP OF STORE BUILDING—REAL HEROISM SHOWN.

When the water began rising so rapidly early Sunday morning the lives of a number in the Quaker Meadows section were greatly endangered. So suddenly and surprisingly did the water rise, many feet in a few seconds time, that several families were caught and but for prompt work would probably have been drowned. Shortly after midnight Saturday night the family of Mr. McK. Kincaid, living near Fleming's ford, saw that they would be compelled to get out. So surrounded even then was the house by the water that they telephoned for help. Thereupon Messrs. Leith Gordon, R. W. Pipkin, Thompson Gillam, Steve Lowdermilk, John Small, Charlie Moffit, Ted Gordon, Webb Estes and probably others built a boat as quickly as possible, the lumber having been secured at the plant of the M. M. & T. Co., and about six o'clock Messrs. Leith Gordon and R. W. Pipkin went after the danger-threatened family. They made several trips and finally succeeded in bringing them all to safety. Guests at the Kincaid home were Mrs. Kincaid's sister, Mrs. J. J. Hefner and her children, of Hickory. Also Mr. John Fox was one of those rescued from the Kincaid home. He had gone there to telephone to his son and while in the house the water rose so rapidly that he could not get away. He was the last one brought away by the rescuing party. Fearing the house might go he climbed a tree and was found there by Messrs Gordon and Pipkin when they made the last trip.

The water reached the second floor of the home and though often it seemed that nothing could keep the house from moving it remained at the same place.

The most sensational rescue of the day was that of Mr. Fons Duckworth, who was brought to land about 10 o'clock Sunday morning from the top of his father's store where he had spent the greater part of the night. Early Saturday night water began rising in the store, which was probably 200 yards from the original bank of the river. Mr. J. L. Duckworth and his two sons wese in the store and decided they should leave. The father and one son got out but Fons remembering some chickens which he thought ought to be let out stopped to attend to them and the rapid rise of the water caught him. When daylight came he was seen by those on the shore to be signalling for help. A reward was offered for anyone who would go to his assistance, the amount reaching about $1200. Gordon and Pipkin who were exhausted from their rescue of the Kincaid family were not able to go. The water was angry and dangerous looking. Duckworth seemed doomed to death and an effort to save him meant a risk of life. Will Clark volunteered to take the chance. He went quite a distance up the stream and came down with the current at which was judged to be about 20 miles an hour, and let his boat, the same in which the Kincaid family had been rescued, hit the store building in such a way as to halt it. He succeeded in bringing Duckworth to land, amid the cheering of the spectators who were lined along the water's dege. Very unselfishly he refused to accept the reward that had been offered, and received the praise of those who had witnessed his deed in a very modest manner. He has been acclaimed a hero, and his name will live as long as the memory of the 1916 flood.

The home of Mr. J. H. Parks went down the stream about 7 o'clock, the family leaving the house just about 20 minutes before it began to move. Miss Bessie Parks, the last to leave waded out in water several feet deep. The house was owned by Mr. J. T. Perkins. It is reported to have washed to Rocky Ford and there dashed to pieces.

Those suffering great loss in the Quaker Meadows section were Olin Avery, George Kanipe, Henry McGhinnis, Mose Corpening (col.,) Charlie Clark, L. A. Clark, Durant Williams, Joe Allman, John Parks, C. M. McDowell, McK. Kincaid and J. T. Perkins. The Edmonson farm at the lower bridge suffered considerable damage and large sections of it are still under water.

SITUATION IN CATAWBA AS BAD AS IN BURKE.

Telephone messages and a few travelers from Hickory tell a story that is just as fearful as that of Burke's loss. Every bridge in Catawba county is gone except one over South Fork river. The cotton mill at Rhodhiss has been damaged possibly irreparably. It is said 500 bales of cotton were washed out of the mill. A number of the mill houses went in the flood, and water in the company store building reached to the second floor. The Brookford mill was damaged to the extent of eight or ten thousand dollars, possibly much of the machinery completely ruined. Hickory and Newton, like Morganton, have been cut off since Saturday from communication with the outside world. Yesterday afternoon connection was re-established between Hickory and Newton, thereby connecting Morganton and Newton.

THE FLOOD IN LOVELADY.

For The News-Herald:

The flood struck us heavily. Hoffman's bridge is gone. At Mrs. J. H. Hoffman's two out houses and a barn were moved about 200 feet, and the water was in 3 feet of Mrs. Hoffman's dwelling. The entire crop of wheat and hay on the place was lost and there will practically be no corn made. Mr. H. P.Holler lost his wheat crop. Water was up in his barn and in 3 feet of his house.

I hope our county commissioners will issue bonds at once sufficient to replace the bridges in the county. Then the member of the next Legislature can pass an act covering the same. By so doing employment can be given many men and teams now out of work. We must act speedily!

S. M. ASBURY.

EVERY EFFORT MADE TO GET OUTSIDE NEWS UNSUCCESSFUL.

The News-Herald Tried Unsuccessfully to Get Outside News But Morganton is Yet Cut Off Completely.

This special edition of The News-Herald was begun in the hope that last night communication could be established in some manner with Charlotte or Asheville and telegraphic news from the outside world be obtained to act as a substitute in the absence of daily papers on which our people have learned to depend. Every effort that could possibly be put forth was made without any success whatever. We had hoped to get through the Hickory Daily Record messages from Charlotte, but it was found that no connection at all could be made. The Record sent to Lincolnton but a message from Editor Farabee last night stated that they had to content themselves with local news exclusively.

We hope to get messages sometime tomorrow; in fact, we feel sure we can get them tomorrow night and another special edition will be issued tomorrow morning which we feel safe in promising will carry news from the out side world. We want to serve the community as best we can and shall do everything in our power to get for our people the best news service possible.

Manager Matthews, of the Bell Telephone, is sending out a squad of men this morning to work on the line between Morganton and Marion. It is said 31 poles are down at Bridgewater, but even at that we may possibly get in communication with Asheville late today.

Trainmaster Leonard was here yesterday and said probably a train could be put through from Asheville to Morganton by Wednesday noon.

AN EXCITING TRIP.

Mr. R. W. Pipkin made a rather exciting trip to Hickory yesterday afternoon. The shower about noon caused one of what are known as the Double Branches near Valdese to get up considerably. He decided he would not try to ford it and for part of the distance between Valdese and Connelly Springs his Ford traveled the railroad track. Mr. Pipkin says that as he came back he saw some unknown motorist who had not used his caution in the stream with the water above his wind shield and he making a desperate effort to get the machine out of the stream.

Mr. Pipkin made the trip to bring Judge Lane to Morganton, but in some way missed him and Judge Lane came by horse and buggy to Morganton. Judge Lane also had to use the railroad track as a highway.

Judge Walter Clark and Miss Eugenia Clark, of Raleigh, are spending several days with Judge Clark's daughter, Mrs. J. Ernest Erwin.

HOW THE MERCHANT

Can Encourage the Farmer and What the Farmer Can Do.

Mr. Merchant and Business Man you now have before you the greatest opportunity in your life to help your farmer friends. The fact that you have fallen is not what counts, but how you take it. There's no question but that the farmers of Burke county, and especially those on the water courses, are in a very distressful situation. The farmers as a rule are the easiest people on the face of the globe to become discouraged when a calamity such as the flood has befallen them. For this reason I am writing this insist on the business men to take an interest in the farmers and cheer them up just a little. In cases of this kind the initiative part of the farmer's mind fails to work. As a rule he simply gives up when he could go ahead and make good.

The writer lives on Johns river and has gone through conditions very similar to the conditions that now prevail on the river today. One of my neighbor's farm was in a way destroyed from a visionary standpoint and he made a bigger howl than a man that lost his fortune in a mind. He was almost heartbroken. It seemed that he was broken up, and to hear him tell it, you would think that there would never be another chance for him. We bought millet seed and sowed the lands that looked as if they were destroyed for that season, and the yield from the millet hay was something enormous. The neighbor was so discouraged that he could not be persuaded to spend a few dollars for seed to make a crop that would take the place of the crop that he had planted in the spring. He spent the summer growling about how nature had broken him up. That fall and winter this neighbor bought ton after ton of the millet hay that we had grown on the land that was seemingly destroyed by the overflow of the river.

Now there is still a chance for the farmers to grow a heavy crop of hay. If millet is sown by the first of August and even a little later it will make a very fair crop to take care of the live stock on the farm this winter. Peas and cane will also make a heavy hay crop yet this year. Sudan grass is one of the fastest growing grasses we have, makes an excellent hay, and will make a good crop sown as late as the middle of August.

Now I think it behooves the business men to take this up with every farmer they come in contact with, and not only cheer them up, but give them a little real advise in regard to getting them to sow some kind of crop to grow feed to take the place of that which was washed away by the river. In fact you should press the question so strongly upon their minds that they will go right home and do something. They can even make a good crop of forage by sowing corn for hay if they should be unable to get the seeds as I have named above.

As I have described above, will take care of the live stock till next spring, and if they will sow a liberal acreage in winter oats to be cut next spring for hay, will carry them far into the summer. Crimson clover and vetch will also make an early hay crop for next summer.

Now le; every business man in town get right in behind the farmers in the flood zone and make this proposition to them so strong that they will take right hold and make next summer one of our most prosperous years.

Opportunities are scarce in this world, and remember that a neglected opportunities never come back again.

There should be about 45 to 50 pounds of millet seed sown per acre.

Sedan grass should be sown at rate of 20 to 25 pounds per acre.

E. L. PERKINS,
County Agent.

PLANS FOR RELIEF.

In a Union meet held Sunday evening, July 16, on motion Rev. E. E. Williamson, a committee was appointed to devise ways and means of providing for the needs of those who suffered loss of the necessities of life by reason of the recent storm and flood. The following were chosen on this committee: Messrs. B. F. Davis, A. C. Kerley, E. M. Hairfield and J. Ernest Erwin. The committee was asked to meet Monday at 10:30 a. m.

The committee met at the appointed hour and elected Hon. B. F. Davis, chairman and treasurer, E. M. Hairfield, secretary.

After organization and a brief discussion of the situation E. M. Hairfield made the following motion which was passed:

Resolved, that a sub-committee of three be appointed to make full investigation and to ascertain, as nearly as possible, the damage done and loss sustained, and the actual needs to be met in specific and individual cases; and to report the same to the public meeting to be held in the Court House on Thursday evening at 8 o'clock.

The chair appointed the following committee: I. T .Avery, Chm., R. T. Claywell and E. M. Hairfield.

On motion of Rev. E. E. Williamson a Publicity Committee was named as follows: Rev. J. R. Williams, Rev. E. E. Williamson and Miss Beatrice Cobb, aided by the Boy Scouts.

On motion made by I. T. Avery that a Farmers' aid committee be appointed. The chair named on this committee, J. Ernest Erwin, E. L. Perkins, J. C. McDowell.

On motion offered by J. E. Erwin a committee on household needs was appointed as follows: Mesdames A. C. Avery, Jr., I. Lazarus, J. Ernest Erwin, H. L. Millner, W. A. Leslie.

Meeting adjourned.

B. F. DAVIS, Chm.
E. M. HAIRFIELD, Sec.

July 17, 1916.

WHAT WE HAVE BEEN ABLE TO LEARN FROM OTHER COUNTIES

In talking with the Hickory Record last night we learned that the Monbo mill in Iredell has been swept away. The old Turner mill is gone and the report is that the new Turner mill was submerged and damaged considerably.

Morganton people are especially interested in the last named mill, different individuals here owning $17,000 worth of stock in the mill.

Over 100 feet of the Lookout dam, near Statesville, is gone, and over 300 feet of the embankment was swept away.

All the bridges to Charlotte, the railroad, interurban and highway were demolished and it is impossible to reach Charlotte by any route.

In February 1917, German submarine attacks resumed.

In the two months before the official U.S. declaration of war, German submarines had sunk eight U.S. vessels, killing forty-eight Americans. It also had been revealed that the German foreign secretary, Alfred Zimmerman, was seeking Mexican help against the United States.

War was declared on April 6, 1917.

Congress passed the Selective Service Act and almost five million men were enrolled for military training. More than two million reached France after General Pershing was appointed head of the American Expeditionary Force.

Over there:

Saint-Mihiel.

Château-Thierry.

Aisne-Marne.

Meuse-Argonne.

For the United States alone, there were 53,500 battle deaths.

For Germany, Austria-Hungary, Turkey, Russia, Britain, and France, combined casualties ran into the tens of millions.

The armistice agreement was signed on November 11, 1918.

(The *Denver Post*'s Armistice issue was printed on pink paper. The vertical lines of type, "War's Over" and "Surrender," were in bright red ink.)

The Des Moines Register

(Formerly The Register and Leader)

OL. 68, NO. 280. DES MOINES, IOWA, FRIDAY MORNING, APRIL 6, 1917.—FOURTEEN PAGES. TWO CENTS

EXTRA!

HOSTILITIES ARE BEGUN

FIRST ACT OF WAR BY UNITED STATES SEIZURE OF INTERNED GERMAN SHIPS

WASHINGTON, D. C., April 6.—It is understood hat orders for the seizure of all German ships in merican ports went out this morning immediately pon the passage of the war resolution by the house. The vessels will be held for the present as a measure of afety. So far there has been no decision as to whether the government shall take them over and pay for them fter the war.

BOSTON, April 6.—Five German steamships which ave been in refuge at this port were ordered seized nd their crews dispossessed by Collector of the Port dmund Billings early today. The vessels taken over re the Amerika and Cincinnati, passenger ships, and he Wittekind, Koln and Ockenfels, freight steamers.

NEW LONDON, Conn., April 6.—The North German Lloyd steamer, Willehad, which came here from oston last August in order that accommodations ight be provided for the members of the crew of the erman merchant submarine, Deutschland, was ordered ized this morning by Collector of the Port James A. cGovern.

BALTIMORE, Md., April 6.—Three German steamhips the Rhine, Nekar and Bulgaria were ordered eized at this port this morning. United States marshal, ssisted by a company of national guardsmen, have oarded the vessels.

EXICANS MARCH ON BORDER

arranza Troops Start General Movement Northward.

EL PASO, Texas, April 5.—De facto troops in the states of Nuevo Leon, Coahuila and Chihuahua have begun a general movement toward the American border, according to highly reliable information received here tonight. The movement in these three border states has been officially reported to Washington and is being watched closely.

In Chihuahua a movement is being made in a northwesterly direction by General Murguia's troops, the reason given by Carranza officials being that it is an offensive campaign against Villa.

Reports have already been received here that Francisco Villa's men were closer to the border than had been thought.

A Villa courier arrived today from the field with information from Villa. He crossed the border at Marfa, Tex., east of El Paso, and expected to start late tonight on his return to rejoin his command. He refused to reveal the location of the main Villa command. He derried, however, that any Germans were with the Villa forces. ...res was said to be Villa's objective.

FRENCH SOLDIERS CHEER U. S.

Wilson's Speech Arouses Great Enthusiasm.

(From a Staff Correspondent of The Associated Press.)

BRITISH FRONT IN FRANCE, Wednesday, April 4.—The soldiers who are facing the Germans in the front line did not learn until this evening of President Wilson's address to congress foreshadowing the entry of the United States into the war. Even the most distressing weather conditions, with heavy snow, did not check their enthusiasm.

American volunteer aviators who have earned the high esteem of the French fighters with whom they have been in service for many months, and members of the American ambulance units, who are encountered on every part of the front, were cheered enthusiastically.

President Wilson's decisive utterance was almost the sole topic of conversation among the soldiers tonight. It was felt that in addition to furnishing war supplies the United States could give invaluable assistance to the allies by sending specialists in all branches in which that country is pre-eminent and undertaking organization of railroads and other transport behind the lines.

British Cabinet Officer Welcomes America As Ally

BY THE RT. HON. ARTHUR HENDERSON.

Member of the British War Cabinet.

(Special Cable to The Register.)

LONDON, April 5.—Since the outbreak of the war in the fateful month of August, 1914, the mass of the people in this country, no matter to what class of the community they belonged, have regarded the conflict as one waged by the powers of humanity and justice against the domination of an overweaning minority, who would lead the bulk of their fellow countrymen to believe in the omnipotence of force in the world war wherein we have now been engaged for nearly three years.

It has been looked upon here as essentially a war of democracy against tyranny.

That being so, we have watched with the greatest interest the attitude of the United States of America has adopted in the various stages of the struggle. We have seen their notes flouted by the enemy, their intentions deliberately misunderstood, the rights of their citizens ridiculed and their liberties destroyed.

Not only that, but we have seen that American citizens can no longer rely upon their rights as members of a neutral nation to preserve them from outrages perpetrated by an unscrupulous belligerent.

Now that it has been decided that the United States will take part in the efforts which the allied nations—now happily in the pursuit of true democracy—are making to bring the struggle to a victorious conclusion, we can welcome our comrade nation whose patience and forbearance in the past will, we are confident, be matched in the future by its loyalty, courage and devotion to the cause of international liberty.

In the closest co-operation, the free democracies of Europe and America must continue to struggle with courage and determination until the greatest menace to the peace of the world has been destroyed, and replaced by a league of those sufficiently powerful to enforce peace.

British Want Chance to Cheer American Troops

LONDON, April 5.—The Spectator, discussing the military aspect of American intervention into the war, appeals for the immediate dispatch of a small American force to this side as a "visible pledge and bond of union."

"A single brigade would be enough," it says. "We venture to say that if an American brigade marched through the streets of London before re-embarking for France our houses would almost crack with the cheering."

NEW PEACE BAIT IS PUT OUT BY AUSTRIA ACTING FOR KAISER

BY JOHN CALLAN O'LAUGHLIN.

(Special to The Chicago Herald and Des Moines Register)

WASHINGTON, D. C., April 5.—I am informed on high authority that Austria-Hungary, through her embassy in Washington, is about to present a peace proposal to President Wilson.

The proposal contemplates the opening of negotiations with all the belligerents with a view to securing a durable peace.

It is suggested in connection with the proposal that the president should play a prominent part in bringing the warring nations to the council table. There is no intention that he shall act as mediator—the United States now is regarded as an enemy by Germany and as having precisely the same status as Great Britain, France, Italy, Russia and Japan.

No offers as a basis of peace are said to be contained in the proposal.

Germany does not appear as one of the responsible principals in urging peace. She is, according to the statement of the president, in a state of war with this country and formal proclamation to this effect will be made tomorrow.

Therefore, Germany has used her ally to sound out the United States. As the proposal contains no guarantees, according to the information in the possession of the authorities here, it is not likely to be accepted by the president or referred to the governments at London, Paris, Petrograd, Rome and Tokio.

The object of the proposal is believed to be that which has been apprehended for some time—division in American counsels. In spite of the fact that the United States is at war with Germany, the Teutonic governments are hopeful of moving in such fashion as to make ineffective American aid to the allies. By constantly harping on peace, they hope to encourage the pacifists and thereby prevent the dispatch of troops to Europe and make half hearted American participation in the war.

From the Teutonic point of view, peace should be more acceptable today to the allies than has been the case hitherto. It is asserted that the Russian revolution has tremendously weakened the allied strength. Instead of the new government at Petrograd being stronger, or than that of the czar it is declared to be in fact weaker. Officers are said to be deserting their regiments because of the attitude of the men. It is claimed Russia can no longer be counted upon as an effective factor in the war. This claim is not justified according, to some authorities.

Nevertheless the situation in Russia does not make for effective military operation. Germany knows the situation as well as Great Britain and France do. If she should consider Russia no longer as a factor in the war, it will be possible for von Hindenburg to keep a thin line on the eastern front and to concentrate troops for an invasion of Italy. The coal situation in Italy is exceedingly acute, due to the operation of German and Austro-Hungarian submarines. Lack of fuel will seriously handicap the Italian troops, for it will be impos-

CONTINUED ON PAGE 2, COLUMN 4.

American Sailor Lost.

WASHINGTON, D. C., April 5.—Gunner Kopeiucci, one of the twelve bluejackets on the American steamer Aztec, sunk off the coast of France, was reported still missing in dispatches to the navy department today from Naval Attache Sayles at Paris.

U. S. GIVES ALLIES BIGGEST RESOURCES IN WORLD'S HISTORY

WASHINGTON, D. C., April 5.—Actual and potential resources which, all told, probably never have been equaled by any other nation in the history of the world, are brought into the great war under the American flag.

Into the balance against Germany are thrown a navy in strength and efficiency among the foremost afloat; an army comparatively small but highly efficient, backed by a citizenry of upwards of 20,000,000 capable of military duty; industrial resources incomparably the greatest in the world, already mobilized for public service; and the moral force of more than 100,000,000 Americans awakened to their country's peril and united behind their president with a patriotic ferver reincarnating the spirit of '76.

Nation's Destinies Secure.

Although much remains to be done, officials believe the nation's destinies are secure now, no matter how stubborn or prolonged may be the pressure of German militarism or how wide the scope of German intrigue.

The slowly maturing preparedness sentiment has borne fruit in military, naval and industrial preparations which already have put the United States on a defense basis not even hoped for two years ago.

The navy, always the first line of defense, has cleared its decks of antiquated incumbrances, has added new units modernized to meet German tactics, and the patriotic co-operation of ship and material makers is hurrying to completion other mighty fighting craft that will be the last word in power and efficiency.

Authorized but ten days ago to recruit to the full war strength of 87,000 men, the navy already has almost attained the total. To provide additional officers a class of midshipmen has been graduated three months ahead of its time.

A newly organized coast patrol of submarine chasers is on duty and hundreds of small craft to augment it are under construction.

Army preparations are less complete because of the uncertainty over what congress will authorize. The regulars, numbering nearly 120,000 and trained and equipped in a way which their officers believe matches unit for unit the boasted efficiency of Germany's best, are ready to respond overnight to whatever call may come.

Guard Now in Service.

The national guard, 150,000 strong and hardened by months of service at the border, already has many units in active service for police duty throughout the country and can be fully mobilized on short notice.

Without additional authorization by congress the regulars and guardsmen could be recruited to a combined strength of 400,000 and detailed plans for whatever larger army may be authorised have been made and large quantities of equipment purchased for it.

Industrial preparations have produced a great compact scheme of national resources with almost unlimited possibilities. The council of national defense, in daily conferences with the nation's leading financial, commercial, scientific and labor chiefs, not only has worked out a definite and detailed industrial mobilization plan, but has secured the indorsement and pledges of the men which can put it into effect at a moment's notice, bringing to the military arms of the service the full resources of the nation.

For military reasons only a small part of the detail of these preparations has been made public. It

CONTINUED ON PAGE 2, COLUMN 6.

THE NEW RECRUIT

STARS AND STRIPES DISPLAYED IN PARIS

PARIS, April 5.—This was America's day in France. Besides the parliamentary manifestation and the great display of the Stars and Stripes throughout the capital, the municipal councils met in cities both large and small and passed resolutions acclaiming the United States.

The crowded subway cars were more animated than at any time since the war began with general conversation about the new American ally. Knots of soldiers and civilians in front of all cafes and at all street corners discussed the great event with manifest satisfaction. Newspapers containing American developments were eagerly purchased.

The appearance of the American flag at windows in different parts of the city multiplied rapidly as the day advanced and soon the available supply was exhausted.

Extraordinary scenes of enthusiasm for the United States were witnessed in both houses of parliament. Not since the historic session of Aug. 4, 1914, has there been a parallel.

Alexandre Ribot, the venerable premier, arose immediately after the chamber came to order and began an address in solemn and impressive tones to the silent assemblage which filled every part of the house. The deputies listened with unbroken attention until the first mention of the United States. At first there was a decorous clapping of hands and then the whole house spontaneously arose, cheering for the United States and President Wilson.

The American ambassador, William G. Sharp, was in the diplomatic gallery. The deputies turned toward him and the demonstraton continued. The ambassador stood up and bowed and the cheering was redoubled.

Premier Ribot continued his address but almost every phrase was interrupted by applause. Mr. Sharp was again obliged to rise and acknowledge an ovation when the premier said, "The United States wishes neither conquest nor com-

CONTINUED ON PAGE 2, COLUMN 4.

TEUTONS CUT WILSON SPEECH

Strike Out Reference to Conduct of German Agents.

COPENHAGEN, April 5.—The German public, to the present, has had no opportunity to hear the full story of the reasons leading up to the entry of the United States in the war, as only condensed and expurgated versions of President Wilson's message appeared in German newspapers yesterday under headings indicating that this was virtually the complete text.

This in part is apparently due to the fact that the first versions of the speech telegraphed from England to neutral countries on the continent on Tuesday were sharply condensed, whole sections having been eliminated, particularly from the latter part of the message.

But a comparison of this tabloid of the speech received in Copenhagen with that published in Berlin shows that the German censor's pencil had been vigorously employed to strike out reference to the conduct of German agents which constitutes one of the main items of President Wilson's indictment of the autocratic German government.

FINE CONGRESSMANELECT

Convicted of Corrupt Practices in Election.

PITTSBURGH, April 5.—O. D. Bleakley, republican congressman elect from the twenty-eighth Pennsylvania district was sentenced in the United States District court here today to pay a fine of $800 and costs for violating the corrupt practices act by spending more than $5,000 in his election.

He was indicted by a federal grand jury in Erie last week. Congressman Bleakley announced today that he had resigned his seat.

EXPLOSION KILLS FOUR

Another Missing and Sixty-seven Hurt in Chicago Accident.

CHICAGO, April 5.—Four persons were killed, a fifth is missing and sixty-seven were injured by an explosion in a one story brick building in North Halsted street today.

The structure, occupied as a restaurant, was fairly occupied by patrons at the time of the explosion, which is believed to have resulted from leaking gas in the basement. It was said tonight that several deaths might result among those most severely injured. Search of the ruins has not been completed.

THREE FROM IOWA VOTE AGAINST WAR

WASHINGTON, D. C., April 5. Special. The Iowa delegation in the house aligned tonight 8 to 3 in favor of the war resolution. Those who came out for it this evening prior to the voting were Towner, Green, Good, Dowell, Kennedy, Scott, Sweet and Ramseyer. Those opposing it included Woods, Hull and Haugen.

Representative Hull in a speech declared strongly against the resolution. He said until war was declared, it was not disloyalty for a member of congress to stand by the people. He declared the vast majority of the people were against it. He referred to the "mad cry of the minority who are drowning the voice of the majority."

Says It Is Railroaded.

"An awful mistake," was Mr. Hull's characterization of the war. He said one reason he opposed the resolution was the manner in which it was being railroaded through congress at the dictates of one man, meaning the president.

"It is dangerous to plunge a free people into an unpopular war," said he, "but if war comes I pray God that the United States may fight with all its might through to victory."

Mr. Ramseyer, though bitterly opposed to the war policy, said this evening he had concluded to vote for the resolution. Though he would seek to amend it, he pointed out the country had been in a sort of a limited war for weeks. He gave out this statement:

Would Make the Rich Pay.

"I favor billions for defense but not one cent for European alliances; general training for our national defense, but not one American soldier for the European trenches. Profit must be taken out of war, therefore all incomes above a certain limited per cent after making allowances for local and state taxes, expenses and reasonable salaries, should be taken in this emergency by the national government as taxes. Each generation should pay for its own wars."

THE WEATHER TODAY

WASHINGTON, D. C., April 5.—Following is the official forecast of the United States weather bureau:

Iowa—Fair and somewhat ... or Friday; Saturday unse... probably showers and ... por...

CONGRESSMEN PAS... WAR RESOLUTION... VOTE OF 373 T...

Ballot Taken at 3 o'clock ... Seventeen Hours ... Hot Debate

...tween the United States and Germany, ... senate, passed ... ly after 3 o'clock ... by a vote of 373 ...

President Wilson ... the resolution ... President Marshall ... tached his signature ... ate.

It formally declares ... of belligerency forced ... man aggression and ... izes and directs the president to employ the military and ... forces and all the resources of the nation to bring war against Germany to a successful termination.

Without roll calls the house rejected all amendments, including proposals to prohibit the sending of any troops overseas without congressional authority.

Passage of the resolution followed seventeen hours of debate. There was no attempt to filibuster, but the pacifist group, under the leadership of Democratic Leader Kitchin, prolonged the discussion with impassioned speeches declaring conscience would not permit them to support the president's recommendation that a state of war be declared.

Miss Rankin of Montana, only woman member of congress, sat through the first roll call with bowed head, failing to answer to her name, called by the clerk.

On the second roll call ... rose and said in sobbing ... "I want to stand by my country, but I cannot vote for ...

For a moment ... ...

WORLD AT PEACE

WAR'S OVER

SURRENDER

FLAMING BATTLE FRONTS SILENCED AT 11, PARIS TIME

(By Associated Press.)

WASHINGTON, Nov. 11.—The greatest war in history ended Monday morning at 6 o'clock, Washington time, after 1,567 days of horror, during which virtually the whole civilized world has been convulsed.

Announcement of the tremendous event was made at the state department at the capital at 2:45 o'clock Monday morning, and in a few seconds was flashed thruout the continent by the Associated Press.

The terse announcement of the state department did not tell anything of the scene at Marshal Foch's headquarters at the time the armistice was signed. It was stated, however, that at 6 o'clock, Paris time, the signatures of Germany's delegates were fixed to the document which blasted forever the dreams which embroiled the world in a struggle which has cost, at the very lowest estimate, 10,000,000 lives.

ARMISTICE TERMS MAKE HUN PAY FOR EACH DROP OF BLOOD

Left Bank of Rhine to Be Held by Allies, Great Part Of Hun Fleet Seized, All Territory Evacuated In 14 Days and Sufferers Indemnified.

Following in brief are the terms of the armistice as announced by President Wilson Monday afternoon in an address to congress:

German armies to evacuate France, Belgium, Alsace-Lorraine and Luxemburg within fourteen days.

German armies must evacuate left bank of Rhine, that territory to be administered by allies.

In connection with the evacuation of the left bank of the Rhine it is provided that the allies shall hold the crossings of the river at Coblenz, Cologne and Mayence, together with bridgeheads in a thirty-kilometer radius.

The right bank of the Rhineland, that occupied by the allies, is to become a neutral zone and the bank held by the Germans is to be evacuated in nineteen days. The armistice is for thirty days, but the president spoke of the war as "coming to an end."

Germany must surrender 160 submarines, 50 destroyers, six battle-cruisers, ten battleships, eight light cruisers and other miscellaneous ships.

Among the financial terms are restitution for damage done by the German armies; restitution of the cash taken from the national bank of Belgium and return of gold taken from Russia and Rumania.

The military terms include the surrender of 5,000 guns, half field and half light artillery; 30,000 machine guns, 3,000 flame throwers and 2,000 aeroplanes.

(Turn to Page 16—Col. 1.)

POST BOMBS CRASH NEWS OF GREATEST DAY THRU DENVER

(By LUTE H. JOHNSON.)

At 12:45 the flash came; the armistice was signed.

At 12:46 the first bomb went up from The Post. It cracked upon a sleeping Denver.

Denver woke up. As bomb followed bomb citizens tumbled from their beds; hotels began emptying their rooms into the corridors.

Peace!

At 12:47 the cry of the newsboy was heard on the streets.

"The War Is Over!"

It was the headline of the first Post extra; it became the cry of the waking city.

At 12:48 a bareheaded man came running. He stopped at The Post window and whispered as a prayer: "The war is over." His boy is in France.

In five minutes from downtown hotels and sleeping apart-

(Turn to Page 7—Col. 1.)

TEUTONIC MONARCHS BURIED AMID RUINS.

When the war began the Teutonic alliance was headed by two of the proudest houses in history—the Hohenzollerns and the Hapsburgs. Today, William II, of Germany, is a fugitive in Holland and Charles I, of Austria, while he still may be in his country, has been stripped of power and has seen his empire shattered. Ferdinand of Bulgaria, another of the rulers in the Teutonic combination, has fled from his country and Mohammed V of Turkey who also joined in the attempt of Germany to dominate the world, is dead, slain, it is said, by the hand of an assassin.

(By Associated Press.)

Washington, Nov. 11.—President Wilson issued a formal proclamation at 10 o'clock Monday morning announcing that the armistice with Germany had been signed.

PROCLAMATION ISSUED BY PRESIDENT WILSON.

The proclamation follows:

"My Fellow Countrymen:

"The armistice was signed Monday morning. Everything for which America fought has been accomplished. It will now be our fortunate duty to assist by example, by sober, friendly council and by material aid in the establishment of just democracy thruout the world.

"WOODROW WILSON."

The world war was ended at 6 o'clock Monday morning, Wash-

(Turn to Page 7—Col. 7.)

THE HUN IS DOWN

(By WALTER L. CHINNECK.)

BLEEDING Civilization wipes her righteous sword upon the cloak of Peace.

The greatest, the most portentious hour in the history of the world beats out its thunderous note today for all creation to hear, and its echo will reverberate thru all Eternity.

From a bondage worse than death, from shackles that sought to bind us heart and soul, from a burden that would have bowed us down into the very dust and mud churned up by Prussian boots, we stand today delivered. Generations to come will mark this as the birthday of their liberty and freedom—as the corner-stone in a new and glorious era of time.

THE HUN IS DOWN

[illegible] greatest vindication of Right over Might that History [illegible], has come to pass, and Civilization lifts her maimed [illegible] and swears a new allegiance.

[illegible] night of misery and anguish, unutterable for those [illegible] on the fronts of France and Belgium and Siberia, is eclipsed by the morning, and splendidly, magnificently breaks the dawn.

THE HUN IS DOWN

At our feet lies the monster that has assailed us with every bloody and treacherous design conceived in the brains of devils. What shall we do with this stinking yet terrible carcass of Prussia? Shall we resurrect it with forgiveness, with offers of new friendship; shall we staunch the black blood ebbing from its venomous heart?

Stricken now to the death, inert and bloody at our feet, what does it stand for, this beaten body of Prussia? You soldiers of the Great Republic who dealt this monster its mortal wound, kick the body over onto its back and look into that face, so full of lust, rapacity, Satanic greed, brutality! What said those cruel lips, now dripping with the slaver of death?

Here is what they said and would say again if aught could resurrect this shameful carcass of iniquity:

In the days of its might this monster cried thru the lips of its kaiser: "I am the salt of the earth."

(Turn to Page 3—Col. 1.)

LAST EDITION
FAIR AND WARMER
Sunrise, 6.24 Sunset, 4.34

THE INDIANAPOLIS NEWS

First Ten Months 1918 { Daily average circulation City and County...66,080 Grand Total...123,173

VOL. XLIX { NUMBER ... WHOLE NO. ... Entered as second class matter at Postoffice, Indianapolis, Ind. Issued six days a week. MONDAY EVENING, NOVEMBER 11, 1918. TWENTY-TWO PAGES {TWO CENTS} MAIL BY ZONES 4½c TO 90c A MONTH BY LOCAL CARRIER $5.20 A YEAR

FULL TEXT OF TERMS

FOURTH EXTRA FOURTH EXTRA

WITHDRAWAL TO LEFT BANK OF RHINE, AND SURRENDER OF SHIPS REQUIRED

Conditions Call for Reparation for Damage Done by German Army, Restoration of Money Taken From Banks of Belgium and Roumania, Repudiation of Treaties With Roumania and Russia and Surrender of Vast Quantities of Material.

HUNS CAN NOT RENEW WAR—WILSON

WASHINGTON, November 11.—The terms of the armistice with Germany were read to the congress by President Wilson at 1 o'clock this afternoon.

The strictly military terms of the armistice are embraced in eleven specifications which include the evacuation of all invaded territories, the withdrawal of the German troops from the left bank of the Rhine and the surrender of all supplies of war.

The terms also provide for the abandonment by Germany of the treaties of Bucharest and Brest-Litovsk.

The naval terms provide for the surrender of 160 submarines, fifty destroyers, six battle cruisers, ten battleships, eight light cruisers and other miscellaneous ships.

Vessels to Be Given Up.

All allied vessels in German hands are to be surrendered and Germany is to notify neutrals that they are free to trade at once on the seas with the allied countries.

Among the financial terms included are restitution for damage done by the German armies; restitution of the money taken from the National Bank of Belgium and return of gold taken from Russia and Roumania.

Surrender of Guns.

The military terms include the surrender of 5,000 guns, half field and half light artillery; 30,000 machine guns, 3,000 flame throwers and 2,000 airplanes.

The surrender of 5,000 locomotives, 50,000 wagons, 10,000 motor lorries, the railways of Alsace-Lorraine for use by the allies and stores of coal and iron also is included.

The immediate repatriation of all allied and American prisoners without reciprocal action by the allies also is included.

In connection with the evacuation of the left bank of the Rhine it is provided that the allies shall hold the crossings of the river at Coblentz, Cologne and Mayence; together with bridgeheads and a thirty kilometer radius.

Becomes Neutral Zone.

The right bank of the Rhineland, that occupied by the allies, is to become a neutral zone and the bank held by the Germans is to be evacuated in nineteen days. The armistice is for thirty days, but the President spoke of the war as "coming to an end."

German troops are to retire at once from any territory held by Russia, Roumania and Turkey before the war.

The allied forces are to have access to the evacuated territory, either through Dantzig or by the river Vistula. The unconditional capitulation of all German forces in East Africa within one month is provided.

Huns Become Prisoners.

German troops which have not left the invaded territories, which specifically includes Alsace-Lorraine within fourteen days, become prisoners of war.

The repatriation within fourteen days of the thousands of unfortun-

Continued on Page Fourteen.

ENTHUSIAM IN HOUSE WHEN PRESIDENT SPOKE

STATESMEN, DIPLOMATS AND JUSTICES CHEER.

TODAY AND APRIL 6, 1917

The Indianapolis News Bureau,
33 Wyatt Building.

WASHINGTON, November 11.—A happy, wildly enthusiastic crowd of congressmen, senators, supreme court justices, cabinet officers, diplomats and just plain citizens greeted the President today when he read to the joint session in the house a list of the terms on which Germany has surrendered to the allies.

In remarkable contrast to the serious-minded, grave and anxious audience that heard his demand for a declaration of war on Germany one year ago last April, today's audience was exhilerated to the last degree and tumultously proud of every single sentence that the President uttered.

Cheer after cheer rang out as the President enumerated one by one the drastic terms that the once military mad Germany was forced to submit to as a means to peace. Even the supreme court justices, ordinarily the embodiment of calm and sober thought, joined in the spirit of the occasion. Chief Justice White acted almost as cheer leader for the assembly.

Smiled, Rubbed His Hands.

Sitting directly in front of the President this veteran of the civil war smiled and rubbed his hands continuously and could hardly contain himself for joy.

"Bravo! Bravo!" he would call out as the President went on with his address.

The entire diplomatic corps of the allied and neutral nations hung on every word the President uttered, and it was remarked that even the neutral diplomats seemed to grow most enthusiastic over the end of the war and announcement of the terms imposed on Germany.

Charles E. Hughes occupied a seat on the floor and was an enthusiastic, if not more so, than the congressmen that surrounded him.

He cheered and applauded as loudly as any one and paid the most earnest attention to what the President had to say.

Major Fiorella LaGuardia, the New York aviator congressman, occupied a seat on the floor and led his colleagues in applause for the peace terms.

Wears Chrysanthemum.

Mrs. Wilson, becomingly attired in a dark suit and with a great yellow chrysanthemum on her coat, smiled and smiled at those around her and seemed to take immense delight in the ovation that was paid her husband. The President's daughter, Mrs. McAdoo, sitting next to Mrs. Wilson, entered into the spirit of the occasion and vied with the other women in the executive gallery in applauding the armistice terms.

Of all the times that President Wilson has ever addressed the congress, today's address was by far and away the happiest occasion. The President is always cheered and applauded when he addresses the congress, even if it is on a partisan mission that he comes. But today the applause and cheering were

Continued on Page Fourteen.

FOCH'S FAMOUS ORDER

LONDON, November 11.—Marshal Foch issued the following to allied army commanders today:

"Hostilities will cease November 11, at 11 a. m., along the French front.

"The allied troops will not, until further orders, go beyond the line reached at that hour."

INDIANAPOLIS SETS NEW JOY RECORD

Everybody Turns Out to Send Noisy News to Huns and William Hohenzollern.

STORES AND MILLS CLOSED

Only Work Performed Was Effort to Raise More Steam to Make a Greater Din.

GOVERNOR CELEBRATES

Governor Goodrich called on every one who could to suspend business and celebrate the great allied victory.

"While I have no authority to issue a proclamation making it a holiday, the Goveryor said, "let's us all stop and celebrate the triumph of our just cause."

The Governor then set an example and closed his office and went out to take as joyous a part in the celebration as his health permitted.

A new record for joy was set in Indianapolis today.

Never in the history of the city has the spirit of high carnival held such sway as since the hour the news came of Germany's surrender. Every noise-making device that ingenious Hoosier brains could invent began a mobilization in the downtown streets early and unless sheer fatigue calls a halt—well, nobody knows when calm will come again.

Bands, drum corps, cans, pans, bells, tinkling cymbals, circular saws, automobile horns, squawkers, guns, revolvers, torpedoes, whistles, trumpets, calliopes, accordeons, skillets, fire engines—everything that had anything louder than a sigh in it—participated in the outburst of American happiness. There was no formality. A fellow with formal ideas had about as much chance in that crowd as a snowball in a Turkish bath. Dignified business men melted into boyhood's happiest mood and marched beside the humblest man in his employ. Mary and John and the baby came downtown in anything that served for transportation. If the transportation were lacking—walking still was good! The idea was to get downtown!

Flag Venders Busy Merchants.

At every downtown corner flag venders reaped harvests. Men with toy balloons and squawkers also found their business better than $2.20 wheat. Every factory and shop turned loose its ten or its thousands of men and women. In the shops where women are employed the overall-clad females marched right out in their working clothes and joined in the victory-mad throng. Enthusiasts in office buildings tore paper into bits and sailed the confetti over the heads of the paraders. A giant Old

Continued on Page Fourteen.

AT TOMLINSON HALL

Under the auspices of the Church Federation of Indianapolis, a great mass meeting will be held in Tomlinson hall Tuesday night to give formal expression to the joy and gratitude in the hearts of all because of the end of the world war, according to an anonuncement by the Rev. Morton C. Pearson, secretary of the federation.

The hall will be open at 7:30 o'clock and until 8 o'clock The Indianapolis News Newsboys' Band will play. Governor James P. Goodrich will make a brief address. The Rev. O. W. Fifer will speak on "The Spiritual Element in the Great War." The Rev. O. D. Odell will give an address on experiences at Verdun and St. Mihiel. The Y. M. C. A. quartet will sing and a song service will be led by A. H. Godard, general secretary of the Y. M. C. A.

Thomas C. Day, president of the Church Federation, will preside.

HERE ARE THE SURRENDER TERMS GERMANS SIGNED

WASHINGTON, November 11.—The President spoke as follows:

"Gentlemen of the congress:

"In these anxious times of rapid and stupendous change it will in some degree lighten my sense of responsibility to perform in person the duty of communicating to you some of the larger circumstances of the situation with which it is necessary to deal.

"The German authorities, who have, at the invitation of the supreme war council, been in communication with Marshal Foch, have accepted and signed the terms of armistice which he was authorized and instructed to communicate to them. Those terms are as follows:

"I. Military clauses on western front:

"1. Cessation of operations by land and in the air six hours after the signature of the armistice.

"2. Immediate evacuation of invaded countries: Belgium, Francec, Alsace-Lorraine, Luxemburg, so ordered as to be completed within fourteen days from the signature of the armistice. German troops which have not left the above mentioned territories within the period fixed, will become prisoners of war. Occupation by the allied and United States forces jointly will keep pace with evacuation in these areas. All movements of evacuation and occupation will be regulated in accordance with a note annexed to the stated terms.

"3. Repatriation beginning at once and to be completed within fourteen days of all inhabitants of the countries above mentioned, including hostages and persons under trial or convicted.

"4. Surrender in good condition by the German armies of the following equipment: Five thousand guns (2,500 heavy, 2,500 field), 30,000 machine guns, 3,000 minnewerfer, 2,000 airplanes (fighters, bombers—firstly D, seventy-three's and night bombing machines). The above to be delivered in Simmstu to the allies and the United States troops in accordance with the detailed conditions laid down in the annexed note.

"5. Evacuaton by the German armies of the countries on the left bank of the Rhine.

"These countries on the left bank of the Rhine shall be administered by the local authorities under the control of the allied and United States armies of occupation. The occupation of these territories will be determined by allied and United States garrisons holding the principal crossings of the Rhine, Mayence, Coblenz, Cologne, together with bridgeheads at these points in thirty kilometer radius on the right bank and by garrisons similarly holding the strategic points of the regions. A neutral zone shall be reserved on the right of the Rhine between the stream and a line drawn parallel to it forty kilometers to the east from the frontier of Holland to the parallel of Gernsheim and as far as practicable a distance of thirty kilometers from the east of the stream from this parallel upon Swiss frontier.

"Evacuation by the enemy of the Rhine lands shall be so ordered as to be completed within a further period of eleven days, in all nineteen days after the signature of the armistice. All movements of evacuation and occupation will be regulated according to the note annexed.

"6. In all territory evacuated by the enemy there shall be no evacuation of inhabitants; no damage or harm shall be done to the persons or property of the inhabitants. No destruction of any kind to be committed. Military establishments of all kinds shall be delivered intact as well as military stores of food, munitions, equipment not removed during the periods fixed for evacuaton. Stores of food of all kinds for the civil population, cattle, etc., shall be left in situ. Industrial establishments shall not be impaired in any way and their personnel shall not be moved. Roads and means of communication of every kind, railroad, waterways, main roads, bridges, telegraphs, telephones, shall be in no manner impaired.

"7. All civil and military personnel at present employed on them shall remain. Five thousand locomotives, 50,000 wagons and 10,000 motor lorries in good working order with all necessary spare parts and fittings shall be delivered to the associated powers within the period fixed for the evacuation of Belgium and Luxemburg. The railways of Alsace-Lorraine shall be handed over within the same period, together with all prewar personnel and material. Further material necessary for the working of railways in the country on the left bank of the Rhine shall be left in situ. All stores of coal and material for the upkeep of permanent ways, signals and repair shops left entire in situ and kept in an efficient state by Germany during the whole period of armistice. All barges taken from the allies shall be restored to them. A note appended regulates the details of these measures.

"8. The German command shall be responsible for revealing all mines or delay acting fuses disposed on territory evacuated by the German troops and shall assist in their discovery and destruction. The German command shall also reveal all destructive measures that may have been taken (such as poisoning or polluting of springs, wells, etc.), under penalty of reprisals.

"9. The right of requisition shall be exercised by the allies and the United States armies in all occupied territory. The upkeep of the troops of occupation in the Rhineland (excluding Alsace-Lorraine) shall be charged to the German government.

"10. An immediate repatriation without reciprocity according to detailed conditions which shall be fixed, of all allied and United States prisoners of war. The allied powers and the

Continued on Page Thirteen.

NOVEMBER DRAFT CALL CANCELLED

President Orders Provost Marshal-General Crowder to Take Action.

300,000 MEN ARE AFFECTED

Outstanding Calls Stopped, Holding Up Movement of 252,000 During Next Five Days.

WASHINGTON, November 11.—By order of President Wilson Provost Marshal-General Crowder today directed the cancelation of all outstanding draft calls, stopping the movement during the next five days of 252,000 men and setting aside all November calls for more than 300,000 men.

A small number of men in eastern states started entraining at 6 a. m. today for cantonments under the calls, and the cancellation comes too late to affect their status. They will be regarded as in the army until demobilized. Men not entrained, whether specially inducted or assembled by general call, for whom the day and hour of service has been set by draft boards, will be regarded as honorably discharged, and so paid.

Calls for the navy and marine corps are not affected by the cancellation, and entrainments of men for these services will continue as ordered. Draft boards will continue classification of registrants of September 12.

Secretary Baker later announced that so far as practical, all men who have been called and who have not completed their training will immediately be turned back to civilian life.

Orders Sent to Boards.

Telegrams to the more than 4,500 odd local draft boards, canceling the calls were prepared two days ago, at General Crowder's orders, and only the word of the general staff was needed to release them. The draft executive has been urgent in recommending the suspension

Continued on Page Nineteen.

LIGHTLESS ORDER IS SUSPENDED FOR NIGHT

GARFIELD MAKES EXCEPTION TO RULE.

FOR VICTORY CELEBRATION

WASHINGTON, November 11.—Fuel Administrator Garfield today suspended the lightless night order for tonight only, for celebrations of peace throughout the country.

LIGHTLESS NIGHTS NO MORE.

Instructions Sent to Fuel Administrators By Woollen.

The federal lightless night ruling as it applies to Indiana is discontinued. Instructions were sent to county fuel administrators in the state by Evans Woollen, state fuel administrator. He announced that the federal fuel administrator had told him to use his discretion in the matter of continuing the ruling and he had determined to discontinue the practice. However, light produced by fuel must not be used extravagantly or wastefully for outdoor illumination, he said.

The order, as it applied to Indiana, provided that on Monday and Tuesday nights of each week no outdoor sign lights nor window display lights should be burning.

ANOTHER PRESIDENT.

Professor Masaryk Made Head of Czecho-Slovak Republic.

WASHINGTON, November 11.—Prof. Thomas G. Masaryk, president of the Czecho-Slovak national council, has been elected president of the Czecho-Slovak republic. News of his election was conveyed today in a message from the foreign minister of the national council at Paris, who urged that he proceed at once to Prague to take up his duties.

GOOD TIME PROGRAM

At 8 o'clock tonight, in Monument Circle, official celebration of the surrender of the Huns will begin, with the singing of the Doxology, the words of which follow:

Praise God from whom all blessings flow,
Praise Him all creatures here below,
Praise Him above ye heavenly hosts,
Praise Father, Son and Holy Ghost.

The singing will be accompanied by the chimes of Christ church and by a great band, made up of all the principal band organizations of the city.

Community singing, motion pictures and fireworks are a part of the program. From the roofs of all the buildings facing the Circle redfire pots will be lighted. Aerial bombs and skyrockets will be fired.

The celebration will end with the singing of "The Star-Spangled Banner" and the unfurling of the Stars and Stripes from the top of the Monument. There will be no speaking.

The meeting will be held under the auspices of the special committee appointed by Mayor Charles W. Jewett and the war camp community service.

PEOPLE'S MOVEMENT TAKES ALL GERMANY

Revolutionary Uprising Spreads Like Wildfire, With Berlin, Cologne, Leipsic and Other Big Cities in Control of Socialist Forces—Different States Proclaim Themselves Independent Republics, Following Example Set in Austria-Hungary.

INTERNATIONAL EMBLEM FOR EBERT

AMSTERDAM, November 11.—Emperor William, it is reported here, was on his way to the British lines to surrender, when he was headed off by German revolutionists and forced to seek safety in Holland.

COPENHAGEN, November 11 (by the Associated Press).—The revolution in Germany is today, to all intents and purposes, an accomplished fact.

The revolt has not yet spread throughout the whole empire but fourteen of the twenty-six states, including all the four kingdoms and all other important states, are reported securely in the hands of the revolutionists.

The twelve small states which apparently are not yet affected can not hope, it is believed here, to stay the triumphal progress of the Socialists.

LONDON (2:35 p. m.), November 11.—Field Marshal von Hindenburg has placed himself and the German army at the disposition of the new people's government at Berlin, says a dispatch from the German capital by way of Copenhagen.

The field marshal asked the Cologne soldiers' and workers' council to send delegates to German main headquarters at once. A delegation left Cologne this morning. Field Marshal von Hindenburg said he had taken this action "in order to avoid chaos."

LONDON, November 11.—With Berlin, Leipzig, Stuttgart, Cologne, Hamburg, Frankfort and many other cities in the hands of revolutionists, who followed the lead set at Kiel, when the red flag was raised last week, a soldiers' and workmen's council has taken over the government of the empire.

As in Austria-Hungary, different independent governments have been set up. Wuerttemberg, Schleswig-Holstein and Hesse-Darmstadt have declared themselves independent republics, following the action of Bavaria last Friday. Wilhelm II of Wurttemberg has announced he will not stand in the way of any movement demanded by a majority of the people.

The free cities of Hamburg, Bremen and Lubeck are ruled by Socialists. In the grand duchies of Oldenburg, Baden, Hesse, Mecklenberg-Schwerin and Mecklenberg-Strelitz the power of the rulers is gone. The grand dukes are conferring with delegates and promising all reforms demanded, but their thrones are tottering.

The grand duke of Oldenburg has been dethroned and the grand duke of Mecklenberg-Schweirin has abdicated, according to dispatches from Hamburg to Copenhagen. The Hamburg Nachrichten, which reports the abdication of the grand duke, says that a government for Mecklenberg has been formed by a workers' and soldiers' council.

In Berlin great street demonstrations took place Sunday, according to the Copenhagen correspondent of the Associated Press. The marchers carried banners with the inscription, "Freedom, Peace and Bread" and sang the workmen's "Marseillaise." The Socialist leaders, Goehre and Sudekum, who are officers in the landwehr, have issued an appeal to all officers not to provoke useless bloodshed.

Deputy Ebert and other party leaders have formed a committee of twelve men, representing the larger political factions, to facilitate co-operation with the soldiers' council. No German press comment on the situation has reached Copenhagen over the Socialist controlled wires, except a brief appeal by Germania, the Centrist organ, to the people to remember that the adoption of Bolshevism would mean continued war with the allies and misery for the people.

Germany's navy apparently is scattered into disjointed units, each seeking sanctuary in Danish ports or waiting in German harbors for the latest turn of events.

MAKEUP OF GOVERNMENT.

According to a Wolff bureau message, the Social Democratic party "invited the Independent Socialist party to enter the government with equal rights." A Copenhagen dispatch to the Exchange Telegraph Company said that in the new government there will be only three representatives for the majority

Continued on Page Thirteen.

1921

President Warren G. Harding proclaimed November 11 Armistice Day, a national holiday. The first burial ceremony was held at the Tomb of the Unknown Soldier at Arlington National Cemetery in Virginia.

These are excerpts from the Pulitzer Prize-winning account of the interment of the first unknown on that day. It was written by Kirke L. Simpson, the first AP reporter ever given a byline. The Pulitzer he won was the first awarded a news service writer.

By KIRKE L. SIMPSON
Associated Press Writer

WASHINGTON (AP)—Under the wide and starry skies of his own homeland, America's unknown dead from France sleeps tonight, a soldier home from the wars.

Alone, he lies in the narrow cell of stone that guards his body; but his soul has entered into the spirit that is America. Wherever liberty is held close in men's hearts, the honor and the glory and the pledge of high endeavor poured out over this nameless one of fame will be told and sung by Americans for all time.

Scrolled across the marble arch of the memorial raised to American soldier and sailor dead, everywhere, which stands like a monument behind his tomb, runs this legend: "We here highly resolve that these dead have not died in vain."

The words were spoken by the martyred Lincoln over the dead at Gettysburg. And today with voice strong, with determination and ringing with deep emotion, another president echoed that high resolve over the coffin of the soldier who died for the flag in France. . . .

U. S. Census, 1920—RICHMOND, 171,667

Weather Forecast: Rain tonight or Saturday; colder Saturday.
NEWS LEADER THERMOMETER AT NOON, 55.

News Leader Want Ads. Yesterday

HOME EDITION
Delivered By Carrier, 10c a Week.
MARKETS COMPLETE.

THE NEWS LEADER

EXCLUSIVE AFTERNOON ASSOCIATED PRESS REPORTS.

Circulation Yesterday
48,745
No Incomplete Extras Included.

NUMBER 7,635. Randolph 7 Calls The News Leader. 30 PAGES TODAY. RICHMOND, VA., FRIDAY, NOVEMBER 11, 1921. Delivered by Carrier, 10 Cents a Week. Single Copy, 2 Cents

LAY HERO TO REST WITH HIGHEST HONORS

NATION'S CHIEFS WALK BEHIND UNKNOWN'S BIER; CHEER WILSON AS HE PAYS TRIBUTE TO DEAD

BUSINESS HERE HALTS; HONOR WAR'S HEROES

Silent Tribute to Memory of Richmond's Dead Paid as Armistice Hour Strikes on Third Anniversary.

As a silent tribute to the memory of those heroes who gave their lives for a victorious peace, RICHMOND virtually ceased all activity at noon today. The bells in every fire house began tolling at noon, and continued their peals for ten minutes, by order of Director of Public Safety Myers.

At five minutes to 12 the chimes of Centenary Methodist church rang out to herald the two minutes of silent prayer which was generally observed by the pople of RICHMOND at noon. In accordance with instructions issued by President Thomas S. Wheelwright, the master switches in the power house of the Virginia Railway and Power Company were pulled at 12 o'clock, halting all current on its lines and stopping every street car on the tracks of its system. The switches were held open for two minutes.

Telegraph Wires Stop, Too.

Simultaneously, the telegraph wires of the entire Postal and Western Union systems in this division were closed by special order.

What few industries were in operation today checked their work promptly on the stroke of noon, and hardly a wheel turned in all of RICHMOND for "the silent moment."

Even motor cars drew to the nearest curbings and cut their engines in respect to the proclamation of President Harding that the dead of the American and allied forces be thus honored. The "Armistice Angelus" was heard in every section of the city.

R., F. and P. Trains Halt.

At noon all trains of the Richmond, Fredericksburg and Potomac, Atlantic Coast Line, Chesapeake and Ohio, Norfolk and Western and the Seaboard Air Line railroads stood still for two minutes in memory of the American soldiers who made the supreme sacrifice.

Eppa Hunton Jr., president of the R., F. and P., in an Armistice Day message to the employes of the road, said:

"It is suggested that we offer thanks to Almighty God for these and other blessings, and pray that He make us as steadfast and sincere in peace as were those who gave their lives for the preservation of civilization, to the end that when the King of Glory calls the sleeping hosts from the dust we may meet with clean hands and the knowledge of duty conscientiously performed."

Memorial Tribute.

At the city auditorium at 2:15 o'clock thousands of RICHMOND citizens will gather in a memorial tribute to the soldier dead and for a reconsecration to the principles of everlasting peace. The tears and anguish of the stirring war days are still fresh in the hearts of RICHMOND'S folk—the people here, like all of America, see no glory in war save the preservation of the ideals for which this city's sons gave their lives.

The principal feature of the Armistice Day celebration today will be the parade of young veterans of the world war, who at 1:30 o'clock will march from Capitol square to the city auditorium.

In the line will be many who have seen war in all its horror, and as they march by in the procession this afternoon the hearts of the thousands who line the sidewalks will swell with

LONDON HALTS WALK TO PAY HEROES HONOR

Great Throngs Fill Open Spaces With Bared Heads. Stillness Broken Only by Stifled Sobs.

(By Associated Press.)

London, Nov. 11.—On the stroke of hour marking the third anniversary of the armistice in the world war London today paused in a mute two-minute testimony to the nation's grateful remembrance of the victory and reverent tribute to the fallen.

A few minutes before 11 o'clock all vehicular traffic was diverted from Whitehall, Piccadilly Circus, Stock Exchange Place, Trafalgar Square and other public open spaces. Into these places corwded great concourses of people.

As the hour approached the throng joined in singing "O, God, Our Help in Ages Past," and then, at the sounding of maroons in the distance, imitating the booms of guns, hats were raised, flags went to halfmast and every head was reverently bowed in a stillness broken only by a stiffled sob from a woman here and there among the quiet masses. Throughout the city ever wheel had stopped turning at the signal, and all activities were suspended.

In the bustling financial district, just before the hour struck, the tapes ticked off the request: "Prepare to do honor to the glorious dead!" and here, as elsewhere, there was a total cessation of business.

Crowds Remain Motionless.

The crowds remained motionless until "God Save the King" was played. Then the whir of motors, the clatter of hoofs and the movement of pedestrians was resumed.

The observance of the day centered about the cenotaph in Whitehall where representatives of King George, Prime Minister Lloyd George and all the members of the cabinet, together with delegations from the dominions and other portions of the empire added wreaths to the hundreds already resting on the base of the empty tomb. Throughout the day lines of those who desired to pay tribute passed four abreast by the flower burdened monument.

Religious and other ceremonies commemorating the day were held throughout the country. In Westminster Abbey, a permanent slab hewn from marble found near the battlefield of Waterloo was placed over the body of the unknown warrior. The inscription upon it concludes with the words:

"They buried him among kings because he had done good towards God and towards His house."

WHITLER 'NOT GUILTY' OF DANVILLE MURDER

(Special to The News Leader.)

Danville, Va., Nov. 11.—A. A. Whitler was found "not guilty" by a jury at 12 o'clock last night of the charge of killing John R. Cassell, property owner, who had leased a house to Whitler.

Whitler, in his testimony, which was supported by that of his wife, said that Cassell went into the yard of the Whitler home and started a quarrel over the possession o fthe house. He also said Cassell attacked him with a hoe. In a fight, which ensued, Whitler used a razor, inflicting a wound in Cassell's throat, it was alleged.

Cassell insisted on being taken home, where he treated his wound. Blood poison developed and he died within a few days after leaving a local hospital.

HALF MILLION OFFERED FOR NEW MASON HOME

Acca Temple, Ancient Arabic Order, Nobles of the Mystic Shrine, will hold a business session at the Masonic teemplpe tonight at 8 o'clock. On Nov. 29, a ceremonial session will be held.

Reports are to be made tonight on the progress of the fund for a new mosque to be erected by Acca Tempple on the lot recently acquired at Laurel and Main streets. It is understood that approximately $500,000 has already been subscribed and that a building costing from $800,000 to $1,000,000 will be erected, containing an auditorium seating between 4,000 and 5,000 people.

SECRETARY OF WAR WEEKS PLACING WREATH ON BIER OF AMERICA'S "UNKNOWN HERO" IN NATION'S CAPITOL

—Copyright by Underwood & Underwood, N. Y.

ANDERSON ON VA. ELECTION

Defeated Candidate, in Statement, Says He Sees "Nothing Abnormal" in Tuesday's Democratic Victory.

Declaring that the Republicans have "sown the seed of the truth in the fruitful soil of the minds and hearts of the people, and can abide our time for in due season it will bring forth the fruits of freedom and reform," Henry W. Anderson, of RICHMOND, defeated candidate for governor, in Tuesday's election, today made public a statement, in which he says he sees "nothing abnormal in the results."

Asserting that his party entered the campaign "with no illusions either as to elections in Virginia or as to the sacrifices which the fight would entail," Mr. Anderson held that the Democratic victory was the "natural outcome of the political conditions which have prevailed in Virginia for years."

The Statement.

This statement, in full, reads as follows:

"A severe illness which has kept me confined to my bed since Sunday has made it impossible for me to consider the election results or anything else until today. The circumstances seem to call for a brief statement from me as to the election.

"I see nothing abnormal in these results. They are the natural outcome of the political conditions which have prevailed in Virginia for years.

"We entered this campaign with no illusions either as to elections in Virginia or as to the sacrifices which the fight would entail. We regarded the immediate election day results as of secondary importance; but thought then and think now that the larger ends in view fully justify the effort.

A Drastic Program.

"We proposed a very drastic program at Norfolk, both for the state and the Republican party. That program united the thoughtful people of that party as they have not been united for years, but it brought confusion and denial to others, and caused others, though not a material element, to leave the party entirely. This affected to some extent the immediate vote, but it placed the party on a sound moral and political basis and made it possible for it to become a great constructive agency for service to Virginia.

"So as to the state. The reforms

(Continued on Second Page.)

CROWDS CHEER WILSON AS HE APPEARS IN PROCESSION

Ex-President Makes His First Public Appearance Since Inauguration Day.

BY DAVID LAWRENCE.

(By News Leader's Leased Wire.)

Arlington Amphitheatre, Va., Nov. 11.—Three years ago to the hour the big guns on the western front stopped firing, and the world took count of the horrible toll of a great war. Today, as if by symbolic parallel, the president of the United States stood before the casket of America's unknown dead and preached a sermon of peace. The thought and inspiration of the moment conveyed by the president was that the living should not forget the sacrifices of the dead.

Mr. Harding, with deliberate significance, staged the armament conference to begin coincidentally with the ceremonies attending the burial of the unknown dead. He made it the great reminder of what have the war had wrought, the great reminder of what remains to be done to save the world from further destruction of human life.

Mr. Harding's formula for the future is as yet undefined. Today he gave expression merely to the principle of world concord. Tragically enough, there rode in the procession, behind the unknown warrior, another soldier, enfeebled and decrepit, who once rose to lofty heights as he, too, presented a formula for world peace—the league of nations—only to have it rejected at home after a historic political battle.

Outburst of Cheering.

Down Pennsylvania avenue rode the silent figure of Woodrow Wilson in the back seat of a victoria drawn by two horses. Twice had Mr. Wilson ridden thus through the main thoroughfare of the nation's capital, bowing right and left in response to the plaudits of two inaugural crowds.

Today's solemnity was, however, no exception. The hundreds of thousands of people who had stood in reverent silence while President Harding, General Pershing and the other notables trudged on foot behind the casket, gave vent to an outburst of cheering as the former president broke into view.

"It's Woodrow Wilson!" the crowd shouted, revealing both its surprise at his appearance on such a cold day and the commendation, too, for the rugged courage which made Woodrow Wilson defy a physician's advice and pay homage to the soldier whom he commanded to war.

Mr. Wilson wanted to participate. There was hesitation about inviting

(Continued on Sixth Page.)

WOODROW WILSON.

H. G. WELLS' FOURTH ARTICLE SATURDAY

In tomorrow's News Leader will appear the fourth article, in a series, by H. G. Wells on the armament conference. "The Unknown Soldier of the Great War" is his topic Saturday.

MAY ADOPT BABY LEFT BY WOMAN AT HOTEL

Members of the Employes' Welfare Association of Kaufmann & Company, Inc., will hold their second informal dansant next Thursday evening in the auditorium of the Jefferson hotel, 8:30 to 12 o'clock. From the number of invitations already issued, the affair will be largely attended. The association has arranged for a special orchestra to play for the dancing.

TOBACCO MEN GET $200,000

Checks Sent Today to Virginia Growers in Sun-Cured Association Who Pooled Crops for Selling.

Checks aggregating nearly $200,000 are being mailed out of RICHMOND today to approximately 900 tobacco farmers, members of the Sun-Cured Tobacco Growers' Association, representing their 1920 crop, which was pooled last fall because of the low prices, which, in some instances, were less than the actual transportation and warehouse costs of moving and selling the weed. At least $3 per 100 pounds were realized by holding the crop for more favorable conditions, J. H. Quisenberry, of Louisa county, president of the association, declared today.

The checks range from $1,800 to the largest grower to about $50 for small crops, and the growers are located pincipally in Caoline, Louisa, Hanover, Goochland and Fluvanna counties, although the association also has members in King William, King and Queen, Essex, Powhatan, Cumberland and Chesterfield counties.

About 12 per cent. of last year's sun-cured Virginia crop was pooled with the association, officers said today, and so successful was this system of co-operative marketing, made necessary partly because of the fact that fully 85 per cent. of the buying was concentrated in the hands of one buyer representing one of the largest companies in this city, that the pool will be operated again this year. Approximately 65 per cent. of the 1921 crop already has been signed under contract, and this is expected to be materially increased.

The executive committee which worked out the plan was composed of President Quisenberry, W. S. Garrett, of Goochland, secretary and treasurer; W. W. Green, of Caroline, and J. C. Stiles, of Ashland, Hanover county.

In RICHMOND, the tobacco was handled by F. D. Williams & Co., which concern acted as sales agent for the association.

P. C. WOOTERS STILL IN BED.

P. C. Wooters, who underwent an operation at St. Elizabeth's hospital, has been removed to the home of his sister. He is still in bed.

THANKFUL NATION BESTOWS ITS GREATEST HOMAGE ON GALLANT SOLDIER OF U. S.

President, Clad in Mourning, Walks With Gen. Pershing at Head of Procession. Minute Guns Boom Salute as Cortege Passes From the Capitol to Arlington.

[The text of President Harding's Arlington address will be found on page six.]

(By Associated Press.)

Washington, Nov. 11.—Laid to rest with all the honors a grateful nation could pay, the unknown hero from France was bivouacked among the [illegible] dead today in Arlington National cemetery.

The highest officers of the army and navy walked beside his coffin; [illegible] but the hands of gallant comrades of the great war laid hands upon it.

President Harding walked behind the bier to do him homage. Former President Wilson made his first public appearance in months; General Pershing turned aside an opportunity to ride and trudged beside the body to its last resting place.

Representatives of foreign governments reverently laid their highest military decorations on his casket, and with soil from France where he fell unknown, he was laid away.

Minute guns at Fort Myer boomed their continuous tribute as the funeral procession was passing from the capital to the great marble amphitheatre at Arlington, where the ceremonies were opened with the playing of the Star Spangled Banner by the marine band.

Walking in single file before the caisson, strode the highest officers of the army and the navy and the marine corps, generals and admirals, all, who are honored in their place as bearers for this plain soldier of the ranks, who died for the flag. They were headed by Major-General Harbord, deputy chief of staff, and first behind the casket walked President Harding, abreast with General Pershing, chief mourners in this funeral procession.

Clad in Mourning.

The president and the man who led the American armies overseas walked almost alone. Over toward the roped sides of the avenue, their aides moved in line, but the places these two held in the cortege as head of a mourning nation and head of the army was distinct.

The president was clad in black mourning dress with silk hat and walked step for step with General Pershing, who wore of his many war decorations, only the victory medal that every comrade of the war may wear.

An open carriage followed close on the heels of the group of valiant, young and old. It contained former President Wilson and Mrs. Wilson. It was the first time since he left the White House that Mr. Wilson has appeared publicly, and a spatter of hand-clapping ran along the crowded street as he passed with a cheer or two and shrill call of salute now and then to which he doffed his hat.

Row on row behind the carriage, marching to muffled drums, came the hosts of others gathered in honor of the dead. Veterans of the war between the states were in that line, group after group of the dead man's comrades at home or overseas in the great struggle, men from every state, from every patriotic society in endless rows, proudly walking to the grave of the nameless hero.

Pershing Walks On.

At the White House President Harding turned aside with the senators and representatives and judges, but General Pershing walked on behind the casket, Secretary Weeks and Secretary Denby joining him for the long road over the river to Arlington.

While the president was reviewing the procession, there came a moment's delay and he stepped into the street and shook hands with the medal of honor man. When former Presient Wilson passed in his carriage Mr. Harding saluted him by taking off his hat and the former president returned the salute. The crowd cheered. The revent silence all along the line had only been broken by handclapping and some cheers as the former president passed by. After passing the White House, Mr. Wilson's carriage turned out of the procession and drove him home.

It was Mr. Wilson's first public appearance since March 4, when he rode up Pennsylvania avenue with President Harding. The comment was heard in the crowd that the former president, long a sick man, looked better than many folk expected.

While the remainder of the procession was winding its way to Arlington, the great ampitheatre was filling with the guests invited to the ceremony. The body was to arrive there, according to program, at 11:15 o'clock.

Arrival at Arlington.

After winding its way between the long lines of a reverent multitude in the streets of the capital, the funeral procession toiled upon the long hill leading to Arlington, arriving at the main gates a little after 11 o'clock.

The invited guests long before had begun to assemble within the marble walls [illegible] looking the [illegible] capitol [illegible] in the haze of a fall day. The invited [illegible] including great chieftains of [illegible] were seated on the long rows of marble benches, and thousands [illegible] standing. Thousands more stood [illegible] side, or anywhere to merely be [illegible]

Just before 11:15 o'clock the [illegible] son bearing the flag draped coffin [illegible] ed up to the west entrance and [illegible] removed by the bodybearers, [illegible] ceded by the choir and the [illegible] was borne tenderly along through [illegible] west entrance around the right [illegible] lonade to the apse and was placed [illegible] the catafalque. The great audience rose and stood uncovered as [illegible] in followed by General Pershing, the distinguished officers of the [illegible] and navy as mourners.

Foreign Chiefs There.

Marshal Foch and his staff, in full uniform of the French army, blue coat and red trousers, came with all his war medals across his breast. General Jacques, Belgian [illegible] also came and the two strolled [illegible] the marble colonnade behind the boxes, exchanging greetings. General Diaz, of Italy, joined them during the wait. Together the three moved [illegible] the Japanese mission to a place in front of the stage, where the [illegible] lies.

Ambassador Geddes, in full [illegible] diplomatic uniform came, [illegible] visited the crypt below where [illegible] offerings for the dead from [illegible] king, waited with a guard of [illegible] officers.

Chief Plenty Coos, of the Crow Indians, attired in full war [illegible] feathered bonnet, furs and [illegible] variegated colors, was seated [illegible] platform, joining the group of [illegible] tinguished military leaders from [illegible] rope. Thus the uniform of the Americans took its place with [illegible] of its allied powers in the last [illegible]

A group of American Indians [illegible] appeared in the audience, [illegible] their beaded moccasins down the [illegible] and into their places.

Premier Briand, of France, [illegible] among the last to arrive.

With the party of distinguished [illegible] complete and the body of the unknown hero on the catafalque, the [illegible] waited for the arrival of President Harding.

Amplifiers Carry Song [illegible]

The first strains of "[illegible] Funeral March" had heralded the coming of the unknown to his [illegible] honors.

Far out among the trees [illegible] fort, the dull dun-color of [illegible] troops, had showed and marching [illegible] step to the throbbing, muffled beat of the drums, the marine band and [illegible] slowly out to circle the great [illegible] made to the entrance where the [illegible] plieed choir waited.

As the casket was lifted from the gun carriage the solemn chords of the hymn was joined by the deep [illegible] of the band. The choir sang "The Son of God Goes Forth to War" [illegible] the telephone amplifiers caught the chords and threw them out [illegible] land to the thousands standing [illegible] away as San Francisco.

Secretary Weeks came in with Secretary Denby and took his [illegible] master of ceremonies. [illegible] kept trickling in to the [illegible] through every entrance and [illegible] simple, bare, a hundred [illegible]

(Continued on Sixth Page.)

1923

In the summer of 1923, President Harding left on a cross-country trip. During a stopover in San Francisco on July 28, he was taken ill with ptomaine poisoning. Five days later, he died of a stroke.

Vice-President Calvin Coolidge became President, sworn in by his father, a local Vermont magistrate.

UY THE DENVER POST IF YOU WANT LATEST NEWS 12 TO 24 HOURS AHEAD OF OTHER PAPERS

THE DENVER POST

THE PAID CIRCULATION OF THE DENVER POST YESTERDAY WAS 140,420

EARLY MORNING **EXTRA**

DENVER, COLO., FRIDAY, AUG. 3, 1923

HARDING DEATH STUNS NATION
COOLIDGE TAKES OATH 2:47 A. M.
MRS. HARDING RALLIES BRAVELY

COOLIDGE SWORN IN BY FATHER WHO IS NOTARY PUBLIC; HARDING POLICIES WILL BE CARRIED OUT

[illegible], Vt., Aug. 3.—President Calvin Coolidge received the news of the death of President Harding [illegible] his own elevation to the presidency at ten minutes before midnight, standard time.

[illegible] Friday morning, the new president was sworn in by his father, John C. Coolidge, who is a notary [illegible] Coolidge leaves for Washington at 7:30, catching a train at Rutland for New York at 9:35.

[illegible] Coolidge received the first news of the death [illegible] Harding thru telegrams from George C[illegible] secretary to President Harding, and from [illegible] whose telegram [illegible] as the notification from Mr. Christian [illegible]

Coolidge heard the news of President Harding's death and his own [illegible] elevation to the nation's highest [illegible] from his aged father, who had [illegible] to take Secretary Christian's telegram from the [illegible]

(Turn to Page 2—Col. [illegible])

[illegible] Coolidge issued the following statement:

"[illegible] have reached me, which I fear are correct. [illegible] President Harding is gone. The world has lost a [illegible] good man. I mourn his loss. He was my chief [illegible] friend. It will be my purpose to carry out the [illegible] which he has begun for the service of the American [illegible] and for meeting their responsibilities where[illegible] may arise.

"[illegible] this purpose, I shall seek the co-operation of [illegible] who have been associated with the president [illegible] term of office. Those who have given their [illegible] to assist him, I wish to remain in office, that [illegible] assist me.

"[illegible] faith that God will direct the destinies of [illegible]."

[illegible] concerning the time when he would assume office, [illegible] said:

"[illegible] my intention to remain here until I can secure the [illegible] for the oath of office, which will be administered to [illegible] father, who is a notary public, if that will meet the [illegible] requirements. I expect to leave for Washington dur[illegible]."

[illegible] following telegram was sent to Mrs. Harding:

"Plymouth, Vt., Aug. 3, 1923.

"[illegible] G. Harding, San Francisco, Calif.:

"[illegible] offer you our deepest sympathy. May God bless you [illegible] you.

"(Signed) "CALVIN COOLIDGE,
"GRACE COOLIDGE."

[illegible] telegram announcing the death of the president was [illegible]:

"Palace Hotel, San Francisco, Calif., Aug. 2, 1923.

"[illegible] Coolidge, Plymouth, Vt.:

"[illegible] president died instantly and without warning and while [illegible] with members of his family at 7:30 p. m. His physicians [illegible] death was apparently due to some brain embolism, [illegible] an apoplexy.

"GEORGE B. CHRISTIAN, JR.,
"Secretary."

[illegible], Vt., Aug. 3.—(By Associated Press.)—Galvanized by Secretary Hoover, had hardly left the [illegible]

APOPLEXY STROKE ENDS LIFE OF PRESIDENT AT 7:30 THURSDAY EVENING

San Francisco, Aug. 3.—(By the Associated Press.)—[illegible]

The American people from coast to coast and from [illegible] their heads in grief, for their president was dead. [illegible] had brought renewed hope of recovery, death came [illegible] of cerebral apoplexy.

The end came instantaneously and without even a [illegible] to summon additional physicians [illegible]

[illegible]

[illegible] for the physicians to come quickly.

Brigadier General Sawyer, chief of the staff of physicians who have been attending the chief executive, [illegible] and the two nurses present, Miss Ruth Powderly and Miss [illegible], did all they could but it availed nothing.

The president had fought and won one victory against [illegible] but it appeared in a more insidious form and he lost the battle.

Great as was the shock to all who dwell under the American flag and to peoples in many lands, for Mr. Harding, by virtue of his office, his kindly and his lovable personality, had become a world figure, the great shock came to his wife, reading by his side. But she did not collapse.

"She was shocked, of course, and at first unable to realize that she had lost the husband who had made up all the interest in her life for so many proud and happy years," said General Sawyer later. "But there was no collapse, no hysteria. Just a brave rally to face her sorrows and the duties devolving upon her at this hour."

Mrs. Harding was standing the shock well early Friday but whether she could stand up under the grief that bore down upon her as the sad journey back to Washington is made was another question. Those who knew her best say that she will.

When dawn crept over the mountains and lighted up the Golden Gate Friday morning almost all of the arrangements for this trip—the saddest transcontinental journey in the history of the nation—had been made. The trip will be started about 7 o'clock Friday evening, and should end in Washington Tuesday morning. From that point the arrangements have not been definitely made, but it is expected that the body will lie in state in the rotunda of the capitol, where a sorrowing people have oftentimes before paid their last respects to the leaders and the heroes they have lost.

(Turn to Page 2—Col. 1.)

'THAT'S GOOD, GO ON; READ MORE' ARE LAST WORDS SPOKEN BY HARDING

San Francisco, Aug. 2.—(By the Associated Press.)—"That's good. Go on. Read some more."

These were the last words uttered by President Harding to Mrs. Harding.

Mrs. Harding was at his bedside reading aloud when she paused and looked at the president, according to Alfred Holman, San Francisco publisher and close personal friend of the president, who visited the sick room a few moments before the end came.

Mr. Holman told interviewers that the president's hand raised as he asked Mrs. Harding to continue reading. Instantly his expression changed. He was dead.

STROKE TAKES LIFE WHILE MRS. HARDING IS READING ALOUD TO CHIEF EXECUTIVE

Wife of the President Bears Up Under Shock With Remarkable Fortitude, Rallying to Face Duties And Sorrows Devolving Upon Her.

San Francisco, Aug. 3.—(By Associated Press.)—Mrs. Harding was as brave and strong after the end as she had been [illegible] the end. Altho not strong and still affected by her illness of nearly a year ago, she declared she could not break down, and she did not break down in the hour of her greatest grief.

The hastily summoned members of the president's cabinet, [illegible] by Secretary Hoover, had hardly left the room, which had become a death chamber, before the cry of newsboys telling the extras rose from the streets far below.

Mingled with those calls was heard the soft crying of a woman. It was not Mrs. Harding, tho for as much as she desired to give expression to the greatest grief that can come to a woman, she met the situation calmly.

Mrs. Harding was reading aloud to the chief executive an article entitled, "A Calm Review of a Calm Man," in which he was the man reviewed, when the stroke of apoplexy brought an end to his life, according to Mrs. E. E. Remsberg, sister of Mr. Harding.

Mrs. Harding Thursday night received Capt. Allen Buchanan, commander of the navy transport Henderson, on which the president sailed to Alaska and returned to the continental United States, who came to offer his condolence.

After the meeting, Captain Buchanan said:

"Mrs. Harding is a woman of remarkable qualities. She is bearing up with great bravery and courage."

Captain Buchanan said the sailors and marines on the Henderson would march without arms in the procession when the president's body is taken from the hotel tomorrow, beginning the trip to Washington.

"The ship will march every man of its personnel," Captain Buchanan said. "We could not do less for the commander-in-chief, particularly one who was as good as Mr. Harding was to us of the Henderson all the while he was aboard."

"Mrs. Harding has a firm grip upon herself," said Herbert C. Hoover, secretary of commerce, when questioned by interviewers as to her condition, as he emerged from the presidential suite.

Mrs. Herbert Hoover, wife of the secretary of the commerce department, was with Mrs. Harding almost continuously for hours after the president's death. She declared that the first lady was bearing up extremely well under the shock of the tragedy.

"Mrs. Harding is perfectly well," said Mrs. Hoover. "Of course she cries, but there is nothing like a collapse. She is going [illegible]

(Turn to Page 2 —Col. 1.)

BODY LEAVES SAN FRANCISCO FOR THE CAPITAL FRIDAY NIGHT

[illegible] to Pass Thru Cheyenne—Special Car to Be Lighted at Night and Two Soldiers and Two Marines to Stand Guard Over Casket.

San Francisco, Aug. 3.—The body of President Harding will [illegible] San Francisco on a special train at about 7 o'clock Friday [illegible] and go direct to Washington, by way of Reno, Ogden, [illegible] Omaha and Chicago.

[illegible] announcement was made Thursday night after a conference participated in by the four members of the president's official [illegible] San Francisco and was approved by Mrs. Harding.

[illegible] train will make no stops en route except those necessary for its operation. The body of the president will be borne in the rear car, probably the same in which he made the trip from the capital to the Pacific coast.

The car will be lighted at night and at all times two soldiers and two sailors, a part of a naval and military guard of sixteen enlisted men, will stand at attention guarding the casket.

The train will carry the presidential party as composed during the trip across the country to Alaska and also General Pershing, Attorney General Daugherty and Mr. and Mrs. E. E. Remsberg and family, Mrs. Remsberg being a sister of the president.

The body will not be taken from the hotel except to go direct[illegible]

(Turn to Page 2 —Col. 7.)

Death Bulletin Comes As Blow To Reporters Waiting At Sick Room

San Francisco, Aug. 2.—The newspapermen had an engagement with General Sawyer for 8 o'clock Thursday night. He was to tell them then of how the president was progressing toward recovery. In view of what he had said on prior occasions during the day and statements in two official bulletins, the newspapermen had every expectation that they would be able to record that Mr. Harding was one more step nearer the goal of recovery.

"There will be a bulletin," said one of the White house messengers gathered in the corridor of the presidential suite. In a few minutes copies of the bulletin, on thin white paper, were handed to the waiting reporters. Instead of informing them that the president's condition continued to improve, it gave them the astounding information that he was dead.

1925

From July 10 to July 21, 1925, in the small town of Dayton, Tennessee, world attention focused on a trial in which two of the nation's best-known attorneys debated whether the Bible or modern science offers the truth of mankind's creation.

The case involved a young biology teacher, John T. Scopes, who had been arrested for violating a Tennessee law that prohibited the teaching in public schools of "any theory which denies the story of the Divine creation of man as taught in the Bible. . . ."

The defense attorney was Clarence Darrow, the prosecuting attorney William Jennings Bryan. Scores of newsmen converged on Dayton, including H. L. Mencken, whose reporting of the trial became a classic of American journalism.

Scopes was eventually found guilty and fined $100, a verdict later overturned on technical grounds by the Tennessee Supreme Court.

Although generally unenforced, the Tennessee law remained on the books and was not repealed until 1967.

Bryan died of a heart attack a week after the trial.

Daily June Paid Circulation 160,782

The Des Moines Register

The Newspaper Iowa Depends Upon

CITY FINAL

VOL. 77, NO. 30. DES MOINES, IOWA, TUESDAY MORNING, JULY 21, 1925.—SIXTEEN PAGES. PRICE 3 CENTS

DARROW VS. BRYAN ON BIBLE

Scopes' Lawyer Puts Commoner on Stand As Witness

SAYS RAILWAYS DISCRIMINATE AGAINST IOWA

Wylie Declares Rate Increases Help the Chicago Jobbers.

The petition of seventy-three western railroads for a general increase of 11 per cent in all freight rates would, if granted, discriminate against Des Moines and other Iowa jobbing centers in favor of Chicago, Milwaukee and points east including cities as far east as the Atlantic coast, E. Wylie, freight commissioner of the Greater Des Moines committee, announced yesterday.

Mr. Wylie had just prepared a comparison table comparing present freight rates by classes with the proposed increases, distances from 1 to 500 miles, to be used when he takes part in the hearings on the petition of western roads which the interstate commerce commission has called in Chicago beginning Sept. 1.

The table discloses that the proposed adjustment and increase of freight rates ranges from eight per cent to increases as high as [illegible] cent. The bulk of the increases [illegible] are for intrastate short hauls [illegible] the highest increases asked for long hauls of carload lots [illegible] Wylie said yesterday, would [illegible] a hardship on Iowa jobbers and give eastern shippers a further advantage that they recently received when the interstate commerce commission reduced rates from Indiana to Missouri river cities and interior cities in Iowa.

Would Hurt Farmers.

...obbers in Des Moines, Waterloo, ...kaloosa, Ottumwa, Burlington, ...t Dodge, Mason City, Cedar ...pids, Red Oak, Boone, Dubuque, ...rton, Marshalltown, Grinnell ...other Iowa cities would suffer ...the increase, Mr. Wylie said. ...increase would be reflected in ...increase in the consumer cost ...the products which would add to ...burden on agriculture, which ...ady estimates, according to the ...erican Farm Bureau federation, ...$95,000,000 of the direct in...ase of $190,000,000 would be ...e by farmers.

To illustrate the effect of the ...oposed rates on Iowa jobbers, ...Wylie cited the change which ...uld result on articles shipped ...m Chicago in carload lots for ...tribution from Council Bluffs, ...d articles shipped from the Des ...ines jobbing center to a mer...ant in Council Bluffs.

The western trunk line railroad ...mmittee is authority for the ...tement that 50 per cent of the ...pping is done by carload lots, ...ich comes under class 5. He ...d the statement of E. B. ...yd, chairman of the commit..., in an oral argument made in ...ashington before the interstate ...mmerce commission in 1917 ...d said that a recent check on ...Boyd's figures, made in his ...ice, disclosed that the same fig...s hold good now.

"A check was made of the two ...ssifications in 1915, in detail, ...every item," Mr. Boyd said, ...d we find that in the official ...ssification 50.7 per cent of the ...al number of carload ratings ...found in the fifth class, and in ...western classification 50.6 per ...t of the carload ratings is ...nd in the fifth class."

...laim 64 Per Cent Increase.

The carriers' recent proposal ...rates between Omaha and ...nsas City on the one hand," ...Wylie said yesterday, "and ...cago and Milwaukee on the ...er hand, was to increase the ...sent fifth class rate of 41.5 ...ts per 100 pounds only to the ...ent of ½ cent, or up to 42 cents ...100 pounds.

Fifth class rates are sub...tially limited to full carlot ...vements and not made to apply ...such shipments as may be de...bed as jobbing or distributing ...pments that are made in less ...n carlots. Third class and also ...th class rates are especially ...resentative of charges made ...jobbing or distributing less ...n carload business.

The present third class rate ...m Des Moines to Council ...ffs is 29½ cents and the in...ased rate proposed being 34½ ...ts the added burden in the ...e is 19 cents per 100 pounds ...ch shows that the proposed ...third class rate for distances ...41 to 145 miles is 64 per cent ...her.

Figuring on the basis of the ...important fourth class, the ...posed increase in the Iowa ...e is 11½ cents per 100 pounds, ...in round numbers a proposed ...rease of 50 per cent.

This would mean that the Chi...jobber under the proposed ...rease would get his fifth class ...vement of carload freight from ...ago into Council Bluffs, to be ...re redistributed, for a rate ...½ cent greater than the pres... figure. But the interior Iowa ...ber, as illustrated by the dis...ce between Des Moines and ...ncil Bluffs, would have to ...y an increase, not of ½ cent ...100 pounds, but of 19 cents ...third class or 11½ cents on ...rth class, increases respective... of 64 per cent and 50 per cent ...pared with an increase of ½ ...cent for the Chicago jobber.

...ndits Get $[illegible] Payroll.

...uskegon, Mich., July 20 ...)—Two men in an automo... held up a messenger with the ...ey Foundry company payroll ...y and escaped with approx...tely $33,000.

Jardine Pledges His Support for Co-operatives

Sees Need for Leadership Among Farmers.

Philadelphia, July 20 (A.P.)—Secretary Jardine placed the support of the department of agriculture behind the principle of co-operation in an address today before the American Institute of Co-operation.

"It must be constantly kept in mind," he said, "that the problems confronting agriculture cannot be solved from the outside, but by the farmers themselves, who know the problems. This obviously does not mean exclusively farmers, although they must take the lead in co-operative effort for agricultural purposes.

"The principle of co-operation I consider to be so important not only to agriculture, but to the national life as a whole, that I am happy to place the United States department of agriculture at the service of this great movement.

Need for Leadership.

"The need for leadership was never greater than at the present time. Agriculture has just passed through a period of depression [illegible] While improvement has been made and the prospects for the future are encouraging, we must at the same time recognize the fact that much remains to be done to place agriculture on a satisfactory basis. We wish to prevent a recurrence of the conditions of 1921.

"The idea that co-operative organizations will eliminate middlemen was regarded by the secretary as a mistaken one, resulting largely from lack of information as to the services necessary to carry farm products from the producer to the ultimate consumer.

"The failures of co-operative associations, although the proportion of failures probably has been no greater than in other business enterprises, point to the need for a study of business methods. We find that, generally, co-operative associations are wrecked because of business mistakes — the same mistakes that have wrecked business concerns for hundreds of years. Insufficient capital, an insufficient volume of business, and poor management are the principal causes of failure. There is nothing in the history of co-operative failures which need cause discouragement. Rather an analysis of the mistakes of the past should contribute to the development of more sound and stable organizations.

Co-Operation Advantageous.

"It must be recognized that in an industry like farming, co-operation possesses certain distinct advantages over the older methods of trading in commodities. The agricultural co-operative takes the whole crop of its members. It tries to market this to the best advantage. It avoids depression of prices because it does not aim to buy the commodity at the lowest possible price and thus exert a bearish influence on the market, nor does it resort to the practice of dumping surpluses. Furthermore, in the co-operative organization we have a producers' agency, which permits of greater freedom of technical improvement, both in production and in distribution methods, thus benefiting society as a whole. Co-operation does not work only to the benefit of a producing class.

"As the need for supplemental statistics becomes apparent, they can be collected, in most instances, by the department and other agencies now engaged in this work. But all this statistical information must be interpreted and made available to the producers by the co-operative associations. I do not wish to minimize other contributions which the co-operative organizations have made and may make to agriculture. However, the opportunity for service they have in bringing about a more stable production is to me of prime importance.

Limitation Unnecessary.

"It should be made clear, at this point, that stabilization of production does not mean necessarily the limitation of production. It most assuredly does not mean a production smaller than is necessary to supply the wants of our own people. What we seek by stabilization is a condition of equilibrium, a condition that will avoid, first, wastes incident to the production of farm crops in excess of market requirements, and secondly, artificially high prices to an insufficient supply.

"A realization by leaders in the co-operative movement that co-operation is not merely a means for obtaining a better price for a single year's crop but that it is a means for gradually adapting production to market demands, for insuring less wasteful distribution, for reducing the spread between what the farmer receives and what the consumer pays, for aiding in the solution of agricultural credit problems as they arise, for improving the rural life of the nation, for insuring a better understanding of national and international problems—this realization, implanted by leaders and future leaders, such as I see before me, in the minds and hearts of the farm people of the United States, will do much to insure not only the success of co-operation, but increased prosperity and stability for the nation."

WAITING

COOLIDGE SENDS CHINA DEBT BACK

Wipes Boxer Indemnity Off the Slate.

Washington, July 20 (A.P.)—China's debt of $6,137,552, the final instalment of the indemnity for the Boxer outbreaks, was wiped off the slate today by the United States government.

The money will be used for educational purposes under direction of a board appointed by the Chinese government, made up of American and Chinese citizens.

President Coolidge, in remitting the debt at this time to the troubled nation, acted under authority granted by congress more than a year ago. The Chinese legation, taking note of the action today, declared it would go far toward further cementing the friendship of the two nations.

"The Chinese people," the legation said, "will never forget this act of justice and good will on the part of America. It is safe to say that the gratitude of the Chinese people for this generous act will not fail to manifest itself in various ways in the future relations of the countries."

The statement declared that twenty-four years ago, when the powers exacted the indemnity, "the American government protested strenuously against this unjust proceeding, but without avail," and that ever since it had maintained that the indemnity should be returned to China solely for that nation's benefit.

China's indemnity to the United States originally was fixed at $24,000,000, but congress in 1908 ordered a large part of it eliminated.

Patrolman Groff Is Ill.

Patrolman Gus Groff became ill yesterday while performing his duties in the downtown section and was taken to his home by a friend. He lives at 818 Eighth street.

The Weather Today

LOCAL—Probably fair today and tomorrow, not much change in temperature.

IOWA—Generally fair Tuesday and Wednesday; not much change in temperature.

ILLINOIS—Mostly overcast Tuesday with showers in south portion; Wednesday partly overcast, cooler in extreme north portion.

MISSOURI—Unsettled Tuesday, with showers in east and south portions; Wednesday partly overcast, but much change in temperature.

MINNESOTA—Fair Tuesday and Wednesday, not much change in temperature.

SOUTH DAKOTA—Fair Tuesday; Wednesday probably showers, not much change in temperature.

NEBRASKA—Partly overcast Tuesday; Wednesday probably showers, not much change in temperature.

KANSAS—Mostly overcast Tuesday; Wednesday probably showers, not much change in temperature.

Hourly temperatures at Des Moines yesterday:

Total accumulated deficiency of precipitation at Des Moines since Jan. 1 is 4.10 inches.

The normal precipitation at Des Moines Jan. 1 to date is 18.60 inches.

Relative humidity ...

Sun rises at Des Moines today at 4:51 a. m. and sets at 7:50 p. m.

Japan Warns China Against Treaty Talk

Note Suggests Cessation of Anti-Foreignism.

Tokio, July 21 (A.P.)—The foreign office announced today that it had sent a note to China through Kenkichi Yoshizawa, Japanese minister to China, on July 10 advising her in a friendly manner that the agitation for the revision of treaties was inappropriate at present.

The note suggested the cessation of anti-foreign agitation and the restoration of order before taking up the matter of the treaties. It added that Japan felt "deep sympathy with China prompted by the fact that she once suffered the same experience from unequal treaties with foreign powers."

CAR LEFT PARKED AT WAKONDA RUNS AMUCK ON LINKS

The motor car of Mr. and Mrs. Davis S. Chamberlain II ran wild without driver or passengers at Wakonda club yesterday morning, scattering girl golfers and caddies, touring most of hole No. 1 fairway and finally crashing into a tree.

The car, a sedan, had been left standing in the drive near the clubhouse. It is still a mystery how it started off the roadway as no one was near it at the time and none saw it move until one of the caddies in the group playing behind the caddy house cried out as he saw it rushing toward him.

It circled the caddy house and raced down the lane between No. 1 and No. 4 tees, narrowly missing Miss Doris Green and Miss Louise Koetts, who, with Jack Welsh, the club professional, jumped aside to let it pass.

Finally it swerved to the side and struck a large oak tree head on, smashing the front of the car and twisting the frame. It is estimated that $300 damage was done.

Held for Staging "Mad Scene" at Cemetery

Three patrolmen, answering an emergency call yesterday evening from persons living near Woodland cemetery, found Sylvester Kirwin, 54 years old, standing near the cemetery entrance, alternately pulling his hair and tossing his shoes into the air, according to reports submitted by them.

When the patrolmen arrived at the scene of the alleged disturbance a crowd had congregated near Kirwin and he was reported to be shrieking: "They're trying to kill me; take them away."

Kirwin will face a charge of intoxication when he appears in municipal court today. He lives at 1030 Twentieth street.

King Boris Pardons.

Sofia, July 20.—King Boris of Bulgaria today pardoned fifty-eight convicts here and reduced the sentences of 164.

IOWANS TESTIFY IN RUM EXPOSE

Federal Attorney Withholds Customers' Names.

New York, July 20 (Special)—Granted immunity from prosecution by a provision of the Volstead act, customers of the Broadway mail order liquor firm raided last Friday testified today before the federal grand jury. Federal District Attorney Emory R. Buckner said they came from Illinois, Iowa and Nebraska, but declined further to identify them. They were among the 20,000 clients to whom the $2,000,000 corporation shipped liquor from this city in wardrobe trunks.

A list of "prospects" found on George Fox, one of the corporation's salesmen arrested in Des Moines, Ia., included the names of all of the members of the [illegible] Country club.

"But that does not mean," hastily asserted Mr. Buckner, "that those people ordered or bought liquor. Neither can I say that records of shipment to persons in twenty-nine states, which we found in the files and books kept by the raided Broadway offices are positive proof that those persons actually bought liquor in violation of the prohibition law.

"For me to give out the names of any of these persons without further investigation might work great injustice. Fictitious names undoubtedly were used in many cases. Liquor very likely was consigned to persons other than it was intended for. The trunks were called for at express offices."

William Gilbert, general prohibition agent, working directly under Field Chief R. C. Yellowley at Washington, went before the grand jury and told of his nation-wide investigation, which resulted not only in Friday's raid on offices at 1133 Broadway with the arrest of seven men and one woman, but also in previous raids at 7 West Twenty-second street and 634 Broadway. All places were shipping liquor in wardrobe trunks to customers in inland cities.

Cutting plants, where smuggled liquors were adulterated with alcohol and resealed with counterfeit strips and stamps, were found operating in connection with the shipping rooms on Twenty-second street and at 634 Broadway, according to Mr. Gilbert. Mr. Buckner said he was convinced that all three establishments were united in a bootleg syndicate headed by Jacob Kirschenblatt, who was arrested in the raid at 1133 Broadway and is held for the federal grand jury in $5,000 bail.

Asks Police Aid in Hunt for Daughter

Mrs. A. Franz, 3904 First street, asked police yesterday to search for her 12-year-old daughter, Evelyn Demmons, who left home Sunday afternoon with the intention of visiting a chum, who lives at 1214 Pleasant street. The girl did not appear at her playmate's home and did not return to her home Sunday night.

She was described as being tall for her age. At the time of her disappearance she wore a brown silk dress, white silk hose and black and tan shoes.

DARROW CITED FOR CONTEMPT, BUT GETS OFF

Court Is Moved to Open Air to Avoid Peril From Throng.

Dayton, Tenn., July 20 (By The Associated Press)—The first sensation of the seventh court day in the Scopes case came when Judge Raulston, immediately after the opening of court, cited Clarence Darrow for contempt of court as a result of remarks made Friday by the Chicago lawyer. He was ordered to appear before the bar of the court to answer tomorrow morning.

At the opening of the afternoon session, however, Mr. Darrow gained the floor and extended an apology for his remarks. The overture from the visiting attorney was accepted and Judge Raulston and the lawyer shook hands.

Moves Court Outdoors.

Before this outcome of the contempt citation incident could be [illegible] as news through the court room, packed far beyond its capacity, Judge Raulston announced that the crowd was endangering the safety of all, and, to avoid a possible break down of the floor, court would be adjourned to an open air platform on the lawn below. There the court sat for the rest of the afternoon.

Statements of eight scientists and two clergymen were placed in the record of the case by the defense during the day. These statements set forth what testimony would be given if scientific and expert testimony had been permitted in the case.

Judge Raulston, Mr. Darrow, William Jennings Bryan, Attorney General Stewart, Dudley Field Malone and Arthur G. Hays posed for a "good fellowship" photograph as the crowd fought its way out of the courtroom onto the lawn below.

The exchange of kind words between the judge and Mr. Darrow seemed to restore a general spirit of good cheer among counsel on both sides of the case, and the court and attorneys were in rare good humor as the scene was shifted.

Raulston Cites Darrow.

As court opened for the afternoon session Mr. Darrow was recognized by the court to make a statement. He said that he did not know how hard his words of Friday looked until he had seen the minutes. He said that he was sorry. He said that in his stay in Dayton and vicinity he had been treated with great kindness and appreciated this consideration.

"I don't think any such occasion ever arose before in my practice," he said. "So far as intending to insult the court, I never meant anything of the kind. I have been sorry I made the remarks ever since I had a chance to read them.

"Of course, your honor will remember," said Mr. Darrow, "that whatever took place was hurried, one thing following another and the truth is, I did not know just how it looked until I read over the minutes as your honor did and when I read them over I was sorry that I had said it.

"On Friday I determined immediately on reading it over to tell the court just what I thought this morning. In the meantime I had seen one paper which stated that the court thought that I was trying to get in position where I would be held in contempt.

"Now, I want to say that what I say is in good faith regardless of what your honor may think is right for you to do. I have been practicing law for forty-seven years and I have been pretty busy most of the time in court, and I have had many a case where I have had to do what I have been doing here, fight the public opinion of the people, in the community where I was trying the case—and I never yet have had any criticism by the court for anything I have done in court."

Sorry He Made Statement.

He added that he thought he had gone further than he should have gone and "so far as its having been premeditated or made for the purpose of insult to the court, I had not the slightest thought of that."

He continued that he had never, perhaps, been in a community where his religious ideas differed as widely from the great mass as here, but nevertheless he had never been treated better, kindlier or more hospitably.

"Personally, I don't think it constitutes a contempt, but I am quite certain the remark should not have been made and the court could not help taking notice of it and I am sorry that I made it, ever since I got time to read it, and I want to apologize to the court for it."

"If this little incident had been personal between Colonel Darrow and myself," said Judge Raulston, "it would have been passed by unnoticed, but I could not pass them by when I represent the great state of Tennessee."

Judge Accepts Apology.

After telling of some of the great men of Tennessee, Judge Raulston said:

"My friends and Colonel Darrow, the man that I believe came

(Continued on Page 3, Col. 3)

Biggest Day of the Trial at a Glance

The following were the developments in the Scopes case at Dayton, Tenn., yesterday:

Clarence Darrow put William Jennings Bryan on the stand as a witness for the defense. Mr. Bryan testified to a literal belief in the bible.

Mr. Darrow was cited for contempt for a remark about the court, but was freed after he had apologized.

Court was moved into the open air because the throngs flocking into the building aroused fears that it would collapse.

Scientists' statements on creation and evolution were read into the record of the trial, though barred from the jury.

Dr. Shailer Mathews of the University of Chicago divinity school explained in a statement why there is no conflict between the biblical and scientific interpretations of Genesis.

EXPLAINS BIBLE CREATION STORY

Shailer Mathews Says Genesis Accounts Differ.

Dayton, Tenn., July 20 (A.P.)—"A correct understanding of Genesis shows that its account of creation is no more denied by evolution than it is by the laws of light, electricity and gravitation," said a statement of Dr. Shailer Mathews, dean of the divinity school of the University of Chicago, read into the record of the Scopes trial today.

"The bible deals with religion. There are two accounts in Genesis of the creation of man. They are not identical and at points differ widely. It would be difficult to say which is the teaching of the bible. The aim of both, however, is clear and wonderfully inspired.

"Each shows that God created man and how man differs from beasts in resembling God, in that he possesses a moral and spiritual nature.

"In the first account in Genesis it is said that God made beasts, cattle and all creeping things by having the earth bring them forth as living creatures. The Hebrew expression here used, 'Nephesh chayah,' is the same as that used in the second chapter of Genesis to describe man when created.

Man Part Animal.

"The first story then continues with the creation by God of man in the divine image, male and female being created on the sixth day. In the second account God is said to have formed man from the dust of the ground and to have breathed into him the breath of life.

"Man thus became a living soul. In the Hebrew, the same word is used as that previously used to describe the animals which the earth brought forth.

"This living creature, Adam, is placed by God in a garden which he is to till. He is forbidden to eat of the tree of knowledge of good and evil. He, however, disobeys and eats the fruit. God then declares that man has become 'one of us knowing good and evil.'

"Genesis thus says that an animal life, produced by God from the earth by his spirit, came to be like God through a development born of experience. Thus, so far from opposing the Genesis account of the creation of man the theory of evolution in some degree resembles it.

Religious Interpretation.

"But the book of Genesis is not intended to teach science, but to teach the activity of God in nature and spiritual value of man. It is a religious interpretation of nature and God's relation thereto, in which the inspired writers use the best of the then current knowledge of the universe to show how God was in the creative process and how that process culminated in man possessed of both animal and divine elements.

"The theory of evolution is an attempt to explain the process in detail. It does not take place in a vacuum, but in an environment in which is God. Genesis and evolution are complementary to each other, Genesis emphasizing the divine cause and science the details of the process through which God works. This view that evolution is not contrary to Genesis is held by many conservative evangelical theologians such as Hall, Strong, Micou, Harris and Johnson. Mullins also holds to a theistic evolution."

And the Radio, Too

Several pieces of furniture, along with a radio, were easily disposed of when Mrs. S. R. Pemberton, 1618 York St. advertised them in the Household Goods columns of The Register and Tribune-News.

JOSHUA COULD STOP THE SUN, BRYAN AVERS

He Hotly Calls Questioning a Ridiculing of God.

Dayton, Tenn., July 20 (A.P.)—Admitted agnosticism met fundamentalism here today as Clarence Darrow, counsel for the defense in the Scopes evolution case, drew out William Jennings Bryan, associate counsel for the prosecution, upon the witness stand.

Hundreds of men and women, drawn from the peaceful hills and valleys for miles around, pushed close to the rough wooden platform behind the courthouse as the verbal swords of the two clashed time and again, sending off flashes that drew volleys of handclapping and booming mountain fox calls.

A silence, broken only by the rustling of the maple trees, settled over the crowd as Arthur Garfield Hayes announced the intention of the defense to call Bryan to the witness stand.

The purpose was explained later by Mr. Darrow as an effort to "show the people what fundamentalism is." Bryan arose from the witness stand to tell Darrow, the judge and the assembled spectators that its purpose was to cast "slurs upon the bible."

CLARENCE DARROW.

The nature of the examination brought Atty. Gen. A. T. Stewart and other members of counsel for the prosecution to their feet time after time to interpose objections. Frequently it even caused Darrow to arise with objections as the witness proceeded to direct the course himself.

Faces grew strained and lips tightened among the spectators at the apparent irreverance of some of the questions and they arose to cheer as the witness waved aside the protection of the judge with the declaration:

"These gentlemen have not had much chance. They did not come here to try this case. They came here to try revealed religion. I am here to defend it and they can ask me any questions they please."

W. J. BRYAN.

As it proceeded insinuations ceased to be insinuations and became either unveiled sarcasm or pointed irony, until argument succeeding argument, a fresh one threatened to arouse more controversial remarks than any of the preceding ones, and Judge Raulston adjourned for the day with several members of both the prosecution and the defense counsel on their feet and hot words on their tongues.

The questioning began with the usual qualifying questions for the expert witness and after Bryan had announced his intention of calling to the stand Mr. Darrow, Dudley Field Malone and Mr. Hays.

The witness said that he had made considerable study of the bible, including its interpretation on the particular question involved.

"Do you claim that everything in the bible should be literally interpreted?"

Accepts Bible Literally.

"I believe that everything in the bible should be accepted as it is given there. Some of the bible is given illustratively. For instance, 'ye are the salt of the earth.' I would not insist that man was actually salt or that he had flesh of salt, but it is used in the sense of salt as saving God's people."

"But when you read that Jonah swallowed the whale—or that the whale swallowed Jonah—excuse me please, how do you literally interpret that?"

"When I read that a big fish swallowed Jonah it doesn't say whale."

"Doesn't it? Are you sure?"

"That is my recollection of it. A big fish, and I believe it, and I believe in a God who can make a whale and can make a man and can make both do what he pleases."

Other interrogations along the same line followed until the query:

"You don't know whether [illegible] was the ordinary run of [illegible] made for that purpose?"

"You may guess. You evolutionists guess," responded the witness.

"But when we [illegible]

(Continued on [illegible])

1926

Rear Admiral Richard E. Byrd, then a thirty-eight-year-old naval commander, made history on May 9, 1926, when he made the first flight over the North Pole.

Floyd Bennett was his copilot.

Byrd later led his first Antarctic expedition in 1928 and set up the base camp that he named "Little America." He also flew over the South Pole and led four more Antarctic explorations, pioneering in the aerial mapping and scientific investigation of Antarctica.

Robert Goddard launched the first liquid-fuel rocket, from a farm in Auburn, Massachusetts. It went up 184 feet.

EXTRA

THE INDIANAPOLIS STAR.

EXTRA

ALWAYS FIRST—ALWAYS FAIR—ALWAYS COMPLETE.

VOL. 23. NO. 339. Entered as Second Class Matter at Post Office, Indianapolis, Ind. Issued Daily and Sunday. MONDAY MORNING, MAY 10, 1926. Daily by Carrier 15 Cents Per Week. Sunday 10 Cents Per Copy. Mail by Zones 75c to $1.00. THREE CENTS.

BYRD MAKES FIRST FLIGHT OVER POLE

Intrepid American Naval Aviator and Floyd Bennett, Pilot, Circle Top of World in Air Trip Lasting Fifteen Hours and Thirty Minutes.

BY WILLIAM BYRD,

The New York Times Correspondent With the Byrd Expedition.

(Copyright, 1926, by the New York Times Company and the St. Louis Post-Dispatch.) By Wireless to the New York Times.

KINGS BAY, SPITZBERGEN, May 9.—America's claim to the north pole was cinched tonight when, after a flight of fifteen hours and thirty minutes, Commander Richard E. Byrd and Floyd Bennett, his pilot, returned to announce that they had flown to the pole, circling it several times and verifying Admiral Peary's observations completely.

They were favored by continued sunlight and there was never the slightest fog, enabling Commander Byrd to use his sun compass and bubble sextant and obtain the most accurate observations possible.

There were three magnetic compasses in the plane, but all of them deviated eccentrically after reaching high latitudes.

Bennett declared that when he was piloting the magnetic compasses were wholly useless and would swing almost a quarter turn, turning very slowly.

Without the sunlight, navigation would have been almost impossible. Bennett and Commander Byrd alternated in the piloting, Bennett refilling the gasoline containers while the commander piloted and navigated.

PROCEED WITH LEAKY OIL SYSTEM.

Commander Byrd found that the Bumstead sun compass worked perfectly, even when held in the hand, so when he was in the pilot's seat he held the joystick in one hand while he got his direction from the sun compass held in the other.

When they were within sixty miles of the pole the oil system of the right-hand motor began leaking badly, and it seemed necessary to choose between proceeding with two motors or attempting a landing to make repairs.

In the neighborhood of the pole numerous stretches of smooth ice were visible and a landing was favored by Bennett, but Commander Byrd, remembering his difficulties in starting at Kings Bay, vetoed this proposal.

ALL MOTORS WORK SMOOTHLY.

Both agreed, however, to continue the flight to the pole, even if they went on with only two motors. To their surprise, the right-hand motor continued to work effectively, despite the rupured oil tank, and when the Fokker returned to Kings Bay all three motors were hitting perfectly.

The Josephine Ford, after making three circles over Kings Bay, landed at the lake off the runway and taxied to the original starting position.

Commander Byrd and Bennett hurried a mile and a half to the shore, where a motor boat rushed them to the Chantier. The crew aboard her went wild with joy, waving flags and their caps. Many of the crew completely broke down with emotion and, with tears streaming from their eyes, embraced the fliers.

BY WILLIAM BYRD.

KINGS BAY, Spitzbergen, Sunday, May 9, 6 P. M. Greenwich (1 p. m., Indianapolis time). Lieutenant Commander Richard E. Byrd, United States Navy, leader of the Byrd polar expedition, returned from his flight to the north pole in the airplane Josephine Ford at 4:20 this afternoon, Greenwich time (11:20 a. m., Indianapolis time).

The commander reached the north pole. He started at 12:50 o'clock this morning, Greenwich time (7:50 p. m. Saturday, Indianapolis time), which is full daylight at this time of the year in the arctic, so that his flying time on the dash to the pole and back was fifteen and a half hours.

The Josephine Ford had as its pilot on the trip Floyd G. Bennett, the American pilot of the Byrd expedition. The two were welcomed on their return by Capt. Roald Amundsen, Lincoln Ellsworth and the entire crew of the airship Norge, now awaiting her chance to fly over the north pole from Spitzbergen to Alaska, and the entire summer population of Kings Bay, all of whom had been asleep when the airplane took off fifteen hours previously.

BYRD'S FINGERS FROZEN AT POLE.

Commander Byrd's nose and several fingers were frozen while he was taking observations in zero temperature (Fahrenheit) above the north pole, but treatment here speedily restored circulation, and the commander is all right now.

Lieutenant Commander Byrd completed his first flight six days before he planned to make it. His schedule called for his flights to begin on May 15.

He intended first to fly to Peary Land to establish a landing base, then back to Spitzbergen for more supplies, then to Peary Land again and then to the pole. Thus in his first flight he has accomplished the objectives which he outlined for himself in the first four scheduled air journeys. After reaching the pole, it was Commander Byrd's plan to return to Peary Land. His next flight was to be a wide loop to the northwest in search for unknown land in the great area which previous explorers have been unable to penetrate.

ONE FLIGHT TAKES PLACE OF FOUR.

By accomplishing his polar objective and the exploration of tens of thousands of square miles of unknown area on his first flight, the explorer frees himself for a series of flights into the "blind spot" or unknown area of the arctic.

Commander Byrd believed, from Admiral Peary's description of Peary Land, that fields suitable for landing could be found there, but Stefansson, Prof. W. H. Hobbs and other experts expressed the opinion that an attempt to descend there would be extremely dangerous.

With the great cruising radius of the Fokker thoroughly tested Commander Byrd is now in a position to make the 425 mile flight from Spitzbergen to Peary Land and fly all over that country in search of landing fields, and if no level spaces appear, fly back to Spitzbergen.

NEXT OBJECTIVE IS PEARY LAND.

If he finds a base on Peary Land, Commander Byrd will probably try to fly to Alaska. That has always been in his mind as one of the possibilities of his expedition. With the confidence in his plane and in his own navigating ability which his successful trip to the pole has inspired, the likelihood that he will make the attempt to cross the arctic basin to the Alaska or northwest Canadian coast is strongly increased.

He has shown that he can make a nonstop flight of [illegible] miles in the Fokker. That is sufficient to take him from Peary Land to Point Barrow. Such a flight would carry him through the great unexplored area which lies between the Beaufort sea and the north pole. His great mission ahead is to search in this area for new land.

Each day gained is of great importance, as the arctic atmosphere, clear in the early spring, is obscured by mists and then by heavy fogs as the season advances, and the temperature rises.

Fog is the worst peril that faces arctic airplane fliers. The risk of attempting a landing on the snow and ice of an unknown region is next. The time in which Commander Byrd can fly is limited. By the end of the present month he expected that the fog would be such as to render flight impossible.

PUTS UTMOST FAITH IN COMPASS.

The arctic aviator believes that his improved instruments of navigation insure him against losing his way, even if he gets in that part of the arctic where the compass needle points south instead of north, or gyrates erratically about the dial.

His chief reliance against mishap is that his Fokker carries three motors, the first two for ordinary service and the third for reserve.

Calculating the hazard of flying from the known statistics, he estimates that, with the third motor, there is not one chance in more than two thousand of his being compelled to descend through motor trouble.

Scientific attention to the problem of nonfreezing engine oil is another factor of safety. The experience of Commander Byrd and his pilot, Bennett, in more than two thousand miles of arctic flying at various heights and in many different temperatures, is another great asset.

MAY LAND ON HIS NEXT FLIGHT.

If Commander Byrd finds land, his schedule will probably be dis-

CONTINUED ON PAGE THREE.

ALL KINGS BAY OUT TO GREET NAVY MAN ON HIS SAFE RETURN

U. S.-Built Monoplane Miss Josephine Ford Accomplishes Perilous 1,600-Mile Journey in Single Day —Amazement Caused in New York by Change of Plans That Results in Daring Dash in One Stretch

AMUNDSEN AND ELLSWORTH IN RECEPTION

NEW YORK, May 9.—(AP)—Lieutenant Commander Richard E. Byrd, United States Navy aviator, flew over the north pole today, the New York Times and the St. Louis (Mo.) Post Dispatch announced. Commander Byrd, first to accomplish this feat, made the flight in 15 hours and 30 minutes, leaving his base at Kings Bay, Spitzbergen, at 12:50 o'clock this morning (Greenwich time) and returning safely at 4:20 o'clock this afternoon. Byrd was accompanied on his flight by Floyd Bennett, chief petty officer in the naval air service.

The entire population of Kings Bay turned out to welcome the American's return. Capt. Amundsen, Lincoln Ellsworth and the crew of their airship Norge, on which they plan a similar flight, greeted Commander Byrd upon his descent.

ACCIDENTS AT START.

The American-built monoplane, Miss Josephine Ford, in which Lieutenant Commander Richard E. Byrd flew over the pole, was taken to Spitzbergen aboard the steamer Chantier after several false starts and near accidents in New York harbor. The three-engine Fokker plane, named after the daughter of Edsel Ford, was endangered by a falling beam while the Chantier was being loaded at the Brooklyn navy yard. Readjustments of cargo were made, and the ship left the yard April 5, but had to anchor again off Staten island to allow the crew to make fast other pieces of cargo which threatened the airplane.

RICHARD E. BYRD

BRAVES ICE HAZARDS.

The motors of the Miss Josephine Ford and the expedition's second airplane, a Curtiss Oriole, were taken from the hold and fastened on deck, and the Chantier crossed the bar on the night of April 6. The expedition arrived at King's bay, Spitzbergen, on April 29. The following day, braving the ice hazards, the crew landed the airplanes, and began their reassembling. On May 4 tests were made of skiis attached to the Miss Josephine Ford, but one of them snapped. A successful trial flight was made the next day, and Commander Byrd announced on May 6 that he was ready for his dash to the pole.

Vilhjalmur Stefansson tonight expressed enthusiasm for Commander Byrd's successful flight over the north pole.

"I am delighted with Byrd's success," he said. "There have heretofore been two schools of opinion as to the arctic flight, one maintaining that it is not more difficult than any other kind and the other that it is extremely difficult and dangerous. I feel sure that when Byrd's story comes in it will bear out the opinion of the former school, to which Byrd himself belongs.

"Byrd had two objectives. He has attained one of them—flying to the north pole and back. This clears the decks for his more ambitious and more important flight to the northwest of Peary land in search of unknown land, and I hope he will be equally successful there."

A message to Commander Byrd was broadcast tonight from WMCA in the hope that he would be able to pick it up at his base at King's bay. It follows: "New Yorkers send their congratulation on your flight over north pole."

The message was sent by Stefansson, John David, Carol Lomen and Arthur L. Lee.

COVERED 1,600 MILES.

Byrd was able to know that he had reached the north pole by making observations of the sun's position. Using a new sextant carrying an artificial horizon, he was able to locate the pole within twenty miles. Before sailing north, he explained that he would know he was over the pole when the altitude of the sun above the horizon equaled the sun's declination, which was given in the nautical almanac he carried.

Commander Byrd demonstrated that wings could do in less than a day what Admiral Peary, discoverer of the north pole, consumed eight months in negotiating by dog sled. This also made Byrd's the first of nine expeditions attempting the feat, to reach the north pole this year.

His giant three-motored airplane carried him safely over wastes which Amundsen last year pronounced unsafe for airplane flights, and the distance traveled, roughly 1,6000 miles, was equal to more than a month's mushing in the arctic under the most ideal conditions for dog teams.

The flight and return of Commander Byrd, recounted by wireless, were far different, both in the act and the transmission of news, from the departure of Admiral Robert E. Peary from Sydney, N. S., July 7, 1918.

CONTRAST WITH PEARY.

Peary hardly had cleared the harbor and was just beginning to fight some of the worst of the Atlantic ocean's storms in the little schooner Roosevelt, in the time Byrd went to and returned from the pole.

The report that Byrd, who last year accompanied MacMillan into the north, actually had reached the pole before returning to his base, was received with amazement here, as the announced plans for his first flight called only for negotiating the 400 miles to Peary land and return, a total of 800 miles.

This in itself was considered a daring feat because of the paucity of landing places on the jagged arctic ice plains, but the flight of at least 1,600 miles involved in a round trip hop to the pole rivaled the most optimistic hopes of observers of this flight.

In four months after setting out, Peary had only reached Etah, Greenland, and there still remained a dash of hundreds of miles to the pole. During the following months, until June of 1909, no word was received concerning Peary, except here and there a multitude of rumors. It seemed for awhile that Peary would be robbed of the honor, for on Jan. 9 of 1909 Dr. Frederick A. Cook descended from the northern wastes with the claim that he had been the first. This later

CONTINUED ON PAGE THREE.

BRITAIN DEBATES MOVE TO ARREST STRIKE LEADERS

Moderates in Cabinet Vigorously Oppose Action for Fear of Inflaming Public Mind.

CIVIL SUIT PLANNED

LONDON, May 9.—(Universal Service)—The general strike enters the second week with the government debating the possible effect of a move to arrest all the strike leaders. This step has been under consideration since Thursday, when Sir John Simon, in a speech in the House of Commons, declared the strike to be illegal and the leaders guilty of conspiring against constitutional government.

The moderates in the Cabinet have, up to date, prevented the execution of the plan and are vigorously opposed to its adoption at any future date on the ground that it would inflame the public mind and create sympathy for the unions.

Alternative civil proceedings have been suggested and are now being considered. It is to make a test case of the legality of the strike immediately by a claim for damages against one of the strike leaders, and to expedite appeals to the highest court—the House of Lords.

KING HOLDS COUNCIL.

King George held a council at Buckingham Palace tonight, which was attended by Lord Balfour, Attorney General Hogg and Home Secretary Joynson-Hicks. The King has kept in close touch with all developments since the beginning of the strike, but there was nothing to indicate that he personally would intervene, as has been hinted in several quarters. He has been advised against such a course, which also is contrary to his personal wishes.

His Majesty's intervention in the case of Ireland during the treaty negotiations was entirely successful, but the present situation is very different, and there is no certainty that royal intervention would be effective.

The members of the privy council who met with the King tonight included no labor representatives, although Ramsay MacDonald, J. H. Thomas and other former labor ministers belong to the council.

Cardinal Bourne today described the strike as unChristian and disloyal.

CONTINUED ON PAGE TWO.

DREAMED 20 YEARS OF TRIP, BYRD SAID

NEW YORK, May 9.—(Universal Service)—Just before sailing on the Chantier for the north pole expedition, Commander Byrd turned to Vilhjalmar Stefanson, himself a veteran arctic explorer, and said:

"I have dreamed of making this trip for twenty years, ever since as a boy of 17 I read of Admiral Peary's expedition."

John D. Rockefeller Jr., Godfrey Cabot and Lorillard Spencer were three of a group of business men who had faith enough in Commander Byrd to finance his expedition.

No scientific expedition, it was said, ever started out under such favorable auspices as that of Commander Byrd.

$50,000 GIFT BY BOYDS TO FUND

Committee Plans to Push $1,000,000 Riley Memorial Hospital Drive.

Hugh McK. Landon, president of the James Whitcomb Riley Memorial Association and chairman of the governing body of the James Whitcomb Riley hospital for children, announced last night a gift of $50,000 to the building fund by Mrs. Linnaes C. Boyd, her daughter, Mrs. William Higgins of Woodstock drive, Indianapolis, and Mrs. Boyd's son, Philip, now a resident of California. The gift was made in memory of the husband and father of the donors, Linnaes C. Boyd, for many years one of the best known business men of Indianapolis and former president of the Indianapolis Water Company. Mr. Boyd died about three years ago.

The gift, it was announced, is one of the largest to be made to the hospital fund.

INTERESTED IN HOSPITAL.

Mr. Boyd, before his death, was deeply interested in the hospital for children and was one of the first men to become identified in the plan when first broached to him by Dr. Lafayette Page, generally credited with having been the originator of the idea which has now grown into one of the finest children's hospital in America. Mr. Boyd, according to Dr. Page, frequently expressed the hope that plans would progress far enough to enable him to make a substantial subscription but he died before this opportunity came. The subscription by Mrs. Boyd and her son and daughter carries out the desire of the husband to play a part in the construction of the hospital.

"The members of the governing board are overwhelmed by this generous gift," Mr. Landon said last night.

CONTINUED ON PAGE TWO.

FAMILY DECLARES BYRD WAS ALWAYS BRAVE ADVENTURER

Brother, Now Governor of Virginia, and Mother Proud of Explorer.

RICHMOND, Va., May 9.—(AP)—A message from Lieutenant Commander Richard Evelyn Byrd stating that he had "returned safely" was received here this afternoon by his brother, Governor Harry Flood Byrd, and his mother, Mrs. Richard Evelyn Byrd Sr. It was interpreted to mean that the aviator had flown over the North Pole and returned to his base. The message was received by Mrs. Byrd as a sort of Mother's day greeting. "I am proud of Dick," she said. Governor Byrd said: "I am tremendously gratified and proud to hear of my brother's success in reaching the pole."

The family of the naval flier expressed relief at the news.

"Dick has been so lucky all his life that he believes he will come through even though ninety-nine of a hundred chances might be against him," his brother said. "I am proud of him. He has always been such an adventurous fellow that we are somewhat relieved, though proud, that he has made the flight. If he had not and believed there was a ghost of a chance to do so, he would try again as soon as possible."

"TERRIBLE 24 HOURS."

"We couldn't understand the message," Mrs. Byrd declared. "All that we really heard was that he was safe, and we did not hear that the trip had been successful, but in my heart I knew it was successful—I feel that Dick could not fail.

"It has been a terrible twenty-four hours," she said. "I had asked my friends not to mention it to me, and I've said nothing about it because I knew that was the only way I could stand it. And, now that I know he is successful, and safe, I've gone all to pieces. I really am weak as a kitten with emotion.

"Nevertheless, I must confess that I am glad to know it is successful because if this flight had been a failure I know Dick would have tried until he discovered the pole. That's the kind he is, and so I was especially interested. He was born that way—an adventurer, an explorer, absolutely without fear. I think most every one knows now that he went around the world by himself when he was only 12 years old, but long before he was 12 fear had been eliminated from his composition. Indeed, I don't believe that he ever knew fear."

DISCOVERER OF ORE IN MESABA RANGE IS DEAD

DULUTH, Minn., May 9.—(AP)—Leonidas Merritt, 82 years old, discoverer of the first iron ore on the Mesaba range, died today at his home of heart disease.

SUCCESS OF FLIGHT OVER POLE SHOWS YEARS OF PREPARATION

(International.)

LIEUTENANT COMMANDER RICHARD E. BYRD (LEFT) AND LIEUT. G. O. NOVILLE, PHOTOGRAPHED IN THEIR ARCTIC COSTUMES BEFORE LEAVING NEW YORK.

Lieutenant Commander Byrd Planned on Arctic Dash When Academy Student—Later Decided on Trip by Airplane.

(By Associated Press.)

When Commander Richard Evelyn Byrd set sail from New York April 6, the occasion marked the realization of a dream which had been with him since boyhood days—an expedition of his own into the arctic regions.

With him was Floyd Bennett, chief petty officer in the naval air service, who flew over three thousand miles with the commander last year when the two accompanied the MacMillan party in the north. He became Byrd's "right-hand" man and the two of them planned to share the most dangerous and important work of the expedition.

"Bennett is a man of the greatest energy, endurance and skill, both as a navigator and as a mechanic," Byrd wrote of him. "I would not like to be in the arctic without him and I would take him before any other man in the world."

In outlining his plans, the commander said that after reaching King's bay, Spitzbergen, the airplane would be made ready for the flights while William C. Haines, the United States Weather Bureau official, studied and reported on weather conditions.

OIL EXPERT HELPS.

Here the skill of Lieut. G. O. Noville, expert on gasoline and oils, came into play. Working out oil problems and providing mixtures to lubricate at low temperatures without becoming thin and at higher temperatures useless was his task.

"The objective of our first flight," Byrd said, "will be the first landing field we can find on Peary Land, the northernmost known land in the world. It is at the extreme north tip of Greenland, about four hundred miles northwest of Spitzbergen. The northernmost point of Peary Land is

CONTINUED ON PAGE THREE.

'WE ARE OFF IN HIGH HOPE,' SAID BYRD ON LEAVING

"No Man in World I Would Rather Make Flight With Than Bennett," He Declared Before Hop-off.

TOLD EXPLORING PLANS

BY WILLIAM BYRD.

(Copyright by the New York Times Company and St. Louis Post-Dispatch.)

KINGS BAY, Spitzbergen, May 8.—"We are off for the pole," said Commander Byrd this morning just before the Josephine Ford started for the coveted goal. "Our intention is to fly due north 720 miles in a beeline, the distance from Kings Bay to the top of the world, and without stopping the motors to fix position.

"Having done this, our purpose is to turn leftward and circle back within sight of the north Greenland coast on the return course, which because of the curve is somewhat longer, approximately nine hundred miles."

CHANGES FLYING PLAN.

"We intend to explore by going to Peary land via the pole rather than to the pole via Peary land. The reason for the change is our experience up here in flying. Landing on the snow with skiis with a large three-motored plane indicates that it is inadvisable to land in unknown territory with a heavy load, as we would have to do if we went direct to Peary land. Under the present plan, when we get there it will be quite light.

"The course to the pole is for the most part over the area already explored by Amundsen and Ellsworth last year. But from 87.44 degrees onward we shall be passing over regions never before seen by man, except the points where we cross Peary's course of 1909.

LAND NEVER SEEN BEFORE.

"Between the pole and Peary Land the territory is unexplored, and from the plane, if the air is clear, we can survey perhaps 60,000 square miles

CONTINUED ON PAGE THREE.

WEATHER FORECAST

Jim Crow says:

Time wasted is always 100 per cent loss, no matter which side thinks it wins that British strike.

Forecast for Indiana for Monday and Tuesday:

Rain Monday and possibly Tuesday; cooler; fresh shifting winds.

Forecast for Indianapolis and vicinity for Monday and Tuesday:

Rain Monday and possibly Tuesday; cooler, fresh shifting winds.

ADVICE TO FRUIT GROWERS.

FORECAST (United States Weather Bureau, Chicago)—Rain Monday and possibly Tuesday; cooler, fresh shifting winds. COMMENT (Supplied by Purdue University and Indiana Horticultural Society)—Strawberries should receive frequent and thorough cultivation throughout the first growing season in order to conserve moisture and kill the weeds. The cultivation need be only deep enough to maintain a dust mulch. For further information on strawberries, write to Purdue university agricultural experiment station, Lafayette, Ind., and ask for bulletin No. 200.

United States Weather Bureau Special Report for The Indianapolis Star.

ALMANAC OF THE DAY.

Sun rises at...4:34 | Sun sets at...6:48

WEATHER CONDITIONS YESTERDAY.

—Relative Humidity.—

7 a. m. 63 pct | Noon 31 pct | 7 p. m. 87 pct

—Precipitation.—

Amount during twenty-four hours ending at 7 p. m. .... .30

Total amount since Jan. 1, 1926.. 12.70

Accumulated departure from normal since Jan. 1 (deficiency)... 3.83

—Temperatures.—

7 a. m...Dry 66 Wet 58 | Maximum... 80

Noon... Dry 80 Wet 60 |

7 p. m...Dry 61 Wet 59 | Minimum... 60

—For the Same Date Last Year.—

7 a. m.......... 55 | Maximum...... 66

7 p. m.......... 60 | Minimum...... 53

1927

Attracted by an offer of $25,000 prize for the first New York-to-Paris nonstop flight, Charles Lindbergh interested a group of St. Louis businessmen in backing his entry.

He took off in a trim, silver Ryan monoplane named *The Spirit of St. Louis*, early the morning of May 20, 1927. He landed at Le Bourget Field in Paris 33½ hours later, the first solo nonstop transatlantic flight in history.

On his return, Lindbergh received the Medal of Honor and was promoted to the rank of colonel. Tumultuous crowds greeted the "Lone Eagle" wherever he went.

HOME EDITION

New York Evening Post

HOME EDITION
With Opening Prices
Five Sections 60 Pages

FIVE 5 CENTS FOUNDED 1801 MEMBER OF THE ASSOCIATED PRESS SATURDAY, MAY 21, 1927 FIVE 5 CENTS

REPORT LINDBERGH OVER ERIN

SHARKEY WINS FROM MALONEY BY KNOCKOUT

Boston Boxer Victor in Fifth Round When Referee Stops the Battle

40,000 SEE HIM ANNEX RIGHT TO MEET TUNNEY

Loser Makes Game Battle, Torn and Battered by Victor's Right Hand

By JACK KOFOED

Boston, smug citadel of moral and literary endeavor, highbrow Boston, which became the cradle of modern pugilism when John L. Sullivan belted his defiance to the world, has again returned to the fistic limelight. A swarthy son of hers—though of a different race than Sullivan—has lifted himself to within touching distance of the world's heavyweight championship.

Jack Sharkey knocked out Jim Maloney in five rounds at the Yankee Stadium last night before 30,000 people.

The boxer turned fighter. The cream-puff hitter became a slugger. That fifth round was as dramatic a picture as the prize-ring can produce. The men battled on fairly even terms for the first three. Then Sharkey's stabbing left ripped Jim's defense to shreds and a sharp right sent him to the floor just before the bell.

Maloney, his left eye dripping blood, his face creased with foreboding and desperate determination, rushed from his corner at the start of the fatal round. He pulled and missed again. Then those short hooks that Sam Langford used to teach him.

[illegible]

Boston though he was, the courage had not been hammered out of him. He reached back and seized the ropes, hauling himself to his feet in a blind effort to continue the fight that had become so unequal.

His gameness was greater than his strength. The count had reached six when he found his feet, but that was a lost feeble gesture. Referee Louis Magnolia intervened to save him.

Thus Jack Sharkey, once Josef Cukoschay of Lithuanian parentage and a product of Lithuanian training, became the outstanding contender for the championship held by Gene Tunney, who sat placidly in a ringside watching.

Jack showed himself a masterful boxer. He showed the utmost confidence in himself. Even Tunney, who proclaimed himself "the man of Destiny," was never more sure, though Sharkey never proclaimed it as offensively as Sharkey has.

The miracle of it, though, was where the winner found his punch. Maloney had never been knocked out. He seemed tough and rugged, but the smashing punch of the Lithuanian's right knocked the foundations out from under him, and, prior to this Sharkey had never knocked out a good man.

Was at His Best

Sharkey was better than he showed, then beating Wills or McTigue. The psychological advantage was with him, speed and cleverness, too, were on his side. Maloney had only his aggressiveness and unquenchable courage. His one right hand and his hooking left eventually missed. [illegible]

The man who pounded Jim Maloney to the canvas in five rounds last night would have easily beaten [illegible]

(Continued on Page Ten)

EX-BRAZILIAN HEAD HISSED

Rio Janeiro, Brazil, May 21 (AP).—Former President Arturo Bernardes was the object of hostile demonstrations when he alighted from a train here last night. In spite of strong police measures a large crowd at the railway station shouted epithets at the former President and hissed him.

Five Sections

The Evening Post today comprises five sections as follows:

1. News, Sports, Travel, Editorial, Religious.
2. Financial, Real Estate.
3. Literary Review.
4. Rotogravure.
5. Society, Drama, Art, Music, Fashions, Resorts, Antiques, Radio, Automobiles.

Heads Dry Forces

DR. JAMES M. DORAN

NATION CHANGES DRY EXECUTIVES

Appointment of Lowman and Dr. Doran After Andrews Resigns Forces Haynes Out

MELLON PRAISES GENERAL

By a Staff Correspondent

Washington, May 21—The big shake-up in the Federal Prohibition Enforcement Bureau, so long anticipated, finally has come.

General Lincoln C. Andrews, Assistant Secretary of the Treasury and head of prohibition enforcement for the past two years, has resigned to leave the service August 1; Seymour W. Lowman of Elmira, N. Y., former Lieutenant-Governor, will succeed him.

Major A. A. Haynes, temporary as-[illegible]

[illegible] staged in the capital, most religion or be forced out.

Dr. James M. Doran, for twenty years in the Treasury and chief chemist of the prohibition unit, has been made prohibition commissioner. Commissioner Doran will name Major E. H. White, former prohibition administrator for Washington, assistant commissioner in place of Haynes.

Haynes Resignation Waited

Haynes, focal point of the battle which has had the prohibition bureau in turmoil months on end, had not formally tendered his resignation last night.

Secretary of the Treasury Mellon and Under Secretary Ogden Mills were in a quandary concerning when Haynes would bow to the mandate of Mr. Mellon that he must get out. General Andrews, also inacquainted with Haynes's prospective action, said that it would not be necessary for him to resign, that he would be automatically forced out when Dr. Doran takes over the reins today.

It has been known for weeks that Haynes had lost out in the fight staged to be named permanent commissioner of prohibition, a fight in which he had the backing of Wayne B. Wheeler and the Anti-Saloon League of which Mr. Wheeler is so much a part.

Haynes's fall began when it was learned that while the Anti-Saloon League was heart and soul for him, other dry organizations and leaders were opposed to him.

No Changes in Policy

The resignation of General Andrews was more or less of a surprise, though his quitting the service has been a matter for conjecture for some time past. Then it became almost a certainty and Lowman also has been thought to be the man undergoing grooming for Haynes's place, was mentioned for the first time as probable successor to Andrews.

There are to be no changes in policy in enforcing prohibition or administering the new reorganization law, Secretary Mellon declared in announcing the changes. Commissioner Doran is to have full responsibility for enforcement. Assistant Secretary Lowman is to be contact man between the Secretary and Commissioner Doran.

The new assistant secretary, fifty-nine years old, a contractor and an out-and-out dry, is coming to Washington [illegible]

(Continued on Page Five)

POLA AND PRINCE SAIL

Coming Here on Aquitania From Chateau Near Paris

Paris, May 21 (AP).—Pola Negri and her new husband, Prince Serge Mdivani, started back for America today, she to resume her film screen work and he to engage in the oil business. They entrained this morning with a compartment full of baggage, for Cherbourg, where they will sail aboard the Aquitania.

Miss Negri and the young Russian Prince were married a week ago today at her Chateau near Seraincourt, about thirty miles from Paris.

FRANCE THRILLS FOR ARRIVAL OF CAPT. LINDBERGH

All Arrangements for Landing at Le Bourget Complete—Crowds Wait at Field

TO LIGHT ALL AIRWAYS WHEN DARKNESS FALLS

Every Precaution Taken to Prevent Disaster—Great Welcome I Planned

Evening Post Foreign Service
Copyright, 1927, by N. Y. Evening Post, Inc.
Paris, May 21 (By Cable).—Paris again is thrilled over the possibility of a successful transatlantic flight—and the best wishes of all Frenchmen are with Captain Charles Lindbergh, whose sportsmanship and daring are of the kind that already has won much praise.

The betting in Paris sporting centers is even money.

Due to the Nungesser-Coli tragedy, which still is fresh in the minds of Frenchmen, the reception of the American flyer will be whole hearted, although not spectacular.

International aviation circles, however, will accord the young flyer a rousing welcome with the co-operation and collaboration of French airmen. Beacon lights will shine as soon as darkness falls tonight.

Every precaution has been ordered by the French Ministry of Marine. Le Bourget flying field will be well cleared and the runways will be glaring from dusk on throughout the night to mark a path for the flyer plane.

Coast Guard lookouts will be posted tonight and aviation authorities and the American Embassy have made every [illegible] be signalled off France. Weather bulletins [illegible] weather.

Paris Enthusiastic

Paris, May 21 (AP).—France was waiting with bated breath today for the first signs of the gallant Lindbergh when he nears the close of his lonely flight from New York to Paris.

Although the experts may shake their heads over the daring of the youth, the Frenchman's readily kindled imagination has caught the fire of his intrepidity and spirit in seizing unhesitatingly what appeared to him an excellent chance to achieve his ambition.

There was genuine relief when the cables announced that he had negotiated successfully the first stage of his adventurous trip and headed out over the ocean from Newfoundland, and there is no doubt he will get a welcome such as is vouchsafed few visitors to France.

Having seen to it that everything possible has been done to guide Lindbergh after he reaches the French coast by means of signals and powerful searchlights, the authorities were completing arrangements today, aided by the military to handle record crowds which will flock to Le Bourget flying field to witness the landing. The landing space will be kept absolutely clear. Only the reception committee, officials and a few privileged persons will be allowed on the ground, but powerful floodlights will make the arriving plane visible for considerable distance.

Herrick to Greet Him

With a view to preventing confusion and possible collisions, the air authorities have requested, or, where possible, ordered that no planes take the air tonight during the hours the aviator is expected, realizing that after the grueling journey and many sleepless hours he will be in no condition for social amenities. The welcome will be cut to a minimum. Lindbergh will be rushed in an automobile to a Paris hotel, where a suite is waiting for him.

(Continued on Page Two)

COURVILLE TO WED EDITH KELLY GOULD

Producer and Bride to Be Married on Wednesday in London

London, May 21 (AP).—Announcement was made today that Edith Kelly Gould, former wife of Frank Jay Gould, will be married to Albert de Courville, London theatrical producer, at the London Registry Office next Wednesday.

"BUTCH" AND "FLO" JOSHED

South Hadley, Mass., May 21—Mount Holyoke College girls are stirred by the romance of "Butch" and "Flo." "Butch" is the nickname for John Coolidge given in the Amherst Junior Yearbook. The Mount Holyoke Senior year book in joshing Miss Florence Trumbull, daughter of the Governor of Connecticut, tells of an increasing number of telephone calls to Amherst.

Flyin' Fool Streaks for Paris

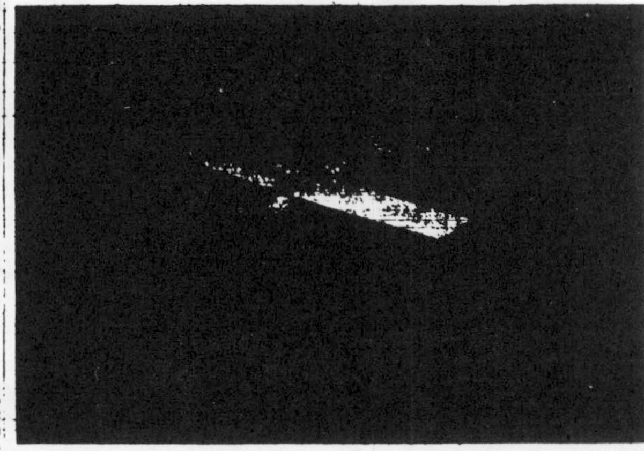

P. & A. Photo

This photo, taken from an accompanying plane, shows Captain Charles Lindbergh in his Paris-bound monoplane more than an hour after he had hopped off from Roosevelt Field yesterday morning.

FEAR MISSISSIPPI SHIFTS ITS COURSE

Federal Engineers Think River May Cut Shorter Channel to Gulf Through Atchafalaya

NEW PARISH IS MENACED

New Orleans, May 21.—Fears that the Mississippi River might change its course cut out a new and shorter channel to the Gulf of Mexico through the Atchafalaya Basin, permanently flooding Louisiana's "sugar bowl," were engrossing Federal engineers today while frantic efforts were being made to save Pointe Coupee, the last parish of the sugar country, from inundation.

Rapid disintegration of the levee at McCrea, on the east bank of the Atchafalaya, is threatening to inundate about 3,000,000 acres in Pointe Coupee and parishes immediately to the south, and Former Governor John M. Parker, State relief director, has ordered 50,000 people residing in that fertile section of the original "Sugar Bowl" to evacuate at once.

This, many are refusing to do, but Army officials, the State Highway Department and leading business houses of the State are rushing trucks and automobiles into the area in the hope the people will be induced to leave without the use of troops.

River's Movement Surprising

Although State Engineers and Dr. I. M. Cline, head of the New Orleans weather bureau, scouted suggestions the Mississippi was shifting its route, Major John Ootwals of the Mississippi River Commission, insisted the river was behaving in a manner entirely unfamiliar in the light of previous floods.

"We can't tell what is taking place, but unquestionably something unusual is happening," he remarked. The break in the levees at Milliken Bend, on the west bank of the river, would be the start of the new channel, he believed.

State engineers scouted at the mere suggestion New Orleans, Metropolis of the South, might be deprived of port facilities, asserted the mighty flood now pouring down the Atchafalaya Basin was merely the accumulation of waters released through the Bayou des Glaises breaks into the Atchafalaya, and declared that if any such thing as a change of course should occur, it would be a comparatively simple engineering project to close the Milliken Bend gap as soon as the flood has passed and divert the water back into its old channel.

Spillway advocates took advantage of

(Continued on Page Two)

Last Bulletins on Paris Hop

Cherbourg, France, May 21 (AP).—Strong winds from the southwest caused heavy naval seaplanes to suspend maneuvers here today, but as soon as Captain Lindbergh's plane is reported approaching the French coast they are expected to go aloft and convoy him in.

Havre, France, May 21 (AP).—It was somewhat cloudy over the English Channel this morning, but with a brisk wind from the west and northwest, the weather was regarded as extremely favorable for Captain Lindbergh. All vessels and wireless stations are keeping the sharpest lookout for the "flying fool" [illegible] caught him.

DARROW PREPARES CARUSO'S DEFENSE

Veteran Chicago Criminal Lawyer Says Sicilian Does Not Deserve to Die

Chicago, May 21.—An ignorant Sicilian today awaited electrocution in the death house of Sing Sing and a thousand miles away one of the world's most famed lawyers prepared to save him—in the name of justice.

The prisoner is Francesco Caruso, who last February in his poor Brooklyn flat killed the physician who failed to save Francesco's six-year-old bambino, Joey, who died of diphtheria. The lawyer is Clarence Darrow, who snatched Leob and Leopold from the gibbet; who spoke for science and evolution at the Scopes' trial in Dayton, Tenn., and whose voice ever has been raised for the defense in the courtrooms of the country.

"Now this Caruso is sentenced to die," Darrow said today in his office here. "He was a father who loved his son, loved his son too well—loved him to the point of killing. Should we execute a father because he loved his son? Would justice thus be served?"

Darrow said he stood ready to make a plea for Caruso before the Supreme Court of New York, before Governor Al Smith, or whatever agency can review the case, and the plea will be based on the insanity of Caruso already condemned to death by the trial court.

Mrs. Brown of New York, a daughter of Robert Ingersoll, whom Darrow greatly admired, first turned to Darrow and asked he intervene for the Sicilian.

(Continued on Page Five)

BELLANCA WAITING ON LINDBERGH HOP

Won't Take Off for Paris If Flyin' Fool Makes It—Injunction Denied

BYRD CHRISTENING TODAY

By CHARLES MURPHY
Staff Correspondent of Evening Post
Curtiss Field, Long Island, May 21.—The Bellanca monoplane, that everlasting [illegible] in the New York-to-Paris race, [illegible] is in its hangar today after a projected "surprise" hop-off, decided upon shortly before midnight, had dissolved into mist as indefinite as that which settled, damp and chilling, about the hangar itself.

She may take off late this afternoon, if the fickle winds of the North Atlantic seaboard give the word, or if Captain Charles Lindbergh, now believed streaking in his silvery "Spirit of St. Louis" over the Atlantic, is not heard from.

Then again this promise—it has the voices of Clarence Chamberlin, pilot; Giuseppe Bellanca, builder, and Charles A. Levine, financial backer—may be just another phase of the "On Again, Off Again, Gone Again, Finnegan, conundrum into which the Bellanca definitely seems to have resolved itself.

Two Factors Enter

For the take-off is contigent upon two most important factors, weather and the success of Captain Lindbergh. If the blond Westerner settles down in Paris, the Bellanca, it was again announced, will not stir from its roost upon a trans-oceanic quest.

Meanwhile, Commander Richard E. Byrd's giant Fokker America, drew to itself the attention of the spectacular-loving crowds. Byrd had drawn broken over the field, before the Long Islanders began to arrive at Roosevelt Field for a day-long education in how one prepares for a transatlantic flight.

At 5:30 A. M. mechanics wheeled the

(Continued on Page Five)

4 KILLED AS AUTO STALLS ON TRACKS

Three Others, All From One Family, Gravely Hurt as N. Y. C. Train Crushes Car Up State

Sodus, N. Y., May 21 (AP).—Four of a family of seven were killed late last night at The New York Central crossing two miles east of here, when their automobile stalled on the tracks and was hit by an eastbound passenger train.

The dead are Mrs. William Blankenburg, her daughter, six and four and a baby two months old. Blankenburg, driver of the machine was pinned against a tree and may die. He and the other children, all seriously injured, were brought to a hospital here. All were residents of Sodus.

MEXICO MAY EASE CREDITS

Partial Moratorium Recommended Due to Business Depression

Mexico City, May 21 (AP).—Recommendations implying a sort of partial moratorium, have been made by the permanent commission appointed at the recent business men's meeting called to study the economic situation.

The commission proposes that, because of business depression, tight money and difficult collections, Mexican commercial houses be as liberal as possible in not enforcing collections from reliable establishments and in extending credits to such concerns.

JUST FIVE YEARS OLD, HE MAKES GOOD AS POLICEMAN

"Patrolman" Arnold Toner, Rescuer of Lost Kids, Dons Uniform for Duty With Traffic Officer Pal

It isn't very often that a mere patrolman walks into Commissioner Warren's office at Police Headquarters, but today "Patrolman" Arnold Toner strolled through the mahogany door and the Commissioner jumped up and shook his hand and patted him on the head.

"Patrolman" Toner in the glittering pride of a new uniform, wasn't a bit abashed. He grinned up at Commissioner Warren and took the congratulations like a veteran.

Arnold Toner is the youngest patrolman who ever joined the department. He is five, the mascot of the East 104th street precinct, a full-fledged traffic man, and missing persons specialist.

He has been all of these things for the past four months ever since he found the parents of a missing child and saved the detectives of the precinct a lot of trouble. But today he got his uniform bought for him by the cops of the 104th street district and came down to pass the inspection of the Commissioner and Chief Inspector Lahey.

Besides, he wanted to see Police headquarters where he had never been

(Continued on Page Five)

WATCHERS SIGHT SPEEDING PLANE IN SOUTH IRELAND

Policeman at Dungarvan, County Waterford, Says Ship Passed Over Town at 6:22, New York Time—Earlier Reports Put Plane Off Coast

RADIO MESSAGE SAYS LINER SIGHTED PARIS PLANE 25 MILES OFF THE SHORE

St. Louis Flyer Has Crossed Atlantic at Phenomenal Speed—Rains Reported in Ireland, but Weather in France Is Ideal

Captain Charles Lindbergh has leaped through the night from Newfoundland to the Irish Coast and may, if the three brief reports received here this morning are accurate, arrive in Paris early this afternoon.

The three reports, contradictory in some details, agree that the slim winged silver plane has been sighted by the Empress of Scotland this morning.

The first message, coming to the Commercial Cable Company office here from Cape Race, Newfoundland, said that a relayed radio message from the Empress of Scotland, 500 miles off the coast of Newfoundland, reported seeing the solitary bird of passage scudding eastward at 2:30 A. M.

An airplane, believed to be Lindbergh's monoplane, swooped over Dungarvan, County Waterford, in the south of Ireland, at 11:22 this morning by their time—6:22 by New York daylight time—the police superintendent there reported, according to the latest dispatch from the Associated Press. This was confirmation of earlier scant reports.

Seen Off Coast

The second report came from the Independent Wireless Corporation, which said it had picked up a relayed message from an unnamed ship which had seen Lindbergh 25 miles toward Ireland at 4:30 this morning. [illegible]

On the basis of this slim announcement [illegible] the Empress of Scotland and to [illegible] 500 miles from the west coast of Ireland, and that from this the liner's master had computed that the light-hearted young Missourian would be in Paris around noon.

The third report came, ostensibly from a British Government station on the Irish Coast, to the Radio Corporation of America. This again had the Empress of Scotland sighting the swiftly streaming monoplane, but gave the liner's position as within twenty-five miles of the coast, and set the time at 8:30 New York daylight time.

From these conflicting messages came the single heart-lifting impression that Lindbergh had, in truth, been seen by the Empress of Scotland, somewhere, how far out at sea unknown, but safe.

Speed Phenomenal

Aviation experts who had gone to bed with no later word of the lonely boy's adventure than his passage over St. John's, Newfoundland, at 7:15 last evening, doubted when they heard these reports that he could have approached Ireland so swiftly, for it is a distance of nearly 2,000 watery miles from Newfoundland to Ireland and with slight wind on the tail of the "Spirit of St. Louis," they were skeptical that he could have travelled 1,700 miles or more in eleven hours—a rate of better than 150 miles an hour.

Yet they, too, believed that, somewhere, at some time in the night or dawn, Lindbergh had been seen and was safe.

Four British destroyers are waiting off Cobh, the Queenstown of yore, stationed there to flash the first word of "Lucky Slim's" bridging of the Atlantic, the Associated Press reported, and added that the Canadian Pacific offices in London had not received any word of Lindbergh from the Empress of Scotland.

Many Ships Off Coast

Definite word should come soon from the swarm of shipping off the Irish coast or from Ireland itself, where thousands are waiting to see the audacious young American cross.

Before this series of messages from the liner there is the last definite word of the Spirit of St Louis came from St John's.

Until then Lindbergh had headed north and east, but there he winged off almost straight to the east, flying low between the hills girding the town, sprinting along the unseen path that Hawker and Greeve followed unsuccessfully and which later Alcock and Brown successfully negotiated between Newfoundland and Ireland.

The weather, all important to men who challenge distance with man-made wings, is partly in his favor, partly against him.

The Navy Department hydrographers at Washington reported this morning that "Lucky Slim" has found ideal flying weather in his passage over the North Atlantic.

But the Navy weather experts added that, once across the 1000 miles of sea and with 800 miles to go—a hard, bitter weaving 600 miles, when the man's strong young body will be nearly exhausted from a day and a night and a day in the stuffy little cabin—the young Missourian will encounter light rain. According to the Army and Navy Press report, the Navy experts do not think these will be heavy enough seriously to impede Captain Lindbergh or menace his safe landing.

Rains in Ireland

But from Dublin, Ireland, came a dispatch telling of heavy rains in all parts of that island and little of the westerly wind which has pushed Lindbergh along all the way up the Atlantic Coast from Roosevelt Field and eastward from Newfoundland.

This dispatch added that if the rainstorms in the west coast of Ireland had been extended [illegible]

[illegible]

France, where still mourns Nungesser and Coli, is watching Lindbergh's light-hearted essay with grave admiration.

The French newspapers already have adopted the attitude of America as to him, with good-nature and astonishment, as "le fou volant"—the flying fool.

The obscurity of his stepping off jaunt with two hours' sleep and a sandwich to sustain him started their interest.

And Lindbergh is not content, it seems, for a friend in St. Louis revealed today that this flight from New York to Paris is to Lindbergh only a training test for a far more dangerous venture—a flight from the United States to Australia via Hawaii in the great hops.

Harry Knight, one of his backers in the flight, in revealing this, added that Lindbergh plans to challenge single-handed, the fifty-one-hour flight record established by Clarence Chamberlin and Bert Acosta in the Bellanca Columbia.

With the weather neither all in his favor nor altogether against him, Lindbergh is gaining the constant advantage of decreased weight of his plane. The wood-and-metal bird, laden to the tank-tops with gasoline and oil when she lifted her wheels from the Long Island mud at 7:52 yesterday morning, weighed 5,150 pounds.

As the hours have passed, the great

(Continued on Page Two)

'SHILOH DRUMMER BOY' DIES

Famous Civil War Hero Passes Away—Served Under Grant

Franklin, Pa., May 21 (AP).—[illegible] the "Drummer Boy of Shiloh," during the Civil War, John S. Butler, seventy-seven, is dead at his home here.

Although only twelve, Butler, then a resident of Princeton, Ind., answered President Lincoln's first call for volunteers in 1861 as a drummer boy in the Seventeenth Regiment, Indiana Volunteer Infantry, commanded by the late Brigadier General Ulysses S. Grant. Butler particularly distinguished himself in the Battle of Shiloh in April, 1862, by his [illegible] play. "The Drummer Boy of Shiloh," was based on Butler's [illegible]

SUNDAY NEWS

5 CENTS PAY NO MORE

Vol. 7. No. 5. Published Each Sunday New York, Sunday, May 22, 1927 84 Pages

'LUCKY' WINS!

Story on Page 3

NEWS photo

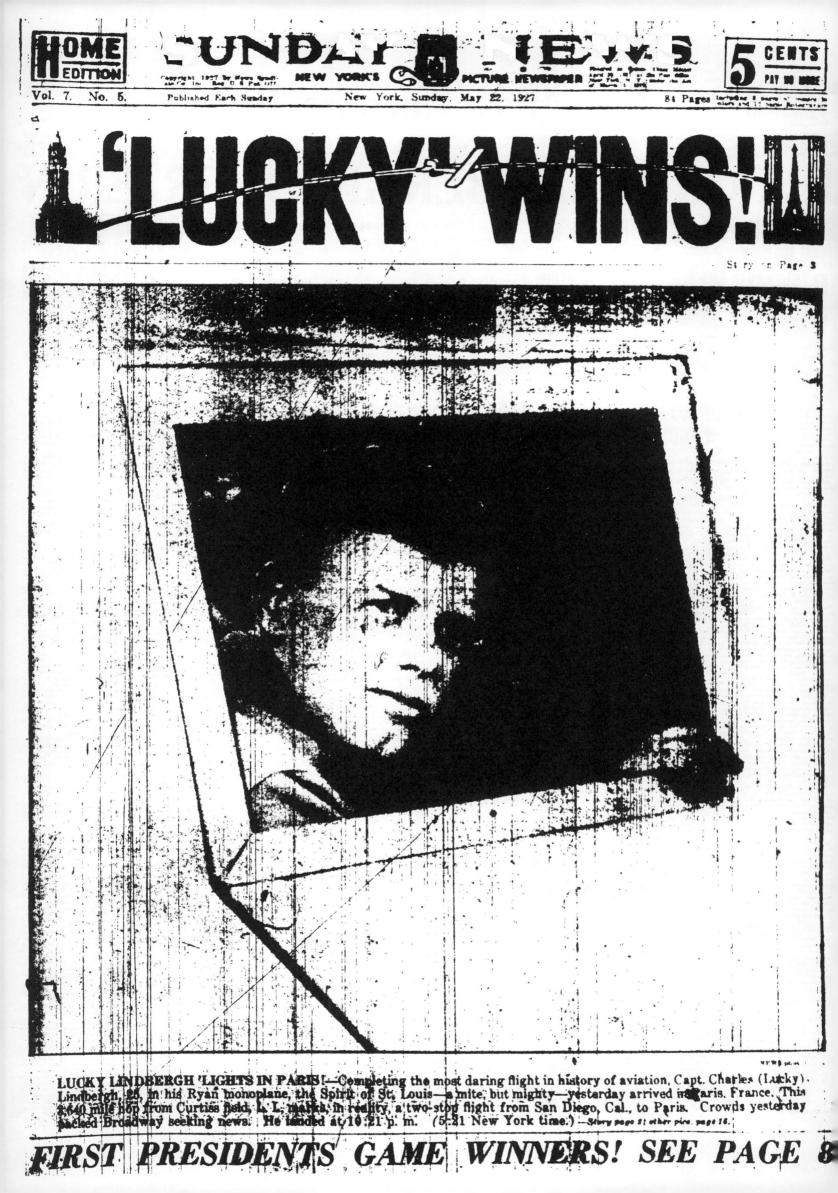

LUCKY LINDBERGH 'LIGHTS IN PARIS!—Completing the most daring flight in history of aviation, Capt. Charles (Lucky) Lindbergh, 25, in his Ryan monoplane, the Spirit of St. Louis—a mite, but mighty—yesterday arrived in Paris, France. This 3,640 mile hop from Curtiss field, L. I., marks, in reality, a two-stop flight from San Diego, Cal., to Paris. Crowds yesterday packed Broadway seeking news. He landed at 10:21 p. m. (5:21 New York time.) —Story page 3; other pics. page 16.

FIRST PRESIDENTS GAME WINNERS! SEE PAGE 8

The Boston Daily Globe

Reg. U. S. Pat. Off.
VOL CXII NO 54 — Entered as second class mail matter at Boston, Mass., under the act of March 3, 1879—242 Washington St.
BOSTON, TUESDAY MORNING, AUGUST 23, 1927—TWENTY-FOUR PAGES
COPYRIGHT, 1927, BY THE GLOBE NEWSPAPER CO. (3) TWO CENTS

MADEIROS, SACCO, VANZETTI DIED IN CHAIR THIS MORNING

Electrocuted in That Order Soon After Midnight—All Reject Religious Consolation to the Last—Two Make Statements

POLICE TAKE 156 OF "DEATH WATCH"

Sacco and Vanzetti Demonstration in Front Of State House Is Broken Up Several Times—Some Rearrested

With the taking into custody of 23 adults and three juveniles shortly after 5 o'clock police brought the total number of arrests of State House pickets yesterday to 156, there having been 130 persons arrested previously.

Some of those arrested early returned to the State House after being bailed and were arrested again. Thousands of persons gathered on the Common and Beacon st to watch the pickets and the activity of the police.

All the prisoners were bailed out at police stations and released by Commissioners Joseph Fahey and William Brophy, with the exception of Helen Crowe, who refused bail but later accepted it when she was taken to the City Prison.

Men Locked in Cells

The men were locked in cells, while the women were detained in the guard

Continued on the Ninth Page.

TODAY'S GLOBE CONTENTS

TODAY'S GLOBE CONTENTS

PRISON IS GUARDED BY VERITABLE ARMY

Six Establishments of Police on Duty

Riot Squads and Machine-Gun Groups at Stragetic Points

Mobilized silently and quickly, with the precision of a well-trained army, police of six different establishments representing the Boston and Cambridge departments, the Metropolitan District Commission, State Police Patrol, Boston & Maine Railroad detectives and the prison force united last night to guard the State Prison at Charlestown and its vicinity during the straining hours preceding and following the execution of Sacco, Vanzetti and Madeiros.

Allowing no one not properly accredited within 150 yards of the prison walls, the police, numbering close to 800 armed men, established a cordon of steel about the area, ready to handle any disorder.

Floodlights set up on the prison walls virtually turned night into day, riot and machine guns were carried by capable looking officers, high-presure fire hose was in the hands of picked firemen at strategic points, and the greatest concentra-

Continued on the Seventh Page.

TODAY'S GLOBE CONTENTS

WINTHROP JOKER SETS OFF FIRECRACKERS AS A SCARE

WINTHROP, Aug 23—Shortly after midnight, when the executions were in progress, two loud reports were heard at Cottage Cove and Horn Bar avs. The sound was heard over Winthrop. People rushed to the scene; the explosion was but 200 feet away from the huge standpipe, containing 1,000,000 gallons of water, which supplies the town. There had been threats, according to the police, that the standpipe would be blown up.

Arriving at the scene police found that the reports came from two giant firecrackers, tossed in the road by some practical joker with a distorted sense of humor.

RADIO PROGRAMS PAGE 21

CELESTINO MADEIROS — NICOLA SACCO — BARTOLOMEO VANZETTI

LAST-MINUTE PLEAS BOMBARD GOVERNOR

Wife and Sister of Men Beg Mercy And Lawyers Ask More Time In Long Day at Office

PARADERS DISPERSED AT CHARLESTOWN

Police Feared March on Prison Imminent

Eight Arrested and Others Break Their Formation

The much-feared march of Sacco-Vanzetti sympathizers to the Charlestown Prison, which accounted for the extraordinary guard of nearly 800 police about its walls all last night, seemed imminent just before midnight, when a formation of 50 Sacco-Vanzetti sympathizers started through the streets of Charlestown in the direction of the prison.

Quick work by the handful of police left in the Charlestown Police Station at City Square prevented what might have been a serious disturbance, although the paraders were in no position to threaten the armed guards.

The police made eight arrests, each on the technical charge of violation of the City Ordinance relative to the carrying of placards, and dissolved the parade without untoward incident.

Passed Police Station

The arrested persons include those who gave their names as Isadore Lovett, Helen Peabody of Cambridge, Frederick Beade of Lawrence, Frank Zito, John Horn, John Gorman, Dora Dolavitch and Amellia F. Borris.

The procession marched over the new Charlestown Bridge from the direction of Boston proper and circled City sq.

It seemed that the paraders purposely passed the City-sq Police Station, and it was this fact that proved their undoing. They were carrying placards making known their sympathies and a cheer here and there aroused the police.

Six Others Arrested

Sergt Kuhlman and special officer William J. Bonner rushed outside and attempted to stop the parade, and succeeded in placing two men, who seemed like leaders, under arrest.

They thought then that the parade was broken up, but the others formed into line of fours again, raised their placards and headed toward the prison. At Union and Washington sts, near the prison, another detail of police stepped in and arrested the other six and completely routed the marchers.

There was never any danger at any time and the police were satisfied that the parade was simply a demonstration rather than any effort to march on the prison.

Although continuously besieged for nearly 14 hours to grant a respite or otherwise exercise executive clemency, Gov Alvan T. Fuller left the State House at 12:12 this morning without taking any action toward intervention in the execution of Sacco and Vanzetti. When he left he made no statement. As he passed through the group of waiting newspaper men he said, "Good night."

There was not a moment from his arrival at 10:40 yesterday morning when he was not engrossed in the details of the case. He remained in his office all the time and twice had lunches brought to him.

His day was given over to listening to appeals in behalf of the condemned men. Not the least trying was an interview, late yesterday evening, with Mrs Rosa Sacco, wife of Nicola Sacco, and Miss Luigia Vanzetti, sister of Bartolomeo Vanzetti.

Kane Last to Appear

The last person who saw the Governor in behalf of the men was Francis Fisher Kane of Philadelphia, an attorney retained by one committee of Sacco-Vanzetti sympathizers. Mr Kane left the State House at 11:57, after a few minutes' talk with the Governor.

William G. Thompson, formerly counsel for Sacco and Vanzetti, was with the Governor for some time, leaving at 11:45. Mr Thompson said when he left the Governor's office, "I was trying to do my full duty by my former clients whom I believe to be innocent and who have not had a fair trial. If I had not believed it I would not have been here tonight."

At 9 o'clock last evening Mrs Sacco and Miss Vanzetti had a long audience with the Governor when they went to the State House. With them were Gardner Jackson, chairman of the Sacco-Vanzetti Defense Committee, his sister, Miss Edith B. Jackson, Aldrico Felicanni, treasurer of the committee, and Michael A. Musmanno, who has been associated with Arthur D. Hill in the recent handling of the case for the accused men.

Three Go Into Office

Of these, only Mrs Sacco, Miss Vanzetti and Mr Musmanno, who acted as interpreter, went into the Governor's office, where, besides Gov Fuller, were Lieut Gov Frank G. Allen, Joseph Wiggin, the Governor's personal counsel, and Herman A. MacDonald, the Governor's private secretary. Atty Gen Arthur K. Reading was at times in the room.

The conference lasted for an hour and a half. Both women spoke through Mr Musmanno. Mrs Sacco urged the Governor to be merciful. She said her husband had been convicted largely through the evidence of a witness who said she saw Sacco lying under an automobile soon after the murder, trying to make repairs on the car. Mrs Sacco declared that her husband had

Continued on the Sixth Page.

MEN REITERATED THEIR INNOCENCE

Atty Thompson Quotes Sacco and Vanzetti

Ex-Chief Counsel Denies He Had Access to Federal Files

After a surprise visit to the death house early in the evening, William G. Thompson, for four years chief counsel for Sacco and Vanzetti, gave out a statement to the newspapermen, quoting both men in reiteration of "their absolute innocence" and declaring that Vanzetti stated:

"No lawyer who has ever been concerned in my defense has any right to say or hint that I, in any form of words whatever, said anything which could possibly be interpreted as an admission of any guilt whatever."

Mr Thompson branded as "absolutely untrue" statements that he has had access to the files of the Department of Justice.

Opinion Not Altered

Regarding the action of Gov Fuller, Mr Thompson said: "I cannot with due regard for professional propriety engage in any public discussion or

Continued on the Fourth Page.

Will Rogers' Dispatch

(Special to Boston Globe—Copyright, 1927)

TOPEKA, Kan, Aug 22—This is Topeka, the home of both Kansas Senators. Capper's life has been dedicated to the farmers and Curtis' to the helping of the Indians. Both denominations, the farmers and the Indians, are now destitute.

Tonight in Kansas City I am to be made president of a large body of men, the ex-Mayors' Association, an earnest bunch of men trying to come back, all placed where they are by the honesty of the ballot.

What this country needs is more ex-Mayors.

Yours, the President of the ex-Mayors' Association,

WILL ROGERS

DUMB-BELLS

Madeiros in Stupor—Other Two Face Death Calmly

Judges Holmes, Anderson And Lowell Refuse Final Appeals

VANZETTI FORGIVES, SACCO SAYS GOODBY

Nicola Sacco and Bartolomeo Vanzetti are dead.

Between midnight and 12:30 this morning, at the Charlestown State Prison, they paid with their lives for a crime of which they had been convicted by a jury of their peers.

Sacco marched to his death at 12:11:12, with defiance on his lips for the social order which executed him, and a farewell for his family and friends. He was dead seven minutes and 50 seconds later. Vanzetti's last words were a cry of innocence and forgiveness. He was brought into the death chamber at 12:20:38, and was dead at 12:26:55.

Woodenly, without word or sign, Celestino Madeiros had been executed a few minutes before. His life was the penalty for a murder and robbery, a penalty which would have been paid long before except for the

Continued on the Eighth Page.

SEVEN-YEAR BATTLE IN COURTS FAILURE

The seven-year legal battle to save Sacco and Vanzetti continued with unabated vigor last night until within two hours of the expiration of the respite when defense counsel had exhausted every legal recourse.

In the last few hours before midnight the battery of defense counsel appealed for a second time to Justice Oliver Wendell Holmes of the United States Supreme Court, to Judge James A. Lowell and to Judge George W. Anderson, both of the United States District Court. All of these last minute efforts, however, were unavailing.

These appeals supplemented those of the past few days during which three justices of the United States Supreme Court were appealed to, also the full bench of the Massachusetts Supreme Court and several judges of the Supreme Court.

The United States Supreme Court Justices who were visited with an

Continued on the Ninth Page.

THE WEATHER

Forecast for Boston and Vicinity: Tuesday partly cloudy, probably light local showers. Wednesday partly cloudy and cooler. Moderate southeast and south winds.

Washington Forecast for New England and Eastern New York: Tuesday cloudy, probably showers. Wednesday partly cloudy and cooler.

The Temperature Yesterday at Thompson's Spa: 3 a m, 64; 6 a m, 64; 9 a m, 67; 12 m, 74; 3 p m, 72; 6 p m, 78; 9 p m, 71; 12 mid, 69. Average temperature yesterday, 69 1-6.

THE WEATHER ELSEWHERE

	Temperature High	8 P M	Weather
Boston	78	70	Clear
San Francisco	66	64	Clear
Williston	86	60	Pt Cloudy
St Paul	70	66	Cloudy
St Louis	86	80	Clear
Chicago	82	74	Clear
Nantucket	72	62	Cloudy
Portland, Me	74	62	Cloudy
Eastport	66	56	Cloudy
New York	72	66	Cloudy
Washington	78	72	Rain
Jacksonville	88	86	Pt Cloudy

1928

Ruth Snyder and her lover, Judd Gray, had been convicted of murdering her husband, Albert, in 1927.

They were executed at Sing Sing prison on January 12, 1928.

Photographs were forbidden, but Tom Howard, a photographer for the Pacific & Atlantic agency, strapped a tiny camera to his ankle and took his picture just after Mrs. Snyder was electrocuted.

The New York *Daily News* front page of January 14 published the photo, noting, "The only unofficial photo ever taken within the death chamber, this most remarkable, exclusive picture shows closeup of Ruth Snyder in death chair at Sing Sing as lethal current surged through her body at 11:06 Thursday night. . . ."

This was also the year in which Ben Hecht and Charles MacArthur wrote the play *Front Page*.

Average net paid circulation of THE NEWS, Dec., 1927:
Sunday, 1,357,556
Daily, 1,193,297

DAILY NEWS

Copyright 1928 by News Syndicate Co. Inc. Reg. U. S. Pat. Off.

NEW YORK'S PICTURE NEWSPAPER

Entered as 2nd class matter Post Office New York N. Y.

FINAL EDITION

Vol. 9. No. 174 28 Pages | New York, Saturday, January 14, 1928 | 2 Cents IN CITY LIMITS

CROWDS Follow Ruth and Judd to GRAVE

Story on Page 3

© 1928 by Pacific & Atlantic Photos

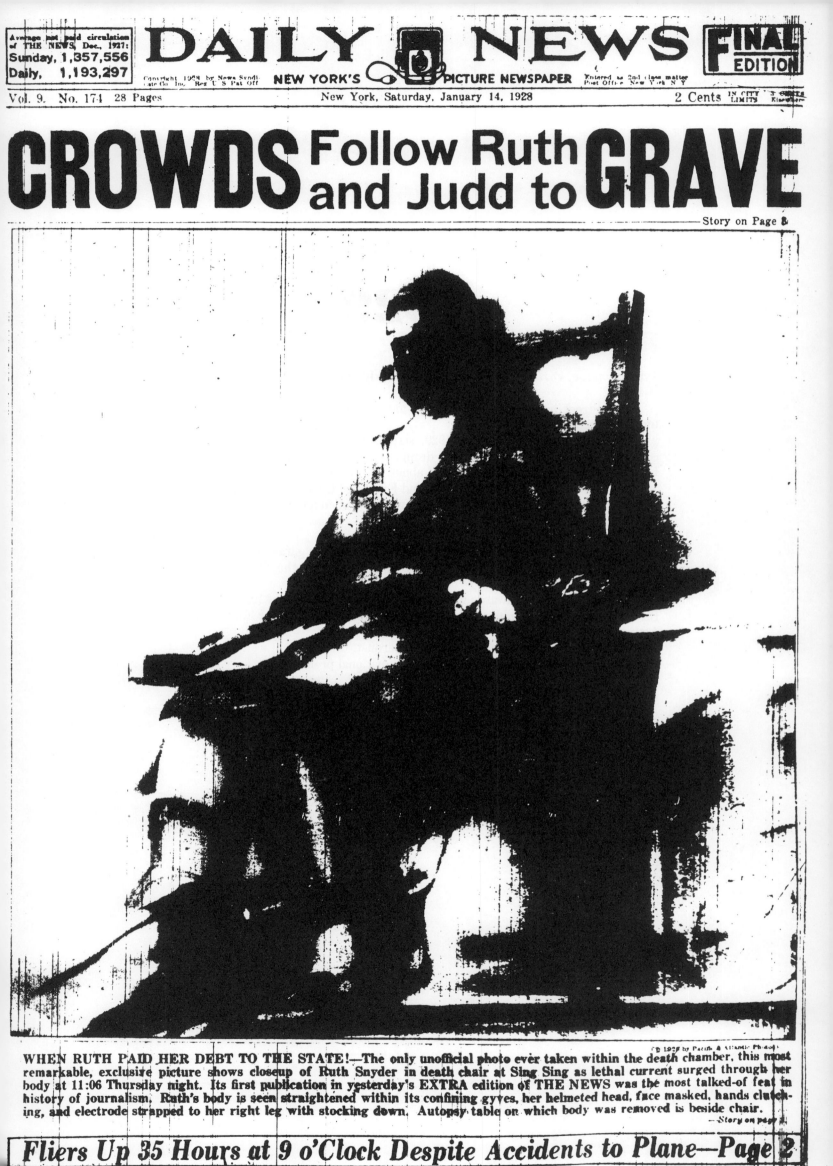

WHEN RUTH PAID HER DEBT TO THE STATE!—The only unofficial photo ever taken within the death chamber, this most remarkable, exclusive picture shows closeup of Ruth Snyder in death chair at Sing Sing as lethal current surged through her body at 11:06 Thursday night. Its first publication in yesterday's EXTRA edition of THE NEWS was the most talked-of feat in history of journalism. Ruth's body is seen straightened within its confining gyves, her helmeted head, face masked, hands clutching, and electrode strapped to her right leg with stocking down. Autopsy table on which body was removed is beside chair.

—Story on page 3

Fliers Up 35 Hours at 9 o'Clock Despite Accidents to Plane—Page 2

1929

Typically terse, *Variety*, the show business weekly, summarized the stock market crash of 1929.

Wall Street had indeed laid an egg, and it took years to put the country back together again.

In a single day, October 29, 1929, sixteen million shares were sold off. In the continuing selling panic, stock values dropped some $15 billion by the end of the year. By mid-1932, stock losses increased to about $75 billion.

With the creation of the Securities and Exchange Commission, in 1934, and other legislation, the country's security industry was controlled and regulated and the nation was able to work itself out of the Depression.

Other events of 1929:

Six members of the Moran gang were lined up against a garage wall in Chicago and shot dead in Chicago's gang wars. It became known as the St. Valentine's Day Massacre.

The first Academy Awards were presented, honoring films of 1927-28. *Wings* was Best Picture, Emil Jannings won Best Actor, and Janet Gaynor was named Best Actress.

Composer Hoagy Carmichael wrote "Stardust."

The radio show *Amos 'n' Andy* made its national premiere.

STAGE | BROADWAY | SCREEN

VARIETY

PRICE 25¢

Published Weekly at 154 West 46th St., New York, N. Y., by Variety, Inc. Annual subscription, $10. Single copies, 25 cents
Entered as second-class matter December 22, 1905, at the Post Office at New York, N. Y., under the act of March 3, 1879.

VOL. XCVII. No. 3 NEW YORK, WEDNESDAY, OCTOBER 30, 1929 88 PAGES

WALL ST. LAYS AN EGG

Going Dumb Is Deadly to Hostess In Her Serious Dance Hall Profesh

A hostess at Roseland has her problems. The paid steppers consider their work a definite profession calling for specialized technique and high-power salesmanship.

"You see, you gotta sell your personality," said one. "Each one of we girls has our own clientele to cater to. It's just like selling dresses in a store—you have to know what to sell each particular customer.

"Some want to dance, some want to kid, some want to get soupy, and others are just 'misunderstood husbands'."

Girls applying for hostess jobs at Roseland must be 21 or older. They must work five nights a week. They are strictly on their own, no salary going with the job and the house collecting 10 cents on every 35 cent ticket. To keep her job, a girl must turn in at least 100 tickets a week during the cold season and 50 in the summer months. In a dull week girls buy their own tickets to keep up the record.

If a partner wishes to sit out a dance, he must pay for the privilege. "Sitting-out time" sells at eight tickets an hour, or $2.80. It's usually a poor sport who will come across with less than $3, many kicking in heavier for a little genial conversation.

The girl who knows her professional dancing trade will keep an alert eye open for potential "sitter-outers," ascertain their hobbies and talk herself into a whole string of tickets. In this way she not only earns money easily, but saves wear and tear on her evening dresses and slippers.

Big money rolls in if she has a good line. One of the most successful girls at Roseland takes this part of her work so seriously that she reads up on current events (sports and stock market included) and has a smattering of current literature and art.

"There are two types of hostesses at Roseland," she said, displaying high brow leanings. "They are the 'mental' and the 'physical.' Surprisingly enough the physical ones are not those who make the most money. One customer will buy three tickets from them at the most. They rely on their sex appeal and go dumb between dances—and that's the surest way to lose a partner, going dumb.

Mental Girls

"The 'mental' girls, being good conversationalists, can wise-crack with the flippant, sympathize with the lonely and know how to salt the fresh boys and make them like it. I have one client who has been coming up every Monday night for two and a half years. Some times he dances all evening, other times we sit out every dance and just talk. He's a good spender, but his wife doesn't understand him."

Usually the hostesses change every two years, although one or two girls have been there for eight years. Some marry, some go into the chorus, others get hat-checking

(Continued on page 63)

Hunk on Winchell

When the Walter Winchells moved into 204 West 55th street, late last week, June, that's Mrs. Winchell, selected a special room as Walter's exclusive sleep den for his late hour nights. She shusshed the Winchell kidlets when her husband dove in at his usual eight o'clock the first morning.

At noon, Walter's midnight, his sound proof room was penetrated by so many high C's he awoke with but four hours of dreams and a grouch. Investigated at once, after having signed the lease of course.

Right next door, on the same floor, is the studio of the noted vocal instructor, Kinney. Among his pupils are Ona Munson, Irene Delroy and Marjorie Peterson. They love Winchell like you love carbolic acid.

And Miss Munson is reported to have requested that an amplifier be started hereafter when she runs up the scale.

Demand for Vaude

Springfield, Ill., Oct. 29.

Petitions requesting Publix theatres to resume vaudeville in Decatur, Ill. are in circulation in that city.

Petitions specify that vaudeville at one or more of the three larger Publix houses would furnish employment to a number of Decatur musicians and stage hands and provide larger variety of local entertainment.

Paul Witte, Publix manager in Decatur, states that he believes vaudeville will find a place in Decatur before the season is over.

Pickpocketing Dying Out

Chicago, Oct. 29.

Some 1,000-odd pickpockets who used to make Chicago what it was are no more. A confidential list in the hands of government revenue men shows them to be operating in bottles.

In the last eight months there has not been a complaint or an arrest for pocket picking.

Flirting Contest

Paris, Oct. 29.

New idea here: "flirting contest" at the Bal Tabarin cabaret.

Gals are permitted to flirt only to a limited degree with a committee of judges regulating their manner of approach.

DROP IN STOCKS ROPES SHOWMEN

Many Weep and Call Off Christmas Orders — Legit Shows Hit

MERGERS HALTED

The most dramatic event in the financial history of America is the collapse of the New York Stock Market. The stage was Wall Street, but the onlookers covered the country. Estimates are that 22,000,000 people were in the market at the time.

Tragedy, despair and ruination spell the story of countless thousands of marginal stock traders. Perhaps Manhattan was worst hit in the number of victims. Many may remain broke for the rest of their lives, because the money that disappeared via the ticker tape was the savings of years.

Many people of Broadway are known to have been wiped out. Reports of some in show business losing as much as $300,000 is not hearsay. One caustic comment to that was that the theatre is enough of a gamble without its people to venture into Wall street.

Prominent showmen, several identified with the picture industry

(Continued on page 64)

FILTHY SHOW OF SHUBERTS GOOD FOR SCREEN

Chicago, Oct. 29.

Shubert's latest musical of their "Night" series, now in Chicago, is so filthy that one of the cast admits embarrassment while in the performance.

The second act of this scramble called "Broadway Nights," is the

(Continued on page 63)

Soft Drink Smuggling

Chicago, Oct. 29.

Bootlegging charged water and ginger ale into the main Loop hotels is recent.

Water, at hotel prices, is 45 cents a bottle. Under the new plan a legger brings in a case at 25 cents a bottle. Ginger ale coming through these channels retails at 15 cents. Hotels get 50 the bottle.

Kidding Kissers in Talkers Burns Up Fans of Screen's Best Lovers

Talker Crashes Olympus

Paris, Oct. 29.

Fox "Follies" and the Fox Movietone newsreel are running this week in Athens, Greece, the first sound pictures heard in the birthplace of world culture, and in all Greece, for that matter.

Several weeks ago, Variety's Cairo correspondent cabled that a cinema had been wired in Alexandria, Cleopatra's home town.

Only Sodom and Gomorrah remain to be heard from.

HOMELY WOMEN SCARCE; CAN'T EARN OVER $25

No homely ones on Broadway!

And now it looks as if Crosby Gaige may have to postpone production of "One Beautiful Evening" because the Main Stem is devoid of the non-beauts necessary for the casting of the show.

Arthur Lubin, caster for the producer, for several weeks has been trying to land the right type of women. A most unusual piece, the drama has an all-women lineup, and, although as many as 28 are needed, all must be homely—and middle age or over, except for two who can be young.

Vera Caspary wrote the play and it centers about conditions at a club for girls where requirements of residence demand that the girls must not earn over $25 per week in order to live under its roof.

That's why they must be homely.

Ads for Execs

Chicago, Oct. 29.

Newspaper ad calling for potential executives for the Publix-B. & K. organization here, drew heavy response, with over 100 applicants.

From all walks of life, with several $20,000-a-year men among the mob, seeking a chance to break into the show business.

Studio in Church

A new Roman Catholic Church, Holy Angels, newly opened on East 47th street near 1st avenue, New York (Italian Parish), has rented out its upper story as a motion picture studio.

Visugraph, industrial producing concern, has established its headquarters there.

Boys who used to whistle and girls who used to giggle when love scenes were flashed on the screen are in action again. A couple of years ago they began to take the love stuff seriously and desisted but the talkers are reviving the ha ha for film osculators.

Heavy loving lovers of silent picture days accustomed to charming audiences into spasms of silent ecstasy when kissing the leading lady are getting the bird instead of the heartbeat. The sound accompaniment is making it tough.

Such a picture romancer as John Gilbert is getting laughs in place of the sighs of other days, and the flaps who still think he's grand are getting sore. One little flap had to be quieted by an usher when making a commotion during a Gilbert picture at the Capitol, New York. The person sitting next to her like many others in the house, took Gilbert's passion lightly. The girl jumped to his defense and started to bawl out the Gilbert derider.

Not only has Gilbert received the bird lately, but all of the other male screen players who specialize in romance. Charley Farrell in "Sunny Side Up" draws many a giggle from his mush stuff.

In the silents when a lover would whisper like a ventriloquist, lips apart and unmoved, and roll his eyes passionately, preparatory to the clinch and then kiss, it looked pretty natural and was believable. The build-up to the kissing now makes a gag of the kiss.

When the kiss is with serious intent, the laughs are out of order. It's burning the impressed female fans to see their favorite kissers kidded when kissing.

In Reverse

Seems the only type of love stuff received as intended since advent of the talkers in the comedy love scene. The screen comics are becoming the heavy lovers and the heavy lovers comedians.

The normal kiss, delivered with the usual smack, sounds like an explosion. For that reason clinch scenes in the early talkers had them rolling in the aisles.

Toning down their kissing to make it noiseless has made bum kissers of the screen's best lovers, but, audible or silent, the kisses are getting laughs that don't belong.

Hollywood, Oct. 29.

Soft pedal on dialog in romantic love scenes in the future. Hereafter, the sacchrine stuff will be

(Continued on page 63)

BROOKLYN EDITION

DAILY NEWS

Copyright, 1929, by News Syndicate Co., Inc. Reg. U. S. Pat. Off. NEW YORK'S PICTURE NEWSPAPER Entered as 2nd class matter, Post Office, New York, N. Y.

EXTRA EDITION

Vol. 11. No. 107 56 Pages New York, Tuesday, October 29, 1929 2 Cents IN CITY LIMITS | 3 CENTS Elsewhere

LOSS IN STOCK COLLAPSE 10 BILLION

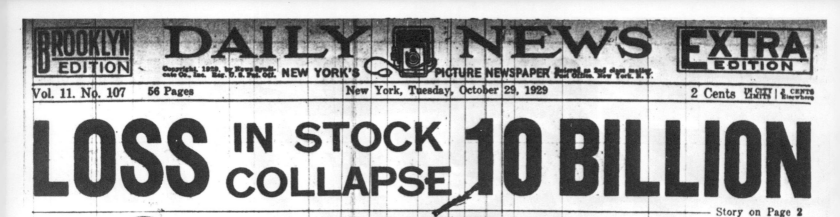

Story on Page 2

(NEWS photo)

NO, NOT MARRIED!—Well, not legally, anyhow. That's what Irene Bordoni (above), who interprets IT in a multitude of languages on the musical comedy stage, claims in an annulment suit she filed in Chicago yesterday against E. Ray Goetz, producer, her husband and former manager. She says he married her less than a year after he divorced Ethel Johnson Goetz in 1918. —*Story on page 3.*

(By Pacific & Atlantic)

PANTAGES SWINGS MOP.—Dejected at conviction on assault charge by Eunice Pringle, 17, Alexander Pantages (with cigar), theatrical magnate, is forced to mop up like other prisoners while awaiting sentence in Los Angeles jail. He is unable to eat prison fare. Here he is entering jail with deputy sheriffs. —*Story on page 3.*

(NEWS photo)

CLOUDS HAD GOLDEN LINING.—Mrs. Edith Murphy Belpusi Healy (above), came back from west yesterday with Reno divorce from Percy C. Healy, wealthy broker, and $500,000 alimony. Healy wooed her in plane. —*Story on page 21.*

(NEWS photo)

MAN DIES IN SUSPICIOUS FIRE.—Body of Joseph Sinascalchi was found in ruins of fire that swept apartment house nearing completion in West 183d st. yesterday. Flames shot high above roof. Firemen are shown at work. Damage was $250,000. Police seek disgruntled former employe. *Story on page 20.*

Mail Plane and 5 Lost in Western Storm

PAGE TWO

Chicago Daily Tribune

THE WORLD'S GREATEST NEWSPAPER

VOLUME LXXXVIII.—NO. 40 C [REG. U. S. PAT. OFFICE: COPYRIGHT 1929 BY THE CHICAGO TRIBUNE.] FRIDAY, FEBRUARY 15, 1929.—42 PAGES THIS PAPER CONSISTS OF THREE SECTIONS SECTION ONE * * * PRICE TWO CENTS

SLAY DOCTOR IN MASSACRE

Snub Sanitary Board's Plea for 27 Millions

[E]LIMINATE "BAD [E]GGS," DEMAND [O]F LEGISLATORS

[Sh]y at Bonds Without a Referendum.

BY OSCAR HEWITT.

[Chicago Tribune Press Service.]

Springfield, Ill., Feb. 14.—[Special.] A delegation from the sanitary district board found out today how far its district record has dropped into disrepute at the state capitol.

It was given a cold shoulder on the ... by Speaker David Shanahan and a hot tongue lashing by members of the executive committee of the senate side.

All that was asked by President Edward W. Elmore, Trustees Ross A. Woodhull and Henry A. Berger, and Attorney Walter E. Beebe was authority to issue $27,000,000 in bonds without a referendum, so that the district may comply with the requirements of the federal government in building sewage treatment plants. It admitted fear that voters would not approve bond issues.

"Nothing doing on removing the referendum," said Speaker Shanahan to the trustees. "I am opposed to tax increases or the removal of referendums on bond issues."

Senate Group Hears Trustees.

The hearing of the trustees on the senate side came at a session of the executive committee, which was considering a resolution of Senator Harry Starr of Chicago which provides for the appointment of a committee of five to investigate the district and ... for turning over to the federal government the Illinois waterway, including that part under the control of the sanitary district.

"The special grand jury which commented on the rotten condition at the district," said Senator Starr, "suggested that the district be turned over to the city. That's taking the valuables from Jesse James and turning them over to Frank James."

The executive committee, after two hours of debate, voted to report out the Starr resolution "without recommendation," so that there will be a full discussion of the district's affairs on the floor of the senate.

Shows Feeling of Senators.

The committee session indicated not only what some senators will say later but the position they will take on the district's request. The request is embodied in a bill presented to the senate today by Senator James J. Barbour of Chicago.

Senators Starr, Henry M. Dunlap of Savoy and William R. McCauley of Olney—which is Gov. Emmerson's district—asked questions and made comments which indicated that they believed it against public policy to give the present trustees power to issue bonds without a referendum. Before giving that authority they wanted some or all of the six holdover trustees off the board.

Three times Senator Dunlap suggested that the legislature should pass a law permitting the residents of Chicago to recall the "half dozen bad eggs," as one senator phrased it.

Demands They Resign.

"They should resign," asserted Senator Starr. "The public has lost confidence in them. If they resign there will be fewer to watch."

"What can prevent the six old trustees from electing a new president and forming a new organization, if we grant the power to issue $27,000,000 in bonds without a referendum?" asked Senator McCauley.

"Nothing," answered Senator Roy Woods of Chicago. "They have managed the organization several times in the last few years."

"What guarantee have we that the management will not continue corruption, fraud and graft if we do not give the people the power to recall the drainage trustees?" Senator Dunlap added.

"No one stands for the intolerable and criminal conditions by which the people have been looted out of millions," observed Senator Barbour.

Starr Interrupts Elmore.

"With the president and cashier of a bank straight it would be hard to put over crooked deals on a bank," argued President Elmore.

"But if you found a crooked condition in a bank," interposed Senator Starr, "the bank examiner would insist that the five or six directors responsible for the crookedness be removed and new directors substituted

[Continued on page 6, column 8.]

NEWS SUMMARY of the Tribune

(And Historical Scrap Book.)

Friday, February 15, 1929.

Average net paid circulation of THE CHICAGO TRIBUNE January, 1929:

Daily - - - - 824,633

Sunday - - 1,251,304

CERMAK ENLISTS COUNTY IN FIGHT ON GAS TAX BILL

City to Get Nothing, Simpson Says.

President Anton J. Cermak of the county board yesterday joined the fight against Gov. Louis L. Emmerson's 3 cent gasoline tax bill. From Miami Beach, Fla., where he is recuperating from an attack of intestinal inflammation, the county executive sent a telegram to his office, urging the use of every influence to block a tax that would not give Chicago and Cook county its share of the revenue.

At the same time James Simpson, chairman of the Chicago plan commission, who has asked the Association of Commerce to oppose Gov. Emmerson's gas bill, presented new arguments for fighting inequitable distribution of the revenue. He pointed out that Chicago motorists, through the vehicle tax, are now paying the state $6,000,000, of which none is spent in Chicago and only a small percentage on the roads of Cook county.

City Gets Nothing, He Says.

"With the gasoline tax added to the vehicle tax," said Mr. Simpson, "Chicago automobile owners would be turning over $13,500,000 to the state. Under the bill as presented to the legislature, none of this money would be applied to the city's streets and little to the county's roads.

"Under the present vehicle tax of $8 to $20 a year, the motorist is paying the equivalent of approximately 2 cents a gallon to the state. The legislative bill would add 3 cents to this, making a total of 5 cents a gallon levied against Chicago motorists for roads they wouldn't get."

Cook county would pay about 45 per cent of the gas tax under the measure proposed by the new governor, it was estimated by President Cermak. To show what the county would get in return, Mr. Cermak pointed to the $60,000,000 highway bond issue as a precedent, in which Cook county was allowed only 3 per cent of the new roads. Another precedent was the $100,000,000 bond issue in which the county was allotted 5 per cent of the road mileage but didn't get it, according to Mr. Cermak.

City's Share $7,500,000.

Gov. Emmerson would return to each of the state's counties a third of the tax paid by its residents. The other two-thirds would go to the state for building roads, principally down state. Chicago would pay $7,500,000 annually, it is estimated.

Down state legislators argue that Chicago motorists should help pay for their roads because city residents frequently drive through the rural communities. Mr. Cermak in a survey made to oppose Gov. Len Small's gas tax, showed that eighteen automobiles from down state entered Cook county to every one Cook county automobile that traveled over down state roads.

President Cermak's telegram read in part:

"Instruct Chicago and Cook county legislators not to sacrifice their constituents in the gas tax legislation. Our community must be treated fairly in this legislation if we are to support the measure. I am for a proper gas tax, apportioning the revenue, because it will make it possible to build more roads in Cook county without adding to the general tax bill."

Paying for Own Roads.

Cook county's $15,000,000 road building program is nearing completion. It was financed by bonds for which Cook county residents are paying. Another bond issue, boosting Cook county general taxes will be necessary Mr. Cermak's office pointed out, unless it gets its fair portion of the revenue from the proposed gasoline tax.

Ald. John S. Clark [30th], chairman of the council finance committee, made the same argument in behalf of the city, pointing out that Chicago is too badly in need of money to repair its streets to afford to be taxed for county roads. He will present a resolution Monday, he announced, asking the council to take a stand opposing Gov. Emmerson's bill.

Andrew L. Sanger, manager of the Cartage exchange, representing owners of 2,000 trucks which do most of the hauling for loop stores, voiced the opposition of his association to the tax bill as it now stands.

"For each five ton truck," he said,

[Continued on page 16, column 3.]

J. RAGLAN PATCHMORE COMES TO TOWN

Heavy Snowfall Caused Untold Suffering

South Side Teems with Anguish

J. Raglan Patchmore Makes History for Two Hours

At 4 o'clock all was quiet in the newspaper office. At three minutes past four every telephone in the place was ringing furiously as reports came in from many parts of the south side that terrible howls of anguish were rocking the whole district.

SCENE OF GREAT ACTIVITY.

"It's an earthquake or a race riot," reported one informant.

A reporter was dispatched posthaste to the scene of the disaster and at once located the cause of the excitement.

Mr. J. Raglan Patchmore, chaperoned by a hard boiled policeman, was engaged in shoveling snow, and from time to time his whole soul was concentrated in a 100 per cent protest.

"I'm not responsible for putting this

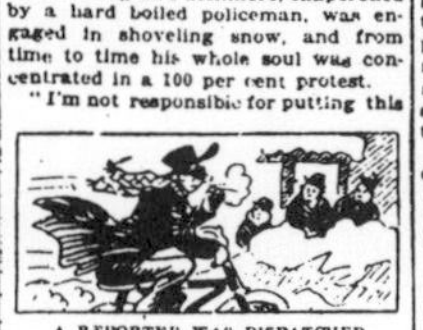

A REPORTER WAS DISPATCHED POSTHASTE.

snow here," he cried, "and why should I have to take it away?"

This was unanswerable.

Every few seconds the policeman endeavored to persuade Mr. Patchmore to resume his labors. He was working much harder than Mr. Patchmore. His total output of perspiration was greater than the total amount of snow shoveled by Mr. P., thereby presenting an interesting problem in economics.

"This is the greatest indignity I have ever suffered" panted the noted Apostle of Repose as he leaned against his shovel, "but it serves me right for

A 100% PROTEST.

staying in the city while snow shoveling is epidemic. It nearly happened once before, back in 1907, but a January thaw saved me."

For many years Mr. Patchmore, who is the inventor of static, has constituted one-half of the city's leisure class, rated by output, and so to see him engaged in work of any kind was epochal to say the least.

"What does a man think about when he is shoveling snow?" asked the reporter, desirous of adding something to the sum total of human knowledge.

"Of the utter futility of it," answered Mr. Patchmore, ruefully regarding the calluses on his hands, the first he had ever acquired on that part of his body. "And the heartlessness of it," he added. "When I shovel snow I take the work away from some poor, deserving fellow who wants to work more than I do."

As the reporter was jotting this down while it was still fresh, Mr. Patchmore expounded in a more violent vein.

"It's an outrage! The country is going to the dogs. There is not enough unemployment. I hope to see it increased at once."

"By about how many?"

"By one. This is the first time I have worked, outside of an institution where they specialize in it, since the panic of 1893, when I lost my entire fortune of eleven dollars. Since then I have avoided accumulating money for fear of losing it in another panic."

"You should take these cataclysms philosophically," suggested the reporter.

By this time it was 6 o'clock and the policeman exhausted from his labors told Mr. Patchmore he could lay off for the day.

"Come back tomorrow," he said; "we'll have some more snow for you."

"Can you trust him to return to the scene of his labors?" queried the astonished reporter.

WHERE HE WEARS HIS CALLUSES.

"No. He'll leave the city by the first southbound freight. He can't stand the physical torture of shoveling snow. You know there's a heavy reward for getting Patchmore out of town."

The newspaper reading public has been unable to follow Mr. Patchmore's inactivities. He moves so slowly it is almost a physical impossibility to follow him.

It is only when he is actuated by some compelling motive, such as a constable or a watchdog, that he accelerates his activities to something approaching third speed.

After such bursts he rests so intensively that he manages to keep his average below that of all his fellow men.

"Where do you purpose going when you leave the city?" Mr. Patchmore was asked.

"I shall study a weather chart," relighting an Inperfecto, "and hope to get below the snow line as soon as possible."

SOUTHBOUND.

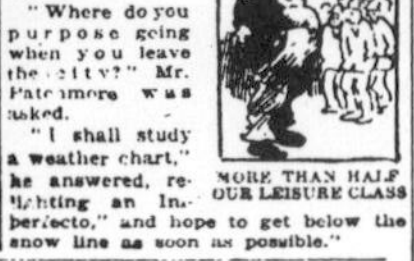

MORE THAN HALF OUR LEISURE CLASS

FORMER RUSSIAN PRINCESS TAKEN TO PSYCHOPATHIC

Mrs. Mabel Rogers Blakely, once the wife of Prince Kropotkin of an aristocratic Russian family, was taken from her room in the Hotel Sherman last night to the county psychopathic hospital for observation. Police took her to the hospital on a warrant issued several days ago by County Judge Edmund K. Jarecki on the recommendation of Dr. William Hickson, municipal psychiatrist, who said he found her mentally unbalanced.

Mrs. Blakely, who had lived until recently at the Rogers Park hotel, has been involved in civil suits over her fortune, reputed to exceed $1,000,000. Several judges, among them Judge Philip J. Finnegan, reported she had telephoned them, making threats and complaining of their decisions in the civil suits. She charges her relatives with instigating a suit to have her declared incompetent in order to gain control of her wealth.

REPORT WRIGLEY SHIFTS PROXIES TO COL. STEWART

New York, Feb. 14.—(AP)—The New York Herald-Tribune tomorrow will say it was reported in Wall street that William Wrigley Jr., chewing gum manufacturer, has shifted his support from John D. Rockefeller Jr. to Col. Stewart in the Standard Oil company of Indiana proxy fight.

Wrigley holds a large block of Indiana Standard stock and previously had signed proxies in favor of Mr. Rockefeller.

At Mr. Rockefeller's office it was said no notification had been received from Mr. Wrigley and that Mr. Rockefeller still had proxies of more than 51 per cent of the stock.

Brewing Plant in Foreign War Veterans' Post Seized

Revere, Mass., Feb. 14.—(AP)—A room fitted out to represent a dugout of world war days in France, even to French inscriptions and artistic decorations, in a building said to be the home of Revere post, Veterans of Foreign Wars, was raided today by federal prohibition officers. A brewing plant, a liquor "splitting" plant, and a quantity of liquor were seized. Jack Wheeler, commander of the post, and Benjamin Waxler, in charge of the bar, were summoned to appear before the United States commissioner tomorrow on charges of violating the dry laws.

Clerk Is Found Dead in Room of Loop Hotel

A. N. Hamilton, 48 years old, 5430 Ellis avenue, a clerk employed in the claim department of the Illinois Bell Telephone company, was found dead in his room at the Sherman hotel last night, supposedly of heart disease

Parliament of Canada Buries Royal Titles

BY GEORGE SMITH.

[Chicago Tribune Press Service.]

[Copyright: 1929: By The Chicago Tribune.]

OTTAWA, Ont., Feb. 14.—The issue of the restoration of titles for Canadians was buried apparently for the duration of this generation when the Canadian house of commons this afternoon refused to allow a special committee to reconsider to any extent whatsoever the Canadian parliament's 1919 address to the king of Great Britain, which asked the king not to bestow titles upon Canadians.

The resolution of Charles Cahan, Montreal Conservative, asking for such committee consideration was defeated almost two to one, by 114 to 60 votes, in spite of the fact that the leaders of both major parties, Premier Mackenzie King and Richard Bennett, supported it and voted for it.

Cabinet Is Split.

The King cabinet of Canada split on the issue and the poll of the vote found Premier King, Finance Minister Robb, Health Minister Dr. King, Secretary of State Rinfret, Marine Minister Cardin, and Solicitor General Cannon voting for the resolution, while Postmaster General Veniot, Minister of Agriculture Motherwell, Railways Minister Dunning, Public Works Minister Elliott, Defense Minister Ralston, Immigration Minister Forke, and Labor Minister Heenan voted against it.

Even the chief whips of both parties, who are supposed to round up party men behind their leaders, voted against their own leaders in this queerest of all house divisions in Canadian parliament.

The rank and file of the major parties split wide open, although most Liberals voted against reconsideration of the titles and most Conservatives for reconsideration of them. Progressives and Laborites voted solidly against.

Nobody Defends Titles.

Another astonishing feature of the debate, which has lasted three days in parliament, was that not a single member in parliament would voice his approval of a return to titles in Canada. Mr. Cahan was assumed to favor a return to them because he fathered the resolution, but today when that sentiment was attributed to him he indignantly demanded to be shown where in his speech he had favored a return to titles. The whole house laughed at this retreat of the last protitular parliamentarian in the Canadian commons.

Titles opponents throughout the afternoon again spurned any suggestion of titular appendages for Canadians. Mr. Brown of Manitoba effectively dampened any lurking titles enthusiasm with a fervent rendering of Bobbie Burns' "A Man's a Man for a' That."

George Spotton, Ontario Conservative, declared that not with his vote would any of the Canadian mothers of dead soldier sons bow the knee to titled women and call them "lady."

Denounces "Empty Heads."

Tom Bird of British Columbia denounced those "vain and empty headed Canadians" who would seek titular distinction and, like Mr. Spotton, he proclaimed against any return to medievalism. Where was there a knight of today, Mr. Bird demanded heatedly, who fulfilled the precepts of ancient knighthood of either fighting wrong, defending the weak, fearing God, or honoring the king.

"Why," he exclaimed, "they dishonor the king, these empty headed Canadians, who wear foreign honors contrary to the king's wishes."

THE WEATHER

FRIDAY, FEBRUARY 15, 1929.

Sunrise, 6:46; sunset, 5:23. Moon sets at 12:07 a. m. Saturday. Saturn and Mercury are morning stars; Jupiter, Mars, and Venus are evening stars.

Chicago and vicinity—Increasing cloudiness and slightly warmer Friday; snow Friday night and probably early Saturday, followed by clearing Saturday; moderate westerly winds, becoming variable.

Illinois—Increasing cloudiness Friday; possibly rain in extreme south portion, slightly warmer; rain or snow in south, and possibly snow in north portion—Saturday, somewhat colder in south portion.

TRIBUNE BAROMETER

TEMPERATURES IN CHICAGO

MAXIMUM, 2 P. M. 26

MINIMUM, 8 A. M. 13

3 a. m....21	Noon....20	8 p. m....21
4 a. m....20	1 p. m....24	9 p. m....20
5 a. m....17	2 p. m....26	Unofficial—
6 a. m....15	3 p. m....25	10 p. m....20
7 a. m....14	4 p. m....24	11 p. m....20
8 a. m....13	5 p. m....23	Midnight....20
9 a. m....15	6 p. m....22	1 a. m....19
10 a. m....18	7 p. m....21	2 a. m....19
11 a. m....19		

For 24 hours ended at 7 p. m., Feb. 14: Mean temperature, 20 degrees; normal, 26; deficiency since Jan. 1, 287. Precipitation, 0; excess since Jan. 1, 1.26 inches.

Barometer, 7 a. m. 30.03; 7 p. m. 30.03.

[Official weather table on page 36.]

Ruth Roland, Former Film Star, Weds Screen Actor

Beverly Hills, Cal., Feb. 14.—(AP)—Ruth Roland, former star of motion picture serials, and Ben Bard, film actor, were married at a brilliant ceremony here tonight. Billie Dove, screen star, was maid of honor and Robert Z. Leonard, a director, best man. The couple declined to reveal their honeymoon plans.

The bride has made a fortune in real estate since leaving the films

CONGRESS ACTS TOMORROW ON ALIEN KILLERS

BY ARTHUR SEARS HENNING.

[Chicago Tribune Press Service.]

Washington, D. C., Feb. 14.—[Special.]—A move to rid Chicago and other large cities of alien gunmen and "pineapple" tossers is to be made in the house Saturday, when the deportation bill and other proposed legislation affecting immigrants will be considered under a special rule.

Representative Albert Johnson [Rep. Wash.], chairman of the immigration committee, will offer an amendment, adding to the enumerated classes of deportable aliens the following:

"An alien who is convicted of carrying, transporting, or possessing any weapon or explosive bomb, for which he is sentenced to imprisonment for a term of one year or more; but only if the offense is committed after the enactment of this act."

Follows Sabath Amendment.

The amendment was proposed originally by Representative Adolph J. Sabath [Dem., Ill.], a member of the immigration committee, who has been pressing for action that would enable the federal government to deport the alien gangs that have been terrorizing Chicago.

Inability to break up these gangs by the deportation process has been attributed to defective deportation and naturalization laws. When these gangs are rounded up by the police it is found that many of their members are naturalized, and hence not subject to deportation. Many of the aliens are not deportable under the present law, which provides for deportation for an offense involving moral turpitude committed within five years of entry, for which the alien has been imprisoned one year or more, or for more than one such offense at any time after entry.

First offenders who have been in the country more than five years slip through the net, as do others by virtue of varying construction of the term "moral turpitude."

Aim to Close Loopholes.

The Sabath amendment closes these loopholes and makes it possible to deport alien gunmen and bomb throwers for first offenses at any time after the enactment of the law.

The bombings and gang shootings in Chicago have caused the immigration service to dispatch several additional inspectors to that city for a checkup of alien criminals. These inspectors have been investigating the records of aliens among the 3,000 recently caught by the police, but so far as Washington has been informed they have not found many who are deportable.

The immigration service is planning to increase the Chicago force of inspectors from the half dozen now stationed there to fifty as rapidly as congress will appropriate for the expansion.

"The majority of the so-called alien gunmen are not aliens at all," said Congressman Sabath tonight. "They are American citizens by birth or naturalization. But so far as aliens do constitute these gangs they should be deported. The present law is inadequate for the purpose and I believe that my amendment will go far toward breaking up the alien gangs."

Drug Peddlers Included.

The bill also provides for the deportation of alien violators of the Mann white slave and Harrison narcotic acts, aliens who harbor or aid deportable aliens, aliens who enter the United States unlawfully, and aliens who assist them, aliens convicted of two felonies and aliens who are habitual criminals, having been given three or more sentences, aggregating two years or more, within ten years after entry.

Deported aliens who reënter the United States are declared guilty of a felony, with punishment fixed at imprisonment for not more than two years or a fine of not more than $1,000, or both.

An alien who gains entry into the

[Continued on page 2, column 7.]

OFFICIALS PROBE BOOZE DEALS IN GANG SHOOTING

Inquest Today in Seven Deaths.

[Pictures on back page.]

In the state's attorney's investigation last night of the "north side massacre" in which seven men were shot dead against a wall in a garage at 2122 North Clark street yesterday morning a covetailing of underworld rumors developed a double motive.

It is the police belief that the gangsters who were killed paid the penalty for being followers of George Moran, successor to Dean O'Banion. The historic antagonist, as history goes in the swift careers of gangsters, of the O'Banion-Moran crew, is Alphonse Capone, otherwise Al Brown.

See 20th Ward Motive.

While that historic antagonism furnished the police a background of hate, jealousy, and revenge, it was also reported that a more immediate reason for the seven murders lies in a campaign of Moran's alcohol sellers to take liquor from Detroit sources and with it penetrate the Bloody Twentieth ward, the booze territory of the Capone gang.

While the police under Commissioner Russell and State's Attorney Swanson were hunting evidence a special coroner's jury was impanelled by Coroner Bundesen to investigate the murders of the men listed and described as follows:

Dr. Reinhardt H. Schwimmer, resident of the Parkway hotel, an optometrist with offices in the Capitol building. Had no criminal record, but was known as the companion of hoodlums and was said to have boasted recently that he was in the alky racket and could have any one "taken for a ride."

Peter Gusenberg, 434 Roscoe street, for 27 years a criminal and one of the leaders of the Moran gang.

Albert R. Weinshank, owner of the Alcazar club, 4207 Broadway, and an official of the Central Cleaners and Dyers company, 2705 Fullerton avenue.

Adam Heyer, alias Frank Snyder, alias Hayes, 2024 Farragut avenue, owner of the S. M. C. Cartage company, where the murders took place.

John May, 1249 West Madison street, father of seven children and an ex-safe blower.

James Clark, brother-in-law of Bugs Moran, and said to have a reputation as a hardened killer.

Frank Gusenberg, brother of Peter, who died in the Alexian Brothers' hospital after refusing for an hour to give any information to the police about his assailants.

The members of Coroner Bundesen's special jury which will meet at 10 a. m. today are:

Bert A. Massee, president of the Palm Olive company.

Walter E. Olson, president of the Olson Rug company.

Fred Bernstein, manager of the Covenant club.

Dr. John D. McCormick, dean

1931

The "Star-Spangled Banner" was officially declared the national anthem of the United States.

Unemployment topped four million in the United States as the bank panic spread.

Ruth Judd surrendered in a sensational murder case in Arizona.

Chicago gangster Al "Scarface" Capone was sent to prison for income-tax evasion.

In Arizona 5c per copy, 60c per month — PAY NO MORE — Out of Arizona 10c per copy, $1.00 per month

Extra PHOENIX EVENING GAZETTE Extra

ARIZONA'S CAPITAL NEWSPAPER + AGGRESSIVE AND INDEPENDENT

VOL. LI. PHOENIX, ARIZONA, Friday Evening, October 23, 1931 NO. 306.

RUTH JUDD SURRENDERS

SELF DEFENSE CLAIM MADE BY WOMAN; HAND SHATTERED BY BULLET

(Exclusive Gazette Dispatch)

LOS ANGELES, Oct. 23.—Mrs. Winnie Ruth Judd, sought in the trunk murders of two girl friends in Phoenix, surrendered to officers here tonight.

She was critically injured, her right hand being virtually shot off.

She confessed to the dual killing and pleaded self defense.

Officers found her when they were sent to an undertaking establishment at Court and Olive street, four blocks from the county jail.

She surrendered without resistance or discussion.

She was in a state of collapse.

This was believed due to lack of food and loss of blood from her injury. She had had nothing to eat in four days, or since she left Phoenix Sunday.

She was taken immediately to the jail.

Radio reports of the capture, broadcast by Los Angeles stations, sent throngs surging toward the scene of the surrender and the jail.

Her surrender climaxed not only five days of intensive searching, but an afternoon of anxiety during which it was believed she might surrender any minute.

TALKS TO JUDD

First warning that Mrs. Judd might be getting ready to surrender came late this afternoon when it was learned that one of the defense attorneys had arranged telephonic communication between her and Dr. Judd.

Richard Cantillon, the attorney, in revealing the communication said he believed Mrs. Judd might be ready to surrender.

He said he had had two telephone calls, one of which came shortly after noon.

A woman's voice was excited and nervous. She said Mrs. Judd was [illegible] and wanted to get in touch with her husband, answering an appeal he issued through the morning papers.

Cantillon did not question the woman further, but gave her a telephone number at which he said she could reach Dr. Judd. The woman called a second time shortly before 2 p. m., and said she could not get the other number.

Cantillon repeated it for her. Several hours later he announced that Mrs. Judd's attempt to communicate with her husband had been successful and that they had [illegible].

"Dr. Judd has contacted and talked with his wife," the attorney's statement said. "He instructed me to stay in the office all night if necessary, to make the final arrangements."

BROTHER IS GLAD

[illegible] that Mrs. Judd had communicated with her husband, her brother, Burton J. McKinnell, her brother with whom she went to the Southern Pacific station last Monday in an unsuccessful attempt to reclaim the murder trunks, exclaimed:

"Thank God she's alive. I know she's innocent."

Although Cantillon announced that Mrs. Judd's surrender was imminent, it was several hours before she actually surrendered. It was learned this was because of a controversy between the Los Angeles county sheriff's office and those over who was to have jurisdiction.

Inspector Davidson ordered police officers to stand guard outside the hall of justice in case she appeared and an attempt was made to take her to the sheriff's office.

Cantillon later announced:

"Dr. Judd has instructed me to stay in the office all night if necessary to make final arrangements for Mrs. Judd's surrender."

It, however, was not necessary, as the surrender came shortly afterward.

[illegible] officers over the entire West breathed a deep sigh of relief as soon as word of Mrs. Judd's surrender was flashed.

For five days they had been conducting one of the most intensive searches in the history of the West.

Their hunt began the moment the two trunks shipped from Phoenix with their gruesome contents, were opened by officers in Los Angeles.

DENIES HAVING KEYS

The trunks were not obtained early in the afternoon by Mrs. Judd because baggagemen, noticing blood oozing from them, thought they contained contraband deer meat.

They asked Mrs. Judd and her brother to open the trunks.

Mrs. Judd hesitated, then said she did not have the keys; that they were in her husband's possession. She and the youth left the place immediately, driving away in his collegiate flivver.

Later, baggagemen decided to call police and have the trunks opened under official supervision.

The locks were broken, instantly revealing their grisly contents. One trunk contained the body of Mrs. LeRoi and part of the body of Miss Samuelsen. The other was found to contain still other parts of Miss Samuelsen's body.

Part of the latter was still missing. It was discovered some hours later in a suitcase in the woman's rest room of the station. It was with a hatbox which, opened, disclosed surgical instruments with which Miss Samuelsen might have been dismembered, and the 25 caliber automatic with which the two women might have been shot.

Immediately an alarm was broadcast for the arrest of Mrs. Judd and McKinnell. McKinnell was found by officers, but said he had let his sister out of his car early in the afternoon and did not know where she was.

Dr. Judd next was taken into custody but he denied knowledge of his wife's whereabouts and said he had not seen her in several months.

Both he and McKinnell were kept in custody for many hours while they were grilled thoroughly.

Officers here meanwhile established that the two women had been killed in their home at 2929 North Second street, probably Friday night. Their bodies were packed in a trunk dragged from their garage.

Saturday night the trunk was taken to Mrs. Judd's apartment, where the dismembering of Miss Samuelsen's body apparently took place.

Sunday the trunks were taken to the Union station by H. U. Grimm, owner of Mrs. Judd's apartment, who had no suspicion of their contents.

Shaw Says Justice Corruption Insufficient To Oust Dry Law

LONDON, Oct. 23.—(AP)—Bootlegging in the United States results in corruption of police and law courts, but that is no reason for doing away with prohibition George Bernard Shaw told the World Prohibition federation yesterday.

He attacked tipplers who utilize alcohol to obtain jollity or courage, saying he should feel ashamed if he had to resort to such aids. [illegible] And he also accused Gilbert Chesterton of being a "secret teetotaler" because Mr. Chesterton "is very loud" in singing the praises of wine.

"The direct results of prohibition in the United States have been excellently successful in every way," Mr. Shaw said, "but some of the indirect results are very curious.

"There's an industry called bootlegging in America, and its profits are so large that the people who take part in it [illegible] the corruption of justice. In some of the eastern states this corruption of the police and the bench has reached the point that the work of the bootleggers has become quite safe.

"That is a very serious result, but it is not a reason for going back on prohibition. Rather is it a reason for the reorganization of law and order."

In Soviet Russia, he said, the bootlegger or gangster would last about 10 minutes. "Over there they would shoot the profiteers just as they deal with gangsters. One day the profiteer disappears and his relatives are informed that he won't be back."

The way to cure drunkenness, G. B. S. continued, is to "make the people not want to drink." He added:

"I believe a greater proportion of the people of this country are not [illegible] of drinking [illegible] actually are [illegible]"

Trunk Murder Mystery Principals

Mrs. Winnie Ruth Judd (right) against whom first degree murder charges stand in the trunks slaying of Mrs. Agnes Anne LeRoi (left) and Miss Hedvig Samuelsen (center). Dr. W. C. Judd, husband of Mrs. Judd (below) was the first to get in communication with his wife, who eluded capture for five days although sought throughout the West.

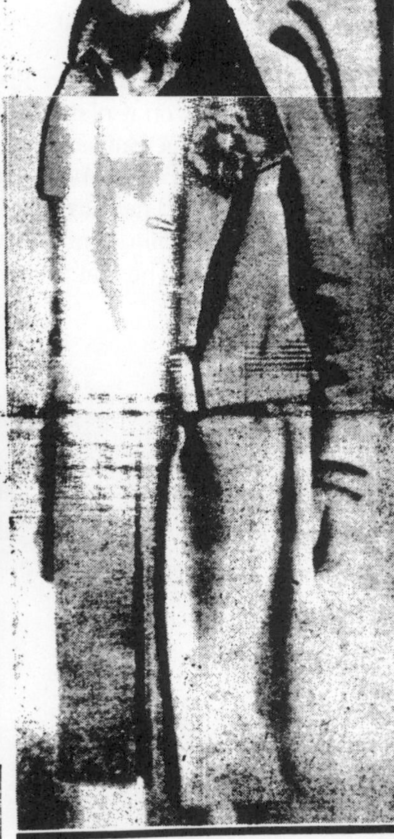

New York Man Unable To Give Crime Motive

ELBERON, N. J., Oct. 23.—(AP)—Thomas Frelinghuysen, of New York and Elberon, writer of a letter found among the effects of Miss Hedvig Samuelsen, one of the trunk murder victims whose bodies were found at Los Angeles, said last night his acquaintances with her was of a casual nature.

He could throw no light on her murder or that of her friend.

Frelinghuysen, son of the late Frederick Frelinghuysen, New York broker, said he did not know the girl intimately and the "dear sweetheart" letter found among Miss Samuelsen's effects was just "one of those things."

"I met her last summer on a tour in Alaska," he explained. "She was such a pathetic creature that I sent her some books."

Less Tension Is Manifest In Trade Circles

NEW YORK, Oct. 23.—(AP)—Bradstreet's tomorrow will say:

"Fair seasonal activity in some lines is evident in most of the reports to Bradstreet's from 50 leading cities. Cooler weather has been a factor here although some reports complain that temperatures still are too high for best results. There also are here and there disappointing complaints that volume of trade is not up to last year but, in general, an encouraging amount of cheerfulness is expressed—another indication that business is coming to expect less activity than in other recent years and is adjusting itself accordingly."

Dun's tomorrow will say:

"Sentiment was further improved this week. Evidence of greater stability in commodity prices was accompanied by more active trading in some of the primary markets. The volume of sales in dry goods increased both at wholesale and retail, much of the increase in the wholesale division being traced to the filling of long deferred needs in cotton goods. A lessening of the tension in financial conditions in the country as a whole was clearly reflected in this renewed trading."

Silver Prices Are Subject Of Conference

SALT LAKE CITY, Oct. 23.—(AP)—Mark L. Requa, Republican national committeeman from California, stopped here yesterday on route home from the East and conferred with a group of Utah men concerning the silver situation.

"I am naturally concerned with silver," he said, "since I am a mining engineer and a former resident of Nevada."

He met with Sen. Reed Smoot, Harold F. Fabian, Republican national committeeman [illegible] (Utah) [illegible] W. Mont Ferry, president of the American Silver Producers association and a member of the international silver organization and with George W. [illegible] and Frank E. Cook, other [illegible]

DEPOT TRIP DESCRIBED IN TRUNK CASE

"I hope nothing like this ever happens again in my life. No siree, I got all of it I wanted on this job."

So was expressed the sentiment of H. U. Grimm, impromptu "trunk murder" expressman who, with his 19-year-old son, hauled to the Union station here the two trunks of Mrs. Winnie Ruth Judd in which were the bodies of Mrs. Agnes Anne Le Roi and Miss Hedvig Samuelsen, it developed when the trunks were opened in Los Angeles.

But the 49-year-old contractor, builder and landlord, from whom Mrs. Judd rented her apartment, added as an afterthought: "—and that woman still owes me $1.50."

Not only did Grimm haul Mrs. Judd's trunks to the railway station, but it was he and his son who drove her to the train when she carried with her the suitcase, a hatbox and another small grip, Grimm said.

Grimm, father of six children, came here six years ago from Portland, Ore. He has engaged in Sunday school and church work for 24 or 25 years.

Grimm's story of the trip of the trunks from the Judd apartment to the railway station follows:

"About 5:30 o'clock my boy and I came to the apartment and took the two trunks out. She didn't say anything about how we should handle the trunks and she didn't seem to care.

"The big trunk was so heavy and hard to handle that I said to my boy that we wouldn't put it in the car—just rope it on the running board. The boy went back and carried the little trunk out by himself.

"In the meantime Mrs. Judd carried out the suitcase, a hatbox and another small grip. We started toward the station, she sitting in front with me and my boy was in back with the smaller trunk.

Short Of Funds

"I don't remember just what we talked about . . . nothing important, I guess. When we got to the station she said, 'Well, I just as well pay you for this dray bill.' Then she opened her purse and gave me a paper dollar. She also had a silver dollar which she took into the depot to get changed and pay me the other half dollar.

"When she went in she took the hatbox with her. She didn't let me get ahold of that at all.

"She went back to the baggage room and I heard her ask how much her baggage would cost to ship. A moment later she came out to the car where I was and asked if it was alright if she paid the dray bill when she came back—that she was short of funds. When I said it would be alright she took the dollar bill.

"She said she'd be back Wednesday or Thursday . . . [illegible] owes me $1.50—[illegible]"

FRENCH DOLLS HOLD SECRETS IN SLAYINGS

Where two vivacious Phoenix girls met brutal death last Friday night and were shipped as baggage to Los Angeles, two equally lifeless and gawky, floppy French dolls yesterday reigned supreme.

It was the home of Mrs. Agnes Anne LeRoi and Miss Hedvig Samuelsen.

The milling throng of curious poured into the neighborhood of 2929 North Second street by the hundreds, in automobiles, on foot and even by street cars nearby.

Many were content to drive or walk by and scan the modern little duplex with its unimpressive surroundings.

But others surged around the house from early yesterday morning until well after dusk last night—peeking in windows, knocking on doors, exploring the grounds and garage and, above all, seeking souvenirs.

To the souvenir hunters in the past four days has gone anything outside the house not under lock or nailed down, and even some things which were nailed down. Two of the four numbers, "2929" disappeared Thursday morning from the front of the home. The visitors have beaten a path through the uncut grass in the front yard to the front door.

Many came just to see what is believed to have been the "death chamber," the bedroom in the rear of the house in which Mrs. LeRoi and bed-ridden Miss Samuelsen are believed to have been shot to death.

Amateur detectives daily make much ado over their search for "clues." Strangers join in heated discussions in the yard of the house as to theories of the double slaying.

An eerie, unexpected thrill caught a number of the curious off-guard Thursday morning.

In the front living room of the home, several blankets had been carelessly tossed over a straight-backed chair which stood near enough to the window of the room so that it could be seen through the hallway leading to the bedroom. Over the blankets, carelessly or otherwise, had been thrown a dress belonging to one of the two slain women. Atop the back of the chair, resting on the blankets, were two women's hats.

At a casual glance through any one of several lace-curtained windows in the home, it appeared that a woman sat in the chair.

A young boy stood peering in through a bedroom window. His attention suddenly focused on the "scarecrow" in the living room. "My gosh, there's a woman sitting in the front room," he exclaimed.

The curious crowded around . . . intent upon missing nothing. For a few moments they gazed in awe . . . it did look like a woman.

Then, like a bolt out of the blue, came a remark from another youngster, "Gosh, she hasn't any legs!"

A woman screamed, others paled. The curious dropped back as though suddenly confronted by a spectre. But it was broad daylight, and the sudden fright passed off quickly.

Throughout the day the two French dolls sat silently, serenely in the "murder house." One's slim legs dangled nearly a foot below a black satin dress. The flaming red of the other doll's dress was a brilliant contrast. One had been found on Mrs. LeRoi's bed—undoubtedly her doll." The other sat stoically on a small stand beside the front door when officers first entered the house.

If dolls could only talk . . .

The LeRoi-Samuelsen dwelling was deserted last night, as lonely and foreboding as it has been every night as soon as shrouded with darkness.

EX-HUSBAND SAYS VICTIM ROMANTICIST

PORTLAND, Ore., Oct. 23.—(AP)—William Mason, automobile dealer here, revealed yesterday that he was the first husband of Agnes Imlah LeRoi, one of the victims in the Phoenix trunk murders.

"I married her in 1925," he said, "while she was in training at a hospital here. The ceremony was performed at Kelso. We lived together about 18 months. We did not quarrel but it was a case of incompatibility and we agreed on a settlement and divorce.

"At the time of our marriage," he continued, "she wanted it kept secret so she could complete her training. We were not successful in this and she left the hospital soon after.

"When we were divorced I assisted her in re-entering the hospital. We saw each other occasionally and were friendly. Following her marriage to LeRoi Smith I saw but little of her. She divorced him, I recall, and nursed in Albany for a time and then went to Alaska."

Later, he said, while he was working in Seattle, she telephoned him from a down-town hotel. He called to see her. "She had a girl with her whom she was taking to Arizona from Alaska," Mason said. "I presume this was Miss Samuelsen.

"Since then I have heard but little of her.

"She was a fine little girl, very sweet, very pretty, but romantically inclined. She was exceedingly bright and of an outstanding personality."

Mason said he had had no word from her from Phoenix and until he read of the tragedy was not familiar with her activities there. He had never heard of Ruth Judd, sought as her slayer.

STIMSON, LAVAL OUTLINE VIEWS ON WORLD ILLS

U.S. BANS GUARANTEE OF FRENCH SECURITY

Senator Borah Tells Of 'Musts' Regarding Commitments

BY CHARLES M. M'CANN

WASHINGTON, Oct. 23.—(UP)—Premier Pierre Laval of France and Secretary of State Henry L. Stimson basked in the sunshine on the south porch of the state department this afternoon and participated in a polite exchange of opinions on the world crisis and methods of overcoming it.

There were three developments in the first real "working day" of the French statesman's visit to Washington. They were:

An intimate talk between Laval, president of the council of ministers of France, and Secretary of State Stimson on the south portico of the state department. Looking out over the beautiful monument grounds to the Potomac river, they talked for half an hour, in a warm autumn sun.

BORAH GIVES VIEWS

Laval and his pretty daughter, Josette, went to the White House later in the afternoon for an overnight visit. The French premier, Stimson, Undersecretary of the Treasury Mills and Jacques Dinet, interpreter, went at once to the Lincoln study to talk with President Hoover. There was an informal dinner tonight at which Mrs. Hoover, Mrs. Stimson, Josette and Reine Claudel, daughter of the French ambassador, joined the conference for an hour. Then the men went back to the Lincoln study for more talk.

Senator Borah of Idaho, Progressive leader and chairman of the foreign relations committee which must approve all treaties, in a frank, forceful talk with French newspapermen told them first that this country would not and could not guarantee France's security; second that disarmament must follow, not precede, solution of European political and territorial problems; third, that the Versailles treaty must be revised "by peace or war."

LAVAL OUTLINES IDEAS

The premier's day, and that of his daughter, was a potpourri of formal and informal visits, shopping tours, hurried motorings to the tomb of the Unknown Soldier and such things.

For Laval the high lights were his balcony conference with Stimson and the visit to the White House, where it had been arranged to discuss world questions until late in the night.

Most colorful was the talk with Stimson. Silk-hatted, escorted by aides, Laval went to Stimson's office. Within a couple of minutes he and Stimson were alone out on the great gray granite balcony; Laval with his cigaret, facing a noon-day sun as they talked.

Laval, swarthy, self-contained, gesticulated eloquently if deliberately as he opened the conversation by outlining the French view of things, as Stimson had hoped he would. Stimson would comment briefly at intervals, occasionally pausing for the right French word, then talking on, holding his coat lapels or waving a forefinger at Laval. Thus they talked back and forth. At the end of half an hour, bareheaded in the sun, they seemed to begin talking personalities — they became fast friends during the recent Paris-London debt conference—and then they moved reluctantly indoors.

DISCUSS GUARANTEES

It seemed obvious to observers that Laval was trying to persuade Stimson of the justice of France's demand for a guarantee of her security against attack before she disarmed; that Stimson was keeping a brake on any hope Laval might have of an American guarantee.

After the conference it was learned that both Laval and Stimson were fearful of raising too much hope, here or in France, of any specific agreement now on debts, reparations, disarmament or anything else. It would be better, the view was taken, for the United States and French governments to make agreements later on the basis of the ideas each absorbed from the other.

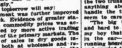

Jabby

[illegible]

1932

The infant son of Charles and Anne Morrow Lindbergh was kidnapped and killed. National anger over the tragedy forced the passage of the death penalty in federal kidnapping cases.

Franklin Delano Roosevelt was elected President and John Nance Garner Vice-President on a platform promising a New Deal.

Amelia Earhart became the first woman to fly alone across the Atlantic Ocean.

Radio City Music Hall opened in New York City.

In the landmark *Powell* v. *Alabama* decision, the U.S. Supreme Court overturned the conviction of nine young blacks convicted the previous year of rape at Scottsboro, Alabama. The court ruled that the defendants had been denied adequate counsel.

"All the News That's Fit to Print."

The New York Times.

5 A.M. EDITION

WEATHER—Rain today; tomorrow fair and colder. Temperatures Yesterday—Max., 54; Min., 38.

VOL. LXXXII....No. 27,318. Entered as Second-Class Matter, Postoffice, New York, N. Y. NEW YORK, WEDNESDAY, NOVEMBER 9, 1932. ***** TWO CENTS In New York City | THREE CENTS Within 200 Miles | FOUR CENTS Elsewhere Except in 7th and 8th Postal Zones

ROOSEVELT WINNER IN LANDSLIDE! DEMOCRATS CONTROL WET CONGRESS; LEHMAN GOVERNOR, O'BRIEN MAYOR

IG VOTE FOR M'KEE

'Brien Is 245,464 Behind Ticket as Protests Rise

UT FINAL LEAD IS 616,736

ounds Concedes Defeat Early, Saying 'Day of Miracles Is Past.'

KEE TOTAL IS 137,538

ousands of "Write-In" Votes re Wasted as Backers Fail to Record Choice Properly.

LLQUIT POLLS 248,425

ts Greatest Vote in History of City for a Socialist—Runs Far Ahead of Party.

urrogate John P. O'Brien, Tammy's candidate, was elected Mayor New York yesterday, but overdowing his victory, which was a one conclusion, was the tremen'write-in" vote cast for Acting or Joseph V. McKee.

inal returns from the city showed ge O'Brien to have received a rality of 616,736 over his nearest onent, Lewis H. Pounds, Repub- n. Judge O'Brien's vote was 5,768, Mr. Pounds polled 439,032, Morris Hillquit, Socialist, polled highest vote ever given a candi- e of h's party in the city by re- ..g 24..425 votes.

Vote Listed by Boroughs.

, boroughs, the totals were as ows:

	O'Brien.	Pounds.	Hillquit.
hattan	309,256	113,278	39,398
ıx	181,349	48,284	67,949
klyn	358,605	155,478	112,740
ens	176,237	105,481	25,821
mond	30,321	16,511	2,517
total........	1,055,768	439,032	248,425

ne vote for Mr. McKee, put early morning at 137,538, actually was more than that, if ballots in ch the voters had abbreviated his ne, or used initials, or spelled it ngly, were counted.

ne vote was unprecedented, par- larly as the use of voting ma- nes made it much more difficult a name to be writen in than on old paper ballots.

dge O'Brien had a clear majority 215,000 votes over the combined of Pounds, Hillquit and McKee, the McKee ballots cast aside as would have reduced this, it was ted out last night.

ne vote for Mr. McKee by oughs was as follows:

nhattan, 26,336, with ten election dis- missing.
onx, 24,483, complete.
oklyn, 43,328, complete.
eens, 36,303, complete.
hmond, 6,790, complete.
y total, 137,538.

ne vote for Mr. McKee, made hout any campaign on his part, in the face of his own disavowal the movement, kept him in the tical picture as a candidate to be koned with for the full four-year n, to be voted on in 1933.

ne term for which Judge O'Brien elected starts on Jan. 1, 1933, ends on Jan. 1, 1934.

ie vote for Mr. O'Brien indicated ran 381,263 votes behind Gover- Roosevelt in the city, in actual es cast, though his plurality was 245,464 smaller than that given he Presidential candidate.

r. Pounds conceded Mr. O'Brien's ory as early as 9:30 in the eve- , and he sent the latter a tele- m of congratulation.

said later he could have been ted only by a miracle, and that days of miracles were past. Mr. Kee, receiving election returns at Park Lane, also sent a short

Continued on Page Seven.

THE GOVERNOR-ELECT.

© New York Times Studio.

Colonel Herbert H. Lehman.

JUDGES IN 'DEAL' WIN; PROTEST VOTE HEAVY

Steuer and Hofstadter Elected With Lydon and Leary to Supreme Court Bench.

290,000 FOR INDEPENDENTS

Bar Leaders Elated by Big Count for Deutsch and Alger—Call It 'Warning to Bosses.'

City Court Justice Aron Steuer and State Senator Samuel H. Hofstadter were elected yesterday over their independent opponents, Bernard S. Deutsch and George W. Alger, by a vote of about 2 to 1.

The protest vote against the so-called deal by which Senator Hofstadter and Justice Steuer received bipatrisan nominations for two of four vacancies on the Supreme Court bench in the first judicial district exceeded all expectations, but it was not enough to upset the combined strength of the Republican and Democratic organizations.

Justice Richard P. Lydon, who was nominated by both major parties for re-election, and Municipal Court Justice Timothy A. Leary, who had the Democratic nomination for the fourth vacancy on the bench, were elected with comfortable margins. Municipal Court Justice George L. Genung, who had the Republican nomination, trailed far behind the independent candidates.

Since Justice Lydon's re-election was virtually uncontested, his totals were not computed in the early returns. Of the other, Justice Steuer and Judge Leary were running slightly ahead of Senator Hofstadter, whose lead was large enough, however, to preclude the possibility of his being overtaken by Mr. Deutsch, his nearest rival.

The Complete Returns.

The complete returns for the entire first judicial district, comprising the boroughs of Manhattan and the Bronx, follow:

Steuer	565,405
Leary	547,112
Hofstadter	544,032
Deutsch	293,125
Alger	287,167
Genung	205,222

The totals recorded for the judiciary candidates in Manhattan follow:

Steuer	367,295
Hofstadter	357,430
Leary	331,442
Deutsch	147,886
Alger	145,346
Genung	138,304

Final returns from the Bronx, where the independent candidates ran strongest, showed the following totals:

Leary	215,670
Steuer	198,110
Hofstadter	186,602
Deutsch	145,239
Alger	141,821
Genung	66,918

The independent candidates did not

Continued on Page Twelve.

STATE VICTORY SOLID

Lehman Gets Record Party Plurality of 887,000.

WAGNER CLOSE TO HIM

National Ticket Has Margin of 615,000—Full Slate Is Elected.

RELIEF BONDS ARE VOTED

Republicans Have Narrow Edge Up-State—Hill Admits 'Protest' Defeated Them.

By JAMES A. HAGERTY.

Lieut. Gov. Herbert H. Lehman, Democratic nominee for Governor, defeated Colonel William J. Donovan, Republican, yesterday, in the Democratic whirlwind that swept New York State, by a plurality of about 887,000, a record for a Democratic candidate in this State.

Governor Franklin D. Roosevelt and Speaker John N. Garner, the Democratic candidates for President and Vice President, carried the State by a plurality of about 615,000, as against Governor Roosevelt's heretofore record Democratic plurality of 725,000, which he received as candidate for re-election to the Governorship two years ago.

With Governor Roosevelt and Colonel Lehman were swept into office the other Democratic candidates on the State-wide ticket, United States Senator Robert F. Wagner, candidate for re-election; M. William Bray, for Lieutenant Governor; State Controller Morris S. Tremaine, Attorney General John J. Bennett Jr. and the two candidates for Representatives-at-Large, Elmer E. Studley and John Fitzgibbons.

Colonel Lehman led Governor Roosevelt by 88,279 in actual votes cast in New York City and also led the Governor in many cities and counties up-State. His indicated plurality exceeded that of Governor Roosevelt by more than 250,000, but exceeded the indicated plurality for Senator Wagner by only about 35,000.

Returns on the proposition and proposed constitutional amendment were slow in coming in, but a large majority for the proposal to issue $30,000,000 in bonds for unemployment relief was indicated, and scattering returns indicated that the constitutional amendment to throw open the forest reserve to the development of recreational facilities had been beaten.

The vote for President and State-wide candidates follows:

FOR PRESIDENT.

New York City, complete—Roosevelt, Democrat, 1,437,231; Hoover, Republican, 575,031; Thomas, Socialist, 120,486; actual plurality for Roosevelt, 862,200.

Up-State, 431 election districts missing—Roosevelt, 1,022,121; Hoover, 1,254,032; actual plurality for Hoover, 231,911; indicated plurality for Hoover, 247,107; indicated plurality for Roosevelt in the entire State, 615,093.

FOR GOVERNOR.

New York City, complete—Lehman, Democrat, 1,525,510; Donovan, Republican, 542,492; plurality for Lehman, 983,018.

Up-State, 561 election districts missing—Lehman, 1,056,088; Donovan, 1,141,735; actual plurality for Donovan, 85,647; indicated plurality for Donovan, 95,817.

Indicated plurality for Lehman in the entire State, 887,201.

FOR UNITED STATES SENATOR.

New York City, complete—Wagner, Dem., 1,438,343; Medalie, Rep., 517,733; plurality for Wagner, 920,610.

Up-State, 1,301 districts missing—Wagner, 915,699; Medalie, 964,418;

Continued on Page Sixteen.

The President's Message To the President-Elect

From a Staff Correspondent.

PALO ALTO, Cal., Nov. 8.—President Hoover conceded his defeat for re-election at 9:17 o'clock tonight, Pacific Time, and dispatched this telegram of congratulations to Governor Roosevelt:

Palo Alto, Cal., Nov. 8, 1932.

The Hon. Franklin D. Roosevelt,
Biltmore Hotel,
New York, N. Y.

I congratulate you on the opportunity that has come to you to be of service to the country and I wish for you a most successful administration. In the common purpose of all of us I shall dedicate myself to every possible helpful effort.

HERBERT HOOVER.

Governor Roosevelt had not received President Hoover's message when he left for his home shortly before 2 o'clock this morning. Pending its receipt he said he preferred not to make reply or comment on the message.

DEMOCRATS CONTROL STATE SENATE, 26-25

Republican Margin in Assembly of 6 Votes Is Reduced to 2 —Lose by 4 Up-State.

ALSO TWO SENATE SEATS

Moffatt Is Re-elected, While Hastings and Dr. Love Are Defeated in City Race.

The slender working majority of two votes by which the Republicans control the present State Senate was swept away in yesterday's Democratic landslide. The next Senate will be made up of 25 Republicans and 26 Democrats, giving the Democrats a majority of one. The present Senate has 27 Republican and 25 Democratic members. Twenty-six votes are required to pass a bill in that branch of the Legislature.

In the Assembly, where 76 votes are required to control legislation, the Republican majority of six is cut down to two in the 1933 Legislature. The Republicans won 77 seats and the Democrats 73 at yesterday's elections for the Assembly.

The Democrats won four Assembly districts north of the Bronx away from the Republicans; one district in Monroe County, one district in Oneida and two in Sullivan and Schoharie counties. The Republicans, however, reduced the up-State Democratic gains by recapturing from them Schuyler county in the southern tier, where last year they succeeded in electing their candidate for the Lower House.

Post Is Defeated.

The Republicans also managed to strengthen their New York City representation by electing Herbert Brownell Jr. in the Tenth (Manhattan) District. This was the district where Langdon W. Post, Democratic incumbent was turned down by Tammany for supporting legislation to broaden the powers and continue the Hofstadter Committee and ran as an independent, polling 5,053 votes. Mr. Brownell defeated his Tammany opponent by a scant plurality of 307 votes. He received 8,907 votes, Sylva La Chappelle, the Democrat, 8,600.

The Democrats gained two Senate districts up-State, the Thirty-first, made up of Rensselaer County, and the Thirty-sixth, made up of Oneida. In the Thirty-fourth, composed of St. Lawrence and Franklin Counties, Warren T. Thayer, the present Republican incumbent, managed to win again after a hard fight.

The New York City Republicans will have three representatives in the Legislature, Senator-elect George Blumberg, who won by a plurality of approximately 500 over Senator John A. Hastings, Democratic incumbent in the Seventh Senatorial

Continued on Page Five.

OVERTURN IN SENATE

Bingham, Watson, Moses and Smoot Are Defeated.

DEMOCRATIC MAJORITY 12

Party Adds to Control in House—May Rule Both Branches This Winter.

LA GUARDIA LOSES SEAT

Mrs. Pratt Defeated, Wadsworth Wins—Texas Sends Garner Back to the House.

The Democratic wave of victory yesterday gave that party complete control of Congress and in its onrush carried down to defeat the four Republican leaders of the Senate.

Senator Smoot of Utah, Republican dean of the Senate and chairman of the powerful Finance Committee; Senator Watson of Indiana, floor leader; Senator Moses, president pro tempore and Senator Jones of Washington, chairman of the Appropriations Committee, all were relegated to the ranks of "lame ducks." No such upset has occurred in recent history.

While returns early this morning showed the new Senate will be Democratic by a majority of twelve and the House overwhelmingly Democratic, there was a possibility that in the session of the old Congress convening on Dec. 5, the Democrats will achieve a slender control of the whole body.

Changes in Coming Session.

They now have a majority of one in the House, in the old Congress that still is to hold a "lame-duck" session; in the Senate the numbers were evened with the defeat of Senator Barbour of New Jersey for the short term beginning next month, and there was, early this morning, an even chance that Colorado would elect Walter Walker, a Democrat, also for the short term. In that event the Senate in December would be: Democrats 49, Republicans 46, Farmer-Labor 1.

On the basis of incomplete returns, the new Senate stood at Democrats 54, Republicans 34, Farmer-Labor 1, and seven States still in doubt.

The next Congress not only will be Democratic; it will be wet.

New York Republicans fared especially ill in the election, which saw Representative La Guardia, fiery "liberal" Republican who led a bloc that controlled the House temporarily in the last session, defeated by J. J. Lanzetta, Democrat. Representative Ruth Pratt also failed of re-election.

Moses Loses in Close Race.

Of the most prominent Republicans who were unseated, Senator Watson went down first, conceding his defeat by Frederick Van Nuys, Democrat.

Senator Moses ran nip and tuck with Fred H. Brown, Democrat, until after midnight in the poll of ballots, when returns from Manchester, N. H., spelled his certain defeat.

Senator Smoot was defeated by Professor E. D. Thomas and Mr. Jones by Homer T. Bone. Both of the victors were Democrats. Senator Jones, who is better known as the author of the "five-and-ten" law than for his important committee chairmanship, was defeated coincident with adoption of a State referendum in Washington repealing that State's prohibition law.

An important Republican defeat in the House was that of Representative Haugen of Iowa, co-author of the McNary-Haugen bill, who went down before F. Bierman, Democrat.

McAdoo Wins Seat.

William Gibbs McAdoo, former Democratic Secretary of the Treasury, who was credited with switching the Democratic National Convention to Franklin D. Roosevelt through

Continued on Page Six.

THE PRESIDENT-ELECT.

© New York Times Studio.

Franklin D. Roosevelt.

The Electoral Vote

ROOSEVELT 448.

Alabama	11	Nebraska	7
Arizona	3	Nevada	3
Arkansas	9	New Jersey	16
California	22	New Mexico	3
Colorado	6	New York	47
Florida	7	North Carolina	13
Georgia	12	North Dakota	4
Idaho	4	Ohio	26
Illinois	29	Oklahoma	11
Indiana	14	Rhode Island	4
Iowa	11	South Carolina	8
Kansas	9	South Dakota	4
Kentucky	11	Tennessee	11
Louisiana	10	Texas	23
Maryland	8	Utah	4
Massachusetts	17	Virginia	11
Minnesota	11	Washington	8
Mississippi	9	West Virginia	8
Missouri	15	Wisconsin	12
Montana	4	Wyoming	3

HOOVER 59.

Connecticut	8	New Hampshire	4
Delaware	3	Pennsylvania	36
Maine	5	Vermont	3

DOUBTFUL 24.

Michigan	19	Oregon	5

Votes in Electoral College, 531; needed to elect, 266.

Wets in Control in Both Houses, But Short of Two-Thirds in Senate

Modification of Volstead Act Appears Certain, and House Has Easy Majority for Repeal, but Upper Chamber Support Is Uncertain on Basis of Returns.

Complete control of the next Congress by forces opposed to Federal prohibition was one of the results which came with the political upheaval that took place with yesterday's election.

With full returns from the major portion of the country and definite trends established in the remainder, it appeared certain that those demanding a change in the dry laws would hold between fifty and fifty-five seats in the Senate and 300 or more in the House of Representatives.

Up until an early hour this morning, only nineteen outspoken drys had been returned definitely to the House, while twenty-four Senators, most of whom did not come up for re-election this year, remained among the prohibitionists. Around 100 House seats still were in doubt, and several Senators and re-elected Representatives were yet undecided how to align themselves on the question.

The aggregation chosen yesterday represented a veritable checker-board of views on prohibition reform, but the extent of the majorities indicated a good chance for immediate modification of the Volstead act to allow light wines and beer. The gains in both Houses were chiefly among Democrats, whose party has been pledged to that course.

Modification in the next Congress appeared much more probable on the basis of yesterday's election than outright repeal of the Eighteenth Amendment. Sixty-four Senate seats and 290 in the House will be required for the latter, whereas only a bare majority of 49 in the Senate and 218 in the House would be needed to change the national prohibition (Volstead) law.

The House was sure of the necessary two-thirds for repeal, as early this morning the anti-prohibitionists had already captured 292 seats; the

Continued on Page Eight.

SWEEP IS NATIONAL

Democrats Carry 40 States, Electoral Votes 448.

SIX STATES FOR HOOVER

He Loses New York, New Jersey, Bay State, Indiana and Ohio.

DEMOCRATS WIN SENATE

Necessary Majority for Repeal of the Volstead Act in Prospect.

RECORD NATIONAL VOTE

Hoover Felicitates Rival and Promises 'Every Helpful Effort for Common Purpose.'

Roosevelt Statement.

President-elect Roosevelt gave the following statement to THE NEW YORK TIMES early this morning:

"While I am grateful with all my heart for this expression of the confidence of my fellow-Americans, I realize keenly the responsibility I shall assume and I mean to serve with my utmost capacity the interest of the nation.

"The people could not have arrived at this result if they had not been informed properly of my views by an independent press, and I value particularly the high service of THE NEW YORK TIMES in its reporting of my speeches and in its enlightened comment."

By ARTHUR KROCK.

A political cataclysm, unprecedented in the nation's history and produced by three years of depression, thrust President Herbert Hoover and the Republican power from control of the government yesterday, elected Governor Franklin Delano Roosevelt President of the United States, provided the Democrats with a large majority in Congress and gave them administration of the affairs of many States of the Union.

Fifteen minutes after midnight, Eastern Standard Time, The Associated Press flashed from Palo Alto this line: "Hoover concedes defeat."

It was then fifteen minutes after nine in California, and the President had been in his residence on the Leland Stanford campus only a few hours, arriving with expressed confidence of victory.

A few minutes after the flash from Palo Alto the text of Mr. Hoover's message of congratulation to his successful opponent was received by THE NEW YORK TIMES, though it was delayed in direct transmission to the President-elect. After offering his felicitations to Governor Roosevelt on his "opportunity to be of service to the country," and extending wishes for success, the President "dedicated" himself to "every possible helpful effort * * * in the common purpose of us all."

This language strengthened the belief of those who expect that the relations between the victor and the vanquished, in view of the exigent condition of the country, will be more than perfunctory, and that they may soon confer in an effort to arrive at a mutual program of stabilization during the period between now

OVER 60,000 DAILY READERS

The Daily Home News family of readers is large and growing. Over 60,000 people read this newspaper every day.

THE DAILY HOME NEWS

For a Greater New Brunswick

WEATHER

Cloudy tonight; Thursday rain; not much change in temperature.

Temperature at Noon 50

Founded in 1878 Late Edition

New Brunswick, N. J., Wednesday Afternoon, March 2, 1932.

16 Pages—Three Cents.

POST CARD STATES 'BABE SAFE'

CHINESE FORCES RETREATING FROM SHANGHAI TO WEST

Chinese, However, Explain They Are Preparing New Fighting Lines

NO PROGRESS MADE IN TRUCE EFFORTS

By MORRIS J. HARRIS
Associated Press
Staff Correspondent
Copyright, 1932
By The Associated Press

SHANGHAI, March 2.—China's now world famous 19th Route Army was retreating westward tonight after five weeks of stubborn fighting at Shanghai, closely pressed by a powerful Japanese war machine.

The Japanese claimed that the Chinese soldiers, unable to stand any longer the terrible force of their artillery, aerial and naval attacks, broke their lines and beat a retreat, which they said, was rapidly turning into a rout.

Chinese military officials, however, said it was a "tactical retreat" and that they planned to establish new defense lines at Nanziang, ten miles west and renew the battle there.

They were falling back, they said, to protect their communications which were endangered by the landing of a large force of Japanese troops at Liuho, twenty miles up the Yangtze River. The Liuho Japanese force immediately began a drive southward after they landed.

Although it was impossible to determine the number of Chinese troops participating in the retreat, observers here estimated there were 50,000 of them. There were additional Chinese troops two miles west but these were not falling back, the Chinese said.

The Japanese, freshened by the addition of thousands of reinforcements during the last two or three days, followed up their advantage closely. From Liuho, on the southern bank of the Yangtze, the Japanese line formed a giant arc bulging westward and ending in the vicinity of Chapei, adjacent to the Shanghai international settlement. This long line crept slowly westward tonight on the heels of the Chinese.

Chapei, which has been reduced to a mass of wreckage since the hostilities began, was deserted by the Chinese by 6 o'clock tonight. A number of huge fires roared in the battered city demolishing whatever was left.

COMMISSION WILL MEET TOMORROW

Raritan Township to Vote Acceptance of Offer of Edison Interests

With the signature of Governor A. Harry Moore now safely affixed to Assembly bill 281, the commissioners of Raritan Township are in readiness to go ahead with the final adjustment of the back taxes on the potash plant, and a resolution authorizing acceptance of the settlement offer of the Edison interests will be passed at an adjourned meeting tomorrow night.

Counsel for the Metropolitan Cement Corporation, Edison subsidiary, which plans to take over the plant and reopen it for the manufacture of cement, will be present to witness the proceedings tomorrow evening, and a large audience of township employes is also expected to watch the completion of a transaction which they hope will enable the township to pay at least a part of the salaries due them from the first of the year.

The deal will bring $177,500 into the township treasury, $102,500 for back taxes and interest, $15,000 in advance for 1932 taxes, and $60,000 for a like amount of tax revenue bonds of the township.

The first amount will probably be applied exclusively to the reduction of funded debt, but $75,000 will remain to catch up on the current obligations of the municipality, one of the largest of which is the payroll, now two months in arrears.

DRIVER FINED $5 FOR RECKLESSNESS

Joseph Scheighardt, 22, of 7 Ellen street, was fined $5 by Recorder Charles E. Tindell in police court this morning when charged with reckless driving on Livingston avenue. Scheighardt, who received his first driver's license this year, said he did not know how fast he was driving when arrested shortly after 4:30 p. m. yesterday near the Roosevelt Junior High School. Patrolman Rudolph Valdato estimated the speed of the car at forty miles an hour.

Patrolman Valdato testified that he noticed Scheighardt's car at Suydam street and watched it proceed toward Welton street. The officer said the driver passed another machine on the way.

EFFICIENCY

The Minister of Finance at Bagdad, Irak, has issued orders to all departments that there must be only one chair in the rooms of bureau heads. This order was given to discourage visitors wasting time in governmental offices.

METUCHEN TAX RATE JUMPS 200 POINTS, NOW HIGHEST IN COUNTY

Officials' Decision for 'Clean' Budget Causes $7.99 Rate To Be Struck for Borough; Metuchen Paying Debts Of Previous Administrations

A tax rate of $7.99 per $100 assessed valuation, an increase of 200 points was struck this morning by the Middlesex County Board of Taxation for the Borough of Metuchen.

It is the highest rate ever struck for a municipality in the county and means the borough property owners will pay an increase of $20 per $1,000 assessed valuation. On every $1,000 assessed valuation, the borough taxpayer will pay $79.90.

The $7.99 rate establishes a new record for taxes in Middlesex County. The rate for 1931 was $5.99 per $100 assessed valuation which was the fifth highest but this year, Metuchen takes first place without a struggle.

The rate does not come as a surprise to the taxpayers of Metuchen for they have been apprised for some time that the rate would approach the $8.00 mark.

Metuchen is paying today for the sins committed by previous administrations. The present administration has tackled the tax problem in the borough in a business like manner. Deficits in appropriations which remained unpaid for three and four years are being met this year, anticipated revenues of other years which failed to materialize are being funded and in adopting a "clean" budget, the "Borough Fathers" are placing Metuchen on a sound financial basis.

An analysis of the items in the budget reveals that the "Borough Fathers" have attacked the borough financial problem in a manner which other taxing districts have feared. It is not popular from a political viewpoint to increase taxes but the conditions that faced the present administration upon

Continued on Page Eleven

GARAGEMEN FORM NEW ORGANIZATION

Fred H. Ramhorst Elected President of Maintenance Committee

Protection of the rights of independent garage owners was stressed at the opening meeting of the Independent Automotive Maintenance Committee of Middlesex County, held at the Ramhorst garage on Jelin street last evening. Close to fifty independent garage owners of this city and vicinity attended the meeting. The organization is a part of the State wide unit devoted to the protection of the rights and privileges of independent garage owners.

Fred H. Ramhorst, one of the prominent independent garage owners in the city, was elected president of the organization at the enthusiastic assemblage. Mr. Ramhorst promised his wholehearted support in bringing about a strong organization. Other officers elected include George Baxter as vice-president, Leonard N. Flomerfelt, secretary and George Bailey, treasurer.

Like organizations in other fields a unit has been sought by the independent garagemen where they could meet for discussions of the everyday problems. As a result a group of energetic garage owners in this city met for a forum on the subject of instituting a subsidiary organization of the State Automotive Maintenance Association. Fred Ramhorst, George Baxter, Harry Jamison, Kurt Gil-

(Continued on Page Eleven)

GEORGE KOJAC ENGAGED TO WED NEW YORK DANCER

NEW YORK, March 2.—George Kojac, champion swimmer, and Katherine Fogarty, 20, a dancer, announced their engagement last night. Kojac is 22 years old today.

World's champion in the fifty-yard backstroke and the 440-yard free-style distance, Kojac will take part in the Olympics next summer at Los Angeles.

No wedding date was announced. Kojac broke the world's 100-yard backstroke record at the new Central High School pool in Trenton Monday night.

FIREMAN OVERCOME DURING FIRE AT PRINCETON BANK

PRINCETON, March 2.—The explosion of accumulated gas in the cellar of the Princeton Bank and Trust Company, Nassau and Bank streets, caused a fire last night which was extinguished after three fire companies were in action for several hours. Dense smoke poured from the cellar. George Durner, a volunteer fireman, was overcome and taken to Princeton Hospital.

125 MEN EMPLOYED BY LINDEN FIRMS

LINDEN, March 2.—One hundred and twenty-five men were given employment at the American Cyanamid Company, manufacturers of sulphuric acid, and the General Aniline Works, Inc., German dye workers, during the past week, it was learned today.

PLAN AIR SEARCH

NEW YORK, March 2.—Famous airmen of the east fellow members of Col. Charles A. Lindbergh in the fraternal organization known as the Quiet Birdmen, formed an aerial posse today to attempt to discover from the air the hideout of the kidnapers of the flying colonel's baby son.

FIREMEN TO PROBE BLAZE STARTED IN PIERESENTE HOME

Italian Family Visiting Relatives When Fire Is Discovered

CONTAINERS FOUND IN DAMAGED ROOMS

An investigation is being made by the fire department of a fire of apparent incendiary origin which ruined several rooms in a one-story frame dwelling at 66 Comstock street, shortly after 2 o'clock this morning. Romeo Pieresente, owner of the building, his wife and their four children were at the home of a sister-in-law when the blaze started. He cannot explain the presence of containers in the damaged building, or the heavy odor of an inflammable liquid.

Pieresente said he knew nothing of the fire until told about it this morning by a relative. He left the Comstock street place about 7 o'clock last night, "because his sister-in-law has heart trouble" and he wanted to be with her.

About 11 o'clock last night, Pieresente said he returned to his home and "everything was all right."

"I heard my dog moaning," said the property owner, "and I knew it meant bad luck."

Mrs. Edith Meserole of 64 Comstock street, was awakened by the odor of smoke coming from the Pieresente dwelling. She aroused her husband, Ernest, who turned in an alarm at 2:08 o'clock from box 231, Jones avenue and Delevan street.

The fire broke out in a bed room of the comparatively small structure, and dense smoke arose as the firemen arrived.

"I thought it was snowing when I looked out of my window," remarked Mr. Meserole this morning.

Meserole said he banged against the front door of the house, thinking that the Italian family was at home. It was definitely ascer-

Continued on Page Nine

LACK OF FUNDS HALTS ROAD WORK

Money for Made-Work Not To Be Available After March 15

Between 500 and 600 men employed on State highway in Middlesex County will be thrown out of work on March 15 when funds available for emergency relief work in New Jersey at the disposal of the State Highway Commission will have become exhausted, it was announced yesterday at a meeting of the State Highway Commission.

State Engineer Jacob L. Bauer reported to the commission that no funds will be available for made-work jobs after March 15, and it was decided to inform the men on the jobs at once. The action was taken with reluctance by the Highway Commission but there was no alternative.

All during the winter months squads of men have been engaged on routes throughout the State doing grading work, widening shoulders and installing drainage structures. The board established a rule for the use of hand labor rather than mechanical inventions where such an arrangement would be consistent with efficiency in carrying out the various improvements.

In several instances the board made arrangements with contractors to take over the grading on newly constructed routes to place larger forces of manual labor under the unemployment relief policy.

Several gangs were placed on widening the super highway between Trenton and New Brunswick in preparation for laying an additional lane of concrete on that thoroughfare during the approaching summer. The majority of the men on this project are from Middlesex County.

The excavation for Route S-28 between Tanner's Corner and Rue's Lane was done under the special program and among the other major projects were widening the White Horse Pike, between Berlin and Absecon, and Route 25, from Camden to Bordentown. On practically every route improvements were made to distribute employment throughout the State for the benefit of all municipalities.

Commissioner Abraham Jelin declared this morning that 570 men were employed under the work relief program last week, and throughout the winter the average has been between 500 and 600 men. Most of the men were employed on the super highway and the Tanner's Corner job.

JOB DRIVE HERE AIDS ANOTHER MAN

International Motor Co. Puts Man Back to Work; Total Now 415

With twelve more days remaining for the national American Legion war against depression campaign, the local committee reports 415 jobs obtained in this city, and fully expects the total to reach 500 before the drive comes to an end.

Another job was reported by Neal Reardon today at the International Motor Company, which

AMERICAN LEGION HONOR ROLL

The International Motor Company has taken one more man back to work, it was announced today at the American Legion war against depression headquarters, Room 408, Citizens National Bank building, bringing the total number of jobs obtained since the opening of the drive here to 416. The campaign will end March 15.

Wednesday

International Motor Company—One Man.

Tuesday

College Drers Company—200 women.

Monday

Chaskes and Kulbach—30 persons.

Umansky Knee Pants Company—6 persons.

Tydol Service Gas Station—One man.

Photo Electric and Engraving Company—20 men.

helped swell the remarkable number of positions filled since February 15. New Brunswick leads the State of New Jersey in the number of unemployed citizens put back to work, and the various teams are entitled to every credit for their efforts, Attorney Louis Hendler, local chairman, announced today.

There are many employers of labor who have not been solicited, and the teams in charge of the drive will make certain that every possible source is visited.

The second phase of the American Legion war against depression campaign — the man-a-block system, will be discussed with Ernest G. Webb, head of the Unemployment Relief Committee, tomorrow afternoon at 5 o'clock, at the office of Attorney Louis L. Hendler. A committee has been appointed to represent the American Legion at the conference with Mr. Webb.

The Women's Division is expected to begin its work in finding jobs for the unemployed, under the leadership of Mrs. Ethel Kirkpatrick.

Through the efforts of the American Legion Auxiliary, whose women are working side by side with the Legion in the great campaign to return prosperity, three of the most influential national women's organizations have pledged their support to the war against depression. The National Council of Federated Church Women, Daughters of the American Revolution, and Women's League of the United Synagogue of America are the organizations which have sanctioned the movement.

MRS. ANNA HAFFETT DIES AT HOSPITAL

Mrs. Anna Haffett, 37, of Orchard street, Franklin Township, died yesterday at Middlesex Hospital after having apparently recovered from a surgical operation. A blood clot caused almost sudden death, according to hospital reports.

Through a letter mailed to the patient at the hospital it was possible to locate George Haffett of 848 Columbus avenue, New York City, husband of the deceased.

At the request of Mr. Haffett the body was sent to New York City for burial.

LOCAL HOSPITAL REPORTS BIRTHS OF FOUR BABIES

Two boys and two girls were born yesterday at St. Peter's Hospital. Mr. and Mrs. Walter Bennett of Jamesburg and Mr. and Mrs. James Wright of 236 South Third avenue, Highland Park, are the parents of sons, while daughters were born to Mr. and Mrs. Henry Mc Cauley, 165 Baldwin street, and Mr. and Mrs. John Kuhn, Jamesburg.

Seek Lindbergh Baby in Newark After Card is Discovered in Mails; $50,000 Ransom Note Left at House

BABY IN HANDS OF KIDNAPERS

It was the camera of his famous father that pictured Charles Augustus Lindbergh, Jr., as you see him here. This photo of the world's most famous baby—now 20 months old—was made shortly after his birth at his mother's former home in Englewood, N. J., in June, 1930. Kidnaped from his crib in the nursery of his parent's present home at Hopewell, the child became the object of one of the greatest police hunts in history.

Note Demanding Ransom So Threatening Contents Are Denied

FEAR FOR BABY BECAUSE OF ILLNESS

Famous Baby Snatched From Crib at Home Near Hopewell

(By The Associated Press)

NEWARK, N. J., March 2.—A plain post card addressed to Colonel Charles A. Lindbergh was found in the mails in the Newark post office and read "Babe safe. Instructions later. Act accordingly."

The card, picked up in the noon collections from a box at the corner of Plane and Central avenues, in the heart of the city, was spotted by a distributor in the post office.

The words on the card were printed.

The address read:

"Colonel Charles Lindberg.
"Princeton, N. J."

The card was taken to Newark police headquarters, where it was photostated and scrutinized by finger print experts.

Although post office officials violated the law in taking the card out of the mails, they did so without hesitation, knowing their act would be condoned.

The post office officials said they intended replacing the card in the mails for delivery to Col. Lindbergh after they had finished their examination.

Director of Public Safety William Egan immediately called out the entire police force and a house to house search of Plane street and Central avenue was begun.

Finding the card strengthened the belief the abandoned sedan found early today in Hillside, a suburb, may have been used by the kidnapers in their flight from the Lindbergh home.

The car, unlighted, the bearings of its motor burned out from lack of oil, was found in Field Place near the Newark line. The street is within a few blocks of a detour in Route 29, which runs directly to Somerville, linging there with Route 21, a straight road to Princeton.

The car bore license plates "New York 3K-35-29," and was reported stolen yesterday afternoon from Brooklyn. The owner of the car was given by police as S. Mandel of 1519 East Third street, Brooklyn.

(By The Associated Press)
(Copyright, 1932)

HOPEWELL, N. J., March 2.—Ransom has been demanded for the Lindbergh baby, kidnaped from its nursery last night, and Col. Charles A. Lindbergh is willing to pay if he can get the infant safely back to its mother's arms.

It was learned shortly before noon today that a note found pinned to the sill of the window through which the baby was taken from its sick bed by the kidnapers, made a definite ransom demand.

It also threatened harm to the child if the money was not paid, if the contents of the note was divulged, or if the method of payment suggested in the noat was revealed.

So threatening was the note that for hours its very existence was denied by police investigating the crime.

It was finally determined with absolute definiteness, however, that the ransom demand had been made and that Col. Lindbergh had decided to meet any demand if by so doing he would get his baby back.

No one would say how large the demand was but a report that it was $50,000 went undenied by sources close to the Lindbergh family and to the widespread search.

It was impossible to gain any information as to what instructions may have been contained in the ransom note or to find out just what steps Col. Lindbergh was taking to follow those instructions.

Mrs. Lindbergh, who is reported to be expecting another baby in the spring, was inconsolate today and aside from the brief at having the baby kidnaped she was made additionally anxious because of its illness.

The baby had been suffering from a severe cold and had been on a strict diet. It was feared that exposure to the cold and damp night air in scanty clothing and lack of its carefully prepared and selected food might have serious effect on the child's health even thought it was unharmed by the kidnapers.

Police spread today through the wild country surrounding the Lindbergh estate, up over Sourland hill and into the dense tangle around Devil's Cave and Roaring Rocks, an isolated region which rumor says is inhabited by numerous moonshiners.

Close watch was kept at eastern airports, but nothing was expected fro mthis as no one believed the kidnapers would be so foolhardy as to attempt to secu

(Continued on Page Three)

MOORE HALTS PLAN FOR STATE REWARD

Action Deferred to Offer $25,000 After Conference With Lindbergh

(By The Associated Press)

TRENTON, March 2.—Governor A. Harry Moore and Republican Legislative leaders, after conferring by telephone with Colonel Charles A. Lindbergh, today abondoned plans to offer a reward for apprehension of the kidnapers of the Lindbergh child.

Colonel Lindbergh they said, asked that such action be deferred for the time being while initial efforts to capture the abductors were being made.

All plans for issuance of a proclamation and Legislative action to increase the reward from $10,000 to $25,000 were held in abeyance.

Police officials arriving for a conference with the Governor to organize activities to apprehend the kidnapers and recover the child included: Thomas Wolfe, police chief of Jersey City, police inspectors Harry Walsh and Charles Wilson and police captains Henry Gauphier and Patrick Brady, all of Jersey City, and Col. H. Norman Schwarzkopf, Superintendent of State police.

Arrangements were made to keep in touch with Colonel Lindbergh during the conference.

After brief discussion, the police officials agreed the conference should be transferred to Hopewell where opportunity to interview the Lindbergh family would be offered. They determined to proceed to Hopewell as soon as James McRell, Newark chief of police, arrived.

Governor Moore, remaining in Trenton, said his purpose in calling in the officials was to place at the disposal of the Lindberghs the police facilities of the State.

The police officials left for Hopewell shortly before one p. m.

BLAMES PROFESSIONALS

WASHINGTON, March 2.—An opinion that the kidnaping of 20-months-old Charles A. Lindbergh, Jr., was "obviously the work of professionals" and possibly was done by an organized kidnaping ring from the midwest, was expressed today by Frank J. Loesch, who was a member of the Wickersham commission.

KIDNAPER CAN GET LIFE IN PRISON IN NEW JERSEY

(By The Associated Press)

NEWARK, March 2.—Kidnapping is a high misdemeanor in New Jersey and any person found guilty of it is subject to a life sentence in State Prison at hard labor. A lesser sentence may be imposed at the discretion of the judge but the minimum is five years.

Lindbergh Kidnaping Bulletins

WATCH BORDER LINE

(By The Associated Press)

NIAGARA FALLS, N. Y., March 2.—Search for Charles Augustus Lindbergh, Jr., and his kidnapers extended to the international border today. United States immigration and customs authorities here received instructions from Washington to keep close watch on the border to prevent the escape of the abductors to Canada.

Instructions from Washington were to pay particular attention to automobiles bearing New Jersey license plates. All cars licensed in that state crossing the bridge were subjected to thorough search and their occupants closely questioned.

BLAMES ONE MAN

HOPEWELL, March 2. — Untrained in conventional police methods by wise in woodlore Oscar Bush, veteran trapper neighbor of Col. Charles A. Lindbergh, has decided that the Lindbergh baby was kidnaped by one man, and not by one or more men and woman as detectives believed.

MAKING AIR SURVEY

TRENTON, March 2. — Major Charles H. Schoffel, deputy superintendent of state police, today said an airplane had been brought

(Continued on Page Three)

LINDBERGHS CALM IN TELLING STORY

Baby Had Heavy Cold and Possible Exposure Worries Parents

HOPEWELL, N. J., March 2.—It was a calm husband and wife that the first two officers to reach the Lindbergh mansion found when they reached the house to investigate the kidnapping of the chubby Lindbergh heir.

Patrolman Charles E. Williamson of the Hopewell police and his chief, Harry H. Wolfe, were the first to answer the colonel's distraught alarm of the kidnaping, and Williamson today described to an Associated Press reporter just what took place in those first agonized hours.

The two officers found the Lindberghs in the dining room of their home, with the three servants about them. The colonel's face showed a steely calm, and his pale, anxious-eyed wife, the former Anne Morrow, was also self-possessed, but the self-possession was obviously the result of great effort, Williamson said.

The couple answered the police questions readily, with Mrs. Lindbergh, tremulous in her solicitude over the child. The baby had been suffering from a heavy cold, she told Williamson, and they were nursing him for it. She was worried lest the child, who was clad only in night clothes, suffer from exposure.

Williamson said he conducted

Continued on Page Nine

Lindberghs Reported Worth From Two to Three Million

Fortune Kidnapers Apparently Seek One of Largest in New Jersey as Baby's Grandmother Was Recently Left $19,000,000 Morrow Estate

(By The Associated Press)

NEW YORK, March 2.—The fortune on which the kidnapers of the Lindbergh baby apparently seek to lay hands constitutes one of the largest in New Jersey.

Col. and Mrs. Charles A. Lindbergh are believed in aviation circles here to be worth between $2,000,000 and $3,000,000 while the fortune which the late Senator Dwight W. Morrow, a former Morgan partner, left to Mrs. Lindbergh's mother has been popularly estimated at nearly $19,000,000.

Col. Lindbergh was a poor boy when he hopped off in a borrowed plane for Paris in a flight that made him the world's foremost birdman. Fortune smiled.

He got the $25,000 Orteig prize for the flight and the St. Louis group which backed his venture gave him the "Spirit of St. Louis" plane in recognition of his success. He received an undisclosed sum from Daniel Guggenheim for making a tour of the United States after his return, later becoming technical adviser to Pan-American Airways and T. A. T., as well as serving in an advisory capacity for the Airways Division of the Department of Commerce. His salaries from the two aviation concerns are reported to total $50,000 yearly.

Large sums came to him from newspaper syndication, and from a book he wrote. The first check he received for the book was $100,000, aviation circles said, and royalties are still coming in. Miscellaneous awards in recognition of his flight swelled the total, while in 1929 newspapers said the then Ambassador Morrow had established a $1,000,000 trust fund for their daughter Anne, Lindbergh's wife.

The 50,000 Readers of The Sunday Times Have More Time to Read Ads on Sunday

The Sunday Times

Weather Outlook for Week
North and Middle Atlantic States: Generally fair except rain over south and rain or snow over north portion about middle of week. Continued cold Monday and Tuesday, rising temperature Wednesday and Thursday and colder Friday.

Established 1792. | Five Sections—30 Pages | NEW BRUNSWICK, N. J., SUNDAY MORNING, MARCH 13, 1932. | Fair, moderately cold | City Edition—Five Cents

LINDBERGH "FIXER" SAYS KIDNAPED BABY WELL
WANTS TO BE "SANE" FOR DELICATE WORK AHEAD

Morris Rosner Bases Statement on Definite Knowledge After Talking With Lindberghs at Their Home

Former Government Agent Grants Interview to A. P. Reporter but Does Not Reveal Whether He Has Had Direct Communication With Abductors; Returns Home for Some Relaxation.

By MORRIS WATSON
Copyright, 1932
(By The Associated Press)

NEW YORK, March 12—Morris Rosner, the "fixer" appointed by Col. Charles A. Lindbergh, announced today that he had definite knowledge that the kidnaped Lindbergh baby is alive and safe and will be returned to its parents.

Rosner came from the Lindbergh home this afternoon to his apartment at the corner of 7th avenue and 16th street and after some hesitation agreed to see a reporter.

He said that he was not able to reveal whether he had had actual conversation or other direct communication with the kidnapers, but that his statement that the baby was safe and well and would be returned was based on actual knowledge and was not in any way a mere matter of opinion.

Rosner came to his apartment in the automobile of Douglas Craik of 1111 Park avenue, which was driven by Craik's chauffeur. The chauffeur said that Craik was a friend of Rosner and Rosner had been using the car on the Lindbergh case for a week.

When the reporter first asked Rosner for an interview he showed great reluctance and only agreed to talk when reminded of the great public interest about the Lindbergh baby, which throughout the conversation he referred to as "our baby."

"I have some delicate work to do this afternoon and in the next few days," said Rosner. "I have been on the go for the last 103 hours with no rest. I just came home for a little relaxation, because it is absolutely imperative that I be 'sane' for this very delicate work.

"The kidnapers can be absolutely sure that nothing will ever be done toward prosecuting them either by Col. Lindbergh or myself, but we are pleading with them not to be afraid to rush negotiations. After this thing is over they know where they can find me."

Once Rosner referred to the kidnapers as "that family."

"That family made a mistake," he said, "they'll never make it again."

"Are you certain you will get the baby back?" Rosner was asked.

"There is absolutely no question about that," he replied.

Rosner complained of the publicity brought upon him by his acceptance of Col. Lindbergh's request that he try to find the baby.

"I have absolutely lost my value in my line of work through this publicity," he said.

He complained also about the distinction made in the press between the underworld and the upperworld and pointed out that no such distinction was shown in war time. He said the so-called underworld has only one uniform —"its word of honor and what it knows."

Rosner reached his apartment about 2 o'clock this afternoon and it was not until almost two hours later that he finally agreed to talk.

He made it perfectly clear that it was extremely distasteful to him to be interviewed and that he submitted only because of the great public interest in the baby and because he thought that what he said might in some way help speed up the child's return.

Rosner described himself as a former government agent and said he was responsible for cleaning up the bucket shop situation in New York a dozen years ago and was active in the case of the late William J. Fallon, noted New York criminal lawyer, who was acquitted on charges of jury tampering several years ago. Otherwise, he would say little about himself, except that "I have served my country as much as anybody in uniform ever did."

He said he was called into the Lindbergh case on recommendation of Senator Elmer Thomas of Oklahoma and others "high in the political life of the nation."

ROSNER STORY CALLED UNTRUE BY POLICE

TRENTON, March 12.—Lieut. Walter J. Coughlin said tonight that Col. H. Norman Schwarzkopf, head of the State police, in response to inquiries had authorized a statement both on behalf of the Lindberghs and the police that "there is absolutely no truth in the story Morris Rosner told late today in New York."

Pen and Ink Portrait of Missing Lindbergh Baby

—Drawn especially for Sunday Times by Paul Kroesen.
Charles Augustus Lindbergh, Jr., 20 months old. . . . Has blue eyes, curly, golden hair, fair complexion. . . . Weighs 30 pounds. . . . Is 2 feet 9 inches high. . . . At toddling age. . . . Speaks a few words. Resembles Lindy. . . . Likes dogs. . . Doesn't like strange people. . . . Answers to name of Charles.

Betty Gow, Lindbergh Nurse, not in Vancouver in 1930 With Henry Johnson, Police Say; Man Held in Newark Is Charged With Violation of Immigration Laws.

TRENTON, March 12.—Virtual elimination of information that Betty Gow, Lindbergh nursemaid, and Henry (Red) Johnson were together in Vancouver, B. C., in 1930, was announced today by State police, who said, however, that fingerprints of both had been forwarded to a European agency for complete investigation and checking.

The complete text of the statement by Col. H. Norman Schwarzkopf was as follows:

"Information was received that Betty Gow and Henry Johnson were together in Vancouver, B. C., some time during the period, July to December, 1930. This has been thoroughly investigated by local authorities and also Royal Northwestern Mounted Police, and it was determined that the girl referred to was not Betty Gow of this household, but Betty Cox, and there is nothing definite to link the Henry Johnson now held in Newark, N. J., with the circumstances.

"All angles of Johnson's activities in connection with the Lindbergh case have been thoroughly investigated by various enforcement agencies of the cities mentioned by him and nothing definite has been established which would indicate he was responsible or implicated in the case. He is being held and formally charged with violation of the immigration laws; to wit,

"In 1927, being a subject of Norway, he deserted a Norwegian ship which was docked in New York, thereby entering the country illegally.

"While this offense is bailable, the bail is set by the United States Department of Labor. Said department has been notified of his detention and they have advised that he be held for further action.

"Further information concerning this charge of illegal entry into the United States should be obtained from the assistant secretary of labor in charge of immigration violations in Washington.

"Fingerprints of Betty Gow and Henry Johnson have been forwarded to a European agency for complete investigation and checking."

BETTY GOW TELLS HER MOTHER SHE'S 'NUMBED' WITHOUT THE DARLING

London Sunday Express Publishes Her Letter Home; Declares Mrs. Lindbergh Has Been Very Brave About It All

(By The Associated Press)

LONDON, March 12—Betty Gow, nursemaid to the Lindbergh baby, told her mother in Glasgow in a letter received today that she felt "numbed and terribly lost without that darling."

In the letter, which was printed in the Sunday Express, the nursemaid reported that Mrs. Lindbergh was being "very brave about it." The letter follows:

"Dear Mother:

"You will have heard long ago about this terrible thing that has happened to us. It is the most cruel thing I ever knew.

"I do not feel the least like writing, but I knew you would be anxious to hear from me. I discovered that the baby had gone when I went to lift him at 10 o'clock as usual.

"The Lindberghs were here for the week-end along with the baby, but he caught cold and Mrs. Lindbergh sent for me to come down rather than move the baby.

"His cold had gone to his chest a little bit and I made him a little flannel vest, rubbed his chest and got him fixed up and left him asleep peacefully.

"We guess they took him while we were all having dinner. They got in through one of his windows on a home-made ladder but didn't leave any clues. They wore gloves and socks over their shoes.

"The object is evidently ransom in a big way and in that case they will take good care of him. I hope to goodness we have him back by the time you get this letter. I just feel numbed and terribly lost without that darling. I love him so.

"Reporters are just swarming around the house. The whole country is roused. Mrs. Lindbergh has been very brave about it. She's wonderful.

"Well, dear, I will write you soon again. Hope you are all well. Love to everybody.

"BETTY."

SWEDISH MATCH KING ENDS LIFE IN PARIS

Ivar Krueger Reputed to Be One of World's Richest Men; Act Caused by Burden of work, Announcement Says

(By The Associated Press)

STOCKHOLM, March 12.—Ivar Kreuger, head of the Swedish match trust, committed suicide in Paris, officials of the match company announced tonight.

The announcement read:

"The regrettable death by suicide of Ivar Kreuger was due to the superhuman burden of work he had borne in the past few months and which resulted recently in a nervous breakdown while he was in New York.

"An investigation has begun into the position of the Kreuger companies."

NEW YORK, March 12.—Large-scale liquidation of the stock of Kreuger and Toll in the New York Stock Exchange has been in progress for several days.

This company is one of the chief holding and financing companies of the Swedish match trust, headed by Ivar Kreuger, reported after the close of today's market to have committed suicide in Paris.

Ivar Kreuger, head of the Swedish Match Company since 1917, was reputed to be one of the richest men in the world.

He was 52 years old and unmarried.

The head of the match trust is generally regarded as one of the most powerful business figures in Northern Europe. His company is Kreuger & Toll, the holding and finance company, which controls, among other things, the match monopoly.

It is a vast organization with ninety manufacturing plants in various parts of the world outside of Sweden and with a controlling interest in the leading match concerns of nearly a dozen countries in Europe, America and Japan.

RECLUSE, WHO HAD HID $1,000,000, IS DEAD

NEW YORK, March 12.—Mrs. Ida E. Wood, ninety-three-year-old recluse in whose rooms $1,000,000 in cash, jewelry and securities was found in the last year, died of pneumonia this afternoon in the Herald Square Hotel.

Pneumonia developed only yesterday after Mrs. Wood had suffered a heart attack on Thursday. Four nurses were in constant attendance and both her private physician and her nephew and guardian, Otis F. Wood, made frequent visits to her bedside.

JAP, WHO BEAT WOMAN, IS SENTENCED TO JAIL

SHANGHAI, March 12.—The Japanese consulate announced today that a fifteen-day jail jail sentence had been imposed on a Japanese civilian responsible for the beating administered a week ago to Miss Rose Marlowe, an American missionary teacher.

In a letter to the United States consulate, the Japanese authorities expressed regret about the incident and asserted they had warned their nationals against any repetition.

Reports from the front indicated everything was quiet but the Japanese were moving in large reinforcement units with great quantities of war material. The defense line from Nanziang northward to the Yangtze was strengthened by detachments from the 3,000 reinforcements landed early this morning at Woosung.

The troop movement was impeded by a torrential rainstorm, the first of the spring downpours on which the Chinese had depended for assistance in their defensive action.

ARAKELIAN FAMILY VISITING ILL RELATIVE

Mr. and Mrs. Harry Arakelian and three children, whose home at 10 Oakwood place, North Brunswick Township, was destroyed by fire of unknown origin early Saturday morning, are reported to be visiting relatives in Massachusetts. The Arakelians left their home about 4 o'clock Friday afternoon after receiving a telegram stating that a relative was seriously ill, it was said.

The Arakelian home burned to the ground in less than a half hour, and the residence of Mr. and Mrs. John Dailey next door was damaged beyond repair by the flames.

Friends of the Arakelians report that the head of the household displayed the telegram he received from a relative, and made known his intension of leaving here with his family.

WOULD PERMIT STATES TO BIND DELEGATES

WASHINGTON, March 12. — A bill to permit States to bind their delegates to national political conventions by popular vote was introduced today by Senator Lafollette (R., Wis.), with an expression of hope that it could be passed in time to apply to the forthcoming presidential nominations.

Three Chicago Policemen Shot In Street Fight

Alleged Gunman Is Beaten And Placed in Jail

CHICAGO, March. 12.—Three policemen were shot, one possibly fatally, as alleged Communitst staged a demonstration against the Shanghai fighting in front of the Japanese consulate today.

Twice refused a license to hold a protest meeting in front of the Tribune tower, home of the consulate, a crowd gathered shortly after noon and attacked sixty police who had been stationed there in anticipation of their coming.

Mounted police patrolled Michigan boulevard between the Tribune tower and the Wrigley building, attempting to keep those carrying banners and passing communistic circulars from crossing the avenue.

A policement whacked one placard with his billy and the crowd attacked. Half a dozen shots rang out and three policemen standing in front of a restaurant on the west side of the street, fell squirming to the pavement.

The officers seized the gunman, Stephen Chuck, who said he came here from Canada a few months ago, beat him unconscious, and hurried him to jail. Riot ensued in the middle of the boulevard, attracting hundreds of home-going office workers.

ANOTHER BOARDING HOUSE DESTROYED

BELMAR, March 12. — Levy's Mansion, the fifth big boarding house in the resort to be destroyed by fire of suspicious origin during the month, went up in flames today. The loss is about $25,000.

The structure, a 3-story, 30-room affair, was closed for the winter and the windows boarded up. Firemen fought the flames for six hours.

Police Now Have Counterfeit Bill Given in Change

Four Young Men Said to Have Been Original Passers

A counterfeit $5 bill, which is believed to have been passed last Wednesday at the Green Parrot roadstand near Stony road on the super highway in Raritan Township, has found its way into the hands of the police. The fake money had been given as change to Dr. Lillian French, Old Post Road, Raritan Township, on Friday and was revealed as counterfeit when the osteopath presented it at the First National Bank of Highland Park.

Mrs. George Kyriazis, attendant at the Green Parrot roadstand, is reported to have admitted giving the bill to Dr. French, and is certain that the spurious bank note was tendered her by one of four well dressed young men last Wednesday.

The bill is made to resemble an old bill and is a dull yellow color. It has a photograph of Lincoln on the face and bears the number B 85089435 A.

Mrs. Kyriazis, who speaks broken English, told Patrolman Harold Peterson of the Raritan Township police that she received the fake $5 bill in payment for eight cups of coffee and four hot roast beef sandwiches. She gave the young men $3 charge.

On Friday, Dr. French purchased ten gallons of gasoline and gave a $10 bill in payment for the fuel. She was given the counterfelt $5 bill as part of the change, police reported.

Quesioned as to the identity of the four young men, Mrs. Kyriazis said they were well dressed and wore felt hats. They had an automobile believed to bear Camden County license tags.

Cut of $58,000 In Budget Meets Big Opposition

Club Women of N. J. to Attend Appropriations Hearing

A lively session is expected tomorrow morning when the joint appropriation committee of the Legislature takes up the appropriation for the New Jersey College for Women at a public hearing. Statewide opposition will be voiced against the projected cut of $58,000 in the budget of N. J. C.

The college authorities will ask that no cut be made in allotment of funds to continue teacher-training at the N. J. C. and they will be supported by a large delegation representing the State Federation of Women's Clubs.

The club women are opposed to the proposed cut and also to any movement which has for its motive the reducing of the autonomy of the college, and also to the proposed elimination of the courses for teacher-training given at the college.

Although the club women have expressed determined opposition to the general outline of the Sate Board of Regents plan for reorganization of higher education as it touched the women's college, they at the same time have declared they would oppose the bill for ending the board.

It is reported that, in the event the appropriations committee supports the regents and eliminates the appropriation for teacher-training, an effort will be made to raise funds through private channels to assure the retention of the courses.

The regents claim there is overlapping in respect to teacher-training courses in the State and that the training of teachers should be left to the State Normal Schools supported by the State.

SEABURY RETURNS

NEW YORK, March 12.—Samuel Seabury, counsel to the Hofstadter Legislative Committee, returned today on the liner Monarch of Bermuda from a trip to Bermuda.

Position of Woman Is In Danger

Mrs. Anita Bloomfield's Term as Jury Commissioner Expiring

MAY BE SUCCEEDED BY A. CHRISTENSEN

Incumbent Has Support of County Republican Organization

The term of Mrs. Anita Bloomfield of Metuchen, the only woman jury commissioner in New Jersey, expires on March 24 and there is considerable speculation in political circles over her reappointment. The job pays $750 per annum and the appointment rests with the Governor.

Mrs. Bloomfield has the support of the Republican leaders of Middlesex for reappointment and it is reported that Governor Moore will be requested by the G. O. P. to give her another term. It is not likely, however, that Governor Moore, a Democrat will accept any recommendation made by the Republican organization.

Governor Larson appointed Mrs. Bloomfield after she was turned down for a post in the State Labor Department. It was understood she would be named Director of the Bureau for Women and Children but this appointment was given to Mrs. Isabella M. Summers of Paterson.

When it became apparent that Mrs. Bloomfield would not be given a State job, Governor Larson named her jury commissioner replacing Arnold Christensen of Perth Amboy who was filling the job temporarily at the time.

It is now reported that Christensen is in line for the appointment although he is not an active candidate. There is considerable political "wire pulling" being done for Christensen who is a brother of Township Commissioner Walter Christensen of Raritan Township. Democratic leaders have refused to comment on the appointment. Chairman Edmund A. Hayes declared last night that he had given no serious consideration to the appointment while it was learned from Republican sources that the county organization is united behind Mrs. Bloomfield.

Christensen was a candidate for the assembly last November and met with defeat. He is looked upon as an organization Republican in Perth Amboy.

Shot Gun Is Used by Man To End Life

Body of Grover Applegate, Monroe Township, Found In Shed

NO REASON GIVEN FOR SUICIDAL ACT

Two-Foot Stick Utilized To Pull Trigger of Weapon

MONROE TOWNSHIP, March 12.—Grover C. Applegate, 58, a farmer residing on Hightstown-Freehold road, this township, ended his life today by shooting himself in the head with a shotgun.

Anxious over his disappearance, Peter Patacki, a farmhand, on searching the premises found Applegate's body in a chicken shed. The door had been fastened with a string, but was left partly open so that the farmhand's attention was called to the building.

No reason could be advanced for the act of the farmer, who was born in this section. He was last seen about 7 o'clock this morning.

Coroner Eugene J. Mullen of Perth Amboy conducted an investigation and gave permission for removal of the body to Undertaker A. S. Cole and Sons of Cranbury.

Applegate used a single-barrel shotgun to commit suicide. He used a two-foot long stick to trip the trigger of the weapon after placing the end of the barrel against the side of his head. No one on the farm heard the shot.

The deceased was single and lived with his aunt. He is survived by two brothers, Charles Applegate, who lives on a nearby farm, and Russell Applegate of Allentown; also a sister, Mrs. Alice Tindall of Hamilton Square.

Funeral services will be held from the Applegate residence at 11 o'clock Monday morning. Rev. Powell Norton, pastor of Hightstown Baptist Church, will have charge of the services. Interment will be in Hightstown Cemetery.

Drys Will Put Full Ticket in G.O.P. Primary

Announcement Follows Shift of N. J. Delegation on Issue

Announcement by Edmund Halsey, Essex, dry candidate for governor last year that the New Jersey drys will put a complete dry ticket in the field at the Republican primaries, May 17, for delegates to the Republican National convention, for Congress members, and for the New Jersey Legislature came yesterday following the sensational switch on Friday of Congressmen Randolph Perkins of Bergen County, Charles A. Eaton of Somerset, and Charles A. Wolverton of Camden, all Republicans, from the bone-dry side to the wet side.

This shift makes the entire New Jersey Congress delegation solidly wet for the first time since prohibition was ratified in 1920. Congressman William H. Sutphin of the Third Congressional District was among the first of the delegation to announce he would vote with the wets when the "show down" takes place on Monday.

The change in front of the three dry Congressman came just as the House of Representatives was getting ready to vote on Monday on the motion to relieve the judiciary committee from further consideration of the Beck-Linthicum resolution that aims at alteration of the 18th Amendment.

If both the Senate and the House pass this resolution then the proposal will get to a special national convention for ratification, this convention being made up of delegates chosen in each state to consider this proposal and nothing else.

Halsey's announcement about a complete dry ticket in New Jersey is to "fight the wets" in the primaries came after hurried conferences among New Jersey Anti-Saloon League leaders who were admittedly chagrined by the surrender of the remaining drys in the New Jersey delegation.

"The drys of New Jersey have had their minds on the kidnapers and other law breakers and they have forgotten about the dry cause," said Mr. Halsey.

Twenty-Two Are Placed at Work In Local Drive

Chaskes and Kulbach Take On 20; Reliable Hatchery Two

The total number of unemployed persons put back to work through the American Legion war against depression campaign, since the opening of the drive on February 15, is now 502, according to reports from campaign headquarters. The firm of Chaskes and Kulbach Manufacturing Company will give jobs to twenty persons, and the Reliable Hatchery Company will employ two men, it was announced Saturday. Attorney Samuel M. Adler of Team No. is responsible for the twenty-two jobs.

But two days remain for the American Legion war against depression, which has been conducted throughout the country. The drive was instituted by the American Legion to aid in restoring normal times by putting 1,000,000 unemployed back to work. In all forty-three employers of labor are on the American Legion honor roll in this city as having given jobs to one or more unemployed persons.

Attorney Louis L. Hendler, chairman of the local American Legion committee, again expresses his thanks to all who cooperated in the worthy undertaking. New Brunswick leads the State in number of jobs obtained for the unemployed.

Firms and individuals on the honor roll here are:

Burns, Lane, Richardson; Jay Drug Store; Three Star Cap Company; Unger Cigar Box Company; Somerset Duco and Refinishing Company; Swift and Company; United Cigar Stores Company; Armour and Company; De Angelis Brothers; International Motor Company.

Sandler and Davis; Charles T. Valesi; Arctic Ice Company; Dr. A. L. Morris (Raritan Animal Hospital); Merckens, Inc; Morris Payensen; Spinelli Motor Company; John F. McGovern and Son; New Brunswick Window Cleaning Company; Lowenthal Meat Market.

La Salle Manufacturing Company; Russell Playing Card Company.

Continued on Page Five

NOMINATION OF EVANS IS CONFIRMED

(By The Associated Press)

WASHINGTON, March 12. — The Senate today confirmed the nomination of Frank Evans of Utah as a member of the Farm Board.

1933

The Tennessee Valley Authority, one of President Roosevelt's most ambitious New Deal programs, was created by Congress in 1933.

The job of the TVA was to develop the largely untapped resources of the Tennessee River and its tributaries—some forty thousand square miles in seven states—an area particularly hard hit by the Depression.

In the same year, Roosevelt also declared a national bank holiday, suspended the activity of the Federal Reserve System; appointed Frances Perkins as secretary of labor, the first woman Cabinet member; and began his radio "fireside chats."

"All the News That's Fit to Print."

The New York Times.

LATE CITY EDITION
WEATHER—Occasional light rain, warmer today and tomorrow.
Temperatures Yesterday—Max., 43; Min., 35.

L. LXXXII....No. 27,442. Entered as Second-Class Matter. Postoffice, New York, N. Y. NEW YORK, MONDAY, MARCH 13, 1933. P TWO CENTS In New York City. | THREE CENTS Within 200 Miles | FOUR CENTS Elsewhere Except in 7th and 8th Postal Zones

IANY BANKS IN THE CITY AND NATION REOPEN TODAY FOR NORMAL OPERATIONS, BUT WITH HOARDING BARRED; ROOSEVELT APPEALS ON THE RADIO FOR FULL CONFIDENCE

DENBURG DROPS AG OF REPUBLIC; ZIS CARRY CITIES

dent Orders Black-White- of Empire and Swastika ner Flown Side by Side.

ISTS WIN IN PRUSSIA

ure Majorities Alone or h Allies in Local Polls, weeping 'Red Berlin.'

ER CURBS FOLLOWERS

ands Them to Cease Petty secutions — All Germany arches on Memorial Day.

REDERICK T. BIRCHALL.
al Cable to THE NEW YORK TIMES.

LIN, March 12.—This was rman Memorial Day, the day ich all Germany, mourning ar dead, might theoretically pected to meditate upon the nd take warning therefrom. n this day the whole Reich ormal farewell of the Weimar ic and the régime built t.

other interpretation can be on the outstanding incident day, which was the promulga- a Presidential decree pro- that henceforth the colors hall fly upon all public build- Germany shall be the black, and red of the former im- sm and the Nazi swastika— oked cross- side by side. red, black and gold ensign e republican Germany has waved its last, for a time at and the new era has begun in t.

National Socialists further dated their position in to- municipal and communal elec- throughout Prussia, polling gest vote in most of the im- t cities and generally obtain- ajorities with their National- es.

Is and Allies Win Berlin.

ter Berlin returned the Nazis ationalists with an absolute ty, leaving the Socialists, nists and Centrists combined inority. This ends "Red Ber- d terminates fourteen years ination by the parties of the

tly what the new era sym- by the flag ruling will bring and whither it will lead be- the realm of prophecy. The news is that the fourteen- d structure of the republic being dismantled and left wreckers, and upon its foun- something quite new is be- gun.

dent von Hindenburg's de- as read to the whole nation the government radio by llor Hitler, who in so doing ced himself for the first the authorized mouthpiece President.

decree says:

this day, when throughout ny the old black-white-red floating at half-staff in of our war dead, I decree ginning tomorrow and until initive regulation of the na- colors the black-white-red e hooked cross flags are to played together.

se flags unite the glorious the German Reich and the t rebirth of the German na- Unitedly they shall embody wer of the State and the im- interconnection of all the l sections of the German Military establishments will only the Reich war flag."

l the definitive regulation of tional colors" may be taken shadowing a constitutional on for a new flag altogether. probability it will be made orporating the swastika in black-white-red stripes. In antime it is ordered that the gs shall be flown alongside ther for three days contin-

Hitler Curbs Followers.

her highly important incident day was the issuance by llor Hitler to his followers rect command to end imme-

Continued on Page Six.

Two More Americans Beaten By Bands of Nazis in Berlin

By The Associated Press.

BERLIN, March 12.—Two more Americans were the victims of assaults here yesterday. Julian Fuhs, a New York musician, was beaten by men in Nazi uniforms who demanded money. A storm troop leader interfered, calling the police

Herman Roseman of Brooklyn, a medical student in the University of Berlin, was attacked as he was coming out of a department store with a package. He showed his passport, but a policeman refused to intervene. At the police station the police told him they could not interfere with the Nazis.

Both Mr. Fuhs and Mr. Roseman made affidavits at the United States Consulate.

QUAKE ZONE BEGINS TASKS OF RECOVERY

Central Agency Created—Use of R. F. C. Funds Sought for California Relief.

TREMORS STILL GO ON

Long Beach Under Rehabilitation Dictator—Check-Up Cuts Death List to 110.

Special to THE NEW YORK TIMES.

LOS ANGELES, March 12.—The count of human lives lost in the earthquake disaster in Southern California beginning Friday evening was reduced today, following an official check by Coroner Nance of Los Angeles County and deputy sheriffs.

The known loss of life from the earthquake is now put at 110 persons, of whom ninety-eight died of injuries and twelve of shock.

In Long Beach, where the check-up revealed duplicated reports, the dead numbered fifty-one with the death of a hospital patient today. The bodies of three, a woman and two men, were unidentified at Long Beach.

With the estimate of damage remaining at nearly $50,000,000, the tasks of recovery through local, State and Federal effort were begun under centralized direction.

Minor shocks occurred through the day and this evening, continuing to shake down weakened structures.

New Direction of Shocks.

Last night the more pronounced shocks changed to the opposite direction in stress from those of the previous twenty-four hours, residents of Long Beach reported.

Friday night's tremors rocked the surface of the earth from north to south, but last night the direction changed from west to east. What the change in direction of the shocks may signify is problematical.

One arrest for looting at Long Beach was reported by the police. The authorities locked up a man who gave the name of Terence Morgan, after he had been discovered, they asserted, in a wrecked residence with various articles of value in his pockets.

Public schools throughout Los Angeles will remain closed all this week to check all buildings for damage, the Board of Education has ordered. In the county outside of Los Angeles only those schools in the heavy earthquake area will be closed until further notice, County Superintendent of Schools Clifton announced. About 50,000 children will be out of school because of the orders.

Three cities have formally requested Reconstruction Finance Corporation aid through Rolland A. Vandegrift, State Director of Finance, to start rehabilitation. Santa Ana requested $750,000 for reconstruction and unemployment, its estimated property loss being $1,250,000, with only 10 per cent of buildings insured against earthquake.

Compton, with estimated property damage of $5,000,000, asked for $125,000 to start immediate reconstruction of business houses and private residences. Mayor Pomeroy of South Gate stated that $25,000 would see the city through the preliminary period and $125,000 more would restore its original status.

Mr. Vandegrift sought information from Washington as to how far the State may use R. F. C.

Continued on Page Ten.

ECONOMY VICTORY LOOMS

Measure Up in Senate Today, With Passage Predicted This Week.

VETERANS FIGHTING CUTS

8 or 10 Democrats Champion Cause, but Republicans Will Offset Defections.

EMPLOYMENT PLANS NEXT

Roosevelt Also May Submit Emergency Farm Relief Bill Before Congress Recesses.

Special to THE NEW YORK TIMES.

WASHINGTON, March 12.—Passage by the Senate of the $500,000,000 economy bill voted by the House yesterday was predicted today by Senate leaders. They told President Roosevelt that vigorous opposition to the reduction of veterans' benefits was indicated but that they expected the measure to be accepted by a substantial majority after three or four days' debate. The bill will come up in the Senate tomorrow.

The President was informed that eight or ten Democratic Senators were opposed to the proposed reductions in the veterans' budget. The opposition of some Senators has become so pronounced against the scaling down of Federal aid to veterans that Senator Robinson of Arkansas, majority floor leader, has decided to abandon any attempt to bind Democratic members by a caucus, although a conference may be held tomorrow to exchange views before the Senate begins consideration of the economy bill.

Senator Pittman of Nevada, who, with Senator Robinson of Arkansas, was expected to lead the administration battle for the bill, which would empower the President to effect the economies, said tonight that before the end of the present week the measure would be passed by the Senate and put into legal effect.

Pittman Predicts 2-to-1 Vote.

"As far as I can learn, there are from eight to ten Senators who will vote against the veterans' cut and may finally oppose the bill if there is not some modification of the reduction to the veterans," Senator Pittman said. "Because of this situation there will be a full discussion in the Senate, lasting three or four days. Despite the opposition it is my belief that the measure will be passed by the Senate by a 2-to-1 majority."

President Roosevelt has refused compromises suggested by some Senators to make a cut of 10 per cent in appropriations for veterans not disabled in the service. He has insisted that there is no justice in such expenditures in the face of increasing deficit and that the only way to balance the budget is through the drastic reductions he proposes.

Messages received at the White House today from Governors, business leaders and others strongly commended the President for his prompt action looking to balancing the budget. Some of the Governors offered to submit resolutions to their Legislatures urging their State representatives in the Senate to stand solidly behind the administration. While the telegrams and letters were chiefly of a congratulatory nature there were plenty of protests from American Legionnaires. On the other hand, many veterans of the World War, among them men who have been prominent in Legion affairs, strongly endorsed the President's stand.

Republican Help Expected.

Opposition to the reductions on veterans has been strengthened over the week-end by the activities of lobbies and the flood of protests received by Senators from the veterans in their States. Latest surveys of the Senate, however, indicate that the administration's program will be accepted by the Senate without substantial change.

It is expected that the administration may lose some Democratic support but that the losses will be more than made up by the promised Republican accessions. Senator McNary, minority Senate leader, believes that fully two-thirds of the Republicans will go along with the administration. He has called a

Continued on Page Five.

Opening of Stock Exchange Awaits More Bank Facilities

The New York Stock Exchange, the New York Curb Exchange and the various commodity markets of New York will remain closed today, according to latest advices, in order to await a resumption of fuller banking operations.

In the absence of definite knowledge as to the number of banks that will be open on Wednesday under the schedule for reopening sound institutions on three successive days this week, it is not expected that transactions in securities or in commodities will be resumed until then.

A meeting of Stock Exchange executives held last night considered a series of additional regulations governing the conduct of affairs by members. The rules will be made public today after they have been communicated to the members.

M'COOEY DISAVOWS SLAP AT ROOSEVELT

Repudiates Action of Kings Delegation in Not Backing Federal Economy Bill.

HE WIRES THE PRESIDENT

Curry Plans No Similar Step—Says He Did Not Know How Tammany Men Would Vote.

John H. McCooey, veteran Kings County Democratic leader, last night took the unprecedented step of repudiating the action of the Brooklyn delegation in Congress, which voted on Saturday against the Roosevelt economy bill. Mr. McCooey sent a personal telegram to President Roosevelt, informing him of his action, and made public the statement here, at the same time.

Tammany Leader John F. Curry, asked last night if he intended to take the same step as Mr. McCooey did, said he had no such plans at present. He said that he, and Mr. Cooey as well, were on their way home from the Cermak funeral in Chicago when the House voted on the bill, and he did not know how the New York delegation voted until he returned late Saturday night.

Mr. McCooey's telegram to President Roosevelt said that he repudiated the action of Brooklyn Representatives in voting against the economy bill and that a statement in the press this morning explained his stand.

Expects Fairness on Pensions.

The statement itself follows:

"The action of the members of the House of Representatives from this county in voting against legislation proposed by the President does not meet with my personal approval and I am confident it is likewise displeasing to the people of Brooklyn.

"I know that the President will deal in a fair and impartial manner in the matter of veterans' pensions and I am firmly convinced that those who are not of this opinion are unduly alarmed.

"Never has our country been in the sad plight which has enveloped it for over three years and the President is entitled to and must receive the support of every American citizen and their representatives in Congress in his efforts to end the depression and restore the country to its former prosperous condition."

The line-up of the Representatives from New York City on the economy program had been the topic of conversation in political circles from the time the roll-call was printed in newspapers here, and Mr. McCooey's statement last night added fresh fuel to the flames.

Seen as Political Move.

It was construed generally as a bid by Mr. McCooey to keep "in" with the Roosevelt camp, now in control of the State and Federal Governments, and it renewed the talk of the possibility of Mr. McCooey being won over to join forces with Edward J. Flynn, the Bronx leader, instead of sticking to Tammany Leader Curry.

In quarters close to the Roosevelt camp, however, it was said that resentment over the vote of the New York Representatives is strong. It was pointed out that Mr. Curry

Continued on Page Two.

NEAR NORMAL HERE TODAY

52 Members of Reserve and All State Banks in This City to Open.

SAVINGS GROUP INCLUDED

They Waive 60-Day Clause, but Are Ordered to Limit Withdrawals at Present.

NEW CURRENCY IS AMPLE

Federal Reserve to Function as Usual Except for Rules Safeguarding Gold.

New York City banks which on first examination by the Federal and State authorities have been found to be completely sound will reopen in full today. Authorization to resume full banking functions were issued at 12:30 o'clock this morning by the Federal Reserve Bank of New York to its member banks and a half hour later by Superintendent of Banks Joseph A. Broderick to institutions under his jurisdiction which are not members of the Federal Reserve System.

The licenses to Federal Reserve member banks were sent out immediately after President Roosevelt's radio address to the people explaining the banking situation and the Administration's program of gradual re-openings. The list of those licensed, as made public by the Reserve Bank, comprises fifty-two institutions. All of the important member banks are included.

As soon as the Federal Reserve list was issued, Superintendent Broderick began notifying institutions under his jurisdiction in Greater New York, but not members of the Federal Reserve, that they had been licensed "to perform the usual banking functions, except as restricted by executive order of the President and regulations of the Secretary of the Treasury."

Banks Licensed by Broderick.

The list of banks licensed by the Superintendent of Banks included all twenty-four of the State-chartered non-member banks in the five boroughs. The fifty-nine savings banks in the city were authorized to open without invoking the protection of the sixty-day clause, but they will limit withdrawals for the time being to $25 weekly for each depositor, under a ruling of the State Banking Board.

Simultaneously with the licensing of banks here to reopen, Federal Reserve and State banking authorities in the eleven other Federal Reserve Bank cities throughout the country issued permits to banks in their respective cities which had been examined and found in good order. In this way the first step in President Roosevelt's program for a staggered reopening of banks will bring about the resumption of normal business today by all the principal banks in the leading cities of the country.

In succeeding steps, banks in the 250 cities of the country having recognized clearing house associations and which have been examined and found sound will be opened tomorrow and banks in other sections of the country will be licensed to resume business on Wednesday.

Lehman Issues Proclamation.

Earlier, Governor Lehman had issued a proclamation authorizing the State banking authorities to make regulations for the resumption of business by State-chartered institutions. His proclamation follows:

Whereas the President of the United States issued on the tenth day of March, nineteen hundred and thirty-three, an executive order prescribing methods whereby banking institutions could commence the performance of their functions:

Now, therefore, I, Herbert H. Lehman, Governor of the State of New York, by virtue of the authority vested in me by chapter forty-two of the laws of nineteen hundred thirty-three, and by virtue of all other authority vested in me, hereby proclaim, order and direct that each of the appropriate authorities of the State of New York having immediate supervision of institu-

Continued on Page Four.

Banks Opening Today

The Federal Reserve Bank of New York at 12:30 o'clock this morning made public a list of the New York City member banks which it had authorized to open for business at the usual banking hours today.

This list was as follows:

FEDERAL RESERVE MEMBERS.

Manhattan.

Amalgamated Bank of New York.
Bankers Trust Company.
Bank of the Manhattan Company.
Bank of New York & Trust Company.
Bank of Yorktown.
Central Hanover Bank & Trust Company.
Chase National Bank.
Chemical Bank & Trust Company.
Clinton Trust Company.
Colonial Trust Company.
Commercial National Bank & Trust Company.
Continental Bank & Trust Company.
Corn Exchange Bank Trust Company.
Dunbar National Bank.
Federation Bank & Trust Company of New York.
Fifth Avenue Bank of New York.
First National Bank of New York.
Fulton Trust Company of New York.
Grace National Bank.
Guaranty Trust Company
Harbor State Bank.
Irving Trust Company.
Manufacturers Trust Company.
Marine Midland Trust Company.
Merchants Bank.
National Bank of Yorkville.
National City Bank.
National Safety Bank and Trust Company.
New York Trust Company.
Public National Bank and Trust Company.
J. Henry Schroder Trust Company.
Sterling National Bank and Trust Company.
Trade Bank of New York.
United States Trust Company.

Brooklyn.

Bensonhurst National Bank of Brooklyn.
Brooklyn Trust Company.
Flatbush National Bank of Brooklyn.
Fort Greene National Bank of New York.
Kingsboro National Bank of Brooklyn.
National Exchange Bank and Trust Company.
Peoples National Bank of Brooklyn.

Queens.

Bayside National Bank of New York.
College Point National Bank of New York.
National Bank of Far Rockaway.
National Bank of Queens County in New York.
Forest Hills National Bank of New York.
Springfield Gardens National Bank of New York.
Woodside National Bank of New York.

Bronx.

National Bronx Bank.

Richmond.

Mariner Harbor National Bank.
Staten Island National Bank & Trust Company of New York.
Tottenville National Bank.

NON-MEMBERS OF FEDERAL RESERVE.

State commercial banks in New York City authorized by State Bank Superintendent Broderick to open today:

Manhattan.

Anglo-South America Trust Company.
Banca Commerciale Italiana Trust Company.
Banco di Napoli Trust Company.
Bank of Athens Trust Company.
Bank of Sicily Trust Company.
City Bank Farmers Trust Company.
Corporation Trust Company.
County Trust Company.
Empire Trust Company.
Equitable Trust Company.
Fiduciary Trust Company.
Hellenic Bank Trust Company.
Hias Immigrant Bank.
Lawyers Trust Company.
Pennsylvania Exchange Bank.
Title Guarantee and Trust Company.
Trust Company of North America.
Underwriters Trust Company.

Brooklyn.

Citizens Bank.
Kings County Trust Company.

Queens.

Boulevard Bank, Forest Hills.

Bronx.

Bronx County Trust Company.

Richmond.

South Shore Bank.
West New Brighton Bank.

SAVINGS BANKS.

All savings banks throughout the city will be open for business today. Under an order by the State Banking Department, however, depositors will not be permitted to withdraw more than $25 a week. The savings banks have decided not to invoke the sixty-day clause against withdrawals.

News of the opening of banks throughout the country will be found on Page 2.

The President's Speech

Special to THE NEW YORK TIMES.

WASHINGTON, March 12.—The text of President Roosevelt's radio address on the banking situation, delivered at 10 o'clock tonight from his study in the White House, was as follows:

My friends, I want to talk for a few minutes with the people of the United States about banking—with the comparatively few who understand the mechanics of banking, but more particularly with the overwhelming majority of you who use banks for the making of deposits and the drawing of checks. I want to tell you what has been done in the last few days, and why it was done, and what the next steps are going to be.

I recognize that the many proclamations from State Capitols and from Washington, the legislation, the Treasury regulations, &c., couched for the most part in banking and legal terms, ought to be explained for the benefit of the average citizen. I owe this in particular because of the fortitude and the good temper with which everybody has accepted the inconvenience and the hardships of the banking holiday.

I know that when you understand what we in Washington have been about, I shall continue to have your cooperation as fully as I have had your sympathy and your help during the past week.

First of all, let me state the simple fact that when you deposit money in a bank, the bank does not put the money into a safe deposit vault. It invests your money in many different forms of credit—in bonds, commercial paper, mortgages, and many other kinds of loans.

In other words, the bank puts your money to work to keep the wheels of industry and of agriculture turning around. A comparatively small part of the money you put into the bank is kept

Continued on Page Three.

SOUND BANKS CLASSIFIED

Reserve Board Flooded by Applications to Enter System.

R. F. C. ALSO WILL RESUME

President Declares That Ample Currency Will Be Provided for Needs of All.

STATE BANKS WILL GET AID

His Address Emphasizes This Point After Governors Lehman and Ritchie Protest.

Special to THE NEW YORK TIMES.

WASHINGTON, March 12.—President Roosevelt explained the banking situation to the people of the United States in a fifteen-minute radio address tonight. The President's appeal for confidence in the government's program was made after preparations had been completed for the progressive reopening, beginning tomorrow morning, of banks classified as sound by Federal and State officials.

The banks to open tomorrow are member banks of the Federal Reserve System in the twelve Federal Reserve Bank cities, licensed by the Treasury, and non-member State banks which have received the approval of the State banking superintendents.

On Tuesday licensed banks will reopen in cities having recognized clearing house associations, and on Wednesday will come the reopenings in other communities of banks in other categories.

Officials, headed by Secretary Woodin, labored all day and all night at the Treasury to make the necessary arrangements and several new regulations were issued. The Executive Offices at the White House remained open also.

Woodin Defines Banks' First Duty.

Secretary Woodin shortly before 11 o'clock tonight issued the following statement:

"The first duty of the banks reopening under license of the Secretary of the Treasury for the performance of their usual functions is to see that the primary needs of the people for funds for necessaries of life and for normal business undertakings are met.

"Accordingly, withdrawals for hoarding have been prohibited, and the Secretary of the Treasury suggests that until more normal conditions have been established, transfer of funds by banks or their customers be limited to necessary purposes."

Instructions went forth from the Federal Reserve Board to the Reserve Banks to release locally the names of member banks and State banks licensed to open tomorrow. When it was reported that the Cleveland Federal Reserve Bank had declined to give out the list the Reserve Board sent peremptory instructions that this should be done in Cleveland as elsewhere.

A flood of applications by State banks not members of the Federal Reserve System for membership were being received by the Federal Reserve Board by mail and telegraph. They came from almost every section of the country, where they had first been passed upon by the Federal Reserve Banks.

The rush of applications began almost immediately after the emergency banking legislation was adopted, and the Federal Reserve Board will pass upon them as rapidly as possible. There is every prospect that one result of the national banking holiday will be a very considerable increase in the membership and resources of the Reserve System.

Among Treasury Department regulations issued today was one granting permission to private banking houses and other financial institutions which do not come under Federal or State supervision, to resume normal operation, with restrictions, however, as to the release of gold or gold certificates and transactions in foreign exchange.

Another regulation of major importance permitted the Reconstruction Finance Corporation to renew its operations tomorrow. An effort will be made to have the corpora-

Continued on Page Three.

1934

The fast and luxurious passenger liner *Morro Castle* was nearing the end of her Havana-to-New York cruise when fire broke out. Within a short time, much of the 11,500-ton ship was a mass of flames.

In the confusion that followed, 134 of the 548 passengers died, either by drowning or incineration in the floating crematorium.

Later investigation also was to reveal much negligence and stupidity on the part of the crew, many of whom were the first ones to flee the ship.

In the same year, bank robber and murderer John Dillinger, public enemy number one, was shot and killed by agents of the FBI.

Outlaw Clyde Barrow and his companion, Bonnie Parker, were killed by a sheriff's posse in Louisiana, ending an eight-year trail of murder and robbery.

And the Dionne quintuplets, five girls, were born in Callender, Ontario, Canada.

When the winds came, noon turned to darkness and dirt was everywhere. When it stopped, the fields were gone, leaving only drifting sands.

The dust storms in the Midwest and Great Plains in the 1930s destroyed about 150,000 square miles of farmland in the heart of the country, blowing the drought-weakened topsoil hundreds, even thousands, of miles away.

One storm alone, in May 1934, blew away an estimated 300 million tons of topsoil.

Latest List of Ship Passengers and Survivors in This Edition

THE WEATHER
Rain and Easterly Gales, Diminishing Tomorrow. (See Page 3.)

ASBURY PARK EVENING PRESS

FINAL EDITION

FORTY-EIGHTH YEAR. NO. 212. ASBURY PARK, N. J., SATURDAY, SEPTEMBER 8, 1934 PRICE THREE CENTS

199 RESCUED, 359 FEARED LOST WHEN LINER BURNS OFF BELMAR

ERSEY STRIKERS BASE PEACE HOPE ON MILLS' STAND

ook for Speedy Settlement Based on New Jacquard Contract — Believe Others Will Follow.

CORE OF MILLS REOPEN UNDER PROTECTIVE MOVE

PATERSON, Sept. 8. (AP) — Union aders in the Paterson silk and rayon strict, looking to a speedy and favorable settlement of the strike here, sed their hopes today chiefly on the illingness of Jacquard silk manufacturers to sign a new contract giving organized workers definite concessions.

Approval of the agreement by the ational textile strike committee would nd 4,000 of the 13,000 strikers in this strict back to their looms, and would, the opinion of Eli Keller, general anager of the Associated Silk Workers, probably induce Jacquard silk anufacturers elsewhere to sign similar contracts.

Joseph M. Harrison and Julius Bruer, embers of the Master Weavers institute, were to go to Washington today confer with the national strike committee. Alexander Williams and Henry ss, business agents of the Associated Silk Workers local 1716, branch of the American Federation of Silk orkers, and William Leech, recording cretary, were also going to Washington to attend the conference.

Under the terms of a contract signed the union and the institute last year cquard workers have been working 5 weekly shifts of 40 hours each. The w agreement of the Jacquard manufacturers, however, calls for only one ft of 40 hours.

No change in the basic rates of pay included in the proposed contract, ce the Jacquard workers, union ders and manufacturers say, consid- themselves highly paid. The present ntract expires Oct. 24. While the nference between manufacturers and ion leaders was in session yesterday, institute made application in Jersey y before Vice Chancelor John O. gelow for an injunction restraining union from "forcing" workers to ve the mills.

Unions Must Defend Strike

Vice Chancelor Bigelow signed an er compelling the union to show se why it should not be restrained m calling a strike. The order is urnable next Wednesday.

All silk and rayon mills in the Paton area were closed today for the urday and Sunday holiday. A series mass meetings of union workers are eduled at union headquarters over weekend in preparation for a more centrated form of picketing on Mon- .

Under the new picketing plan every rker will report in front of the build- where he or she has been work- The massed workers will picket mill at opening time, and will then rch to union headquarters.

Efforts will be directed mainly to- rds bringing out some 5,000 unor- nized throwsters, and the 2,000 broad workers who are still at their looms. Whether the 20,000 silk and rayon rs in the area will be called on to ke was still doubtful today. George

(Continued on page six)

COUPLE FOUND SLAIN

dies of Kansas Oil Worker and Wife Found in Culvert.

EL DORADO, Kas., Sept. 8. (AP)— e bodies of Frank Kelly, 25, an oil ker, and his wife, 20, were found night in a concrete culvert eight es west of Augusta, their throats cut m ear to ear.

Police immediately began qustioning fford Kelly, brother of Frank who, ice Chief Charles Parton, said, was olved in a fight with Frank, Sat- ay night.

The Press Today

SPECIAL FEATURES

Survivor Searches Vainly For Trace of His Sister

Dr. Charles Cochrane, Prominent Brooklyn Physician, Looks for Relative—Avon Man Seeks Brother and Wife, Also Aboard.

Avon was the center today of a pathetic effort of two men to locate relatives they fear may have gone down with the S. S. Morro Castle.

Dr. Charles Cochrane, a survivor, looked with waning hope for his sister, Miss Katherine Cochrane; A. C. Vosseler and his wife, summer residents at 204 Norwood avenue, Avon, searched fruitlessly for a trace of Vosseler's brother and his wife, Dr. and Mrs. Theodore Vosseler. Aiding in the search were Mr. and Mrs. Chester A. Peake, summer residents at 213 Woodland avenue, Avon.

All are close friends, as the three doctors are all associated on the staff of the Carson C. Peck Memorial hospital, Brooklyn, which was founded in memory of a former Rumson summer resident. Dr. Peake is also associated with the staff at the Pitkin hospital.

Dr. Cochran, near exhaustion after three hours in a small boat, with only a coat to protect him from the raging storm, came ashore at Spring Lake. He telephoned the Peake's, who rushed clothes to him at the Spring Lake police headquarters and almost immediately began a round of hospitals seeking his sister. He tried the beaches where survivors were drifting in. Then he scanned the growing lines of bodies that were beginning to drift ashore.

Little Hope Held Out

The Peakes, meanwhile, had summoned the Vosselers, and, after a council of war, went out with Dr. Cochrane while the Vosselers sat at a telephone, to call various points where survivors might be, and to await word from others.

The searchers came back to the Peake house, discouraged, after a search of several hours. Little hope was held out that the three might be alive.

As he paused, near exhaustion, at the Spring Lake police headquarters, the six-foot Dr. Cochrane told his story.

"I was asleep in my cabin when, it seemed to me about 3 a. m., I awoke to smell a pungent odor of smoke. I heard a banging on the door and rose quickly.

"The passageway outside my cabin was a mass of flames thru which there

(Continued on Page Three)

50 HURT AS SHIP LURCHES ON LAKE

Rochester Excursionists Are Thrown from Chairs in Ferry Accident.

CRAFT RETURNS SAFELY TO PORT AT ROCHESTER

ROCHESTER, N. Y., Sept. 8. (AP)— Fifty persons were reported injured, several seriously, when an excursion ferry suddenly lurched forward as it was returning to Rochester early today from a trip on Lake Ontario.

About 500 passengers were on board. It was not learned immediately what caused the ferry to lurch.

The accident happened about 12 miles off the entrance to the port of Rochester. Word was sent ahead to have ambulances and physicians ready at the docks to care for the injured.

The boat leaped forward so suddenly that most of the passengers were hurled from their chairs, it was reported.

The Canadian national railways car ferry, a regular lake vessel, was chartered by the group for the excursion. Most of the passengers were residents of Rochester.

Most of the accident victims were treated at the docks when the vessel arrived. Two were taken to hospitals.

Capt. Charles E. Redfern said that when the ferry was about seven or eight miles off shore a sudden wind came up and increased almost to gale velocity. He said he finally decided to turn back and that it was while the vessel was turning that the accident occurred.

It suddenly rolled violently, he stated, as if struck by the rough waters. He attributed the rolling of the

(Continued on page six)

FLAMES DESTROY COOLING SYSTEM

Refrigeration Unit in Local High School Burns—Loss Is $2,000.

CAFETERIA WILL OPEN MONDAY DESPITE BLAZE

A large wooden refrigerator and its metal freezing unit burned this morning in the cafeteria of the Asbury Park high school. Damage to the cooling apparatus was estimated at $2,000 by Capt. William E. Taggart, acting chief of the fire department.

The fire was discovered at 8.55 when Miss Dorothy Smith, cafeteria manager, entered the building with Frank Hulick and Calvin Patterson, school janitors, to prepare the cafeteria for its opening Monday when school begins.

The three smelled smoke, and on entering the cafeteria found the room filled with bluish smoke. Using chemical extinguishers, Hulick and Patterson put out the blaze before the flames had spread beyond the ice box. The fire started in the motor and spread to the wooden containing unit

The blaze presumably started thru defective wiring or thru lack of lubrication in the motor which had not been in use since last spring. Smoke damage to the room was negligible, Captain Taggart said. The fire will not prevent the opening of the cafeteria Monday.

To avoid possible escape of freezing fluid from pipes damaged by the fire, Captain Taggart called upon the Jersey Central Power and Light company to empty the freezing fluid from the machine. Such fluid gives off a suffocating odor when allowed to escape, Taggart said.

(Continued on page six)

Carton Continues Lottery Hearing, Rejects Toolan's Dismissal Move

Because "the case is not apparent," U. S. Commissioner James D. Carton, sr., yesterday continued for two weeks the federal hearing of six men and a woman arrested Aug. 29 in Sheriff Howard Height's raid on a $1,000,000 Keansburg lottery ring.

Another defendant, Joseph Arnold, Newark, was released from $2,000 bail, because the youth, a medical student in Switzerland, had been working at the plant only a day and a half. It was not believed he would have sufficient knowledge of the allegedly illegal activities of the place to sustain a case. Arnold is still under $1,000 bail on the state charge.

Carton granted the continuation after V. D. Garvey, department of justice agent, had put only one witness, Undersheriff Paul Kiernan, on the witness stand to prove that the eight were engaged in interstate commerce and therefore liable under the federal statutes.

Attorney for the prisoners, State Sen. John E. Toolan, Middlesex, immedately asked for a dismissal on the grounds that nothing in the written complaint had been proven by Kiernan's evidence.

The prisoners are: Benjamin B. Lustgarten, Atlantic City, Morris Winniman, Newark, alleged leader of the gang, Michael Maguire, Middletown township, Benjamin Byer, Philadelphia, George Silverman, New York, Miss Mary Posta, Reading, Pa., and Joseph Wolfe, Keansburg.

Mrs. Laverne Matthews, held under state bail but not on the federal charge, also attended the hearing.

"Very Important Case"

Toolan said that under the federal statute, and because of court rulings,

(Continued on page six)

S. S. Morro Castle Swept by Flames

Here is a broadside view of the S.S. Morro Castle which was built in 1930. She was raked by fire off Belmar early this morning.

List of S. S. Morro Castle Survivors

(See Page 3 for Passenger List)

Clarence Monroe, seaman.
John Caldwell, waiter.
Felix Seijo, waiter.
Morris Namerosky, waiter.
Albert Gasch, steward.
Max Hassien, waiter.
Nicholas Capaz, fireman.
Richard Kopf, steward.
Joseph Ferr, steward.
Benjamin Mezer, steward.
Donato Varelo, oiler.
John D'Uva, steward.
William Lockmier, seaman.
John Smith, steward.
Florenzio Rodriquez, steward.
Ellis Beaumont, fireman.
Antonio Georgio, oiler.
Norman Witherspoon, waiter.
David Vinck, porter.
Thomas Charles, seaman.
Morris Weisberger, seaman.
Walter Sunkins, oiler.
Andrew Zabala, fireman.
William Wright, wiper.
Walter Cody, junior cadet.
Colin Houston, fireman.
Henry Harris, third electrician.
Joseph Garcia, carpenter.
William Bernhardt, seaman.
Gerald Dunn, seaman.
Fred Walker, seaman.
Sydney Davis, bell boy.
Joe Davis, bell boy.
Carl Pyron, waiter.
Herman Seerkin, bell boy.
James York, oiler.
Valentine Muney, mess man.
Jaun Suarez, waiter, Tampa, Fla.
Leroy Kilsey, seaman.
Irwin Coln, cadet.
Paul Arneth, passenger, Brooklyn.
Peter Krusher, seaman.
Ferdinand Zark, steward.
Paul Molnar, bell boy.
Hans Strowm, steward.
Ernest L. Abbot, engineer.
Solomon Miller, waiter.
William Torres, seaman.
Edward Jansen, waiter.
Joseph Mantanvales, oiler.
Addis Daly, bell boy.
Milton Stephenson, waiter.
James McManus, seaman.
John Saulters, fireman
Joseph Fernandez, seaman.
Joseph O'Connor, steward.
Charles Brink, waiter, Phillipsburg.
Joseph Spilgas, seaman.
Dr. Charles Cochrane, Brooklyn, passenger.
Frank Carey, waiter.
Percy Mille, electrician.
Sinclair J. Henderson, waiter.
Mrs. Renee Mendez Capote, passenger, Havana, Cuba.
Miss Ann Conway, passenger, New York city.
Miss Florence Roberts, Pawtucket, R. I.
Charles Eichler, steward.
Thomas Noves, fireman.
Gustaf F. Hanrin, quartermaster.
George Gonzalez, waiter.
Charles Bruns, seaman, New York city.
John Gross, seaman, New York city.
Arthur Bagley, ordinary seaman, New York city.
Walter Clody, seaman, New York city.
Andrew Zabala, fireman, New York city.
Leroy Kelsey, seaman, Albany.
Charles Jackson, 33, member of crew, Buffalo, N. Y., in Fitkin hospital.
Daniel Conduicus, seaman, New York city, in Fitkin hospital.
Joseph Marko 20, steward, Flushing, L. I., in Fitkin hospital.
William Kitchen, 54, Cleveland, O., seaman, in Fitkin hospital.
Emma LaRoche, Providence, R. I., passenger, in Fitkin hospital.
Mrs. Pearl Panimo, 38, passenger, Bangor, Pa., in Fitkin hospital.
Rocco Viola, member of crew, New York city.
John Barrow, fireman, New York city.
Charles Brick, pantryman, Phillipsburg, N. J.
Artulo Mata, Havana, Cuba, in Fitkin hospital.
Mr. and Mrs. Lloyd Gene Barnstead, passengers, 1891 Harrison avenue, Bronx, N. Y.
George Whitlock, passenger, assistant vice president National City bank, New York.
Mrs. Mary Robenson, 45, passenger, Richmond Hill, N. Y.
Miss Lillian Davidson of the Presbyterian hospital, New York city.
Miss Carolyn Carey, Philadelphia.
Dr. and Mrs. Jules Blondeau, 17th and Chestnut streets, Philadelphia.
Dr. and Mrs. Morris Philips, 255 East 79th street, New York city.
Mr. and Mrs. Abe Cohen, 11 King Terrace, Hartford, Conn.
Dr. Amelio Giro, Cuba.
Miss Diane Levy, 1334 Grant street, Bronx, N. Y.
Mrs. Peter Grady, 1902 East 18th street, Philadelphia.
Miss Marjorie Ehrman, 401 Elbernarle street, Hempstead, L. I.
Miss Rose Biren, 1521 Spruce street, Philadelphia.
Mr. and Mrs. Stephen Bodner, 15 Summit road, Elizabeth.
Miss Jane Adams, 6205 Lunekin Heights, Philadelphia.
Edward J. Brady, 704 Overbrook avenue, Philadelphia.

Same Steamer in Distress Year Ago

NEW YORK, Sept. 8 (AP)—The steamer Morro Castle, burning off the New Jersey coast today, was in distress just a year ago on a voyage from Havana to New York when she ran into a hurricane off Cape Hatteras.

For two days the vessel battled the storm, her radio silent. Finally on Sept. 18 she emerged from the storm and finished the trip safely. At that time the ship carried 140 passengers and a crew of 200.

The Morro Castle, a vessel of about 11,000 tons gross tonnage was launched in August, 1930, and on her first trip from Havana to New York broke the record for that run.

SYLVAN FORUM POSTPONED

HOLMDEL, Sept. 8.—Assemblyman Theron McCampbell announced today that the Democratic meeting slated for his Sylvan forum this Sunday has been postponed until Sept. 21 because of inclement weather. Gov. A. Harry Moore, Democratic candidate for the United States senate, and Judge William L. Dill, the party's candidate for governor, are scheduled speakers.

GREATEST DISASTER SINCE VESTRIS SANK

NEW YORK, Sept. 8. (AP)—The burning of the Morro Castle is the second major shipping disaster off the eastern coast of the United States in the past 80 years.

The Vestris foundered in a storm off the Virginia Capes on Nov. 12, 1928, with the loss of 110 lives.

Greater disasters have occurred on inland waters. The excursion steamer General Slocum burned in the East river, New York, in 1904 with the loss of 1,021 lives and the excursion steamer Eastland capsized in the Chicago river with the loss of 812 persons 11 years later.

In 1865 a boiler explosion destroyed the steamboat Sultana, killing approximately 1,700 on the Mississippi near Memphis. Most of the victims were exchanged union prisoners.

Ship's Dog Saved

SPRING LAKE, Sept. 8. (AP)—A mongrel puppy, mascot of the crew of the Morro Castle which was burned off shore today, jumped to the beach as one of the first life boats grated on the sand. An unidentified seaman, proffered a blanket by a Red Cross worker, solemnly wrapped up the drenched puppy.

Havana Probes For Sabotage

HAVANA, Sept. 8. (AP) — Maj. Hilario Gonzalez, chief of the Havana port police, began an investigation this morning into the loading of the S. S. Morro Castle in order to determine whether there were any signs of sabotage and if all cargo-loading rules had been complied with.

Dudley Thomas, Havana passenger agent of the Ward line, denied rumors that sabotage might have been responsible for the burning of the ship and said he blieved the fire resulted from lightning.

STUDENT LIST SWELLS

Early Enrollment at Matawan Forecasts New Record for Year.

MATAWAN, Sept. 8—A total of 1,030 pupils are enrolled in the Matawan school system so far this year. School authorities say today that this early enrollment in the local schools indicates that before the school year is over the figure of 1,200 reached last year will be exceeded. The students enrolled today are divided as follows: High school, 210; grammar school in Matawan, 570, and Cliffwood school, 150.

Victor Papa, son of Mr. and Mrs. Phillip Papa, 708 Seventh avenue, left yesterday to attend Georgetown university.

Bodies Wash Ashore; Many Survivors Land

Morro Castle, Inbound from Havana, Gutted from Stem to Stern. Cause Not Determined

RESCUE CREWS BATTLE HEAVY SEAS TO REACH BLAZING SHIP

Flames Sweep Decks in Few Minutes, Trapping Passengers in Cabins. Many Tales of Heroism

BULLETIN

At 1 p. m. this afternoon two lifeboats from the steamship Morro Castle were heading for the Spring Lake shore with a few survivors of the fire which swept the liner. The cutter Tampa was attempting to get a line aboard the ship and planned to tow it to New York harbor. The fire was still burning.

One hundred and ninety-nine out of 558 persons aboard the Morro Castle had been rescued this afternoon following a fire that swept thru the giant Ward liner off Belmar earlier in the day.

Fears were held for all of those unaccounted for. It was believed the toll taken by the dread terror of the sea would reach 359.

Bodies Float Ashore

The first grim remains of the catastrophe, floating bodies, began washing ashore from Allenhurst to Spring Lake three hours after flames broke out in the steamer's library at 4.23 a. m.

Eighty-five of those saved, some hysterically screaming and waving, came ashore in five of the vessel's lifeboats. Six were believed to have been launched. An airplane hovering over the catastrophe dropped a note at Spring Lake saying the remaining boat was making its way towards shore in a heavy sea. Some aboard the liner were still alive.

A small group, after having been in the water for five hours, were able to swim ashore at the same beach. As the weary men and women came into view thru the half-fog and misty rain, rescuers struggled thru the booming surf or put out in coast guard boats.

The first picked up were Mr. and Mrs. Abraham Cohen, Hartford, Conn. The couple had one life preserver between them, and they collapsed as they were lifted from the sea and taken to Fitkin hospital, Neptune.

The others swimming either had lifebelts or were desperately clinging to bits of wreckage.

Many Panic-Stricken

As the last boats were beached some of the men and women became frantic, and attempted to leap into the water. First aid squad workers and other volunteers were hampered by the reckless survivors.

Alongside the burning Morro Castle, the steamers Andrea F. Luckenbach and Monarch of Bermuda were picking up survivors. About 9.30, officials of the Luckenbach line reported their vessel had left the scene, with 22 survivors aboard, and would dock at the foot of 35th street, Brooklyn, at 11.30.

The Furness-Bermuda line reported the Monarch had rescued 65 and was still standing by in the forelorn hope of finding more of the living among the floating debris.

"Rescued 65 from Morro Castle in own boats," reported the master of the Monarch. "Am still standing by in hopes of getting more."

As the morning progressed, other steamers arrived at the scene. A radio told the fearfully waiting world that some passengers still were on the burning hulk, the superstructure of which long since had gone up in flames. A coast guard cutter, the Tampa, from New York, was vainly endeavoring to come in close to the wrecked liner in an effort to take them off.

Hampered by Storm

The heavy seas and strong northeasterly gale hampered workers somewhat. Earlier in the morning, the raging gale, reported to have reached hurricane proportions further out in the Atlantic, obliterated the terrible picture from the horrified eyes of shore watchers.

Besides the Luckenbach, Monarch of Bermuda and the cutter, it was known that two other vessels, the City of Savannah and the President Cleveland, were also near the rescue point but it could not be learned whether they had yet taken survivors off.

All rescue resources of the north Jersey shore, from Sandy Hook to Barnegat, were swung into rapid action within a few minutes after the fateful message was picked up at the Tuckerton station of the Radio Corporation of America:

"SOS — SOS — Morro Castle afire 20 miles south Scotland light . . . fire near wireless room . . ."

Sinister silence dropped down and not another code message came thru from the vessel. It was feared that either fire had wiped out the transmitting apparatus or a part of the super-

The Weather
For Shreveport and Vicinity—Partly cloudy tonight and Thursday, about 80 to 85 degrees for highest temperature Thursday. Red river local stage, 9.2 feet. Noon temperature, 86 degrees.

Shreveport Journal

FINAL EDITION

VOL. 38.—NO. 115. SHREVEPORT, LA., WEDNESDAY, MAY 23, 1934 Price 5 Cen

BARROW AND PARKER WOMAN SHOT DEAD NEAR GIBSLAND

MUSICIAN INJURED HERE

HAMLIN KEYSER IS FOUND UNCONSCIOUS ON SIDEWALK HERE

Son of Former Natchitoches Mayor Is in Extremely Grave Condition.

OFFICERS SCOUT FOUL PLAY THEORY

Police Believe Young Man Fell and Sustained Fracture of Skull.

Mr. and Mrs. Steve Grunaart, both 27, are being held in the city jail as suspects in connection with the critical injury of Hamlin Keyser, 24, son of John H. Keyser, former mayor of Natchitoches, who was found Wednesday morning, about 3 o'clock, in an unconscious condition, lying on the sidewalk in front of the Tullos hotel, 609 Louisiana avenue, Capt. C. R. Kent said, shortly after 2 p. m. Willie Hamilton, negro porter at the Tullos, also is being held as a suspect, as it is believed by police that he can give information before Keyser was hurt, it was stated.

Police investigating the case said that Keyser had been visiting in the room of the Grunharts and there had been a drinking party going on. They said, in their opinion, he either was thrown or fell from the balcony of the hotel, which accounted for his skull being fractured. Keyser's condition Wednesday afternoon was pronounced as very critical.

Hamlin Keyser, 24, son of John H. Keyser, former mayor of Natchitoches, and member of a local orchestra, was in the Charity hospital Wednesday in a critical condition, suffering from a fracture at the base of the skull.

Police were at a loss to determine how the injury was sustained, but advanced the theory that the young man fell to the pavement, striking his head.

Keyser was found in an unconscious condition on the sidewalk near the Tullos hotel, 609 Louisiana avenue about 3 o'clock Wednesday morning by Walter Payne, a night watchman. Blood was coming out of his ears. Payne reported the discovery to police and Keyser was taken to the hospital in a McCook Brothers ambulance.

He had not regained consciousness several hours later and his

PAGE SIX, COL. FIVE.

Hero Pilot and 3 Others Perish In Plane Wreck

LOS ANGELES, May 23.—The pilot of an airplane which crashed with the loss of three lives here last night, was disclosed today as the hero of another aerial accident in which he was credited with saving several lives.

Victims of the crash here were Kenneth P. Gardner, 25, second lieutenant in the air corps reserve; Ruth H. Converse, 21, daughter of William I. Converse, treasurer of a large retail drug company, and Robert G. Sitzman, Jr., 23, Los Angeles. The ship fell from an altitude of 1,000 feet and burst into flames.

Gardner formerly was with the air corps at March field, Riverside, Cal., and during his service a bombing plane which he was piloting caught fire. He continued to fly the craft until several enlisted men leaped to safety with parachutes and then abandoned the craft himself.

SEEK TO RESTRAIN 12 FOR CODE VIOLATIONS

Bill of Complaint and Petition in Equity Filed by Federal Prosecutor Here.

Bills of complaint and petitions in equity, seeking to restrain 12 Shreveport cleaners and dyers from further alleged violations of the NRA code, were filed Wednesday by Federal District Attorney Philip H. Mecom. The documents were delivered to Judge Ben C. Dawkins in Monroe during the afternoon for his signature.

Those named in the complaint are: Herman Lieber, doing business under the trade name of Lieber Cash & Carry; Hilliard Woods (Central Cleaners); D. A. Rials (Barrel Cleaners); A. T. Kirkland, Max Goldberg and W. G. Casten (O. K. Hatters & Cleaners); John Demopolis (Stag Cleaners & Hatters); Antonio Leberta (Leberta shoe shop); Henderson Ford (City Dye Works); R. H. Himes (Holly-

PAGE FIFTEEN, COL. ONE.

Extension of 'Tick Tax' Is Proposed in House

Would Prolong Levy to 1938—Bill to Hang Kidnapers Offered at Session.

(Associated Press.)

BATON ROUGE, La., May 23.—The legislature was asked to extend the meat and dairy products tax dedicated to tick eradication today in a bill introduced by Representative Lester, West Feliciana, when the house convened at 11 a. m.

The Lester bill would amend the 1932 "tick tax" act to extend the tax's time duration from 1936 to 1938 to provide more funds for the state tick eradication campaign.

Kidnaping Bill Offered.

A bill by Representative Madison, Morehouse, kidnaping punishable by death or life imprisonment was included among measures introduced.

Resignation of Representative Hammon, Jackson, as a member of the house public roads and highways committee was followed by announcement by Speaker Ellender of the appointment of Representative Wilkinson, West Baton Rouge as his successor.

Lively discussion was precipitated when Representative Madison vainly asked adoption of a resolution for the house to employ "20 stenographers to write bills and letters for us."

The resolution failed of passage without a record vote—although one was asked by the author—amended humorously by Representative Peyton, Caddo, to provide that "four of the said stenographers shall be redheads, 10 brunettes, and eight blondes."

"This is the only legislature I know of that doesn't provide such facilities," Madison asserted.

Ellender Opposes.

Speaker Ellender explained that he could obtain as many stenographers as necessary from various state offices to do any necessary clerical work for the representatives, and said he opposed the resolution.

Asked by Representative Hoffpauir, Acadia, and Representative Bordelon Avoyelles, where the money would come from, and how much salaries would be paid, the speaker said he "didn't know."

The house later adopted unanimously a resolution by Madison urging congress to provide assistance for the "jake paralysis" victims of 1930.

Hamiter Bill to Committee.

The bill by Representative Hamiter, Caddo, to prohibit state board of liquidation borrowing, was referred to judiciary "B" committee of which Representative Bauer, St. Mary, an antiadministration house leader, is chairman.

A resolution by Representative Lester calling upon the Louisiana highway commission to supply full information about the status of its "farmer's road" program, was unanimously adopted after Representative Hoffpauir said Chairman A. P. Tugwell of the commission had told him he would be glad to furnish the data.

The house passed, 94 to 0, and sent to the senate, the Wimberly bill to appropriate $160,000 to pay the expenses of the session.

Three-day leave of absence was granted Representative Lucas, Rapides, with the legislature planning week-end adjournment tomorrow at noon. The house adjourned until tomorrow at 9 a. m.

SURGEON SENT BY PLANE TO AID OF NOTED EXPLORER

(Associated Press.)

WASHINGTON, May 23.—Navy department officials said today that a navy plane had left the Panama Canal zone at 6:15 a. m. for the Galapagos islands, carrying a surgeon to the aid of William Albert Robinson, noted explorer.

Robinson was stricken with acute appendicitis while aboard a small boat and was reported critically ill.

The navy plane was piloted by Lieut. Commander Herman H. Halland. The surgeon, Lieut. Commander Rollo W. Hutchinson, was the only passenger.

Department officials said the Galapagos islands were more than 500 miles from the Canal zone.

WRANGLE DEVELOPS IN LA. STATE SENATE AT BRIEF SESSION

Major Discussion Over Time Chamber Will Reconvene Tomorrow.

(Associated Press.)

BATON ROUGE, La., May 23.—Ending a 15-minute session marked principally by a scattering row over what time it will reconvene tomorrow and the introduction of a bill which would throw open to the public the records of the office of supervisor of public accounts, the senate adjourned today until 10 a. m. tomorrow.

Records of the supervisor of public accounts, presently closed to public inspection under a law adopted in 1912, would become public documents after having been officially audited under terms of a bill presented by Senator Paul Chasez, New Orleans.

Exactly 15 minutes after Lieut. Gov. John B. Fournet rapped his gavel calling the senate to order, Senator Coleman Lindsey, newly-designated administration floor leader, moved to adjourn until 9 a. m. tomorrow.

Senators Waldo H. Dugas and Chasez jumped up.

"I move to amend that to adjourn

PAGE SIXTEEN, COL. EIGHT.

DEATH OF A VETERAN.

(Special to The Journal.)

MAGNOLIA, Ark., May 23.—C. N. Robertson, aged 89, a former resident of this county and a Confederate veteran, died recently at the home of his daughter, Mrs. J. A. Lamb at Winthrop, following a decline in health for a year. He is survived by three sons, G. P. Robertson, Livingston, Texas; John Robertson, Texarkana; Bob Robertson, Waldo; one daughter, Mrs. J. A. Lamb, Winthrop; one sister, Mrs. T. E. Parker, Texarkana; 16 grandchildren, and nine great grandchildren. Funeral services were held at Winthrop.

News Tabs!

Yoo Hoo, Dillinger.

* * *   * * *

Straight Shooter.

* * *   * * *

Lucky 13.

* * *   * * *

Won by a Nose.

TUCSON, ARIZ.—ONE TOUGH ASSIGNMENT, THAT'S WHAT EDMUND ATKINSON, PIMA COUNTY DEPUTY SHERIFF, SAYS IT IS.

HE HAS BEEN TOLD TO SERVE A SUBPOENA ON JOHN DILLINGER.

THE FUGITIVE GUNMAN IS CITED TO APPEAR IN SUPERIOR COURT HERE MAY 25 TO ANSWER TO A CIVIL ACTION BROUGHT AGAINST HIM BY VARIOUS BANKS WHICH LAY CLAIM TO ABOUT $24,000 IN LOOT, IMPOUNDED AFTER THE CAPTURE—AND BEFORE THE ESCAPE—OF DILLINGER.

* * *

OSHKOSH, Wis.—Motorcycle Officer Irving Stilp is being reprimanded—not for his marksmanship, but for his choice of a place to display it.

A markeep told Stilp he couldn't hit the broad side of a barn with his undersized revolver.

Accepting the challenge, the officer smashed a beer glass on a window 50 paces away.

Now he has been deprived of his day off for the next five weeks.

* * *

HUTCHINSON, Kan.—That No. 13 may be unlucky to some, but not to inmates of the state reformatory.

The reason: For the last year every No. 13 boy who has had a hearing before the state board of administration has been paroled.

* * *

PHILADELPHIA.—HOTEL EMPLOYEES WON A RACE AGAINST DETATH BY A NOSE—A GUEST'S NOSE.

THEY HALTED GEORGE HAINES OF WOODFIELD, W. VA., AS HE SNIPPED HIS NOSTRILS WITH A PAIR OF SCISSORS IN WHAT POLICE SAID WAS AN ATTEMPT TO END HIS LIFE.

DOCTORS SAID THE CUTS WERE NOT SERIOUS.

NEWSPAPER WORKER IS VICTIM OF HOLDUP

Josh Jones, employe of a morning newspaper, was accosted by a white hi-jacker Wednesday morning about 1 o'clock in the 400 block of Marshall street, near the Post Office cafe, and relieved of $2 in cash, according to a police report. Jones told police that the man held a gun on him which he thought to be of Spanish make. The hi-jacker was described as being about 35 years old, five feet nine inches tall, weighed about 140 pounds and was wearing a gray cap, dark coat and light trousers.

PAIR SURPRISED BY OFFICER ON BIENVILLE PARISH HIGHWA

Widely-Sought Outlaw Pair Killed

Clyde Barrow, notorious Southwestern outlaw, and his cigar-smoking woman companion, Bonnie Parker, pictured at right, who were slain by officers in Bienville parish, between Sailes and Gibsland Wednesday morning.

According to report received here six officers, including one former Texas ranger, concealed on a hill awaited the car in which Barrow and Parker were riding, and as they did so the officers commanded the pair to stop.

When they failed to do so, officers fired into the car killing the pair and riddling their car with bullets.

Barrow Blazed Bloody Trail in the Southwest

Career of Dangerous Outlaw and Woman Companion Ended by Officers' Fire.

(Associated Press.)

DALLAS, Texas, May 23.—The criminal career of Clyde Barrow, furtive killer, shot to death with Bonnie Parker, his woman companion, in a clash with officers in Louisiana, became one of the nation's most dangerous outlaws through his ruthless resort to firearms whenever he encountered difficulties in carrying out the robberies he undertook.

Started as Auto Thief.

Most of the victims credited to his deadly machine-gun and pistol fire, fell without having a chance to protect themselves. Barrow, who started out as an automobile thief in Dallas, and blamed his subsequent depredations on officers mistreating him, displayed a bitter hatred of the law and its enforcers, especially in the last two years, when he has been hunted incessantly throughout the Southwest.

Blazed Bloody Trail.

He was first arrested in Dallas for automobile theft in December, 1926, but got off lightly. In 1930 he was convicted of automobile theft at Waco and sentenced to 14 years. Ross S. Sterling, former

PAGE ELEVEN, COL. SEVEN.

CORONER'S JURY BRINGS IN REPORT IN SLAYING OF 2

Holds Officers Who Killed Barrow and Woman Acted in Line of Duty.

ARCADIA, La., May 23.—After hearing the six officers who took part in the slaying of Barrow and the Parker woman, the jury empaneled by Coroner P. L. Wade Wednesday afternoon brought in a verdict, in effect, that Barrow and the woman came to their deaths by gunshot wounds in the hands of officers in the line of their duty. It required more than an hour to hear the testimony.

Following the report of the jury's

PAGE EIGHT, COL. EIGHT.

EL KARUBAH BAND TO PLAY IN PARADE FOR BEAUTIES SATURDAY

March Will Begin at Municipal Auditorium Promptly at 11 o'Clock A. M.

The El Karubah Shrine band of 40 pieces, under the direction of Frank Fuhrer, will participate in the parade of the 35 most beautiful girls in the land of Ark-La-Tex in the downtown section of Shreveport Saturday morning, it was definitely announced Wednesday.

The El Karubah band is one of the finest musical organizations in the entire country, and in addition to their stirring martial music, their striking colored uniforms and snappy step, make a most inspiring sight.

The parade will start from the Municipal auditorium Saturday morning at 11 o'clock promptly. The route will be down Milam to Spring street, Spring to Texas and Texas street to Common, and Common to Milam, and then back to the auditorium.

Through the co-operation of C. D. Evans, commissioner of streets and parks, the city of Shreveport will

Shreveport Agog as Imp Horde Starts Invasion

Latest Type of Puzzle Has Mayor Already as Victim and Will Capture Many Others.

The Imp is on the loose here. Heh! Heh!

Medical officers, who are authority on insomniacs, megalomaniacs, and those jittery souls whose neuronic gymnastics are geared to the mad course of a squirrel in a wobbly revolving cage, did their best to head him off, but the Imp eluded them with a diabolical flirt of his forked appendage and romped into town.

With IMPudent nonchalance, Imp chose as its first victim Mayor Geo. W. Hardy of Shreveport. His honor, fascinated by the game, is pictured on page 18.

And Imp is here to stay and grow in stature, for he has more than a trillion, three hundred billion (1,300,000,000,000) tricks in his little red envelope.

The Imp's first leering bow to this section of the South, which he will soon number among his conquests, is made today in The Shreveport Journal.

To make it plain—or at least as plain as Milligan's theory of cosmology or Herr Einstein's childishly lucid exposition of his relativity premise—there are only 15 pieces in the Imp puzzle. But there is an ace in the hole—and that ace is a grim and empty square where a sixteenth piece would be put. The little pieces, numbered from 1 to 15, are so constructed and inte-

Desperado and H Woman Compani Are Instantly Kill

Order of Concealed Posse to Halt Disrega and Two Are Riddled With Missiles From Guns of Possemen.

The eight-year trail of murder and robb Clyde Barrow, dangerous bandit of the South was ended Wednesday morning at 9:15 o'clock b Bonnie Parker, his woman companion in crime hail of bullets from a sheriff's posse, 50 miles e here near the Sailes community in Bienville p several miles from the town of Gibsland.

Both the man and woman were killed inst before they could fire a shot and their bodies automobile were riddled with bullets. They into a posse's ambush, arranged by the former tain of Texas rangers, Frank Hamer, who ha lowed Barrow's trail relentlessly, and by Sheriff derson Jordan of Bienville parish.

With the posse, heavily armed, hiding in the grass the paved highway, Barrow's car broke over the horizon, at an 85-mile rate. As the car approached, an officer "halt." Barrow and the woman answered by reachi their guns and they were met by a fusillade from guns hands of six officers. Bonnie Parker died with her he tween her knees and a machine gun on her lap. slumped behind the steering wheel with a gun in his grip

The autimobile careened from the road and crushe an embankment.

The bandits' trail was picked up Tuesday by offic Bossier parish, near Benton.

In the wrecked bandit car officers found army rifle ed-off automatic shotguns, machine guns, pistols and a quantity of ammunition. First news of the slaying r Shreveport about 9:45 a. m., coming in a long-distance m to The Journal from an Acadia correspondent.

Governor Told of Matter.

Gov. O. K. Allen was given a graphic description slayings over long-distance telephone by Sheriff Jorda Governor Allen officially congratulated the officers name of the state.

The governor was told that shortly after 9 a. m., th cers, who were hidden in the grass along the roadside, nized the grey sedan in which they knew the two were ing. Barrow was driving.

Some of the officers quickly walked out into the ro called for a halt but Barrow reached for a sawed-off and stepped hard on the accelerator. As the car, A Fo sport sedan, leaped forward, the officers poured a barr fire into the car and the two inside slumped over and careened into a ditch and against an embankment.

Hundreds of people from the countryside swarmed scene to see an end of two of America's most-criminals.

Sheriff Jordan of Bienville parish said that he had received a tip that the First National bank of Arcadia was to be robbed Wednesday or Thursday. He immediately notified Texas officers, as he suspected that the contemplated job might be one of Barrow and his gang.

Sheriff Jordan said that the pair came from Benton Tuesday afternoon and passed through Gibsland about 4 or 5 o'clock in the afternoon and again Wednesday morning shortly before the killing, which occurred about 9:15 a. m.

In the group of officers who awaited the pair on the highway were: Sheriff Jordan, his deputy, Paul M. Oakley, both of Bienville parish; former Ranger Captain Frank Hamer of Austin, Texas; Bob Alcorn of the sheriff's department at Dallas, Texas; B. M. Gantt, Austin, member of the Texas state highway officers' department, and Officer Hinton. Oakley was credited with firing the first shot.

The officers were stationed in a ring on top of a hill.

The oficers were concealed in high grass over a distance of about half a block when they sighted Barrow's car approaching the hill. There were two trucks on the Castor-Gibsland road, going in opposite directions. These trucks served as an extra shield against discovery by Barrow and his companion, who were first fired upon by Deputy Sheriff Oakley. He used a shotgun loaded with buckshot, and he fired quickly after ordering Barrow to stop, which warning Barrow ignored.

Barrow opened a door of the car, evidently to fire a sawed-off shotgun which he held in one hand, but Deputy Oakley and other officers, who imm joined in the shooting, quick.

Sheriff Jordan said it sible Barrow or the Parker fired one time, each of the ing a sawed-off shotgun shooting occurred, but the had not examined their sufficiently to establish th

Barrow's car, after movi half a block from the poi Deputy Oakley opened fi into the enbankment, but seriously damaged exce wheel which had been s posely and the body of which was peppered with from the officers' guns.

The Barrow car, when th

PAGE ELEVEN, COL.

BEVERLY HILLS, Cal 23.—Senator Norris wa abolish the electoral colleg is a bad time to try and with anything connected w lege." We will have to the lowbrows get in. We not a man to get discoura was years trying to get abolish the lame-duck sess

When you get down to sense, and level-headedne answerable to nobody but conscience, you just about definition of that quiet-figh senator.

The Weather

SATURDAY—Cloudy. Friday's high 81, low 51. Weather detail on Page 17.

THE DAILY OKLAHOMAN

Entered at the Oklahoma City, Oklahoma, postoffice as second class mail matter under the act of March 3, 1879

Daily April Paid Circulation 193,359 Morning 99,651 Evening 93,708 Sunday 116,449

VOL. 42. NO. 124. (AP) MEANS ASSOCIATED PRESS TWENTY PAGES—OKLAHOMA CITY, SATURDAY, MAY 12, 1934. (AP) MEANS ASSOCIATED PRESS SINGLE COPY PRICE Daily 5c; Sunday 10c

POST TO TRY HIGH FLIGHT HERE

Hey, You! It's Opera, A Grand Kind, Too

Madhouse Is Tame Affair When It Is Compared To Dress Rehearsal Night.

By PAUL KENNEDY

NIGHTMARES come and go in the lives of mortal men until you've sat through a dress rehearsal of a grand opera you've missed most thoroughgoing nightmare that ever trampled the tranquillity of normal existence.

Take the dress rehearsal of Madama Butterfly, for example, compared to that the daybreak on a big guinea farm would be as serene as Lord Dunsany's Wednesday afternoon tea. "Lights! Lights! In the name of heaven give me some lights! This is supposed to be in Japan."

"Very well, Mr. Edwards." "There, that's better. All right, here we go."

Carlo Edwards

The beautifully tragic story of Japan's jilted Butterfly begins to unfold to the strong, yet tender strains of Puccini's genius. Pinkerton and Goro have used up a couple of minutes each discussing the good old U. S. A. when ......

"NO! NO! STOP IT. You see, I waved at you. I coaxed you. I warned you three bars ahead. Then Madama Butterfly begins to ... a human can do. Why didn't you come in on time? Why didn't you? All right, let's have it from Number 79."

After a couple of slugs of Nippon gin, Pinkerton thinks the Nagasaki situation is definitely looking up. Then Madama Butterfly begins giving them the musical works and Pinkerton is certain he's going to like the part.

FOLLOWED by a bevy of beautiful girls, Madama Butterfly flutters in, lifting a dozen high "C's" on the way in when......

"Hey! Wait a minute! Hold everything. Where are the umbrellas for the girls? These girls have umbrellas. Where are the umbrellas? Somebody answer me!"

"They're on the way from Chicago, Mr. Edwards."

"Chicago! Chicago! This is Oklahoma City. Why didn't somebody tell me the girls didn't have umbrellas? Well, let's go. Number 92."

You couldn't fool a sailor, even in Japan's time and this Butterfly person looks like the real McCoy to Mr. Pinkerton. Although Butterfly is a bit cagey about it all, she lets it be known in no mean aria that Nagasaki's cherry blossoms are old stuff to her since his arrival. It looks like the tenor, soprano and the orchestra are going to finish in a dead heat when......

"NO! No! Where is the chorus offstage? Are they all in the lobby? Is something wrong with the ... with the music? The general idea is for the voices to sing along with the music. All right let's go. Number 120."

Darkness begins to fall on Nagasaki harbor. It begins to pour down. As a matter of fact, Pinkerton and Butterfly are hard put to wind up their love scene while they can still remember their general locations to each other when......

"Hey! Hey, you electricians. Where's the twilight? You've skipped the twilight. It takes 20 whole minutes of twilight to fade in . . . you've got it flashing down. Take it easy . . . 20 minutes. All right let's go. Number 150."

The electricians begin putting Japanese English on the twilight ... and twilight moves down to Nagasaki. Soon little lights begin blinking across the bay. Beneath the cherry blossoms the old, old story of the color's love and a trusting maiden reaches its tender climax.

Throbbing violins, cooing oboes, piping piccolos all attest the beauty of a passion that bloomed and died. In a stirring duet the scene ended ......

"Curtain! Give us the curtain! We can't sing out there all night! All curtain! Well, ladies and gentlemen of the orchestra and the chorus, concluded Carlo Edwards, director "we've done a fine job. It looks like we're going to put an opera that will be a credit to the city and the state. I'm proud of you . . . all of you.

"Hey! Hey you stage hands. Strike the set. Ready for act two.

"Great heavens, here I've just got two hours for the show and nobody's doing anything. Where are the props fellows? Hey . . . . ."

Hickox Discusses Astronomy

Prof. J. O. Hickox, of the staff at Mount Wilson observatory in California, Friday night discussed astronomy in a lecture at Epworth Methodist church.

BOARD TO ACT IN FIGHT OVER BALLOT NAMES

Ruling May Strip Group From Election Lists After Hearing.

MONEY IS PUT UP

Turley Farmer Says He Will Make Campaign For Governor.

Politicians were left in doubt about the outcome of the fight over the muddle of candidates' names Friday when the state election board virtually completed testimony in the trick filing cases, but gave no decisions.

Predictions both ways were current, but many seasoned political followers believed the administrative board will strike a severe blow at the newly developed fad of filing "shadow" names to confuse the voters on well known names.

Good Faith Is Claimed

Testimony in the mix-up cases was climaxed Friday by the declaration of Ezra Jackson Walton, of Turley, who claimed to be better known as Jack Walton, that his candidacy for the Democratic nomination for governor is in good faith. He declared he filed to be a candidate for the working class of people. His filing is challenged by J. C. "Jack" Walton, corporation commissioner, who also filed as Jack Walton.

Attorneys for the Waltons were given until Monday to file briefs, which means the case will not be decided until next week. The only testimony that remains to be taken in the wholesale challenges is in the contest of the Will Rogers (congressman and Ardmore's Will) in the filing for congressman at large.

The election board will meet Saturday and may pass on the challenge of the filing of Robert L. Stewart, Jones farmer, for the Democratic nomination for corporation commissioner as "Robert L. Stewart."

Walker Deposits $250

His filing was challenged by Paul Stewart, state senator, a candidate in the race. Senator Stewart Friday filed petitions signed by about 2,000 persons in support of his declaration that his candidacy is in good faith.

Paul A. Walker, Rocky farmer, who leaped into the crest of the political wave created by the name filing, Thursday made his $250 "good faith" deposit. His name is identical with that of Paul A. Walker, chairman of the corporation commission, who is not up for re-election this year.

C. N. Nunn, Porter, widely known farmer and stockman, who is one of the leading candidates for president of the state board of agriculture, introduced testimony of two sisters of his "shadow" name opponent in challenging the filing.

He challenged the filing of John D. Nunn, 601 East Ninth street, on the grounds that it was not in good faith and that Nunn is not qualified to hold the office, as he has never been a farmer.

Decision Is Reserved

Mrs. Fannie Hickock, 1504 Northwest Eleventh street, a sister of John D. Nunn, said that her brother never had any experience as a farmer and that his wife told her he filed to split the vote. Sarah Nunn, another sister, testified he never had lived or worked on a farm.

The board held it would reserve its decision while John D. Nunn attempts

(Continued on Page 2, Column 5)

Davis Resigns Baptist University Presidency Because of Ill Health

Hale V. Davis

Bartlesville Minister Is Considered As Successor—Board To Act May 22.

SHAWNEE, May 11—(Special)—Dr. Hale V. Davis, president of Oklahoma Baptist university, resigned Friday and will seek to regain his health, impaired by strenuous labors in the school and church.

The resignation, accepted reluctantly by the board of trustees, will be effective in July. Although his future plans are indefinite, it was indicated Doctor Davis would take a complete rest this summer and later probably would resume an active pastorate. He is suffering from nervous exhaustion, friends said, and while his condition is not at all alarming, rest and relaxation are necessary.

Successor to Be Named

Trustees will meet May 22 to select a successor, with indications Friday pointing to Dr. J. W. Railey of Bartlesville as the most likely man for the post. Doctor Railey, chairman of the board of trustees for the last year, also is pastor of the First Baptist church of Bartlesville. He has been there about four years.

Another possibility is Dr. E. Godbold of Kansas City, secretary of Baptist missions in Missouri. Doctor Godbold, however, has rejected two previous offers to head the university and is considered as a possibility only.

Former City Pastor

Virtually "drafted" from the Exchange Avenue Baptist church in Oklahoma City, Doctor Davis began his university regime here in November, 1932. He had served the Oklahoma City church for 14 years, building it up from a small beginning to one of the largest and most active in the state. His organization and executive ability as demonstrated at the church was needed, the Baptists were convinced, at the university which was having hard financial sledding.

An educational loan drive for $40,000 was launched immediately and is nearing completion. Doctor Davis will continue with this, it was announced, and expects to wind it up within 60 days or so. He will delay his vacation until this task is complete.

WELCOME SET FOR DEBATERS

National Champions Will Arrive by Plane, Be Greeted by Group.

Alice Sutton and Jack Durland will be welcomed in style befitting national debate champions when they return to the city Saturday morning.

The pair who won the national title at Topeka, Kan., Thursday night will land at municipal airport at 11:30 a. m. or soon after and an escort of hundreds of cars loaded with Central highschool students and patrons will be on hand to accompany them to the school.

Students of the three city senior highschools riding in floats, each decorated to recall one of the schools' numerous athletic and forensic victories during the year, will join the state band parade through the downtown district.

The two debaters and their coach, Harold Netherton, spent Friday night in Topeka, after returning there from Omaha, Neb., where they appeared on a National Broadcasting Co. radio program Friday morning.

Burrell Tibbs, flying a Black Gold Refining Co. ship, will leave at 5 a. m. Saturday for Topeka, to return the trio to Oklahoma City.

CLOUDY SKIES DUE TO BRING RAINS SUNDAY

More cloudy weather is due for Oklahoma Saturday, followed by cooler temperatures and thundershowers Sunday, according to Harry F. Wahlgren, federal weatherman.

No rain is expected Saturday and the extent of Sunday's predicted showers cannot be foretold yet, Wahlgren said.

Temperatures slipped into the low eighties over most of the state Friday, and a driving south wind, carrying clouds of dust, did its best to eliminate benefits of recent moisture. City temperature ranged from low of 51 to high of 81.

According to state reports, Oklahoma has not been hit as hard by heat and drouth as much of the remainder of the winter wheat belt Rainfall, however, has been confined to small areas, leaving stricken sections scattered throughout the entire western part.

Convicts Try New Serum Experiment

CANON CITY, Colo., May 11—(AP)—A second injection of a newly-discovered serum, which it is hoped will prevent tuberculosis, was given Friday to two Colorado prison convicts here by Dr. H. J. Corper, of the National Jewish hospital at Denver, who discovered the serum.

After a quantity of the new serum is given to the subjects of the test, tuberculosis bacilli will be injected into their bodies to determine if the serum will prevent them from getting the disease.

CITY CLUB HEARS CRISMORE EXPLAIN GARNISHMENT LAW

Evert Crismore, peace justice, Friday night explained operation of the garnishment law at the monthly meeting of the West Side Civic club at Second Methodist church. The club also heard report on the progress of work by the city in cleaning out the old riverbed near the city waterworks. This project has been urged for two years, according to C. E. Day, president.

LIGHT SCHOOL LEVY VOTE IS LIKELY TODAY

Citizens Asked to Back Extra 10 Mills For Education Needs.

PAY RAISE AT STAKE

Board Says More Cash Required to Assure Full Term.

(List of voting locations, Page 2)

Light voting is expected Saturday as Oklahoma Citians again go to the polls to decide whether the extra 10 mills, which the school board has said are needed for operation of the schools next year, will be levied.

The election has aroused little interest and there is no organized opposition. The few outspoken opponents of the increased budget have said they will not fight the extra levy, which is to help provide increases in salary for school employes.

Voting the 10 mills will be the first step in returning the school system to normalcy and will assure a nine-month term in the city for next year, school board members said.

Failure Means Short Term

Failure to vote the excess levy Saturday would mean a three-month school term next year, board members warned in their circular advertising the election.

The school budget for next year is $2,069,000, which is $225,000 greater than this year. The increase was made to give the teachers and other school employes a 7 percent increase in wages.

The money would be raised by the 10-mill extra levy and the schools' 5-mill allotment which it expects from the county excise board. The schools share with the city and county in a 15-mill levy, apportioned by the excise board. The extra levy has been voted here for the last 10 years.

All Citizens May Vote

Every citizen is eligible to vote, the attorney general has held. Registration is not necessary and neither is it required that the voter be a taxpayer.

If a voter is challenged, all he need do to cast his ballot is to prove that he is a qualified elector, J. G. Stearley, school clerk-business manager, said Friday.

Stearley, with the county election board, will count the ballots at the courthouse soon after the polls are closed and the school board will meet early next week to canvass the ballots.

Only a majority of the votes cast in the election is needed for it to carry.

The polls, which are in school houses, will be open from 6 a. m. to 7 p. m.

Woodward Farmers Ask Cotton Permit

WASHINGTON, May 11.—(AP)—The farm administration was asked Friday to "stretch" the cotton acreage reduction program to permit farmers in the drouth-stricken and dust-storm plagued section around Woodward, Okla., to grow cotton instead of their customary wheat.

Senator Thomas (D., Okla.) put the problem to administration officials after receiving appeals from farmers in the area, who said their wheat prospects virtually had been destroyed, and that they must turn for the time being to some other staple.

Pact on Municipal Debt Bill Reached

WASHINGTON, May 10.—(AP)—The bill setting up machinery by which more than $1,000,000,000 of municipal debts may be compromised with consent of creditors Friday received approval of senate and house conferees, with a more liberal provision for certain taxing districts inserted in the measure.

The conference report will be considered first in the house, probably early next week.

Wells Dines with Roosevelt

WASHINGTON, May 11.—(AP)—H. G. Wells, who has written much about the future, dined Friday night with Franklin D. Roosevelt, who is having a hand at shaping it.

How Well Do You Know Geography?

CAN you name, in their order from north to south, the first tier of states on the west side of the Mississippi river? The tier on the east. If you are well grounded in the geography, you can. If you cannot, you need a five-color map of the United States, available for 10 cents.

Use This Coupon

The Daily Oklahoman Information Bureau, Frederic J. Haskin, Director, Washington, D. C.

I enclose herewith TEN CENTS in coin (Carefully wrapped) for a copy of the MAP OF THE UNITED STATES.

Name ....

Street ....

City ....

State ....

(Mail to Washington, D. C.)

GULLIBLE ARE THOSE POLICE, AND NICE, TOO

Guy Mitchell, police sergeant, was nice about letting a man arrested at Northwest Sixteenth street and May avenue Friday go home after monay to pay a fine for running a boulevard.

And the man was nice about leaving his car in the police alley while he went after the fine.

Then to spoil all these niceties, some men came down from a local motor company and said the car in the alley had been stolen from their service floor. The nice man did not return to pay his fine.

Corey, Once Head Of U. S. Steel, Dies

NEW YORK, May 11.—(AP)—William Ellis Corey, 68 years old, widely known industrialist leader and a former president of the United States Steel Corp., died at his home Friday night.

Corey, who virtually had been retired for the last five years, became ill about two months ago. Death was attributed to pneumonia.

Corey succeeded Charles M. Schwab as general superintendent of the Homestead Steel works before attaining presidency of United States Steel.

Murder, Maybe; Larceny Barred

NEW YORK, May 11.—(AP)—Danny Ahearn, Hollywood scenarist and author of a book called "Murder and How to Get Away with It," pleaded guilty Friday to a charge of attempted grand larceny before Judge Owen W Bohan.

"That's one thing you couldn't get away with," the court remarked as Ahearn was led away.

Airman Will Seek His New Altitude Record In Next Three Weeks

Oklahoma City Airport to 'See Good Show;' 50,000-Foot Level Will Be His Goal.

By WILEY POST

(Copyright, 1934, by North American Newspaper Alliance and The Daily Oklahoman. World rights reserved).

NEW YORK, May 11.—Within the next three weeks the Winnie Mae, which took me around the world twice to new records, will be called on to take me at least 50,000 feet into the air.

According to present plans we'll take off from the Oklahoma City municipal airport. That's my home town and we have never given the boys there a good show. I don't know just what the date will be, but it will be pretty soon.

We're not going up for a thrill. This flight will represent one more battle in the campaign aviators all over the world have been waging to raise man's ceiling and increase the amount of space he can put to practical use.

The unofficial altitude record for airplanes is 47,500 feet. The Winnie Mae, at the most conservative estimate, ought to beat that by half a mile. I think it probable we shall get to 55,000 feet and highly possible Winnie may go even higher. I'll not stop going up until I stop feeling comfortable, or until Winnie can't climb anymore.

Altitude records are not entirely like sporting records. There is a good deal of the idea of being first and best in it, but there is also a practical purpose and a high, even noble, vision.

Future Flights Will Be "Out of Sight"

PLANES of the future will fly out of sight of earth. Up there in the thinner part of the earth's atmosphere, there's a new world seemingly made for airplane travel. No head winds, no storms, no rain, no snow, cloudless, limitless visibility. Bullet speeds are normal up there. A ship with an average cruising speed of 150 miles an hour could do 300 there without breathing heavily.

That new world has been penetrated, but it is by no means tamed to our purposes. On my flight with the Winnie Mae—the first of a long series I am planning—I am bringing into the war against space four new guns.

The problem of breathing up there has been solved by the oxygen tank. But pressure remains unsubjected. I think I have something that will chop it down to our size.

Pressure has taken its toll of pioneers. Many have lost their lives to it. And up to now every man who has gone higher than 40,000 feet in an airplane has given years of his life to do it. He has suffered hurts to his body medical science cannot repair. It has been a bitterly true joke that high fliers die young.

Pressure at sea level is 15 pounds to the square inch inside the body and outside. That enables us to exist comfortably. At 40,000 feet, there are three pounds of pressure to the square inch outside the body and 15 pounds inside. That means every muscle, every tissue, every organ in the body is strained and agonized. Pictures of Maj. Rudolph W. Schroeder's heart, taken a few hours after his ascent to 36,130 feet, showed it dilated to three times its normal size. Eventually it came back into shape, but he was not the man he used to be and I fear he never will be.

Rubberized Suit Will Control Air Pressure

ON my flight I am going to use a rubberized silk suit designed to equalize this pressure. This suit will work exactly opposite from a diving suit—that is, it will push down on the body instead of pushing out from it. In order to insure complete flexibility of movement, I am going to get five pounds of pressure from the suit, although it is designed to give me any amount up to 25 pounds. The five pounds coupled with the three pounds of the atmosphere will give me a pressure I can expect at 15,000 feet. I have often flown at this altitude without any discomfort.

The second new device I am trying out is a specially built propeller with extremely variable pitch. At high altitudes I will be able to slant the propeller to scoop more air under the Winnie Mae's wings.

I believe the two new superchargers I have put on the plane will conquer the ignition problem at these altitudes. An army aviator flying over Washington almost gave his life to show us what was wrong with our superchargers.

At high altitudes, the spark refuses to leap the spark gap. It runs wild, jumping over into the magneto and outside the cylinder. The supercharger's purpose is to control the spark in its leap.

This army man's supercharger was faulty and the spark exploded his motor right out of the plane. He landed in one piece, but his cylinders didn't. They rained down over the city. With the improvements on the Winnie Mae, the ignition can be expected to behave at any altitude. The outside supercharger at first gave us carburetor trouble. But now we have reinforced all connections with packing glands and I think we're ready.

There are a thousand other details we have worked out. We have built on the past toward the future. And I sincerely hope this first of my projected series of high altitude flights will bring closer the day when passengers will ride in hermetically sealed cabins and pilots in hermetically sealed suits at three or four hundred miles an hour in perfect safety and in perfect comfort.

That world up there belongs to us and some day we will have it.

Beaten in Court Battle To Keep Wife, Man Kills Self

Grimly keeping a promise to take his life if he failed to regain his 18-year-old wife who said she would rather attend highschool than keep house for a middle-aged husband, Orie Kalivoda late Friday left the courtroom of R. P. Hill, district judge, went to his home ten miles south of Wheatland and killed himself.

Kalivoda lost a final legal bout to keep his wife when Judge Hill granted her a divorce in a contested action. Stern-faced, the Bohemia-born man took the witness stand and told of his love for the young woman who refused to live with him.

"I want her," he said, "and I thought she loved me. I have begun to doubt it."

Earlier, the wife, Laura, said she had married Kalivoda because he threatened to commit suicide on the front porch of her parents' home if she refused. She said she did not love him and didn't want to live with him.

Kalivoda was grim as Judge Hill rendered his verdict. His jaws clamped tightly, he shook hands with his former wife and her parents, Mr. and Mrs. W. T. Morava, who live three miles southwest of town. Then he stalked from the courtroom.

His attorney, J. S. Estes, saw him go with misgivings. Kalivoda had told him that if he lost his wife he would kill himself.

About 8 p. m. Estes received a telephone call at his home. Kalivoda had kept his promise.

TWO DEMANDS LEAVE GETTLE SEARCH IN AIR

Family Agrees to Pay $75,000, Then Gets $40,000 Order.

POLICE OUT OF WAY

All Law Agencies to Stand Aside Until Victim Is Returned Safely.

(Picture on Page 5)

LOS ANGELES, May 11.—(AP)—While negotiations for the release of William F. Gettle from the hands of kidnapers apparently were progressing on the basis of a $75,000 ransom demand to which the family attorney quickly agreed, the invalid wife of the victim Friday night received an entirely different demand for $40,000.

Further complicating the situation, a second mysterious telephone call was made to the office of the attorney, Ernest E. Noon, late in the day, the anonymous informant demanding that if he was "ready to talk" he should "put an ad in the personal column of one of the morning papers tomorrow."

The new aspects of case broke while authorities, who had called off all official activity to allow the negotiations to proceed without police hindrance, were predicting the release of Gettle "within 24 hours."

Call Starts Developments

Starting the series of developments, a telephone call was made to Noon's office Friday morning in which the caller demanded $75,000 and to which Noon reputedly agreed with little hesitation.

The exchange of a millionaire-sized ransom for the life and freedom of the wealthy business man was envisioned as the trust officer of a bank figured in a conference with Noon, and the attorney made several mysterious trips out of his office, stopping at the bank on one of them.

The letter to the seriously stricken Mrs. Gettle, although arousing doubts in the minds of onlooking officers as to authenticity, threw another iron in the fire. Mailed from San Bernardino, 60 miles east of here at 6 p. m., Thursday night, 18 hours after Gettle had been seized by two smooth working masked gunmen, it said:

"Get $40,000 in used bills in tens and twenties and keep ready. Don't tell the law. We'll get in touch with you later."

Written on Cheap Paper

It was written upon cheap paper in an ordinary hand.

The second telephone message to Noon's office, center of the negotiation activities, came while the attorney was out on one of his secret trips.

"Is this Mr. Noon's office?" The anonymous male caller asked when the attorney's secretary, Miss Grace Hundley, answered.

"Is Mr. Noon in?" The caller went on.

"He's out but is due back any minute," Miss Hundley answered.

"Well, do you know if he's ready to talk?"

"I'm sure that he'll be only to glad to talk to anyone. I suggest that you call back in a few minutes."

Conversation Is Broken

"Just tell him," the voice continued, "that if he is ready to talk he should put an ad in the personal column of one of the morning papers tomorrow."

Before Miss Hundley could reply the man hung up.

Some time before the second telephone call came, Noon said he had the money ready and would make payment as soon as he ascertained that Gettle would be freed without injury.

"The welfare of Mr. Gettle is the first consideration," he said. "We will pay if Mr. Gettle is released unharmed."

All Officers Withdraw

The case seemingly began moving toward a cold cash climax after the first telephone call to Noon and as all arms of the law figuring in the case were called off as the result of a conference between the attorney and Buron Fitts, district attorney.

During the day Mrs. Gettle, who is recuperating from an attack of pneumonia, reputedly collapsed under the increasing tension of the case and fears were expressed for her life. She was reported somewhat improved Friday night, however. The four Gettle children, all under 10 years of age, were taken for a ride in the family automobile during the afternoon, under the eyes of an armed chaufeeur and a bodyguard.

At mid-morning, the attorney received the first telephone call "from a party who informed him they had

(Continued on Page 3, Column 6)

You Should Vote Today for Extra 10-Mill Levy to Assure Full School Term and Raise Salaries

1935

During his turbulent political career, Huey Long made Louisiana something of a personal fiefdom.

He had been elected governor of that state in 1928, campaigning on the slogan, "Every man a king, but no man wears a crown." During his four years as governor, Long won the support of the people and made himself the virtual dictator of Louisiana, stifling political opposition with his autocratic rule.

He was elected to the Senate and started a "Share the Wealth" movement. He was considered a possible third-party candidate for the presidency in the 1936 presidential election.

But, on September 8, 1935, Long was shot by a young doctor, Carl Weiss, as the senator walked along the Capitol corridor in Baton Rouge, Louisiana. He died two days later.

EXTRA **MORNING ADVOCATE** EXTRA

ASSOCIATED PRESS. (AP) Baton Rouge, Louisiana, Sunday, September 8, 1935.

HUEY LONG CRITICALLY WOUNDED BY LOCAL DOCTOR WHO IS SLAIN

...torm Dead ...re Burned in Florida

...nger of Pestilence Lessens as Decomposed Bodies Are Consumed by Funeral Pyres.

...IEF SERVICES ARE CONDUCTED

...emation Order Issued Over Wish of Roosevelt; Sheriff Estimates 150 Bodies Affected.

Miami, Fla., Sept. 7 (AP)—...anger of pestilence in Flor...a's tragedy-stricken coral ...ays was lessened tonight as ...ames twinkled from scattered ...uneral pyres of storm dead.

...quickly as Protestant, Cath... and Jewish clergymen could ... to their church's farewell to ... dead, workers applied the ...h to the oil-drenched, badly ...omposed victims of Monday's ...ricane.

...heriff D. C. Coleman, heading ... workers in the storm area, ...mated 150 bodies were affected ... the cremation order, issued ... the wish of President Roose... when health officers saw dis... imminent.

Latest Tabulation

...he latest tabulations of the ...rm's toll by the FERA and ... Cross disclosed these figures.

...eterans in three key camps 716.
...nidentified dead or missing 281.
... hospitals 128.
...dentified dead 46.
...escued uninjured or slig... 244.
...o record 7.
...ivilians:
...issing and unaccounted for 90.
...ead identified 8.
...ead unidentified 21.
...njured 286.

Bodies Stacked High

...he first mass burning—36 ...ies—was at Snake Creek, with... a few hundred feet of the jum... wreckage of Camp 3.

...ational Farm Survey Pleases Henry Wallace

...cretary of Agriculture Well Satisfied with Investigation Looking to Planned Program.

...thens, Ga., Sept 7 (AP)—Ex...ssing himself as "well pleased" ...n information gathered so far ... a nation-wide survey looking ...ard a planned agricultural pro...m for the United States, Henry ...llace, secretary of agriculture, ... here today after a conference ... the southern farm situation.

...he secretary came here Thurs... for the third of his regional ...ferences with agricultural ex... and educators.

...e first such conference was ...d recently at Ames, Ia., for ... Middle West. Other meetings ...e held at Logan, Utah. for ... Far West, and here, for the ...th. Next week, agricultural ...ders will meet at Storrs, Conn., ... discuss the eastern agricultural ...ation.

Royal Union Is Annulled by Pope Pius

...ondon, Sunday, Sept. 8 (AP)—...e newspaper Sunday Referee ...ay printed a story on "High ...thority" that Pope Pius had ...ulled the marriage of former ...g Alfonso and former Queen ...toria Eugenia of Spain.

...he newspaper said the annul...nt had been handed down in ... Holy Roman Rota, a proce...e which excludes publicity in ... form.

...he belief was expressed by the ...er that the former queen will ...tinue to live in London.

...iver Ship Organization Asks 3 Million Loan

...t. Louis, Sept. 7 (AP)—The ...ssissippi River Motor Ships ...dicate today asked the PWA ... a loan of $3,979,100 to con...uct six steel-hulled river boats ... open up a new ERA of ex...sion and tourist travel on in...d waterways."

SENATOR LONG IS WOUNEDED BY LOCAL DOCTOR WHO IS SHOT DEAD BY GUARDS

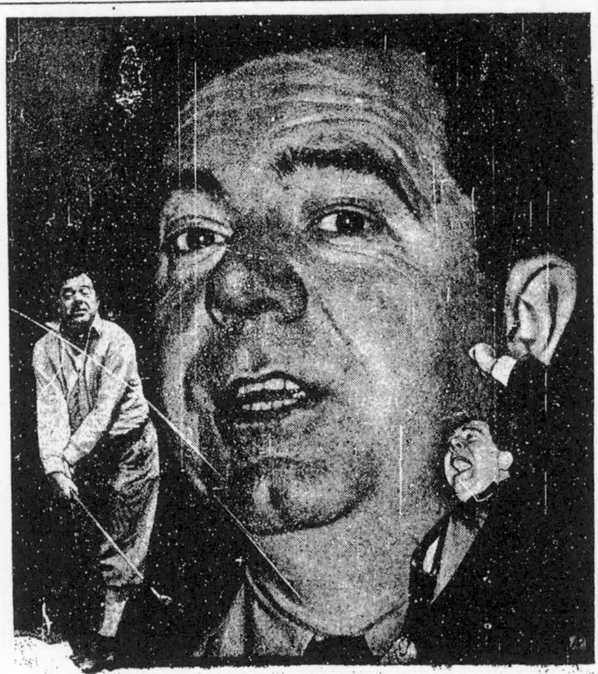

...uey P. Long was shot through the abdomen and seriously wounded here tonight by Dr. Carl Weiss, prominent Baton Rouge eye specialist, who was shot dead by Long's guards. The senator's condition was termed grave, but not critical by Dr. Arthur Vidrine, head of the New Orleans Charity hospital.

Merchants Plan Many Values for Big Dollar Day

Electric Company to Co-operate Tuesday by Letting Shoppers Ride Free from 9 to 11 A. M.

Many merchants of the city will co-operate in a big Dollar Day next Tuesday. A wide variety of fall fashions will be offered.

Termed a "Town-wide Dollar Day," the sale will in reality be a city-wide affair, with many merchants co-operating.

New, fresh merchandise at "prices you can't resist" will be offered to shoppers. There will be school supplies and school clothes, fall wearing apparel for grown-ups, house furnishing articles, gifts, and a hundred and one other classes of merchandise.

As a courtesy to shoppers, the Baton Rouge Electric company and the merchants offering Dollar day bargains will provide for free transportation on street cars between the hours of 9 and 11 a. m. Tuesday.

Advance reports from the co-operating merchants bring the word that the sale Tuesday will eclipse all other sales in value-giving opportunities to the consumer. Store windows are already crammed full with bargain wares and merchandise and are now attracting the attention of the passers-by.

All of the bargains being offered

(Continued on Page 2.)

Vets Claim Overstay of Leave Saved Lives

Key West, Fla., Sept. 7 (AP)—Thirteen veterans in Key West today credited the fact they were alive to their absence without leave from Florida Key rehabilitation camps when Monday night's tropical hurricane demolished them.

The men came to Key West Saturday with others—about 50 in all—to spend the week-end.

When their companions returned Sunday night, they decided to stay over in Key West for Labor Day, even though they had no leave. Monday afternoon they entrained for the Keys. The train was held in Key West because of the hurricane threat.

"We knew we would be docked one day's pay for overstaying our leave," said Claude W. Brown of Cincinnati, "but we realize now how fortunate we were that we wanted to spend Labor Day here.

"We see listed among the dead some of the men who were in Key West with us and returned Sunday."

The Great Game of Politics

By FRANK R. KENT

Copyright, 1935, by Baltimore Sun

One of That Kind

Washington, Sept. 7.

SO LONG as what Professor Moley has so felicitously described as the "gentle rain of checks" continues to fall upon the farmers, there is slight chance they can be weaned from Mr. Roosevelt or that they will, until the inevitable bump comes, cease to regard AAA as other than beneficent and noble. They would hardly be human if they didn't.

SO LONG as the bonuses roll regularly in and the prices prove blithely up, arguments about the inequity of regimentation, the inevitable trend toward complete socialism and the loss of individual freedom fall upon deaf ears. For example, after a week's survey of the State, it is reported in the Des Moines Register-Tribune, by Mr. Richard Wilson, that "a boom-like Iowa, happily spending its money, moves into the year of a great decision, its 1932 faith in the New Deal shaken but by no means dissipated." Mr. Wilson thinks the reaction against Mr. Roosevelt has

(Continued on Page 2.)

Man Admits Growing Marijuana in His Backyard at Home

Confessing that he had raised the drug bearing "weed" in his own back yard, C. M. Powers, 1733 North boulevard, was arrested at his home last night by Capt. Mc B. Heard and Detective M. V. Raborn, city police department, and charged with sale and possession of marijuana cigarettes.

Powers was caught in the act of selling three of the drug laden cigarettes to Charles Hays, 370 South Seventeenth street, according to police reports.

A search of the home revealed six more cigarettes and a quantity of the loose drug.

When questioned, Powers admitted possession of the marijuana and said he raised and cultivated it in his back yard, police stated.

He is lodged in the parish jail awaiting trial.

War Department Initiates Probe of Crab Fishing

Engineering Aid Sent to Morgan City to Investigate Water Blocking Charge.

New Orleans, Sept. 7 (AP)—The U. S. war department took a hand today in complaints that crab fishermen in the Morgan City, La., area were interfering with navigation and locking navigable waters in that vicinity, and sent Grover C. Rackerby, chief engineering aide in charge of the permit section of the war department for this district to Morgan City.

United States Atty. Rene A. Viosca announced that the war department was beginning an investigation into the complaints against the Morgan City crab fishers.

Citizens Asked for Aid

The action by the government followed an appeal on Thursday to Mr. Viosca by Dist. Atty. L. A. Pecot of Franklin and other St. Mary parish citizens for protection in the "crabbers' war."

The St. Maray parish delegation charged that members of a fishermen's organization in the area had been "shooting into crab boats of rival crabbers" and had also gone so far as to block progress of rival crabbers' boats in ...wick bay and other navigable waters in the trouble zone.

The war department interceded today in its capacity as supervisor of inland navigable waterways in the United States.

Two Men and Boy Killed by Gas in Well Bottom

Cleveland, Tenn., Sept. 7 (AP)—Two men and a boy were killed by gas at the bottom of a 47-foot well near here today.

William Parker, 54, the father of 12 children, was overcome by a heavy gas known as "black damp." One of his sons, D. C. Parker, 14, who rushed to his aid, also succumbed, as did a neighbor, Jake Cranfield, 51, who was summoned by the Parker family.

Pakrer had been digging the well for some time and had experienced difficulty with gas as he neared the water level.

Last night he sought to burn out the gas with pine knots and went today to ascertain whether his efforts had succeeded. His wife pleaded with him not to go down into the well, but when he insisted she and the son let him down with a windlass.

Prominent Local Eye Specialist Shoots Senator in Stomach; Condition Reported Serious, But Not Critical by Medics

Long's Attacker Prominent Local Eye Specialist

Dr. Carl Weis Survived by Wife and 3-Months-Old Son.

Dr. Carl Austin Weiss, well-known physician of Baton Rouge, was killed last night the instant after he fired upon and hit Senator Huey P. Long in a corridor of the state capitol. The shooting occurred at 9:20 o'clock and police state dthat some 25 shots entered the body of Dr. Weiss.

Dr. Weiss was one of the prominent younger physicians of the city and was associated in practice with his father, a well-known, eye, ear, nose and throat specialist of the state. He was the son-in-law of Judge B. H. Pavy of Opelousas, political enemy of Huey P. Long. His widow, who survives him, was the former Yvonne Pavy and has been a member of the French faculty of the Louisiana State university.

Dr. Weiss was an honor graduate of Tulane university medical school and following his graduation studied at a hospital in Vienna, Austria. Later, he was at the American hospital of Paris, France. On his return from abroad he spent two years in special study at the Bellevue hospital of New York city.

Several years ago he returned to Baton Rouge to take up his practice here. He married Miss Pavy on December 27, 1933, in Opelousas.

Surviving Dr. Weiss are: his wife and young son, Carl A. Weiss, Jr., aged three months; his parents, Dr. and Mrs. C. A. Weiss; a sister, Mrs. A. C. Broussard of New Orleans, the former Olga Weiss; and a brother, Tom Ed Weiss, now a student at the Louisiana State university.

Dr. Weiss was 29 years of age, his date of birth having been December 28, 1905.

Suspect Admits Brutal Attack on Small Girl

Cafe Worker Confesses Attack After Being Spirited Away from Gulfport to Jackson.

Gulfport, Miss., Sept. 7 (AP)—After being questioned here last night in connection with a brutal attack on an 11-year-old girl, a Gulfport cafe worker, booked by police as Louis Boudreaux, alias George Burke, 25, was spirited away to the Hinds county jail at Jackson where B. F. Cruthirds, Gulfport chief of police, said he confessed to the attack.

Boudreaux, or Burke, was arrested by Gulfport officers after his movements had been watched since the attack early Friday morning. Because of high feeling on the coast he was questioned in the woods here and then carried away secretly to Jackson in a police car. There Burke was formally charged with assault.

Victim in Critical Condition.

The victim of the attack, Lillian Stiglets, was in a critical condition today suffering from head wounds inflicted upon her by an attacker who lured her from her home after midnight and left her in an apparent dying condition behind a billboard on a vacant lot near her home.

Her aunt and uncle, Mr. and Mrs. Clarence Goodson, discovered her condition and rescued her

(Continued on Page 2.)

Old Age Pension Group Will Ask for 5 Billion

Washington, Sept. 7 (AP)—Dr. J. E. Pope, head of the National Old Age Pension association, said today his organization would ask congress to provide $5,500,000,000 annually for old age pensions.

"We are asking $30 a month for every man and woman over 55," said Dr. Pope. "There are approximately 15,000,000 persons over that age."

The association, which claims a membership of between 15,000,000 and 20,000,000, woul dtax the smallest incomes at one and one-half per cent and incomes of $1,000,000 at nine per cent, in order to provide funds for the program "to supplant the social security law."

Friends Volunteer Blood as Long Suffers from Internal Hemorrhage.

WOUNDED SOLON STILL CONSCIOUS

Condition Said to Be Good Although Senator Is in Great Pain.

A rush of volunteers were being typed at 10:30 to obtain proper classification for a blood transfusion. Senator Long was shot through the right side, the bullet traveling through the base of the right lung and passing out the back just below the left lung, causing an internal hemorrhage.

Given Transfusion

Senator Huey P. Long, wounded in the stomach tonight by an assassin who was killed by bodyguards, was given a blood transfusion at 11 p. m. tonight.

Senator Long, while apparently in extreme pain, was conscious. After being rushed into the Our Lady of the Lake sanitarium amid pandemonium which alarmed all other patients in the institution, he was hurriedly placed in bed in room 314 and given first aid. His condition was stated to be good at the time and a corps of medical experts were being rushed to the sanitarium to aid in his treatment and to help administer the blood transfusions.

Senator Long remembered to have Lieutenant Governor Noe call his wife, telling her he was going to recover and to drive slowly in coming to the hospital. Some difficulty was had in notifying Mrs. Long, due to the inability to obtain phone service through central, and it was about 20 minutes before Mrs. Long arrived.

Senator Long, Justice of the Supreme Court John B. Fournet had just left the senator's office, and Dr. Weiss was standing back against the wall as they went to pass him and the shooting occurred.

Dr. Weiss presented his weapon, a 32 calibre automatic of outlaw make, and apparently attempted to jam it against the senator's side. Justice Fournet attempted to slap the gun from his hand but Dr. Weiss had already fired.

A struggle ensued and another shot was fired, apparently into the floor by Dr. Weiss. Then a fusillade cut Dr. Weiss down, riddled with scores of bullets.

Mobile Ballot Boxes Held Up Pending Probe

Investigators Uncover Names of Four Dead Negroes Used to Obtain Absentee Votes.

Mobile, Ala., Sept. 7 (AP)—Following evidence turned up by investigators in a campaign prior to Mobile's municipal election Monday, Circuit Solicitor Bart B. Chamberlain today ordered City Clerk S. H. Hendrix to hold ballot boxes to be used in the election, intact for investigation by the October term of the county grand jury.

Investigators have uncovered the fact names of four dead negroes in one ward have been used to obtain absentee ballots and two of these ballots already have been been cast by mail.

Three persons listed on an absentee ballot list have complained they did not apply for or obtain such ballots.

Votes of two of the persons who said they did not obtain ballots were turned into city hall, along with 113 othefs, by Harry Drys-

(Continued on Page 2.)

Federal District Judge Upholds Connally Act

Sherman, Tex., Sept. 7 (AP)—Judge Randolph Bryant in federal district court today upheld the constitutionality of the new Connally oil act.

This federal measure, enacted by congress last February, was designed to prevent the movement in interstate commerce of oil produced or withdrawn from storage in excess of the amount permitted by state laws.

Bullet Fired by Physician Passes Entirely Through Political Senator's body, Failing to Hit Any Vital Organ.

BILL EFFECTING FATHER-IN-LAW OF ATTACKER IS CAUSE OF SHOOTING

Bodyguards Accompanying Senator Riddle Body of Doctor; Assailant's Gun Jammed as He Attempted to Fire Again.

Senator Huey P. Long is living tonight because a small calibre pistol of an outlaw make jammed as Dr. Cary A. Weiss, Jr., an eye, ear, nose and throat specialist of Baton Rouge, shot twice at the senator from close range just after he had come off the floor of the house tonight.

Dr. Weiss himself was killed. He was identified by Dr. Thomas B. Bird, parish coroner, a practicing physician here.

At 11 o'clock tonight it was reliably learned that Senator Long's condition was serious, though not necessarily critical. He was shot one time through the body, the bullet having pierced the lung, according to most authentic reports.

Seventeen doctors were summoned from various parts of the state and the Baton Rouge airport lights were ordered kept on for any arriving planes. One of the famous Mayo Brothers of Rochester, Minn. was summoned.

Justice Fournet obviously prevented Long from being instantly killed as Dr. Weis attempted to pres his weapon against the senator's heart.

The National Guard was being mobilized in New Orleans presumably to be brought to Baton Rouge tonight.

Long started back with death almost upon him and began wildly flinging his arms, attempting to ward off a further and possibly fatal wound. The bullet which cut through his lung slashed a gash in the senator's finger.

Long continued flailing his arms until the volley from nearby bodyguards cut Dr. Weis down. Then grasping his side he walked slowly out, was hurried down an elevator and to the sanitarium. He was conscious at all times.

The mystery of the shooting earlier was the circumstances of the second shot. Probably it was fired by Dr. Weiss as one bystander said he saw the young psysician doubled over, "trying to hide or protect his gun and shooting into the floor."

Dr. Weiss is the son-in-law of Dr. B. H. Pavy of Opelousas, against whom proceedings of removal were instituted in the legislature Saturday. He was married to Yvonne Pavy a little over a year ago and has a 3-months-old son.

She was heartbroken over the tragedy and apparently near collapse last night at the home of relatives.

Dr. Weiss is the son-in-law of Judge B. H. Pavy of Opelousas, whose position as district judge was jeopardized by an act introduced in the present session of the legislature to "gerrymander" his district so that Senator Long would have a majority and thereby defeat him.

"My God, we were all anti-Long, but I didn't think my son would do that," Mrs. C. A. Weiss, Sr., mother of the dead man, declared when she was informed of the killing.

The act introduced in the special session and which was being pushed through in clock-like manner transferred St. Landry parish, the home of Judge Pavy, out of a judicial district, composed of Evangeline and St. Landry parishes and put it in a district with

(Continued on Page 2.)

Reporter Saw Shooting.

Charles E. Frampton, reporter and statistician of the attorney general's office, said he witnessed the shooting and declared that Murphy Roden, a state policeman assigned to Senator Long's guard, prevented the senator's assailant from firing additional bullets into him.

"I had just come out of the governor's office," Mr. Frampton said, "and heard a muffled shot. I looked down the corridor, and saw Roden grappled with a man. Another shot was fired, and Roden was shot in the thumb of his left hand.

"Roden broke loose from the man and started firing at him. A number of other men also began shooting at the man, who fell in the corridor about 10 feet from the door leading into Governor Allen's office."

Carl Weiss Lay in Wait to Kill Long

Dr. Weiss waited grimly for Senator Long, with death in his heart and a gun in his pocket—a small automatic of outlaw make.

Two residents of the Highland road, Fred Watkins and N. A. Shelton, passed the small hallway in which the shooting took place and noticed Dr. Weiss, a small man dressed all in white, standing against the wall. They heard him say, "It won't be Long now" and said he smiled wanly as he muttered the words, which possibly were addressed to two men talking together down the hall, or possibly to himself.

The crack of two sharp shots followed a few moments later, they said, followed by stumbling noisy confusion and then the volleying of many pistols as Dr. Weiss was cut down.

Tax Suspension on Refiners Is Kept in Effect

Governor Issues New Proclamation Extending Four-Cent Rebate Until December 8.

A three months' extension of the suspension of four cents of the five cents tax on oil refiners and the tax on the business of manufacturing in the state was issued through proclamation of Governor Allen yesterday.

The tax of five cents a barrel and the tax on manufacturers was levied at the third extra session of the Louisiana legislature held in 1934 and resulted in the announcement by the Standard Oil company that nundreds of employees would be dropped from the payrolls.

Another session was called authorizing the governor to suspend the tax on refiners and the license tax on other manufacturers and, under that authority, the governor suspended the tax until September 8. The proclamation issued today extends the suspension to December 8.

Dixie Captain Refuses Offer to Leave Ship

New York, Sept. 7 (AP)—In an exchange of radiograms today with General Manager S. Ira Cooper of the Morgan Line, Capt. E. W. Sundstrom declined to leave his stricken steamship Dixie to seek shore rest and attention to his injuries.

Cooper ordered him to take respite from direction of salvage operations on the Florida reef.

The captain replied:

"There is no physical reason why I should go ashore. I can get all rest necessary. With your permission I remain on ship."

Cooper commented: "I guess the captain will have to have his way."

A resolution of appreciation to the crew was drafted by passengers.

The Weather
MONDAY—Cloudy, Colder
Sunday's high 86, low 57
(Weather detail on page 15.)

The Only Morning Newspaper in Oklahoma With Associated Press Wirephoto

THE DAILY OKLAHOMAN

Entered at the Oklahoma City, Oklahoma, postoffice as second class mail matter under the act of March 3, 1879

Daily March Paid Circulation
192,698
Morning 99,366 Evening 93,332
Sunday 117,962

VOL. 43. NO. 97. (AP) MEANS ASSOCIATED PRESS SIXTEEN PAGES—OKLAHOMA CITY, MONDAY, APRIL 15, 1935. (AP) MEANS ASSOCIATED PRESS SINGLE COPY PRICE Daily 5c; Sunday 10c

POST LANDS FAR SHORT OF GOAL

THE strong timber of Oklahoma language is being whittled on by Gertrude Steinisms. It has become the sad, alas too bad, to prattle, prattle, prattle in the way the rattles. Not only are the highschool boys and gals carrying on all their conversation that way, but sedate oldsters are trying their hand at it as well. Alas how sad, alas too bad, alas what a fad. Something ought to be done about it.

• • •

Fred Jones has ten stray dogs around his house.

The old taxicabs John Evans recently sold out of service are headed for Japan, where they'll think they are some pumpkins. . . . A lot of the used cars ferried from all parts of the country to California eventually find a ready market in Nippon.

When Rose Mary Butler went off to Soochow, China, mission she found 250 steamer letters awaiting her. Postage for individual letters would have cost $25. So she mimeographed a long letter, mailed copies second class to each friend.

BUS passengers laughed and nudged each other when W. J. Caldwell made his morning dash to the bus

stop. Someone had pinned one of his wife's dresses to the back of his overcoat, and the dress was fluttering madly behind him in the morning breeze.

Luther Harrison has carried one pencil for 12 years. Right, he's Scotch.

THE new regime: Mayor Martin's first name has been amputated officially. . . It's Frank Martin now—not J. Frank Martin nor John Frank Martin. . . . And orchids to Mrs. Martin for keeping her only political promise: To have Frank slicked up for inauguration. . . . C. T. (Cassius) Lockwood overwhelms the mayor when it comes to having a hearty laugh. . . . Jack Moore is a worthy oratorical successor to J. E. Taylor, who never missed a chance to make a speech before voting on a controversial question. . . . Joe Campbell, torch-bearer for organized labor, learned to take it while playing professional football. . . . Barlow Gers stole the inaugural show by declaring, "If I have as little trouble in office as I did getting in office, everything is going to be O. K."

Charles W. Offutt is limited to two cigars a day, but he always carries six in his outside coat pocket along with a pencil and a pen.

If you think women aren't coming to the front, just glance at the names of Oklahoma City streets . . . Alice Louise, Olie, Lottie, Beatrice, Mable, Florence, Daisy, Eldora, Eleanor, Georgia, Hattie, Trena, and so on.

Milton Slosser, who coaxes swelling melodies from the Wurlitzer at the Criterion, studied for the priesthood for five years.

THERE is a young popular song sheet seller here who can throw his 10-year-old tenor into the bass register at will. What makes it so

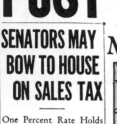

alarming when he eases up to you on the sidewalk, is that he does.

John R. Hardcastle, in full grin, would pass for Al Smith.

Things we like—Peanut butter and cracker sandwiches at midnight . . . George Key's slouch . . . dustless days . . . moonlight nights. . . . Our new spring suit . . . Sunday afternoon naps . . . Pete Gracey's Tennessee drawl . . . Mrs. O. F. Rothmeyer in that shimmery white dress . . . Glenn Taylor's accordion playing.

Phoebe Jo Schull said she didn't know what she would do if her name appeared in this column again. Now we shall see.

WE'VE never seen a football player who thought the glorious game was worth the cost, once the bands stop playing. We asked the great Cash Gentry what he thought about it. "It'll never be worth what it's cost me. I've got a knee that will never get well, I've lost most of my teeth and my health was practically ruined," answered O. U.'s contribution to all-American football. "By the way," he added, "Do you know where I can get a job?"

Mrs. E. Guy Owens says they don't use the bathtub at her house anymore, just dust themselves off with the whisk-broom.

Little Bill Finney, 5 years old, who refers to himself on the phone as "Mr. Finney," greeted his kindergarten teacher last week with this one: "Miss Blank did you know your pants are on fire? April fool!"

SENATORS MAY BOW TO HOUSE ON SALES TAX

One Percent Rate Holds Favor Despite Move To Double Levy.

IT IS 'SHOWDOWN DAY'

Leaders Seek Agreement On Revenue Measures With 'Trades.'

The state senate may bow to the house Monday and pass the sales and service tax at 1 percent, despite plans of leaders to raise the rate to 2 percent and reduce the scope of taxable services.

Rapid developments are expected Monday, which is the "showdown day" on revenue bills. Many conferences between leaders of the two houses and efforts to "trade" on the tax bills, with each house vying for advantage, will be the order of the day.

It was reported leaders were attempting to negotiate agreements, and the administration will attempt again to break the hold of Leon C. Phillips, red-haired speaker, in the house.

House Threatens Emergency

Threat of the house to refuse to attach the emergency clause to a 2 percent bill, as voiced by Phillips, plainly had the senate leaders befuddled Sunday on the eve of the battle in the upper house to pass the bill.

If the senate votes the tax bill with a 2 percent rate, it will be thrown before conference committee for a struggle, which leaders say will bring the numerous attempts to agree upon a rate and the scope of taxation.

Administration backers of the 2 percent rate declared a 1 percent tax would mean a reduction in appropriations for common schools and adjournment of the legislature without provision of sufficient revenues to meet the ordinary expenses of government.

Conferences Held Sunday

Conferences were held Sunday by senate leaders in attempts to map strategy for the contests Monday, as Governor Marland urged the 2 percent rate.

"I think the senate will pass the bill with a 2 percent rate," said James C. Nance, senate floor leader.

"If we don't pass it at 2 percent we will have to reduce the appropriations for common schools," said Allen G. Nichols, chairman of the appropriations committee. "If the house won't pass a 2 percent tax bill it will have to take the blame for not giving enough money for schools. We are going to try to pass the 2 percent rate."

Phillips Outlines Plans

Despite the prediction of leaders, observers noted an undercurrent of sentiment to pass the bill with a 1 percent rate in view of the stand of the house.

"Monday is showdown day," commented Phillips in his blunt way. "We'll have to finish the sales tax, income tax and drivers' license tax. We want the repeal of the gasoline tax diversion law too. We want $8,200,000 for schools, too, if we leave funds from the beer law and the school land department to schools as they are now."

"We want the old age pension and homestead exemption resolutions for vote on constitutional amendments, too, before we adjourn," he added.

Efforts of Governor Marland and the senate to pass the housing board bill in some form also will figure in negotiations. Phillips still declared the house will not pass the housing board bill.

Conferees of the two houses on the drastic net income tax bill will meet Monday, with house members plan-

(Continued on Page 16, Column 2.)

★ ★

More Dust, Cold Ride Into State on High Winds

GREEN PASTURES—Normal and in some areas better than normal rainfall will assure good pasture lands in all of Oklahoma but the panhandle and far west this year, according to K. D. Blood, federal crop statistician. Not dust, but the recent moisture-absorbing winds have been the cause of damage in the western areas, Blood said.

THRUST FROM NORTH SLATED TO BE SHORT

Rapid Temperature Drop Accompanies Storm Over Wide Area.

A north wind driving dust and cold out of Colorado and Kansas whipped into Oklahoma Sunday night.

Harry Wahlgren officially predicted a cold wave on the strength of an expected 50-degree drop in temperature from the near-record maximum of 86 degrees here Sunday afternoon. The temperature early Monday morning was 54 degrees.

Although not expected to go below freezing, minimum temperature of 34 to 40 degrees is slated here by Monday night, with the thermometer climbing upward again Tuesday under fair skies.

Dust May Continue

Wahlgren warned that a dust pall may hang over most of Oklahoma Monday, but he believed the plague would be of short duration.

Skies may be partly cloudy to cloudy, but no hope of rain came from the weather bureau.

A duster threw the entire Texas panhandle, half of New Mexico, part of Colorado, the Oklahoma panhandle and western Kansas into almost total darkness late Sunday afternoon.

Dust swirled into Oklahoma City about 7:15, carried by a 25-mile an hour north wind, but the haze lightened as the capricious wind shifted into the northeast. Wahlgren predicted it would swing around to the northwest, racing out of the parched areas, early Monday.

45-Mile Wind Reported

Northeasterly gales of 45 and 56 miles an hour were reported at Waynoka, Canadian, Texas, and Tucumcari, N. M. They were laden with dust, sending a billowing black cloud rolling over the plains country. Vision at Kansas City, Mo., was three miles.

Light haze was reported in southern and eastern Oklahoma.

Guymon was darkened by the dust shortly after a large crowd had packed the Methodist church in prayers for rain.

The high wind at Beaver enshrouded the town in dust and the temperature fell from 80 to 63 degrees in 15 minutes.

When the onrushing black cloud struck Woodward at 4:30 p. m., frightened residents scurried to cellars. Hammon residents also took refuge underground when the menacing cloud rolled out of the northwest at 5:45 p. m.

A terrifying tornado funnel, 50 feet wide at the top, bore down on Sayre, but broke and scattered dust in every

(Continued on Page 2, Column 2)

BREAD BASKET—Major part of Oklahoma's wheat lands will produce an average crop this year despite the wind erosion in the panhandle, according to the federal crop statistician. Crop conditions in the state's wheat belt, though poor in the panhandle, become progressively better to the east, as shown by the map.

Prison Cruelty Charges Are Cited as Prosecution Cause

THREE ESCAPE DALLAS PRISON

Sheets Tied Together For Long Climb From Sixth Floor.

DALLAS, Texas, April 14.—(AP)—Three prisoners, one of them identified by officers as a recent associate of Raymond Hamilton, sawed their way out of the Dallas county jail early Sunday.

Jail records gave the names of the trio, John Bratcher, the former Hamilton associate, held for federal officers; Olin Tyler, charged with murder; and Tommy Bryant, charged with burglary.

Officers were reluctant to discuss the case, but said the men obtained saws from some source and cut the bolt off the lock of their cell on the sixth floor.

They made their way along a hall to a window, cut out two bars, and slid to the ground on a rope made of bed sheets. They used 26 sheets to negotiate the six floors.

The watchman at the courthouse just across the street noticed the hanging sheets shortly before 4 a. m. and notified officers.

A large force of deputies was sent in search of the men.

Matlage Defense Attorney Says Proof Will Be Given at Trial.

MANGUM, April 14.—(Special.)—G. Gordon McBride, attorney for George Matlage, former Granite reformatory inmate, Sunday declared that he will prove Matlage is being prosecuted "solely because he tried to tell the state what conditions are in the reformatory."

Matlage, 25-year-old Oklahoma City resident, faces trial here Monday on a charge of assault with intent to kill W. E. Parkey, reformatory night sergeant.

Early Quiz Is Cited

"This assault that they charge took place last August was investigated then by county officials, and no charge was filed," said McBride. "But when Matlage came down here in February to testify in the investigation of the reformatory, they dug up this old incident and filed the charge."

It was Matlage who claimed that both his wrists were broken while he was handcuffed to bars as punishment for violating prison discipline. Three state investigations followed, and in two of them the warden, Mrs. George A. Waters, was exonerated. She was replaced, however, by Fred Hunt, now warden.

Waters to Prosecute

McBride said he will summon as witnesses some of the Greer county officials themselves in his attempt to show the prosecution is not in good faith. He will call 25 witnesses, most of them reformatory inmates and guards.

Victor Waters, county attorney and son of Mrs. Waters, said he will use less than six witnesses in the prosecution. He said the state will prove that Matlage cut the prison sergeant several times with a knife as Parkey attempted to remove him from a punishment cell.

Carl Clark, charged jointly with Matlage, never has been arrested.

SANTA'S MAIL RELAYER HAS EVEN CHANCE

SANTA CLAUS, Ind., April 14.—(AP)—The man who has proved to thousands of expectant children throughout the world that there really is a Santa Claus, was given a 50-50 chance to live here Sunday.

For years James F. Martin, genial 60-year-old postmaster of this diminutive settlement nestled in the friendly hills of southern Indiana, has relayed Christmas gifts and requests to such places as Palestine, Egypt, the Philippines, Canada, England and to most of the United States.

Saturday, while at work in the commonplace shop which has enlivened Yule festivities every year, Martin was stricken with a paralytic stroke.

Hyde Park Studies Linen Production

HYDE PARK, N. Y., April 14.—(AP)—Home-grown linen and manufacture of rope from flax were being considered Sunday by the Hyde Park association to help unemployed.

Mrs. Franklin D. Roosevelt, wife of the president, is a member of the association and has taken an active part in its work. A survey is being conducted to see if flax can be raised in the vicinity.

RHODE ISLAND MILL UNIONS URGE NEW POLITICAL PARTY

PROVIDENCE, R. I., April 14.—(AP)—The Rhode Island Textile council, representing unions of the United Textile Workers of America, Sunday recommended formation of a third party. It condemned failure of the Democratic majority in the Rhode Island legislature to pass measures sought by labor.

Board Steps Mexican Strikes

MEXICO, D. F., April 14.—(AP)—Strikes of light and power company employes in nine cities ended Sunday as the result of a ruling by the labor board that they were illegal.

Long Again Calls Legislature Term

BATON ROUGE, La., April 14.—(AP)—Members of the Louisiana legislature were notified Sunday to assemble in special session Monday night as Senator Huey P. Long returned from New Orleans to the state capital to write new laws for them to enact.

It was generally understood that one purpose of the session would be to set up state machinery for administration of funds Louisiana is expected to derive from the federal relief bill.

Insurance Executive Dead

KANSAS CITY, April 14.—(AP)—Riddelle L. Gregory, president of the Postal Life and Casualty Insurance Co. here, died Sunday.

WHALE SHOW LEAVES $822 FOR CHARITY

"Colossus," the giant whale, rolled out of Oklahoma City Sunday night but he left $822.42 behind him for The Daily Oklahoman and Oklahoma City Times Milk and Ice fund.

A record crowd poured through the marine exhibit at First street and Walker avenue Sunday. Officials estimated that total attendance reached 18,000 for the ten-day exhibition.

Receipts for the show totaled $2,056.05. Forty percent of this amount was given the Milk and Ice fund. Cold weather the first week handicapped the show but attendance Friday, Saturday and Sunday was heavy. The whale show this week will be at Ada.

Davis Visits Stricken Mother

NASHVILLE, Tenn., April 14.—(AP)—The serious illness of his mother, Mrs. M. H. Davis, Sunday brought Norman H. Davis, American ambassador at large, by airplane from New York.

Detroit Housewives Push Grand Jury Price Probe

DETROIT, April 14.—(AP)—Housewives of Detroit will desert their dishwashing and dusting Thursday to attend a grand jury investigation into the rising price of bread, milk, meat and other items in the household budget.

Housewives' complaints have swelled to a citywide clamor over a cent-a-quart jump in milk and a 2-cent jump in bread, with other commodities moving skyward in proportion.

Prosecutor Duncan McCrea, in petitioning Judge Henry S. Sweeny for the grand jury session, expressed his belief that the increased prices are a result of price fixing conspiracies and combinations in violation of the state anti-trust laws.

Judge Sweeney recognized the housewives' interest and announced that the one-man grand jury will be as "open as possible." He will conduct the investigation.

The cent-a-quart increase in the price of milk will be the first topic of inquiry. Bread will be next.

"Other situations," McCrea said, "will be inquired into."

Officials pointed out that the language of the petition was broad enough to cover an investigation of the price of meat, gasoline or any other commodity distributed by dealers banded together in a trade organization.

Pact of Three Powers Seen As Key to League's Session

Council Gathers to Study French Protest To German Arms.

(Additional details on Page 11)
(By The Associated Press)

The united stand of three great World war Allies against a rearmed Germany, the outcome of the historic Stresa conference, was in back of the league council Sunday as statesmen gathered at Geneva to consider France's memorandum of protest.

A united front for peace rather than a stand against the reich was considered, however, to be the future attitude of the powers.

Stresa—The premiers of Italy, France and England announced full and cordial agreement on six points calculated to insure the peace of Europe. A communique summarizing the conference blamed Germany for "undermining public confidence in security," expressed willingness to continue with peace efforts and pact making, and on behalf of Italy and England, reaffirmed adherence to the Locarno treaty in protection of Germany in case of attack.

Geneva—On the eve of the council meeting the league published France's memorandum, an appeal in the name of peace against Germany's violation of the Versailles treaty which did not, however, call for punishment. The council was asked to provide measures, possibly application of sanctions, against any further violation.

Berlin—An official communique was interpreted as attempting to turn the tables on France in answer to her league memorandum by citing the alleged "coercion" of Germany by the arming of other powers, especially France.

Moscow—Reports from Czechoslovakia that a delegation was coming to Moscow to draw up an air pact were published in the newspapers. The press expressed the belief that the Stresa conference will result in clarification of the British attitude toward continental affairs.

Addis Ababa—Emperor Haile Selassie announced compulsory military conscription of both men and women in answer to Italy's mobilization of troops in Ethiopia's neighboring African colonies.

Twin of Mother May Seek Gloria

NEW YORK, April 14.—(AP)—The Daily News says in a copyright story that Lady Furness, twin sister of Mrs. Gloria Vanderbilt, will attempt to gain custody of 10-year-old Gloria Vanderbilt herself should Mrs. Vanderbilt lose her court battle with Mrs. Harry Payne Whitney.

Should Mrs. Whitney retain custody of the child through a decision on the pending appeal, the News says, Lady Furness will counter with a new court action to obtain her sister's daughter for herself.

MISSING SOCIETY WOMAN'S KIN OFFER $100 FOR RETURN

FARMINGTON, Conn., April 14.—(AP)—The family of Mrs. Anne Booth Gordon, pretty 25-year-old society matron missing four days from her home here, Sunday authorized the posting of $100 for her safe return.

U. S. to Build More Homes

WASHINGTON, April 14.—(AP)—Contracts awarded Sunday for building 112 houses in subsistence homesteads communities brought the total under construction or contract to 1,311. Of these, 624 have been completed.

Tree Honors Sam Houston

NEW YORK, April 14.—(AP)—A tree transplanted from its old home at Huntsville, Texas, was dedicated in Central park Sunday in memory of Gen. Sam Houston, first president of the republic of Texas.

DEFENSE SET BY BARNETTS

Clearance Receipt Claimed On Records Involved In Ardmore Case.

W. J. Barnett, former state bank commissioner, and his brother, N. S. Barnett, will combat charges that they removed records from the American Bank and Trust Co., Ardmore, with a clearance receipt issued to N. S. Barnett, Sid White, their attorney, said Sunday.

The two accused former officials conferred with White here Sunday and will return Monday to go with him to Ardmore to be arraigned on the felony charge and post bond.

Howard Johnson, new bank commissioner, March 6 removed N. S. Barnett, who had been in charge of the Ardmore bank, largest state institution placed under a moratorium. He had been appointed by W. J. Barnett.

"At the time N. S. Barnett was checked out, he insisted on a complete audit being made," White declared. "When it was finished, Barnett was given a receipt which stated that all records were present and proper."

White said that the Barnett brothers had gone to Tishomingo "on business," and that they would return to their home at Shawnee before coming here Monday.

UPSIDE DOWN STOMACH TRIO DOING NICELY

FALL RIVER, Mass., April 14.—(AP)—Jimmy Neilson's temperature rose two degrees Sunday but doctors reported the 13-year-old San Jose, Calif., boy "slightly more comfortable" Sunday night.

Alyce Jane McHenry, the 10-year-old Omaha, Neb., girl of upside down stomach fame, spent a quiet Sunday at the nurses' home and William Spiegelblatt, 9 years old, of Newport, R. I., was progressing favorably from his operation for diaphragmatic hernia performed Saturday.

SPEED FLIGHT IS HALTED BY BROKEN GEAR

Supercharger's Clutch I Stripped, Forcing Him To Come Down.

NEW PLANS IN DOUBT

Flier Refuses to Make Comment on Future Experiments.

LAFAYETTE, Ind., April 14.—(AP)—Wiley Post's third attemp to crack the transcontinenta airplane speed record by way o the stratosphere ended here lat Sunday when, plagued by super charger trouble, he brought th Winnie Mae down to a "bell landing" at the Purdue univer sity airport.

Streaking away from the Burban Union air terminal at 5:27½ a. n Pacific coast time, Post nurtle through thin air at speeds which ap proximated 300 miles per hour.

Over this college community th sturdy ship which has set two around the-world marks, failed him. Afte circling the university field four o five times, the flier came down i what airport attaches termed "sweet landing."

Plans Are in Doubt

"Get my hat off," were Post's firs words. He was wearing a visore aluminum helmet and a 16-poun rubber fabric suit in which he re ceived oxygen.

"Will you try again?" he was aske

"I don't know," Post answered, " don't want to talk about it at all."

Post averaged 231.48 miles per ho in his 1,900-mile flight to Lafayet On his second record attempt he ave aged 279.36 miles per hours from Bu bank to Cleveland.

A crowd of Purdue students ar townspeople jammed around the plan Souvenir hunters displayed bits paint they had scratched off the shi Within a short time traffic wa tangled for blocks about the field.

Flew at 33,000 Feet

Post said a clutch on one of h superchargers was stripped. He re mained at the field for some time su perintending the placing of woode skis on the wheelless ship so that could be towed into a hangar. He i dicated he would remain here awai ing arrival of landing gear.

The Oklahoma flier carried no rad sending equipment and was not hear from or seen from the time of h takeoff until he was forced down.

He flew through the stratosphe at an average altitude of approximat ly 33,000 feet. He depended main on a radio receiving set for plottin his course 900 miles by tuning broadcasting stations enroute.

Post was forced down February in the Mojave desert 125 miles o of Burbank by motor trouble whic later he alleged was caused by sab tage. On his second attempt came down at Cleveland because depletion of his oxygen supply. had hoped to make the third tr in seven or eight hours.

Post said flying conditions Sunda were unusually bad.

POST READY FOR BED AFTER STRAIN OF FLIGHT

NEW YORK, April 14.—(AP)—"T supercharger just quit on me," Wil Post, forced down Sunday at LaFa ette, Ind., on a transcontinental fligh told his backers here by telephone.

"It got colder than it ever got be fore," Post told a representative Frank Phillips, Oklahoma oil ma backing the flight.

"The oxygen made me feel goo It isn't a good idea to breath oxyge with a cold. I had a cold befo starting and I didn't feel so dar well when I landed.

"The wind was mostly north high altitude, and I was up ove 36,000 feet at one time.

"I didn't see the ground fro Denver until I landed at LaFayett I had a tailwind from Burbank the Grand Canyon.

"When the supercharger quit, flew blind for an hour and the dropped 23,000 feet through clou to about 7,000 feet and cut the moto

"I knew there was a landing fiel at LaFayette which I liked, and I landed there."

Post was asked whether he wante to come to New York.

"I want to go to bed, he replied.

Bashful Nudists Seek Colony Sit

ARCADIA, Fla., April 14.—(AP)—Wanted—By a Missouri nudist colon—a large tract of land for coloniza tion, provided it is remote from pry ing eyes.

Dale Foster of Arcadia has report receipt of several inquiries from th colony. He replied the only land h had for sale was too close to neigh bors.

Hugo Lumber Plant Burns

HUGO, April 14.—(AP)—Fire at t R. M. Fry Lumber Co. and sawm here Sunday caused damage estimat at $10,000.

Weather Forecast
PROBABLY SHOWERS
Sunrise, 4:57. Sunset, 6:41.

THE INDIANAPOLIS NEWS

LAST EDITION

VOL. LXVI NUMBER (WHOLE NO. 20,528) Entered as second-class matter at postoffice, Indianapolis, Ind. Issued daily. FRIDAY EVENING, AUGUST 16, 1935. THIRTY PAGES BY LOCAL CARRIER 12c A WEEK; MAIL BY ZONES 25c TO $1 A MONTH THREE CENTS

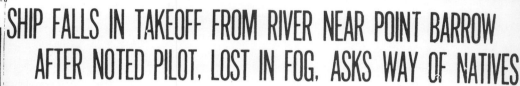

WILL ROGERS AND WILEY POST DIE IN ALASKA WHEN PLANE CRASHES AFTER FORCED LANDING

SHIP FALLS IN TAKEOFF FROM RIVER NEAR POINT BARROW AFTER NOTED PILOT, LOST IN FOG, ASKS WAY OF NATIVES

4th Extra

Other news and pictures of the Rogers-Post tragedy are on Pages 7, 8 and 9, Part 1, and Pages 1, 7 and 15, Part 2.

WASHINGTON, August 16 (A.P.)—Charles A. Lindbergh was said this afternoon to be handling arrangements for Mrs. Will Rogers to obtain the body of her husband. She so informed officials who contacted her at Skowhegan, Me.

Lindbergh, reported at Northhaven, Me., offered to place planes at the disposal of her and Mrs. Wiley Post, or others interested in assisting them.

SEATTLE, August 16.—Will Rogers, cowboy philosopher, actor and air travel enthusiast, and Wiley Post, who circled the earth alone in a plane, were killed last night when their plane crashed in fog fifteen miles south of Point Barrow in northernmost Alaska.

The word of their death came today to the United States Army Signal Corps headquarters here from their Point Barrow station.

The first terse message said:

"Post and Rogers crashed fifteen miles south of here (Point Barrow) at 5 o'clock last night. Have recovered bodies and placed them in care of Dr. Griest (in charge of a small Point Barrow hospital). Standing by on Anchorage (Alaska) hourly."

The message was signed by Staff Sergeant Morgan, the only army man on duty at the small Point Barrow settlement.

Crashed From Fifty Feet.

Later, he wirelessed the plane crashed from only fifty feet in the air after taking off from a small river.

"Navy runner reported plane crashed fifteen miles south of Barrow," he said.

"Immediately hired fast launch, proceeded to scene, found plane complete wreck, partially submerged two feet water. Recovered body of Rogers then necessary tear plane apart extract body of Post from water. Brought bodies to Barrow, turned over to Dr. Greist, also salvaged personal effects which I am holding. Advise relatives and instruct this station fully as to procedure.

"Natives camping small river fifteen miles south here claim Post and Rogers landed, asked way to Barrow. Taking off engine misfired on right bank while only fifty feet over water. Plane out of control, crashed, tearing right wing off and toppling over forced engine back through body of plane. Both apparently killed instantly. Both bodies bruised. Post's wrist watch broken, stopped 8:18 p.m."

Henry W. Greist operates the Presbyterian Hospital at Point Barrow, which is maintained primarily for the care of Eskimos.

Post and Rogers were on an aerial vacation which Post had planned would take him to Moscow, but Rogers had not decided whether he would accompany him further than Nome, where Wiley planned to establish a base for his projected flight across Siberia.

Early plans for the flight included arrangements for Mrs. Post, the flyer's wife, to accompany them. At the last moment Mrs. Post withdrew.

Mrs. Rogers, wife of the humorist-philosopher, and Mrs. Post were notified of the tragedy by Captain Frank E. Stoner, of the signal corps headquarters, here.

Cutter to Pick Up Bodies.

A coast guard cutter, the Northland was ordered to turn back to Point Barrow, which it left yesterday, to pick up the bodies and bring them to Seattle.

The crash occurred as Post was pointing his pontoon-equipped plane toward Point Barrow, 500 miles away, on a flight from Fairbanks.

The plane took off from Fairbanks late yesterday, but when Post learned that a dense fog shrouded Point Barrow, he set his ship down on the small stream.

The department of commerce at Washington ordered inspectors to proceed at once to the scene of the wreck. The inspectors, however, lack jurisdiction to act as the accident did not occur on a regular airline and the plane was privately owned.

As soon as word of the death of the two men was received President Roosevelt, a good friend of Rogers and Post, was informed.

The territory south of Barrow is

Continued on Page 7, Part 2

HUMORIST AND FLYER FAST FRIENDS

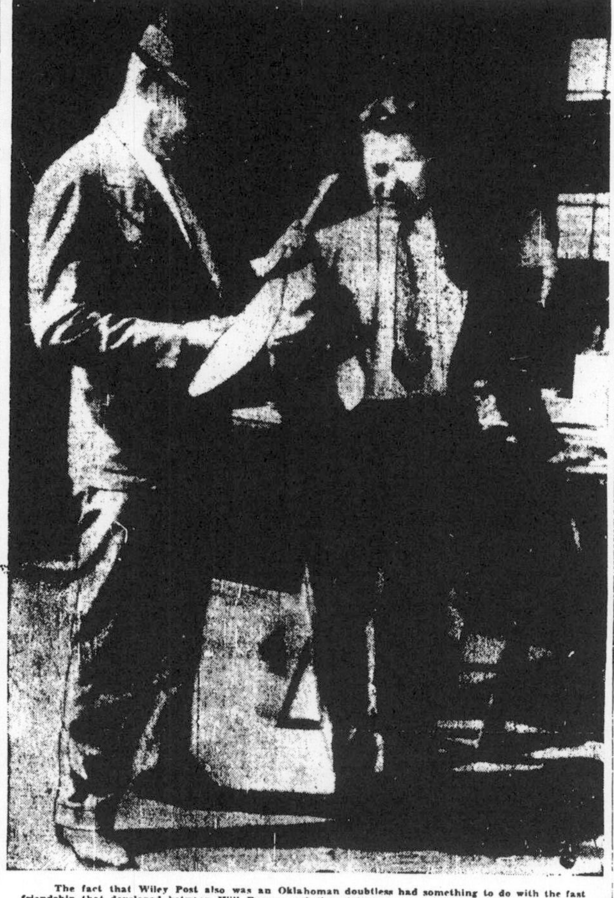

The fact that Wiley Post also was an Oklahoman doubtless had something to do with the fast friendship that developed between Will Rogers and the plainsman-turned-philosopher and the one-eyed well-digger who became one of the world's most noted aviators and explorers.

Here are the two in a characteristic pose, taken at Seattle just a day or so before departure on their fateful trip. Rogers is inspecting a paddle fashioned by Post for use in the event of a forced landing on the water.

LAST TIME TOGETHER

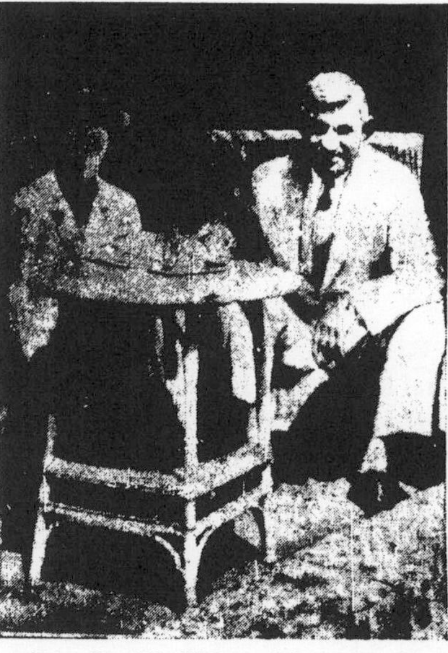

Here are Mr. and Mrs. Will Rogers enjoying a restful period at their home in Beverly Hills shortly before the famous humorist left on his flight to Alaska with Wiley Post.

WILL ROGERS SAYS:

[Herewith is the daily Will Rogers dispatch which has been appearing in The Indianapolis News for years. It is the last dispatch that came from the noted humorist, and was received in The News office just about an hour before word of his death, along with Wiley Post, stunned the news room.

In these few paragraphs each day, the kindly humorist has long entertained readers of The News with his apt comments on current events. Each Saturday he wrote a longer article for the last page of The News describing his activities of the preceding week.]

To the Editor of The News:

FAIRBANKS, Alaska, August 16.—Visited our new emigrants. Now this is not the time to discuss whether it will succeed or whether it won't; whether it's a farming country or whether it is not, nor to enumerate the hundreds of mistakes and confusions and rows and arguments and management in the whole thing at home and here. As I see it, there is only one problem now that they are here and that's to get 'em housed within six or eight weeks.

Things have been in a terrible mess. They are getting 'em straightened out, but even now not fast enough. There are about 700 or 800 of 'em. About 200 went back. Also about half that many workmen were sent here from the transient camps down home (no CCC) and just lately they are using about 150 Alaskan workmen, paid regular wages.

But it's just a few weeks to snow now and they have to be out of the tents, both workmen and settlers. Plenty food. Always has been and will be. They can always get that, but it's houses they need right now and Colonel Hunt, in charge, realizes it.

You know, after all, there is a lot of difference in pioneering for gold, and pioneering for spinach. Yours,

WILL ROGERS.

CLIPPER STARTS WAKE ISLAND HOP

Pan-American Plane Takes Off on 1,191-Mile Flight Over Mid-Pacific.

MIDWAY ISLANDS (By Pan-American Airways), August 16 (A.P.)—Heading for desolate Wake island, 1,191 statute miles southwest of here over mid-Pacific, the Pan-American clipper seaplane took off today.

RAIL, FARM BANKRUPTCY BILLS TO BE CONSIDERED

WASHINGTON, August 16 (A.P.)—Plans to consider rail pension and farm bankruptcy legislation before congress adjourns were disclosed today by Senator Joseph T. Robinson (Dem., Ark.), floor leader.

Holding Compromise Fails.

WASHINGTON, August 16 (A.P.)—Compromise offers submitted by house and senate conferees on the public utility bill failed today in another vain effort to get together on the provision for compulsory abolition of "unnecessary" holding companies.

Senator Burton K. Wheeler (Dem., Mont.), insisting on some form of dissolution of surplus holding companies, asserted, however, that prospects for agreement were "a little brighter."

The conferees spent two hours in debate over compromise proposals and adjourned, subject to a call for a meeting Monday.

News First on Tragedy Flash

SEATTLE, August 16.—News of the death of Wiley Post and Will Rogers in an airplane crash near Point Barrow, Alaska, today was first flashed to the world by the Associated Press.

Its report at 8:48 a. m. central standard time from the United States army signal corps was 40 minutes or more ahead of all other press associations.

The Indianapolis News is a member of the Associated Press and the United Press.

TAX WEALTH BILL FACES NEW FIGHT

Senate-House Conference Is Certain to Produce Controversies Over Proposals.

NEW LEGISLATIVE RECORD

Democratic Leaders Rush Measure to Passage by Vote of 57 to 22.

WASHINGTON, August 16 (A.P.)—After streaking through the senate in record time, the tax bill designed to raise $250,000,000 from new levies on million-dollar incomes, large corporations, estates and gifts dropped today into a senate-house conference in which several controversies threaten.

Democratic leaders hoped these disputes could be settled in time to adjourn congress next week.

One controversy started even before the senate, by a 57-to-22 vote, passed its finance committee's bill late yesterday at the end of only two days of debate.

It centered around an amendment, which the senate approved at the urging of Senator William E. Borah (Rep., Idaho), to prohibit the federal government from issuing any more tax-exempt securities. The treasury was fighting this and there is opposition in the house.

Another Stumbling Block.

Another stumbling block facing the senate-house conferees who will seek to reconcile the senate bill with a markedly different measure already passed by the house was the question of taxes on estates and inheritances. The senate substituted increases in the present estate taxes for the brand-new inheritance levies approved by the house.

The senate also voted for higher gift taxes on donors, instead of the house's new levies on recipients of gifts; it raised the surtax rates on individual net incomes over $1,000,000, where the house started the rates at $50,000; it increased the house graduated corporation income rates, reduced the other chamber's excess profits rates, increased existing capital stock taxes and imposed a new tax on dividends received by one corporation from another.

The Borah amendment, approved 46 to 30, would make the income from future issues of government bonds subject to the income tax. Treasury officials immediately objected. They argued it would seriously handicap the Roosevelt financial program and place the government at a disadvantage in borrowing since states and municipalities would still have the right to issue tax-free securities.

Would Raise Money Cost.

Besides making it difficult to obtain funds to finance the $4,000,000,000 work relief program, officials said, the amendment would raise the cost of all money obtained by the government.

President Roosevelt in his tax message had recommended a constitutional amendment to permit simultaneous taxation of income from both federal and state bonds.

The senate's scrapping of inheritance levies was expected to encounter strong house opposition in conference. The proposed inheritance taxes ranged from 4 per cent on the first taxable $10,000 to 75 per cent on that part over $10,000,000. In these, the senate substituted increases in existing taxes on estates. These new levies would rise from 2 per cent on the first taxable $10,000 to 70 per cent on the excess over $50,000,000.

President Roosevelt recommended the inheritance tax to be imposed on existing estates levies as a means of breaking up large fortunes.

Silver Amendment Added.

Another amendment added to the bill yesterday without a record vote was the plan of Senator Pat McCarran (Dem., Nev.) to repeal three sections of the silver purchase act. These levy a 50 per cent. tax on silver trading profits, provide for nationalization of the metal and licensing of imports and exports. The legislators said this was headed off a doubtful fate in conference.

Seven Republicans, forty-eight Democrats, one Farmer-Labor and one Progressive senator voted "aye." The tax bill passed the senate. In opposition were ten Democrats, twelve Republicans. Both Frederick VanNuys and Sherman Minton, Indiana, voted for the bill.

Before the final roll call, Senator Elmer Thomas (Dem., Okla.) re-urged the soldiers' bonus issue, but failed to get Democratic leaders on record in favor of giving this legislation a preferred status early next January.

Thomas offered the Patman inflationary bonus bill to pay the bonus immediately with new money but withdrew it when Senator Joseph T. Robinson (Dem., Ark.), majority leader, announced the subject would

Continued on Page 7, Part 1

THREE MEN WEIGH FATE OF ETHIOPIA

Conference May Result in Alteration of Map in East Africa.

ITALY WANTS OCCUPATION

Demand Arouses Fear That It Will Be Impossible to Avert War.

PARIS, August 16 (A.P.)—Three men met today in a secret session which may result in the alteration of the map of Ethiopia and a change in the African empire's economic life.

The men were Premier Pierre Laval, of France; Baron Pompeo Aloisi, of Italy, and Anthony Eden, of Great Britain. They conducted their talk in the ante-chamber of the clock room of the foreign ministry, where their countries, in 1928, signed the Kellogg-Briand pact "outlawing war."

Their avowed intention is to prevent war between Italy and Ethiopia.

For a few minutes, Robert G. Vansittart, British permanent foreign undersecretary, sat in on the conference, but, for the remainder of the meeting, the three diplomats were alone.

Assistants Wait Outside.

A group of twelve other experts and secretaries sat outside the antechamber until an hour and a half had elapsed and they were all called in for lunch.

After lunch, Premier Laval came out from the room alone and said: "We have no declaration to make. We worked hard all morning and will continue throughout the afternoon."

The three negotiators resumed their secret talk, their accompanying experts remaining outside in case they were needed.

The demand for Italian occupation of Ethiopia to enforce any concessions given Italy aroused fear today among the tripartite conference representatives that they would be unable to prevent war in east Africa.

Occupation Is Il Duce's Demand.

Armed occupation was Mussolini's demand as presented to the representatives of France, Great Britain and Italy in their conversations for the settlement of the Italo-Ethiopian dispute.

Premier Laval was expected to seize on Mussolini's terms as a starting point for negotiations which he hoped would close the gap between the British and Italian viewpoint.

Emperor Haile Selassie, not represented at the parleys, remained an uncertain factor since the three powers' problem is to find a way of making Italian control of Ethiopia acceptable to him.

Their hopes lay in the possibility that he would accept Mussolini's minimum demand when he is convinced war is inevitable.

Ethiopian Troops Speeded.

ADDIS ABABA, August 16 (A.P.)—Movements of Ethiopian troops and munitions toward the frontier were speeded up today as the first reports from the Paris peace conversations failed to revive hopes that war between Ethiopia and Italy might be averted.

Dedjazmatch Abarrah, son of Ras Kassa, governor of Condar left with reinforcements for the northern army, now estimated at 425,000.

Emperor Haile Selassie held further war councils with chieftains after a reception to the army press correspondents.

3 FIREMEN HURT AT PAPER PLANT

Spontaneous Combustion of Rags in Basement Believed Cause of Flames.

LOSS ESTIMATE $5,000

Stock in Basement Ruined and Smoke Damages Other Property.

Fighting a $5,000 fire in the smoke-filled, three-story building of the Indianapolis Paper Container Company, 217 West Tenth street, this morning, three firemen from Engine House 5 were overcome.

Six others were affected by the smoke, but after a short rest continued in their line of duty.

Originating in the basement from an unknown source about 4 a. m., the fire filled the concrete and steel structure with smoke and firemen fought for three hours before it was entirely extinguished. Companies from Engine Houses 1, 5, 7 and 8 were called.

150 Window Panes Broken.

Most of the damage was in the destruction of paper products in the basement by water, and the breaking of 150 window panes by firemen in an effort to reach the flames which were confined to the basement and first floor.

Those overcome were Lafe Pease, Eli Lucas and John Craw. Pease and Lucas were unable to continue their work, and were sent home, while Craw recovered and remained on duty.

Firemen donned gas masks to protect themselves from the choking fumes, and groped through the smoke for an hour before they were able to find the flames. After the fire was found, the basement was flooded with water three and a half feet deep.

The fire first was noticed by Radio Patrolmen Charles Springer and Bernard Miller, who saw smoke escaping from the building.

The company is owned by Carl Shafer, 5515 North Pennsylvania street, and Paul Denny, 3744 North Meridian street. Don Shafer, son of Carl Shafer, said he was the last one in the basement Thursday evening and there was no indication of fire at that time. It was believed the flames may have been caused by spontaneous combustion in some rags.

Two colored motorists, who were watching the fire instead of the street, drove into a pumper hose, cut it in two and caused a policeman to be doused with water. The motorists were arrested.

Machinery Undamaged.

The building is of steel and cement construction, with large glass windows. The company manufactures various kinds of paper containers and much of its product was stored in the basement where it was flooded with water. Several tons of paper, recently bought by the company, also were destroyed. Several dies were damaged, and wiring was impaired.

Machinery on the second and third floors escaped damage, but a large number of cardboard boxes, stored on upper floors, were ruined. The loss is covered by insurance, owners said.

Fire Company No. 2 had a call Thursday night when Floyd Caylor, 1822 Hillside avenue, went to sleep in his car with a lighted cigarette in his hand, setting fire to upholstery. Damage was slight.

Tragedy-Stunned City Recalls How Rogers Endeared Himself on Numerous Occasions Here

BY WILLIAM L. TOMS

"The lines are all busy—all trunks in use—yes, Rogers and Post both were killed—no further information—the lines are all busy."

Working feverishly at the switchboard in The News office, two operators were attempting to clear the jam of calls as the world spread that the beloved Will Rogers and his pilot, the globe-circling Wiley Post, had been killed in an aviation accident in Alaska.

"I've been worried to death since they left on that trip," sobbed one of the hundreds of women whose calls came in at one of those infrequent times when one of the switchboard plugs was not in use.

It seemed only yesterday when Rogers came to town, that time by train, to do his big bit toward making this little corner of the world a little happier, a little more cheerful, and a little more thoughtful. And it seemed only the day before when the intrepid Post was here to relate experiences on his record swing around the great globe the two now have left.

Spoke at Hospital.

Of the scores of visits paid Indianapolis by Rogers, none stands out in greater relief than the one last January—the one which proved to be his farewell to Indiana. Just for a change in his program, Will decided to come by train here and it was the train he chose that crashed into an automobile in Irvington and killed two women. Of all the passengers on that train, none seemed more affected than Rogers and the incident was deplored in Rogers's daily column in The News the following day.

But he had been summoned here to speak for the Indianapolis Junior League in behalf of the James Whitcomb Riley Hospital for Children and Rogers knew that amusement was what the people expected. Casting aside for the moment the sorrow that was his, Rogers, the old trouper, became at once the Oklahoma cowboy of the past, the crisp commentator of intermediate years and the philosopher of the current day.

Among the thousands of close friends of the famous humorist, Indianapolis contributed the man he reputedly admired most, Kin Hubbard, who created Abe Martin in his early days with The News. Years ago, in New York, when Rogers was on the stage and Hubbard at the peak of his popularity, the Oklahoma cowboy espied Hubbard in an audience and stopped the show to introduce his Hoosier friend as "the greatest humorist in the world today." When Hubbard passed on a few years ago, one of the most touching telegrams received came from Rogers.

Kings and presidents figuratively knelt at the feet of Rogers, yet all the acclaim that was his never seemed to bother the warm-blooded Claremore man, who was proud of an Indian strain. It always seemed, in fact, that Rogers was just a little more thrilled even than those privileged to meet him. With all his fame, Will never seemed to outgrow the boyishness that made him an instant favorite with Indianapolis years and years ago when he first tossed a lariat and chewed gum on the stage of the old Keith's theater.

And when he appeared here for the Junior League last January to twit the lawmakers, poke jokes at the wealthy and otherwise indulge in the verbal pranks his audience craved, wasn't it natural for some one to demand a few tricks with the ropes? And was it merely a coincidence that Rogers had brought those lariats

Continued on Page 7, Part 1

Purdue Airport End of Post's Third Stratosphere Attempt

Hoosiers, saddened by the death of Will Rogers and Wiley Post, recall the famous, globe-girdling pilot's last visit in Indiana in April on his third unsuccessful attempt to span the United States in record-breaking time by way of the stratosphere.

Taking off from Burbank, Cal., in the Winnie Mae, he had dropped his landing gear and headed east. Near Lafayette, his supercharger "quit" as he subsequently explained, and he made a "belly landing" with his silver and blue monoplane at the Purdue University airport.

Word of the flyer's forced landing spread rapidly and fifteen minutes after he had brought his plane down, hundreds of University students and Lafayette residents were at the airport.

He declined invitations of University officials to stay at the Union building and went to a downtown hotel. Disappointed and apparently semi-dazed after the removal of his sixteen-pound rubber fabric suit and visored aluminum helmet, worn for protection in the stratosphere, he was reluctant to discuss his flight.

Smoking one cigarette after another, he met reporters and photographers with a tired smile and the comment, "You won't get much out of me."

Only one among the scores of telegrams that came to him from all parts of the country did he accept. That one was from his wife.

"I thought the third time would be a charm," he said, referring to his attempts to span the country. He said he was getting tired of making emergency landings without landing gear.

Indianapolis extended a royal welcome to Post on his visit here in September, 1933, shortly after he completed his solo round-the-world flight. He appeared before the Kiwanis state convention.

Witty, shy and unassuming, he related his various experiences on his flight which set a new record. He was the guest of honor at a dinner given for him by the aviation bureau of the Chamber of Commerce, prior to his address at the Kiwanis assembly.

11:30 A. M. Saturday

That's the deadline for the big Saturday want ad section of The News. Two days' results, Saturday and Sunday, for one day's cost!

On Saturday The News carries more rent ads and merchandise than all the other Indianapolis papers put together! Selection means reader-interest, and reader interest means results.

So if you have a room or house for or for rent phone Ri. 5441, before 11:30 a. m. Saturday.—The Indianapolis News.

1936

President Roosevelt was reelected for a second term, and:

Bruno Richard Hauptmann was convicted of kidnapping and killing the Lindbergh baby.

Civil war raged in Spain.

Boulder Dam was completed, creating Lake Mead.

Margaret Mitchell published *Gone With the Wind.*

WEATHER FORECAST
Rain early today; colder tonight; fair and and moderately cold tomorrow.
Yesterday's Temperatures: Max., 48; Min., 40.
(Details on Page 29)

THE SUN

Secret Of King's Struggle Bared Before House Of Commons By Premier Baldwin —Page 3

Registered United States Patent Office

ol. 200—D. PAID CIRCULATION NOVEMBER MORNING, 144,371 EVENING, 152,703 297,074 || SUNDAY 207,267 BALTIMORE, FRIDAY, DECEMBER 11, 1936 Entered as second-class matter at Baltimore Postoffice Copyright, 1936, by The A. S. Abell Company, Publishers of The Sun. 30 Pages 2 Cents

YORK WILL BECOME KING TODAY; CROWDS CHEER EDWARD'S NAME; MRS. SIMPSON WAITS SILENTLY

.ONDON CROWD .LL BUT MOBS TS KING-TO-BE

'ork Wildly Greeted 'pon Return From Fare- ell Dinner With Edward

·ENSE THRONG BARS ·ATH OF AUTOMOBILE

.hange In Rulers Occurs 248 Years To Day After James II Fled England

New King Took Part In Jutland Battle

New York, Dec. 10 (AP)—The new King of England has faced death in battle under the Union Jack.

The Duke of York was under fire in the greatest naval engagement of the World War—the battle of Jutland.

Aboard the flagship of Admiral Jellicoe, the Collingwood, he served in a fore turret, as an officer. He was mentioned in dispatches for coolness and valor.

[By the Associated Press]

London, Friday, Dec. 11—Great Britain's new Monarch—the man who will come either King Albert I or King George VI—was all but mobbed by a ildly enthusiastic crowd of Londoners early today when he returned to s home from his farewell dinner ith his brother as King Edward VIII.

So dense was the crowd that it took me minutes for the Royal automobile bearing the new King to force path through the throng. After he ighted in front of his home, 145 Piccadilly, the so-called "palace with a amber," across Green Park from ickingham Palace, he had great difficulty in making his way from the rb into the house.

Bears Edward's Approval

He returned with recollections of a allenge once voiced by his elder other when he occupied the throne. e former King Edward then said: "My brother Bertie," said ex-King lward, when he was Prince of Wales, would make a better King than I ould."

The sallow-cheeked "Bertie," who ce wryly complained in a public atement that his chief claim to fame emed to be that he was the father two small, golden-curled princesses effect took over the reins of dynasty 10 A. M.—the moment a thin ribbon ink traced the signature "Edward I." on the formal document of abdication.

Actually King From 10 A. M.

At that historic moment, as Edward's n dotted the last period of his signare as Rex-Imperator, the erstwhile uke of York stepped out of his lifeng role of "second fiddle" and beme sovereign of the greatest empire earth—subject only to the formal pproval of the British and dominion arliaments.

And for the first time in exactly 248 ears to the day, since James II fled ngland on December 10, 1688, the rone changed hands without the elancholy cry ringing through the reets:

"The King is dead! Long live the ing!"

Other English Kings have been deed or died, but never before has a ing voluntarily abdicated as Edard has done in his last precedentaking act of a precedent-breaking ign.

Londoners Are Dazed

Tonight, while London crowds wanred aimlessly—in dazed bewilderent—through nearby Piccadilly Circus, the King-to-be hurried home. hen he returned to Fort Belvedere, dward's country retreat, for a farell dinner—perhaps the last time he ill ever see his brother.

As the 40-year-old Duke emerged om his London home, no thrillvered crowds waited outside to heer, as they had cheered the new ing Edward VIII on a bitterly cold inter's day last January.

No patient thousands stood hour fter hour, hoping for a glimpse of e new ruler, as they had stood out-

Continued on Page 4, Column 8)

Ernest Simpson Fails In Effort To Avert Edward's Abdication

London, Dec. 10 (AP)—Ernest Aldrich Simpson, divorced husband of King Edward's betrothed, was disclosed tonight to have made a poignant, lastminute attempt to stave off abdication of his sovereign.

Late last night, Simpson's friends disclosed, the London ships' broker made overtures, through intermediaries, in the hope his former wife would renounce Edward's proffered hand so definitely that the swift march to abdication would be halted.

The appeal was not in any way a plea for reconciliation with the American-born divorcee. It constituted devotion to King and country, which he once served as a member of the King's Coldstream Guards. He is a personal friend of the King.

However, like the rest of the immense pressure brought upon the sovereign, his effort failed.

CANADA FEELS PERSONAL LOSS IN ABDICATION

King Edward Had Endeared Himself To People Of Dominion

By J. A. STEVENSON

[Special Correspondence of The Sun]

Ottawa, Ont., Dec. 7—The strange and moving drama which has kept the whole Canadian people in common with the rest of the British Commonwealth under an intense strain for the past week came to a tragic denouement today when news was flashed from London and immediately broadcasted all over the Dominion that the Speaker of the British House of Commons was reading King Edward's message of abdication.

All night long officials had been decoding long cable messages from London and Ministers were apprised well beforehand of the impending tragedy. The general public had also been prepared for it by pessimistic cables from London published in yesterday's evening papers and many households sat up almost all night discussing what today would bring.

People Abroad Early

People were abroad early this morning and by the time the first broadcasts of the proceedings in the British Commons were due to arrive, there were thousands of quiet, solemn audiences gathered round radios awaiting the fateful words. Many business men did not go to their offices at all but stayed at home, and merchants found that even the calls of Christmas shopping were being neglected by the women.

The news soon spread that the King actually had made formal abdication of the throne and soon special editions of the papers were selling like hot cakes on the street.

Endears Self To Public

King Edward during his three visits to the Dominion has made scores of personal friends of high and low estate

(Continued on Page 3, Column 7)

WOMAN IN CASE BANS COMMENT ON KING'S ACT

Holds Herself Virtual Prisoner In Her Haven At Cannes, France

GUARDED BY FRENCH AND ENGLISH POLICE

Plans Undisclosed, But Reunion Of Lovers Will Not Occur On Riviera

[By the Associated Press]

Cannes, France, Dec. 10—Wallis Warfield Simpson waited tonight for her unthroned King.

She held herself a prisoner in her Riviera haven, whence she came December 3 from England when the waves of controversy surrounding King Edward's intention to marry her began to beat about her head.

Today she knew before the world learned that the monarch had given up his imperial charge in order to make her his bride.

She had been in telephonic communication with London during the morning.

Refuses All Comment

The way cleared for their marriage, she refused through her spokesmen to comment on Edward's world-shaking pronouncement: "I have determined to renounce the throne." Then she retired to seclusion.

Eight French detectives and officers from Scotland Yard in London stood guard inside and outside the grounds of Lou Viei villa to see that her withdrawal into privacy is observed.

A crowd gathered during the afternoon in a soaking rain, but the officers had little to do. There was no sign of the striking brunette divorcee.

No Statement, None To Come

She "has nothing to say," brokenly declared Lord Brownlow, gentleman-in-waiting to the King, who came out, head bowed, to meet newspaper men after the world knew love had triumphed over duty in the heart of the world's mightiest monarch.

"There has been no statement, and there will be no statement," concluded Brownlow as he turned and slowly retraced his steps to the stuccoed villa nestling near terraces of orange groves and pine trees beside the sea.

It was a poignant moment as the spokesman turned away.

Dusk was falling. Lengthening shadows fell across Mrs. Simpson's bedroom windows, which look out upon a lighthouse standing sentinel-like in Riviera Harbor. The howl of a neighbor's dogs echoed across the countryside.

Will Not Meet Edward At Cannes

Wallis' plans were undisclosed tonight, but it was announced she would not meet Edward here.

Before Brownlow disclosed that she would not comment on the dramatic action of the man who loves her, another spokesman, Herman Rogers, of

(Continued on Page 2, Column 8)

Britain's New Rulers With Queen Mother

DUKE OF YORK DUCHESS OF YORK QUEEN MARY

LONDON—The prospective King and Queen are shown as they appeared with Queen Mary last year at the British Industries Fair at Olympia.

Lady Astor Says King Has Caused Unhappiness To All His Subjects

Virginia-Born M. P. Asserts Mrs. Simpson Was Rejected Because Of Her History—Claims No Class Issue, Only Moral One

[By the Associated Press]

New York, Dec. 10—Her voice audibly breaking in sobs of emotion, Nancy, Lady Astor, said in a broadcast from London tonight that King Edward's placing of "personal affection above public duty" has caused "unhappiness in the hearts of all his Majesty's subjects."

"But underneath that unhappiness," said the American-born woman who was the first of her sex admitted to Parliament, "remains the same spirit of calm determination which has characterized the Anglo-Saxon race in every emergency.

"Those who will not obey the rules, can't rule," she said, "and believe me, in this crisis, tragic though it has been, it has left us not weaker, but stronger."

The daughter of the Virginia Langhornes, who made her life career in England, added that all parties stood solidly behind the Government. "There was no class issue but fundamentally, a moral one," she said. "Mrs. Simpson was rejected because of her previous history," said Lady Astor. "The Prime Minister made it quite clear that the Dominions showed objection to the King's marriage to Mrs. Simpson. . . . . Not because she is not of royal blood nor because she was an American."

She said "you must understand that in the reign of George V, the crown became in a very special legal sense the bond of the empire . . . our kind of monarchy is not out of date, for it appeals to the heart as well as the head."

Of Edward, she said: "We all loved him and still do. But we hoped great things of him and today we mourn that he has let these opportunities pass from him."

Edward Expected To Fly To Austrian Alps, Leaving Britain Tomorrow Morning

Likely To Be Given Title Of Duke Of Inverness, Settlement, Believed Already Decided Upon, May Be Announced In New Year's List

By PHILIP WAGNER

[London Bureau of The Sun]

London, Dec. 10—King Edward VIII intends to leave England as soon as convenient, after he has given royal assent to the new Act of Settlement which is expected to pass both houses of Parliament by tomorrow night.

It is believed that Edward will not retain the title of either Duke of Cornwall or the Duke of Lancaster, but a new title will be conferred upon him by the new King, which is expected to be either a new dukedom or an old one revived. The title Duke of Inverness has been mentioned.

The settlement upon him, which is assumed already has been determined, will be included in the new King's Civil List. It is not intended that the settlement shall be made until New Year's Day.

Expected To Leave Saturday

The belief is that Edward, after signing the Act of Settlement, officially designated as His Majesty's Declaration of Abdication Act, 1936, will leave for the Austrian Alps. As he is making a world-wide broadcast tomorrow night, and as Edward customarily travels by plane, the assumption is that he will leave the following morning.

The Accession Council will be held at 11 A. M. Saturday and the proclamation will be made at noon. At 2.45 P. M. Saturday, both houses of Parliament will begin taking the oath of allegiance to the new King and the swearing in will continue Monday. One aspect of the changing of the Kings is the vast amount of swearing in of all public servants, which, in the case of some of the dominions, was not completed for six months after Edward's accession and must now be begun all over again.

Not To Change Coronation

It was earlier believed that the coronation would be deliberately postponed until June in order to avoid any unpleasant reminders of the sudden termination of Edward's reign. It now has been determined that the coronation date will remain unchanged—though it is the new King who makes the formal announcement of the date after his accession and hence this decision is subject to change.

In the balance, it is felt more would be lost by postponing the date than by keeping May 12. This decision comes as a tremendous relief, particularly to the hotel and travel trade.

Abdication Not Surprise

Prime Minister Stanley Baldwin's message announcing the end of one of the shortest and less glorious reigns of modern times, was not a surprise by the time it was delivered.

The way had been prepared by the morning papers, all of which indicated strongly that the abdication was pending, though none said so. The prevailing opinion is that Baldwin acquitted himself well in his speech of explanation which was made *extempore* from a few notes.

And there are those saying tonight that Baldwin has regained again the pinnacle of popularity from which he has been gradually slipping throughout the past twelve months. It is almost exactly a year since he began to slip after the revelations following the Hoare-Laval scheme to divide Ethiopia and end the war in Africa.

Called "Savior"

Now in a day he has become not only the savior of the nation's symbolic virtue, but the savior of the constitutional monarchy as well—that is, if the innumerable loose ends still left to be woven together do not get snarled in the weaving.

Undoubtedly the sentence in his speech which is going home to the public with the biggest impact is his quotation of the King's own words: "I am going to marry Mrs. Simpson and I am prepared to go."

The popular reaction to this remark as derived from dozens of conversations is definitely not the romantic

(Continued on Page 5, Column 3)

FREE STATE DUE TO SEVER LAST TIE WITH CROWN

Dail Eireann Expected Today To Drop King From Constitution

[By the Associated Press]

Dublin, Irish Free State, Dec. 10—Usually informed persons said late tonight the Irish Free State Parliament probably would sever its last direct connection with the British crown tomorrow.

These sources said proposals would be submitted to Parliament—called the Dail Eireann—to amend the constitution of the Free State, which has the status of a British Dominion, so as to completely eliminate the King from the charter and vest all executive authority in the Dail and the Irish Cabinet.

Such a move, it was said in these quarters, would be in line with President Eamon De Valera's program of cutting out of the constitution elements which, in his words, "create a source of irritation to the Irish national feeling."

Move For Republic Unlikely

Authoritative sources said a sudden declaration of the Free State as a republic cannot be expected, however.

Other legislative proposals to be raised in the Dail, it was reported, would provide for contact and cooperation with Australia, Canada, New Zealand, Great Britain and South Africa as long as the Irish people wish.

The Government indicated it would agree with the British Parliament in accepting the abdication of King Edward as "King of Ireland."

The net result of this action, usually informed sources said, would be recognition of the next King, the present Duke of York, as a symbol of cooperation.

Dail Eireann Would Advise

Under the action which these persons said the Dail would take tomorrow, the new monarch would act upon the advice of the Irish Cabinet on behalf of the Free State in such matters as the appointment of diplomatic and consular representatives and in certain

(Continued on Page 3, Column 8)

MONARCHY IS ATTACKED BY LABOR IN COMMONS IN ABDICATION BILL DEBATE

Left-Winger Booed As He Declares System Has Outlived Its Usefulness—People Appear Uneasy Following Edward's Abdication

RULER EXPECTED TO GO INTO EXILE WHEN LAW IS PASSED

Hushed Parliament Hears Reading Of Message And Baldwin's Explanation Of Negotiations Extending Over Several Months

U. S. To Hear Edward's Address

New York, Dec. 10 (AP)—King Edward's message to the British Empire which he is to deliver tomorrow over the British Broadcasting Company, will be carried in this country by both the National Broadcasting Company and Columbia Broadcasting System. The announced time is 5 P. M. (E.S.T.).

[By the Associated Press]

London, Friday, Dec. 11—Edward VIII renounced the throne of the British Empire for a woman's love and today the Duke of York, his brother and successor, took on his shoulders the problems of a troubled world.

Thus forces were set in motion which may not be fully judged in this generation.

Still King and Emperor, Edward awaited one last document, the law of abdication, before becoming David Windsor, who would marry Wallis Warfield Simpson, American born and twice divorced.

Brothers Have Dinner Together

The King and the King-to-be had probably their last dinner together in Edward's retreat at Fort Belvedere. There Edward gave what counsel he could to the brother who will succeed him when the law dethroning the one and enthroning the other is passed by Parliament and signed by Edward today. That will end his role as King.

Farewell to his 495,000,000 subjects will be spoken by Edward in a broadcast tonight. It was announced he will speak as a simple citizen. He may not even speak from England. He may speak from France, where he is expected to fly when he formally lays down his scepter and starts his new life.

Edward Expected To Leave Country

He will be an exile in fact for a time, if not by legal requirement. His abdication, read in Parliament yesterday, gave his decision as "irrevocable" and surrendered rights to the throne in the name of any descendants. He cut himself off for all time for the woman he loves and who waits for him at Cannes, where from the villa Lou Viei she looked out through drizzling rain, under dark clouds at an uneasy sea.

"Long live the King," shouted many tonight but many also were quiet, disturbed and uneasy. They symbolized the world's unrest, the changing times that shadow the universe with war and threat of war, political upheavals, economic changes and grave doubt of what the future may bring.

While "Long live the King" echoed the British Parliament heard predictions of the end of kings.

Three members attacked the Government, the King and monarchic system.

Laborite Assails Monarchy

James Maxton, Left-wing Laborite, declared the "institution of monarchy has outlived its usefulness" and pointed to the present crisis as a lesson.

Socialist George Buchanan spoke of "pampered royalty" which is "surrounded by a set of flunkies."

"If the King was one-tenth as good as you say he was, why does everyone want him to be unloaded? It is because you know he was a weak creature and you want to get rid of him."

William Gallacher, only Communist in Parliament, called the crisis "an issue between two groups who were fighting continually for domination."

Damage "Irrepairable"

"It will not be possible," he said, "to repair the damage that has been done to the monarchical institution of this country."

These minority voices, raised amid a floodtide of satisfaction and approval, expressed publicly and boldly the anxieties business men and politicians have spread in mild terms as they questioned the future.

The crisis halted factories making souvenirs for the coronation May 12 and it will cost great sums in replacing objects labeled with Edward's name and face.

The crisis went, economists said, deeper than that.

Commons Hears Decision

Prime Minister Stanley Baldwin himself touched on the seriousness of the case Monday when he told the House of Commons "any considerable prolongation of the present state of suspense and uncertainty would in-

1937

At about 7 P.M. on the night of May 6, 1937, Captain Max Pruss of the *Hindenburg* received word that he could land the airship at the naval air station at Lakehurst, New Jersey.

The German-made *Hindenburg*, "the silvery queen of the skies," was about to complete its first transatlantic flight of the season. It had taken three days to carry the thirty-one passengers and a crew of sixty-nine from Frankfurt, Germany.

As the ground crew waited below, the *Hindenburg* dropped its landing lines and approached the mooring mast nose first.

Then, suddenly, a dull explosion near the tail and a bright flash of light.

In forty-seven seconds, fire completely devoured the zeppelin and reduced it to a flaming skeleton.

Thirteen passengers died, as did twenty-three of the crew, including one on the ground.

Some, somehow, survived.

Investigations determined a probable cause—static electricity touching off some leaking hydrogen gas.

See Pages 18, 19, 20 and 21 for Stories and Pictures on Zeppelin Disaster

THE WEATHER
Fair Today and Tomorrow. Slightly Warmer Tomorrow. (See Page 2.)

ASBURY PARK EVENING PRESS

FINAL EDITION

FIFTY-FIRST YEAR. NO. 108 | ASBURY PARK, N. J., FRIDAY, MAY 7, 1937 | PRICE THREE CENTS

HINDENBURG TOLL IS SET AT 35

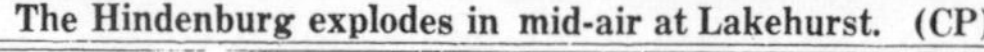

The Hindenburg explodes in mid-air at Lakehurst. (CP)

A stricken giant falls to her doom. (CP)

Shore Squads Race to Scene

150 Men Answer Call for Aid as They Did in Morro Fire.

Minutes after a belch of smoke and flame sprang from the stern of the majestic Hindenburg, shore first aid squads were racing thru the downpour of the season's first severe thunder storm, reenacting the scene they played on a late summer morning, Sept. 8, 1934, when the Morro Castle suddenly caught fire eight miles off Belmar.

Thruout Monmouth and Ocean counties whistles, bells, horns and sirens sounded a call to action for more than 150 men. Some left dinners unfinished, others forgot sports pages and the news columns of the evening papers, in another home the baby sat half washed in the bath tub, in still another a family argument remained unsettled.

Somewhere, someone lay injured. Duty called the first aid squad.

"What, t'e Hindenburg?"

While alarms still sounded thruout the Jersey shore, racing motors and howling sirens faced the pelting rain. Here and there was lightning and thunder, foretelling death and suffering; just as a roaring east wind predicted death when the luxury liner met its fate.

Ambulances Converge on Lakehurst

From Matawan and Atlantic Highlands at the northern extremities of Monmouth county to the southern reaches of Ocean county, speeding, red white and brown messengers of mercy converged on the Lakehurst station.

Manned by four, five and six men, the ambulances sped toward the scene of the disaster with other squad members, unable to reach the cars in time to ride, starting to the field in their own autos.

In this city the alarm brought the response of the fire department first aid squad. Dr. Daniel F. Featherston and Fire Chief William S. Taggart hurried to the scene in the chief's car. Close behind was the city ambulance manned by Capt. William Tighe and Firemen Wynn Graham and William Palhaeber.

From Avon, Belmar, Bradley Beach, Eatontown, Oakhurst, Wanamassa, Manasquan, Lakewood, Spring Lake, Toms River, Point Pleasant, Ocean

(Continued on Page 20)

Press Reporter, Witness, Tells of Horrible Scene

Sight of Staggering Passengers and Crew, Flesh Whitened by Burning Gases, Appalling—Shock Written on Faces of Survivors.

By CARL L. KEMPF
Staff Correspondent

LAKEHURST—The spectacle of the Hindenburg, majestic queen of the skies, bursting into flames 100 feet in the air as it coasted up to within 300 feet of its mooring mast at the Lakehurst Naval Air station last night, was appalling. The sight of the injured passengers and crew, their flesh whitened by the burning gases, being carried or staggering from the wreckage was horrible.

Shock was written on the faces of the few who were able to sense the danger and leap from the ship as it fell in flames. Their tongues were mute from their brush with death.

Officials, ground crew, photographers and reporters had been impatient as the ship hovered off the coast and over Barnegat bay in the sunshine while showers drenched the landing field. Twice the men were placed to the east of the mast, shortly after 6 o'clock, in preparation for grabbing the mooring lines to pull the air giant to the mast it never was to reach. Twice the men were driven shivering to the inadequate shelter of the planking of the mast's platform while the rain swept across the field.

At last, out of a bank of clouds to the southwest, the ship approached. By now the wind had shifted to the south and dropped to four knots, according to the huge neon letters set at the edge of the field to guide the navigators.

The Hindenburg floated across the field, its commander awaiting an opportunity to come down. It swung to the south again, and headed toward the mast, bore off toward the west and valved water from the stern as the propellers roared in reverse. The ground crew rushed the mooring lines toward the new position.

I could imagine the hustle of the passengers gathering belongings together in preparation of debarkation. I could imagine the crew at stations awaiting the commands which would bring the ship to its berth.

Mooring Lines Drop

In the nose a porthole opened and a sand bag with guide line attached dropped out to the ground. I looked at my watch. It was 7:20 p. m. A few seconds later, and a second porthole opened and another mooring line hit the ground. The 150 ground crew men ran to grab the lines. The front propellers idled. The left rear blades roared in reverse holding the ship steady for its first contact with the ground since the take off at Frankfort on Main. It was a thrilling sight. Then:

POOFF.

A mass of flames burst from the rear of the silvered structure about 100 feet from the stern fins. God! Can they make it?

POOFF! Another burst of flames about the middle of the craft. And the stern started to settle slowly.

A gasp went up from those on the ground.

Then the ground crew ran, as the 800 foot mass of blazing fabric and hydrogen came down upon them. The ship started to drift toward the mooring mast and the group of officials. They broke and ran.

(Continued on Page 20)

Fred G. Hurley Hurt By Ambulance Jolt

POINT PLEASANT.—Fred G. Hurley, president of the New Jersey State Council of First Aid Squads, was injured last night at the Lakehurst Naval Air station as the Point Pleasant Beach first aid ambulance in which he was riding struck a raised railroad crossing on the grounds.

Hurley suffered dislocation of several vertebrae and was recovering today at Beach Boros hospital here. He was thrown from his place in the front seat against the windshield. Claude Asay, another member of the aid squad, suffered a slight leg injury in the same mishap.

The ambulance was slightly damaged.

Hospital Patients

The following passengers and crew members were admitted to four shore hospitals during the night following the Hindenburg disaster. Their names and condiion as reported today follow:

At Paul Kimball hospital, Lakewood:

Passengers

Philip Mangone, 25 East End avenue, New York.

George Hirschfeld, 36, Bremen and New York.

William G. Leuchtenberg, 64, Larchmont, N. Y.

Hans Hugo Witt.

Hans Vinholt.

Clifford Osbun, 904 Vine avenue, Park Ridge, Ill.

Otto Ernst, Hamburg cotton broker.

Lt. Col. Nelson Morris, Chicago meat packer.

Crew

Commander Max Pruss, 46, badly burned.

Captain Ernst Lehmann, 52, condition serious.

Albert Samnit, 44, Frankfort.

Theodore Ritter, 25, mechanic.

Franz Herzog, navagation officer, critical.

Adolph Fisher.

Ralph Stahler.

Joseph Leibrecht, 33, electrician.

August Deutschler, 28, mechanic.

Ludwig Felber, died at 11:50.

Dr. Retiger, ship's doctor, first and second degree burns.

William Speck, 46, chief radio operator.

Walter Bernholzer, died 2:45 a. m.

Charles Axel, ground crew, Lakehurst.

Schoenherr.

(Continued On Page 20)

Motorists Must Keep Away From Lakehurst

TRENTON, (AP)—Col. Mark O. Kimberling, state police superintendent, appealed to motorists today to remain away from Lakehurst, scene of the Hindenburg disaster, this weekend "unless they have important business in that territory."

Expressing fear of the hazards of traffic snarls, Colonel Kimberling said about 100 state troopers had been assigned to keep automobiles moving away from the Naval Air base.

"They will not allow sightseers near the reservation," he said, and added: "Curios persons will not be able to see anything anyhow."

34 Survivors Are Treated At Four Shore Hospitals

Pruss and Lehmann at Paul Kimball, Lakewood, Suffering Second Degree Burns—Crew, Passengers Mutter Tragic Stories—Luther Visits Them.

Four shore hospitals today ministered to the searing wounds of 34 Hindenburg survivors—among them Capt. Max Pruss, commander of the mighty German airship that crashed in flames at Lakehurst last night, and Capt. Ernst A. Lehmann, former skipper of the dirigible, who sailed in an advisory capacity on the Hindenburg's last crossing.

Captain Pruss, Captain Lehmann and 19 other officers, members of the crew and passengers are in the Paul Kimball hospital, Lakewood; seven are being cared for at Fitkin hospital, Neptune; four are confined to the Beach Boros hospital, Point Pleasant, and four more to the Royal Pines Hotel and Clinic, Pinewald.

Pruss and Lehmann were reported in "fair" condition this morning, but hospital authorities feared that serious second degree burns might seal forever the lips of the two men who might be able to shed some light on the mysterious explosion which demolished the air queen.

Two men, both members of the crew, died at Paul Kimball during the night. They were Ludwig Felber, who expired shortly before midnight, and Walter Bernholzer, who succumbed at 2:45 a. m.

Irene Doehner, 13-year-old daughter of a Mexico City pharmacist who perished in the blaze, died at Beach Boros hospital at 3:30 a. m.

Others in critical condition at the Lakewood hospital include Franz Herzog, navigation officer of the Hindenburgh and Dr. Retiger, the ship's surgeon.

Nurses and doctors had difficulty establishing the identity of the injured and dying as most of them spoke only German. They were aided in the early morning hours, however, by Capt. Carl Weigand of the S. S. Deutschland of the Hamburg-American line, and the Rev. Father Humbert Osterman, Seaside Park, both of whom talked to all the officers at the Lakewood hospital.

Additional Workers Help

The entire day staff remained on duty at Paul Kimball, while 25 additional nurses and 13 physicians treated the suffering survivors. A supply of tannic acid, used in the treatment of severe burns, was rushed to the hospital by the Lilley Pharmaceutal company.

George Hirschfeld, 36, a Bremen cotton broker with offices in New York city, was comfortable enough to tell of his escape from the burning airship.

"I was standing about in the middle of the promenade deck," he told his New York representative, Adam T.

(Continued on page twenty-one)

Possible Causes of Hindenburg Disaster

(Staff Correspondent)

LAKEHURST—The possibility that the Hindenburg was heavily charged with static electricity which discharged a spark into the ship's hydrogen gas when a wet mooring line made contact with the ground was a theory held by many observers here today.

The ship would have gathered static in the electrical storm which developed over the Jersey shore yesterday afternoon.

A flash of lightning as the ship's cables struck the ground might have caused the explosion. Prof. John C. Albright, professor of physics and meteorology at the Case School of Applied Science in Cleveland, said the lightning would have struck at the highest point in the bag and probably would have not been noticed in the confusion.

Gill Robb Wilson, state aviation commissioner, said he believed leakage of gas within the ship had been ignited by a motor backfire when the ship reversed her motors. He said he was certain the fire started within the ship.

Many Survivors Badly Burned

Twenty-Six Bodies Recovered From Wreckage of Sky Queen--Investigations Launched as Sabotage Is Hinted--Spectator Victim.

LATEST DEVELOPMENTS

Death toll in Hindenburg disaster was set at 35 today.

Sixty-six survivors, several of them near death, were accounted for. Four shore hospitals were caring for 34 passenger and crew members.

In Germany Dr. Hugo Eckener, famous dirigible skipper, declared we "must make an about face and abandon hydrogen." (Story on page 21)

Loss of Hindenburg causes Lakehurst to fear for future of naval air station. (Story on page 20)

(Staff Correspondent)

LAKEHURST.—The cold ashes of the once mighty Hindenburg, Germany's proud queen of the skies, lay on the landing field of the Naval Air station at Lakehurst today mute testimony to the ferocity of the explosion and fire which racked her early last night, killing 35 of her passengers and crew and leaving 64 others horribly burned and injured.

Sorrow settled over this town of airships, which has seen the Akron, the Shenandoah and the Macon sail away to their doom, as the German and American governments took swift action to determine the cause of the disaster.

Washington officials and Dr. Hans Luther, soon to retire as German ambassador to the United States, opened inquiries—all, however, relating to the highly inflammable hydrogen gas used in the big ship for lifting.

Rosendahl Reports

Commdr. Charles E. Rosendahl, commandant of the air station, said in his report to the navy department "about four minutes after the ropes had been dropped a fire appeared in the after part of the ship and worked progressively forward."

"The ship settled to the ground tail first and was practically completely ablaze for her entire length by the time the ground was reached. . . ."

Dr. Raymond A. Taylor, Lakewood, Ocean county coroner, said he would decide, after a conference with officials, whether or not there would be a county inquest.

Gathered at the administration building for the conference were Dr. Luther, General von Boettischer, military attache of the German embassy; Rear Admiral Arthur B. Cook, chief of the bureau of aeronautics of the United States; Col.

THE WAR YEARS, II

War began in Europe.

Germany, without warning, invaded Poland in a *blitzkrieg* of surprise air and tank attacks.

Great Britain and France declared war on Germany.

The Soviet Union invaded Poland from the east, splitting the nation in two.

President Roosevelt declared U.S. neutrality.

The Academy Award nominations for Best Picture were *Gone With the Wind, The Wizard of Oz, Dark Victory, Of Mice and Men, Goodbye Mr. Chips, Ninotchka, Love Affair, Mr. Smith Goes to Washington, Stagecoach,* and *Wuthering Heights.* (It was also the year *Gunga Din* was released.)

Suddenly, early on the morning of Sunday, December 7, 1941, in Hawaii, fighters and bombers of the Japanese Navy swooped down on the American naval base at Pearl Harbor. They destroyed scores of U.S. planes, sunk or severely damaged seven battleships, and crippled three cruisers and three destroyers.

The surprise assault took 2,330 lives and left more than 1,000 wounded.

The next day, President Roosevelt stood before a joint session of Congress. Characterizing the Pearl Harbor attack as a "a day that will live in infamy," he called for a declaration of war against Japan.

First war issues of the Honolulu *Star-Bulletin* said that the Honolulu *Advertiser* was unable to publish December 7 or early December 8 because of a break in its press. The *Advertiser* denied it was because of sabotage.

In addition to printing its own regular and extra editions, on the morning of December 8, the *Star-Bulletin* printed the regular morning edition of the *Advertiser.*

Days later, Germany and Italy joined Japan in declaring war against the United States.

In 1940, the United States started preparing for the inevitable.

Congress created the Selective Service System, the first peacetime draft. It required all men between the ages of twenty-one and thirty-six to register for military service.

German armies invaded Denmark, Norway, Holland, Belgium, and Luxembourg.

Italy declared war on Britain and France.

Germany started its bombing of London.

Winston Churchill was named prime minister of Great Britain and spoke of the "blood, toil, tears, and sweat" to come.

[*text continued*]

ON TODAY'S EDITORIAL PAGE
A Tribute to Lloyd C. Stark: Editorial.
The President's Speech: Editorial.
Collusion in High Building Costs: Mirror of Public Opinion.

ST. LOUIS POST-DISPATCH

The Only Evening Newspaper in St. Louis With the Associated Press News Service

FINAL
(Closing New York Stock Prices)
**

VOL. 93. NO. 116. (63rd Year.) ST. LOUIS, MONDAY, DECEMBER 30, 1940.—22 PAGES PRICE 3 CENTS

DEMOCRATS WILL CONTEST DONNELL'S ELECTION, TO ASK LEGISLATIVE INVESTIGATION

UNDER THIS PLAN NO WINNER WILL BE NAMED UNTIL INQUIRY IS ENDED

Decision Reached After Chairman Hulen Presents Evidence Gathered by Special Investigators on Technical Errors in Vote.

JEFFERSON CITY, Dec. 30.—The Democratic State Committee this afternoon decided to petition the Legislature to conduct "a general and sweeping investigation of the vote cast for Governor." This is the method of contesting the election described in yesterday's Post-Dispatch, which would keep Forrest C. Donnell from taking the governorship, pending decision on the investigation.

By CURTIS A. BETTS
Staff Correspondent of the Post-Dispatch.

JEFFERSON CITY, Dec. 30.—The Democratic State Committee met at noon today in the Senate lounge to hear a report from C. Marion Hulen, State Democratic chairman, on which, it is expected, the committee will direct that a contest be instituted in the Legislature in an effort to seat Lawrence McDaniel, Democrat, in place of Forrest C. Donnell, who was shown by the election returns to have been elected Governor by a plurality of 3613 votes.

The contest procedure will be to appoint a legislative committee with power to hear testimony and recount the ballots in disputed precincts. It is probable that several months would be required to take the testimony.

Some of Objections.

An issue of the legality of the election in some precincts will be based on the ground that the voting places were not provided with booths, and that voters were forced to mark their ballots in public. There is a report that the Democrats will ask that the total vote of these precincts be thrown out, holding that failure to have booths did not conform to the constitutional requirement for a secret ballot.

In other precincts, it is said, there is a large number of ballots which were counted for Donnell illegally. These ballots, it is said, contained crosses in the circle at the top of the Democratic ticket, a line was drawn through McDaniel's name, and crosses placed in the square to the left of Donnell's name.

Hulen has refused to make public any of the evidence gathered by 10 investigators he has had at work since the election, but it is reported the evidence consists entirely of technical irregularities and that no evidence of intentional fraud has been found.

It is known that several members of the Legislature are opposed to proceeding with a contest in the absence of a showing of fraud and are opposed to exercising the Legislature's

Continued on Page 3, Column 2.

'CITY' FINANCIAL DISTRICT IS PART OF LONDON LYING WITHIN ANCIENT BOUNDARIES

LONDON, Dec. 30 (AP).

THE City is that part of London which lies within the boundaries of ancient London. It has a population of about 11,000 persons, but in the daytime this number is swelled by many thousands of workers and business men from the rest of London and areas as far as the south coast. The Bank of England is situated there.

British Government offices, Buckingham Palace, the houses of Parliament and the main shopping center of London are in the City of Westminster, which lies west of the City of London.

The Guildhall, which dates from the early fifteenth century, has been hit before by German raiders. It is a hall where great city functions are held and adjoining it are a library, museum and art gallery.

TODAY'S WAR NEWS

LONDON—Great fires set in heart of London in worst incendiary bomb attack of war; ancient City (financial) district hardest hit; many firemen and wardens killed battling flames; damage heavy; R. A. F. attacks invasion ports and objective in Germany.

BUDAPEST — Hungary begins mobilizing army as Germany masses troops on Bulgarian border; force moving through Hungary into Rumania now estimated at 800,000.

ROME—British bomb Naples, killing seven persons; British attack reported repulsed on Egyptian-Libyan frontier; Italian warships bombard Greeks in southern Albania.

ATHENS—Greeks report strong Italian counterattacks repulsed north of Chimara and in Klisura region.

BERLIN—Germans report English Rolls-Royce plant bombed; say bombers sank one ship, set another afire in attack on British convoy.

U. S. PRODUCING 700 PLANES, 2400 MOTORS A MONTH

More Than 10,000 Semi-Automatic Rifles and 100 Tanks, Says Defense Commission Report.

WASHINGTON, Dec. 30 (AP).—The Defense Commission reported today that the country's arms output was up to 2400 aircraft motors, 700 planes, more than 10,000 semi-automatic rifles and 100 tanks a month.

The defense program, the commission said, already has put a million persons to work in the last two months, and "several million more will be needed by next November."

The agency likewise reported that it had approved contracts totaling more than 10 billion dollars and that the army and navy had awarded nine-tenths of these, including $3,300,000,000 for ships, $1,500,000,000 for factory expansion and housing, $1,300,000,000 for planes and parts, $400,000,000 for ammunition, $500,000,000 for guns and $400,000,000 for trucks and tanks.

These contracts, plus those placed by the British and other nations, commit American industry to produce 50,000 airplanes and 130,000 airplane motors, 9200 tanks, 2,065,000 guns of all kinds and their ammunition, 380 navy ships, 200 merchant ships, 210 camps and cantonments, clothing and equipment for 1,200,000 men and 50,000 trucks.

Factories Under Contract.

Also under contract are 40 Government factories, among them the first mass-production tank factory in the world, five explosive plants, six ammunition plants and five machine-gun plants.

Gun contracts embrace 400,000 automatic rifles, 17,000 heavy guns, 25,000 light guns, 13,000 trench mortars, 300,000 machine guns. Other contracts call for 33,000,000 loaded shells.

Another item was that a new

Continued on Page 3, Column 2.

TREND OF TODAY'S MARKETS

Stocks firm; industrials extend rally. Bonds improved. Foreign exchange quiet. Cotton firm. Metals steady. Wheat firm. Corn firm.

HUNGARY BEGINS MOBILIZING ARMY AS NAZIS MASS ON BULGARIA BORDER

Action Viewed as Possible Move to Bolster German Flank Against Russia If Hitler Strikes South toward Greece and Turkey.

BUDAPEST, Dec. 30 (AP). — Hungary began mobilizing additional troops today in a movement reported designed to lead to total mobilization by next Jan. 15.

The action was interpreted in some quarters as a sign of one more step in German preparations for war in the Balkans, where Hungary's army might help strengthen the German flank against Soviet Russia while the Nazis struck south toward Greece and Turkey.

Mobilization cards reached thousands of Hungarian men of military age last night and this morning.

This coincided with reports of renewed Russian military activity on highways running from Lwow (Lemberg), in Russian Poland, to the Slovak frontier.

The flow of German troops and equipment continued at top capacity of the Hungarian and Rumanian railroads, some of the forces going as far as the Bulgarian frontier.

New Nazi Thrust Expected

Hungary's action, with several other signs in the Balkans, strengthened the belief of observers that a new German thrust was in preparation.

Many were of the opinion that Germany, now reported to be increasing its forces in Rumania to some 800,000 men, is preparing its own Balkan army and the armies of its Balkan and Central European allies for double duty—striking south against Greece and Turkey, but at the same time protecting the northern flank against a possible Russian thrust.

This was taken to mean Berlin had not received Moscow's promise to stay neutral if the Germans drove deeper in to the Balkans or, if such a promise had been given, that the Germans were taking no chances.

Bulgaria Uneasy Over Move.

Adding to the Balkan tension was the presence of an advance guard of German troops on the Rumanian-Bulgarian frontier and the resignation of Hungary's Minister of Agriculture, Michael Teleki, because of a reported difference with his Government over the mass movement of German soldiers through his nation.

Reports from Sofia, the Bulgarian capital, said King Boris III was expected to make an important radio speech on New Year's day. It was believed he would give the nation the key to his policy on the presence of German troops at Bulgaria's front door.

Nervous Bulgars, knowing well that their country constitutes a potential avenue to Greece, to Turkey or to the Russian-dominated Black Sea, wondered where and how far the steady surge of Nazi troops would spread.

Informed quarters said Bulgaria probably would permit passage of German forces only under protest, recognizing the "futility" of armed resistance, if the Nazis attempted such a movement.

German troops moving to aid

Continued on Page 4, Column 2.

GERMANS SET FIRE TO HEART OF LONDON IN FIERCE RAID

Worst Incendiary Attack of War Causes Heavy Damage to Financial District — Thousands Fight Flames.

LONDON, Dec. 30 (AP). — The smashed, blackened ruins of many buildings littered London's ancient "City," the heart of the capital, today after Nazi fire bombs had rained down last night in the fiercest incendiary raid of the war.

Scarcely a street in the busy business district stretching eastward from the Strand was unmarked by fire or undamaged by high explosives.

Damage was expected to run into millions of pounds sterling. Casualties in the center of London were said to be few, but the toll throughout the London area was unestimated.

In contrast to last night's operations, a Government communique this evening announced: "During daylight today bombs have been dropped by single enemy aircraft at one point in East Anglia and a place in Kent. The damage done was slight and casualties few."

Scores of landmarks were damaged or destroyed in last night's attack. Among them were the Guildhall and the Church of St. Lawrence Jewry in the Guildhall Yard, which Sir Christopher Wren built and where Dick Whittington worshipped.

Night Fighters Effective.

Royal Air Force fighters were credited with saving London from still worse destruction.

When the German bombers first flew over the city and scattered their incendiaries, ground defenses shot up a heavy anti-aircraft barrage.

But their guns ceased firing when the glow of fires began to light the sky and the roar of fighter planes swooping in to smash and scatter the German formations was heard.

While firemen and police battled the flames with dynamite and tons of water, the R. A. F. patrolled the sky and gave them a chance to work unmolested by the high explosive bombs usually thrown into a fire area.

Broad areas of London were hit, but the raid centered on the City. The Government described the assault as a "deliberate attempt" to burn out Britain's hub of empire.

The fires were the greatest threat to the ancient City since it was rebuilt after being laid waste by its great fire in the seventeenth century.

Rain Checks Flames.

Rain which swept over England after London's water pressure began to fail at the height of the fire-fighting helped keep the flames in check.

St. Paul's Cathedral, menaced before by delayed-action bombs and fires, was saved when firemen, working through a hail of explosives which killed some of their number, prevented flames from spreading from neighboring buildings.

Continued on Page 4, Column 4.

RAIN LATE TODAY OR TOMORROW; NOT MUCH CHANGE

THE TEMPERATURES.

1 a. m.	38	8 a. m.	37
2 a. m.	38	10 a. m.	37
3 a. m.	38	11 a. m.	37
4 a. m.	38	12 noon	38
5 a. m.	37	1 p. m.	38
6 a. m.	37	2 p. m.	38
7 a. m.	37	3 p. m.	39

Normal maximum this date, 39; normal minimum, 24.

Yesterday's high, 46 (1 p. m.); low, 36 (12:10 a. m.).

Weather in other cities—Page 4B.

Official forecast for St. Louis and vicinity: Cloudy with occasional light rain beginning late tonight or tomorrow; not much change in temperature.

Missouri: Occasional light rain in west portion tonight and tomorrow, and beginning in east portion late tonight or tomorrow; somewhat warmer in southwest and south central portions tonight.

Illinois: Cloudy tonight, followed by rain tomorrow night and Wednesday, and in west and south portions tomorrow; slightly warmer in south portion tomorrow.

(All weather data, including forecast and temperatures, supplied by U. S. Weather Bureau.)

14,685 Marriage Licenses in City This Year Establish New Record

The marriage license bureau at City Hall has issued 14,685 licenses this year—the highest number since the bureau was opened 60 years ago, and an increase of 24.5 per cent over the previous record year of 1936, when 11,796 were issued.

Bureau clerks expressed the opinion that causes of the record were the draft; better times, which permitted many couples to marry after long delay, and the continuing demand for licenses by Illinois residents avoiding that State's marriage health law which became effective in 1937.

In the last 25 years, the smallest number of licenses—4615—was issued during the depression in 1932. Since then there has been a gradual increase. In 1930 the number was 11,332. In 1917, the year the United States entered the World War, 8528 licenses were issued.

Issuance of licenses at the East St. Louis bureau dropped precipitously after the Illinois marriage law went into effect—from 1196 in 1936 to 607 in 1937 and 232 in 1938, the lowest in memory of Clerk Thomas Murphy. Last year, 245 were issued, this year, 176.

ROOSEVELT DECLARES U.S. IS IN DANGER, CALLS FOR MORE AID TO BRITAIN, ASSERTS AXIS IS NOT GOING TO WIN WAR

Making Momentous Declaration

—Associated Press Wirephoto.

PRESIDENT ROOSEVELT faced this battery of radio microphones when he delivered his talk on national security in the Oval Room at the White House. He read from the looseleaf notebook on the table before him.

TALK OF GRANTING BRITAIN A BIGGER PORTION OF ARMS

WASHINGTON, Dec. 30 (AP).—Secretary of the Treasury Morgenthau disclosed today that President Roosevelt's "lease-lending" plan for financing war materials "might apply" to Greece, China and other countries.

WASHINGTON, Dec. 30 (AP).—President Roosevelt's declaration that United States experts would determine how best to use American armament production "to defend this hemisphere" gave rise today to belief that an upward revision was contemplated in the present 50-50 formula governing aid to Britain.

"The decision as to how much shall be sent abroad and how much shall remain at home must be made on the basis of our over-all military necessities," Roosevelt said in his address last night.

Heretofore, a "rule of thumb" limited British aid to approximately 50 per cent of United States arms production and the intimation that this policy might be abandoned for a higher percentage was one point commanding congressional attention as legislators studied and commented on the speech.

Those believing the 50-50 formula would be abandoned cited another passage of the speech which they considered pertinent. In this, Roosevelt said:

"It is a matter of most vital concern to us that European and Asiatic war-makers should not gain control of the oceans which lead to this hemisphere . . . If Great Britain goes down, the Axis powers will control the continents of Europe, Asia, Africa, Australasia and the high seas and they will be in a position to bring enormous military and naval resources against this hemisphere."

Senator Austin (Rep.), Vermont, the acting minority leader, said his impression was that the President "kept his hands untied" on the amount of defense production to be sent to Britain and had left the administration "free to take any position which our military necessities make obvious."

Senator Wheeler (Dem.), Montana,

Continued on Page 6, Column 2.

JAPANESE ADMIT 100,000 MEN KILLED; SAY CHINA LOST 1,800,000 IN WAR

TOKYO, Dec. 30 (AP).

THE Japanese War Department announced today that 1,800,000 Chinese and 100,000 Japanese have been killed since hostilities began in July, 1937.

Of the total casualties, the War Department said in a review of the conflict, 580,000 Chinese and 13,000 Japanese were killed in 1940.

AXIS TOLERANCE IS LIMITED, GAYDA REPLIES TO PRESIDENT

'OFF TO THE WARS,' SAYS SENATOR HIRAM JOHNSON, LEAVING FOR WASHINGTON

SAN FRANCISCO, Dec. 30 (AP).

SENATOR HIRAM W. JOHNSON, departing yesterday for Washington and the opening of the Seventy-seventh Congress, remarked he was "off to the wars."

"The President said he hates war, so maybe he won't get in it," said the Republican isolationist. "Of course, he's only going to have an army of four million men. Maybe he'll send them down to Tierra del Fuego."

Johnson will start his fifth term as Senator when Congress convenes Jan. 3.

REACTION TO SPEECH GRATIFIES ROOSEVELT

'Tremendously Pleased,' Aid Says—Messages Favor His Views, 100 to 1.

WASHINGTON, Dec. 30 (AP).—President Roosevelt was described today as "tremendously pleased" by the reaction to his defense address, in which he told the nation that it faced an emergency comparable only to war.

Stephen Early, a White House Secretary, said the President was gratified that leaders of both parties had praised the speech, because he had called for national effort and realized that it could be "attained quicker and more effectively by unity."

Last night's address, Early said, brought a greater response than any other Roosevelt had made. Messages ran about 100 to one in favor of the views expressed in it, he added, saying that the total was not yet available.

As a possible follow-up to the address, which advocated even more aid to Britain, Roosevelt had a luncheon engagement today with Secretary of the Treasury Morgenthau and Arthur B. Purvis, chairman of the British Purchasing Mission.

Purvis told reporters afterward that it was a "general talk on sup-

Continued on Page 6, Column 1.

Fascist Editor Calls Roosevelt a 'Man of Undeclared War' — No Indication of Nazi Reaction.

ROME, Dec. 30 (AP).—Virginio Gayda, authoritative Fascist editor, replied to President Roosevelt's fireside address today with a warning that the "tolerance" of the Rome-Berlin Axis is limited. He called the President "a man of undeclared war against the Axis."

Writing in Il Giornale d'Italia, Gayda cited two specific actions which, he said, would mean "open United States intervention for which no excuse could be created." But he indicated the Axis would not take any action until they had been put into effect.

The steps which Gayda said would bring America close to war were any attempt by American flag ships to force a counterblockade or the cession to Britain of German and Italian ships now taking refuge in United States harbors.

"Nothing New."

Gayda asserted that, in itself, the President's speech had produced "nothing new." He said it only confirmed the passage of the United States first from neutrality to nonbelligerency and from that to a state "short of war."

"It is not without significance that President Roosevelt showed he gives due consideration to that current of American public opinion which manifests considerable reluctance to be involved in war," one high Fascist said.

He reported Italy was "remaining faithful to her policy of intimate collaboration with her ally, Germany."

"Conscious of the tasks for which she is fighting in Europe and Africa, she looks with faith to the future with her war efforts bent toward victory and without worrying more than necessary about the attitude third parties may assume in favor of powers which are enemies of the Axis," he asserted.

Other Reaction.

Italian newspapers had anticipated the President's call for more aid to Britain. La Stampa of Turin raised the possibility that the United States might go so far in aiding Britain that it would become involved in war.

"One day when the White House

Continued on Page 6, Column 2.

Famous Matador Gored to Death Before Crowd of 30,000 in Mexico

MEXICO CITY, Dec. 30 (AP).—Pitched into the air and gored three times by a bull, Alberto Balderas, famous Mexican bullfighter, was killed yesterday in Mexico City's bull ring only a few minutes after 30,000 spectators had cheered his artistry in dispatching another bull.

He was the first matador and the third member of a bullfighting troupe to be killed in the arena since it was opened in 1906. Balderas was 29 years old.

THIS COUNTRY 'MUST BE THE GREAT ARSENAL OF DEMOCRACY'

President Says Expeditionary Force Will Not Be Sent — No Mention of Navy Nor Explicit Pledge to Stay Out of Conflict.

TEXT ON PAGE 1B.

By RAYMOND P. BRANDT
Chief Washington Correspondent of the Post-Dispatch.

WASHINGTON, Dec. 30.—In the bluntest language he has used to the American people and the rest of the world, President Roosevelt last night denounced "the unholy alliance" of the Axis dictators with their "pious frauds," and proclaimed that this country "must be the great arsenal of democracy."

Speaking from the White House over virtually every radio station in this country, including the short waves to foreign nations, Roosevelt called for a mightier effort than the United States has ever yet made to defend this country by further aid to Great Britain and its allies.

With solemn emphasis of every word, he declared:

"I believe that the Axis powers are not going to win this war. I base that belief on the latest and best information."

"We have no excuse for defeatism. We have every good reason for hope—hope for peace, hope for the defense of our civilization and for the building of a better civilization in the future."

Reply to "Appeasers."

The President's 37-minute address was the announcement of a policy, not a blueprint for action. It was a reply to what he called the "American appeasers" who are clamoring for a "negotiated peace," and an announcement to the European and Asiatic dictators that there will be no "bottlenecks" in our determination to aid Great Britain.

"No dictator, no combination of dictators," he asserted, "will weaken that determination by threats of how they will construe that determination."

The President declared that the sending of every ounce and every ton of munitions this country could spare to Britain would not necessarily be unneutral.

"It is no more unneutral for us to do that than it is for Sweden, Russia and other nations near Germany, to send steel and ore and oil and other war materials into Germany every day in the week."

As in his campaign speeches, the President promised that no American expeditionary force would be sent beyond our own borders, but he did not categorically promise that this country could stay out of war, nor did he mention any action the navy might take.

"Frankly and definitely," he said, "there is danger ahead—danger against which we must prepare. But we well know that we cannot escape danger or the fear of it, by crawling into bed and pulling the covers over our heads."

If Britain Falls.

Predicting that if Great Britain is defeated, this country would live at the point of a Nazi gun, the President said:

"Thinking in terms of today and tomorrow, I make the direct statement to the American people that there is far less chance of the United States getting into war, if we do all we can now to support the nations defending themselves against attack by the Axis than if we acquiesce in their defeat, submit tamely to an Axis victory, and wait our turn to be the object of attack in another war later on.

"If we are to be completely honest with ourselves, we must admit there is risk in any (the President placed great emphasis on "any") course we may take. But I deeply believe that the great majority of our people agree that the course that I advocate involves the least risk now and the greatest hope for world peace in the future."

The President did not discuss further details of his new "lease-lend" policy of aid to Britain—these probably will be revealed in his message to Congress—but he likely

Continued on Page 8, Column 6.

Honolulu Star-Bulletin 1st EXTRA

Evening Bulletin, Est. 1882, No. 11270
Hawaiian Star, Vol. XLVIII, No. 15380

8 PAGES—HONOLULU, TERRITORY OF HAWAII, U. S. A., SUNDAY, DECEMBER 7, 1941—8 PAGES

★ PRICE FIVE CEN

WAR!

(Associated Press by Transpacific Telephone)

SAN FRANCISCO, Dec. 7.—President Roosevelt announced this morning that Japanese planes had attacked Manila and Pearl Harbor.

OAHU BOMBED BY JAPANESE PLANES

SIX KNOWN DEAD, 21 INJURED, AT EMERGENCY HOSPITAL

Attack Made On Island's Defense Areas

By UNITED PRESS

WASHINGTON, Dec. 7. —Text of a White House announcement detailing the attack on the Hawaiian islands is:

"The Japanese attacked Pearl Harbor from the air and all naval and military activities on the island of Oahu, principal American base in the Hawaiian islands."

Oahu was attacked at 7:55 this morning by Japanese planes.

The Rising Sun, emblem of Japan, was seen on plane wing tips.

Wave after wave of bombers streamed through the clouded morning sky from the southwest and flung their missiles on a city resting in peaceful Sabbath calm.

According to an unconfirmed report received at the governor's office, the Japanese force that attacked Oahu reached island waters aboard two small airplane carriers.

It was also reported that at the governor's office either an attempt had been made to bomb the USS Lexington, or that it had been bombed.

CITY IN UPROAR

Within 10 minutes the city was in an uproar. As bombs fell in many parts of the city, and in defense areas the defenders of the islands went into quick action.

Army intelligence officers at Ft. Shafter announced officially shortly after 9 a. m. the fact of the bombardment by an enemy but long previous army and navy had taken immediate measures in defense.

"Oahu is under a sporadic air raid," the announcement said.

"Civilians are ordered to stay off the streets until further notice."

CIVILIANS ORDERED OFF STREETS

The army has ordered that all civilians stay off the streets and highways and not use telephones.

Evidence that the Japanese attack has registered some hits was shown by three billowing pillars of smoke in the Pearl Harbor and Hickam field area.

All navy personnel and civilian defense workers, with the exception of women, have been ordered to duty at Pearl Harbor.

The Pearl Harbor highway was immediately a mess of racing cars.

A trickling stream of injured people began pouring into the city emergency hospital a few minutes after the bombardment started.

Thousands of telephone calls almost swamped the Mutual Telephone Co., which put extra operators on duty.

At The Star-Bulletin office the phone calls deluged the single operator and it was impossible for this newspaper, for sometime, to handle the flood of calls. Here also an emergency operator was called.

HOUR OF ATTACK—7:55 A. M.

An official army report from department headquarters, made public shortly before 11, is that the first attack was at 7:55 a. m.

Witnesses said they saw at least 50 airplanes over Pearl Harbor.

The attack centered in the Pearl Harbor, Army authorities said:

"The rising sun was seen on the wing tips of the airplanes."

Although martial law has not been declared officially, the city of Honolulu was operating under M-Day conditions.

It is reliably reported that enemy objectives under attack were Wheeler field Hickam field, Kaneohe bay and naval air station and Pearl Harbor.

Some enemy planes were reported shot down.

The body of the pilot was seen in a plane burning at Wahiawa.

Oahu appeared to be taking calmly after the first uproar of queries.

ANTIAIRCRAFT GUNS IN ACTION

First indication of the raid came shodtly before 8 this morning when antiaircraft guns around Pearl Habor began sending up a thunderous barrage.

At the same time a vast cloud of black smoke arose from the naval base and also from Hickam field where flames could be seen.

BOMB NEAR GOVERNOR'S MANSION

Shortly before 9:30 a bomb fell near Washington Place, the residence of the governor. Governor Poindexter and Secretary Charles M. Hite were there.

It was reported that the bomb killed an unidentified Chinese man across the street in front of the Schuman Carriage Co. where windows were broken.

C. E. Daniels, a welder, found a fragment of shell or bomb at South and Queen Sts. which he brought into the City Hall. This fragrent weighed about a pound.

At 10:05 a. m. today Governor Poindexter telephoned to The Star-Bulletin announcing he has declared a state of emergency for the entire territory.

He announced that Edouard L. Doty, executive secretary of the major disaster council, has been appointed director under the M-Day law's provisions.

Governor Poindexter urged all residents of Honolulu to remain off the street, and the people of the territory to remain calm.

Mr. Doty reported that all major disaster council wardens and medical units were on duty within a half hour of the time the alarm was given.

Workers employed at Pearl Harbor were ordered at 10:10 a. m. not to report at Pearl Harbor.

The mayor's major disaster council was to meet at the city hall at about 10:30 this morning.

At least two Japanese planes were reported at Hawaiian department headquarters to have been shot down.

One of the planes was shot down at Ft. Kamehameha and the other back of the Wa-

Turn to Page 2, Column 1

Hundreds See City Bombed

Hundreds of Honolulans who hurried to the top of Punchbowl soon after bombs began to fall, saw spread out before them the whole panaroma of surprise attack and defense.

Far off over Pearl Harbor the white sky was polka-dotted with anti-aircraft smoke.

Rolling away from the navy base were billowing clouds of ugly black smoke. Sometimes a burst of flame reddened the black sources of the smoke.

Out from the silver-surfaced mouth of the harbor a flotilla of destroyers streamed to battle, smoke pouring from their stacks.

Turn to Page 2, Column 3

Schools Closed

All schools on Oahu, both public and private, will remain closed until further notice, Edouard L. Doty, territorial director of civilian defense, announced at 11 a. m. today. This does not apply elsewhere in the territory.

Names of Dead and Injured

The city emergency hospital reported at 10:30 a list of 6 killed and 21 injured.

The complete list will be carried later. Here is a partial list:

Peter Lopes, 34, of 2041 Kamanaiki St., was reported at 9:30 a. m. to be in serious condition from wounds in the upper abdomen.

Bernice Gouveia, 12, 2706 Kalihi St., is suffering from a mangled thigh, lacerations on the right leg and left arm.

A Portuguese girl, unidentified, 20 years old, died on arrival from puncture wounds.

Another victim who died on arrival was Frank Ohashi, 20, 2706 Kamanaiki St., from puncture wounds in the chest.

Cecelia Broadly, 28, Moanalua gardens, was released from the hospital after treatment for lacerations.

Three were reported injured and one reported killed from the bomb that fell at Fort and School Sts.

Editorial

HAWAII MEETS THE CRISIS

Honolulu and Hawaii will meet the emergency of war today as Honolulu and Hawaii have met emergencies in the past—coolly, calmly and with immediate and complete support of the officials, officers and troops who are in charge.

Governor Poindexter and the army and navy leaders have called upon the public to remain calm; for civilians who have no essential business on the streets to stay off; and for every man and woman to do his duty.

That request, coupled with the measures promptly taken to meet the situation that has suddenly and terribly developed, will be needed.

Hawaii will do its part—as a loyal American territory.

In this crisis, every difference of race, creed and color will be submerged in the one desire and determination to play the part that Americans always play in crisis.

BULLETIN

Additional Star-Bulletin extras today will cover the latest developments in this war move.

THE MILWAUKEE JOURNAL

Copyright, 1942, by The Journal Company

ixtieth Year | Circulation Yesterday ...... 285,760 Circulation One Year Ago ... 272,110 | Thursday, April 9, 1942 | Daily 3 Cents Sunday 10 Cents | 46 Pages—Latest Edition

Bataan Defense Crushed by Japs

WPB Puts Sharp Curb on New Construction

Residential Building Held to $500 Limit

ork Now in Progress May Be Halted Under Broad Order to Protect Vital Materials

ashington, D. C.—(AP)—A dras- government order blocking vir- ly all new construction work, ate and public, except for the effort, went into effect Thurs-

e war production board's order, ed late Wednesday, prohibited residential construction other maintenance and repair work e cost was $500 or more, for- any new agricultural construc- of $1,000 or more, and specified no other types of construction mmercial, industrial, recreation- stitutional, highway or utilities, ther publicly or privately fi- ced—could be started if the cost more than $5,000.

e only exceptions were in cases re specific government permis- might be granted.

arther, said WPB, projects now er construction are being ex- ined individually, and may be ped "if the scarce materials to sed in them can be put to more ctive use in the war program."

$500 Limit for Full Year

WPB Chairman Donald M. Nelson the action would virtually "sus- the civilian construction in- ry" for the duration. The la- department estimated previous- that nondefense construction d amount to $3,650,000,000 this

e $500 limit on residential con- tion applies to a full year, that owner may not spend $500 on eling and later make another

Turn to WPB Bans, page 4, col. 3

20,000 Workers Here Affected by Stoppage; Small Contractors to Feel the Pinch

The jobs of 20,000 construction trades workers in Milwaukee were at stake Thursday as a result of the war production board's ban on building. In addition, hundreds of small contractors face hard times.

Milwaukee county rolled up a construction total of more than $32,000,000 in 1941, and building has been almost as active so far this year. Under the WPB order, only construction essential to the war effort will be permitted after Thursday.

"We hope that war construction will absorb a large number of building workers, but the order is sure to result in unemployment," said Peter T. Schoemann, president of the Milwaukee Building and Construction Trades council.

"If a large number of building workers whose families live in Milwaukee have to migrate to Merrimac, Madison and other places where war plants are under construction, they will have to maintain temporary living quarters, at additional expense."

Thinks Order "Helpful"

The belief that the WPB order "will be helpful," although it will cause temporary dislocations, was expressed by A. G. Schmedeman, state director of the FHA office in the federal building. The FHA is in charge of priority applications for building materials and has been close to the construction situation in the defense areas of the state.

Schmedeman said the order would result in "building where it is needed" and would stabilize the building industry for the duration of the war. He said that the materials situation has been bad in some cities where the housing demand has boomed because of war plant expansions, while materials were relatively plentiful in other cities without war work.

Because the FHA has been handling priority applications for defense housing, it is expected that the office here will act as a clearing house for construction authorizations. WPB approval will be necessary to obtain a building permit.

Defense Housing to Go On

"The order does not stop defense housing construction, and that is a move in the right direction," said George L. Faber, president of the Milwaukee chapter of the Home Builders' institute. "At least the period of uncertainty is over. We know where we are."

Faber said that many small house projects have been held up because of uncertainty over how far government restrictions would go. He said the order was a green light for needed small houses in defense areas.

Construction volume in Milwaukee is still far under the peak of 1929, but it has been on the upgrade in the last three years. The total for 1941 in the city and suburbs was $22,400,000, compared with $23,600,000 in 1940.

So far this year, building permits have been issued for 606 dwelling units with a valuation of $2,833,700. In the first three months of 1941 permits were issued for 579 units. In 1941 Milwaukee county residents built a total of 3,834 dwelling units, averaging $4,654 in cost. The average for the 606 units this year has been $4,677.

The increase in average cost of dwelling units has been due to the

Turn to Workers, page 4, col. 1

Still Issue Permits

Leon M. Gurda, city building inspector, was doing business as usual Thursday. He told numerous telephone callers that he had received no official notice of a ban on building permits. Permits issued here Thursday included one for a duplex flat, two for single family dwellings and about a dozen for garages.

Milwaukee

Where Civil Service?

least two positions of some im- ance soon are to be filled by the One is that of harbor manager, other that of superintendent of et sanitation.

both instances requests have made that the jobs be filled r the so-called "expert clause" e civil service regulations—that promotion without examina-

rare instances such a course be justified. In most instances t. And, we think, the city serv- commission will pretty definite- ark itself, and establish its cali- by what it does in these two s.

it easily permits the elevation en individuals under the "expert se," it will be evading normal service procedure. If it insists xaminations—either promotion- restricted to city employes, or open to all competitors—it will llowing the principles it is cre- to uphold.

ere is little excuse for singling one man in the public service, ting him to a higher position, skirting around civil service to

e individual involved may be petent and deserving or he may e political favorite of a supe- or a group. To let down the in one or two or a dozen cases be to break down sound, non- ical and properly protective civil ice.

may be to invite the entrance political favoritisms and pres- into almost all cases of job g.

y political scramble for jobs ht to be scotched. Every public ought to be filled by men or en of ability, competent not only e the jobs but to compete against s for them.

ere is nothing peculiarly "ex- about the management of Mil- kee's harbor or the supervision s street sanitation. Both jobs ire ability, but it well may be somebody in New York, New eans or San Francisco has great- arbor managerial ability than e preselected Milwaukeean. Or ard foreman here, an engineer where, may have the best qualifi- ons for the street superintend-

[illegible] the city service commis- [illegible] on some sort of fair ex- [illegible] in the two cases now be- [illegible] it will cast doubts on its own [illegible] importance as a pro- [illegible] body.

The Weather

Compiled by U. S. Weather Bureau

Milwaukee—Little change in temperature Thursday afternoon; somewhat warmer Thursday night; light rain Friday forenoon, possibly beginning Thursday night.

Hour	5	6	7	8	9	10	11	12	1	2	3
Temp.	37	37	37	37	37	37	37	38	38	38	38

Wisconsin—Slightly warmer in west and north central portions; light rain in south portion and rain or snow in northeast portion Thursday night; rain in south and rain or snow in north portions Friday forenoon.

Temperature range Wednesday, 40 at 2 p. m. and 34 at 6 a. m.; precipitation for 24 hours ending at 6:30 a. m. Thursday, none.

Temperature range a year ago Wednesday, [illegible] and 36; precipitation, none.

Sunrise Friday, 6:18; sunset, 7:26.

Moonrise, [illegible] a. m. Friday; moonset, [illegible] p. m. Friday.

Weather summary and vital statistics, page 6, Part 2.

Store Burglar Sends Back Loot With an Apology

On the night of Mar. 26 burglars broke into the store of the Milwaukee Aquarium & Model Railroad Co., 3316 W. Lisbon av., and stole $19.65 in cash.

On Thursday the company received this unsigned typewritten letter from one of the burglars:

"I committed a wrong. Something that I never did in my life before. I shared in the $19 that was stolen from your store. I will never again be involved in such wrongdoing. Although I only shared in half of what was taken, I am enclosing the full amount. I have a guilty conscience and want to do the right thing. Please forgive me."

Enclosed were a $10 and two $5 bills—$20 in all, or 35c more than the amount stolen.

Dorsey Loses Draft Position

Negro Attorney Is Ousted as Appeal Agent; Says Order Is Surprise

James W. Dorsey, Negro attorney, was served Thursday with an order removing him as government appeal agent of Draft Board 6.

James Dorsey

The order was issued by Brig. Gen. L. B. Hershey, Washington, D. C., national selective service director, on recommendation of Gov. Heil. The effective date as stated in the order was Mar. 26.

The order was served by a deputy United States marshal at the request of the state selective service office at Madison. It gave no reason for the removal of Dorsey, whose offices are at 635-A W. Walnut st.

Gov. Heil could not be reached here for comment.

"For Good of Service"

At Madison, Bentley Courtenay, in charge of the state selective service office in the absence from the city of Col. John F. Mullen, acting state director, said that he was at liberty to say only that Dorsey's removal had been ordered "for the good of the service."

Courtenay explained that Col. Mullen, who is in Washington, and Gov. Heil had personally handled the Dorsey matter.

Courtenay said that the removal was a "routine proposition" and that "no implications should be drawn from it."

Surprised, Dorsey Says

Dorsey said he was "completely surprised" by the removal order.

"I knew nothing about it," he said, "and I know of no reason why I should have been removed."

Dorsey explained that when the reporter telephoned, he was talking to Paul G. Zedler, chairman of Draft Board 6, in his (Dorsey's) office about the removal order.

Zedler told the reporter:

"I can't for the world imagine what this is all about. I have often complimented Mr. Dorsey for his diligence in handling draft cases. He has worked hard. There has been no criticism of his work. The board is very well satisfied with his work."

Dorsey has been appeal agent ever since the selective service system was established. He was appointed by Gov. Heil. As appeal agent in the sixth ward, where Milwaukee's Negro population lives, he has handled many draft matters involving Negroes.

Agent's Duties Outlined

The duties of the appeal agent, as described in the selective service regulations, follow:

"The duties of the appeal agent are twofold. He shall protect the interest of registrants and their dependents by assisting them in the furnishing of information to the local board and by advising them concerning appeals. In order to protect the interests of the government or of registrants, he shall appeal any classification he thinks should be appealed."

Dorsey lives at 1730 N. 7th st. He has practiced law here since 1929. He formerly belonged to the Republican party. He twice failed of election as alderman of the sixth ward.

Autos, New Tires Stolen

Theft of his automobile which has four practically new tires was reported to police Wednesday by Joseph Saffro, Astor hotel. The car was taken at N. 17th st. and W. North av.

Two British Cruisers Sunk in India Battle

Lost in Aerial Attacks, London Says; Japanese Claim Big Toll of Ships in Bay of Bengal

From Press Dispatches

A grim naval-air showdown—with the fate of Ceylon if not India at stake—appeared Thursday to be under way in the Bay of Bengal between British warships and Japanese naval and air forces.

The British admiralty admitted the loss of the heavy cruisers Cornwall and Dorsetshire, sunk by Japanese planes off the coast of India.

Japanese broadcasts claimed that 44 Allied merchant ships had been sunk or damaged in the Bay of Bengal, and dispatches from Ceylon told of an enemy air raid on Trincomalee, British naval base on the east side of the island.

The Bengal bay naval fight was the first definite word on previous Axis radio reports of a British naval squadron led by the 31,100 ton battleship Malaya steaming into the Indian ocean to challenge the Japanese fleet.

Japs Step Up Activity

The sinking of the Cornwall and Dorsetshire was a blow to British naval strength immediately available to cope with Japanese aircraft carriers and warships reported increasing their activities astride the sea lanes to Calcutta in the bay between the bombed coast of India and invaded Burma.

There was no confirmation of a Berlin broadcast quoting dispatches purportedly from Tokyo that Japanese expeditionary forces supported by cruisers and destroyers landed last Sunday on the Burma west coast and were within 30 miles of the Bengal border of India. That would place them between the border and the big Burmese port of Akyab.

Earlier roundabout reports that the Japanese had forced their way ashore at Akyab have been denied by the British headquarters at New Delhi.

Other Ships Near, Belief

The admiralty's announcement did not say when the Dorsetshire and Cornwall were sunk, and there was no intimation what other warships were operating with the cruisers. The fact that 1,100 crew members were reported saved indicated that other ships were on hand. The crews of the two ships normally totaled about 1,330 men.

The Dorsetshire was a 9,975 ton ship. Its torpedoes finished off the German battleship Bismarck in the Atlantic little less than a year ago. The Cornwall displaced 10,000 tons.

The Rome radio reported that the remaining units of the British squadron were engaged in a running sea fight with stronger Japanese naval forces.

Informed sources in London believed the British Indian ocean squadron probably was operating from Trincomalee.

Systematic Japanese air reconnaissance is being maintained over the Bay of Bengal and, according to Tokyo broadcasts, Japanese submarines are operating in the Ganges estuary.

Tokyo broadcasts avoided mention of an offensive against India and said that these operations are being carried out with the objective of securing the flank of the Japanese forces fighting in Burma.

The Japanese Account

A communique broadcast from Tokyo said:

"During naval operations in the Indian ocean up to Apr. 7 the Japanese have sunk two British cruisers, one of the London type, 9,850 tons, and one of the Cornwall type, 10,000 tons.

"Forty-four merchant ships have been either sunk or damaged and 60 enemy planes have been shot down. The merchant ships included 21 vessels, approximating 140,000 tons, sunk and 23 others, approximating 102,000 tons, badly damaged.

"Three hangars and one repair factory and other important enemy facilities were seriously damaged.

"During the operations the Japanese forces lost five planes but sustained no damage to warships."

Survivors Are Landed

A New Delhi communique said that combined enemy naval and air attacks had resulted in the sinking of several Allied merchant ships in the Indian ocean area, and added that 400 to 500 survivors had landed on the Orissa coast.

Of the land fighting in Burma, dispatches Thursday said merely that Japanese were keeping up pressure against Chinese forces north of Toungoo.

English Trip for Morehouse

Milwaukeean to Be Guest at Enthronement of Temple as Archbishop

Clifford P. Morehouse of Milwaukee, editor of the Living Church, Episcopal weekly magazine published here, will leave for England this week by clipper plane as one of an official delegation of four Americans who will attend the enthronement of Dr. William Temple as the new archbishop of Canterbury.

Morehouse, who is vice-president of the Associated Church Press, and Dr. Henry Smith Leiper, New York, secretary of the Universal Christian council, will be in England as guests of the British ministry of information.

Also in the delegation are the Rt. Rev. James De Wolf Perry, Providence, R. I., the bishop of Rhode Island, who is being sent by Bishop Henry St. George Tucker of Virginia, the presiding bishop of the Episcopal church in this country, and Dr. William Adams Brown, retired professor of the Union Theological seminary, New York, who is being sent by the Rev. Dr. Luther Weigle, president of the Federal Council of Churches.

It is unprecedented to send a non-Anglican, or a "nonconformist," like Dr. Brown, who is a Presbyterian, to an enthronement.

Go to Other Enthronement

The delegation will also attend the enthronement of Dr. Cyril Garbett, who will succeed Dr. Temple as the archbishop of York. In addition, Morehouse and Dr. Leiper will attend meetings of the new British Council of Churches, which is the federation of the Protestant churches in England, and various Anglican church meetings. They will carry the greetings of American churches in the form of expressions of solidarity.

Morehouse and Bishop Perry will consult with the archbishop of Canterbury and other church leaders concerning the correlating of the mission work of the Church of England and the American Episcopal church. Before the war the two churches divided the territory in which they did missionary work, so as to prevent overlapping of endeavor.

Pool Resources, Plan

For the last two years members of the Episcopal church in this country have raised more than $300,000 a year to support the foreign missions of the Church of England. Now it is proposed to pool the resources of the two churches, to make plans jointly and to centralize work so as to avoid waste. Because of the war the Church of England is having difficulty supporting its missions and in getting its missionaries from one place to another. The pooling of work will mean that the American church will extend its work in the western hemisphere

A True 'War Mother'

New York, N. Y.—(AP)—Mrs. Mary A. Zraick lost her husband in World War I. Her three sons, Alick, 33, George, 30, and Edward, 28, will enter the army together Apr. 17.

Gen. Wainwright

—Acme

Lieut. Gen. Jonathan Wainwright was in command of the American-Filipino defenders of the Bataan peninsula whose lines were broken Thursday by the Japanese. He now is on Corregidor, island fortress in Manila bay.

British Striking Back in Desert

Italy Admits Counterblow Against Threat of New Offensive by Axis

By the Associated Press

Britain's desert armies, swiftly countering the threat of a new drive by 125,000 troops under Field Marshal Erwin Rommel, were reported seizing the initiative Thursday with attacks on advanced Axis positions in north Africa.

Premier Mussolini's high command acknowledged that the British were counterattacking on the Libyan front, but asserted they had been beaten off.

British headquarters at Cairo said that British troops were engaging Axis forces at Sidi Bregisch, about 75 miles southwest of Tobruk, and that other British columns had captured a number of Axis troops between Tmimi and El Gazala.

El Gazala is 40 miles west of Tobruk; Tmimi 20 miles farther west.

"The enemy did not attempt to advance further yesterday," British headquarters said.

The British reported the sinking of a 10,000 ton Italian cruiser in the central Mediterranean.

A London admiralty communique said that a British submarine torpedoed the cruiser, which was escorted by destroyers and aircraft.

A British communique told of continued heavy Axis air attacks against the bomb battered island of Malta throughout Wednesday and said "There was some damage to service property."

Four Junkers 88 bombers and four Messerschmitt 109 fighters were shot down "and many other enemy aircraft were probably destroyed or badly damaged," the communique said. Two British planes were listed as missing.

Berlin broadcasts quoted Nazi military quarters as saying the 10 hour bombing of Malta Tuesday was the greatest of the war, leaving the principal city of Valletta "a spectacle of utter destruction," its docks and supply depots aflame, its antiaircraft guns silenced.

Reds Pierce Orel Line, Beaten Back, Nazis Say

Berlin, Germany—(From German Broadcasts)—(AP)—A break-through by massed Russian infantry and tanks in German lines northeast of Orel was reported Thursday by the Berlin radio, but it said that several days of hard fighting had restored the German line.

The daily high command communique said only that "in the central and northern sectors of the eastern front various powerful attacks by the enemy were repulsed."

Orel is about 200 miles south of Moscow and slightly west.

The radio account said that the Russians managed to push back the Germans advanced lines by pressure on three sides.

The radio, quoting the high command on still other action not included in Thursday's communique, said that isolated attacks by reinforced German infantry units had succeeded against Russian fortified positions, including one which lasted four days, in which 100 fortified points were taken and a wooded area cleared of the Red army.

Russian attacks in the Gulf of Finland on the island of Tytarsaari, occupied by German and Finnish troops, collapsed and the Russians lost 270 dead, the German communique said.

On the Caucasian coast, the Germans said, Nazi bombers successfully attacked harbor installations and an oil refinery.

More Typhus Told

Moscow, USSR—(AP)—More than 1,250 cases of typhus have been registered in Berlin in the last two weeks, creating an epidemic that is "daily assuming more threatening proportions," Tass, Soviet news agency, reported Thursday. At Kuestrin, Germany, Nazi military authorities were compelled to delay the dispatch of reinforcements to the front because of an outbreak of typhus among the troops, the agency declared.

Down 545 Planes

Kuibyshev, USSR—(AP)—Soviet fliers and ground gunners were reported Thursday to have destroyed 139 Nazi transport planes, assigned to supply isolated northwestern front units, in three days of a 10 day period which cost the Germans a total of 545 aircraft.

Evidence that Germany is rushing new aircraft into war service was announced in a communique.

"Antiaircraft men of one unit shot down a Junkers 88 dive bomber which was released from the factory Feb. 22, 1942," it said. "Men of this group a few days later shot down

Turn to Russ, page 2, col. 6

36,853 Face Choice of Capture or Death

Roosevelt Gives Gen. Wainwright Free Hand to Decide Future Action; War Secretary Stimson Discloses Some Supplies Got In to Besieged Forces at a High Cost in Shipping

Washington, D. C.—(AP)—Capture or death at the hands of invading Japanese hordes faced the bulk of 36,853 gallant American-Filipino defenders of Bataan peninsula Thursday, closing a heroic four month battle on Luzon against numerically overwhelming forces.

Exhausted by short rations and disease, and virtually cut off from supplies despite costly efforts which provided some ammunition but did not relieve the food shortage, the doughty defenders fell back before the Japanese who already had overrun the rich Dutch Indies and Britain's Singapore and Malaya.

Secretary of War Stimson related the first details concerning the defenders Thursday after a special communique had announced that the defense of Bataan had probably been overcome, and said President Roosevelt had authorized the Philippine commander to make any decision he deemed necessary in the light of events.

There was a roundabout radio report from Berlin quoting a Shanghai newspaper report that Lieut. Gen. Jonathan M. Wainwright, commander on Bataan, had sought an armistice, but this was not confirmed in any other quarter.

Corregidor Believed Holding Out

Latest reports, Stimson said, indicated that Corregidor and other fortresses guarding Manila bay were still in United States hands, as was about half of the area of the Philippines, but he declined to predict how long the forts could be held.

Military quarters here saw little hope, however, that any sizable portion of Wainwright's exhausted troops could be evacuated to the island fortresses in the face of an enemy pounding at them by air and land.

(Wainwright's forces included two tank battalions, some of whose personnel included former Wisconsin national guardsmen from Janesville and the adjoining area.)

Stimson said he saw no reason why resistance by small isolated forces in the Philippines would not continue.

"This is only a temporary loss," Stimson said. "We shall not stop until we drive out the invaders from the islands."

Stimson disclosed that under the direction of Brig. Gen. Patrick J. Hurley, former secretary of war who is now minister to New Zealand, urgent efforts were made beginning last Jan. 11 to reinforce the besieged Philippine forces.

Stimson said the efforts were undertaken as soon as Gen. Douglas MacArthur had taken his position on the peninsula, when "we began to take steps to make his stay as long as possible."

(On orders of President Roosevelt, Gen. MacArthur relinquished active command in the Philippines to Gen. Wainwright in March and traveled to Australia to take over supreme United Nations command in the southwest Pacific.)

American army officers who set up a base in Australia had as part of their duty the assignment to attempt to break the Japanese blockade.

Some Supplies Got In

"To make sure that special efforts were put into the task, former Secretary Hurley was put in charge and authorized and directed to make every effort possible," Stimson continued.

"Very large sums of money were placed to his credit and also to the credit of Gen. MacArthur. It was proposed that MacArthur put in the Philippines what he could.

"Gen. Hurley was very successful. He secured several shipments of supplies which got into the Philippines and part of which reached Corregidor and Bataan. But for every ship that arrived, we lost nearly two ships.

"I am glad to say the defenders were never short of ammunition, owing to these efforts. Up until the last word from them, they had plenty of small arms and artillery ammunition.

"But they had been on short rations since MacArthur put them into effect Jan. 11. This fact and the long strain were a very potent factor in wearing down our troops, making them unable to rebound to the counterattack as at first."

General Given Free Choice

President Roosevelt sent a message to Gen. Wainwright Wednesday. In the message, Stimson said, the chief executive expressed his "full appreciation of the enormous difficulties confronting Gen. Wainwright and told him he had nothing but praise for his method of conducting the defense and for his soldierly conduct throughout.

Stimson said the president told Wainwright that "any decision he reached now would be in the interests of the country and the splendid troops he commanded."

The war department's somber early morning communique stating the probability that the defenses on Bataan have been overcome was the latest word the war department had received up to 10:30 a. m. eastern war time, Stimson said.

Praise for Gallant Defense

"Our troops, outnumbered and worn down by successive attacks by fresh troops, exhausted by insufficient rations and the disease prevalent in that peninsula, fought and [illegible] [illegible] and [illegible] for [illegible]," the secretary said.

"We do not know the details of what has happened since then [illegible] [illegible] but it is evident [illegible] [illegible]

Turn to Philippines, page 2, col. 3

Text of Latest Communique on Bataan Fighting

Washington, D. C.—The war department in a communique issued at 5:15 a. m. Thursday said:

"A message from Gen. Wainwright at Fort Mills just received at the war department states that the Japanese attack on Bataan peninsula succeeded in enveloping the east flank of our lines, in the position held by the 2nd corps. An attack by the 1st corps, ordered to relieve the situation, failed due to complete physical exhaustion of the troops.

"Full details are not available but this situation indicates the probability that the defenses on Bataan have been overcome."

Late Wednesday a communique announced:

"Fresh Japanese troops are continuing their forward drive in Bataan with great vigor.

"A heavy attack on our new positions is now in progress. Dive bombers and attack aircraft are bombing and machine gunning our front lines. Heavy bombers are continuing their attacks on our rear areas near the southern extremity of the Bataan peninsula.

"The present Japanese attack is the longest sustained drive of the enemy since operations began in Bataan. Waves of shock troops have attacked almost continuously, without regard to casualties, which have been heavy on both sides. American and Filipino troops, including naval and marine contingents, have stubbornly resisted every advance. Repeated efforts of the enemy to land troops behind our lines have been frustrated by our beach defenses, manned largely by naval and marine personnel."

Wainwright Thought He'd Miss the War, Going to Philippines

Dallas, Tex.—(AP)—When Lieut. Gen. Jonathan Wainwright—now leading the American-Filipino forces in Bataan in the battle for their lives—received orders to go to the Philippines he was disgusted because he was afraid he'd miss the war.

Col. C. A. Dougherty of the Dallas ROTC, an old friend, saw Wainwright at Fort Clark on the Mexican border just after the latter had received orders to report for the Philippines.

"He was regretting those orders," Dougherty said. "He was afraid that something might break over here and there he would be stuck in the Philippines missing everything."

Whipped for Tire Theft

Wilmington, Del.—(AP)—Chief Justice Daniel J. Layton sentenced Horace Purnell, 29, a Negro of Roxanna, Va., to 10 lashes at the whipping post and two years in prison after his conviction on charges of stealing automobile tires from a garage.

Not Quite so Cold

Boston and vicinity—Not quite so cold today; moderate winds. High tide—4:21 A. M., 4:31 P. M. Low tide—10:28 A. M., 10:57 P. M. Full report on page 2.

THE BOSTON HERALD

6 A. M. EXTRA

VOL. CLXXXXIII, NO. 153 (Copyright, 1942) Boston Herald-Traveler Corporation BOSTON, SUNDAY, NOVEMBER 29, 1942—EIGHTY-EIGHT PAGES ★★★★★★ With "THIS WEEK" Colorgravure Magazine TEN CENTS

450 DIE AS FLAMES AND PANIC TRAP COCOANUT GROVE CROWD

Scores of Service Men Lost, Fire Worst in City's History, Few Victims Identified

Hospitals Jammed With Dead, Injured

The frightful disaster at the Cocoanut Grove quickly taxed the facilities of every hospital within 15 miles of the scene of death and desolation. Scores of ambulances called from neighboring communities engaged in shuttle service as they freighted their loads of dead and injured to hospital wards and morgues.

Bodies of victims beyond aid were piled in the lobbies of the hospitals as doctors and nurses turned their attention to relieving the sufferings of those still alive. The city's North and South morgues were quickly packed with dead.

Attendants at the morgues even went to the extreme of clearing out the garages to provide space.

(Continued on Page Thirty-one)

Bill Cunningham's Special Story appears this morning on page 34.

Madame Grabs the Dust Cloth As War Job Lures Housemaid

By LAWRENCE DAME

Because a lot of women have changed their names from "kitchen canaries" to defense workers since Pearl Harbor, housemaid's knee is becoming an occupational disease of the elite. The hand of your hostess often may be as rough as that of a woman mechanic. And the lady who answers the doorbell these days, with duster in hand and a cloth round her permanent, is known by her accent rather than her garb as the mistress of the house.

Ladies who once had three servants now are doing the housework themselves and are leading their children along the Esplanade where once they paraded their dogs.

(Continued on Page Five, Section B)

Massachusetts State Guard Ready to Tangle with Invader

By CAPT. KARL M. FROST

Unfortunately, it would require an actual enemy invasion of Massachusetts to make many of our neighbors wake up to the fact that we have a State Guard armed and drilled to stand up to the invaders. Federal Army demands have not taken all of Massachusetts' fighting men, by any means, and until that sorry day when women have to shoulder a gun, Massachusetts will always have a State Guard.

Look over the rank and file of the State Guard, and you will

(Continued on Page Five, Section B)

HERALD FEATURES

Index to Classified Advertisements

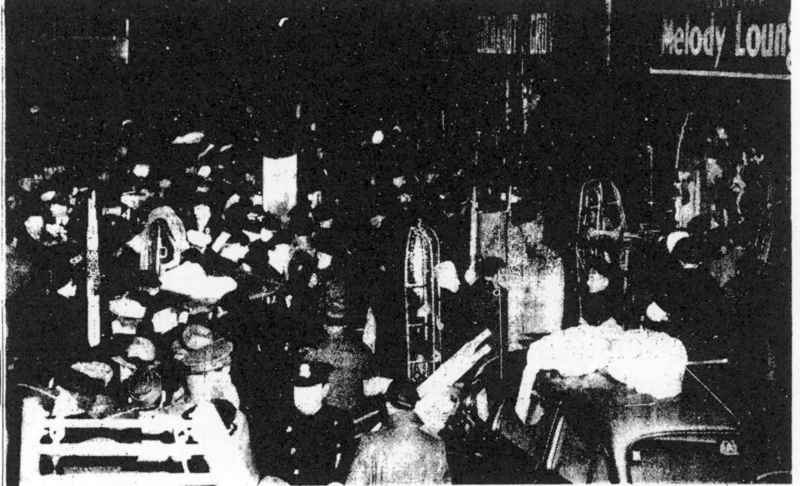

STRETCHERS AT SCENE OF DISASTER held in readiness for victims being taken from the fire box. Priests, nurses, civilians and sailors helped firemen and police in heroic rescue efforts and even in fighting blaze at Cocoanut Grove.

NAZIS RETIRE IN TUNISIA

Blow up Bridges as They Go; on Defensive

U. S. Communiques--Page 24

ALLIED FORCE HEADQUARTERS IN NORTH AFRICA, Nov. 28 (AP)—The Germans were today trying to stem the Allied advance in Tunisia by blowing up bridges, railroads and highways after being hurled back into their defense line near Bizerte and Tunis.

They fell back after losing 10 tanks in a futile counter-attack at Tebourba, 15 miles west of Tunis. It was the third such tank loss for the Germans in fights against the British in northern Tunisia. The Nazis were now believed to have retired into the lines ringing the two cities to await the Allied onslaught.

"It is significant that the Germans are now definitely on the defensive while at first it was not sure whether they were strong enough for a plan-

(Continued on Page Twenty-four)

Throngs Seek Identification As Inquest Board Convenes

List of Injured, Page 30

As throngs poured into Boston early today in a frantic attempt to identify missing relatives, a board of inquest was convened at the scene of the fire with plans to transfer operations to the Statler Hotel for further deliberation.

The board was composed of Mayor Tobin, Fire Commissioner Reilly, Building Commissioner Mooney, Health Commissioner Gately, State Fire Marshall Garrity and Fire Chief Pope. Members of the board were at the night club while the embers still burned.

Hotel lobbies in the vicinity of the night club were thronged with frantic relatives of victims seeking information while officials were helpless to aid them.

VIVID ACCOUNT OF FIRE START

Heroic Rescues; Exciting Scenes

John Walsh, chairman of the Boston committee of public safety, helped to save 14 members of his party of merrymakers at the Cocoanut Grove and left two inside the night club whose fate was unknown at 1 A. M. today, he told Mayor Tobin during an interview in the charred ruins.

"I don't know where John Gill, alumni secretary of Boston College, is, nor his wife," said Walsh, "They

(Continued on Page Thirty-two)

2 MEN VICTIMS ARE IDENTIFIED

Identified dead at Cambridge Hospital, Mt. Auburn street.

VINCENT H. PREZIUSO, 35, 289 Lowell street, Somerville.

HOWARD R. JOHNSON, 40, 52 Vernon street, Somerville.

One man and three women unidentified.

One unidentified woman on the danger list.

All suffered from smoke and second and third degree burns. Deaths due to asphyxiation.

Marshal Law Is Set At Scene---Priests, Nurses, Sailors Aid

Fire Stories and Pictures—Pages 30, 31, 32 and 33.

At least 450 persons perished late last night and early today as flames roared through the Cocoanut Grove nightclub on Piedmont street, in the heart of downtown Boston. Most of the fatalities came when 700 inside the club were crushed in screaming panic as they fought to get outside.

It was the worst fire in the history of Boston.

The disaster had mounted to such proportions by 1:35 A. M. that martial law was clamped down on the fire area as firemen and police continued to take bodies from the club.

Two hours later the police department said the dead numbered 463.

Bodies May Not Be Seen Pending Inquest

The Red Cross disaster service started early today to compile a list of the dead at the various hospitals. Officials at many of the hospitals announced that "no one" would be allowed to view the bodies for possible identification until the bodies had been examined by the medical examiner.

A 3 A. M. the navy started removing sailors from civilian hospitals to the Chelsea Marine Hospital.

Many of the merrymakers at the club when the fire broke out were celebrators from the Boston College-Holy Cross game yesterday afternoon.

There were varying versions of the fire's origin, some placing it in the basement, others in the kitchen adjoining the Melody Lounge, and others by a drapery catching fire from a match.

Commissioner Reilly said an eyewitness told him the fire started just inside the main entrance to the night club near the steps leading to Melody Lounge. This same eye

(Continued on Page Thirty-three)

Firemen Hunting Bodies Amid Black Relics on Dance Floor

An eerie scene of death and disaster met the eyes of horrified observers who penetrated police and military lines inside the Cocoanut Grove at midnight. Bodies were still being carried out on stretchers. A few twitched feebly in the light of still-burning rafters on the once-gay dance floor. Most were limp in death.

Firemen's floodlights marked paths across the warped floor, which in spots was knee-deep in water and in other places showed the debris of catastrophe.

A woman's hat, as sodden as a napkin underfoot a broken string of imitation pearls; a litter of broken highball glasses, smashed chairs, blackened linen and even the black dinner jacket of an ill-fated member of Mickey Alpert's orchestra were included in the litter over which a motley but earnest and self-sacrificing throng of rescue workers tramped.

GRUESOME BODY HUNT

In two corners of the dancing room, where burned-out, decorative palms drooped and water dripped from the scarred room, firemen, naval officers, army men, police and civilian defense workers raked without conversation in the wreckage, still hunting for bodies.

Once in a while the almost hysterical yells of a stretcher bearer, trying to make way for victims still being taken out of the flooded, smoke-filled cellar where night club employes died in a terrible trap, blanketed the horror-struck whispers and the ceaseless dripping of the ceiling.

Outside, as the blear-eyed firefighters and bearers toiled within, a mixture of civilians, police, firemen, sailors, soldiers, air raid wardens, and relief workers formed

(Continued on Page Thirty-two)

Known Dead At Hospitals In Fire, Panic

The counted dead at vario[us] hospitals and morgues at 3 A.[M.]

Massachusetts General 6
Peter Bent Brigham 2
Carney
St. Elizabeth's
Cambridge City
Cambridge Hospital
Southern Mortuary 21
Northern Mortuary 5
St. Margaret's
Faulkner
Chelsea Naval
Massachusetts Memorial
Beth Israel
U. S. Marine

Total

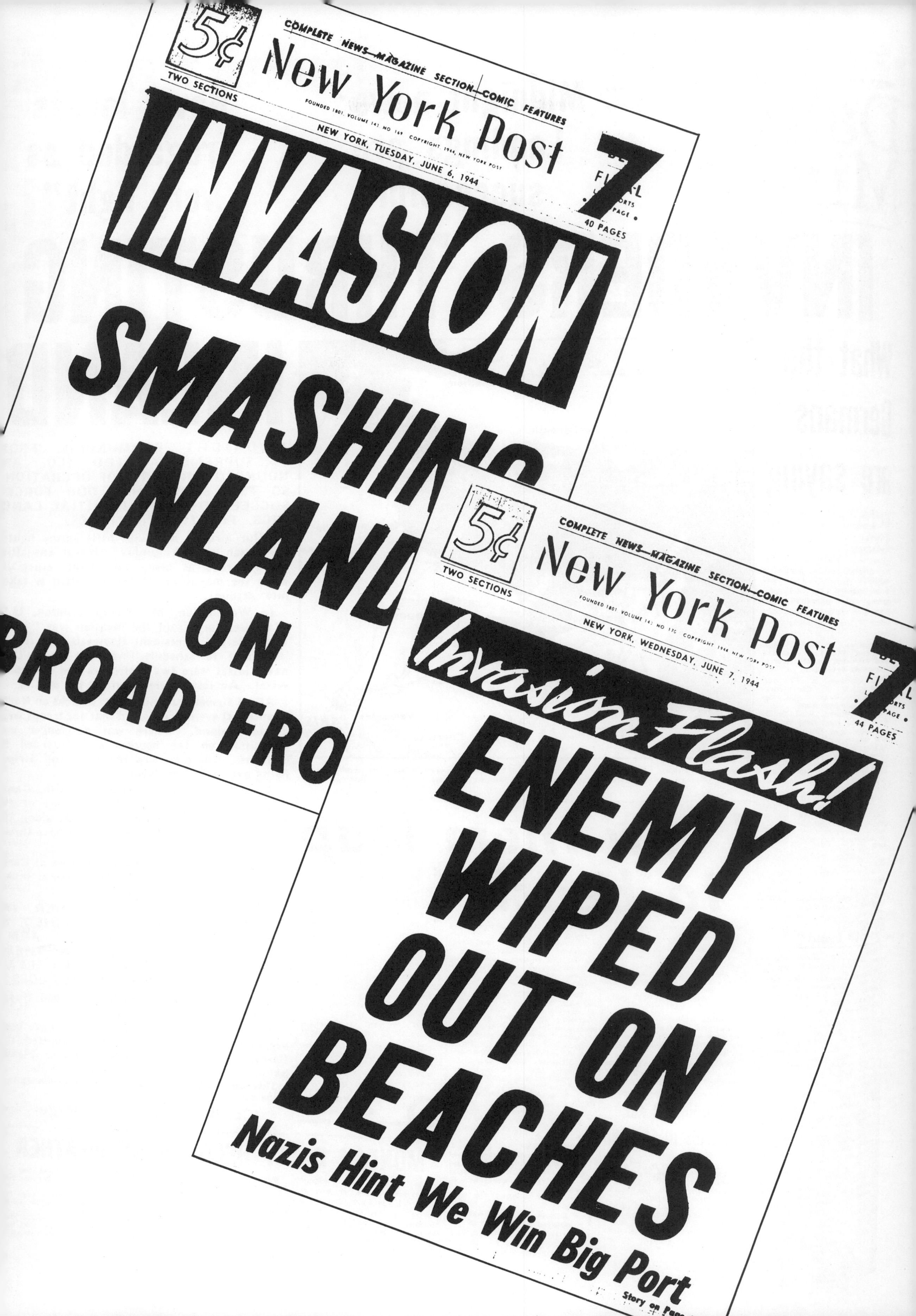
5¢

COMPLETE NEWS—MAGAZINE SECTION—COMIC FEATURES

TWO SECTIONS

New York Post

FOUNDED 1801. VOLUME 143 NO 169 COPYRIGHT 1944, NEW YORK POST

NEW YORK, TUESDAY, JUNE 6, 1944

7

40 PAGES

INVASION

SMASHING INLAND ON BROAD FRO

5¢

COMPLETE NEWS—MAGAZINE SECTION—COMIC FEATURES

TWO SECTIONS

New York Post

FOUNDED 1801 VOLUME 143 NO 170 COPYRIGHT 1944 NEW YORK POST

NEW YORK, WEDNESDAY, JUNE 7, 1944

7

44 PAGES

Invasion Flash!

ENEMY WIPED OUT ON BEACHES

Nazis Hint We Win Big Port

Story on Page

DAILY MIRROR, Wednesday, June 7, 1944.

Daily Mirror

JUNE 7

No. 12,627 ONE PENNY Registered at the G.P.O. as a Newspaper.

Midnight news: Landings are successful

• Naval losses "regarded as very light"

INVADERS THRUSTING INLAND

What the Germans are saying

GERMAN radio last night reported new Allied landings at Calais and Boulogne.

Powerful paratroop formations dropped behind Boulogne and north of Rouen were said to be engaged in "vicious" fighting. Other paratroops had a firm grip on a nineteen mile stretch of the Cherbourg-Caen road.

Sertorius, military commentator, said the offensive had extended to the entire Normandy peninsula.

Paris claimed a German counter-attack in the Cherbourg region was "still developing" late last night.

Our bridgehead, said to be [illegible] miles long and several miles deep, was first reported to be between Villers-sur-Mer and Trouville.

Later broadcasts corrected this to further west on both sides of the River Orne and north-west of Bayeux, between Caen and Isigny.

A British-American group, with light tanks and tank reconnaissance cars, was operating on dunes north-east of Bayeux "trying to link up with the larger bridgehead," said Berlin.

Other enemy radio reports were:

Allied reinforcements "pouring in."

Except for the beachhead at Caen, all invasion troops landed from the sea thrown back. This beachhead narrowed down in some places.

"Navy Off Dunkirk"

Strong Allied naval forces were off Dunkirk and Calais.

Fifteen cruisers with fifty to sixty destroyers operating off Le Havre last night, with landing craft apparently waiting to attack.

Allied airborne troops on the Cherbourg peninsula "wiped out to a man" at Barfleur and La Pernelle, but more airborne troops pressing against Caen.

Allied landings on Channel Islands. Troops from 280 ships attacking Arromanches and [illegible] between Cherbourg and Le Havre. Cliffs scaled by ladder and tanks landed.

Allied landing craft penetrated Orne and Vire Estuaries, main centres of the landing between St. Vaast [illegible] la Hogue and the Cherbourg peninsula tip.

In heavy artillery duel with coastal batteries off St. Vaast, [illegible] cruiser and troop-carrying landing craft were sunk.

Paratroops made twelve landings in all from Cherbourg to [illegible]. First and Sixth British and 82nd and 101st American airborne divisions engaged. [illegible] troops tried to break [illegible] Germans west of Isigny.

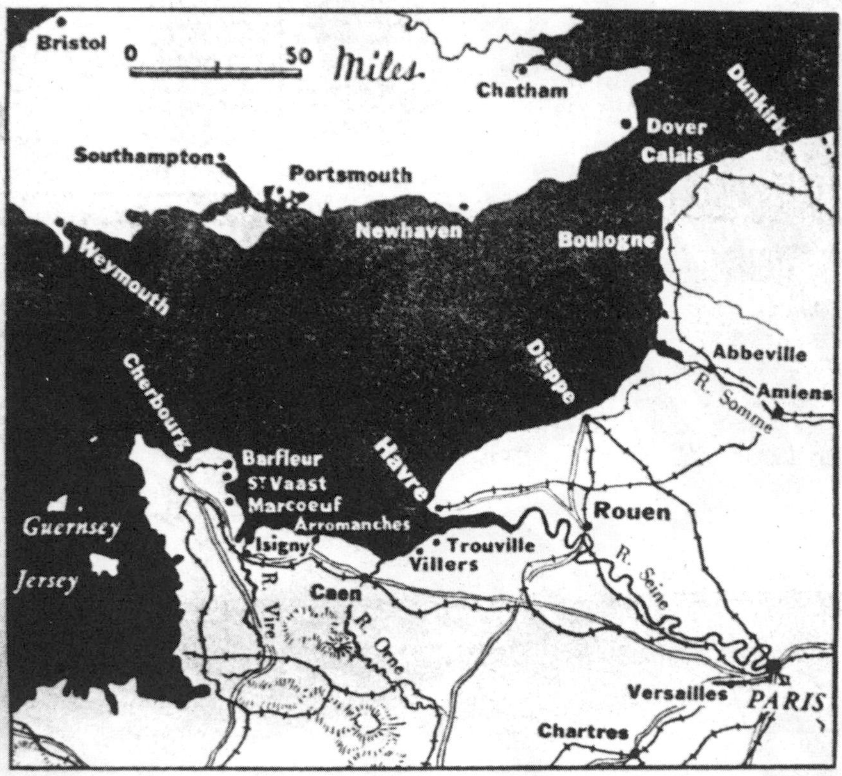

The invasion coast, showing the chief centres of activity between Cherbourg and Havre. Latest German radio reports suggest new Allied landings further north near Boulogne and Calais

MIDNIGHT COMMUNIQUE FROM SUPREME ALLIED H.Q. ANNOUNCED: "REPORTS OF OPERATION SO FAR SHOW THAT OUR FORCE SUCCEEDED IN THEIR INITIAL LANDINGS. FIGHTING CONTINUES.

"Our aircraft met with little enemy fighte opposition or AA gunfire. Naval casualtie are regarded as being very light, especiall when the magnitude of the operation is take into account."

In Washington, Mr. Henry Stimson, U.S War Secretary, said the invasion was "goin very nicely." President Roosevelt said it wa "running to schedule." Up to noon, U.S naval losses were two destroyers and a landin vessel. Air losses were about one per cent.

Allied airmen returning from attacks on Nort France last evening reported that our troops wer moving inland. There was no longer an opposition on the beaches now guarded b balloons. One pilot saw the Stars and Stripe flying over a French town.

According to earlier reports, British, Cana dian and American spearhead troops of th Allied Armies have gained footholds along th Normandy coast, and in some places have thru several miles inland.

Fighting is going on inside the town of Caen seven miles from the coast, and several intac bridges have been captured.

BATTLING STILL FURTHER IN LAND, AND WELL ESTABLISHED, I THE GREATEST AIRBORNE ARM EVER FLOWN INTO ACTION. THES TROOPS WERE LANDED WITH GREA ACCURACY AND VERY LITTLE LOSS.

The airborne fleet consisted of 1,000 troop carrying planes, including gliders.

But though several vital obstacles have bee overcome with much less loss than expected, th Germans will concentrate their reserves. Heav battles are looming.

This was the situation outlined in the Commons la night by Mr. Churchill.

(Continued on Back Page)

I saw them leap to beach

ABOARD A BRITISH DESTROYER OFF NORTH FRANCE, Tuesday

GUNS are belching flame from more than 600 Allied warships. Thousands of bombers are roaring overhead, and fighters are weaving in and out of the clouds.

The invasion of Western Europe has begun.

Rolling clouds of dense black and grey smoke cover the beaches south-west of Le Havre, writes Desmond Tighe, of Reuter.

We are standing some 8,000 yards off the beaches of Berniere-sur-Mer, seven miles east of Arromanches, and from the bridge of this destroyer I can see vast numbers of naval craft.

In ten minutes more than 2,000 tons of H.E. shells have gone down on the beach-head.

It is now exactly 7.25 a.m., and through my glasses I can see the first wave of assault troops touching down on the water's edge and fan up the beach.

Under the supreme command of Admiral Sir Bertram Ramsay, Allied Naval Commander, Expeditionary Force, two great forces are taking part.

An eastern task force, mostly British and Canadian warships, is led by Rear-Admiral Sir Phillip Vian, of Cossack fame.

A western task force, mainly of American warships, is commanded by U.S. Rear-Admiral Alan G. Kirk.

The weather for the landings was not perfect, but despite high running seas and a strong north-westerly wind a bold decision was taken to go ahead.

The plans allowed for four phases:

1. —*Landings by airborne paratroops in the rear.*
2. —*A tremendous night bombing by the RAF on the landing beaches themselves.*
3. —*A bombardment by more than 600 Allied warships from battleships, cruisers, monitors and destroyers.*
4. —*A daybreak bombing attack by the full force of the U.S. Air Force just after dawn and before the first troops went in.*

Events moved rapidly after 4 a.m., and I will put on record the diary kept on the bridge:

5.7 a.m.—Lying eight miles from the lowering position for invasion craft.

5.20.—Dawn. Innumerable assault ships appear smudgily.

5.27.—Night bombing has ceased, and the great naval bombardment begins.

5.33.—We move in slowly.

5.36.—Cruisers open fire. We

Continued on Back Page

FIRST WOUNDED ARE BACK IN ENGLAND

The first Allied wounded were landed back in England yesterday. Some were taken to an East Anglian hospital.

Despite their wounds, many were smiling cheerfully.

Officially recorded next-of-kin of a wounded soldier on the danger list in a hospital at home will be sent a telegram, production of which at a police station will secure travel warrants for two persons.

MONDAY D-DAY HELD UP BY WEATHER

The invasion was delayed twenty-four hours, it was revealed at S.H.A.E.F. last night.

With his D-Day fixed for Monday morning, General Eisenhower was told by weather experts that conditions would be too bad.

But they forecast that by Tuesday there would be an improvement.

Eisenhower had to make a decision knowing that, once launched, the invasion could not be called off.

He took the decision to go in on Tuesday—and though the weather was not kind, the e perts' forecast was largely fu filled.

The landing craft, except fo four, were able to battle on t the other side.

Rain fell in the Straits las night and the outlook was un settled. The sea was smoot

ARIZONA REPUBLIC

INDEPENDENT — THE STATE'S GREATEST NEWSPAPER

55th Year, No. 263, Phoenix, Arizona
112 N. Central Ave. Telephone 3-1111

Monday Morning, February 5, 1945
5c Copy; 10c Out of State. 14 Pages

U.S. TROOPS REACH HEART OF MANILA

Santo Tomas Camp, Palace Are Captured

By C. YATES McDANIEL

GENERAL MacARTHUR'S HEADQUARTERS, Luzon, Feb. 5—(Monday)—(AP)—Just 26 days after their initial Luzon invasion, American troops speared to the heart of Manila yesterday, freed thousands of civilian war prisoners, seized the governmental palace and pressed against little more than sniper fire toward complete control of the Philippines capital.

Gen. Douglas MacArthur announced the virtual achievement of his prime goal in a triumphant communique today. A dynamited bridge on the northern outskirts prevented the general from entering Manila immediately. He turned back to find another route.

Santo Tomas Seized

Veteran First Cavalry Division forces made an encircling drive in darkness Saturday night to seize the Santo Tomas internment camp from the east. About 3,000 civilians, mainly American women and children, have been held at Santo Tomas since May 1, 1942.

A sharp engagement occurred at the camp. Frontline reports said the guards were killed and the prison was taken over completely after room-to-room fighting. Removal of the prisoners by ambulance began.

The mechanized cavalrymen then captured Malacanan Palace, former governmental headquarters of the Philippine commonwealth. Japanese officials had fled.

Surprise Airborne Landing

Paratroopers of the 11th Airborne Division executed a neat surprise landing—first of its kind in the Philippine campaign — behind enemy lines to move onto Manila from the south, only 18 miles away.

These paratroops landed Friday ahead of Yanks who had invaded the coast to the west last Wednesday. This gave the Americans command of a 2,000-foot height on a fine highway to the Cavite naval base and Manila itself.

Elements of the 37th Division entered Manila from the north, capturing the Grace Park airdrome, and pushed cautiously toward the wide and deep Pasig river which runs through the center of the city. Most of the bridges over the Pasig appeared intact.

The Americans held the northern half of Manila, but south of the Pasig, in the commercial center, the Japanese may put up a bloody fight. Demolition explosions were heard and fires were seen in the southern section.

No Major Stand

The enemy offered no major stand in the northern part of Manila. The main threat was harassing machine-gun and sniper fire from houses.

Fred Hampson, Associated Press correspondent, with the First Cavalry troops, said the liberated Filipinos were deliriously happy as the Yanks poured into their city.

"Victory!" "The Americans are back!" "God bless the Americans!" These were the cries of the liberated.

Hampson walked for five miles toward the Manila waterfront, and wrote that "a few buildings were smashed and burned, but on the whole that part of Manila was not greatly damaged. However, off in the distance we could see huge fires and columns of smoke. The dock area was burning fiercely."

(President Roosevelt messaged Philippine President Sergio Osmena that "The American people rejoice with me in the liberation of your capital.")

(Santo Tomas is perhaps the area in Manila closest to the hearts of American and British people. Within Santo Tomas the American and British civilians—3,000 men and women at one time—have waited deliverance for three long years.

(Front line reports said ambulances already were bringing out the Santo Tomas prisoners.)

Malacanan Palace, in Yank hands, was the historic residence succes

(Continued On Page 4, Col. 2)

Invasion Dates In Philippines

(By Associated Press)

Here are the invasion dates and places in the Philippine campaign climaxed with the entry into Manila:

October 20, 1944 — American troops land on Leyte island.

October 26 — Yanks seized southern coast of Samar island, just east of Leyte.

December 15—Americans land on southwest coast of Mindoro. Immediately south of Luzon.

January 6, 1945 — Marinduque island, east of Mindoro, invaded.

January 8 — Amphibious hop puts Yanks in northwest coast of Mindoro.

January 9 — Luzon island invaded at Lingayen gulf.

January 29—Second invasion of Luzon, on Zambales coast 60 air-line miles northwest of Manila.

January 31—Third invasion of Luzon, on Batangas coast below Manila bay.

February 3 — Americans enter Manila.

Few Fires Scar City Of Manila

SAN FRANCISCO, Feb. 4—Most of Manila appears intact, with only 10 fires burning in Japanese ammunition dumps, piers and warehouses, correspondents of American radio networks reported today after the American penetration of the capital.

Royal Arch Gunnison of Mutual, who flew over the city, said Manila "is not in as bad condition as might be expected." He reported Pier 7, largest dockside on either side of the Pacific, is aflame, however.

Most of the public buildings, including the Bay View and Manila hotels, appeared intact, he added.

Pat Flaherty of the National Broadcasting Company likewise reported no evidence of wholesale destruction by the retreating Japanese.

William J. Dunn, Columbia Broadcasting System broadcaster, said he saw a large enemy cargo ship afire in Manila bay, apparently ignited by its crew because of the futility of escape into the U. S. controlled outer waters.

City Natives Weary

John Adams of Blue Network reported flying over captured Grace Field and said "it appears that the field could be put in operation in short order."

Gunnison said a "great pall of smoke" still hung over Manila but that there appeared to be more smoke than fire.

Thousands of war-weary Filipinos lined the routes of the American troops, he continued. He said the city dwellers, in contrast to the country Filipinos, appeared weary and dejected.

Some, he added, even bowed to the Americans, a habit they had learned under long Japanese subjugation. Some cried to the Americans: "You will never know how we have missed you."

"It was a happy but pitiful sight," Gunnison said.

Flaherty declared "there is fighting going on right now in Manila for control of the city."

Ex-Inmates See Prison

Adams reported that there were "few people on the streets" and that the many lining the American entry routes were on the outskirts.

Gunnison, who with two other correspondents on Luzon, Russell Brines of the Associated Press and Carl Mydans of Life magazine, was in the Santo Tomas concentration camp before being exchanged, flew over the camp:

"A woman in red slacks and a white blouse waved from the roof of a building," he said. "Children were swinging from swings I built when I was a prisoner two years ago. The 500 grass and bamboo huts about the camp were intact, but seemed empty. It's obvious that of the 3,800 people who were there when I left, some have been moved."

Crippled Yanks Land Behind Soviet Lines

LONDON, Feb. 4—(AP)—Several of the American Flying Fortresses crippled over Berlin yesterday headed toward the Oder river to make forced landings behind Russian lines.

"Probably be seeing you in Berlin," one radioed.

Iwo Jima Air Bases Are Hit

U. S. PACIFIC FLEET HEADQUARTERS, FORWARD AREA, Feb. 5 — (Monday) — (Via Navy Radio) — (AP) — Army Liberators bombed Iwo Jima in the Volcano Islands Friday and Saturday, concentrating on air installations and storage areas, Adm. Chester W. Nimitz announced today. Ofte bombed Iwo Jima is 750 miles south of Tokyo.

On the Friday strike intense antiaircraft fire was encountered and one escorting Lightning fighter was lost. Chichi Jima in the near-by Bonin Islands also was bombed Friday.

Navy search Venturas in the North Pacific made machine-gun and rocket attacks on buildings and radio installations at Kurabu Saki on Paramushiru and at Shimushu Islands in the Kuriles. All participating aircraft returned.

Far-ranging marine aircraft bombed installations on Yap in the bypassed Western Carolines, Babelthuap in the Palau Islands and installations on Rota in the Marianas Friday.

"There were seven Japanese fighter aircraft in the air over Iwo Jima. The antiaircraft and fighter resistance at Iwo Jima was the sharpest noted in recent weeks of almost daily hammering at the important enemy [illegible]

Russians Outflank Hun Forts

By W. W. HERCHER

LONDON, Feb. 4—(AP)—Russian forces marching on Berlin moved northward today to outflank the Oder river bastion city of Kustrin and captured Barwalde, 38 miles from the capital.

Farther south, another flanking movement apparently aimed at bypassing the second large Oder line fortress town, Frankfurt, was begun with the capture of Ziebingen, 13 miles southeast of Frankfurt and 51 from Berlin.

On the road to Barwalde, troops of Marshal Gregory K. Zhukov's First White Russian Army also took Neudamm, 10 miles northeast of Kustrin.

The regular nightly communique broadcast from Moscow announced these advances toward Berlin, but said nothing of a push toward the German Baltic port of Stettin which the German high command reported had reached Pyritz, 22 miles southeast of Stettin.

Moving around Kustrin and Frankfurt, guardians of the last 40 miles to Berlin, Zhukov captured more than 100 towns and villages, the Soviet communique said, adding that 1,500 prisoners had been taken in this sector.

Baltic Hold Extended

An order of the day by Marshal Joseph Stalin announced earlier the capture of the East Prussian towns of Landsberg and Bartenstein, south of the capital, Konigsberg, where Gen. Ivan Cherniakhovsky's Third White Russian Army is squeezing tighter its ring around the last trapped Nazi defenders.

The communique added that Soviet troops had completely cleared the enemy from the Kurische Nehrung, the strip of land separating Kurisches bay from the Baltic sea which extends northward from Cranz, also captured today, to Memel.

The Russians also took more than 70 other towns and, with the fall of Cranz, occupied an eight-mile stretch of the Baltic coast, extending southwest from Cranz to Alknicken.

Of East Prussia's 14,283 square miles, the Germans now hold only approximately 800 square miles west and southwest of Konigsberg.

Frontline dispatches reaching London from Moscow said street fighting already was underway in Kustrin and that Frankfurt, 16 miles to the south, was in Soviet artillery range.

Rail Lines Severed

At Barwalde, the Russians cut the railroad between Kustrin and Stettin, and at Neudamm the rail line from Kustrin to Soldin, nearest Russian approach to Stettin officially reported, was severed. At Ziebingen, the railroad from Frankfurt southeastward was cut, hampering German communications with the Silesian front.

Both Barwalde and Ziebingen are approximately four miles from the east bank of the Oder and there was no indication from Moscow that the Russians had crossed the river in either sector, despite German reports that attempts to force the river northwest of Kustrin had been repulsed.

One German war reporter said in a broadcast that the Russians had established several bridgeheads across the Oder, including one 10 miles deep. He did not give the locations of these bridgeheads, but indicated that one might be at Steinau, 34 miles northwest of besieged Breslau, where the Germans have acknowledged several penetrations by Marshal Ivan S. Konev's forces.

Great air battles swirled over the Oder front. A quick thaw in a 30-degree rise of temperature hampered Zhukov's movements, Moscow said.

Kobe Blasted By Superforts

TWENTY-FIRST BOMBER COMMAND, GUAM, Feb. 4—(Via Navy Radio) — (AP) — A "sizable" strike by American Superfortresses on the main Japanese island of Honshu today is meeting "weather which is preventing visual bombing", 21st Bomber Command Headquarters announced.

The city or cities under attack were not mentioned, nor was the number of planes participating revealed in the headquarters statement.

(A Japanese Imperial Headquarters communique broadcast by Tokyo radio said 100 Superforts raided the Kobe and Osaka industrial areas and admitted "some losses."

(The broadcast said 85 B-29s hit Kobe within 45 minutes and 15 other Superforts bombed Kishiwada in the Osaka prefecture and Matsuzaka in the Mie prefecture. The latter is about 50 miles north of Kobe. Kishiwada is on Osaka bay.)

(The daylight attacks were preceded by overnight forays by B-29s apparently flying singly over the Osaka and adjacent Wakayama prefectures, Tokyo said.)

Destruction In Berlin Is Very Great

By CHARLES CHAMBERLAIN

LONDON, Feb. 4 (AP)—German broadcasts warned of four separate forces of bombers winging over the reich tonight, possibly indicating a Royal Air Force Mosquito attack on Berlin, whose heart was scourged by 1,000 U. S. Flying Fortresses Saturday.

The record American assault scored eight direct hits on the German air ministry, and poured 18 concentrations of bombs into the area occupied by the war office, Hitler's reich chancellery, Goebbels' ministry of propaganda, and Gestapo headquarters, an American communique disclosed.

Heavies May Be Out

Tonight the German warning system reported fast bomber formations—a term that fits Mosquito bombers with their two-ton blockbusters—over the Hannover and Brunswick areas and farther east in Berlin's Brandenberg province. Another warning told of a bomber formation approaching Western Germany—perhaps RAF Lancasters and Halifaxes headed for freight yard or oil targets.

Buildings in the very heart of Berlin were left gutted and charred from one of the war's best jobs of bombing marksmanship. Badly-disrupted radio broadcasting services provided one indication of the confusion wrought in the refugee-filled capital, less than 40 miles from Russian lines.

The 1,000 Flying Fortresses left an almost unbroken mass of fire and smoke over an area two miles long and a mile wide in the core of the city, and smoke boiled up more than two miles high through the clouds, U. S. Strategic Air Force Headquarters said.

Losses Are Reduced

The cost was 19 bombers and five fighters, including losses in a simultaneous strike on Magdeburg to the southwest. Revised figures showing 16 of the 35 first reported lost actually had landed in safe territory.

The huge pall of smoke rising after the air ministry building was stricken made it impossible for photograph interpreters to plot direct hits on the other key buildings nearby, the communique said.

Bombs damaged the Potsdamer, Friedrichstrasse, Anhalter Gorlitzer, and Schleischer railroad stations and adjacent rail lines, severely mauled the Tempelhof freight yards and the Deutsche Gesellschaft gas works near the center of Berlin.

German radio services returned to an approximation of normal broadcasting today but apparently their foreign language services still were awry. Transocean's morning service consisted of only two messages.

Strange Signal Unexplained

There was no clarification of DNB's mysteriously-signalled words, "schluss, schluss," meaning "the end, the end," last night. The word, sometimes used to terminate transmission, had never before been interpolated during broadcasts.

A DNB home broadcast today assured shaken Berliners that the Russians would be stopped at the Oder river, declaring it "must be clear to everyone that there will be a first battle of the Oder before there could be a question of a battle of Berlin. Therefore, it is obvious that Berliners should continue to live and work with the greatest calm."

Canned Goods Lost In Warehouse Blaze

TANEYTOWN, Md., Feb. 4—(AP)—Between 28,000 and 30,000 cases of canned vegetables stored for the government at Fefser's canning factory were destroyed today when fire swept three warehouse sections.

The canning machinery was saved through the efforts of the Taneytown, Union Bridge and Westminster fire companies.

Freezing of the water supply hampered the firemen in combating the blaze in the frame structure.

Wide Gap Ripped In Westwall

By AUSTIN BEALMEAR

PARIS, Feb. 4—(AP)—The U. S. First Army ripped a hole all the way through the westwall southeast of Aachen and 29 miles from the Rhine today, bending back the south flank of the enemy's powerful Roer river defenses which block an Allied drive to the Ruhr and Rhineland.

The north wing of four assaulting divisions swung east 4½ miles, knifing through two villages—one of them a mile and a half from the vital Roer river dams beyond the westwall, where the enemy has been opening gates, flooding the valley and balking a push farther north.

A front dispatch said the doughboys struck in snow, sleet and freezing rain, overpowered the last system of German pillboxes at a point eight miles east of Monschau. They fought out into open country within a mile of a five-mile-wide fir forest, one of the last barriers to the Cologne plain.

Youth Camp Taken

(A Blue network correspondent reported from the front that the Americans reached the south bank of the lake formed by the dams, overrunning a big Nazi youth training camp which had been a project of Hitler, Gobbels and Himmler.)

To the south the U. S. Third Army broke into the main Siegfried Line system 5½ miles inside the reich and 3½ miles from the fortress of Prum, in a drive that may be the forerunner of a big push from the west.

The Third Army seized at least three German villages southeast of St. Vith and pushing into the Schnee Eifel forest was outflanking Brandscheid, 4½ miles west of Prum and a key to the Siegfried Line defenses.

Battle Nears End

The battle of Southern Alsace appeared nearing its final phase as French and American forces squeezed the Colmar pocket from north and south.

They were within nine miles of a junction between Colmar and Mulhouse and the Germans were trying frantically to extricate an estimated 2,500 troops from the Vosges foothills to the west.

The U. S. Seventh Army in Northern Alsace was hammering a stubborn German last-stand position in Oberhoffen, 15 miles north of Strasbourg, and to the west in the Northern Vosges scored a gain against the enemy in the Bitche salient.

Heavy Fight Rages

Heaviest fighting raged in Western Germany, however, where the Germans were trying to salvage a deteriorating situation which might undermine their powerful Cologne plain first line of defense on the Roer.

Lt. Gen. Courtney H. Hodges' First Army troops now were through a 12-mile section of the double Siegfried Line in the Monschau sector, were as deep as 12 miles into the reich, and besides piercing the last fortified wall on the north flank were within three quarters of a mile of duplicating that feat in the center of the push.

The Ninth Infantry Division first captured Einruhr, six miles northeast of Monschau and two miles from the Roer dams, in a four mile drive along the Upper Roer.

Town Is Seized

Then just to the south another blow carried through the last main fixed fortifications of the second belt of defenses.

Meanwhile, the Ninth's right wing was running into heavy fighting two miles to the southeast at Herhahn, two miles from the road junction of Gemund. The Germans need the lateral roads running out of Gemund and they threw a counterblow that was warded off.

Two miles farther south the Second Division drew up its assault lines a mile from a second road center—Schleiden—capturing the village of Ettelscheid, three fourths of a mile from the last main belt of the Siegfried Line of which Schleiden is a part.

Air Troops Advance

The First Division, seizing Hollerath, five miles southwest of the Second Division, struck some of the rockiest resistance as the Germans fought back from fortified villages.

At the western loop of the Siegfried Line some two miles farther south, the 82nd Airborne Division broke through the pillbox-studded westwall's first defense line south of Udenbreth, then swung around and began attacking pillboxes from the rear in a bruising battle.

Lt. Gen. George S. Patton's Third Army, despite another 2½ mile advance into Germany had yet to reach the main fortifications of the Siegfried Line, which becomes a single defense belt on this front and stands somewhat farther east of the border.

Berlin Is Cautioned Of Airborne Invasion

STOCKHOLM, Feb. 4—(AP)—The Swedish newspaper Aftontidningen in an undated "private" dispatch said today that residents of Berlin have been alerted to the possibility of an early Allied attempt to land air-borne troops in the capital area.

The dispatch gave no authority but said the purpose of such a landing would be to "roll up the defenses of Berlin from the rear."

Vital War Decisions Predicted This Week

WASHINGTON, Feb. 4 (AP) The capital expects that this week will be one of the most eventful of the war.

Three developments appear probable:

1. Conclusion of the Roosevelt-Churchill-Stalin talks—accompanied or closely followed by momentous announcements of military and diplomatic decisions bearing on the end of the wars in Europe and Asia and the beginnings of peace.

2. More definite information on how long and tough the Nazi death struggle probably will be. Development of Allied assaults along the Oder river before Berlin, and along the Siegfried Line in the west, is undergoing constant analysis by Allied military chiefs for any evidence of fatal German weaknesses.

3. Completing the conquest of Manila, intended American base for breaking the Japanese empire in half and also for building up forces for the next great moves against Japan. Beyond Manila, except for possible invasion of secondary islands in the Luzon area, lie the China coast and the Japanese homeland.

About the Big Three meeting there is nothing official on which to base expectations. It is known that Harry Hopkins and Edward Stettinius, secretary of state, left Italy several days ago for unannounced destinations at the conclusion of what Hopkins called an information tour for the President preliminary to his meeting with Winston Churchill and Joseph Stalin. Also, Hopkins told reporters in Europe that the meeting would very likely be brief, which led to speculation that it would be over before many days passed. Numerous European sources have speculated that it already is going on.

The swift pace of the war in Europe is believed to have brought to the top of the agenda various military questions connected with the co-operation of Russian and Anglo-American forces inside Germany, assuming prolonged resistance there. But the great decisions, believed to foreshadow an unprecedented new role of the United States in European affairs, are expected to deal with long-range international problems.

Those who assume success for efforts of the Big Three to assure future co-operation predict that out of the talks will come machinery for Allied instead of lone-hand settlement of international European problems.

Failure to arrive at a basis for co-operation, with assurances from Britain and Russia to respect American aims for liberated Europe, would be interpreted here as a signal failure of the conference and a bad omen for the future of efforts to prevent war.

How far present and future developments of the Pacific war may enter into general discussions of the Big Three is debated. Unofficial insistence from London that Russian participation against Japan is not likely to be sought meets even more definite assertions from American sources that the subject will come up.

Meanwhile the stage is being set for the final campaigns against Japan with the Manila area of Luzon as the key to future strategy. It is from there that American forces soon will operate, according to plans completed many months ago, to sever the ocean supply lines between Japan's war industries and their raw materials sources in Malaya and the Indies.

Also it seems certain that around Manila will be built the massive forces of men, planes and ships that will be needed to breach the enemy-held China coast and come to grips with the Japanese armies.

Canada Faces Vital Draft Ballot Today

By HARRY T. MONTGOMERY

OWEN SOUND, Ont., Feb. 4—(AP)—Prime Minister W. L. Mackenzie King's compromise conscription policy will be judged directly by the people for the first time tomorrow in the eagerly-watched Grey North by-election, in which Gen. A. G. L. McNaughton, defense minister, is seeking a seat in parliament.

The prime minister won a 2-1 vote of confidence in parliament last December on his policy of sending abroad limited numbers of Canada's drafted home army to fill depleted infantry ranks in the dominion's volunteer army. Tomorrow, however, will bring the first appraisal of the policy directly by the electorate.

Although other issues are involved, including the popularity of the socialistic CCF (Co-operative Commonwealth Federation), the by-election campaign has pivoted mainly and bitterly around the conscription question.

In addition to Canada's future man-power program, the dissolution of the present parliament and the date of the dominion's forthcoming general election also hinge upon the outcome of the balloting by the 23,000 members of this relatively remote rural community.

General McNaughton and his two opponents are contesting a seat in a parliament which may never meet. **If the defense minister is defeated, Prime Minister King is expected to dissolve parliament at an early date without a further session. But if McNaughton wins the seat, for which the government arranged the by-election, King may summon a short session for enacting routine measures for the coming year.**

The defense minister is opposed by Garfield Case, a former mayor of Owen Sound, on the progressive conservative ticket, and by Air Vice Marshal A. Earl Godfrey, well-to-do member of an industrial firm, the CCF candidate. The CCF has directed its appeal principally to the farmers, comprising a majority of the constituency and having a history of support of progressive farmers' movements.

Eleven-Year-Old Killed By Auto

GLORIA FRANKHOUSER, 11-year-old daughter of Mr. and Mrs. B. W. Frankhouser, 202 East Indianola avenue, was struck and killed by an automobile last night when she stepped from behind a street car at Third street and Indianola avenue.

It was the 18th fatality resulting

1945	This Date	1944
18	Feb. 4	47

from motor vehicle accidents in Arizona since January 1.

W. O. Ruth, state highway patrolman, said the Frankhouser girl, with two other girls, left an Indian School street car. They walked to the rear of the car and were walking west across Third street when the accident occurred.

The driver of the auto was identified as Gustave Breithauer, 802 North Second street. He was driving south, Ruth said.

The two unidentified girls escaped injury.

Asia Air Leader Named

LONDON, Feb. 5 (Monday)—(AP)—Air Marshal Sir Keith Park, air officer commander in chief of the Middle East Command since January, 1944, has been appointed air commander in chief in Southeast Asia, replacing Air Chief Marshal Sir Trafford Leigh-Mallory, who was lost en route to his post.

British Surround Satpangon Units

SOUTHEAST ASIA COMMAND HEADQUARTERS, Kandy, Ceylon, Feb. 4—(AP)—British 14th Army troops, driving the Japanese from the area west of Mandalay, have surrounded and subjected to air attacks the enemy garrison at Satpangon west of Myinmu, it was announced today.

Forty miles above Mandalay British troops protecting a bridgehead on the east bank of the Irrawaddy river at Singu have repulsed two Japanese attacks, the Allied headquarters communique said.

On the west coast heavy fighting continued at Kangaw, 30 miles east of Akyab, where the Japanese are battling to keep open their escape route to the south. The war bulletin said the mopping up of remaining enemy forces was being carried out above and below Minbya, 30 miles northeast of Akyab.

In Northern Burma American troops of the Mars task force took a strongly defended hill just west of the Burma road after a two-day battle, the communique said.

[W]inter May [S]et Record [i]n New York

[A]LBANY, N. Y., Feb. 4 (AP) [New] York is brewing a new winter [for] the old folks to hand down to [their] great grandchildren, a winter [that] may replace the blizzard of [Ma]rch, 1888, as the standard of [comparison].

[Th]e venerable chestnut, "Can't [comp]are with the blizzard of '88", [may] get a well-earned rest. But [Empire] State's sons and daughters [may] get just as sick of the new [one].

[...] Think this is bad? Child, you [sh]ould have seen the winter of [...]

[St]ories of service and heroism [came] from all sections. There was [a] Troop B state trooper from [...] who tramped three miles [thro]ugh heavy drifts to an isolated [farm] and carried back a sick [...]th-old baby to a waiting ambulance.

[In] Genesee county a state police [...] used sleds to bring supplies [to] families in a hamlet shut off [from] the main highway.

[Th]ere there are humorous stories. [O]ne Wayne county farm wife [sudd]enly faced with the staggering [prob]lem of accommodating more [than] 125 stalled motorists for the [night]. She pulled through, with [the] help of supplies from a bakery [truck] stalled with half a hundred other vehicles.

[...] area in the state [...] the focal point of official trans[port]ation clearing operations was [Buff]alo and western counties.

[...] by repeated blizzards and [snow]storms since December 11, the Buffalo railroad yards were [...] repeatedly. [...] [...] Association of America [...] said it was "possibly the worst tieup in Buffalo [history]." [...] Volunteers and state [...] mobilized by Gov. [Thomas] E. Dewey concentrated on [...] the yards.

[...] areas had food shortages, [...] and increased school[...]. An under sheriff of On[...] county drove 100 miles over [...] roads to take a [stric]ken farm wife to a hospital 10 miles away.

[Wh]eeler R. Farr, 62 years old, [of C]anandaigua, driving home after 48 [contin]uous hours on a New York [...]ral plow, fell asleep and col[lided] with a vehicle driven by [Willi]am J. Wolfe of Churchville. [He] was so exhausted that he [was] found still asleep after the im[pact].

[Wi]th good weather, railroad of[ficial]s said the fuel crisis may end [n]ext week, but closing of stores, [scho]ols, churches and amusement [place]s will continue for several [days] in most upstate cities. Al[bany] will lend a week-long store [holi]day Wednesday. Elmira and [Bin]ghampton started four-day [com]mercial recesses today.

[H]ighways have been most af[fect]ed in Central New York. At [one] time there were 4,000 miles [of] closed highways in the Syra[cus]e area alone.

[Me]al deliveries in Syracuse are [on a] cash and carry basis, 100 [poun]ds to a customer. Four chil[dren] in one family stayed in bed [for] days before the family se[cure]d emergency fuel.

[On]ondaga county sheriff's men [have] been so busy fighting drifts [to g]et expectant mothers to hos[pital]s that residents are making ["rese]rvations". A Manlius Center [wom]an phoned to tell the sheriff [she e]xpected to go to the hospital [a]bout 10 days".

[G]ermany Potato [R]ation Reduced

(By Associated Press)

[T]HE WEEKLY RATION of pota[toes] for German civilians has been [redu]ced by half a kilogram (about [1.1] pound), the German DNB [agen]cy reported yesterday in a [broa]dcast recorded by the Federal [Com]munications Commission. It did [not] say what the total ration now [woul]d be.

[Th]e broadcast said the cut had [been] necessitated by a "difficulty [whic]h has particularly affected the [tran]sport of potatoes," and that [pers]ons who had stored more than [...] kilograms must return 25 kilo[gram]s of their potato stock.

[La]st Friday DNB reported that [prese]nt German food ration cards [had] been extended to April 8, in[stead] of April 1, forcing consumers [to m]ake their present rations of all [...] last nine weeks instead of [...]

Extra

MALONE EVENING TELEGRAM

MEMBER OF ASSOCIATED PRESS

MALONE, N. Y., THURSDAY, APRIL 12, 1945

PRESIDENT DIES

Victim of Massive Cerebral Hemorrhage

Death Comes Suddenly at Warm Springs, Georgia

LIFE SKETCH OF PRESIDENT

By The Associated Press

The tradition-shattering presidential career of Franklin Delano Roosevelt spanned turbulent years of peace in which he worked to lift the Nation out of a depression and tumultuous years of war when he played a dominant role in charting an Allied victory.

While he gained the adulation of millions, the unprecedented moves he made and the political theories he embraced made him the frequent target for blistering criticism.

Accusations ranged from "demagoguery" to "dictatorship." The public debt jumped to a record peacetime high, then to even greater wartime peaks. Critics charged the President with trying to "pack" the Supreme Court after that tribunal had thrown out several of his favorite projects and he sought to inject "new blood" by reorganizing the membership. Some party stalwarts forsook him.

But he became the first President in history to be elected to a third term—and by a smashing majority—and then won the nomination for a fourth.

An International Statesman

Mr. Roosevelt had attained a substantial international stature in the years when he was concerned primarily with applying revolutionary remedies to an economic blight rooted in World War I.

And after the flames of a second global conflict were kindled, he became the pivotal statesman of more than 30 United Nations which pooled their might to smash a German-Italian-Japanese Axis.

Kings and queens, presidents and prime ministers, travelled to the White House to consult him.

The military strategy of nations representing 75 per cent of the earth's surface and 60 per cent of its population—a strategy that sent American fighting men, American war weapons, American food and American dollars to combat the Axis—was mapped at conferences in which he took a leading part.

In Unprecedented Parleys

He constantly shuffled and revised a prodigious war production program, framed stupendous war budgets to be met by taxes that hurt and, also at home, fought an inflation peril hardly less dangerous to the Nation than its enemies at arms.

He drew up with United Nations colleagues, as the war progressed, blueprints for peace—a peace designed to avoid the hasty mistakes of the Versailles treaty.

International conferences on a scale never before seen in history helped the President to formulate his war plans. Rising to a pinnacle of world attention with him in these councils was Britain's sturdy Prime Minister, Winston Churchill.

His intimates said nothing less than the threat of war, and finally war itself, could have prompted Mr. Roosevelt to stir up political turmoil in tremendous proportions by shattering the 150-year-old two-term presidential tradition begun by George Washington, and then running for a fourth term.

Says He Preferred to Retire

In 1940, the Chief Executive told the Democratic National Convention he was accepting renomination for a third term only because of a "storm" raging in Europe. He was re-elected overwhelmingly over Wendell L. Willkie, the Republican candidate.

Four years later Mr. Roosevelt said his preference was to retire to the family estate at Hyde Park, N. Y., where he was born January 30, 1882. He told Democratic Chairman Robert E. Hannegan in a letter:

"All that is within me cries out to go back to my home on the Hudson River, to avoid public responsibilities, and to avoid also the publicity which in our democracy follows every step of the Nation's Chief Executive.

"Such would be my choice. But we of this generation chance to live in a day and hour when our Nation has been attacked, and when its future existence and the future existence of our chosen method of government are at stake.

Accepts As 'Good Soldier'

"To win this war wholeheartedly, unequivocally and as quickly as we can is our task of the first importance. To win this war in such a way that there be no further world wars in the foreseeable future is our second objective. To provide occupations, and to provide a decent standard of living for our men in the armed forces after the war, and for all Americans, are the final objectives.

"Therefore, reluctantly, but as a good soldier . . . I will accept and serve in this office, if I am so ordered by the commander-in-chief of us all—the sovereign people of the United States."

His Republican opponent was Gov. Thomas E. Dewey of New York.

A tremendous figure of a man, despite legs left withered and useless by infantile paralysis in 1921, Mr. Roosevelt shouldered burdens as heavy as any Chief Executive ever carried. While he stood up under a job which had wrecked the health of many a predecessor, the years naturally left their mark on him

Forced to Take Rest

Influenza, sinusitis and bronchitis weakened him in the winter of 1943-44 and rumors spread about his health. In April, 1944, he bundled up his old clothes and took a month off to convalesce in shirt-sleeves on the languorous plantation coast of South Carolina. When he returned to Washington, his physician said he was in as good shape as any man of 62 could hope to be and that his condition offered no bar to another four years in the White House.

Mr. Roosevelt accepted the fourth-term nomination by radio from a naval base at San Diego, Calif. Immediately, he boarded a cruiser for his first wartime trip into the Pacific and consultations in Hawaii—where a sneak punch brought America into the war on December 7, 1941—with top commanders in the battle against Japan.

He long since had broken all Presidential travel records, and war did not deter him from pushing the mileage up around 300,000.

Momentous Decisions

Time after time, he or Mr. Churchill dared the dangers of Atlantic crossings for epochal conferences which shifted the Allies from the defensive to the offensive and changed the course of combat around the world.

Standing out in sharp relief, in the light of events the next summer, where their meetings at Cairo and Teheran, Iran, at the close of 1943. In a series of parleys they talked with Premier Joseph Stalin of Russia, Generalissimo Chiang Kai-shek of China and President Ismet Inonu of Turkey.

(To Be Continued)

Harry Truman Becomes President

BULLETIN

Washington —(AP)— Harry S. Truman of Missouri was sworn in as thirty-second President of the United States tonight at 7:09 p. m. (EWT).

By ERNEST B. VACARRO

Member of the Associated Press Senate staff, who traveled with President Truman during Truman's campaign for the Vicepresidency last fall.

Washington — (AP)— Vicepresident Harry S. Truman entered the White House tonight in one of the most critical periods in his nation's history with humble confidence that he is big enough to meet the burdens of a war-time presidency.

He entered it with a determination to call upon the best brains of the country to help guide him through the perils of war, peace negotiations and reconversion.

Those of us who travelled with him on a transcontinental speech-making tour for the vicepresidency last fall and who were in daily conference with him before and after his election, think of him as a man:

1. Whose courage has been demonstrated time and again as a campaigner and as chairman of the Senate War Investigating Committe who never hesitated to lambast those high in administration favor.

2. Whose knowledge of his own limitations is such that he never hesitates to call on others whose qualifications on matters of high importance he may consider superior to his own.

3. Whose ability to "pick the brains" of others raised the Truman committee to a status rarely enjoyed by a congressional committee.

4. Whose friendliness and modesty is the same as it was when he entered the vicepresidency and as it probably was when he was a farmboy down in Missouri.

Bells, Fire Siren Ring As FDR Dies

Though it was only a coincidence this evening, April 12, as the startling news of the death of President Roosevelt was flashed across the nation, the bells of the Congregational Church and the local fire siren lifted their voices into the air in a combined tolling and wailing suggestion of tragedy.

Many local people thought the news of the President's death was being announced by this means.

The church bells sounded the "Angelus." The fire department had been called to the home of Mrs. Vina Supernault, 41 Water St.

Conference Will Be Held As Planned

Washington — (AP)— President Truman announced tonight that the United Nations Conference called for April 26 will go on as scheduled.

FRANKLIN DELANO ROOSEVELT.

HARRY S. TRUMAN

TRIBUTES

Congressman Kilburn

"I am deeply shocked. I think every American feels a great sense of loss that our President should be taken when his leadership is so badly needed to finish victory and his immense world-wide influence used for a lasting peace."

Mayor Henry W. Badore

"As Mayor of the Village of Malone I wish to publicly express my personal sorrow and that of the community upon the death of our great leader, President Franklin D. Roosevelt.

"His administration of the conduct of the present world-wide struggle, his sponsorship of social and economic reforms, his aims and ideals for a just and lasting peace have earned for him a position among the outstanding leaders in the history of the world, and only the future can foretell his great and numerous contributions to mankind.

"Though his death at this time imposes a great burden upon his successor and upon the American people, we can pattern ourselves after him and taking to ourselves his courage, his great faith in America and in the American people, and his firm desire for peace among men and nations, unite as he would wish us under his successor, Harry Truman and strive through and with our every effort to accomplish the aim for which he truly gave his life, an early victory over our enemies and a lasting peace."

Executive Suffers Attack While Posing for Sketch; Dies Two Hours Later

Washington - (AP) - The death of President Franklin D. Roosevelt shocked Washington to its foundations today.

From the man who now will become President -- Vice President Harry Truman -- down to the least of the city's people the news was overwhelming.

Mrs. Roosevelt, after dispatching a widowed mother's message of strength to their four sons in service, prepared to fly to Warm Springs.

The capital prepared for a funeral in the East Room of the White House Saturday.

The burial of the only man to serve three terms as President -- only to die in the third month of his fourth term -- is to be at Hyde Park, N. Y.

That is the home for which he said last year all that was within him cried out for.

A cabinet meeting was called immediately and Truman was present—10 years ago an obscure county judge in Missouri. He would become the 32nd president.

The President's death was announced by his secretary, Stephen Early, who on Dec. 7, 1941, gave the world the news of the Pearl Harbor attack that plunged this country into war.

The White House called the three major news services at about 5:45 p. m., (EWT), on a conference call. There was a long pause.

Then Early came on the wire and made the electrifying announcement. His voice sounded fairly calm and measured but he obviously was laboring under intense emotion.

His first words were:

"Here is a flash.

"The President died suddenly early this afternoon - -"

There was a sudden flurry among his listeners.

"You mean President Roosevelt," someone shouted over the line.

"Of course," Early replied. "There is only one President."

Although interrupted several times, he continued to recite what he called "notes for the story."

"I have no statement," he explained.

Mr. Roosevelt had not been in the best of health for some time, it was disclosed tonight.

Last week at a banquet for Associate Judge Hugo Black of the Supreme Court, Mrs. Roosevelt disclosed to Senator Barkley of Kentucky, the Democratic leader, that the food the President had been eating recently had no taste for him.

Barkly said he remarked that Mr. Roosevelt looked thin and haggard and Mrs. Roosevelt said she also felt he was too thin.

Mrs. Roosevelt said that for several days previous the President had been taking only gruel because he had no taste for other foods.

When the death became known here, several hundred gathered outside the iron railing of the White House grounds. They questioned guards through the fence, without success. The lowering of the flag atop the White House to half staff attracted scores of other passersby late in the afternoon.

On Capitol Hill, the telephone switchboards were "hopelessly" jammed with calls.

Two physicians were at the President's bedside when death came at 4:35 p. m., Washington time. They were identified by Admiral Ross T. McIntyre, the President's personal physician, as Dr. James Paullin of Atlanta, and Dr. Howard Bruen, a Navy commander who was at Warm Springs with the President.

Physician Tells of President's Last Hours

By D. Harold Oliver

Warm Springs, Ga. — (AP)— President Franklin Delano Roosevelt died suddenly at 3:35 p. m., central time today of a massive cerebral hemorrhage.

Commander Howard Bruenn, naval physician, made this announcement to reporters shortly after White House Secretary William D. Hassett called a hurried news conference to announce the death of the nation's only fourth-term chief executive.

Mr. Roosevelt died in the "Little White House on top of Pine Mountain where he had come for a three-week rest. He was 63 years old.

Dr. Bruenn said he saw the President this morning and he was in excellent spirits at 9:30 a. m.

"At one o'clock," Bruenn added, "he was sitting in a chair while sketches were being made of him by an architect. He suddenly complained of a very severe occipital headache (back of the head.)

"Within a very few minutes he lost consciousness. He was seen by me at 1:30 p. m., fifteen minutes after the episode had started.

"He did not regain consciousness and he died at 3:35 p. m.

Only others present in the cottage were Comdr. George Fox, White House pharmacist and long an attendant on the President; Hassett, Miss Grace Tully, confidential secretary, and two cousins, Miss Laura DeLano and Miss Margaret Suckley.

Bruenn said he called Vice Admiral Ross T McIntyre, Navy's surgeon general and White House physician in Washington and that McIntyre in turn called Dr James E. Paullin, of Atlanta, an internal medicine practitioner and honorary consultant to the Navy surgeon general.

NICE-MARSEILLE EDITION

THE STARS AND STRIPES

Daily Newspaper of U.S. Armed Forces in the European Theater of Operations

Vol. 1—No. 32 Saturday, April 14, 1945 ONE FRANC

KIDS WILL PLAY

ROSEVILLE, Ga.—A city operated recreation center for children folded after four months because a nearby pool-room had absorbed all the juvenile customers.

MEXICO IRISH

SEATTLE, Wash.—Judge J. Neergaard released all Irish who traced their drinking back to St. Patrick's Day sprees, including a Mexican named Francisco Gallagher.

FDR's Death Stuns Nation

Yanks Drive Toward Reds

3rd Army Men Break Into Jena

Stars and Stripes Paris Bureau

Tanks of three American armies were driving down the last 100 miles toward link-up with the Russian armies yesterday as U. S. forces throughout Europe dipped their flags to half-mast at 0800 in silent tribute to the passing of their Commander-in-Chief.

Lt. Gen. William H. Simpson's 9th Army was across the Elbe River and unofficial reports said Magdeburg on the Elbe had fallen. Simpson's tanks and infantry pressed on toward Berlin, 50 miles away, their movements hidden under a veil of security.

Miles behind armored columns driving on the capital, U. S. 17th Airborne Div. troops captured Duisburg in the shrinking Ruhr Pocket.

Tanks of Lt. Gen. Courtney H. Hodges' 1st Army slashed 35 miles across the German heartland, crossed the Saale River and reached the Weisse River 17 miles from Leipzig.

On Hodges' right flank, armor of Lt. Gen. George S. Patton's 3rd Army entered Jena, scene of one of the decisive actions in the Napoleonic wars. The 76th Inf. Div. cleaning up behind the tanks cleared 55 towns and crossed the

(Continued on Page 4)

The New First Family

PRESIDENT TRUMAN leaves the White House with his wife and daughter Mary Margaret. Picture was taken last January at inauguration time. —PA

Many Riviera Restees Couldn't Believe News

By JAMES J. HARRIGAN
Stars and Stripes Staff Writer

News of the death of President Roosevelt shocked and appalled American and Allied servicemen here in Nice

First reports cast a pall over the gaiety which characterizes this Riviera soldier-playground. Many restees refused to believe the President had passed away. Many declares it to be a rumor or instigated enemy propaganda.

But headlines in The Stars And Stripes yesterday cleared all doubt.

Along Nice's Avenue Victoire, on Victor Hugo Boulevard, and on the Promenade Des Anglais, everywhere American soldiers gathered, the death of the President was the topic of conversation.

In front of the Le Patriote newspaper building where The Stars and Stripes is published, Pvt. Woodrow

(Continued on Page 4)

VIENNA TAKEN AFTER 7 DAYS

Stars and Stripes Paris Bureau

Fall of Vienna after seven days of bitter street fighting was announced yesterday by Marshal Stalin as the Red Army pushed deeper into Austria and Czechoslovakia along three possible routes for a linkup with Anglo-American forces.

Along the Oder River, approximately 40 miles east of Berlin, Russian artillery hammered German defenses.

In the battle for Vienna and its approaches, the Russians announced, more than 130,000 prisoners were taken.

People Cry In Streets; Rites Today

NEW YORK, April 13—The people wept today.

In little groups, they gathered on the streets of the villages and the big towns and talked haltingly of the loss of a great friend, and leader.

"It's like one of my family dying," said a soldier as he turned away from the side of St. Patrick's Cathredral. A woman walked down Fifth Avenue reading a newspaper to her companion who was crying. Nearby a sailor tried to comfort a young girl who was weeping.

Radio chains cancelled all comic programs and light music, and stopped broadcasts of advertising matter. In New York, many night-clubs closed immediately.

Body On Way North

Even as a wave of sorrow spread throughout the nation, a ten-car special train bearing the President's body left Warm Springs, Ga., where he died, at 10:15 AM CWT. Aboard it were numbers of friends and relatives associates who had hurried South upon hearing the news.

From Warm Springs the train was scheduled to go to Atlanta, then up through the Carolinas past Greenville and Spartanburg, S. C., and Charlotte, N. C.

Meanwhile President Harry S. Truman took the oath of office and immediately conferred with Army and Navy chiefs on latest developments in the global war. He proclaimed tomorrow a day of mourning throughout the Nation.

The President's body was taken to the train through a lane of soldiers from Fort Benning Ga. Two thousand soldiers from the Fort Benning Infantry school and Parachute School under the command of Maj. Gen. Fred Walker arrived early this morning to provide the honor guard.

Mrs. Roosevelt In Seclusion

Fifty picked MPs from Benning formed a lane at the little village through which the funeral cortege passed.

Mrs. Eleanor Roosevelt, accompanied by Stephen Early, the President's press secretary and Rear Adm. Ross T. McIntyre, his personal physician, arrived in Warm Springs early today in an army plane. Mrs. Roosevelt, who was described as bearing her grief "very nobly," went into seclusion at the "Little White House."

The funeral will be held in the East room of the White House tomorrow at 4 PM. At 10 PM the funeral party will leave Washington by train for Hyde Park, where the President will be buried Sunday at 10 AM in the garden between his home and the Franklin D. Roosevelt Library. President Truman will attend the Hyde Park services. Mr.

(Continued on Page 3)

PRESIDENT DIED WITH NO PAIN

WARM SPRINGS, Ga., April 13—President Roosevelt's last spoken words were: "I have a terrific headache." They were addressed to an artist who was making sketches of the President before the fireplace of the "Little White House," on top of Pine mountain.

He placed his right hand on the back of his head, laid his head back on his chair and closed his eyes, lapsing quickly into unconciousness. His Negro valet and a Filipino messboy carried him to his bedroom.

Fifteen minutes later, at 1:30 PM Central War Time, his attending physician, Cmdr. Howard Bruenn of the Navy, reached his side. The President never regained conciousness and died painlessly at 3:35 PM CWT (10:35 PM Paris time).

Dr. Bruenn said the President succumbed to a "massive cerebral hemorrhage," Bruenn said that at 9:30 AM President Roosevelt "was in excellent spirits and showed no evidence whatever of feeling ill."

'We Have Lost Wise Leader' —Marshall

WASHINGTON, April 13 (ANS) Gen. George C. Marshall, in a special message to army personnel on the death of the President, said today:

"We have lost a great leader. His far seeing wisdom in military counsel has been a constant source of courage to all of us who have worked side by side with him from the dark days of the war's beginning.

"No tribute from the Army could be so eloquent as the hourly record of victories of the past few weeks."

Secretary of War Stimson added: "We have lost a great president and a great commander-in-chief. Throughout these years of crisis when the nation was plunged into war by powerful enemies, the faith and dauntless courage of Franklin Roosevelt have never faltered. Nor has his broad vision, with which he supported his military commanders, ever failed. He believed unswervingly that the right and strength of free nations would triumph over the evils of despotism. The American people have upheld his faith."

Secretary Forrestal told the Navy: "The world has lost a champion of democracy who can ill be spared by our country and the Allied cause."

DBS CANCELS FDR MEMORIAL

Plans made for special memorial services to President Roosevelt today in Nice, Cannes and Marseille were cancelled late last night following instructions received from Washington.

A cablegram sent by the War Department to Riviera District of Delta Base Section ordered postponement of all memorial services.

It was explained that at a future date uniform memorial services would be arranged for all army installations.

As a sign of respect to the late Commander-in-Chief, flags came down to half mast yesterday and GI bars and night clubs closed up throughout DBS for a three-day period ending Sunday midnight.

SUICIDE PILOTS SINK U. S. SHIP

GUAM, April 13 (ANS)—A strong Japanese air fleet, including suicide pilots bent on self-destruction in crashes against choice targets, sank an American destroyer and damaged several other ships off Okinawa yesterday in a fierce engagement in which 118 enemy aircraft were destroyed.

All evidence suggested that most of the attacking force was wiped out by suicide crashes if not by American interceptors and anti-aircraft guns ashore and afloat.

The attack was directed against ships and supply dumps at the U. S. Tenth Army's beachhead, established Easter morning near Hagushi on the west coast. Seven planes were destroyed in the morning and 111 in a furious afternoon engagement.

For the eighth successive day, no American advances in Okinawa's southern sector were reported.

STETTINIUS IS NEXT IN LINE

WASHINGTON, April 13 (ANS)—Accession of Vice-President Harry S. Truman to the Presidency moves Secretary of State Edward R. Stettinius, Jr., up next in line for the office.

The Vice Presidency itself remains vacant, but Senator Kenneth D. McKellar (D.-Tenn.), president pro tempore, becomes presiding officer of the Senate.

Congress long ago provided for Presidential succession ranging through seven cabinet positions.

In the event of the death or resignation of a Vice President who has succeeded to the Presidency, the line is this: Secretary of State, Secretary of the Treasury, Secretary of War, Attorney General, Postmaster General, Secretary of the Navy and Secretary of the Interior.

French Vets Attack In Alps

By PAUL S. GREEN
Stars and Stripes Staff Writer

WITH FRENCH FORCES IN THE MARITIME ALPS, April 13—The Maritime Alps front, quiet since American troops drove to the Italian border last September after the Riviera "champagne campaign," has blazed into sudden action as French units took to the offensive, French headquarters disclosed today.

The offensive on the Franco-Italian border comes when Gen. Mark W. Clark's veterans are beginning their push from the other end of the Italian front

French troops, many of whom fought with the Free French at Bir-Hakeim in Africa and recently took part in the Alsace campaign, are engaged in small-scale but heavy fighting for the mountain peaks on this side of the French frontier which dominate roads and valleys inside Italy.

For seven months there was no action on this front but routine patrolling and artillery exchanges. The positions were originally taken by Yanks and Canadians of the 1st Special Service Force, now disbanded, and paratroopers of the 82nd Airborne Div. after the invasion of southern France.

Pulled out last December, they were replaced by Japanese-Americans of the 442nd Combat Team, now back with the 5th Army and artillery outfits turned infantry. The French took over more than a month ago.

Barely 30 airline miles northeast of American combat men who thought they were getting away

(Continued on Page 4)

PAPER, BUDDY?
TACOMA, Wash.—Agitated by a temporary shortage of toilet paper throughout the paper-making Northwest, wholesalers have started a "Share the Roll" campaign.

NICE-MARSEILLE EDITION
THE STARS AND STRIPES
Daily Newspaper of U.S. Armed Forces in the European Theater of Operations

LAST ROLL
CHERTSEY, England—Carrying out the deathbed request of Thomas Elston, mourners drove in his funeral procession the steam roller he had driven and loved for 38 years.

Vol. 1—No. 33 | Sunday, April 15, 1945 | ONE FRANC

3rd 40 Mi. From Dresden

BRIEF SERVICE HELD FOR FDR IN EAST ROOM

WASHINGTON, April 14—Simple funeral services for Franklin D. Roosevelt were held today at 4 PM in the East Room of the White House while the nation observed a day of mourning.

The brief service of the Episcopal Church was read by Bishop Angus Dun of the National Cathedral, assisted by the Rev. Howard S. Wilkinson of St. Thomas Church and the Rev. John G. McGee of St. John's Church.

There was no state funeral, and in accordance with the family's wishes, the body did not lie in state.

The same simplicity will mark graveside services tomorrow at 10 AM when Mr. Roosevelt will be buried in the hedge-walled family garden at Hyde Park, N. Y.

Thousands of citizens stood silently on the street and on the lawn of the White House, while inside, Mrs. Eleanor Roosevelt, Mrs. Anna Boettiger, Mr. Roosevelt's only daughter, Brig. Gen. Elliott Roosevelt, his son, and President Harry S. Truman and other members of the official family listened to the traditional prayers and hymns.

The funeral party is to entrain for Hyde Park where the Rev. Dr. George W. Anthony, rector of St. James Church, where Mr. Roosevelt was a senior warden, will hold a private burial service tomorrow.

The burial place is in a flower garden enclosed by a high hedge, between the family home overlooking the Hudson and the Roosevelt library on the estate.

In contrast to the simplicity of the services, elaborate ceremony marked the progress of the funeral train from Warm Springs, Ga., to the White House. Marines and soldiers stood vigil along the route of the 22-hour train passage, and re-

(*Continued on Page 4*)

MAJORS PLAN FDR TRIBUTE

WASHINGTON, April 14 (ANS) The opening game of the 1945 baseball season here Monday between the New York Yankees and the Washington Senators will be played as scheduled and dedicated to the memory of Franklin Delano Roosevelt.

This is really President Roosevelt's game. For several years the Senators played their opening game a day ahead of the rest of the teams for the convenience of Mr. Roosevelt.

Senator officials said the crowd will stand a full minute in silent prayer and tribute to the man who frequently befriended the game.

No changes will be made in the inaugural day program "because Mr. Roosevelt would have wanted things to go on as usual," a spokesman for Clark Griffith said.

President Truman who, as vice president two months ago, promised he would "throw out the first ball if President Roosevelt cannot do it," may not be able to keep his promise. He is scheduled to address a joint session of Congress at 1 PM that day.

Peace Rumors Sweep U. K.

Reports that Hitler's Reich was about to fall swept Britain yesterday, after the receipt of important news from the front had caused Prime Minister Churchill to cancel his plans for flying to Washington to attend President Roose-

Eisenhower Orders 30 Days Mourning

In honor of President Roosevelt, Gen. Eisenhower has ordered 30 days of mourning by American troops in the ETO, and wherever military operations permit the colors will be displayed at half-staff for 30 days.

The supreme commander sent Mrs. Eleanor Roosevelt a message in which he called the commander-in-chief's passing "a personal loss and grief to millions of American fighting men." He promised that his troops would "continue and intensify our efforts in order that the great task which he undertook is fulfilled in complete victory."

TORNADO TOLL REACHES 100

OKLAHOMA CITY, April 14 (ANS)—As reports filtered in from isolated areas, the toll of Thursday's tornado in Oklahoma, Arkansas and Missouri rose above 100.

Oklahoma had 80 deaths, with the most disastrous storm at the town of Antlers in the southeast section, where 58 were known dead.

Twenty were dead and five were missing in northwestern Arkansas. Five were killed in the Missouri Ozarks. The injured ran into hundreds, property damage into thousands.

Fewer than half the dead at Antlers had been identified, chiefly because the bodies were taken to nearby cities before relatives had time to view them. Antlers has only one funeral home and two of its employees were killed in the storm.

Many of the 600 soldiers who came in from Camp Maxey, Tex., to do medical work, aid the police and provide food from field kitchens were being withdrawn.

All utilities were working, but were overburdened. The Red Cross has set up a headquarters to aid in rehabilitation, but no definite plans for rebuilding have been made.

Things Are Looking Up

WITH SMILES on everybody's faces, Lt. Gen. George S. Patton, Jr., explains a point to Gen. Eisenhower while Gen. Omar N. Bradley and Lt. Gen. Courtney Hodges look on. They were photographed somewhere in Germany recently.

B29s Fire Tokyo Anew; Japs Say Palace Hit

GUAM, April 14 (ANS)—Huge explosions and fires devastated Tokyo today after hundreds of Superfortresses, in their greatest raid of the war, poured incendiary bombs on the city. Tokyo said the Imperial Palace of Emperor Hirohito was set afire.

A Japanese communique also said the main building and sanctuary of the Meiji shrine, one of the great Shinto shrines in Japan, had been "burned to ashes."

A U. S. correspondent who rode over Tokyo in a B29 said flames and blasts of explosions spread through a five-square-mile target area as the great fleet of bombers hit the concentrated munitions production zone. One tremendous blast threw a Superfortress 5,000 feet upward.

The roar of explosions could be heard more than 100 miles away from Tokyo as the Marianas-based Superforts swung away from Japan after the war's 16th heavy raid on the enemy capital.

Knifing Into East Front Rear Areas

BULLETIN

A SHAEF flash last night announced the capture of Franz von Papen, German ambassador to Turkey and one of Adolf Hitler's diplomatic advisers. No details were given. Von Papen was attached to the German embassy in Washington during the first World War and was expelled from the U. S. after the Black Tom explosion.

Stars and Stripes Paris Bureau

Three American armored divisions were driving into the rear areas of German armies fighting on the Russian front last night after thrusting up to 47 miles east of Jena to within 40 miles of Dresden and 90 miles of Gorlitz on the eastern front.

No opposition has materialized to stop this armored rush between Leipzig and Czechoslovakia and there were no indications reported that Germans facing east have turned around to meet the Americans driving into their rear from the west.

Supreme Headquarters reports up to midafternoon yesterday, lagging 16 hours behind front reports in some cases, placed the 9th Armd. Div. of the 1st Army 15 miles south of Leipzig and the 4th and 6th Armd. Divs. of Lt. Gen. George S.

(*Continued on Page 4*)

RUSSIAN TRICK TOOK VIENNA

LONDON, April 14 (AP)—Russian troops today fought west and north of Vienna which was captured yesterday after discovery of an underground passage permitted the Red Army to move under the German defenders and attack them from the rear without reducing the city to rubble.

Today, strains of "The Blue Danube," played by the Soviet conquerers floated over the captured Austrian capital while Russian field kitchens fed hungry children and mothers.

Tolbukhin's forces, pushing along the Danube valley toward Linz and Munich and across southern Austria toward Graz, smashed enemy resistance and captured the railway station of Hagenbrunn, about six miles north of Vienna.

Before Berlin, Russian artillery hit German positions along the Oder river. Berlin broadcasts said German recon photos indicated the Russians are getting set for a large attack in this sector although main troop movements have not yet started.

B17S HIT NAZIS NEAR BORDEAUX

Stars and Stripes Paris Bureau

Eighth Air Force yesterday hurled more than 1,150 heavies in a two-hour bombing attack against an estimated 35,000 German troops concentrated in the Gironde River pocket, north of Bordeaux.

The Forts and Liberators flew unescorted for the first time in months. Five heavies are missing.

The bombers dropped more than 3,500 tons of explosives on AA batteries and other installations in the German-held area which commands the Atlantic port.

Armored Units Cutting Reich In Two

MOVING FASTER than the map-maker's pencils, 3rd Army's 4th Armored Division was officially reported yesterday 40 miles west of Dresden and 1st Army's 9th Armored was 15 miles south of Leipzig. Farther south, Gen. Patton's 11th Armored entered the outskirts of Wagnerian Bayreuth, 25 miles from Czechoslovakia.

COOLER
Scattered Showers and Cooler; Moderate Winds Monday

The Detroit Free Press

MONDAY, MAY 7, 1945 — On Guard for Over a Century — Vol. 115—No. 3 — Five Cents

METRO FINAL

"Augsburg Germans Want to Hang Nazis"—See Jack Bell on Page 18.

Weird Tale of International Peace Intrigues Bared

ROME—(UP)—Allied headquarters disclosed the inside story of the surrender in northern Italy, a tale as fantastic as ever appeared between the covers of a work of fiction.

It detailed two months of secret negotiations carried on by German commanders without the knowledge of Adolf Hitler and introduced a dachshund named Fritzel and a midnight train named The Cloak and Dagger Special as elements in the real-life story of international intrigue.

The 10,000-word announcement titled "The Story Behind the German Surrender" revealed that the late Benito Mussolini, during his last days, was "led around by the nose" by his late mistress, Clara Petacci, and that only as late as April 18 did Adolf Hitler begin worrying about his future.

Mussolini, it said, wanted to die a hero's death in battle, but was prevented from doing so by his mistress. One of the Germans who participated in the negotiations said, "Mussolini is being pulled this way and that way by the women around him."

THE ACCOUNT revealed that the replacement of Field Marshal Albert Kesselring as commander in Italy by Col. Gen. Heinrich von Vietinghoff almost upset the plans for surrender but that Gen. Mark W. Clark's thunderous offensive which started April 9 did the trick.

Heinrich Himmler learned that SS Gen. Karl Wolff, commander of SS forces in Italy and Austria, had been to Switzerland and almost halted the negotiations with a telephone call.

Flying weather was precarious and negotiating German generals almost were killed several times by Allied planes. But in the end the surrender was signed at Caserta, near Naples, last Sunday.

THE NEGOTIATIONS began when Allied agents in Switzerland reported that they had received feelers in February from a highly placed Nazi military commander.

Headquarters here simply watched the back-door maneuvering until March 2, when the Allied agents reported that two German officers had arrived at the Swiss frontier and were desirous of establishing a communications channel with the Allies.

One of those Germans said he would return March 8 with credentials and definite proposals after consulting with Wolff at Fasano, Italy. As a test of his ability to produce results, the officer was asked to release certain Italian patriots held by the Germans. He did.

On March 8, Wolff and two officers arrived at the same Swiss border town and Allied agents reported that they were prepared for surrender discussions.

FIELD MARSHAL Sir Harold R. L. G. Alexander, Allied

Turn to Page 3, Column 4

★ ★ ★ ★ ★ ★ ★ ★ ★ ★ ★ ★ ★ ★ ★

London Reports:

COMPLETE SURRENDER NEAR

'Gen. Bor', Polish War Hero, Freed

Yanks Find Winant in Secret Cell; Schuschnigg's Fate Is in Doubt

BY EDWARD KENNEDY

PARIS—(AP)—Lt. Gen. Tadeuz Komorowski ("Gen. Bor"), who led the bloody Polish underground uprising in Warsaw, and Lt. John G. Winant, Jr., son of the United States Ambassador to Britain, have reached an American command post in Austria from a camp for prized prisoners of war.

Reliable officials at Rome said Kurt Schuschnigg, former Austrian chancellor; former French Premier Leon Blum, and German Pastor Martin Niemoeller had been in Allied hands for at least two days.

EARLIER, SUPREME headquarters at Paris had said Blum and Schuschnigg were spirited away from a secret Alpine prison camp at Itter Castle in Austria by the Germans just before Americans of the United States Seventh Army arrived there.

Apparently the prominent captives were liberated by the United States Fifth Army driving up from Italy.

Schuschnigg and Blum have been rumored several times to have been killed.

European leaders liberated from the Castle of Itter included former French Premiers Edouard Daladier and Paul Reynaud and former Generalissimos Maurice Gamelin and Maxime Weygand.

Komorowski, who directed the unsuccessful sixty-three-day revolt in Warsaw under hispseudonym of "Gen. Bor," was brought to the command post with Winant and liberated British notables.

They were escorted by Swiss representatives, who had taken over the special prison camp as protectors of Allied interests in enemy territory.

EXISTENCE OF the prison at Itter Castle was disclosed when the famous Basque tennis ace Jean Borotra escaped in disguise and got through German lines to Seventh Army tank forces which fought their way to the castle

Turn to Page 5, Column 1

Associated Press Wirephoto
GEN. TADEUZ KOMOROWSKI
Led Polish resistance

British Find Bock's Body

WITH BRITISH SECOND ARMY—(AP)—The riddled body of Fedor von Bock, who as a field marshal commanded the Central Army Group in the German invasion of Russia in June, 1941, was found north of Hamburg by British troops.

He had been dead about a week, and may have been caught in a strafing raid. Von Bock's body either had been ignored or was not recognized by German troops. It was left for a burial squad to pick up.

Von Bock was relieved of his army command after German failures to take both Moscow and Stalingrad.

Lewis Silent

NEW YORK — (AP) — John L. Lewis, president of the United Mine Workers, remained silent regarding resumption of work in the Government-seized Pennsylvania anthracite mines. The Government has ordered the miners to return to work Monday.

Portugal Ends German Ties

LISBON—(AP)—Portugal severed relations with Germany Sunday and sealed the German Legation, Chancery, Consulate and German Propaganda Bureau.

The decision was taken because Portugal considers that a German Government no longer exists.

A note delivered to the German minister said Portugal will hold all German property to be delivered when a new legal government is recognized.

Yanks Blast 20 Jap Ships Off Korea

Land-Based Planes Sweep Foe's Waters

BY FRANK TREMAINE

GUAM — (UP) — Navy land-based planes struck enemy shipping in the narrow waters separating Japan and the Asiatic mainland Saturday and Sunday.

They sank or damaged more than 20 Japanese merchant ships, Fleet Adm. Chester W. Nimitz disclosed.

• • •

SEARCH aircraft of Fleet Airwing No. 1 made a daring raid in coastal waters of Korea on the Asiatic mainland.

They also hit the narrow Korean straits and the Straits of Tsushima, scene of the famous Japanese naval victory over Russia 40 years ago.

Enemy ships sunk were two large oilers, a medium freighter and a small cargo ship. Two oilers were among the 16 vessels damaged.

The United States Pacific Fleet continued to bombard Jap positions on Okinawa.

But no word was received from Lt. Gen. Simon Bolivar Buckner's 10th Army on progress of the land operations.

• • •

NIMITZ'S communique reported a total of 29 Japanese aircraft downed over the week-end in addition to 199 reported in the two previous communiques.

Heavy units of the British fleet bombarded enemy airfields at Hirara and Nobara on Miyako Island, in the Sakashima group of the Ryukyus on Friday.

The force included battleships and cruisers.

British carrier aircraft attacked airfields in the Sakashima group, destroying 15 enemy planes in the air and three on the ground.

12 Lodgers Die in Fire

MOBILE, Ala. — (AP) — Twelve persons burned to death and two others were critically injured in a fire that destroyed a three-story brick lodging house.

The house, known as "Victory House," accomodated war workers.

Four guests jumped from second and third stories to the pavement. Two of these died and the others were seriously hurt.

Michigan Leads in Clothing Drive

Michigan, with a contribution of 8,334,509 pounds, led the nation Sunday in the United National Clothing Collection campaign.

Henry J. Kaiser, national chairman, disclosed 71,675,695 pounds of clothes, shoes and bedding for overseas relief had been gathered

Associated Press Wirephoto

NO HONOR—Nazi supermen once drank from super duper beer glasses like the one on the table beside Wilhelm Guillon, 76, a janitor in the Sterneckesbrauhouse, Munich. It was here that the eight original members of the Nazi Party once met. Guillon served as a waiter for Hitler in 1921. The table in this meeting room is the original Nazi council table.

Gas Refund Date Is Set

Rebates May Equal Half of 1944 Bill

The average domestic and commercial user of natural gas in the Detroit area should receive a refund equal to half the 1944 gas bill when the $20,000,000 in rate cuts is distributed.

Richard A. Sullivan, City utilities rate consultant, estimated that amount as the average return to householders. He expressed the hope that the return would be made within two and a half months.

• • •

THE MICHIGAN Public Service Commission has called a conference for 10 a. m. Wednesday in the Fort Shelby Hotel.

Representatives of the City, the County, the Consumers Power Co. and the Michigan Consolidated Gas Co. will discuss the method of distribution.

The refund is the largest in the history of utilities. It has been piling up for three years.

Sullivan believes that a formula, based on gas consumption over a test period should be adopted.

To be legally safe, however, James H. Lee, assistant corporation counsel, believes that each bill and rebate should be computed.

"The next step will be to have the Panhandle Eastern Pipeline Co. file new rates, in accordance with the reduction, with the Federal Power Commission," Sullivan said.

"All the rates from Nov. 1, 1942 to June 1, 1945 will have to be refigured on the basis of the reduction. About $8,000,000 of the $20,000,000 will be refunded to Detroit consumers."

DEATH IS THE RINGMASTER

Ringling Circus Aerialist Plunges to Her Doom

Free Press-Chicago Tribune Wire

NEW YORK—Death played ringmaster at 11 p. m. Sunday in the circus at Madison Square Garden. It struck down a famed and pretty woman aerialist from her precarious perch 60 feet above the tanbark.

The dark-haired, bespangled victim was thirty-year-old Victoria Rumlina, of the husband-and-wife team of Torrence and Victoria, Viennese aerialists who had been with the circus for eight years.

The pair had just finished a daring act in which Torrence, hanging by a foot from a rope with a revolving pole in his teeth, swung Victoria around.

• • •

THE COUPLE had just begun to make their descent—described as one of the most graceful in the repertory of any circus performers—when Victoria's grasp on her husband's arm was somehow loosened.

Other performers reported that she had been ill during the day and might have become dizzy.

She fell, face downward. The audience was too horrified even to gasp. Several persons fainted.

Clowns and half-dressed acrobats hastily placed her body on a litter and carried her across the street to Polyclinic Hospital. She died a few minutes later.

• • •

OTHER PERFORMERS said Victoria's death bore out an old circus superstitution — that accidents come to the show in cycles of three.

Little more than a week ago eight girls fell from aerial ladders and five were injured. Just four days ago Esterina Repensky, a horsewoman, fell during the big riding act and broke her right arm.

The circus went on to its end Sunday night, in accordance with trouper tradition.

BULLETIN

By the United Press

A British Broadcasting Co. report of a broadcast by the Flensburg radio in Demark said early Monday that Adm. Karl Doenitz, new German Fuehrer, had ordered all Nazi U-boats to cease hostilities and return to their bases.

The broadcast said that Doenitz told the U-boat men that a continuation of the struggle was impossible.

Jeeps for Sale

ROME — (AP) — Negotiations are reported under way here for the sale to the Italian Government of a large number of jeeps, trucks, bulldozers and other equipment used by American forces in the Italian campaign.

Robbed of $800

John Sarfan, 52, of 3119 E. Jefferson, reported to police Sunday night that he had been robbed of $800 by two men as he was about to enter his apartment.

Purse Snatched

Mary Tademoru, of 280 E. Kirby, told police that her purse containing $350 was snatched at 10 a. m. Sunday at John R and Kirby.

Patton Smashing Ahead to Prague

Hurls 10 Divisions into Czech Fight; Pilsen Falls; 5th Enters Austria

LONDON—(AP)—In big, black type, the London morning newspapers forecast the end of the European war within a few hours.

"It May Be Today," said the Daily Mail's front-page banner line.

"All Over in Europe at Any Hour," said the Daily Herald.

"Germany's Final Surrender Imminent," said the Daily Telegraph.

"The Last Hour," declared the Daily Express.

"Germans Ready to Surrender to Russians," said the News-Chronicle, with a sub-head, "V-Day May Be Announced at Tea Time."

Nazi Army Falls Back

BY ROBERT EUNSON

PARIS—(AP)—Gen. George S. Patton hurled at least 10 infantry and armored divisions into the battle of Czechoslovakia Sunday.

His Third Army seized the great munitions city of Pilsen in a power-laden offensive designed to crush the last German army now fighting the Allies of the West.

Simultaneously, the United States Fifth Army from Italy invaded Southern Austria at two points.

It applied pressure from the south while the Third Army was ripping 45 miles deep into that dismembered nation from the north.

The German Seventh Army fell back toward the Czech capital of Prague, 50 miles northeast of Pilsen.

• • •

THE THIRD ARMY struck along a 175-mile front from Eger, in Northwestern Czechoslovakia, to Steyr, 20 miles southeast of Austria's third city of Linz.

The fall of Pilsen, second city in Czechoslovakia and home of the famed Skoda Munitions Works, carried the Third Army 45 miles inside Czechoslovakia.

Field dispatches said the flood of American tanks and men was being met by only sporadic resistance.

Broadcasts from Prague said the capital was torn by confused fighting.

German tanks were reported racing through Prague, shooting up Patriots who earlier had

Turn to Page 2, Column 1

News to Come from Capitals

New York Times Foreign Service

LONDON—Grand Adm. Karl Doenitz and his German henchmen were reported without confirmation Sunday to have decided to surrender immediately on all fronts including the Russian.

London expected formal announcement of the European victory possibly within hours.

(The Swedish newspaper Dagens Nyheter said early Monday, in an unverified dispatch from the Norwegian frontier, that Hans Thomsen, German minister to Sweden, was en route to Stockholm with German surrender documents, according to the United Press.

(The documents, it was reported, will be delivered to Allied legations Monday morning and the capitulation announcement will follow.

(The dispatch did not say whether the purported documents provided for the surrender only of Norway or for all German-held areas.)

• • •

LENDING credence to reports, mainly from Stockholm, that the Germans had decided not to make Norway a battlefield was the silence of the Oslo radio except for a brief message in which Doenitz told the Germans not to scuttle their ships.

Both the British Press Association and the Exchange Telegraph Agency reported that the hour of surrender on all fronts was "approaching at unforeseen speed."

Prime Minister Winston Churchill worked at No. 10 Downing St.

Turn to Page 2, Column 6

IN DER FUEHRER'S CELLAR

Detroiter Drinks on Hitler

Chicago Tribune Foreign Service

BERCHTESGADEN — Said Pvt. Clyde Wilcox, of Detroit, in the basement of Adolf Hitler's retreat in Berchtesgaden:

"It takes too long to pull a cork."

With that he knocked the top off a bottle of 1928 vintage champagne with his gun butt.

He and two comrades drank a toast—to the war's end. Just a few minutes before, the First and Nineteenth German Armies had surrendered.

"It's been a long time," Wilcox said. "But we never doubted the end. I hope it's not the Pacific for me now."

On Inside Pages

An Editorial of Significance

"Freedom Still Lives" is the theme of a brilliant, full-page editorial by Malcolm W. Bingay in today's Free Press. Many readers will want to retain as a souvenir this illustrated editorial dealing with the conquest of Germany. It appears on Page 8.

VINSON ASKS COMMON SENSE

Sober V-E Rejoicing Urged

WASHINGTON—(AP)—The Government Sunday left to the "common sense" of the American people and local officials the manner of celebrating when V-E Day comes.

A statement of War Mobilizer Fred M. Vinson said Federal authorities asked that war production continue uninterrupted with the formal ending of hostilities in Europe and that there be "no greater interruption of normal activity than the peoples' sense of sober rejoicing demands."

The statement said that "numerous citizens and local officials have inquired whether the Federal Government looks with favor upon local celebrations, following the termination of hostilities in Europe, which interrupt the normal course of business."

It added that "the Federal authorities will not attempt to prescribe a rigid rule of conduct. . . ."

EUROPE WAR ENDS

EXTRA

ROCHESTER TIMES-UNION

This newspaper is supplied daily with complete telegraphic reports of The Associated Press, United Press, International News Service, The Gannett National and Empire State Services and full photo coverage.

VOL. XXVIII. NO. 49 ROCHESTER, N. Y., MONDAY, MAY 7, 1945 6 PAGES Daily Entered as Second Class Matter, Postoffice, Rochester

NAZIS QUIT

In Remaining Pockets

Reims, France--(AP)--Germany surrendered unconditionally to the Western Allies and Russia at 2:41 A. M French time today (8:41 P. M., EWT Sunday). The surrender took place at a little red school house which is the headqurarters of Gen. Eisenhower. The surrender which brought the war in Europe to a formal end after five years, eight months and six days of bloodshed and destruction was signed for Germany by Col. Gen. Gustav Jodl, chief of staff of the German army.

It was signed for the Supreme Allied Comman by Lt. Gen. Walter Bedell Smith, chief of staff for Ge Eisenhower. It was also signed by Gen. Ivan Suslop roff for Russia and by Gen. Francois Sevez for Franc

Before the European war ended the men who start it, Benito Mussolini and Adolf Hitler, were dead and was Franklin D. Roosevelt, who had mobilized the wo against them.

President Roosevelt, one of the first leaders to recog nize the ultimate meaning of the Rome-Berlin Axi died Apr. 12, 1945, while working on plans for world re habilitation. He lived to see the Allied armies burst int Germany for the kill. He was mourned by freedom-lovir peoples everywhere with an almost personal grief.

Unmourned and unhonored, his final clay battered the boots of his former subjects, Mussolini was execu by Italian Partisans. He had been little more than a ba ground shadow in the final days of the war he entered w dreams of empire.

On May 1, a few hours after Mussolini was buried, Hamburg radio broadcast that Hitler had died in the Ber Reichschancellery, fighting Bolshevism with his last brea There were some doubts as to the manner, but the All world seemed disposed to accept the fact of death.

The collapse of Germany was foreshadowed last July when at attempt was made to kill Hitler and seize power what the dictator said was a small clique of "foolish, crimina nally stupid" German officers.

This revolt among Hitler's entourage, coming alm exactly a year after the sorry lackey Benito Mussolini been broken in Italy; the rapid advances of Russian arm in the east, the drive of Allied armies in Italy, and the s cess of the most difficult amphibious invasion in history, invasion of Normandy, all suggested that the German ar was approaching a debacle.

At the start, the war looked to the world, grossly und rating German preparations, like the throw of a mad adv turer.

Allies Narrowly Escape Defeat

It turned out that the Allies snatched victory only af hairbreadth escape from defeat.

Hitler opened it with a razzledazzle of propagand secret weapons, armored spearheads, bombing armada parachute troops, Fifth Columns and political sleight-o hand which quickly established him as a sinister Barnum war.

Before it ended, merged with the war in Asia and Pacific by the Japanese attack on Pearl Harbor, it had be fought on all the oceans and continents.

"In this war there will be no victors and losers, merely survivors and annihilated." Hitler threatened, a accordingly he set a pace for ruthlessness and cruelty precedented in modern war.

The conflict became:

A War of Secret Battles—Long, silent struggles to sm his invasion fleet off Britain, to master the submarine wh imperiled the United States as never before, to crush ro bomb launching sites in France.

New Inventions, Techniques Used

A War of Secret Weapons—In which the Allies w radar, a brand new conception of massed fleets of invas barges, the technique of mass bombing through clouds, many other inventions, outdid Hitler.

War in the Air—In which whole armies of millions gaged. For the first time the capitals of great nations scores of other cities were marked for methodical destruct

A War of Cities—Stalingrad, Liningrad, Odessa, Se topol, Cassino—whose streets and houses were turned trenches and forts. A new technique of battle in the ru of cities developed. London was blitzed, and Berlin shatte

A war underground between Quislings and armies resistance, and a war of psychology in which the four fr doms and the Atlantic Charter were used to combat Na idealogy.

(Please Turn Page)

U. S., Britain Call For Evidence in Seizure of Poles

By JOHN M. HIGHTOWER

San Francisco—(AP)—The United States and Britain were reported by United Nations Conference officials today to have demanded of Russia that she supply her evidence against the 16 arrested leaders of the Polish underground.

The aim is to break the latest Big Three deadlock over Poland. It is part of a strategy sidetracking the Polish row from the main line of the conference so the Big Three may try for maximum unity in designing a world organization for future peace.

The goal is to shift the dispute to Washington, London and Moscow getting from the Russians a full explanation of the arrests. President Truman and Prime Minister Churchill are reported to have intervened directly with Marshal Stalin.

Russian Foreign Commissar Molotov is now slated to quit San Francisco for Moscow around mid-week. So long as he is here, speculation continues that Russia may give the conference a sensation by making known her future plans toward Japan. The collapse of German armies has stimulated this speculation. For any such momentous move, either Stalin, or Molotov in his present situation here, might serve as an announcer.

Latin Issue Rises

On the main line of conference developments, word spread today that Stalin may have replied favorably to Molotov's request for instructions on the review and regional arrangements amendments to the Dumbarton Oaks charter, left over from last Friday night's meeting of the Big Four.

If this information proves correct, then a scheduled meeting of foreign ministers today could produce complete harmony on the changes which the Big Four want in the Dumbarton Oaks plan.

This would not solve all the problems before the conference by any means. Perhaps the greatest developing issue is the demand of the Latin American countries that the Pan American security system be allowed to be independent of the proposed world security council in using force to block aggression.

The Latin American nations also are reported upset by a big-power amendment which says that in selecting the six non-permanent members of the security council, the world assembly may take into account their ability as warring nations and also their locations in the world.

Times-Union Extra!

THIS Times-Union is an EXTRA edition, printed early today because of major news developments which have been received ahead of regular publication hours.

DUE to curtailment of newsprint, both by governmental restriction and manufacturers' allowance, this EXTRA edition lists SIX pages. Only by limitation to this size could an extra be published for YOUR convenience and information.

ADVERTISING and many news and feature columns have been eliminated for which The Times-Union expresses regrets to readers and advertisers. The Times-Union believes service to its readers most important in flashing this news, hence the curtailed editions.

LATER editions of The Times-Union, complete in every detail, are available at regular distribution points.

Remember '18? This Time War Only Half Over

This was joyous Rochester when the Armistice was announced Nov. 11, 1918. That time the war was all over and the shouting had begun. This time, with fighting ended in Europe, another major war remains to be won against the Japanese. Picture shows 1918 crowd at Main and North streets. Note time on clock on Sibley Tower.

Yanks Pound Jap Sea Lanes; 33,462 Nips Die on Okinawa

Guam—(AP)—Hammering at Japan's shrinking sea lanes, land-based American bombers sank or damaged 20 enemy ships Saturday at the entrance to the Sea of Japan, the Navy reported today. The planes came from Okinawa, where U. S. ground forces have killed 33,462 Nipponese—15 for every Yank slain.

While U. S. bombers harried shipping in the straits linking Japan and Korea, the British Fleet shelled Southern Ryukyu Islands, 800 miles to the south, in its first announced bombardment while operating with the U. S. Fifth Fleet. One major British ship was damaged, but was able to resume operations.

Adm. Chester W. Nimitz' communique today made no mention of ground action on Okinawa, where Yanks resumed a general offensive Saturday after killing off 3,000 Japanese who made a futile tank-led counterattack.

Failure of the Nipponese attack brought their losses since the beginning of the Okinawa campaign Apr. 1 to 3,462 killed and 700 prisoners. U. S. ground casualties up to last Thursday were 14,283, including 2,337 killed, 11,432 wounded, 514 missing. Including Navy losses this brings the American casualty total for the Okinawa operation to 19,834, of whom 3,468 were killed.

Japanese planes made new attacks on U. S. shipping around Okinawa Saturday and Sunday, damaging one light unit. Four attacking aircraft were shot down. Eighteen others were destroyed by British carrier planes supporting the naval bombardment in the Southern Ryukyus.

Another Huge Murder Camp!

London—(AP)—The Moscow radio said today that more than four million persons of various European nationalities were killed by the Germans in the Oswiecim concentration camp in Poland.

The broadcast quoted the Soviet Extraordinary State Commission describing the camp as "far surpassing all hitherto known German death-camps in its elaborate equipment, technical organization and mass-scale extermination of people."

"German professors and doctors conducted here mass experiments on perfectly healthy men, women and children" the report said. "They conducted experiments in sterilization of women, castration of men, experiments on children, experiments on artificial infection of masses of people with cancer, typhus and malaria and they tested poisons on live people."

Text of German Broadcast on Capitulation

By United Press

The text of a speech by German Foreign Minister Count Ludwig Schwerin von Krosigk as broadcast by the Flensburg radio and recorded by the British Broadcasting Company.

German men and women: The high command of the armed forces on orders of Grand Admiral Doenitz has today declared the unconditional surrender of all German fighting troops.

As leading minister of the Reich government which the Admiral of the Fleet has appointed for dealing with war tasks, I turn at this tragic moment of our history to the German nation.

After a heroic fight of almost six years of incomparable hardness, Germany has succumbed to the overwhelming power of her enemies.

To continue the war would only mean senseless bloodshed and futile distintegration.

The government, which has a feeling of responsibility for the future of its nation, was compelled to act on the collapse of all physical and material forces, and to demand of the enemy the cessation of hostilities.

B-29s Pound Kyushu Fields

Guam—(AP)—Airdromes on Kyushu, southernmost of the Japanese mainland islands, were pounded by about 60 Marianas-based Superfortresses today. Good bombing results were obtained in clear weather.

The B-29 raid was the 17th on Kyushu since Mar. 27, when Superforts began their campaign against staging bases from which the Japanese have launched attacks on American positions and shipping at Okinawa, 325 miles to the south.

Three B-29s were lost and between eight and 15 enemy interceptors shot down in Saturday's triple raid against Kyushu air fields and the Hiro naval aircraft plant near Kure. Tokyo reported 25 Superforts laid mines in the Inland Sea Saturday night.

Poultry Dealers Call Holiday

New York—(AP)—A poultry holiday, starting today and continuing until retailers can "buy and sell poultry at ceiling prices," has been called by unanimous resolution of representatives of 5,000 retail kosher meat and poultry dealers.

VICTORY ISSUE
May 8, 1945

News Chronicle

4 a.m. EDITION

No. 30,881 TUESDAY MAY 8 1945 ONE PENNY

TODAY IS V DAY

Today and tomorrow are national holidays: Churchill speaks at 3 p.m., the King at 9

TODAY IS V DAY AND A PUBLIC HOLIDAY. TOMORROW IS V DAY PLUS ONE AND IS ALSO A PUBLIC HOLIDAY.

THIS WAS ANNOUNCED LAST NIGHT IN THE FOLLOWING OFFICIAL STATEMENT:

"It is understood that in accordance with arrangements between the three Great Powers an official announcement will be broadcast by the Prime Minister at three o'clock tomorrow afternoon, May 8.

"In view of this fact, tomorrow, Tuesday, will be treated as Victory in Europe Day and will be regarded as a holiday. The day following, May 9, will also be a holiday.

"His Majesty the King will broadcast to the peoples of the British Empire and Commonwealth tomorrow at 9 p.m.

"Parliament will meet at the usual time tomorrow."

The unconditional surrender of Germany was first announced to the world at 2.9 yesterday afternoon by the Germans themselves.

Broadcasting then, von Krosigk, the Foreign Minister, said: "The High Command of the armed forces, at the order of Grand-Admiral Doenitz, has today declared the unconditional surrender of all fighting German troops."

FULL CEREMONY IN BERLIN TODAY

The surrender had been signed at 2.41 a.m. in the small red school-house near Rheims which Gen. Eisenhower uses as his headquarters. Col.-Gen. Jodl signed for Germany.

The total surrender will be made today to Gen. Eisenhower, representing the Western Allies, and to Marshal Zhukov, representing the Soviet Union.

The German representatives are not yet known, but it is understood that Guderian, Chief of the Imperial Staff, will be the signatory. It is expected that the signing will take place in Berlin.

Boehme, commander of the Wehrmacht in Norway, announced last night that his troops would have "to bow to the dictate of our enemies in the interests of the German cause as a whole."

The Swedish radio last night reported an Allied fleet of 48 ships cruising off Oslo Fiord.

London lit its victory fires last night

News Chronicle Reporters

LONDON decided last night to celebrate V Day without waiting for further orders.

Scenes in the West End assumed a fantastic air, rivalling Boat Race celebrations and recalling the Armistice Night of 1918.

With nightfall, hundreds of bonfires threw a lurid glow into the clouds over the city, reminiscent of the "fire-raising" raids on London of 1940-41.

And above the roar of cheering, singing and shouting, was heard the hum of aircraft circling overhead—making even more vivid the memories of the "blitz" days.

All the Allies

East End and West End—neither waited for official news

Victory bonfires burned in the East End and the West End last night. The people of Havering Street (above), in blitzed Stepney, made theirs from the debris of wrecked houses. ... celebrators set fire to a pile of

Helpless P.C.

FULL SURRENDER WAS SIGNED IN A SCHOOLROOM

RHEIMS, Monday.

AT 2.41 a.m. today Col.-Gen. Jodl, German Chief of Staff, signed the unconditional surrender of Germany in the little red schoolhouse which is Gen. Eisenhower's H.Q.

Gen. Eisenhower was not present. For Britain and the U.S. Gen. Bedell-Smith signed the surrender document; Gen. Ivan Susloparov signed for the Soviet Union and Gen. Francois Sevez for France.

The German emissaries were repeatedly asked: "Do you understand the significance of the terms?" The Germans said that they did.

When the signing was completed Gen. Jodl said: "With this signature the German people and the German armed forces are, for better or worse, delivered into the victors' hands."

Reuter and B.U.P.

"SENSELESS FOR US TO CONTINUE"—Krosigk

Firelit dancers

German cruisers surrender

The King to Gen. Eisenhower

Spain and Sweden break with Nazis

Fighting goes on in Prague

Lublin wants to try arrested Poles

News and Pictures only

[THE WAR YEARS, II *continued*]

It was the most destructive war in human history.

In the six years since Hitler's armies marched into Poland, sixteen million soldiers were killed. Some eighteen million civilians died. Untold millions were wounded or never accounted for.

Although America did not enter the war until 1941, nearly 300,000 Americans gave their lives.

On May 7, 1945, a formal surrender document was signed in the headquarters of General Dwight D. Eisenhower in Rheims, France. The treaty required the surrender of all German forces and marked the end of the war in Europe as of midnight, May 8, 1945.

On August 6, 1945, the United States dropped the first atomic bomb on the city of Hiroshima, Japan. Three days later, another atomic bomb was dropped on Nagasaki.

On August 14, Emperor Hirohito announced that Japan would surrender, and on September 2, 1945, the Japanese signed the formal surrender document aboard the U.S. battleship *Missouri* in Tokyo Bay.

SANTA FE NEW MEXICAN

The Oldest Newspaper in the Southwest, Founded in 1849

MEMBER AUDIT BUREAU OF CIRCULATIONS | SANTA FE, NEW MEXICO, MONDAY, AUGUST 6, 1945 | ASSOCIATED PRESS UNITED PRESS | Price 5c

os Alamos Secret Disclosed by Truman

TOMIC BOMBS DROP ON JAPAN

PITOL

ILL HARRISON

Deadliest Weapons in World's History Made In Santa Fe Vicinity

Santa Fe learned officially today of a city of 6,000 in its own front yard.

The reverberating announcement of the Los Alamos bomb, with 2,000 times the power of the great Grand-Slammers dropped on Germany, also lifted the secret of the community on the Pajarito Plateau, whose presence Santa Fe has ignored, except in whispers, for more than two years.

Decision to locate the Atomic Bomb Project Laboratory on mesa an hour's drive from Santa Fe meant that it was necessary for the Army Engineers to construct an entirely new town to house the workers and their families. Primary reason for selection of the isolated site was security.

Ranch School Site

When the Army took over the property early in 1943 there were a few buildings which had been occupied by the Los Alamos Ranch School. New buildings began going up at once. Today there are 37 in the main technical area and about 200 others on the property used for the project itself. Three hundred buildings containing 620 family units, also were constructed, as well as military barracks, hospital buildings and structures for administrative offices.

Dr. J. R. Oppenheimer, one of the foremost physicists in the country and director of the laboratory, came to the site during early stages of construction. Other scientists and technical workers followed soon after.

Scientific groups which had been working on the project elsewhere in the country moved in rapidly, bringing their equipment with them. The Harvard cyclotron was in operation six weeks after it had reached the site.

Tortuous Route

Nearest railroad facilities are at Albuquerque and Santa Fe. This made it necessary to truck everything from those cities, at least. The road from Santa Fe is a tortuous one, and in the beginning, the last 18 miles were not paved. This was bad enough for passenger cars, and presented a particularly tough problem in hauling heavy loads.

Today the community has more than 6,000 residents. Slightly less than two-thirds are civilian men, women and children and the remainder military personnel. The post commandant is Col. Gerald R. Tyler.

First need of arriving personnel in mess halls, or in a large cafeteria. was housing. Various types were constructed, to meet different needs. There are three-room prefabricated, individual houses; three-room apartments, eight to a building, and four- and five-room apartments, four in a two-story unit. There are some hutments, Quonset-type huts and government and personally-owned trailers.

Bachelor Dorms

Dormitories have been constructed for unmarried personnel, or persons who do not have their families with them. Rents, for family groups, are based on earnings. Apartments are unfurnished and family groups ordinarily bring their furniture with them, although some items of government furniture have been available.

Housewives shop for food for daily meals at an army commissary where ration points are as important as elsewhere. A "trading post" offers items needed in everyday life and there are the usual post exchange stores.

Personnel living in dormitories eat There is also a dining room with waitress service.

City Dads, Too

A "town council" of eight elected members serves in an advisory capacity, meeting with representatives of the project and of the commanding officer. There is a school board, appointed by Colonel Tyler and Doctor Oppenheimer, which oversees operation of an accredited elementary school and high school. There

(Continued on Back Page)

REVOLUTIONARY

News of the development at Las Alamos of an atomic bomb immediately raised conjecture regarding the potential industrial uses of the energy.

The power of the atomic force harnessed by scientists in the secret projects is almost beyond comprehension—one bomb packing the wallop of the bomb loads of 2,000 Superforts. Talk was at once heard of the possibility of the newly controlled energy replacing coal, electricity, gasoline, water as a source of power.

That the study of the subject will continue was assured by the appointment by the Secretary of War of a committee to carry on investigation of atomic energy.

Spokesmen for the Las Alamos project said they had not been informed if this meant post-war continuation of the mountain project.

TERRITORIAL CHANGES OF WORLD WAR II—Black areas on map are those parts of Germany which the Big Three proposes will come under Polish rule. Shaded area is territory which Russia has taken control over since the start of hostilities on the continent. Northern East Prussia, proposed as Russian by the Big Three, is the newest addition to Soviet territory. There still remains some question as to final disposition of the port of Stettin. Note the large section of Baltic coastline of the proposed new Poland.

4 More Nippon Cities Now Smoldering Ruins

By The Associated Press

American airmen said they turned four more forewarned Japanese cities to ashes today as 750 Superforts and Mustang fighters reportedly swept the enemy's sacred islands with fire bombs, rockets and parachuted mines.

B-29 crewmen returning to their Marianas Island bases told of setting fires visible for 150 miles at sea. Some ran into intense antiaircraft fire and strong interception including rocket planes as they raided cities Tokyo described as "defenseless".

Waves of B-29s from the Marianas Islands and Mustang fighters from Iwo Jima struck as American commanders reported 17 Nipponese ships and small craft and 61 locomotives were destroyed or damaged in previous aerial blows, reaching over 4,500 miles from Paramushiro to Singapore.

Terror-ridden China carried the brunt of ground actions. Elsewhere land armies hunted for Japanese generals in the northern Philippines, drove toward trapping the largest Japanese force remaining in New Guinea and counted 13,000 Nipponese dead in recent fighting in monsoon-swept south Burma.

Superforts warned 12 more cities Sunday morning they were on their fire list. A formation of 580 followed up today by lighting towering fires in four of the 31 forewarned cities.

Today's targets include Nishinomiya, noted in prewar days for producing Japan's best sake, favorite alcoholic beverage of Nippon. The other industrial targets were Maebashi, 60 miles from Tokyo, saga on northern Honshu Island, and Imbari, on the southern island of Honshu. One B-29 unit hammered the Ube coal liquefaction plant with high explosives.

Japanese also reported Mustangs from Iwo raked the capital with rockets, bombs and machinegun bullets in daylight for the third time in four days.

For consolation, Japanese propagandists reported: Americans "lead a starvation life;" Nipponese raiders caught U. S. planes lined up wing to wing on two Okinawa air fields; a U. S. submarine was sunk off the coast of Japan; Nipponese subs sank two Allied vessels in the central Pacific.

Chinese reports told of new terror in China. Once-beautiful Kweilin, former southeast China air base city, was left thoroughly sacked. Fifty-thousand Chinese were killed or missing from Kanhsien in east central China. A thousand civilians were reported killed by forced poisonous injections at Ichang, enemy-held central China river port.

Americans and Filipinos eliminated an ambushing Japanese company and beat back two desperate counterattacks on northern Luzon island, running last week's toll in the Philippines to 4,740 Japanese killed and 444 taken prisoner. U S losses for the week were 27 killed, 61 wounded.

Maj. Gen. William Gill offered a 45-day furlough to any member of the 32d Division who captures an enemy general alive. Chief prize is Gen. Tomoyuki Yamashita, onetime "Tiger of Malaya" variously reported cornered, killed or flown from northern Luzon mountains.

Hi Johnson Dies at 79

WASHINGTON, Aug. 6 (AP)—Sen. Hiram W. Johnson of California, militant opponent of the League of Nations and the San Francisco Charter for a United Nations organization, died today.

The veteran Republican senator succumbed at Naval Hospital, where he had been confined for 2½ weeks. His physician, Capt. Robert E. Duncan, USN, said he died from a thrombosis of a cerebral artery.

The 79-year-old Californian died at 6:45 a. m. after having been in ill health for some time.

His political activities extended over a third of a century covering some of the most stirring events in the nation's history.

A striking figure in the Senate since first elected to Congress in 1916, he played a leading part in defeating President Wilson's League of Nations Covenant and later in opposing United States' adherence to the World Court.

His wife, whom he referred to as "the boss" was with him at the time of his death.

Senator McKellar (D.-Tenn.), President of the Senate, today will appoint a committee to attend the funeral of the silver-haired veteran.

'Utter Destruction,' Promised in Potsdam Ultimatum, Unleashed; Power Equals 2,000 Superforts

WASHINGTON, Aug. 6 (AP)—The U. S. Army Air Force has released on the Japanese an atomic bomb containing more power than 20,000 tons of TNT.

It produces more than 2,000 times the blast of the largest bomb ever used before.

The announcement of the development was made in a statement by President Truman released by the White House today.

The bomb was dropped 16 hours ago on Hiroshima, an important Japanese army base.

The President said that the bomb has "added a new and revolutionary increase in destruction" on the Japanese.

Mr. Truman added:

"It is an atomic bomb. It is a harnessing of the basic power of the universe. The force from which the sun draws its power has been loosed against those who brought war to the Far East."

The base that was hit is a major quartermaster depot and has large ordnance, machine tool and aircraft plants.

The raid on Hiroshima, located on Honshu Island on the shores of the Inland sea, had not been disclosed previously although the 20th Air Force on Guam announced that 580 Superforts raided four Japanese cities at about the same time.

The city of 318,000 also contains a principal port.

2 Billion Gamble

The President disclosed that the Germans "worked feverishly" in search of a way to use atomic energy in their war effort but failed. Meantime American and British scientists studied the problem and developed two principal plants and some lesser factories for the production of atomic power.

The President disclosed that more than 65 000 persons now are working in great secrecy in these plants, adding:

"We have spent $2,000,000,000 on the greatest scientific gamble in history — and won."

"We are now prepared to obliterate more rapidly and completely every productive enterprise the Japanese have above ground in any city. We shall completely destroy Japan's power to make war."

The President noted that the Big Three ultimatum issued July 26 at Potsdam was intended "to spare the Japanese people from utter destruction" and the Japanese leaders rejected it. The atomic bomb now is the answer to that rejection and the President said "they may expect a rain of ruin from the air, the like of which has never been seen on this earth."

Process Secret

Mr. Truman forecast that sea and land forces will follow up this air attack in such numbers and power as the Japanese never have witnessed.

The President said that this discovery may open the war for an entirely new concept of force and power. The actual harnessing of atomic energy may in the future supply the power that now comes from coal, oil and the great dams, he said.

"It has never been the habit of the scientists of this country or the policy of this government to withhold from the world scientific knowledge," Mr. Truman said. "Normally therefore everything about the work with atomic energy would be made public." That will have to wait, however, he said until the war emergency is over.

MADE IN SANTA FE

WASHINGTON, Aug. 6 (AP)—The atomic bomb disclosed by President Truman today was developed at factories in Tennessee, Washington and New Mexico.

Mr. Truman said that from 65,000 to 125,000 workers were employed on the project at Oak Ridge near Knoxville, Tenn., at Richland near Pasco, Wash., and at an unnamed installation near Santa Fe, New Mexico.

He said the work was so secret that most of the employes did not know the character of it.

WILL SHORTEN WAR

WASHINGTON, Aug. 6 (AP) — Secretary Stimson predicted today that the atomic bomb will "prove a tremendous aid" in shortening the war with Japan.

The war secretary made his statement as the Army reported that an "impenetrable cloud of dust and smoke" cloaked Hiroshima after it was hit by the new weapon from the air.

An accurate assessment of the damage inflicted by the bomb is not yet available, however, the War Department said. As soon as details of its effectiveness are learned, the department added, they will be released.

PUNCH CATASTROPHIC

WASHINGTON, Aug. 6 (AP) — The atomic bomb announced by President Truman today packs a punch equivalent to that normally delivered by 2,000 B-29s.

The President said the missile has an explosive force equal to 20,000 tons—40,000,000 pounds—of TNT. Assuming a B-29 carries a bomb load of 10 tons of TNT, four 500-plane raids by the world's biggest bombers would be necessary to equal in destructive power the exploding fury of one atomic bomb.

The atomic bomb dwarfs by 2,000 times the blast power of the British "grand-slam" bomb, which weighed approximately 11 tons.

LONDON, Aug. 6 (AP)—Germany possessed some atomic power secrets, Winston Churchill said tonight, but "by God's mercy, British and American science outpaced all German efforts."

Tomato Juice Off Rationing

WASHINGTON, Aug. 6 (AP)—Grocers scratched point values today from canned tomato juice, mixed vegetable juice and grapefruit-orange juice blends.

OPA's action in making those products ration-free yesterday followed a recommendation from Secretary of Agriculture Anderson based on lowered military demands.

Anderson also announced that civilian store shelves will get 10,000,000 more cases of canned vegetables from this year's pack than had been expected.

Despite the 10 per cent increase, however, the Agriculture Department said the total still will be less than last year's.

SENTENCED

Pat Chaves, 333 Urioste Street, faced a 100-day jail sentence and $100 fine today on conviction before Peace Justice A. E. P. Robinson of assault and battery on a woman taxi driver. The court reported the case Saturday as involving a Pat Lopez and called attention today to the correct name of the defendant.

May Be Tool To End Wars; New Era Seen

Mankind's successful transition [illegible] a new age, the Atomic Age, was ushered in July 16, 1945, before the eyes of a tense group of renowned scientists and military men gathered in the desertlands of New Mexico to witness the first hand results of their $2,000,000,000 effort. Here in a remote section of the Alamogordo Air Base 120 miles southeast of Albuquerque the first man-made atomic explosion, the outstanding achievement of nuclear science, was achieved at 5:30 a. m. of that day.

Mounted on a steel tower, a revolutionary weapon destined to change war as it has been known, or which may even be the instrumentality [illegible] end all wars, was set off with an impact which signalized man's entrance into a new physical world. Success was greater than the most ambitious estimates. A small amount of matter, the product of a chain of huge specially constructed industrial plants, was made to release the energy of the universe locked up within the atom from the beginning of time.

Credit J. R. Oppenheimer

This phase of the Atomic Bomb Project, which is headed by Maj. Gen. Leslie R. Groves, was under the direction of Dr J. R. Oppenheimer, theoretical physicist of the University of California. He is [illegible] be credited with achieving the implementation of atomic energy for military purposes.

Tension before the actual detonation was at a tremendous pitch. Failure was an ever-present possibility. Too great a success, envisioned by some of those present, might have meant an uncontrollable unusable weapon.

Final assembly of the atomic bomb began on the night of July 12 [illegible] an old ranch house. As various component assemblies arrived from distant points, tension among the scientists rose to an increasing pitch. Coolest of all was the man charged with the actual assembly of the vital core, Dr. R. F. Bacher, in normal times a professor at Cornell University.

Lightning Threatens

On Saturday, July 14, the unit which was to determine the success or failure of the entire project was elevated to the top of the steel tower.

The ominous weather which had dogged the assembly of the bomb had a very sobering effect on the assembled experts whose work was accomplished amid lightning flashes and peals of thunder.

Nearest observation point was set up 10,000 yards south of the tower where in a timber and earth shelter the controls for the tests were located. At a point 17,000 yards from the tower at a point which would give the best observation the key figures in the atomic bomb project took their posts. These included General Groves, Dr Vannevar Bush, head of the Office of Scientific Research and Development, and Dr. James B. Conant, president of Harvard University.

Lie Face Down

Actual detonation was in charge of Dr. K. T. Bainbridge of Massachusetts Institute of Technology. He and Lieutenant Bush, in charge of the Military Police Detachment, were the last men to inspect the tower with its cosmic bomb.

At the Base Camp, all present were ordered to lie on the ground, face downward, heads away from the blast direction.

Tension reached a tremendous pitch in the control room as the deadline approached. The several observation points in the area were tied in to the control room by radio and with 20 minutes to go, Dr. S. K. Allison of Chicago University [illegible]

(Continued on Back Page)

Now They Can Be Told Aloud, Those Stoories of 'the Hill'

By WILLIAM McNULTY

The secret of Los Alamos is out and The New Mexican staff and other newspapermen through New Mexico can heave a sigh—sigh, nothing; it's more of a groan—of relief.

President Truman's revelation today that it was an atomic bomb THEY were working on on The Hill ended what was probably the strictest censorship ever imposed upon the press of this state. There was practically no limit to the lengths that the guards went to and the situation at times became fantastically involved including the famed "Battle of the MPs."

Notwithstanding the censorship, the news of Los Alamos had scarcely raced about the Plaza this morning when the membership of the "I-Knew-It-All-Along" club began growing by leaps and bounds. As a matter of record, the most recent rumor, No. 6,892—straight from the horse's mouth last week—was that Alamos was working lickety-split, night and day, in the production of windshield wipers for submarines.

The taboo on the mention of Los Alamos was final, complete and until today, irrevocable and not susceptible to any exceptions whatsoever.

A whole social world existed in nowhere in which people were married and babies were born nowhere. People died in a vacuum, autos and trucks crashed in a vacuum and the MPs baseball team materialized out of a vacuum, trained in a vacuum and after their games at Fort Marcy Park, returned to the vacuum. Even the graduates of Los Alamos Ranch School, the institution which preceded Uncle Sam's Atomic Bomb Project Laboratory, ceased to be graduates of Los Alamos; they bounded direct from Public School No. 7 clear into the classrooms of Harvard and Yale.

And on days when the Alamos experimenters threw their atomic bombs about a little too vigorously and the windows of Santa Fe rattled ominously, this paper's phones would ring but the whole staff could just "no speak English".

The chain of secrecy about the project was maintained from the big cities of the East where workers were recruited clear through to the delivery of these same workers on The Hill. The Alamos Bus stop was at Sena Plaza and people laden with luggage and youngsters clinging to their arms, frequently barged into offices of that Plaza and inquired "Where do we go to work?" One of the earliest bits of Alamos lore was that of the dude Wac who had never been farther west than Albany, N. Y.; she chose the moment when The Hill bus was turning the highest point on the Jemez mountains to peek out and fainted dead away.

Under these conditions of secrecy rumors multiplied like maggots in one of Mel Hagman's garbage cans. Gas warfare, rockets, jet propulsion, death rays and — atomic bombs — were among the guesses most frequently voiced. During the last Presidential campaign, Alamos—no foolin'—was sometimes a Republican internment camp.

In the early days of the project, even the "outside employes" who knew no more of what was going on than the Japs in the foxholes of Guadalcanal, were sworn never to reveal what they didn't know anyway, for the rest of their lifetime. Our own B. B. Dunne got tangled in the wringer for so much as mentioning that "there were a lot of scientists in town".

Then there was the time when the New York Daily was whipping up a Sunday feature on Nobel prize-winners "in the U. S. It queried The New Mexican for a brief summary of what Prof X was doing now. The staff recognized the Alamos postoffice box number—that famous postal box where babies were born and to which whole crateloads of furniture assigned—but it was decided to give the professor a whirl anyway on the old "You can't shoot me for trying" principle. A letter went out to Professor X in which an interview was asked.

The next morning at 8:09 their watches must have been slow—two guards jumped the cityroom. After a heap of protestations and avowals of innocence, it was agreed that the following telegram could be sent the News:

"Your man working for Mr Whiskers on extremely hush-hush project. No soap."

The telegram was delivered in New York by a Western Union boy flanked by a covey of guards. These men then began spilling all over the News cityroom like oranges out of a busted crate.

How, they wanted to know did the News staff explain such Dick Tracy huggermugger stuff?

The News' difficulty was that the girl who had sent the telegram had gone on vacation and couldn't be reached. The News explained it after two clouded weeks in which, by report, you couldn't toss a cigaret in a wastepaper basket without setting fire to a guard.

The tantalizing little that Santa Feans knew about The Hill, only heightened their interest. There were the lights to be seen from miles away; there were the days when fires raged and smoke billowed in the mountains and always the mysterious explosions — (Lad) Holmes moved to Tesuque and had moments when she thought she was back in bomb-shattered London!

The payoff, however, came in the "Battle of the MPs". More than a year ago a boxing card was arranged in which the Santa Fe High athletes took on the Alamos MPs. The sluggers from The Hill must have been missing out on their vitamins or the Demons were packing an atomic punch because the MPs were knocked cold, two or three of them in one round and one punch practically.

Unfortunately for Mel Rhine and his Santa Fe MPs—as distinct from the Alamos MPs—soldiers read the sports pages and the next Saturday night, there was an epidemic of free-swinging in the bars and restaurants.

Frantically Rhine demanded that The New Mexican print an explanation that the one-round pushovers were decidedly NOT his MPs but he ran smack into the Alamos secrecy ban.

For hours Rhine sweated over a document which, by the time it complied with censorship requirements, rambled for no less than 700 words or so—and meant exactly nothing to anybody. It was a masterpiece of obfuscation. Of course, the boys were still swinging at the so-called "one-round MPs" for weeks before they discovered their mistake.

The Weather

New Mexico: Partly cloudy with widely scattered thunderstorms mostly over mountains during afternoon and evening; otherwise fair tonight and tomorrow; no important change in temperature.

City

High 90, low 56.

Airport

High 82, low 63.

Weather Forecast
Virginia—Generally fair Wednesday and Thursday. A little cooler Wednesday.
North Carolina — Cloudiness, few showers, little change in temperature Wednesday and Thursday.
Full U. S. Weather Bureau report on Page 2.

Norfolk Virginian-Pilot

Sun and Tides
Sun rises, 6:14 a. m. Sun sets, 8:06 p. m.
High water, 10:21 a. m. and 10:41 p. m. Low water, 4:19 a. m. and 4:23 p. m.

Vol. CLXXVIII. No. 39 — Norfolk, Virginia, Wednesday, August 8, 1945 — Five Cents the Copy

Big Jap City 60 Per Cent Razed By Atomic Bomb; Crew Tells Story

Tuck Wins, Fenwick Leads As Running Mate

Plunkett Concedes Defeat; Collins Is 2nd; Muse Trails

Administration Candidates Win in All Except Few Cities, Counties

Richmond, Aug. 7.—(AP)—William Tuck, of South Boston, was nominated today by Virginia Democrats as their candidate for Governor.

With 1,267 out of 1,715 precincts in the State tabulated, Tuck had 957 votes to 30,379 for Moss A. Plunkett, of Roanoke, a lead of almost two and a half to one which held consistently from the first returns. The returns came from virtually every area of the State and Tuck was leading in all except a few of the counties and cities.

In the three-cornered contest for the nomination for Lieutenant Governor, Charles A. Fenwick, delegate from Arlington County, held a slight lead over Lewis Preston Collins, of Marion, while State Senator Leonard F. Muse, of Roanoke, was trailing far behind and apparently was out of the race. The 76 precincts gave Fenwick 40,795 votes to 36,208 for Collins and 24,— for Muse.

Plunkett conceded defeat on the basis of incomplete returns and sent a message of congratulations to Tuck.

"My congratulations upon your winning the nomination for Governor," the message said.

Mr. Plunkett said the incomplete returns indicated he had been given about 30 per cent of the vote cast in the primary.

Tuck long has been a leader in the State Democratic Organization headed by United States Senator Harry F. Byrd and was strongly backed in the race by that organization. Plunkett, a veteran advocate of repeal of the poll tax, campaigned against what he termed machine misrule" in Virginia and asserted that "penny-pinching" by the organization had dragged Virginia near the bottom of the list of States in education, health and welfare work.

Tonight in South Boston, Tuck issued a statement asserting that Associated Press returns showed his nomination by a big majority and that he interpreted this to mean that the people of Virginia wanted

See Tuck Wins, Page 12, Col. 1

William M. Tuck

Charles R. Fenwick

Snowden Snows Under Plunkett and Collins

Amherst, Aug. 7.—(AP)—Snowden precinct in Amherst County, the first to report in today's Democratic primary, gave William M. Tuck eight votes to none for Moss A. Plunkett for the nomination for Governor. The precinct, counting before the polls closed when all eight voters had voted, gave L. P. Collins and Charles R. Fenwick 8 and Leonard G. Muse 0 in the race for lieutenant governor.

Halsey Gets Back on Job Off Jap Coast

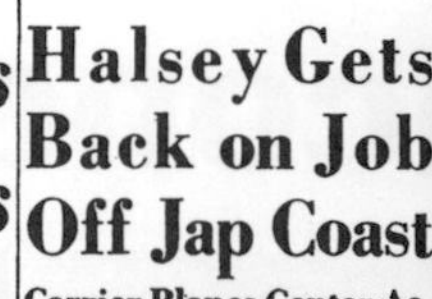

Carrier Planes Center Assaults on Life-Lines; Blockade Air-Tight

Guam, Wednesday, Aug. 8.—(AP)—Today, as reports came in on the effect of the most deadly bomb ever invented, Adm. Chester Nimitz disclosed that the fleet is back in action. It sent carrier planes Monday against the former American base of Wake. Another task force on the same day wound up three days of searching for enemy shipping off China but was able to report only small successes, so effective has been the blockade between Japan and the Asiatic mainland.

A large barge and a small coastal vessel were listed as destroyed off China. At Wake small craft also were the victims.

Carrier planes under the overall command of Vice Adm. Jesse B. Oldendorf, centered their China coast attacks on the island of Ting Hoi, 75 miles southeast of Shanghai. They damaged buildings in a seaplanes area.

Halsey Back off Japan

(In Washington, the Navy said that Admiral Halsey's Third Fleet, after dodging a threatening typhoon, is back off Japan ready to "let loose more and more destruction on vital costal installations." This suggested more devastation such as that Halsey's force visited on more than 1,300 vessels and 1,000 planes in July during which Japan's fleet virtually ceased to exist.)

In Monday's attack on Wake, an unspecified number of small craft were destroyed or damaged. On the same day, four small enemy cargo vessels were sunk in the Tushima Straits between Korea and Japan by Search Privateers of Fleet Air Wing One. The Navy raiders strafed a four-masted schooner off Korea and strafed a radar station in the Danjo Islands, west of the southern Japanese island of Kyushu. The following day, before dawn, a Navy Mitchell rocketed an unidentified enemy vessel in the Tsushima Straits.

Ship Sunk off Honshu

On Tuesday, Fleet Air Wing 18 Privateers sank a 300-foot cargo ship off the southern coast of Honshu.

Sunday, Privateers of Fleet Air Wing Four swept over the Northern Kuriles. They left two small vessels burning and sinking, bombed and strafed installations.

More than 300 Liberators, Mitchells and Invaders of the Far East

See War on Japan, Page 3, Col. 6

TENNESSEE PLANT WHERE ATOMIC BOMBS ARE MADE AND CITY WHICH BOMB HIT—A view of the gigantic production plant (above) of the Clinton Engineer Works at Oak Ridge, Tenn., where part of the atomic bomb project is located. Existence of the new secret weapon was disclosed by President Truman 16 hours after the first atomic bomb fell on Hiroshima, Japanese Naval Base. The bomb has the explosive force of 20,000 tons of TNT, its use will shorten the Japanese war or wipe out Japan. British and American scientists collaborated for more than five years in the development of the bomb. The new atomic bomb was used for the first time Sunday. An American plane dropped one on the city of Hiroshima (lower photo), a Japanese Army base. (U. S. Army Air Forces photos by radio from International News Soundphotos. Additional pictures on Page 11.)

Blast Rocks B-29 Ten Miles Away, Awed Fliers Say

Superfort Crewmen Dump Explosive Right in Center of Hiroshima, They Believe City Wiped from Face of Earth, Area Wrapped in Smoke

Guam, Wednesday, Aug. 8.—(AP)—Four and one-tenth square miles "or 60 per cent" of Hiroshima were wiped out by the devastating atomic bomb dropped Monday by a B-29, the U. S. Army Strategic Air Force Headquarters reported.

Five major industrial targets were wiped out in the city of six and nine-tenths square miles.

"Additional damage was shown outside the completely destroyed area," said a communique based on reconnaissance photographs made over the city of 343,000 on the morning of the day the bomb was dropped by a Superfort which felt the concussion of the parachute-dropped weapon while 10 miles away.

The men who participated could give no estimate of the damage other than that it "must have been extensive."

Equals 2,000 B-29's or 12,000 Tons of Bombs

Photographs, taken a few minutes after the atomic bomb blasted Hiroshima, showed a spectacular formation of white smoke rising like a long-necked mushroom over the city. Only several dots were perceivable in the target city—the remainder was obscured by clouds or smoke.

So, with a single bomb, a single Superfort accomplished as great damage as normally is inflicted by a large force of B-29's. Actually, the force of the atomic bomb is reported equivalent to 2,000 B-29's, which themselves carry a tremendous wallop in an average of six tons of bombs each.

U. S. Army Strategic Air Force Headquarters maintained its high degree of secrecy regarding operation of the revolutionary weapon and there was no indication when the next atomic bomb will be delivered to Japan.

The five major industrial targets reported destroyed at Hiroshima were not listed by Spaatz.

Crewmen related that the lone bomb struck squarely in the center of the industrial-military city of 343,000 on southern Honshu in the Japanese mainland August 6 (Pacific time) with a flash and concussion that brought an exclamation of "My God" from a battle-hardened Superfortress crew 10 miles away.

For following up on other enemy targets, there are more B-29s ready to carry more of the same awesome bombs. This was announced by Gen. Carl S. Spaatz, commander of the U. S. Army Strategic Air Force.

Crewmen who carried the awful new bomb which is declared to have an explosive power the equivalent to bombs that 2,000 Superfortresses would have had to carry previously although they were far away, felt the concussion like a close explosion of antiaircraft fire.

Col. Paul W. Tibbets, Jr., of Miami, Fla., who piloted the Superfortress and Navy Capt. William S. Parsons, of Santa Fe, N. Mex., Navy ordnance expert, described the explosions as "tremendous and awe-inspiring."

Make as Much Distance as They Could

"It was 0915 (9:15 a. m.) when we dropped our bomb and we turned the plane broadside to get the best view," said Captain Parsons. "Then we made as much distance from the ball of fire as we could.

"We were at least ten miles away and there was a visual impact even though every man wore colored glasses for protection. We had braced ourselves when the bomb was gone for the shock and Tibbets said 'close flak' and it was just like that—a close burst of antiaircraft fire.

"The crew said 'My God' and couldn't believe what had happened.

"A mountain of smoke was going up in a mushroom with the stem coming down. At the top was white smoke but up to 1,000 feet from the ground there was swirling, boiling dust. Soon afterward small fires sprang up on the edge of town but the town was entirely obscured. We stayed around two or three minutes and by that time the smoke had risen to 40,000 feet. As we watched the top of the white cloud broke off and another soon formed."

Spaatz Highly Elated at New Weapon

Details of the bombing were disclosed at a press conference attended by Gen. Carl Spaatz who termed the new bomb the "most revolutionary development in the history of the world."

Spaatz was obviously highly elated at the new bombing weapon. He said if he had had it in Europe "it would have shortened the war six to eight months." Maj. Gen. Curtis LeMay said that if this bomb had been available there would have been "no need to have had D-Day in Europe."

Just what damage was done to Hiroshima was not known. Photographs taken at the time of the bombing showed only smoke. Photo-

Crew Tells Story, Page 8, Col. 4

Tokyo's Papers Silent on Bomb But Radio Isn't

Japanese Warned to Get Out of Cities; Cabinet In Emergency Session

San Francisco, Aug. 7.—(AP)—The dire news that an atomic bomb has hit Japan still was withheld from the Nipponese in their Wednesday morning papers (Tokyo date) but—

The Japanese cabinet was reported in emergency session.

All morning papers admitted grave concern and bitterly denounced the "new-type bomb attack."

In London, The Daily Mail listening post reported hearing the Japanese people warned to evacuate big cities.

No domestic broadcast referred to the explosive as "atomic" although "atomic bomb" was mentioned in a broadcast to the American zone.

Tokyo's Wednesday morning papers all reported the "new type" attack, called it "barbarity" and "masacre tactics" but refrained pointedly from dealing extensively with the damage inflicted on the target city of Hiroshima.

Throughout the day the Japanese had broadcast repeated accounts of the new bomb, carefully refraining from using the word "atomic" or admitting the breadth of destruction, but branding it a "diabolic weapon."

"Since it is presumed that the enemy planes will continue to use this new bomb," the Osaka radio said in a domestic broadcast, "the authorities will point out measures to cope with it immediately."

Japanese accounts said "several bombs" fell on the big military base Monday, coming from the bomb bays of only a few Superforts, and Osaka added: "Even if the enemy does raid with a small number of planes we must be careful not to look at the raids lightly."

Another broadcast beamed to the United States declared that the use of the atomoc bomb branded "the enemy for ages to come as a destroyer of justice and mankind."

Destructive Power Admitted

All train travel into Hiroshima—which the Japanese conceded was "considerably damaged"—was forbidden.

"The destructive power of the new weapon can not be slighted," warned Domei agency, which said "a few" of the annihilating bombs floated in over the military city by parachute and burst "before reaching the ground."

Apparently the Japanese could not believe that a single atomic bomb, which President Truman disclosed yesterday had hit Japan for the first time Monday (Tokyo

See Nips Skeptical, Page 11, Col. 3

Garrett Trails Norfolk County House Contest

On the face of incomplete returns last night the election of the Walton-Humphries legislative ticket in Norfolk County's Democratic primary election yesterday was indicated, in what was one of the hottest contests with the largest qualified list (12,128) in the county's history.

Unofficial returns from 27 of the 30 precincts in the Norfolk County-South Norfolk District gave E. T. Humphries 3,869 votes; T. G. Walton 4,081 and James N. Garrett 3,188.

Garrett led the ticket in South

See Garrett Trails, Page 12, Col. 4

Tito Tells Yugoslavs Peter Can Not Return

Belgrade, Aug. 7.—(AP)—Premier Marshal Tito told the Peoples Front Congress today that King Peter would not be allowed to return to Yugoslavia. Tito said the decision was based on the grounds that Gen. Draja Mihailovic and Milan Nedic acted in the King's name during the German occupation.

Atom Bomb Damage To Be Told Today

Experts Now Analyzing Pictures of Hiroshima Strike; New Jap Surrender Ultimatum Hinted

By Douglas B. Cornell

Washington, Aug. 7.—(AP)—Results of the first atomic bomb strike on Hiroshima, which prompted unofficial predictions of a new surrender ultimatum to Japan, will be disclosed tomorrow. The War Department so announced tonight. It said reconnaissance planes had photographed the Japanese army base city, or what is left of it, and that experts now are analyzing the pictures.

A report on the damage caused by this new terror from the skies will be issued here or in Guam. An "impenetrable cloud of dust and smoke" hid Hiroshima immediately after the attack Sunday.

Japanese broadcasts warned the people to be ready for more superbomb raids, and the Japanese cabinet was reported meeting in special session.

Tokyo Cabinet Meeting

The National Broadcasting Company in New York picked up a British Broadcasting Company's broadcast which said Radio Tokyo indicated the cabinet had been summoned to discuss the new menace.

How soon the use of atomic bombing may be followed by a new surrender ultimatum, or a Japanese decision to fight or or quit now, was highly conjectural.

But one able military authority here said "inevitably" Japan will be told—quickly—that she must quit or face the onslaught of the most terrible weapon ever devised. And another declared the Japanese may be expected to make up their minds within six weeks whether to get out of the war or see their home islands devastated from the air.

Navy Department Statement

A prepared Navy Department read on the Navy Hour radio program (NBC) said this about the bomb:

"It is too early yet to tell what effect the atomic bomb will have on Japanese morale. We may have to destroy four or five cities befoer they actually believe we have such a bomb. But we will bring them the proof. With the destruc-

See Bomb Damage, Page 3, Col. 2

Date Set Over Year Ago For Dropping New Bomb

Guam, Aug. 7.—(AP)—Brig. Gen. Thomas F. Farrell, Albany, N. Y., disclosed today that the August 5 (United States) date for dropping the first atomic bomb on the enemy was set "well over a year ago." Farrell, aide to Maj. Gen. Leslie R. Groves, Pasadena, Calif., veteran Army construction engineer who was in charge of the bomb development program said at a news conference the goal was set in order to lay out a schedule for completing the huge project. For a while, he indicated, American and British scientists thought they were racing against time with the Germans who had been known to have started work on an atomic bomb of their own. "One of our major worries over in Europe was that some secret weapon was being developed by the Germans comparable to this," said Gen. Carl A. Spaatz, commander of Strategic Air Forces in the Pacific. "We were vitally concerned. All of the stories were that they were ahead of us."

Soldiers May Bring Pet Dogs Across Now

Rome, Aug. 7.—(AP)—Previous frantic efforts of American soldiers to stow away their pet dogs on transports headed for the U. S. will not be necessary any longer. Allied headquarters said today that pet dogs could be shipped home on War Shipping Administration vessels provided the owners obtained approval from their regimental commanders and paid the freight. The pets still will be banned from Army transports, however.

25 B-29's Blast Pittsburgh of Japan

140 Thunderbolts Escort Sky Giants; 1,500 Tons Of Bombs Hit Yawta

By Murlin Spencer

Guam, Wednesday, Aug. 8.—(AP)—Two hundred and twenty-five Superfortresses, escorted by 140 Thunderbolt fighters, spilled 1,500 tons of demolition bombs, Wednesday on Yawata, "the Pittsburgh of Japan," in the third attack in as many days on the enemy homeland. Yawata had been warned only three days before it was marked for destruction.

Returning pilots brought back word they started large fires which spread to conflagrations—noteworthy because it was a demolition and not an incendiary attack.

Yawata, on the north tip of Kyushu, has a population of 261,000.

The big sky dreadnaughts, flying from the Marianas covered by Thunderbolts from Okinawa, hit a city which had been warned on August 5 it was listed for a B-29 bomb treatment.

First Target Hit on Japan

Yawata was the first target ever hit on Japan by the B-29s, having been attacked June 14, 1944, again

Yawata Bombed, Page 8, Col. 3

All Promises To Be Translated Into Action, Tuck Pledges State

South Boston, Aug. 7.—(AP)—With Associated Press returns indicating his nomination for governor in today's Democratic primary, Lieut. Gov. William M. Tuck tonight issued a statement expressing his appreciation and interpreting the vote to mean "that the people of Virginia want me to translate my promises into action." "I intend to respect them all," he said, adding that it would be his firm purpose to finance adequately any program sponsored.

"No tax program, however, will be recommended by me unles and until the welfare of Virginia and the continuation of sound progressive government demands it, and then until every possible source of saving through efficiency in the State government has been explored," he said.

The nominee voted in his home precinct here this morning, about 10 o'clock, spent a good part of the day conversing with friends and well-wishers.

In his statement tonight he said: "The incomplete returns indicate my nomination by a large majority. I am most grateful for the confidence which my friends and fellow Democrats all over Virginia have shown in me.

Many Projects Listed

"I interpret my nomination to mean that the people of Virginia want me to translate my promises into action to the end that we may have a stronger and more progressive school system, co-ordinated with an equally progressive department of public health, expanded to serve the needs of all Virginians; better marketing facilities and communications for our farmers; a speedy completion and improvement of our highway system; the execution of our program for public buildings; and with a special emphasis for the proper care of those who suffer from mental difficulties, and other afflictions

See Tuck Promises, Page 13, Col. 1

More Superforts Ready to Drop 'Atoms' on Nips, Says Spaatz

Strategic Air Force Chief Declares Leaflets Will Tell Japanese Truth About New Danger

By Morrie Landsberg

Guam, Aug. 7.—(AP)—Gen. Carl A. Spaatz announced today that more B-29s are in readiness to follow the "Enola Gay" which dropped the first atomic bomb on the Japanese city of Hiroshima with awesome explosive force. The U. S. Army Strategic Air Force commander added that the atomic bombers would operate from 20th Air Force bases in the Marianas.

To all questions as to how the bomb is carried, how large it is or from what altitude it was dropped, the general said "no" crisply and "definitely," or waved the query aside altogether.

He told a news conference that the force behind the single atomic bomb dropped on Hiroshima was the equivalent of the bombing power of 2,000 Superforts.

Spaatz, at the conclusion of the meeting, announced there would be a leaflet campaign to let the Japanese people know they had been atom-bombed and could expect more in the future. Whether this meant that specific cities will be warned in advance, as with the B-29 fire raids, was not made clear but it seemed unlikely in view of the special nature of the new explosive.

Granting the tremendous power of the atomic bomb, General Spaatz refused to conjecture specifically on how it would affect the end of the war with Japan.

But the lean, tough general declared:

"It won't be pleasant for the Japanese to absorb."

Asked whether the atomic bomb is still in the experimental stage, Spaatz said "the experiment was over July 16," the date when the

See B-29's Ready, Page 11, Col. 2

SECOND EXTRA

NORFOLK LEDGER-DISPATCH

SECOND EXTRA

VOL CXXXIV—NO. 38 NORFOLK, VA., TUESDAY AFTERNOON, AUGUST 14, 1945 PRICE FIVE CENTS

WAR OVER

Japan Surrenders Unconditionally

Army To Cut 5,000,000 Within Year

Washington, Aug 14.—(AP)—President Truman tonight forecast that 5,000,000 to 5,500,000 men now in the Army may be returned to civilian life within the next 12 to 18 months.

Furthermore, he said in announcing Japan's surrender, only the lowest age groups will now be drafted into the Army. Preliminary estimates indicate only those under 26 will be called, Mr. Truman added.

His recommendation was that Selective Service reduce inducting immediately from 80,000 a month to 50,000.

Too Early For Definite Figure

"It is too early to propose a definite figure for the occupation forces which will be required in the Pacific 12 months from now or what reduction it may be possible to make in the strength of the Army force now allotted to occupation duties in Europe," the President said in a statement.

"It is apparent, however, that we can release as many men as can be brought home by the means available during the next year."

Army releases will be speeded by air and sea transportation in an effort to attain that 5,000,000, to 5,500,000 figure, he said.

Mr. Truman said that in justice to millions of men who have given "long and faithful service under the difficult and hazardous conditions of the Pacific war and elsewhere overseas a constant flow of replacements to the occupational forces is thought to be imperative.

He added that inductions of 50,000 per month in the lowest age groups "will provide only sufficient men to support the forces required for occupational duty and to permit the relief of long-service men overseas to the maximum extent transportation makes possible."

Does Not Mention Navy Call

The present problem, he said, centers on the readjustment of personnel now in uniform and induction of new men through Selective Service to "permit the earliest possible release from the Army of those men who have long records of dangerous, arduous and faithful service."

The President did not mention the Navy draft call, currently about 20,000 men a month.

Selective Director Lewis B. Hershey said he had no word of the Navy's plans, but that it would "reasonable to expect a cut there too."

SAILORS CELEBRATE VICTORY—Uncle Sam's Navy men who have borne the brunt of Pacific warfare joined Marines and Soldiers on Granby Street in tonight's wild celebration. (Vollmer photo.)

City Celebrates Joyfully; Noisy Crowds Pack Streets

Norfolk started a great celebration late today when Japan's acceptance of the allied surrender terms was announced officially at 7 o'clock.

Whistles, sirens, church bells and automobile horns contributed to the din, accompanied by the shouting of crowds in the streets.

At first the news was given a mixed reception and there was doubt until word spread that this time the announcement had been made officially.

"It was about time," said one spectator.

"Wonder if it will turn out to be another false alarm," said another.

Finally the crowd was convinced the war had ended and the celebration gained momentum.

All Norfolk policemen were summoned to duty to help keep the crowds as orderly as possible.

Beer retailers closed their places of business immediately.

Stores will be closed tomorrow and tomorrow night at 8 o'clock services thanksgiving for victory will be held in many local churches.

The Public Information Office at the Naval Base reported a brief celebration. The whistle on the power plant was sounded, flares were set off, and men cheered, but within half an hour all was quiet again.

By 8 o'clock Granby street from the post office to Main Street was packed with a milling, shouting, sweating throng of men, women and children. Motorists helped with the noise making but made little progress as traffic was brought virtually to a standstill. Traffic moved with little or no delay, however, on Boush Street and other important thoroughfares.

Lt. Comdr. C. Burke Hewitt, public relations officer at the Norfolk Navy Yard, said the yard let off all employees on the night force to join in the celebration except those refitting transports or engaged in maintenance work. The crowd at the navy yard was orderly, he said, but in downtown Portsmouth the tumult was described as "terrific."

AMG Ready To Move In

Washington, Aug. 14.—(AP)—The Army's Military Government forces are ready to go into Japan with the first troops landing after the Nipponese surrender, it was learned today.

Officers now on Okinawa and in the Philippines are only awaiting the signal to move, and others will be speeded from the Monterey staging base for civil affairs officers. Within a few weeks some 2,000 or more are expected to be on the job.

The Navy also will send in military government officers for a joint administration similar to the setup on Okinawa where the task is shared by the two services.

Details of the military government plan for Japan had not been disclosed but informed forces say it calls for a stern rule similar to the administration effective in Germany.

The military government is expected to establish headquarters only in key areas, largely on the large Japanese island of Honshu.

Spain Protests Tangier Conference

Paris, Aug. 14—(AP)—The French government consulted with Britain today after receipt of a Spanish note protesting the exclusion of the Franco government from the Paris conference to determine the status of Tangier, the international zone opposite Gibraltar which Spain occupied June 14, 1940.

The Spanish note was handed to the French yesterday.

Japanese Report Two New Wonder Drugs

San Francisco, Aug. 14. (AP)—Japanese claimed today their scientists have developed two wonder drugs, "koha" and "shiko," which rapidly are curing thousands of persons burned in air raids. A Domei news agency broadcast said the pills also are good for chilblains.

Chinese, Russ Sign Treaty of Friendship

London, Aug. 14—(AP)—The Moscow radio said tonight the Soviet Union and the Chinese Republic had signed a treaty of friendship today.

Keep Peace, Says Truman

Washington, Aug. 14.—(AP)—In an impromptu speech on the White House lawn early tonight President Truman told a large crowd of spectators that this was a great day for democracy.

He said it marked the final triumph over Fascism and would go down in history as one of its most noteworthy days.

The whole country now should unite, the President said, in efforts to preserve the future peace of the world.

America, said Mr. Truman, now can start "on our real task of implementation of free government in the world."

When thousands of spectators who had waited patiently in Lafayette park across the street from the executive mansion began a chant: "We want Truman," the President appeared on the White House steps with Mrs. Truman.

Surrounded by Secret Service men, the President and his wife walked down the steps, across the lawn and around a fountain to the high iron fence which fronts the White House on Pennsylvania Avenue.

There the President waved and smiled to the crowd.

As the throng continued cheering, Mr. and Mrs. Truman returned to the White House porch where he spoke into a microphone that had been set up there hastily.

The text of his extemporaneous speech, as transcribed from shorthand notes:

"Ladies and gentlemen, this is the great day. This is the day we have been looking for since December 7, 1941.

"This is the day when Fascism and police government ceases in the world.

"This is the day for the democracies.

"This is the day when we can start on our real task of implementation of free government in the world.

"We are faced with the greatest task we ever have been faced with. The emergency is as great is it was on December 7, 1941.

"It is going to take the help of all of us to do it. I know we are going to do it."

BRITISH DIPLOMAT DIES

London, Aug. 14. (AP)—Sir Eric Phipps, 69, British ambassador to Berlin from 1933 to 1937 and ambassador to Paris when war broke out in 1939, died last night.

Indianapolis Lost; All Hands Casualties

Washington, Aug. 14.—(AP)—The heavy cruiser Indianapolis was lost recently in the Philippine Sea from enemy action with 100 per cent casualties to her personnel totalling 1,196 officers and men.

Announcing this today, the Navy said the famous vessel was lost shortly after completion of her last mission, sailing from San Francisco July 16 on a high-speed run to Guam to deliver essential atomic bomb material. She was lost after safely delivering her cargo.

The Navy gave no details of her final, fatal action.

Casualties included five Navy dead, including one officer; 845 Navy missing, including 63 officers; 307 Navy wounded, including 15 officers; 30 Marine Corps missing, including two officers; and nine enlisted Marine Corps wounded.

Truman Orders Hostilities Ended on All Fronts

Washington, Aug. 14—(AP)—President Truman tonight dispatched through Secretary of State Byrnes an order for the Japanese government to stop the war on all fronts.

The dispatch was sent through the Swiss government, being turned over to the Swiss legation here a few minutes after 7 o'clock.

The President ordered:

1. That the Japanese government "direct prompt cessation of hostilities by Japanese forces." Gen. Douglas MacArthur, as supreme Allied commander, must be informed by the Japanese of the effective date and hour for hostilities to cease.

2. That the Japanese government send emissaries immediatel to MacArthur with information on the Japanese forces and with full power to make arrangements as MacArthur directs for the formal enemy surrender.

3. That the Japanese government stand ready to receive from MacArthur information on "the time, place and other details of the formal surrender."

The text of the President's message was released by the State Department about half an hour after it was placed in the hands of Swiss Charge d'Affaires Max Grassli.

Mountbatten Prepares To Accept Surrenders

Kandy, Ceylon, Aug. 14. (AP)—Adm. Lord Louis Mounbatten, returning to his headquarters today from conferences in Potsdam and London, was ready in the event of a Japanese capitulation to convert his invasion units to occupation forces and to accept surrenders locally in southeast Asia and the East Indies. Several hundred thousand enemy soldiers are involved.

Russians Invade Jehol; Smash Karafuto Defenses

London, Aug. 14 (AP)—Russian troops made a sensational spurt of 93 miles from Outer Mongolia, invading Jehol province and capturing Linsi and Tapanshang, 260 miles north of Peiping in North China, the Soviet communique announced tonight.

London, Aug. 14 (AP)—The Russians have landed troops on the Japanese half of Sakhalin Island (Karafuto) and pierced the enemy's defenses, the Soviet communique announced tonight.

Troops of the First Far Eastern front advancing into Manchuria from the east crossed the Mutankiang river and captured the fiercely defended town of Mutankiang, 270 miles east of Harbin. Mutankiang is the junction of the main railway to Harbin and the line connecting Korea and Manchuria.

CROWDS SING IN STREETS

Sydney, Australia, Aug. 14 (AP) Large cheering crowds gathered in the streets tonight and danced and sang as newspapers carried large headlines saying Japan had accepted the Allies surrender terms.

B-29s Strike Final Blow

Guam, Wednesday, Aug. 15. (AP)—Between 950 and 1,000 Superforts and fighter planes smashed heavily in dreaded fire, demolition and strafing attacks against Japanese war industries yesterday and early today while the world awaited the emperor's answer to Allied surrender demands.

About 6,000 tons of bombs were dropped on six military targets in the last 24 hours, Strategic Air Forces headquarters announced. This made that period one of the busiest days in the history of the 20th Air Force.

The B-29s hurled their might against the enemy hard on the heels of devastating attacks by carrier aircraft of Admiral Halsey's Third Fleet and attached British warships, still hovering off the Japanese coast.

725 B-29s in Attack

More than 725 B-29s from the Marianas and 180 fighters based on Iwo Jima participated in the Superfort smash.

Targets for the assault included war industries at Isezaki and Kumagaya, only an hour's automobile ride from the emperor's palace, and the Nippon oil refinery at Akita.

Kumagaya was one of the cities on the Superforts "death list."

Other targets were the Marifu railroad yards on the Tokyo main line, the giant Osaga arsenal and the naval arsenal at Tokuyama.

Flying the longest non-stop mission from the Marianas on record, more than 150 B-29s bombed Akita refinery on northern Honshu in the darkness early today.

A couple of hours earlier an even larger Superfort fleet set fire to Isezaki, 75 miles northwest of Tokyo, and Kumagaya, 42 miles northwest of the capital city.

None of these targets had been hit previously.

The night-time assaults were a round-the-clock extension of the attacks which opened against the Marifu railway yards on southern Honshu shortly after noon Tuesday. During Tuesday afternoon the Hikari and Osaka arsenals were bombed.

Biggest Assault Since August 1

The night and day raids constituted the first maximum effort of the 20th Air Force since August 1 when 824 Superforts carried out the biggest assault on record.

Bombing the Nippon oil refinery near Akita was the longest mission ever undertaken from Guam without a stopover at Iwo for fuel.

MacArthur To Accept Capitulation

Washington, Aug. 14.—(AP)—Japan has surrendered unconditionally President Truman announced at 7 p. m tonight.

General of the Army Douglas A. MacArthur has been designated Supreme Allied Commander to receive the surrender.

Offensive operations have been ordere suspended everywhere.

V-J Day will proclaimed only after the surrender has been formally accepted by MacArthur.

President Truman said he regarded the surrender as "unconditional." The Japanes note, however, directly followed one from Secretary of State Byrnes in which the Allie agreed that the Japanese would be permitte to keep their emperor, at least for a time. Th Byrnes note prescribed that the emperc should be completely controlled by the Allie also that the Japanese people should have o opportunity later on to decide by ballot th kind of government they want.

Mr. Truman read the formal message relayed from Emperor Hirohito through th Swiss Government in which the Japanese rul pledged the surrender on the terms laid dow by the Big Three Conference at Potsdam.

"I have received this afternoon a messag from the Japanese Government in reply to th message forwarded to that government by th Secretary of State on August 11.

"I deem this reply a full acceptance of th Potsdam declaration which specifies the u conditional surrender of Japan.

"In this reply there is no qualification.

"Arrangements are now being made for th formal signing of surrender terms at the ea liest possible moment.

"Great Britain, Russia and China will represented by high ranking officers.

"Meantime, the Allied armed forces ha been ordered to suspend offensive action.

"The proclamation of V-J Day must wait until the for signing of the surrender terms by Japan."

Simultaneously, Mr. Truman disclosed that Selective S ice is taking immediate steps to slash inductions from 80, to 50,000 a month.

Henceforth, Mr. Truman said, only those men under will be drafted for the reduced quotos.

. . . . The White House made public the Japanese governme message accepting that ended the war which started Decem 7, 1941.

The text of their message, which was delivered by Swiss charge d'affaires, follows:

"Communication of the Japanese government of Au 14, 1945, addressed to the governments of the United St Great Britain, the Soviet Union, and China:

"With reference to the Japanese government's not August 10 regarding their acceptance of the provisions of Potsdam declaration and the reply of the governments of United States, Great Britain, the Soviet Union and China, by American Secretary of State Byrnes, under the date of gust 11, the Japanese government have the honor to comm cate to the governments of the four powers as follows:

"1. His Majesty the Emperor has issued an imperial rescrip

(Continued on Page 3)

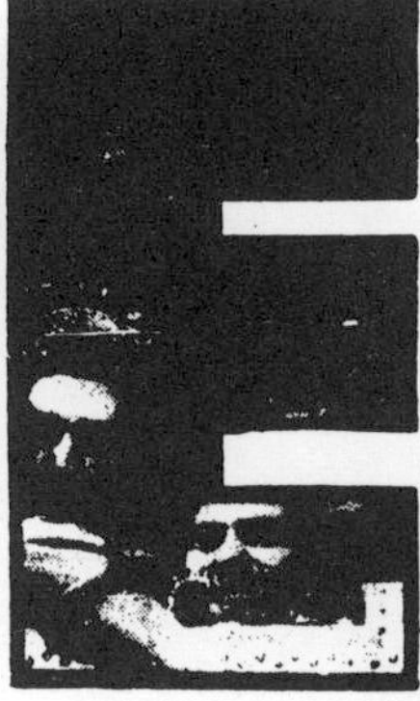

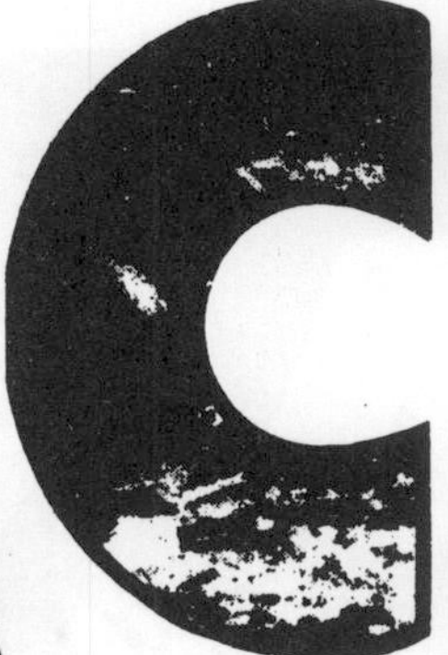
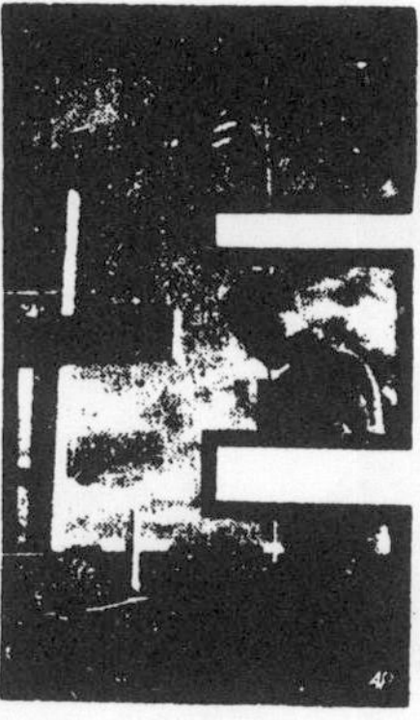

PEACE!

THE INDIANAPOLIS STAR **EXTRA**

FAIR AND FIRST

VOL. 43. NO. 71. ★★★ WEDNESDAY MORNING, AUGUST 15, 1945 Entered as Second-Class Matter at Post Office, Indianapolis, Ind. Issued Daily and Sunday. FIVE CENTS.

WAR IS ENDED—TRUMAN

Nip Sub Sinks Cruiser Indianapolis Carrying Atom Bomb Load; 883 Killed

315 Survive Blow; 5th. Fleet Flagship Hit Off Philippines

Peleliu, Palau Islands, Aug. 5 (Delayed)—(AP)—The 10,000-ton cruiser Indianapolis was sunk in less than 15 minutes, presumably by a Japanese submarine, 12 minutes past midnight July 30—and 883 crew members lost their lives in one of the Navy's worst disasters.

She went down in the Philippines Sea, within 450 miles of Leyte, while on an unescorted high-speed run from San Francisco.

She had completed the trip to Guam and was bound for the Philippines.

There were 315 survivors.

Washington, Aug. 14 (AP)—The heavy cruiser Indianapolis was lost recently in the Philippine Sea from enemy action with 100 per cent casualties to her personnel totaling 1,198 officers and men.

Announcing this today, the Navy said the famous vessel was lost shortly after completion of her last mission, sailing from San Francisco, Cal., on July 16, on a high-speed run to Guam to deliver essential atomic bomb material. She was lost after delivering her cargo safely.

The Navy gave no details of her final, fatal action.

(The Navy Department told the Indianapolis Star Washington Bureau last night that the Indianapolis still was carrying atomic bomb material when struck.)

Casualties included five Navy dead, including one officer; 845 Navy missing, including 63 officers; 307 Navy wounded, including 13 officers; 30 Marine Corps missing, including two officers; and nine enlisted Marine Corps wounded.

Her casualties placed her near the top in weight of losses on a single vessel in this war. The ill-fated aircraft carrier Franklin suffered 341 dead, 431 missing and more than 300 wounded. The battleship Arizona, with a total of 1,104 officers and men lost in the Pearl Harbor attack, leads the list in personnel killed.

THE INDIANAPOLIS, traditionally the flagship of the powerful Fifth Fleet, had been at the Mare Island Navy yard for repairs just before her last run. She had been damaged by a Japanese suicide plane off Okinawa March 31, 1945. Adm. Raymond A. Spruance was aboard at the time of the suicide attack, but he escaped injury.

Skipper of the Indianapolis was Capt. Charles B. McVay III, of Washington. He is listed as wounded.

The Indianapolis, first naval vessel laid down and completed after the London Naval Conference of 1930, was commissioned at the Philadelphia navy yard on Nov. 15, 1932. After a shakedown cruise to Central American waters, she was assigned to special duty with President Roosevelt, embarking him and his party at Campobello on July 9, 1933, and cruising with them until Aug. 1. In September of that year she sailed from Annapolis with Secretary of the Navy Claude Swan-

Turn to Page 6, Column 3

Big Draft Cut Is Forecast

5 Million Vets To Be Released—Truman

Washington, Aug. 14 (AP)—President Truman tonight forecast that 5,000,000 to 5,500,000 men now in the Army may be returned to civilian life within the next 12 to 18 months.

Furthermore, he said in announcing Japan's surrender, only the lowest age groups will now be drafted into the Army. Preliminary estimates indicate only those under 26 will be called, Mr. Truman added.

His recommendation was that Selective Service reduce inductions immediately from 80,000 a month to 50,000.

IT IS TOO early to propose a definite figure for the occupation

Turn to Page 2, Column 8

Stores To Stay Closed Today, Tomorrow

Stores will remain closed today and tomorrow, Murray H. Morris, manager of the Merchants Association, said last night after formal announcement by President Truman that Japan had surrendered.

The Weather

Jim Crow says:

From now on Hirohito, Son of Heaven, will be free to do just as the "honorable" Allies tell him.

Indianapolis—Fair Wednesday and Thursday; cooler south portion Wednesday.

Indiana — Wednesday partly cloudy and considerably cooler.

Two Holidays With Pay Are War-End Gift

Washington, Aug. 14 (AP)—Tomorrow and Thursday are days off for government workers, and holidays for pay purposes for workers in general.

And V-J Day, when it comes, will be a premium pay day, too.

President Truman announced both rulings tonight.

He directed agency heads throughout the government to cut their forces down to a bare skeleton staff Aug. 15 and 16 and not to charge the two days against the employes' annual leave. He said it was in "inadequate" recognition of the four-year efforts of "one of the hardest working groups of war workers."

FOR OTHER workers under wage control, Wednesday and Thursday count like Christmas and the few other accepted holidays for purposes of overtime pay and in figuring the number of days worked in a week. Many employers already have gotten approval for regular time pay to workers who take the day off.

Postal service for the next two days will "approximate holiday

Turn to Page 2, Column 2

Hoosiers Get Two Days Off

Gates Proclaims State Holiday

Today and tomorrow were declared legal holidays by Governor Ralph F. Gates in a proclamation issued last night. He urged thanksgiving for return of peace to the world.

The proclamation:

"Whereas, It has been officially announced by the President of the United States that the Imperial Japanese Government has advised the Government of the United States of its unconditional

Turn to Page 2, Column 1

Gas Rationing To End Quickly

Here's good news for motorists gasoline rationing will be ended "very quickly."

James D. Strickland, Indiana district OPA director, announced yesterday motorists can order filling station attendant to "fill 'er up" within a matter of a few days.

"Gasoline rationing will end very quickly after the President proclaims V-J day, Mr. Strickland said. The director also disclosed rationing of tires, shoes and most processed foods will be terminated "quickly."

Many persons yesterday forsook the crowded, noisy streets to celebrate quietly in the city's churches the end of the war. Typical was this reverent worshiper in Christ Episcopal Church giving thanks in the peace of the hushed church.

The tumult and the shouting dies,
The captains and the kings depart,
Still stands thine ancient sacrifice,
An humble and a contrite heart.
Lord God of Hosts, be with us yet.
Lest we forget, lest we forget.

—Budyard Kipling

V-J Comes, Rain Pours; 'Midst Din, City Celebrates

By MARY E. BOSTWICK

After two false starts, Indianapolis really blew its top at the third—and this time official—celebration of V-J Day last night.

The celebration got under way a few seconds after 6 o'clock, when, to the accompaniment of as fine a display of heavenly artillery as has been seen around here in a long time, the official word came over the radio.

The thunder rumbled and crashed in terrific salvos, the lightning flashed and flickered, the rain came down in sheets, and everybody who had any sort of vehicle that would still travel, dashed out into the tempest and with braying horns, clanging cow bells, shrill whistles and any other noise-maker available, cruised the flooded streets. One car was equipped with a locomotive bell.

About 7:30 o'clock the rain died to a drizzle, and as darkness began to fall the sky was suffused with a lurid crimson glow.

INTO MONUMENT Circle poured a milling, yelling throng. The motorized part of the celebration—the thousands of automobiles that, bumper to bumper, crept through the streets, was barred from the Circle. More people kept coming all the time, converging into the Circle from all points of the compass to yell, cheer, blow whistles and ring bells. They thumped on lard cans, oil cans, dishpans and tin wash-

Turn to Page 2, Column 2

Jap Surrender Brings World-Wide Rejoicing

Washington, Aug. 14 (AP)—The second World War, history's greatest flood of death and destruction, ended tonight with Japan's unconditional surrender.

Formalities still remained—the official signing of surrender terms and a proclamation of V-J Day.

But from the moment President Truman announced at 6 p.m. (CWT) that the enemy of the Pacific had agreed to Allied terms, the world put aside for a time woeful thoughts of the cost in dead and dollars and celebrated in wild frenzy. Formalities meant nothing to people freed at last of war.

To reporters crammed into his office, shoving now useless war maps against a marble mantle, the President disclosed that:

Japan, without ever being invaded, had accepted completely and without reservation an Allied declaration of Potsdam dictating unconditional surrender.

Gen. Douglas MacArthur had been designated supreme Allied commander, the man to receive surrender.

There is to be no power for the Japanese Emperor—although Allies will let him remain their tool. No longer will the warlords reign, through him. Hirohito——or any successor—will take orders from MacArthur.

Allied forces were ordered to "suspend offensive action" everywhere.

From now on, only men under 26 will be drafted. Army draft calls will be cut from 80,000 a month to 50,000. Mr. Truman forecast that five to five and a half million soldiers may be released within 12 to 18 months.

The surrender announcement set in motion a whole chain of events. Among them:

To a Japanese government which once had boasted it would dictate peace terms in the White House, Mr. Truman dispatched orders to "direct prompt cessation of hostilities," tell MacArthur of the effective date and hour, and send emissaries to the general to arrange formal surrender.

The War Manpower Commission terminated all man power controls.

The Navy piled a $6,000,000,000 cancellation of contracts on top of a previous $1,200,000,000 cut in its shipbuilding program.

Congress was summoned back to work on Sept. 5, more than a month ahead of schedule, to get busy on unemployment compensation, surplus property disposal, full employment, government reorganization and the continuation of abolition of war agencies.

The Office of Censorship said it was getting ready to

Turn to Page 2, Column 1

Petain To Die, Jury Rules

Gets Death Verdict In Treason Trial

Paris, Aug. 15 (Wednesday)—(AP) Marshal Henri Philippe Petain, 89 years old, was convicted and sentenced to death early today by three judges and a 24-man jury, who deliberated almost seven hours.

The jury recommended clemency because of his great age. This recommendation for clemency presumably will be considered by Gen. DeGaulle, President of the French provisional government.

Besides condemning the former chief of the Vichy state to death for "plotting against the internal safety of France," the court also sentenced him to national indignity and ordered confiscation of all his property.

The lengthy judgment, read by Judge Mongibeaux, president of the court, went over the acts of collaboration of the Vichy government with Germany point by point and laid their responsibility at Petain's feet. Mongibeaux said the marshal instituted "a veritable regime of terror" in France.

THE COURT found Petain guilty of attacking the security

Turn to Page 2, Column 8

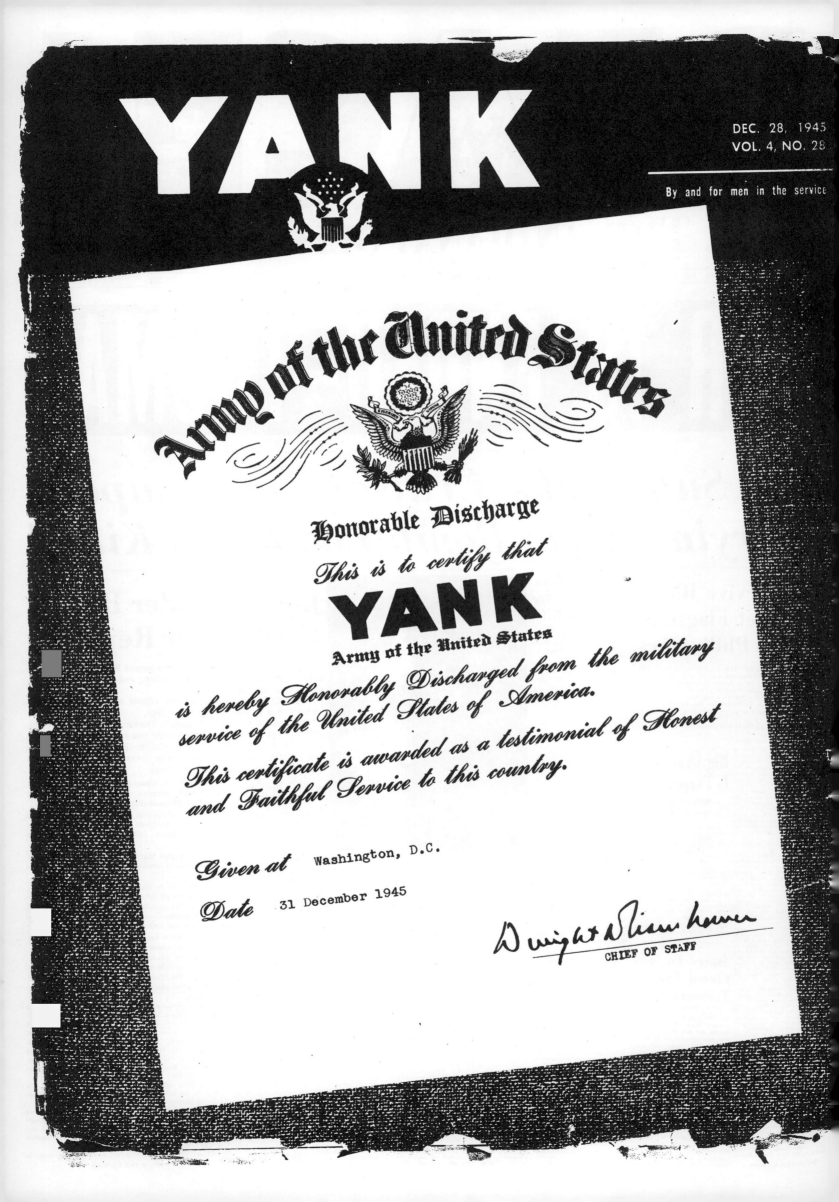

YANK

DEC. 28, 1945
VOL. 4, NO. 28

By and for men in the service

Honorable Discharge

This is to certify that

YANK

Army of the United States

is hereby Honorably Discharged from the military service of the United States of America.

This certificate is awarded as a testimonial of Honest and Faithful Service to this country.

Given at Washington, D.C.

Date 31 December 1945

Dwight D Eisenhower
CHIEF OF STAFF

SUNDAY NEWS
Copr. 1945 by News Syndicate Co. Inc. NEW YORK PICTURE NEWSPAPER Trade Mark Reg. U. S. Pat. Off.
Vol. 25. No. 13 New York, Sunday, July 29, 1945 Main Section, 84 Pages

13 KILLED AS BOMBER HITS EMPIRE STATE

Story on Page 3

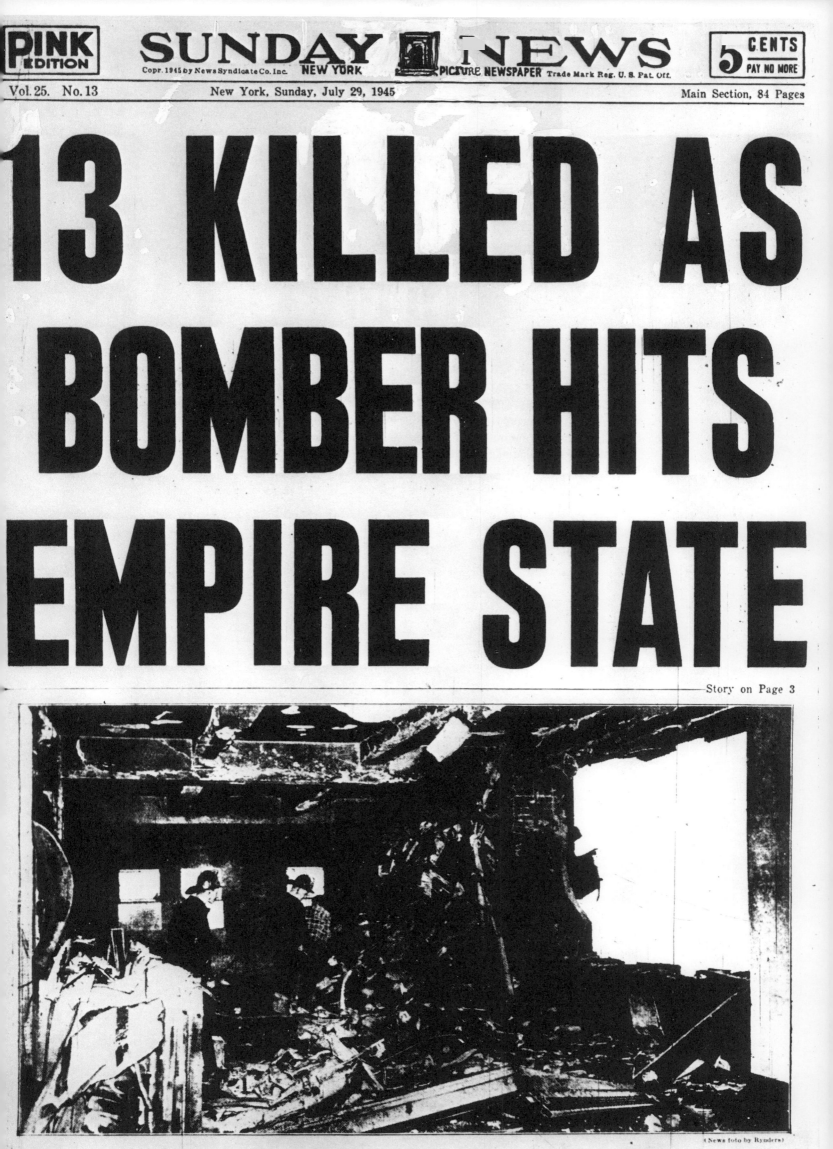

(News foto by Rynders)

Wreckage-strewn 78th floor of Empire State Building. Bomber tore 18-foot hole in wall. Propeller is embedded in wall at left.

1946

With the war over, the U.S. government lifted most price and wage controls and things started to get back to a peacetime footing.

It was the year of *Annie Get Your Gun*, the movies *The Big Sleep* and *Notorious*.

A fire in the Winecoff Hotel in Atlanta, Georgia, killed 127 people and injured 100 others. The hotel had no outside fire escapes and no sprinkler system.

Winston Churchill spoke at Fulton, Missouri: "From Stettin in the Baltic to Trieste in the Adriatic, an iron curtain has descended across the continent." He warned of the expansionist tendencies of the Soviet Union.

WEATHER
[illegible] Fair, [illegible] slightly [illegible]. Details on Page 34.

The Atlanta Journal EXTRA

"COVERS DIXIE LIKE THE DEW"

VOL. LXIV, NO. 286 | Full Associated Press Service | ATLANTA (2), GA., SATURDAY, DECEMBER 7, 1946 | PRICE FIVE CENTS

40 FEARED DEAD IN WINECOFF FIRE

ATLANTA FIREMEN RESCUE SURVIVOR FROM BURNING WINECOFF HOTEL HERE

An unidentified woman, guest of the Winecoff hotel, her face drawn with anxiety, is helped to safety by Atlanta firemen during the early morning holocaust at the hotel Saturday. The hotel's marquee shows in the background.—Journal Photo by Jack Young.

Many Leap to Their Deaths As Flames Sweep Hotel Here

At least 40 persons were believed killed and scores were injured as flames swept the 15-story Winecoff hotel here shortly before dawn Saturday in what may prove to be the worst hotel fire in Atlanta's history.

Police said an undetermined number of bodies, trapped by the surging flames, are still inside the hotel at an early hour.

Ambulances were shuttling between the hotel and hospitals as fast as trips could be completed, and Grady hospital called in every doctor, nurse and orderly available.

Several persons leaped to their deaths before the eyes of horrified spectators.

The first person to plunge to death was a girl of about 14. She dangled for a while from a rope fashioned of a sheet and towels, then fell as it tore apart.

The casualty lis was mounting almost by the minute.

More than 50 persons had been treated for varying degrees of burns by 7:30 a. m.

Police Capt. L. J. Carroll and Officer N. W. Smith said they had made their way through smoke-filled stairways to the seventh floor 30 minutes after the fire was discovered shortly before 4 a. m. (E. S. T.), but were driven back by the quickly-spreading flames.

One fireman in a rescuec rew said many bodies were strewn in the upper floors and that in one room on the top floor he found a woman's body and the bodies of five children.

A police lieutenant said he could see from a window of an adjacent building the hands and feet of several victims on window ledges. The remainder of these bodies were not visible, the officer said.

The origin of the fire was not immediately known, firemen said.

At 5:15 a. m., about 20 guests could still be seen through the flames as they crouched along ledges at the tenth, eleventh and twelfth floors of the stone and brick structure.

With several floors beneath them a raging, billowing mass of flames, their position appeared hopeless to firemen except for those who might leap to safety into firemen's nets.

Red Cross Official Hurt

J. W. Gates, Red Cross safety director, his head wrapped in a blood-stained towel, was assisting in the rescue work. He said a falling brick had struck him on the head, opening a deep gash. He continued, however, to aid firemen and police who sought to reach the trapped guests.

There was no way immediately to fix the death count. Every available ambulance in the city was doing shuttle service removing the dead and terror-stricken injured.

The hotel faces on two streets and an alley, and from the fourth floor overlooks an adjoining roof.

Hopelessly trapped, the guests leaped from all sides of the burning structure. About 25 or 30 escaped by descending fire ladders to the adjacent roof.

General Reaches Safety

Among them were Maj. General P. W. Baade, of Washington, who commanded the Thirty-Fifth Division overseas during World War II. Mrs. Baade and Captain D. C. Waelde also escaped down ladders lifted to them by firemen. General Baade credited firemen with saving "many, many lives."

E. J. Hosch, one of the Associated Press reporters sent to the fire, said it "was all flame and no smoke all red flames simply eating out the interior of the hotel."

Hosch said that of nine women he saw leap from the hotel's upper stories upon his arrival at the fire, six were caught in nets by firemen. Three, however, missed the net and crashed to their deaths on the pavement.

At 4:40 a. m. (E. S. T.) guests were still grouped in windows of the hotel's upper rooms and were screaming and pleading for rescue.

Ambulances rushed the injured to hospitals.

The flames were dense on the Peachtree side of the structure.

Reds to Shun UN If Frisco Made Site

Special to the New York Times and The Atlanta Journal

LAKE SUCCEESS, N. Y., Dec. 6.—In a bitter attack charging that the United States had "interfered inexcusably" with the United Nations site deliberations the Soviet Union delivered a flat ultimatum here Thursday night that if San Francisco were selected as the world capital Russia and "other member states" would not attend conferences held there.

Czech Attache Routs 4 Brooklyn Assailants

NEW YORK, Dec. 6 (AP) Joseph Forman, 60-year-old head of the information service for the Czechoslovak consulate, fought off four assailants on a dark Brooklyn street early Friday, police said, and escaped with a superficial knife wound in a leg.

Police said Forman, a Czech citizen and a powerfully built man, swung his weight behind his fists when two men seized him and started searching for his wallet. As the fight went against the assailants, two other men emerged from a doorway and jumped Forman, police said.

A woman in a nearby apartment heard the scuffle, opened a window and screamed for police. A patrolman responded and the four fled.

U. S. Flotilla Reaches Piraeus in Heavy Storm

ATHENS, Dec. 6 (AP) A United States naval squadron which is making a series of informal calls at eastern Mediterranean ports reached Piraeus, the port of Athens, in the midst of a heavy thunderstorm and high winds Friday. The squadron includes the aircraft carrier Randolph, the light cruiser Fargo, the landing ship Donner and the destroyer Perry. The commander is Vice-Admiral Bernhard H. Bieri, chief of U. S. naval forces in the Mediterranean.

Packers Say Supplies Not Yet Endangered

CHICAGO, Dec. 6 (U.P.) Spokesmen for the nation's "Big Four" meat packers said Friday supplies will remain plentiful unless the coal strike is prolonged for another three weeks or a month.

List of Dead And Injured

Known Dead

Following is a partial list of dead in the Winecoff hotel fire:

WILLARD JONES, Oak Ridge, Tenn.

MAXINE WILLIS, Bainbridge, Ga.

V. R. MOODY, no address.

PAUL D. LAIN, 3606 Cliff Road, Birmingham, Ala.

CARL C. RASMUSSEN, MD., 810 Sixty-Third St., Des Moines, Iowa.

Known Injured

The following were reported injured in the hotel fire:

MILDRED LEON JOHNSON, 19, Atlanta.

MRS. T. S. LEDBETTER, 27, Atlanta.

DOROTHY MOEN, 16, Columbus.

HENRY H. LEMON, Atlanta.

CHARLES GRAY, Rome.

RAY DICKERSON, Conley.

IMA DELL INGRAM, Rockford, Illinois.

MRS. W. E. TRIBBLE, Rockford, Ill.

F. J. JONES, Atlanta.

ROBERT E. MUNNS, Augusta.

ANDREW J. BURNHAM, Atlanta.

RADNA GREEN, address unknown.

EDITH BURCH, Chattanooga.

CHARLES BOSCHUNG, Cullman, Ala.

EVELYN DUBERRY, Atlanta.

DELILAH JOSEPHINE CHAMBERS, Murphy, N. C.

RANDOLPH A. TOLLISON, Atlanta.

A. C. TAYLOR, Atlanta.

SAMUEL DUNCAN, Athens.

MRS. JOHN L. HARRIS JR., Columbus.

BASIL WOLFE, Toronto, Canada.

MRS. ELIZABETH TARVER, county public health nurse, Albany.

ED WILLIAMS, 16, high school youth, Cordele.

Ship Cited for Heroism

NORFOLK, Va., Dec. 6 (AP)—For outstanding heroism in action against enemy Japanese forces in the Pacific war area, from October 12, 1944, to June 19, 1945," the 29-year-old battleship Mississippi was Friday awarded the Navy Unit commendation.

REPORTER STUMBLES OVER BODIES; SEES WOMAN LEAPING TO DEATH

By CHICK HOSCH, Associated Press Writer

I saw four women leap to their deaths from the burning Winecoff hotel in chill predawn darkness Saturday.

I reached the scene of the in[illegible] famous Peachtree Street [illegible] than 45 minutes after the [illegible] was discovered in time to see [illegible] women leap to their [illegible] and others to mortal in[illegible]

Flames were shooting from the [illegible] fifth and sixth floors and [illegible] the smoke and blazes dozens of guests could be seen clinging to the ledges or leaning from [illegible]

[illegible] made of sheets and other [illegible] were hung down the sides [illegible] building. These fragile life[illegible] to safety were buffeted by [illegible] and streams of water.

Body Landed at Feet

[illegible] to the hotel entrance, [illegible] standing in the doorway when a woman's body hurtled through the marquee and landed in the street at my feet. One body could be seen draped grotesquely over the ledge of a balcony which the marquee covers.

I started up the stairs, but at the second floor heard that several of the trapped were jumping from the rear of the hotel into an ally. I ran to the rear of the hotel, but tripped over something and fell sprawling. Recovering, I turned to see several bodies lying on the walk. An elderly man sobbed hysterically at the side of a woman he was trying futileyl to lift.

It was too dark to get much of a picture of the scene there so I returned to the front of the building again. Several other guests, most of them women, came hurtling down into the outstretched firenets.

Of the 15 or 20 that I saw jump, none walked away. They hit the nets with such force that firemen couldn't hold them in most cases, managing only a check their leap.

Woman on Ledge

City Detective E. B. Brooks told of seeing one woman descend a sheet-rope three floors to an extension ladder hoisted by firemen. As we stood talking, we watched a woman back over the ledge of a night-floor window and start down a rope of twisted bed clothing.

Between floors she lost her footing against the water-drenched building and her body started swaying and slowly turning in the light of flames lapping at her feet. We watched as she turned loose and hurtled down, flat against the walls, screaming.

Her body hit the marquee with a sickening thud.

"God!" muttered Brooks, "I knew she couldn't clear that marquee."

Frantic fear seemed to catch the trapped at that point and as fast as firemen could clear the net of a broken body, another would smash into it. A moanful, piercing wail traced the descent of those who jumped, tapering off like the eerie scream of a shell disappearing into the distance.

It chilled you to the depths of your soul. It left you sickened and weary.

One firemen after another stumbled blindly from the building, overcome by smoke. Some collapsed in the street. Ambulances from every city hospital and nearby towns and Army posts shuttled through the night.

Saw no Children

Strangely, I saw no children among the trapped and Brooks and other officers with whom I talked said they had heard of only one child, but did not know its fate. I saw no men leap from the ledges.

In an alley I encountered Maj. General P. W. Baade, of Washington, D. C., who commandeered the Thirty-fifth division overseas in the recent war. He told how he and Mrs. Baade, awakened in their sixth floor room, escaped down a firemen's ladder to an adjoining roof. Captain D. Waelde, of Atlanta, said he and dozens of others escaped by the same ladder. They praised the efforts of firemen and credited them with saving many lives.

IT WAS AT 3:40 A. M.

Girl Elevator Operator Gives First Warning

A Negro girl elevator operator was credited Saturday with being the first person to report the disastrous fire which swept through the Winecoff hotel.

Comer L. Rowan, the hotel's night manager, said the girl, identified only as Rosita, told him the hotel was on fire at 3:40 a. m.

"I sent her to find the bellboy who was making a routine floor check," Mr. Rowan said, "and asked her to aid him in arousing the guests.

"I mayself ran to the switchboard and began phoning the rooms, warning the guests of the fire. I couldn't say much to each guest time was short with me—but I told those I talked to to get to safety and to be certain to close the doors to their rooms to keep a draft from spreading the flames."

Mr. Rowan said about 280 guests were registered and that this registration was near capacity.

1947

On the morning of April 16, 1947, Texas City, Texas, a small but bustling port community on Galveston Bay, almost ceased to exist.

A French freighter, the *Grandcamp*, with a load of ammonium nitrate, blew up in the harbor and set off a series of devastating explosions.

One of the worst explosions in U.S. history, it left 512 people dead, more than 3,000 injured, two-thirds of Texas City destroyed, and more than $51 million in damages.

HOME EDITION
Price 5 Cents

THE HOUSTON CHRONICLE

VOL. 46 NO. 186 HOUSTON, TEXAS, THURSDAY, APRIL 17, 1947 SIXTY PAGES

THE WEATHER

Houston and vicinity: Cool tonight, warmer Friday. Lowest tonight 45 degrees.
East Texas: Slightly warmer Friday.
More data on page 12, Sec. C.

FIVE FIRES RAGE IN BLAST RUINS; RED CROSS SAYS DEAD 700 TO 900

Sorrow, Suffering and Death Stalk Texas City

The wartime boom town of exas City lay in warlike devastation Thursday.

A pall of horror clouded the y, cradled on the west shores Galveston Bay. Sorrow, suffer g and death stalked the city. erves were keyed to a ragged ge, with citizens and hundreds out-of-town volunteer workers ady to believe any rumor.

A young mother, wounded and with blood streaming from her face, roamed the streets, clutching a small baby in her arms. The baby was dead. The mother did not seem to realize it, for she violently fought off all attempts to take the baby from her. She seemed unaware of her own injuries, even after a nurse led her to a first aid station and began tending the wounds.

This was typical of the situation from the first few minutes after the original blast and continuing Thursday.

Fear-haunted relatives wandered about, seeking their kin who had been in or near the ravaged area.

In Galveston, where most of the seriously injured were taken, men with one or both arms missing stepped from ambulances and walked into hospitals.

Men blinded by the blasts—doctors said many of them will never see again—stumbled from the ambulances and groped toward the hospitals until aides would tend them.

As the citizens and out-of-town workers milled about Texas City and the dock area, they obviously were jumpy and ready to duck for cover at the first indication of a new series of blasts. They glanced worriedly at the fires still burning along the docks.

Would the city be completely demolished before it was all over? The thought apparently was in every mind and was expressed by many.

Tales of human destruction were legion.

B. M. Squyres, Houston policeman, said the blast of the High Flyer threw him beside an old man. He saw a piece of steel slice off the man's head.

B. P. Jansan, Harris County Emergency Corps worker, was loading a first-aid truck when the second blast occurred. Nearby, he said, he saw a man's jugular vein severed by a piece of flying debris.

"I pinched off the vein and packed it with sterile pads," Jansan said.

A mother of 15 children, who lives adjacent to the worst blast area, fled the area Wednesday with 12 of the children (the other three are married and live in other parts of Texas), but the father was missing. The mother, Mrs. Mercedes Oliveros, 56, said the last she heard of the father, Raphael Oliveros, he was in the original

(See SIDELIGHTS, page 17.)

Top left: Final rites being administered to 30 victims of the tragic blast laid out in a Texas City cafe. Administering the last sacraments are Father Norman Reuss, in the center at the rear, and Father Frank Macarty, on the right. The two Catholic priests were sent to the disaster scenes from St. Thomas High School in Houston.

Top right: Rescue workers use a blasted piece of timber to pry up a section of rail as they seek more bodies amid the debris of the explosion at Texas City.

Bottom: Graveyard of cars blasted by explosion. In the foreground is a lifeboat that was blown from a ship far inland.

Total Injured Estimated At "About 3000"

Second Ship Explodes and More Blasts Follow, Adding to Devastation in Town.

A sad and shattered Texas City was trying to identify its hundreds of dead Thursday, while five great fires still raged along the waterfront, blocking a search which might disclose an additional "several hundred" bodies.

Chronicle reporters counted 240 dead Thursday morning. Literally thousands of injured filled every avalable hospital bed in Galveston, Houston and adjacent areas. Hundreds are missing.

The national Red Cross set up an initial appropriation of $250,000 for Texas City relief, and Chairman Basil O'Connor advised Governor Beauford Jester that "more will be available if needed." Maurice Reddy, veteran disaster official from national headquarters, was sent to direct activities at the scene.

All bodies in Texas City's debris-strewn streets and blasted buildings outside the fire area have been collected, Police Chief W. F. Ladish announced.

"There may be several hundred more in that dock area," Chief Ladish said. "We just won't know until we can get in there."

The tragedy broke at 9:12 a.m. Wednesday when the Grandcamp, a burning nitrate vessel docked at Texas City, exploded with a terrific blast. Explosions in the giant Monsanto chemical plant and at the Stone Oil refinery followed. Flames still raged throughout an area several miles square. Early Thursday morning two more vessels at the Texas City dockside, the Wilson B. Keene and the High Flyer, exploded and sank.

W. H. Sandberg, vice-president of the Texas City Terminal Railway Company, termed the situation "still dangerous" Thursday. The fires apparently were being held within the dock area, however, and although precautions against and additional explosions were redoubled there was no immediate indications of such possibility.

Meanwhile a generous state and nation, shocked by the tragedy, rallied quickly to pour relief supplies and personnel into Texas City. The Red Cross, the army, the navy, doctors and nurses from a 200-mile radius, and peace officers from near-by cities were on hand.

An Associated Press dispatch from Austin quoted Governor Beauford Jester as announcing the Red Cross had given an estimate of "positive" dead totaling 400, with 364 embalmed, and an additional 200 to 250 "probable" dead. These figures were based on a count made by the Red Cross at 5 a.m. Thursday.

The Red Cross at that time also reported 350 to 400 persons hospitalized with injuries, and estimated the total injured at 3000.

A later estimate from the Red Cross national headquarters in Washington put the "known dead" at 714, with an additional 200 "believed" dead buried in debris along the water-front area. The information, headquarters said, came from John C. Wilson of St. Louis, manager of the Red Cross Midwestern area, who is receiving reports from organization workers in Texas City.

Most public utilities were functioning, Chief Ladish reported, although a number of water mains which had withstood the shock of Wednesday's explosions were broken in the 1:15 a.m. Thursday blast of the Ss High Flyer and water could be seen bubbling up at various spots in the streets.

As a precaution against a contaminated water supply—although no contamination has yet been reported definitely—health officials began giving typhoid shots to everyone in Texas City Thursday.

Property damage was estimated roughly Thursday at between $22,000,000 and $27,000,000, including the loss of the steamers Grandcamp, the High Flyer and the Wilson B. Keene, valued at about $2,200,000 for the three. The values on the vessels do not represent preesnt day replacement cost, it was emphasized.

Of the counted bodies, 192 are in Texas City, 28 in Galveston and 20 in Houston.

Only some 50 or 60 had been identified, but at 7 a.m. Thursday Texas City city officials opened the doors of the Central High School gymnasium, where 189 bodies were laid out in six long rows, and bade Texas Citians to enter and begin the heart-rending task of putting a name to the nameless ones. One body had been removed during the night by relatives.

Some 150 embalmers, including students from as far away as Dallas, had worked throughout the night in an emergency mortuary set up in the McGar Garage, to have the bodies ready for inspection Thursday.

Some 1500 out-of-town policemen, deputy sheriffs, Texas Rangers, state highway patrolmen, and army, navy and national guard personnel were on hand to patrol the area. Although practically every store building and warehouse in

(See TEXAS CITY DISASTER, Page 23.)

njured Walk In Daze Into Hospitals

BY EDDIE KRELL.
Staff Correspondent.

Galveston, April 17.—They entered the Galveston hospitals—ore than 700 of them—still azed and bewildered after the errific explosion that rocked exas City.

Some of them walked in with oody stumps where arms used hang. Some were carried in ith shattered legs. Some were ver to see again.

But the John Sealy, St. Mary's, arine and Fort Crockett hospitals were ready for them, and everything humanly possible was ne to aid the hundreds of injured men, women and children om Texas City.

o o o

udent Nurses Called.

Doctors and nurses from every y in Southeast Texas were re. Five hundred students m the University of Texas hool of medicine were taken out their classrooms and pressed to service.

Blood plasma from cities as far St. Louis was flown in. Lifeving drugs were rushed in in undance. The Red Cross was here it was needed.

Housewives, office workers d bobby-soxers flocked to the spitals to help if they could. any had the benefit of nursing perience learned during the ar. Others had never even lled a bandage, but they all anted to help. And did.

o o o

ozen to Be Blind.

Doctors at John Sealy and St ary's hospitals considered well ough were sent home to make om for the blast victims.

More than 400 entered the emergency room of the John Sealy ospital, Dr. Chauncy Leake, viceesident of the University of exas and dean of the medical hool, said.

"Those who were not very seris were sent to Fort Crockett," octor Leake said.

"It appears that about 12 of the ctims in our hospital will be toly blind. There is no estimating e number of amputees except say that it will be dozens.

"We had 10 operating tables going constantly and they were being manned by operating teams on ree-hour shifts. Most of the inries were broken limbs, body ts and chest injuries. We had rprisingly few burns."

o o o

ildren Moved Out.

Doctor Leake said the children tients in the hospital were taken the Stuart Convalescent Home make room for the Texas City ctims.

"It was inspiring to witness the unanimous response of the public in this catastrophe," Doctor eake said. "Help of all types was mediately available. I think the ar experience of the hospital staff and students helped immensely. The staff clicked right from the beginning and the students knew what to do and how to do it."

Doctor Leake said the explosion served as a good example for the need of a blood bank. He said the supply the hospital had on hand took care of the situation at the beginning and more arrived when it was needed.

Approximately 15,000 units of blood were sent to the John Sealy Hospital, which diverted some of it to other Galveston hospitals, Doctor Leake said. He added the response for donors of whole blood was excellent but said there still is a need for Type O blood.

He estimated that the majority of the patients in the hospital would be there for at least 10 days.

Doctor Leake said the army and navy proved a great aid to the hospital, sending blood plasma, drugs and blankets.

There were approximately 600 patients in the hospital Wednesday night, in addition to the blast victims.

Seven blast victims had died in John Sealy Hospital by Wednesday night.

Mary Ann Allen, 19, student nurse, said the injured were very co-operative with the doctors and nurses but relatives gave hospital attendants some difficulty.

Miss Allen said she was stationed at the door of the emergency room and two medical students had to help her all day long control the anxious crowd of relatives and friends trying to get in.

"Some times they jammed so thick at the door we had difficulty getting the patients in. Hysterical women looking for husbands screamed and shouted. It seemed the patients were still too dazed and bewildered to raise any fuss, even if they wanted to. One

(See KRELL, page 29.)

A. P. Writer Reminded Of Nagasaki A-Bomb

(Editor's note: The following eyewitness account of the scene in Texas City, stricken by a series of blasts and oil fires, was written by Hal Boyle, Pulitzer prize-winning Associated Press staff correspondent. As a war correspondent, Boyle served on all of the active fronts in World War II.)

BY HAL BOYLE,
Associated Press Writer.

Over Texas City, April 17.—In four years of war coverage, I have seen no concentrated devastation so utter, except Nagasaki, Japan, victim of the second atom bomb, as presented Thursday by flaming Texas City.

The damage along the waterfront of Texas City exceeds in intensity that inflicted on Bari, Italy, in the fall of 1943 when German bombers hit that port and 17 vessels went up in flames, including three ammunition ships whose titanic explosions killed hundreds of American troops and Italian civilians.

From the air the burning industrial port looks like a peacetime parallel to war-bombed Ploesti, Roumanian oil capital.

It is now 7:15 a.m. We are making our third flight over the burning town.

The fire-ravaged industrial section and the peaceful residential areas offer the contrast between life and death.

One is a two-mile wide torch. The other is the living pattern of a deserted village, its fate still dependent on whether the present favorable wind holds.

Angry smoke towering to 3000 feet spreads from the city like a gigantic black wing—deep and dense where it joins the ground,

(See BOYLE, page 13.)

TODAY'S INDEX

Partial List Of Dead

A partial list of dead in the Texas City explosion included the following:

AT TEXAS CITY.

John Gibson, Texas City.
Dave Mitchell.
T. B. Lewis.
William H. Falkenhagen.
Irma Torres.
Antonio Torres.
Mose Jones, negro.
T. B. Lewis.
Ernest Stork.
Arthur H. Cannon.
A. D. Masters.
Dave Mitchell.
C. Q. Wells.
Bennie Gerson.
D. W. Hayes.
Jess De Leon.
Joseph McCorr.
Fred Brumley, 16, of La Porte.
Benny La Salle, 45, Pan-American Refinery employe.
A negro woman, decapitated.
A white girl about 6 years old.
A white man, about 35.
A white man, about 40.
A white man, about 45.
F. L. Lutterman.
Antonio Torres.
Thomas A. Womack.
Fred Womack.
Charles K. Gilcrease, 29, of La Marque.
Mrs. Pearl Davis.
A white woman about 30.
A white girl about 14.
Jesse Jones.
Austin Edwards.
Lucio Salazar.
V. O. Nieto.
George F. DeBoer.
E. E. May, Texas City constable.
Joseph DeWitt Meek.
Gonzales Garcia.
T. B. Warren.
Gregory H. Perez.
Antonio A. Garonzuay.
Robert Lee Smith.
Isaac Burton Goar.
George Williams, Galveston.
Pete Dello.
Hugh Matthew Frilaux.
E. J. Katzmark.
Thomas Franklin McIntyre.
Dale D. Wells of Galveston.
William Hightower.
George Azala, 1001 Woodring, Houston.
O. T. Evans.
Bertie E. Turner.
Edward P. Campbell.
L. A. Oliver.
Bill Phillips.
Clarence William Green.
Louis Eugene Griffin.
R. L. Pelosi.
Joseph LeCain.
W. S. Bellow.
John L. Kelly.
Alfred S. Gusam.
Joe Richardson.
Clarence W. Green.
L. Q. Brown, Palestine.
M. Evans.
L. J. Armatta, Lissie, Texas.
Harry E. Cox.
A. D. Masters.
Melvin John Kunkel, 110½ Seventy-First, Houston.
Earl Clinton Hartnett.

(See LIST OF DEAD, page 13.)

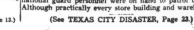

1948

Democratic President Harry S. Truman won reelection over Republican Governor Thomas E. Dewey, although readers of an early edition of the *Chicago Tribune* weren't sure for a while.

Many pollsters, politicians—and, apparently, the Washington bureau of the *Tribune*—had expected Dewey to win.

Truman saw a copy of the newspaper when his "Victory Special" train, returning him to Washington from his Independence, Missouri, home, stopped in St. Louis.

The *Tribune* had it right in the next day's issue, which stressed a double murder over coverage of the election.

AN AMERICAN PAPER FOR AMERICANS

Chicago Daily Tribune

THE WORLD'S GREATEST NEWSPAPER

54 PAGES CITY ★★ HOME

VOL. CVII.—NO. 264 ... WEDNESDAY, NOVEMBER 3, 1948

DEWEY DEFEATS TRUMAN

G. O. P. Sweep Indicated in State; Boyle Leads in City

REPUBLICAN TICKET AHEAD OF 1944 VOTE

Downstate Balloting Gives Trend

Probable Winners

SENATOR—Wayland Brooks (R.)*
GOVERNOR—Dwight H. Green (R.)*
LT. GOV.—Richard Yates Rowe
SECRETARY OF STATE—William G. Stratton (R.)
AUDITOR—Simon A. Murray (R.)
TREASURER—Elmer H. Droste
ATTY. GEN.—George F. Barrett
*Re-elected.

BY ARTHUR EVANS

Early returns last night indicated that the Dewey-Warren Republican ticket and the state ticket headed by Sen. Brooks and Gov. Green would carry Illinois. Returns from downstate, fragmentary but typical, showed G.O.P. candidates running stronger than in 1944. Brooks and Green downstate were running neck and neck up with Dewey.

Most of the first reports were from Chicago, and as usual they were overloaded with returns from Democratic ward strongholds. President Truman was leading Gov. Dewey, and both Brooks and Green were trailing the national ticket. Green was behind Brooks.

FROM DOWNSTATE

The first seven down state precincts to report gave Truman 27.3 per cent, Dewey 72.7. The same precincts gave Paul H. Douglas for senator 26, per cent, Brooks (R) 74. Adlai E. Stevenson for governor 25.6 per cent, and Green 74.4. These seven precincts were from Knox county, a Republican center; from Rock Island, old Democratic stronghold, and from Franklin county, old Democratic coal mining territory.

In Chicago 308 precincts out of 4,142 gave Truman 61 per cent, Dewey 39 per cent. In Chicago 266 precincts gave Douglas 65 per cent, Brooks 35; Stevenson 66 per cent, and Green 34.

The battle of the ballots was the old battle between Chicago, one of the big city Democratic machine, and the rest of the state, which since 1944 has been rolling up Republican majorities.

... in 20 years, or ... since ... 1... ... ha...

[Continued on Page 3, Col. 1]

Tops Coghlan in Hot Race for Attorney

Probable Winners

STATE'S ATTORNEY—John S. Boyle (D.) or Malachy J. Coghlan (R.)
RECORDER OF DEEDS—Victor L. Schlaeger (D.)
CIRCUIT COURT CLERK—John E. Conroy (D.) or Mrs. Mabel Reinecke (R.)
CORONER—A. L. Brodie (D.) or Frank Kalteux (R.)
SUPERIOR COURT CLERK—Henry Sonnenschein (D.)
SANITARY DISTRICT TRUSTEES (3)—Frank W. Chesrow (D.), John A. Cullerton (D.), and Casimir Griglik (D.) or Walter E. McCarron (R.)
MUNICIPAL COURT BAILIFF—Albert J. Horan (D.)
MUNICIPAL COURT CLERK—Joseph L. Gill (D.)
*Re-elected.

BY GEORGE TAGGE

Heavy Democratic leads in Chicago wards darkened the outlook last night for Republican candidates for state's attorney and other Cook county offices.

John S. Boyle (D.) was running ahead of Malachy J. Coghlan (R.) in what had been billed as a sizzling race for state's attorney. Most other G.O.P. candidates trailed Coghlan's share of the Chicago vote.

The suburbs in slower returns were delivering for Coghlan about what had been expected. But in normally Republican territory in the city Coghlan was getting about a 5 to 4 break while Democratic strongholds slammed thru for Boyle with votes of from 2 to 1 all the way to 10 to 1.

HEAVY BOYLE VOTE

From the first 204 city precincts Boyle got 51,665 votes or 62.1 per cent, against 30,082 or 36.9 per cent for Coghlan. Municipal Judge Samuel Heller of the Progressive party got 1,369 votes or 1.6 per cent in these precincts.

It was a battle for survival by the Democratic machine. Thousands of Democratic door bell ringers concentrated on begging votes for Boyle during the closing week of the campaign.

PATRONAGE A LURE

Most of Boyle's running mates had the patronage of their offices to throw into the battle to save the Democratic county ticket. Coghlan lacked this advantage. In 1946 the G.O.P. captured 12 out of 17 county-wide offices but none of these was at stake yesterday.

Mayor Kennelly was a major campaign factor for the first time since the election in 1947. Boyle was one of

[Continued on Page 2, Col. 3]

RECORD CITY VOTE SEEN IN LATE TALLIES

Suburban Ballot Near 375,000

A new high record vote seemed certain for Chicago yesterday in the first post-war Presidential election.

A turnout of 1,900,000 was indicated in the final sampling of precincts in each of the 50 wards, according to Chief Clerk John S. Rusch of the Chicago election board. This prediction was based on a projection of 1,789,776 one hour before the polls closed.

TOPS 1944 RECORD

The old record was established in 1944, the Chicago vote was 1,856,460. Since then the voting registration has increased 7.7 per cent.

Earlier checks of one precinct in each ward indicated 1,062,644 persons had voted at 11:30 a.m., halfway mark in the day's balloting, and that 675,309 had voted by 8:45 a.m., end of the first quarter of the voting period.

HEAVY COUNTY VOTE

Heavy balloting also was reported in suburban Cook county. Experts predicted the all-time record for suburban area—371,192 votes in 1944—would be approached and possibly exceeded.

George McCullom, chief clerk in the election division of County Clerk Flynn's office, said a spot check of 636 county precincts under Flynn's jurisdiction in the early afternoon showed an average of 300 votes a precinct had been cast. He estimated that the day's total for these precincts at 275,000. No samples were taken from the 10 suburban communities under jurisdiction of the Chicago board of election commissioners.

RAINS OVER STATE

Whether the state's record vote of 4,262,196 in 1944 was exceeded remained problematical.

Rains moved north into Illinois during the night, with precipitation of .25 to .50 of an inch reported in most parts of southern and central Illinois by early afternoon. The rainfall was expected to curb the vote somewhat, particularly in the sparsely settled rural areas.

BULLETINS ON ELECTIONS

COOK COUNTY

President—749 pcts. of 5023 in Cook county: Truman D 182,780, Dewey R 128,916, Wallace P 575.

Senator—481 pcts. of 5023 in Cook county: Douglas D 128,596, Brooks R 70,465.

Governor—481 pcts. of 5023 in Cook county Stevenson D 133,374, Green R 68,973.

Lieutenant Governor—14 pcts. of Cook county: Dixon D 3,968, Rowe R 1,495.

State's Attorney—524 pcts. of 5023 in Cook county: Boyle D 134,682, Coghlan R 80,100. Heller P 3,959.

Secretary of State—14 pcts. of 4143 in Chicago: Barret D 4,003, Stratton R 1,494.

State Treasurer—14 pcts. of 4,143 in Chicago: Smith D 3,994, Droste R 1,475.

State Auditor—14 pcts. of 5,023 in Cook county: Cooper D 5,... Murray R 1,382.

Attorney General—14 pcts. of 4,143 in Chicago: Elliott D 3,977, Barret R 1,499.

Circuit Court Clerk—12 pcts. of 4,143 in Chicago: Conroy D 3,153, Reinecke R 1,385, Lawson P 96.

Coroner—12 pcts. of 5023 in Cook county: Brodie D 3,225, Kalteux R 1,309, Doyle P 99.

Congress—7th Dist.—1 pcts. of 412 Sabath D 286, Sperry R 57.

Congress—10th Dist.—2 pcts. of 422: Peters D 251, Hoffman R 515.

Superior Court Clerk—17 pcts. of 4143 in Chicago; Sonnenschein D 4,655, Reddy R 1,933 McKenzie P 122.

Recorder—17 pcts. of 5023 in Cook county: Schlaeger D 5569, Polnar R 1924, Eiger P 122.

ILLINOIS

President—600 precincts of 9,231 in Illinois (76 downstate, 524 in Cook county) Truman 139,724, Dewey 97,675.

Senator—172 precincts of 9,231 in Illinois (22 downstate and 150 in Cook county) Douglas 42,137, Brooks 25,035.

Governor—... precincts of 9,231 in Illinois (... downstate ... in Cook county) Stevenson ...,808, Green 40,755.

... ... in Illinois ... ...

Auditor—... precincts of 9,231 in Illinois. Cooper ...400, Murray 635.

Secretary of State—4 precincts of 9,231 in Illinois, Barrett D 415, Stratton R 633.

NATION

Birmingham, Ala., Nov. 2 (AP)-Gov. Thurmond, the State Rights Democratic candidate, won Alabama's 11 electoral votes.

Alabama 2 boxes of 2,408, Thurmond 116. Dewey 37, Wallace 3.

Arkansas—2 districts of 2,217 Truman 85; Dewey 2, Wallace 2.

Florida—60 ... precincts of 1,523, Dewey 8,983, Thurmond 3,173, Truman 11,657, Wallace 1,151; governor, 39 precincts, Acker R 2,369, Warren D 9,743.

Georgia ...5 out of 1,736 ...ts Truman 2,27... stretcheey 325, Thurmond ..., Wallace ...

Kansas—Nov. 2 (AP) Returns from precincts in 15 cities in Kansas: President, 185 precincts: Dewey 8,772; Truman 6,840; governor, 176 precincts: Carlson (R) 8,225, Carpenter (D) 6,064; senator, 180 precincts: Schoeppel (R) 8,002; McGill (D) 5,703.

Connecticut—17 towns of 169, Truman 132,772; Dewey 100,771.

Indiana—349 precincts of 4,058, Dewey 81,347, Truman 89,583; governor, 311 precincts Creighton R 67,182 Schricker D 88,203.

Kentucky 332 of 4066 precincts, Truman 66,171 Dewey 62,980; senator, Chapman D 53,323, Cooper R 72,224.

Massachusetts 5 precincts of 1,879, Dewey 257, Truman, 169, Wallace 7.

Maryland, 26 polling places of 1347, Truman 7,556, Dewey 4,008, Wallace 326, Thurmond 43.

Michigan—1 precinct out of 4,202, Truman 131, Dewey 89, Wallace 3; senator, Hook, D 137, Ferguson R 93; governor Williams D 144, Sigler R 90.

Mississippi—... precincts of 17..., Thurmond ...57, Truman 8..., Dewey 4.

New Hampshire—3 districts of 2..3, Truman ..., Dewey ...

Massachusetts—7 precincts of 1,87..., Truman ..., Dewey 650, Wallace 10; governor, Bradford R 634, Dever ... ... R 674, Fitzgerald ...

New Mexico, senator, ... precincts of 884, ... 1,911, Anderson ...,008.

Ohio—1... polling places of 9,..10, Truman 187,830, Dewey 221,233, Wallace 1,389; governor, 32 polling places Herbert R 3,264, Lausche D 2,978.

Oklahoma—senator 2 precincts of 3701 Kerr D 164 Rizley R 89.

Rhode Island—4 districts of 266, Truman 345, Dewey 1,294, Wallace 9.

Rhode Island senator. 4 districts of 266; Green D 557, Hazard R 1,237.

Columbia, S.C., Nov. 2-(AP)-Gov. J. Strom Thurmond, States' rights presidential candidate, captured his home state's eight electoral college votes today.

South Carolina—500 precincts of 1,296, Dewey 2,462, Thurmond 43,018, Truman 16,168, Wallace 56; senator 307 precincts, Maybank D 36,800, Gerald R 1,171.

South Dakota—2 precincts of 1,942, Truman 210, Dewey 282; senator, Mundt R 137; Engel D 64.

Tennessee—421 districts 2,300, Dewey 11,258, Thurmond 5,472, Truman 22,629, Wallace 116; Senator, Kefauver D 24,181, Reece R 10,043; governor, 2,300, Acuff R 11,739, Browning D 27,596.

Texas—133 precincts Truman 6,485, Dewey 7,887, Thurmond 5,314, Wallace 185; senate, Johnson D 6,..., Porter R 9,701.

Vermont—1 out of 246 districts, Dewey, 74, Truman, 15.

Virginia—13 precincts of 1,755, Truman 480, Dewey 158, Thurmond 56, Wallace 8; Senate, 10 precincts, Robertson D 452, Woods R 158.

Wisconsin—49 of 3,143 precincts, Truman, 6,418, Dewey 7,216, Wallace 163; governor, 14 precincts, Rennebohm R 1,056, Thompson D 453, Borquist P 21.

THE WEATHER

Wednesday, Nov. 3, 1948

CHICAGO AND VICINITY: Partly cloudy, not much change in temperature; high 60, low 44; southeast winds 10 to 15 miles per hour. Thursday fair and warmer.

ILLINOIS: Rain ending early today. Partly cloudy in afternoon and a little warmer.

TEMPERATURES IN CHICAGO

1 a.m.	[illegible]	11 a.m.	[illegible]	6 p.m.	[illegible]
2 a.m.	[illegible]	Noon	[illegible]	7 p.m.	[illegible]
3 a.m.	[illegible]	1 p.m.	[illegible]	8 p.m.	[illegible]
4 a.m.	[illegible]	2 p.m.	[illegible]	9 p.m.	[illegible]
5 a.m.	[illegible]	3 p.m.	[illegible]	10 p.m.	[illegible]
6 a.m.	[illegible]	4 p.m.	[illegible]	11 p.m.	[illegible]
7 a.m.	[illegible]	5 p.m.	[illegible]	Midnight	[illegible]
10 a.m.	[illegible]				

Sunrise, 6:27. Sunset, 4:43. Moonset, 7:26 p.m. Thursday. Evening stars: Jupiter and Mars. Morning stars: Saturn, Venus, and Mercury.

Other reports on page 18.

Early Count Gives G.O.P. Senate Edge

BY WALTER TROHAN

Republicans took an early lead in one of the hottest campaigns in history for control of the senate. G.O.P. retention of control of the senate seemed assured when New Mexico appeared to be deserting solid Democratic rule.

Patrick J. Hurley, Republican, took an early lead over former Agriculture Secretary Anderson in New Mexico, one of eight pivotal states. This offset what was expected to be a certain Democratic gain in Oklahoma, where former Gov. Kerr, Democrat, leaped ahead of Rep. Rizley (R.). The G.O.P. was also ahead in Kentucky where Sen. Cooper (R.) led Rep. Chapman (D.).

5 VACANT SEATS

The present house has 243 Republicans, 185 Democrats, and two American Labor party members. There are five vacancies.

There was no indication of the outcome in West Virginia, Wyoming, Minnesota, Colorado, and Montana, the other five pivotal states.

In West Virginia, Sen. Revercomb R took a lead over former Sen. Matthew M. Neely D after the latter had taken the first precincts reporting.

G.O.P. HOPES HIGH

Altho the result of the fight to retain control of the senate, which the G.O.P. won in 1946, may not be known until the last ballot is counted, G.O.P. hopes soared high on first returns.

It was indicated that the G.O.P. might hold the present 51 to 45 majority as returns showed Gov. Dewey piling up a large vote in doubtful states. There was a possibility that the G.O.P. might even gain a seat or two.

House control was not in doubt from the earliest returns. The Republicans took an early lead, which promised a measure of control even greater than that enjoyed in the 80th congress. A gain of more than 10 seats was indicated.

BALL TRAILING

In Minnesota Sen. Ball (R., Minn.) was trailing popular Hubert Humphrey, Democratic mayor of Minneapolis in a ...

[Continued on Page 9, Col. 8]

Daily Average Net Paid Circulation
FOR SEPTEMBER, 1948
DAILY 985,000
In Excess of
THE CHICAGO TRIBUNE

PUTS G.O.P. BACK IN THE WHITE HOUSE

Sizable Electoral Margin Seen

BY ARTHUR SEARS HENNING

Dewey and Warren won a sweeping victory in the Presidential election yesterday.

The early returns showed the Republican ticket leading Truman so that the complete returns would disclose that Dewey won the Presidency by an overwhelming majority of electoral votes.

Herbert Brownell, manager of the Dewey campaign, claimed on the basis of the incomplete returns that "we will wind up by sweeping two-thirds of the states for the Republican ticket."

ILLINOIS IS INCLUDED

As states definitely in the Republican column in the light of the fragmentary returns Brownell named Illinois, Ohio, Indiana, Connecticut, Delaware, Maine, Maryland, New Hampshire, Vermont, and South Dakota. Four years ago the Republicans carried only five of these states.

"At this moment," said Brownell, "the polls have closed in 12 of the 48 states outside the solid south. These states have a total of 120 votes in the electoral college.

"On the basis of reports which I have been receiving from organization leaders thruout the country, I am confident that the Dewey-Warren ticket has already carried 10 of these 12 states with a total of 102 of the 120 electoral votes.

"In the two other states Kentucky and West Virginia returns are not yet conclusive but the trend to the Dewey-Warren ticket is heartening."

... DEAL REPUDIATED

The Republican victor brought to a close the 16 year reign of the New Deal which began in the country's most devastating depression, introduced a collectivist economy, produced a ... ...

Chicago Daily Tribune

THE WORLD'S GREATEST NEWSPAPER

WEDNESDAY, NOVEMBER 3, 1948

AN AMERICAN PAPER FOR AMERICANS

VOL. CVII—NO. 264

54 PAGES CITY ★★ FINAL

FOUR CENTS—PAY NO MORE

EARLY DEWEY LEAD NARROW DOUGLAS, STEVENSON WIN

DEMOCRATIC SWEEP TAKES STATE POSTS

Dewey Has Slim Illinois Lead

BY ARTHUR EVANS

Boyle Victor; Democratic Ticket Wins

Probable Winners

BULLETINS ON ELECTIONS

COOK COUNTY

VOTE UPSETS PERIL G.O.P. SENATE RULE

Margin in House Is Pared

BY WALTER TROHAN

Truman Gets Slight Edge in N.Y. State

FARMS, CITIES GIVE TRUMAN A HEAVY VOTE

Key States Still in Doubt

BY ARTHUR SEARS HENNING

FARM VOTE LIGHTER

CREDIT KENNELLY

THE WEATHER

Chicago Daily Tribune

THE WORLD'S GREATEST NEWSPAPER

THURSDAY, NOVEMBER 4, 1948

AN AMERICAN PAPER FOR AMERICANS

VOL. CVII—NO. 265

48 PAGES CITY ★★ FINAL

FOUR CENTS—PAY NO MORE

CONFESSES DOUBLE KILLING

Home Town Turns Out for Truman Victory Celebration

DEMOCRATS WIN PLUMS IN STATE SWEEP

Springfield Due for Social Fling

BY GEORGE TAGGE

Slew Young Couple on Golf Course

SETTLING POLITICAL DIFFERENCES

TELLS CROWD PARTY CAN PUSH AIMS

Plans Holiday In Florida

BY WILLARD EDWARDS

U.N. Excited, Red Amazed by Election

BY CHESLY MANLY

TRUMAN WINS BY PLURALITY OF 2 MILLION

Dewey Asks for U.S. Unity

BY ARTHUR SEARS HENNING

Life Insurers Study 6 Block Home Project

BOOKIES TAKE LICKING ON TRUMAN; HANNEGAN CLEANS UP AT 15 TO 1

B-29 Strikes Peak; Fear 13 Killed

Howard White Elected Judge Of Circuit Court

Willkie's Son Elected to Indiana Legislature

JUBILANT DEMOCRATS TELEPHONE TRIBUNE TO BOAST OF VICTORY

THE WEATHER

Tribune Features

130 G. O. P. CLOCKS STOP IN CITY HALL AS DEMOCRATS RE...

FOR SEPTEMBER, 1948 DAILY 985,000

WEATHER
Risk of general light snow, little change in temperature tonight and Saturday.
Weather Details on Page 1, Part 2

THE INDIANAPOLIS NEWS

LATEST EDITION

VOL. 78 | 78th YEAR | FRIDAY EVENING, JANUARY 30, 1948 | 42 PAGES | 5 CENTS

GANDHI MURDERED BY HINDU ASSASSIN

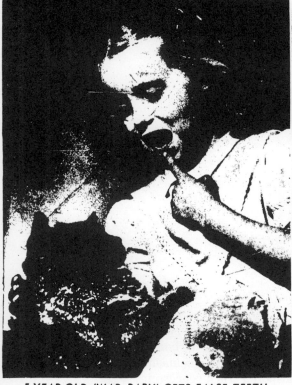

5-YEAR-OLD 'WAR BABY' GETS FALSE TEETH

Frances Ann Shelland, who at age 5 will soon have a pair of false teeth, enlists the sympathy of her best animal friend, a cat named Foxy. Daughter of 8th Air Force Sgt. and Mrs. Maynard W. Shelland, 38 S. Hawthorne Lane, Frances An nwas born in 1942 in London, where her mother was able to obtain one egg a month, two ounces of butter a week and four or five oranges in as many years. This diet left Frances Ann, who wasn't brought to America until she was 4, with insufficient nourishment to grow healthy teeth. Picture shows her natural teeth which are all badly decayed. Her false oens will be so made that there will be room for her next real teeth when they come in.—The News Photo, George F. Tilford.

House Group Cuts Agency Budgets 6%

By the Associated Press

WASHINGTON, Jan. 30—The House Appropriations Committee brought in the first big money bill of the 1948 session today with a 6% cut in President Truman's spending estimates.

Among other things, the committee whacked the President's own emergency fund from $1,000,000 to $700,000. It said he has been using it for things which "cannot be classified on any reasonable basis" as emergencies.

The bill is to provide funds for the Presidential office and 22 other government agencies for the fiscal year starting July 1. The committee recommended a total of $991,583,551. The President's estimate, through the Budget Bureau, was $1,047,798,864.

The committee cut $100,000 from the $400,000 requested for the President's Council of Economic Advisers.

It threw out a $504,000 item to get ready for any possible emergency which might make it necessary to draft men into the Army again.

Exceeds '47 Total

The committee said it does not believe the draft training by the Office of Selective Service records is "warranted" at this time.

Explaining the cut in the President's emergency fund, the committee said the money is supposed to provide for emergencies affecting the national interest of security."

It said the money should not be spent to establish "boards or commissions" or for other non-emergency uses to which similar funds have been put "during 1948 and in previous years."

The $700,000 recommended was still $200,000 more than the President got last year.

As drawn by the committee, the bill carries these funds for the larger agencies:

Executive office of the President, $6,142,312 asked, $5,589,312 recommended, cut $553,000.

Civil Service Commission, $287,598,098 asked, $243,294,098 recommended, cut $44,304,000.

Federal Communications Commission, $6,540,000 asked, $6,300,000 recommended, cut $240,000.

Federal Power Commission, $4,220,000 asked, $4,049,550 recommended, cut $170,540.

Federal Trade Commission, $3,975,000 asked, $3,478,035 recommended, cut $496,965.

Federal Works Agency, $529,454,554 asked, $525,863,944 recommended, cut $3,590,610. ($459,588,854 of the total recommended is for the Public Roads Administration.)

General Accounting Office, $33,161,000 asked and recommended.

Interstate Commerce Commission, $11,299,000 asked, $10,819,317 recommended, cut $409,683.

National Advisory Committee for Aeronautics, $47,995,000 asked, $47,905,000 recommended, cut $90,000. (In addition, the committee receives contract authority for $18,200,000.)

Philippine War Damage Commission, $95,000,000 asked and recommended.

Securties and Exchange Commission, $6,000,000 asked, $5,826,140 recommended, cut $173,860.

Bobs Hutton Better, Say Bern Doctors

BERN, Switzerland, Jan. 30 (AP)—Doctors reported Princess Troubetzkoy, the former Barbara Hutton, "rather better" today. But they said she is not yet out of danger.

An examination this morning, the doctors said, disclosed no complications from a serious intestinal operation performed in a Bern clinic Tuesday.

The Princess, heiress to the Woolworth dime-store fortune, has been married to Prince Igor Troubetzkoy of France a year.

Truman Aids Polio Drive

WASHINGTON, Jan. 30 (AP)—President Truman will speak over the radio at 10:54 p. m. (C. S. T.) tonight in behalf of the annual March of Dimes campaign.

TEEN TERMS

2 Robbers Sentenced

Two 18-year-old youths, one an admitted armed robber and the other a confessed burglar, were sentenced to the Indiana Reformatory by Judge William D. Bain in Criminal Court, Division 1, today.

James Russell Parry received two 10-year terms, to be served concurrently, after he reversed a not guilty plea and admitted to Detectives Harold Goodman and Elmer White the perpetration of 14 armed robberies last June and July.

John Sullivan, who a year ago received a six-month term for illegal possession of an automobile, was sentenced to 3 to 5 years for a series of burglaries committed since he served the sentence.

Perry was sentenced for robberies at the Toddle House, 907 N. Pennsylvania St., June 19 and at a Hoosier Pete filling station July 21. The detectives said Perry specialized in holding up filling stations and food markets. He obtained $45 and a wrist watch at the Toddle House and $40 from the filling station.

Also sentenced was Robert E. Lee Anderson, who wil servee 2 to 14 years on a sex charge and 2 to 21 years for incest, the terms to run concurrently.

Creighton Enters Governorship Race

By EDWARD H. ZIEGNER, The News Staff Writer

Hobart Creighton, Warsaw, Speaker of the Indiana House of Representatives, today announced he will be a candidate for the Republican nomination for Governor at the G. O. P. state convention in June.

The Warsaw Republican, a member of the House since 1933 and Speaker in the 1943, 1945 and 1947 General Assembly sessions, became the second G. O. P. candidate to make a formal announcement. Lieutenant Governor Richard T. James announced earlier this month he would seek the nomination.

Mr. Greighton and his brother Russell are operators of the largest Leghorn chicken breeding farm in the nation.

"Now that I have announced my candidacy for the Republican nomination for Governor," he said, "I wish to make it plain that I will be in the race until the end. Rumors I have made a 'deal' or would accept second place on the ticket are completely and totally without foundation. I am a candidate for the nominaiton for Governor and for no other office." presently an active member of

It had been reported for several weeks that Mr. Creighton would seek the Republican gubernantorial nomination, and his home district, the Second, recently endorsed him for that office.

C. Reuben Williams, of the Warsaw Daily Times, one of his friends who are supporting Mr. Creighton in his bid for the G. O. P. gubernatorial nomination, today issued a statement which in part said:

"His (Creighton's) one promise,

HOBART CREIGHTON

if elected Governor, is to give all that is in him in devotion to the interests of the state and its people. A simple promise that cov-

Continued on Page 18, Col. 1

Feeney Halts Payments on Sewer Survey

Engineering Firm Called to Consult on Contract With City

Mayor Al Feeney today ordered the Board of Sanitary Commissioners to withhold payments to Moore & Owen, Indianapolis engineering firm, on its contract to provide plans for a $35,000,000 sewer modernization program.

A sum of $77,125 has been paid to the firm thus far, according to James F. Cunningham, Sanitary Board president, and $18,300 now is on deposit, earmarked for payment.

Mayor Feeney said he would ask Russell B. Moore, partner in the firm to come to his officec for a discussion of the contract. He also ordered Mr. Cunningham to investigate the terms of the contract and the performance of its duties by the firm.

Mr. Cunningham said records in the Sanitary Board's office showed that $18,300 was paid to Moore & Owen August 11, and $58,825 December 10. The money has been advanced by the Federal Works Administration and is to be returned to the federal government when the bond issue is granted for carrying out the work that has been planned.

This contract between the city and the firm was severely criticized by Mayor Feeney in his campaign for the office last fall.

Moore & Owen presented a voluminous report to the city administration and City Council last year on the work that had been done up to that time. Illustrated with numerous maps, diagrams and charts, it proposed a long-range sewer improvement program for the Indianapolis area, and outlined work that needed to be done immediately.

Mihai-Anne Wedding in May, Says Father

ST. MORITZ, Jan. 30 (UP)—Prince Rene of Bourbon Parma said today his daughter, Princess Anne, will be married to former King Mihai of Romania in May.

The prince said the marriage would take place in Copenhagen, Paris or Villefranche on the French Riviera.

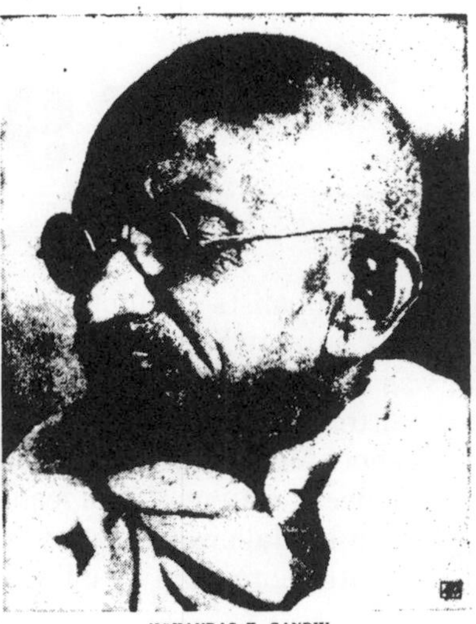

MOHANDAS K. GANDHI

'ANYTHING MIGHT HAPPEN IN INDIA'

By the Associated Press

LONDON, Jan. 30—A government official said today almost anything might happen in the Indian subcontinent as a result of Mohandas K. Gandhi's death, but observed:

Thank God the assassin was not a Moslem, or all hell certainly would break loose."

This official, who spent many years in British government service in India, said authorities there would have to move fast to keep the situation in hand.

Prime Minister Clement Attlee is expected to appeal tonight to India and Pakistan to bury their differences in the crisis caused by the assassination. Mr. Attlee will broadcast a tribute to Gandhi on behalf of the British Government and people.

George Bernard Shaw, long a friend and admirer of Gandhi, commented sadly:

"It shows how dangerous it is to be good."

Lord Pethick-Lawrence, former secretary of state for India and Burma, said:

"It is a great shock to learn of the cruel assassination of my intimate friend, Gandhi, beloved teacher of India. I know that there is one wish that he would have had above all else. That is that his death should not be avenged or made the occasion for further bloodshed and violence, but should lead to reconciliation among all the peoples in the great subcontinent of Asia."

Pethick-Lawrence led the British Cabinet mission to India in 1945.

FAVORITE SONS TO FRONT

Eisenhower Withdrawal Helps Halleck Talk

By DON UNDERWOOD, The News Washington Bureau

WASHINGTON, Jan. 30—The Republican national convention will meet just five months hence to choose the G. O. P. nominee for the Presidential nomination.

Politically-wise observers are content that, as of this time, no one of the half-dozen candidates possesses enough first-ballot votes to consider himself definitely "in."

Acknowledged as the two leading candidates, now that Gen. Dwight D. Eisenhower has taken himself from the race, are Governor Thomas E Dewey, New York, and Senator Robert A Taft (R., O.).

Others prominently mentioned as possibilities include former Governor Harold E. Stassen, Minnesota; Speaker of the House Joseph W. Martin, Jr.; Arthur Vandenberg, president pro tem. of the Senate; Earl Warren, Governor of California, and possibly Gen. Douglas MacArthur, who still has not declared his intentions.

Then there are the "favorite sons" of several states.

In Indiana, political observers concede that Majority Leader Charles A. Halleck is the choice for favorite son of the Hoosier state. He has not yet taken cognizance of the sentiment in that direction, although he repeatedly has been approached on the designation.

One purpose of supporting a favorite son is to provide leeway in the early balloting for jockeying by various state delegations until they can see which way the tide is running. As soon as they think they can determine who the eventual nominee might be, then the delegations start swinging on to the band wagon.

Moreover, a favorite son always has a dark horse chance of winning. Representative Halleck is highly regarded in the House. He now holds the highly important post of majority party leader.

The provisional roll call by the G. O. P. national committee shows 1,093 delegates apportioned among the 48 states, the District of Columbia, Alaska, Hawaii and Porto Rico. This number includes 29 from Indiana. The total of 1,093 is 36 more than in the 1944 convention because of G. O. P. victories in the 1946 congressional elections.

For nomination, a candidate will need 547 delegate votes—that's for a one-vote majority. At present, the Dewey forces are claiming nearly 400 delegate votes, a figure at which the Taft supporters scoff. The Ohioan's backers are inclined to figure their own strength after the first ballots at around 300 votes, including most of the Southern states and possibly Pennsylvania.

Political leaders in Ohio, recoiling from the audacity of Mr. Stassen in challenging Senator Taft on his home grounds in the Ohio primary, contend that the Minnesotan will get fewer than four delegate votes.

A compilation of the states with admitted favorite son candidates

Continued on Page 18, Col. 4

Shirley Temple Mother

SANTA MONICA, Cal., Jan. 30 (AP)—Shirley Temple, who not so long ago was a famous movie child star, became a mother today.

While husband John Agar paced a waiting room, Shirley gave birth to a daughter. Dr. William C. Bradbury said both were doing nicely.

The child, to be named Linda Susan, weight 7 pounds 6 ounces.

HEY, FANS, GET HEP ON RECORDS

You won't be up to date on the latest records or Indianapolis's favorite songs, singers and orchestras, unless you read The News record features today on Page 2, Part 2. William L. Herman, a member of The News staff, has been especially assigned to cover the record beat. His comments on the popular tunes, along with reviews of clasical records by Herbert P. Kenney, Jr., will appear each Friday exclusively in The News.

Tragedy Stuns India; Political Foes Blamed

By the Associated Press

NEW DELHI, Jan. 30—A Hindu tonight shot to death Mohandas K. Gandhi, apostle of nonviolence and father of Indian independence.

Police said the frail spiritual leader of India's hundreds of millions of Hindus was killed for "political reasons—because some persons did not agree with his appeals against violence."

Gandhi, 78, was walking to his prayer meeting grounds, on the lawn of the Birla mansion, to appeal again for an end of communal violence. Three shots rang out at close range. One found his heart. Death came quickly to his emaciated body, wasted in a recent fast in the cause of peace amid the rival religious sects of India and Pakistan.

The assassin was held incommunicado. Police said he was a civilian from Poona, although he was wearing Army clothes. Earlier this month a bomb had exploded near the spot where Gandhi was holding his prayer meeting.

Dr. G. L. Qamara, a Hindu physician, who was in the prayer meeting crowd, pronounced Gandhi dead shortly after the shooting. Death came within a few minutes, but the doctor was not certain of the exact time.

Tens of thousands of Indians streamed to Gandhi's bier in his quarters in the palatial residence of G. D. Birla, an industrialist who long had supported Gandhi. They passed sadly in single file.

Sobbing bitterly, Gandhi's personal secretary, S. Kalyanam, told the Associated Press:

"Bapu is dead."

Bapu is the affectionate name for Gandhi, meaning father. To millions of his followers, he was known as Mahatma, or great-souled one. His full name was Mohandas Karamchand Gandhi.

Biography of Mohandas Gandhi on Page 3.

Bystanders said Gandhi slumped forward as the third shot rang out. He seemed unconscious as he was carried to his quarters in Birla House.

Triumph or Failure

Death came less than a year after he achieved his life's main goal of independence from Great Britain for the teeming subcontinent of India. Paradoxically, however, Gandhi considered his triumph a failure because India and her 400,000,000 people were divided into separate dominions of India (Hindu) and Pakistan (Moslem). The partition resulted in bloody, destructive communal warfare between Moslems on one side and Hindus and Sikhs on the other.

It was in an effort to end the bloodshed that Gandhi undertook this month the last of his many fasts. After five days in which he threatened to starve himself to death, Gandhi broke his fast January 18 on the "pledge and counsel" of friends in both dominions. He said they had assured him of "complete unbroken friendship" between all communities.

Opposed by Minority

During the tense days of his fast, some of the more militant shouted bitterly in the streets and before his living quarters:

"Let Gandhi die."

But there was every indication that this was the view of a tiny minority, embittered by the communal warfare.

Some Hindus, their womenfolk violated in the communal upheavals, had resented Gandhi's pleas for peace with the Moslems.

Laid Down 7-Point Program

Gandhi undertook the fast against the advice of his physicians.

The effects of his gesture became noticeable at once. Peace, however uneasy, settled over New Delhi. Two days later, January 21, the bomb exploded near Birla house.

Gandhi asked police to be lenient with the young Hindu who threw it.

"We should not harbor hatred," he said. "I will request the police not to trouble him but to have compassion toward him and make him see the righteous path."

Even as he spoke, the Hindu spiritual leader was too weak to walk from the effects of his long fast. He had been carried to that prayer meeting on a chair.

At one of his last prayer meetings a listener asked Gandhi to proclaim himself a reincarnation of God. Gandhi laughed. The speaker persisted and Gandhi, becoming impatient, told him to sit down and be quiet.

Gandhi had laid down a 7-point program as a formula for peace in India—his terms for sparing his own life through ending his fast. He required that Hindus should fraternize with Moslems on the

Continued on Page 18, Col. 5

HINDU HORROR

Anguished Cry Rises at Slaying

By the Associated Press

LONDON, Jan. 30 — Robert Stimson, BBC correspondent, witnessed the assassination of Mohandas Gandhi.

He cabled these impressions:

"The shots did not sound very loud—they reminded me of firecrackers. When they were fired, Gandhi fell back.

"Immediately after this I saw some of Gandhi's entourage grappling with a heavy set man in a khaki bush coat. He had blood on him, no doubt from wounds inflicted by his assailants."

"Gandhi was picked up by some of his followers and carried into Birla House, where he was taken a back room." Mr. Stimson said.

"Suddenly realization of what had happened swept through the crowd and a terrific cry of grief arose.

"The crowd of 400 or 500 people waited with a grief most moving to see.

"Men and women wept and beat their breasts."

Gandhi had arrived a few minutes late for his prayer meeting. But when he walked across the lawn from Birla House, Mr. Stimson said, "he was looking healthier and sprightlier than he had since his recent fast."

"He was supported by two members of his entourage" Mr. Stimson said.

He reported Gandhi had just mounted the covered dais from which he conducted his prayer meetings and the crowd was pressing around him when the shots were fired.

Schuman Wins OK on Bank-Note Recall

By the United Press

PARIS, Jan. 30—The National Assembly tonight adopted a government measure establishing a free gold market and authorizing the conversion of foreign holdings.

By the Associated Press

PARIS, Jan. 30—Both houses of France's Legislature approved today the government's bill withdrawing all 5,000-franc notes from circulation.

The Finance Ministry announced that everyone holding the 5,000-franc notes will be repaid. The announcement said the operation is not "an expropriation." An official source had indicated yesterday that some of the bills might be confiscated as a blow at the black market if holders could not explain their possession.

Premier Robert Schuman's drastic money program cleared another hurdle when the Council of the Republic ratified by a vote of 167 to 126 the bill abolishing the 5,000-franc note as legal tender.

Earlier the National Assembly approved the bill, 308 to 288, after an all-night debate. The Premier had staked the life of his two-month-old coalition Cabinet on his program.

About 66,000,000 of the 5,000-franc notes were in circulation, valued at $1,540,000,000 at the new rate of 214 francs to the dollar.

"There is not and will not be any withdrawal of other notes of the Bank of France," the Finance Ministry announced.

Another administration bill, to free the gold market, hopped a preliminary hurdle. The Assembly turned down the unfavorable recommendation of its own Finance Commission. The tally was 328 to 240.

After that, the Assembly adjourned. Further debate was scheduled on the gold bill. The measure was believed to have a good chance of assembly approval.

The step also may cut down the total amount of money in circula-

Continued on Page 18, Col. 7

NEWS FEATURES

1950

Two Puerto Rico nationalists attempted to kill President Truman at Blair House, where the President was living while the White House was renovated.

Truman was unhurt, but a White House guard was killed.

One of the attempted assassins was killed, the other wounded.

Senator Joseph McCarthy charged that the State Department was harboring Communists. He became an unofficial leader of a national crusade against communism.

Seven gunmen in Halloween masks held up the Brinks armored truck concern in Boston and fled with more than $1 million.

Snow and Rain
BOSTON AND VICINITY—Snow changing to sleet and rain. Highest temperatures in the middle 30's. Clearing tonight. Tides: High—10:56 A. M., 11:34 P. M. Low—4:41 A. M., 5:23 P. M. Sunrise—7:09. Sunset—4:40. Full report on Page 2.

THE BOSTON HERALD

6 A. M. EXTRA

VOL. CCVIII, NO. 18 LATE CITY EDITION BOSTON, WEDNESDAY, JANUARY 18, 1950—THIRTY-TWO PAGES ★★★★★★ FIVE CENTS

Nine Bandits Steal $1,500,000, Leave Another Million at Brink's

BIGGEST ROBBERY IN U. S. HISTORY

SCENE OF LAST NIGHT'S MILLION-DOLLAR-PLUS ROBBERY of Brink's, Inc., armored car firm, on the second floor of the company's garage on Prince Street in the North End. At left (AP Photo) is Herman C. Pfaff, one of the five employes held up and disarmed by the seven masked bandits who entered the room where the money was. Beside him is the rope with which he was tied. At right is the opened vault from which the gunmen scooped more than $1,500,000 and then swore angrily because they were unable to carry away any more. (Photo by Julian Carpenter)

5 Armed Guards Bound, Gagged

Page of photos, Page 30

Nine gunmen seized an estimated $1,500,000, at least $1,000,000 of it in cash, last night from the second floor office of Brink's, Inc., armored car firm, at the company's North End garage.

The final check-up of the theft will show the total robbery "will go $1,500,000 all right," Police Commissioner Sullivan said. At 4 A. M., he and the Brink's manager announced that as nearly as could be determined, the bandits had taken $1,000,000 in cash and $500,000 in checks.

The gunmen left another million dollars behind because they culdn't carry it.

It was the biggest cash robbery in the nation's history.

Seven of the bandits, disguised by Halloween masks, cowed and disarmed five employes and scooped the money from an open vault. They carried it away in two large-sized canvas Federal Reserve Bank money bags, and cursed because they were unable to carry away more.

Driven Away by Confederates

The seven entered the scond floor office at Prince and Commercial streets at 7:10 P.M. Twenty minutes later they were driven away by confederates who had waited outside with two cars. They left the five Brink's workers bound and gagged on the floor, and they left police bewildered by the suddenness of the million-dollar-plus theft.

(Continued on Page Ten)

Victims Tell How Gang Cowed Five

Still shaking with emotion an hour after he had been freed of his bonds following the $1,500,000 holdup at Brink's, Inc., in the North End, James C. Allen of 26 Crandall street, Roslindale, gave the following account of what happened in this greatest haul by bandits in the United States:

"There were five of us in the vault and in the outer cage by the vault. Six or seven men, all armed, all of medium size, and all wearing masks like the kids use at Halloween, stepped through the door in the rear and right up to the door of the cage.

"One of them said, 'Don't move, boys, or we'll let you

(Continued on Page Ten)

150 Police 'Brass' Confer on Holdup

Supt. of Police Edward W. Fallon, addressing about 150 captains, lieutenants, sergeants and detectives from all divisions of the Boston department, in the fourth floor hearing room at police headquarters last night, described how nine bandits took "over one million dollars" in the North End robbery.

The superintendent and Police Commissioner Sullivan ordered all police captains, lieutenants, sergeants and detectives to headquarters for an extraordinary meeting after the Brink's holdup climaxed a series of recent Boston robberies. Fallon explained in detail what had happened, and told the department's officers they "must" solve this largest of the robberies.

(Continued on Page Ten)

FIN COM ASKS 595 JOB CUT

Public Works Saving Set at $1.3 Million

Savings totaling approximately $1,350,000 a year could be made by more efficient operation of the Boston public works department and elimination of 595 unnecessary jobs, the Boston Finance Commission estimated in a report to be made public today.

Greatest opportunity to cut down the department's expenditures, which totaled approximately $18,000,000 in 1949, lies in the sanitary division, the commission found. It was recommended that 423 positions in the division be eliminated, providing an annual payroll saving of $932,000.

This division's street cleaning

(Continued on Page Five)

Police Blast Brink, Charge 'Inside Job'

Too Many Had Access to Keys

Police investigating last night's million-dollar holdup worked on the theory that it was an "inside job" and blamed the Brink company for loose protection of the huge amounts of money it handled.

They said a spokesman for the company admitted that several employes had passkeys to the company's offices, and that probably several former employes still have them.

'Poor Security'

It was Edward W. Fallon, superintendent of police, who criticized the company's security methods.

"They got more than $1,500,000," Fallon said, telling an emergency meeting of police officials about the robbery, "and they missed another

(Continued on Page Ten)

Truman Calls For Showdown On Civil Rights

WASHINGTON, Jan. 17 (AP)—President Truman declared today that the administration will press the bitterly fought civil rights program to a showdown vote in Congress "if it takes all summer."

The President served notice, in effect, that he wants every member of Congress to be put on record for or against the proposals which caused a split in Democratic party ranks during the 1948 presidential election campaign.

Lashing out at a coalition of Southern Democrats and Republi-

(Continued on Page Six)

(Herald Staff Photo by Julian Carpenter)

MILLION IN CASH LEFT BEHIND—Detective Walter J. Armstrong inspects canvas sacks containing thousands of dollars overlooked by masked bandits in $1,500,000 robbery of Brink's, Inc., garage in the North End last night.

Biggest Manhunt Seeks 'Cream of Crime World'

Nine men completed the largest cash robbery in American history in 20 minutes last night and then disappeared from the face of the earth, along with their more than $1,500,000, as far as the Boston police were concerned.

At 1 A. M., today, the greatest concentration of Boston police officers ever assembled to investigate one robbery was working without a known clue. There were only sketchy descriptions of seven masked men, each of the seven weighing "about 180 pounds" and a description of two cars which were both "shiny black."

The cars raced away from Brink's, Inc., and went up Prince street, it was known. From there? Nobody apparently had the slightest idea.

The police tried, with every known method, to pick up something, someone, anything, which would give them a lead to the bandits. Detectives and uniformed policemen swarmed into the railroad stations, bus terminals and hotels, on watch for anyone acting suspiciously or appearing as if they were on anything but legitimate business.

Trail Ends

Police Commissioner Sullivan and Supt. Edward W. Fallon both were at the holdup scene a few minutes after the robbery was reported. They ordered the captains of all police divisions, along with their lieutenants and sergeant inspectors, to headquarters for a conference.

There Supt Fallon reported the robbery in detail, and told the assembled men they were on trial before the entire nation, which would note whether the Boston police department could solve the greatest holdup ever engineered in America.

Supt. Fallon, after inspecting the robbery scene, sharply criticized the armored truck firm for "the poor security measures it takes to protect such huge sums of money." But this did not alter the fact that Boston had been the scene of the nation's largest cash robbery.

"The robbery was so neatly executed," Capt. John D. Ahern of the special service squad said, "that it must have been engineered by the cream of the crime world."

Today's Herald

	Page		Page
Amusem'nts	26,27	Lyons	25
Bridge	31	Mark Trail	25
Class Ads	27-29	Mullins	22
Comics	31	Obituaries	23
Commodities	15	Radio	10
Courts	18	Society	21
Cunningham	11	Ships	31
Dahl Cartoon	22	Sports	11-13
Editorials	22	Women's Pages	19-21
Fashion	20		
Financial	13-15		

STEEL PLANTS CURTAIL AS COAL STOCKS SHRINK

PITTSBURGH, Jan. 17 (AP)—The spreading strike of more than 81,000 soft coal miners bit into the nation's steel production today amid signs the government soon may seek a court order against John L. Lewis.

Coal shortages, which already have curtailed railroad service, threatened to close 300 big Pittsburgh area industrial plants by cutting off electrical power.

General Counsel Robert Denham of the National Labor Relations Board indicated he may ask tomorrow or Thursday for a court order against the three-day week which Lewis fixed for miners last July 1.

Coal operators have filed charges of unfair labor practices against Lewis. They say the short work week is the United Mine Worker president's way of controlling production.

Steel production at the nearby Midland, Pa., plant of Crucible Steel Company of America was reduced 25 per cent. A thousand of

(Continued on Page Six)

Korean War

At the end of World War II, the United States took charge of Korea south of the 38th parallel, the Soviet Union occupied the area north. In 1948, rival governments were formed.

On the rainy summer morning of June 25, 1950, the Communist forces of the North invaded South Korea in an attempt to force unification.

No match for the North Korean armies, South Korea appealed for help. President Harry S. Truman committed U.S. troops to Korea on June 30, with General Douglas MacArthur in command of a United Nations force.

North Korean forces drove south almost at will at first, pushing U.S. and South Korean forces into a small area around the port of Pusan. But MacArthur boldly ordered an amphibious landing at Seoul's seaport of Inchon, in a desperate attempt to cut enemy supply lines.

It worked and MacArthur pursued the retreating North Koreans into North Korea itself and pushed toward the Yalu River on the border with Communist China.

On November 26, Chinese Communist troops entered the war and forced allied armies back south.

Another year of offensives and counteroffensives resulted in something of a stalemate, and MacArthur suggested bombing Chinese supply depots inside China itself. Finding himself in basic conflict with the plans and strategies of President Truman, MacArthur was relieved of his duties in April 1951.

In the 1952 presidential campaign, Dwight D. Eisenhower promised to "go to Korea" if he was elected. He was and he did.

On July 27, 1953, an armistice was signed providing for a cease-fire and the establishment of a demilitarized zone at about the 38th parallel—North and South Korea remained separate.

Good Morning

Omaha and vicinity: Partly cloudy and warm; thunder showers late afternoon or evening. High near 90.

Weather map, weather other cities, Page 19-B.

Sunday World-Herald

Nebraska's Only Full Wirephoto Service. Eight News Services Cover the World.

OUR 65TH YEAR—No. 44. OMAHA, NEBRASKA, JUNE 25, 1950.—ONE HUNDRED EIGHTY-FOUR PAGES. SECTION A, TWENTY-EIGHT PAGES. 6 FIFTEEN CENTS

North Korean Red Invasion of South Is Reported Slowed

More State Patients Voluntary

Four Mental Hospitals Report Such Cases Most Easily Cured

First of a series telling new developments in the treatment of the mentally ill in Nebraska.

By Harold Andersen

World-Herald Lincoln Bureau, 503 Federal Securities Building.

A steadily increasing number of Nebraskans are offering themselves as voluntary patients for treatment at state mental hospitals.

In the last 11 months, 40.6 per cent of all patients admitted to our state mental institutions went there voluntarily.

This is a highly significant trend, the experts declare.

W. H. Diers of the State Board of Control, which supervises the mental hospitals, calls it "a great step forward" in the treatment of mental illness in Nebraska.

Quietly, a law enacted by the 1947 Legislature has wrought this important change. The law for the first time provided that persons might be admitted as voluntary state hospital patients.

Law Changed

No longer is it necessary for a mentally sick person to be haled before the "insanity board" and sent to the hospital by order of the board.

The 1947 law changed the name of each county's board to County Board of Mental Health and struck the term "insane" from the law books.

Dr. Juul C. Nielsen, superintendent of the State Mental Hospital at Hastings, told The World-Herald that these are some of the benefits stemming from the increasing percentage of voluntary patients:

Voluntary patients are better patients who, by and large, are more easily and quickly cured. They want to be cured or they wouldn't have come to the hospital.

Are More Receptive

They are more receptive to treatment, don't feel the resentment or shame which often goes with being ordered to the hospital by county authorities.

Voluntary patients are, for the most part, persons who would have come to the hospital eventually anyhow, under a legal order. By coming earlier, before their troubles are further advanced, they can be treated more quickly and easily.

The hospitals are enabled to treat more patients—voluntary patients are relatively quickly treated, so the patient turnover is much faster.

Most of the voluntary patients are referred to the hospital by private doctors, Dr. Nielsen said.

Gains Related

In four of the first five months of this year, he reported, more patients have entered Hastings voluntarily than have been sent by legal order. Example:

In May, the hospital received 52 volunteer patients, but only 23 by county authorities.

If this trend continues, Dr. Nielsen said, the Hastings hospital this year for the first time in its 63-year history will take in more voluntary patients than patients committed under legal order.

Some Have Waiting Lists

Board of Control figures for the last 11 months show these percentages of voluntary patients among all patients admitted at our state mental institutions:

Hastings, 50.4 per cent, or 326 of 647 patients.

Lincoln State Hospital, 9.1 per cent, or 27 of 297 patients.

Norfolk State Hospital, 18.4 per cent, or 38 of 207 patients.

Psychiatric unit in Douglas County Hospital in Omaha, 86.7 per cent, or 143 of 165 patients.

Total, 1,316 patients, with 534, or 40.6 per cent, voluntary admissions.

Mr. Diers and Board of Control Chairman Forrest R. Johnson pointed out that Norfolk and Lincoln hospitals have a waiting list of patients. This is why they can't take as many voluntary patients as Hastings, they said.

They also pointed out that the psychiatric unit at Omaha was designed to specialize in voluntary patients.

Poor Sport

Chicago Tribune Press Service.

Reading, England—A pig bit the judge of a stock show after it was awarded a second prize.

In Your Newspaper

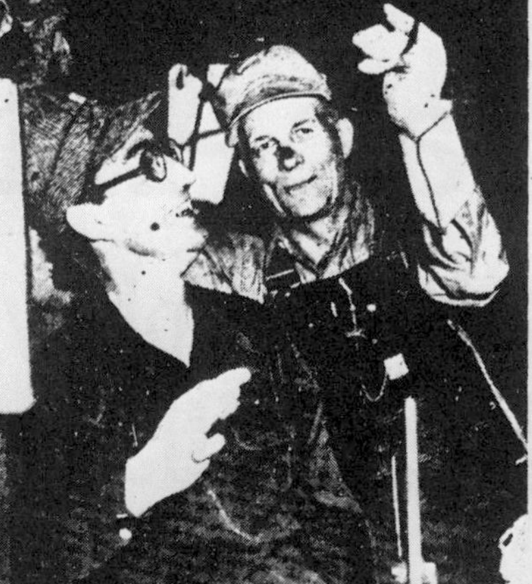

—World-Herald Photo.

Casey Jones Duncan . . . meets real engineer.

Symphony Conductor Meets Rail Interrupter of Concerts

The conductor of the Omaha Symphony Orchestra Saturday met the engineer who has interrupted his Pops Concerts for three years with train whistles.

Richard Duncan, dressed in overalls and an engineer's cap, went to the Chicago and North Western yards Saturday to greet Gay Crotty of Norfolk, Neb., pilot of the train which passes Peony Park at 9:15 p. m., 15 minutes after the concerts begin.

At last week's concert, the orchestra, with perfect timing, broke into "Casey Jones" just as the train reached the double crossing that calls for whistle signals.

"We've been annoying each other for three years," Mr. Duncan shouted to the engineer over the very unmusical hissing of the steam engine.

Mr. Crotty invited the orchestra conductor aboard.

"A childhood ambition," Mr. Duncan admitted, as he leaned from the window of the cab.

He pulled the cord that blows the whistle a few times, decided there was nothing he could do to improve its tonal quality.

Messrs Duncan and Crotty exchanged notes. Mr. Crotty has been on the same run from Norfolk to Omaha for three years. He works Tuesdays, Thursdays and Saturdays.

The Pops Concerts have been held on Thursdays in previous years. The 1950 weekly concerts are on Tuesdays.

So Mr. Crotty is definitely the man responsible for an annoyance that has turned into a weekly source of amusement for summer concert fans.

"I can't see your downbeat from the window of my cab," Mr. Crotty said. "But maybe we can rig up a light signal that will keep us in step on the 'Casey Jones' number."

Mr. Crotty promised to give concert fans a few extra signals of greeting at next Tuesday's Viennese Night waltz program.

Air Hunt Halts for Lost Plane

To Resume at Daylight on Lake Michigan

Chicago Tribune Press Service.

Chicago, Ill.—A dawn-to-dark search Saturday by more than 50 planes and a smaller number of surface craft failed to find any trace of a missing Northwest Airlines plane with 58 persons aboard.

The plane is presumed to have crashed in Lake Michigan.

The air search was abandoned at nightfall, to be resumed Sunday, but six Coast Guard boats continued the quest throughout the night.

If all aboard perished, as seemed virtually certain, it would be the nation's worst aviation accident.

The search centered about a large oil slick in the lake about six miles offshore from South Milwaukee, Wis.

A diver descended to the bottom in 66 feet of water and reported no trace of wreckage, however.

Several other oil slicks were reported by crews aboard search planes, but it was pointed out that oil slicks are not uncommon in that area, which is traversed by many lake freighters.

The missing plane, a DC-4 en route from New York to Seattle with a stop scheduled at Minneapolis, was last reported heading out over the lake at 12:15 a. m. Saturday.

You Are Reading 'The First Fifty'

The First Fifty!

That is the fitting name given to this edition of The Sunday World-Herald, which supplies many answers to these questions:

"How have Nebraska and Western Iowa fared during the first half of the Twentieth Century?" "What lies ahead during the second half of an epochal century?"

Included with this edition of The World-Herald are three special sections that carry out "The First Fifty" theme. These sections contain hundreds of articles and pictures dealing with this prosperous area's business and agriculture, with its customs and its culture, with its hobbies and its recreations.

On Page 22-G an erroneous figure is used in describing activities of the Fairbury Windmill Company. The company's annual pay roll amounts to more than 500 thousand dollars, not 35 thousand dollars as the article states.

Theater 'Smear' Brings No Arrest

By Reuters, Ltd.

Stockholm—A 55-year-old man Saturday asked the police to arrest an actress in a variety theater here who had come down into the audience and kissed him during her act.

Grinning policemen refused to arrest the actress but rubbed the lipstick marks off the man's face.

Truman Wins Convert to Air

Mayor of Baltimore Is Pleased by Trip

Baltimore, Md. (AP)—Mayor Thomas D'Alesandro of Baltimore, who has long quaked at the mere thought of flying, was converted to the air age Saturday by President Truman.

As Mr. Truman himself put it in his dedication speech at Baltimore's new International Friendship Airport, he initiated Mr. D'Alesandro's "first flying lesson."

Mr. D'Alesandro, in an agonized moment, had accepted the President's invitation to accompany him on the flight from Washington to Baltimore.

The Mayor conceded shortly before his first airplane ride that he had prayed for rain so the 30-mile flight could be avoided.

He repented, though, and later prayed for sunshine—which materialized—lest ceremonies at the airport be dampened, the Mayor said.

Once inside the plane, Mr. Truman showed Mr. D'Alesandro around. He told him when to fasten the seat belt and invited him in conversation. "I didn't even notice when we left the ground," said a grateful Mr. D'Alesandro.

Airborne, the Mayor relaxed, discovered that:

1. The countryside looks like a map from on high.
2. There are "air pockets" which need "paving."
3. Planes are "like little homes."

Back in Baltimore, Mr. D'Alesandro called the trip "delightful." A reporter asked if he would fly again. "Of course," said the Mayor airily.

East Berlin Police Arrest 2 Americans

Berlin (AP)—The Communist People's Police of East Berlin arrested two American soldiers Saturday night in a subway station in the Soviet sector of the city, West Berlin police said.

Police said the two soldiers were seized after they allegedly had torn down Communist propaganda posters from the station wall.

Man in Jail Is Questioned in May Deaths

Truth Serum Brings Startling Data; No McClelland Mention

Is the case of the double murder of Mr. and Mrs. R. L. May, 2d, about to be reopened?

County authorities are questioning a new suspect in the County Jail in connection with the case, it was learned Saturday.

They conceded that the suspect has revealed startling information while under the effects of truth serum. Checks on outside sources put him at the scene of the abandoned death car at the strategic time.

Does Not Confess

He admits leaving Omaha the day after the double killing of the young couple on the West Dodge Highway on August 28, 1947. Under the influence of the serum he discusses being with a couple similar to the newly-married young persons.

The suspect does not mention Charles McClelland, carnival worker, who pleaded guilty and was sentenced to life on two charges of second degree murder. McClelland is now in the State Penitentiary.

The new suspect does not deny the killings or confess them. Under questioning when not under influence of the serum, he says:

"You're the cops. It is your job to prove that I'm guilty."

Cited Tough Route

The suspect describes the seating arrangement in the murder car but says he did not do the actual shooting, that his "buddy" became panicky.

He had been living in the vicinity of Sixteenth and Locust Streets where the blood-stained murder car had been found behind a building in the forenoon after the night of the killing.

The location of the murder car had puzzled every one who had anything to do with the investigation. Many of them thought a person from that neighborhood must have been implicated in the murders. They pointed out the complicated route the car had to travel to be placed in the rear of the building.

McClelland Recants

McClelland, a man of many stories, now claims he had nothing to do with the murders. Repeated questionings have failed to shake him.

One official said he is positive that the suspect knows who did the killings or had a part in them.

The suspect's story under the serum often trails off in the assertion that "I don't remember that part—I was drunk then."

Officials have often said they believe McClelland had an accomplice.

Asked for a statement, County Attorney James J. Fitzgerald said: "I have no comment at this time. The May case has never been closed because we have been satisfied from the start it was more than a one-man job."

Schrempp Called

Attorney Warren Schrempp was called into the case Saturday night by the suspect's mother. He went to the Courthouse and demanded that he be permitted to see the suspect as his lawyer. He was told that orders had been issued that no one was to see the suspect.

Mr. Schrempp, after unsuccessfully trying to contact County Attorney Fitzgerald, called District Judge James T. English and was given permission to see the suspect.

Mr. Schrempp said he talked to the suspect who told him that he was innocent of the charges but that he had submitted voluntarily to the truth serum test in the presence of his mother.

Mr. Schrempp said that he had told his client that he need not answer any questions unless he (Mr. Schrempp) was present.

Mr. Schrempp said that his client told him he knew nothing about the May murder.

Foe of President Wins Senate Race

Raleigh, N. C. (AP)—Willis Smith, Raleigh lawyer who campaigned as an opponent of President Truman's program, was nominated in North Carolina's Democratic Senatorial Primary Saturday.

Returns from 1,940 of 1,990 precincts gave Mr. Smith 277,672 votes to 257,156 for Senator Frank Graham, a supporter of the President.

Mr. Smith, who made President Truman, Negroes and communism paramount issues of a bitter campaign, led virtually from the start of the tabulations.

The vote reversed the count in the May 27 primary in which Senator Graham led. He failed, however, to get a majority of the ballots cast and Mr. Smith requested a runoff.

American Teachers Find Queen Charming

Cliveden, England (AP)—Ninety-seven American teachers shook hands with Queen Elizabeth Saturday and afterward pronounced her charming.

The Americans and 133 more teachers from British dominions met the Queen at Cliveden, home of Viscount and Viscountess Astor.

Envoy Asserts Attackers Had Russian Help

U. S. Calls on U. N. to Hold Meeting on Issue Immediately

Compiled from Press Dispatches.

John Myun Chang, Korean Ambassador, declared in Washington that the North Korean attack on Southern Korea "could not have been carried out without Soviet direction."

After a 20-minute conference with State Department officials early Sunday, he told the United Press "I don't think the United States will abandon us."

Mr. Chang took the same position as Senator Knowland (Rep., Cal.) who a few minutes earlier told the Associated Press the invasion must have been with Soviet support.

U. N. Meeting Asked

The United States early Sunday formally called for an "immediate meeting" of the United Nations Security Council to deal with the Communist invasion.

Press Officer Lincoln White said that "we asked that this meeting be held this afternoon."

Mr. White, a State Department spokesman, made this formal announcement, saying that the American action had been taken at 1:30 a. m., Eastern Standard Time:

"The United States has asked the Secretary General of the United Nations to notify the President of the United Nations Security Council that the United States Government requests an immediate meeting of the Security Council to consider the Korean situation."

The Secretary General at the United Nations Headquarters in New York is Trygve Lie. The President of the Security Council for the present month, State Department officials said, is B. N. Rao, of India.

Truman Gets Word

Secretary of State Acheson was at his farm in near-by Maryland and was being kept informed of developments by telephone.

Word also was being sent to President Truman, who is spending the week end in Independence, Mo.

United Nations officials said at Lake Success, N. Y., the U. N. has no official word of the reported war. But they pointed out the U. N. has a commission in South Korea.

Sing Is Tonight if Weather Good

Tonight at 8:15, Omahans will gather in World War II Memorial Park for the season's first Community Sing.

That is, unless the weather interferes, as it did last week. Director Billy Meyers has asked all sing fans to tune in to Station KOWH at 6 p. m. today for last-minute reports on the songfest.

This is the thirteenth season of Community Sings, sponsored by The World-Herald.

Special buses will be assigned to the Dodge Street runs. They will unload and load at the monument atop the hill.

These songs are on tonight's program:

National Anthem. The More We Get Together. We're Here for Fun. Grand Night for Fun. Grand Night for Singing. Onward Christian Soldiers. Omaha. Marines Hymn. Bells of St. Marys. Riders in the Sky. Dearie. It's a Big Wide Wonderful World. Long, Long Trail. Down by the Station. Moonlight and Roses. Cruising Down the River. There's No Tomorrow. Dear Hearts and Gentle People. On the Road to Mandalay. Blue Skirt Waltz. Clementine. Darktown Strutters Ball. There's Yes. Yes in Your Eyes. My Wild Irish Rose. Clancy Lowered the Boom. Tipperary. When You're Smiling. Marching Along Together. Stars and Stripes Forever. Now Is the Hour. Taps. Good Night Neighbor.

The Weather

U. S. Weather Bureau.

Nebraska: Partly cloudy, scattered thunder showers over state and cooler west. Highs, 75 to 80 west, 90 east. Partly cloudy Monday; cooler west and north.

Iowa: Partly cloudy and rather warm and humid with scattered thunder showers north. Highs, 85 to 90 east, 90 to 95 west. Partly cloudy Monday with scattered showers and cooler west and central.

Temperatures

(Readings taken at Omaha airport.)

12:30 p. m.	87	7:30 p. m.	87
1:30 p. m.	90	8:30 p. m.	85
2:30 p. m.	89	9:30 p. m.	84
3:30 p. m.	91	10:30 p. m.	82
4:30 p. m.	90	11:30 p. m.	82
5:30 p. m.	90	12:30 a. m.	81
6:30 p. m.	89	1:30 a. m.	79

Summary of 24 hours ended at 12:30 a. m., Sunday:

Temperatures: High, 92; low, 72; mean, 82; normal, 72; deficiency since January 1, 183; high year ago, 89; low, 65; record for same date: High, 101 in 1931; low, 53 in 1928.

Wind velocity at 12:30 a. m., 15 miles an hour, southeast.

Barometer at 12:30 a. m., 29.71 inches (sea level pressure).

Precipitation: Total 24 hours, 0; total this month, 1.69; since January 1, 11.29; deficiency, 1.66. Total to date last year to midnight, 16.63.

Relative humidity (percentage): 6:30 a. m. 77; noon, 58; 6:30 p. m., 55; 12:30 a. m., 80.

Missouri River level Sunday: 9.9 feet; normal, 12.3.

Sun sets Sunday at 8:01 p. m. Sun rises Monday at 4:52 a. m.

MANCHURIA
MUKDEN
Liaoyang
Yingkow
Seishin
Hamheung
Wonsan
Pyongyang
(U.S.S.R.)
KOREA
38°
Haeju
Kaesong
Kangmung
Seoul
Samchok
Onjin Peninsula
KOREA
(U.S.)
Taikyu
Yellow Sea
Pusan
Moppo
Sunchon
Posong
Yosu
0 100
STATUTE MILES

—AP Wirephoto.

Where Communist Forces Invaded

Communist forces from North Korea invaded South Korea. The border city, Kaesong (arrow), was said to be partly occupied. Two amphibious landings were reported on the east coast at Kangmung and Samchok (arrow), 20 and 40 miles south of the border. Onjin Peninsula was reported being evacuated.

It Happened in Omaha—

Even 'Ladies' Are Unladylike

The Omaha police radio allows considerable benefit of the doubt when it tells the cruiser men about female law violators.

In an order to make an investigation came this comment: "Lady with a knife attempting to attack another lady."

Tax Cut Bill Is Criticized

Butler to Go Along, Hopes for Better

State spending to set record. Page 3-A. Taxes here comparatively low. Page 10-A.

By John Jarrell

World-Herald Washington Bureau, 1374 National Press Building.

The hottest issue in Washington during this sultry week end is the tax bill reported out by the House Ways and Means Committee.

Right now it looks like it stands a good chance of passage. Administration sponsors are openly gleeful because they say it has what it takes, from a political standpoint.

It reduces war-time excise taxes in many categories by one billion dollars, and makes up the difference by closing some loopholes and increasing the taxes on corporations earning more than 167 thousand dollars. Smaller corporations will pay less.

Martin Calls It Phony

Described as a "phony tax relief bill" by House Republican Leader Joseph W. Martin it is, nevertheless, going to get a number of Republican votes because of the excise tax reductions.

The two Nebraska members of Congressional tax-writing committees, Senator Hugh Butler and Representative Carl Curtis, both found fault with the increased corporation tax feature, but both indicated they will support the measure because of what they described as "overdue" excise tax relief.

Said Mr. Butler of the Senate Finance Committee, which will begin hearings on the measure as soon as the House has acted:

"I'm disappointed the House Committee doesn't give the people a real tax reduction bill. I think the reduction is way overdue on war-time excise taxes but the House bill, in effect, nullifies all of the good that came from that reduction by increasing corporate taxes which, actually, are paid by the consumer and not by the corporation.

Not Much Reduction

"In effect, it is a tax reduction bill without much reduction. But I will be inclined to go along with it with the hope that it won't be too long before a Republican Congress will have a chance to give the people a real reduction in taxes and governmental expenses."

Mr. Curtis, who belongs to the House Ways and Means Committee, declared:

"The excise relief the bill grants is long overdue. In some instances I am disappointed, but I am supporting the excise relief that this bill includes.

"It will make considerable difference to many industries. And I think speed of action is essential, because as long as uncertainty exists over what Congress will do, business makes no sales and the Government collects no taxes."

2 of 5 Spurn Vote Signup

Lack of Interest Stirs Club Campaign

By Lou Gerdes

Two out of every five Omahans apparently are too indifferent even to register so they can vote.

Of 157 thousand Omahans eligible to vote, 60,390 were unregistered as of last week.

Shocking facts like these on democracy have once again awakened the Presidents Round Table. This group is made up of the leaders of 15 Omaha service clubs. They organized about 15 years ago, became pretty much dormant during the war and now act subject to call.

Clinton Urged Revival

Glenn L. Cavanaugh Saturday credited C. E. Clinton, president of the Downtown Kiwanis Club, with the revival.

Mr. Clinton became interested in a "Get Out and Register the Vote" campaign. It was a job for the round table, he decided.

Mr. Cavanaugh, president of the Omaha Safety Council and also a Kiwanis leader, is pinch-hitting temporarily for Mr. Clinton. Monday the round table leaders will meet at 6 p. m. in the Fontenelle Hotel, on Mr. Cavanaugh's call, to hear progress of several interesting ideas to spur registrations.

One already is producing results.

Cards to All Members

All Downtown Kiwanis Club members have received cards to sign vowing that they and every eligible member of their family has voted. So far 155 of 221 members have signed.

Through the round table similar cards have gone out to the memberships of the other service organizations. Reports will be made on each group Monday.

Plan No. 2 calls for writing every other organization in the city and urging that each follow the same pattern.

The big pay-off may come in Plan No. 3, still being worked out.

In short, it would be to have every member of every non-political organization in Omaha write, call or personally visit five other persons in the effort to get them to register.

Registration is an easy, swift process. The Courthouse is open from 8:30 a. m. to 4:30 p. m. each working day except Saturday when the colsing is noon. Special registration booths for various areas also are announced from week to week.

In County 40 Days

Eligibility requirements are:

You must be over 21, a citizen of Nebraska six months, have lived in the county 40 days and at your present residence at least 10 days before election.

You must register if you wish to vote. Signing of a poll book does not meet the requirement.

If you have moved or changed your name since you last registered, you must re-register.

If you were naturalized by court order, you must bring your citizenship papers.

Briggs, CIO Workers Initial Pension Pact

Detroit, Mich. (UP)—Briggs Manufacturing Company and the CIO United Auto Workers initialed a three-year pension-and-pay-raise contract Saturday night.

They thus avoided a strike of 30 thousand key parts workers set for Monday.

Artillery Fire Heavy Along Wide Front

Strange Planes Over Seoul but No Bombs Dropped by Attackers

Compiled from Press and Cable Dispatches.

The Communist invasion from North Korea into South Korea virtually was stopped by Sunday afternoon, United States military authorities told the Associated Press at Seoul.

The North Koreans had invaded at dawn on a wide front at probably 11 points.

Though the advance was almost stopped, heavy artillery fire continued.

The advisers said the Northerners pushed three miles south of the border at one point before they met the first strong resistance.

No Bombs Dropped

Strange planes droned over the capital, but no bombs were dropped.

It was believed likely the Northerners will wait for clear skies before sending over their Russian-made fighters.

Defense Minister Sihn Sung Mo announced reinforcements were being rushed to the front.

One report said two Northern tanks had been knocked out by South Korean pillboxes.

Amphibious landings were reported on the east coast, as much as 40 miles south of the dividing line.

City Partly Taken

The border city of Kaesong, only 40 miles to the northwest, was said to be partly occupied by the invaders.

First accounts said attackers encountered only minor resistance in the surprise attack. Progress by the Reds was reported all along the line.

The Communists have made numerous raids into the south in the past.

Already Onjin Peninsula, northwest of Seoul, was reported being evacuated.

Southern troops were getting out as best they could.

Peninsula Evacuated

United States advisers never have considered the peninsula defensible. It is cut off entirely from the remainder of South Korea except by sea.

The greatest Northern assault was reported in regiment strength in the Chunchon area (Shunsen), about 50 miles northeast of Seoul.

The first amphibious attack came at Kangmung, 20 miles to the south of the border, at 6 a. m. The second hit Samchok, 40 miles south of the border, at 9 a. m. The two invading forces were estimated at six hundred men each.

Both the United Press and the International News Service reported the North Korean Government had declared war, six hours after 60 thousand troops attacked along the two hundred-mile front.

Doug's Help Asked

A Korean spokesman told INS his Government is asking the aid of Gen. Douglas MacArthur's occupation headquarters in Japan and particularly seeks airplanes.

There are about five hundred American officers and men of a military advisory mission in Seoul. In addition there are many American officials, business men and missionaries.

The last United States combat troops were withdrawn from South Korea in 1949.

John Foster Dulles, special United States State Department adviser, who has been making a tour of the Far East, telephoned Washington from Kyoto that he was rushing back to Tokyo to see General MacArthur.

Showers Expected Late in Afternoon

It'll be good weather for picnics and outings around Omaha most of today, according to the Weather Bureau.

Toward late afternoon or evening, however, thunder storms are expected. The high temperature will again hover around 90.

Much the same weather is predicted for the rest of the state, except that in the west it will not get quite so hot. Highs there are not expected to exceed 80 degrees.

ALBUQUERQUE JOURNAL
NEW MEXICO'S LEADING NEWSPAPER
Good Morning
71st Year [illegible] Wednesday Morning, April 11, 1951 Published Every Morning 28 Pages in Two Sections Price [illegible]

Truman Ousts MacArthur

Planes, Guns Wipe Out Big Red Base

Policy Disput[e] Blamed; Helm To Ridgway

WASHINGTON, Wednesday, April 11 (INS)—Pres[ident] Truman early this morning relieved Gen. Douglas A. [Mac]Arthur of his entire command in the Far East and im[me]diately appointed Lt. Gen. Matthew B. Ridgway as [his] successor.

The White House, in an extraordinary presidential st[ate]ment issued shortly after 1 a. m. announced the Presid[ent's] decision.

Reporters were summoned secretly to the White H[ouse] and handed the following statement by the President:

"With deep regret I have [con]cluded that General of the A[rmy] Douglas MacArthur is unab[le to] give his wholehearted supp[ort to] the policies of the United S[tates] Government and the United [Na]tions in matters pertaining [to his] official duties.

"In view of the specifi[c re]sponsibilities imposed upo[n me] by the Constitution of the U[nited] States and the added respon[sibili]ties entrusted to me by the [Unit]ed Nations I have decided [that I] must make a change of com[mand] in the Far East.

"I have, therefore, relieved [Gen.] MacArthur of his command[s and] have designated Lt. Gen. [Mat]thew B. Ridgway as his [succes]sor."

Gen. Douglas MacArthur

Lt. Gen. Matthew B. Ridgway

Must Follow Orders

The President added:

"Full and vigorous deb[ate on] matters of national policy [is a] vital element in the constit[utional] system of our free democr[acy. It] is fundamental, however, [that] military commanders m[ust be] governed by the policies a[nd di]rectives issued to them [in the] manner provided by our law[s and] [illegible]

"Gen. MacArthur's place [illegible]

Widely Criticized

[illegible]

Named by Roosevelt

[illegible]

Continued on Page [illegible]

Colder Weather Rides Into City On Wind and Dust

High winds and dust swept New Mexico Tuesday. It was the worst dust storm so far in 1951 at Albuquerque, where gusts up to 60 miles an hour were recorded. The winds were expected to continue most of the night here, and to be followed by much colder weather today.

The cause is a cold front which [moved] into eastern New Mexico [from the] North. The storm brought eight inches of snow to Denver, and disrupted airplane [schedules] to that Colorado city Tuesday morning.

Temperatures around the state dropped sharply Tuesday night after a day during which wind-swept dust slowed traffic to a crawl and caused a number of minor traffic accidents.

Snow at Raton

Three of the accidents were west of Lordsburg in the southwest corner of the state. In the fringe area of the storm, Lordsburg may have escaped the cold as reports there Tuesday night said it was still warm.

But diagonally across the state northeast, Raton was under a four-inch blanket of snow and roads in the area were reported slick and icy.

The wind dropped at Raton early in the evening after blowing with gusts up to 50 miles an hour throughout the day. Las Vegas and Wagon Mound had snow but the snow storm apparently to have missed Tucumcari and swept on into west Texas.

Snow was reported at Amarillo and Dalhart in the Texas Panhandle and placed escaping snow were hit by dust storms. Dust was blowing generally all down the east side of New Mexico and at El Paso, Portales reported the wind [illegible] of 60 miles an hour [gusts].

Worker Is Killed

At El Paso, Juan Aundiz, a lumber yard employe, was killed when the wind toppled lumber on him.

Reports from around the state were generally the same. Visibility was almost zero at times.

Tucumcari reported the temperature was 25 Tuesday night [and] expected to go lower. Las

Continued on Page Two.

Winter Hits Wide Area Once More

By the Associated Press

Heavy snow and strong northerly winds brought a return of wintry weather Tuesday to a wide area in the rockies and western plains.

Two to eight inches of new snow were reported in northern Colorado and over most of Wyoming, Western Kansas and northern New Mexico also were struck.

In contrast, California's interior valleys baked in temperatures around 100.

Meanwhile, the flood-stricken area in the Midwest reported its rampaging rivers were dropping, although the estimated 12,000 persons made homeless by the waters still were unable to return to their homes.

The snow storm left roads either slick or sloppy. Some telephone lines in Colorado were down. Boulder, Colo., had more than nine inches. Wyoming reported a maximum of four inches.

Motorists in western Kansas bucked hard blowing snow and zero visibility. Airports were shut in.

The storm was reported ended or petering out by mid-afternoon Tuesday. Ranchers and farmers viewed the moisture it deposited as a blessing for livestock pastures and winter wheat fields.

Meanwhile, the Weather Bureau reported the heat wave in California's interior valleys will continue Wednesday. Some sample high temperatures have included 96 at Red Bluff, 90 at Bakersfield and Paso Robles, and 100 at Indio.

Scattered light rains fell over parts of the great lakes area, the Virginias, New England, the delta region in Louisiana, and in southern Florida. Miami reported the heaviest 24-hour rainfall—2.16 inches.

Moderate to heavy frost was reported in extreme southern Missouri, and Memphis, Tenn., had light frost.

Mechem Signs Releases for 3

SANTA FE, April 10 (AP)—Gov. Edwin L. Mechem today signed conditional releases, with the recommendation of the parole board, for three prisoners at the state prison.

Ordered released were:

Charles Roy Campbell, sentenced May 1, 1950, from McKinley County to 1-3 years for taking a car for temporary use without the permission of the owner.

Antonio Rodriguez, sentenced Nov. 4, 1950, from Dona Ana County to 7 months to 1 year and $[illegible] court costs for breaking and entering in nighttime. He was remanded to custody of the U. S. immigration and naturalization service.

Felix Moses Woolley, sentenced [illegible] 1950, from Chaves County to 1-3 years for assault with a deadly weapon.

Light-Hearted Guy Took By Light-Fingered Gal

PITTSBURGH, April 10 (AP)—What George Matthews thought was love at first sight turned out to be nothing more than a "twist" in the pickpocket game.

He told police he was standing on a downtown corner when a good-looking woman ran up to him, flung her arms around him, and kissed him on the mouth. Then she swirled away in an auto. When he recovered, George found his wallet and $190 gone.

House Slashes Agency Funds, Requests Cut by 44 Per Cent

[illegible] reductions recommended by the Appropriations Committee [illegible] the agencies involved still have an opportunity to persuade the Senate to restore some of the [illegible]

[illegible] Cannon (D., Mo.), of the House committee struck the [illegible] when he demanded [illegible] on the bill that Congress [illegible] abandon a policy of "business as usual." With [illegible]

Paul Firm Gets Contract to Pave District No. 59

City Commission Also Approves Big Arterial System

M. M. Paul & Son, Albuquerque contractors, Tuesday night were awarded contract for Paving District 59, located north and east from Rio Grande Park, on a low bid of $[illegible].

The bid is for three inch paving and amounts to $[illegible] a square yard. Allison & Haney had the second lowest of six bids made, $[illegible].

[illegible] tracted in the current long-range paving program.

Back County Plan

The commission also approved a recommended arterial highway system in a move to obtain $1,800,000 in federal assistance. The [illegible] two segments of the system, similar to one approved earlier in the day by the county commission, envisages construction of the Lead-Coal-Zuni-West Mesa limited access highway and the extension of Coors Road north to Bernalillo.

Commissioners gave four-to-one approval of the arterial system after Commissioner Clyde Tingley assailed the Lead-Coal-Zuni proposal. "The right-of-way would cost $1,000,000 and that's low," Tingley said.

Commissioners approved a proposal from the Armored Motor Service to pick up the monies from parking meters for a fee of 7½ cents a meter a month. The service would include winding of the meters.

Believes It Reasonable

City Manager Charles E. Wells [illegible] the proposal reasonable [illegible] the cost to the city [illegible] meters have been installed.

The commissioners also approved [illegible]

Continued on Page Sixteen

School Buildings Decision Deferred

The Albuquerque Board of Education Tuesday night deferred decision on which of many needed school buildings to construct first pending notification of the status of its application for $1,240,000 of federal funds.

The board has been informed all such applications from New Mexico are being turned down for the present fiscal year.

[illegible] of the construction program [illegible] of the turndown, was [illegible] board's agenda Tuesday night. But when Supt. John Milne [illegible] he believed any reshuffling of the building program [illegible] would slow up federal [illegible] board members decided not to discuss the matter.

Affects Four Projects

The federal funds would go to construct [illegible] elementary school for the Inez Addition, an elementary school at Georgia and Truman, another on Gonzales Road, a junior high on South San Pedro and to pay part of a proposed addition for Highland High School.

The application is separate from the $[illegible] of federal funds [illegible] Tuesday by the U. S. Office of Education for a new [illegible] elementary school at Sandia Base.

Promises No Relief

School officials reported this project will not aid the overcrowded Albuquerque schools. It would accommodate 380 pupils children who will live in the Wherry Housing project now under construction and those now attending the school at Kirtland Base which would be closed.

The new school would be located west of the present gate of Sandia Base [illegible] Gibson, a mile south, three-quarters of a mile southwest of the present Sandia Base school. This school would continue [illegible]

As at the present Sandia and Kirtland base schools, the Albuquerque school system will furnish teachers and school supplies. The federal government will maintain the building and furnish [illegible]

Rio Commissioners Continue El Vado Conferences Today

SANTA FE, April 10 (AP)—Rio Grande compact commissioners meet here again tomorrow in another attempt to decide if El Vado reservoir shall be drained.

The commission met most of today but tonight members announced that they still had not reached a decision.

Facing the compact commission is this question:

Shall the commission go ahead with the proposed draining of 4000-plus acre feet now in El Vado to pay a Middle Rio Grande project water debt to the Elephant Butte irrigation district in southern New Mexico and Texas?

[illegible] John Bliss, the New Mexico compact commissioner, said the commission will meet again Wednesday morning in a closed session.

"We are going to try to work out a solution to this and several other matters," Bliss said. He did not say what other questions would be discussed.

Claim First Right

Indian spokesmen, fighting the draining of El Vado, told the commission today they have first claim to water in the upper Rio Grande.

Opposing the El Vado draining were William Brophy, Albuquerque attorney, representing the Pueblo Indians in the Middle Rio Grande conservancy district, and Diego Abeita, a spokesman for six Indian pueblos.

Urging the commission to let the draining order stand were John L. Gregg, manager of the Elephant Butte irrigation district, and M. B. Phillips, manager of the El Paso county water improvement district No. 1.

Would Share Payment

Hubert Ball of Albuquerque, chief engineer for the Middle Rio Grande conservancy district, [illegible]

[illegible]

Gov. Edwin L. Mechem, who [illegible]

Continued on Page Two

Mortician Gets Divorce When Hubbies Revive

LOS ANGELES, April 10 (AP)—He could forgive his wife, William A. Crim told the court today, for not telling him she had five divorced husbands.

But he drew the line, Crim added, when some of them began calling on her.

"One of them even tried to beat me up when I objected," the 33-year-old mortician testified.

He was given a divorce from Carmen Crim, 35, whom he married last September.

Irrigation Water Topic of Session Here Next Friday

An attempt to [illegible] will be available in the Rio Grande valley this season and to [illegible] of the water will be made at a meeting here Friday of federal, state and local officials.

The meeting will be the second annual one of the Rio Grande Water Forecast Committee, started a year ago under sponsorship of the Soil Conservation Service. The meeting will be in the Federal Building court room, beginning at 9 a. m.

A new topic for this year's agenda is a discussion of progress of artificial rain-increasing efforts in the watershed.

Other topics will be the usual: Outlook for the 1951 water supply [illegible]

Continued on Page Two

County Asks Aid From U. S. on Two Urban Road Plans

The proposed Lead-Coal-Zuni-West Mesa limited access highway and a northward extension of Coors Road Tuesday were recommended [illegible]

[illegible]

As proposed the highway would join U. S. 66 at the intersection of Zuni and East Central. It

Continued on Page Nineteen

Castner Cites Residence Law In Move to Bar Tourist Chief

From The Journal's Santa Fe Bureau

SANTA FE, April 10—State Auditor Bob Castner said today he will ask the state Highway Commission for an explanation of its reasons for hiring as state tourist bureau director a non-resident of New Mexico. Castner said he would act as soon as a paycheck voucher for new director, Melvin Drake, came to his office. Drake will take over his new post on May 1.

Castner said he would ask Drake for a certificate of employment which would require a statement that the employe has been a resident of New Mexico for one year prior to his receiving the state job.

Drake will not be a legal resident until August. He says he arrived in Albuquerque last July from Minnesota where he was connected with a Minneapolis radio station.

Castner said that the law allows for exceptions only in cases where the state cannot find competent personnel in New Mexico but [he] felt that there appeared to be a number of competent persons available for the post who are legal residents of the state.

[illegible]

[illegible] Charles Jones and Gov. Edwin Mechem [illegible] that the one-year residence requirement of state employes does not apply to Drake since he is a professional.

[illegible]

Determination of what constitutes a special skill or profession is a "common sense consideration," according to an attorney in the attorney general's office.

"This legal adviser did not think that a publicity man could come under the heading of a professional as implied in the law."

Official opinion by the attorney general's office can be given only to state officials and departments. Castner is expected to ask for such an opinion.

Both Jones and Mechem Tuesday agreed with Drake's plan to call in all advertising agencies in the state to allow them to present their wares. Mechem said that in the past many agencies have not been allowed to bid for the job of handling some $[illegible] worth of advertising a year. At the regular 15 per cent commission, the contract is worth some $37,500 a year. (See additional story on Page 19.)

Rallying Center For Three Armies Reported Smashed

Chinese Continue To Hold Electric Plant at Big Dam

TOKYO, Wednesday, April 11 (AP)—Allied planes and artillery were reported today to have wiped out Chorwon, the rallying center of three Chinese Red armies in west-central Korea.

The ruined western base of the big Communist assembly triangle is 17 miles north of the 38th Parallel. Its destruction was reported in a field dispatch.

But Chinese defenders of the [illegible] Hwachon power dam, at the eastern base of the triangle, still clung to that hydroelectric plant today. The Reds opened some of its flood gates Monday in a futile attempt to swamp advancing American forces.

AP Correspondent Tom Bradshaw reported from the front that Allied troops last night pushed closer to the dam—third largest in Korea. But he said powerful Red resistance made it slow going.

Each of the Hwachon powersite, the Reds were reported to have abandoned the town of Inje. Inje, four miles north of 38 and 25 miles east of the town of Hwachon, is in a sector where the Reds have been putting up a stiff fight.

Allied ruining of Chorwon deprived the Reds of one of their most important supply and assembly centers. Artillery began pounding Chorwon three days ago.

General MacArthur's intelligence officers estimated last week that the Reds were massing up to 600,000 men in the Chorwon-Kumhwa-Hwachon triangle for an expected counter-offensive.

[illegible] MacArthur's mid-morning communique said UN forces held the initiative all across Korea Tuesday and scored gains.

Just north of the 38th Parallel on a highway leading up to Chorwon, Turkish infantry crossed the Hantan River Tuesday. Brushing aside light Red resistance, the Turks seized a hill southeast of Yonchon. Yonchon is 13 miles southwest of Chorwon.

Paint Store Fire Damage Is Heavy

Komac Paints, Inc., [illegible] East Central, was heavily damaged Tuesday night in a spectacular fire of undetermined origin.

Assistant Manager Gene [illegible] said most of the stock [illegible] stock of paints was destroyed by the blaze.

Two explosions of [illegible] flammable paint [illegible] but no one was injured. [illegible] who battled the [illegible] two and a half hours [illegible] tered with paint.

The fire started about [illegible] the rear of the [illegible] according to the [illegible] Water and smoke [illegible] to the adjoining [illegible] 3107 East Central.

The building is owned by [illegible] Hicke.

It was the [illegible] evening. Earlier [illegible] were called to the Four H [illegible] near [illegible] gate-caused fire [illegible] barns and corrals.

Apodaca's Claim For Back Wages Denied by Court

Dist. Judge R. F. Deacon Arledge Tuesday denied A. L. (Happy) Apodaca's claim of $1464.67 in back wages during the time he was suspended as sheriff of Dona Ana County.

At the same time Judge Arledge held there were no shortages to justify Apodaca's suspension by the then state comptroller, J. D. Hannah.

Hannah had suspended the officer for a three-month period in 1949 pending disposition of various charges against him.

Judge Arledge ruled that since the Dona Ana County Commission, defendants in the suit, had paid A. B. Martinez who temporarily replaced Apodaca, for his services, Apodaca could not recover duplicate salary payments.

Court observers indicated the ruling would not prevent Apodaca from suing Martinez or Hannah or both, for the amount he sought.

Ouster Is Great Surprise In Tokyo

TOKYO, Wednesday, April 11 [illegible]

We Can Shuck off All Cont[rols] In 2 Years, Johnson Belie[ves]

CHICAGO, April 10 (AP)—Eric Johnston, economic stabilizer, said tonight "I believe we can shuck off controls in two years and maybe sooner."

Johnston put it this way:

"With decent luck, with hard slugging, with patience plus a helping of confidence, I believe we can shuck off controls in two years and maybe sooner.

"I believe with all my heart it can be done and if we do it sooner, why that's so much the better. Whenever controls are no longer needed, I am going to be the first to suggest they be removed."

Johnston's remarks were prepared for a dinner meeting sponsored by the State Street Council and the Chicago Assn. of Commerce.

"There's a widespread impression, and I get it every day in my office, that the worst of it is over," Johnston said.

But, he added, "we w[ill need] more and tighter sandbag[s of con]trols when we're actually [spend]ing 54 billion dollars for [defense] as we will be by next Ch[ristmas]. Less steel, less rubber, le[ss] [illegible] less copper, tin and le[ad for] civilians spell the necessit[y for] stronger stabilization dike[s].

"There'll be shortages, [short]ages and more money [illegible] right up inflation's alley."

He told the businessm[en the] whole readjustment progra[m must] rest on a sound foundati[on of] stabilized economy.

"If we succeed—and I [illegible] we will—the rewards will [be] solid and enduring," he [said.] [illegible] will have an unmatchable [illegible] We will have a producti[ve ma]chine of bountiful capaci[ty.]

Then, he predicted, [we] can "shuck off controls."

Good Morning
Omaha and Council Bluffs: Mostly sunny, not so warm. Northwest winds 20 to 30 miles per hour afternoon. High near 58. Cooler tonight.
* Weather map, weather other cities on Page 21.

MORNING WORLD-HERALD

Election Special

Nebraska's Only Full Wirephoto Service. Eight News Services Cover the World.

OUR 88TH YEAR—No. 30. Entered as Second-Class Matter at Post-office, Omaha, Nebraska, under Act of 1879. OMAHA, NEBRASKA, WEDNESDAY, NOVEMBER 5, 1952.—THIRTY-SIX PAGES. Published every week-day morning at World-Herald Square, Omaha, Neb. 6 FIVE CENTS

Eisenhower Wins 39 States; Senate and House Undecided; Republicans Hold Nebraska

Program for Streets, Two-Mill Garbage Levy Plan Approved

Air Terminal Issue Lagging in Voting Here

Both Firemen's Plans Are Ahead; Decision Indicates a Stalemate

Douglas County returns, Page 8.

Omahans had balloted in a $1,500,000 street improvement program and a 2-mill trash and garbage disposal levy, it appeared early Wednesday.

As unofficial election returns mounted from the 204 city precincts, these two issues showed fat margins of approval.

But a $1,685,000 airport terminal bond issue was lagging by a sizable margin. And it looked as if the Fire Department advancement items were stalemated.

Court Edict Seen

The civil service proposal of Fire Commissioner William D. Noyes was getting hearty approval. But the firemen's counter proposal for a sliding seniority also had a margin of approval.

Both will be approved if both get a majority no matter what the ratio, according to City Attorney Edward F. Fogarty.

If both plans are approved it would probably mean that they will be disregarded and the present advancement system continued, said Mr. Fogarty. Final decision might rest with the courts.

101 Miles in Plan

Under the street improvement program, which was getting a 3 to 2 approval, 101 miles of streets would be resurfaced with 1½ to 2 inches of asphaltic concrete during the next 10 years. Another ... miles of streets would be sealed in the same period.

Omahans were promised trash and garbage pickup and disposal if the City Council if the 2-mill levy were voted. This proposal was leading by a 4 to 3 ratio.

Mayor Cunningham said if the levy were approved the present method of grinding and drying garbage for animal feed probably would be continued.

Will Ask Committee

He said he would turn to the Citizens Trash and Garbage Disposal Committee to advise him on what type of garbage and trash collection should be developed.

There seemed little indication that a 4 to 3 negative ratio on the airport bonds would reverse itself in the final tally.

The Airport Commission proposed the bond issue with the belief the Federal Government would match the money for a new terminal, proposed north of the present building.

The News in Brief

For Wednesday, Nov. 5, 1952

Foreign	Page
Indonesia Suggests Neutral Commission on POW Issue	32
Quake Sends 13-foot Tidal Wave Smashing at Oahu	1
MK's Smash at Triangle Hill Leads	2
Yugoslav Vice-Premier Ousted for Views	23
National	
Nixon Sweep National Balloting	1
Astronomer Finds Star Bridges Join Galaxies	3
Kansas Has World's Most-Bombed Spot	32
Doctor Warns Against Athletics After 40	32
Rioting Convicts Surrender in Ohio	15
Local	
German Robs Loan Company of $200	14
Omahan in Crew of Record-Breaking Korea Bomber	19
Pottawattamie County Picks ..., Beardsley, Jensen	8
Omahans Favor Garbage Levy	1
Sports	
Swamped Husker Lineup to Face Kansas	27
Deer Herds in Nebraska Reported Too Large	27
200 Oklahoma Fans to Trail Team to Notre Dame	27
Tom Vacanti, Now 30, Stars for Paris Island Marines	27
Keeps to Offer Afternoon Program Friday	27
Miscellaneous	
Amusements	30
Comics, Features	24, 25
Crossword Puzzle	18
Deaths	31
Editorial	22
Household Arts	20
Markets, Financial	31
Picture Page	36
Radio and TV Programs	25
Test Your Facts	29
Want Ads	31 to 33
Women's News	22
Special Writers	
Hal Boyle	26
Herman Bundesen	24
George Crane	24
Dorothy Dix	22
Goren on Bridge	17
David Lawrence	26
F D	21
George E. Sokolsky	26

Tidal Wave Hits Islands After Quake

13-Foot Wall of Water Does Oahu Damage; Shock One of Biggest

Honolulu (AP)—A thundering 13-foot wall of water, powered by one of recorded history's mightiest earthquakes 3,500 miles away, struck the evacuated northwest shore of Oahu in the Hawaiian Islands Tuesday.

It was the fourth and largest tidal wave to hit Hawaii in little more than an hour.

The waves were built by a seismic shock that raced through the Pacific at more than four hundred miles an hour from a point in the Sea of Okhotsk between Siberia and Japan.

The shock also threw nine-foot waves at Adak in the Aleutians and Midway in the Central Pacific.

Phone Lines Downed

The 13-foot wave on Oahu knocked down telephone lines and bowled over a United States Navy photographer but he was reported uninjured.

In Honolulu Harbor, on the Oahu southern shore and in the lee of the seismic shock, rising water tore a cement barge from its moorings. The barge struck the Matson freighter Hawaiian Packer a glancing blow amidships and caved in 25 feet of the freighter's rail and stanchions.

At Hilo on Hawaii Island a recently-completed 13-thousand-dollar territorial boathouse was demolished by a wave, the Coast Guard reported.

Coast Guard buoys, weighing 10 to 12 tons, were torn from their moorings.

Hilo police ordered the evacuation of Keauhaha Beach, badly hit by a tidal wave in 1946 when 169 died.

Hangars Flooded

A spokesman for the United States Coast and Geodetic Survey at Honolulu said radio reports from Midway said 1½ feet of water stood on airplane hangar floors there and that electric generators were out of commission. He said the radio apparently was operating from emergency generators.

"All personnel (on Midway) apparently had been moved to safety in advance of the wave," the spokesman said.

Transocean Airlines in San Francisco said the wave had passed Wake Island and had caused no damage. About one hundred people on Wake took to high ground, about 15 feet above sea level, to escape the rising water.

At Oahu, successive waves struck savagely at sea walls and other beach installations for about 10 minutes, then receded. At some places water swept inland 75 yards, marooning automobiles and flooding yards.

Polls Closed

Warned of worse waves to come, owners of beach property began moving furniture and belongings off lower floors.

Reports that waves would strike the Western Coast of the United States were termed false by the Thirteenth Coast Guard District headquarters at Seattle but not before several polling places in Pacific County, Washington, hurriedly had closed.

'Really Great One'

Navy headquarters at Honolulu issued a tidal wave alert a few hours after a "very big quake" was reported centered at Paramushiro, just south of Kamchatka's spear-like peninsula jutting out of the Siberian mainland.

At the California Institute of Technology, Pasadena, Dr. Charles Richter said it showed a magnitude of 8, placing it in the category of "really great earthquakes."

Lincolnite Casts His 20th-Ballot

Lincoln (UP) — A 98-year-old Lincoln man, T. I. Gifford, voted Tuesday in his twentieth Presidential election — and said he cast a ballot for Dwight Eisenhower.

Mr. Gifford first voted in 1876 and said he has not missed a Presidential election since.

Nine Judges Stay in Front

Stauffer Eighth; Morgan in Also-Ran Spot

All nine of the District Judges seeking re-election were marching along in front with 136 out of 228 precincts counted.

Judge James T. English was leading the ticket, followed closely by Judge James M. Fitzgerald.

Running in eighth spot was Judge Carroll O. Stauffer, who holds the office by appointment.

Judge Stauffer had received widespread support from Omaha attorneys who feared that because of his relatively unknown name, he might have trouble in the election.

Judge W. A. Day, in ninth spot, was well ahead of the tenth place candidate, Former County Attorney Kelso Morgan.

Carnazzo, O'Connor in Tight Struggle

Judge Louis T. Carnazzo and Patrick W. O'Connor are in a tight struggle for the fifth seat on the Municipal bench.

With 136 out of 204 precincts reported, Judge Carnazzo was 363 votes behind. The score: Carnazzo, 25,164 and O'Connor 25,527.

Judge Carnazzo had been appointed to the bench to fill the vacancy caused by the death of Judge Dennis O'Brien earlier this year.

The other four incumbent judges were well ahead with Judge Lester Palmer leading the ticket. He was followed by Judges Frank Nimtz, Patrick W. Lynch and Perry M. Wheeler.

One School Board Incumbent Trails

All but one of the incumbents on the Omaha Board of Education seemed headed back into office early today as election returns mounted.

Leo J. Dworak, John S. Engdahl, Evelyn W. Lucas, Harry D. Barber and Robert C. Hastings were the old board members leading the field for the long term.

However, Incumbent John M. Thomas had slipped behind Louis Kavan.

None of the other five candidates appeared to be offering much of a threat to the top six.

For the two short terms, Isabella Carter was comfortably ahead and Richard Swenson held a narrow edge on E. F. Fill Gwynne-Vaughan.

The Weather

U. S. Weather Bureau.

Iowa: Partly cloudy, turning cooler today. West to southwest winds 20 to 25 miles per hour shifting to northwest. Little change in humidity. Highs 48 to 55 northwest, 55 to 63 southeast.

Nebraska: Generally fair, much colder today, tonight. Northerly winds 30 to 35 miles per hour. Minimum humidity 10 to 20. High in 40's.

Temperatures

(Readings taken at Omaha Airport.)

12:30 p. m.	42	8:30 p. m.	59
1:30 p. m.	45	9:30 p. m.	49
2:30 p. m.	47	10:30 p. m.	48
3:30 p. m.	48	11:30 p. m.	54
4:30 p. m.	49	12:30 a. m.	52
5:30 p. m.	51	1:30 a. m.	49
6:30 p. m.	50	2:30 a. m.	44
7:30 p. m.	58	3:30 a. m.	41

Tuesday's high temperature, 70; low, 44; mean, 57; normal, 44. Total departure from normal since January 1, +635.

Record temperatures this date: High, 76 in 1909; low, 14 in 1951.

Temperatures year ago this date: High, 19; low, 14.

Wind velocity at 12:30 a. m., 5 miles an hour, south-southwest.

Barometer at 12:30 a. m., 29.81 inches (sea level pressure).

Precipitation: Total 24 hours, 0; total this month, 0; since January 1, 26.82; excess, .83. Total to date last year to midnight, 39.13.

Relative humidity (percentage): 6:30 a. m., 37; noon, 26; 6:30 p. m., 32; 12:30 a. m., 39.

Missouri River level: 4.3 feet; normal, 6.5.

Sun sets Wednesday at 5:15 p. m. Sun rises Thursday at 7:02 a. m.

Traffic Fatalities

November 4—1952	1952	1951
Deaths in Nebraska	288	276
Deaths in Omaha	20	22
Deaths in Iowa	471	521

Crosby Leads 5 to 3; Butler Has 3-1 Edge

Eisenhower Handed Lopsided Victory by Voters in Nebraska

By Harold Andersen

Led by Dwight D. Eisenhower and Hugh A. Butler, Republican candidates Tuesday smashed to one of the most one-sided triumphs in Nebraska policital history.

Nebraska voters swept every major Republican candidate to victory, most by lopsided margins.

With two-thirds of the state's precincts reported, General Eisenhower was assured Nebraska's six electoral votes by an apparent margin of about 2½ to 1.

Polling 71 Per Cent

The Republican candidate was polling around 71 per cent of the Presidential vote. If this ratio holds up through the final, official vote tallies, it could be the most one-sided Presidential margin in Nebraska history.

The record has stood since 1872 when Ulysses S. Grant copped nearly 71 per cent of the total vote.

Republican candidate Thomas E. Dewey got 54 per cent of the Nebraska vote in 1948.

Hruska Wins

In what Republicans had felt would be their closest race, the Second Congressional District, Republican Roman L. Hruska, 48, Omaha attorney, beat Democrat James A. Hart.

Mr. Hart conceded defeat early today. He wired Mr. Hruska: "Congratulations and best wishes on your fine victory. May God bless you and your work as our next Congressman."

Dwight Griswold made Nebraska political history by becoming the first former Nebraska Governor

Turn to Page 8, Column 1

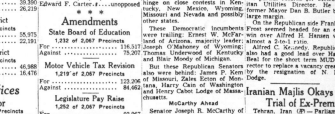

Robert Crosby . . . Governor.

America Likes Ike

—AP Wirephoto.

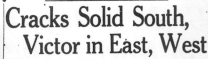

A New York crowd chanted, "We want Ike!" And when they got him, General Eisenhower wore this radiant smile.

Popular and Electoral Vote

At 2:10 A. M. (Central Standard Time)
(By the Associated Press)

State—	Voting Units	Units Reporting	Popular Vote Stevenson	Popular Vote Eisenhower	Trend of Elec. Vote Stv.	Trend of Elec. Vote Eis.
Alabama	2,505	1,942	217,327	124,700	11	...
Arizona	505	310	53,551	82,135	..	4
Arkansas	2,382	1,242	99,058	68,035	8	...
California	20,746	10,591	789,450	1,014,893	..	32
Colorado	1,650	316	41,388	64,105	..	6
Connecticut	169	169	481,482	610,989	..	8
Delaware	278	191	40,990	43,215	..	3
Florida	1,684	1,343	374,960	476,744	..	10
Georgia	1,814	759	253,389	117,879	12	...
Idaho	865	458	52,019	100,748	..	4
Illinois	9,680	6,291	1,284,723	1,367,005	..	27
Indiana	4,202	2,455	557,884	743,104	..	13
Iowa	2,481	1,389	261,111	448,080	..	10
Kansas	2,851	1,277	90,113	211,870	..	8
Kentucky	4,135	2,654	346,056	333,700	10	...
Louisiana	2,118	914	192,685	187,662	10	...
Maine	625	617	118,545	232,622	..	5
Maryland	1,428	1,411	389,452	489,955	..	9
Massachusetts	1,967	1,087	581,873	656,858	..	16
Michigan	4,480	1,023	229,722	386,264	..	20
Minnesota	3,793	1,046	268,622	300,598	..	11
Mississippi	1,790	1,396	143,226	98,389	8	...
Missouri	4,771	3,137	481,893	525,163	..	13
Montana	1,137	349	49,938	52,935	..	4
Nebraska	2,067	482	31,072	80,775	..	6
Nevada	353	170	9,152	15,241	..	3
New Hampshire	297	290	99,218	155,819	..	4
New Jersey	3,840	3,080	843,940	1,079,764	..	16
New Mexico	894	291	36,150	43,904	..	4
New York	10,348	10,181	3,044,648	3,851,975	..	45
North Carolina	2,036	1,763	563,138	471,740	14	...
North Dakota	2,299	355	15,804	37,904	..	4
Ohio	10,877	4,613	646,649	833,347	..	25
Oklahoma	3,859	3,468	360,168	420,120	..	8
Oregon	2,269	967	52,474	98,289	..	6
Pennsylvania	8,472	7,027	1,725,871	1,904,682	..	32
Rhode Island	284	284	193,152	200,551	..	4
South Carolina	1,563	1,426	165,126	154,380	8	..
South Dakota	1,950	1,393	55,454	108,157	..	4
Tennessee	2,495	2,059	268,147	271,397	..	11
Texas	254	236	648,904	756,788	..	24
Utah	969	471	62,180	101,476	..	4
Vermont	246	246	43,220	109,239	..	3
Virginia	1,795	1,722	255,043	330,532	..	12
Washington	4,381	308	35,457	40,324	..	9
West Virginia	2,841	1,481	234,531	220,214	8	..
Wisconsin	3,225	2,036	356,218	554,369	..	12
Wyoming	677	325	11,063	20,714	..	3
Totals	146,347	87,033	17,156,236	20,589,351	89	442

Returns From Nebraska

National Offices

President

1,372 of 2,067 Precincts

Dwight D. Eisenhower-R. 243,329
Adlai E. Stevenson-D. 101,345

* * *

Senator, Full Term

1,371 of 2,067 Precincts

Hugh Butler-R. 235,620
Stanley D. Long-D. 87,674
Dwight Bell-I. 10,451

* * *

Senator, Short Term

1,372 of 2,067 Precincts

Dwight Griswold-R. 209,584
William Ritchie-D. 117,908

Congressman

First District

478 of 615 Precincts

Carl T. Curtis-R. 76,594
Samuel Freeman-D. 30,249

Second District

167 of 314 Precincts

Roman L. Hruska-R. 39,390
James A. Hart-D. 26,219

Third District

353 of 495 Precincts

R. D. Harrison-R. 55,975
Alan A. Dusatko-D. 22,191

Fourth District

344 of 643 Precincts

A. L. Miller-R. 46,988
Francis D. Lee-D. 16,476

State Offices

Governor

1,372 of 2,067 Precincts

Robert B. Crosby-R. 205,804
Walter R. Raecke-D. 128,269

* * *

Lieutenant Governor

1,331 of 2,067 Precincts

Charles J. Warner-R. 202,350
A. Clifford Anderson-D. 108,506

* * *

Secretary of State

1,331 of 2,067 Precincts

Frank Marsh-R. 202,082
Harry R. Swanson-D. 110,446

* * *

State Auditor

1,331 of 2,067 Precincts

Ray C. Johnson-R. 217,701
Gustav F. Beschorner-D. 84,337

State Treasurer

1,263 of 2,067 Precincts

Frank B. Heintz-R. 177,711
J. R. Farris-D. 104,435

* * *

Attorney General

1,271 of 2,067 Precincts

Clarence S. Beck-R. 178,476
Michael T. McLaughlin-D. 100,558

* * *

Railway Commissioner

1,271 of 2,067 Precincts

Joseph J. Brown-R. 176,380
J. C. McReynolds-D. 95,809

* * *

Supreme Court

Second District

John Yeager unopposed

Fourth District

Fred Messmore unopposed

Sixth District

Edward F. Carter unopposed

* * *

Amendments

State Board of Education

1,232 of 2,067 Precincts

For 116,517
Against 75,207

Motor Vehicle Tax Revision

1,219 of 2,067 Precincts

For 123,206
Against 84,462

Legislature Pay Raise

1,252 of 2,067 Precincts

For 93,967
Against 95,030

Reduced Publication

1,232 of 2,067 Precincts

For 134,253
Against 48,628

Bigger Constitutional Convention

1,232 of 2,067 Precincts

For 110,046
Against 65,328

Revised Pay Procedure

1,219 of 2,067 Precincts

For 108,223
Against 78,019

Iowa Bellwether Counties Repeat

Des Moines, Ia. (AP)—The four Iowa counties which have been on the winning side in every Presidential election since 1900 were all tending that way again in latest tabulations from Tuesday's general election.

They are Jasper, Palo Alto, Monona and Decatur. Jasper and Palo Alto have gone to the winner each time since 1896.

All gave a Republican outlook after Jake More, Democratic state chairman, had conceded the Presidency to Republican Dwight D. Eisenhower.

Duke Soon Will Start Training With RAF

London (AP)—The Duke of Edinburgh has passed his medical test and will start flying lessons with the Royal Air Force when official engagements permit, it was said Tuesday night.

The Queen's husband, 31, will train at the RAF station at White Waltham. Flight Lieut. C. R. Gordon has been appointed his instructor.

Cracks Solid South, Victor in East, West

Democrats Defeated After 20 Years; GOP Makes Gain in Senate

Washington (AP)—Republicans made gains Tuesday in a tough battle to give Dwight D. Eisenhower a GOP Congress but the outcome still was in doubt in both House and Senate.

Two Senate seats now held by Democrats, in Connecticut and Maryland, were captured by Republicans. But this still was one short of the net gain of three needed to assure GOP control of that branch in the Eighty-third Congress.

In the House the Republicans had a net gain of five seats up to 4 a. m. (CST). But they needed a pickup of 16 to win a majority there.

14 in Doubt

The Senate race, where the Democrats had a mathematical edge before the voting began, promised to be exceedingly close.

Twenty-one Senate races had been decided at 4 a. m.; the Republicans won 15 of them. That left the Senate tally 41 to 41 because the Democrats will have 35 holdovers and the Republicans 26 in the new Congress.

Of the 14 races in doubt, Republicans were leading in nine and Democrats in five. If the candidates who were leading proved to be the victors, the Republicans would control the Senate.

Moody Trailing

Vice-President Nixon would cast the deciding vote in cases of ties in the Senate.

The Senate race appeared to hinge on close contests in Kentucky, New Mexico, Wyoming, Missouri and Nevada and possibly other states.

These Democratic incumbents were trailing: Ernest W. McFarland of Arizona, majority leader; Joseph O'Mahoney of Wyoming; Thomas Underwood of Kentucky and Blair Moody of Michigan.

But these Republican Senators also were behind: James P. Kem of Missouri, Zales Ecton of Montana, Harry Cain of Washington and Henry Cabot Lodge of Massachusetts.

McCarthy Ahead

Senator Joseph R. McCarthy of Wisconsin, who became a top campaign issue because of tactics in pressing charges of Communist infiltration into the Federal Government, was far ahead in his bid for re-election.

In Ohio, Senator Bricker, Republican, was leading Michael DiSalle, former Office of Price Stabilization chief.

In Indiana, Republican Senator Jenner defeated Henry Schricker.

The Democrats clung to an edge in the House but many of the marginal districts were yet to be heard from.

The House tally stood at 168 Democrats and 165 Republicans. This included 80 Southern Democrats and 15 Republicans who were unopposed.

One of the Republican House gains was made in traditionally Democratic Virginia which voted for Republican Dwight D. Eisenhower this time.

Compiled from Press Dispatches.

Gen. Dwight D Eisenhower will be the next President of the United States.

He and his many millions of supporters brought down in ruins the 20-year-old structure of the New Deal and Fair Deal Tuesday.

Gov. Adlai Stevenson, Democratic nominee, conceded at 1:10 a. m. after he had seen even his own state fall into line in the general's column.

The Republicans broke the Solid South by capturing Florida and Virginia with ease.

Takes Midlands

They blitzed the New England States, surrounded New York and Pennsylvania, captured the industrial Midlands and swept the Midwest.

The fire kindled in the East swept to the West where everything from Canada south to Mexico was safely Republican.

Even Texas was falling.

Thirty-nine states with 442 electoral votes were Republican.

Only the Deep South, and West Virginia, Kentucky and Arkansas stayed with the Democrats.

Nixon Goes Along

With him to victory General Eisenhower carried Senator Richard Nixon of California, the man who exposed Alger Hiss.

In upstate New York, General Eisenhower had almost a million lead over his opponent.

From the first reports, Florida was leading for General Eisenhower and every report brought a widening margin.

"Doubtful" states such as Massachusetts, Minnesota, Maryland and Washington left no doubt: America likes Ike.

Returns from 102,030 of the country's 146,347 voting units showed the popular vote:

Eisenhower 24,265,754
Stevenson 19,936,707

Vice-President-Elect Nixon . . . his vote may be decisive in even Senate.

Metcalfe Leads Race for OPPD

Ted W. Metcalfe, present Omaha Public Power District Director, led the field in the OPPD director vote returns early today.

William Kunold was the other top OPPD candidate. Both seemed to have safe margins over Harry Knudsen and Gus A. Dworak.

Attorney James F. Green, Democrat, polled the largest vote in the partial returns for Metropolitan Utilities District. He led former Mayor Dan B. Butler by a large margin.

On the Republican side Frank L. Frost seemed headed for an easy win over Alfred H. Hansen with almost a 2-to-1 ratio.

Alfred C. Kennedy, Republican, also had a good lead over Harry Beal for the short term MUD director to replace a vacancy created by the resignation of N. Phil Dodge.

Iranian Majlis Okays Trial of Ex-Premier

Tehran, Iran (AP)—Parliament Tuesday gave the third and final reading to a bill authorizing the Justice Ministry to prosecute former Premier Ahmed Qavam as responsible for the deaths in last July's riots. The rioting ended Mr. Qavam's four-day term and returned Premier Mohammed Mossadegh to power.

Deputies of the Majlis (lower house) passed the measure by a standing vote and sent it to the Government for enforcement. Mr. Qavam is in hiding.

Woman Has to Doff Ike Skirt to Cast Ballot

Miami Beach, Fla. (AP)—An unidentified woman had to take off her "I Like Ike" skirt Tuesday before election officials would allow her to vote.

So she calmly removed her skirt, stood in line in her slip for 15 minutes, then voted.

★★ THE NEW MEXICAN ★★

...th Year, Issue No. 203 SANTA FE, NEW MEXICO, MONDAY, JULY 27, 1953 Price 7 Cents

Fighting Stops In Korea

U. N. Sets Meeting On Korea Aug. 17th

UNITED NATIONS, N. Y. (AP)—The U. N. General Assembly will meet three weeks from today ...cide the next big hurdle in the Korean problem—setting up the special political conference. The ...ference provided for in the armistice agreement must meet within 90 days. Its chief job will be ...y to transform the armistice into a permanent peace. Just what subjects will come up remain ...e decided. The 60-nation General Assembly will determine which nations will have a seat at the ...erence and will fix the time and place it will meet. Some delegates want the Assembly to work ...the conference agenda too, but others have indicated they want to leave that to the conference itself. The call for the Assembly meeting on Aug. 17 went out quickly last night, but Assembly President Lester B. Pearson of Canada and other leaders thought it best to allow ample time for private consultations before the formal meetings begin.

May Agree Early

Pearson expressed the hope that some plans might be agreed upon informally before the session opens. If this is done, Pearson said, the meeting might be concluded in a week or a little more.

The U. N. received formal notification of the armistice at 6:48 p.m. (MST) ... minutes after the conclusion of the Panmunjom signing. U. S. Delegate Henry Cabot Lodge Jr. informed Secretary General Dag Hammarskjold orally and later, before television cameras, handed him a letter with the notification.

"Let us thank God and fervently pray that this armistice heralds a lasting peace," Lodge said.

Hammarskjold said:

"I wish to express the firm conviction that all parties by abiding by the armistice will contribute to paving the way to a peaceful settlement of the political and economic problems still facing us in Korea. . . . The United Nations will devote the best of its endeavors to the great tasks of reconciliation and rehabilitation that lie ahead."

Hails Truce

... [illegible] ... political problems still unsettled.

"The signing of the armistice is the end of one chapter—of bloodshed and conflict," he said, "but it is only the beginning of a new and difficult one—the making of peace.

"This new chapter can only be completed successfully in Korea if the armistice terms are faithfully and scrupulously observed by all concerned.

"If this is done, we can move on to the next stage toward political settlement and reconstruction in a free, democratic and united Korea—a goal which the Korean people have fought so valiantly to reach. Such a settlement could in its turn lead to a solution of outstanding issues in the whole of the far east."

$82.3 Million State Budget Under Study

...budget of $82,300,000 as the ...ll cost of running the state ...nment in the current 42nd ...year was recommended to the Finance Board today.

...e Comptroller Edwart Hart... said this total included 32 ...n for the Highway Department and $15,600,000 million for educational institutions. The ...t workers made no recom... ...tions on either of those figures. The Highway Commission ...been held to have complete ...rity over its own funds and ...Board of Education Finance ...mmended adoption of its figures for the schools.

...e remainder of the total re... ...d recommended outgo of ...0,000 million for all other ...departments, agencies and ...s.

...increase of approximately 8 ...n over the previous esti... ...d total was attributed to ... [illegible] ... during the Legislature's consideration of the budget means ... are starting now at such ... level it would be difficult ... them further."

...r state institutions, total ...3,518,000 was recommended ...st requests of $3,969,000, ...nan said a cut of about $100,... ...vas indicated for the penitentiary because estimated revenue ...been overstated by about that ...

...e, in reply to a question from ...rd member, the comptroller ...rked that the highway bud... ... [illegible] ... in view of that ...y's independence from fi... ...board control. And, he added, ...are running into the same ...with the Land Office."

Baca Violates Law's Intent —Robinson

...Mexico State Atty. Gen. ...Robinson said today that ...Liquor Director Elfego Baca ...lating the intent" of the state ...law by permitting the trans... ...a license into Farmington.

...Baca is taking advantage of ...tentional loophole in the ...re act, but I am afraid his ...is legal," Robinson.

...inson said he and members ...staff discussed the liquor ...length this morning and de... ...that it technically prohibits ...the issuance of new licenses in ...which already have one liquor ...for every 1,500 residents. Rob... ...said the Legislature provided ...o licenses be "issued" in com... ...es which have the legal max... ...of liquor licenses.

...word "issued" apparently ap... ...only to new liquor licenses, al... ...that undoubtedly was not ...tent of the Legislature," Rob... ...said. "Mr. Baca is violating ...t of the New Mexico Leg... ...with his decision to permit ...ransfers as the one at Farm... ...but it is apparently legal."

The Weather

...per's Old Men ...ain Threatens

...when we get the old men of ...Mexican staggering through ... ... turn rainy. ... show... ...s due in this ...cons and ... through ... under ... cloudy ... Tempera... extremes ... the ... the next 24 ... compared ... today were ... and 68 yesterday. The rain... ...d to .3 inch downtown, and ...at the mercury stood at 61.

...Cosmetic Specials at Capital ...ncy. Listen to Calla Hay ...tomorrow, KVSF. (Adv.)

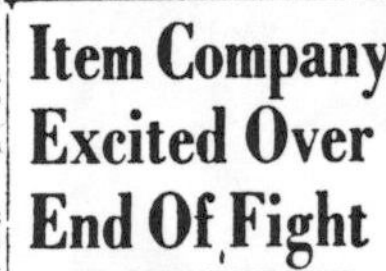

Item Company Excited Over End Of Fight

By JOHN RANDOLPH

CENTRAL FRONT, Korea (AP)—I had promised Item Company I would bring them a bottle of whisky the minute that agreement was reached on the armistice.

They didn't see me coming until the last 20 yards on the steep and muddy hill northeast of Kumhwa.

Under my arm, like a football, I was carrying the fifth of 100-proof bond, wrapped safely in a dirty GI khaki towel.

Sgt. Ippolito spotted me floundering and gasping up the final slope. He looked a long moment—then he started to yell, his voice breaking with excitement.

"He's got it! He's got the bottle! It's an armistice, by God—they've got an armistice!"

Helmeted heads craned out of bunkers and foxholes and dirty bearded faces turned my way and Ippolito ran down the slopes to meet me.

A horrible suspicion of doubt crossed his face and he stopped short.

"You wouldn't kid us, would ... [illegible] ..."

"It's true. It's official. The U. N. Command ... announced an armistice had been agreed upon. They sign it tomorrow at 10 a. m. The cease-fire is 12 hours later—10 p. m. tomorrow."

Another and deeper shadow crossed Ippolito's face.

"Tonight . . . You mean we got to sweat out tonight . . . Jesus Christ. I hope we make it." Then he shoved the awful fear out of his mind, brightened again and shouted:

"The lieutenant! Lieutenant! They got an armistice—he brought the bottle just like he said."

The others were crowding around now, maybe a dozen of them, and I was escorted to the muddy hole covered with logs that was the company command post. Lt. Don C. Patton, the company executive, leaned out from under the sandbagged logs. Patton is a bronzed young man with a big brown mustache and a sweaty, mud-stained face.

We shake hands. Ippolito explains our bargain. I hand over the bottle.

"Whenever you think best," I tell him.

Patton considers.

It is 8 p. m. now, Sunday evening. For 26 hours still these men will be at war—while all the world relaxes and rejoices. Twenty-nine hours, 29 eternities, on a hill in North Korea, where death counts out the seconds, one by one.

"We'll drink it tomorrow night—at 10 o'clock" Patton decides, and he puts the bottle carefully in an old ammunition box underneath his field telephone and the mud-stained battle map.

"Thank you very much," he said.

I am invited into the tiny bunker and the small group gathers around as the news is relayed to other company positions and outposts on the field telephone.

I have come back to Item Company at a terrible moment. Only two ... before, in a tragedy almost ... end hearing in the last hours of the war, two rounds of American artillery have landed by accident in the middle of the company. In two seconds a sergeant was dead and 10 other men were wounded, some very seriously.

Just the night before, this company and King Company, its neighbor, fought back a savage Chinese attack that was launched with 6,000 rounds of Communist shellfire.

These men are bone weary . . . filthy . . . dirty . . . soaked to the skin by unending summer showers. They have been living in holes like rats since the U. S. 3rd Division was jerked from only three days of reserve and flung into the Kumsong front to plug the gap left by the collapse of the ROK Capitol Division.

Now these men are told that the war is over—except that they must go through one more night of fear and ... on this hill position, the Chinese lines.

The ... of a Chinese shell ... from the hill where Love Company is waiting across the valley to our left.

These men, with their angers, their ... their hope, their ...

(Continued on Page Two)

Queen Rites Will Precede Zozobra Fete

For the very first time, the coronation of the Queen will precede the burning of Zozobra to mark the general opening of the 241st Santa Fe Fiesta, the evening of Aug. 28.

As another new feature of the four-day annual celebration here, the enthronement ceremony is to take place in the Cathedral of St. Francis at 7:30 that Friday evening.

Archbishop Edwin V. Byrne of Santa Fe will place the crown on the 1953 Fiesta Queen—Miss Maria Cristella Romero—at the ceremony in the historic Cathedral.

Also for the first time, a colorful procession of the Queen, her court, other Fiesta personalities and a marching orchestra will precede the coronation. The procession is to start from the archbishop's residence in Cathedral Place at 7 p.m., proceeding down Water Street to Don Gaspar, then to San Francisco Street and east to the Cathedral.

The Rev. Msgr. C. C. Schoeppner, pastor of Guadalupe Church and a member of the archbishop's administrative staff, will be in charge of the coronation and the several other details of church participation in the 1953 Fiesta.

The burning of Zozobra at Fort Marcy Park is scheduled at 9 p.m. following the coronation ceremony at the Cathedral, with other Fiesta events programmed for the next three days and nights.

Members of the Fiesta Council will meet at 8 p.m. Wednesday to settle further details of this annual observance, known as the oldest community celebration in the United States.

Dr. L. A. Turley Dies In Oklahoma

Dr. L. A. Turley, dean emeritus of the University of Oklahoma Medical School, died Saturday at Oklahoma City, it was learned here today.

Dr. Turley, well known here, was a regular summer visitor in Santa Fe for the past 40 years, and was brother of Walter G. Turley, Santa Fe, consulting engineer, who left yesterday for Oklahoma City, where the funeral is to be held.

W9SNAFU CALLING CQ—Columnist Will Harrison goes "on the air" with his own "ham" mobile station. He chose call letters W9SNAFU. Burro power is furnished by Skitow (left and underneath), property of James Riley of Santa Fe. Harrison was host to 70 licensed New Mexico radio amateurs Sunday as outgrowth of a column in which he criticized their efforts to obtain special license plates with station call letters instead of regular numbers.

River Water Plans Buried In Congress

WASHINGTON (UP) — Congress raced toward adjournment today with two bills to authorize construction of the huge Shiprock irrigation project and San Juan transmountain diversion canal buried hopelessly in committees.

Measures to authorize construction of the billion-dollar reclamation projects were introduced in both the House and Senate last spring. Both still remain buried in House and Senate interior committees.

The bureau of reclamation, however, is continuing its investigations and preparation of a feasibility report on the San Juan-Chama diversion project despite objections from residents of Farmington, N.M.

The proposed diversion canal would divert a maximum of 235,000 acre feet from the San Juan water shed to the Rio Grande across the continental divide.

Also included in the project would be construction of the Navaho dam and some 100 miles of irrigation canals to feed water to the Navaho Shiprock irrigation project and the South San Juan irrigation project.

GOP Leader Sets His Plan

DEXTER (AP) — Frank Wortman, elected Saturday as chairman of the state GOP said yesterday that a "reasonable facsimile" of a plan of party action suggested by retiring Chairman Harry Robbins would be adopted by the party.

Robins suggested in a farewell address during the meeting in which Wortman was elected that the party set up a permanent state headquarters and hire an executive assistant to the chairman, maintaining the chairman's present $12,000 salary.

Robins also suggested that the women and Young Republicans be given an operating budget.

Wortman did not say if all these suggestions will be incorporated into the plan.

Saying he will not at present devote all his time to the duties of his new job, Wortman said he does not plan to move to either Albuquerque or Santa Fe to set up permanent headquarters.

He said he will travel through the state as much as is necessary.

City Cops Arrest Algodones Man

Carl Andrew Allen, 29, of Algodones, and a woman companion, Tillie Montoya, were arrested by Santa Fe police yesterday at the De Vargas Hotel.

City police had been alerted for the pair by state police, who said they were wanted in Albuquerque for investigation of passing bogus checks. They were turned over to state police who last night delivered them to the Bernalillo County sheriff's office.

Radio Hams Get Even With Will Harrison

By GUY LEMMON

New Mexico radio amateurs climaxed a meeting in Santa Fe Sunday with a free feed at the expense of a newspaper columnist who cheerfully ate his words. More than 70 licensed "ham" operators showed up for the good-natured ribbing of Will Harrison, who had said in a column that no radio amateurs had mobile sending and receiving apparatus in their cars. The statement was in connection with the amateurs' successful efforts during the last Legislature to obtain authorization for special license plates with their station call letters rather than regular numbers.

A total of 43 of the cars at the celebration carried mobile transmitters and receivers, according to G. Merton Sayre of Roswell, sectional communications manager for the American Radio Relay League.

A. David Middleton, Albuquerque, West Gulf director of the American Radio Relay League, presented Harrison with an honorary membership in the New Mexico Amateur Mobile Radio Assn. The certificate gave him the title of "admiral of the mobile fleet" with juridictoin over "the commonwealth of New Mexico, the vast unsettled areas of Texas, and the independent, sovereign state of Socorro."

Roy Self of Roy, New Mexico director for the Military Affiliate Radio System, also presented Harrison with an honorary membership in that organization.

With the honors went a mobile station for Harrison's own use. A sad little burro named Skitow furnished the mobility. Harrison said he would adopt the call letters W9SNAFU.

The party climaxed a two-day meeting of the amateurs with civil defense officials in Santa Fe, during which they took part in a disaster test Sunday morning.

John Harvey of Santa Fe, who had charge of the test operations pronounced it a success. Three emergency communications networks were on the air within an hour after the foothill reservoirs serving Santa Fe "burst," and the Santa Fe River flooded the city, he said. A Naval Reserve mobile radio unit from Albuquerque served as control point for one of the nets and relayed messages throughout the state, Harvey said.

After the test the "hams" gathered at Harrison's home for the mock ceremonies. Harrison served ham sandwiches and Hamm's beer.

Harrison himself, for the benefit of photographers, dined on one of his old newspaper columns.

HOME CLUBS MEET

PORTALES (AP) — The New Mexico Assn. of Home Extension Clubs will hold its tenth annual meeting at Eastern New Mexico University Aug. 17-18.

Ike Requests $200 Million For S. Korea

WASHINGTON (AP) — President Eisenhower today formally requested Congress to provide an initial 200 million dollars for Korean relief. He said security interests of the United States "clearly indicate the need to act promptly."

Acting less than 24 hours after signing of the armistice at Panmunjom, the President said:

"The extent of devastation suffered by the people and the economy of Korea is staggering."

In a special message to Congress Eisenhower spoke of a confidential survey of Korean economic conditions made more than three months ago by Henry J. Tasca, the President's special representative on Korean economic affairs.

"The completed survey has been reviewed by the National Security Council," Eisenhower said. He added:

"On the basis of its analysis and recommendation, I am convinced that the security interests of the United States clearly indicate the need to act promptly, not only to meet immediate relief needs but also to begin the long-range work of restoring the economy to health and strength."

Indian Liquor Okayed By House

WASHINGTON (AP) — The House passed unanimously and sent to the Senate today a bill to repeal laws prohibiting sale of intoxicants to Indians.

The House Interior Committee, in recommending House approval of the bill, expressed hope that "all legislation discriminating against our Indian citizens may be abolished."

GOP LIKES EMMONS

ALBUQUERQUE (AP) — The Republican State Central Committee adopted without dissent a motion by Manuel Otero of Albuquerque endorsing nomination of Glenn Emmons, Gallup banker, as Indian commissioner.

Last Barrage Ends Killing

By FORREST EDWARDS

SEOUL (AP)—Shooting stopped along the Korean battlefront at 10 p.m. tonight (6 a.m. Monday MST), bringing to an abrupt halt 37 months of death and destruction. While ground fighting was all but nil the final hours, mounting Communist artillery fire took its toll of Allied soldiers up to the last minute. At 10 p.m., a hush fell over the front. The last man to die may never be named. Nor, perhaps will the last hero. The front, usually aflame at this hour of night, just grew dark.

Men heaved sighs of relief, but with great caution.

As the clock ticked off the seconds, they grew more brave.

The last reported barrage—the final one of the Korean war on the Central Front—lifted at 9:43 p.m.

Ends in Silence

The fighting there, at least, ended in silence.

AP Correspondent John Randolph said the cease-fire came on the Central Front amid silence after a smashing artillery duel between Allied and Red guns that began in mid-afternoon and built up a deafening crescendo shortly before 10 p. m.

Randolph said all firing stopped at 9:43 p.m. ...

A few seconds after 10 p.m. wild yells broke out from American GIs.

All day and into the night the Reds sent artillery and mortar barrages screaming into Allied lines east of Kumhwa on the Central Front.

The barrages mounted in fury as the hours went by. Sometimes shells ripped front and rear line positions at the rate of four a minute.

Allied artillery boomed back trying to silence the guns.

Even as the shooting ended, litter jeeps and ambulances wound down dusty hill trails from outpost ridges, bringing moaning, broken men to rear hospitals.

1,000 Rounds

Correspondent Randolph reported that between 6 a. m. and 9 p. m., a U. S. division east of Kumwha had been hit by 3,000 rounds of Chinese artillery.

Only five minutes before the guns fell silent, American and South Korean artillerymen tried to muffle the Red guns once and for all with a ... barrage.

Using massive supercharges of powder, nearly 12 battalions of Allied artillery opened simultaneously.

Flames gushed from the muzzles battery after battery fired in salvo.

The valleys roared and shook as the shells burst deep behind the Red lines.

The Communist shelling stopped—at about the same moment the Allied barrage lifted.

If the Reds had not insisted on an attack, there would have been little or no firing on the closing day.

The 8th Army had warned division commanders only to fire defensively. The order was meant to save lives.

From the Red side, there was no sound. Some of their men died, too, in those last frenzied moments.

Last Plane Bagged

The last Communist plane shot down was bagged at 12:25 p.m., more than two hours after the truce was signed. Capt. Ralph Parr of Apple Valley, Calif., destroyed a Russian-made IL-12 transport just south of the Manchurian border.

American Sabre jets swept to the Yalu in the afternoon, but Red MIG fighters scurried back to their Red China sanctuary.

At the front, nervously exhausted Allied infantrymen got out of their bunkers, shook hands, and brought out bottles hoarded for the big day.

On the Western Front, in the Marine sector, AP Correspondents George McArthur and Fred Waters reported the Allies were firing "one for one."

When a Red shell splashed in Allied territory, American big guns sent one screaming back.

Correspondent Robert Gibson, on the East-Central Front, reported heavy shelling by the Reds and said Allied artillery answered in kind.

Now, the Allied and Communist armies are to pull back within 72 hours 1¼ miles, forming a 2½-mile-wide buffer strip.

Diplomats Take Over

The diplomats now take over in an attempt to bring lasting peace to this war-torn land.

While Americans and other U. N. troops waited for darkness—the usual time for Red attacks, the air war continued.

Fifth Air Force said 400 Air Force, Marine and carrier-based planes unloaded bombs on Red troops and supply concentrations in the Kumsong Bulge sector. It was at this East-Central Front strip that the Communists two weeks ago hurled their greatest attack in two years.

They will get to keep the few miles won at a staggering cost in human life. A map released by the U. N. Command after the armistice signing showed the Reds were given almost all the Kumsong Bulge, plus some other ridges and outposts whose ...

(Continued on Page Two)

Wife Awaits Nervously For PW Exchange

The big guns of slaughter have quieted and a young Santa Fe wife has learned to hope again.

It has been three years since her husband sailed for Korea and more than a year since he became a prisoner of the Communists, but Mrs. Roger Hartman said the armistice, and with it the exchange of prisoners, has boosted her hopes.

"I'm so nervous I'm scared," she said today. "It's been three years and so many things can happen in that length of time."

She said her 28-year-old husband, 2nd Lt. Roger Hartman, who was held a prisoner of the Germans for six months during World War II, sailed for Korea July 4 three years ago.

The last letter she had from him was written in July, 1952, but by the time she received it, the young lieutenant had already fallen into enemy hands.

Since then, except for two telegrams from his Communist captors Mrs. Hartman has heard no word from her husband.

But he's a prisoner, she's sure of that. And soon he will be freed...

Then the young artillery officer can come home to his wife and three children, one of whom he has never seen.

Thanksgiving Period Set For Santa Fe

Mayor Paul Huss has set aside 6 p.m. today as a time for prayer of thanksgiving for the armistice in the Korean war.

In a proclamation issued early today, Huss proclaimed the hour as "a time for prayers of thanksgiving and of hope that our boys will soon and safely return home."

The mayor has requested all churches in Santa Fe to join in tolling their bells at 6 p.m. in observance of the end of the 37-month war in Korea.

In further observance of the armistice, the office of Archbishop Edwin V. Byrne has announced that special prayers will be said Sunday in all Catholic churches for the safe return of Santa Fe's sons ... in Thanksgiving.

Tot Has Wild Ride On Car Bumper

LITTLETON, Colo. (AP)—Red light flashing and siren screaming, State Patrolman Kenneth Thomason chased a pickup truck for two miles south of here Friday night. When he finally halted Mrs. Albert Lynes, the Lynes' 3-year-old daughter, Mary Margaret, climbed from the front bumper of the truck and greeted her parents.

Thomason said the tot evidently had ridden on the front of the truck for 10 miles at speeds between 45 and 50 m.p.h. The parents thought the girl was home in bed.

JAIL REFUGE

CARLSBAD (AP) — Police ... J. S. McCall offered the city ... as refuge to a man who had ... arrested on drunk charges. ... judge figured he would be safer in jail than on the outside where his angry wife could get hold of him. Said Judge McCall "I know if I were in your boots I wouldn't want to go home; so I thought you'd like it better in jail."

OUR HOME TOWN

...s Cruces lends its hopes to ...s of five families of area ...men who are either prisoners ...ar or missing in Korea that ...return may be speedy.

Las Cruces Sun-News

AN INDEPENDENT DAILY AND SUNDAY NEWSPAPER SERVING SOUTHERN NEW MEXICO

THE WEATHER

LAS CRUCES AREA: Partly cloudy today, tonight and Tuesday. Little change in temperature. High [illegible] 90-100; low tonight [illegible]. Last 24 hours: Las Cruces [illegible]; State College, 95-62.

...—No. 166 ASSOCIATED PRESS LEASED WIRE — LAS CRUCES, NEW MEXICO, MONDAY EVENING, JULY 27, 1953 — CENTRAL PRESS PICTURES — PRICE FIVE CENTS

...rmistice Silences Booming Korean Guns Today

...Negotiators Promise To Return ...36 Prisoners Of War, Including ...3 Americans Within Next 60 Days

...SAN, July 27 (AP)—The ...cords of the Panmunjom ...egotiations released today ...that the Communists have ...Allies they will return 12,... ...oners of war — including ...mericans.

...ommunists gave this break... ...the captives they will re-

...Americans.
...Koreans.
...ritish.
...ench.
...rks.
...stralians.
...ipinos.
...nadians.
...lombians.
...th Africans.
...k.
...gian.
...anese.

...akes a total of 4,877 pris- ...non-Korean nationality to be returned.

The Allies informed the Communists that about 5,000 Chinese prisoners and 69,000 North Korean captives will be returned to the Reds in the big exchange of prisoners.

Information Exchanged

The information was exchanged in a secret staff officers session held at Panmunjom July 22. Marine Col. James C. Murray spoke for the Allies and North Korean Col. Lee Pyong Il for the Reds.

The U. N. said that about 7,800 North Koreans and 14,500 Chinese captives will be turned over to the neutral nations repatriation commission. These prisoners have renounced communism and do not want to return to their homelands.

300 Per Day

The Communists said yesterday they would return 300 prisoners a

(Continued on Page 4)

Korean War Costs United States Dearly; 140,000 Casualties, $15 Billions In Cash

WASHINGTON, July 27 (AP)—What did the Korean War cost the United States?

More than 22,000 dead on the battlefield, part of a 140,000 casualty total.

More than $15 billions to help pay for over 1,135,000 tons of artillery ammunition; over 1,800,000,000 bullets and grenades; 800 tanks and 40,000 trucks used up in battle; more than two million shells for naval guns; hundreds of thousands of tons of bombs.

General Rearmament

It triggered a general rearmament program for which the government has spent to date over 101 billion dollars.

The shooting and the casualty lists will stop.

But the boys won't start home tomorrow or next week. Secretary of Defense Wilson says, "It will be a long time before we can with safety withdraw our troops from Korea." A long time can mean six months or more, depending on how fast prisoners are exchanged—and how soon peace, instead of mere armistice, can be assured.

U. S. Cautioned

Everyone—President Eisenhower, Secretary of State Dulles, Wilson hurried to caution the country that a Korean truce should not be a signal for demobilization or letdown of the defenses against a bigger war by Russia.

The government is obviously worried lest industry think that the truce means quick and wholesale cancellation of munitions orders.

Production To Continue

Hardly had the truce signing announcement been made when Wilson issued a statement saying current productions plans would be continued "until such time as an orderly production plan can be worked out that will take into account the changed Korean requirements." He did not, however, give a hint of whether than plan would be ready soon or at some distant date.

Some Trimming

On the day the war started—June 25, 1950—the United States had under arms 1,460,000 men in the Army, Navy, Marines and Air Force. Less than half a dozen Army divisions were manned and equipped to a point where they were ready for battle.

Today the military manpower counts up to about 3½ million, although it is being trimmed some under the economy program. The Army has 20 divisions.

Death, Destruction Cease After 37 Months Of War

SEOUL, July 27 (AP)—Shooting stopped along the Korean battlefront at 10 p. m. tonight (6 a. m. Monday MST), bringing to an abrupt halt 37 months of death and destruction.

While ground fighting was all but nil the final hours, mounting Communist artillery fire took its toll of Allied soldiers up to the last minute.

Hush Falls

At 10 p. m., a hush fell over the front.

The last man to die may never be named. Nor, perhaps will the last hero.

The front, usually aflame at this hour of night, just grew dark.

Men heaved sighs of relief, but with great caution.

As the clock ticked off the seconds, they grew more brave.

Last Barrage

The last reported barrage—the final one of the Korean war on the [illegible] 9:43 p. m.

The fighting there, at least, ended in silence.

AP Correspondent John Randolph said the cease-fire came on the Central front amid silence after a smashing artillery duel between Allied and Red guns that began in mid-afternoon and built up a deafening crescendo shortly before 10 p. m.

Randolph said all firing stopped at 9:43 p. m.

Wild Yells

A few seconds after 10 p. m. wild yells broke out from American GIs.

All day and into the night the Reds sent artillery and mortar barrages screaming into Allied lines east of Kumhwa on the Central front. [illegible]

The barrages mounted in fury as the hours went by. Sometimes shells ripped front and near line

(Continued on Page 4)

Hope Increases In Las Cruces Area For Two Known Prisoners, Three Men Reported Missing By Army

By THE ASSOCIATED PRESS

For many New Mexico families, including several in Las Cruces and area, hopes were a little brighter that they would see loved ones in the Armed Forces again soon now that the Korean truce is signed.

The Communists' promise to start prisoners of war on their way home bolstered that hope.

Known Prisoners

Twenty-five New Mexicans are known to be in Korean prison camps while another 51 are listed only as "missing."

One New Mexico prisoner, Cpl. [illegible] of La Madera, came home early this year when a prisoner exchange was made.

The following New Mexicans were listed by the Communists as prisoners of war in December, 1951:

Prisoners Listed

Alamogordo — Pfc. Rudolfo C. Guerra.

Albuquerque — Pfc. Curtis A. Thompson, Pfc. Celso J. Montoya, Pfc. Jose Mares, Pfc. Lloyd E. Osborn, Pfc. Antonio J. Sanchez, Pfc. Franklin O. Gillreath. Relatives of Thompson and Gillreath have since moved to Texas.

Capitan — Pfc. Margarito Trujillo.

Clovis — Cpl. Dan L. McKinney.

(Continued on Page 4)

...w Mexico's Radio Amateurs ...ngle Business With Pleasure

...A FE, July 27 (AP)—Just ...a newspaper columnist said ...ide things about amateur ...New Mexico, this ancient ..., theoretically doused with ...billion tons of water yes-...

...than 100 amateur radio ...s from all parts of the ...scended on the city early ...y in about half that many ...eet columnist Will Harri-... ...ight aobut their hobby.

...w Hams

...on said there were only ...ams in the state and only ...number of these had trans-... ...in their cars. In the re-... ...uproar, Harrison offered ...ents and food to any mo-... ...s who would pay him a ...

...e hams it was a big party. ...the largest gathering of ...amateurs — that is, hams ...ansmitters operated completely from their cars — in the state's history.

Dry Run

And part of the show was a simulated civil defense test in which "due to sabotage, accident or enemy action" the highest of the three Santa Fe reservoirs broke, taking out the two lower ones and dumping tons of water on the city.

The biggest group taking part was a 17-car cavalcade that left Albuquerque about 8:30 a. m. As the cars raced along the highway in a string stretching over a mile, the lead cars kept those behind advised of approaching traffic conditions and the air crackled with steady banter among the stations.

Police Escort

A police escort led the cavalcade through Santa Fe to the rendezvous point at the federal building, headquarters for the

(Continued on Page 4)

Garbage Disposal Needs More Care, Sanitarian Says

Las Crucens were called upon today by Hi Miller, county health department, to exercise more care in the disposal of garbage. And he laid down several rules of procedure for them to follow.

The sanitarian said if residents would wrap garbage before putting it in the can, and then make certain the lid was on tight, it would aid the city in their fight to eliminate flies in the municipality.

Commends Action

Miller commended the action of local authorities in fighting flies and their breeding places. He be-

(Continued on Page 4)

Weather Balloon Falls Undamaged In Cruces Today

An army weather balloon floated down from the skies over Las Cruces at 9:15 a. m. today, landing near Sheriff's Conoco service station on West Picacho.

Capt. J. Moore, who picked up the apparatus, said it was dropped on the end of a red parachute.

Differing from other weather balloons that have fallen in the area, the equipment, as nearly as could be determined, was undamaged in the descent.

State Feed Meet Wants Committee To Advise On Aid

Approximately 50 members of the New Mexico Grain and Feed dealers association today went on record as favoring establishment of an advisory committee to act in conjunction with the state drought relief committee. The proposal was made to the group by Austin Brooks of the El Rancho Milling co., Clovis.

In a talk to the session shortly before noon, B. B. Atchley, Clayton, state chairman of the Production Marketing administration, told the gathering he "strongly favored formation of such a committee."

Slight Dent

Atchley said he believed that, although recent moisture throughout the state has made a slight dent in drought conditions, the season for growing crops to supplement range feeding is over.

The general role of grain and feed dealers in the state will be to augment and aid distribution of feeds to stricken areas.

Under the program, the Com-

(Continued on Page 4)

State Finance Board Approves $82,300,000 New Mexico Budget

SANTA FE, July 27 (AP) A budget of $82,300,000 as the overall cost of running the state government in the current 42nd fiscal year was recommended to the State Finance board today.

State Comptroller Edwart Hartman said this total included 32 million for the Highway department and $15,600,000 million for the educational institutions. The budget workers made no recommendations on either of those figures. The Highway commission has been held to have complete authority over its own funds and the Board of Education Finance recommended adoption of its figures for the schools.

For All Departments

The remainder of the total represented recommended outgo of $35,100,000 million for all other state departments, agencies and boards.

An increase of approximately 8 million over the previous estimated total was attributed to growth in earmarked funds expected to be available.

Cannot Trim

Hartman told the board that cuts made during the Legislature's considerations of the budget meant that "we are starting now at such a low level it would be difficult to trim them further."

For state institutions, a total of $3,818,000 was recommended against requests of $3,959,000. Hartman said a cut of about $100,000 was indicated for the penitentiary because estimated revenue had been overstated by about that much.

Purely Academic

Once, in reply to a question from a board member, the comptroller remarked that the highway budget "is interesting information but purely academic" in view of that agency's independence from finance board control. And, he added, "we are running into the same situation with the land office."

Funeral Services Set Here Tuesday For Cruces Man

Joaquin M. Archuleta, 39, will be buried in San Jose cemetery here following funeral services tomorrow.

Mr. Archuleta, of Las Cruces, died July 21 in the Veterans hospital at Phoenix.

He is survived by his mother, Mrs. Guadalupe Archuleta, Las Cruces; two sisters, Mrs. Robert A. Montoya and Mrs. Marcilino Estrada, both of Las Cruces, and four nieces.

Mr. Archuleta served in World War II and was in the South Pacific theater four years. He was awarded several citations for bravery, including one for action in the Philippines.

Rosary services will be at 8 p. m. tonight at Nelson's Funeral home. Funeral mass will be said at St. Genevieve's church at 9 a. m. Tuesday.

Double Services Held For Victims Of Traffic Crash

Final rites for Mrs. Iva Jean Moore, 28, Pecos, Tex., were conducted at 10:30 a. m. today from the Mesilla Park Baptist church. Mrs. Moore died Monday, July 20, from injuries incurred in an automobile accident July 18 on highway 80 about eight miles south of Las Cruces.

Three ministers officated at the services. They were, Rev. Nathan Maloy, La Mesa, Rev. Ted Trent, Mesilla Park, and Rev. Pat Brock, Anthony.

Pallbearers Listed

Pallbearers were: Eddie Foreman, Stanley Shoup, Paul Sullivan, Buddy Dyer, Roy Alverson and Clifford Anderson. Burial was made in Masonic cemetery.

Mrs. Moore is survived by her husband, Pvt. William Moore; her parents, Mr. and Mrs. Henry C. Tanner, Pecos, Tex., and three

(Continued on Page 4)

...Cruces Firm ...Hold Banquet ...30 Tonight

...Mesilla Valley Motor com-... ...ll hold a banquet at 7:30 ...ay at Vonnie Lee's to cele-... ...e firm's winning the Four-... ...ward, and also the Ford ...company's 50th anniver-...

...s the fifth straight year ...firm has won the award, ...d to a dealer annually for ...ing work.

...will be employees of the ...y and their wives, Ford ...y officials from Denver, ...ral Las Cruces dignita-... ...their wives, including ...Apodaca and the Las ...barber shop quartet.

...any officials said they ex-... ...etween 75 and 80 persons ...affair.

Market Declines Nominally In Face Of Korean Truce

NEW YORK, July 27 (AP)—stock market took the Korean truce in stride today with only a nominal decline.

Prices were marked down at the start in many key areas. At the same time, however, resistance appeared in a variety of sections, and a gradual improvement from the lows was apparent everywhere.

The decline went to between 1 and 2 points at the outside with most of the minus signs in the small fractions. Gains extended to around a point. Volume was fast right at the start of trading and then turned quiet. The pace was a bit better than a million shares for the entire day.

EL PASOAN WOUNDED

WASHINGTON, July 27 (AP)—The Defense department announced yesterday that Sgt. 1/C Roger T. Holman, son of Mr. and Mrs. John J. Holman, El Paso, was wounded in Korean fighting.

Infant Hurt In Fall From Car At College

Frankie Abernathy, 14-month-old son of Mr. and Mrs. William Abernathy, box 206, Fairacres, was released by Memorial General hospital after treatment for head injuries.

Authorities at the institution said the youngster was injured when he fell from an automobile near New Mexico A&M.

Funeral Services Set For Las Cruces Baby

Graveside services for Felix Contreras, Jr., were set at 4 p.m. Tuesday in San Jose cemetery. Father J. M. Gonzales is to officiate at the rites.

The two-month-old child of Mr. and Mrs. Felix Contreras, 615 South Espina, died Sunday night in Memorial General hospital.

In addition to his parents, he is survived by one sister, Cecilia.

Fulmer Memorial Chapel is in charge of arrangements.

Cruces Red Cross Chapter To Meet In Annual Session

The Dona Ana county chapter of the American Red Cross will hold its annual meeting at 8 p.m. today in the WIA building at the corner of Reymond and Court.

Main item of business will be the election of three new members to the board of directors of the organisation. They will fill present vacancies.

Chapter personnel also will give annual reports. A film on Red Cross activities will be shown.

Mrs. Berniece Lytle, executive secretary of the local chapter, said "All persons holding current membership cards received during the 1953 fund campaign are urged to attend."

Publicity-Happy Burglar Writes Notes To Sheriff

LUFKIN, July 27 (AP)—A publicity-happy burglar who leaves typewritten notes calling himself "The King of Safecrackers" says he knows something about the unsolved million-dollar Brinks robbery in Boston.

The burglar visited here again Saturday night and left his usual calling card: a four-page letter to the Angelina county sheriff. That is, he left it after taking between $250 and $400 from two safes broken open in a wholesale grocery.

In his note Saturday "The King" detailed 53 safecracking jobs he said were his handiwork this year.

The pen-wielding thug added: "If you can bring me in I'll tell you some things about the Brinks job." He said he even knew how the door to the offices of the armored car services was opened—"a pick and squeeze was used."

Eisenhower Seeks $200 Millions Aid For Korea Relief

WASHINGTON, July 27 (AP)—President Eisenhower today formally requested Congress to provide an initial $200 millions for Korea relief. He said security interests of the United States "clearly indicate the need to act promptly."

Acting less than 24 hours after signing of the armistice at Panmunjom, the President said:

"The extent of devastation suffered by the people and the economy of Korea is staggering."

In a special message to Congress Eisenhower spoke of a confidential survey of Korean economic conditions made more than three months ago by Henry J. Tasca, the President's special representative on Korean economic affairs.

"The completed survey has been reviewed by the National Security council," Eisenhower said.

Area Sends Big Group To State Republican Meet

One of the largest county contingents ever to attend a state GOP convention has returned with the satisfaction of knowing that one of their delegation nearly got a state office.

One of the delegates, Mary Lou Alvarez, tied for runnerup spot for the job of state secretary of the central committee. Her strong showing was excellent in view of the fact that her campaign didn't get under way until a half-hour before the sessions started at Albuquerque.

Other Delegates

Other delegates from Las Cruces and the Dona Ana area were: Mrs. A. D. Dinsmore; Mrs. J. M. Carriege; Mrs. Tito Ledesma; Bob Jacobsen, Hatch; Herbert Boyer, Vado; Jim Baird; Cruz Alvarez;

(Continued on Page 4)

Services Are Pending For Mesilla Resident

Funeral services are pending for Mrs. Louis T. Lucero, 87, Mesilla, pending arrangements by relatives. She died yesterday.

Nelson's Funeral home is in charge of arrangements.

...n Reports Beer ...n From Car Here

...Coonce, 1821 California, re-... ...to city police Saturday ...at someone had stolen a ...beer from his car. He told ...it was parked at the ...Stull's Liquor store on ...Main st.

...Treated For Cuts ...wing Wreck Here

...an was treated late Satur-... ...Memorial General hospital ...and bruises received in ...collision at Griggs and ...streets. He was Paul Grant, ...North Mesa.

...'s vehicle collided with one ...by Adolfo Soto, 19, 320 ...Tornillo. His car was de-... ...by city police as a "total

COTTON MARKET

...(Courtesy Hoover Cotton Co.)

33.87	33.76	33.84-86
34.17	34.05	34.16-17
34.20	34.23	34.20
34.47	34.37	34.47
34.24	34.10	34.24
33.61	33.40	33.56-57
33.60	33.39	33.53-57

Wonderful, But What Of Future?

Most Congressmen Express Happiness At Armistice; Warn Of Communist Trick

WASHINGTON, July 27 (AP)—Practically to a man, members of Congress who commented on the signing of the Korean armistice said in effect: Wonderful, but what of the future?

"We have only opened a new chapter in a long book—the fight for peace," was the reaction of Senator Wiley (R-Wis.), chairman of the Senate Foreign Relations committee.

Applaud Truce

Wiley and many of his fellow Republicans applauded the truce agreement, but generally in terms highly tempered with caution.

Others, like Chairman Short (R-Mo.) of the House Armed Services committee, were even more pessimistic. Short said he was "anything but pleased."

Democrats, like Senate Minority Leader Lyndon B. Johnson of Texas and Assistant House Leader McCormack of Massachusetts, called for vigilance against any Communist ruse during the post-truce period.

And Senator Douglas (D-Ill.) questioned whether admission of Red China to the United Nations "may well be . . . the informal understanding that lies behind the whole armistice."

Much Surprised

However, Representative Vorys (R-Ohio), appearing on the same CBS television program with Douglas, said he would be "very much surprised" if that was the case.

Washington greeted last night's news of the Korean truce signing quietly.

A crippled newsboy, shuffling through a small crowd of soldiers and young men waiting at a bus stop, kept shouting, "War's over." He got a few looks but sold no papers.

Embassy Closed

Just before the truce hours, a reporter called at the Russian embassy. An aide poked his head around the door and, to all questions, said, "Embassy closed—nobody here—tomorrow please."

A South Korean emissary greeted the truce with harsh words. "Nothing but a crumble of trash," said Col. Ben C. Limb, South Korea's representative to the United Nations, in a filmed appearance on a CBS television program. He

(Continued on Page 4)

Paper Mill Awards Four Door Prizes At Grand Opening

Four door prizes were given away Saturday night by the Paper Mill to celebrate its grand opening.

First prize, a pen and pencil set, went to Myrtle Raley. Second prize, a sports blanket with a plastic carrying case, was given W. A. Sutherland. An aluminum lazy susan, third prize, and a masterpiece paint set, fourth prize, were won by Mary Frances Vercher Roark and Dean Alvin D. Boston of New Mexico A&M.

Cruces Court To Hear Drunk Driving Charge

One case was on the docket today as District Court resumed its session.

The trial of John Engler, charged on a count of driving while intoxicated, was scheduled to be presented to a court jury sometime today.

A court source said jurymen for the trial were to be chosen about 11:30 a. m. today, and would probably get underway following a noon recess.

Engler is being defended by Las Cruces attorney T. B. Raphsch.

Police Chief, Editor Disgraced

Berlin Reds Hit By Purge Resulting From June Riots

BERLIN, July 27 (AP)—East Germany's Communist bosses unveiled today their first big purge of the party high command since the June 17 workers revolt.

They plastered deposed Police Chief Wilhelm Zaisser with further disgrace, throwing him off the party Central committee and Politburo.

Editor Fired

They also kicked Rudolf Herrnstadt, editor of the official newspaper Neues Deutschland, off the committee and dropped three officials from both the Politburo and the list of "candidates" for committee membership.

The latter trio were Acting Foreign Minister Anton Ackerman; his former wife, Elli Schmidt, president of the Women's League, and Hans Jendretzky, union chairman in East Berlin.

Secret Meeting

The decisions were reached yesterday at the windup of a two-day secret meeting of the committee in East Berlin. They were announced in a communique issued in the names of Premier Otto Grotewohl and Walter Ulbricht, party secretary general and deputy premier.

Ulbricht, often rumored as a likely purge target since the workers outbreak, won unanimous reelection as secretary general, the post of real power in Red politics. He had to share the principal speeches and announcements with Grotewohl, however, which seemed to discount recent reports that these two top cogs in the East

(Continued on Page 4)

Las Cruces Receives Air Force Commission

James A. Blevins, Las Cruces, has been commissioned as a second lieutenant in the Air Force. Maj. Gen. Walter C. Sweeney Jr., 15th Air Force commander, presented Lieutenant Blevins his commission during a graduation ceremony at the Air Force ROTC summer camp, March Air Force base, Calif.

Lieutenant Blevins entered the ROTC program at New Mexico A&M.

Two Vehicles Damaged In Down-Town Wreck

Two vehicles were slightly damaged at [illegible] today when they collided in the [illegible] block on West Las Cruces ave.

City patrolman [illegible] investigated the accident, said a truck driven by [illegible], North Mesquite, collided with a jeep driven by Donald R. [illegible], 405 South Church.

1953

Tornadoes spread death and destruction through parts of the United States, killing hundreds in Texas, Ohio, Michigan, and Massachusetts.

Queen Elizabeth II, daughter of King George VI of Great Britain, was coronated with traditional pomp and ceremony.

Georgi Malenkov succeeded Josef Stalin as Soviet premier. Lavrenti Beria, former chief of Soviet secret police, was expelled from the Communist Party, arrested for conspiracy, tried secretly, and shot.

Major Charles Yeager reached an airspeed of more than 1,600 mph in an X-1A rocket-powered plane.

The New York Yankees became the first team to win five consecutive World Series.

Golfer Ben Hogan won the Masters Tournament, the U.S. and British Open championships.

Nineteen-year-old Maureen Connolly became the first woman to win the grand slam of tennis—the British, U.S., Australian, and French singles championships—in one year.

THE DAILY TELEGRAPH AND MORNING POST, WEDNESDAY, JUNE 3, 1953

The Daily Telegraph

and Morning Post

24-PAGE PICTURE SUPPLEMENT

4 A.M.

No. 30,548 LONDON, WEDNESDAY, JUNE 3, 1953 Printed in LONDON and MANCHESTER Price 2d.

ELIZABETH II IS CROWNED

SPLENDOUR IN ABBEY SEEN BY MILLIONS

QUEEN 6 TIMES ON PALACE BALCONY: VAST CROWDS

ROYAL BROADCAST: PLEDGE TO SERVICE OF HER PEOPLES

WITH THE SPLENDOUR AND SOLEMNITY OF AN HISTORIC RITUAL INSIDE WESTMINSTER ABBEY, WITH TRADITIONAL POMP AND COLOUR AND PAGEANTRY ALONG THE ROYAL ROUTE OUTSIDE, ELIZABETH II WAS YESTERDAY CROWNED QUEEN AMID THE AFFECTIONATE ACCLAIM OF MILLIONS OF HER PEOPLE IN THIS COUNTRY AND THROUGHOUT HER GREAT COMMONWEALTH OF NATIONS.

The assembly of nearly 8,000 in the Abbey, Princes and premiers, peers and commoners, heard her in a clear, sweet voice take the Coronation Oath which binds her to the service of her peoples and to the maintenance of the laws of God; saw her, clad in a robe of gold, receive from the Archbishop of Canterbury, Dr. Fisher, the Crown of St. Edward; and joined in the heartfelt cry, oft-repeated, of "God Save the Queen." For the first time, through the agency of television, millions of people in their homes were spectators of the impressive rites.

The Duke of Edinburgh, first after the Archbishop to kneel and place his hands between those of her Majesty in the act of homage, was at her side during the Communion.

At the end of the long ceremony the Queen, invested with robe of purple velvet, wearing the Imperial State Crown, and carrying the Orb and Sceptre, drove in a 2½-mile-long cavalcade back to Buckingham Palace. The streets were lined by nearly three million people, many thousands of whom had waited all night in rain and cold. The coolness of the showery weather seemed to emphasise the warmth of their welcome as roar after roar of thunderous applause surged round the Royal coach.

THE BELLS PEAL OUT

With the bells of London pealing joyously and the vast multitude cheering itself hoarse, the radiant Queen neared the Palace. Here there was one of the greatest demonstrations of popular enthusiasm ever witnessed in the capital.

It was repeated and increased when at 5.42 p.m. her Majesty came out on the balcony to acknowledge the tumultuous loyalty of the crowd —the first of six appearances during the evening. With her were the Duke of Edinburgh, the Duke of Cornwall, Princess Anne, Queen Elizabeth the Queen Mother and Princess Margaret.

The rain had stopped and the sun was struggling through the clouds as three minutes later jet fighters of the R.A.F. flew over to salute the newly crowned Sovereign.

In a moving and intimate broadcast last evening to the Commonwealth, the Queen pledged herself again to the service of her peoples "as so many of you are pledged to mine. Throughout all my life and with all my heart I shall strive to be worthy of your trust."

NIGHT SCENES AT THE PALACE

The huge, cheering throng remained outside the Palace till long after dark. Their repeated calls brought the Queen and the Duke of Edinburgh out again five more times, at 7.20, 9.45, 10.40, 11.30 and midnight.

SPLENDOUR AND PIETY IN THE ABBEY

By NORMAN RILEY

In the Abbey Church of St. Peter, Westminster, endowed richly by the first illustrious Elizabeth, Her Most Excellent Majesty Queen Elizabeth II dedicated herself yesterday to the service of her people.

...gold beneath the incandescent fire of fifty floodlights slung high in the vaulted transept and above the sanctuary. The Abbey pillars were well-nigh hidden beneath pale blue and silver hangings into which were woven the shamrock, the Tudor rose, the thistle and the leek. In each section of the transept were three galleries, each gallery holding an average of 300 people, with the peers and the peeresses on tiered blue and gold chairs.

In the middle of the ceremonial theatre, on a rostrum approached by five steps, the throne gleamed really in the flood of light, isolated, ignored, until the Queen had received, at the hands of the Church, the emblems of majesty which entitled her to take her place there as God's anointed.

This was the setting when the singing of Parry's version of the Psalm "I was glad" heralded the Queen's arrival at the Great West Door.

SCHOLARS' SALUTE

"Vivat Regina"

ELIZABETHAN COMPARISON

THE DUKE'S ENTRY

Midshipman Page

(Continued on P. 11, Col. 3)

ON THE BALCONY. The Queen, the Duke of Edinburgh, the Duke of Cornwall and Princess Anne on the balcony at Buckingham Palace when they came out to acknowledge greetings from the crowd.

"DECLARATION OF OUR HOPES FOR FUTURE"

The Queen's Broadcast to Empire

The Queen broadcast to the Commonwealth last night from a sitting-room in Buckingham Palace. Her Majesty's message was as follows:

When I spoke to you last, at Christmas, I asked you all, whatever your religion, to pray for me on the day of my Coronation—to pray that God would give me wisdom and strength to carry out the promises that I should then be making.

Throughout this memorable day I have been uplifted and sustained by the knowledge that your thoughts and prayers were with me. I have been aware all the time that my peoples, spread far and wide throughout every Continent and ocean in the world, were united to support me in the task to which I have now been dedicated with such solemnity.

Many thousands of you came to London from all parts of the Commonwealth and Empire to join in the ceremony, but I have been conscious too of the millions of others who have shared in it by means of wireless or television in their homes.

• • •

All of you, near or far, have been united in one purpose. It is hard for me to find words in which to tell you of the strength which this knowledge has given me.

The ceremonies you have seen to-day are ancient, and some of their origins are veiled in the mists of the past. But their spirit and their meaning shine through the ages never, perhaps, more brightly than now.

...than a thousand years, but the living strength and majesty of the Commonwealth and Empire; of societies old and new, of lands and races different in history and origins but all, by God's will, united in spirit and in aim.

Therefore I am sure that this, my Coronation, is not the symbol of a power and a splendour that are gone, but a declaration of our hopes for the future, and for the years I may, by God's grace and mercy, be given to reign and serve you as your Queen.

• • •

I have been speaking of the vast regions and varied peoples to whom I owe my duty, but there has also sprung from our island home a theme of social and political thought which constitutes our message to the world and through the changing generations has found acceptance both within and far beyond my realms.

Parliamentary institutions, with their free speech and respect for the rights of minorities, and the inspiration of a broad tolerance in thought and its expression—all this we conceive to be a precious part of our way of life and outlook.

• • •

During recent centuries, this message has been sustained and invigorated by the immense contribution, in language, literature and action, of the nations of our Commonwealth overseas.

RIVER MIRRORS LONDON'S FEU-DE-JOIE

£12,500 FIREWORKS

DAILY TELEGRAPH REPORTER

Britain's biggest firework show, a traditional feu-de-joie to celebrate the Queen's crowning, opened on the South Bank site last night with the thunder of a Royal Salute of 41 maroons and was reflected in the Thames.

Hundreds of thousands of people, 20 deep along the Victoria Embankment pavements, saw the £12,500 display. Towards the end hundreds of people, chilled by the exceptionally cold night, started dancing along the Embankment.

At the 12th maroon a 30ft portrait in fireworks of the Queen appeared at ground level. It burned for about 30 seconds, and then, on either side, blazed pictures of the Duke of Edinburgh, the Duke of Cornwall and Princess Anne. The portraits had barely faded from sight when a barrage of 200 rockets filled the sky with coloured stars.

Gigantic catherine wheels, the largest producing a circle of light 100ft across, were matched by gold and silver rockets hissing upwards, some releasing screaming devices, others red, white and blue stars. Set-pieces on the ground included an 800ft colonnade of white, fiery spray.

LATE ABBEY DEPARTURE

PROCESSION HALTED

Daily Telegraph Reporter

The return procession fell behind time. As a result the Queen, who was due to reach Buckingham Palace at 4.31 p.m., did not arrive until 4.56 p.m.

BAKERLOO CHAOS

ROYAL DRIVE TO-DAY

QUEEN ON BALCONY WAVES AT MIDNIGHT

LONDON LIGHTS SWITCHED ON

DAILY TELEGRAPH REPORTERS

The Queen, accompanied by the Duke of Edinburgh, appeared on the balcony at Buckingham Palace at midnight to wave for three minutes to a wildly cheering crowd.

It was their sixth appearance on the balcony. People waved bowler hats, women's hats, balloons and closed umbrellas.

The Queen waved her right arm continuously. Each time the Duke raised his hand high above his head the crowd went wild.

As the Queen waved, the singing of "God save the Queen" spread through the crowd. Following the Queen off the balcony, the Duke turned in the doorway and waved vigorously again.

At 12.10 the balcony floodlights went out. Then a few seconds later the whole Palace floodlighting dimmed away.

...illuminations were greeted with a wave of cheers.

Singing and dancing broke out and fireworks were exploded. Streamers and gaily coloured balloons appeared while workmen were still clearing street stands of piles of dismantled barriers.

When the Queen appeared she had exchanged her Imperial State Crown for a tiara. She wore a white gown and ermine wrap. The Duke of Edinburgh was in dinner jacket. They remained on the balcony, cheered continuously by the great crowd, for six minutes.

LIGHTS SWITCH ON

Signal for Gaiety

30,000 CHEER

Royal Family Appear

(Continued on P. 11, Col. 6)

U.S. GOOD WISHES

MR. MOLOTOV'S TOAST TO QUEEN

EMBASSY BALL

LATE NEWS

PICCADILLY DANCING TILL 3.30 a.m.

LONDON THANKED

ILL IN ABBEY

Index to Other Pages

To-day's Weather

Broadcasting: Page 4, Cols. 6 & 7

WEATHER TODAY
Partly Cloudy
Temperature Forecast
Low, 30; High, 48

THE INDIANAPOLIS STAR

"Where the spirit of the Lord is, there is Liberty."—II Cor. 3:17

VOL. 50. NO. 274 ★★★★ FRIDAY MORNING, MARCH 6, 1953

STALIN, MOST POWERFUL DICTATOR IN HISTORY, DIES

The Day In Indiana

By Maurice Early

Solons Eye Auto Tax
Bonding Limit Peril
Hurts Local Units
Cut Property Value
New Schools Doomed

MANY COMMUNITIES in the state would receive a blow that would reduce their power to borrow money, under an Indiana House of Representatives measure ready for action in the Senate.

THIS IS THE MEASURE that would do away with the assessment of automobiles and other motor vehicles this year. It provides that the State Board of Tax Commissioners shall establish rules for the assessment of motor vehicles next year.

UNDER THE RULES fixed by the State Tax Board, owners of motor vehicles would pay their taxes on the cars at the time application is made for license plates.

ALL OF THIS is designed to make certain that all car owners pay property taxes. There have been various studies which indicate that thousands of car owners escape property tax.

OBJECTIVE of the bill, to make certain that every car owner must pay property tax before he can obtain a license, is good.

BUT IN THIS proposed change the property tax system would receive a staggering blow. Under the State Constitution, local units of government are limited in their bonding power to 2 per cent of the assessed valuation of their property.

MANY OF THEM are up to their bonding power limit now and others are approaching the limit. Many communities needing new schools do not have enough bonding power to provide the new buildings.

IF ALL the automobiles and other motor vehicles are taken off of the property tax assessment list, the bonding limitation of the communities will be reduced drastically.

IN THE LAST report of the county assessors to the State Tax Board it is estimated that motor vehicles of the state are assessed $485,000,000. All this valuation would be wiped out by the terms of the pending measure.

IF THIS valuation is removed from the books, that aggregate bonding power of the communities would be reduced at least $10,000,000. Such a reduction would be a body-blow to many of the communities badly in need of new schools.

CLEAN UP of restaurants and all eating places, especially in the rural communities, proposed under a new licensing measure, may be postponed for another two years.

UNDER A MEASURE backed by the Indiana Restaurant Association, it is proposed to license all eating places and charge a $10 annual fee. The fees, to raise about $120,000, would be used to hire State Board of Health restaurant inspectors.

THIS BILL, which has passed the House and is ready for second reading in the Senate, has been attacked by Senator Roy Conrad because "it is a new tax" and both political parties, promised there would be no new taxes.

CONRAD was defeated in an effort to reduce the license fee from $10 to $5. He insisted there are thousands of small operators, such as hamburger stands and drugstores serving lunches, which would find the license fee a burden and regard it as a new tax.

VERY FEW eating places get any sort of inspection at present. Only nine cities have restaurant ordinances and issue licenses. The fees range from nothing to $20.

OF THE 12,000 eating places in the state, the association estimates there are only 7,000 that get any kind of inspection to protect the public. Many of these are taverns. Those in rural sections are not subject to any effective sanitary regulations.

What He Wanted And The Part He Got!

Boy Charged In Slaying

Shoots Playmate Fatally With Rifle

A 14-year-old boy was charged with manslaughter yesterday after he was accused of "showing off" with a .22 caliber rifle which discharged and killed a playmate.

Juvenile Aid Division officials said they filed the charges against Frank Rush, 1006 Oliver Street, when they said he told five conflicting stories of the fatal wounding of Larry R. Whitlow, 13, in the Rush home.

Police said, however, that James Mahaney, 12, 610 Birch Street, a witness, declared that Frank had put a cartridge in the rifle and had ejected it several times by snapping the rifle bolt, despite warnings that such play was dangerous.

JAMES SAID he went to the Whitlow home at 554 Drover Street yesterday morning. There was no school because of the teachers' curriculum conference, and they wandered around the neighborhood until Larry suggested:

"Let's go see what Frank's doing."

They watched television and talked basketball at the Rush home for a while, when Frank went to a rear bedroom and returned carrying his rifle, James said.

Frank stood in the dining room, snapping the bolt to throw

Turn to Page 2, Column 6

$3,446,000 Lopped Off Proposed Budget

By FARWELL RHODES JR.

Working in almost continuous session, the Indiana Senate Finance Committee announced last night that it had slashed a net $3,446,000 off of the proposed state biennial budget.

This lowered the total proposed expenditures to $602,199,738 for operating the state government during the 1953-55 period.

MAJOR REDUCTIONS made by the committee, according to Chairman Clem McConaha, Centerville Republican, were:

1 A $2,016,000 cut in the allocations for personal services and operating expenses of all state departments except the mental institutions. This included the four state schools, Indiana and Purdue Universities and Ball State and Indiana State Teachers' Colleges.

2 A $1,180,000 slice off the proposed operating budgets of the eight state mental hospitals.

3 An approximate $250,000 reduction in appropriations for constructing new buildings at the state institutions.

The term "personal services" refers to salaries of state employes.

Senator McConaha explained that the committee proposes to restore $100,000 of the funds it cut from the budget to serve as a contingency fund with which to make "emergency" salary adjustments and meet other unanticipated needs.

THE CONTINGENCY fund would be administered by the Governor and State Budget Committee.

The budgets of the state colleges and universities were trimmed about 2 per cent and the mental hospital budgets were pruned approximately 8 per cent, Senator McConaha said.

He explained, however, that the mental hospital budget-cutting would not mean lowering of the salaries of attendants and other personnel, but simply elimination of some new jobs that had been provided for originally in the budgets. Present employes still are due for substantial pay raises, he said.

The Finance Committee still was working early this morning to wind up its consideration of the three budget bills so they can be reported out of committee by noon today.

The Senate then will sit in committee as a whole this afternoon and make its final decision on what the budget should be.

The budget bills probably will be passed immediately under rules suspension and Senate and House of Representatives conferees will go into session to iron out final adjustments.

Ike Clears Way To Oust Demos Frozen In Jobs

Washington (AP)—President Eisenhower cleared the decks yesterday for ousting at least several hundred holdover Democratic officials from their government jobs.

Eisenhower directed that an executive order be drafted immediately "to provide the heads of agencies with greater freedom in determining" who should occupy a number of jobs now under civil service protection.

White House Press Secretary James C. Hagerty said in answer to questions this would make it possible to fire the present holders of the jobs concerned. All of the jobs, in some degree, are policy-making posts.

There have been complaints that when the new Republican administration went into office, it found that in many agencies the new chief could appoint only a handful of the top policy makers.

EISENHOWER also told the Civil Service Commission to review the whole question of employes in "Schedule A" of the civil service rules. Schedule A jobs are those of a policy-making nature.

Hagerty said a number of office holders who should have been put in Schedule A, and thus made subject to dismissal at the administration's pleasure, instead were "frozen" in their jobs by the Roosevelt and Truman administrations.

Officials said the assistant administrator of the Federal Security Administration, the agency's number two post, is a good example of an official who was given civil service protection improperly.

They didn't name names, but John L. Thurston has had this $15,000-a-year job. Thurston served under Oscar R. Ewing who headed the agency during the Truman administration. Ewing left with the end of President Truman's term.

House To Zip Through 2 Administration 'Musts'

The Indiana House of Representatives will shift into high gear today to push through two major administration bills streamlining the state's health and penal programs.

Representative Norman J. Neely, Bloomington Republican and House majority leader, announced last night that rules will be suspended to pass Senate Bill 205 this morning.

Previously passed by the Senate, this bill would set up a new State Department of Health embracing all the mental institutions.

Neely added that Senate Bill 258, which would establish a new State Department of Corrections, also will be passed under suspension of the rules either late today or early tomorrow.

THE TWO MEASURES represent the only important action left before the lower chamber as it heads into the final three session days of the 1953 General Assembly.

They would give Governor George N. Craig some of the tools to carry out his pledges to revamp and modernize Indiana's mental health and prison systems.

Neely said he anticipates no serious trouble in pushing the two key measures through the House, which is dominated by Republicans loyal to the administration.

The Department of Corrections would be headed by a full-time, three-member board. The department would include three divisions, Administration, Classifications and Treatment and Industries and Farms. The board would have direct charge of administration, while assistant directors would head the other two divisions.

THE HEALTH BILL would centralize supervision of all mental and other medical state hospitals. Three divisions, each to be headed by directors, would be Mental Health, Health and Preventive Medicine and Medical Institutions.

A single director would head the department but most supervisory powers would be vested in heads of the three divisions.

Today is the last day in which bills can be passed in the House but that rule could be waived to pass the corrections bill tomorrow.

Neely said that about 18 Senate bills remain to be acted on and the House then will be done except for acting on conference committee reports and motions for concurrence or dissent from Senate amendments.

No Mention Made Of Successor In Soviet Broadcast

By THE ASSOCIATED PRESS

Moscow (Friday)—Josef Stalin died last night behind the 12-foot-thick walls of the Kremlin. He dominated a third of the world's peoples as the most powerful dictator in history.

The prime minister of the Soviet Union and the supreme chief of the Communist Party succumbed at 9:50 p.m. (12:50 p.m. CST), four days after suffering a brain hemorrhage (stroke).

He had been in coma since he was stricken Sunday night, and his condition grew progressively worse. Yesterday his 10 physicians said his heart was faltering.

The announcement of his death was broadcast here at 4:07 a.m. (Moscow time) today—more than six hours after his doctors had given up their struggle.

The official announcement said:

"The heart of the comrade and inspired continuer of Lenin's will, the wise leader and teacher of the Communist party and the Soviet people—Joseph Vissarionovitch Stalin has stopped beating."

THERE WAS NO immediate indication in Moscow who was taking over control of the country, but the announcement was issued in the name of the Communist Party's Central Committee, the Council of Ministers and the Presidium of the Supreme Council. All these are organs

Half Page of Pictures on Page 48

gans which Stalin dominated, and among those next to him in power have been Georgi Malenkov, L. P. Beria, V. M. Molotov and Nicholas Bulganin.

As if appealing for unity, the official statement said:

"In these sorrowful days all the peoples of our country are rallying even closer in a great fraternal family under the tested leadership of the Communist Party created and reared by Lenin and Stalin."

THE MOST prominent leader of the Communist Party, next to Stalin, has been Malenkov. He keynoted the All-Party Congress last October, laying down the law to all segments of the party in matters of discipline.

"The Soviet people have boundless faith in and are permeated with a deep love for their Communist Party, for they know that the supreme law governing all the activity of the party is service in the interests of the people," the announcement said.

The announcement concluded:

"The immortal name of Stalin will live forever in the hearts of the Soviet people and all progressive mankind."

THERE WAS NO mention at any place of any of Stalin's lieutenants—Malenkov, Beria, and so on. The signature was merely:

"The Central Committee of the Communist Party of the USSR; the USSR Council of Ministers; the USSR Supreme Council Presidium."

Stalin's fatal illness became known on Wednesday, more than two days after he was stricken in his Kremlin apartment. An official announcement issued from the ministry of health and signed by the 10 physicians said Stalin "had a sudden hemorrhage of the brain" the night of March 1. This "affected vitally important parts of the brain" and paralyzed his right leg and arm. He lost consciousness and the power to speak.

Stalin ruled Russia as undisputed dictator for nearly 30 years. Through Communism, he extended his sway beyond the borders of the Soviet Union and its 200 million people to areas encompassing another half billion people.

HE REACHED the height of his power when he led the Soviet Union against the Nazis of Adolf Hitler as an ally of the United States and Great Britain. He was one of the "big three" of the world—with Britain's Winston Churchill and America's Franklin D. Roosevelt.

Stalin made a deal with Hitler in 1939 which shocked the rest of the world. The deal unleashed the war, but it granted Stalin precious time. When the Nazis struck at him, he was ready. He scorched the earth of Mother Russia and he fought. He fought so well that he punctured the myth of Nazi invincibility.

At Stalingrad, 10 years ago, the Russians fought for a city, block by block, house by house and room by room. There they smashed a great Germany army. In Russian history Stalingrad is known as the turning point of the war. From there the way led straight to victory and the world cheered Stalin and his countrymen.

BUT THERE WERE clouds in the bright sky of allied cooperation. When the war ended, the wartime store of good will

Turn to Page 10, Column 5

Body Of Premier To Lie In State

Moscow (Friday) (AP)—The Moscow Radio announced today that Prime Minister Stalin will lie in state in Moscow's famed Hall of Columns.

The broadcast said seven party leaders, headed by N. S. Khruschev, a secretary of the Central Committee of the Communist Party, will make funeral arrangements.

In Today's Star

TODAY'S CHUCKLE

If a man removes his hat in an elevator he has one of two things—good manners or hair.

Communists Lose Leader

JOSEF STALIN
Death Ends Long Career As Dictator

Craig Wins In House, Keeps License Bureau

By JEP CADOU, JR.

Governor George N. Craig scored a decisive victory yesterday when the Indiana House of Representatives dealt a death blow to a bill that would have taken the Bureau of Motor Vehicles from his control.

An effort by a coalition of Democrats and anti-administration Republicans to "blast" the measure out of committee was beaten 59 to 34 after an hour and a half of fiery debate.

All concerned conceded the bill now is dead for the session. It would have returned control over license bureau patronage to Secretary of State Crawford F. Parker.

THE GOVERNOR was supported by 57 Republicans and 2 Democrats who voted against the motion. He was opposed by 19 GOP members and 15 Democrats who were for it. Listed as not voting were five Republicans and two Democrats.

Probably the prime political issue of the 1953 session, the bill excited oratory which at times approached the boiling point.

Representative Norman J. Neely, Bloomington Republican and House majority leader, blamed the bill on "a small group of willful men playing politics in the Senate." The bill has passed the Senate Feb. 24 by a vote of 30 to 16.

Neely also blasted the Senate for failure to take prompt action on House bills which are stacked up in committees of the upper chamber.

"We've been diggin' and doin' the work while most of the Senate were shootin' off their big bazoos," he shouted.

"THEY'VE BEEN spending their time in hotel rooms trying to find ways to embarrass the Governor instead of considering bills," he added.

The GOP leader admitted "the Republican Party is a little bit torn to shreds" by the vehicles bureau dispute.

Robert S. Webb, Arcadia Republican, led the anti-administrative forces with a fire-and-brimstone speech in which he lambasted Craig for taking over the bureau from Parker last Jan. 12.

"It was an insult to the secretary of state, an insult to the Republican Party and an insult to the voters of Indiana," Webb thundered.

Webb hit particularly at the employment of Framcen Gruesbeck, as assistant commissioner of the bureau, and the alleged use of H. Dale Brown, Marion County clerk, as "unofficial patronage distributor."

WEBB RECOUNTED that

Turn to Page 2, Column 6

Van Fleet Rips Ammo Lack

Tells Senate Korea Fighting Hindered

Washington (INS) Gen. James A. Van Fleet testified yesterday that "serious shortages" of ammunition have beset United States forces in Korea and Senator Byrd (D-Va.) demanded that Defense Secretary Charles E. Wilson punish officials guilty of "criminal inefficiency."

Byrd asserted that Van Fleet's disclosure of a 22-month shortage of some types of ammunition, including hand grenades, proved that the Korean War has been "improperly prosecuted."

The former Eighth Army commander told the Senate Armed Services Committee the United States has not been doing "what it takes" to win the Korean War. He cited shortages not only of vitally needed ammunition but of skilled manpower.

Van Fleet declared the United States has lost "prestige, honor and influence" among its Allies, which can be regained only by a clear-cut military victory. He warned that signing an armistice with the Communists "would be a defeat."

BYRD ACTED AFTER hearing Van Fleet testify that he had made "almost daily" protests against the ammunition shortage. In asking punishment for those responsible for the shortages, he indicated he had court-martial in mind.

The Defense Department said "the situation" has been receiving the "urgent attention" of Wilson since the Secretary took office Jan. 20.

Byrd pointed out that Congress has appropriated $103,000,000,000 to the armed forces since the Korean war started. He said it is therefore "outrageous" that United States lives have been lost through ammunition supply failures.

The general declared that the United States has had neither the ammunition nor the men to "carry out a limited mission." He said the shortage of "junior leaders"—platoon commanders and non-coms—is 50 per cent, and the over-all manpower shortage 11 per cent.

As for ammunition, Van Fleet disclosed that shortages of some types have been so acute that it had to be flown from Japan for U.S. artillery on the Korean front.

The Weather

Joe Crow Says: Little Charlottes Ille in tends to "C" that the "A's" —Attucks, Alexandria and Amo —don't have it tomorrow at the Fieldhouse.

Indianapolis — Party cloudy and warmer today, turning colder tonight. Mostly fair tomorrow.

Indiana — Partly cloudy today turning colder in south portion. Mostly fair tomorrow.

Christ's Life Told

The daily Lenten feature, Memo to Caesar, will be found on Page 3.

THE WEATHER
Louisiana and Mississippi: Clearing and cooler Sunday. Monday fair and cool strong northerly winds on the coast. Sunday.

The Sunday Post-Herald

COMPLETE LEASED WIRE REPORT OF THE ASSOCIATED PRESS AND AP NEWS FEATURES.

Central News and Feature Service — VICKSBURG, MISSISSIPPI, SUNDAY, DECEMBER 6, 1953 — (Price 10 Cents) — No. 290

TORNADO DISASTER HITS CITY

Trapped Children Dug From Theater Debris Last Night

escue workers are pictured above digging into the debris of the aenger Theater which collapsed in the tornado late Saturday. hree children died in the theater, and three were still missing t midnight last night.

At Least 15 Killed, Injured Mounts Into Hundreds; Hits From River, Moves Through Heart Of Business District

A tornado swirled out of the southwest late yesterday, and in five awful minutes it etched a patch of death and destruction across Vicksburg from the river front diagonally through the heart of the business district, then hit its final punch on residential areas in the northwestern part of the town.

At least fifteen were killed.

The number of injured mounted into hundreds. Property damage was in the millions.

LISTED AS DEAD

Listed as dead by the funeral homes of Vicksburg were:

White—

Nick Cassino, Sr.

Lindsey Groves, two year old daughter of Mr. and Mrs. Thomas Groves.

Harlow Fried, Five year old son of Mr. and Mrs. Saul Fried.

Alvin Harwood, about 10 years old.

Robert Stanley Glatt, son of Mr. and Mrs. Dalton Glatt.

L. M. Langren of Dallas, Tex.

Colored—

Joe Winn

E. C. Parker

Monney Powell, Jr.

Susan Hebron

Henry Brown

Emma Pearl Johnson

Claudia Lewis Varnado

The twister struck with a mighty fury and deadly suddenness.

It churned its way from Levee Street up the west slopes and hit Washington street in the heart of town.

Four blocks, from Veto to China street were ravaged.

Then it twisted its way northeastward, smashed into the Saenger Theatre where nearly hundred people were watching a matinee movie; moved on across Courthouse Square and won through the residential areas of Adams, Fayette, Randolph and adjacent streets.

PEOPLE TRAPPED

In addition to the victims whose lives were snuffed out almost instantly scores were trapped in collapsing buildings.

The most tragic of these situations was at the Saenger Theatre where the massive roof of the building collapsed and buried over half the big auditorium.

Scores of people were in the theater at the time the twister struck, and frantic workmen struggled to move away the debris and dig out the victims.

At least three people died in the theater, and last night, there was still a few people missing.

Another theater, the Strand, suffered a less-serious collapse of its roof, but occupants were reported moved out safely.

The Happyland Nursery on Grove and Cherry streets was wrecked and two children died in this disaster.

On Washington street the Mississippi Hardware Company was a total wreck, and ten employees were trapped in the basement for three hours.

According to Manager V. W. Logan, they heard the tornado coming and as the building started caving in they ran to the basement.

The entire force at Palermo's Men's Shop was trapped when this building collapsed. They too remained under the debris for hours and at least two people from this store, Joseph Palermo, Sr., and Preston Gough were badly hurt.

Last night, young Jack Palermo, who was in the store at the time the storm struck, has not been found.

FIRES BREAK OT

Adding to the terror of the catastrophe were fires which broke out in the debris.

The big Union Compress, with an estimated thousand bales of cotton, caught and the blaze it made lighted the western sky.

Other fires raged in residential areas, and the Sears Roebuck Warehouse on Mulberry Street also had a fire, according to the fire department.

Mayor Pat Kelly said damage would run into the millions.

HELP FROM AFAR

Within an hour after disaster struck, relief agencies were mobilized, and soon help came from surrounding towns and cities.

The Red Cross set up headquarters in the telephone exchange with emergency stations at the Carr Central High School. The Y. M. C. A. and other public buildings were also staffed for emergency care of injured and homeless.

From surrounding towns and cities, ambulances, fire-fighting and emergency rescue equipment and personnel were rushed. Among those furnishing help were Tallulah, Jackson, Greenville and others.

The National Guard was called out and a state emergency clamped over the stricken area.

Other military reserves, particularly local companies of the Army, Navy and Marine Corps, furnished manpower and facilities, and the U. S. Engineers pressed men and equipment into service.

STRIKES SUDDENLY

The tornado blew in from the southwest at 5:35 p. m.

Several resident reported seeing it strike the city. Mrs. George Smart said it was visible from her home on Bazsinsky Road, and she could hear it roar.

Others reported hearing the tremendous noise which it made.

Mr. Logan at the Mississippi Hardware said he heard it coming and recognized the sound.

"I shouted it's a tornado," he said, "and tried to get to the front door to close it."

About that time, he continued, the front of the building began caving. He turned and shouted for everyone to go to the cellar.

He said they remained under a concrete stairway for added protection. They were in the building almost three hours.

Warrens Trapped Seven Hours

Mr. and Mrs. Leonard Warren were trapped under the debris of their store for seven hours before they were rescued.

As rescue workers dug toward them, they conversed with Mr. and Mrs. Warren. Mr. Warren told them he and Mrs. Warren were trapped by falling timber. A girder across his chest had pinned him to the floor.

Escape For Palermos

At Palermo's men's shop, the story was almost the same.

"The Lord was with us," said Joe Palermo, owner of the store,

(See Page Three)

Bill Logan Tells Of Escape From Miss. Hardware

Bill Logan, hardware dealer, leaned against the wall of his demolished store tonight and sighed.

"A half hour ago," he said, "I wouldn't have given three cents for my chances in there."

He had been in the store in the middle of the business district, when Vicksburg's worst tornado ripped through the city and in five minutes caused a million dollars damage.

"There were 10 of us in there," he said, pointing to the pile of stone, brick and lumber that once was a retail-wholesale hardware store.

"I heard the wind and said 'That's a tornado.' Then I heard the front glass blow in. I decided the best thing to do would be to go out back.

"We couldn't. The back door was jammed shut with debris. The building was shaking so we went down into the basement and hid under a concrete staircase. We listened to the building falling down."

Finally, after what seemed like a lifetime. Logan said he and the others decided the blow was over and left by the rear basement door.

"I don't know," he said wearily. "the Lord was with us, I guess. My warehouse in the next block was flattened. I guess it just wasn't my turn.

Small Tornado Hits In Area Near Sterlington, La.

STERLINGTON, La., Dec. 5 (AP)—State police said tonight that a small tornado struck a community about four miles from here on Louisiana highway 815, destroying five houses and damaging a store.

Police said 21 Negroes were made homeless. No serious injuries were reported.

Sterlington is in Ouachita Parish.

rench Premier Laniel l; Not Present At econd Big-3 Meeting

UCKER'S TOWN, Bermuda, . 5 (AP)—French Premier Joseph iel, officially reported to have n taken down with a chill and r, absented himself tonight n the second meeting of the Three.

resident Eisenhower and Prime ister Churchill were loaded for session with arguments for ication by France of the European army treaty. French Foreign Minister Georges Bidault, ng in for Laniel, heard them

n official French bulletin late ght said Laniel was under the of Lord Moran, Churchill's own doctor, and was running a high fever. French sources said he might have to stay in bed over the weekend—which would just about be the duration of the conference. He was said to have taken to his bed in mid-afternoon after being about in the morning and lunching with Eisenhower.

News photographers encountered him strolling just before noon looking well and pleased.

A "bar of secrecy," lowered over the proceedings as the conference turned to the delicate European Defense Community pact, prevented newsmen from learning whether

(See Page Three)

Only Nine Years Old, He Looked Like An Old Man

Roger Powers is only nine years old. But, his eyes tonight looked dead with the dullness you see sometimes in old men.

Roger got that look in 15 minutes inside Vicksburg's Saenger Theater tonight. It was Vicksburg's tornado look.

His voice was clear, however, when he said:

"I was in the front row when the roof fell in."

He paused for a second, his eyes wandering here and there, one hand going to the bandage that covered a big gash on his head. His other hand was clutched tightly in the comforting hands of his mother.

"It pinned me under the seats with a lot of other guys. It seemed like a long time before they pulled me out. Just my head was sticking out."

Those shocked eyes watched his mother. Roger was quiet now but his mother's anguished face told the story of that twitching body they pulled from the wreckage of the Saenger.

The boy's voice rose again. "The men came and began digging me out. When they dug out my seat they found another guy."

The voice rose a bit, hysteria haunting it. "Just his hand was sticking out.

"He was dead, I think."

"No, he wasn't," replied his mother as her son's voice died away.

She looked at reporters and you knew she lied.

Child Tells Of Destruction Of Saenger Theatre

Twelve - year - old Dalton Glatt brushed death tonight in a movie theater.

He was one of 34 boys and girls engaged in the American pastime of watching a Saturday night movie in the Saenger Theater in Vicksburg.

He was sitting on the back of his spine, relaxed and enjoying himself with his brother, Robert, 9.

Suddenly the screen on which unwound a drama from Hollywood began to whip and quiver. The building shook and a great roaring drowned out the words of the hero.

Dalton sat up straight. He looked from side to side. Others were doing the same thing.

"I saw the wall falling in," Dalton said later. "I jumped under a seat."

He winced in pain as a doctor worked with his broken arm.

"I thought my brother, Robert had jumped under too." he said after a little.

The doctor grimaced as if he had the broken arm. He opened his mouth, then closed it without words.

Robert didn't make it under the seat. He was killed by the falling wall.

But, no one could bring himself to tell Dalton.

xpect State Solons o Pass Most Of School rogram By Christmas

ACKSON, Miss., Dec. 5 (AP)—Mississippi's special legislative session xpected to pass before Christ- most of Mississippi' extenprogram to equalize Negro white schools.

wmakers are attempting to de- a working solution to the segtion problem facing this deeph state where whites barely umber Negroes.

o lawmaker has expressed op- tion to the idea behind the pron but some argue they ought vait until the U. S. Supreme rt hands down a decision on constitutionality of segregation he public schools

ly a small portion of the 33- multi-million-dollar project is ed specifically at equalizing arate grammar and high school ities.

e majority of the bills seek orrect ills in the school system modernize existing laws.

ost of the bills passed in six s of floor debate are describe 1 "a package program" some observers feel the representatives of the committee are doing just that.

Nevertheless, most of the lawmakers are doing their best to provide a program that will stand no matter what the U. S. Supreme Court rules.

The only bill passed by both

(See Page Three)

ov. Hugh White as necessary. if the equalization bills fail ass.

e exception, however, is Senbill 1204 which sets up a proof state aid for the construcschool buildings and auzes 30 million dollars in state s from which the counties l borrow to finance their buildprograms. A similar House bill is in the ways and means comce.

move by Rep. Ney Gore Jr., uitman County to suspend the s and remove the bill so the e could consider it failed by de margin.

hough the governor, in his ing message to a joint assemthe lawmakers the 11-member slative recess study committee not offering the program as

Tragedy Takes Two Lives At Local Nursery

A small group of volunteers worked frantically against time to save the life of a woman buried beneath five feet of brick, mortar and other debris at the Happyland Nursery on Jackson Street, but the bodies of two lifeless children were found nearby.

Mrs. Tommy Groves, wife of a Herald Linotype operator, was rescued but her small daughter and Harlow Fried, son of Mr. and Mrs. Saul Fried, perished as the tornado Saturday ravaged the nursery.

The workers dug with hands and shovels working in close quarters always facing the danger that the shell of the building would collapse.

At first, Mrs. Groves' voice, a bare whisper, was heard. Then an arm and finally her face was uncovered. After an agonizing hour, she was then pulled from the debris.

Miraculously, Mrs. Groves suffers only minor injuries. According to her husband, she has a fractured ankle, cuts and bruises.

G. Ross Freeman, Rural Authority To Be Speaker At Community Meet Here

The south's leading expert on rural development work will be the principal speaker for the annual round-up meeting of the Community Development program, according to an announcement Saturday by W. M. Covington, chairman of the Chamber of Commerce Agriculture Committee.

G. Ross Freeman of Atlanta, director of the Town and Country Church development program

The meeting will be held Thursday night at the Carr Central High School, with a barbecue supper sheduled at 7 o'clock and the business program set for 7:45.

The highlight of the banquet will be the presentation of nearly 5,500 in awards to the winning communities and individuals for work of the past year.

Six Vicksburg organizations which are sponsoring communities in the competition and the six communities will team to stage the barbecue dinner, and tickets may be purchas from any of the civic clubs, the community grous or the Chamber of Commerce.

Mr. Freeman is director of the Town and Country Church Development Program. This program is interdenominational and inter-racial. It is sponsored jointly by Emory University, of Atlanta, thirteen Southern state committees, and the Sears Roebuck Foundation.

"Mr. Freeman is considered to be one of the finest speakers in this section of the nation" declared W. M. Covington, chairman of the Chamber of Commerce Agricultural Committee, which is sponsoring the annual awards program. "We feel especially honored to have his as our speaker for this year. We earnestly hope that every member of the rural communities, every civic club member in Vicksburg, every member of the Ministerial Association, and all other interested persons will attend this meeting to hear Mr. Freeman's inspiring message on how to develop stronger communities through stronger churches."

Competing rural communities are Jeff Davis, Bovina, Jett, Culkin, Redwood, and Oak Ridge. Civic club sponsors are: Kiwanis, Lions, JayCees, Elks, Civitan, and Rotary Clubs.

Negro Porter Helped From Palermo's Where One Person's Missing

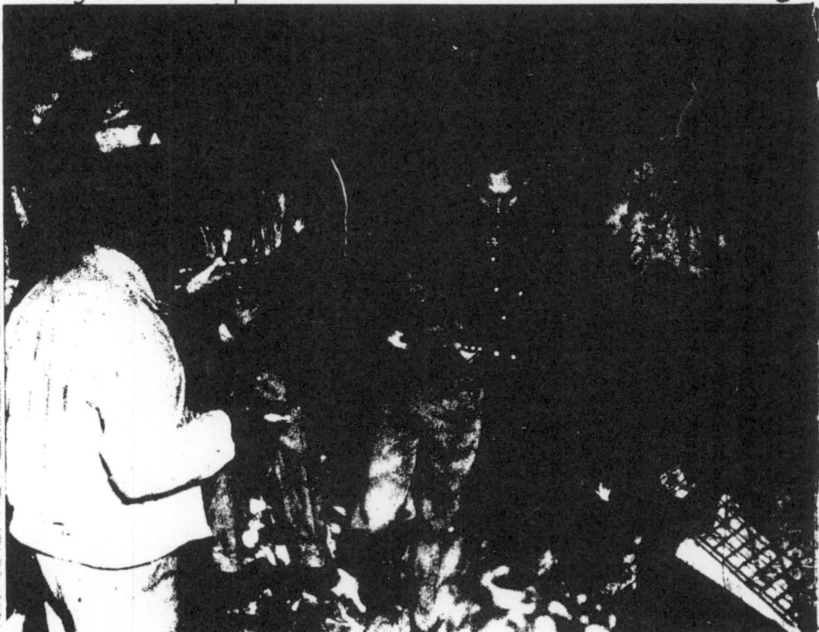

The negro porter is helped from Palermo's Clothing Store after the tornado struck. One person, Jack Palermo, is missing in the store.

1954

In a ruling of historic consequences, the U.S. Supreme Court held unanimously that racial segregation in public schools is unconstitutional.

The suit that began it all had been brought by the National Association for the Advancement of Colored People on behalf of an eleven-year-old schoolgirl, Linda Brown, who by order of the Topeka, Kansas, School Board had to attend a school exclusively for blacks.

The Supreme Court decision, on May 17, 1954, reversed an 1896 ruling that held that "separate but equal accommodations" for the races did not violate the Constitution. Speaking for the court, Chief Justice Earl Warren now said "that in the field of public education the doctrine of 'separate but equal' has no place."

There was some resistance to in fact ending the segregation of schools in some places, but by the end of the 1960s, court decisions and federal civil rights acts had attained at least token compliance with the 1954 ruling.

In the same year, Communist forces of Ho Chi Minh defeated the French at Dien Bien Phu in northern Vietnam, marking the end of French power in Indochina. A Geneva settlement separated Vietnam into North and South.

STATE **THE TOPEKA** JOURNAL

AN INDEPENDENT NEWSPAPER

By Stauffer Publications, Inc.

Topeka, Kansas, Monday, May 17, 1954—Twenty-four Pages

Home Edition

Official City Paper

FIVE CENTS

SCHOOL SEGREGATION BANNED

Supreme Court Refutes Doctrine of Separate but Equal Education

High Tribunal Fails to Specify When Practice of Dual Schools Must Be Dropped by States

Washington, May 17 (AP)—The Supreme court ruled unanimously Monday that segregation of Negro and white students in public schools is unconstitutional. But it said it will hear further arguments this fall on how and when to end the practice.

Thus many months — perhaps more time will elapse—before the historic ruling actually wipes out the separate schools now in existence in many states.

Chief Justice Warren read the court's opinion which declared:

"We conclude that in the field of public education the doctrine of separate but equal (sic) has no place. Separate educational facilities are inherently unequal.

* * *

"THEREFORE, we hold that the plaintiffs (Negro parents) and others similarly situated for whom the action has been brought are, by reason of the segregation complained of, deprived of the equal protection of the laws guaranteed by the fourteenth amendment.

"This disposition makes unnecessary and any discussion whether such segregation also violates the due process clause of the fourteenth amendment."

The fourteenth amendment was adopted after the Civil war, primarily for the benefit of slaves freed by President Lincoln. It says no state may deny any person due process and equal protection of the law, nor abridge their privileges of immunities.

* * *

THE CASES decided Monday—with the court's finding that segregation is unconstitutional—involved five states: South Carolina, Virginia, Kansas, Delaware and the District of Columbia.

But lawyers said a ruling against segregation would affect a total of 17 states which have laws requiring separation of the races in schools, plus three other states having laws which permit—but do not require—segregation.

* * *

THE COURT was told the 17 states and the District of Columbia had 70 per cent of the nation's Negro population, or 10,522,495 Negroes out of a 15,042,692 total. States with permissive segregation had an additional one per cent.

States whose laws require segregation were listed for the court as Alabama, Arkansas, Delaware, Florida, Georgia, Kentucky, Louisiana, Maryland, Mississippi, Missouri, North Carolina, Oklahoma, South Carolina, Tennessee, Texas, Virginia and West Virginia.

States with permissive segregation were listed as New Mexico Wyoming and Kansas.

* * *

AFTER reviewing a long line of decisions bearing on the "separate but equal" doctrine, Chief Justice Warren wrote:

"We come then to the question presented: Does segregation of children in public schools solely on the basis of race, even tho the physical facilities and other 'tangible' factors may be equal, deprive the children of the minority group of equal education opportunities? We believe that it does."

★ ★ ★ ★ ★ ★

Court Ruling Hailed

Segregation Already Ending Here, Say School Officials

Jacob A. Dickinson, president of the Topeka Board of Education, hailed the Supreme court's segregation ruling Monday as "in the finest spirit of the law and true democracy.

"In my opinion, the court has been very wise in deciding the basic question and then calling for further discussion by all parties as to orderly and reasonable application of the ruling," Dickinson said.

* * *

"**THE TOPEKA** Board of Education will, of course, continue the implementation of its policy to terminate the maintenance of segregation in the elementary grades as rapidly as practicable.'

For further details on segregation, see stories on page 6.

"The acceptance of this policy by the people of Topeka is a fine example for the rest of the country which I am sure will honor this decision of the Supreme court with temperate action and genuine compliance."

* * *

SUPT. WENDELL GODWIN said: "This action will have no effect upon Topeka schools because segregation already is being terminated in an orderly manner.

"During 1953-54, Randolph and Southwest schools were integrated. During 1954-55, Central Park, Clay, Crestview, Gage, Grant (partial), Oakland, Polk (partial), Potwin, Quincy, Quinton Heights, State Street and Sumner schools will be integrated.

"Subsequent steps will be taken in the light of experience accumlated during the first two steps. I've not had the opportunity to examine the court's ruling but I imagine that segregation will be terminated in Topeka before the Supreme court decides when and how it should be done."

Summary of Court's Segregation Ruling

Washington, May 17 (AP)—Here is the meat of the Supreme court's ruling Monday in the school segragation cases:

Segregation is unconstitutional—it violates the constitutional guarantee of equal protection of the laws.

A formal recree ordering it stopped will be postponed until after arguments on special points are heard at the fall term.

Attorneys general of the states involved will be invited to fill briefs by October 11 and to appear later before the court for further arguments on fixing an effective date when Negro students shall be admitted along with white children, and on how the order should be issued. This could be done either (1) by having a special master recommend specific terms for a final decree by the Supreme court or (2) by sending the cases back to lower federal courts for action.

Rainfall Spread Far Over State

Oakley Is High With 2.08 Inches

More rain is predicted for the Topeka area Monday night after intermittent showers Sunday brought .60 inch to the city.

Beneficial rains fell Sunday over wide areas of Kansas, with northwest and eastern portions getting the most.

Oakley was high with 2.08.

Other rainfall reports:

Chanute	.61	Frankfort	.43
Emporia	.62	St. Francis	1.09
Lebo	.78	Atwood	1.46
Garnett	1.15	Colby	1.35
Paola	1.45	Oberlin	1.06
Osage City	1.23	Hoxie	1.56
Herington	.76	Cedar Bl'ff dam	1.63
Willard	.66	Ellis	.99
Lecompton	.61	Norton	.72
Lawrence	.75	Hill City	.85
Valley Falls	.58	Garden City	.28
Holton	.68	Dodge City	.03

TODAY'S CHUCKLE

"So you are building a new house, eh? How are you getting along with it?"

"Fine. I've got the roof and the mortgage on it already, and I expect to have the furnace and the sheriff in by fall."

FOLKS AND THINGS

By 2054 This Bill Should Be Terrific

By GORDON F. MARTIN (State Journal Staff Writer)

LIKELY it was that Jim Lane and his Free State army raiders figgered it weren't no crime to steal a hoss from a Kentuckian nohow.

A Kentucky man couldn't be nothin' but a Southern sympathizer. And even if he had no slaves hisself, he couldn't be nothin' but a no-good Democrat who didn't deserve to own a hoss anyway.

So just go on out to his place southeast of town and git a hoss anytime you need one, boys. And don't bother to pay for it.

* * *

NOW MAYBE that's the way old Jim Lane used to counsel his Free Soil militia when "the boys" were ridin' around roughshod over anybody who got in their way. And maybe Lane's riders didn't have to be told about how to "git a hoss" without paying for the animal.

However it was, some of Jim Lane's men stole a couple of valuable horses from James R. Warren. They also took some guns, clothes and shoes, and some blankets too. James Warren itemized his losses when he filed a claim with the Shawnee county Probate judge against the Territory of Kansas.

Lane's men, he swore, took property with a value of $268.50, and took it at the point of a gun.

* * *

THAT WAS in 1856. Warren's claim was processed a year later but never paid.

Now nearly 100 years later, Warren's grandson, who is Frank J. Warren, former Topeka mayor, figures that $258.10 claim has earned compound interest which makes it worth $84,873.93 today.

A bill for that amount was presented to Governor Arn Monday by Warren who said, in a letter:

"The State of Kansas has owed the original amount of this claim for approximately 100 years and I feel sure my native state will want to make some arrangements to pay an honest debt that is long past due. In any event, I hope it will not be allowed to accumulate for another Centennial, lest my grandchildren will have claim on all the state income and half the land value."

* * *

WARREN said with a grin that he didn't expect to hold his breath until the state paid off. But he indicated that what the Centennial needs is a gag or two along with its historical aspect, and he says that he has had some enjoyable moments digging into family history in the state's Centennial year.

Warren's grandfather, James Warren, was a wagon boss on the old Santa Fe trail, and after his bullwhacking days, he moved from his native Kentucky to a homestead on Deer creek. That was in 1854.

Frank Warren remembers how his father used to tell of Grandfather Warren's precautions against Free Soilers' raids on his farm home.

"Grandfather always had a horse saddled and ready," said Warren, "because they used to run him off periodically. I guess it was because he was a Kentuckian and a Democrat. His homestead was in the Deer creek area north of old Vinewood park."

* * *

THIS WAS Warren's letter to Governor Arn, outlining his Grandpa's claim, as shown by photostatic copies of records of the territorial probate court:

"I am enclosing herewith a claim as part of the estate of my grandfather, James R. Warren, in the amount of $84,873.93 for livestock, merchandise and equipment taken by force of arms by Jim Lane and his Free State army during the month of September, 1856, approximately 100 years ago. This claim was properly processed and accepted by the state (Kansas Territory) on December 10, 1857.

"The claim at first glance may seem out of proportion to the original amount ($268.50). I figured the amount on the basis of compound interest which I believe is the only fair method that could be used in computing the amount due. I am not sure you are the proper official to burden with this just and unfortunate claim. While the original amount may not seem large, I am sure it was a tremendous loss to my grandparents who were striving desperately to eke out a living on the claim they homesteaded on Deer creek 3½ miles southeast of Topeka on October 10, 1854.

"**ANYWAY**, two or three hundred dollars was a lot of money in those days, and $84,873.93 is a lot of money in these days, as far as I am concerned."

Warren indicated he didn't expect to get the state to rush to the treasury and write a check.

"I would like very much to know," his letter concluded, "before the close of this centennial year, what disposition is made of this claim."

And he must have grinned when he wrote this postscript: "Unless this claim is returned in 30 days, I will assume it is being processed for payment."

Turnpike Bonds Authorized So Suit Can Start

Supreme Court Will Clear Legal Air in Friendly Action

The Kansas Turnpike authority Monday formally approved issuance of 140 million dollars in revenue bonds for the 234-mile proposed Kansas turnpike.

In so doing, the KTA deliberately stuck its neck out in a legal way to become a target of a friendly-type quo warranto suit by the state to determine the legality of the KTA's actions and the law under which it operates.

A quo warranto action in substance inquires of the defendant: By what right do you act in this matter?

The state agency also incorporated in resolutions other actions and a set of bylaws thought necessary to offer Atty. Gen. Harold R. Fatzer something to challenge.

* * *

WILLIAM TIMMERMAN, assistant attorney general, said the suit would be filled within a few days.

The suit, to be filed as an original action in the Kansas Supreme court, is being brought to make sure no legal hitch develops after the turnpike gets under construction, and to facilitate the huge bond sale.

Altho the court has never ruled directly on any phase of the KTA, lawyers believe the high tribunal has ruled favorably on similar questions in other unrelated suits.

* * *

BESIDES AUTHORIZING the bond issue, the KTA named Topeka as headquarters for the turnpike, and specified regular meetings as the second and fourth Mondays of each month at 10 ah. Special meetings can be called any time, with proper notice.

The KTA also approved entering a trust agreement with financial institutions to secure the bond issue, and receiving a proposal from the First Boston Corp. and Smith, Barney and Co., both of New York, Kansas municipal bond companies and six Kansas City, Mo., firms for sale of such bonds.

Topeka Can Hear Centennial Star on Monday Night

Topekans will get a chance to preview the singing of Lucille Norman, feminine singing star of the Centennial pageant, Monday night.

Miss Norman will sing as a guest star in an original operetta on "The Railroad Hour" at 7 pm. The operetta has been written by Jerome Lawrence and Bob Lee, producers of the radio program.

The program will be carried by radio station WDAF.

It takes a lot of calculating with an adding machine to figure compound interest, Frank J. Warren says, on his grandfather's claim for two horses stolen by Jim Lane's men in 1856.

State Journal Photo

Laying Track at the Fairgrounds for 'Cyrus Holliday'

This special crew from the Santa Fe railroad was hard at work Monday morning putting down a 300-foot strip of track on which the 1880 Cyrus K. Holliday locomotive and one car will chug into the Centennial pageant. The operaion was almost identical to the type of work done in early days to move the tracks across native prairie—rough-hewn ties, light rail and tracks laid directly to bare earth.

Future of Probe Uncertain After President Rules

Eisenhower Cloaks Top-Level Meeting on Army's Charges

BULLETIN

Washington, May 17 (AP)—Senators investigating the McCarthy-Army row Monday recessed until next Monday to give time to try to clarify a Presidential order forbidding further inquiry into high-level administration conferences.

Washington, May 17 (AP)—The future of the McCarthy-Army hearings was thrown in doubt Monday by a Presidential order—denounced by Senaor McCarthy as an "iron curtain"—shutting off inquiry into whether "higher-ups" directed the Army's charges against the Senator.

The Senate Investigations subcommittee recessed its public hearings at 11:55 am. to consider in closed session what stand it might take on Eisenhower's order.

McCarthy, claiming that "this cover up" made it impossible to get at the truth, declined to say, when asked by reporters, whether he might walk out on the hearings if the subcommittee accepts the order.

* * *

THE PRESIDENT'S order was laid before the subcommittee when it convened, and received a calm reception at the time.

But later, Senator Jackson (D-Wash.), McClellan (D-Ark.) and Symington (D-Mo.) fired a few critical volleys at it.

McCarthy asked for a five-minute recess to confer with his aides, Roy M. Cohn and Francis P. Carr, about their course in the light of what he termed this "almost unbelievable situation."

* * *

RTURNING, he told the subcommittee: "I must admit I'm at somewhat of a loss as to what to do at this moment."

"For some fantastically strange reason," he said, "the iron curtain is pulled down" forbidding testimony concerning what was said or done at a meeting last January attended by Attorney General Brownell, top White House aide Sherman Adams, and others.

McCarthy said:

"The American people will not stand for a cover-up half way thru these hearings."

* * *

McCARTHY described the January 21 meeting as one at which the charges the Army has fired at hime of "improper" pressures to get favored treatment for Pvt. G. David Schine, "were instigated and conceived."

Workmen Busy at Fairgrounds Setting Stage for Biggest Show

By BOB ROTER (State Journal Staff Writer)

There was plenty of action at the Kansas Free fairgrounds Monday as workmen tackled the job of getting the area ready for the Centeninal pageant.

Immediately in front of the grandstand, carpenters were rapidly putting up a 32x64-foot stage. Lighting equipment was rolling in from all directions.

Members of the Topeka stagehands union were installing the lighting equipment and moving scenery bracing out to the front of the grandstand.

To the last of the stage, a 15-man crew from the Santa Fe railroad were laying ties and rails for the Cyrus K. Holliday train.

* * *

AND THAT WAS a rather large operation in itself. The section gang doing the job was under the direction of John Laris of 705 Jefferson.

Trucks were moving second-hand ties into the area and dump ing the mon the ground. Periodically a truck with several rails would drive up and dump off the

TOPEKA 1954 1854 CENTENNIAL

rail lengths.

Standing by to watch the proceedings and make suggestions were John Urlacher of 1641 Buchanan, Sante Fe roadmaster, and Herb Miller of Emporia, division engineer from Emporia.

"We are trying to lay this rail as aeuthntically as we can," Miller and Urlacher commented.

* * *

THEY POINTED OUT the ties have been laid on bare earth, just as was done in the early days.

"We're putting rails right across 'prairi sod' just like they used to do it," Urlacher said.

The rails were spiked directly to the rough-hewn ties instead of being set on leveling plates as is now done. There were no fancy machines to set the ties, ballast them or put down the rails. It was all hand work.

e Th heavy rails—heavier than were originally used to bring the railroad to Topeka—were manhandled by the crew is the same fashion original track-laying crews worked.

* * *

BECAUSE OF the muddy condition of the track where the train will run for part of the distance, plans were being made to put in a little chat for ballasting. None of the rest of the 300 feet of track will be ballasted.

Tuesday, the 1880 Cyrus K. Holliday locomotive, tender and one car will be switched down to about Nineteenth and Harrison. There it will be loaded on a truck and moved to the fairgrounds, unloaded and put on the specially-laid rails.

Meanwhile right in front of the grandstand, the carpenters were hard at work getting the framework for the specially-built stage in place. They, too, were hampered some by the mud of the track.

* * *

THE STAGE will be elevated 3 feet from ground level and have scaffolding and bracing at the rear for the scenery built by stagehands during the past few weeks.

William Meader, produced-director of the pageant, and Allen Cooke, his assistant, were sitting in the stands going over last minute details on the stage and its construction.

Lighting equipment occupied a large area just to the west of the regular fairgrounds stage. Most of it is yet to be installed.

However, some of the heavy lighting equipment was already going up on decks attached to the grandstand.

Buy Parade Seats Now, Committee Urges

Four thousand bleacher seats will be set up on the south side of the statehouse grounds along Tenth for Saturday's Centennial parade, but this number will be augmented if necessary.

Early demand has been brisk.

Ed Dyer, whose committee is carrying out this project, said an additional 1,800 seats will be brought from Kansas State college if demand warrants. Those wanting parade bleacher seats are asked to buy them not later than Tuesday, at $1 apiece, at the municipal auditorium.

Tickets for the Centennial pageant at the fairgrounds May 22-25 are also on sale at the auditorium.

Centennial Street Decorations Will Go Up on Tuesday

Decoration of downtown streets for Topeka's Centennial celebration, May 22-25, will begin Tuesday.

The decorations which include red, white and blue banners, 6 by 10 feet, will be placed on electric light poles on Kansas from Fourth to Tenth; the 100 block east and west on Sixth and the 100 block on West Eighth.

* * *

THE DECORATIONS, furnished by the merchants' division of the Chamber of Commerce, feature the word "welcome."

They are of nylon and were ordered especially for the Centennial.

REVIEW DENIED

Washington, May 17 (AP)—The Supreme court Monday denied six Kansas City firms a review of their unsuccessful suits to collect about a million dollars from the United States for damage caused by the 1951 Kaw river flood.

The Forecast . . .

Forecast for Topeka and vicinity: Partly cloudy Monday afternoon, considerable cloudiness Monday night with thundershowers in the Topeka area. Tuesday partly cloudy, cooler Monday night and Tuesday, low Monday night 50, highs Tuesday in 70s.

For Kansas: Partly cloudy extreme east, elsewhere considerable cloudiness Monday afternoon and night, with scattered thunderstorms extreme west late Monday afternoon or evening, spreading to west and central by night; Tuesday considerable cloudiness with scattered showers central in morning and scattered thunderstorms developing over most of state in afternoon or night; slightly cooler northeast and extreme east Monday night; low night 45 to 50 extreme northwest, elsewhere in 50s.

Hourly Temperatures

(At Municipal Airport)

Midnight	57	8 am	61
1 am	56	9 am	62
2 am	56	10 am	63
3 am	56	11 am	64
4 am	55	Noon	66
5 am	56	1 pm	65
6 am	57	2 pm	67
7 am	60	3 pm	66

Temperature extremes Sunday: In the nation 103 at Presidio, Tex., 25 at Frasier, Colo.; in the state: 80 at Dodge City, 50 at Goodland.

Precipitation in last 24 hours, .60; normal precipitation to date, 9.93; amount received, 6.42; deficiency, 3.51.

High here Sunday, 69; low, 55; normal, 64; average, 2 degrees below normal.

Highest temperature on local record for this date, 92 in 1907; lowest, 39 in 1945.

Day Before Big Celebration Starts

Friday Night's Street Dance Will Climax Beard-Bonnet Era

Topeka's bearded and bonnetted clans will have their big day Friday according to Frank Harwi, Centennial executive director.

Harwi reported judging of beards and bonnets will take place about 9 pm Friday at the parade reviewing stand at Tenth and Van Buren. Three cash prizes will go to winners in both the beard contest and the bonnet contest, he said.

* * *

THE JUDGING will be held during the intermission of the huge street dance being planned for Friday night.

He asked all persons wanting to enter either of the contests meet at the rear of the reviewing stand at 8:30 pm.

Harwi also said the winners of the two contesst will ride near the front of the parade Saturday in a convertible.

No requirements for entry have been set other than the beard or bonnet.

1955

Shifts in world leaders:

President Juan Perón was ousted in a bloodless coup d'etat in Argentina.

Sir Anthony Eden succeeded Winston Churchill as prime minister of Great Britain.

Georgi Malenkov resigned and was succeeded by Nikolai Bulganin as premier of the Soviet Union.

Ngo Dinh Diem became ruler of South Vietnam.

In the United States, polio cases, which had been rising for almost a generation, dropped sharply as a result of a vaccination for children.

The vaccine had been developed by Dr. Jonas Salk and first administered to schoolchildren in Pittsburgh, Pennsylvania, before the nationwide program began.

Blacks boycotted segregated bus lines in Montgomery, Alabama, and the Reverend Dr. Martin Luther King, Jr., the boycott leader, gained national prominence by advocating passive resistance to segregation in public places.

SCRIPPS-HOWARD

The Pittsburgh Press

VOL. 71, No. 291 | TUESDAY, APRIL 12, 1955 | WEATHER—Mild and wet.

—Baseball—
FINAL
Latest Stocks
70 Pages—5 Cents

POLIO IS CONQUERED

Public Airing Urged on Transit Bill

County Legislators Advocate Hearings

[Feigel joins transit bill supporters, Page 23; an editorial, "Let's Have a Hearing!" Page 2, Sec. 2.]

A drive to hold public hearings on the mass transit authority bill was rolling in high gear today.

Three Allegheny County legislators, who are members of the committee that has pigeonholed the bill, came out in favor of airing the proposal.

Urging that the bill be put under the public spotlight so that all of the various viewpoints can be heard are:

Rep. Joseph P. Rigby, Shadyside Republican.

Rep. Maurice H. Goldstein, Squirrel Hill Republican.

Rep. David M. Boies, Clairton Democrat.

Want Hearings in City

Both Republican assemblymen think the hearings should be held here in Pittsburgh instead of Harrisburg where they normally are held. Dr. Boies did not specify any particular location.

This was the first "thaw" in the legislative ice-jam that has piled up around the bill since it was introduced last February.

It came on the heels of mounting public pressure to give the voters a chance to decide whether they want a County-wide authority to take over the mass transportation lines.

Business and civic leaders strongly endorsed the referendum over the week end. This was followed yesterday by declarations of support from County Commissioner John M. Walker, Oakmont Republican, and Pittsburgh's Democratic Mayor David L. Lawrence.

"Neutrals" Encouraged

Meanwhile, the two majority commissioners, Democrats John J. Kane and Harry W. Fowler, who have been standing pat on a "neutral" position, said they are "encouraged by the new show of interest in the transit bill."

Chairman Kane even went so far as to say that he "personally favors the bill." But he "won't push it until it's clear there is substantial support from the public."

Commissioner Fowler commented that he would "like to get an expression of opinion from the various boroughs and townships in the County."

The Allegheny County Assn. of Townships is slated to discuss the bill April 20. The counterpart association of boroughs has no plans at this time to even consider the bill.

Both Commissioners Kane and Fowler were instrumental in setting up the two study committees which proposed the creation of a transit authority and drafted the enabling act.

Because of lack of public enthusiasm, they adopted a strategy of "watchful waiting and withheld giving it all-out support. The bill has been tied up in committee ever since it was introduced.

In the latest proposal for pub-

Continued on Page 13, Column 1

Biggest Thrill Came 31 Months Ago

It's Anti-Climax for Dr. Salk

He Was Confident of Success After Blood Check in 1952

It was strictly an anti-climax for Dr. Jonas E. Salk to learn today that his polio vaccine had passed its crucial tests.

He experienced his big once-in-a-lifetime thrill exactly 31 months ago.

It came shortly after Labor Day, 1952, when blood samples taken from the first children to be inoculated with the vaccine were being checked at his University of Pittsburgh laboratory.

As Dr. Salk peered through a microscope at the test tubes which contained the blood specimens, he saw the evidence he was looking for.

Cells planted in the tubes were growing normally despite the fact they had been infected with deadly polio virus. This meant only one thing:

The vaccine was working.

From that day on, Dr. Salk never wavered in his conviction that the vaccine could prevent polio under natural conditions as well as in the laboratory.

That's why today's official verdict "didn't come as any surprise—it was something that was to be expected."

How does he feel now that the suspense is over?

"Well, there's little to say," Dr. Salk observes, "other than it would be nice to take a week end off."

Week-end holidays have been a rare luxury for Dr. Salk since he plunged into polio research here seven years ago.

The 40-year-old scientist is a human dynamo. He often spends seven days a week in the lab at Municipal Hospital and sometimes puts in as many as 18 hours a day.

"But he's no different now

Continued on Page 2, Column 1

—United Press Telephoto

LIFE-SAVER in wording off crippling polio is this little bottle. It contains enough Salk vaccine for complete immunization of one child.

—United Press Telephoto

DR. THOMAS FRANCIS JR. DR. JONAS SALK
Polio fighters flash victory smiles.

Rain Forecast Today, Tomorrow

Thunderstorms To Hit District

Raincoat weather is forecast for the Pittsburgh district for today and tomorrow.

It will be mostly cloudy with scattered showers or thunderstorms today, tonight and tomorrow.

But the temperature will be mild, the high today 72, low tonight, 52, and high tomorrow, 72.

Istanbul that Dingbat is shadowing? Nein; is not a bull. Is how a matador ducks out of the rain.

Salk Medal Urged

NEW YORK, April 12—Rep. Steven B. Derounian, Republican of New York, said he would introduce legislation in Congress tomorrow to award Dr. Jonas E. Salk an appropriate medal for developing the anti-polio vaccine.

Took Pictures at Courthouse

Photo Ban Violators Guilty of Contempt

Publishers, Cameramen to Appeal 5-Day Jail Terms, $100 to $500 Fines

GREENSBURG, April 12 (Special)—Publishers and cameramen who defied the "photo ban" at Westmoreland County Courthouse today were found guilty of criminal contempt.

They were sentenced to five days in jail each with fines ranging from $100 to $500.

However, President Judge Richard D. Laird stayed the sentences when the defendants filed immediate notice of appeal to the State Supreme Court.

The defendants are David W. Mack, publisher of the Greensburg Tribune; William Block, publisher of the Pittsburgh Post-Gazette; Andrew Bernhard, Post-Gazette editor; Vince Johnson, reporter; James G. Klingensmith and Don Bindyke, photographers, and Robert Purdy, a free-lance photographer hired by the Tribune.

Each was released on his recognizance pending the appeal.

They had taken pictures last Dec. 28 of John Wesley Wable, condemned "Phantom Killer" of the Pennsylvania Turnpike, as he walked to the courtroom to hear his sentence.

During Wable's trial months before, Judge Edward G. Bauer had forbidden news photographers from the courthouse limits. His order was upheld by Judges Laird and John M. McConnell.

Photographers were kept, at that time, from snapping any pictures of Wable, adhering to the judges' rule.

The photo ban says, in part:

"No picture or photographs shall be taken, immediately preceding or during sessions of this court or recesses between sessions, in any of the

Continued on Page 2, Column 6

Official Report Given to Leader

Drug Scandal Costing State Millions Charged

GOP System Invited Bribery, Graft, Deputy Attorney General Tells Governor

By L. R. LINDGREN, Press Harrisburg Writer

HARRISBURG, April 12—A State drug-buying scandal broke wide open today when Gov. George M. Leader received an official report showing "wilful negligence" had cost the State at least one million dollars a year.

The Governor termed the disclosure both "startling" and "fantastic."

He took immediate steps to speed up an over-all investigation of State buying practices to plug loopholes that might involve losses running into millions more.

The report was made by Deputy Attorney General John Sullivan.

He charged that the purchasing system used by previous Republican Administrations was "an open invitation to graft" manipulation, bribery, extortion, price rigging and favoritism.

Attorney General Herbert B. Cohen declared the report confirms charges made last week by Democratic State Chairman Joseph M. Barr that Republicans were guilty of "financial manipulation for political profit."

Two Allegheny County Republicans — Sen. Robert D. Fleming and Assemblyman Joseph P. Rigby — have served notice that they intend to demand proof of Senator Barr's

Continued on Page 13, Column 3

Blizzard Hits Northern Plains

By THE UNITED PRESS

Winter howled back into the Northern Plains today with a surprise April blizzard which piled up more than a foot of wet snow and marooned scores of motorists amid fast-piling drifts.

The freak storm hit Wyoming, Colorado and Nebraska without warning last night and was going strong today.

A school bus containing two children and the driver was missing somewhere in the snowy wastes along the Wyoming-Colorado line. At Kendall, Neb., zero visibility and impassable drifts forced a snow plow to give up its attempt to rescue uncounted scores of marooned drivers.

Rain Postpones Pirate Opener

The Pittsburgh Pirates-Brooklyn Dodgers National League opener scheduled in Brooklyn today was postponed because of rain.

The two teams will open the season at Ebbets Field tomorrow, originally an open date, after which the Pirates will fly here to open the Bucs' home season Thursday.

Vietnamese Flee Reds

SAIGON, Indo-China, April 12—A record number of 8000 refugees from Communism in the north arrived here to seek safety in free South Viet Nam yesterday.

Vaccine To By-Pass Wholesalers

Doctors, Hospitals, Druggists to Get It

The Salk polio vaccine will be rationed out to doctors, hospitals and druggists as fast as it can be produced.

To speed up the process and prevent possible piling up in warehouses when the vaccine is needed elsewhere, wholesale drug firms will be by-passed in the first crucial months of distribution.

At least two of the drug manufacturers already making the vaccine are ready to start commercial shipments — which will retail at $2 per shot plus the doctor's fee — as soon as the Government licensing agency gives the go-ahead signal.

It almost came today.

Changed Mind

The Federal Department of Health, Education and Welfare first announced it would license the vaccine for commercial use at 4 p. m. today.

Then it changed its mind and said the licensing had been postponed.

The delay was ordered to give the experts more time to study today's report on the vaccine's effectiveness, a spokesman said.

The department then said an announcement will be made "later" on whether or not the vaccine will be licensed for general use.

Won't Take Long

Once the Government stamps its okay on the vaccine, it could be available commercially in Pittsburgh within 48 hours.

Harry J. Loynd, president of Parke, Davis and Co., said the pharmaceutical industry can produce enough vaccine to immunize all of the 61 million Americans under the age of 21 by the end of this year.

Within two years, he added, there will be enough available to inoculate everyone in the world who needs it.

With official release of the report verifying success of the Salk preparation, Eli Lilly and Co. announced that it has stockpiled "millions of doses" of the vaccine, which will be shipped directly to doctors, hospitals and druggists who have placed "provisional" orders.

And Parke, Davis and Co. announced at the Ann Arbor, Mich., meeting today that it will build a new plant at Detroit specifically to manufacture the Salk vaccine.

Company officials said they hope to be producing 900,000 anti-polio shots a week before the end of this year.

One Pittsburgh drug wholesaler estimated the direct shipment from manufacturer to doctors will continue for "at least" a month "until the confusion dies down."

Right at the outset, although drug firms have been preparing for more than a year for today's news, there is going to be a commercial "shortage" of the vaccine, since the National

Continued on Page 2, Column 1

Mayor, Governor Laud Dr. Salk

Medical Society Sends Tribute

"A prophet is not without honor, save in his own country and in his own house."

That ancient sentiment went down the drain today as the City of Pittsburgh, the Commonwealth of Pennsylvania, and the Pennsylvania Medical Society hailed Dr. Jonas E. Salk for the success of his polio vaccine.

In rapid-fire style, they sent tributes to Ann Arbor, Mich., where Dr. Salk saw the official world unveiling of his vaccine.

Mayor David L. Lawrence lauded Dr. Salk and his coworkers as "a prideful example of Pittsburgh's ever-growing importance as a center of medical care and research."

Gov. George M. Leader immediately announced the young scientist will be given Pennsylvania's highest award —the Medal of Meritorious Service.

And with a mingling of pride and humility, President Dudley P. Walker announced:

"The Medical Society of the State of Pennsylvania and its 11,000 members gratefully accept this new weapon against a disease which has caused such sorrow and tragedy to so many families."

As the rest of the world laid

Continued on Page 2, Column 6

THE WEATHER

Tuesday, April 12, 1955

Eastern Standard Time

Local—Mostly cloudy and mild with scattered showers and thunderstorms late this afternoon, tonight and Wednesday. High temperature today and tomorrow 72 degrees. Low tonight 52.

Temperatures at Pittsburgh 24 hours ending at 7:30 a. m. today—Highest 74, lowest 55, mean 65.

Highest and lowest temperatures a year ago 51 and 41. Partly cloudy.

Downtown temperature readings reported by the United States Weather Bureau.

Midnight	59	9 a. m.	59
1 a. m.	60	10 a. m.	62
2 a. m.	60	11 a. m.	65
3 a. m.	60	Noon	66
4 a. m.	58	1 p. m.	67
5 a. m.	58	2 p. m.	69
6 a. m.	58	3 p. m.	70
7 a. m.	58	4 p. m.	69
8 a. m.	58		

Highest temperature this date since 1874, 84 in 1878.

Lowest temperature this date since 1874, 22 in 1910.

Barometer reading at 3 p. m., 30.02, rising.

Humidity at 3 p. m., 50%.

Sunrise 5:47 a. m., sunset 6:55 p. m.

River stage at 3 p. m., 16.7, Fal.

FIVE-DAY FORECAST

Wednesday, April 13, through Sunday, April 17—Western Pennsylvania, Ohio, West Virginia and Western New York—Temperatures will average two to three degrees above normal. Turning cooler Wednesday afternoon and night. Cool on Thursday. Warmer Friday and Saturday. Showers and thunderstorms Wednesday and Saturday will total one-third inch. The average daily normal temperature for Pittsburgh for the five-day period is 49 degrees, the average daily maximum temperature is 59 degrees and the average daily minimum temperature is 38 degrees.

MAP AND DETAILED REPORT, PAGE 42

Salk Shots 80 to 90% Effective

[Other pictures and stories, Pages 2, 18 and 19; texts of reports on polio vaccine tests, Page 5; an editorial, "The Victory Over Polio," Page 2, Sec. 2.]

By JOHN TROAN, Pittsburgh Press Staff Writer

ANN ARBOR, Mich., April 12—Medical science has triumphed over polio, a dread disease that has scourged mankind for more than 160 years.

The dramatic victory, so sweeping it overwhelmed even the scientists who had gathered here, was scored by the vaccine developed by Dr. Jonas E. Salk at the University of Pittsburgh.

Dr. Thomas Francis Jr., of the University of Michigan, announced here that the vaccine prevents paralyzing polio in 80 to 90 per cent of the children who get it.

"There can be no doubt now that children can be inoculated successfully against polio," Dr. Francis declared.

"The vaccine works. It is safe, effective and potent."

Dr. William G. Workman, chief of the government bureau which licenses medical preparations, announced immediately that the vaccine will be released to the public as quickly as drug houses can cut through the necessary red tape.

Some Scientists Weep

The impact of Dr. Francis' announcement was terrific.

Some of the scientists actually wept at the news.

The report was handed out first to newsmen assembled in a giant makeshift newsroom on the University of Michigan campus. The scene was packed with drama that is equaled only on momentous occasions.

Copies of the report, 113 pages long, were brought in on a big dolly.

An armed guard from a secret printing room where the material had been impounded since the report was completed Sunday afternoon accompanied it.

Newspaper reporters, radio and television men scrambled to get their copies. Then came a wild dash for phones and typewriters to spread the news to the world.

People leaped over tables and slapped each other on the back. Scientists in the corridors en route to the start of a formal scientific meeting didn't even have to wait for Dr. Francis to say a word.

"It works, it works," newsmen shouted.

Called 'A Planned Miracle'

Doctors began shaking each other's hands and passing out congratulations to Doctor Salk and members of his research team, virtually all of whom were present for the historic occasion.

Even as the scientists were shaking their heads over what one outstanding researcher termed "a planned miracle," Dr. Salk stepped up to electrify them with a new report concerning the effectiveness of the vaccine.

He disclosed that tests on children in Allegheny County in the past two years showed that only two shots are needed instead of three, to build up immunity to polio.

He recommended, therefore, that youngsters be given two injections spaced two to four weeks apart, with a booster shot seven months or so later.

He said the booster seems to offer protection for years afterward but he still isn't sure how many.

Right now, it looks like boosters will be needed only once every two to 2½ years.

If Dr. Salk's two-shot schedule is substituted for the three-injection timetable that has been used up to now, it means there will probably be enough vaccine to inoculate 45,000,000 persons this year.

This would be sufficient to immunize every child

Continued on Page 2, Column 7

Means More Vaccine Will Be Available

2 Shots Enough to Prevent Polio

ANN ARBOR, Mich., April 12 (Special)—Two instead of three shots of Salk vaccine can prevent polio.

This was announced this morning by its discoverer, Dr. Jonas E. Salk, after hearing the historic announcement of the vaccine's success at the University of Michigan.

Dr. Salk said studies on children in Allegheny County during the past two years have convinced him it is best to give two injections of vaccine two to four weeks apart, followed by a booster dose seven months or so later.

The booster shot, he explained, "triggers" a person's resistance to polio to a "remarkably high level."

In the 1954 field trials of the vaccine, nearly two million school children received three inoculations over a five-week period.

By reducing the number of shots, enough of the Salk vaccine will be available to protect 45 million children—all those in the nation under 15 years of age—before the end of this year, if no adults ask for the shots.

Dr. Salk's talk followed a report by Dr. Thomas Francis Jr. on the effectiveness of the vaccine in which the drug was called 80 to 90 per cent effective.

The researcher spoke from a paper prepared before he was told of Dr. Francis' findings.

Dr. Salk asserted that the maximum effect of the booster shot can be gotten only if it is given at least seven months after the first inoculations.

How long the booster will last, he said he didn't know as yet. But he said it should be good for "years."

Dr. Salk further urged that all children who had received polio shots during the 1954 field trials be given an additional booster dose this year.

This is necessary, he explained, because the three shots given over a five-week period during the field trials could not have produced more than a primary effect — short term immunity to polio.

Long term immunity to the disease, he said, can only be accomplished by a booster shot given months after the first two doses of the Salk drug.

Special Section In Press Today

With today's Press there's a special 24-page section for Gimbels.

On Inside Pages

Press Telephones

Want-Ads —COurt 1-4900
Other Depts. —COurt 1-7200

1956

The fog was thick the night of July 25, 1956, off the New England coast.

The Italian liner *Andrea Doria* was about 45 miles south of Nantucket, Massachusetts, headed for New York. Outbound, just five miles from her, was the Swedish liner *Stockholm*.

They collided that night, the *Stockholm* tearing a hole in the starboard side of the *Andrea Doria*.

The French liner *Ile de France* sped to the accident scene and helped in the rescue of nearly seventeen hundred people. Fifty-one others died.

The *Andrea Doria* went down to a watery grave.

FAIR PLAY
THURSDAY—Fair, highest in mid-80s.
FRIDAY—Same.
Full Report on Page 2

The Boston Daily Globe

Reg. U. S. Pat. Off.
VOL. CLXX No. 26
Copyright 1956 By GLOBE NEWSPAPER CO.
BOSTON, THURSDAY MORNING, JULY 26, 1956
36 PAGES—FIVE CENTS

GUIDE TO FEATURES

2 Liners Crash Off Nantucket

Andrea Doria Abandoned; Hundreds Are Picked Up; Stockholm's Bow Crushed; Fog Hampers Rescue

Over 2500 Passengers on Stricken Vessels

Ile de France at Scene; 3 Injured on Stockholm

The Andrea Doria was listing badly but still afloat, with her passengers and crew being removed, at 4 this morning.

Two hundred were taken aboard the vessel Cape Ann, 200 had been transferred to the Isle de France, some 50 are aboard the Army vessel Thomas and 425 on the Stockholm.

The liner Stockholm reported "three serious casualties" and asked for a helicopter to remove them.

Two crack ocean liners collided in fog 45 miles southeast of Nantucket late last night and most of the 1700 passengers and crew of the Italian Line's Andrea Doria had abandoned the listing ship by 3 this morning.

The SS Stockholm, her bow shattered and taking water in forward holds, was limping toward New York at slow speed, four hours after the crash.

Passengers and crewmen of the 27,000-ton Doria were transferred to the liner Ile de France and the fruit ship Cape Ann in those vessels' lifeboats after the Doria's were rendered useless by the heavy list.

LINERS CRASH Page Seven

TWO LINERS IN COLLISION OFF NANTUCKET—Italian luxury cruiser Andrea Doria, top, and Swedish SS Stockholm.

$50 Million Project Periled by Toll Road

Prudential to Abandon Back Bay B. & A. Yard Site If Restricted

By WILLIAM J. LEWIS

The chairman of the Massachusetts Turnpike Authority favors extension of the East-West Toll Road into the Back Bay over the Boston & Albany line and engineering studies began yesterday.

This route may endanger a planned multi-million dollar development in the railroad's soon-to-be-abandoned Back Bay yards.

The Prudential Insurance Co. intends to erect a $20 million office building on the B. & A. site as part of a $50 million development project. It may now decide to look elsewhere than Boston for a site.

Should any appreciable amount of land beyond the present roadbed be required by the Turnpike Authority, a Prudential spokesman said, "it is very likely" that his company's full plans could not be realized.

Fred Smith, vice president of Prudential, said that "in the event our entire development cannot be built on this site we are not interested in the project at all."

Mayor Hynes, Boston Chamber of Commerce officials and other interested parties have indicated they will demand an alternate route for the toll road be selected, should the Prudential project be jeopardized.

TOLL ROAD
Page Twenty-one

$3.7 Billion Compromise On Foreign Aid Wins OK

WASHINGTON, July 25 (UP)—House and Senate negotiators agreed today on a compromise $3.7 billion foreign aid money bill with a ban on nearly all future military aid to Communist Yugoslavia.

The measure now goes to the Senate and House for final approval. The $3.7 billion is half way between the Senate-voted $4 billion aid fund and the House's $3.4 billion.

The conferees alloted $2 billion for direct military aid, nearly $1.2 billion for "defense support" indirect military aid, $260 million for economic assistance, $152 million for "point four" technical assistance and $185 million for miscellaneous programs.

President Eisenhower originally had requested $4.9 billion. The compromise was more than $1 billion less than that, but about $1 billion greater than the $2.7 billion in new funds voted last year.

The compromise also authorizes the Administration to spend about $240 million in left-over aid funds from previous years. This would bring the total available this year to nearly $4 billion, compared to the $3.2 billion available last year.

President Eisenhower earlier today was described as "most pleased" by the Senate action yesterday in approving the full $4 billion.

FOREIGN AID
Page Three

NHRR Surveying 39 Lines; Seeks to Drop Losing Ones

(See Also Page 20)

The New Haven Railroad will begin a study of 39 branch lines today to determine which are losing money and will request permission to abandon those that are.

A railroad spokesman said that he was sure the parts of the Old Colony branch would come under the study.

He said the road has a request pending to drop passenger service in Connecticut on the Waterbury to Winsted line.

Alpert said the petition was made to the Connecticut Public Utilities Commission, which already is considering a petition to drop service on the line from Hartford to Boston, by way of Putnam and Willimantic.

NEW HAVEN
Page Five

Baseball Results

AMERICAN LEAGUE
Kansas City 9, BOSTON 6.
New York 10, Chicago 1.
Detroit 6, Baltimore 2.
Cleveland 11, Washington 3.

NATIONAL LEAGUE
Milwaukee 7, New York 4.
Brooklyn 2, Cincinnati 1.
Pittsburgh 9, Chicago 8.
St. Louis 8, Philadelphia 7.

RED SOX TODAY
At Kansas City (Sullivan vs. Herriage). 4 p.m. Radio-WHDH.

Comic Dictionary

BRAINS

What a really clever girl hides behind a low neckline.

Blood Test On Sgt McKeon Showed Alcohol

By ROBERT S. BIRD

PARRIS ISLAND, S.C., July 25—A medical test on S Sgt Matthew C. McKeon 3½ hours after he led a night march into a tidal stream where six recruits drowned, showed a measurable quantity of alcohol present in his blood, a Navy Medical Corps man testified today.

MARINE TRIAL
Page Five

Nixon-vs-Herter Choice Put Up to Ike

Salem Man Dies, 7 Hurt in Fall Of N.H. Chair Lift

By CHARLES TARBI

GILFORD, N.H., July 25—Three investigations into the collapse of an aerial chairlift, which plunged a Salem, Mass., man to his death and injured seven passengers, will be launched tomorrow morning.

Structural engineers, insurance investigators and state officials will inspect the litter of steel cable and damaged chairs lying along the 3200-foot sloping side of Rowe Mountain, in the Belknap Recreation Area.

William M. Kirby Jr., 33, of 70 Lawrence st., Salem, was dashed onto a rock ledge 20 feet below his swaying chair when the lift's 6400-foot cable broke at 10:30 this morning.

CHAIR LIFT
Page Six

Stassen to Fight on for Bay Stater Unless President Backs Californian

By DON WHITEHEAD

WASHINGTON, July 25—Presidential aid Harold E. Stassen said today he will drop his "dump Nixon" drive in the event President Eisenhower says in unmistakable terms he wants Vice President Richard M. Nixon as his running mate.

Stassen made this statement to reporters at the end of a political stormy day during which:

1. He bluntly accused Republican National Chairman Leonard W. Hall of trying to bar the door of the Vice Presidential nomination to all save Nixon.

2. He declared Nixon, in confidential polls of public sentiment taken during the last four weeks, had emerged as the weakest of eight potential Republican candidates for the Vice Presidency.

3. He disclosed he had called Gov. Christian A. Herter by telephone last week and told Herter he would seek the nomination for him. He said the Massachusetts governor did not try to dissuade him.

4. He hinted broadly that prior to the Republican convention in San Francisco next month the President "will make his position clear. The statement implied that Stassen clung to a hope of support from the President although most politicos here regarded it as "whistling in the dark."

STASSEN—NIXON
Page Eight

Passengers On Doria

Among those reported to be aboard the Andrea Doria were the following:

MAYOR RICHARDSON DILWORTH of Philadelphia and Mrs. Dilworth.

MORRIS NOVAK, president of radio station WOV, New York city and his wife.

GEORGE P. KERR, European manager of Proctor and Gamble and family.

ROBERT T. YOUNG, principal surveyor for the American Bureau of Shipping, and family.

ISTZAN RABOVSKY and his wife Nora Kovach, international dancers.

LIST
Page Six

Exchange of Radio Calls

Here is the dramatic story of a collision at sea as snatched by the Coast Guard radiomen from a series of distress messages flashed from ship to ship:

★ ★ ★

11:22 p.m.—(From the Stockholm). We have collided with another ship. Please. Ship in collision.

★ ★ ★

12:08 a.m.—(From the Stockholm). Collided with other vessel in position 40 34N 69 45W. But still undetermine our damage.

★ ★ ★

12:09—(From the Stockholm). Badly damaged. Full bow crushed. Our No. 1 hold filled with water. We have to stay in our position. Help if you can.

MESSAGES
Page Seven

Parents of 6 Teen-Agers Face Auto-Ban Hearings

Parents of six teen-agers are scheduled for hearings before Registry of Motor Vehicles officers today in the second round of a statewide crackdown on motorized juvenile delinquency.

In each instance parents will be asked to show cause why registration of the family automobile should not be revoked because of irresponsibility evidenced by the young drivers.

First round in the campaign was conducted in the Malden Registry of Motor Vehicles yesterday by Registrar Rudolph F. King.

Parents of three youths were heard privately by King.

King said after the hearing that he would announce in a few days his decision as to whether registrations of the parents would be revoked.

TEEN-AGERS
Page Nine

Ruth Roman, Son Aboard Stricken Liner

Ruth Roman, Boston actress who achieved Hollywood stardom was among passengers aboard the Andrea Doria. She was returning home from a vacation with her son Richard Hall.

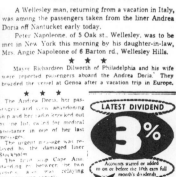

RUTH ROMAN

ROMAN
Page Seven

Natick Sailor Found Guilty of Maine Murder

BATH, Me., July 25—A Superior Court jury after only 41 minutes of deliberation early tonight found Richard B. Woods, 21-year-old Natick, Mass., sailor guilty of first degree murder.

He was convicted of murdering Wilfred Blais, 47, in a $140 holdup in his Topsham grocery store on April 7.

Under Maine law the mandatory sentence is life imprisonment, but Justice Leonard F. Williams deferred sentencing. Defense counsel Harold J. Rubin, who presented no witnesses, said he would appeal the conviction to the State Supreme Court.

WOODS GUILTY
Page Three

Pay Raise Bill Enacted; Herter Veto Predicted

The Massachusetts Legislature enacted a bill last night for a 10 percent, across-the-board pay raise for 34,000 state employees, but a veto by Gov. Herter is predicted within the next few days.

Herter has declared his unalterable opposition to this Democratic-sponsored measure—especially its $300 minimum and $500 ceiling.

PAY RAISE
Page Six

BULLETINS

A Wellesley man, returning from a vacation in Italy, was among the passengers taken from the liner Andrea Doria off Nantucket early today.

Peter Napoleone, of 5 Oak st., Wellesley, was to be met in New York this morning by his daughter-in-law, Mrs. Angie Napoleone of 6 Barton rd., Wellesley Hills.

★ ★ ★

Mayor Richardson Dilworth of Philadelphia and his wife were reported passengers aboard the Andrea Doria. They boarded the vessel at Genoa after a vacation trip in Europe.

★ ★ ★

The Andrea Doria, her passengers and crew abandoning ship and her radio knocked out by the list, called for medical assistance in one of her last messages.

The urgent message was relayed by the damaged liner Stockholm.

The fruit ship Cape Ann, standing by between the two vessels, also was relaying messages and reports.

BULLETINS
Page Seven

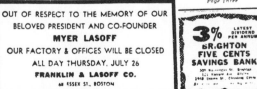

1957

After the U.S. Supreme Court had, in 1955, ordered an end to segregated school systems "with all deliberate speed," many districts in the South began making plans to comply. But in other areas, there was resistance.

In Little Rock, Arkansas, Governor Orval Faubus called out the state National Guard in September 1957 to prevent the integration of Central High School.

President Eisenhower sent federal troops to Little Rock to enforce the court order.

Nine black students entered the school guarded by troops.

A foreign word—*Sputnik*—became common to much of the world.

The Soviet Union launched this baby satellite on October 4, 1957, providing the first manmade object to orbit the earth.

The beep-beep-beep from Sputnik's radio transmitter sent the United States scurrying into the space race.

Arkansas Gazette.

Registered U. S. Patent Office

VOL. 138—NO. 259. LITTLE ROCK, SUNDAY, SEPTEMBER 15, 1957.—112 PAGES—NINE SECTIONS ★ ★ ★ ★ PRICE 15c

Little Rock Forecast

Partly cloudy with isolated thundershowers today and tonight; a little cooler tonight. A high of 86 is predicted today and a low of 56 tonight. Yesterday's high 89, low 64.

(Details, Weather Map on Page 3C.)

Faubus Asks Compromise; Ike Refuses Commitment

In the News

Andrei Gromyko, Russian Foreign minister, landed at McGuire Air Force Base, N. J., in a new Russian jet airliner to take personal charge of his country's embattled United Nations delegation, and told a crowd of 200 persons: "The 12th session of the UN General Assembly is to consider a number of international problems of paramount importance toward maintenance and strengthening of peace and development of international co-operation. The correct settlement of these problems will enhance the authority of the United Nations."

Secretary of State John Foster Dulles will fly from Washington to New York today to debate cold war issues with the Russian delegation in the UN Assembly.

Crooner Frank Sinatra was reported by the London Evening Standard to be planning to marry actress Lauren Bacall, widow of actor Humphrey Bogart, "within six months."

Chief Justice Earl Warren is taking a three-day course in Jewish judicial processes, dating back more than 2,000 years, at the Jewish Theological Seminary of America at New York.

Wladyslaw Gomulka, Polish Communist boss now in Yugoslavia for talks with President Tito, ignored the United States exhibit and visited the Russian pavilion at the International Fair at Zagreb.

Mayor de Lesseps S. Morrison of New Orleans said at Chattanooga that even with integration taking place rapidly by legal means there would "never be more than 3 or 4 per cent of the Negro population in integrated schools and parks."

Mrs. Franklin D. Roosevelt, 72, was reported suffering a mild stomach upset at Moscow after several days of strenuous touring Russian provinces.

Elsa Cardenas, 22, Mexican actress who appeared in the motion picture "Giant," was married at Houston to Guy Preston Patton, 36, independent oil operator.

Mrs. Dorothy Paul, 26, a polio victim, was removed from an iron lung at Shreveport, La., in time for the birth of her six-pound, 4-ounce son.

William Maynard, 23, was fined $100 at Ukiah, Cal., for starting a forest fire that cost $30,000 to control when he set signal fires to attract help while lost on a deer-hunting trip.

Actress Lilli Palmer, divorced in February from British actor Rex Harrison, said at Paris she would marry Carlos Thomson, an Argentine actor, within the next three weeks.

Rt. Rev. Henry Knox Sherrill, president bishop of the Protestant Episcopal Church, will receive an honorary degree of doctor of civil law in a special convocation at the University of the South at Sewanee, Tenn., today.

Rev. Gerald H. Kennedy, Methodist bishop of Los Angeles, urged the denomination to abolish its special administrative agency for Negro churches, telling a Church conference at Los Angeles: "It doesn't work, it is impractical and it is wrong."

Thor Heyerdahl, adventurer-scientist of Kon-Tiki fame, has a new book out on his latest expedition seeking proofs for his theory on ancient migration from South America to Polynesia, his publishers said at Oslo, Norway.

Pope Pius XII, in a speech made public at the Vatican, urged members of Roman Catholic religious orders to abstain from smoking, public vacations and extended "pleasure trips," declaring that elimination of such "superficial articles" from their lives was necessary as a symbol of priestly humility.

William C. Spire, 34, a combat pilot in World War II who is on active reserve status despite a crippling attack of polio in 1954, received the customary "greetings" from his Selective Service board at Omaha, Neb., and jubilantly sat down and wrote this chatty thank-you note: "Ever since the enactment of the Selective Service Act of 1939 I have been consistently ignored. This can, you know, lead to the conclusion that people just don't want me. I am both pleased and honored to return herewith your questionnaire."

Admiral Jerauld Wright, supreme Allied commander in the Atlantic, said at Norfolk, Va., he thought it was "extremely unlikely" that big-scale fleet maneuvers by Russia and Allied nations might produce contact of ships or planes, thus causing incidents.

On the Inside

Governor Reiterates Views at Mansion

By CHARLES T. DAVIS
Of the Gazette Staff

After he returned to the Mansion last night at 11:15 Governor Faubus chatted amiably for a half hour with this representative of the Arkansas Gazette.

While he added little to his previous public statements, Mr. Faubus said:

1. That he simply hadn't made up his mind what he would say at his press conference today about maintaining the National Guard troops around Central High School.

2. That it is possible that he will have something definite to say about the Guards around the Mansion.

3. That his basic attitude was still that first expressed in Pulaski County Chancery Court when he said that he had no objection to integration so long as it was peacefully accomplished. "Remember," he said, "We went ahead and integrated three other schools in Arkansas."

4. That he had no official reports of the trouble at Ozark, one of the schools referred to, where Negroes had entered the local schools but are now out of school again as a result of local pressures.

5. That he could not comment on any conversations at Newport yesterday with President Eisenhower and other members of the Administration.

The weary governor conducted this informal interview at a table in the Mansion breakfast room over a cup of coffee. Also present were Mrs. Faubus and members of the governor's staff.

Turkey Tells Syria It Won't Attack

Damascus, Sept. 14 (AP).—Turkey has sent assurances that its Army is not poised to attack Syria, Foreign Minister Salah Bitar said today.

Bitar, said Turkey had notified the Syrian government that troop movements in Turkey were routine maneuvers carried out every year at this time.

Syria hopes, Bitar said, the Turkish operations "will only be maneuvers and not be followed by something else."

As tension over Syria's leftward moves seemed to be relaxing, the Russian government announced yesterday a new warning to Turkey that an assault on Syria would lead to world war. This warning came from Russian Premier Nikolai Bulganin in a letter charging that Turkish troops were massed at the Syrian border for an assault.

New Reports on Troops

A government spokesman said Syria had received new reports of Turkish troop concentrations at the border but that "it does not bother us."

"We don't expect an attack," he said, but "we have to be ready in case of any emergency."

For the last few days only Army officers have been recalled to duty, the spokesman said. "It's not even partial mobilization. We have been calling up officers just to be ready • • • When everybody concentrates on your borders you try to prepare for defensive measures."

He said Syria was studying—but "not taking very seriously"—Egyptian reports that American armored units had arrived secretly in Israeli and were massing there.

Blast at Israel

President Shukri Kuwatly was quoted by Damascus radio as saying Israel represented the greatest threat to Syria and other Arab nations and was "looking to usurp more Arab lands."

The spokesman said Syria had dropped the idea of asking her neighbors whether they really expressed anxiety to the United States about events here. He said all the neighbors had already "denied expressing anxiety."

Pledges of Aid

Syria got further assurances of friendship today from Saudi Arabia and Iraq.

At New York, Ahmed Shukairy, the Saudi minister of State for United Nations affairs, said Saudi Arabia would stand by Syria in an attack "from whatever quarter." Here at Damascus, Jamil el Madfai, former Iraqi premier and now chairman of Iraq's upper house, told newsmen that any aggression against Syria "will be regarded as directed against Iraq."

Twisters Kill 2 in Oklahoma

By the Associated Press

Tornadoes smashed through rural communities in Central Oklahoma last night, killing a farmer and his wife, injuring several persons and destroying a number of houses.

Police reported at least 15 buildings damaged or destroyed at Sacred Heart, Okla., about 50 miles southeast of Oklahoma City. Another twister at Bethel, Okla., destroyed or damaged 25 to 30 houses, they said.

Haskell Campbell, 48, and his wife, Jewell, 42, were killed when their house was destroyed near the Sacred Heart school. Their daughter, Nancy, 10, was injured.

The funnels, rare at this time of the year, dipped out of a disturbance moving over Oklahoma, Texas and Arkansas. Large hailstones fell in several areas and damaging winds whipped across level prairieland.

To the South, a wind described by some observers as a tornado struck Wichita Falls, Tex., destroying a service station and damaging a drive-in cafe and several houses. The wind was accompanied by heavy rain and hail.

Hailstones the size of baseballs pounded Oklahoma City. Union City, Okla., also was hit by hail.

Arkansas Area Alerted

A severe weather warning including the possibility of tornadoes in parts of Arkansas, Oklahoma and Texas had been issued by the United States Weather Bureau at Little Rock last night.

The Bureau said:

"Scattered severe thunderstorms accompanied by large hail, tornadoes, and locally damaging surface winds are expected over most of southeast and eastern Oklahoma, extreme west central Arkansas, most of north central and northeast Texas this evening and early Sunday from 8 p. m. this evening until 2 a. m. Sunday.

"The approximate area is bounded by Abilene, Tex., Tulsa, Okla., Hot Springs, Ark., Palestine, Tex., and back to Abilene."

Going to the Moon? Hurry! Reds Say They'll Do It by '65

Moscow, Sept. 14 (UP).—A leading Russian scientist said today that Russia planned to send manned rockets to the moon, Mars and Venus by 1965. Y. C. Khlebtsevich, a missile expert, outlined detailed plans for interplanetary flights in an article in the Literary Gazette.

Khlebtsevich said the project called for an assault on each of the planets in turn—the moon between 1960 and 1965 and Venus and Mars between 1963 and 1965.

He estimated the trip to Venus would take 146 days and to Mars 258 days.

The article said Russian scientists planned to attack space in these three stages:

1. Unmanned rockets guided by radio from the earth will first blaze the interplanetary trail.

2. Unmanned "armored laboratories" would then be fired to positions on the planets to reconnoiter them by television.

3. Multi-stage rockets would deliver a manned "scientific station" to each of the planets.

Khlebtsevich referred to Russia's recent announcement that it has successfully tested an intercontinental ballistics missile as evidence it possesses "all the necessary means to build cosmic rockets."

He said Russia is prepared to launch space conquest on the basis of principles worked out by the late Russian rocket pioneer Konstantin Tsiolkovsky, who has been credited with laying the groundwork for the intercontinental ballistic missile three decades ago.

—United Press Telephoto

Does This Handshake Seal Agreement?

President Eisenhower and Governor Faubus say goodby after their conference on the Little Rock integration crisis while Attorney General Herbert Brownell Jr. (center) and Representative Brooks Hays (Dem., Ark.) converse in the background.

Status of Troops Still Unanswered

By MERRIMAN SMITH
Of the United Press

Newport, R. I., Sept. 14.—Arkansas Governor Faubus went to President Eisenhower with a compromise plan for settling the Little Rock school crisis today and then appealed to federal authorities to be patient in enforcing desegregation.

After a two-hour and 10-minute conference with the president, Mr. Faubus was asked if the meeting had materially changed the situation in Little Rock, where National Guard troops are keeping Negro students out of Central High School at the governor's command.

"I wouldn't know," Mr. Faubus replied.

The United Press was informed that Mr. Faubus had presented a compromise to the president under which integration of the Little Rock schools would be delayed for a year-long cooling-off period.

In return, it was said, Mr. Faubus offered to co-operate fully to help prepare the people of Little Rock for integration.

President Eisenhower was said to have listened to Mr. Faubus' plan without making any commitments. He made no reference to it in a brief statement issued after Mr. Faubus had given his version of the meeting to newsmen.

The two men talked privately for 20 minutes in Mr. Eisenhower's vacation office and then were joined by their aides for an hour and 50 minutes more. Among those at the meeting was Attorney General Herbert Brownell Jr. who is behind an effort to get a federal court injunction against Mr. Faubus halting his use of troops in Little Rock.

Attending with Brownell were Sherman Adams, chief White House aide, and Gerald D. Morgan, the president's chief counsel.

With Mr. Faubus at the conference were Representative Brooks Hays (Dem., Ark.), who arranged the meeting, and Arnold Sikes, the governor's executive secretary.

Left Smiling

When Mr. Faubus entered the meeting he was reportedly "ready to go to jail" if a solution could not be found. He left smiling and rushed to his hotel to prepare his statement.

The Supreme Court school desegregation ruling must be carried out, Mr. Faubus said, but changes cannot be made overnight.

"I entertain the hope that the Department of Justice and the federal judiciary will act with understanding and patience in discharging their duties."

Mr. Faubus pledged he would abide by the United States Constitution and by any "valid" court orders. Mr. Eisenhower said he recognized that Mr. Faubus had the "inescapable responsibility" of preserving law and order in his state. "I am gratified by his constructive and co-operative attitude at our meeting," the president said.

No mention was made of the National Guard troops that the governor sent to Little Rock's Central High School September 2 to keep Negroes from enrolling. He has defied three federal court orders to call off the troops and is under subpoena to appear in court September 20 to fight a proposed injunction against him.

When asked whether he would withdraw the Guard from the School Monday, Mr. Faubus said:

"I'll have to take care of that problem when I return home."

Solution Outlined

It was learned Mr. Faubus outlined to the president a possible solution to the crisis without a "direct showdown" between the federal and Arkansas governments over the use of troops.

At a news conference after his meeting with Mr. Eisenhower, Mr. Faubus would not comment on any compromise proposals. But it was learned that Mr. Faubus did offer a compromise that would include suspension of any federal court action pending a one-year cooling-off period. That also would mean a one-year delay in integrating Little Rock's public schools.

An understanding resulting from the conference would have to meet the approval of Federal Judge Ronald N. Davies, who has ordered three times that integration go into effect in Little Rock, only to be defied by Mr. Faubus.

Meeting Cordial

The meeting between Mr. Faubus and Mr. Eisenhower was cordial. The two men smiled and shook hands when they met and when they said goodbye.

"Good luck," Mr. Eisenhower said beaming, "and I hope this all works out."

The Arkansas governor flew to

(See MEETING on Page 2A.)

Texts

Texts of the statements issued in Rhode Island yesterday by President Eisenhower and by Governor Faubus will be found on Page 2A along with the transcript of Governor Faubus' press conference at Providence.

Home Again, Faubus Has No Comment

Governor Faubus returned at 10:40 p. m. yesterday to Little Rock from his meeting with President Eisenhower. But he would say nothing about their Rhode Island talk.

Asked about the conference, the governor said "no comment."

Mr. Faubus appeared extremely tired after the long flight from Providence, R. I. He said nothing about the status of the Arkansas National Guard troops which have been at Little Rock Central High School for two weeks.

Asked about a copyrighted article in the Detroit News last night to the effect that the governor agreed with Mr. Eisenhower to "gracefully" remove the troops in exchange for easy treatment in a federal court suit, Mr. Faubus smiled faintly.

"The Detroit News is perfectly free to speculate," he said, "and if they're lucky it's fine. If not it's their responsibility."

The governor agreed after prodding by a horde of newsmen to hold a press conference between 1 p. m. and 2 p. m. today. No hint was given as to whether he would further clarify the result of his talk with Mr. Eisenhower.

Plane 4 Hours Late

Mr. Faubus' two-engine plane landed at Adams Field more than four hours after it had been scheduled originally. The governor's party stopped at Covington, Ky., about 6 p. m. to eat and was delayed on takeoff by bad flying conditions.

A crowd of 150 persons containing many of the same persons who have showed up in front of Central High School during the two weeks of the integration impasse, cheered several times when the governor walked from the newsmen toward the administration building at Adams Field. Mr. Faubus removed his hat and waved greetings. Finding that he was going in the wrong direction, an aide led him back to the landing apron where two sedans and a State Police car awaited. Although tired, Mr. Faubus was smiling and cheerful.

The crowd began gathering at the airport before 8 p. m. and remained despite the governor's late arrival.

Hays Flies to Texas

Representative Brooks Hays of Little Rock, who accompanied the governor to Rhode Island, left Mr. Faubus' party at New York city to take another plane to Texas on a speaking mission for the Southern Baptist convention.

Confusion Remains

The lack of any definite statement by the governor left confusion as to what he actually had said earlier in a press conference after meeting with the president.

Key figures on both sides of the integration battle line during the afternoon had awaited hopefully the governor's return and hoped for clarification.

They noted that Mr. Faubus had pledged to obey the law on

(See REACTION on Page 2A.)

See Editorial On Page 4F

Did Faubus Gain or Lose In Duel With Government?

By ELIZABETH CARPENTER
Gazette Washington Bureau
1302 National Press Building

Washington, Sept. 14.—What has Governor Faubus gained—or lost—in his duel with the federal government?

In adding up the score, Washington observers note these side effects of the governor's use of the National Guard to bar Negroes from attending Little Rock Central High School:

1. Mr. Faubus' appearance in the spotlight of controversy has revived interest in charges of vote fraud in the 1954 Democratic primary which saw him elected governor by a 5,000-vote margin.

2. Segregationists, hailing the Arkansas governor as their new champion, are booming him for chairmanship of the Southern Governors Conference.

3. If Mr. Faubus has gained vote support among Arkansas segregationists, by the same token he has lost the backing of Negro voters which many political observers think put him in office in 1954 and may have kept him there in last summer's primary.

Francis A. Cherry, unseated by Mr. Faubus in the 1954 gubernatorial primary, has told friends that a switch of the Negro vote, which he says went almost totally for Mr. Faubus, would have reversed the outcome. There are about 65,000 Negro voters in Arkansas. Asked to comment on Mr. Faubus' action in the Little Rock integration dispute, Cherry refers to his statement as governor when the Supreme Court decision against school segregation was handed down in May 1954:

"Though I do not approve of the Court decision, as long as I am governor I will never lead Arkansas into a lawless course. Arkansas will obey the law. It always has."

Cherry now is a member of the Federal Subversive Activities Control Board.

Negro Vote Sold?

An editorial of the State Press, a Little Rock Negro newspaper, charging that Negro votes were sold to put Mr. Faubus in office in 1954, is being widely circulated here. Several national news exposes are in the making concerning not only an alleged sale of Negro votes but the 1954 returns from Madison County, Mr. Faubus' home county.

While the federal government has no power to probe an election of a state ticket, it now has two investigations of 1956 general elections underway in Arkansas: The West Memphis vote probe which will be brought before the Grand Jury in September, and a preliminary probe into vote charges on the national ticket in Madison County. If these materialize, a state investigation could expand the probe into the Madison County returns.

Incidentally, Mr. Faubus' request in Rhode Island today for "patience and understanding" from the Justice Department and federal courts was interpreted here as a plea for the government to hold back an FBI report which will support a Justice Department petition for an injunction against the governor. The report is considered fatal to the governor's claim that the threat

(See EFFECTS on Page 2A.)

Red Feather Drive Has Record Goal

A record goal of $611,840.35 has been set for the 35th annual Red Feather campaign in Pulaski County.

This is an increase of $25,712 over last year and includes 32 agencies in health, welfare and youth training and the Arkansas Children's Hospital.

The fund-raising campaign will get underway September 23.

Edward M. Penick, general campaign chairman, said that no out-of-town fund-raising organization would assist in the campaign this year. The appeal will be made by the Chest's staff and over 5,000 volunteers for a saving of over $12,000.

Penick emphasized that there was no "cushion" in the goal. "It represents the minimum needs of our agencies," he said.

Four per cent of the goal has been set aside for collection losses and emergencies and 2.9 per cent for campaign expenses.

Campaign headquarters have been opened at 208 Louisiana. The telephone number is FRanklin 2-3355.

Take $1,000 and Multiply by . . .

General Chairman Edward M. Penick holds a fraction of the Red Feather goal—a $1,000 bill.

Detroit News Says
Faubus Set To Pull Guard 'Gracefully'

Detroit, Sept. 14 (UP).—Governor Faubus and President Eisenhower made a deal in which the Arkansas governor agreed to "gracefully" withdraw National Guard troops from embattled Little Rock Central High School, the Detroit News said tonight.

In return, said the News, the Justice Department will "exercise restraint" in its prosecution of a pending Federal Court order requiring Governor Faubus to show cause why he should not be enjoined from using guardsmen to block racial integration at the school.

The copyrighted article by Robert S. Ball said the information came from the "highest possible authority" after the president and Governor Faubus met today at Newport, R. I.

Under the agreement, said the News, Faubus would pull out National Guard troops "and turn policing powers over to a possibly augmented state police and to the local municipal authorities."

The News quoted its source as saying, "the greatest accomplishment today was that the president and his top advisers came to a realization that there is a peculiar problem in enforcing federal statutes in touchy areas of the South and at the same time the Arkansas governor acknowledged the fact court decrees must be complied with."

There is hope the injunction now sought against Faubus will not be issued, the News source said.

City Edition

ARKANSAS DEMOCRAT

Today's News Today

EIGHTY-SIXTH YEAR—No. 357 · Entered as Second Class Matter Post Office, Little Rock, Ark. · LITTLE ROCK, MONDAY EVENING, SEPTEMBER 23, 1957 · 16 PAGES · ★ ★ · PRICE 5¢

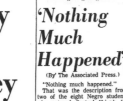

COULDN'T GET AWAY — This Negro newsman was unable to escape a crowd of irate segregationists at Little Rock Central High School today as violence broke out when Negro students entered the school. The white man riding the Negro's back is unidentified. The newsman was identified as Alex Wilson, a reporter from the Tri-State Defender, Memphis. (Democrat Photo by Counts.)

Growing Violence Forces Withdrawal of 8 Negro Students at Central High

By ROBERT TROUTT.
(Democrat Staff Writer.)

Eight Negro students entered Central High School this morning amid uncontrolled violence that grew so swiftly school and law enforcement officers decided to withdraw them shortly after noon. A milling, shouting mob of more than 1,000 persons ringed the school area.

Two city police cars took the Negro students to their homes shortly after noon.

Earlier they had entered by a side door while a diversionary group of Negroes appeared at the front.

Numerous fights broke out immediately and an appeal for state police brought 50 troopers racing to the scene to aid city patrolmen in battling the crowd. Acting Gov. Nathan Gordon said state troopers were withdrawn about 12:30 p. m. when Chief Marvin Potts phoned that they were no longer needed.

Shortly after the Negro students slipped in and went to the principal's office, many white students began leaving the building.

One of the Negro adults was knocked down, beaten and kicked. Women screamed and men cursed and tried to breech the line of officers thrown around the huge school ground.

Several fights broke out among Negro and white students in the corridors of Central High School after the Negroes entered, a student who left the school building said today.

The youth said he saw three Negroes with blood on their clothing. He said Negro students were chased through the hallways inside the building, and that "several fights had broken out."

School Supt. Virgil Blossom confirmed that the Negroes had been withdrawn after Mayor Mann had radioed an announcement on the police network: "Tell the crowd the Negroes have been removed from Central High School."

The announcement came to the growing crowd, which numbered [illegible]

The policemen escorted the Negroes to city police cars at the back entrance on 14th and drove away, without the knowledge of the crowd.

Blossom said the decision to take the Negroes out of school came after a conference with Assistant Chief of Police Gene Smith, who was in charge of the officers at the school.

"I asked Smith if he thought it would be best for the children to be taken out of the school and returned home," Blossom told the Democrat.

"Smith told me he thought it would be best and I told him to tell (Jess) Matthews, (CHS principal) to let him take the Negro students home."

After a police officer announced to the crowd that no Negro students remained in the building, another announcement followed that City Attorney O. D. Longstreth had authorized the police to allow one member of the crowd to go into the school and see for himself there were no Negro students present. The officer expressed a desire for someone to go whom the crowd would believe, and called for a minister.

Shortly before the announcement was made, members of the mob began hurling rocks and bottles indiscriminately at passing cars, which contained white persons.

Police blocked streets around the school and routed traffic on other streets, to stop the crowd from attacking motorists.

The crowd grew more violent.

See VIOLENCE on page 2.

RUNNING A GANTLET — This newsman ran a gantlet of anger at Central High School as violence broke out today when Negro students entered the school. Men in the crowd slugged at the Negro as he ran and one unidentified man kicked him in the stomach. (Democrat Photo by Counts.)

★ ★ ★

Faubus May Fly Back From Parley

By GEORGE DOUTHIT.
(Democrat Staff Writer.)

Governor Faubus told the Democrat from Sea Island, Ga., today that if integration troubles warranted it he would fly back to Little Rock.

He is attending the Southern Governors' Conference in Georgia. Mr. Faubus told the Democrat he had no immediate plans to return ahead of time because Lt. Gov. Nathan Gordon, now in charge, "is a man of good judgment and I have faith in his judgment."

Mr. Faubus was critical of Little Rock city and school officials and Negro leaders, [illegible] should have had the good sense to do what I urged them to do—allow for a cooling off period."

"I think this could have been worse the first day (September 3) and because I didn't want this to happen I acted in the way I did in calling out the National Guard," he said.

"I wanted to avoid this sort of thing; this violence; it is repulsive to me, to have it happen in my state."

"I think that Mayor Mann and Chief Potts should certainly see that the Negro students and their parents should have protection at their homes," Governor Faubus told the Democrat when informed later of the withdrawal of the students from Central High school.

Mr. Gordon moved into the governor's office at 8 a. m. today and was surrounded by several of Mr. Faubus' aides to help him keep touch on the situation.

One of these was Adj. Gen. Sherman Clinger, head of the Arkansas National Guard, which Mr. Gordon said he would call if the situation re-

See FAUBUS on Page 2.

★ ★ ★

Blossom Defers To Potts

Supt. Virgil T. Blossom, who Saturday promised newsmen he would try to have reports on conditions inside Central High School an hour after Negroes began attending classes, did not hold a press conference this morning.

The superintendent was in the school board offices but was "unavailable" to reporters by telephone. With him in his offices was Wayne Upton, school board secretary.

When finally contacted by the Democrat, Blossom would offer no comment on reports of violence within the school building itself but referred all such questions to Police Chief Marvin Potts.

He would say only that under the law no child can be compelled to stay in a school building if he is a student in any class above the 8th grade.

Chief Potts said that no violence inside the school had been reported to him.

★ ★ ★

'Nothing Much Happened'

(By The Associated Press.)

"Nothing much happened."

That was the description from two of the eight Negro students who entered Central High for three hours today.

Reached by telephone at his home, Terrance Roberts, 15, one of the Negro students, said:

"Nothing really happened. We went to classes as scheduled but after the third period, we were taken out and driven home.

"Some school officials came and took us out. There was not a whole lot of trouble.

"I was pushed but I don't know that anybody got hit.

"It was [illegible] after we got [illegible] classes. Some of the white students walked out. Just a few of them."

Another student, Thelma Mothershed said: "Nothing much happened at all.

"I went to three classes. There was no shouting or anything. Neither the teachers nor most of the students acted like they resented having us there. We didn't pay too much attention to the commotion going on in the halls.

"Then the registrar came and got us out of the classes.

"We weren't told why."

"Some of the students spoke to me and some ignored me.

"I was the only Negro girl in my class."

She said she was not told if she could go back to the school or when.

AEC Fires Half-Sized Atom Bomb

Atomic Test Site, Nev. (AP)—A relatively small atomic device was fired today from a 500-foot tower on the Yucca Flat testing grounds. It was the oft-postponed "Whitney" shot, 22nd in the 1957 series.

The Atomic Energy Commission said the energy yield was more than half nominal, which means the blast would have the equivalent of something more than 10,000 tons of TNT.

★ ★ ★

Crowd Is Dispersed At School

Police Break Up White Group At Negro Institution

Little Rock police broke up a crowd of white boys during the noon hour at St. Bartholomew's School, 1622 Marshall.

"I was eating my lunch when it all happened," said Father Lawrence M. Friedel, SVD, pastor of the church to which is attached the Catholic school for all Negro students from kindergarten through senior high school grades.

The priest said the sisters in charge of the school told him "some white boys with maybe one or two grownups started throwing rocks at the children as they were on the sidewalk edging the campus during the noon lunch period."

One Negro girl was hit on the leg by a white boy with "a stick, I think," the priest told the Democrat.

The police came quickly, he added, "and we were very grateful. We rang the bell for the classes 10 minutes early and they are all in their classrooms. No one was hurt seriously."

Attorney Chased.

City Attorney O. D. Longstreth and a group of men with whom he was apparently arguing were ordered to break up and leave a residential yard at 2124 W. 14th shortly after noon.

A woman residing in the house went across the street to the school grounds and returned with Assistant Police Chief Gene Smith, who ordered Longstreth and the others to disband and leave.

'Here They Come'

Crowd's Yell Touches Off Brutal Fighting

[illegible] is an eye witness account of the violence at Central High School this morning.

By WILMER COUNTS.
(Democrat Staff Photographer.)

I was standing at the corner of 16th and Park when I heard some of the crowd yell out "here they come."

I looked down 16th to the east and there was a Negro man and a Negro boy being confronted by a large crowd of white men. The police were still at the school.

I went around the crowd through a vacant lot and as I got to where the men were, the Negro boy had run on east on 16th and was being chased by several white men.

The Negro man started walking in that direction when white men came up and started hitting him and pushing him down. One man kicked him in the face while he was down. Others were using abusive language.

I followed in front of the Negro man with the crowd behind him. They kicked and hit him for approximately a block. One man with a stone the size of a softball in his hand kept saying "I am going to give you three minutes."

As I recall the Negro man said nothing nor did he resist in any way.

Attention of these men was diverted back toward the school where the Negro students were entering and the white men ran back in that direction.

The Negro man was left at this point in a standing position. I went back up to the school where this same group of men, and others, were trying to storm the police lines and get into the school and "get those Negroes."

They were referring to the Negro students who had entered the school building.

All during this fight policemen were patrolling down the street on motorcycles but were making no attempt to help out the Negro man nor to stop the agitators.

School Spat No Problem For Jurors

Pulaski Circuit Judge William J. Kirby today told members of the new grand jury that he felt there were sufficient law enforcement agencies handling the situation at Central High School today, and he did not think it would need their attention at this time.

Judge Kirby made the remarks as he charged the new jury. He read a routine charge. Judge Kirby said he had been asked by two or three persons if he would give the grand jury a special charge in view of the trouble at Central High this morning.

Newsmen Victims Of Mob

Five newsmen, including two Life photographers, were attacked in the melee that accompanied outbreaks at Central High School today.

Francis Miller, who had been slugged in the mouth, was brought to Little Rock police headquarters and docketed. Details could not be learned immediately.

A few minutes later, police brought in two more Life staff members—Paul Welch, a writer, and Gray Villet, a photographer. Welch had a cut on his neck, and he told a reporter that he thought he had been slugged. Both Welch and Villet were booked on an open charge.

Ed Planer, reporter for WDSU-TV, New Orleans, reported to his station that he and a cameraman were attacked.

As he was being docketed, Miller was asked what happened. "Well, they hit me in the mouth and now they're locking me up." Miller said. He did not identify "they."

Pallner told his office that he and M. J. Gauthier, a cameraman for the station were attacked when they took pictures of a girl coming out of the school.

He said a small crowd advanced on the TV crew, kicked him and tore off Gauthier's shirt.

Neither was hurt.

Negroes Out Until Ike Acts

"The Negro children will not return to Central High School until they have assurance from the President of the United States that they will be protected against the mob," Mrs. Daisy Bates, president of the Arkansas division of NAACP, said this afternoon.

The told newsmen she had issued an appeal to the president.

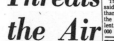

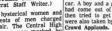

High Court Has First Meeting

The Arkansas Supreme Court convened today after its summer recess to admit 14 new lawyers to the bar, hear one oral argument and take a number of pending cases under submission.

The court will not hand down any opinions until next Monday.

The new lawyers were among the 22 who passed the bar examinations in July. They were sworn in by Chief Justice Carleton Harris.

The Weather

Little Rock, North Little Rock and Vicinity—Fair and mild this afternoon, tonight and Tuesday. High this afternoon in the mid 70's; low tonight, in the mid 50's.

Arkansas — Partly cloudy and mild this afternoon, tonight and Tuesday. High this afternoon in the 70's. Low tonight in the mid 40's to mid 50's. Highest Tuesday afternoon low 70's to low 80's.

Extended Forecast—Monday p. m. to Saturday p. m.—Temperatures will average 2 to 4 degrees below normal with little change until warming trend latter part of week. Little or no precipitation.

River Forecast—The Arkansas and Ouachita will rise slightly. Other streams in the Little Rock District will change little.

6 a. m.	58	10 a. m.	70
7 a. m.	59	11 a. m.	73
8 a. m.	61	12 noon	73
9 a. m.	66	1 p. m.	75

Maximum yesterday 73
Minimum yesterday 62
Maximum a year ago today 82
Minimum a year ago today 65
Sunset today .... 6:05 p. m.
Sunrise tomorrow ... 5:58 a. m.
Precipitation 24 hours to 7 a. m. today, .09 inches.
Precipitation since January 1, 1957, 31.77 inches.
Departure from normal since January 1, 1957, plus 15.83 inches.

★ ★ ★

Wails, Threats Pierce the Air

By PHYLLIS DILLAHA.
(Democrat Staff Writer.)

Wails of hysterical women and fearful threats of men charged the tense air. The Central High School scene was marked by chaos and frustrated anger.

"Turn in your badge and join our side," a hysterical woman cried as she clung to the arm of a city policeman.

"Get another job," members of the crowd shouted at both state and city enforcement officers.

"This is all we need," a man told several companions. "Let's go home and get our shotguns."

The big and unruly crowd gradually edged the police-guarded barricades along the sidewalks out into the street. The shoving and pressing within the crowd was terrific.

A screaming woman was hustled down the street to a police car. A boy and a girl student, who had come out of the school and then tried to get back inside, were also taken by police to a car.

Crowd Applauds.

The crowd began watching the doors, applauding each time students left the building. Dozens poured outside. Those who left were not permitted to get back inside.

Parents swamped the school office with telephone calls demanding that their children be permitted to leave. Many of the parents said they were afraid their children would get hurt if violence broke out inside the building. Others wanted their children released as a protest against the Negro students' being in the school.

Students coming out of the building said that teachers and football coaches were at the entrances trying to keep them from leaving.

The Democrat received several calls from irate persons who said they had heard that the students were locked in their classrooms so that they could not leave. The reports apparently were false.

There was no evidence that teachers and coaches at the entrances did more than try to talk the students into staying. No physical force was used, according to reports.

Auto Traffic Scoreboard

Death Toll.

To Date:	1957	1956
Little Rock	6	9
N. Little Rock	3	6
Pulaski Co.	22	36
Arkansas	344	320
1956 Total for Little Rock		17
1956 Total for N. L. Rock		6
1956 Total for Pulaski Co.		55
1956 Total for Arkansas		482

POLICE PUSH BACK CROWDS—A line of Little Rock policemen push back the crowd that tried to break through after it was announced "they are in" after eight Negro students entered Central High School. (Democrat Photo by Counts.)

Long Island Daily Press

FINAL

137th YEAR No. 275 SATURDAY, OCTOBER 5, 1957 Entered as Second Class Matter At Postoffice, Jamaica, N. Y. 24 PAGES 5 CENTS

Soviet 'Moon' Spotted Over US

By FRANK CAREY

WASHINGTON (AP) — U.S. scientists announced early today that they have computed an approximate orbit for the Russian Earth satellite.

They predicted the baby moon will whiz over the Philadelphia vicinity, with succeeding orbits passing over midwestern states and over the Pacific Coast.

Dr. Richard W. Porter, chairman of the technical panel on Earth satellites for the International Geophysical Year, said the approximate orbit was figured out by piecing together "miscellaneous bits of information from amateur, commercial and government radio receiving stations both in this country and Japan."

Porter said the satellite signals on 20 and 40 megacycles "should be strong enough to be heard on amateur communications receivers throughout most of New England and the North Atlantic States" at 11 a.m.

★ ★ ★

Reds Win the Race Into Outer Space

MOSCOW (AP) — The Soviet Union announced today it has launched the Earth's first man-made satellite 560 miles out in space and it now is circling the globe at tremendous speed.

The dramatic claim that Russia had beaten the United States in the satellite race came in an announcement saying the artificial moon was launched yesterday by multiple-stage rockets. The site of the launching was not given.

The instrument-laden globe was described as 23 inches in diameter and weighing 185 pounds. The announced weight is about nine times that of a projected 22-inch U. S. Earth satellite.

The man-made moon carries no propellant. The thrust of the last rocket sends it speeding off at about 18,000 miles an hour. This speed is sufficient to offset the pull of gravity. It thus keeps circling the Earth just like the real moon does.

AN ANNOUNCEMENT by the official agency Tass said the moon was circling the globe every hour and 35 minutes. It transmits radio signals back to the earth as it hurtles along.

The launching came just three months and four days after the opening of the International Geophysical Year (IGY), a concerted program by the world's scientists to learn more of the Earth's secrets.

Tass said the moon can be observed by simple optical instruments in the evening or early morning. Soviet scientists tracked the tiny satellite by radar and radio.

(The Defense Department in Washington said Navy researchers Friday recorded three passes of the Soviet satellite over the United States, one in the vicinity of Washington. Radio signals were picked up from the satellite elsewhere in the United States, Britain and Canada.)

• • •

THE ORBIT of the man-made moon was not given. Soviet scientists said previously they expected to launch a satellite on a north-south path around the Earth.

"The successful launching of the first man-made satellite makes a tremendous contribution to the treasure house of world science and culture," the Tass announcement said.

"Artificial Earth satellites will pave the way for space travel and it seems that the present generation will witness how the freed and conscious labor of the people of the new socialist society turns into reality the most bold dreams of mankind."

• • •

THE ANNOUNCEMENT, coming close on the claim Aug. 26 that the Soviet Union had successfully tested the first intercontinental ballistics missile, is expected to have an impact both in the Soviet Union and abroad.

U.S. scientists still are making plans to launch their first Earth satellite next spring after test shots this fall.

The announcement by Tass was spread over the front pages of Pravda and Izvestia without comment.

No comment was necessary, however, to tell the Soviet people that their leaders again had carried off a feat whose propaganda value may far outweight its scientific contributions to IGY studies.

• • •

IN ANNOUNCING Soviet plans to launch several artifical moons, Soviet IGY Chairman Ivan P. Bardin and his associates said June 18 the first would be sent aloft within the geophysical year.

At the same time they protested they were not in a race with the United States to be first. But the propaganda value of being the first is great in these days when many nations are inclined to choose between the two leading powers of the world.

The Tass announcement said the Russians plan to launch several even heavier Earth satellities in the next year.

It reported the satellite is fitted with radio transmitters sending continuous signals to Earth on the 15 and 7.5-meter wave lengths. It added the signals could be received easily by amateurs.

• • •

THE ANNOUCEMENT said the satellite was appearing over Moscow this morning but

(Turn to Next Page)

Is Red 'Moon' Sending Code?

PASADENA, Calif. (AP) — A scientist at the California Institute of Technology said last night the Russian Earth satellite is transmitting coded information in addition to the steady "beep" radio signals.

Dr. Henry L. Richter Jr. of the electronic research section of Caltech's jet propulsion laboratory said special equipment intercepted the transmission of coded information from the satellite.

"Unless the Russians give us a clue," he said, "we may not be able to decipher the messages."

★ ★ ★

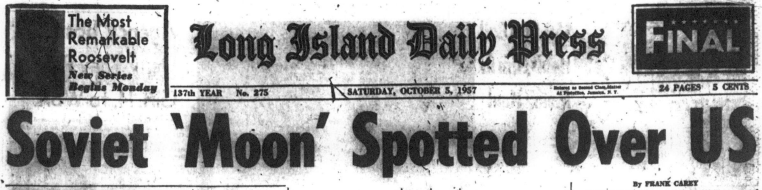

Russians Hope Satellite Can Stay Up for 3 Weeks

FROM THE PRESS WIRES

WASHINGTON — With the first flush of victory dimming out, Russian scientists admitted soberly today that their pioneer step into outer space depends on a multitude of ifs.

The biggest if was the expected life-span of the 185-pound orb the Soviet Union launched into space, whistling from Pole to Pole at 5 miles a second, some 558 miles straight up.

It could be destroyed today or tomorrow by colliding with the meteors which continually bombard every planet in the universe, burning up as they enter the atmosphere.

And it may stay on its elliptical orbit as long as its momentum holds out, said Russia's Dr. A. A. Blagonravov at the Soviet Embassy here.

If the satellite lasts three weeks, or longer, he said, it would certainly provide invaluable knowledge of the mysteries of outer space and the unknown outer reaches of the earth's atmosphere.

It was at an Embassy vodka party yesterday that Blagonravov and other top Red space experts announced that the Soviets had taken the first step into man's last unexplored region—space.

From U. S. scientists who are cooperating with the Russians and other nations in the International Geopyhsical Year, the announcement drew unqualified congratulations. But the political ramifications of the venture had many U.S. officials more worried than they have been since the Cold War began.

It was admitted everywhere that the Reds had scored a great propaganda victory, and the implication was clear that the Russians would certainly claim they now excel the Free World in military prowess.

A Defense Dept. spokesman said the "stunning" development indicates the USSR is "well along" the road to perfecting an intercontinental

(Turn to Next Page)

The arrows circling the globe indicate the path of the Earth satellite which the Russians launched yesterday.

They Were Siamese Twins

Virginia Kate, left, and Theresa May Horton, born joined at the forehead 14 months ago, play happily in their Mountain City, Tenn., home. The twins made medical history 10 months ago when surgeons at the National Institute of Neurological Diseases, Bethesda, Md., successfully separated them. (AP Wirephoto)

Troops Smash New Polish Riot

WARSAW (AP) — Angry students and other Poles battled police, security troops and militia in Warsaw's streets last night in the second violent anti-government demonstration in two days.

The street battling rolled up to the doors of Communist Party headquarters, where the Central Committee was reported in emergency session, before the demonstration was smashed.

Unlike the fighting of Thursday night, which was confined to an area around Polytechnic School, the violence this time spread to three sections of Warsaw. And for the first time, other Poles joined the 2,000 students in their defiance of government force.

THE DEMONSTRATORS hurled bricks and shouted "Gestapo, Gestapo," a reference to the Nazi secret police. They tossed back tear gas bombs thrown by the police.

Government forces beat the demonstrators with rubber truncheons, scattered them with tear gas and rubber bombs and finally restored order after five hours of fighting.

THE RIOTING began after students had met peacefully and demanded the return of Po Prostu, a student newspaper banned Wednesday.

The paper had become a symbol of the limited freedom won by Poles when Wladyslaw Gomulka was restored to Communist Party leadership a year ago.

LI Siamese Twins In Philadelphia, Surgery Weighed

Long Island's Siamese twins, born nine days ago in Mercy Hospital in Rockville Centre, are undergoing extensive examination by four bone specialists in Children's Hospital, Philadelphia, Pa.

The doctors will decide in three to four days whether the babies—both girls—can survive an operation to separate them.

They are joined at the base of the spine, a Children's Hospital spokesman said today.

The twins, whose combined weight is now 13½ pounds, were taken to Philadelphia Thursday night.

AUTHORITIES, at Mercy Hospital and the doctor who delivered the babies—Dr. William Dolan of Hempstead—refused earlier to discuss the case at the request of the parents, Marie and John Schatz of 135 Park Ave., Carle Place.

The four specialists examined the infants, Patricia and Pamela, all day yesterday. The babies are reported in "good health."

IT WAS FIRST reported that the babies were joined at the pelvis. However, Mercy Hospital immediately blanketed their birth Sept. 26 at 7:25 p.m. in a shroud of secrecy. Not even other mothers who were roommates of the twins' mother knew it was a Siamese birth.

A drawn curtain hid them from the sight of visitors and most of the hospital staff.

Pamela and Patricia are

Long Island's first living Siamese twins. Three years ago a Cedarhurst woman bore Siamese twins. One was stillborn and the other died after an operation was performed to separate them.

Coinword Jackpot $1,600

Who's going to win the COINWORD jackpot?

The Press has been trying to give it away for several weeks.

But again, no one rang up a perfect score in this week's COINWORD Number 97.

So another $300 has been added to the $1,600 jackpot to make next week's COINWORD Number 98 worth $1,900.

Two contestants came close this week. They had only one word wrong. Their names will appear in Monday's edition, along with the new puzzle and official entry blank for COINWORD Number 98.

Hoffa Vote Puts Labor On the Spot

WASHINGTON (AP) — James R. Hoffa's election as president of the giant Teamsters Union appeared certain today to spur moves for federal legislation to crack down on labor racketeering.

Sen. John McClellan (D-Ark), chairman of the Special Senate Rackets Investigating Committee, called Hoffa's election a challenge that he said Congress will accept and meet.

"The need for federal legislation is now greatly accentuated," McClellan said shortly after delegates to the Teamsters convention in Miami Beach overwhelmingly elected Hoffa yesterday in defiance of a directive from the AFL-CIO to clean house.

• • •

SECRETARY of Labor James P. Mitchell said in Chicago he saw a strong possibility that Hoffa's election may bring about passage of what Mitchell termed "repressive labor legislation."

Leaders of the AFL-CIO obviously have been concerned about just such a possibility, although a spokesman for the labor federation said that President George Meany would have no comment on Hoffa's election.

In advance of the Teamsters convention, the AFL-CIO Executive Committee called on the union to rid itself of "corrupt influences" and the officers responsible for them, or face expulsion.

The Executive Council took this stand last month on the basis of a report from the federation's Ethical Practices Committee, which had aimed charges of wrongdoing at Hoffa and several other top Teamsters officials.

• • •

THE TEAMSTERS were given until Oct. 24 to undertake cleanup action, and to report back to the Executive Council. Any ouster action would be taken by the AFL-CIO convention in Atlantic City, N.J., starting Dec. 5.

In issuing a call yesterday for the Atlantic City meeting, the AFL-CIO said "determinations by the Executive Council to rid the labor movement of all corrupt influences, and the entire matter of labor's ethical standards, will be before the second constitutional convention."

In Miami Beach, Hoffa said the Teamsters want to remain in the AFL-CIO. But he said that if they are expelled and efforts are made to raid the union's membership, "we will be ready to defend ourselves."

He promised to make the Teamsters Organization "a model of trade unionism."

THREE TIMES NO

TOKYO (AP)—The Japanese Foreign Office announced today the Soviet Union has rejected Japan's third request for suspension of Russian nuclear tests.

Nab Doctor In Blue Cross Gyp

A New Hyde Park physician appeared in Nassau County Court yesterday accused of collecting $612 from a health insurance plan for services he never performed on nine Sperry Gyroscope Co. employes.

Dr. Albert O. Rossi, 39, of 2035 Lakeville Rd. was arraigned before Judge Paul J. Widlitz on 19 counts of larceny and presenting false proofs for an insurance claim.

His lawyer, Albert A. Oppido of New Hyde Park, asked the judge to postpone the arraignment for one week to give him time to examine the indictment. The request was granted.

Dr. Rossi is accused of accepting seven $72 checks, one $60 check and a $48 check from the United Medical Service Inc. between May 7 and Dec. 31, 1956, for treating a bone ailment for nine employes at Sperry's Lake Success plant.

He did not perform the service, according to the indict-

(Turn to Next Page)

Djilas Jailed 7 More Years

SREMSKA MITROVICA, Yugoslavia (AP)—Milovan Djilas, former vice-president of Yugoslavia, was sentenced today to seven additional years in prison for writing hostile propaganda against communism and the Yugoslav government abroad.

He was brought into court here—after a one-day trial yesterday—from the penitentiary where his is serving a prison sentence of three years for a similar offense. The court decided to combine his previous sentence and today's into nine years.

The specific charge was publication of a book in the U.S. called "The New Class." In the book, Djilas said communism, like capitalism, creates an elite class.

"The New Class," was published after the manuscript was smuggled out of prison.

Sewer Fumes Kill 3, Gas Masks Checked

Gas masks worn by the Public Works crew that investigated a faulty Long Island City sewer were being analyzed for defects today at Pittsburgh in an effort to determine the cause of three workmen's deaths.

The dead were Joseph Messina, 3?, of 48-56 186th St., Flushing, who died at 5:40 p.m. yesterday, Stephen Guarino of Brooklyn, 38, who died yesterday morning and John Rooney of Staten Island, 30, who died from fumes in the sewer Wednesday afternoon.

They were among five other Public Works men and seven firemen overcome by fumes in the 30-foot deep sewer at Vernon Blvd. and 43rd Ave., Long Island City.

• • •

THE FUMES were a deadly combination of accumulated sewer and marsh gases which had forced police earlier to close off a four-block area around the sewer.

The tragedy is being investigated by the Queens District Attorney, the Consolidated Edison Co., and the New York City Public Works and Air Pollution Control Depts.

District Attorney Frank D. O'Connor said the gas masks worn by the Public Works crew and the firemen were sent back to the manufacturer in Pittsburgh for tests and he should have the results Monday. He said further that:

1. The sewer, which had not been opened for service, contained 20 feet of water, overflow from an adjoining sewer, and the contractor had opened a bulkhead between the two drains to draw off the overflow.

2. But when the contractor saw that the water was "cloudy and dirty," he had two men close the bulkhead on Tuesday—and they were overcome by gas.

It was then, O'Connor said, that Public Works staffer

(Turn to Page 3)

Asian Flu Continues Slow Climb, Expected to Strike 1 Out of 10

The Asian Flu epidemic was expected today to continue a slow climb throughout the New York-Long Island area, with 5,244 new cases including hundreds among hospital personnel in New York City and scattered cases in the suburbs.

But as they have been doing since the situation was declared epidemic, health officials continued to stress that it is a "relatively mild" respiratory ailment and deaths have been few and far between.

Attendance in the New York City schools dropped again yesterday, partly due to the epidemic and partly to the fact that Jewish students were being kept home for the High Holy Day observance of Yom Kippur.

Yesterday in Nassau, there was a moment of alarm when the Freeport-Mepham High School football game scheduled for today was called off because "12 out of 24 players" on the Freeport team had a "flu-like" disease during the week.

But Dr. Earle G. Brown, the Nassau Health Commissioner, said there was no epidemic in the Freeport school and the cancellation was only "a precautionary measure."

A soccer game at Jamaica High School was called off yesterday for the same reason, but the figures on how many players were ill were not available.

Health officials predicted that before the end of the epidemic at least one person out of 10 in the area it affects will come down with the disease. At the same time, they pointed out that almost all those who have had the disease were only in bed "for two days at the most."

"Presumed" fatalities from the disease — or from other diseases it brings on by lowering the victim's resistance — included a 9-year-old girl in Brooklyn whose "immediate"

(Turn to Next Page)

Inside The Press

THE WEATHER Mostly fair and seasonably cool today, with highest temperatures in the low 60's. Partly cloudy tonight, the low in the 50's. Mostly fair tomorrow with temperatures in the 60's.

1958

Memorial Day was first observed in 1865, when black schoolchildren of Charleston, South Carolina, commemorated the neglected graves of Union soldiers near their city.

On May 30, 1868, John Logan, commander of the Grand Army of the Republic, designated May 30 as a national Memorial Day and ordered GAR posts to decorate the graves "of comrades who died in defense of their country."

State by state, Memorial Day was legalized until, after World War I, it was officially set to honor the fallen in all U.S. wars.

On Memorial Day in 1958, President Eisenhower took part in ceremonies at the Tomb of the Unknowns in Arlington National Cemetery as two other nameless soldiers were buried alongside the unknown of World War I. The two represented those who died in World War II and the Korean War.

A federal law in 1971 provided for observance of the holiday on the last Monday in May.

In the face of early Soviet successes with artificial satellites, President Eisenhower established the National Aeronautics and Space Administration to direct the U.S. space program.

NASA organized Project Mercury, a long-range plan to put a man in orbit.

The Weather

RICHMOND: Sunny, warm, humid; chance of afternoon shower. Sunday, increasing cloudiness.

Local Data on Page 1

Richmond Times-Dispatch

Vees Sweep

Virginians defeat Columbus twice, 6-1, 3-2. Pages 11, 13.

108th Year | Volume 108, Number 151 | Published Morning and Sunday | Richmond 11, Virginia, Saturday, May 31, 1958 | Milton 4-1851 | Second Class Mail Privileges Authorized at Richmond, Va. | 5 Cents

—AP Wirephoto

President, Vice President, Other Leaders Stand in Silent Salute to Heroes of Two Wars

IN ARLINGTON CEREMONY

Unknown Soldiers at Rest

By Douglas B. Cornell

ARLINGTON NATIONAL CEMETERY, May 30 (AP)—United in death and glory, the unknown servicemen of two wars were enshrined Friday in Arlington and in the hearts of their countrymen.

A grieving but proud nation laid to rest the unknown heroes of Korea and World War II, on a sun-drenched Virginia hillside.

They were placed beside the Unknown Soldier who died in World War I, the war that America hoped 40 years ago would be the last.

Friday night they slept in eternal peace beneath the stars, honored as symbols of all the thousands who gave their lives for liberty on the battlefields of 1941-45 and 1950-53.

From their President, an old soldier himself, they received the nation's highest award, the Medal of Honor, reserved for the valorous and for deeds which defied death.

President Eisenhower laid the coveted medals on the flag-draped bronze caskets in funeral ceremonies in the colonnaded marble amphitheater of Arlington Cemetery across the Potomac from Washington. And he held the position of honor at committal services beside the graves.

Mr. Eisenhower spoke only 26 words: "On behalf of a grateful people I now present Medals of Honor to these two unknowns who gave their lives for the United States of America."

No one knew the names of these unknowns, no one knew their rank, service, color or how they died for the flag.

Thousands of their fellow Americans and the great of the nation poured out accolades for the unknown—and the yet renowned—all the day through.

They had lain in state, these unknowns, in the rotunda of the Capitol in Washington, for two full days of honor and acclaim. They made their last journey in a funeral procession from the Capitol to the heights of Arlington.

Twin black caissons drawn by six matched gray horses took them along the route between rows of uniformed men and civilians, young and old, offering their homage.

Metropolitan and park police estimated jointly that 115,000 watchers lined the route. The crowd in the vicinity of the amphitheater was estimated at 25,000. In the heat, about 400 persons collapsed, including Supreme Court Justice Charles E. Whitaker.

Beloved, familiar hymns, from bands and the Arlington carillon, were the musical tribute to the dead.

The President, other leaders of government, members of Congress and the Supreme Court and the diplomatic corps awaited them at Arlington.

The national anthem rang out. A brisk breeze tugged at flags between the white marble columns and rustled those on the caskets resting on the amphitheater apse.

The chief of army chaplains, Maj. Gen. Patrick J. Ryan, offered an invocation and a tribute to those who gave their lives on the altar of freedom.

Three times, a trumpet called out "Attention."

For two full minutes there was silence.

A child in the audience cried. Off in the distance could be heard the wail of a siren, the drone of a plane.

Mr. Eisenhower stood immobile, squinted into the afternoon sun.

The funeral services went on, with hymns, the reading of a psalm, the reading of a Scripture lesson—"Let not your hearts be troubled"—and a benediction.

Reverently then, the audience stood while the unnamed warriors were carried by their pallbearers to the spot in front of the amphitheater where the unknown of World War I has slept for nearly 37 years.

An honor guard of all the uniformed services came to present arms on command, their gleaming bayoneted rifles pointing to the sky as sentinels of the dead.

The President and Vice President Nixon walked slowly forward and took their places, the chief executive at the head of the unknown of World War II, the Vice President at the foot of the Korean unknown.

Army, navy and air force chaplains said the committal services of the Catholic, Protestant and Jewish faiths. Each offered up a prayer that God grant eternal rest and peace to the unknown heroes.

With the bells of the carillon ringing softly, Mr. Eisenhower marched to the tomb of the World War I unknown with

Continued on Page 3, Col. 1

Holiday Weather Is Perfect As Thousands Leave City

Virginians enjoyed perfect weather yesterday and thousands took advantage of the first of the vacation season's long week ends to escape from the city.

The weatherman forecast continued pleasant weather today and tomorrow, with only the chance of afternoon or evening thundershowers to mar the 78-hour holiday period. The chance of afternoon showers today is slim, the weatherman said, but Sunday will be rather cloudy, continued warm and humid, and showers are expected later in the day. The high expected today is about 86.

The five-day forecast for the state through Wednesday is for the temperature to average near or slightly above normal. The normal high and low readings for this period are 83 and 60.

Yesterday's sunny skies and high of 81 degrees lured many motorists to the highways, and picnics, trips to the beach and visits to relatives were the order of the day. Many Virginians, however, settled for just loafing around the house and puttering in the backyard.

The state's program to prevent deaths on the highway during the long week end seemed to be getting results. Only one traffic death was reported in Virginia in the first 24 hours. (See accident story, Page 3).

A Newport News man, Woodrow Wilson Bloxom, 42, was killed when he was struck by a speeding Chesapeake & Ohio Railway passenger train.

It was the first accident involving the new self-propelled Budd train units which went into service between Richmond and Warwick several weeks ago.

Thomas W. Rowe, 73, of Richmond, the engineer, said Bloxom ran from a wooded area and onto the track in front of the train. Rowe told police the man made no effort to get out of the way of the train.

An Arlington youth, Maurice Franko, 14, drowned yesterday in Black pond near Madeira school in Fairfax county.

Witnesses told police the boy failed to make shore when he tried to swim the 50-yard width of the pond. Two companions tried to rescue young Franko.

The nation's toll of accidental deaths reported yesterday included 91 traffic fatalities, 30 drownings and 19 from miscellaneous causes.

The traffic fatality toll was slightly less than the expected number at the end of the first day of the week end.

Safety officials called the fall-off in auto fatalities a hopeful trend, but restated their plea that motorists exert extra caution.

The slower death pace followed an early spurt that had brought predictions of near-record killings on America's highways.

Ned H. Dearborn, president of the National Safety Council, said the slowdown gave cause to expect an auto death toll somewhat under the prediction of 350 during the period from 6 p.m. Thursday to midnight Sunday.

Several ceremonies were held

Continued on Page 2, Col. 1

MEDAL WINNERS GREETED

WASHINGTON, May 30 (AP) President Eisenhower shook hands with 216 great fighters Friday and said he hoped they would help him fight for his defense reorganization bill.

The President greeted that many winners of the Medal of Honor, this nation's highest military award, in the sun-drenched rose garden at the White House.

"Because you have been such great fighters, I am quite certain that all of you feel a great compulsion to be a fighter for peace," Mr. Eisenhower said in an informal talk.

Expressing hope that each of the medal winners will "find it within his power and within his desire to help," Mr. Eisenhower said:

"We need a clean-cut bill that makes it possible to have a security that is not only sound and strong but also leaves the country solvent."

For each of the 216 privates, sergeants and on up to generals and admirals who have won the coveted medal, old soldier Eisenhower had a warm smile and a hearty handshake. For most of them he had a word of reminiscence about their outfits.

Swing by Socialists To DeGaulle Is Seen

General Arrives in Paris; Riots Erupt in Capital

From AP Dispatches

The hour of decision on giving Gen. Charles deGaulle the job of premier of France on his terms arrives in Paris today.

A day of swift moving political events and a night of disorders in the heart of Paris set the stage for a possible key Socialist party switch to insure deGaulle's triumph.

The party's leaders sped the 150 miles to deGaulle's country home at Colombey-les-deux-Eglises Friday to talk with him, then they returned to report to a party caucus. They were said to have told their followers they were impressed with deGaulle's program to save France and with the men he proposed to name in the cabinet to help him.

The caucus applauded the report but deferred final decision until today. It was reported, however, that the Socialists with their 97 decisive assembly votes were swinging around to deGaulle's support.

The tall, somber general and his wife—their car significantly loaded this time with luggage—drove into Paris shortly before midnight and lodged in a hotel near the Arc de Triomphe.

Early Saturday the prospective premier was reported planning a final roundtable session with leaders of the parties he wants represented in his cabinet.

The Communists and the extreme rightwing Poujadists are to be left out of those talks, it was reported.

Socialist sources, who oppose Communist penetration, said the discussions would be only with leaders of what are called the national parties. In France the adjective national excludes the extremists of both sides.

Reliable reports said that among those deGaulle wants in his cabinet are Socialist ex-Premier Guy Mollet, outgoing Premier Pflimlin and Conservative leader Antoine Pinay. Mollet, who resigned last June 10 after setting a postwar cabinet record of 16 months in office, was one of the men who conferred with deGaulle Friday

Continued on Page 7, Col. 1

Dog Gone!

CHICAGO, May 30—(AP) If your Chihuahua pup likes to nestle in your hip pocket and travel with you, that's fine. Beware, though, of pickpockets. That's the advice of Frank de Rosaire, 70, who says his Chihuahua was lifted from his pocket in a Chicago taproom recently.

City Budget Is Approved By Council

By Ed Grimsley

A general fund budget providing for expenditures of $35,789,000 during the 12 months beginning July 1 was approved yesterday by City Council.

Council acted at a brief session held at 8:30 in the morning. There were no dissenting votes, although the budget has become a matter of dispute in the councilmanic campaign.

Council has been criticized for failing to grant the full request of the School Board. The school budget of more than $11,200,000 is $185,000 less than the board requested.

But councilmen who favored the reduced school budget contend that the school program should not suffer, because the budget, despite the reduction, is about $600,000 higher than estimated expenditures for the current year.

Actually, yesterday's meeting was a formality. It was too late for changes, and Council either had to adopt the budget as it was amended a week ago or the City Manager's budget recommendations would have become effective automatically.

Council required seven rath-

Continued on Page 2, Col. 5

Turnpike to Save Time, Reveal New Scenery

By Allan Jones

The 75-million dollar Richmond-Petersburg Turnpike, the largest toll project ever undertaken in Virginia, will be a great timesaver for north-south traffic when it opens in about a month.

At the same time, motorists using the 35-mile project will see new views of Richmond's downtown skyline and some pleasant countryside—uncluttered by outdoor advertising—in Chesterfield county.

All but small portions of the superhighway in the Hermitage road area of North Richmond and near the interchange at U. S. 460-301 in Petersburg have been hard surfaced.

It is now possible to travel the length of the facility, but not at the maximum speed limit of 60 miles an hour. Some sections of the highway, while they are hard surfaced, haven't received their final coating of asphalt.

Ready to Accept 12 Miles

The turnpike authority is on the verge of accepting 12 miles of roadway, all of it in Chesterfield county. Authority engineers will inspect every inch of the highway, culverts and shoulders before they will recommend that the facility be accepted.

The turnpike's consultants have estimated motorists will save 27 minutes by using the toll road instead of the existing U. S. Rt. 1 at non-peak traffic periods. They say it takes 65 minutes to travel U. S. Rt. 1 from north of the city to south of Petersburg, compared to 38 minutes on the toll road.

The consultants have said it requires 83 minutes to travel U. S. Rt. 1 from Richmond to Petersburg at peak traffic hours, and 40 minutes on the toll road during the same periods. This would be a saving of 43 minutes.

There are 65 traffic lights from north of Richmond to the southern terminal of the toll road along U. S. 1. Motorists traveling the length of the toll road must stop four times to pay fares.

Accurate Timing Impossible

It was impossible yesterday to make an accurate timing along the toll road because it was necessary to slow down to 5-10 miles an hour for construction workers, and because one complete section of the road in Chesterfield is barricaded.

But it took 74 minutes to travel U. S. 1 from the northern (actually on U. S. Rt. 301) to the southern terminus of the toll road on yesterday's holi-

Continued on Page 2, Col. 5

Airline Cancels Buzzing Charge

SAN FRANCISCO, May 30 (AP) United Air Lines Friday withdrew its charge, based on a pilot's statement, that an air force B47 "deliberately buzzed" a UAL airliner with 57 passengers and a crew of five.

The airline had protested to the Civil Aeronautics Administration after Thursday's incident near Salinas, Kan. Friday, it accepted the air force's denial that any buzzing was involved.

A spokesman said UAL's Denver office had checked with the air force pilot involved, Maj. Eugene Mathis of Schilling Air Force Base near Salinas and "accepted his statement that he had our airplane in sight and was maneuvering to avoid collision."

COMING IN SUNDAY'S T-D

Davis and His 'Good Samaritan'

Tuesday is the 150th anniversary of the birth of Jefferson Davis. The Times-Dispatch's Washington correspondent, Frank van der Linden, tells the little known facts about the President of the Confederacy during his confinement at Fortress Monroe, including his meeting his "Good Samaritan," Brevet Lt. Col. John J. Craven, M.D.

What Is the Future of U. S. Air Travel?

On the threshold of the commercial jet age, the collision of still another military jet with an airliner—the third this year—has stirred grave misgivings over the immediate future of American air travel. The Associated Press' Roger Greene gives some authoritative answers to the question: Will it be safe to travel by air?

Who Owns the South Pole?

Rep. Steven B. Derounian of New York says let's not lose our stake in the South Pole. Derounian, who has been to Antarctica, tells what we must do if the President's "international treaty" plan fails. It's in This Week Magazine.

IN TODAY'S T-D

HENRICO Rescue Squad's campaign falls far short of goal. Page 2.

VIRGINIA submarine commander says atom sub could stay down for a year. Page 3.

JIMMY Bryan wins Indianapolis 500. Pat O'Connor killed. Page 11.

Here Are Views of U.S. Rt. 301 at Toll Road Entrance, Chamberlayne Ave. and Cowardin Ave.

1959

Since the original thirteen states formed the Union, Congress had admitted thirty-seven others. Five—Vermont, Kentucky, Tennessee, Maine, and West Virginia—had been created from parts of already-existing states. Texas had been an independent republic before admission. California had been admitted after being ceded to the United States by Mexico. Each of the other thirty had entered the Union only after spending some time as an organized territory.

By 1912, with the admission of New Mexico in January and Arizona in February, the United States consisted of the "contiguous" 48—each bordering at least one other state.

It was to be another forty-seven years before the Union would grow—and it grew away from the mainland.

Alaska, bought from Russia in 1867 for $7.2 million, was organized as a territory in 1912. It was admitted to the Union as the forty-ninth state—the first noncontiguous state—on January 3, 1959.

Hawaii, the first overseas and second noncontiguous state—was admitted as the fiftieth and last, on August 21, 1959.

WRONG FOOT
Cloudy and mild today; low tonight near 12, high tomorrow near 20.
Details on Page 19

THE INDIANAPOLIS NEWS

The Great Hoosier Daily Since 1869

"Where the Spirit of the Lord Is, There Is Liberty"—II Cor. 3-17

HOME EDITION

90th YEAR | MElrose 8-2411 | FRIDAY EVENING, JANUARY 2, 1959 | 36 PAGES | 7 CENTS 40c per week delivered by carrier

First Castro Forces Enter Quiet Havana

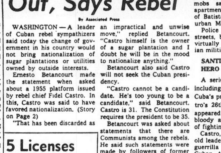

Mobs Riot in Cuba

HAVANA—A Havana policeman aims his rifle at members of a mob that looted and wrecked a gambling casino in the Plaza Hotel. The looting followed Cuban dictator Fulgencio Batista's flight to the Dominican Republic. Mobs ransacked casinos and burned the debris in the streets.—AP Wirephoto

New President, Rebel Chief Delay Arrival

From the Press Associations

HAVANA—Advance spearheads of Fidel Castro's revolutionary forces entered Havana peacefully today.

Truckloads of bearded guerrilla fighters rolled triumphantly into the city from the eastern provinces of Matanzas and La Villas toward the former military headquarters of deposed President Fulgencio Batista at Camp Columbia.

Castro and Dr. Manuel Urrutia, who was named provisional president, are expected in the capital tomorrow. Col. Ramon Barquin, head of the armed forces, sent a plane to Santiago de Cuba to pick up the new leaders. Castro earlier had said he would arrive from the provisional capital today.

DR. MANUEL URRUTIA . . . named president.—AP Wirephoto

Barquin said he was "placing all armed forces of the republic at the disposition of Castro." Other insurgent groups also were cooperating with Castro. Former President Carlos Prio Socarras, who was deposed by Batista in March, 1952, arrived in Havana from the United States.

PARTISANS KEEP CITY QUIET

The Castro forces entered Havana unopposed. Partisans who emerged from underground yesterday kept the city quiet today, save for occasional shots. It was a different scene from yesterday, when hooligans took advantage of celebrations by Castro's followers to run wild. A general strike called by Castro paralyzed the city.

There were no disorders during the night or in the morning hours today. However, the large-scale looting and pillaging continued as late as 10 o'clock last night when mobs sacked a brand new apartment house owned by one of Batista's daughters in suburban Miramar.

Police were patrolling the streets, but in company of—virtually in custody of—civilian militiamen.

SANTIAGO WELCOMES HERO FROM HILLS

A series of rebel victories, including the capture of Cuba's principal cities by Castro's 26th of July movement, appeared to have brought the bloody and costly 2½ years of fighting to an end.

Castro, the bearded, 32-year-old leader of the rebels whose guerrilla tactics bested the Cuban Army, Air Force and Navy, received a thunderous ovation in Santiago when he emerged from the hills to begin the takeover of government.

Santiago is the capital of Oriente province in the extreme eastern end of Cuba and from the first was a Castro stronghold.

Batista, who fled to the Dominican Republic before daylight yesterday, left behind a military junta led by Maj. Gen. Eulogio Cantillo.

But the rebels said they would have no dealings with the junta and quickly seized power.

The 40,000 Americans in Cuba appeared safe. U.S. Ambassador Earl T. Smith said arrangements had been made to send planes and a ship to Havana today to take home tourists and students here for the Christmas holidays.

The Castro command also instructed rebel forces not to attack Cuban troops near Guantanamo Bay, site of a U.S. naval base.

FREE PRISONERS OF BATISTA

Mobs in a 4-hour orgy of rioting yesterday destroyed thousands of dollars worth of property, smashed two downtown night spots, the casino at the Plaza Hotel and Sevilla Hotel, wrecked a dozen airline offices and stormed into other buildings.

Other mobs wrecked the fifth police precinct station, which was the strongpoint of the antirebel movement in Havana and where rebels said political prisoners were tortured. Other groups freed hundreds of political prisoners—and criminals—from the Municipal Jail.

Among those freed were two Americans who told an almost hysterical story of spending many months there undergoing daily beatings. They identified themselves as Jonathan Graham, 30, of Hollywood, Fla., a chemical manufacturer, and Dean Leon Gleaves, 23, of Portland, Ore.

(Other stories on Page 2).

FIDEL CASTRO . . . as rebel leader appeared in 1957.—AP Wirephoto

Grills Outlines Proposed Way to Reapportion

By EDWARD ZIEGNER

Senator Nelson Grills (D., Indianapolis) today outlined a plan whereby he believes the 1959 General Assembly not only can but must reapportion the state in accordance with population gains and losses.

Grills, in a letter to Samuel Lesh, director of the state Legislative Reference Bureau, cited an 1895 decision of the state Supreme Court which, he said, gives the Assembly authority to make an enumeration of citizens and then a reapportionment, despite the fact such acts would be out of "sequence."

The Indianapolis attorney proposed:

1 That the 1959 General Assembly repeal an 1865 act making it the duty of township trustees to enumerate male voters.

2 That the Assembly then adopt a law establishing an enumeration committee of the General Assembly, with its members to be appointed by the speaker of the House and the president of the Senate.

3 This committee would then determine, through examination of the 1950 federal census for the state, the number of males over 21 in each county. With this determined, the committee would then report back to the full Assembly, this constituting the enumeration of inhabitants required by Article 4, Section 4 of the state Constitution.

4 The 1959 Assembly would then apportion the membership of House and Senate on the basis of the enumeration provided by the committee.

"Accepting the principles set down by the Supreme Court," Grills said in his letter, "it would be not only desirable but the legal duty of the General Assembly after it has received the enumeration to immediately reapportion the state."

Normally, the state should have been reapportioned in 1957, with an enumeration having been made in 1956. However, the last enumeration was in 1919 and the last reapportionment in 1921, and the assembly has ignored the constitutional mandate to do so each six years since then.

The Grills plan appeared to offer a solution toward reapportionment, although its favorable reception by the 1959 Assembly would remain a question. Many legislators have felt the only valid solution is amendment of the state Constitution, and such amendment cannot even be begun in 1959, because of other proposed amendments that are pending.

Because of the 37-year delay in reapportionment, urban areas in the state have far less representation than their population entitles them to, and rural areas far more. Marion County, which now has 11 state representatives, would have at least 14 under a reapportionment.

Herman Hoglebogle Says:

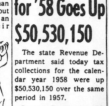

One of my policeman friends complains about car owners who attach an emblem denoting their profession, lodge, politics or auto club to license plates so that a letter prefix or number is hidden. He says he's even seen emblems of the FOP (Fraternal Order of Police) hiding part of the license. This can handicap police in their hunt for a stolen car or for one wanted in a hit-run accident. Let's keep those plates clear.

Winter Coming Back to Town

Winter is heading back to Indianapolis tonight with snow flurries borne on 20 to 30 mph winds and the promise of near-zero temperatures over the weekend.

The mercury is expected to drop to near 12 here tonight, but possible lows tomorrow night through Wednesday could fall in the 5 above zero range.

Predicted low for the northern part of the state tonight is 8 above zero. However, the five-day forecast calls for temperatures averaging 10 to 15 degrees below normal, which could push the mercury as far as 3 below zero before Wednesday.

Normal lows for the period range from 12 to 26 and normal highs range from 27 to 44.

Tomorrow will be cloudy and cold with an expected high near 20. Highest temperature predicted for the state tomorrow is 25.

Clerk Shot by Gunmen in Store Holdup

A 23-year-old clerk at the M & H liquor store, 301 W. McCarty, was wounded critically this afternoon when two gunmen held up the store.

Taken to General Hospital with a .38-caliber wound in his right side was Donald Hemelgarn, 1626 S. Delaware.

Lee Mitchell, 37 E. Palmer, owner of the store, told police that he and Hemelgarn were in the back of the store taking inventory when the two men entered the front about 12:15 p.m.

When they were unable to open a swinging door to go behind the counter, one of the gunmen shot Hemelgarn without warning.

One of the men took Mitchell's billfold containing $40 while the other took $60 from the cash register.

As the gunmen ran south on Senate, Mitchell fired three shots at them with a .32-caliber revolver. He said he apparently missed them.

State Revenue for '58 Goes Up $50,530,150

The state Revenue Department said today tax collections for the calendar year 1958 were up $50,530,150 over the same period in 1957.

Revenue Commissioner Edwin Beaman said most of the whopping increase resulted from a 50% boost in the gross income tax, effective July 1, 1957, and a 2c-per-gallon boost in state gasoline tax, effective March 15, 1957.

Total collections for the year were $301,460,613, the first time in state history collections for a single year exceeded $300 million.

DECREASE BLAMED ON RECESSION

Gross income tax collections totaled $186,745,419, compared with $145,378,077 in 1957. Collections during the last three months of 1958 were down more than $1 million compared with the same 1957 period.

Beaman attributed the decrease mainly to recession conditions existing this year.

Other collections:

Motor fuel, $100,583,133, up $9,368,049; store license, $626,435, up $16,592; inheritance, $5,879,649, up $57,206; intangibles, $5,718,782, down $253,920; oil inspection, $1,549,578, down $13,058; petroleum severance, $353,713, down $12,310, and employment agency licenses, $3,900, up $250.

Beaman said the number of employers withholding gross income taxes has increased about 3,000 in 1958, and that a special drive on delinquent diesel fuel taxes picked up an extra $10,000 in the last four months.

TODAY'S DEFINITION

WOMAN—A creature that's expensive when picked up, but explosive when dropped.

BIRTHDAY SOON? CHECK YOUR LICENSE

If your birthday is in January and your driver's license is two years old, it must be renewed before the end of this month. The fee is $1.50.

And if you were born before January 1, 1922, you must pass a written and vision test at an auto license branch before you can get your license renewed.

Driver manuals, on which written tests are based, are available at license branches.

Driver permits, under state law, must be renewed every two years during the driver's birth month and the tests, once taken, must be taken again every four years.

Drivers born after January 1, 1922, must start taking the tests in July, whenever they apply for renewal.

Connie May Be Ready for Trial Soon

Minnie B. (Connie) Nicholas has undergone a second operation on her left arm and may be ready to stand trial for the murder of Forrest Teel in February, her attorney disclosed today.

Attorney Charles W. Symmes said, "We are ready to try the case. We will know definitely about Connie's arm in a few weeks, and will be ready for trial in February."

Mrs. Nicholas, 42, under indictment for the pistol slaying last July of the wealthy business executive after a lovers' quarrel, underwent her second operation at General Hospital.

Symmes said the operation was comparatively minor. Tendons were treated to correct a condition that has caused Mrs. Nicholas' fingers on her left hand to curl, he said.

Symmes said demand for an early trial will be made before Judge Thomas J. Faulconer in Criminal Court 2 as soon as results of the second operation are definitely determined.

Property Seizure Out, Says Rebel

By Associated Press

WASHINGTON—A leader of Cuban rebel sympathizers said today the change of government in his country would not bring nationalization of sugar plantations or utilities owned by outside interests.

Ernesto Betancourt made the statement when asked about a 1955 platform issued by rebel chief Fidel Castro. In this, Castro was said to have favored nationalization. (Story on Page 2)

"That has been discarded as an impractical and unwise move," replied Betancourt. "Castro himself is the owner of a sugar plantation and I doubt he will be in the mood to nationalize anything."

Betancourt also said Castro will not seek the Cuban presidency.

"Castro cannot be a candidate. He's too young to be a candidate," said Betancourt. Castro is 31. The Constitution requires the president to be 35.

Betancourt was asked about statements that there are Communists among the rebels. He said such statements were made by followers of former President Fulgencio Batista to try to discredit the rebels.

"We are against the Communists," Betancourt said. "We don't want to have anything to do with them."

5 Licenses of Driver Investigated

The five driver licenses found on a 39-year-old Indianapolis man arrested on a disorderly person charge are under police investigation.

The arrested man, Frank Stokes, 4609 Kingman Dr., was charged with two others after a disturbance at the Stone restaurant, 228 N. Illinois.

Arrested with Stokes were William Lemon, 26, 906 Arbor, and Scott (Blackie) Warren, 35, also of 4609 Kingman. Warren is the brother of William Warren, a member of the Board of Public Safety.

The three men were found not guilty yesterday by Judge Ernie S. Burke, Municipal Court 3.

On Stokes when he was arrested Wednesday was a driver license and four copies, all bearing the name of Edward Eugene Barnett, Terre Haute.

The arresting officer, Patrolman Raymond Stratton, kept the five licenses for checking with the Motor Vehicle Bureau.

The original of the license showed a date of July 7, 1955. The four copies showed an issue date of July 7, 1957.

Cuban Rebels Quiz Newsmen

By Associated Press

HAVANA—Armed Cuban rebels fired today on the Havana Post building and temporarily detained three Associated Press men covering the city's post-revolt convulsion. The three were released after questioning.

Larry Allen, roving AP correspondent; George Kaufman, Havana AP bureau chief, and Harold Valentine, AP photographer from Miami, were taken to a police station but were freed 30 minutes later.

Rebels carrying machine guns, rifles and other weapons opened fire on the Post building at 10:30 a.m. (CDT). Several bullets smashed through the windows and into the walls of the Post editorial office adjoining the AP headquarters on the second floor. The Post is an English-language newspaper.

The front door of the building was smashed in and six rebels pounded up the stairs and leveled rifes at the AP men. They escorted them into the Post composing room, where they claimed to have found a pistol and attempted to pin ownership on the AP.

"We were herded downstairs and into an automobile and taken to a police station where young rebels were running the show," Allen said.

"After much protesting and explaining that we were Americans the rebels decided to release us and permit us to return to the Post building."

NEWS FEATURES

COMPLETE 1958 STOCKS

The News today carries a complete list of transactions on the New York Stock Exchange for 1958. Included are sales, high, low, closing prices and net change from the close of 1957. On Page 28.

ALL FOR ONE, ONE FOR ALL

8 Resolutions Proposed for Keeping Family Happy

By JOHN SEMBOWER
WNS Reporter

ANN ARBOR, Mich.—A ready-made set of New Year's resolutions, guaranteed to produce happy family living in 1959, is suggested by a noted husband-wife lecture team here at the University of Michigan.

It is based on specific suggestions developed by Harry and Bonaro Overstreet at the annual parent education institute, attended by more than 600 persons at the university, and aimed at eradicating juvenile delinquency and other ills.

The proposed family resolutions follow.

1 To show deep affection to all family members during the entire coming year.

2 To show respect for the individuality of others in the family group.

3 To cultivate interest in learning and acquiring knowledge. This applies to all family members, not just the ones still going to school.

4 To seek opportunities for many cooperative, shared experiences.

5 To cultivate respect for a general framework of law and order within the home.

6 To extend understanding and to help the members who must learn to handle the "unwanted experiences" of life—disappointments, failures, loneliness and grief.

7 To cultivate strong bonds with the outside world.

8 And finally, to seek an appreciation for the values of life, including recognition of the self as part of a broad universe.

Parents who doubt that they wield much influence on the lives of their children ought to concentrate on raising family life to the highest plane, say the Overstreets.

"It is the one place where parents can make a big difference. It is the one place where they cannot possibly feel that they are too small to count."

The family living experts urge that parents, by their own example, show youngsters how to make an acceptable life through the development of their natural talents and resources.

They warn, however, that children should not be subjected to constant unfavorable comparisons by their elders.

In the home, each individual should develop some skill where he can work off and work out his inner tensions and particular insights, they continue.

As far as discipline is concerned, the Overstreets insist that even the smallest child can begin to develop standards of conduct and a sense of the common welfare of the family. And no one in the family should be "above the law."

The first constructive step in many families toward a richer and better experience, say the Overstreets, often is a conference to develop some common principles or goals—say, some New Year's resolutions. They may get considerably bent during coming months, but they should never be broken!

STATEHOOD!

House Sends Bill to Ike

WASHINGTON, D.C., March 12—Congress ended decades of procrastination today and sent to the White House a bill to give Hawaii the Statehood it has so long deserved.

The House overwhelmingly approved the bill this afternoon.

The vote was 323-89. The time was 3:04 p.m. E.S.T. (10:04 a.m. H.S.T.).

It was the same bill that passed the Senate 76-15 last night.

More Statehood . . .

The House action sent the bill on to President Eisenhower whose signature was assured.

The actual admission will be delayed for several months by the mechanics of procedure which includes holding an election in Hawaii.

It likely will be late July, possibly as late as October, before the 50th State formally joins the Union.

President Eisenhower has 10 legislative days—not counting Sundays—to sign the bill after it formally is presented to him, possibly tomorrow.

Under the terms of the bill, the Governor of Hawaii has 30 days after formal notification of the President's approval to issue a proclamation of elections.

. . . On the Inside

The primary election could be held no less than 60 or more than 90 days after the proclamation. A general election could be held no later than 40 days after the primary.

After the results of the elections are officially certified to the President—assuming Hawaii elects to accept Statehood—the President would issue his proclamation admitting Hawaii as a state.

Governor Quinn of Hawaii said today he was not prepared to say how soon he could be ready to proclaim elections or what time interval would be allowed for them.

As the House roll call reached the 218 affirmative votes needed for passage, Governor Quinn, who was waiting here, telephoned a signal for celebrations to be touched off in Hawaii. This was about 2:57 p.m. (9:57 a.m. Hawaii Time.)

It was a moment the residents of the last incorporated territory under the American flag had awaited for more than 50 years.

Hawaii will be the first island state. But Alaska's admission as the 49th state had already broken through a long argument from some Congress members against admitting territories not joined geographically to the other states.

Congressional opposition, which had kept the door slammed shut on Hawaii, melted in the final hours of House debate.

Speaker Rayburn, Texas Democrat, who once said the Statehood Bill would pass over his dead body, came over in the last hour.

Representative Rogers, Texas Democrat, in the day's first major

Turn to Page 1-D, Column 8

Stocks Late

Because of transmission delay, the New York Stock Exchange quotations are not included in this edition.

Honolulu Star-Bulletin

HONOLULU, TERRITORY OF HAWAII, U. S. A., THURSDAY, MARCH 12, 1959

Honolulu Star-Bulletin, Vol. 48, No. 61 ★★★★ Phone 57-911

Special Radio, Phone Lines Flash News

Sirens, Bells Herald Statehood Arrival

The wail of civil defense sirens informed Honolulans today that Statehood, long awaited, had finally been approved.

Immediately afterward church bells pealed, ships' whistles tooted and motorists leaned on their horns.

From 8 to 9 p.m. tonight there will be street dancing at Iolani Palace, on Kalakaua Avenue, at the Moiliili Community Center, Waialae-Kahala Shopping Center, Kailua Shopping Center, Kaneohe, Wahiawa Civic Center, Waipahu, Moanalua Shopping Center, Kalihi Shopping Center and in Pauoa.

At 7:25 p.m. the international bonfire will be lit at Sand Island.

From 7:30 to 9 p.m. the Armed Forces will set off pyrotechnics off Leeward Oahu.

Tomorrow, legislators and other Government officials are scheduled to proceed from Iolani Palace at 9 a.m. to Kawaiahao Church, where an interdenominational service is to be held.

A joint concert by the Royal Hawaiian Band and Armed Forces bands is scheduled for 10 a.m. at the Palace.

At 11 a.m. a Statehood Commemoration Ceremony is to be held there.

At noon a 50-gun salute is to be fired from the Palace grounds. Simultaneously, Hawaii Air National Guard planes are to fly in formation over the legislative chambers.

Turn to Page 1-D, Column 7

DIRECTORY

Faubus's Telegram

Statehood support and congratulations came from many sources, including areas in the Deep South from where they weren't expected.

As an example, the United Press released a telegram today sent by Governor Orval E. Faubus of Arkansas, undated but held up until Congress had completed action.

Governor Faubus's telegram reads:

"For years I have favored and have openly supported Statehood for both Hawaii and Alaska. Please accept my sincere congratulations on soon becoming the 50th State of the Union."

★ ★ ★ First Class Citizens Now ★ ★ ★

Anchorage Daily Times

EXTRA

READ BY ALASKANS EVERYWHERE

ORTY-THIRD YEAR | PHONE 58201 | ANCHORAGE, ALASKA, MONDAY, JUNE 30, 1958 | 20 PAGES | PRICE 10 CENTS

WE'RE IN

★★★★★★★ ★★★★★★★ ★★★★★★★ ★★★★★★★ ★★★★★★★ ★★★★★★★ ★★★★★★★

64-20 VOTE MAKES ALASKA 49th STATE

Historic Vote Ends 6 Days Of Debate

By A. ROBERT SMITH
Times Washington Correspondent

WASHINGTON (AP) — Alaskan statehood forces won their most historic congressional battle tonight by pushing the statehood bill through the Senate in a whirlwind finish. Opposition forces utterly collapsed tonight after six days of debate.

The historic moment came at 8 o'clock EDT. (2 p.m. Anchorage time). The vote was 64-20. Victory came on the vote of 33 Republicans and 31 Democrats. Opposing it were 12 Democrats and 8 Republicans.

Fighting off all amendments and efforts to sidetrack the bill to a committee for further study, Senator Jackson led statehood backers to the victory they have waited many years to celebrate. At his side throughout the long debate was Alaskan Delegate Bob Bartlett.

The bill now goes to the White House for the signature of President Eisenhower making it the law of the land. This act will trigger the machinery of statehood, allowing Gov. Mike Stepovich to set election dates. After the election, the President will proclaim Alaska the 49th State. The President is expected to sign the bill Wednesday or Thursday and to notify Gov. Stepovich immediately. The governor is in Washington and undoubtedly will be present at the White House to receive the news personally, along with a large contingent of Alaskans who have been in Washington urging passage of the statehood bill.

Final passage came quickly after the defeat of a surprise proposal for sending the bill to the Armed Services Committee 55-31. For an anxious hour or two, this move had statehood backers sweating. It had both Republican and Democratic sponsorship from senators who said they were concerned about national security.

Just before the vote that passed the bill, senators crowded into the chambers, visitors jammed the galleries and there was a feel of history in the making for everyone present. Senators one by one arose to congratulate the many persons in Congress whose efforts were rewarded by tonight's action. When the vote was announced by Senator Neuberger of Oregon, who was presiding at the time, the chamber was filled with applause.

The opposition collapsed after the Senate slapped down an amendment by Sen. Thurmond, 62-22, and followed by shou ing down a second Thurmond amendment.

Senator Eastland, the other chief holdout then threw in the sponge and said he wasn't going to even bother to try to send the bill to his Judiciary Committee as he had intended. He said he knew he was licked.

By this time the bandwagon for statehood was rolling in high gear. It had been gathering speed all day in

(Continued on Page 11)

'Great Day' In History Of Alaska

WASHINGTON, (AP) — Senate action, completing Congressional consideration of Alaskan statehood, tonight provoked the following comment:

Delegate E. L. (Bob) Bartlett (D-Alaska) — "This is a great day. This is the greatest day in Alaska's history. The Congress has acted wisely and in the national interest. We of Alaska will justify what has been done this day — we shall make there a state mighty in every way."

Gov. Mike Stepovich of Alaska:

"Thank God for everything that's happened here. We will show the people of the United States they have not made a mistake."

Territorial Sen. John Butrovich — "It's the American tradition. We've seen it work today."

Sen. William A. Egan, one of Alaska's unofficial Congressional delegation — "Passage of the Alaska statehood bill by the Senate assures that the American citizens of Alaska have won the long fought battle to enjoy their rightful heritage as one of the great states of our Ameri-

(Continued on Page 11)

Victory Brings Quick Reactions

eaders of the Anchorage mmunity could hardly contain ir exuberance today as the s came from Washington, ., that the Senate had passthe statehood bill.

eactions ranged the entire nut of phrases of joy and ght in every phase of Anrage life.

The sirens blaring out the ws that Alaska had become e 49th state drew spectators iting for the Edna Lee Deers murder trial to resume t onto the steps of the U.S. urthouse.

udge J. L. McCarrey Jr., o had just entered the courtm, adjourned the court. Mrs. ders sat in the corridor n her mother, unmoved as rt house employes, lawyers, visitors surged along the ways of the courthouse.

n his chambers, minutes la- Judge McCarrey seemed nned.

He expressed concern over the trend of events. He said he had no comment to make on the passage of statehood. He said only, "My concern is will they allow us to go into this state in an orderly manner."

City Manager George Shannon could only say, "Whoopee! I'm very happy. It means we'll have more home rule. We won't have to go to Washington now for insignificant items of local affairs.

Richard Kennard, president of the Chamber of Commerce, added, "Hallelujah! That's wonderful. I think that's terrific. It's the greatest day of our life."

City Councilman Roy Nigh found he couldn't describe his reaction. "It's wonderful. Words can't describe it." And William Besser, also a councilman, cried out, "Hurrah, I'm delighted."

(Continued on Page 11)

She Goes Up Tonight

BONFIRE CELEBRATION IS TONIGHT

The biggest bonfire in Alaska will be lit tonight to celebrate statehood. Explorer Scouts who have been on guard at the park strip site at Ninth and H will light the fire with torches in an all-out celebration of statehood bill passage by the Senate. The bonfire will spark other similar celebrations throughout Alaska. Forty-nine tons of wood went into the historic pile — with an extra ton for Hawaii. The big celebration at the bonfire will be at 8 p.m. There will be band music, singing, dancing, prayers. Firemen will be on hand to keep the fire under control. Traffic will be kept from the immediate scene. All roads are expected to lead to the park strip for the historic program. This view of the huge pile of wood shows the L Street Apartments in the background.

Anchorage Blows Its Lid

Anchorage blew the lid off today.

Alaska's largest city rocked and rolled as the air was split by the sound of sirens, horns, bells, firecrackers, guns — and everything else that could be used to make a noise.

Sirens sounded first as the official word came through that the Senate had, at long last, passed the statehood bill. Then came the eruption of noise.

Pent-up emotions were released in a spontaneous burst of excitement that penetrated everywhere.

Employes s t r e a m e d from their places of business and an immediate holiday was declared.

Although most of the activity was uncontrolled, there was some with a definite purpose. Members of the Elks Lodge hurried with their huge American flag to the federal building. There Fur Rendez-

(Continued on Page 11)

First 49-Star Flag Goes Up

Within minutes after word was received here of Senate passage of the statehood bill, Federal Electric Corp. claimed it was flying, before anyone else, a flag with 49 stars for the new state. The flag was flying at its Fifth and Barrow building.

1960

John F. Kennedy was elected as thirty-fifth President of the United States. At forty-three, he was the youngest man ever elected to the office and the first Roman Catholic.

Lyndon B. Johnson was elected as Vice-President.

A U-2 spy plane flown by Gary Powers was shot down over Soviet territory. Powers was imprisoned and exchanged by the Soviets the next year for convicted Soviet spy Rudolf Abel.

Premier Fidel Castro of Cuba confiscated U.S. property in his Caribbean island nation. The United States then embargoed exports to Cuba.

Two commercial airliners crashed over New York City, killing 134 in the air and on the ground.

--Five Pages of Stories and Pictures of Plane Crash--

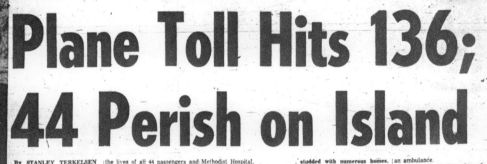

Staten Island Advance

THE WEATHER — Tonight: Snow flurries, low in teens. Tomorrow: Mostly fair and cold.

VOL. 75. NO. 13,061 STATEN ISLAND, N. Y., SATURDAY, DECEMBER 17, 1960 5-STAR FINAL 22 PAGES 5 CENTS

Plane Toll Hits 136; 44 Perish on Island

By STANLEY TERKELSEN

The death toll in yesterday's air crash over Staten Island — the worst air tragedy in history—climbed today to 136. Nine of them were bystanders in a thickly populated neighborhood of the Park Slope section of Brooklyn.

The crash of the four-engine Trans World Air Lines Constellation which disintegrated in a thunderous explosion over New Dorp and plummeted in parts onto Miller Field — a few hundred feet from a built-up section of one-family homes — claimed the lives of all 44 passengers and crew.

It was almost certain that a Staten Islander, 40 - year - old Michael Hotinski of 11 Simonson Ave., Mariners Harbor, was aboard the second plane, a United Air Lines DC-8 jet that set off a nine-alarm fire when it plunged to earth amid a row of brownstone dwellings in Brooklyn.

The only survivor among the 127 persons aboard the planes was another DC-8 passenger, an 11-year-old Wilmette, Ill., boy who was conscious but in critical condition today in Brooklyn's Methodist Hospital.

* * *

THE LARGEST group of investigators ever assembled by the Civil Aeronautics Board was working around the clock in an effort to determine how the paths of the liners crossed over Staten Island when their approach routes should have placed them 10 miles apart.

South Shore residents who watched in horror as the Constellation exploded at low altitude over New Dorp and separated at low altitude into three large sections said it was miraculous the aircraft missed plowing into neighborhoods studded with numerous homes, schools and stores.

Several said they were sure the pilot had made a last-minute effort to steer the severed plane into the New Dorp airfield or the Lower Bay.

* * *

FRANTIC rescue efforts by scores of individuals extricated two men and a woman from the Miller Field wreckage alive.

The men were flown by Coast Guard helicopter to the U.S. Public Health Service Hospital, where both died within an hour.

The woman died while being rushed to the same hospital in an ambulance.

Investigators had no immediate evidence how the midair collision occurred, or that there was any direct contact between the two aircraft at all.

None of the scores of witnesses who saw the constellation separate and explode in a ball of flames over New Dorp said they actually saw a collision.

* * *

THERE was a possibility one of the planes exploded first, shooting heavy remnants into the second aircraft.

Part of an aileron of the United

(Continued on Page 2)

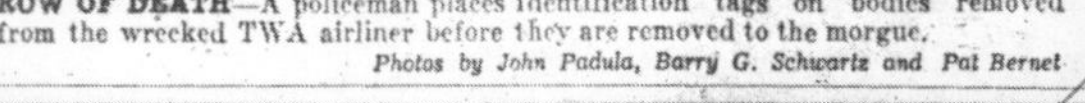

ROW OF DEATH—A policeman places identification tags on bodies removed from the wrecked TWA airliner before they are removed to the morgue.

Photos by John Padula, Barry G. Schwartz and Pat Bernet

LAST REMAINS—Water is poured onto the burning sections of the TWA Constellation where it crashed in Miller Field.

COCKPIT OF DEATH—The top of the Constellation's cockpit remains intact amidst other twisted wreckage at Miller Field.

Miller Field: Death Takes Over

By RAYMOND A. WITTEK

Death left a bloody imprint in the snow in a corner of Miller Field yesterday.

Everywhere there was destruction and the sight of bleeding, mutilated bodies—some with parts of clothing burned off—sprawled in the snow.

And the air was filled with the sickly sweet odor of those who perished in the flames.

The living picked their way among the dead.

A priest, seeing a body, dropped to his knee, and gave the last rites of the Roman Catholic Church.

* * *

EVERYWHERE there were soldiers, civilians and firemen and policemen, some in uniform

(Continued on Page 2)

'I Baptized a Tiny Child . . .'

By ALAN CHRISTOFFERSEN

One after another, the Rev John J. Lennon administered last rites over the charred remains of the air-crash victims at Miller Field.

Dead or alive, he didn't know. He administered the rites so many times he lost count.

"I can't even say how many persons there were . . . I know there was a tiny child I baptized," said the assistant pastor of Our Lady Queen of Peace R.C. Church, New Dorp.

Other clergymen of various faiths also sped to the scene to do what they could.

The Rev. Joseph T. Riordan, assistant pastor of St. Joseph's R. C. Church, Rossville, and St. Thomas R.C. Church, Pleasant Plains, rode to the scene in a St. Vincent's Hospital ambulance. He joined with priests from St. Char-

(Continued on Page 2)

Even the Hardened Are Numb

By ROBERT J. POPP

Dozens of men worked quietly yesterday with the stamp of tragedy on their face.

Each of them had seen violent death in some form, had seen many grief-stricken people. But the very immensity of this numbed them.

They carried bodies into the morgue at Farm Colony on stretchers. They carried them in on cots. One was even lifted in wrapped in a blanket.

When the morgue proper became filled, the bodies were laid out in rows in an adjacent garage. There was a stillness about the scene. Policemen, detectives, morgue workers—all seemed to be wrapped in their own thoughts.

* * *

MANY turned their eyes for a time to a large red stain in the snow—a stain that was common 16 years ago yesterday during the Battle of the Bulge.

Here specialists in identifying bodies worked quietly and quick

(Continued on Page 11

Islander Went On Death Flight At Final Minute

By GEORGE O. REDDY

A 40-year-old Mariners Harbor businessman's name was included on the passenger list of the United Air Lines jet plane that crashed in Brooklyn yesterday after colliding with another airliner over Staten Island, United said.

He is Michael Hotinski of 11 Simonson Ave., the father of two sons.

His wife, Gertrude, was under sedation last night after being treated by a doctor.

A friend and a business acquaintance both phoned United's office in Chicago to confirm that Hotinski was on the plane. A ticket agent informed them that although Hotinski did not have a reservation his name was on the passenger list for the flight.

Despite his name being on the

(Continued on Page 11)

MICHAEL HOTINSKI

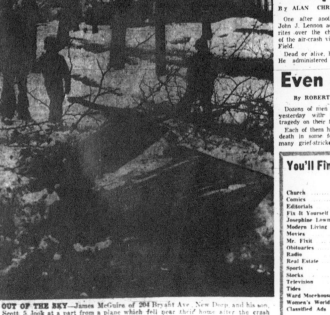

OUT OF THE SKY—James McGuire of 204 Bryant Ave., New Dorp, and his son, Scott, 5, look at a part from a plane which fell near their home after the crash of a DC 8 jet and a four-engine Constellation.

You'll Find It . . .

Bandits Get $11,000 in Stickup

By ALFRED G. HAGGERTY and ROBERT J. LYONS

Two armed men, wearing women's clothes walked quietly into a West Brighton bank yesterday afternoon and ordered two women tellers to fill a paper bag with money. They walked out with $11,723 in cash after slugging the manager with a gun butt.

The employes of the New Brighton-Staten Island Savings and Loan Association branch at 741 Castleton Ave. said one of the men was in his 30's and was wearing a woman's fur coat and a "peculiar hat."

The other, they said, was in his 20's and wearing dark glasses, but in the excitement they didn't notice what clothing he was wearing. "I think he had on a women's coat," one of them said. Both men were about six feet tall, they added.

William Ford of Sea View, the branch manager, and the two tellers, Ada Egbert of Stapleton and Catherine Lenza of Mariners Harbor, were the only ones in the bank when the robbers walked in about 1:30.

* * *

THE TELLERS knew they were men immediately, Ford said, but thought it was a belated Halloween joke and weren't too concerned.

Their lack of concern quickly turned to fear when the men whipped out guns and one of them said, "Stand back."

Ford, who was working in a rear office, said:

"I heard some commotion. Just as I got to the door one of the men leaped over the partition at the back and ordered me to lie down. When I didn't get down right away, he hit me with the gun. Then I went down, flat."

At the same time, the man told the women not to touch the alarm.

Then the same man handed

(Continued on Page 11)

1962

Seventeen days in October were fraught with the ultimate danger—the possibility of nuclear war.

In Cuba, United States spy planes had discovered missile bases under construction by the Soviets. President Kennedy ordered a naval blockade of the island.

Finally, Soviet Premier Nikita Khrushchev agreed to dismantle the bases and remove the missiles.

John Glenn became the first American to orbit the earth, with a three-orbit flight aboard *Friendship 7*. Later in the year, Scott Carpenter went three orbits aboard *Aurora 7*, and Walter Schirra completed six orbits aboard *Sigma 7*.

Rachel Carson published *Silent Spring*, about insecticides. . . .Barbara Tuchman wrote *Guns of August*, about the beginnings of World War I. . . .Stanley Kubrick directed *Lolita*, based on Vladimir Nabokov's book. . . .Edward Albee wrote *Who's Afraid of Virginia Woolf.*

5 FINAL EDITION
© 1962 NEWSDAY INC
CENTS

Newsday

LONG ISLAND
Tues., Feb. 20, 1962 Vol. 22, No. 142

GLENN FLIES! 'FEELS FINE'

Shot Perfect; Try 3 Orbits

(Story on Page 3)

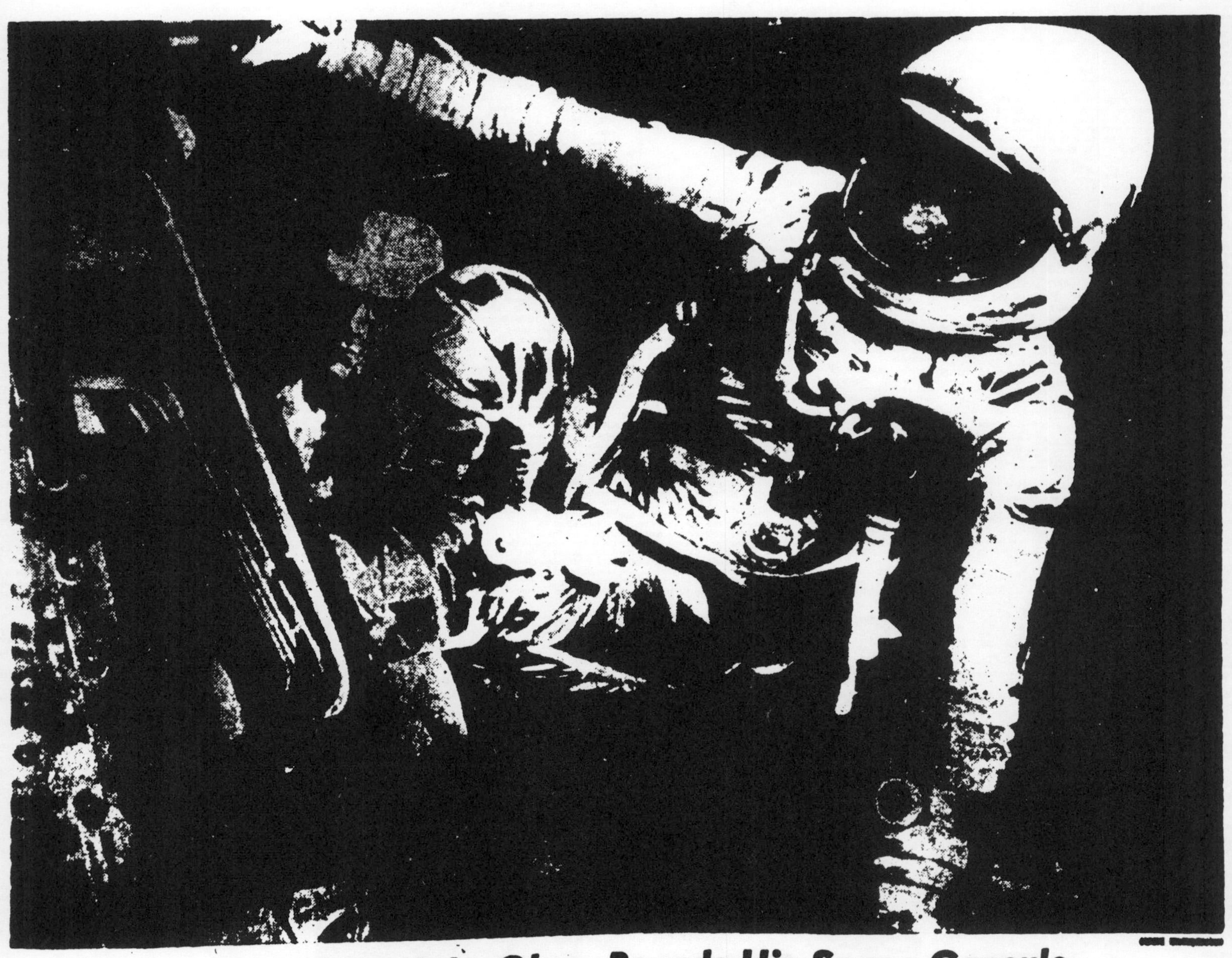

Astronaut John Glenn Boards His Space Capsule

FINAL THE COMMERCIAL APPEAL FINAL

23rd YEAR—No. 274 C***** MEMPHIS, TENN., MONDAY MORNING, OCTOBER 1, 1962 32 PAGES PRICE 7 CENTS

Two Men Are Dead In Campus Rioting After Meredith Is Escorted To Dormitory; Soldiers Try To Restore Order At Ole Miss

Barnett's Plea

Governor Concedes Negro On Campus—Urges All To Avoid Violence

By KENNETH TOLER

From The Commercial Appeal Jackson, Miss., Bureau

JACKSON, Miss., Sept. 30. — Gov. Ross Barnett Sunday night virtually conceded that Negro James Meredith would be enrolled at the University of Mississippi and urged Mississippians to avoid violence.

At the same time he said "Mississippi will continue to fight the Meredith case and all similar cases through the courts.

"Surrounded on all sides by the armed forces and oppressive power of the United States of America," the governor said, "my courage and convictions do not waver . . . but we must at all odds preserve the peace and avoid bloodshed."

Governor Barnett spent the day at the governor's mansion, the oldest governor's mansion in the nation, set back about 50 feet from a busy downtown Jackson street.

An arch-segregationist who had fought hard on four previous occasions to prevent James Meredith from entering the university, Governor Barnett did not fight Sunday.

By doing nothing to prevent the Negro's entry on the campus Sunday or to prevent his registration when it comes, Governor Barnett could purge himself of contempt of the United States Fifth Circuit Court of Appeals in New Orleans. He has until Tuesday to purge himself or become liable for a civil contempt fine of $10,000 a day.

Governor Barnett modified his course only after receiving a personal telegram from President Kennedy demanding he do so, and after having had several telephone conferences over the past few days with Atty. Gen. Robert Kennedy, the President's brother.

Governor Barnett's statement, handed to the press Sunday night by state highway patrolman guarding the mansion, follows:

"As Governor of the State of Mississippi, I have just been informed by the attorney general of the United States that Meredith has today (Sunday) been placed on the campus of the University of Mississippi by means of Government helicopters and is accompanied by Federal officers.

"I urge all Mississippians and instruct every state officer under my command to do everything in their power to preserve peace and to avoid violence in any form.

"Surrounded on all sides by the armed forces and oppressive power of the United States of America, my courage and my convictions do not waver. My heart still says 'never,' but my calm judgment abhors the bloodshed that would follow. I love Mississippi. I love her people. I love those 10,000 good Mississippians in the National Guard who have been federalized and requested to oppose me and their own people. I know that we are physically overpowered. I know that our principles remain true, but we must at all odds preserve the peace and avoid bloodshed.

"To the officials of the Federal government, I say:

"Gentlemen, you are tramping on the sovereignty of this great state and depriving it of every vestige of honor and respect as a member of the union of states. You are destroying the Constitution of this great nation. May God have mercy on your souls. Mississippi will continue to fight the Meredith case and all similar cases through the courts to restore the sovereignty of the state and constitutional government."

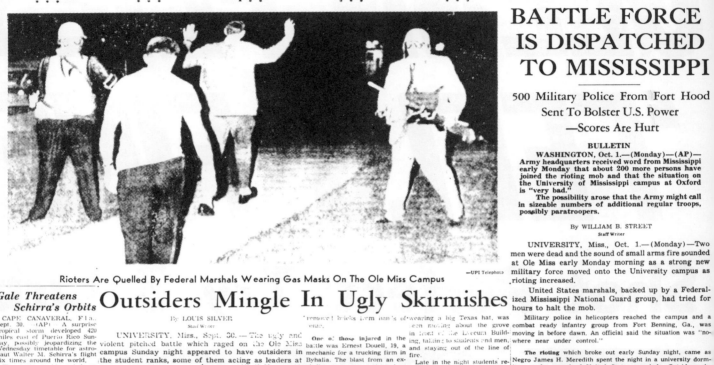

Rioters Are Quelled By Federal Marshals Wearing Gas Masks On The Ole Miss Campus —UPI Telephoto

Gale Threatens Schirra's Orbits

CAPE CANAVERAL, Fla., Sept. 30. —(AP)— A surprise tropical storm developed 420 miles east of Puerto Rico Sunday, possibly jeopardizing the Wednesday timetable for astronaut Walter M. Schirra's flight six times around the world.

The storm, packing winds up to 54 miles an hour late Sunday, is traveling on a track which would carry it across the impact area for Schirra's third orbit at about launch time.

A Weather Bureau advisory said winds inside the storm are expected to increase over the next 12 hours, raising the spectre of a fullfledged hurricane.

Present plans call for Schirra to be sent on his 17,500-mile-an-hour trip between 6 a.m. and 8 a.m. Wednesday (Memphis time). The flight plan calls for perfect weather in all possible recovery areas before takeoff.

NASA scheduled a weather briefing for Monday morning.

The Weather

U. S. DEPARTMENT OF COMMERCE

FOR MEMPHIS and Vicinity— Monday mostly cloudy with showers ending before noon. Partly cloudy and cooler in the afternoon. High Monday 70. Winds southerly at 10 miles per hour becoming northerly at 10 to 15 miles per hour in the afternoon. Partly cloudy and cool Monday night and Tuesday. Low Monday night 54.

Sun rises 5:54; sets 5:44

FIVE-DAY OUTLOOK

FOR THE MID-SOUTH—Temperatures will average 4 to 6 degrees below normal. Cool through the middle of the week, then slowly rising temperatures through the week end. Normal high 80. Normal low 57. Precipitation will total less than one-fourth inch occurring the first of the week.

YESTERDAY'S REPORT

Highest, 82 degrees at 2:30 p.m.

Lowest, 54 degrees at 5:30 a.m.

Mean (midway between high and low), 73. Normal mean for date, 70.

HOURLY READINGS

4 a.m.	57	4 p.m.	79
6 a.m.	55	6 p.m.	76
8 a.m.	64	8 p.m.	71
10 a.m.	72	10 p.m.	70
Noon	78	Midnight	67
2 p.m.	81	2 a.m.	67

Temperature 7 a.m., 57; 7 p.m., 74. Precipitation at Airport, none. Dewpoint (condensation temperature) at midnight 57, barometer reading at midnight [illegible], falling. Precipitation Jan. 1—Sept. 29, 36.78 inches which is .57 inches below normal.

A YEAR AGO YESTERDAY

Maximum temperature, 90; minimum, 66; rainfall 17. Precipitation Jan. 1—Sept. 30, 31.74 inches which was 4.76 inches below normal.

(Map, Forecast on Page 18)

Outsiders Mingle In Ugly Skirmishes

By LOUIS SILVER

Staff Writer

UNIVERSITY, Miss., Sept. 30. — The ugly and violent pitched battle which raged on the Ole Miss campus Sunday night appeared to have outsiders in the student ranks, some of them acting as leaders at times.

During the skirmishes, mob members hurled brickbats and slabs of stone at the steel-helmeted marshals.

The marshals responded by firing tear gas which choked the area in the vicinity of the Lyceum Building where the fight raged.

The crowd was estimated at about 2,000 centered by a militant core of about 400.

Angry young men clutching bricks, soft drink bottles and rocks made two unsuccessful attacks on the marshals ringing the administration building. The men, many of whom appeared not to be students, massed at the base of a statue of a Confederate soldier.

They moved toward the Lyceum Building in the first surge and were turned back by a heavy barrage of exploding tear gas shells fired by the marshals.

After scattering, they reassembled for the second surge. And again were met by a second tear gas barrage.

Col. T. B. Birdsong, chief of the Mississippi Highway Patrol, was gassed when a tear gas bomb exploded at his feet. He was moved inside the Lyceum Building.

The gas temporarily put out of action this newspaper's Bill Street, but he later returned to the scene. Street earlier had been a tear gas victim during the Montgomery freedom-rider conflict.

Several injuries were reported, including three students who said they were hit by pellets from a shotgun blast. They were unidentified, but witnesses said pellets struck one in the hand, another in the cheek and a third in a leg.

Many persons with tears streaming from their eyes took refuge in the campus YMCA building located about 300 yards from the administration building.

Former Army Maj. Gen. Edwin Walker was conspicuous on the campus. He was routed with about 300 students by a tear gas barrage.

Between the two volleys of tear gas was a brief and unsuccessful effort to **arrange a** truce which would end the clouds of tear gas from the marshals and the hail of brickbats from the mob. Three students handled negotiations, but their talks with the marshals were interrupted by shouts of "Get the Nigger out." The negotiations ended when other students crowded around.

Before the first mob advance began, General Walker addressed a crowd of 400 students. He told them any blood that was shed was "on the hands of the Federal Government." He also quoted an aide of Gov. Ross Barnett as telling him Mississippi had "been sold out." After the speech, the mob advanced on the Lyceum Building.

Quite a few students who weren't rioting left the campus. Girls streamed out of dormitories, some half dressed, got into cars and fled the campus.

Two Episcopal clergymen appeared on the campus to try to bring the violence to a halt. The Rev. Duncan Gray Jr., rector of St. Peter's Church, and the Rev. Wofford Smith, episcopal chaplain at the university, approached students, urged them to throw down their bricks, and removed bricks from hands of some.

One of those injured in the battle was Ernest Douell, 19, a mechanic for a trucking firm in Byhalia. The blast from an exploding tear gas canister hospitalized him with a severe wrist laceration.

"I dodged the first one of those things, but the second one got me." He said he came down with about 55 friends in eight cars from Byhalia and Olive Branch area. He insisted they did not come to participate, but only to watch.

Highway patrolman Weldon Brunt of Ackerman was reported to be seriously injured, and was being flown to a hospital in Jackson.

Meanwhile in Starkville, more than a thousand persons, many of them Mississippi State University students, hoisted a Confederate flag to the top of the campus parade grounds, and burned a paper dummy, apparently representing James H. Meredith. The crowd cheered.

Students then piled in cars and rode through Starkville streets. City police said no damage was done and that the youths were "just letting off steam."

Most of the street lights in the circle in front of the Lyceum were broken out, and jagged pieces of soft drink bottles and pieces of metal littered the ground. One youth fired a fire extinguisher into the face of one of the drivers of the trucks used to bring marshals in.

One marshal near the administration building was struck on the leg by a two-foot iron pipe wielded by one of the students.

Chancellor J. D. Williams used a loudspeaker to urge students to go back to their dormitories. As of last night, Chancellor Williams indicated that classes would be held, if possible, today.

Meanwhile, General Walker, wearing a big Texas hat, was seen moving about the grove in front of the Lyceum Building, talking to students and men, and staying out of the line of fire.

Late in the night students resorted to different tactics. They rolled up a fire truck, stretched out a hose, and aimed a stream of water at the Lyceum. They were repulsed by tear gas.

Army trucks driving up to the marshals' line-of-defense in front of the Lyceum were peppered with rocks, stones, and bricks.

Seven marshals stood at one end of Baxter Hall where James Meredith is staying. The manager of Baxter Hall pleaded with Federal officials to remove Meredith. But marshals stood firm and refused.

The number of people in the grove seemed to increase. A public official said a good part of the crowd were non-students.

More cars of outsiders arrived, one bearing a sign "Arkansas Volunteers."

Chancellor Williams asked the staff of the campus daily, "The Mississippian" to put out a special edition for Monday, although it is ordinarily not printed that day. An editorial appearing said: "This is a battle between the State of Mississippi and the United States Government; the University is caught in the middle . . . the Federal Government is once again showing its strength and powers to uphold the laws of our country.

"No matter what your conviction you should follow the advice of Gov. Ross Barnett by not taking any action for violence . . ."

The Lyceum was made a command post. Injured marshals were taken inside, where a physician treated them. Physicians were standing by at Oxford Hospital for additional injured. Students receiving minor injuries were treated at University Health Center.

Even in the early morning hours, General Walker remained on the campus.

BATTLE FORCE IS DISPATCHED TO MISSISSIPPI

500 Military Police From Fort Hood Sent To Bolster U.S. Power —Scores Are Hurt

BULLETIN

WASHINGTON, Oct. 1.—(Monday)—(AP)— Army headquarters received word from Mississippi early Monday that about 200 more persons have joined the rioting mob and that the situation on the University of Mississippi campus at Oxford is "very bad."

The possibility arose that the Army might call in sizeable numbers of additional regular troops, possibly paratroopers.

By WILLIAM B. STREET

Staff Writer

UNIVERSITY, Miss., Oct. 1.—(Monday)—Two men were dead and the sound of small arms fire sounded at Ole Miss early Monday morning as a strong new military force moved onto the University campus as rioting increased.

United States marshals, backed up by a Federalized Mississippi National Guard group, had tried for hours to halt the mob.

Military police in helicopters reached the campus and a combat ready infantry group from Fort Benning, Ga., was moving in before dawn. An official said the situation was "nowhere near under control."

The rioting which broke out early Sunday night, came as Negro James H. Meredith spent the night in a university dormitory under guard of United States marshals. Outside mobs flocked on the campus and engaged the marshals in swirling combat.

Mississippi Highway Patrolmen and sheriffs and city police officers moved in and set up blockades at campus entrances early this morning.

A foreign newsman, Paul Guihard, was found dead near a women's dormitory with a "penetrating back wound" and Ray Gunter, 23, of near Oxford, died with a bullet wound in the head.

A marshal clubbed a white youth entering the dormitory where Meredith was housed.

Three other persons were hurt during the shooting on the campus and a number of persons were hurt by exploding tear gas cartridges, including this reporter.

Two Federal marshals were shot and a coed was hurt slightly when she was hit in the stomach by an exploding tear gas shell. Marshal Graham Same was in serious condition with a gunshot wound in the neck and another marshal was hit in the thigh by a bullet fired from the mob. The coed was identified as Ann Gillespie.

About 75 students were treated for cuts, bruises and tear gas burns. Bill Crider of the Associated Press Bureau in Memphis was injured, apparently not seriously, when he was hit in the back by shotgun pellets.

Many members of the mob obviously were not students. They carried soft drink and beer bottles filled with gasoline to make Molotov cocktails to hurl.

The combat-ready Second Battle Group of the 2nd Infantry, en route from Fort Benning, Ga., to Memphis was ordered to Oxford at 1 a.m. today. At 12:10 a.m., A Company of the 503rd Military Police Battalion was air-lifted by helicopter to the campus. The remainder of the unit and the 716th MP Battalion moved by truck.

The battle group will begin arriving in Oxford at 4 a.m. today, Army officials said. The entire unit will be on the campus by 5:30 a.m.

To replace the units ordered to Oxford, a 500-man MP Battalion from Fort Hood, Texas, the 720th began moving to Millington.

Lt. Gov. Paul B. Johnson was reported en route from Jackson to the campus. A number of the students were upset and leaving the university. One coed had tears streaming down her face as she wrote the riot story for the university newspaper.

Meredith was in Baxter Dormitory and the force of marshals around the dormitory was increased. Many students refused to stay in the dormitory with the Negro.

Among the outside demonstrators on the campus was former Maj. Gen. Edwin Walker of Dallas. He was accompanied by a relatively small number of demonstrators.

Guihard's body was found by students and the Oxford Hospital administrator said his death probably was caused by the "penetrating wound" in the upper part of his back. He was a correspondent for the London Daily Sketch.

There were no details about Gunter's death. The wounded marshal was flown to Memphis Naval Air Station at Millington.

Crider, struck in the back by the shotgun blast, said shots rang out sporadically around the campus.

He said they came from guns in the hands "of kids rushing around and not enrolled here."

Crider said he saw seven or eight teenagers shooting.

The firings in the night followed a tear gas barrage by marshals holding back a mob of 2,000 screaming, jeering persons.

The tragic turn of events on the 114-year-old campus rich with traditions followed a plea by President John F. Kennedy and Gov. Ross Barnett for peaceful compliance with desegregation orders.

Mississippi Highway Patrolmen were ordered returned to their home districts at 7 Sunday night in an order broadcast on the patrol radio network. The order said the "university campus has been taken over by Federal forces."

Chancellor J. D. Williams used a loudspeaker system to ask all students to refrain from rioting.

(Additional stories on the Ole Miss integration crisis are on Pages 17, 4 and 24, with pictures on Pages 17 and 32. Kennedy text Page 5.)

Army Trucks Take United States Marshals Down Sorority Row On Ole Miss Campus —UPI Telephoto

On The Inside Pages—

Pennant Race Ends In Tie

SAN FRANCISCO VICTORY and Los Angeles defeat forces playoff for the National League pennant. —Page 20.

A TRANSFORMATION TAKES PLACE every week at Whitehaven YMCA. A lounge with jukebox disappears, and an altar table and electric organ are added, to make a religious sanctuary. —Page 3.

CHEATING THE GOVERNMENT isn't difficult under the ADC welfare program. One woman receiving checks was told the Welfare Department had no records on her payments. —Page 11.

One Sunday Magazine

The Miami Herald

Sunday, October 28, 1962 No. 331 Florida's Most Complete Newspaper 52nd Year 212 Pages 20 Cents
A Latin American Edition is Published Daily

JFK Tells Nikita Missiles Must Go; U.S. Plane Missing

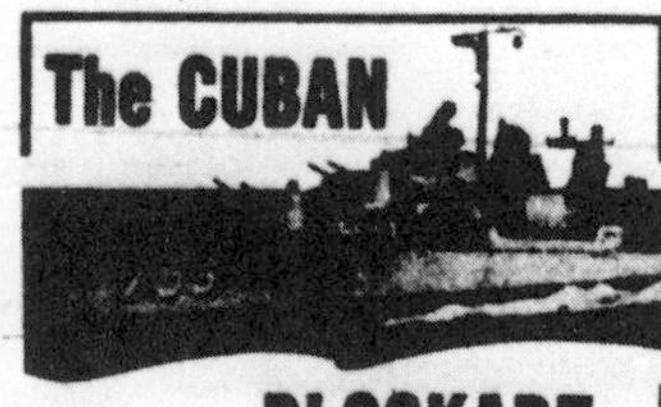

At a Glance

KENNEDY-KHRUSHCHEV

President Kennedy rejected Premier Khrushchev's deal to swap missile bases in Cuba for U.S. bases in Turkey. Kennedy said Khrushchev must defuse the nuclear missile buildup in Cuba before there can be "sensible negotiation" or a peaceful settlement of the Cuban crisis.

* * *

CUBA

A U.S. reconnaissance plane was missing and presumed lost Saturday night, after the Cuban government had announced its anti-aircraft guns had fired on unidentified warplanes.

* * *

KEY WEST

Army rocket men threw up machine gun emplacements facing Cuba on Key West beaches Saturday and said they were "ready to go" if called into action as the nation's first line of defense.

* * *

CIVIL DEFENSE

U.S. officials laid Civil Defense plans before the governors conference in Washington. State executives received Pentagon and White House briefings on the crisis.

* * *

MOSCOW

Soviet propagandists whipped up big anti-American demonstrations outside U.S. embassy in Moscow. Some 3,000 Russians broke windows and splattered ink, and then quietly dispersed.

* * *

LONDON

British Foreign Secretary Lord Home warned the Soviet Union that the danger of war is increased by Cuban buildup.

* * *

CASTRO

Fidel Castro is reported stewing in his bared role as a Russian pawn. Indications are he's taking action on his own.

* * *

GUANTANAMO

Admiral reports all's "going along quietly" at U.S. Navy base at Guantanamo. The base can be defended, he said.

* * *

TURKEY

Diplomatic circles feel Khrushchev's cleverly-worded offer to make a Cuba-Turkey missile base deal may have put the U.S. on the propaganda defensive. But Kennedy had no choice. Any other reaction would have had the effect of abandoning the U.S. moral and legal position that the Cuban bases constitute a new Red peril in the Western Hemisphere.

* * *

SCHIRRA

Astronaut Wally Schirra Jr. said that South Florida is the safest place to be in case of a missile attack. Grinning, Schirra said, "if they ever do get mad, you can watch the things going overhead."

* * * * * *

The Full Cuban Story

Aircraft Missing Over Cuba

Cuba Claims Ack-Ack Attack

WASHINGTON — (UPI) — The United States reported one of its military reconnaissance planes missing Saturday night after the Cuban government had announced its anti-aircraft batteries fired on unidentified warplanes.

In a terse statement, the Defense Department said the U.S. plane was presumed lost.

Assistant Defense Secretary Arthur Sylvester added a stern warning that air surveillance of Cuba would continue and "appropriate measures" would be taken to protect U.S. aircraft.

Sylvester gave no other details and did not say where the U.S. plane was missing. But he said they might be made available later.

Earlier in the day, the Cuban armed forces general staff reported that anti-aircraft guns had driven off unidentified planes which penetrated deeply into Western Cuba.

All Cuban government radio stations broke into their programs to read the following communique from the general staff:

"At 10:17 a.m. Cuban anti-aircraft batteries drove off unidentified warplanes which had amply violated Cuban air-space and had penetrated deeply into national territory over the western part of the republic.

"The Cuban armed forces are in a maximum state of alert, a maximum combative disposition, and prepared to defend the sacred rights of the fatherland."

The reference to "western Cuba" in the Cuban communique presumably refers to Pinar del Rio Province.

The Cuban government Saturday ordered the creation of 26-man stretcher-bearer teams in every neighborhood and work center. The National Directorate of Revolutionary Defense Committees said the first aid teams were needed "in these moments in which the threat of direct aggression looms over us from the number one enemy of the peoples of the world, Yankee imperialism."

—Associated Press Wirephoto

Soldiers Man Machine Gun Beside Anti-Aircraft Rocket Position
. . . ready on the beach at Key West, 90 miles from Cuba

'U.S. Plans Military Action Soon,' Adlai Tells Allies

New York Times Service

UNITED NATIONS, N.Y. — Adlai E. Stevenson told the Western allies Saturday that **the United States intends to take military action to eliminate Soviet missile bases in Cuba "in a brief space of time"** unless work on them was halted.

Sources said that Stevenson made clear in his statement to our allies that the military action contemplated, if no way is found to stop the development of the bases, would be in the form of an air strike to put them out of action, not an invasion of Cuba.

The U.S. representative told U.N. delegates of 15 countries that the development of the Cuban bases was threatening to change the nuclear balance of power in favor of the Soviet Union.

He emphasized that, according to the latest U.S. reports, work on the bases was continuing at increased speed.

Stevenson spent half an hour with Thant discussing Premier Khrushchev's letter to President Kennedy offering to give up Soviet missile bases in Cuba in exchange for the withdrawal of American missile bases in Turkey.

Later in the day Thant received Valerian A. Zorin, the Soviet representative, for a talk of an hour and a half. Zorin handed Thant a copy of Khrushchev's letter making the Cuba-Turkey offer.

That's last caller was Mario Garcia-Inchaustegui of Cuba, who gave him a letter from Premier Fidel Castro inviting Thant to visit Cuba "with a view to direct discussions on the present crisis, prompted by our common purpose of freeing mankind from the dangers of war."

Slight optimism for a break-through in the crisis was stirred by the assurances of Kennedy and Khrushchev Friday night to take temporary steps to avoid a "direct confrontation" in the high seas around Cuba. The assurances were in response to appeals from Thant.

U.S. sources emphasized that the continued military buildup in Cuba was the main and immediate concern of the United States and that cessation of the buildup was a preliminary to consideration of any proposals.

* * *

Air Force Calls 14,000

WASHINGTON — (AP) — Secretary of Defense Robert S. McNamara ordered 24 troop carrier squadrons of the Air Force Reserve into active duty Saturday night after Cuban guns fired upon unarmed American reconnaissance planes.

Troop carriers are planes used to transport paratroopers and other combat men. More than 14,000 men are involved in the callup.

In his announcement, McNamara confirmed for the first time that Cuban anti-aircraft guns actually had fired upon American planes.

McNamara said that he was activating associated support units for the troop carrier squadrons.

Haitian Troops Set to Aid U.S.

PORT AU PRINCE, Haiti — (UPI) — All Haitian armed forces were ordered on the alert and at the disposal of the U.S. commander of the naval blockade of Cuba by the Haitian government.

Haiti also ordered its delegates at the Unite Nations and the Organization of American States to support the United States actions against Castro Cuba.

Czech-Cuba Flights Full

VIENNA — (AP) — Passenger flights from Communist Czechoslovakia to Cuba are solidly booked up for the next five weeks, Prague headquarters of National Czech Airlines said Saturday.

An official, reached from Vienna by telephone, said all tickets to Havana had been sold out "since earlier this month for official and private travel."

The airline declined to explain whether the heavy bookings were in any way connected with the Cuban crisis. The line operates two weekly Prague - Havana flights via Shannon and Gander. Cubana, the Cuban air line, flies once a week.

Why Nik Picked Turkey

WASHINGTON — (UPI) — Turkey, at the crossroads of three continents, has been a target of Russian expansionism for more than 200 years.

It was a pro-Allied neutral during the second world war, and one of the first to join the U.S. in sending troops to fight the Korean War in 1950.

President Harry S. Truman and Secretary of State George Marshall decided in 1948 to come to the aid of Greece and Turkey in their struggle to fend off communism.

Since then, the United States has given Turkey more than one billion dollars in economic aid and more than a half billion dollars in military aid.

American intermediate range ballistic missiles — the Jupiters — have been on station in Turkey since 1958, guarding approaches to the underbelly of Europe and to the strategic oil fields of Arabia. These latter contain more oil reserves than any other area in the world.

The United States has about 30 Jupiters, with a range of 1,700 miles, in Turkey and a similar group in Italy. It is these missiles the Soviet Union hopes to eliminate.

The U.S. attitude in recent days has been:

THE U.S. Jupiters in Turkey and Italy were placed there under NATO agreement as defensive weapons against the threat of Soviet nuclear missiles which Khrushchev has said are zeroed in on members of the NATO alliance.

THERE WAS no secrecy about NATO's decision to put

Turn to Page 2A Col. 1

President Sees Hope In Letter

U.S. Will Not Trade Bases

By Herald Wire Services

WASHINGTON — President Kennedy told Soviet Premier Khrushchev Saturday night he believes the United States and Russia could negotiate a solution to the Cuban crisis but said again the possibility depends on prompt dismantling of Soviet missile sites in Cuba.

The White House made public a letter from Kennedy to Khrushchev which termed proposals made by the Soviet leader Friday "generally acceptable."

These proposals, White House sources said, did not include the deal set forth by Khrushchev Saturday in which Russia would withdraw its offensive arms from Cuba and the United States would do the same in Turkey.

This new development to the diplomatic front followed hard on the heels of an announcement by the Pentagon that a U.S. military plane helping to keep watch over the Communist missile buildup in Cuba is missing and presumed lost.

Havana Radio had boasted a few hours earlier that Cuban anti-aircraft batteries had driven off invading planes.

In his letter, Kennedy summed up Khrushchev's previous suggestions as requiring Russia to remove offensive weapons from Cuba under U.N. observation and stop sending weapons to the Castro regime, while the United States would — with U.N. safeguards — halt its weapons blockade of Cuba and pledge not to invade Cuba.

But Kennedy insisted that Russia must first stop work on missile sites in Cuba and render offensive weapons there incapable of operation "under effective international guarantees."

Khrushchev's letter of Friday did not contain any reference to the deal the Soviet premier proposed in a separate message broadcast Saturday by Moscow Radio under which Russia said it would take offensive weapons out of Cuba if the United States pulled missiles out of Turkey.

The Khrushchev letter to which Kennedy referred was not made public, but in his reply Kennedy said the key elements were "generally acceptable as I understand them."

Kennedy said he regarded these points the principal elements of the Soviet premier's proposals:

1—Russia "would agree to remove these weapons systems from Cuba under appropriate United Nations observation and supervision and undertake, with suitable safeguards, to halt the further introduction of such weapons systems into Cuba."

2—The United States "would agree upon the establishment of adequate arrangements through the United Nations to insure the carrying out and the continuation of these commitments (A) to remove promptly the quarantine measures now in effect and (B) to give assurances against an invasion

Turn to Page 2A Col. 6

Reds Advance

Nehru Makes Plea To World for Arms

NEW DELHI — (UPI) — Prime Minister Jawaharlal Nehru appealed to the world Saturday for arms as Chinese Communist invaders drove back Indian troops defending a key mountain pass guarding the plains of India.

A government spokesman said Indian forces broke off contact with Chinese troops at Jang, five miles east of the fallen monastery town of Towang and retreated to high ground along the Towang-Bomdilla road.

Bomdilla, some 50 miles east of Towang, is the site of an Indian army headquarters, and a key Northeast Frontier Agency center controlling an invasion route to the rich Assam plains 14,500 feet below.

On the far northeastern front, the spokesman said, Indian troops hurled back two more Chinese Communist attacks on the outskirts of Walong, a principal town of the Luhit division of the Northeast Frontier above the Burmese border.

Indian defenders had previously beaten back two Chinese Red assaults in the same sector.

The Indian embassy in Moscow announced it had delivered a message from Nehru to Soviet Premier Nikita Khrushchev but said it could not reveal the note's contents. Nehru sent a message to President Kennedy Friday.

(In London, a spokesman at the commonwealth relations office said Britain will send Indian a quantity of small arms as soon as possible. He said the arms would be shipped in response to an Indian request received within the past 24 hours.)

Red China called anew for troop disengagement along the Sino-Indian border and a summit meeting between the Indian and Chinese Communist premiers. It rejects as "absolutely unacceptable" India's stipulation that the border situation must be restored to the status of Sept. 8, 1962, before the Indians would consent to such talks.

Today's Chuckle

Many people who complain about being up to their ears in work are just lying down on the job.

—Arnold Glasow

JACKSONVILLE
MIAMI
NASSAU
X MARUCLA—BOARDED
HAVANA
CUBA
CAPE MAISI
MEXICO
HAITI DOM. REP.
JAMAICA
HONDURAS

INTERCEPTION AREA defined by the United States Saturday is enclosed by circles. X shows where Lebanese ship Marucla was boarded by the Navy Friday. U.N. Ambassador Adlai Stevenson told Acting Secretary General U Thant, who will relay the information to Premier Khrushchev, that the Navy will board Soviet vessels within 500 nautical miles of Havana and Cape Maisi, Cuba.

Where To Find It

1963

BULLETIN
DALLAS, NOV. 22 (AP)—PRESIDENT JOHN F. KENNEDY, THIRTY-FIFTH PRESIDENT OF THE UNITED STATES, WAS SHOT TO DEATH TODAY BY A HIDDEN ASSASSIN ARMED WITH A HIGH-POWERED RIFLE.

The tragedy shocked and benumbed the nation.

Television and print images recounted the horror.

The motorcade . . . the "crack!" of a shot . . . the race to the hospital, in vain. The blood-splattered widow, Jacqueline Kennedy, her grief veiled as she was handed the flag that covered the casket.

BULLETIN
DALLAS, NOV. 24 (AP)—LEE HARVEY OSWALD, ACCUSED SLAYER OF PRESIDENT KENNEDY, WAS SHOT TODAY APPARENTLY IN THE STOMACH AS HE LEFT THE CITY HALL UNDER HEAVY GUARD EN ROUTE TO AN ARMORED CAR FOR TRANSFER TO THE CITY JAIL.

Shot by a local club owner named Jack Ruby.

The news transcended tragedy.

EXTRA **Register** STAR EXTRA

—To-day's News To-day—

VOLUME 11 Number 5386 Hudson Register-Star; Hudson, N. Y., Friday, November 22, 1963 Eighteen Pages Price Five Cents

PRESIDENT IS DEAD

Murdered By Assassin's Bullet In Dallas

Flags At Half Mast: Mayor

Mayor Samuel Wheeler expressed "great shock" over the assassination of President Kennedy.

Wheeler said it was "shocking" for every American. He expressed deep sorrow to the Kennedy family.

Wheeler asked all citizens, out of respect for our President, to display the American Flag at half-mast until the funeral.

City People Express Shock, Disbelief

Shock and disbelief were on the faces of Hudsonians today as they learned of the murder of President Kennedy.

Many expressed the view of ... of 216 Warren St.: "It doesn't seem possible that anything like this could happen in our country."

Mary Whitbeck of 24 Spring St., said it was a "great loss for our country." Philip Garafalo, sitting alone in his H. and ... Restaurant, said, "the shock has still got me."

Lester Haight of 128 Green St., remarked that "it's a terrible thing. It strained by heart to hear it."

Roy Wolcott of Hudson called it "horrible" and wondered how something like this could happen in this day and age.

Mrs. Sylvia Mann of Hudson told a reporter she burst into tears when she heard that the President had been killed. Other reactions were "unbelievable," "Why."

Edson Snyder, former head of the County American Legion said it was a great national calamity." "I have not sufficiently recovered to make any further comment."

Bill Diver of Hudson called it a terrible tragedy and remarked that the Kennedy's were a "representative American family."

Philip Pomerantz remarked that it was a "tradegy of the worst degree." I'm overwhelmed, I can't believe it."

"A very black day in our history," said John McEvoy, Hudson American Legion Commander. McEvoy added that all Legion activities had been suspended for tonight.

Rev. Wilhelm Baer of Hudson said he had "just heard it." I

(Continued on Page 12-A)

Now President of United States

(Nov. 22) — NEW PRESIDENT OF THE UNITED STATES—With the death of President John F. Kennedy from an assassin's bullet in Dallas today, Vice President Lyndon B. Johnson, above, will become the new President of the United States. Johnson is shown in his office in the Capitol building in Washington in 1962. (AP Wirephoto) (See AP wire story.)

DALLAS (AP) — Lyndon B. Johnson was sworn in as President of the United States at about 1:38 p.m. (CST) today.

Johnson took the oath aboard the presidential plane at Dallas' Love Field. He was preparing to fly to Washington to take over the government.

DALLAS, TEX., NOV. 22 — PRESIDENT SHOT — President John F. Kennedy slumped down in back seat of car after being shot today. Mrs. Kennedy leans over President as unidentified man stands on bumper. (AP Wirephoto)

BULLETIN

FORT WORTH, Tex., (AP)—Soon after President Kennedy was assassinated today in Dallas, a white man in his mid 20s was arrested in the Riverside section of Forth Worth in the shooting of a Dallas policeman.

The man who has black curly hair and who wore a red shirt, denied that he was connected with the assassination of the President.

His hands were handcuffed and he was taken to the Fort Worth City jail.

DALLAS (AP) — The Dallas Police Department today arrested Lee H. Oswald, 24, in connection with the slaying of a Dallas policeman shortly after President Kennedy was assassinated.

He was also being questioned to see if he had any connection with the slaying of the President.

Oswald was pulled screaming and yelling from the Texas Theater in the Oak Cliff section of Dallas.

He brandished a pistol which officers took away from him after a scuffle. Police officer M. N. McDonald, who was cut across the face in the scuffle, quoted Oswald as saying after he was subdued, "Well, it's all over now."

Shocked Senate Adjourns Until Monday

WASHINGTON (AP) — A shocked Senate adjourned today until noon Monday after a prayer by its chaplain for President Kennedy, shot in Dallas, Tex.

The House was not in session.

The President's younger brother, Sen. Edward M. Kennedy, D-Mass., was presiding over the Senate when he received word of the shooting.

He went to his office but left there almost immediately. His staff said they do not know where he had gone.

Atty. Gen. Robert F. Kennedy, the President's other brother and closest adviser, was having lunch at home when word of his brother's shooting reached him.

Kennedy's personal secretary said the attorney general was remaining at the Kennedy estate in McLean, Va.

All activity at the White House—as, apparently, in every office of the government—came swiftly to a stop when news of the ambush shooting in Dallas arrived.

White House staff members, from the President's closest confidants to lowliest ushers, stood clustered around radio and television sets and news tickers waiting for news from Dallas.

The same was true in government departments and agencies throughout the capital.

When word reached the White House that the President was dead, the tension gave way to tears. Women wept unashamedly and the knots of anxious watchers before the television sets broke up quietly.

Church bells in the neighborhood began to toll, and people began drifting toward the White House to stand silently on the sidewalk, or in Lafayette Park across Pennsylvania Avenue, just to stare.

Occasionally, a passerby would ask a White House guard what the news was, then stand dumbly when told the President was dead.

DALLAS, TEX., Nov. 22—KENNEDY AND CONNALLY SHOT — President John Kennedy grasps his chest after being shot in Dallas today during parade. Next to Kennedy, back to camera, is Texas Governor John Connally. Arrow shows President moment after he was hit. (AP Wirephoto)

DALLAS (AP) — President John F. Kennedy, thirty-sixth president of the United States, was shot to death today by a hidden assassin armed with a high-powered rifle.

Kennedy, 46, lived about 30 minutes after a sniper cut him down as his limousine left downtown Dallas. Newsmen said the shot that hit him was fired about 12:30 p.m. (CST). A hospital announcement said he died at approximately 1 p.m. of a bullet wound in the head.

Automatically, the mantle of the presidency fell to Vice President Lyndon B. Johnson, a native Texan who had been riding two cars behind the chief executive.

There was no immediate word on when Johnson would take the oath of office.

Kennedy died at Parkland Hospital where his bullet-pierced body had been taken in a frantic but futile effort to save his life.

Lying wounded at the same hospital was Gov. John Connally of Texas, who was cut down by the same fusillade that ended the life of the youngest man ever elected to the presidency.

Connally and his wife had been riding with the President and Mrs. Kennedy.

The First Lady cradled her dying husband's bloodsmeared head in her arms as the presidential limousine raced to the hospital.

"Oh, no," she kept crying.

Connally slumped in his seat beside the President.

Police ordered an unprecedented dragnet of the city, hunting for the assassin.

They believed the fatal shots were fired by a white man, about 30, slender of build, weighing about 165 pounds, and standing 5 feet 10 inches tall.

The murder weapon was reportedly a 30-30 rifle.

Shortly before Kennedy's death became known, he was administered the last rites of the Roman Catholic Church. He had been the first Roman Catholic president in American history.

Even as two clergymen hovered over the fallen President in the hospital emergency room, doctors and nurses administered blood transfusions.

Kennedy died of a gunshot wound in the brain at approximately 1 p.m. (CST) according to an announcement by acting White House press secretary Malcolm Kilduff.

The new President, Lyndon Johnson, and his wife left the hospital a half hour later. Newsmen had no opportunity to question them.

Asst. presidential press secretary Malcolm Kilduff said Johnson was not hit. The new President previously had been reported wounded.

The horror of the assassination was mirrored in an eyewitness account by Sen. Ralph Yarborough, D-Tex., who had been riding three cars behind Kennedy.

"You could tell something awful and tragic had happened," the senator told newsmen before Kennedy's death became known. His voice breaking and his eyes red-rimmed, Yarborough said:

"I could see a Secret Service man in the President's car leaning on the car with his hands in anger, anguish and despair. I knew then something tragic had happened."

Yarborough had counted three rifle shots as the presidential limousine left downtown Dallas through a triple underpass. The shots were fired from above—possibly from one of the bridges or from a nearby building.

One witness, television reporter Mal Couch, said he saw a gun emerge from an upper story of a warehouse commanding an unobstructed view of the presidential car.

Kennedy was the first president to be assassinated since William McKinley was shot in 1901.

It was the first death of a president in office since Franklin D. Roosevelt died of a cerebral hemorrhage at Warm Springs, Ga., in April 1945.

Roosevelt had been enjoying a vacation when he died. McKinley had been shaking hands at a reception at an exposition in Buffalo, N.Y.

Kennedy and his wife had just passed the halfway point in a three-day speaking tour through Texas.

The President already had prepared a luncheon address for a Dallas audience before he died. In his prepared text, he assailed his ultraconservative critics.

Dallas is considered a center of conservative philosophy and finance.

Here, on Oct. 24, Adlai E. Stevenson was spat upon by one heckler and struck by another after making a United Nations Day address.

It was believed that Kenneday's body would be moved shortly to Washington.

Traditionally, funeral services for presidents who die in office are held in the capital city.

Kilduff told newsmen that Gov. Connally, a Democrat, was wounded in the right chest in the same ambush that felled the President.

Connally was rushed into sur-

(Continued on Page 12-A)

Cancel Opening Of Parkway

Official ceremonies marking the completion of the Taconic State Parkway to the Berkshire Spur of the Thruway, scheduled in the Town of Chatham Monday morning, were cancelled late this afternoon because of the assassination of President John F. Kennedy.

The announcement was made by Alexander Ald-rich of Chatham Center, personal representative of Gov. Nelson Rockefeller in the scheduled county ceremony.

R. Burdell Bixby of Hudson, chairman of the Thruway Authority, was to have presided at the ceremony.

The connecting roads will be opened as scheduled, but there will be no official ceremonies marking the historic event.

Johnson Takes Nation's Helm, Pages 4 and 5

The Dallas Morning News

John F. Kennedy Life History, Pages 16 and 17

VOL. 115—NO. 54 TELEPHONE: Riverside 7-4611 DALLAS, TEXAS, SATURDAY, NOVEMBER 23, 1963—50 PAGES IN 4 SECTIONS ★★★★ PRICE 5 CENTS

KENNEDY SLAIN ON DALLAS STREET

★ ★ ★ ★ ★ ★ ★ ★ ★ ★ ★ ★ ★ ★ ★ ★

JOHNSON BECOMES PRESIDENT

Receives Oath on Aircraft

By ROBERT E. BASKIN
Washington Bureau of The News

In a solemn and sorrowful hour, with a nation mourning its dead President, Lyndon B. Johnson Friday took the oath of office as the 36th chief executive of the United States.

Following custom, the oath-taking took place quickly—only an hour and a half after the assassination of President Kennedy.

Federal Judge Sarah T. Hughes of Dallas administered the oath in a hurriedly arranged ceremony at 2:39 p.m. aboard Air Force 1, the presidential plane that brought Kennedy on his ill-fated Texas trip and on which his body was taken back to Washington.

Mrs. Johnson and Mrs. Kennedy, her stocking still flecked with blood from the assassination, flanked the vice-president as he raised his right hand in the forward compartment of the presidential jetliner at Love Field. About 25 White House staff members and friends were present as Johnson intoned the familiar oath:

"I do solemnly swear that I will perform the duties of President of the United States to the best of my ability, and defend, protect and preserve the Constitution of the United States."

The 55-year-old Johnson, the first Texan ever to become President, turned and kissed his wife on the cheek, giving her shoulders a squeeze. Then he put his arm around Mrs. Kennedy, kissing her gently on her right cheek.

Mrs. Kennedy, in tears, was wearing the same bright pink suit she wore on the fatal ride, a ride in which she had been wildly acclaimed by friendly, cheering crowds in Dallas before rifle shots rang out and the President collapsed in the seat of the car beside her.

Johnson had deliberately delayed the ceremony to give Kennedy's widow time to compose herself for one of the gruelling aspects of her husband's assassination.

CONTINUED ON PAGE 15

Lyndon B. Johnson

Gov. Connally Resting Well

By MIKE QUINN

Gov. John Connally — felled Friday by a sniper's bullet in the back—rested in "quite satisfactory" condition late Friday night at Parkland Hospital following nearly four hours of surgery in the afternoon.

An aide for the governor reported at 10:30 p.m. that the governor was asleep and resting comfortably following the incident which claimed President Kennedy's life.

Meanwhile, Dr. Tom Shires, chief of surgeons at University of Texas Southwestern Medical School, said Connally barely missed a fatal wound:

"After consulting with Mrs. Connally and others on the scene, the consensus is that the governor was quite fortunate that he turned to see what happened to the President. If he had not turned to his right, there is a good chance he probably would have been shot through the heart—as it was, the bullet caused a tangential wound."

Dr. Shires rushed to Dallas by Air Force jet after word of the shooting was flashed.

Connally was operated on by Dr. Robert R. Shaw, thoracic

CONTINUED ON PAGE 2.

Impact Shattering To World Capitals

By the Associated Press

Word of President Kennedy's assassination struck the world's capitals with shattering impact, leaving heads of state and the man in the street stunned and grief-stricken.

While messages of condolence poured into the White House from presidents, premiers and crowned heads, the little people of many lands reacted with numbed disbelief.

Pubs in London and cafes in Paris fell silent, as the news came over radio and television.

IN MOSCOW, a Russian girl walked weeping along the street.

At U.N. headquarters in New York, delegates of 11 nations bowed their heads in a moment of silence.

In Buenos Aires, newspapers sounded sirens reserved for news of the utmost gravity.

Britain's Prime Minister Douglas-Home sent condolences, and Sir Winston Churchill branded the slaying a monstrous act.

"The loss to the United States and to the world is incalculable," Sir Winston declared. "Those who come after Mr. Kennedy must strive the more to achieve the ideals of world peace and human happiness and dignity to which his presidency was dedicated."

Douglas-Home issued this terse statement:

"The Prime Minister has learned with the most profound shock and horror of the death

CONTINUED ON PAGE 2.

Pro-Communist Charged With Act

A sniper shot and killed President John F. Kennedy on the streets of Dallas Friday. A 24-year-old pro-Communist who once tried to defect to Russia was charged with the murder shortly before midnight.

Kennedy was shot about 12:20 p.m. Friday at the foot of Elm Street as the Presidential car entered the approach to the Triple Underpass. The President died in a sixth-floor surgery room at Parkland Hospital about 1 p.m., though doctors said there was no chance for him to live when he reached the hospital.

Within two hours, Vice-President Lyndon Johnson was sworn in as the nation's 36th President inside the presidential plane before departing for Washington.

The gunman also seriously wounded Texas Gov. John Connally, who was riding with the President.

Four Hours in Surgery

Connally spent four hours on an operating table, but his condition was reported as "quite satisfactory" at midnight.

The assassin, firing from the sixth floor of the Texas School Book Depository Building near the Triple Underpass sent a Mauser 6.5 rifle bullet smashing into the President's head.

An hour after the President died, police hauled the 24-year-old suspect, Lee Harvey Oswald, out of an Oak Cliff movie house.

He had worked for a short time at the depository, and police had encountered him while searching the building shortly after the assassination. They turned him loose when he was identified as an employe but put out a pickup order on him when he failed to report for a work roll call.

He also was accused of killing a Dallas policeman, J. D. Tippit, whose body was found during the vast manhunt for the President's assassin.

Oswald, who has an extensive pro-Communist background, four years ago renounced his American citizenship in Russia and tried to become a Russian citizen. Later, he returned to this country.

Friendly Crowd Cheered Kennedy

Shockingly, the President was shot after driving the length of Main Street through a crowd termed the largest and friendliest of his 2-day Texas visit. It was a good-natured crowd that surged out from the curbs almost against the swiftly moving presidential car. The protective bubble had been removed from the official convertible.

Mrs. Connally, who occupied one of the two jump seats in the car, turned to the President a few moments before and remarked, "You can't say Dallas wasn't friendly to you."

At Fort Worth, Kennedy had just delivered one of the most well-received speeches of his ca-

CONTINUED ON PAGE 2.

FUNERAL FOR PRESIDENT WILL BE HELD ON MONDAY

WASHINGTON (AP)—President Kennedy's funeral will be held Monday at St. Matthews Roman Catholic Cathedral, the White House announced Friday night.

The body of the slain President will lie in repose at the White House Saturday and will lie in state in the rotunda of the Capitol on Sunday and Monday.

The President's body will be taken a couple of miles to the cathedral at 11 a.m. (EST) Monday. There, Richard Cardinal Cushing, Archbishop of Boston and close friend of the Kennedy family, will celebrate a pontifical requiem Mass at noon.

Acting White House Press Secretary Andrew T. Hatcher said he did not know where Kennedy will be buried. There has been one report, still unconfirmed, that burial would be in the family plot in Brookline, Mass.

The President's body will be moved from the White House in an official cortege to the Capitol rotunda at 1 p.m. Sunday. This ceremony will be attended by members of the

CONTINUED ON PAGE 12.

John F. Kennedy

GRAY CLOUDS WENT AWAY

Day Began as Auspiciously As Any in Kennedy's Career

(Robert E. Baskin, chief of the Washington Bureau of The News, was one of four persons representing the world press in the motorcade which resulted in the President's assassination. This is his account of what happened.)

By ROBERT E. BASKIN
Washington Bureau of The News

It was a day that started as auspiciously as any in the career of John F. Kennedy.

When we boarded the Presidential jetliner, Air Force One, at Fort Worth at midmorning, the White House party was in high spirits. The Fort Worth welcome had been a tremendous one. Shortly before the 15-minute flight to Love Field, ugly gray clouds were swept away by a brisk breeze. The sun was out, and the Texas sky was a vivid blue.

President and Mrs. Kennedy, she strikingly attired in a pink suit with a pert matching hat, made an instant hit at Love Field as they shook hands with hundreds of persons along the fence line.

Then the last journey began.

The big open Lincoln car moved out smoothly, carrying Mr. and Mrs. Kennedy and Gov. John Connally and his wife, Nellie.

Three cars back was the press pool car, in which three other newspapermen and I rode. Just ahead of us were Dallas Mayor and Mrs. Earle Caboll and Rep. Ray Roberts of McKinney.

Malcolm Kilduff, assistant presidential press secretary, was with us, and as we moved into the heart of the city Kilduff expressed elation over the friendly nature of the welcome and the great outpouring of people.

Everyone in the press car agreed it was one of the most cordial receptions the President had received in quite a while.

Buoyed by the cheers of the multitudes on Main Street, our motorcade moved on past the courthouse. Then came the approach to the Triple Underpass, with the leading cars picking up speed as the crowd thinned out somewhat. Over to our right loomed the gaunt structure labeled the Texas State School Book Depositary.

It was 12:30 p.m.

The sharp crack of a rifle rang out. But at that moment we couldn't believe it was just that. "What the hell was that?" someone in our car asked.

Then there were two more shots—measured carefully.

We saw people along the street diving for the ground.

CONTINUED ON PAGE 2.

Night of the Soul
A shocked city numbly grieves—See editorial on Page 2-A

THE DALLAS TIMES HERALD

FINAL EDITION

CONTINUOUSLY PUBLISHED FOR 87 YEARS   THE TIMES 1876   THE HERALD 1886   CONSOLIDATED 1888

87th Year—No. 295 ★★★ ·· DALLAS, TEXAS, MONDAY EVENING, NOVEMBER 25, 1963 Telephones—Classified, RI8-1414 Other Depts., R.I-4355 3 Parts Price Five Cents

Sad Nation Bids Kennedy Farewell

FBI Tipped Oswald Would Be Killed

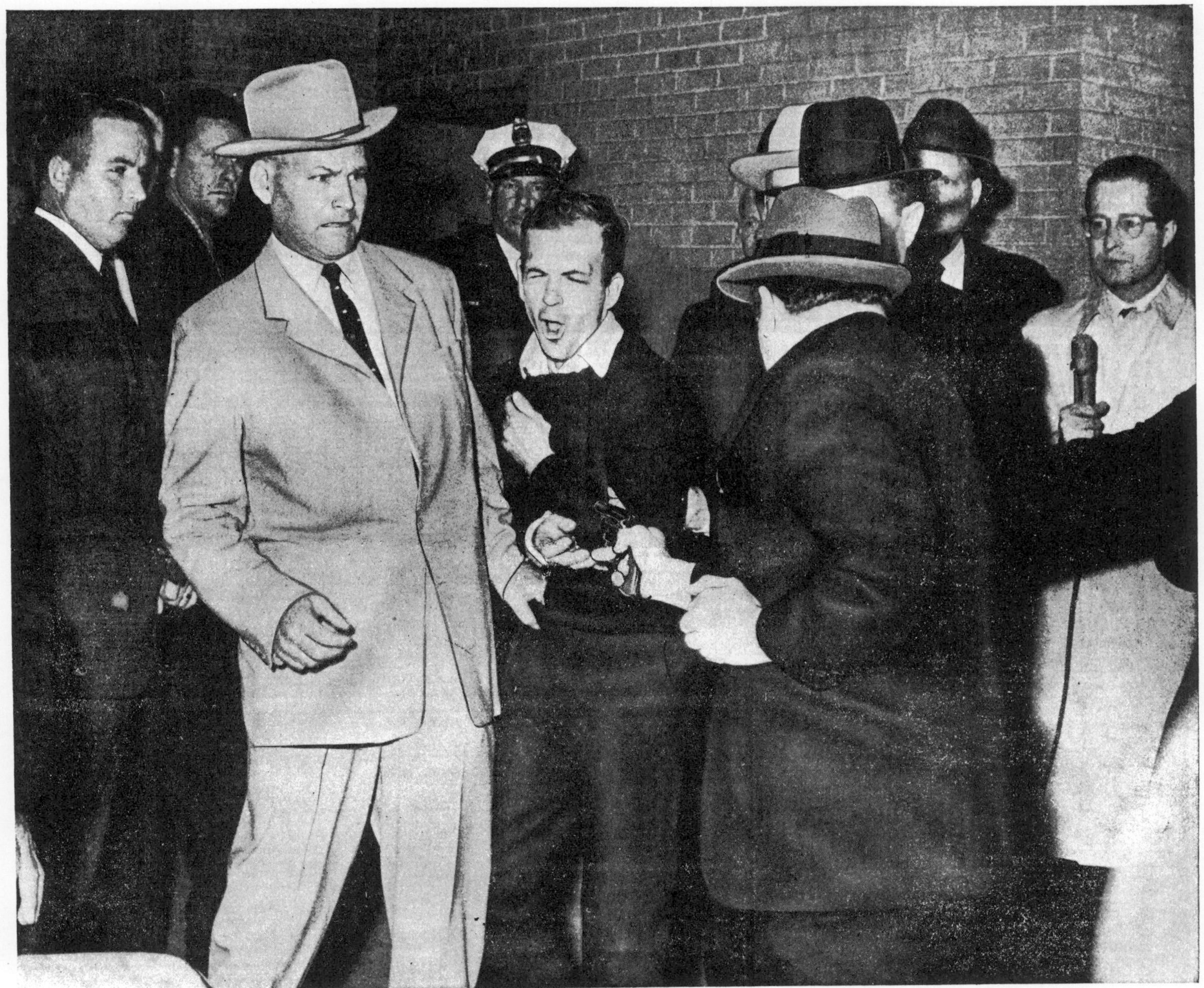

The President's accused killer as executioner's bullet pierces body.

Anonymous Call Forecast Slaying During Transfer

The self-appointed executioner of President Kennedy's accused assassin was the materialization of a blunt warning issued police hours earlier, The Times Herald learned Monday.

An anonymous telephone call to Federal Bureau of Investigation headquarters at 2:15 a.m. warned that Lee Harvey Oswald would be killed during his transfer from the city lockup to county jail.

The FBI immediately relayed the warning to police and the sheriff's office.

Oswald, notwithstanding the warning and dozens of riot-gun armed policemen, was fatally wounded in the basement of the police and courts building at 11:20 a.m. as officers prepared to place him in an armored car for the short ride to the courthouse.

Jack Ruby, nightclub operator and physical culture addict, darted from a crowd of newsmen with cat-like speed, rammed a .38 revolver into Oswald's body and triggered a shot witnessed by the world.

Police stood helpless. One managed only to swear in the split second that added a second explosive chapter in the President's assassination.

Meanwhile, Ruby was transferred from city to county jail without incident about noon Monday.

The transfer took place so casually that neither newsmen covering the county court and records building nor the crowds outside had an inkling of the action.

Nearly an hour after Ruby's transfer Monday, Sheriff Bill Decker held a press conference to inform the news representatives that Ruby had been transferred but he would not reveal which jail cell was used.

The Times Herald learned Monday afternoon that Ruby was with John Holbrook, a Dallas psychiatrist often used by the district attorney's office to determine the sanity of criminal suspects.

Ruby's attorney, Tom Howard, has indicated his client may plead

See OSWALD on Page 24

History Recorded

The historic photograph above was made by Bob Jackson, staff photographer of The Times Herald, from a few feet. It was caught at the precise moment the bullet from Jack Ruby's pistol entered the body of Lee Harvey Oswald, accused assassin of President Kennedy.

Note outstretched arm at right attempting to thwart the killer. Photographer Jackson has recorded for history one of its' most bizarre and dramatic moments.

GRIEVING WORLD WEEPS

Nation Buries Its Chief

WASHINGTON (AP) — Amid pangs of sorrow and with solemn rites, America and world statesmen bade farewell today to John Fitzgerald Kennedy as a grieving world wept.

Following the martyred President closely every inch of travel to the grave in Arlington National Cemetery was his young widow, Jacqueline, bravely bearing up.

Her beautiful face partly obscured in a long veil, she went part of the tragic way on foot—from the White House to St. Matthew's Cathedral for the requiem mass.

So also did one of the greatest arrays of foreign statesmen ever assembled — they came from 53 nations and included 26 heads of state or government.

At the mass, Richard Cardinal Cushing of Boston, old friend of the Kennedy family, offered up the holy eucharist, and prayed:

"Almighty God, may this sacrifice cleanse from sin the soul of your servant, John, who has gone from this world, and so may he receive forgiveness and everlasting rest from you."

Near the flag-enveloped coffin, Mrs. Kennedy knelt before the high altar and received the cardinal's hand the wafer of communion — the wafer which in the Roman Catholic faith had been converted into the flesh of Christ.

Grieving in the cathedral were the new President, Lyndon B. Johnson, and his wife, Lady Bird. They too rode and walked in the procession that took the body from the Capitol, past the White House, to the cathedral, and then to Arlington, across the Potomac River in Virginia.

The Kennedy children, Caroline and John, with whom their father loved to play, were at the great church to say their own goodbye.

When the services ended, Cardinal Cushing stooped and kissed Caroline.

Mrs. Kennedy, her veil floating in the cool breeze, took Caroline and John by their hands. They walked down the cathedral steps behind the casket.

As servicemen put the casket back on the caisson for the three-mile journey to Arlington, John put his hand up in salute.

Little John, 3 years old today, seemed a little bewildered. He turned his head to the side, and looked behind him. Caroline, who will be 6 on Wednesday, was composed but pale.

The church bells tolled. The muffled drums beat.

Mrs. Kennedy and the others rode to Arlington in limousines.

See NATION on Page 26

1964

Lyndon Johnson, who took over as President with the assassination of John Kennedy, was elected on his own over Senator Barry Goldwater. Senator Hubert Humphrey was Vice-President.

On the other side of the world, three North Vietnamese PT boats encountered the U.S. destroyer *Maddox* in the Gulf of Tonkin off the Vietnamese coast.

Congress passed the Tonkin Gulf Resolution giving the President the power to use any action necessary to repel armed attacks on U.S. forces. U.S. jets bombed PT boat bases and an oil depot in North Vietnam.

Earthquake Picture Story Told On Inside Pages

EXTRA **Anchorage Daily Times** EXTRA

49TH YEAR · ANCHORAGE, ALASKA, SUNDAY, MARCH 29, 1964 · PRICE 10 CENTS IN ANCHORAGE AND VICINITY

CITY RALLIES FROM QUAKE

☆ ☆

SHOCKWAVE ONE OF MIGHTIEST

FFICIAL CASUALTY T AS OF 2 P.M.

Seven persons were reported known dead in Anchor- and three seriously injured according to an earth- ce casualty list compiled this morning.

However, no figures were available on the number ersons missing in city areas.

Thirteen persons who are missing were listed by city l Defense Headquarters. Anyone having informa- on any of those listed as missing were asked to call Civil Defense.

Those listed as missing are:

Ruebel Grow, male, age 60, last seen going into drive- at 2016 West Marston Drive.

Andrew J. Chikoyak, male, native, five feet, five es, 130 pounds. Probably on Fourth Avenue at time arthquake.

Louis Wagner, male, age 21, probably in Sand Lake nity and probably riding with party named Burrells.

Georgina Ondola, female, age 20, probably in area of h Avenue.

Pfc. Daneil Bures, possibly in Mt. Alyeska area.

Pvt. Gramby, believed in Palmer area.

Pfc. Richard Barnes.

Pvt. Thomas Hood.

Pvt. Dennis Planing.

M. Sgt. Harold Lord.

Jessie Martin, daughter of Betty Martin.

Pfc. and Mrs. Richard D. Wilson.

Construction workers demolishing the J. C. Penney e are searching for three missing persons last seen he store.

Prononuced dead on arrival at Providence Hospital here all injured from the Anchorage area were n—were: William G. Taylor, 45, 3729 McCain Road, ederal Aviation Agency employe who was in the rol tower at International Airport; Mrs. Virgil E. ght, 2114 Marston Drive; a baby about one year old, tified as the daughter of Mr. and Mrs. Jerry Ware, Whittier, and a man identified only as J. J. Mar- z.

Other victims taken directly to mortuaries were: y Louise Rustigan, wife of Baxter Rustigan, oper- of City Cold Storage who lives on Peck Avenue; Styer, 19, son of Mr .and Mrs. Leroy Styer, 2800 umbia Way, and a man identified only as Clayton er, who was picked up at 3339 Iliamna St.

Only eight persons, of a total of 108 brought to Prov- ce Hospital for treatment, were admitted to the hos- and three of these are reported to be in serious dition.

Mrs. Jerry Ware of Whittier is in very serious con- on with a crushed arm. Virgil Knight, husband of of the dead victims, is in critical condition at the pital.

Also seriously injured is a Mrs. Nona Oberbey, be- ed to have been in the Hillside Apartments on 16th

Providence is still caring for most of some 22 pa- s transferred from Presbyterian Hospital. There indication when the downtown hospital will be ened.

The Air Force Hospital at Elmendorf was evacuated precautionary measure after the large masonry ding was badly damaged by the quake. All patients e moved into bachelor officer quarters and hos- l personnel quarters.

No fatalities were reported, however, and military orities are now preparing a list of injured persons.

Only one natural death has been reported, that of ert I. Smith, 36, of Talkeetna, brother of Theron h of Anchorage. His body is at Evergreen Memor- Chapel.

The bodies of quake victims Martinez, Taylor and er are at Anchorage Funeral Chapel. Mrs. Knight the Ware child were taken to Angelus Mortuary. Rustigan and Styer were taken to Angelus Mor- y.

nsina Due To Dock Here

laska Steamship Com- y's vanship Tonsina is duled to arrive in An- age Tuesday and un- at the city port.

vessel—on its first as a vanship — had originally scheduled ock at Seward but was rted directly 'to Anch- e after Friday's earth- ke.

he Army Engineers ka District let a con- on an emergency bas- his morning to Miller . and the contractor ted work repairing land approaches to the city dock so the ship can be unloaded.

A possible hazard—leaking gasoline from storage tanks — was apparently solved. The Air Force foamed the area and trucks have hauled in gravel and blotted the soaked area with sand.

The Engineers were also probing navigation approaches to the city port to see if there had been any changes in channels due to earthquake.

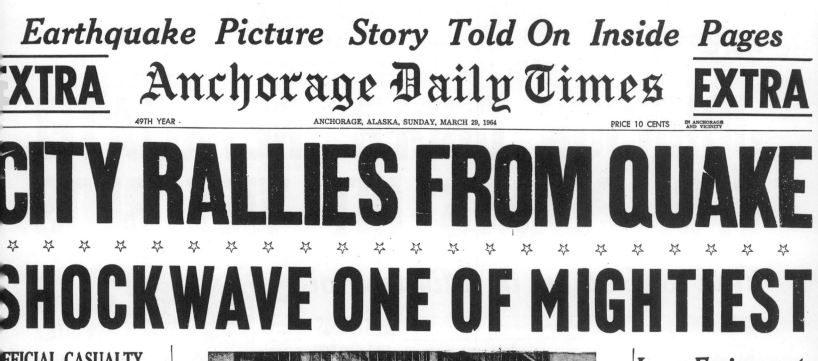

Men Flee Penney's Store As Quake Shatters Wall

The World Was In A Weird Frenzy

Atwood Sees Home Torn Apart By Quake

(Editor and publisher Robert B. Atwood of the Anchorage Daily Times watched his home torn apart in the twisting, tearing movements of Anchorage's disastrous earthquake Friday night. The home was located on Marston Drive in Turnagain, overlooking Knik Arm. Here is his story,)

By ROBERT B. ATWOOD
The Anchorage Daily Times

Mrs. Atwood was leaving for the grocery store when I arrived home from the office about 5:30 Friday evening. I thought of going with her.

Then, I decided to stay home and practice on my trumpet while the house was empty. I could blow loud without disturbing anyone.

I had just started precisely that when the earthquake started. Earthquakes of the minor sort are not uncommom here but they always prompt me to stop what I am doing and watch what happens.

In a few short moments it was obvious that this earthquake was no minor one. The chandelier made from a ship's wheel swayed too much. Things were falling that have never fallen before.

I headed for the door, carrying my trumpet. At the door I saw walls weaving. This was no place for me. Out onto the driveway I went.

I was still carrying my trumpet.

On the driveway I turned and watched my house squirm and groan, as though in last mortal agony. It was as though someone had engaged it in a gigantic taffy pull, stretching it, shrinking it and twisting it.

I was glad my wife was not there to watch. She had designed it, planned it, built it with herself as architect, contractor and superintendent.

I became aware of the falling of tall trees in our yard and I moved to a spot where I thought I would be safe. But, as I moved, I saw cracks appear in the earth. Pieces of ground in jigsaw puzzle shapes moved up and down, tilted at all angles.

I tried to move away, but more appeared in every direction.

I was moving toward my neighbor's house, but I noticed that my house was moving away from me, fast. My neighbor's house was not standing still. All the world was in a wierd frenzy.

As I started to climb the fence to my neighbor's yard, the fence disappeared.

Trees were falling in crazy patterns with staccato crackling. Deep chasms opened up. Table top pieces of earth moved upward to stand like toadstools with great overhangs. Some turned at crazy angles.

A chasm opened beneath me. I tumbled down. It seemed to be an endless fall. Soft sand cushioned the impact. I was quickly on the verge of being buried. I was only one of many bits of debris tumbling into that chasm.

I found I couldn't pull my right arm from the sand. It was buried to the shoulder. Most of the rest of my body was also covered. I let go of my trumpet and my arm pulled free easily.

Somehow, even in that perilous position, I felt keenly the loss. I felt I had just lost my last contact with many things associated with a happy home.

Many thoughts flashed through my mind, but never did I think this was the end for me. I scrambled to stay atop the debris.

I ducked pieces of trees, fence posts, mail boxes and other odds and ends.

Then, I had the awful experience of watching my neighbor's home slowly collapse and slide into the chasm. For a time it threatened to come down on top of me, but the earth was still moving and the chasm opened to receive the house.

I feared for the life of my neighbors.

When the earth movement stopped, I climbed to the top of the wall of my chasm. I found angular landscape in every direction.

I found my neighbor, Warren Hines, carrying his young daughter.

We found his wife atop one of the high mushroom-like promotories. She was standing alone with her auto, marooned.

She said she had stopped outside of the gate of her home and watched the earthquake consume everything. We also found their son. Fate was kind to the Hines.

We climbed up and down chasm walls and under dangerous overhanging pieces of frozen ground to safety.

The children seemed to know we were in deep trouble. They responded marvelously. Never a whimper.

Helicopters were overhead but they couldn't land near us. The ground was too topsy turvy. After what seemed to be endless time, rescuers came to us and helped the party out of the quagmire that had once been a home.

Loss Estimated By Governor At $250 Million

In the incredible aftermath of one of the world's mightiest earthquakes, the people of Anchorage began to rebuild today on a hazy, quiet Easter Sunday.

The survey of damages and loss continued in the largest city of Alaska and throughout the coastal regions of the 49th State devastated by the giant quake which ripped the earth about 5:36 p.m. on Good Friday.

Anchorage counted seven confirmed fatalities early this afternoon and three serious injured—and an untold number of missing. Across the state and down the Pacific Coast, where giant tidal waves battered the shorelines, the death toll mounted—perhaps as high as 80.

Gov. William A. Egan, in Anchorage to direct state assistance, called the quake "the worst disaster Alaska has ever suffered."

"There is nothing to compare with it," the governor said.

"But the people do not consider this a beating or themselves licked," Egan said.

The governor said the Anchorage area suffered a total loss of at least $250 million. He called the figure conservative.

Hard hats and helmets were the Easter parade headgear attire as the big cleanup task got under way.

Anchorage Mayor George Sharrock, on duty almost continuously since the earth trembled with a mighty roar, expressed the confidence of the city as it looks ahead.

"I haven't found anyone who isn't going to rebuild," the mayor said. "It'll be better than before."

Anchorage and Alaska were not alone as the recovery operation began.

At his vacation ranch in Texas, President Johnson was up most of the night receiving reports of the disaster.

He greeted a news conference this morning as a weary-eyed, concerned national leader. He said he had no plans to visit Alaska. Federal orders already have been issued under the President's direction, declaring the quake zone as a disaster area.

Federal officials were quickly on the scene to assess losses and begin setting up procedures on what specific aid could be offered.

Alaka's two United States senators, E. L. Bartlett and Ernest Gruening, were among the first of the Washington officials to arrive.

In the immediate wake of the earthquake, hundreds of homes were shattered.

The Turnagain and West Turnagain areas were devastated along the bluff line overlooking Knik Arm.

Homes fell away as the earth sloughed off. Trees tumbled, cars fell into yawning pits. Mothers sheltered children in churning hallways of homes. Others led youngsters to safety.

The quake slipped buildings, shattered windows, sent grocery and merchandise flying in stores through the city.

Government Hill School split open. West High School was turned into a shambles. The new Four Seasons Apartment building, nearing completion just off L Street, collapsed.

The 14-story Mt. McKinley and 1200 I Street apartment buildings, Anchorage's highest buildings, were twisted and made uninhabitable.

The quake struck with shuddering force just as many offices were closing for the day, and many shops and stores were in the last half hour of the Friday pre-Easter business day.

The grinding force of the wrenching earth tore streets and lawns apart.

The ground heaved and structures buckled.

A thousand personal tragedies unfolded with the opening earth. Without panic, stunned people paused as they became aware of the awful might of what was happening.

J. C. Penney Co.'s five-story, year-old building on Fifth Avenue heaved and buckled. A dozen or more people stood with shock as the walls of Penney's sheared away, crushing half a dozen cars parked at the curb.

One of the first victims of the tragedy died in her car as the walls tumbled.

Across the city, the quake brought the normal life of a great city to a halt—and focused all activity into personal and community efforts to save lives.

The city mustered quickly, with the aid of untold hundreds of personal sacrifices playing a part in a stirring civic performance.

There was severe damage to the Cordova Building,

(Continued to Page 2)

Where to Find It:

Comics	14	TV, Radio	6
Editorials	8	Weather	16
Markets	15	Women	9

*****

THE WEATHER—Mostly fair and a little warmer today and tonight; high today 88, low tonight 68. Thursday fair and warmer. Sunrise 6:13, sunset 8:28.

The Des Moines Register

The Newspaper Iowa Depends Upon

Des Moines, Iowa, Wednesday Morning, August 5, 1964—20 Pages—Two Sections

Price 10 Cents

JOHNSON ORDER: RETALIATE! U. S. PLANES HIT VIET REDS

Find 3 Bodies in Mississippi

RIGHTS AIDES LAST SEEN IN NEARBY TOWN

Had Been Sought Since June 22

PICTURES: Page 7

WASHINGTON, D. C. (AP)—The FBI announced Tuesday night the finding of three bodies in graves at the site of a dam near Philadelphia, Miss., where three civil rights workers disappeared six weeks ago.

The FBI said the bodies were found in a wooded area about 6 miles southwest of Philadelphia, where the three young men were last seen.

The three, Andrew Goodman, James Earl Chaney and Michael Henry Schwerner, were last seen on the night of June 21.

The FBI said a search party of FBI agents turned up the bodies late Tuesday afternoon while digging in thick woods and underbrush several hundred yards off Route 21.

When the area was first searched, officials said, what appeared to be a fresh dam thrown up to catch water in a low area was found. Later, it was noticed that the dam had collected no water despite several showers in the area.

An investigation of the dam was ordered and the excavation uncovered the bodies in the fill of the dam.

The bodies are being removed to Jackson, Miss., where laboratory tests will be made to identify them and determine the cause of death.

Roy Moore, chief of the FBI office in the Mississippi capital, said his agency is "fairly certain" the bodies are those of the missing workers.

Map Locates Philadelphia

The FBI search for the three missing civil rights workers began June 22. The next day their 1963 station wagon was found abandoned and burned on a dirt road off Route 21 about 13 miles northeast of Philadelphia.

The three civil rights workers include a 21-year old Negro, Chaney, from Meridian, Miss., and two white New Yorkers—Goodman, 20, and Schwerner, 24.

They left Meridian late in the morning of June 21 for the purpose, they said, of investigating the June 16 burning of a Negro church in the Philadelphia area.

Chaney was arrested in Philadelphia reportedly for speeding about 4 p. m. The arresting officer, a deputy in the county sheriff office, also held Schwerner and Goodman for investigation.

The three men were released some six hours later.

COUNTY SEAT

Sheriff Vows Probe of Jail Complaints

By Jerry Szumski And Jack Gillard

A former Polk County Jail prisoner complained about jail conditions Tuesday and Sheriff Wilbur T. Hildreth said he intends to "check every bona fide complaint, as has always been my practice."

Hildreth said he has questioned his staff about conditions turned up in a surprise Sunday inspection.

"Very Seriously"

In the wake of a 28-year-old prisoner's complaint that he was denied medical treatment and statements by jailers that reflected on the policies of Chief Jailer Caleb Spangler, the sheriff said:

"I certainly want to go into these complaints very seriously and see if they have any foundation. I'm certainly interested in the welfare of every prisoner."

He declined to say what steps he might take if the complaints are borne out.

The Polk County Board of Supervisors Tuesday made public a letter to Hildreth in which the supervisors said they found the jail "all in good shape" during a Monday visit.

A Des Moines man in his mid-20s who recently completed a four-month term in the jail claimed Tuesday that Spangler segregates Negroes in one cell block and "punishes" troublesome white inmates with confinement in "the colored cell"—cellblock No. 6.

"They put me in there after a light bulb was broken in another cell," he said. "They assumed it was my fault." He said he was confined to No. 6 under "filthy conditions" about six weeks.

A Negro in the cellblock, he said, was denied a request to telephone his family in Wisconsin, where a brother was dying.

"Told to Write"

"They told him to write a letter and they would send it air mail," said the former prisoner. He said he was threatened twice with confinement in No. 6 as punishment.

"They use the colored cell as a threat for violating any of the jail rules," he said.

The former prisoner claimed "it took six weeks of constant complaining to get medical attention for an ulcer."

He said Spangler eventually arranged for him to go to Broadlawns Polk County Hospital, where "I got a three-minute physical and was sent back to jail."

JAIL—*Continued on Page Four*

INSIDE THE REGISTER

Rebels Enter Stanleyville

CONGOLESE REBELS, backed by the Chinese Communists, surge into Stanleyville, then withdraw ... Page 20

A BILL to delay for at least two years court-ordered legislative reapportionments is approved at a closed Senate committee hearing ... Page 4

SENATE investigators are told that a pharmaceutical firm sold stock to doctors with understanding they would prescribe its products to patients ... Page 10

Sale of Land To Squatters Is Ruled Out

By Ed Heins (Register Staff Writer)

MARQUETTE, IA. — Sale of state land along the Mississippi River to cabin owners who have been living on it illegally for years is an "impossibility," the Iowa Conservation Commission chairman said Tuesday.

Chairman Sherry Fisher of Des Moines said the commission can recommend sale of state land under its jurisdiction only when it is of no further conservation value. "Such a statement wouldn't be true in this case," he said.

The commission members scheduled their regular monthly meeting in this northeast Iowa community to get a personal view of two Mississippi River sites on which private cabin owners are squatting. Some of the cabins have been on state land over 20 years.

One of the sites involves a 1½-mile stretch of riverbank between the mouth of the Yellow River and the boundary of the Effigy Mounds National Monument near Marquette. Thirty-one private cabins and trailers are parked on the land.

Thirty-seven cabins are located on a strip of land about two miles south of Harpers Ferry.

20-Day Proposal

The commission staff, which uncovered the squatting problem, has recommended cabin owners be given 20 days to remove their buildings. The state should then develop public river

SQUATTERS—*Continued on Page Ten*

SEEK HARRIS FOR $30,000 SCHOOL POST

Nashville in Bid to Superintendent

Des Moines School Board cuts 1964-65 budget by $107,826—easing the burden to taxpayers and increasing student fees. PAGE 3

By Jack Magarrell

Des Moines School Superintendent John H. Harris said Tuesday he plans to decide today whether to go to Nashville, Tenn., for $30,000 or stay in Des Moines for $26,000.

Representatives of the Nashville School Board were in Des Moines about 10 days ago and Harris visited Nashville last weekend, he said.

HARRIS

Harris said he had not asked for the superintendent's job there, but Nashville officials contacted him and made him the offer over the weekend.

"I'm thinking very seriously about it," Harris said.

"The challenging thing that I'd be interested in is that they have a new form of government there," he said. "It's a new experiment in political science."

City-County

The City of Nashville recently merged with Davidson County to form a single metropolitan government. The city and county school systems also are combined.

The metropolitan unit has a population of about 450,000, Harris said. That is more than double the size of Des Moines.

Harris told the Des Moines School Board members in a closed-door session Tuesday afternoon that he would make his decision within a day or two.

3-Year Contract

If he decides to accept the Nashville job, he will ask the Des Moines School Board to release him from a three-year contract approved last June 2.

That contract gave Harris a $1,500 raise to $26,000 a year. Harris came to the superintendent's job here in 1957 at a salary of $18,500.

IOWA COOLER AFTER RAINS

Iowa's weather ranged from hot to cool Tuesday afternoon in the wake of showers that drew some of the humidity out of the air and put it into the ground.

All the heat was in the north, with Decorah reporting the state high of 97 degrees. By contrast, Ottumwa and Burlington, protected by clouds, had highs of only 78. Des Moines had 86.

More showers and thunderstorms may fall in southern Iowa today and temperatures generally will be a little warmer. The parched northeast may get showers by Thursday, the Weather Bureau said.

Site of Attacks

Map locates Tonkin Gulf, off North Viet Nam, where for the second consecutive day North Vietnamese torpedo boats attacked two U. S. Navy vessels.

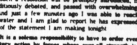

Text of Johnson Speech

WASHINGTON, D. C. (AP)—Following is the text of President Johnson's radio and television speech Tuesday night on the Viet Nam situation:

My fellow Americans:

As President and commander-in-chief, it is my duty to the American people to report that renewed hostile actions against U. S. ships on the high seas in the Gulf of Tonkin have today required me to order the military forces of the United States to take action in reply.

The initial attack on the destroyer Maddox, on Aug. 2, was repeated today by a number of hostile vessels attacking two U. S. destroyers with torpedoes. The destroyers, and supporting aircraft, acted at once on the orders I gave after the initial act of aggression. We believe at least two of the attacking boats were sunk. There were no U. S. losses.

The performance of commanders and crews in this engagement is in the highest tradition of the United States Navy.

But repeated acts of violence against the armed forces of the United States must be met not only with alert defense, but with positive reply. That reply is being given as I speak to you. Air action is now in execution against gunboats and certain supporting facilities of North Viet Nam which have been used in these hostile operations.

In the larger sense, this new act of aggression, aimed directly at our own forces, again brings home to all of us in the United States the importance of the struggle for peace and security in Southeast Asia.

Aggression by terror against the peaceful villagers of South Viet Nam has now been joined by open aggression on the high seas against the United States of America. The determination of all Americans to carry out our whole commitment to the people and government of South Viet Nam will be redoubled by this outrage.

Yet our response, for the present, will be limited and fitting. We Americans know, although others appear to forget, the risks of spreading conflict—we still seek no wider war.

I have instructed the secretary of state to make this position totally clear to friends, to adversaries, and indeed to all. I have instructed Ambassador (Adlai) Stevenson to raise this matter immediately and urgently before the Security Council of the United Nations.

Finally, I have met today with the leaders of both parties in the Congress of the United States and I have informed them that I shall immediately request the Congress to pass a resolution making it clear that our government is united in its determination to take all necessary measures in support of freedom, and in defense of peace, in Southeast Asia.

I have been given encouraging assistance by these leaders that such a resolution will be promptly introduced, freely and expeditiously debated, and passed with overwhelming support.

And just a few minutes ago I was able to reach Senator Goldwater and I am glad to report he has expressed his support of the statement I am making tonight.

It is a solemn responsibility to have to order even limited military action by forces whose over-all strength is as vast and as awesome as those of the United States of America.

But it is my considered conviction, shared throughout your government, that firmness in the right is indispensable today for peace. That firmness will always be measured. Its mission is peace.

Potomac Fever

WASHINGTON, D. C. — The administration has ordered a thorough study of water problems, of which it has several, including, hot, deep, and Gold.

Premier Nguyen Khanh seems to be a lot more excited about getting us into a fight in North Viet Nam than we are. We've had sad experience with pop top Khanhs.

The way German journalists have been operating, when a Republican picks up a newspaper these days he just hopes that Senator Goldwater isn't in deutsch again.

Barry doesn't like U. S. newspapers very much, either. It's pretty sneaky, printing them in a language that almost everybody in the country can read.

President Johnson signs the bill to mint silver dollars. In clip joints out west the customers toss silver dollars to the strippers—putting the cartwheel before the torso.

The Army has a new explosive that a soldier can use to dig a foxhole quickly. We're ready for any kind of war now—we've got pushbutton foxholes.

—Jack Wilson

STRIKE BOAT BASES AFTER NEW ATTACK

Buildup in Asia of U. S. Forces

Leased Wire to The Register

WASHINGTON, D. C.—President Johnson told the nation Tuesday night he had ordered retaliatory action against gunboats and "certain supporting facilities in North Viet Nam," after renewed attacks against American destroyers in the Gulf of Tonkin.

Mr. Johnson said in a radio-television address that the air attacks on the North Vietnamese facilities were taking place as he spoke, shortly after 10:30 p. m. (C. D. T.).

This "positive reply," as the President called it, followed a naval battle Tuesday in which a number of North Vietnamese PT boats attacked two United States destroyers with torpedoes. Two of the Vietnamese boats were sunk. The U. S. ships suffered no damage and no loss of life.

In other developments:

1 **The United States, in accordance with Mr. Johnson's announced intention, asked for an urgent meeting of the United Nations Security Council this morning to inform the council of its actions.**

2 **Robert S. McNamara, secretary of defense, disclosed at a post-midnight news conference that American air strikes against Communist bases were continuing today.**

He also disclosed that a new military buildup is under way in Southeast Asia.

McNamara declined to say where the air strikes by carrier-based U. S. planes were being made.

In answer to a question, he said, "We are not attacking Hanoi," but only patrol craft and the bases which support them. Hanoi is the capital of Communist North Viet Nam.

"The United States has taken the precaution of moving substantial military reinforcements to Southeast Asia," McNamara said.

"It is also making replacement deployments to the western Pacific from the continental United States."

The defense chief said in a formal statement:

"I can tell you some of the action that has already been undertaken. U. S. naval aircraft from the carriers Ticonderoga and Constellation in the Gulf of Tonkin area where our destroyers have undergone two deliberate attacks by the North Vietnamese have already initiated air strikes against the bases from which these PT boats have operated.

"Our naval aircraft have

ASIA—*Continued on Page Five*

Robert Kennedys Expect 9th Child

WASHINGTON, D. C. (AP)—Mrs. Robert F. Kennedy, 35, wife of the attorney general, is expecting her ninth child in December, a friend of the family said Tuesday. The Kennedys now have five boys and three girls.

Their youngest child, Christopher George Kennedy, was born July 4, 1963 in Boston. The Kennedys were married in 1950.

Ethel comes from a family of six brothers and sisters. She often has said she wanted an even bigger family. When she was expecting Christopher, she said she wouldn't mind if she had twins.

Possible Rain
High 55 Low 40

DETROIT DAILY PRESS

ELECTION SPECIAL

VOL. II—NO. 5 | DETROIT, MICHIGAN, WEDNESDAY, NOVEMBER 4, 1964 | TEN CENTS

Landslide Batters GOP

1968 - ROMNEY Vs. LBJ?

★ ★ ★ ★ ★ ★

State Splits Ticket For Romney, LBJ

Gov. Romney bucked the trend in Michigan

By OWEN DEATRICK
Daily Press Political Writer

Michigan voters Tuesday crossed party lines in droves to split their ballots and tell the world they like the kind of prosperity produced by Democratic President Lyndon B. Johnson and Republican Gov. Romney.

They joined the nation in giving the President a whopping majority and provided Romney with enough approval to send him back to Lansing for a second term and sweep him to the top of the Republican heap as the logical presidential candidate in 1968.

Carried along to victory of this same divided tide was U.S. Senator Philip A. Hart, a Democrat, who swamped Mrs. Elly Peterson, the first woman in Michigan to make a run for the U.S. Senate.

PROSPERITY WINS

It was an elemental demonstration that "nobody shoots Santa Claus." The state is prosperous and Michigan voters were convinced that now is not the time for change.

Michigan citizens didn't give a hoot whether it was Washington or Lansing that got the credit for the prosperity as long as the cash was there. They liked the combination and they threw party loyalty to the wind to keep it.

The Romney vote proved he was right in his campaign refusal to endorse his party's presidential nominee, Barry Goldwater. While other top GOP leaders hedged on Goldwater along the campaign trail, Romney never wavered.

THREATEN REVENGE

He introduced Goldwater at a rally in the Cobo Arena, but that was all. He said flatly time and again: "I have not endorsed him and I will not endorse him."

Some Goldwater fans were irked. They threatened revenge by refusing to vote for Romney. But if they acted on their threat, they were not numerous enough to make any difference.

Romney gets a second term as governor of Michigan. He can run for a third term, which will be for four years instead of two under the new Constitution. He is the last governor to be elected to a two-year term in Michigan.

In the middle of the first long term in the governor's office, Romney will be 61 and the logical front-runner when

(Continued on Page Three)

Staebler Smiles In Defeat as Followers Sob

By GEORGE PUSCAS
Daily Press Staff Writer

As his supporters sobbed, Congressman-at-Large Neil Staebler conceded the governor's race to incumbent Republican George Romney at 2:41 a.m. Wednesday.

Staebler conceded with a smile only after a long, hopeless wait and after naming almost every other Democrat as a winner of his respective race in Michigan.

On the verge of conceding defeat at the hands of incumbent Republican Gov. Romney at 1 a.m. Wednesday, Staebler held off for hours when his aides claimed to have found a discrepancy in the vote tally.

"There's an unbelievable gap in the Wayne County figures," insisted Mac McWilliams, chairman of Staebler's campaign committee.

"Some of these figures coming from Democratic strongholds are simply too fantastic. So we're sitting tight."

DEM STRONGHOLD

According to McWilliams, the figures of the official tally and the Network Election Service did not jibe. Instead of the 53 per cent of the Wayne County vote going for Staebler, McWilliams hinted that the figure might be closer to 67 per cent.

He would not say whether any such discrepancy would

(Continued on Page Three)

Poindexter Sails Past Vaughn

Thomas L. Poindexter, foe of the Detroit income tax and spokesman of the Greater Detroit Homeowners Council, Tuesday night emerged the victor over Jackie Vaughn III in the contest for Common Council.

Taking an early lead, he pushed on to an indicated lead of about 75,000 votes as the count of the city's 1,099 precincts neared completion.

Although the city's vote turnout was near 673,000, voting in the city contests was about 425,000. Tabulations for three Detroit Board of Education posts and Recorder's and Traffic Courts were even lower.

JUST LIKE PRIMARY

The Council vote followed the pattern indicated in the primary voting Sept. 1. Poindexter led heavily in predominantly white precincts, particularly in the 21st and 22nd wards, with Vaughn scoring well in mixed and Negro precincts.

Poindexter's share of the vote was close to 60 per cent.

(Continued on Page Two)

Index

Mass. Ballot Defeated

Michigan voters decided Tuesday that they prefer the Michigan ballot and rejected the Republican-backed "Massachusetts Ballot" plan by an almost two-to-one margin.

The Massachusetts plan would have made it impossible to vote a straight-party ticket by marking "X" or pulling one lever.

The GOP-controlled Legislature earlier this year rammed through the change, but Democrats forced a referendum vote by circulating petitions.

Ironically, although voters showed they prefer the opportunity to cast a straight party vote, they split their tickets in this election in record numbers to help elect Democrat Lyndon Johnson as president while re-electing Republican George Romney as governor.

THE VICTORY TEAM—This picture of President Johnson and Hubert Humphrey, taken by Tony Spina, chief photographer of the Detroit Free Press, has been submitted to President Johnson for possible use on the Inaugural Medal. It was sent to LBJ by Benjamin Levinson, Detroit businessman. The President said it would "be given every consideration."

Kennedys Sweep In; Pierre in a Battle

Special to The Daily Press

Although death has twice left the family without a political head, Tuesday's elections made it clear that the Kennedy saga in American politics is far from over.

In races from coast to coast, members and allies of the Kennedy clan swept three U.S. Senate seats. All three are young and Democratic and cast in the Kennedy mold of vitality and charm.

THREE WINNERS

● Robert F. Kennedy, 38, the late President John Kennedy's attorney general, won a New York seat from Republican Kenneth Keating and established a base for what could be a shot at the White House. Kennedy got about 54 per cent of the vote.

● Edward (Ted) Kennedy, 32, the youngest brother, easily won renomination to the Senate seat once held by brother John. His margin was about 4 to 1.

● Joseph D. Tydings, 36, a top aide for Robert in the Justice Department, unseated Maryland Senator J. Glenn Beall, winning approximately 60 per cent of the vote.

OTHER ALLIES

However, the Kennedy forces apparently were in trouble in California, where President Kennedy's press secretary, Pierre Salinger," was trailing in the Senate race against former actor George Murphy.

In yet another race, Utah Senator Frank E. Moss, 53, a Democrat and follower of John Kennedy, secured his shaky

Ted Kennedy

seat by defeating Ernest L. Wilkinson, conservative president of Brigham Young University.

And another member of the Kennedy clan is rumored on the way up in politics. R. Sargent Shriver, Robert and Ted's brother-in-law, is reportedly ready to enter Illinois politics and possibly challenge Richard Daley for Chicago's mayoralty. Shriver is a former president of Chicago's Board of Education and is the leader of President Johnson's anti-poverty war.

The upshot of all this is that the Kennedys will probably wield more political power in the coming years than any family in modern American history.

And this despite the death of the two most promising sons of Joseph P. Kennedy.

JOE SHOWED PROMISE

The oldest, Joe, Jr., was considered the most brilliant by his father. The former ambassador planned to introduce "Little Joe" to politics after World War II ended. But Joe, Jr. was killed at 29 when his bomber exploded over the Belgian coast in 1944.

And, of course, John served as the first Catholic president until his assassination last Nov. 22.

Now Robert has taken up the challenge. He could con-

(Continued on Page Two)

15-Million Loss by Barry Wrecks Party

Lyndon Baines Johnson scored the nation's greatest presidential landslide Tuesday, mowing down almost all the GOP's major leaders except Michigan Gov. George Romney.

In his record-smashing re-election, the 56-year-old Texan was trounced only in segregationist Dixie.

The nation's 36th President, by surrendering the traditionally Democratic South, effected one of the most stunning political victories in history and left the Republican Party in near-ruin.

Johnson and his running mate, Sen. Hubert Horatio Humphrey of Minnesota, rolled up a plurality of almost 15 million popular votes against Arizona Senator Barry Goldwater.

SOUGHT MANDATE

Johnson captured all but 50 of the 528 electoral votes.

The landslide eclipsed that of Franklin Delano Roosevelt over Alf Landon in 1936, when Roosevelt won 60.8 of of the popular vote and all but eight electoral votes.

During his campaign, Mr. Johnson made continuous appeals for a record-setting mandate, and he said at midnight Tuesday that the overwhelming results "were on the nose."

Rov. Romney, New York Rep. John Lindsay and Ohio's Robert Taft, Jr., a Senate contender, managed to salvage victory out of the GOP shambles.

The GOP presidential hopes for Illinois industrialist and gubernatorial candidate Charles Percy were dashed. Veteran Senator Kenneth Keating, of New York, was defeated. From East to West, Democratic candidates coasted in on the Johnson coattails.

FACE REORGANIZATION

Republican Gov. Mark Hatfield, of Oregon, put it succinctly: "Our party now faces an agonizing reorganizaiton."

The chances that Romney would emerge as one of the party standard bearers were bright, for Romney had refused to endorse Goldwater and pleaded in vain for a stronger platform at the San Francisco convention in July.

He also appealed to Goldwater for a "heart-to-heart" policy meeting between the two candidates after the Arizona senator was nominated, but the meeting never materialized.

Romney claimed at his jubilant party headquarters Tuesday night that Republican leadership had pulled Michigan out of the red, and party strategists have been carefully studying the state's economy.

There were no immediate statements from Goldwater, who was in Phoenix, or his

(Continued on Page Two)

●

The Story of LBJ's Landslide

PRESIDENTIAL VOTE
83% tallied

Johnson—35,894,214
Goldwater—22,148,413

ELECTORAL VOTE

Johnson—482
Goldwater—52
Undecided—4

BIG GOP LOSERS

Kennth Keating—N.Y.
Charles Percy—Ill.
J. Glenn Beall—Md.
Edwin L. Mechem—N.M.

U.S. SENATE

	Dem.	Rep.
Old Senate	66	34
New Senate	67	33
Gain	1	—
Loss	—	1
Undecided	—	—

U.S. HOUSE

	Dem.	Rep.
Old House	254	174
New House	297	137
Gain	43	—
Loss	—	37
Undecided	1	—

Barry Heads For Eclipse In Politics

Senator Barry Goldwater gave up his Senate seat to run for the presidency, and his Tuesday defeat leaves his political future uncertain and unpromising.

The next Arizonia Senate race is not until 1968, when Carl Hayden is up for re-election. It is unlikly Goldwater would run for a lesser office.

Early in the campaign Goldwater said if he polled 43 percent or more of the popular vote he would run for president again in 1968.

Goldwater said if Johnson won by a landslide he would retire permanently from politics.

The defeated Republican promised a statement on his future at 10 a.m. Wednesday.

YANKS ABROAD GRIN BROADLY

LBJ Voters Rejoice in London

LONDON—(Reuters) — Streamers fluttered and backs were pounded joyfully Wednesday morning, as the first American presicential campaign ever held on foreign soil ended triumphantly with the election of President Lyndon Johnson.

As returns came by radio to London the Americans Abroad for Johnson, headed by Anthony Hyde, of New York, gaily carried out pre-planned victory parties.

Across from Johnson headquarters, Britain's lords, ladies and legislators attended a more neutral gathering.

Ministers of past and present governments, plus peers and American news correspondents, watched election results tabulated at London's plush Savoy Hotel. The British Broadcasting Corporation called it "Britain's most distinguished gathering tonight."

Also at the Savoy gathering were ambassadors of several nations, including U. S. Ambassador David Bruce who would make no comment on the results.

But at the Johnson party, comments were rife. They ranged from "This is news?" to "Yippee."

Denis Plimmer, formerly of New York City and vice chairman of Americans Abroad for Johnson, estimated that U. S. civilians and servicemen gave Johnson about 75,000 votes in absentee ballots in Britain alone.

1965

The Vietnam war heated up.

U.S. Marines landed in Da Nang. . . .The Vietcong attacked a U.S. military compound in South Vietnam. . . .U.S. troop buildup continued.

In the United States, demonstrations against the war began to grow in number and frequency.

There were also civil rights demonstrations. The Reverend Dr. Martin Luther King, Jr., led a march from Selma to Montgomery, Alabama, to protest discrimination in voting registration. Rioting erupted in the Watts section of Los Angeles and the National Guard was called in to restore order.

The Voting Rights Act was passed, expanding registration opportunities for black voters. Federal offices were set up to prevent abuses.

RIOTS SPREAD

Two More Cities Attacked

LATEST NEWS SPORTS

LOS ANGELES EVENING AND SUNDAY

HERALD EXPRESS EXAMINER

CLASSIFIED ADVERTISING Richmond 8-4111 All Other Calls Richmond 8-1212 or Richmond 8-4141

LARGEST EVENING CIRCULATION IN AMERICA

Del Mar RACES Late Scratches

OL. XCV Four Sections Section A 10 CENTS MONDAY, AUGUST 16, 1965 ★ 10 CENTS NO. 143

LBJ Denounces Riots in Peace Plea to Negroes

By MARIANNE MEANS

Herald-Examiner White House Correspondent With Hearst Headline Service

AUSTIN, Aug. 16—President Johnson, who has ice condemned the Negro riots in Los Angeles and lled upon Negroes to meet the "special challenge" of peaceful progress in civil rights, kept in close touch with the smoldering situation in Los Angeles today.

The President and his family are expected to return to Washington late this afternoon after a four-day weekend here.

As news of the Los Angeles rioting poured in, the President offered Federal help to California and issued two strongly-worded statements. He denounced the rioters for their disregard for law and order and pledged that the violence will not hamper progress toward Negro equality.

The President pleaded with the nation to "Not let anger drown understanding" and to move ahead with efforts to "strike at the unjust conditions from which disorder largely flows."

He declared:

"To resort to terror and violence not only shatters the essential right of every citizen to be secure in his home, his shops and in the streets of his town, it strikes from the hand of the Negro the very weapons with which he is achieving his own eman- own emancipation." cipation."

The President expressed his "deep sense of relief" that order was being restored. He ordered Federal rations, trucks, jeeps, and other help dispatched to the scene at the request of California officials.

The President said California and Los Angeles were meeting the crosis and that the Federal Government had

(Continued on Page 10, Col. 1)

Firemen Fight 25 Blazes

Beleaguered city and county firefighters were on the ve today across the Southland answering alarms from far northwest as Pacoima San Pedro as a result of endiarism.

Fire-bomb attacks were reported on a paper bag factory in Wilmington, a Pacoima beverage company warehouse, a lumber yard in Anaheim and buildings in El Segundo, Inglewood and Hollywood.

Most of the blazes during the night were brought under control as a result of combined efforts of firefighters and armed troops, who were along to protect firemen from possible ambush.

Throughout the day yesterday a total of 74 alarms were received by various fire fighting agencies and actual fires were counted. Ten alarms were false. During the night firemen fought 25 blazes and responded to 25 other calls, those being false alarms.

One of the larger fires in the scorched area, a lumber yard at 51st Street and Long Beach Boulevard was brought under control late Sunday afternoon.

FIREMEN IN ARMOR AGAINST SNIPERS

County firemen, the target of snipers during the riot, had more than police and military protection today when they answered fire calls.

County Fire Chief Keith E. Klinger borrowed 200 flack suits from the U.S. Marine Base at Camp Pendleton.

The flack suits are of heavy mesh material built to give head-to-thigh protection from ground fire when worn by airmen.

Some 120 Guardsmen, under command of Capt. S. A. Douglas, 49th Infantry Division are stationed near field quarters of the county firemen at Firestone Plaza, Alameda Avenue and Firestone Boulevard, to answer fire calls with the firemen and return the fire of any snipers.

Also on loan to the County is a U.S. Forest Service plane called a "scanner," from Missoula, Mont.

From the scanner, a photographer may make infrared pictures through smoke and flames to show the type building on fire. This will help determine what equipment will be needed.

Also on hand is a snorkel platform on which ... men may stand when they use fire hoses.

—Herald-Examiner Photo by TERRY SULLIVAN

LONG BEACH POLICE FRISK NEGROES ON STREET AS RIOTING SPREADS

The Negroes were searched after one officer was killed and a curfew was ordered

Whites Hunted, Seized as Snipers

White snipers today were reported riding in the Los Angeles harbor area, following arrest of two adults and two juveniles in separate incidents.

As police and sheriff units desperately tried to contain the six-day old race riots, whites reportedly were beginning to complicate the situation in what one official described as "stupid attempts at retaliation."

Shortly after midnight, Anthony Meyers and Edward Walter Cornejo, both 21, were arrested in the San Pedro area on charges of shooting at inhabited buildings.

Officers sid the pair were "firing indiscriminately" at houses and buildings, using a .22 caliber rifle that was found in their car. Their addresss were not immediately available, police said.

An hour later, at 10th Street and Pacific Avenue in San Pedro, two juveniles were arrested after police stopped their car. A search of the vehicle uncovered a pellet pistol.

This brings to six the number of Caucasions who have been arrested so far during the riots, all found to be carrying firearms in their ca...

"Th... troubles," said one police official. "Things like this can only lead to more bloodshed or broaden this situation.

"We've already got all the trouble we need without having to worry about a lot of kooky white kids riding around taking pot shots at other people."

Cooler Today --A Little

(U.S. Weather, Tides D-4)

It was a little cooler today as the Weather Bureau predicted a high of 89 degrees compared to yesterday's 89 at Civic Center. The low tonight will be 68.

It was mostly sunny today, tomorrow with some cloudiness.

Beaches will be fairly cool with a high temeprature predicted at 77 degrees. Water temperature was 70 degrees.

Rumors Denied

ALGIERS, Aug. 16 (UPI) — A spokesman for the Algerian government yesterday denied reports ousted President Ahmed Ben Bella was dead, ill, in a psychiatric clinic, or had escaped.

GEORGE MEDAK
Shot in the arm

RICHARD LEFEBVRE
Killed in Long Beach

RESIDENT AID SEEN IN LOOT RECOVERY

Los Angeles police today were optimistic that much of the loot taken from the city's southeastern area will be recovered.

Inspector John W. Powers, commander of the force's field command post, said:

"We have been getting calls from citizens in the area, telling of caches of loot taken by rioters in the past four days.

"We appreciate the help they have been to us and hope many others will cooperate similarly when order is restored.

"It is one of the most optimistic notes of this entire chaotic affair and indicates that the majority of people in the area are opposed to the insurrection."

By late Sunday afternoon, police were too busy responding to calls to recover the loot, estimated to be worth millions of dollars.

Rebel Held

KHARTOUM, Sudan, Aug. 16 (UPI) — Gen. Nicolas Plenga of the Congo Rebel Army was arrested yesterday and questioned about rebel leaders in the Sudan.

Fire Bombs, Snipers Hit New Targets

By HARRY TESSEL

Herald-Examiner Staff Writer

Die-hard rioters fire-bombed and triggered sniper shots throughout mob-ravaged Los Angeles today in the sixth day of hoodlum violence across the Southland.

A Long Beach policeman was fatally shotgunned in front of 100 brick-throwers when a fellow officer's weapon accidentally discharged.

A Negro, Neiti Love, 67, was slain by National Guardsmen when she drove through a barricade at 51st Street and Avalon Boulevard.

San Diego Rioting

Molotov cocktails were thrown in San Diege where 60 cursing, rock-throwing Negroes were arrested after 100 police reservists were pressed inte service.

San Bernardino police broke up several would-be mobs of 50 to 100 persons after flurries of stones and bottles smashed liquor store and restaurant windows.

And a fire bomb lashed flames into a Pacoima brewery at 10717 Sutter St.

The death toll for six bloody and burning days of rioting stands at 30. More than 809 persons have been injured and 2679 arrested.

Fire damage is estimated at $175 million, and undetermined millions more have been lost through looting.

Emergency hospitals reported that many looters cut their heel tendons while climbing through broken windows in shops.

Los Angeles police today gave this situatior report:

"Looting and rioting is totally under contre but there is extensive shooting all over the rie area and in the San Fernando Valley and Highland Park."

Some 15,000 National Guardsmen remained on the alert throughout the barricaded mob-torn section where a curfew was clamped down for the second night.

Electricity Cut Off

Thousands of homes in the pillaged Negro neighborhood were without electricity because of fire and rioter-cut wires.

Food was spoiling in refrigerators or unavailable in burned or looted grocery stores, or riot-shut markets:

Negro Baptist Minister W. H. Johnson complained:

"Every drugstore is either burned or locked up in my neighborhood, and my wife needs medicine every day."

AFL-CIO retail clerks and food industry representatives met today to ararnge "immediate reopening of markets closed by rioting."

This is further dollar cost of the riots:

More than $200,000 a day for National Guardsmen.

More than $1 million in additional police salaries.

There were 24 major fires during the night.

(Cont. on Page 4, Cols. 1-2)

TODAY'S TOP FEATURES

1966

The conflict escalated in Vietnam as the United States increased its military strength there and bombed Hanoi and Haiphong.

Violence, including racially related shootings, robberies, burnings, and lootings, erupted in numerous American cities.

Chinese Chairman Mao Tse-tung ordered a purge of "bourgeois bureaucrats," beginning China's Cultural Revolution.

Indira Gandhi succeeded Lal Bahadur Shastri as prime minister of India.

The staid *Times* of London produced its last issue in its old, traditional format of advertisements on the front page.

ROYAL EDITION

THE TIMES

LONDON MONDAY MAY 2 1966

PRICE NINEPENCE

PERSONAL

MOTOR CARS &c.

ON THIS . . . THE LAST DAY OF TRADITIONAL FRONT PAGE ADVERTISING IN THIS NEWSPAPER

H. R. OWEN LTD

17 BERKELEY STREET, London, W.1. Tel.: MAY. 9060

AGRICULTURE

CRAFTSMEN

SHIPPING

SOUTH AFRICA AUSTRALIA NEW ZEALAND ROUND THE WORLD

GIBRALTAR, TANGIER, MOROCCO

H. R. OWEN LIMITED

47 SLOANE STREET, LONDON, S.W.1.

P & O-ORIENT LINES

BLUE STAR LINE

SOUTH AMERICA

PRE-BUDGET CARPET SALE

MEN AT THE TOP

LONDON TUESDAY MAY 3 1966

THE TIMES

London to be new H.Q. for Nato

Mr. Thomson to pursue talks with allies today

FROM OUR DIPLOMATIC CORRESPONDENT

Mr. Callaghan, the Chancellor of the Exchequer, at work in his study at No. 11 Downing Street, yesterday. With him are Mr. G. Mackenzie, his Parliamentary Private Secretary (left), and Mr. P. Vinter, Third Secretary.

BRITAIN LOOKS AT PROSPECT IN E.E.C.

First of visits

Early decisions

Speed required

MR. BROWN AT PRE-BUDGET CABINET

FROM OUR POLITICAL CORRESPONDENT

New campaign

Clash between the major fuel industries

Minister's role to umpire on rival claims

FROM OUR POLITICAL CORRESPONDENT

Costs compared

Big dollar sale by Britain

11 girls in hospital after Paris trip

BOOMERANG BRINGS A RUGBY BAN

SIR A. FORBES TO REST

DUKE OF EDINBURGH IN OSLO

4,000 U.S. drugs to be checked

FROM OUR OWN CORRESPONDENT

Seamen back decision to strike

12,000 WILL BE LAID OFF

FROM OUR CORRESPONDENT

Priest 'in hands of kidnappers'

FROM OUR OWN CORRESPONDENT

ROB ROY AS LARGE AS LIFE

REBUFF TO RHODESIAN MINISTER

No assurances on 'social visit'

British airlift to Zambia ending

Lord Cameron for print inquiry

STOWAWAY IS TAKEN OFF LINER

POLISH BAN ON FOREIGNERS EASED

PILGRIMS CROWD BLACK MADONNA SHRINE

FROM OUR CORRESPONDENT IN EAST EUROPE—CZESTOCHOWA, MAY 2

Door ajar

Starfighter jet crash

RENAULT HOPE FOR SOVIET FACTORY

ON OTHER PAGES

1968

In a turbulent decade, this may have been the most volatile year.

It started with a Vietcong and North Vietnamese offensive during the Tet holiday at the end of January. More than one hundred cities were infiltrated and attacked, including Hue, Khe Sanh, and Saigon itself.

The U.S.S. *Pueblo*, a naval intelligence ship, was seized by North Korean patrol boats. It took negotiators all year to obtain the release of the ship and its crew.

Civil rights riots continued to plague major cities in the United States.

The Reverend Dr. Martin Luther King, Jr., was assassinated in Memphis, Tennessee. James Earl Ray pleaded guilty to the crime and was later sentenced to ninety-nine years.

Senator Robert F. Kennedy was assassinated by Sirhan Sirhan as he campaigned for the presidency in Los Angeles, California. Sirhan was later convicted and sentenced to life imprisonment.

Richard Nixon and Spiro Agnew were elected to lead the nation after Lyndon Johnson announced he would not seek another term and the Democrats unsuccessfully ran Hubert Humphrey for President.

The Albuquerque Tribune

LOCAL FORECAST: Fair today, gusty afternoon winds with snow in Sandias tomorrow.

HOME EDITION
Closing Stock Prices
PRICE: SEVEN CENTS
30c WEEKLY

Vol. 50, No. [illegible] — Albuquerque, New Mexico, Tuesday, January 30, 1968 — 36 Pages in Four Sections

Reds in Major Attack; Shells Fall on Saigon

[illegible] for Cuba?

Navy Jets Force Albq Pilot Back To Florida Key

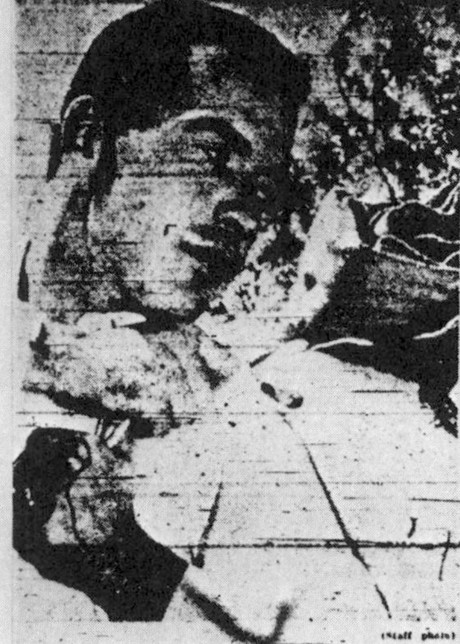

(Staff photo)

BACK IN THE NEWS: Ernest M. Hall, 27-year-old Albuquerque man who was intercepted by Navy jets in a stolen plane over the Florida Keys today, is shown in this 1965 photograph as he prepared to leave Albuquerque on a 13,000-mile foot journey to Brazil — a trip he never finished. He denied today that he was flying the plane to Cuba.

By HOWARD BRYAN
Tribune Staff Writer

27-year-old novice pilot [illegible] Albuquerque, flying a [illegible] plane south toward Cuba, [was] intercepted by Navy jets [over] the Florida Keys this [morn]ing and forced to land at [Key] West.

[Er]nest M. Hall, whom his [moth]er in Albuquerque [illegible] an unstable [illegible] denied that [he w]as headed for Cuba and [told] Florida authorities that he [was] the plane "because I was [in] and out and wanted to [illegible]."

[Hal]l, who was carrying two [illegible] pistols in his duffel [bag], also told the authorities [illegible] the first time he [had] ever landed an airplane.

"By Instinct"

[His] mother, Mrs. W. L. [illegible], 918 Noval Place NW, [told] The Tribune that her son [had] never had more than three [illegible] hours of flying instruction [and had] always claimed that [he could] fly an airplane "by [instinct]."

[Ex]pressing shock and [illegible] over the news, Mrs. [illegible], an attractive, slender, [illegible]haired woman, said she [had] heard from her son last [illegible] from Atlanta, Ga., where [he ha]d gone to find work.

"[I j]ust can't believe that he [would] do this," she said. "I [kn]ow he wasn't headed for [Cuba], for he has always been [very] patriotic, and anti-Com[munist]."

In Jail

[Hall] was being held at the [Monroe] County Jail in Key West. Authorities said they planned to charge him with grand larceny later today in the theft of the plane, a twin-engine Piper Apache.

Authorities said they planned to charge him with grand larceny later today in the theft of the plane, a twin-engine Piper Apache.

The plane was stolen at about 7:30 a.m. (EST) today from a private airport at Marathon, about 30 miles north of Key West. Authorities said the plane was owned by a tourist identified as Ted E. Hellings, Jr.

Calls Center

Police were notified of the stolen plane minutes later when [illegible]

See NAVY, Page A-2

Senate Gets Bills to Hike Income Tax

Measures Would Raise Up To $15 Million

SANTA FE (UPI) — Two major income tax bills were introduced in the Senate today.

Sens. Jerry Apodaca, D-Dona Ana, and George Koran, R-Bernalillo, submitted a measure to provide the state with an additional $13 to $15 million annually in income taxes.

Bills by Sen. Thomas Benavidez, D-Bernalillo, would increase the income tax, and provide that no income tax shall be imposed upon any member of the armed services while on duty outside the United States.

$8 to $10 Million

Benavidez estimated his income tax bill would provide $8 to $10 million additional revenue to the general fund each year.

Senators met for less than one hour, then recessed to go into a closed caucus.

Senators earlier confirmed the nomination of Charles McConnell as state banking commissioner. Confirmation was recommended by the Rules Committee.

Tax Measures

The Benavidez and Apodaca tax measures would raise the tax rate to 2¼ per cent from 1½ per cent on net income not exceeding $20,000; to 6¾ per cent from 4½ per cent on net income not exceeding $100,000, and 8 per cent from 6 per cent on all net income in excess of $100,000.

Corporate Tax

The corporate income tax rate would be raised to 4½ per cent from 3 per cent in both bills.

The Benavidez and Apodaca bills would disallow the federal income tax as a deduction on the state return.

Twin Grins

(Staff photo)

IDENTICAL GRINS: Besides looking alike, the Smith twins, Ann and Amy, both lost both their front teeth on the same day. Their mother says each twin now has one tooth coming back in. The girls are the daughters of Mr. and Mrs. Clark Smith, 810 Morningside SE. Mr. Smith is New Mexico division manager for Horizon Land Co. The 6-year-old twins are the only girls in a family that includes five boys from 3 to 15.

BULLETIN

SAIGON (UPI) — The Viet Cong shelled Saigon itself today in a stunning followup to its attacks on major cities.

First reports said rocket or mortar shells landed near Independence Palace, seat of the government in the heart of Saigon, other government buildings and the U.S. Embassy.

Small-arms fire was heard in the streets.

One building near Independence Palace was set afire.

SAIGON (UPI) — The Viet Cong launched their mightiest offensive of the war today and sent thousands of troops smashing into dozens of towns and villages still celebrating the lunar new year cease-fire. Most attacks were hurled back but fighting was reported tonight in four towns.

The Viet Cong swarming into seven major cities, including Da Nang inflicted millions of dollars in damage on U.S. planes and helicopters in the coordinated attacks.

Fighting [illegible], Hoi An, Nha Trang and Kontum and on the outskirts of Da Nang. Saigon was warned of possible infiltration.

U.S. and allied troops canceled their part of the Tet truce and drove back the guerrillas in daylong fighting that ranged from house to house, from street to street. Seven major cities were hit and many U.S. military installations.

★ ★ ★

Casualty reports were still incomplete but allied forces reported killing at least 441 and capturing hundreds of the guerrillas who blew up $15 million worth of jet planes at Da Nang, damaged dozens of others and destroyed or damaged an estimated 30 helicopters.

Path of death left by Viet Cong raiders, Page D-4

U.S. softens stand on talks, bombing halt, page C-8

Comparatively Light

U.S. and allied losses were comparatively light but figures were incomplete.

U.S. officials said the offensive apparently was plotted by Defense Minister Vo Nguyen Giap of North Vietnam, who has massed 40,000 other troops near the Demilitarized Zone and sent 20,000 of them toward Khe Sanh in a major threat to the U.S. Marine bastion there.

Fighting raged in some of the cities tonight but in most areas the Viet Cong effort failed. Moscow Radio broadcasts reports the Viet Cong had captured Pleiku and Nha Trang but U.S. and Vietnamese forces held both cities tonight.

To "Punish Aggressors"

The clandestine Viet Cong radio said the attack was ordered to "punish the U.S. aggressors" for calling off the cease-fire in the five northern provinces where the enemy threat was greatest. South Vietnam called the attacks "premeditated and callous violation" of the communists' self-proclaimed seven-day truce.

The guerrillas struck at the moment the Buddhist temples rang in Asia's Year of the Monkey and joyful civilian crowds paraded and popped firecrackers in the streets.

From his map-lined war room in Saigon, Gen. William C. Westmoreland, American commander in Vietnam, ordered his forces to forget their 36-hour cease-fire and get back to war.

U.S. spokesmen said the guerrilla attacks centered in central South Vietnam and ob[illegible]

See REDS, Page A-4

LBJ Briefed During Night

WASHINGTON (UPI) — President Johnson was awakened twice during the early morning hours today for special reports from Gen. William C. Westmoreland on the expanding Communist offensive in South Vietnam.

The White House said Johnson remained in the "situation room" until after midnight keeping track of the developments and was roused from bed at 5 a.m. and again at 7 for updated briefings.

Meets With Leaders

Johnson breakfasted with Democratic congressional leaders, Sen. J. William Fulbright, chairman of the Senate Foreign Relations Committee, and Rep. Thomas Morgan, chairman of the House Foreign Affairs Committee, also attended.

White House Press Secretary George Christian said the congressional leaders were filled in on developments in the Communist buildup in the Khe Sanh area and other Viet Cong and North Vietnamese activity in South Vietnam.

UN Reported Making Progress On Sending Mediator to N. Korea

By R. H. BOYCE
Scripps-Howard Staff Writer

NEW YORK — There were signs today that United Nations Security Council members were making progress on a proposal to send a mediator to North Korea to discuss the problem of the captured USS Pueblo.

Intense behind-the-scenes talks centered on a plan to select a representative of a neutral country who would act outside the UN framework.

Key Factor

The key factor in the plan was that, technically at least, it would be a gambit entirely divorced from the Security Council.

If agreed on — and both the Soviet Union and the U.S. were reported closer to "an understanding" of each other's position — it would simply be a matter of concerned governments agreeing privately on this as one possible way of defusing the Pueblo crisis, and using the UN building here as a convenient meeting place.

U.S. to step up aid to S. Korea, page B-8

No Formal Action

There would be no Security Council resolution or other formal council action. As one delegate put it, "the Security Council would be completely out of the picture."

Delegates warned that such a mediator might be unable to effect a successful return of the Pueblo or her crew. There was no indication when any agreement on a mediator might be reached.

Security Council members in twos and threes met late into last night and again today, after a scheduled Security Council session yesterday afternoon was canceled indefinitely.

Not UN Member

It was uncertain whether North Korea would agree to

See UN REPORTED, Page A-4

INSIDE YOUR TRIBUNE TODAY

IS THE U.S. going down Britain's path? See a London Express special analysis on page [illegible]

The Albuquerque Tribune
New Mexico's Significant Newspaper

N.M. Income Up in 1967

New Mexico's per capita income moved upward for the seventh straight year in 1967, the University of New Mexico Bureau of Business Research reported today.

Calling it "probably the best single index of economic welfare" in the state, the bureau estimated that per capita income climbed to $2,443 last year.

The figure is part of a preliminary report on the state's eco[nomy] in 1967 by A. David Sand[oval], economist with the bureau, published in the current issue of "New Mexico Business."

The magazine is published monthly by the bureau which is part of the College of Business Administration at UNM.

Sandoval s[aid] that the $2,443 figure is a ga[in] of 5.6 per cent. The 1966 [figure] was 6.7 per cent.

Part of [the] 1967 increase however, wa[s] the result of an estimated 0.[illegible] per cent decline in the state's [p]opulation, Sandoval wrote.

Ass[um]ptions

Total per[son]al income probably will [be] an all-time high of $2.510 [billi]on for 1967, representing [a] growth rate of about 5 pe[r c]ent, the report says.

The majo[r a]ssumptions used in estimati[ng 1]967 personal in-

[See] N.M., Page A-4

20 Sites Offered

Albuquerque Industrial Development Service Inc. (AIDS) has prepared information on 20 [illegible] sites for a Los Angeles-based trucking firm [illegible] plans to locate here.

Eliminates Bottleneck

Edgewood Road Link To Open This Week

By C. A. HUNDERTMARK
Tribune Staff Writer

State Highway Dept. officials today reported the 6.8-mile stretch of I-40 near Edgewood will be open to traffic sometime this week possibly tomorrow.

The link was completed more than a year ago. However, Highway Department plans originally did not call for opening of the four-lane superhighway until additional sections of I-40 were completed at both ends.

In response to public demand, however, the Highway Commission agreed to connect the completed stretch of road with U.S. Route 66 temporarily.

Tribune Editorial

The action came after The Tribune called attention to the need to link up the highway with old U.S. 66 in an editorial. The New Mexico Motor Club (AAA) was also active in the campaign to get the road opened.

The link runs from a western terminus, just east of Tijeras Canyon, to a point east of Edgewood.

Five sections of the I-40 freeway remain to be completed between Cline's Corners and Albuquerque.

12 Miles

John A. Fairly Jr., head of the Highway Department engineering section, said three projects, covering about 12 miles, remain to be completed in Tijeras Canyon.

Two additional stretches, totaling 10.7 miles, must be completed from a point west

See EDGEWOOD, Page A-4

Committee OKs Gas Tax Bill

SANTA FE (UPI) — The Senate Finance Committee has approved two bills including one that would impose an additional two cent tax on cigarettes.

The [illegible] stamp of endorsement went to legislation requiring cities in disposing of city property to get no less than what they paid for it or at least 5 per cent of the appraised value of the land.

The Tribune's MR. FIX-IT

To Solve Your Problems
Phone 247-3311

Q—Is there a barber in Albuquerque who specializes in trimming and styling beards? I'm a bearded lady and my whiskers are getting a little scraggly.—W.J.

A—Lady, if you got a beard, come down and we'll take your picture and I'll bet somebody will trim it free. Even this item may do the trick — there are probably barbers all over town just dying to trim a lady's beard.

More FIX-IT on page A-2

Snow on Crest, Wind in Town

Ski buffs can scan the Sandia Mountains where the weatherman calls for some snow tomorrow.

It will be fair today with some clouds in the afternoon and winds from 15 to 25 miles an hour. The high today will be 55 and lows tonight will be 26 degrees in the Valley and 30 at the Sunport.

Today's lows were 27 degrees at the Sunport and 22 in the Valley. Humidity at 9 a.m. today was 64 per cent.

AWOL Soldier Charged

Heir to Colorado Oil Fortune Dead

SAN ANGELO, Tex. (UPI) —A rabbit hunter found the body of wealthy young Michael Robineau last night in a cotton field to end a two-day search for the Colorado man.

Officers charged an AWOL soldier from Odessa, Tex., today with murder.

Charged was Miguel Galligas Ybarra, 21, absent without leave from Ft. Sam Houston, Tex., from which Robineau, 21, had just finished six months' duty as an Army reservist Friday.

By His Father

Ybarra, recently back from Korea, was brought to the police station at Odessa, 130 miles northwest of here, by his father yesterday.

Robineau, heir to Colorado oil millions, was shot in the head.

Ybarra was charged with going AWOL Friday, the day Robineau left Ft. Sam Houston.

Members of the Robineau family had said it was not unusual for Robineau to give a hitchhiker a ride.

Heir to $3 Million

Son of the late M. H. Robineau, Denver sportsman and president of Frontier Refining Co., he was reported to be heir to [illegible] million.

Robineau's blood-stained car was found Saturday near Big Lake, 72 miles southeast of San Angelo on a route to Odessa. There was an expended 25-caliber bullet shell in the car.

Michael Robineau

The New York Times Summary of the News

(C) 1968 New York Times News Service

INTERNATIONAL

[WASH]INGTON — The administration has offered to [illegible] North Vietnam and to begin peace talks [illegible] the infiltration of men [illegible] levels. North Vietnam has [illegible]

[illegible] White House conferences [illegible] to include military com[illegible] appeared reconciled [illegible] two or three weeks [illegible] the ship and its crew [illegible] foreign governments [illegible] Union.

[illegible] minister said [illegible] delivery of [illegible] to be used in [illegible]

[illegible]

The Weather

Today—Chance of showers in the morning, then clearing, windy. High in mid 60s. Tuesday—Mostly sunny, cool. Probability of precipitation, 30% today. Temp. range: Today, 55-65; Yesterday, 51-77. Details, B4.

The Washington Post

Times Herald

Index

91st Year · No. 118 · © 1968, The Washington Post Co. · MONDAY, APRIL 1, 1968 · Phone 223-6000 · 10c

Johnson Won't Seek Nomination

Announces Partial Halt In Bombing

President Johnson announced last night that he would not be a candidate for reelection this year.

He made the dramatic announcement after ordering a halt in bombing attacks on North Vietnam and appealing to Hanoi to go to the peace table promptly.

The President's surprise announcements were made in a radio-television address to the Nation from his office in the White House.

Mr. Johnson said "I shall not seek and I will not accept the nomination for another term as President."

President Johnson told the Nation and the world last night that he had ordered a cessation of air and naval attacks on North Vietnam except in the area north of the Demilitarized Zone.

He called this the first step to de-escalate the Vietnam war and appealed to North Vietnam to meet American representatives at Geneva for peace talks.

The President designated W. Averell Harriman, Ambassador at Large, and Llewellyn E. Thompson, Ambassador to Russia, to be available to meet North Vietnamese representatives in Geneva.

"We are prepared to move immediately toward peace through negotiations," the President said in a radio-television talk from his office.

His appeal came two days before the Wisconsin presidential primary in which he faces Sen. Eugene McCarthy who has been sharply critical of the Administration's Vietnam policy.

While promising de-escalation of the war, the President warned that the United States "will not accept a fake solution to this long and arduous struggle and call it peace."

To reinforce his hand and that of the South Vietnamese, the President said that he was sending during the next five months an additional 13,500 men to Vietnam. He called them "support troops" to strengthen forces already there.

Part of these men will come from the active forces and part from reserve units, the President said.

An additional $2.5 billion in appropriations to meet Vietnam war costs will be required in the current fiscal year and $2.6 billion above that already requested will be needed in the fiscal year, the President said.

He again appealed for prompt approval of his tax increase proposal. The Nation faces "the sharpest financial threat" of the postwar years, the President said.

"I cannot promise that the initiative I am announcing tonight will be any more successful in achieving peace than the more than 30 others we have undertaken and agreed to in recent years," Mr. Johnson said.

"It is our hope that North Vietnam, after years of fight-

See PRESIDENT, A15, Col. 4

By Margaret Thomas—The Washington Post

Martin Luther King speaks from Cathedral pulpit.

4000 Hear Dr. King at Cathedral

Leader Reaffirms Intention to Begin March on Schedule

By Bernadette Carey
Washington Post Staff Writer

The Rev. Dr. Martin Luther King Jr. came to Washington yesterday and made an apparent effort to rebuild support for his planned April 22 Poor People's campaign here, shaken last week when his Memphis demonstration erupted with violence.

Speaking to an overflow audience of more than 4000 at National Cathedral, Dr. King declared again his intention to bring 3000 poor people to Washington this month for "a nonviolent demonstration."

"There will be a Poor People's Campaign," Dr. King told his predominantly white audience at the Cathedral.

"But we are not coming to Washington to engage in any histrionic action, nor are we coming to tear up Washington," he said.

"I don't like to predict violence," he added, "but if nothing is done between now and June to raise ghetto hope, I feel this summer will not only be as bad, but worse than last year."

Holds Press Conference

Showing no strain from the events of Memphis, he strode through the packed Cathedral, where normal Sunday attendance ranges from 750 to 1000, wearing a black robe and his usual solemn manner.

During his sermon, laced with Biblical and literary references, his speech was slow, deliberate and restrained.

The same tone prevailed at a short press conference after the church service, in one of the buildings of the Cathedral School.

There Dr. King said that while he had no intention of calling off the demonstration unless the President and Congress took some concrete action, last Thursday's rioting in Memphis had caused him to change some of his plans for the Washington campaign.

To Limit First Wave

To help keep the demonstration under control, he said, it had been decided to limit the first wave of demonstrators, due to arrive the April 22 week, to 3000, and to postpone a planned massive demonstration with additional thousands of poor people until June 15.

Dr. King also acknowledged that because of the violence that took place in Memphis he had decided not to take a planned trip to Nigeria that would have taken him away from Washington during the demonstration.

He said he did not think that the rioting in Memphis

See KING, A4, Col. 4

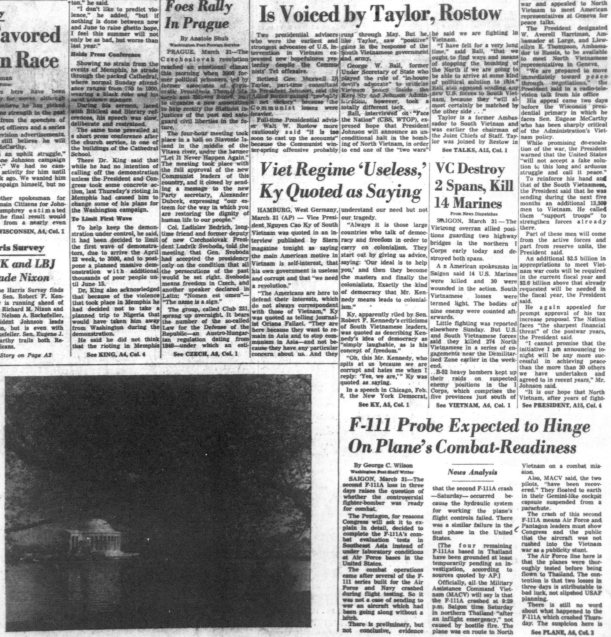

Associated Press

U.S. troops ride past fleeing Vietnamese peasants as they move toward a recent battle northwest of Saigon.

LBJ Supporters Gloomy

McCarthy Favored In Wisconsin Race

By William Chapman
Washington Post Staff Writer

MILWAUKEE, March 31—In his second direct confrontation with President Johnson, Sen. Eugene J. McCarthy is favored to win the Wisconsin Democratic primary Tuesday by veterans in every political camp.

Strong currents of anti-Johnson and antiwar sentiment, the large anticipated crossover voting by Republicans, and the listlessness of the Democratic regular organization are cited to place the President in an underdog's role.

For McCarthy, who won national prominence with his strong showing in the New Hampshire primary, it is almost a do-or-die contest. He must win to maintain the momentum of New Hampshire, his aides concede, and to present a strong alternative to Mr. Johnson and Sen. Robert F. Kennedy through the next important primaries.

On the Republican side, former Vice President Richard M. Nixon is virtually assured of capturing all the state's 30 National Convention votes. However, the large number of Republicans switching to the Democratic side of the ballot probably will leave Nixon running third in the total popular vote.

President Johnson's supporters here have been gloomy for weeks although they believe he has picked up some strength in the past week from the speeches of Cabinet officers and a series of television advertisements. They still believe he will trail McCarthy.

"It's an uphill struggle," said one Johnson campaign leader." We had no campaign activity for him until a week ago. We wanted him to campaign himself, but no luck."

Another spokesman for Wisconsin Citizens for Johnson-Humphrey estimated that the final result would range from a nearly even

See WISCONSIN, A4, Col. 1

Harris Survey

RFK and LBJ Shade Nixon

The Harris Survey finds that Sen. Robert F. Kennedy is running ahead of both Richard M. Nixon and Gov. Nelson A. Rockefeller. President Johnson leads Nixon, but is even with Rockefeller. Sen. Eugene J. McCarthy trails both Republicans.

Story on Page A2

Stalinism Foes Rally In Prague

By Anatole Shub
Washington Post Foreign Service

PRAGUE, March 31—The Czechoslovak revolution reached an emotional climax this morning when 3000 former political prisoners, led by former associates of democratic Presidents Thomas Masaryk and Eduard Benes, met to organize a new association to help rectify the Stalinist injustices of the past and safeguard civil liberties in the future.

The four-hour meeting took place in a hall on Slavonic Island in the middle of the Vltava river, under the banner "Let It Never Happen Again." The meeting took place with the full approval of the new Communist leaders of this country, and it closed by sending a message to the new Party secretary, Alexander Dubcek, expressing "our esteem for the way in which you are restoring the dignity of human life to our people."

Col. Ladislav Bedrich, longtime friend and former deputy of new Czechoslovak President Ludvik Svoboda, told the meeting that Gen. Svoboda had accepted the presidency only on the condition that all the persecutions of the past would be set right. Svoboda means freedom in Czech, and another speaker declared in Latin: "Nomen est omen"—"The name is a sign."

The group, called Club 231, sprang up overnight. It bears the number of the so-called Law for the Defense of the Republic—an Austro-Hungarian regulation dating from 1848—under which an esti-

See CZECH, A8, Col. 1

New Confidence on Vietnam Is Voiced by Taylor, Rostow

Two presidential advisers who were the earliest and strongest advocates of U.S. intervention in Vietnam expressed new hopefulness yesterday despite the Communists' Tet offensive.

Retired Gen. Maxwell D. Taylor, part-time consultant to President Johnson, said the Allied forces gained "probably a net victory" because the Communist losses were heavier.

Full-time Presidential adviser Walt W. Rostow more cautiously said "it is too soon to cast up the accounts" because the Communist winter-spring offensive probably runs through May. But he, like Taylor, saw "positive" gains in the response of the South Vietnamese government and army.

George W. Ball, former Under Secretary of State who played the role of "in-house devil's advocate" to criticize Vietnam policy inside the Kennedy and Johnson Administrations, however, took a totally different tack.

Ball, interviewed on "Face the Nation" (CBS, WTOP), expresed hope that President Johnson will announce an unconditional halt in the bombing of North Vietnam, in order to end one of the "two wars" he said we are fighting in Vietnam.

"I have felt for a very long time," said Ball, "that we ought to find ways and means of stopping the bombing of the North if we are going to be able to arrive at some kind of political solution to this." Ball also opposed sending any new U.S. forces to South Vietnam, because they "will almost certainly be matched by the other side . . ."

Taylor is a former Ambassador to South Vietnam and was earlier the chairman of the Joint Chiefs of Staff. Taylor was joined by Restow in

See TALKS, A15, Col. 1

Viet Regime 'Useless,' Ky Quoted as Saying

HAMBURG, West Germany, March 31 (AP) — Vice President Nguyen Cao Ky of South Vietnam was quoted in an interview published by Stern magazine tonight as saying the main American motive in Vietnam is self-interest, that his own government is useless and corrupt and that "we need a revolution."

"The Americans are here to defend their interests, which do not always correspondent with those of Vietnam," Ky was quoted as telling journalist Oriana Fallaci. "They are here because they want to remain in Asia and to stop communism in Asia—and not because they have any particular concern about us. And they understand our need but not our tragedy.

"Always it is those large countries who talk of democracy and freedom in order to carry on colonialism. They start out by giving us advice, saying: 'Our ideal is to help you,' and then they become the masters and finally the colonialists. Exactly the kind of democracy that Mr. Kennedy means leads to colonialism."

Ky, apparently riled by Sen. Robert F. Kennedy's criticisms of South Vietnamese leaders, was quoted as describing Kennedy's idea of democracy as "simply laughable, as is his concept of freedom."

"Oh, this Mr. Kennedy, who spits at us because we are corrupt and hates me when I reply: 'Yes, we are,'" Ky was quoted as saying.

In a speech in Chicago, Feb. 8, the New York Democrat,

See KY, A5, Col. 1

VC Destroy 2 Spans, Kill 14 Marines

From News Dispatches

SAIGON, March 31—The Vietcong overran allied positions guarding two highway bridges in the northern I Corps early today and destroyed both spans.

An American spokesman in Saigon said 14 U.S. Marines were killed and 30 were wounded in the action. South Vietnamese losses were termed light. The bodies of nine enemy were counted afterwards.

Little fighting was reported elsewhere Sunday. But U.S. and South Vietnamese forces said they killed 274 North Vietnamese in a series of engagements near the Demilitarized Zone earlier in the weekend.

..B-52 heavy bombers kept up their raids on suspected enemy positions in the I Corps, which comprises the five provinces just south of

See VIETNAM, A6, Col. 1

Tidal Basin Breaks Out In Blossoms

The Cherry Blossoms ringing the Tidal Basin were in full bloom yesterday, and more than 90,000 people from the city and from all over the Nation turned out to see them. Their cars rolled around the Basin all afternoon.

For the lucky few who found places to park and a bench to sit on, the city offered contemplation of one of its most celebrated spring spectacles, revealing the sun-splashed marble of the Jefferson Memorial through a delicate screen of pink and white petals.

F-111 Probe Expected to Hinge On Plane's Combat-Readiness

By George C. Wilson
Washington Post Staff Writer

News Analysis

SAIGON, March 31—The second F-111A loss in three days raises the question of whether the controversial fighter-bomber was ready for combat.

The Pentagon, for reasons Congress will ask it to explain in detail, decided to complete the F-111A's combat evaluation tests in Southeast Asia instead of under laboratory conditions at Air Force bases in the United States.

The combat operations came after several of the F-111 series built for the Air Force and Navy crashed during flight testing. So it was not a case of sending to war an aircraft which had been going along without a hitch.

There is preliminary, but not conclusive, evidence that the second F-111A crash—Saturday—occurred because the hydraulic system for working the plane's flight controls failed. There was a similar failure in the test phase in the United States.

[The four remaining F-111As based in Thailand have been grounded at least temporarily pending an investigation, according to sources quoted by AP.]

Officially, all the Military Assistance Command Vietnam (MACV) will say is that the F-111A crashed at 9:29 p.m. Saigon time Saturday in northern Thailand "after an inflight emergency," not caused by hostile fire. The plane was en route to North Vietnam on a combat mission.

Also, MACV said, the two pilots, "have been recovered." They floated to earth in their Gemini-like cockpit capsule suspended from a parachute.

The crash of this second F-111A means Air Force and Pantagon leaders must show Congress and the public that the aircraft was not rushed into the Vietnam war as a publicity stunt.

The Air Force line here is that the planes were thoroughly tested before being flown to Thailand. The contention is that two losses in three days is attributable to bad luck, not slipshod USAF planning.

There is still no word about what happened to the F-111A which crashed Thursday. The suspicion here is

See PLANE, A6, Col. 3

FINAL THE COMMERCIAL APPEAL FINAL
129th YEAR—No. 96 ***** MEMPHIS, TENN., FRIDAY MORNING, APRIL 5, 1968 60 PAGES PRICE 10 CENTS

DR. KING IS SLAIN BY SNIPER

Looting, Arson Touched Off By Death

GUARDSMEN RETURN; CURFEW IS ORDERED

By RICHARD LENTZ

Looting, arson and shooting began minutes after the death f Dr. Martin Luther King Jr. lates last night and in hours 'ennessee National Guardsmen arrived to take over street atrols in riot-torn Memphis.

Negroes began swarming into streets, smashing windows nd setting fires shortly after the announcement of the civil ghts leader's death at 7 p.m.

As the news of Dr. King's slaying flashed, Negroes clashed ith police as far away as Miami, in Jackson, Miss., and in ashville, where another 4,000 guardsmen were called out to eep the peace.

In Memphis, police had arrested 80 persons, including two uveniles and two women by 1 a.m. There were at least 28 ersons reported hurt and a steady flow of injured was being eated at hospitals.

No one had been reported killed in the turmoil.

The most seriously injured person was Ellis Tate of 86 Vest Utah, whom police said was shot while looting. He was in itical condition at John Gaston Hospital.

Officers said he fired at officers with a rifle when they ame into a liquor store he was looting. They returned his fire nd he was hit.

A 24-hour general curfew was ordered last night, with ravel allowed only for emergency or health reasons. Schools, hops and businesses were ordered closed. The curfew will emain in effect indefinitely.

At the biggest fire of the night, policemen armed with ubmachine guns and riot guns guarded firemen who were attling flames that arched 100 feet into the air at O. W. errell Co. at 1001 North Second Street.

Within minutes, 14 pieces of fire equipment were on the ene. There were no incidents.

Black smoke from burning barrels of tar and piles of oofing at the building supplies company rolled over the area.

Earlier, piles of boxes 20 feet high had been set on fire hind Leone's Liberty Cash Crocery at 485 Vance. The flames ere endangering an apartment complex and firemen after urning through live electrical wires. The fire was put out in inutes after Deptuy Fire Chief R. F. Doyle shouted "Knock down, knock it down. Let's get out of here."

Tennessee Highway Patrolmen were reported moving in orce toward Memphis to supplement police and guardsmen. ore than 200 of the state police were sent into Memphis when olence erupted March 28.

Arkansas Gov. Winthrop ockefeller sent state troopers Memphis to observe the riot-g. Last week he ordered 175 kansas guardsmen called for ty in West Memphis.

Officials said firemen from ation One answered eight lls in 20 minutes at one point ring the night.

A store on Firestone Boule-rd was burned so com-etely it could not be immedi-ely identified.

First elements of Guards-en reported no trouble as ey cautiously patrolled Mem-is streets last night. Three tillery batteries were com-itted to the city and nine trols of 16 guardsmen each re deployed on streets.

A spokesman in the gover-r's office said Governor ford Ellingtons also was in ntact with United States ty. Gen. Ramsey Clark, pre-mably to discuss the avail-ility of federal troops for e in Memphis.

A straight line to Washington s kept open last night at lice Headquarters at Second d Adams.

Just minutes after Dr. King d, city offices began receiv-g telephone threats against e life of Mayor Henry Loeb, o was traveling by car to e University of Mississippi a speech. Notified of the ath and outbreak of violence d looting, Mayor Loeb ickly returned to City Hall re.

Governor Ellington, who had dered the 4,000 Guardsmen to Memphis March 28 after outbreak of looting and riot-ing during a march led by Dr. King, said "I can fully appreciate the feelings and emotions which this crime has aroused.

"But for the benefit of everyone, all of our citizens must exercise caution and good judgment."

The curfew immediately closed all liquor stores and establishments selling beer, firearms or ammunition, as it did last Thursday.

Shooting began at 7:17 p.m. when shots were reported in the vicinity of Tillman and Johnson.

The worst sniping appeared to be in the Springdale-Howell area, where two police officers were reported wounded at 8:30 by a gunman shooting from around the corner of a building. At 9:20, police cars were still under fire in the same area.

Condition of the two wounded policemen was not immediately known. They were hit by glass when their squad car windshield was shot out.

Fire and Police Director Frank Holloman said, "Rioting and looting is rampant" in the city.

Mr. Holloman, listening to calls from police radio bands and reports from the field, said his 35 tactical units had the situation fairly well under control by about 9:15 p.m. and looting and other violent incidents had subsided somewhat.

"Remain off the streets, keep your children at home and remain calm," he said. "We are doing everything we can do. I call upon all citizens of Memphis . . . to cooperate fully with officers as they do

(Continued on Page 3)

ARSAW REGIME RAPPED

ore Voice In Government For People Asked

WARSAW, April 4. —(UPI) A pro-government Roman atholic newspaper Thursday iticized the all-powerful rul-g Communist coalition for t allowing the people more ice in government and lled for more democracy in land's socialist system.

The attack by Slowo Pow-echne against the Commu-st-dominated National Unity ront was mild but considered rprising. The editorial came the midst of a wave of dis-issals of high-ranking gov-nment officials and followed udent demands for reforms d more freedom.

Two more officials were cked during the day —Dan-l Kac, chairman of the Office State Economic Reserves, d Welhelm Billig, the gov-nment plenipotentiary for e use of nuclear energy. It ought to 22 the number of gh officials removed since e shakeup began in the wake student demonstrations.

Most of those dismissed ve been Jews. It was not own whether Kac or Billig ere Jewish.

Polish Jews have been amed for helping stir student rest

Firemen Battle Blaze At Ferrell Lumber Co. At 1001 North Second
—Staff Photo by Sam Melhorn

An Editorial—

Memphis Needs Calm

THE assassination of Dr. Martin Luther King in Memphis was a cowardly action. It was a tragedy for Memphis.

The need now is for the community to remain calm and restrained despite the increased tensions which this action has caused. As President Johnson said, all America must "reject blind violence," and "search their hearts."

All citizens should keep in mind that this was the deed of an individual who in some warped-minded way thought he could bring an end to a complex problem with a simple, primitive action.

THE death of Dr. King does not solve any problems in Memphis or in the nation. Indeed, it aggravates the existing problems and makes more urgent the need for settlement of the Memphis dispute that precipitated the assassination. Mayor Loeb and the City Council must move swiftly to that end now.

This is not a time for discussion of the provocations which lay behind this action. Murder has been done. Swift apprehension of the killer and just punishment must follow.

To many who were not aware of the angry forces which have been tearing away at the structure of this community in recent weeks, this should bring understanding. There should be no further divisive actions which we all would certainly regret. Rather, this should serve as an example of what such racial rending causes, and should result in solidifying of sentiment in the community more than ever before.

IT IS time now that those of us in all circumstances and of all attitudes realize in the shock of this emotional action that somehow our difficulties and apparent differences must be resolved without further violence and bloodshed.

Hate has produced its ultimate product at the ultimate price.

THE Commercial Appeal is aware that all law enforcement agencies are doing their utmost to apprehend the killer, but we also realize that information from any source could be helpful. Therefore, The Commercial Appeal offers a reward of $25,000 for information leading to the arrest and conviction of the person or persons responsible for this monstrous crime.

Open Housing Voted

LANSING, Mich., April 4. —(AP) — The Michigan Senate Thursday approved a controversial open housing bill 22-14 after turning down two substitutes for the administration-backed measure. The senators also defeated amendments to provide for a public referendum on the issue and exempt individual home owners.

The Weather

U.S. DEPARTMENT OF COMMERCE

FOR MEMPHIS and vicinity — Fair through Saturday. Cool today and tonight and a little warmer Saturday. High today about 58. winds northwesterly 6 to 12 miles per hour. Low Friday night near 34, with chance of frost.

Sunrise 5:42; sunset 6:25

FIVE-DAY OUTLOOK

Temperatures two to six degrees below normal. Normal high 69, low 48. Warmer over weekend, turning cooler again early next week. Rainfall will average near one inch with chance of locally heavier amounts. Thundershowers most likely near the first of the week.

YESTERDAY'S REPORT

High, 72 degrees at midnight.

Low 44 degrees at midnight.

Mean (midway between high and low), 58. Normal mean for date, 57.

HOURLY READINGS

4 a.m.	70	4 p.m.	57
6 a.m.	70	6 p.m.	55
8 a.m.	64	8 p.m.	50
10 a.m.	57	10 p.m.	46
Noon	59	12 p.m.	44
2 p.m.	59	2 a.m.	42

Temperature 7 a.m., 69; 7 p.m., 53.
Precipitation at Airport, .19.
Dewpoint (condensation temperature) at midnight, 30; barometer reading at midnight 30.13 rising.
Precipitation Jan. 1-April 3, 15.98 inches, which is .36 inches below normal.

A YEAR AGO YESTERDAY

Maximum temperature, 79; minimum, 46; rainfall, none.
Precipitation Jan. 1-April 4, 9.21 inches, which was 7.30 inches below normal.

(Map, Forecast on Page 35)

First Lady Ends Visit

WASHINGTON, April 4. — (AP) — Mrs. Lyndon B. Johnson returned Thursday from two days spent at Mar-a-Lago, the Palm Beach, Fla., home of Mrs. Marjorie Merriweather Post. The First Lady flew back in Mrs. Post's private plane. She plans to leave early Friday for a five-day tour of Texas with 40 foreign editors.

On The Inside Pages—

Humphrey Comes Close

* * *

TELEPHONES:

NEWS AND GENERAL ..526-8811
CLASSIFIED ADS 526-8892
CIRCULATION 525-7001
SPORTS SCORES 525-0651

* * *

Today's 60-page editions of The Commercial Appeal include a 12-page tabloid section for Woolco, featuring an Easter Parade of Values.

Dr. Martin Luther King

Rights And Political Leaders Voice Anguish, Shock, Grief

Johnson Speaks For Saddened Nation And Condemns Violence—Some Express Fear Of Increased Terrorism

From Our Press Services

The nation's civil rights and political leaders reacted with anguish, shock and grief last night at the slaying of Dr. Martin Luther King Jr. in Memphis.

There also was fear that the slaying could lead to more violence.

President Johnson spoke of an "America shocked and saddened" by the assassination as he condemned violence, lawlessness and divisiveness.

The President appeared in the doorway of the White House offices, stern-faced and spoke on all television and radio networks.

"I ask every American citizen," he said, "to reject the blind violence that has struck down Dr. King, who lived by nonviolence."

The President urged prayers for peace and understanding in the land and said:

"We can achieve nothing by lawlessness and divisiveness among the American people."

He said he hopes all Americans would search their hearts.

Vice President Hubert H. Humphrey said the slaying "brings shame to our country. An apostle of nonviolence has been the victim of violence."

The vice president said, however, that his death will bring new strength to the cause he fought for.

Former Vice President Richard M. Nixon sent a telegram to Mrs. King, which said: "Dr. King's death is a great personal tragedy for everyone who knew him and a great tragedy for the nation. "Mrs. Nixon joines me in sympathy and prayers for you and your family in this terrible ordeal."

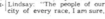

New York Mayor John V. Lindsay: "The people of our city of every race, I am sure, will join hands in paying tribute to him. Our greatest tribute to him will be to bear ourselves as he would want us to — with dignity and prayer."

Senator Wayne Morse (D-Ore.), said Dr. King's death is "one of the saddest tragedies to befall the nation" and warned that the shooting will add to "a very serious domestic crisis. It's going to increase marching across our country."

Fred Meely, a spokesman for the militant Student Non-Violent Coordinating Committee, said, "There is no real comment that we can make. Everybody knows what happened and everybody knows why it happened and the black people in this country know what they have to do about it. That's all I have to say."

Tennessee Gov. Buford Ellington sent a telegram to Dr. King's widow saying he was "deeply saddened and shocked" by the shooting.

Representative Dan Kuykendall (R-Tenn.) in Washington said:

"This dastardly, cowardly act on the part of this unknown person is of great grief to me and, I know, to my city. This is an example of how violence breeds violence. Let's hope and pray that the action and

(Continued on Page 12)

Intensive Manhunt Is Quickly Mounted

President Johnson's Plane Is Reported En Route To Memphis; State Guard Alerted

By JOHN MEANS

A sniper shot and killed Dr. Martin Luther King last night as he stood on the balcony of a downtown hotel.

The most intensive manhunt in the city's history was touched off minutes after the shooting

Violence broke out in Memphis, Nashville, Birmingham, Miami, Raleigh, Washington, New York and other cities as news of the assassination swept the nation.

National leaders, including President Lyndon Johnson, and aides close to the slain 39-year-old Nobel Peace Prize winner, urged the nation to stand calm and avoid violence.

The entire nation was tense.

It was learned early this morning that Air Force One — the President's plane — had left Washington. It may be en route to Memphis.

There was no confirmation that the President was aboard.

The slaying of Dr. King brought Tennessee National Guardsmen back into Memphis. The entire 11,000 men in the state guard were on alert early today.

Memphis was placed under a tight, 24-hour curfew by Mayor Henry Loeb.

All schools will be closed today. Parents were urged to keep their children at home.

A rifle bullet slammed into Dr. King's jaw and neck at 6:01 p.m.

He died in the emergency room at St. Joseph Hospital at 7:05 p.m.

King, the foremost American civil rights leader, was alone on the second-floor walk of the Lorraine Hotel at 406 Mulberry when the bullet struck.

A young white man is believed to have fired the fatal shot from a nearby building.

Looters and vandals roamed the streets despite the imposition of a tight curfew. Shooting was widespread. National Guardsmen were rushed to the North Memphis area of Springdale and Howell after bullets blasted the windshield out of a police car near there.

Police — estimated at more than 150 — descended on the south Memphis hotel, sealed off the area, and almost immediately broadcast a description of the sniper: a while male, 30 to 32 years old, 5 feet, 10 inches tall, about 165 pounds, dark to sandy hair, medium build, ruddy complexion as if he worked outside, wearing a black suit and white shirt.

Frank R. Ahlgren, editor of The Commercial Appeal, announced that the newspaper will pay a $25,000 reward for information leading to the arrest and conviction of Dr. King's assassin.

Dr. King returned to Memphis Wednesday morning to map plans for another downtown march — scheduled for next Monday — in support of the city's striking sanitation workers. He had spent part of the day yesterday awaiting reports from his attorneys, who were in Federal Judge Bailey Brown's courtroom asking that a temporary restraining order against the proposed march be lifted.

The injunction was obtained by the city after Dr. King's first march broke out in violence downtown, brought the National Guard to the city in strength and seriously damaged the Negro leader's reputation for nonviolence. For the first time in his career, he had been present during violence, and it was this picture he was planning to dispel with the march next Monday.

Mayor Loeb declared today, tomorrow and Sunday as days of mourning, and said all flags in the city would be lowered "with appropriate observances."

All ministers, priests and rabbis in the Memphis area have been asked to meet at 10 a.m. today at St. Mary's Cathedral (Episcopal).

Frank Holloman, fire and police director, who took personal command of the murder investigation minutes after the shooting, said "every resource" of city, county, state and federal law enforcement agencies "is committed and dedicated to identifying and apprehending the person or persons responsible."

Mayor Loeb ordered a tight curfew, much stricter than the one imposed after last week's rioting. "All movement is restricted except for health or emergency reasons," the order said.

A few minutes after the shooting, police reported a high-speed chase in which a blue Pontiac was being pursued by a white Mustang out the Austin Peay Highway. Shots were reported fired between the two cars. A white Mustang, seen near the scene of the slaying, was still being sought by police early today.

Officials of Dr. King's Southern Christian Leadership Conference, some of whom were standing near him on the narrow balcony of the hotel when he was shot, continued to urge his nonviolent teachings. His chief lieutenant, Dr. Ralph Abernathy, went to the Mason Temple last night to address a gathering of Dr. King's followers.

"Let us live for what he died for," Dr. Abernathy told the mourning group. "If we respect his leadership, if we appreciate the service that he rendered, then we must do all in our power to carry forth the work that is incomplete.

"If a riot or violence would erupt in Memphis tonight, Dr. King in Heaven would not be pleased."

A few had other ideas. "He died for us, and we're going to die for him," a young man shouted.

Early Friday morning, Mr. Holloman said police believe the murder weapon was a 30-caliber, pump-action Remington rifle equipped with a telescopic sight. Such a weapon was among those stolen Tuesday night from Dowdle Sporting Goods Co. at 2896 Walnut Grove Road.

"The distance over which the bullet traveled before it struck Dr. King was 205 feet, 3 inches, at a down angle," Mr. Holloman said.

He also detailed "other evidence . . . that may help us identify the assassin. The shot was fired from the window of a common bathroom at the end of the hall on the east side of the building at 420 South Main. The suspect checked into the boarding house between 3 and 3:30 p.m. His room was close to the bathroom. The suspect was a white man, 6 feet tall, about 165-175 pounds, between 26 and 32 years of age."

"We do know he bought a pair of binoculars this (Thursday) afternoon in Memphis . . . The man was seen to run from the 420 South Main building and discard the gun and a suitcase at 424 South Main. He simply faded. Nobody saw him get in the car, but a white Mustang was seen to flee the area.

"The evidence we now have indicates that only one man was physically in the area (the bathroom)."

Mr. Holloman would not reveal where the binoculars were purchased, and said he did not know if the name used by the sniper is his real one.

The gun found at the Main street address was turned over to the FBI for ballistics tests. Mr. Holloman said his office is "working closely with the FBI" on other aspects of the investigation.

The former FBI officer also said the investigation was "impaired by the riot situation which developed almost immediately."

"The bullet knocked him off his feet," said the Rev. Jesse Jackson, executive staff member of SCLC. "It sounded like

(Continued on Page 12)

EXTRA

LOS ANGELES EVENING AND SUNDAY
HERALD-EXAMINER
CLASSIFIED ADVERTISING Richmond 8-4111
All Other Calls Richmond 8-1212 or Richmond 8-4141

SUNSET
TODAY'S SPORTS
COMPLETE STOCKS

VOL. XCVIII NO. 72 THURSDAY, JUNE 6, 1968 5 TEN CENTS

RFK IS DEAD

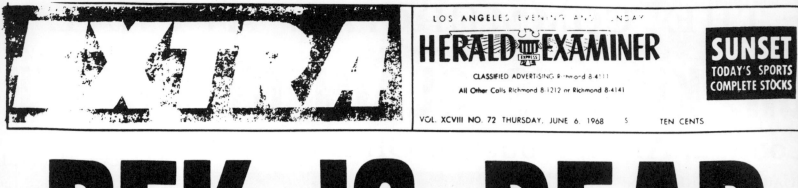

HUNT WOMAN IN SLAYING PROBE

—Associated Press Wirephoto

CASKET BEARING BODY OF ASSASSINATED SEN. ROBERT F. KENNEDY LIFTED INTO JET
Family and close friends accompany remains to New York where slain candidate will lie in state

● *The funeral plans. Page A-2.*
● *A suspect's story Page A-3*

By Conrad Casler
Herald-Examiner Staff Writer

Senator Robert F. Kennedy is dead.

The New York senator died early today 25½ hours after a suspected Jordanian-American terrorist's bullet struck him down at an Ambassador Hotel election victory party.

His wife, Ethel Kennedy, his brother, Sen. Edward Kennedy; sisters Mrs. Stephen Smith and Mrs. Patricia Lawford; his brother-in-law Stephen Smith; his sister-in-law Mrs. John F. Kennedy, wife of the assassinated President, and the senator's three oldest children were at his side when the end came.

He had not regained consciousness after he left surgery shortly after dawn yesterday.

Earlier doctors had given him less than a 10 per cent chance to survive the terrible brain damage caused by the single .22-caliber bullet which crashed through his skull behind his right ear, fragmented and wound up near the center of the brain.

Frank Mankiewicz, Kennedy press aide, said exact time of death was 1:44 a.m. News was withheld from the press for about 20 minutes.

The body along with relatives and close family friends will be flown to New York today where funeral mass will be said at 10 a.m. Saturday in St. Patrick's Cathedral. President Lyndon Johnson provided an Air Force plane for the trip.

An autopsy began at 3 a.m. and lasted seven hours. The team was headed by Coroner Dr. Thomas Naguchi. A neuropathologist and pathologist assisted.

Coroner's Deputy Herbert McRoy said the autopsy took much longer than usual "because of the nature of this case. We are documenting everything as well as photographing as much as possible for a complete file," he said.

Flown in from Washington, D.C., as consultants on the autopsy were an Army, Navy and civilian doctor. They were identified as Col. Pierre Fink, Comdr. Stahl and Dr. Kenneth Earle.

Death was laid to the massive brain damage. "He had insufficient life force to sustain life after the massive trauma," Mankiewicz said. "We never were hopeful after surgery was performed," he said.

The 42-year-old Senator, who moments before he was shot had won victory in the California Democratic presidential preferential primary, became the

(Continued on Page A2, Col. 1)

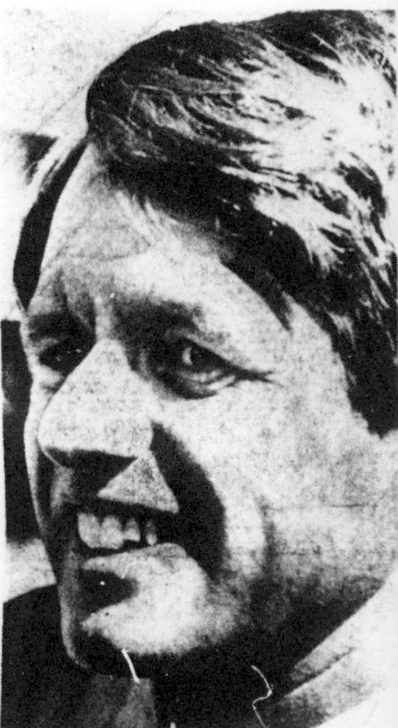

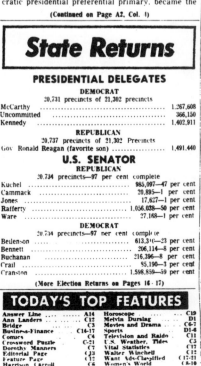

—Herald-Examiner photo by Myron Dub

SLAIN SENATOR ROBERT F. KENNEDY
Assassin's bullet fatal at height of campaign victory

L.A. BIDS FAREWELL TO RFK

Los Angeles said a sad farewell today to Sen. Robert F. Kennedy.

Thousands gathered at Good Samaritan Hospital, where he died early today from an assassin's bullet, and at International Airport, where a Presidential airplane received his mahogany casket from a gray hearse.

There was a voluble outpouring of grief from many of the estimated 4500 persons gathered outside the hospital as his cortege assembled for departure.

Men and women openly wept. Small children, awed by the massive display of emotion, pressed closely to their parents. There were sobs of "Oh Bobby, oh Bobby," and a shower of bright flowers pelted the casket and hearse as many of his admirers paid their final tributes.

Scores of policemen were on hand to control the throng held back by ropes from a cleared traffic lane. The crowd circled the four blocks surrounding the hospital, often seven-deep and overflowing into the street.

Mrs. Ethel Kennedy, the senator's widow, rode in a black limousine directly behind the hearse. With her was Mrs. Jacqueline Kennedy, widow of assassinated President John F. Kennedy. In 12 other limousines were other relatives, his aides, friends and key campaign workers.

The cortege traveled the Harbor Freeway to Imperial Boulevard, then west to the south side of the airport. An honor escort of police and sheriff's oficers on motorcycles preceded the caravan.

Scenes of grief and emotional breakdowns were again evident at the airport, where a crowd estimated at 2500 assembled to say goodbye to the slain presidential candidate.

The crowd was kept well back from the Air Force jet plane—one of three assigned to the White House.

A long red carpet had been laid from the loading step to a spot where the limousines stopped. The carpet was edged by bouquets of red carnations and green fern. The hearse proceeded to an automatic lift forward of the tail section, and the casket was loaded on the platform.

Then Sen. Kennedy's widow

(Continued on Page A2, Col. 1)

LBJ Acts To End Violence

(C) 1968 New York Times News Service

Text of message, A-6

WASHINGTON, June 5—For the second time in five years, Lyndon B. Johnson has undertaken, in the midst of national shock and outrage, to offer prayer, comfort and assistance to his political rivals in the Kennedy family and then to try to heal the country's political and psychological wounds.

The President's first reaction to the shooting of Sen. Robert F. Kennedy was that "there are no words equal to the horror of this tragedy."

But last night, in an emotional and at times even angry statement on television, the President pleaded with all Americans to end the violence in their midst once and for all, to tolerate neither hatred nor the preaching of violence and "for God's sake" to resolve to live under the law.

Johnson said he was appointing a commission of distinguished citizens to investigate both the circumstances and the causes of physical violence of all kinds in the United States in the hope that the nation could learn "how we can stop it" and profit even from its misfortunes.

To the commission, Johnson named Milton Eisenhower, the former president of Johns Hopkins University and the brother of former President Dwight D. Eisenhower, Archbishop Terrence Cooke of New York, Albert Jenner, Chicago attorney who worked for the commission that investigated the assassination of President John F. Kennedy; former ambassador Patricia Harris; Eric Hoffer, the longshoreman turned philosopher, Sens. Philip Hart,

(Continued on Page A2, Col.

Gov. Reagan Proclaims A Period of Mourning

SACRAMENTO (AP)—Gov. Reagan proclaimed a state of mourning throughout California today in tribute to Sen. Robert F. Kennedy and called his assassination "tragic."

"My sympathies go out to Mrs. Kennedy and the senator's children as well as his parents and other members of his family," the Republican governor said in an early morning statement issued by a press aide.

"The tragic, senseless death of Sen. Kennedy affects all Californians and all Americans," Reagan said.

The period of mourning extends until after Kennedy's funeral Saturday. Reagan canceled his public appointments for today, including a helicopter tour of the new California State Exposition and Fair.

At a news conference Wednesday, before Kennedy died, Reagan blamed the shooting in part on "demagogic and irresponsible words of so-called leaders in and out of public office."

State Returns

PRESIDENTIAL DELEGATES

DEMOCRAT
20,731 precincts of 21,302 precincts

McCarthy	1,267,608
Uncommitted	366,150
Kennedy	1,402,911

REPUBLICAN
20,737 precincts of 21,302 Precincts

Gov Ronald Reagan (favorite son)	1,491,440

U.S. SENATOR

REPUBLICAN
20,734 precincts—97 per cent complete

Kuchel	985,097—47 per cent
Cammack	20,895—1 per cent
Jones	17,627—1 per cent
Rafferty	1,056,038—50 per cent
Ware	27,168—1 per cent

DEMOCRAT
20,734 precincts—97 per cent complete

Beilenson	613,3[illegible]—23 per cent
Bennett	206,114—8 per cent
Buchanan	216,396—8 per cent
Crail	85,190—3 per cent
Cranston	1,598,859—59 per cent

(More Election Returns on Pages 16-17)

TODAY'S TOP FEATURES

POLICE SEEKING 'MYSTERY' WOMAN

Police today issued an all-points bulletin for th arrest of a young woman wearing a polka dot dre seen fleeing from the area where Sen. Robert F. Ke nedy was fatally wounded.

This was the first official indication that assassin suspect Sirhan B. Sirhan may have had accomplices in the slaying.

The police bulletin described the woman sought as between the ages of 23 and 27, wearing a white dress with black pol dots.

The order for her arrest we out after Miss Sandy Serran 20, co-chairman of Youth Kennedy in the Pasadena-Al dena area, said on a televisi interview she observed the g running down the steps of terrace at the Ambassad Hoted.

"We shot him!" she quot the girl as saying.

When Miss Serrano asked w was shot, she said the wom replied: "We shot Sen. Ken dy." Miss Serrano said she h seen the girl earlier with tw men, one resembling Sirha She said one of the men w with the girl as she fled.

Muggy Weather

Morning sunshine, pretty much of a stranger of late in the Los Angeles area, played a return engagement today.

Even so, the temperature rose only to the low 70s. It was 68 at Civic Center yesterday.

Tomorrow will be about the same.

House Tax Boost Action Postponed

WASHINGTON (UPI)—House action on President Johnson's 10 per cent income tax surcharge and an accompanying $6 billion spending cut was postponed today from June 12 to June 19.

Rep. Wilbur D. Mills, D-Ark., told the House that he wanted the postponement to give congressmen time to study the report on the legislation which has not yet been filed.

House Sends Crime Bill To Johnson

WASHINGTON (AP) — T House passed and sent to Pre dent Johnson today a crim control bill which includes a b on interstate mail order sales handguns, but not rifles.

Acting only a day after t fatal shooting of Sen. Robert Kennedy, D-N.Y., the House a cepted after about an hour debate the measure whi cleared the Senate last month

Little Change

WEDNESDAY'S TEMPERATURES

2 a.m.	34	10 a.m.	36	6 p.m.	36
3 a.m.	34	11 a.m.	37	7 p.m.	35
4 a.m.	34	Noon	38	8 p.m.	35
5 a.m.	34	1 p.m.	38	9 p.m.	35
6 a.m.	34	2 p.m.	38	10 p.m.	34
7 a.m.	34	3 p.m.	38	11 p.m.	34
8 a.m.	35	4 p.m.	38	Midnight	34
9 a.m.	35	5 p.m.	37	*1 a.m.	33

Details Page 29 *Unofficial

The Minneapolis Tribune

THURSDAY

Vol. CII—No. 167 MINNEAPOLIS, MINN., THURSDAY, NOVEMBER 7, 1968 ★ Single Copy Price 10c Lower Price for Carrier Delivery

NIXON NARROWLY WINS PRESIDENCY

Nixon Faces Democratic Congress

By FRANK WRIGHT
Minneapolis Tribune Staff Correspondent

WASHINGTON, D.C. — The newly-elected 91st Congress fails to give Richard Nixon the "overwhelming mandate to govern" that he sought.

The voters have retained the Democratic majorities that now control the Senate and the House, according to Wednesday's nearly complete unofficial returns from Tuesday's national election.

The people rejected Nixon's appeal, made repeatedly in his campaign, for friendly Republican majorities that would help him put his legislative proposals into effect.

The new line-up in the Senate will be 58 Democrats to 42 Republicans, a net gain of 5 for the GOP. The present split is 63 to 37.

IN THE HOUSE, the Democrats will wind up with 243 or 244 seats to 191 or 192 for the GOP, a gain of 3 or 4 for the Republicans. The present count is 247 Democrats and 188 Republicans, including two vacant seats that were held by the former and one by the latter.

No one ever gave the Republicans more than an outside chance to take over the Senate; but the GOP had hoped to make more inroads than it did, and the Democrats feared it would.

The House was a greater disappointment for Nixon.

GOP Minority Leader Gerald Ford of Michigan had predicted his party would gain at least enough seats to take control, a net of 31.

NIXON'S ADVISERS were less optimistic but did contend last weekend that the GOP would pick up 10 or 12 seats.

In the Senate the Democrats won 18 of the 34 seats at stake and the Republicans 16, although their lead in Oregon was still shaky.

Democrats took two seats held by Republicans:

Alan Cranston, former state controller, defeated Max Rafferty, the state superintendent of public instruction, in California. A conservative, Rafferty had ousted liberal Sen. Thomas Kuchel in the GOP primary.

Gov. Harold Hughes of Iowa won by a slender 9,800-vote margin the spot being vacated by Sen. Bourke Hickenlooper, who is retiring after four terms.

Republicans won at least six seats held by Democrats.

Barry Goldwater, making a comeback to the Senate after his unsuccessful run for the presidency in 1964, easily took the seat of Carl Hayden, who is retiring after having been in Congress since Arizona joined the union in 1912.

Rep. Edward Gurney defeated former Gov. Leroy Collins in Florida for the

Congress Continued on Page 12

Associated Press

NIXON AND WIFE, PAT, JOINED THE REPUBLICANS' VICTORY CELEBRATION IN NEW YORK, N.Y.
The president-elect thanked his supporters at the Waldorf-Astoria Hotel

Nixon Pledges to Seek Unity

By RICHARD P. KLEEMAN
Minneapolis Tribune Staff Correspondent

Richard Milhous Nixon, whose college football coach once advised him to forget about the glories of being a good loser, had no such problem Wednesday.

Before heading for a three-day Florida vacation, the 55-year-old Republican president-elect appeared before some 1,500 campaign workers, backers and newsmen in the grand ballroom of the Waldorf-Astoria Hotel in New York, N.Y.

(TEXT on Page 10.)

He pledged an administration of unity, its guiding philosophy to be that of a placard carried by a teen-ager at a campaign rally in Deshler, Ohio.

"BRING US together," the sign had said, and candidate Nixon quoted it often on the campaign stump.

"That will be the great objective of this administration at the outset—to bring the American people together," said Nixon, clearly pleased at his victory but not demonstratively emotional.

"We want to bridge the generation gap, we want to bridge the gap between the races.

"I am confident that this task is one which we can undertake and one in which we shall be successful."

AFTER accepting his presidential victory, Nixon stopped briefly in Washington, D.C., especially to visit with former President Dwight Eisenhower, confined to Walter Reed Army Medical Center following a series of heart attacks. Nixon was vice-president during Eisenhower's two terms in office.

Nixon arrived in Miami, Fla., at 10 p.m. A crowd of about 250 persons surged onto the runway to greet him as his silver and white Air Force jet pulled to a stop amid numerous security personnel.

Nixon and his wife, Pat,

Nixon Continued on Page 15

Margin Is Smallest in Recent Past

By CHARLES W. BAILEY
Chief of the Minneapolis Tribune Washington Bureau

WASHINGTON, D.C. — Richard M. Nixon won the presidency of the United States Wednesday by the narrowest popular margin in modern times.

The 55-year-old Republican finally emerged as the winner over Democrat Hubert Humphrey of Minnesota after an agonizing wait when Illinois, with 26 crucial electoral votes, fell into his column at midday yesterday.

BUT HUMPHREY'S closing rush—the climax of a one-man battle that carried him far closer to triumph than had seemed possible—left Nixon with a tenuous mandate. And a surprisingly strong Democratic showing in congressional contests not only denied Republicans control of either Senate or House but left Congress almost as strongly Democratic as before.

Thus the president-elect faces the prospect of trying to govern a deeply divided nation with a tiny popular mandate and a hostile Congress. It appeared that he will have to seek to form some kind of coalition — presumably through Cabinet choices — in order to overcome these problems.

Nixon's victory margin in the popular vote appeared last night to be less than 60,000 votes out of a total of 59 million cast for the two men—about one-tenth of 1 per cent. The closest previous popular-vote margin occurred in 1960, when John F. Kennedy beat Nixon by 118,550 votes.

ON THE BASIS of elector-

Election Continued on Page Eight

Snow Possible in Cities Today

Snow may make a slight Twin Cities appearance today, a day expected to be cloudy and cold, the Weather Bureau predicted Wednesday. The high should be 35, with a low tonight of 25.

The precipitation chances (and that means snow) are 20 per cent for today and tonight. That cold predicted for the Twin Cities is expected to be general throughout the region.

Humphrey Says He'll Stay in Politics

By JACK WILSON
Minneapolis Tribune Staff Correspondent

Hubert H. Humphrey told his followers to "go have some fun" Wednesday and then went to his Waverly, Minn., home to begin adjusting to a new future.

He planned to leave in a few days for a vacation hideaway in the Virgin Islands, where he will spend a week or longer before returning to Washington, D.C., where he still has a job as Vice-President of the United States.

In his final words to a crowd of staff workers, Democratic party volunteers and friends at his campaign headquarters at the Leamington Hotel, Humphrey made it clear that he expected to continue in politics, in one way or another.

"I INTEND to continue my dedication to public service and to the building of a responsive and vital Democratic party," he said. "I shall continue my personal commitment to the cause of human rights, of peace, and to the betterment of man."

(TEXT of Humphrey's Concession Statement — Page 17.)

He did not give any sign of how he expected to go about it and his associates insisted he had made no plans beyond Jan. 20, when his term ends.

There will be a seat open in the Senate in two years if Sen. Eugene J. McCarthy carries out his plan not to seek re-election, but Humphrey has given no indication that he would consider running for it. If he were elected to the Senate he would have virtually the same seniority status as any other freshman member, with some

Humphrey Continued on Page 12

Minneapolis Tribune Photo by Kent Kobersteen

HUMPHREYS FACE THE FUTURE WITH SMILES
After Vice-President conceded his loss of presidency

THE HOW AND WHY OF MINNESOTA'S VOTE

By BERNIE SHELLUM
Minneapolis Tribune Staff Writer

The most noteworthy aspect of Tuesday's presidential election in Minnesota was Richard Nixon's failure to recover normally Republican votes lost to President Johnson in 1964.

The president-elect ran slightly better than Barry Goldwater, the 1964 nominee, in the three major cities and in the suburbs, but achieved a significant improvement only in the rural villages.

Had Nixon improved on the 1964 showing statewide at the rate that he did in those villages, Minnesota's 10 electoral votes would have been in doubt.

THIS CONCLUSION was drawn from an analysis of The Tribune's 100-precinct scale model of the Minnesota electorate. The model was built by a scientific method to achieve a balance among the precincts in numbers of voters, geographic location and party affiliation. Once drawn, the precincts were studied to determine population characteristics such as religion, education, race, income level and labor union activity.

Though comprising less than 3 per cent of the state's 3,806 precincts, the model projected the outcome of state presidential balloting within .5 of a percentage point of the actual result.

Humphrey, who lost the presidency to Nixon, won in Minnesota by a landslide in which he took 56 per cent of the DFL and Republican vote.

IN DOING so, he kept Nixon's improvement over Goldwater to 2.4 percentage points in the cities — Minneapolis, St. Paul and Duluth — 4.3 points in the suburbs and 9.7 points in rural farm precincts.

Looked at another way, Nixon gained back one-fifth of the Republican vote lost to Mr. Johnson in the rural villages in 1964, but only 3 per cent of the city voters who fled Goldwater in droves.

In the rural villages tested by the sample, Nixon did 11.1 points better than Goldwater, a rate which, if carried statewide, would have given the former vice-president an additional 90,000 votes, at Humphrey's expense. Nixon had 635,034 votes, to 820,952 for Humphrey, with all but 150 precincts counted.

IN THE FOUR heaviest Republican precincts in the sample—those with at least 75 per cent allegiance to the party—Humphrey got 35 per cent of the vote, compared with 20 per cent for former

Model Continued on Page 12

Almanac

They're Now in Shape for Bargain Day

Thursday, Nov. 7, 1968
312th day, 54 to go this year
Sunrise 6:59 a.m.; sunset 4:54 p.m.

A group of reporters and photographers were trying to top one another's tales about the terrible crush at Democratic National Headquarters Tuesday night.

An editor listened sympathetically and then said, "The trouble is, we sent you in there cold. We should have had you go out to a discount store on three Saturdays running to train for this."

•

Today is the anniversary of the Bolshevik Revolution in Russia. It is called the October Revolution, quite naturally, because it occurred on Nov. 7-8. If you don't feel like celebrating that, it's also National Tuna Week.

TODAY ON THE INSIDE:

Night of Hope Sours

Backers of Hubert Humphrey worked hard Tuesday night at believing they were attending a victory celebration at the Leamington Hotel. After the bartenders and musicians stopped, and Richard Nixon's lead lengthened, hope faded. Staff writer Allan Holbert's report and pictures are on PAGE 17.

TURN THE PAGES TO:

• • • •

Tribune Telephones
News, General .. 372-4141
Want Ads 372-4242
Circulation 372-4343

Rural Voters' Shift Nearly Defeats Langen

By ROBERT FRANKLIN
Minneapolis Tribune Staff Writer

A dramatic shift in rural votes nearly unseated Republican Congressman Odin Langen in northwestern Minnesota's 7th District in Tuesday's general election.

But the 55-year-old Langen held enough city strength to win 51 per cent of the vote and defeat DFLer Robert Bergland of Roseau by about 2,500 votes in the state's closest congressional contest.

Langen's victory, not certain until Wednesday, meant all eight of Minnesota's congressmen were re-elected.

IN THE ONLY contest for state office, DFL incumbent Paul A. Rusmussen used heavy labor support and surprising strength in the 6th District to beat Republican Lyle Nelson of Moorhead for public service commissioner.

MacGregor Fraser
Easily re-elected

An analysis of 100 precincts throughout Minnesota, a scientific scale model of the state's electorate, indicates where some of the candidates showed strengths and weaknesses.

In the 7th District, Langen won two years ago with 63.2 per cent of the vote, an unusually high figure for the normally marginal district. Langen defeated Keith Davi-

Minnesota Continued on Page 16

SADDENED COED FOLLOWS HIS ADVICE

HHH Inspires Future Citizen

By DICK CUNNINGHAM
Minneapolis Tribune Staff Writer

Petra Kelly's blue eyes glistened near tears as she pressed against the backs of the Secret Service men in the Hall of States at the Leamington Hotel Wednesday morning.

Hubert H. Humphrey moved past the officers toward a back door leading to a service corridor.

The job was done.

His voice had nearly broken twice as he told supporters and reporters, some of whom had been with him since April:

"Go have some fun."

HUMPHREY'S face was set in the familiar jut-jawed smile, but his own eyes seemed bright and somehow unseeing as he moved toward the quiet hall.

But suddenly he saw Petra's blonde head past the shoulders of the men, and the eyes came alive.

He reached out for her hand.

"You look so sad. What's the matter?" he asked.

Then Petra's tears came.

"I don't know what to do anymore," she sobbed.

The Vice-President squeezed her hand.

"YOU HAVE to have cheer." He looked squarely into her eyes. Then he was gone.

But it wasn't easy for Petra. She is 20, a German girl in her junior year at American University in Washington, D.C.

In her hotel room Petra had her papers ready to

PETRA KELLY
'You have to have cheer'

file for U.S. citizenship. Hubert H. Humphrey was listed as her sponsor. She had planned to file

Citizenship Continued on Page 16

1969

Man landed on the moon.

The startling simplicity of the statement underscored the wonder, the awe, the inconceivable grandeur of the event.

"It's one small step for man, one giant leap for mankind," said Neil Armstrong as he set the first footprints on lunar soil, July 20, 1969.

Hurricane Camille, perhaps the most destructive storm ever to strike the United States, devastated the Gulf Coast in August.

And the "amazin' " New York Mets won the World Series, their first since their inception in 1962.

SOUVENIR EDITION

SYRACUSE
HERALD-JOURNAL

FINAL
★ ★ ★ ★
NIGHT EDITION

★ Associated Press ★ United Press International ★ Chicago Daily News Service ★ New York Times Service ★ AP Wirephoto ★ UPI Telephoto ★ Complete Local Coverage

SYRACUSE, N.Y., MONDAY, JULY 21, 1969 VOL. 93, NO. 27,682 Published Daily Second class postage paid at Syracuse, N.Y. 10 CENTS (60c Per Week Home Delivered)

MAN ON THE MOON

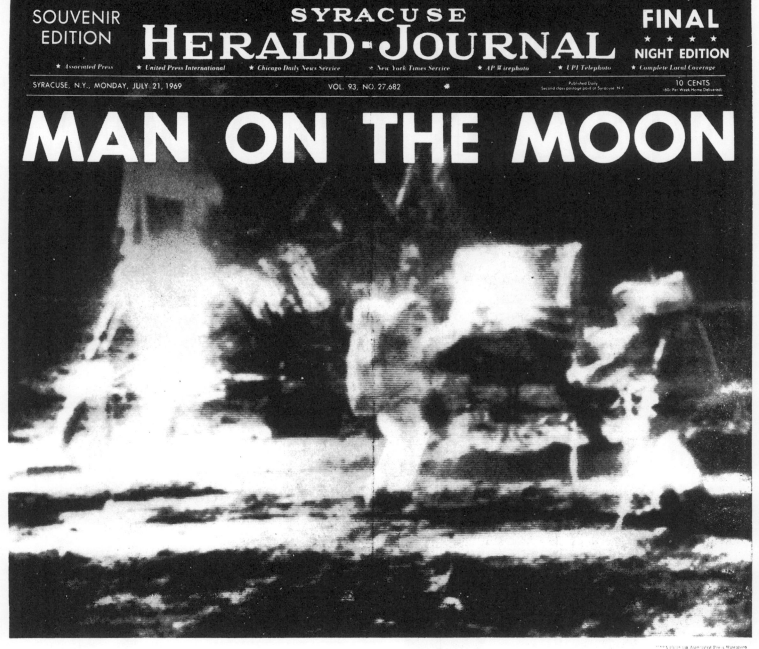

Neil Armstrong, left, and Edwin E. Aldrin Jr. place American flag on surface of moon

'One small step . . . one giant leap'

By B. J. RICHEY and WILLIAM E. HOWARD
Of Our Washington Bureau

MANNED SPACECRAFT CENTER, Tex. — Neil Armstrong and Edwin Aldrin set their sights for home today after opening up the solar system to manned exploration.

Man's first tiny step beyond his world was perfectly executed, breath-taking and short.

Armstrong and Aldrin were poised to blast off from the moon at 1:55 p.m. EDT, today to rejoin Michael Collins, who remained 69 miles above the moon in the main command ship while they spent 21½ hours exploring below.

The two craft should dock late today and start for earth just after midnight.

'Giant Leap For Mankind'

After an exhausting day, the pair was allowed six hours' sleep in the moon ship before ending man's first visit to the moon.

Armstrong and Aldrin, after awaking at Tranquility Base on the moon, plunged into systems checks on the lander and engine on which, again, they were to stake their lives. The bottom section of the craft, with the four landing legs, was to serve as a launch pad and to be left on the moon after they fired the single engine that powers the cabin section of the lunar module called Eagle.

Two phrases will ring down through time when this moment of man's search of the heavens is remembered: "Eagle has landed" and "That's one small step for man, one giant leap for mankind." Both were spoken by Armstrong, commander of Apollo 11.

It was enough to stop earth from turning. First, there was that exhilarating ride from moon orbit, down an untraveled course, then an eerie two hours walking, bounding and digging on the moon while untold millions watched the entire episode unfold on television screens.

"Neil and Buzz, I am talking to you by telephone from the oval room at the White House," President Nixon said to the two moon explorers standing alone in the vast Sea of Tranquility.

"I just can't tell you how proud we all are of you. For every American, this has to be the proudest day of our lives. And for people all over the world, I am sure they, too, join with America in recognizing what a feat this is.

Inspiring

"Because of what you have done, the heavens have become a part of man's world and as you talk to us from the Sea of Tranquility it inspires us to double our efforts to bring peace and tranquility to earth.

"For one priceless moment, in the whole history of man, all the people on this earth are truly one — one in their pride in what you have done, and one in our prayers, that you will return safely to earth," the President concluded.

With emotion choking his voice, Armstrong said:

"Thank you, Mr. President, it's a great honor and privilege for us to be here representing not only the United States but men of peace of all nations, and with interest and a curiosity and a vision for the future. It's an honor for us to be able to participate here today."

Armstrong wiggled out of the lunar module (LM) hatch and backed down a nine-rung ladder to the moon's surface at 10:56 p.m., EDT.

With a television camera trained on him and showing an astounding picture of the epic step, he said:

"That's one small step for man, one giant leap for mankind."

Aldrin followed him to the surface a few minutes later at 11:14 p.m. Both were astounded by the beauty of this strange place.

Once both men were on the moon, they inspected the lunar module. One landing strut was scorched by the rocket engine during landing. Everything else appeared to be in fine form.

Armstrong set up the television camera about 50 feet from the landing craft aiming it at their general working area. He also panned it around the moon to give millions back on earth a quick look at the surface close up.

Attached to the side of the craft was a plaque marking man's first landing on the moon. It read: "Here man from the planet earth first set foot upon the moon, July, 1969 A.D. We came in peace for all mankind."

When Armstrong and Aldrin leave the moon, the bottom stage of the craft bearing this plaque will be left behind. It is signed by President Nixon and the three astronauts.

Also left behind were messages from 73 nations, as well as medallions in honor of three astronauts

(Concluded on Page 5, Col. 1)

Luna lands

JODRELL BANK, England (AP) — Russia apparently landed its unmanned Luna 15 space probe on the moon today just as American astronauts Neil A. Armstrong and Edwin E. "Buzz' Aldrin Jr. prepared to take off, Jodrell Bank Observatory reported.

Astronomer Sir Bernard Lovell said the probe transmitted signals "appropriate to a landing" and it appeared the unmanned craft had left orbit and touched down on the moon.

Exchanges close

New York Times Service

NEW YORK — The nation's stock exchanges and major commodity exchanges were closed Monday in observance of the National Day of Participation declared by President Nixon for the Apollo 11 moon landing.

Associated Press Wirephoto

President Nixon talked by radio hookup from his White House office with astronauts Neil Armstrong and Edwin Aldrin on the moon.

Two full pages of pictures

Men make selves at home on moon . . . Page 6

World hails America's lunar feat . . . Page 7

INDEX . . . Page 2; WEATHER . . . Page 4

Weather Today
Partly Cloudy
75 to 93

TWO SECTIONS
THIRTY-SIX PAGES
105TH YEAR—NO. 202

The Florida Times-Union

A Leader in the Growth and Development of Florida and the South for More Than 104 Years

JACKSONVILLE, MONDAY, JULY 21, 1969

SPORTS
In this section

TEN CENTS

WE'RE ON THE MOON!!

—TIMES-UNION/UPI TELEPHOTO

Old Glory Planted on Moon's Surface

Astronauts Edwin E. Aldrin Jr. and Neil A. Armstrong plant an American flag on the surface of the moon. The deed was performed minutes after they set foot on the alien soil. Since there is no atmosphere — and therefore no wind — the flag is held unfurled by wires.

Armstrong Steps onto Surface

By JOHN BARBOUR

SPACE CENTER, Houston (AP) — Two Americans landed on the moon and explored its surface for some two hours Sunday, planting the first human footprints in its dusty soil. They raised their nation's flag and talked to their President on earth 240,000 miles away.

Both civilian Neil Alden Armstrong and Air Force Col. Edwin E. "Buzz" Aldrin Jr. reported they were back in their spacecraft at 1:11 a.m. EDT Monday. "The hatch is closed and locked," Armstrong reported.

Millions on their home planet watched on television as the pair saluted their flag and scoured the rocky, rugged surface.

The first to step on the moon was Armstrong, 38, of Wapakoneta, Ohio. His foot touched the surface at 10:56 p.m. EDT and he remained out for two hours and 14 minutes.

His first words standing on the moon were, "That's one small step for man, a giant leap formankind."

Twenty minutes after he stepped down, Aldrin followed.

"Beautiful, beautiful, beautiful," he said. "A magnificent desolation."

He remained out for one hour and 44 minutes.

Armstrong stepped cautiously, almost shuffling at first.

"The surface is fine and powdered, like powdered charcoal to the soles of my foot . . ." he said. "I can see my footprints of my boot in the fine particles."

He stepped first onto one of the four saucer-like footpads of his spacecraft. Then the moon. He was in the bitter cold of lunar shadows as the camera caught the sight of his left foot, size 9½, pressing into the lunar soil.

ARMSTRONG SAID THE spacecraft's footpads had pressed only an inch or two into the dusty soil. His foot sank only a "small fraction — about an eighth of an inch" into it, he said.

His first steps were cautious in the one-sixth gravity of the moon. But he quickly reported, "There is no trouble to walk around."

Armstrong was not visible to the third Apollo 11 astronaut, Air Force Lt. Col. Michael Collins locked in a lonely patroling orbit in the command ship Columbia, some 69 miles above them.

"IT HAS A STARK BEAUTY all its own,' Armstrong said. "It's different. But it's very pretty out here."

The television camera on the side of the Eagle was on him constantly.

When he first emerged from the spacecraft, slowly, cautiously, backing out, the world waited, and waited. He took repeated instructions from Aldrin, "Plenty of room to your left."

"How am I doing?" he asked. "You're doing fine," he was answered. Then he told mission control, "Okay, I'm on the porch." It was 10:51 p.m.

AFTER HE TRIPPED THE television camera, the picture of his foot swinging, tentatively groping for the ladder rungs, could be seen clearly.

Minutes later as he scouted the surface for rocks and soil samples he appeared phosphorescent in the sunlight, his white suit blinding. His movements were sort of gross, abnormal leaps, almost like a slow-motion kangaroo. Repeatedly he returned to the spacecraft to perform his many duties.

Armstrong read from the plaque on the side of the spacecraft. In a steady voice, he proclaimed, "Here man first set foot on the moon, July, 1969. We came in peace for all mankind."

At 11:42 p.m. EDT they unfurled the Stars and Stripes and it stood in the airless, windless atmosphere of the moon, held taut by a rod along the top. One of the Americans stood back and saluted.

THE LESSER GRAVITY of the moon, one-sixth that of earth, was no problem for the astronauts. "There's no trouble to walk around," Armstrong said.

They arrived on the moon at 4:18 p.m. Six hours later they were collecting rocks, setting up experiments and stalking the surface as if they belonged there.

PRESIDENT NIXON'S VOICE came to the ears of the astronauts on the moon from the Oval Room at the White House.

"This has to be the most historic telephone call ever made," he said. "I just can't tell you how proud I am. . . . Because of what you have done the heavens have become part of man's world. As you talk to us from the Sea of Tranquility, it inspires us to redouble our efforts to bring peace and tranquility to man.

"All the people on earth are surely one in their pride of

(Continued on A-7—Column 1)

The Moon Edition

Your Times-Union this morning brings you the Moon story right up to the press start time required to get the great outpouring of papers delivered to homes on time.

But The Times-Union team will be on the job and produce an even later run for sale at newsdealers and at the Florida Publishing Co. front entrance. This Street Sale edition will be an expanded souvenir run documenting the historic Apollo 11 adventure.

Look for it today.

Men on Moon Earn Sighs of Pride, Relief

By United Press International

America held its breath Sunday and then let it out in a sigh of pride and relief.

The countdown bringing Neil A. Armstrong and Edwin E. Aldrin to the moon was shared in the homes and hearts of millions of their countrymen.

They prayed for their success at Sunday morning services. Then they stayed close to their television and radio sets, rooting for Armstrong and Aldrin during the last, tense moments of their perilous, incredible journey.

And cheered when they reached the moon.

WHEN THAT WORD came, the waiting back home on earth was just beginning.

The moon watchers in the living rooms settled down to wait for the most dramatic moment of all — Armstrong's first steps on the moon and the chance that they might catch a glimpse of them on their home television sets.

The day man came to the moon was a warm, lazy day in much of the United States — a typical Sunday in July with one tremendous difference, the exhilaration of knowing that two Americans had gone where no man had ever set foot before.

There was a holiday air in the nation. President Nixon's call for a national day of participation meant millions of Americans wouldn't have to show up for work Monday. Even if they came in late, red-eyed and yawning from a night of staring at the television set, they could be pretty sure the boss would be understanding.

AS THE LONG, historic afternoon wore on, Americans went about their usual Sunday ways with the world of space always within ear shot, sometimes before their eyes — the calm, staccato voices of the astronauts and their ground controllers as Armstrong and Aldrin maneuvered their way to the floor of the moon.

The voices from space and their televised images followed Americans to the beaches, the golf courses, the ball parks, the camping sites, all the places where they would normally spend a summer

(Continued on A-3—Column 5)

—TIMES-UNION/UPI TELEPHOTO

Second Man on Moon

Aldrin, lunar module pilot, becomes the second man to set foot on the moon as he gingerly feels his way off the last rung of the LM's ladder and joins Apollo 11 commander Neil Armstrong on the moon's surface.

Eagle's Landing 'Turns On' Globe

LONDON (AP) — Crowds screamed joyously in Trafalgar Square, people danced in Chile, a Russian shouted "Hooray." Almost everyone on Earth was somehow touched by man's arrival on the moon.

Pope Paul VI praised America's three astronauts as "conquerers of the moon" minutes after the Eagle spacecraft touched down on the lunar surface. He said man faces "the expanse of endless space and a new destiny."

Soviet media did not dramatize the landing. Reports of the touchdown were buried in Soviet television and radio newscasts behind other news of the day. But individual Muscovites cheered and expressed congratulations to Americans in the Soviet capital. "Hooray," one yelled. "It's a great day," shouted another.

IN THE WAR-TORN Middle East, Arab radio stations interrupted their bulletins of a major air battle over the Suez Canal to acclaim the event and praise Edwin Aldrin and Neil Armstrong for "making history."

The streets of some of the world's largest cities — Mexico City, Oslo, Belgrade, Rome — were nearly deserted as millions stayed home glued to their television screens.

One Yugoslav teen-ager said: "They have stolen the romance out of the moon and it will never be the same again. Now the moon is real, and lovers won't have it for themselves alone any more."

IN THE MIDDLE OF a war broadcast from Beirut the announcer said: "Ladies and gentlemen. The moon is now within man's grasp." Then Feiroux, one of the Middle East's top singers, began crooning "Oh Moon I am with you."

Poles jammed the lobby of the U.S. Embassy in Warsaw while a crowd of hundreds applauded outside. In Guayaquil, Ecuador, firetrucks blasted their horns to let citizens know of the safe landing.

INDEX

Pat Collins Grins . . .

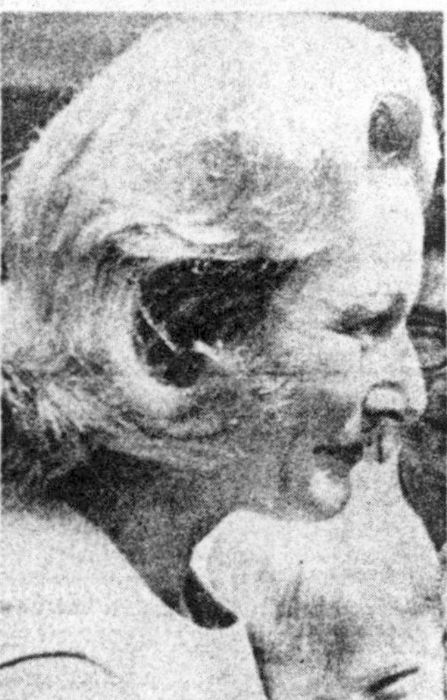

Joan Aldrin Relieved . . .

And Jan Armstrong Signals

Smilin' Through . . .

—TIMES-UNION/UPI TELEPHOTOS

It was all smiles late Sunday and early today for the moon crew's wives. Showing various types of exultation (top to bottom) are Pat Collins, wife of Columbia pilot Michael Collins; and Joan Aldrin and Jan Armstrong, wives of moon walkers Buzz Aldrin and Neil Armstrong, respectively. (See story, A-8.)

INSIDE STORY

WEATHER TODAY
Sunny, Less Humid
High, 82; Low, 65
Yesterday
High, 77; Low, 71

THE INDIANAPOLIS STAR

"Where the spirit of the Lord is, there is Liberty"—II Cor. 3-17

TODAY'S CHUCKLE
One substitute for experience is age—15 or 16 years of age, for example.

VOL. 67, NO. 46 ☆ ☆ ☆ ☆ MONDAY, JULY 21, 1969 633-1240 * 10c

'Eagle Has Landed'

2 U.S. MEN WALK ON THE MOON

Edwin E. Aldrin Jr.
(AP Wirephoto)

Neil A. Armstrong
(AP Wirephoto)

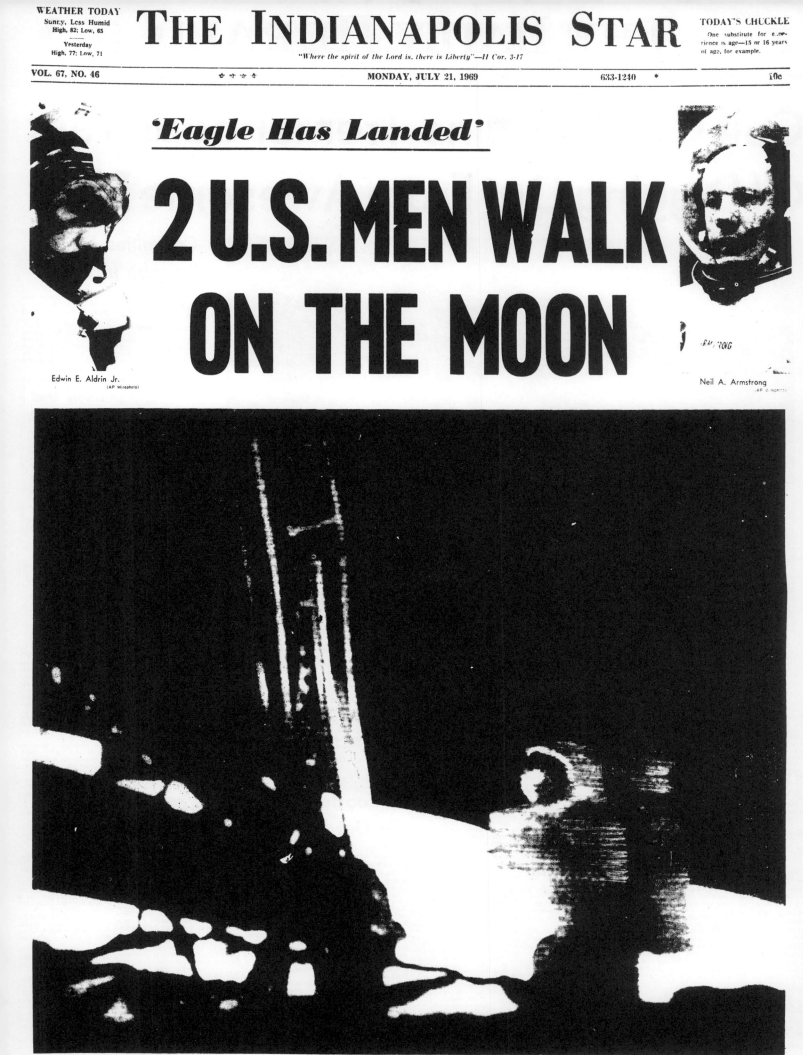

Astronaut Neil Armstrong Stepped On the Surface of the Moon Last Night to Become the First Human to Set Foot on the Planet (AP Wire photo)
Stories of Man's Landing and Walk on the Moon and Pictures Pages 2, 3, 13 and 42.

'One Small Step For Man— One Giant Leap For Mankind'

Neil A. Armstrong's First Words While Standing On The Moon
10:56:31 P.M. EDT July 20, 1969

THE DAILY HERALD

A careful driver who just saw the ahead of him get a tra ticket.

Served By Associated Press Volume 85 — Number 273 Mississippi Coast, Tuesday Afternoon, August 19, 1969 1 Section — 6 Pages Single Copy 10c

Gulf Coast Begins Tremendous Task Of Digging Out From Awesome Blow

This Boat Slammed Into House While Huge Ships Were Tossed Ashore

Casualties Mount; Damage Incredible

By ROBERT McHUGH
RICHARD GLACZIER
and TED O'BOYLE
Herald Staff Writers

The Gulf Coast, left a shambles by one of history's worst storms, began the task of digging out Monday from an awesome and devastating blow.

Early reports listed at least 10 dead and hundreds injured. Many other fatalities are feared as rescue workers clear away debris. Property damage ran into the multiplied millions.

Beach front homes on U. S. 90 were either destroyed or damaged. Scores of them were reduced to rubble.

The storm rubble along the beach was an incredible collection. Dozens of television sets littered the highway and beach, blown by 190 mph winds from a T.V. repair shop that had been destroyed.

The sea wall was cracked in many places. A sports car upside down had been washed up onto a front yard of a destroyed residence.

The recreation room and boiler room of the Veterans Administration hospital was leveled. The American Legion, with its plush Caucus Room Lounge on Gulfport East Beach near the hospital was virtually destroyed.

A fire was smoldering in one gutted beach front house many hours after the storm had passed.

The Parliament House and Masion De Ville Gulfport beach front apartments were torn and battered. Six gasoline pumps were all that remained of a once busy Highway 90 service station.

Mile after mile of beach front showed nothing but wreckage and destruction. Boards and timbers from homes and commercial buildings littered the area in piles that looked as if an unruly giant had been playing jack straws. Downtown Gulfport was littered with glass and tangled power lines. A 26-foot sloop had been washed two and a half blocks from the harbor area into the city and was parked high and dry in front of the First Baptist Church. Office furniture, desks, chairs, filing cabinets, tables and books were in the streets.

Near the devastated State Port of Gulfport a gas main had broken.

The 190 mph winds gouged chunks of brick out of the First Baptist Church, knocked the awning off the Daily Herald building and swept water into the newsroom, advertising offices and press room.

Suburban areas of Gulfport were heavily hit by falling trees, crashing through the roofs of homes.

Three ships ran aground at the State Port, carried ashore by 20-foot tides which accompanied the big storm.

The Hulda, a Liberian flag vessel, the U. S. flag, Alamo Victory and the Silver Hawk were listed toward the water with their keels hard aground in the sand and mud at the north end of the harbor basin.

All three had decided to ride out the monster hurricane, noored to the west pier wharves. The strong winds lashed the ships from the moorings.

All structures except two large marine tanks and the port banana terminal gantries were swept off their foundations.

Buildings, including homes and stores, were shattered where they faced the beach. Tides swept into the downtown area, tearing out walls on concrete and steel structures. Gulf National Bank, located at the junction of U. S. 49 and 90, was

(See Page 2)

Library Shelf Dog's Epitaph

Vicious Hurricane Camille found a frightened German Shepherd dog, carried it on a violent current through downtown Gulfport with other debris.

The dog was deposited, dead, under a fallen book rack in the childrens' department of the public library where it was found Monday afternoon.

The dead dog was under the shelf marked "Animals We Love."

Death Toll May Hit 200

GULFPORT, Miss. (AP) — An increasingly grim picture of Hurricane Camille's devastation emerged today as rescue workers struggled through wreckage looking for dead, injured, missing persons—and missing towns.

"We have 100 confirmed bodies," said state Sen. Ned Cassibry, coordinator of Civil Defense along Mississippi's coastal strip, shattered by 150 mile an hour winds, monster tides and fire.

"We know where there are more bodies," Cassibry added. "We estimate the final toll will be between 150 and 200. There were over 2,000 injured."

Rescue work by 1,500 National Guardsmen, 500 Civil Defense men and volunteers was hampered by the weight of the wreckage left by Camille, the most powerful hurricane ever to hit the American mainland.

"We have enough people to do the work," said Cassibry. "What we need is supplies."

Supplies were coming.

At Atlanta, a dozen C124 Globemasters at Dobbins Air Force Base were assigned to airlift 375,000 pounds of food to Keesler Air Force Base in Biloxi. New Orleans shipped 13,000 gallons of water in tank cars to ravaged Bay St. Louis, just across the state line.

President Nixon declared the state's coastal strip a disaster area, making it eligible for an initial $1 million in federal assistance.

Camille, lashing first at the southeastern edge of Louisiana, shrieked onto the Mississippi coast Sunday night.

The area of maximum force —around the eye—included the port city of Gulfport, with 30,000 residents, and nearby Biloxi with 44,000. Thousands of residents of the coastal strip, warned of coming tides of up to 20 feet above normal, fled inland before Camille arrived.

Biloxi and Gulfport were under 6 p.m. to 6 a.m. curfew. National Guardsmen, armed with rifles, patrolled to prevent looting.

A curfew also was in force at Bogalusa, a city of some 21,500 in Louisiana. Mayor Curt Siegelin said power lines were down, drinking water was scarce and the city in "critical condition."

Martial law was imposed in Louisiana's Plaquemines Parish (county) at sundown Monday. Deputies with cocked shotguns turned back angry residents trying to check on their homes.

The parish is a low delta land, laid down over the centuries by the Mississippi River's silt. Offi-

(See Page 2)

Camille Punches Northward

JACKSON (AP) — Hurricane Camille weaved a path of broken glass, twisted trees and downed powerlines through the south and central part of the state Monday before wasting away into a north Mississippi storm.

After Camille's initial devastating punch over the length of the Mississippi Gulf Coast, the hurricane struck northward, raking populous cities in its path.

The fierce 190 mph winds slowed by the time it reached Hattiesburg and McComb, with 100 mph winds reported at Hattiesburg.

Several store windows collapsed under the windy blast at McComb, observers said, and utility poles, trees and signs were left strewn about the city streets.

Almost every downtown business in Hattiesburg suffered glass breakage, officials said, "and it is impossible to get to downtown Hattiesburg" for the fallen oak trees.

Camp Shelby near Hattiesburg underwent much of the same pounding, with public information officers reporting downed lines, uprooted trees and damaged rooftops. They said, however, no injuries were reported among the hundreds of troops training there.

In Columbia, crushed glass, snapped poles and trees and other debris greeted early venturers into the streets. Officials said no major damage was reported.

As the storm crept slowly northward it lost its big punch.

The Weather Bureau at Jackson reported a record low barometric pressure at its station in adjoining Rankin County with a reading of 29.03 inches. Gusts at the Jackson airport, where the bureau is located, reached 65 mph.

Damaging winds skirted the capitol city, however, as Camille selected a path near Brandon, to the east. Heavy amounts of rain were recorded along the path of the storm as it moved northward through the state.

Mayor Russell Davis of Jackson offered assistance to Gulf Coast towns. Jackson sent firefighting equipment and police personnel to the Coast.

Both Jackson and Hattiesburg became evacuation centers with additional refugees flowing into the cities Monday. Hotels were filled and residents offered homes for displaced families.

In Jackson, the state-owned Robert E. Lee Hotel housed over 1,000 persons while the University of Southern Mississippi at Hattiesburg opened its doors to over 2,000 homeless. Food was offered through the school's cafeteria and the gymnasium quickly became a large dormitory.

Howling winds churned the 33,000-acre Ross Barnett Reservoir north of Jackson as they moved up the state. Officials said several boats broke loose from their moorings.

Blondy Black, manager of the Main Harbor Marina at the reservoir, said a 45-foot houseboat

(See Page 2)

Published In S.C.

The Daily Herald was published again today in Columbia, S. C., and flown to the Gulf Coast to enable residents to stay informed on their stricken area. The Daily Herald staff relayed stories to The State-Record Publishing Company in Columbia where the paper was printed. We will resume normal operations here as soon as possible.

Disaster Area

3 Coastal Counties To Get Federal Aid

WASHINGTON (AP) — President Nixon has declared the three storm-battered coastal counties of Mississippi a federal disaster area, Rep. William M. Colmer, D-Miss., said.

The designation — because of storm damage from Hurricane Camille — makes the counties eligible for an initial $1 million in federal disaster assistance.

Colmer released this text of Nixon's disaster announcement:

. . . "The President has today (Monday) declared that a major disaster exists in Mississippi because of damages due to Hurricane Camille beginning about Aug. 17, 1969.

. . . He has authorized an additional allocation of $1 million for disaster assistance in the affected areas. As additional funds are required for eligible work in the designated disaster area the President will consider further supplemental allocations. This declaration by the President will permit federal aid under the Federal Disaster Act.

. . . The Office of Emergency Preparedness will coordinate federal assistance and administer the funds made available with this declaration by the President. The eligible counties determined so far are Hancock, Harrison and Jackson, the three coastal counties.

. . . Other counties are expected to be added as damage surveys are made."

Patients Flown To Safe Areas

The Mississippi Air National Guard Monday began transferring patients from hospitals here to other areas of the state.

A C-124 Globemaster made a roundtrip flight from Jackson Monday, carrying doctors, nurses and technicians to the Gulfport Veterans Administration Center and returning with 11 patients for transfer to hospitals in Hinds and Rankin Counties.

Gulf Coast hospitals have been crippled by a loss of power and other damage.

Nixon's Guidelines May Set New Mark

WASHINGTON (AP) —Officials in the federal office of Civil Rights say the administration's new guidelines have not slowed school desegregation.

In fact, they predict a record increase this fall.

The proportion of Negroes attending formerly all-white schools is expected to jump from 20 per cent to 40 per cent.

"The desegregation plans keep pouring in," said a spokesman for the Office of Civil Rights—OCR. "The dire predictions have not been borne out."

He referred to criticism that greeted the administration's new desegregation guidelines July 3.

The guidelines call for greater emphasis on court-ordered desegregation than on administrative termination of aid. And they allow districts with problems such as lack of facilities an additional year to complete desegregation.

Pessimists predicted that southern die-hards would use the guidelines as an excuse to delay desegregation further.

But OCR officials say only 12 districts have asked to renegotiate their federally-approved plans since the guidelines were announced. The total for the year is 32. Most asking for renegotiation want additional time to complete desegregation.

"Since July 3 there have been no more or less requests for renegotiation than in similar periods," the spokesman said.

And Robert H. Finch, secretary of health, education and welfare, said recently there would be no renegotiation of agreed plans.

Administrative desegregation actions have been started against 48 additional districts since July 3, the OCR official said.

"It's full-speed ahead as far as we are concerned," he added.

Long Time Resident Beats Storm; Suffers Minor Cut

By RICHARD GLACZIER
Herald Staff Writer

A long time Gulfport resident and businessman rode out Hurricane Camille in his large beach front home Sunday night after securing himself to prevent being swept away by high tides which flowed through his residence.

Tom O. Anderson, 2220 East Beach, sustained only a minor laceration over his eye.

Mr. Anderson, owner of Anderson's Men's Wear on 14th Street, stayed with his two story frame home as 190 mile per hour winds pounded out doors and windows.

He said as tides rose to his doorstep, the windows were blown out. Mr. Anderson said waves then knocked out the front door and water poured in waist deep.

He recalled seeing a police car pass but he was unable to call or signal them for assistance.

He was removed from the residence by a family who came to his rescue about 7 a.m. Monday.

A short time later, he was seen walking to his downtown store, dressed in a fresh suit and straw hat, after an unsuccessful search for his glasses.

He said he was going to have a new set made during the day.

Mississippi Legislature Meets Today

JACKSON, MISS. (AP) — Sessions of the Mississippi Senate and House of Representatives were scheduled today after Hurricane Camille prevented both chambers from obtaining a quorum Monday.

Only 22 of the 52 senators were present Monday and Lt. Gov. Charles Sullivan adjourned the Senate until 10 a.m. Tuesday. Fifty-four of the 122 representatives were on hand and Speaker John Junkin adjourned the House until 2 p.m. Tuesday.

Sullivan told the Senate the absences of lawmakers, from the coast and south Mississippi areas were "certainly understandable."

Renewal Of Religious Warfare

Ireland 'Peace' Threatened

BELFAST, Northern Ireland (AP) — The outlawed Irish Republican Army threatened to renew Northern Ireland's religious warfare as politicians and other leaders worked today to bring lasting peace in the tense, battle-scarred state.

IRA Chief of Staff Cathal Goulding announced in Dublin that volunteers were being mobilized to fight in the North and said some fully-equipped units already had been sent to Belfast. Goulding demanded that the Ulster government disband the B-Specials, the all-Protestant police reserves who have been accused of attacking Northern Ireland's Roman Catholic minority.

Goulding's statement was condemned as ill-timed and inflammatory by the Dublin government and moderate newspapers in the republic. The IRA is illegal in both Northern Ireland and the Irish Republic.

Prime Ministers Harold Wilson of Britain and James Chichester-Clark of Northern Ireland were to meet in London today to discuss ways of keeping the peace and satisfying Catholic demands in the six northern counties still linked to Britain.

Observers said Wilson would demand that the B-Specials be curbed despite strong pressure on Chichester-Clark's Protestant government to stand firm.

The two leaders also were expected to discuss the continuing presence of British troops in Northern Ireland and financial aid for more than 2,000 people left homeless by the rioting. It was thought they also would consider possible changes in the constitutional link between the two governments.

Chichester-Clark's government called a conference Mon-

(See Page 2)

INSIDE
Obituaries ——— Pg. 2
Sports ——— Pg. 13
Editorial ——— Pg. 4

THE DAILY HERALD

WEATHER
Clear to partly cloudy and warm through Friday with widely scattered, mainly afternoon and evening thundershowers. Lowest tonight 70 to 78.

Served By Associated Press Volume 85—Number 275 Mississippi Coast, Thursday Afternoon, August 21, 1969 ★ 1 Section—14 Pages Single Copy 10c

Hurricane Refugees Evacuated; Governor Says Death Toll 230

Old Glory, Midst Destruction, Still Waves In Home Of Brave

Homeless Sent To Other Cities

(From Staff and Wire Reports)

More than 5,500 homeless storm victims from the Gulf Coast were to find temporary shelter today in Hattiesburg and Jackson.

Camp Shelby and the University of Southern Mississippi at Hattiesburg were prepared to take care of 4,000 of them all in need of food, water, clothing and shelter.

Another 1,000 were to be put up at the Robert E. Lee Hotel in Jackson.

Gov. John Bell Williams had ordered the evacuation of Pass Christian, once the jewel of the Gulf Coast with beautiful and stately homes lining the beach and its famed "Scenic Drive."

The community of 4,000 was wiped out by the storm. Long Beach, population 6,000, was virtually destroyed. Many of the storm evacuees were from those two communities.

The stench of death is everywhere in Pass Christian, according to one man who volunteered to assist the body recovery teams there.

Joe Goings, Wiggins, a linotype operator for The Daily Herald who had wartime experienc ience in working with bodies, in working with bodies, said the teams are finding complete families in the debris of some homes destroyed by the storm.

"There is no devastation in Gulfport and Biloxi as compared to down there," Goings said after working in the area Wednesday.

"The stench of death is so terrific the average person could not stand it for long," he said.

He told of helping find three of the five members of one family missing from a beach residence. The father and mother aged 42, and 38, respectively, and one of the missing three daughters were found close together about 75 feet from where their home used to stand. The only son reportedly was blown clear of the house during the storm and floated to safety. The family was identified only by the last name of Smith.

He also noted the lack of safe drinking water over the entire city. If you go in there to help without water you'll dehydrate."

The Navy Seabees are in the area clearing debris with heavy equipment, Goings noted, and are spearheading theevacuation of residents. He said this is being done to prevent the spread of disease.

Commenting on the absolute extent of devastation and the loss sustained by residents who did survive in Pass Christian, Goings reflected: "It's pathetic to see people just sitting around amidst the remains of their homes."

Manwhile, Gov. Williams said the death toll was a minimum 230 on the Mississippi Coast and could be expected to go higher. Counting hurricane-related deaths elsewhere the count was said to be 283.

And Camille, the most intense hurricane to ever hit the U.S. mainland, was far from through.

The drag of land tamed her 200 mile an hour winds to thunderstorm strength soon after she curved inland but her heavy rains set off murderous flash floods in Virginia and West Virginia Wednesday. Officials said 38 already had drowned in Virginia, 2 in West Virginia.

Previously 10 storm dead were reported in Louisiana and 3 in Cuba.

The National Hurricane Center at Miami said Camille's low pressure also had steered Hurricane Debbie, whose 125 m.p.h. winds were far out in the Atlantic, into an ominous turn toward Bermuda.

Camille smashed into the southeastern edge of Louisiana and Mississippi's coast Sunday night. Since then, rescue work had been slow.

"We are finally seeing the light," said Williams. "We finally got some communications set up. This was the biggest problem."

In Gulfport and Biloxi, the city water systems were pumping again with emergency electrical power.

Residents were advised, however, to boil the water or doctor it with chlorine bleach—10 drops to the quart—before drinking it.

State Adj. Gen. Walter Johnson said the order to tighten martial law was aimed at both looting and profiteering.

"Any businessman who is found charging excessive and exorbitant prices for necessities will be arrested on the spot," Johnson said.

Vice President Spiro T. Agnew made a helicopter inspection of the Mississippi and Louisiana storm areas Wednesday. He was accompanied by Williams, Louisiana Gov. John J. McKeithen and George Romney, secretary of housing and urban development.

Biloxi Strip In Shambles Due Camille

By JAMES LUND
Herald Staff Writer

Homes, hotels, motels, gas stations and night clubs were in shambles Wednesday as workman prepared to clear out the beach area. An unofficial count of 205 fixed buildings were destroyed from Hurricane Camille's 150 mile per hour winds and 20 foot tides in the area from the Highway 90 Ocean Springs bridge, to Edgewater Plaza. Shrimp factories on Point Cadet were in shambles and destroyed. Gulf islands refugees building had only a foundation to show its previous existence.

The wooden frames houses on Point Cadet were many shrimp factory workers dwelled were all but washed off the face of the earth. Facto Bake and Winn Dixie were pictures of destruction: only their advertisement signs remained. Church of Redeemer was a total victim of Hurricane Camille, but St. Michael's Church was only slightly damaged.

Only the pilings of the historic Biloxi Yacht Club remained and neighboring George Pattison Pontiac was equally destroyed. Biloxi's small craft harbor and construction being donw on a new harbor remained only in pilings. The area around the Buena Vista hotel was hardly recognizable. The part of the Hotel on the beach was no longer standing. The main segment of the hotel and its convention rooms was damaged from high tide waters but is able to be salvaged.

Baricev's Restaurant was a repeat from Hurricane Betsy as only the pilings stood on the waterfront seafood restaurant. The other Baricev Restaurant was equally destroyed. Farther west on the Biloxi beach destruction prevailed. The amusement park was in shambles with one exception: the giant green dinosaur stood majestically over the ruins as if he was the responsible party. Nightclubs in this area were no longer around. The Beachhouse, a three-walled night-spot on the beach was gone without even a trace of its previous existence. Others were just as unfortunate. The Air Force jet which had stood on the neutral grounds between the sections of highway 90 was on a front lawn. A shrip boat, the Wayde Klein, was perched on a lawn. On the back of the boat a sign, which read do not remove, was scribbled. The ground floors of the Holiday Inn and Admiral Benbow Hotels were also victims of the storm.

Lums, a restaurant that had opened just last week, is permanently out of business. Broadwater Beach Hotel suffered flood damage and the marina was damaged but appeared salvageable. Edgewater Hotel also was flooded but no major damage was apparent. Highway 90 was thickened with debris and most of it was either caven in or askew.

Damage Defies Imagination, Agnew Declares

Vice President Spiro Agnew, after a helicopter tour of Mississippi's coastal area Wednesday, said the damage left by Hurricane Camille would almost "defy the imagination."

President Nixon declared the storm ravaged sections of Louisiana and Mississippi disaster areas earlier this week. Agnew said the federal assistance to the areas would probably "run higher than ever before."

George Romney, Housing and Urban Development secretary, Mississippi's Gov. John Bell Williams and Louisiana's Gov. John J. McKeithen made the tour with the vice president.

Gov. Williams said the evacuation of the coastal area did keep the death toll down but said, "many people, however, refused to leave their homes."

The news conference held here after the tour was a brief one. Gov. McKeithen made no comment.

A spokesman for the Office of Economy Preparedness said it would take about three to five weeks before "any semblance of order is restored."

Agnew said many federal agencies were taking steps to see that residents of the damaged areas are inoculated against tetanus and typhoid, a threat in all disasters.

Prior to thhe briefing, Senator John Stennis Said every effort toward "meeting the need for essential materials' is being given top priority.

He stated recovery operations "are not at a standstill, although it may appear that way."

An Editorial

Heroism was commonplace in our community during the storm. We have printed in the pages of this newspaper in the past few days numerous stories of courage in the face of danger.

But the winds have blown themselves out. The waters have receeded and left us in the midst of rubble and ruin. Spirits are sagging. The shock has worn off. The excitement is gone. We are weary. Our courage is sagging.

Some among us even believe the magnitude of the disaster is too great to overcome. They need leadership. They need guidance.

We are confident that there is enough talent, enough bold spirits on the Coast to provide that leadership. It is beginning to surface here and there even now.

Down on the Gulfport beach, for example, Tom Lambert, owner of Marine Life, Inc., is hard at work clearing out debris and getting ready to rebuild his half-million-dollar tourist attraction, which was virtually destroyed.

The secret to rebuilding our wrecked economy, says Tom, is to give priority to the erection of hotel and motel facilities just as fast as we can.

Tom Lambert says he is going to talk to all of the tourist developers he knows and urge them to "wage a blitzkreig against the aftermath of this storm, to use our efforts and our available money to make Camille pay for itself."

People all over the world are talking about the greatest hurricane in history, Tom notes. Let's get ready to invite them to come on down and take a look at the place it hit.

That's the kind of talk we like to hear. That's the kind of spirit that will help us all endure our burdens and come back stronger than ever.

The natural resources that made the Gulf Coast a great tourist attraction still exist. If there are among us enough men of vision and will, we will not only endure, we will prosper. We will prevail.

Emergency Efforts Ease Water Problem

Water began trickling through the faucets in most areas of Biloxi Tuesday afternoon and Wednesday morning as temporary generators went into operation at the city's wells.

Under the direction of C. A. Davidson, Biloxi building official, six such emergency generators were placed into operation.

"We've got a little water all over town" said Elbert Manuel, general manager of the city's Water Works Department. "But we're losing a lot of water."

He added that about 40 men in his department are busy at work, attempting to repair some of the broken water lines. Commissioner of Finance and Utilities Dominic A. Fallo said the department is also receiving "outside help."

Outside help began arriving in Biloxi Tuesday, assisting in all areas where needed, according to Mrs. Julia Guice, Civil Defense director.

She said Civil Defense assistance came from such areas as Crystal Springs, Corinth, Vicksburg, Natchez, Meridian, Jackson, Boliver County and areas in Louisiana.

Food and clothing for Biloxians who lost their homes are arriving by van-loads. The Red Cross is in charge of distribution at Biloxi Recreation Center, Howard Avenue and Bellman Street, Mrs. Guice said. Six vans of supplies were sent into the D'Iberville area, hard hit by Camille.

Beat Five supervisor Arlan Robinson said some bridges connecting North Biloxi with the peninsula are opened in some areas.

He said the Handsboro, Wilkes and Biloxi River bridges are in use and the main roads to these areas have been cleared by his county workmen who have been on duty since the storm.

Printed Here

Today's edition of The Daily Herald was printed here. However, all type was set and engravings made at the State-Record Company in Columbia, S. C. They were flown here today where the pages were assembled and printed. Today was the first time The Daily Herald was printed here since before the hurricane, although papers were printed daily in Columbia and flown here for distribution.

Death Toll Continues To Mount

BY TOM COOK
Daily Herald Staff Writer

Identification of some bodies is a matter of concern to Gulfport funeral homes as the known area toll from Hurricane Camille mounted to at least 74 as of Thursday morning.

As rescue workers continued to sift through debris, particularly in the hard-hit Pass Christian and Long Beach areas bodies were being uncovered and brought to Gulfport funeral homes.

Lang Funeral Home this morning faced the task of obtaining identifications of ten persons. Riemann Funeral Home was seeking the identity of a young girl, about 12 or 13, whose body was bound near the Broadwater Marina.

Harrison County Coroner Gladys Gorenflo and funeral home officials carefully listed all identifying characteristics in the hopes the information would lead to positive identifications by relatives of friends.

Meanwhile, the list of identified storm victims continued to grow. The bodies most recently recovered include:

At Lang Funeral Home—Mrs. George (Mary) Smith Jr. of Pass Christian; Margaret Rose Smith about 8, her daughter; Mrs. J. C. (Nellie Naomi) Rich., Gulfport; and a U.S. Navy Seabee, identified by the surname of Merrill and said to have resided at Pine View Apartments, Long Beach.

At Riemann Funeral Home—Anneas Saadi Moses Sr., 62, 4512 West Beach, Gulfport, Miss Elizabeth Dambrink, 46, 511 St. Louis St., Pass Christian, George Smith Jr. of Pass Christian, an attorney who practiced law in Gulfport; Roy Moffett, 236 East Second St., Pass Christian.

(Continued On Page Nine)

Victims In Area Listed

Harrison County Coroner Gladys Gorenflo listed 62 known dead as a result of Hurricane Camille which issued the list at 5 p. m. Tuesday.

Only 23 of the bodies were identified by the coroner.

The list:

Renee Bettencourt, age 10-12, found on Biloxi Beach.

Sgt. Irvin Oelke, (ret.), mid-50's, found on Brady Drive, Biloxi.

Mrs. Jeanette Oelke (wife of Sgt. Oelke), found on Brady Drive, Biloxi.

Mrs. Maude Colbert, 79, found at Main Street and East Beach, Biloxi.

John Walter Wozniak, 2½, found at 899 E. Beach, Biloxi.

Rev. G. O'Neill, OSB, found in Ocean Springs.

Mrs. Gloria Halat, no age listed, found on Biloxi Beach.

Unidentified white female early 50's found in North Biloxi at Bay Shore Drive.

Unidentified white male, late 50's, found in North Biloxi at Bay Shore Drive.

Unidentified white male 10-12 years, found on beach in Biloxi.

Unidentified white female, 7-9 years, found on Biloxi Beach.

Unidentified white male, about 40, found on Biloxi Beach.

Bonnie Demtz, no age listed, found at Pass Christian.

Unidentified white female, 19 or 20, found near Wayside Rest Home in Long Beach.

Albin Wagner, 66, found on Azalea Drive, Long Beach.

Mrs. Herry Hale, no age listed, found in pass christian.

Mrs. Lownone Welch, no age listed, found on Lang Avenue, Long Beach.

Victoria Barrett, child, no age listed, found in Pass Christian.

Mrs. Arden Barrett, Victoria's mother, no age listed, found in Pass Christian.

James Chauvin, about 10 or 12, found in Pass Christian.

Katherine Chauvin, about 5, James' sister, found in Pass Christian.

Unidentified child, female, about three, found with the Barretts.

Unidentified white female, about 70, found near the Pass

(Continued On Page Ten)

Searchers Still Find More Dead

Searchhers scouring the hurricane-battered areas of Pass Christian found "a ton of bodies since daylight" today.

Mississippi Gov. John Bell Williams immediately flew to the area which was crushed by Hurricane Camille.

"I can give you no exact number," he said after Executive-Secretary Cecil Yarbro of the state building commission told newsmen of the additional bodies found in Pass Christian. Yarbro is Williams' chief assistant at Pass Christian.

"I can safely say it's over 200," Williams said of the coast's total death toll. "How many more, goodness only knows." Williams earlier estimated the toll at 230 dead and expected it to rise.

A spokesman for the Seabee battalion leading the cleanup in Pass Christian said workers found "many more bodies in trees, under roofs, in bushes, everywhere" Wednesday.

Storms Race For Open Sea

MIAMI (AP) — Hurricane Debbie—apparently too tough for men to tame—and her killer sister Camille raced today for the open sea on courses that would spare Bermuda their devastating winds.

Debbie packed top winds of 110 m.p.h. Camille, called the worst hurricane to hit the U.S. mainland, rekindled after moving back into water off the mid-Atlantic coast and intensified to 50 m.p.h.

Forecasters predicted Debbie would pass well south of Bermuda and buffet the island with gales but spare it of hurricane force winds and tides.

Camille, given a 50-50 chance of again reaching hurricane force, was expected to pass well north of Bermuda. Moving eastward, the storm was located about 250 miles northwest of the mid- Atlantic island.

Red Cross Tells Homes Destroyed

NEW ORLEANS (AP) — The American Red Cross said today an initial survey by building inspectors showed 4,717 homes destroyed by Hurricane Camille along the Mississippi Gulf Coast and in Plaquemines Parish (County), La.

The Red Cross said the building inspectors surveyed only the Gulf Coast area in Mississippi and expected to find more damage when they surveyed north of the immediate coastal area.

Of the homes destroyed, the Red Cross said, about 1,400 were in lower Plaquemines Parish where Camille hit before turning into the Mississippi Coast.

The survey also found 9,718 homes suffering major damage, 8,493 of them in the Harrison County (Gulfport-Biloxi) coastal area; in addition, 22,344 homes suffered minor damage of $75 or more, 19,132 in the Harrison County coastal area.

The Red Cross said 794 trailer homes and 584 small business were destroyed or heavily damaged in the two areas.

1970

Anti-Vietnam War demonstrations reached a peak, with protests against the use of U.S. troops in Cambodia.

At Kent State University in Ohio, four students were killed when the National Guard fired into a crowd of war protestors.

More than four hundred colleges and universities closed or were on strike that spring.

FORECAST
By U.S. Weather Bureau
Chance rain, high 70s. Tonight clearing, low 30s. Wednesday high 50s.
Sun rises 6:26 a.m. Wed.; sets 8:31 p.m.
(Map and Data on Page 15A)

Columbus Evening Dispatch

50 Pages — OHIO'S GREATEST HOME NEWSPAPER — 2 Sections

HOME FINAL
Associated Press News, Wirephotos; United Press International and Chicago Daily News Service

VOL. 99, NO. 309 Phone—461-5000 * COLUMBUS, OHIO 43216, TUESDAY, MAY 5, 1970 **** 10 Cents

PATROL DENIES SNIPER REPORT

SCENE OF DISORDERS — Ohio National Guardsmen line the center of the Kent State University campus. Guardsmen are shown confronted on two sides by a student demonstration. In the foreground is the burned out ROTC building. Behind the building at upper left is where four persons were killed. (AP)

Scheuer

Miller

Krause

Schroeder

KENT, Ohio (AP) — An official of the Ohio Highway Patrol Tuesday disputed reports from the Ohio National Guard that a sniper was spotted by police helicopter before Guardsmen shot four Kent State University students to death Monday during an antiwar demonstration.

Related Stories, 2A and 9A; Page of Pictures, 7B.

The university, ordered evacuated after the shooting, was virtually deserted Tuesday and under heavy police and military guard.

EARLIER, fire destroyed a barn and several farm tractors in one corner of the campus, and fire officials said they believed the blaze was deliberately set.

Sgt. Michael Delaney of the guard public relations staff said after the shootings that, "At the aproximate time of the firing on the campus, the Ohio Highway Patrol — via a helicopter — spotted a sniper on a nearby building."

Tuesday, a patrol official, Maj. D. E. Manly, said "There is nothing on the log on the sighting." Manly said if patrolmen in the helicopter circling the campus had seen a gunman it would have been recorded.

GUARD officials claimed Monday and again Tuesday that the Guardsmen were returning the fire of a small caliber weapon in defense of their lives. A student crowd had surrounded some 30 Guardsmen and were throwing rocks and chunks of concrete at them.

The Justice Department and officials of the National Guard launched separate investigations of the gunfire outburst which took the lives of two girls and two young men.

The dead were Miss Allison Krause, 19, Pittsburgh, Pa.; Miss Sandy Lee Scheuer, 20, Youngstown, Ohio; Jeffrey G. Miller, 20, Plainview, N.Y., and William K. Schroeder, 19, Lorain, Ohio.

PORTAGE County Coroner Dr. Robert Sybert said all four had been shot from the side, "left to right." All died of a single bullet wound, he said.

Miss Krause was hit in the left shoulder, Miss Scheurer in the neck, Schroeder in the left underside of the chest and Miller in the head.

Dr. Sybert said the final autopsy report wouldn't be completed for about a week.

THREE students remained in critical condition Tuesday. One of them, Dean Kahler, of East Canton, Ohio, was paralyzed from the waist down, according to Paul Jacobs, administrator at Robinson Memorial Hospital in Ravenna.

Eight other persons, including two guardsmen were hospitalized. One of the two guardsmen was treated for shock and the other had collapsed from exhaustion.

PRESIDENT Nixon deplored the campus deaths. In a White House statement, he said:

"This should remind us all once again that when dissent turns to violence it invites tragedy. It is my hope that this tragic and unfortunate incident will strengthen the determination of all the nation's campuses administrators, faculty and students alike to stand firmly for the right which exists in this country of peaceful dissent and just as strongly against the resort to violence as a means of such expression."

The campus and the City of Kent were sealed off following the shootings.

SCHOOL officials ordered

See KENT on Page 6A

Turnout Normal To Heavy

By HOWARD HUNTZINGER
Of The Dispatch Staff

Normal to heavy voting was reported in Central Ohio Tuesday as party nominees were selected on the state and county level.

Of the 1.6 million votes expected to be cast in Ohio, 135,600 were to be from Franklin County.

THE REPUBLICAN and Democratic intraparty fights for a place on the November general election ballots attracted major interest in the U.S. Senate and gubernatorial contests.

Voters were choosing between Governor Rhodes and U.S. Rep. Robert Taft Jr. for the Republican senatorial nomination and among three GOP officeholders for the party's nominee for governor.

The latter are Atty. Gen. Paul W. Brown, State Auditor Roger Cloud and U.S. Rep. Donald E. Lukens. The name of Albert Sealy of Dayton remained on the ballot despite the fact he withdrew.

STATE REPUBLICAN Chairman John S. Andrews undoubtedly anticipates many wounds to be healed within the GOP ranks and announced a luncheon would be held Thursday for the

See ELECTION on Page 6A

INSIDE THE DISPATCH

GIs to Quit Cambodia In 7 Weeks, Nixon Says

WASHINGTON (UPI) — President Nixon gave leaders of Congress what was described as a "firm commitment" that all U.S. combat troops now in Cambodia would be pulled back within seven weeks.

Rep. F. Edward Hebert, D-La., reported the president's promise on Capitol Hill following a White House meeting.

NIXON, DEFENSE Secretary Melvin R. Larid and Gen. Earle G. Wheeler briefed congressional leaders and members of the House and Senate Armed Services Committees for about an hour and a half and then answered questions for half an hour on Nixon's decisions to send combat troops into Cambodia and to allow brief, new air raids on North Vietnam.

"They are coming out in five, six or seven weeks at the outside," Hebert said of Nixon's comments on the troops in Cambodia. "That was definitely a firm commitment."

HEBERT IS a ranking member of the House committee.

Blacks Block OSU Building

About 50 black students blocked the entrances to the College of Arts and Sciences building at the Ohio State University campus shortly before noon Tuesday threatening the fragile peace on the campus.

Two attempts to burn buildings during the night had failed and some students were eating cold meals Tuesday because of picketing at student cafeterias.

OBSERVERS SAID as many as 100 students were being kept from entering Denney Hall. No police were called to the scene, but were reportedly alerted to the confrontation.

The building is situated off the Oval behind the Administration Building.

At the same time, students were gathering in the Oval for a non meeting. The crowd exceeded 1,000 as students continued pouring into the area.

Related Stories, Pages 2A and 8A.

Three student leaders called Tuesday for an end to the disruptive boycotts.

TIMOTHY SHEERAN, president of the undergraduate student body, said he was not opposed to nonviolent demonstrations such as Tuesday's boycott of food service facilities, but "the present course of action creates a potentially violent and dangerous situation on the campus, similar to that of Kent State University."

Sheeran was joined in the statement at an 11 a.m. press conference by W. Bruce Achenbach, vice president of the undergraduate student government, and by Stephen Kling, president-elect of the group.

MONDAY NIGHT a storeroom containing duplicating machines in Lord Hall, 124 W. 17th Ave., was badly damaged in a fire at 10:45 p.m. University police said it looked like the fire had

See OSU on Page 6A

Blackmun OKd By Committee

WASHINGTON (AP) — The Senate Judiciary Committee approved by a 16-0 vote Tuesday President Nixon's nomination of Judge Harry J. Blackmun to be a Supreme Court justice.

Chairman James O. Eastland, D-Miss., told newsmen that a report recommending confirmation of the 61-year-old Rochester, Minn., judge will be filed in the Senate Thursday.

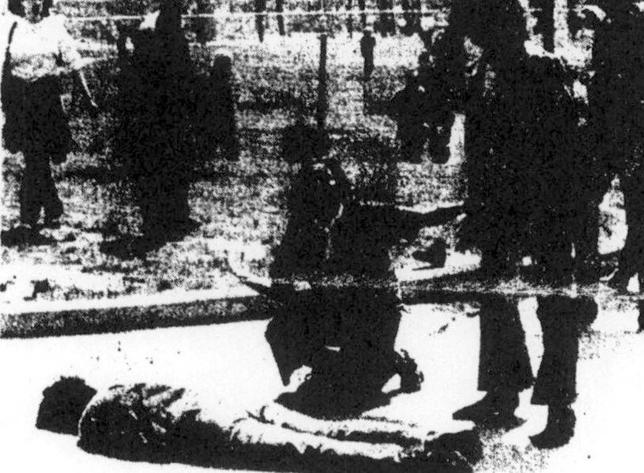

HE'S SHOT—A coed screams as a classmate lies dead on the campus of Kent State University. National Guardsmen fired into a crowd of demonstrators and killed four students. (AP)

HEAVY FIRE, BAD WEATHER STALL THIRD U.S. THRUST

SAIGON (AP) — U.S. troops launched a third offensive into Cambodia Tuesday from the Central Highlands but came under such heavy fire and met such bad weather that helicopters could land but a fraction of the 6,000 men committed to the operation.

On the Fishhook front, 200 miles to the south, U.S. troops met their first serious resistance as a column of tanks blasted its way into the town of Snuol in rubberplantation country eight miles inside Cambodia.

FROM PLEIKU, Associated Press photographer Charles Ryan, covering the new offensive 50 miles to the west, said that two companies of U.S. troops were hit by heavy small-arms fire from both sides of a clearing as helicopters tried to land them. They never made it in.

Sources said that due to the heavy ground fire and a morning haze, which set the operation back several hours, only one battalion of about 500 U.S. troops was landed.

Plans had called for at least two battalions to be airlifted in by the helicopters. The troops that did land began building a semipermanent artillery and patrol base from which to fan out.

A FIELD officers said the better part of a U.S. infantry brigade and a South Vietnamese regiment—estimated at 3,000 or more American troops and an equal number of South Vietnamese — were committed to the new offensive. He said it would be the largest air mobile operation the central highlands of Pleiku in two years.

This was the second major U.S. offensive ordered by President Nixon to destroy Communist sanctuaries and base camps.

Nixon ordered an earlier offensive to the south in the Fishhook region of Cambodia. It was launched last Friday.

THE OTHER offensive was opened last Wednesday by South Vietnamese troops accompanied by U.S. advisers, but with American air and

See INDOCHINA on Page 8A

DELIBERATE DESTRUCTION — Custodian Allan Kitchen, left photo, sweeps up debris outside Ohio State University's Lord Hall, 124 W. 17th Ave., Tuesday after a fire caused extensive damage to a storeroom containing duplicating machines. Robert A. Ulrich, assistant manager of operation at the university facility, looks over an expensive plating machine damaged by the blaze. Firemen were called to the scene at 10:45 p.m. Monday. Police believe the fire was set. (Dispatch Photos)

DEFIES NATIONAL ANTHEM — An unidentified demonstrator at Ohio State University defies the National Anthem and doubles her fist as members of the school's Army ROTC unit salute during ceremonies. (AP)

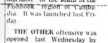

1971

The New York Times had published classified information about U.S. involvement in Vietnam. The Supreme Court upheld the right of *The Times* and the *Washington Post* to publish the information, which became known as the Pentagon Papers.

In Vietnam, the United States blockaded North Vietnam in an attempt to cut off supplies from China and the Soviet Union and mined Hanoi and Haiphong harbors.

The Weather
Today—Partly cloudy, warm, humid, high in the 90s, with a 50 per cent chance of rain decreasing to 40 per cent tonight. Friday—Partly sunny. Temperature range: Today, 70-95; Yesterday, 76-90. Details, Page B2.

The Washington Post
Times Herald

144 Pages 9 Sections

Amusements	C13	Financial	H10
City Life	B 1	Food	D 1
Classified	E 3	Obituaries	B 6
Comics	G 4	Panorama	G 1
Crossword	C10	Sports	H 1
Editorials	A22	Style	C 1
Fed. Diary	G 5	TV-Radio	C12

94th Year · No. 208 · © 1971, The Washington Post Co. · THURSDAY, JULY 1, 1971 · Phone 223-6000 · Circulation 223-6100 Classified 223-6200 · 15c Beyond Washington, Maryland and Virginia · 10c

Court Rules for Newspapers, 6-3

By Charles Del Vecchio—The Washington Post

Post Executive Editor Benjamin Bradlee, in striped shirt, talks to staff after Supreme Court ruling. Next to him is Katharine Graham, publisher, and to left of her is Editorial Page Editor Philip Geyelin. Managing Editor Eugene Patterson is in striped shirt outside glass.

Decision Allows Printing of Stories On Vietnam Study

By John P. MacKenzie
Washington Post Staff Writer

The Supreme Court settled a historic confrontation between government and press by ruling yesterday that The Washington Post and The New York Times are free to publish their stories about the secret Pentagon report on how America went to war in Vietnam.

The decision, which rested on the Bill of Rights guarantee of a free press and the long-standing refusal of Congress to authorize court injunctions against newspapers, was by a 6-to-3 vote.

Deeply divided and venting their differences in nine separate opinions, the justices summed up their action by stating that the government had failed to meet its "heavy burden" of justifying prior restraints against the press in light of cherished First Amendment freedoms.

The court ordered the lifting "forthwith" of stays against both newspapers which have been in effect during most of the three weeks the battle has raged in the courts.

Chief Justice Warren E. Burger, who announced the edict along with his own dissent and the dissents of Justices John M. Harlan and Harry A. Blackmun, then brought to a close the court's brief afternoon session and declared the end, after a two-day extension to settle the newspaper case, of the court's 1970-71 term.

There was widespread satisfaction by the press at the result, though the newspaper industry had wished for a more resounding declaration against even temporary press restraints. The Justice Department had no comment on the court's action, nor did the White House.

Katharine Graham, publisher of The Post, said: "We are extremely gratified not only from the point of view of newspapers, which was not the least of our concerns, but gratified from the point of view of government, good government, and the public's right to know, which is what we were concerned with."

See POST, A15, Col. 1

War File Articles Resumed

By Sanford J. Ungar and George Lardner Jr.
Washington Post Staff Writers

Newspapers throughout the nation, expressing delight over the Supreme Court decision, rushed into print last night with articles based on the once-secret Pentagon papers on Vietnam.

In its own reaction to the court ruling, the Pentagon told Congress at 5 p.m. that it would have enough copies of the full, unedited 47-volume Pentagon study printed for every member of the House and Senate.

Congressmen themselves offered a heavy round of praise for the high court ruling in the cases of The Washington Post and The New York Times, but there were also scattered misgivings.

In Boston and St. Louis, federal district judges immediately lifted the restraining orders they had earlier imposed on The Boston Globe and the St. Louis Post-Dispatch in similar cases initiated by the Justice Department.

The Post-Dispatch, an afternoon newspaper, received the news in time to resume publication of its series based on the Pentagon study in the final edition of its Wednesday paper.

"We're going to continue with our series right where we left off," said A. M. Rosenthal, managing editor of The New York Times, shortly after the Supreme Court ruling. He said that seven to nine installments remained to be printed by that newspaper.

The Post resumed publication of its series with three installments in today's editions. Executive Editor Benjamin C. Bradlee said there would be at least three more articles to follow.

The New York Times had published three articles before the government moved on June 15. The Post published two before it was restrained in the early hours of June 19, and The Globe and Post-Dispatch one each before lower court orders were entered against them on June 22 and June 26.

Other newspapers, including the Chicago Sun-Times and the Los Angeles Times—which published earlier stories based on the Pentagon study but were never sued by the government—indicated last night that they would probably carry the Post series in today's editions.

Many editors and publishers praised the Supreme Court decision.

See PAPERS, A16, Col. 3

Soyuz 11 Deaths Assessed

U.S. Experts Think Oxygen System Failed

By Thomas O'Toole
Washington Post Staff Writer

The three Soviet cosmonauts found dead on their return to earth yesterday almost certainly died from a sudden loss of oxygen in space, either because their oxygen lines broke or because their spacecraft cabin underwent abrupt decompression.

This was the considered judgment of experts in the United States familiar with the Soviet space program and aware of the details so far released by the Soviet news agency Tass. The record-breaking 24-day flight of Soyuz 11 cost the lives of cosmonauts Georgy Dobrovolsky, Vladislav Volkov and Viktor Patsayev.

"Their deaths have all the earmarks of oxygen starvation of the brain," one top U.S. space official said. "I can't think of any other possibility at the moment."

Whatever the reason for the cosmonauts' deaths, it is certain to cast a long and troubled shadow over the future of Soviet manned space flight, at least its immediate future.

"I would have expected a re[illegible] of three other cosmo[illegible] to the Salute space station in the near future," said one high-ranking U.S. space official. "I doubt very seriously if that will happen now, unless they quickly find out what went wrong and can quickly fix it."

Officially, the Soviets said nothing yesterday about the probable cause of the deaths. Tass said only that the three men were found strapped in their seats "without any signs of life" after coming down to a gentle landing in the steppes of Soviet Central Asia just after 2 a.m. Moscow time (7 p.m. EDT Tuesday).

Soviet journalists close to the space program were reported yesterday as saying that the three cosmonauts were found in a state of repose, as if in a deep sleep. Their faces were described as tranquil. They showed no signs of having struggled to survive.

See SOVIET, A26, Col. 1

Vote at 18 Amendment Is Ratified

COLUMBUS, Ohio, June 30 (AP) — The voting age in all elections was lowered to 18 years tonight when Ohio ratified the 26th amendment to the U.S. Constitution, fulfilling the requirement that 38 states do so to make it law.

The Ohio House, with 99 members, ratified the amendment 81-to-9, one day after the Senate passed it 30-to-2.

Ohio House Speaker Charles Kurfess ruled out of order fellow Republican Rep. Jim Thorpe who loudly objected to the quick action as the vote was taken electronically.

North Carolina and Alabama legislatures approved the amendment earlier in the day.

Alabama Gov. George C. Wallace withheld his signature from the measure, hoping to time it so his state would be the one to carry the amendment over. However, Lt. Gov. Jere Beasley and legislators in Ohio said a governor's signature was unnecessary.

The amendment attracted some opposition in the Ohio legislature where some felt such a question should be put to a public vote. Ohio rejected a proposal two years ago to lower its voting age to 19 years.

It took only three months—record time—for 38 states to ratify the amendment, making it law. The process normally takes about 15 months.

Senators Make No Bid to Move

The financial troubles of Senators' owner Robert Short were discussed yesterday at a meeting of American League clubowners in Detroit, but league president Joe Cronin said Short "made no request to move" the franchise.

Details on Page H1.

LBJ Saw de Gaulle as Viet Threat

LYNDON JOHNSON
. . . worried about French

By Murrey Marder
Washington Post Staff Writer

The Kennedy and Johnson administrations in 1963 and 1964 feared that the United States might be forced out of Vietnam without "victory" by "pro-French" factions in Saigon seeking a "neutralist" peace, the Pentagon war study shows.

U.S. strategists had a double concern: that Vietnamese political opponents of American strategy to pursue the war more intensively might negotiate with North Vietnam behind the back of the United States; or that "pro-French" South Vietnamese generals would agree to a "neutralist" end of the war. The highest American officials equated that with a "Communist takeover."

In these critical years before the American role in the conflict had greatly escalated, the United States struggled far more to stay in the war than to get out of it, the secret documents reveal.

By 1964, what the Kennedy and Johnson administrations both labeled a global "test" against Communist expansion also became an unexpected test of another kind, inside the Western alliance. The Johnson administration looked upon French President Charles de Gaulle's attempts to reassert French influence in Indochina and all Asia—especially his call for the "neutralization" of South Vietnam—as the most pernicious portion of the Gaullist plan to break out of American "hegemony" and obtain a larger world role for France.

The American reaction was to dig in deeper in South Vietnam, to avoid at all costs what U.S. strategists perceived as a new double threat of American "humiliation."

Defense Secretary Robert S. McNamara, in a March 16, 1964 memorandum to President Johnson, summarized the U.S. position on negotiations "on the basis of 'neutralization' McNamara reported:

"While de Gaulle has not been clear on what he means by this—and is probably deliberately keeping it vague as he did in working toward an Algerian settlement—he clearly means ont

See JOHNSON, A18, Col. 1

Draft Halts As Congress Snags on Bill

By Spencer Rich
Washington Post Staff Writer

The draft expired last night at midnight after House-Senate conferees on a two-year draft-extension bill reported a deadlock over the Senate's end-the-war amendment.

House Armed Services Committee Chairman F. Edward Hebert (D-La.) told reporters 27 of the 28 differences between the House and Senate versions had been resolved. But "we have no agreement on the Mansfield amendment and we'll come back next Wednesday to try to work it out."

Sen. Henry M. Jackson (D-Wash.) said 20 or 25 compromise proposals on the end-the-war language are kicking around, but "right now it's an impasse."

White House Press Secretary Ronald L. Ziegler said no men will be drafted until Congress completes action on the bill. Ziegler said the President would not exercise emergency authority to call up men who had received student or hardship deferments because "we believe this would cause hardships and dislocations."

The Selective Service System has instructed local boards to stop inductions, preinduction physicals and classification actions. The system is due to call up 16,000 men in July and August.

Hebert told reporters that on the basis of remarks by Dr. Curtis Tarr, Selective Service director, he believed the nation could go "several months" without callups without harming its defense posture.

See DRAFT, A8, Col. 1

Viet Combat Role Urged on JFK in '62

GENERAL LEMNITZER
. . . a grim chart talk.

Chalmers M. Roberts
Washington Post Staff Writer

The year 1962 opened for President Kennedy with the grim word that he had not done enough to save South Vietnam.

According to documents from the Pentagon study available to The Washington Post, the chairman of the Joint Chiefs of Staff had prepared one of those Pentagon flip-chart talks for Mr. Kennedy. Although there is no direct evidence, it seems a reasonable assumption that the talk was delivered. In any case, it is likely that the dreary word reached the President.

Gen. Lyman L. Lemnitzer, then the JCS chairman, was prepared to discuss China's problems (things must be bad because wheat had been purchased from Canada and Australia), the setup of the 16,500-man Vietcong military establishment and the belief that North Vietnam then was running a training center near the city of Vinh "where pro-Vietcong South Vietnamese receive an 18-month military course interspersed with intensive Communist political indoctrination."

"Two 600-man battalions already have completed training," said Lemnitzer's "talking paper" for the Jan. 9 meeting with the President, "and another two battalions began training in May, 1961." Here were signs of danger.

Then Lemnitzer, if he followed the "talking paper" prepared for him, was to quote the President to himself:

"The President on 22 November 1961 authorized the Secretary of State to instruct the US Ambassador to Vietnam to inform President Diem that the U.S. Government was prepared to join the GVN (Government of South Vietnam) in a sharply increased effort to avoid a further deterioration of the situation in SVN (South Vietnam)." Next were listed the military steps the President had approved less than two months earlier.

One chart showed "approved and funded construction projects" including improvements at airfields at Pleiku, Bienhoa and at Tansonnhut (Saigon). Here was the commitment thus far.

See COMMIT, A16, Col. 1

D. A. Jim Garrison Charged in Bribery

By Ken W. Clawson
Washington Post Staff Writer

JIM GARRISON
. . . claims a frame.

Jim Garrison, the New Orleans district attorney who failed to prove a conspiracy in the assassination of President Kennedy, was arrested yesterday on federal charges of taking payoffs to protect illegal gambling operations.

Garrison, released on a $5,000 personal recognizance bond pending a July 9 hearing, said in New Orleans that he was framed but that being arrested was "better than being shot," which he said he had expected since he first started his investigation of the presidential murder.

Charged with Garrison were a New Orleans police captain assigned to Garrison's staff; a police sergeant in charge of the New Orleans vice squad, and seven other persons connected with the pinball machine industry in Louisiana and Mississippi.

All 10 persons were accused of illegal gambling, use of bribery to obstruct law enforcement, interstate travel in aid of racketeering and conspiracy to violate these laws.

See GARRISON, A8, Col. 1

Gravel Goes Undisciplined

Despite outraged comments by Republicans, the Senate yesterday appeared unlikely to discipline Sen. Mike Gravel (D-Alaska) for his Tuesday night performance with the Pentagon papers.

The documents Gravel read aloud at an extraordinary subcommittee meeting, and others he distributed to the press, disclose cables of possible Soviet responses to U.S. moves in Vietnam and depict the Joint Chiefs of Staff as relentlessly pressing for escalation of the war.

Details on Page A15.

U.S. Supported Coup Against Diem

NGO DINH DIEM
. . . U.S. backed ouster

By Don Oberdorfer
Washington Post Staff Writer

At 4:30 p.m. on November 1, 1963, a few hours before he was murdered, President Ngo Dinh Diem of South Vietnam telephoned U.S. Ambassador Henry Cabot Lodge to determine the attitude of the American government toward the coup in progress outside his palace window.

Lodge was noncommittal. He had heard the gunfire, he said, but he did not have all the facts. "Also it is 4:30 a.m. in Washington and the U.S. government cannot possibly have a view."

"But you must have some general ideas," protested Diem. "After all, I am a Chief of State. I have tried to do my duty...I am trying to do now what duty and good sense require. I believe in duty above all."

Lodge replied that Diem had certainly done his duty, and with courage, and no one could take away from him the credit for his contributions to his country. "Now I am worried about your physical safety," the Ambassador continued. Had Diem heard that he had been offered safe conduct out of the country if he resigned?

"No," answered the beleaguered but stubborn Vietnamese President.

"If I can do anything for your physical safety, please call me," Lodge said.

"I am trying to re-establish order," concluded Diem, in the last words he would say to an American. Before the evening was out, he and his brother Ngo Dinh Nhu had fled the Presidential Palace through a secret tunnel. The next afternoon they were captured by the insurgents in Cholon, the Chinese section of the city, and shot to death in an armored personnel carrier rumbling through the Saigon streets.

The refusal to intervene to save the tottering Diem was not a spur of the moment decision by Henry Cabot Lodge. According to a Pentagon study of United States involvement in the war, it was part of a thoroughly planned policy of the United States government, which had decided to back a coup if it appeared likely to succeed.

See DOCUMENTS, A17, Col. 1

1972

Despite the pullout of some of its troops from Vietnam, the United States continued to bomb Hanoi and Haiphong and shell coastal areas of North Vietnam.

Alabama Governor George Wallace, campaigning for the presidency, was shot in Maryland. He was paralyzed from the waist down.

President Nixon and Vice-President Agnew were reelected.

Police arrested five men for breaking into the Democratic party national headquarters in the Watergate office complex in Washington, D.C.

Today's Circulation 10,234

THE NEWS HERALD

Nine Burke Traffic Deaths In '72

Published Daily Monday Through Friday . . . Serving Burke County Since 1885

Vol. 87 | 10c Per Copy, 45c Week Home Delivery | MORGANTON, NORTH CAROLINA, TUESDAY, MAY 16, 1972 | Eighteen Pages — One Section | No. 80

Bullet Leaves Wallace Partially Paralyzed In Lower Extremities

4-H Automotive Winners Leave On Prize-Winning Trip

Sixteen of the grand prize winners in the Burke County 4-H automotive care and safety program left this morning, via Northwestern Bank plane, on a trip to the General Motors assembly plant at Doroville, Ga. They will fly to Atlanta, then go to the plant for a tour and return to the Morganton-Lenoir airport this afternoon. The other top prize winners will go to the World 600 race in Charlotte on May 28. Those making the trip today were (left to right) John Greene, chairman of the steering committee; Duve Carter, chairman of the awards committee; Al Bracey of the Northwestern Bank; Mrs. R. L. Pearson, Salem leader in the program; Jesse Searcy, Oak Hill leader; then (ascending the outer edge of the steps) Wayne Buff, Mary Glassbrooks, Jeannie Sutton, Maria Huffman, Marcia Hunt, Mary Alice Beam, Pam Powell and Larry Starnes. Ascending the inner edge of the steps are Dean Beck, Frank Wallis, Michael Earwood, Randy Oxford, Rose Ross, Penny Walker, Luther Hoilman and Keith Hoyle. (Staff photo)

At Hearing Held By City Council

Carbon City Group Opposes Annexation

By EDNA MAE HERMAN
News Herald Staff Writer

Strong opposition to the Carbon City area being annexed by the City of Morganton was expressed by almost all of the some 25 persons who spoke at the public hearing on the annexation of the Carbon City and Vine Arden areas Monday night.

Approximately 200 persons attended the hearing called by the Morganton City Council. The hearing was convened in the City Council Chambers in Morganton City Hall and then moved to the basement of the Collett Street Recreation Center.

Only one man from the Carbon City area said he wanted to be annexed and he presented a petition with signatures of 26 people in that area stating they want to be admitted to the Morganton city limits.

Leonard Bradley, a leader of those opposing the annexation of Carbon City, presented a petition which he said was signed by approximately 750 persons of Carbon City who are opposed to the extension of the city limits into the Carbon City area west of Morganton.

Although the hearing also involved proposed annexation of the Vine Arden area, only one person spoke up and indicated opposition to this.

Basically the sentiments expressed by those against the Carbon City annexation was that they did not want to be in the city, they had moved where they were to keep out of the city, they didn't feel it was right for them to be taken into the city against their wishes and without letting them vote on it and they claimed the city just wanted the area because of the industry there and the money this would bring in.

The Carbon City Fire Department also was an issue, with those connected with the department concerned about giving it up. They claimed the city didn't want them two years ago when it cut off outside fire protection and they had to start

See CARBON CITY page 6

Next 48 Hours Decisive

By DON McLEOD
Associated Press Writer

SILVER SPRING, Md. (AP) — George C. Wallace, shot down at an election-eve rally, lay gravely wounded and partially paralyzed today on what was to have been the brightest day of his presidential campaign.

The Alabama governor was hit several times by a gunman who pushed a pistol through a shopping-center crowd at Laurel, Md., Monday afternoon and fired point blank. A man identified by police as Arthur Herman Bremer, 21, of Milwaukee, was wrestled to the ground by members of the crowd and arrested immediately.

After five hours of surgery, police and hospital spokesmen said Wallace's life was no longer in danger, but some paralysis was reported. One physician said the outlook for full recovery was not good. The governor's press secretary quoted doctors as saying the paralysis may be temporary, "but we will know more about this in the next 48 hours." He said Wallace will continue his campaign.

Physicians said Wallace came through the night in good spirits despite pain from his wounds. "He says it hurts, and he's feeling fine," Dr. Joseph Schanno said at a morning progress report. He said Wallace's condition remains critical.

Dr. Herman Maganzini, a heart specialist attending Wallace, said his heart is in excellent condition. "He's doing remarkably well considering the extent of his injuries," Maganzini said.

Meanwhile, voters in Maryland and Michigan were balloting today in primaries which Wallace had been favored to win in a double sweep that would have been the high point of his campaign for the Democratic presidential nomination.

"I feel very optimistic about him," Wallace's wife, Cornelia, said after the surgery in Holy Cross Hospital. "As you know, his nature, he didn't earn the title of the 'Fighting Little Judge' for nothing, and I expect him to continue in the same vein."

Doctors said Wallace, 52, was hit by four or five bullets. Only two lodged in his body. One was removed from around his right shoulder. The second, which punctured the stomach and lodged on the lower part of the spine, was left in. Bullets also pierced Wallace's right forearm, grazed the back of his left shoulder blade and grazed

See BULLET page 6

Protestant Bar Bombed In Belfast

BELFAST (AP) — An explosion wrecked a Protestant bar in Belfast late Monday night, injuring 17 persons and sending Protestant youths on a rampage.

It was the second bar bombed in three days. A Roman Catholic tavern was demolished Saturday, touching off a 36-hour Catholic-Protestant battle in which nine persons were killed and more than 70 wounded.

A 50-pound bomb in a parked car shattered the Bluebell Tavern in Sandy Row, a Protestant district in East Belfast. Three girls, 7, 10, and 13 years old, were among the casualties.

Protestant youths threw up barricades around the street, while others charged into a nearby business district, hurling rocks at offices and smashing in widows with clubs.

Police said "older and wiser heads" finally persuaded the youths to return home, and protestant residents removed the barricades.

The two bar bombings and the reaction that followed heightened fears of civil war between the Protestant majority and the Catholic minority. For many months the Protestants have held back, leaving to the British army and the police the task of combatting the Catholic guerrillas of the Irish Republican Army. But since the British government supplanted the Protestant provincial government and made some concessions to the Catholics, Protestant militancy has been increasing.

Amid the escalating Protestant-Catholic violence, gunmen wounded a Catholic father and

See PROTESTANT page 6

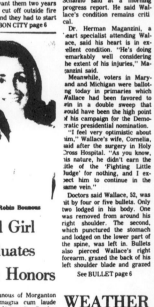

Russell Secrest

Secrest Campaigns In Burke

Russell Secrest, who led a field of six candidates for the Democratic nomination for commissioner of insurance in the May 6 primary but did not get a majority vote was in Burke County Monday to kickoff his campaign for the second primary on June 3.

Secrest led John Ingram of Asheboro by only 73 votes in the first primary and the Randolph County legislator called for a runoff.

A native of Salisbury, Secrest has lived for the past 14 years in Cary where he is currently serving a four-year term on the city council.

The 44-year-old Secrest has been a deputy commissioner with the North Carolina Department of Insurance for 16 years, working under retiring Commissioner Edwin S. Lanier.

See SECREST page 6

Miss Robin Bounous

Local Girl Graduates With Honors

Robin Bounous of Morganton graduated magna cum laude from Duke University Sunday with a B. A. degree in English with secondary school teacher's certification.

Miss Bounous, daughter of Mr. and Mrs. E. P. Bounous, was elected to Phi Beta Kappa and in her senior year was an Alice M. Baldwin Scholar.

Other honors received at Duke included being selected for inclusion in "Who's Who in American Colleges and Universities."

In her senior year she was chairman of the freshman advisory council which has charge of orientation for all incoming freshmen women. She also has served as secretary of her dormitory as well as taking part in a number of other college activities.

More than 1,700 men and women received degrees during Duke's 120th graduation exercises. Walter Cronkite, managing editor and anchorman for CBS News, delivered the commencement address in Duke Indoor Stadium.

Around Burke County

The Hildebran Republican Women's Club meets tonight at Curley's Fish Camp of Hildebran at 7:30 o'clock. Mrs. Alma Burns said all members are invited to attend and to bring guests.

The Burke County Association of Classroom Teachers will have their spring banquet Monday, May 22, at 7 p.m. at the community house. All ACT representatives must have their approximate number of persons attending reported to Miss Betty Brooks, president, by Wednesday morning.

The 1947 class of Glen Alpine High School will hold a reunion Saturday at 6:30 p.m. at Mom 'N Pop's Ham House. All members are asked to be there.

Homecoming will be observed at Mount Olive Baptist Church on Sunday. Rev. Oscar Long, pastor of Shiloh Baptist Church in Watha, will be the 11 a.m. speaker. There will be singing in the afternoon and Sunday school at 10 a.m.

Mrs. Frances Y. Drum, of Hildebran, who is a head nurse at Broughton Hospital, attended the University of North Carolina School of Nursing-NCSNA Psychiatric Nursing Conference group's one-day workshop on group process held at Cherry Hospital in Goldsboro recently.

The focus of the meeting was developing increased awareness of group process and the roles of members functioning within this process. Time was also spent discussing and clarifying the

See AROUND page 6

On Edge Of Hanoi

US Planes Wreck Air Defense Headquarters

By GEORGE ESPER
Associated Press Writer

SAIGON (AP) — American fighter-bombers wrecked North Vietnam's air defense headquarters on the southern edge of Hanoi and cut the main pipeline feeding tanks and supply trucks on the northern front in South Vietnam, the U.S. Command announced today.

Intelligence reports have said Russian technicians and advisers were known to be working in the headquarters, but there was no immediate comment on this from the command.

A six-page communique reporting the assessment of damage done by nearly 2,000 strikes in North Vietnam during the past week said:

"The North Vietnamese Air Defense Headquarters at Bach Mai air field, south of Hanoi, was struck by U.S. Air Force F4s, destroying several structures."

Bach Mai is three miles south of Hanoi.

The command also disclosed that air strikes against North Vietnam have been stepped up to an average of 250 per day in the campaign ordered by President Nixon a week ago to choke off supply routes to the south.

The command had announced earlier that both the northwest and northeast rail lines between Hanoi and China had been cut, and the 7th Air Force reported Sunday that its bombers had destroyed the "Dragon's Jaw" bridge at Thanh Hoa, 80 miles south of Hanoi, a key link in North Vietnam's supply network.

But spokesmen said that the effects of the aerial campaign on the enemy offensive in the south would not be known for at least 30 days. They estimated that the North Vietnamese had a month's supply of fuel close at hand for their tanks and vehicles in the south.

Fighting in the 48-day-old North Vietnamese offensive slowed down, but the reason was not immediately clear. One

See US PLANES page 6

Association Sponsoring Sing, Book

Garland Hamrick, president of the Burke County Law Enforcement Officers Association, said today that the association is definitely sponsoring a gospel sing program at the Morganton High School scheduled for September, and that a book will will be printed with the latest information on drugs.

According to Elmo Fagg, head of the promotion company which is soliciting advertisements for the publication as a benefit for the law enforcement association, one third of the book will be dedicated to discussions of drugs in the hope that this being a souvenir book "people will keep it in front of them and hopefully read it in the hope that it will save a person from becoming a hopeless addict."

Also included in the book, Fagg said, will be four pages

See ASSOCIATION page 6

BLOODSHED BOXSCORE

RALEIGH (AP) — Here is the Motor Vehicle Department's report of highway deaths and injuries for the 24 hours ending at midnight Monday.

Killed	4
Injured (rural)	29
Killed this year	635
Killed to date last year	613
Injured to April 1, 1972	13,732
Injured to April 1, 1971	12,756

Against Galifianakis And Bowles

Jordan And Taylor Call For Runoffs

RALEIGH, N.C. (AP) — Both Lt. Gov. Pat Taylor and Sen. B. Everett Jordan have decided to make a second try — Jordan at winning renomination to his seat and Taylor at capturing North Carolina's Democratic gubernatorial nomination.

Taylor told a news conference Monday that he has decided to "stand and fight" and said he will call for a second primary against Hargrove "Skipper" Bowles, who took 45 per cent of the vote in the May 6 gubernatorial primary. Taylor received 37 per cent of the vote.

Jordan also told a news conference Monday that he would call for a June 3 runoff to give Tar Heel voters another chance for "expression of their views on the man best qualified to represent them" in the Senate.

Rep. Nick Galifianakis, D-N.C., led in the first primary, topping Jordan by about 38,000 votes but failing to win an absolute majority.

The announcements set the stage for another three weeks of vigorous campaigning by major Democratic candidates. Republican Jim Holshouser had already announced that he would seek a runoff with Jim Gardner for the GOP gubernatorial nomination.

Gardner led Holshouser by a slim margin in the first primary May 6. The two Republicans have kept up their attacks on each other while the Democrats spent a week in relative silence waiting for decisions from Taylor and Jordan about the runoffs.

Taylor, a 47-year-old Wadesboro attorney, said he was "out-spent ... out-promised ... and out-fought" in the first campaign. He said since then "most of the state's establishment has been telling me to quit."

But he said he had decided to stand and fight, knowing he was going to be out-spent and put-promised again but not out-fought.

He said he was "going to fight for a decent future for the average citizen of North Carolina" by attempting to improve public schools, helping the mentally ill, the blind, the crippled and the deaf, and by revising state income tax laws."

Taylor admitted that he had personally requested support from two lesser — but potentially important — candidates in his second primary bid, black Charlotte dentist Reginald Hawkins and labor leader Wilbur Hobby.

Hobby and Hawkins together

See JORDAN page 6

WEATHER

NORTH CAROLINA: Some early morning fog, otherwise partly cloudy with a few showers or thundershowers north coast this morning. Clear to partly cloudy tonight and Wednesday. Mild through Wednesday. Highs today and Wednesday 70s. Lows tonight mid to upper 40s mountains to near 60 coast.

IN MORGANTON: Low this morning a cooler and sunny 48 degrees. Rainfall for 24 hours to 8 a.m. today amounted to 0.07 inches.

High for Monday 80 degrees, low 58, with 76 degrees prevailing at reading time at 5 p.m. Rainfall for 24 hours to 8 a.m. Monday was 0.08 inches. Reported by Millard C. Duckworth, U.S. weather observer.

LAKE JAMES: Water today 0.7 feet below spillway or overflow level, compared with 1.2 feet yesterday and 3.7 feet a week ago.

1973

The Watergate scandal reached Senate committee hearings, where former White House counsel John Dean admitted to playing a role in the burglary cover-up and said President Nixon and his aides knew about it.

Taped Watergate conversations were eventually turned over to Judge John Sirica, but there were unexplained gaps in some conversations.

Sirica sentenced seven Watergate defendants to prison terms. The House Judiciary Committee investigated the possible impeachment of President Nixon.

In Vietnam, a cease-fire was signed, ending the Vietnam war for the United States.

Vice-President Spiro Agnew resigned after pleading no contest to charges of income-tax evasion. Republican House leader Gerald Ford became Vice-President.

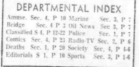

DEPARTMENTAL INDEX

Amuse.	Sec. 4, P 10	Marine	Sec. 3, P 7
Bridge	Sec. 4, P 3	Oil News	Sec. 3, P 7
Classified	S 4, P 12-22	Police	Sec. 1, P 7
Comics	Sec. 4, P 23	Radio-TV	Sec. 2, P 6
Deaths	Sec. 1, P 20	Society	Sec. 4, P 4-6
Editorials	S 1, P 10	Sports	Sec. 3, P 1-6

The Times-Picayune

Serving America's International Gateway Since 1837

CLOUDY

and cold, with northeasterly winds at 12 to 22 miles an hour, is the National Weather Service forecast. High Sunday, 53; low, 47. High Monday, in the mid to upper 40s; low, near 40. Map, details, Sec. 4, Page 2.

136TH YEAR No. 350 — Full Associated Press (AP), National News and Chicago News Wires and AP WIREPHOTO. — NEW ORLEANS, MONDAY MORNING, JANUARY 8, 1973 — Second-Class Postage Paid at New Orleans, La. — SINGLE COPY 10 CENTS

SNIPERS KNOWN TO KILL SEVEN, INJURE 13

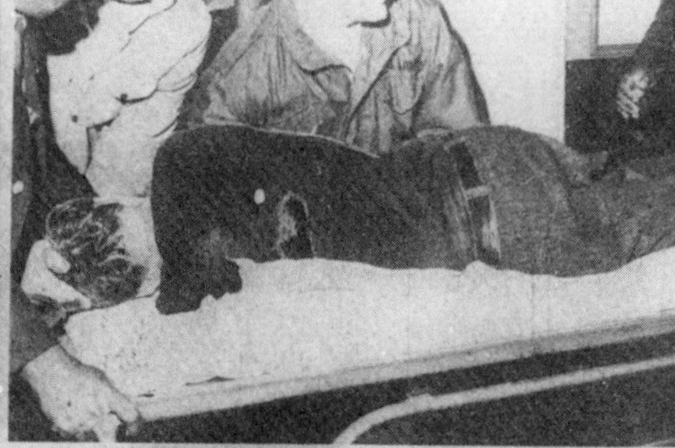

PTN. DAVE M'CANN AIDS WOUNDED PTN. KENNETH SOLIS (LEFT) AND POLICE DEPUTY SUPT. LOUIS SIRGO LIES MORTALLY WOUNDED

—Photos by Times-Picayune staff photographers G. E. Arnold and Ronald LeBoeuf.

One Terrorist Dead; Possibly Two Others at Howard Johnson's

By FRANK L. MARTIN III

One of possibly three sniper-arsonists who terrorized a five-square-block area of downtown New Orleans in a continuing 12-hour shooting spree was killed by police bullets fired from an armored Marine helicopter at 10 p.m. Sunday.

Efforts to flush others—police think at least two—from the Downtown Howard Johnson's Motor Lodge, scene of a police-sniper battle that had left at least seven persons dead and 13 injured, were being halted so city officials could discuss the situation.

Another three persons, probably hotel guests, are thought to be dead inside the hotel. Unofficial sources put the total higher.

FLUSHED BY FIRE

The sniper who was killed was flushed from a cubbyhole by gunfire from the helicopter. Witnesses say he rushed out of a concrete cubicle to fire, retreated, charged out again and was hit.

Police say the ensuing fire from both the helicopter and

PICTURE PAGE IN SEC. 1, PAGE 16.

marksmen on the roofs of surrounding buildings riddled his body.

Later efforts to flush the remaining snipers from the cubicle on the roof, including more helicopter passes, were of no avail.

MEETING CONTINUING

Late Sunday night a meeting among city officials and police was continuing. Police leaving

Cont. in Sec. 1, Page 2, Col. 1

'WON'T DIE,' INJURED OFFICER CONSOLED

Emergency Units Brave Gunfire to Carry Out Daring Rescue

By BRUCE NOLAN

Gerry Arnold crouched behind a tree in Duncan Plaza, cradling the wounded policeman in his arms.

A few feet away, in the open, a stricken sergeant sprawled on the grass.

"I'm gonna die. I'm gonna die," cried the officer near the tree. He was hit in the chest or shoulder.

"No baby, you're not going to die," answered Arnold. "Don't worry about it. They're going to get you out."

Later Arnold, a Times-Picayune photographer, remembered how he hid behind that tree with the wounded policeman, looking for help and shooting pictures at the same time.

Moments later he would see another policeman shot, struck down within an arm's length.

He had gone to cover a fire at the Downtown Howard Johnson's Motor Lodge when the snipers began their deadly work.

The fires apparently were deliberately set, and all apparently designed to lure firemen and policemen into the snipers' sights.

In the beginning, with the shots echoing down Loyola Avenue, Arnold scrambled in a half-crouch from place to place, snapping his shutter and ducking for cover.

For Arnold, policemen, firemen and reporters, those first moments were terrifying. No one could be sure of the snipers' exact position, but each had the sinking feeling that their crosshairs might be trained, unseen, on them.

The shots rang out, reverberating off the sides of buildings with a curiously flat whacking sound, rolling ominously between the walls of a man-made canyon.

"I guess I got there about 11 o'clock," said Arnold," and just as I got there I heard a volley of shots, in succession, like an automatic rifle."

Suddenly, Arnold remembered later, a fireman slumped against his ladder. He was one of the first to be hit outside, and Arnold, snapping pictures, began running in close.

"The fire was continuing," he said, "but the firemen were crouched behind their engines.

"At about the same time someone hollered that a police officer had been shot in a building across the street. So I went across the street, up to the 10th floor in the Traveler's Building, I think, where I found a police officer with his face half blown off.

"Then somebody hollered a police officer's been shot on the mall, across from City Hall.

"So I ran over there and saw a police officer laying prone on

Cont. in Sec. 1, Page 2, Col. 6

Warwick Haven from Gun Battle for a Short Time

By BILL SHEARMAN

If the center of a raging storm is its calmest spot, then, for a while Sunday, the coffee shop and lobby of the Warwick Hotel was a haven for pedestrians and Sunday drivers caught in the midst of the Howard Johnson-based sniper fire.

Located in the very shadow of the hotel at 1315 Gravier St., the Warwick's coffee shop afforded the breakfaster a full view of the besieged hotel and a safe retreat from the gunfire that changed a small hotel fire to a raging gun battle Sunday around 11 a.m.

It was when the gunfire began and two policemen and a fireman fell wounded that the onlookers realized the terrible danger they were in. And they looked for a place to hide.

One such couple were Dr. and Mrs. David Fieselman of 4517 Barnett St., Metairie. The Fieselmans, along with their two-and-a-half-year-old daughter, Baby, were returning from a 9:45 a.m. service at St. Pat-

Cont. in Sec. 1, Page 20, Col. 1

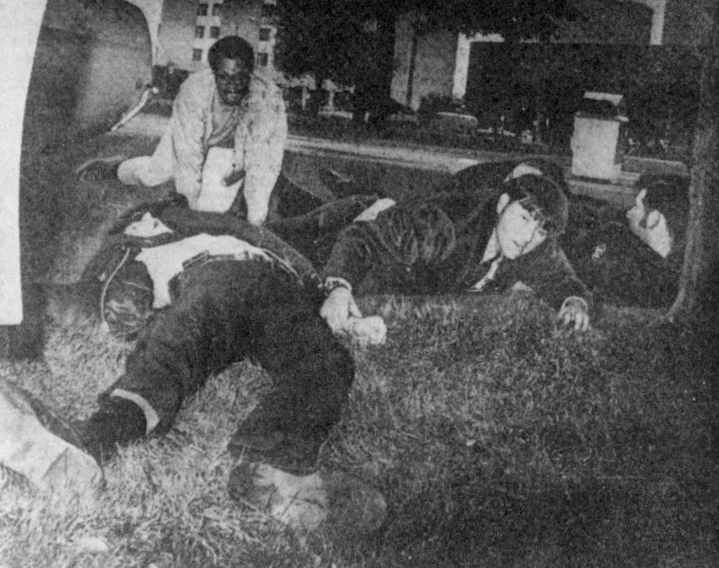

PTN. LEO NEWMAN TAKES PULSE OF DYING PTN. PHILIP COLEMAN

—Photo by Times-Picayune staff photographer G. E. Arnold.

100 POLICEMEN FIRE AT SNIPER

Shots from Copter Add to Fatal Fusillade

By CHRIS SEGURA

One of the snipers on the roof of the Downtown Howard Johnson Motor Lodge was killed Sunday night by police as he ran toward an armored helicopter hovering over the roof. He was cut down by shots from the helicopter and from the Rault Center across the street from the hotel about 10 p.m.

Some 100 policemen fired at the snipers from the center.

The U.S. Marine Corps helicopter had just begun hovering over the building when the sniper stepped out of the concrete cubicle he was using for shelter and fired two quick rounds at the aircraft.

After firing, he jumped out of the line of fire.

RUNS FROM SHELTER

But when a tracer round, fired into the cubicle, lit the area up, the man ran from his shelter toward the helicopter, firing as he ran in zig-zag fashion.

Shots from the Rault Center and the copter cut the man down as he ran and he dropped, apparently dead.

After police in the helicopter had literally riddled the man's body, which lay prostrate by a spinning vent 15 yards from the cubicle, police continued firing from the Rault Center.

Police continued to shoot for about 10 minutes—singly and in volleys.

On subsequent passes by the helicopter, it seemed fire was returned from the cubicle and it was learned from police radio communications that other voices were heard coming from the cubicle.

Police speculated that there were at least two other snipers in the structure.

WEAPON INOPERABLE

Police in the helicopter announced over police radio that gunfire had made the sniper's

Cont. in Sec. 1, Page 3, Col. 3

Battle at Hotel Slows Slightly with Darkness

By ED ANDERSON

The long periods of silence only accentuated the staccato bursts of machine gun fire over the Downtown Howard Johnson's Motor Lodge Sunday night as lawmen of the New Orleans area just waited.

Since early Sunday morning, policemen and firemen were the targets of sniper fire from the upper floors of the hotel.

But Sunday night, it was not all-out warfare as the brunt of the attack was carried out by a Marine Corps armored helicopter which peppered the stronghold of the snipers.

After making four or five passes, drawing fire from the snipers' position, police reported a hit. One police spokesman said the sniper was shot by marksmen positioned in nearby high-rise buildings and the 'copter when he showed himself and fired on the craft.

A little while later, the news came: it was a fatal hit, but

Cont. in Sec. 1, Page 2, Col. 8

SIRGO IS KILLED BY SNIPER FIRE

N.O. Deputy Police Supt. Called Gallant Man

By ED ANDERSON

At least seven persons — including New Orleans Police Department Deputy Supt. Louis Sirgo and two patrolmen — were killed and at least 13 others injured Sunday afternoon during a sniper-police shootout at the Downtown Howard Johnson's Motor Lodge at 330 Loyola Avenue.

There were reports that three other persons died during the shootout, but late Sunday night this had not been confirmed.

Killed in the confrontation — touched off when snipers set fires in the hotel and began shooting at police and firemen who answered the alarm — were:

— Sirgo, who was shot in the back.

—NOPD First District Ptn. Philip J. Coleman Sr., 69 Old Hickory St., Chalmette.

—NOPD Ptn. Paul A. Persigo,

Cont. in Sec. 1, Page 3, Col. 1

Death on a Bloody Afternoon

By DON LEE KEITH

A massive wave of fear mixed with shock at calculated violence rolled through the first few blocks of Loyola Avenue Sunday afternoon, saturating the thick misty air and leaving in its wake, the pall of death.

But as snipers in the Downtown Howard Johnson's Motor Lodge snapped bullets at police and firemen trying to douse fires that had been set in different part of the gripped with both confusion and determination.

Rumors ran rampant through the crowd of spectators, curiosity-seekers and persons merely caught by fate in the vicinity of the shootout.

Even before the first rattle of exchange of fire, men crouched behind vehicles, shrubbery and trees, making do with any available protection. Any movement from the place of safety was head-down and hasty.

By shortly after noon, the swarms of police—both uniformed and plain-clothes—had

Cont. in Sec. 1, Page 17, Col. 1

Gist of the News

(Inside The Times-Picayune Today)

—Monday Morning, January 8, 1973—

International Affairs

National Affairs

Local Affairs

N.O. Emergency Number Created

The City of New Orleans Sunday night established a special emergency telephone service to supply the latest factual information on the sniper-police shootout at the Downtown Howard Johnson's Motor Lodge.

The service—phone number 524-0191—will remain in effect as long as needed, a city spokesman said. Information to be supplied by the special operator includes identities of those persons killed and the conditions and whereabouts of those wounded, he said.

The city spokesman urged, however, that citizens refrain from calling the number unless it is an emergency to avoid tying up the line.

POLICE SHARPSHOO

THE SUNDAY FORUM

Fargo – Moorhead

VOL. 95, NO. 74 — SUNDAY, JANUARY 28, 1973 — Ninety - Six Pages — Price Twenty-five Cents

On Last Day Of War as on First, People Dying in Viet

By HUGH A. MULLIGAN
AP Special Correspondent

SAIGON (AP) — On the last day of the Vietnam war, victory flags flew for both sides in the bright, dry-season sunshine, but men were fighting and people were dying, as they had been since the very first day.

Ellsworth Bunker, the U.S. ambassador, raced through Saigon in a motorcade to attend a morning war briefing at Pentagon East, just like any other Saturday. This time, peace problems were also on the agenda.

Helicopters droned in the sky. Bombers flashed in the sun. Guards dozed on sandbags at bridges. French girls in tiny bikinis splashed in the pool at the Cercle Sportif. An ambulance wailed for attention in a sea of motorbikes.

Downtown Saigon was jammed with shoppers, preparing for Tet the Lunar new year celebration Feb. 3. As they have done since long before the French came and went, women with sidewalk stalls and movable food kitchens showed up just after 6 a.m. to lay out the day's offerings of fried shrimp, noodle soup, brass incense urns and candle holders fashioned from the casings of artillery shells.

Several American GIs wandered past the crowded outdoor markets, looking at garish paintings of nude women and Jesus Christ with slanted eyes on black velvet. They told each other, joyously, without cynicism, that they would be going home in 60 days.

"Free at last . . ."

"Bye, bye, Miss American Pie . . ."

Peace was only hours away, the Armed Forces Radio kept saying, but all over the land war was still here and now.

Peace seemed far away in the Mekong Delta, less real than the mirages cast by the thunderheads in the sky.

On the last day in the war, Capt. Tom Brennan of New York City was up at 5 a.m. as usual, sifting through reports of overnight enemy activities over his first cup of coffee.

As operations officer for My Tho Province in the populous Mekong Delta, Brennan was in his jeep an hour later driving west out of town along National Highway 4 to the Cai Be district where the Viet Cong had tried to cut the vital rice route to Saigon.

Dawn was just breaking over the lush green land as Brennan and his driver, T. Sgt. Ovido Alosta of Mayacuel, Puerto Rico, made their way across open stretches of rice fields interspersed with patches of banana trees and coconut palms.

It was harvest time. Women in conical hats were already in the fields hand-threshing the rice against little canvas screens. Gray water buffaloes plodded ahead of wooden harvesting machines.

By sunup, Highway 4, the wide main road from the capital almost to the tip of the Vietnam peninsula, was the usual chaos of over-loaded province buses, trucks bringing crates of vegetables from the mountain plains of Dalat to the populous Mekong Delta, roadside hucksters selling fresh pineapple, sugar cane, straw hats and black market gasoline stolen from the Americans. But the tree line looked ominous and empty.

Around a bend, past a row of trucks and three-wheeled motorbikes pulled hurriedly off the road, danger waited. There was the familiar crack of automatic weapons, the acrid aroma of cordite, a body or two sprawled grotesquely along the dusty shoulder.

At first light the Viet Cong had tried to cut the road where it turns west to Can Tho, another major delta city, by throwing up an impromptu roadblock of tree branches, stones, mud, old rubber tires, even some surreastically blooming water lilies. From My Tho, the 7th South Vietnamese Division reacted swiftly to join the battle with a task force of armored vehicles and machine-gun laden jeeps. Their commander reported 16 Viet Cong dead.

By 8:15 a.m., Brennan had his first air strike. Two Vietnamese air force Skyraider bombers made lazy looping dives almost to treetop level. They were well into their climb before the earth trembled under 250-pound and 500-pound bombs, and plumes of black smoke rolled above the rice fields. The women bent over their work scarcely bothered to watch.

"A day like any other day, only more so," said Brennan, mopping his red Irish face with a GI handkerchief. "I know it's the last day of the war because they keep telling me so on the radio."

Within an hour, Brennan and Alosta were racing east to investigate more traffic on the other side of town. Highway 4 went about its usual business, ignoring the war as it always has done. Rice trucks lumbered to Saigon, 40 miles away, as if there were no planes in the sky and no percussive thunder of falling bombs.

(See Peace on Page A-13)

F-M Forecast

Mostly fair but colder today; increasing cloudiness tonight with chance of snow flurries Monday; high today 17; low tonight near zero; high Monday 20; precipitation probabilities near zero today and tonight.
(Weather Details on Page A-2)

(AP Wirephoto)

All smiles now, U.S. Secretary of State William Rogers selects a pen before signing the agreement to end the Vietnam War Saturday. Man at left is unidentified aide.

Peace Accord Signed as U.S. Halts Draft

Drink Champagne Toast to Peace

By MICHAEL GOLDSMITH

PARIS (AP) — The United States and North Vietnam formally called an end to their long undeclared war Saturday and their envoys drank a champagne toast to peace and friendship.

They were joined by the South Vietnamese and the Viet Cong in signing the documents that called for a cease-fire, the exchange of prisoners and a withdrawal of all U.S. forces from Vietnam.

The time for the cease-fire on Vietnam's battlefields was midnight Greenwich Mean Time — 7 p.m., EST. The exchange of prisoners and the withdrawal of U.S. troops is to take place within 60 days.

To get around the refusal of South Vietnam and the Viet Cong's provisional revolutionary government to recognize each other, Secretary of State William P. Rogers and North Vietnam's foreign minister, Nguyen Duy Trinh signed a separate set of documents later in the day.

The two ceremonies, the first lasting 18 minutes and the other 10 minutes, in the ornate gray-and-gold ballroom of the former Hotel Majestic, were followed by toasts with champagne provided by France, the host country.

Witnesses said all the envoys taking part clinked glasses, including Foreign Minister Tran Van Lam of South Vietnam and Mrs. Nguyen Thi Binh, the Viet Cong foreign minister.

All four ministers were silent during the signing ceremonies held under the floodlights of television cameras. But while Lam and the other South Vietnamese officials wore grim expressions throughout, Rogers and Hanoi's Trinh twice exchanged nods and a flicker of a smile.

Lam and Mrs. Binh attended only the first ceremony, which began and ended with a noisy "victory" celebration by several hundred Viet Cong and North Vietnamese sympathizers in front of the 700-room building near the Arc de Triomphe.

Lam later called on the French Foreign minister, Maurice Schumann, to lodge a formal protest that the demonstration was tolerated by French police. The demonstrators waved

SIGNING
(Continued on Page 2, Col. 2)

Beats Nixon Draft Goal By 5 Months

WASHINGTON (AP) — Secretary of Defense Melvin R. Laird announced Saturday that "use of the draft has ended."

His action, placing the nation's armed forces on an all-volunteer footing for the first time in nearly 25 years, came five months ahead of President Nixon's goal.

In a message to senior defense officials, Laird said:

"With the signing of the peace agreement in Paris today, and after receiving a report from the secretary of the Army that he foresees no need for further inductions, I wish to inform you that the armed forces henceforth will depend exclusively on volunteer soldiers, sailors, airmen and Marines."

Laird's decision cancels plans to draft about 5,000 men before next June 30, when legal authority to induct young men into the armed forces will expire.

Pentagon manpower officials said that the flow of volunteers, spurred by a series of military pay raises and improved fringe benefits, has encouraged them to believe these 5,000 men can

DRAFT
(Continued on Page 2, Col. 6)

American Death Toll Rises

Attacks Occur to Peace Deadline

By GEORGE ESPER

SAIGON (AP) — A truce shadowed by uncertainties came officially to Vietnam this Sunday morning. Rocket and mortar attacks continued up to the deadline for the fighting to halt, and explosions could be heard even after that.

An American was killed in the last hours of hostilities, bringing to four the number of GIs killed in the last two days. More than a score were wounded.

Church bells rang out in Saigon to signal the start of the cease-fire, and some traffic stopped during a minute of silence.

President Nguyen Van Thieu voiced the Saigon government's gratitude to the Americans who helped it survive. Addressing his people, he said:

"We do not know whether peace will last or not, or will be sabotaged by the Communists.

The cease-fire effective at 8 a.m. Saigon time, was underwritten by orders from both sides for a halt in operations. These in turn reflected the peace agreements signed in Paris about a dozen hours earlier by the governments involved in the 11-year war.

The U.S. Command said it did not know the origin of explosions heard in downtown Saigon after the cease-fire went into effect. Recurring blasts made it sound as if an ammunition dump was blowing up.

Just before dawn, less than two hours before the designated time of the start of the cease-fire, Communist-led forces slammed nearly a score of Soviet-built rockets into Saigon's Tan Son Nhut air base and adjoining areas. Military spokesmen said initial reports indicated one Vietnamese civilian was killed and 15 were wounded.

During the 24 hours preceding the truce, the Saigon command reported 234 North Vietnamese and Viet Cong attacks across South Vietnam. Allied officials described this as a land grab — an attempt to fortify positions.

This was the highest number of attacks ever reported in the war for a 24-hour period.

About half of the attacks were carried out with rockets and mortars. A half hour before the cease-fire the enemy also shelled air bases in the major cities of Da Nang, Pleiku and Can Tho.

The U.S. command would not immediately give out details on the fourth American killed since Friday, nor would it say where he died. Spokesmen said they were awaiting a full report.

Earlier it became known that a 21-year-old Air Force sergeant from Linden, Tex., John Rucker, was among the last Ameri-

ATTACKS
(Continued on Page 2, Col. 3)

Rogers Returns, Asks Prayers for Peace

WASHINGTON (AP) — Secretary of State William P. Rogers arrived from Paris Saturday night where he signed the agreement that brought the United States' longest war to a conclusion.

Rogers' arrival came amid reports that a high ranking U.S. official will be going to Hanoi soon.

U.S. officials said such a trip might not be announced much in advance if at all, but one source said a visit to the North Vietnamese capital sometime by the end of February would be a good guess.

At the moment the cease-fire went into effect at 7 p.m. (EST) Rogers had champagne served to the members of the party on the presidential plane to celebrate the end of hostilities.

As the plane flew over Atlantic City at 15,000 feet the secretary stood in the middle of the aircraft and said, "As of the present moment the cease-fire . . . has become effective."

He then said "Let us raise our glasses to the brave men and

ROGERS
(Continued on Page 2, Col. 3)

Today's Chuckle

TV viewers are still waiting for an announcer who will surprise them with a soap that won't do anything but get the dirt off.

Accident Fatal To Sanborn Man

SANBORN, N. D. (AP) — A Sanborn man was killed Saturday when he apparently lost control of his auto and it rolled over on a county road about a mile south of Sanborn. The Highway Patrol identified the victim as Ralph Budek.

North Dakota [illegible] Vehicle Deaths Jan. to date	
5	10

The funeral for Ralph Budek, 40, will be at 11 Wednesday in St. Mary Catholic Church at Little Falls, Minn. A prayer service will be at 8 Monday in Sacred Heart Catholic Church here.

Mr. Budek was born Feb. 4, 1932 at Little Falls where he was educated and grew to manhood.

ACCIDENT
(Continued on Page 2, Col. 4)

Ervin to Subpoena Nixon Aides in Watergate Probe

By BOB WOODARD and CARL BERNSTEIN
Washington Post Service

WASHINGTON — Sen. Sam J. Ervin (D-N.C.) intends to subpoena some of President Nixon's top aides in the forthcoming senate investigation of the Watergate bugging and an allegedly broader campaign of political espionage and sabotage against the Democrats, according to informed sources on Capitol Hill.

Ervin also intends to investigate the government's inquiry into the Watergate and related matters to determine if it was complete and impartial, the sources said.

Ervin, who will hold the Senate's investigation, is expected to be granted subpoena power to call anyone in the executive branch of the government other than the President himself, the sources reported.

It could not be learned which presidential aides might be called to testify. However, it is known that Ervin believes that any White House officials and and presidential advisers who have been named in news accounts of alleged spying and disruption against the Democrats

WATERGATE
(Continued on Page 2, Col. 4)

Forum Index

(Forum Photos by Colborn Hvidsten III)

Peace Service

About 200 people attended a Service of Celebration and Thanksgiving commemorating peace in Vietnam Saturday night at St. Mary's Cathedral in Fargo. The service was interdenominational and featured Light Team singers from NDSU Lutheran Center, and six local ministers.

The Weather
Variable cloudiness today, fair tonight. High, 78; low, 58. Yesterday's high, 76; low, 63.
(Details and Map, Page C14)

Vol. 273—No. 127—F

THE SUN

FINAL

BALTIMORE, THURSDAY, OCTOBER 11, 1973

66 Pages 10 Cents

AGNEW RESIGNS

Russia resupplies Arabs; U.S. aids Israel

Tel Aviv claims recapture of Golan Heights

Airlift

By JAMES S. KEAT
Washington Bureau of The Sun

Washington — The Soviet Union is flying substantial amounts of munitions to Egypt and Syria, and the United States is supplying Israel with apparently smaller quantities, U.S. officials said yesterday.

The Soviet move has caused deep concern in the administration, because it aggravates both the Arab-Israeli conflict and the diplomatic confrontation between Moscow and Washington over the Mideast crisis.

U.S. officials said about 30 large Soviet transports had been spotted flying toward Egypt and Syria in the past two days. Their cargoes were not known but were presumed to be antiaircraft missiles and ammunition.

At least one El Al Airline Boeing 707, with its seats removed, picked up a load of sidewinder air-to-air missiles at Oceana Naval Air Station near Norfolk yesterday, officials here confirmed. This did not indicate, they said, an administration decision yet to mount a massive resupply operation for Israel.

Want to avoid dispute

[At least two Israeli planes have picked up missiles at Oceana Naval Air Station since Sunday, according to witnesses interviewed by the Norfolk *Pilot*.

[Other witnesses, the paper reported, said a caravan of military trucks drove east along Interstate 64 yesterday morning. Objects described as "apparently missiles" protruded from one of the vehicles.

[The caravan was said to be accompanied by armed guards in military fatigues.]

High administration officials avoided a public challenge to the Soviet Union over the airlift, but privately indicated strenuous diplomatic efforts to dissuade the Kremlin from continuing it.

President Nixon said after a meeting yesterday with President Mobutu Sese Seko of Zaire that the United States is seek-

See AIRLIFT, A2, Col. 4

Mideast

From Wire Services

Israel claimed yesterday that it had recaptured the Golan Heights and that its forces advanced to the edge of the Suez Canal and joined up with an encircled Israeli Army unit.

However, other reports said Egyptian soldiers, tanks and equipment continued to pour across the Suez Canal as the war entered its fifth day.

The reports came from Western correspondents who toured the Sinai yesterday and

A military analysis says Israel must counterattack soon. .... *Page A2*

The Golan Heights fighting is perhaps the biggest tank battle ever. .... *Page A3*

saw evidence that Egyptian forces had reached positions 10 or more miles east of the canal.

Israeli commandos struck across the Suez Canal early today for the first time in the fourth Arab-Israeli war and attacked Egyptian convoys, the Israeli military command said at dawn.

Israeli commandos crossed the 200-foot-wide canal in its southern sector and returned without casualties after attacking "convoys and rear echelons of the enemy," the command said.

Meanwhile, the Israeli Navy shelled Syrian oil installations on the Mediterranean coast more than 300 miles from the Egyptian canal front, a communique said.

Meanwhile, Israel said its jets attacked Damascus airport and other targets deep in Syria and Egypt, and Iraq announced its ground forces had joined the fighting in a major widening of the war.

Earlier press reports in Beirut, Lebanon, said that between 16,000 and 18,000 Iraqi troops and up to 100 tanks had crossed Syria headed for the Golan Heights.

The official Iraqi news agency said Iraqi warplanes carried out more than 80 air

See MIDEAST, A4, Col. 1

Sunpapers photo—Frank R. Gardina

Spiro T. Agnew leaves Baltimore's old Post Office Building after announcing his resignation.

The case against Spiro Agnew

Prosecutors presented to the Federal Court here yesterday a 40-page statement setting forth the evidence they had developed during their investigation of Spiro T. Agnew—a statement accusing him of many other wrongdoings in addition to the one to which the former Vice President entered his "no contest" plea.

Agnew denied the other accusations.

The text of the statement, which was signed by George Beall, United States attorney, and Barnet D. Skolnik, Russell T. Baker, Jr., and Ronald S. Liebman, assistant U.S. attorneys:

INTRODUCTION

The following statement is respectfully submitted to the court by the government at the arraignment of Spiro T. Agnew. It constitutes a detailed recitation of the facts and evidence developed by the investigation to date, which establish in part the source of the unreported funds which constitute the basis of the charge filed today. The presentation of this statement in court today was a material condition, requested by the Department of Justice, to the agreement reached between the government and Mr. Agnew.

SUMMARY

I. The Relationship of Mr. Agnew, I. H. Hammerman 2d and Jerome B. Wolff.

In the spring of 1967, shortly after Mr. Agnew had taken office as Governor of Maryland, he advised Hammerman that it was customary for engineers to make substantial cash payments in return for engineering contracts with the State of Maryland. Mr. Agnew instructed Hammerman to contact Wolff, then the new chairman-director of the Maryland State Roads Commission, to arrange for the establishment of an understanding pursuant to which Wolff would notify Hammerman as to which engineering firms were in line for state contracts so that Hammerman could solicit and obtain from those engineering firms cash payments in consideration thereof.

Hammerman, as instructed, discussed the matter with Wolff, who was receptive but who requested that the cash payments to be elicited from the engineers be split in three equal shares among Agnew, Hammerman and Wolff. Hammerman informed Mr. Agnew of

See TEXT, A9, Col. 1

Tax evasion draws fine, probation

By BENTLEY ORRICK
and THEODORE W. HENDRICKS

Spiro T. Agnew, 39th Vice President of the United States, resigned at 2.05 P.M. yesterday standing in a federal courtroom in Baltimore to plead no contest to a single, negotiated plea of tax evasion.

The resignation—the first under legal fire of a Vice President and only the second vice presidential resignation in U.S. history—officially came with the delivery of a letter from Agnew to Henry A. Kissinger, the Secretary of State, in Washington.

At the conclusion of the 35-minute court hearing here, Judge Walter E. Hoffman fined Agnew $10,000 and placed him on three years' unsupervised probation after accepting his nolo contendere plea on "willfully" evading paying $13,551.47 in federal income taxes in 1967, his first of two years as governor of Maryland.

Agnew's tax returns

The criminal information charging Agnew stated that his 1967 tax return showed a taxable income of $26,099 and taxes owed of $6,416; but, the document added, "as he then and there well knew" his taxable income had been $55,599 and he should have paid $19,967.47 in taxes.

The maximum penalty on the charge is five years' imprisonment and a $10,000 fine.

A 40-page summary of the government case against Agnew stated that for 10 years through "the Christmas season of 1972" while he was Baltimore county executive, governor and Vice President, he regularly received cash kickbacks from consulting engineers who received unbid county, state and, in some cases, federal contracts.

According to the summary, between 1966 and 1973 he received about $87,000 in cash kickbacks from two engineering firms alone, and untabulated thousands more from five other consulting firms and one banking institution.

The summary distinguished these monies from tens of thousands of other dollars in campaign contributions from the same firms.

President Nixon released a letter to Agnew, headed "Dear Ted," saying he was "deeply saddened by this whole course of events."

President to nominate successor

Agnew, in a 40-minute secret meeting in the Oval Office Tuesday night, had informed the President of his decision to resign—a decision reached as a result of intensive secret plea bargaining in Washington concluded Tuesday afternoon with top Justice Department officials and federal prosecutors from Baltimore.

Late yesterday, Agnew said he would address the nation soon about his resignation.

With the Agnew resignation, Carl Albert, the Oklahoma Democrat who is speaker of the House of Representatives, automatically became next in line for the presidency.

Under the so-far untried provisions of the Twenty-fifth Amendment of 1967, President Nixon will nominate a successor who must be confirmed by both houses of Congress voting separately.

The stage was set for the stunning conclusion of the Agnew investigation when he walked into the tightly guarded fifth-floor Courtroom 3 of the old Post Office Building only minutes before the 2 P.M. scheduled start of what was to have been a hearing

See AGNEW, A8, Col. 1

Major news elsewhere

The United Nations Security Council was paralyzed in trying to break the deadlock over finding a political solution to the Mideast crisis with Council members admitting that there was no prospect at present for ending the impasse A2

The Temporary Emergency Court of Appeals upheld the government's Phase 4 controls on retail gasoline prices A6

Charles G. Rebozo, one of President Nixon's closest friends, is likely to be called to testify before the Senate Watergate committee regarding an alleged link between a campaign donation from Howard Hughes and the financing of the presidential estate in California, according to congressional sources A6

In a top-secret meeting the state Commission on Judicial Disabilities heard almost nine hours of testimony relating to the land deal of Judge Dulany Foster ... Back Page

UPI

Orioles stay alive

The Birds won the chance to play today in the fifth and deciding game of the American League play-off by beating Oakland 5 to 4 yesterday. Bobby Grich was besieged by teammates after his tie-breaking homer in the 8th. Andy Etchebarren (arm upraised) belted a three-run homer out of the A's park in the 7th to tie the game. Don Baylor (No. 25), Brooks Robinson (partially obscured by Etchebarren) and an Oriole coach offer thanks. (Details, Page C1)

Reaction:

Nixon talks of successor

By ADAM CLYMER
Washington Bureau of The Sun

Washington—President Nixon started discussing a new vice president with congressional leaders yesterday afternoon, just over two hours after Spiro T. Agnew resigned the post.

He began with four Republicans and then met with two Democrats.

The talks began a few minutes after Mr. Nixon's press secretary, Ronald L. Ziegler, announced that the President would "promptly begin consultations with appropriate national leaders both within and without the administration."

Mr. Ziegler would offer no clues to the President's thinking about a successor to Agnew, but he promised Mr. Nixon would "move expeditiously, and he trusts the Congress will then act promptly to consider the nomination."

The speed of congressional action—each house will act separately—might depend on the sort of nominee Mr. Nixon chooses. Capitol Hill Democrats barely had their dropped jaws back in place after hearing that Agnew had quit before

See NIXON, A7, Col. 1

Capitol Hill is subdued

By ALBERT SEHLSTEDT, JR.
Washington Bureau of The Sun

Washington—Congress, like the rest of the nation, was astonished by resignation of Vice President Agnew yesterday, but quickly went to work setting up procedures to pass upon the qualifications of his nominated successor.

The 25th Amendment to the Constitution, ratified in 1967, states that "whenever there is a vacancy in the office of the Vice President, the President shall nominate a Vice President who shall take office upon confirmation by a majority vote of both houses of Congress."

An hour after the first news bulletin on the Agnew resignation, Senator Mike Mansfield (D., Mont.), Senate majority leader, was holding a meeting in his office laying the prelimi-

See CONGRESS, A6, Col. 1

Index

State leaders sympathetic

By FRED BARBASH

There was sympathy and even open arms and the promise of better things to come for Maryland's native son yesterday in state political and governmental circles.

State Senator Edward P. Thomas (R., Western Md.) chairman of the state Republican party, said Spiro T. Agnew "most certainly would have a political future in Maryland," following his resignation from the vice presidency.

"There still will be a great deal of admiration for the Vice President. He's a very dedicated man and I think he has taken a lot of abuse," Mr. Thomas said.

Governor Mandel, who was informed personally yesterday by the then Vice President, said he believed Agnew had sacrificed his political future for "the stability of the nation, the integrity of the vice presidency and the security of his family."

The decision to resign "must have been a painful one," Mr. Mandel said, but it was "a

See STATE, A14, Col. 1

Other Agnew news

1974

The climax of the Watergate affair occupied front pages across the nation.

For the first time in the history of the United States, a President resigned while in office.

President Nixon had been charged with taking part in a conspiracy to obstruct justice, with failure to fulfill his constitutional oath, and with unconstitutional defiance of committee subpoenas.

Nixon was succeeded in office by Vice-President Gerald Ford, who later pardoned him for all federal crimes he may have committed as President.

Nelson Rockefeller was named Vice-President.

A fad of "streaking"—appearing nude in public—spread across campuses and public places, including the nationally televised Academy Awards presentations.

Hank Aaron hit his 715th career home run, breaking Babe Ruth's record.

Journalists Bob Woodward and Carl Bernstein published *All the President's Men*, about their investigation of Watergate.

The Sears' Tower in Chicago was completed and, at 110 stories, became the tallest building in the world.

WEATHER
Cloudy, showers tonight, low 42. Cloudy Friday, high 52.
(Map, Data on Page 32A)

Columbus Evening Dispatch

100 Pages — OHIO'S GREATEST HOME NEWSPAPER — 5 Sections

HOME FINAL
Associated Press, United Press International, Knight and Copley News Services

VOL. 103, NO. 278 — COLUMBUS, OHIO 43216, THURSDAY, APRIL 4, 1974 — 10 Cents

Tornado Devastates Xenia

(Dispatch Photo by Joe Pasterek)

TORNADO RIPPED THROUGH DOWNTOWN XENIA LEAVING MUCH OF IT IN RUBBLE AND KILLING AT LEAST 35

41 in Ohio Dead; Higher Toll Feared

BULLETIN

President Nixon Thursday declared Ohio a disaster area, U.S. Sen. Robert Taft Jr., R-Ohio, reported after leaving the president's office. The order sets in motion federal relief programs for the specific areas where tornado damage occurred.

At least 41 were killed in Ohio Wednesday by tornadoes that tore through the state, and more were feared dead as rescue workers resumed their search through rubble Thursday.

Other Ohio Tornado Pictures on Pages 26A, 34A, 1B and 25B.

Xenia, the Greene County seat of 25,000 about 20 miles east of Dayton, was the hardest hit area in the Buckeye state.

THIRTY-FIVE persons were known dead in Xenia at dawn, State Highway patrolmen said. Sheriff Russell Bradley predicted the number of fatalities would rise. "I don't think there is any question about it," he said.

One man was killed at the village of Wilberforce near Xenia.

Tornadoes that swept over the Ohio River from Kentucky bit into sections of Cincinnati, killing five and injuring more than 200.

WINDS CAUSED extensive damage in other areas of Ohio, including London, where damage in the business district was so heavy the downtown was evacuated, and in New Albany, in Franklin County, where several houses were demolished.

At least 73 were known dead in Kentucky, some of those in Frankfort and Louisville.

Sixty-three were killed in Indiana, hundreds were injured and thousands were homeless. State officials said at least half a dozen small communities were literally wiped off the map.

SHORTLY AFTER the brunt of the winds hit the Hoosier state, an earth tremor registering 5.0 on the Richter scale, shook wide areas of western Indiana and eastern Illinois.

Samuel Morgan, chief deputy in the Greene County sheriff's department, said 25 to 30 percent of Xenia in Ohio was devastated.

Seven of the 10 school buildings were damaged. Homes by the score were flattened into kindling. Six of the 12 Xenia police cruisers were knocked out of service.

HERMAN MENAPACE, administrator of Green Memorial Hospital, said about 100 injured persons were treated there. About 200 others were taken to hospitals in Springfield and Dayton. The estimate of 300 injured, he said, was conservative.

Many persons who suffered only slight injuries received first aid at the

See OHIO on Page 4A

Death Toll in Storms Over 330

By The Associated Press

Tornadoes struck an area stretching from Georgia to Canada late Wednesday and early Thursday, killing more than 330 persons, the worst tornado death toll in half a century.

Thousands of injuries and millions of dollars in damage resulted from the twisters that hit scores of cities and towns, leaving many in shambles.

ROWS OF bodies were arranged in the rubble-strewn streets. More victims were thought trapped in overturned cars, but heavy equipment was unable to get through the streets to lift the vehicles.

Whole neighborhoods were destroyed, buildings leveled, railroad cars and trucks upended by the vicious winds that struck the Midwest and South.

In Washington, D.C., the American Red Cross said more than 800 disaster workers and nurses were laboring to aid the homeless and injured. Other relief workers and disaster equipment from all over the country were en route to the stricken states.

KENTUCKY APPEARED to be the worst hit, with 77 known dead and hundreds injured after tornadoes skipped across a dozen counties in the center of the state Wednesday, knocking out telephone service and downing power lines.

Five persons were killed and more than 200 injured in Louisville, where twisters ripped up large sections of neighborhoods.

Alabama reported 69 dead, Indiana 63, Tennessee 54, Ohio 41, Georgia 15, Ontario, Canada, 8, North Carolina 4, Michigan 3, Illinois 2, and West Virginia 1.

THE GOVERNORS of Alabama, Ohio and Kentucky asked federal officials to declare all or parts of their states disaster areas.

Early Thursday, two tornadoes hit the town of Meadow Bridge, W.Va., about 50 miles southeast of Charleston, killing one person and injuring several others.

At Radford, in southwest Virginia, high winds flipped over three mobile homes and five persons were injured.

THE RAMPAGE cost more lives than any series of tornadoes since March 18, 1925, when a twister cut through three Midwestern states, killing 689. The 1965 Palm Sunday tornadoes in the Midwest killed 271.

Weather forecasters in Kansas City compared Wednesday's tornado outbreak to a "fast-moving shotgun blast."

"There were twice as many people killed (as the result of tornadoes) in eight

See DEATHS on Page 4A

Capsule Look At the Damage

More than 320 persons were killed, hundreds injured and damage ran into the millions as a result of tornadoes that tore out of the South, roared through the Ohio Valley and into Canada.

The Ohio death toll Thursday morning stood at 41 and it was expected to rise as rescue workers sifted through rubble.

A CAPSULE LOOK AT the damage:

In Ohio the winds gouged Cincinnati, Xenia, London and struck in Franklin County before running out of steam. At least 35 were known dead in Xenia, five in the Cincinnati area and one in Wilberforce. London suffered extensive damage and several New Albany homes were badly damaged.

In Indiana, 63 were known dead and officials said dozens of persons were unaccounted for.

SEVENTY-SEVEN KENTUCKIANS were dead and the governor there said Wednesday was one of the darkest day's in the state's history.

Winds demolished a curling club in Windsor, Ontario, Candada, killing eight persons.

Hearsts Disbelieve Daughter's Message

SAN FRANCISCO (AP) — Sixty days of anguish, effort and hope — and a message from Patricia Hearst to her parents: I reject you; you lie; I cast my lot with my abductors; my name is Tania.

Her father, Randolph A. Hearst, newspaper president and editor, had spent $2 million and promised $4 million more in food handouts for the release of his daughter. There had been a promise that she might be released soon.

"I HAVE CHOSEN to stay and fight," the slim, blonde 20-year-old said Wednesday in a taped message to her family, delivered by a radio station that received it from her captors.

Had the Symbionese Liberation Army won the mind of Patty Hearst?

We don't believe it, her parents, her sisters, her fiance said. That isn't the Patricia we know.

IT WAS the seventh communication — a tape recording that her parents said was definitely of Patricia's voice—that shook the Hearst home.

"Dad, you said that you were concerned with my life, and you also said that you were concerned with the life and interests of all oppressed people in this country," the University of California coed said.

"But you are a liar in both areas and as a member of the ruling class, I know for sure that yours and Mom's interests are never the interests of the people."

"I HAVE BEEN given the choice of being released in a safe area, or joining the forces of the Symbionese Liberation Army and fighting for my freedom and the freedom of all oppressed people.

"I have chosen to stay and fight."

Only one day earlier, her parents had begun to turn to hope [illegible] began

See PATRICIA on Page 4A

AEP to Bring Coal into Ohio

"So far from being needless pains, it may bring considerable profit to carry char-coals to Newcastle."
— Thomas Fuller, 1650

By DAVID LORE
Of The Dispatch Staff

The giant American Electric Power Co. (AEP) — with nary a nod of credit to Fuller — is embarking on its own version of "coals-to-Newcastle," a decision with important ramifications for Ohio's coal industry.

In fact, the small community of Newcastle, Ohio, in western Coschocton County within the next few years will probably be using electricity generated from coal hauled some 1,500 miles from mines in Wyoming, Montana, Colorado and Utah.

NEWCASLTE FALLS within the service area of the Ohio Power Co., a subsidiary of AEP, the nation's largest utility.

AEP in its recently published 1973 annual report discloses plans to buy more than 600 million tons of low-sulfur Western coal to fuel its power plants over the remainder of this century.

"We plan to burn it principally in our plants in Indiana and Ohio," the AEP report states.

WHY IS AEP bringing coal 1,500 miles to Newcastle at a time when Ohio

See COAL on Page 8A

COMPLETE INDEX ON PAGE 2A

Winds Blew Xenia Mail To Mt. Gilead

Hints of the disaster that befell Xenia spread over Ohio in strange ways Wednesday.

Residents in several Ohio counties reported scraps of paper and mail fell from the sky bearing indications they came from the Greene County city.

At Mt. Gilead, 90 miles northeast of Xenia, one homeowner reported finding a gift catalogue in his yard addressed to a Xenia resident. And a woman there said she found mail addressed to Xenia homes.

New Ohio Gas Plant Producing

By TOM FENNESSY
Of The Dispatch Staff

Synthetic gas began flowing into pipelines Thursday from the Columbia Gas System's huge reforming plant at Green Springs, Ohio, near Fremont on the Sandusky-Seneca county line.

Initial production from the $44-million plant is 144 million cubic feet of gas a day. The gas will be piped to gas distribution companies serving 4 million customers in seven states, including Columbia Gas of Ohio which serves Franklin and 61 other Ohio counties.

EVENTUALLY, the plant will supply about 250 million cubic feet of gas daily. J. W. Partridge, chairman of of the Columbia Gas System, said the synthetic gas is needed to offset part of the decline in natural gas deliveries from fields in the southwestern United States. But he added that the supply of the synthetic "will do no more than enable Columbia to maintain service to existing customers."

See NEW on Page 4A

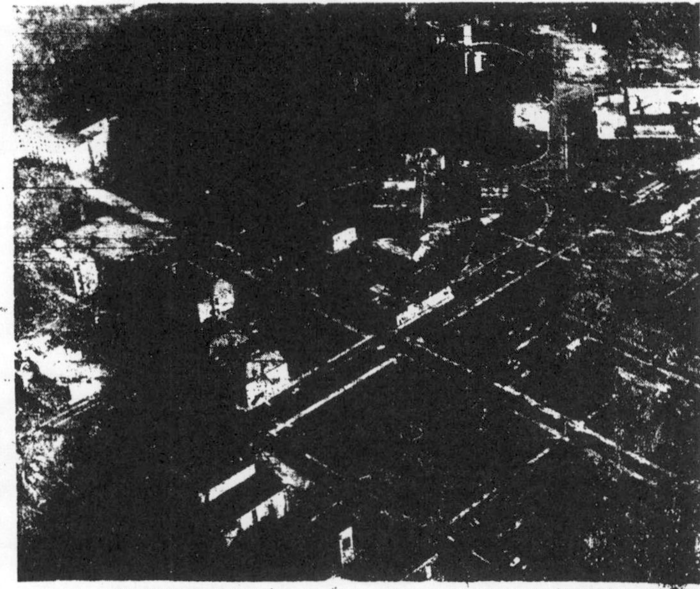

TWISTER'S PATH THROUGH CENTRAL STATE UNIVERSITY CAMPUS MARKED BY ROOFLESS BUILDINGS

The Weather

Today—Rain, high in the low to mid 80s, low in the mid to upper 60s. Chance of rain is 60 per cent today, 40 per cent tonight. Saturday — Cloudy, high around 80. Yesterday's temp. range, 77-68. Details, Page D12.

The Washington Post

Index 112 Pages 4 Sections

Amusements	D 1	Metro	D13
Classified	C14	Obituaries	D19
Comics	D20	Outdoors	C 8
Editorials	A20	Sports	C 1
Fed. Diary	D21	Style	D 1
Financial	C 9	TV-Radio	D 8

97th Year No. 247 © 1974 The Washington Post Co. FRIDAY, AUGUST 9, 1974 Phone (202) 223-6000 Classified 223-6200 Circulation 223-6100 15¢

Nixon Resigns

By Carroll Kilpatrick
Washington Post Staff Writer

Richard Milhous Nixon announced last night he was resigning as the 37th President of the United States.

Vice President Gerald R. Ford of Michigan will take the oath of office at noon today as the new President to fill the remaining 2½ years of Mr. Nixon's term.

After two years of bitter public debate over the Watergate break-in, President Nixon bowed to pressures from the public and leaders of his party to become the first President in American history to resign.

In a televised address from the Oval Office, the President said he had concluded he no longer had "a strong enough political base in Congress" to continue his job.

Declaring that he would have preferred to see the constitutional process of impeachment carried through, he said that he was resigning as of noon today because he "would not have the support of Congress necessary to carry out the duties" of his office.

"I have never been a quitter," Mr. Nixon said. But he said that as President he must put the interests of the nation first.

America needs a full-time President and a full-time Congress, Mr. Nixon said in his final speech as President.

He appealed to the American people to give support and understanding to the new President as he assumes the responsibilities of office.

Mr. Nixon said he was leaving office without bitterness and without placing blame on his critics.

He said he recognized that some of his judgments had been wrong. "I regret deeply any injuries" he may have caused, he said.

However, he said that when he made the mistakes of judgments he did so because he believed at the time they were in the best interests of the nation.

The President said he was gratified by the privilege of serving in the nation's highest office for 5½ years, and he was leaving "with no bitterness to those who opposed me."

He thanked his friends and supporters, ending his 16-minute speech saying he was leaving office "with this one prayer: may God's grace be with you in all the days ahead."

The President's brief speech was delivered in firm tones. He appeared to be in complete control of his emotions. The absence of rancor contrasted sharply with the "farewell" he delivered after being defeated for governor of California in 1962 and almost certainly will help contribute to the healing Mr. Nixon said must now take place.

Mr. Nixon emphasized that world peace had been the overriding concern of his years in office.

He said that when he took the oath, he had made a "sacred commitment" to "consecrate my office and wisdom to the cause of peace among nations.

"I have done my very best in all the days since to be true to that pledge," he said. He said he is confident that the world is a safer place today for the people of all nations.

"This more than anything I hope will be my legacy to you, to my country, as I leave the presidency," the President added.

He observed that he has lived through a turbulent time in American history and recalled the statement of Theodore Roosevelt about "the man in the arena."

Roosevelt had praised the man who strove valiantly to battle in worthy causes and if he fails, "at least fails while daring greatly."

Mr. Nixon placed great emphasis on his successes in foreign affairs. He said his administration had "unlocked the doors" between the United States and Communist China. In that country, he added, millions of people look upon the United States "not as enemies, but as friends."

In the Mideast, he said, the United States must begin to build on the peace in that area. And with the Soviet Union, he said, the administration had begun the process of ending the nuclear arms race. The goal now, he said, is to reduce and finally destroy those arms "so that the threat of nuclear war will no longer hang over the world." The two countries, he added, "must live together in cooperation rather than in confrontation."

Mr. Nixon has served 2,026 days as the 37th President of the United States. He leaves office with 2½ years of his second term remaining to be carried out by the man he nominated to be Vice President last year.

Yesterday morning, the President conferred with his successor. He spent much of the day in his Executive Office Building hideaway working on his speech and attending to last-minute business.

At 7:30 p.m., Mr. Nixon again left the White House for the short walk to the Executive Office Building. The crowd outside the gates waved U.S. flags and sang "America" as he walked slowly up the steps, his head bowed, alone.

At the EOB, Mr. Nixon met for a little over 20 minutes with the leaders of Congress—James O. Eastland (D-Miss.), president pro tem of the Senate; Mike Mansfield (D-Mont.), Senate majority leader; Hugh Scott (R-Pa.), Senate minority leader; Carl Albert (D-Okla.), speaker of the House, and John Rhodes (R-Ariz.), House minority leader.

It was exactly six years ago yesterday that the 55-year-old Californian accepted the Republican nomination for President for the second time and went on to a narrow victory in November over Democrat Hubert H. Humphrey.

"I was ready. I was willing. And events were such that this seemed to be the time the party was willing for me to carry the standard," Nixon said after winning first-ballot nomination in the convention at Miami Beach.

In his acceptance speech on Aug. 8, 1968, the nominee appealed for victory to "make the American dream come true for millions of Americans."

"To the leaders of the Communist world we say, after an era of confrontation, the time has come for an era of negotiation," Nixon said.

The theme was repeated in his first inaugural address on Jan. 20, 1969, and became the basis for the foreign policy of his first administration.

Largely because of his breakthroughs in negotiations with China and the Soviet Union, and partly because of divisions in the Democratic Party, Mr. Nixon won a mammoth election victory in 1972, only to be brought down by scandals that grew out of an excessive zeal to make certain he would win re-election.

Mr. Nixon and his family are expected to fly to their home in San Clemente, Calif. early today. Press secretary Ronald L. Ziegler and Rose Mary Woods, Mr. Nixon's devoted personal secretary for more than two decades, will accompany the Nixons.

Alexander M. Haig Jr., the former Army vice chief of staff who was brought into the White House as staff chief following the resignation of H. R. (Bob) Haldeman on April 30, 1973, has been asked by Mr. Ford to remain in his present position.

It is expected that Haig will continue in the position as staff chief to assure an orderly transfer of responsibilities but not stay indefinitely.

The first firm indication yesterday that the President had reached a decision came when deputy press secretary Garold L. Warren announced at 10:55 a.m. that the President was about to begin a meeting in the Oval Office with the Vice President.

"The President asked the Vice President to come over this morning for a private meeting—and that is all the

See RESIGN, A7, Col. 1

Ford Assumes Presidency Today

By Jules Witcover
Washington Post Staff Writer

Gerald R. Ford Jr., a Grand Rapids, Mich., lawyer who never aspired to national office but had it thrust upon him as a result of two of the greatest political scandals in American history, will become the 38th President of the United States today.

He will be the first American President not elected to national office by the people, having been nominated Vice President by President Nixon last Oct. 12 under provisions of the new 25th Amendment to the Constitution.

The swearing in is to take place either in the Rose Garden, if the weather is good, or in the Oval Office if it is not, sources said last night. In either case, the ceremony will be televised.

President Nixon is not expected to attend the ceremony. Sources said he will already have resigned effective noon and will be on his way with his family to his home in San Clemente.

In the East Room nearly 10 months ago, Mr. Nixon announced his choice of Ford to succeed the resigned Spiro T. Agnew, to the cheering and applauding approval of assembled Republican leaders.

The Agnew scandal, in which the then Vice President resigned before pleading nolo contendre to a charge of federal income tax evasion, put Ford in the line of succession to the presidency. The Watergate scandal, which culminated last night in President Nixon's announcement that he will resign today, has propelled Ford into the White House.

There were reports that the chief justice of the United States, Warren E. Burger, vacationing in Europe, would return to administer the oath of office to Ford.

Sources said the new President is planning to make a brief address to the nation immediately following the swearing in, and to address a joint session of Congress, where he served for 25 years, next Monday or Tuesday.

Ford is expected to ask all members of the Nixon Cabinet to stay on for a time, as well as most White House aides, but associates said yesterday he will move swiftly to enlarge his own staff and integrate it with the holdovers.

According to associates, he will also call for national unity to enhance the prospects of a smooth and orderly transition of power, will praise Mr. Nixon for stepping aside to enable such a transition to take place, and will call on Americans to maintain confidence in their country.

One of the first major tasks he faces is the nomination of a new Vice President under the same 25th Amendment through which he entered the line of succession.

Sources close to Ford said yesterday he is likely to take some time—from several days to a week or more—in making his nomination, which must be confirmed by the House and Senate.

"He's not going to move quickly," one associate said. "He's going to move as quickly as he can, responsibly. He'll get a lot of input from party leaders and friends, and the list will grow before it shrinks. He knows more than most the man he picks may become the next President of the United States."

See FORD, 12, Col. 1

Photo by Harry Naltchayan—The Washington Post

"The first essential is to begin to heal the wounds of this nation . . ."

The Solemnity of Change

Mantle of Power Is Passed Quietly

By Richard Harwood and Haynes Johnson
Washington Post Staff Writers

When the day finally came, the anger and tensions and recriminations that had so enveloped this capital for weeks had been subdued in the solemnity of change. A sense of calm and a tenuous spirit of conciliation began to emerge.

There was no chorus of jubilation in Washington and no cries for vengeance or retribution. There was an absence of turmoil, mobs, violence, massive protests.

The crowds that began gathering at the White House on Tuesday remained quiet, solemn and patient. They were witnesses to history, yes, and someday they would tell their grandchildren about it. But now on this Thursday, Aug. 8, 1974, they seemed more preoccupied by personal feelings of sorrow and sadness.

"Think of it," said a tourist from Wheaton, Ill. "The most beautiful building in the country, right across the street, and the man that lives there, that has worked all his life to get there, has to give it up. . . . It's a sad terrible thing, but he brought it all on himself. But it makes me sad that he has to be humiliated like this."

Another visitor who had driven up from Myrtle Beach, S.C., was philosophical: "Our country will survive. In a way, this is like the Kennedy assassination. It is a sad time for everyone but we'll pull through."

By nightfall, the crowd had swelled to huge proportions, blocking traffic on historic Pennsylvania Avenue, filling up beautiful Lafayette Park with its flower beds, benches and statues.

On Capitol Hill, where the Congress had been engaged in bitter debate for months and engaged, too, in a great constitutional struggle with the executive, there were bipartisan moves to grant immunity for the 37th man ever to serve as President of the United States.

Inside the White House, there were no last-minute theatrics, no public relations gimmicks, no coyness about what was to happen and no rancorous remarks about enemies. Ronald L. Ziegler and Gerald L. Warren, who, as presidential spokesmen, had spent the last months in acrimonious confrontations with reporters, were now emotionally spent. They struggled to keep from crying as they performed their last tasks for the President.

It was an orderly thing, this passing of power. The decision was made

See DAY, A7, Col. 1

A special section on the Nixon presidency—inside today.

An 'Era of Good Feeling'

Congress Expects Harmony With Ford

By Spencer Rich and Richard L. Lyons
Washington Post Staff Writers

From one end of Capitol Hill to the other, members of Congress predicted last night that the presidency of Gerald R. Ford will start with a new "era of good feeling" between Congress and the White House, helping to heal the deep and wrenching blows the nation's government has suffered in the past two years.

The tone was set by the Democratic leaders of the House and the Senate, both of whom have served with Ford on terms of close cooperation during his 25 years in Congress before he became Vice President.

"Jerry Ford is a personal friend," said House Speaker Carl Albert (D-Okla.). "I am sure our relationship will be good."

Senate Majority Leader Mike Mansfield (D-Mont) said, "He's a decent man. He's conservative but you know where he stands. He'd give consideration to congresisonal views. He would get exceptional cooperation."

With little dissent, members of Congress of all shades of opinion gave these views on the likely course of events in Ford's presidency:

- Ford will start with a honeymoon period that will last from a few months to a half year or more, with even his political opponents leaning over backward to help him get a "handle" on the enormously difficult new job he is undertaking. This will fade later but he will start the job with a strong disposition on the part of Democrats and Republicans alike to avoid bitter partisan squabbles.
- The accession of Ford probably will greatly help the GOP in the 1974 elections, by removing Richard Nixon and the Watergate scandal as the immediate central issue of controversy. The GOP may still fare poorly, but a potential disaster has been averted.
- Ford can be expected to consult Congress far more often and far more directly than his predecessor, because Ford is "a creature of the Congress" who has served a quarter of a century and has shown that he respects the legislative process and knows how to get along with members of Congress. "He knows the workings of the Congress, he'll work well with the Congress, and more importantly, he listens and will take political advice from the political sources he respects," said Sen. Edward W. Brooke (R-Mass.).
- The presidency as an instituton won't be weakened by the events cul-

See CONGRESS, A9, Col. 1

The Weather

Today—Partly cloudy, high near 80, low in the 60s. The chance of rain is 20 per cent today and tonight. Sunday—Partly cloudy, high around 80. Yesterday's temperature range, 82-70. Details are on page D2.

The Washington Post

97th Year · No. 248 · SATURDAY, AUGUST 10, 1974 · Phone (202) 223-6000 Classified 223-6200 Circulation 223-6100 · 20c Beyond Washington, Maryland and Virginia · 15c

Ford Becomes 38th President, Promises Openness and Candor

By Jules Witcover
Washington Post Staff Writer

Gerald Rudolph Ford Jr. took the oath of office as 38th President of the United States at noon yesterday and assured a nation torn by the ravages of the Watergate scandal that "our long national nightmare is over."

Mr. Ford, alluding to the fact that he thus became the first American President not elected to national office by the people, asked them "to confirm me as your President with your prayers" and pledged "that I will be the President of all the people."

In a conciliatory address he labeled "just a little straight talk among friends," the new President asked that "as we bind up the internal wounds of Watergate, more painful and more poisonous than those of foreign wars, let us restore the Golden Rule to our political process, and let brotherly love purge our hearts of suspicion and hate."

In asking for the nation's prayers, he requested them as well for the departing President, Richard M. Nixon, and his family, who were flying to their San Clemente, Calif., home aboard the Spirit of '76 as Mr. Ford spoke.

"May our former President, who brought peace to millions, find it for himself," Mr. Ford said, speaking emotionally, his voice cracking at one point. "May God bless and comfort his wonderful wife and daughters whose love and loyalty will forever be a shining legacy to all who bear the lonely burdens of the White House."

The new President was sworn into office in the East Room of the White House at noon, when the resignation of Mr. Nixon, the ultimate political casualty of Watergate, was to take effect. The Chief Justice of the United States, Warren E. Burger, dressed in black judicial robes, administered the oath as Mr. Ford placed his left hand on a Bible held by his wife, Betty.

"I do solemnly swear that I will faithfully execute the office of the President of the United States, and will to the best of my ability, preserve, protect and defend the Constitution of the United States, so help me God."

Then he turned and kissed Mrs. Ford on both cheeks and stood, his arm around her, acknowledging the applause of the audience, which included former Speaker John W. McCormack, Senate Majority Leader Mike Mansfield, and many other senators and congressmen, and one figure prominent in the Watergate scandal, Rose Mary Woods, President Nixon's personal secretary.

After taking the oath, Mr. Ford pledged "an uninterrupted and sincere search for peace" and a policy of "openness and candor" in dealing with the American people.

"I believe that truth is the glue that holds government together, and not only government but civilization itself," he said. "That bond, though strained, is unbroken at home and abroad. In all my public and private acts as your President, I expect to follow my instincts of openness and candor with full confidence that honesty is always the best policy in the end."

Ford said he was making "an unprecedented compact with my countrymen" to engage in "straight talk," especially because he was "aware that you have not elected me as your President by your ballots"—a reference to his selection as Vice President by Mr. Nixon under the 25th

See PRESIDENT, A17, Col. 1

Sad, Emotional Nixon Bids Farewell to Staff

United Press International

"We leave with high hopes."

By Carroll Kilpatrick
Washington Post Staff Writer

Richard Nixon bade a sad emotional farewell to his Cabinet and staff in the East Room of the White House yesterday morning as the final minutes of his presidency ticked away.

"We will see you again," he said as his family, standing beside him, fought to hold back their tears. The former President fought hard, too. He gulped at times, cleared his throat, put on reading glasses he never used in public, and perspired profusely.

He received a standing ovation when he entered the room and another when he and his family departed to board a helicopter to take them to Andrews Air Force Base and his last ride as President aboard the Spirit of '76.

When the presidential craft landed five hours later at El Toro Marine Base near San Clemente, the Nixons were warmly applauded by a crowd of several thousand well wishers. Mr. Nixon spoke briefly, promising to continue to work for peace without saying how. At one point the crowd sang a refrain of "God Bless America."

"We're proud that we have brought this whole world closer to the dream of peace," Mr. Nixon said. "I am going to continue to work for peace."

"We are home again," he concluded before boarding a helicopter for his San Clemente home.

After Mr. Nixon left, some people told why they had come to see him. Ralph Clay of Santa Rosa said he wanted "to thank him for ending the Vietnam war."

Jerome Byrne of Newport Beach said he never supported President Nixon but had come out here today out of respect for the presidency.

Gary Lasley of Los Angeles summed up the feeling of the few anti-Nixon spectators by saying, "He should have made a full confession to the American people instead of blaming the Congress."

For part of his flight to California, Mr. Nixon was still The President. His resignation letter, which he signed before the last ceremonial meetings in the White House, was delivered to Secretary of State Henry A. Kissinger at 11:35 a.m., one hour into the flight to California.

It read: "Dear Mr. Secretary: I hereby resign the Office of President of the United States. Sincerely, Richard Nixon."

Alexander M. Haig Jr., White House staff chief, handed the letter to Kissinger in the Secretary's White House office 25 minutes before Gerald R. Ford took the oath of office as the 38th President of the United States.

The East Room was crowded when the Nixon family entered at 9:32 a.m. Members of the Cabinet and their families, White House staff members and families and old Nixon friends, including Rabbi Baruch Korff, who headed a final citizens' campaign to save the Nixon presidency, applauded loudly and at length.

See NIXON, A20, Col. 5

Ford, Advisers Meet on Inflation

By Peter Milius
Washington Post Staff Writer

President Ford called in his economic advisers two hours after taking the oath of office yesterday and told them he wants to make an immediate and forceful demonstration of his determination to fight inflation.

"He told us he considers this the overall most important problem" the country faces, counselor Kenneth Rush said after the meeting.

"He clearly recognizes the need in the country for a clear statement of policy," said Council of Economic Advisers Chairman Herbert Stein, "a showing of administration leadership."

"What form that showing should take was not decided," Stein said. But "he wants to make such a demonstration."

The advisers, including Federal Reserve Board Chairman Arthur F. Burns, were each asked to submit suggested courses of action through Stein early next week, when they will meet again with the President and possibly make some decisions.

See ECONOMY, A17, Col. 3

General Motors talks of huge price increase. Page A2.

By Frank Johnston—The Washington Post

Chief Justice Warren E. Burger administers presidential oath of office to Gerald R. Ford in the East Room of the White House.

Plain-Spoken Promises and a Level Gaze

By William Greider
Washington Post Staff Writer

Jerry Ford became President without the ruffles and flourishes.

This was a time, he said, for "just a little straight talk among friends." No brassy salute when he walked in, no dramatic drum roll as he became the republic's 38th chief executive.

"My fellow Americans," Gerald R. Ford proclaimed in his dead-earnest manner, "our long national nightmare is over."

The moment of transition, the mystical ceremony of presidential oath-taking, always stirs patriotic emotion when power passes, silently and peacefully, from one national leader to the next. This time, it struck a deeper chord, made more reassuring by Ford's plain-spoken promises.

"In all my public and private acts as President," the man said, "I expect to follow my instincts of openness and candor with full confidence that honesty is always the best policy in the end."

In other times, Gerald Ford's expressions of old-fashioned virtue, honesty and the Golden Rule and a human prayer for help might be brushed aside as political boilerplate. Yesterday, people savored his words and thirsted to believe them. Yesterday, his level gaze and flat Midwestern voice seemed more dramatic than the loftiest rhetoric.

"I have not sought this enormous responsibility," he said, and people knew that was true. "But I will not shirk from it." They believed that, too.

The last bitter drop suddenly vanished from the majestic house on Pennsylvania Avenue when the helicopter went aloft yesterday morning, carrying away the 37th President. The disgraced leader assembled an audience in the East Room one last time before his departure and delivered a maudlin farewell, rambling over the thorns and roses of a whole lifetime.

Still, Richard Nixon left a fragment of poetry behind. "It is only a beginning, always," he said. "The young must know, the old must know it."

"A beginning, always." So it was yesterday in the mansion where Mr. Nixon lived 5½ years as President, shrewd and powerful and, at the end, defenseless. The people who tend to such things scurried around at the appropriate moment and took down the Nixon pictures from the White House corridors. Gerald Ford, framed and in color, went up in his place, a symbolic gesture which confirmed the reality of the event.

An hour or so after Mr. Nixon left, many of the same people came back to the East Room for the second showing. Cabinet officers took their same seats on the left side of the room. The white-suited military ushers guided new

See SCENE, A16, Col. 1

Ford Starts Organizing New Staff

By David S. Broder
Washington Post Staff Writer

President Ford put off the choice of a Vice President until next week and plunged yesterday into the task of recruiting and organizing a White House staff.

Mr. Ford asked all members of former President Nixon's senior staff, including chief of staff Alexander M. Haig Jr., to remain in their jobs for now, but he also clearly signaled that he intends a major changeover as time moves along.

In his first major move, the new President named Jerald F. (Jerry) terHorst, the 52-year-old Washington bureau chief of the Detroit News, as his press secretary, replacing Ronald L. Ziegler, who flew to California with Mr. Nixon.

He also named another former newsman, Robert T. Hartmann, as counselor to the President. Hartmann, head of the Washington bureau of the Los Angles Times from 1954 to 1964, joined Mr. Ford's House staff in 1966 and has been chief of staff of the vice presidential office. He is 57.

TerHorst, at his first briefing, in a crowded, sweltering White House press room, disclosed that the President had named four former colleagues from the House to direct the transition to a new White House operation.

The "transition team," which held its first meeting with Mr. Ford late yesterday, includes:

- John O. Marsh Jr., a former four-term Democratic congressman from Virginia, who was the top Pentagon lobbyist for a year and joined Mr. Ford's vice

See STAFF, A18, Col. 1

President Ford's Address Following the Swearing-in Ceremony

Mr. Chief Justice, my dear friends, my fellow Americans.

The oath I have taken is the same oath that was taken by George Washington and by every President under the Constitution. But I assume the presidency under extraordinary circumstances, never before experienced by Americans. This is an hour of history that troubles our minds and hurts our hearts.

Therefore, I feel it is my first duty to make an unprecedented compact with my countrymen. Not an inaugural speech, not a fireside chat, not a campaign speech. Just a little straight talk among friends. And I intend it to be the first of many.

I am acutely aware that you have not elected me as your President by your ballots. So I ask you to confirm me as your President with your prayers. And I hope that such prayers will also be the first of many.

If you have not chosen me by secret ballot, neither have I gained office by any secret promises. I have not campaigned either for the presidency or the vice presidency. I have not subscribed to any partisan platform, I am indebted to no man and only to one woman—my dear wife—as I begin the most difficult job in the world.

I have not sought this enormous responsibility, but I will not shirk it. Those who nominated and confirmed me as Vice President were my friends and are my friends. They were of both parties, elected by all the people, and acting under the Constitution in their name. It is only fitting then, that I should pledge to them and to you that I will be the President of all the people.

Thomas Jefferson said the people are the only sure reliance for the preservation of our liberty. And down the years Abraham Lincoln renewed this American article of faith, asking: "Is there any better way or equal hope in the world?"

I intend, on Monday next, to request of the Speaker of the House of Representatives and the President Pro Tempore of the Senate the privilege of appearing before Congress to share with my former colleagues and with you, the American people, my views on the priority business of the nation, and to solicit your views and their views. And may I say to the Speaker and the others if I could meet with you right after this, these remarks, I would appreciate it.

Even though this is late in an election year, there is no way we can go forward except together, and no way anybody can win except by serving the people's urgent needs. We cannot stand still or slip backwards. We must go forward, now, together.

To the peoples and the governments of all friendly nations, and I hope that could encompass the whole world, I pledge an uninterrupted and sincere search for peace. America will remain strong and united, but its strength will remain dedicated to the safety and sanity of the enire family of man as well as to our own precious freedom.

I believe that truth is the glue that holds government together, not only our government, but civilization itself. That bond, though strained, is unbroken at home and abroad. In all my public and private acts as your President, I expect to follow my instincts of openness and candor with full confidence that honesty is always the best policy in the end.

My fellow Americans, our long national nightmare is over.

Our Constitution works; our great republic is a government of laws and not of men. Here the people rule. But there is a higher power, by whatever name we honor Him, who ordains not only righteousness but love, not only justice but mercy.

As we bind up the internal wounds of Watergate, more painful and more poisonous than those of foreign wars, let us restore the Golden Rule to our political process, and let brotherly love purge our hearts of suspicion and of hate.

In the beginning I asked you to pray for me. Before closing I again ask your prayers for Richard Nixon and for his family.

May our former President, who brought peace to millions, find it for himself. May God bless and comfort his wonderful wife and daughters whose love and loyalty will forever be a shinning legacy to all who bear the lonely burdens of the White House.

I can only guess at those burdens, although I have witnessed at close hand the tragedies that befell three Presidents and the lesser trials of others.

With all the strength and all the good sense I have gained from life, with all the confidence of my family and friends and dedicated staff impart to me, and with the goodwill of the countless Americans I have encountered in recent visits to 40 states, I now solemnly reaffirm my promise I made to you last December 6: to uphold the Constitution, to do what is right as God gives me to see the right, and to do the very best I can for America.

God helping me, I will not let you down.

Thank you.

1975

After thirty years of war, at times embroiling the French, the Americans, and others, South Vietnam surrendered to the North Vietnamese Communists on April 30, 1975.

In the same year, an American Apollo spacecraft rendezvoused and docked with a Soviet Soyuz. U.S. astronauts and Soviet cosmonauts held a joint news conference from space.

The U.S. merchant ship *Mayaguez* was captured by Cambodian Communists in the Gulf of Siam. U.S. Marines were sent in and recaptured the ship, but thirty-six Americans died in the effort.

The film *One Flew Over the Cuckoo's Nest* became the first movie since 1934 (*It Happened One Night*) to win the four top Academy Awards: Best Picture, Best Actor (Jack Nicholson), Best Actress (Louise Fletcher), and Best Director (Milos Forman).

St. Paul Pioneer Press

Wednesday, April 30, 1975 C☆ Minnesota's First Newspaper Single Copy Price — 15c

S. Vietnam declares surrender to conclude 30 years of warfare

SAIGON — The Saigon government surrendered unconditionally to the viet Cong today, ending 30 years of warfare.

Columns of South Vietnamese troops pulled out of their defensive positions in the city and marched to central points to turn in their weapons.

President Duong Van "Big" Minh spoke to the nation only hours after an armada of U.S. Marine helicopters had completed an emergency evacuation of nearly 900 Americans and thousands of Vietnamese from the besieged capital.

Minh, a retired general and neutralist, was named president Monday in a desperate and unsuccessful attempt to negotiate a peace with the Communist leaders.

In a five-minute radio address, Minh said, "The Republic of Vietnam policy is the policy of peace and reconciliation, aimed at saving the blood of our people. I ask all servicemen to stop firing and stay where you are. I also demand that soldiers of the Provisional Revolutionary Government (Viet Cong) stop firing and stay in place.

"We are here waiting for the Provisional Revolutionary Government, to hand over authority in order to stop useless bloodshed."

Gen. Nguyen Huu Hanh, deputy chief of staff, then went on the air to order all South Vietnamese troops to carry out Minh's orders. "All commanders must be ready to enter into relations with commanders of the Provisional Revolutionary Government to carry out the cease-fire without bloodshed," he said.

The Viet Cong's mission in Paris waited today for the fulfillment of its one remaining demand before accepting the surrender.

Of the last remaining two demands, the dismantling of Saigon war machine and the withdrawal of American ships from South Vietnamese waters, only one remained to be confirmed—the withdrawal of U.S. evacuation ships waiting off the South Vietnamese coast for flights of refugees.

Saigon police and militiamen remained at their posts indicating the Communist-led troops had not yet entered the city.

Some South Vietnamese officers complained that the evacuation of Americans had caused panic in the military, with many top army officers and most of the air force fleeing.

But it had been obvious that the capital would fall. More than a dozen North Vietnamese-Viet Cong divisions were ringing Saigon, which was defended by less than one division of demoralized green troops.

In Washington, White House Deputy Press Secretary John Hushen said when asked for comment on Minh's announcement: "There will be no statement forthcoming from the White House tonight."

One high-ranking official said he got his first word from a reporter.

Associated Press special correspondent Peter Arnett, touring the city, reported nervous soldiers fired occasionally into the air but he saw no dead or wounded.

• • •

Soldiers near the radio station at the northeastern edge of town said Communist-led forces had moved up to the Saigon River bridge and were poised to enter the city.

Minutes after the Americans abandoned the U.S. Embassy, Vietnamese broke inside and looted the fortress-like building, carting off "anything that wasn't nailed down," then burned the building, said United Press International correspondent Alan Dawson, one of those who elected to stay.

As Minh spoke, there was other looting in the downtown area, and soldiers fired over the heads of crowds, creating more panic.

A few more people appeared to brave the around-the-clock curfew minutes after the announcement. But shellfire continued and there was sporadic small arms fire in the heart of the city after the president's brief address.

Hours before the surrender President Ford said in Washington the evacuation of Americans was complete, and he and Secretary of State Henry Kissinger joined in asking the nation to avoid recriminations.

In a statement read by White House Press Secretary Ron Nessen at a nationally broadcast briefing, Ford said removal of the U.S. presence "closes a chapter in the American experience."

The briefing was postponed several times during the day Tuesday until the evacuation was completed at about 4 p.m. CDT (5 a.m. today, Saigon time).

Kissinger briefly sketched the last days before the President ordered the evacuation, saying the U.S. objective was first to "save American lives."

In addition, Kissinger said, "Our purpose was to bring about the most controlled and humane solution possible."

The secretary expressed the hope that last-minute U.S. diplomatic activity "contributed to a political solution . . . but this remains to be seen."

He noted that "Communist demands have been escalating since the military situation has changed in their favor.

"It is clear," he went on, "that what is being aimed

See War, Page 2

Copter crewman helps evacuees up ladder atop Saigon building Tuesday.—AP Wirephoto

30 stranded Marines were last men out

SAIGON (AP) — U.S. Marine helicopters landed on the rooftop helipad of the U.S. Embassy in downtown Saigon this morning and plucked out 30 Marines who had been stranded here after the evacuation of Americans was officially announced as complete.

Shellfire ringed the city as CH46 Seaknights set down on the roof, guided by a red smoke grenade. The Marines raced across the rooftop to climb aboard. They took off again within four minutes, heading out to sea to awaiting U.S. Navy vessels.

In Washington, the Pentagon said the last Marine helicopter left the embassy rooftop at 7:52 a.m. Saigon time (6:52 p.m. CDT) — and that it carried 11 passengers.

North Vietnamese and Viet Cong shells slammed into Tan Son Nhut air base during the night. A big cloud of smoke still was rising at dawn.

To the east, two big fires could be seen in the Long Binh-Bien Hoa area 15 miles northeast of Saigon. One fire was in an ammunition dump. Fiery streamers rose into the air.

The Viet Cong claimed they had captured Bien Hoa, once a big South Vietnamese air base.

As the last Marine helicopter lifted off, it was accompanied by two U.S. gunships flying cover.

Despite a 24-hour curfew, there was moderate traffic in the streets.

Hundreds of Vietnamese waited hopelessly atop some buildings as the last vigil for U.S. helicopters to carry them out of Saigon. In one former U.S. billet near the Caravelle Hotel, 200 Vietnamese sat on the rooftop. The billet had been used as a helicopter pickup point for Americans during the evacuation Tuesday.

Other Vietnamese huddled on the embassy roof.

Looting of buildings de-

See Marines, Page 2

Senate rejects budget demand

WASHINGTON (UPI) — The Senate Tuesday rejected a demand by conservatives to cut deeply into President Ford's budget and reduce the anticipated deficit.

The rebuff to conservatives came as the Senate, acting under 1974 reforms, began debate on the size of the budget for fiscal 1976 which begins July 1.

Led by Sen. James Buckley, R-N.Y., the conservatives offered a budget of $340 billion with a deficit of $34.7 billion. The Senate rejected it 69 to 21.

Ford's budget called for $355.6 billion in spending with an anticipated deficit of $60 billion.

Buckley offered his proposal as a substitute for the budget approved by the Senate budget committee which totals $365 billion and projects a deficit $7.5 billion greater than Ford said he would tolerate.

Final Senate action is not expected before late today.

Also today, the House takes up its budget proposal, including a $73.2 billion deficit.

"I would be amazed if it carried," House Republican leader John Rhodes said Tuesday. He and other Republicans indicated they will vote to send the budget resolution back to the House Budget Committee which drafted it.

During Senate debate, chairman Edmund Muskie, D-Maine, of that body's budget committee urged adoption of the $365 billion version.

Buckley called the proposal a "compromise" because too many programs could not be arbitrarily terminated. But he said adoption of the smaller budget would be "a major step in the direction of fiscal responsibility."

Muskie charged the $340 billion was an "arbitrary figure" which could not be reached without cutting defense spending and social security benefits—two items Buckley said he would not prune.

In his opening speech, Muskie presented the committee's budget and asked, "Could the federal government spend less? Not when the economic stability of the nation is at stake.

"The budget committee's near unanimous judgment is that we cannot spend less and still help millions of unemployed workers and their families weather the worst recession in a generation. We cannot spend less and still meet our commitments in national defense, transportation and other programs."

Sen. Henry Bellmon, Okla., ranking Republican on the committee, backed up Muskie.

The apparent differences between the committee proposal and Ford's are not large, Bellmon said.

See Budget, Page 2

Community corrections program frozen

By Mike Sweeney
Staff Writer

The Governor's Crime Commission Tuesday placed a one-year moratorium on funding new residential community corrections facilities, such as group homes or halfway houses.

Another story on Page 24.

The commission voted 9-6 for the moratorium following presentation of a report which stated such programs have had little or no effect in rehabilitating inmates.

The moratorium is effective immediately and will affect requests for six community facilities, four of which are in rural areas.

Pat McManus, deputy corrections commissioner, said the board's action should have little effect on the department's attempt to move from large security prisons to community-based programs.

"I really would be very surprised if it changed things on the hill (Capitol)," McManus said. He noted the report is critical only of community-based correction residences, not all community corrections programs.

McManus also said the report did not surprise him.

"Even if we had a higher failure rate of people going through halfway houses it would not surprise me," McManus explained. "It (community corrections) is still a babe in the woods and there are no surprises in the report."

The report notes $6 million in federal Law Enforcement Assistance Administration (LEAA) funds have been spent on community corrections in Minnesota since 1969.

McManus said without community corrections facilities, the $6 million would have been spent on larger institutions.

He said community corrections is an experimental idea which is designed to give inmates "a safer way to integrate into the community."

The real issue, McManus continued, is not the success or failure of the programs to rehabilitate, but what would happen to inmates without them.

He said the community residences provide inmates safer custody, away from larger institutions like Stillwater where violence is prevalent and living conditions are at the bare minimum.

McManus called the conclusions of the report "conclusions that are not conclusive" and said it should be eyed as preliminary data.

During discussion of the report, some commission members questioned figures and percentages used and asked if the report gives a true picture of the programs.

The consensus of the commission was to halt funding new programs and study existing facilities to see if they can be improved or should be scrapped.

Weather And Index

It's plain the rain remains a pain

The saying that the "Rain in Spain falls mostly on the plain" doesn't mean a thing, because today — and Thursday — it'll fall all over Minnesota.

The Twin Cities high today and Thursday will be in the mid-50s. Tonight's low will be near 40.

Minnesota highs today and Thursday will be in the mid-40s to mid-50s. Lows tonight will be mostly in the 30s.

Partly cloudy to cloudy skies and the chance of showers or thunderstorms are forecast for most of Wisconsin today. Temperatures will range from low 40s to mid-60s.

Temperatures

1 a.m.	46	9 a.m.	46	5 p.m.	58
2 a.m.	45	10 a.m.	46	6 p.m.	58
3 a.m.	45	11 a.m.	47	7 p.m.	58
4 a.m.	46	Noon	52	8 p.m.	58
5 a.m.	46	1 p.m.	52	9 p.m.	49
6 a.m.	46	2 p.m.	52	10 p.m.	47
7 a.m.	45	3 p.m.	52	11 p.m.	47
8 a.m.	45	4 p.m.	52	Midnight	47

Detailed Report on Page 33

Inside Today

127th Year, No. 2, 2 Sections, 34 Pages.

Telephones

News and General, 222-5011; Want Ads, 222-2844
Metro Circulation, 291-1888

Chicken raiser's giveaway plan lays an egg

PARK RAPIDS (AP) — Chicken raiser Walter Weimerskirchen, caught in the cost-prize squeeze, quit giving away chickens Tuesday and concentrated on force moulting in a gamble for future higher egg prices.

Weimerskirchen has 22,500 hens, and he says he loses 10 cents on every dozen eggs he sells. Weimerskirchen blames "New York meddling in egg prices" for the low return. He says he's disgusted over the "constant yakking about a food shortage."

About 14,500 of the chickens were "spent" — poor producers. Weimerskirchen had planned to sell them to a soup manufacturer. But when he found he would get only about 13 cents a bird, he refused to sell.

"I'm too stubborn an old German," he says, "and I decided I'd give the chickens away before I'd let them go for three cents a pound."

"I thought about just turning them loose in the woods," he said. "But I don't like to destroy food."

Last Friday he began the give-away program which ended at noon Tuesday. He offered two chickens to anyone who wanted them. Two hundred were given away, mostly to older people and others on fixed income. Some people telephoned but didn't come out for chickens, after they found they would have to clean the birds.

"At two or three cents a pound, it doesn't pay to hire the help to load the birds for sale," Weimerskirchen's wife said. "The chickens have to be caught, and it takes a lot of time."

"Maybe the lesson out of this whole thing is to get the hell out of the food business," said Weimerskirchen, 62.

The force-moulting process consists of knocking the poor producers completely out of production by taking away their food, keeping them in dark quarters and giving them very little water for several days. The chickens lose their feathers, and their ability to lay any eggs. By the time they regrow new feathers, they have built up their reserve. In effect, the two-month program recycles the hens to give good egg quality once again. Normally they should be in laying production then for 40 weeks or so.

Mrs. Weimerskirchen and her husband operate a resort, and keep their chickens on a hill nearby. Her husband said they made a profit on the poultry operations last year but the low prices for chickens and eggs, and the high price of feed and other items, are causing a crisis this year.

Weimerskirchen is gambling that egg prices will be better, and he'll be able to sell a lot of eggs to resort patrons later this summer. He reasons that the force-moulting process will have his chickens producing abundantly by that time.

Weimerskirchen doesn't like the talk from politicians and others about a world food shortage.

"What the hell is going on?" he asks. "There's a million pounds of chicken in this area that we can't give away. How can people talk about a food shortage when farmers in the Red River Valley are dumping potatoes because they can't sell them?"

"If any do-gooder comes to me complaining about a food shortage, I'd like to hit him in the mouth," said Weimerskirchen.

1976

It was a Star Spangled year.

The United States celebrated its bicentennial with parades, fireworks, an outpouring of patriotism topped by a fleet of tall ships from thirty-one countries sailing up the Hudson River.

Jimmy Carter, former governor of Georgia, won the presidential election, with Walter Mondale as his running mate.

Today, a special Bicentennial edition

The Philadelphia Inquirer

Historic Philadelphia's Oldest Daily—The Bicentennial Newspaper

Vol. 295, No. 4 ⊙⊙ ©, 1976, The Philadelphia Inquirer Sunday, July 4, 1976 35 CENTS

America's Bicentennial Begins

Israelis liberate hostages

Raiders strike at Uganda airport

Associated Press

TEL AVIV, Israel — Airborne Israeli commandos raided the airport at Entebbe, Uganda, early today and freed all 106 hostages held by the pro-Palestinian hijackers of an Air France jetliner, an Israeli army spokesman said.

An Air France spokesman in Nairobi, Kenya, where the three Israeli military planes stopped over on their way back to Israel, said the commando unit "apparently has eliminated" the hijackers.

He said surgical operations were performed on some wounded persons on the runway of the Nairobi airport. It was not immediately clear how many casualties there were.

The raid took place about 12 hours before the deadline for Israel and four other nations to meet the hijackers' demands of freedom for 53 militants jailed in those nations.

According to the Air France spokesman in Nairobi, fighting was reported around an old terminal building at Entebbe where the hostages were being held captive.

He reported that the Israeli planes flew directly to Uganda from Israel — 2,500 miles — and landed in Nairobi on their return yesterday afternoon.

"Kenyan soldiers surrounded the Israeli planes and prevented our personnel from going near it," the Air France spokesman said, "but one of the Israelis said, 'The operation at Entebbe is over.' From that we gather that the Palestinians have been eliminated."

He reported that the Israeli raiders he saw at Nairobi were wearing civilian clothes.

An Air France plane that had been prepared to take the hostages out of the country was still standing by in Nairobi.

"Tonight Israel defense forces extracted and freed the hostages, including the Air France crew from the airport at Entebbe," an Israeli army communique issued in Tel Aviv said. A military command spokesman told reporters, "As far as we know they were all freed. We do not know if they are all OK."

Most of the hostages, held for a week, were Israelis or Jews of other nationalities. the hijackers had freed 148 other passengers Wednesday and Thursday.

The military command did not say whether the commandos encountered resistance from Ugandan soldiers at the airport.

The French jetliner was commandeered by four hijackers over Greece last Sunday during a flight from Tel Aviv to Paris. After a refueling stop in Benghazi, Libya, the pilot was forced to fly to Uganda, where the hijackers reportedly were joined by three or four others.

Israel said Thursday that it was willing to negotiate with the hijackers. Forty of the prisoners the hijackers wanted released were being held in Israeli jails.

After that, there were meetings of a ministerial group headed by Prime Minister Yitzhak Rabin, and Israel kept secret the efforts it was making.

Philadelphia Inquirer / J. G. DOMKE

Deborah De Medio, holding a toy gun and wearing a sash proclaiming herself a 'Minute Woman,' awaits parade of wagons

Huge throng greets wagons

By Richard L. Papiernik, Tom Masland and Marc Schogol
Inquirer Staff Writers

The Bicentennial wagon trains rolled into Valley Forge yesterday afternoon, and the crowd of 30,000 on hand to greet them swelled to an estimated half-million by the time the day's activities ended with a fireworks display at midnight.

The crowd at first created, then fought its way through a massive traffic jam that built and waned, then built again throughout the day, finally snarling all access roads and causing state police to close off all entrances to the park.

At the time park entrances were closed, police said the crowd numbered "between 400,000 and 500,000 people."

Sitting on chairs set out for the occasion, or sprawling on the grassy hillsides of the natural amphitheater in the park where the official reception stand was placed, the onlookers cheered as the first of the approximately 200 wagons rolled into view shortly after 2 p.m.

And they continued to cheer for hours, especially for home state contingents, as the procession rolled by.

Not even the overturning of one wagon just as it was about to pass the reviewing stand, and a brief but intense altercation on the park's perimeter about whether an "independent" wagon train could enter, marred the day.

The two occupants of the overturned wagon were not injured, and the independents — seven wagons and a buggy from Texas not associated with any "official" train — were finally allowed to take their place in the line of march.

Those in the crowd—some of whom, after getting caught in bumper-to-bumper traffic on the way to Valley Forge, had parked their cars where they could and walked to get there—seemed to be greatly enjoying themselves.

Phil Keisling, a college student from Portland, Ore., who has been

(See WAGONS on 6-A)

Crowds expected at Mall

By John F. Clancy and Howard S. Shapiro
Inquirer Staff Writers

The nation's 200th birthday celebration began in earnest here yesterday as thousands of people greeted wagon trains in Valley Forge, viewed a mammoth birthday cake in Fairmount Park, watched an air show in Willow Grove and visited historic sites in the Independence Hall area.

President Ford will commence today's celebration, which is expected to draw more than a million people to the city's historic area. After the President's first appearance, a spech at 8:50 a.m. at Valley Forge, he will deliver a Bicentennial address at 10 a.m. at Independence Hall.

Also speaking at Independence Hall, where the Declaration of Independence was signed, will be Gov. Milton J. Shapp and Mayor Frank L. Rizzo. The declaration will be read by opera singer Marian Anderson.

Nasty weather threatened to dampen the big day, however. Showers late yesterday cut short the U.S. Navy's Bicentennial air show, which drew a crowd of 125,000 to Willow Grove Naval Air Station. By 8:15, a heavy rain was pounding in Philadelphia, but officials went ahead with a 9:30 p.m. fireworks display at Penn's Landing, on the Delaware River after the rain subsided an hour later.

The National Weather Service, which earlier yesterday had predicted sunny skies for the day, amended its forecast last night to include a 40 percent chance of rain.

The weather notwithstanding, city officials were making final preparations for a multitude of Bicentennial events today. A five-hour parade is scheduled to begin at 12:30 p.m. at Fourth and Market Streets, move through center city and proceed up

(See FOURTH on 8-A)

Unions reject city's proposal

By Ray Holton
Inquirer Labor Writer

Unions representing the city's 24,600 nonuniformed employes have rejected the Rizzo administration's offer of a two-year contract.

The proposal, which did not call for a pay raise until the second year, was turned down as too low, sources said yesterday.

The offer came late Friday in a message to the executive board of District Councils 33 and 47 of the American Federation of State, County and Municipal Employes (AFSCME) from City Managing Director Hillel Levinson.

The executive board then met late into the night, and "never came to an agreement," said a high union source.

"It wasn't sweet enough in the second year," the source added. "By the second year, without a pay raise now, we would be 17 percent behind in the cost of living and taxes alone."

Earl Stout, president of District Council 33, had said he could recommend that his members accept the offer if there were sizable wage increases and a clause giving cost-of-living raises in the second year. Stout was unavailable for comment yesterday.

Meanwhile, a union work slowdown entered its third day, with sanitation workers refusing to accept overtime on the July 4th weekend.

Officials at the Philadelphia Museum of Art decided late yesterday to keep the museum closed tomorrow, when most of the guards refused to work overtime for the holiday.

Other effects of the job action could not be immediately determined, but there were reports of large piles of garbage outside the

(See UNIONS on 4-A)

•

The work showdown was one factor in the decision to close the Bicentennial antique show. Page 7-A.

Philadelphia Inquirer / RUSSELL F. SALMON

AERIAL GYMNASTICS thrilled crowds at the Navy Bicentennial air show in Willow Grove. Story on Page 6-A.

Ford's text: 'Still so much to be done'

Associated Press

President Ford, saluting the nation's 200th birthday, says he welcomes questioning, examination and criticism of society because "the American adventure is a continuing process."

In a Bicentennial text prepared for delivery today at Independence Hall, Ford said:

"As one milestone is passed, another is sighted.

"As we achieve one goal — a longer life span, a literate population, a leadership in world affairs — we raise our sights.

"As we begin our third century, there is still so much to be done."

The President went on to talk about increasing independence and opportunity for all Americans, insurance of the right to privacy, the creation of a more beautiful and safer America and the promotion of a stable international order.

"Each generation of Americans, indeed of all humanity, must strive to

(See FORD on 4-A)

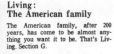

The Bicentennial Inquirer

Washington in Albany

An American Journey

Once it was so common a notice it was a joke: Washington slept here. But progress had crept over the land where Washington slept, and now only determination preserves the presence of the general. This is clear in An American Journey. Section H.

The latest news 200 Years Ago

It is the morning of July 4, 1776. Congress is expected to approve a declaration of independence. But the major story of the morning is the landing of 10,000 redcoats in New York. The Inquirer of today reports the news of 200 Years Ago. Section B.

Business: City's fortunes

The economy of Philadelphia has changed. Gone are the manufacturing jobs. Here now are many more service jobs. The change has not been all for the good. But in Business, there's optimism. Page 7-H.

Review and Opinion: America's future

And so this is the Bicentennial. It is time to recall our history. It is also time to consider the nation's future. In Review and Opinion, scores of Americans do just that. Section F.

Today magazine: Our abiding faith

Americanism might be called a religion. There are shrines. There are creeds. Most of all, there is a deep, abiding faith. A special issue of Today magazine.

Elfreth's Alley

Living: The American family

The American family, after 200 years, has come to be almost anything you want it to be. That's Living. Section G.

Real Estate: The Alley

Famous Elfreth's Alley once was infamous. Grime covered all. But a group of urban pioneers have made it the pride of Philadelphia. A story of Real Estate. Section I.

Arts & Leisure: What to do today

The city is alive today with the Bicentennial. In Arts & Leisure, you'll find maps and listings to help you join the celebration. Section K.

Food: Our tastes

The all-American meal could include a number of courses. But careful research produces this menu: Hamburger, baked potato, corn on the cob and chocolate cake for dessert. That's American Food. Section L.

The weather

Variable cloudiness with a chance of a shower or thundershower. Highs today in the 80s; lows in the 60s. Full weather report, Page 15-E.

Other features

Rocky Mountain News

Denver's Morning Newspaper

Reg. U.S. Pat. Off.

Colorado's First Newspaper—Founded in 1859

METRO EDITION

FORECAST: Possible heavy rain Details, page 9?

15¢

118TH YEAR, NO. 102

Published by Denver Publishing Co. Second class postage paid at Denver, Colorado

DENVER, COLORADO 80201, MONDAY, AUG. 2, 1976

104 PAGES

Scores dead, hundreds hur in Big Thompson flash flood

PAGE

NEWS PHOTO BY BILL PEE

U.S. 34 west of Loveland is no more

This was the scene at the end of U.S. 34 west of Loveland. The road once ran along the left side of the canyon. A corner shows in bottom right.

Flood photos on pages 15, 38 and 65

THE STATES-ITEM

Final Home

Vol. 100—No. 113 Wednesday, October 20, 1976 New Orleans, La. 10 Cents

75 are feared dead in ferry, ship collision

(AP photo by Jack Thornell)

Helicopter circles overturned wreckage of George Prince in river at Luling

More Pictures, Page A-13A.

By WALTER ISAACSON
and LANNY THOMAS

Seventy-five persons may have died today when a 664-foot tanker rammed a fully-loaded Mississippi River ferry between Destrehan and Luling, the St. Charles Parish sheriff said.

Only 11 bodies had been recovered at midday from the ferry George Prince, but Sheriff John St. Amant said he fears at least 35 cars and trucks are at the bottom of the 200-foot-deep river and that as many as 75 persons are trapped either in the cars or inside the sunken ferry.

The ferry was struck by the Norwegian tanker Frosta.

Three of the known dead were identified by St. Amant as:

Anita Poole, about 25, of St. Rose, a student at Nicholls State University.

Edgar J. Holmes, age and address unknown, an employe of the Brown and Root construction firm.

Oscar Green, age, address and occupation unknown.

A fourth victim, also a man, remained unidentified at midday.

AT LEAST 16 survivors were pulled from the swift-running river by a sister ferry boat and taken to the St. Charles General Hospital in Luling.

Many of those feared dead in the collision were workers at the numerous chemical plants and other industries lining the banks of the river in the Luling-Destrehan area.

St. Amant said rescue workers recovered about 50 "hard hat" helmets of the type worn by construction workers and employes of many of the industries in the area.

He said a number of lunch boxes also were recovered in the hours after the 6:30 a.m. collision, which appeared certain to become one of the major tragedies in the history of the river.

The entire crew of the ferry was feared dead.

AFTER THE collision the ferry remained partially afloat for about an hour and all but one corner disappeared in the river. Lines were tied to the vessel and attempts were being made to pull it ashore.

The sheriff said he doesn't believe any more survivors will be found. The passenger section of the ferry is upside down in the deepest part of the river — estimated by the Coast Guard at 200 feet.

A spokesman for the Louisiana State Police said he feared the death toll would grow much higher. "We just don't know how many we have dead," he said.

A sister ferry, the Ollie K. Wilds, rushed to the aid of the George Prince and rescued some of the passengers, taking them to the West Bank ferry landing at Luling. The accident site is about 30 miles upriver from New Orleans.

Jerry Mayo, a member of the Ollie K. Wilds crew, saw the collision.

"We had just docked on the East Bank at about 6:10," Mayo said. "We saw a cargo ship moving up river, approaching the ferry. It blew its horn four or five times.

"The ship hit the ferry broadside. She

Turn to Page A-4, Column 1

(States-Item photo by James W. Guillot)

Collision victims' bodies lie on river bank

Screams of doomed pierced quiet dawn

By WALTER ISAACSON

The terrified screams of the doomed pierced the early morning silence as dawn broke over the Mississippi River near Luling here today.

Charles Chatelain was one of the lucky survivors who did not cry out, but heard the death wails of other ferry travelers, entombed in their automobiles, heading toward their watery graves.

Chatelain, in his pickup truck heading to work aboard the ferry Prince George, was one of the few who survived the river disaster which occurred about 6:30 a.m when the Prince George was struck by a ship.

THE PRINCE GEORGE heading toward the West Bank, slowed up before it should have, Chatelain said, and he looked up. The next thing he saw was the prow of a ship looming over the ferry's deck.

The ship hit the Prince George, drove it upstream and flipped it over immediately, Chatelain said. His pickup and other vehicles were thrown into the icy water and the cars, their windows closed against the biting winds on the river, floated only briefly before they were swept away, headed to the bottom of the river, about 200 feet deep at this point.

Chatelain somehow managed to get out of his truck and heard the screams and shouts of terror from occupants of other vehicles as they went down.

Across the river nearer the East Bank, the other ferry which services the area, the Ollie K. Wilds, was churning toward the stricken vessel after the Ollie K.'s engineer, 43-year-old Joe Landry of Luling, spotted the accident and got the crew heading the Ollie K., which was almost docked on the east bank, rushing, toward the accident.

"I WAS IN THE pilot house on top of the ferry when I saw it happen," Landry said. "I got on the radio and started yelling. I told the captain to get the deckhands to untie the ropes because we were just about to dock. Then we went out to past midriver.

"They (the Prince George) were two-thirds of the way across to the West Bank when it happened," he said. "We saw four to six people stranded on the part of the Prince George that was sticking out of the water and four to six people in the water. Those were the people we were able to bring aboard."

Landry said it took about seven minutes for the Ollie K. to get to the stricken vessel, and it was about 10

Turn to Page A-4, Column 1

16 known survivors

There are 16 known survivors from the ferry George Prince, rammed today in the Mississippi River between Destrehan and Luling. All are hospitalized in St. Charles General Hospital at Luling. Their conditions are unknown.

They were identified as Blair Duhe, Kenneth Bernel, Barry Nayrey, Dan McLendon, Brian Broussard, Leroy Acosta, Nulton Lochney, Charles Chatelain, Richard Respess, Erwin Blue.

Charles Allen, Allen Fisher, David Broussard, Vincent Pardo, Gene Woolverton and George Lingo.

Nameless savior plucked him from river

By WALTER ISAACSON
States-Item staff writer

LULING—Gene Woolverton is not the type who normally drinks at 7 in the morning.

But this morning it was a different matter as he sat in a riverfront barroom belting down straight shots of whisky. He was happy to be there and thankful to a man he doesn't even know for making his early morning binge possible.

Woolverton, 36, of Destrehan, was a passenger on the ferry George Prince when it was rammed by a cargo ship as it crossed the Mississippi River between Destrehan and Luling this morning.

"I HEARD a series of horns and went out to the railing," Woolverton said shortly after being rescued from the George Prince. "I saw a cargo vessel coming. I watched it for about a minute. It appeared at first we had time to make it if we just went straight ahead.

"But then I saw we were going to be hit," Woolverton said. "I grabbed onto a railing. I didn't know what to do. The ship hit us and I was thrown into the river."

Woolverton recounted his ordeal from the time the collision threw him into the river:

"I thought maybe I would swim to the bank. I didn't know how far it was. I started to swim.

"I wasn't thinking. Then I realized how cold it was. I also realized I didn't know how to swim very well.

"I knew I couldn't make it.

"I turned around and saw the railing floating in the water. I decided I had better try to make it back to the ferry. It still hadn't sunk. At that time it looked

Turn to Page A-4, Column 1

1977

President Carter and General Torrijos of Panama signed new treaties regarding the Panama Canal. The Canal Zone would belong to Panama in the year 2000.

A blizzard swept through the Midwest into the East, completely isolating Buffalo, New York.

TV Topics ★ Pause ★ News Magazine ★ Color Comics — **WEEK-END EDITION** — **Storm Special**

WINTRY Extremely cold, windy. Snow flurries today, tonight and Sunday. (COMPLETE REPORT ON PAGE B-10)

BUFFALO EVENING NEWS

Vol. CXCIII—No. 93 | BUFFALO, N. Y., SATURDAY, JANUARY 29, 1977 | 88 Pages | 6 SECTIONS | 30 Cents

Blizzard Paralyzes WNY, Kills 7, Strands Thousands

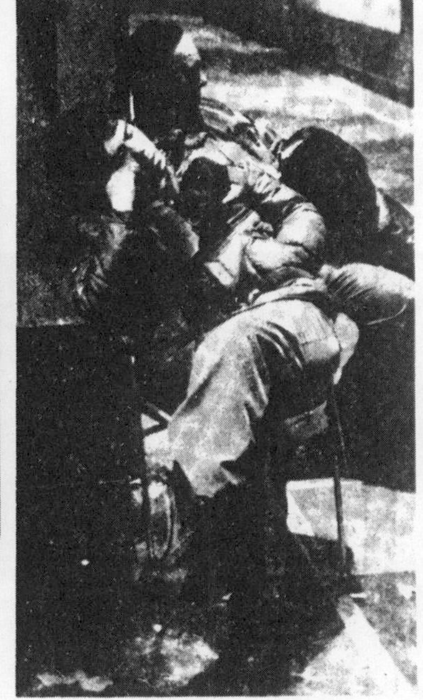

CAUGHT IN CITY HALL — These scenes were typical of what was in store for the thousands of Buffalonians who were stranded downtown Friday by the quick-appearing blizzard which brought zero visibility and 50 mph winds. Above, dozens of civil servants and others stranded in City Hall pass the time in the basement cafeteria late Friday night. Right, two stranded motorists catch 40 winks in a City Hall corridor.

Helicopters, Federal Aid Are Sought

By DAVE STOUT

Winds were easing a bit this morning in what may be the worst storm in Western New York history, a blizzard which killed at least seven persons and disrupted the lives of thousands of others.

The murderous gusts which raked the area hour after hour Friday and early today were subsiding to less-dangerous levels.

Gov. Carey was asked to send in helicopters to search for persons, alive or dead, who may still be in some of the hundreds of vehicles abandoned in the city and suburbs.

"Time is of the essence and we're hopeful that the governor will send in National Guard helicopters from Niagara Falls," said Erie County Sheriff Kenneth J. Braun.

Buffalo has already been promised assistance in the form of two planeloads of snow-removal equipment from the New York Air National Guard. The planes, scheduled to arrive Friday from a Schenectady unit, were now to arrive here around midday.

By 1:30 AM today, the winds had slowed to an average of 30 to 35 mph, compared to the 35-to-45 mph range which raked Buffalo from shortly after noon to 10 PM.

• • •

THE MERCURY had slipped to minus 6 by early morning, breaking by one degree the record low set in 1885 and 1934.

The storm peaked about 6 PM Friday, according to the Buffalo Weather Service, with wind gusts up to 69 mph logged around that hour at Greater Buffalo International Airport.

With the single-digit temperatures, the wind produced a chill factor well under 50 below zero.

Driving horizontal snow before it, the storm roared into Western New York shortly after noon. The temperature, 26 at 11 AM, fell to 3 by 3 PM and kept falling.

Cars, trucks and buses were abandoned all over the area as drivers found themselves in zero-visibility "whiteouts."

• • •

FACTORIES, office buildings, schools and police stations became impromptu hotels for thousands of citizens. Some had never tried to make it to their homes. Others had staggered, red-faced or frostbitten, from their abandoned cars.

For many, perhaps most, Western New Yorkers, transportation was out of the question. Airport flights were canceled, most of the Thruway was closed and other roads were mazes of stalled vehicles.

Forecasters expect winds of 20 to 35 mph to continue through Monday. They should lessen to 15 to 20 mph Tuesday or Wednesday.

• • •

TEMPERATURES are expected to get no higher than 5 today and drop to zero again tonight. Tomorrow, they may climb to 10 or 15. Readings in that range are likely at least until Thursday. Snow flurries are also expected from time to time.

Only about 4½ inches of snow fell over Western New York Friday, but the cold and furious winds made the storm the worst most area residents had ever seen.

The storm not only qualified as a blizzard but, according to the Weather Service, it met the criteria for a "severe blizzard" — winds of 45 mph, great density in falling or blowing snow and temperatures of 10 or under.

Mayor Makowski asked that Buffalo be declared a "major disaster" area. Gov. Carey declared an emergency and asked for federal aid for Western New York.

• • •

THE MAYOR was stranded at City Hall with several hundred persons. County Executive Regan spent the night in the Rath County Office Bldg.

A number of extraordinary steps were taken to combat the storm.

Police used snowmobiles to

(Worst-Ever Blizzard, continued on Page A-5, Col. 2.)

Storm Index

Helping Hands Reach Out to the Stranded As Doors, Hearts Open to Victims of Storm

By RAY HILL and MODESTO ARGENIO

Western New Yorkers, pummeled by the worst blizzard in living memory, opened their hearts and doors Friday night to feed the hungry and shelter the near-frozen.

They came by the thousands, a bedraggled, numbed and nameless cadre — all orphans of the storm.

They slept on the floors of police stations, firehalls, churches, stores, armories and private homes.

And in simple acts of heroism and kindness they wrote a new chapter on human decency to a winter of grim statistics.

News special

It was a night of pipin' hot coffee, hearty sandwiches, of soup thinned by water to feed hungry multitudes.

• • •

FOR THOSE who took shelter, it was also a night to give thanks.

Over soup, sandwiches and dry crackers in an Evans church, the Rev. Raymond L. Morris Jr. reminded 50 storm refugees that they should "remember that it was the Lord who brought us together."

In Sardinia, Father Hubert Reimann, pastor of St. Jude's, cleaned out the rectory cupboards to feed about 30 people who had found a port in the storm in the little church hall.

"We'll take care of each other," he said, "and we'll get through."

Twenty woman manned the kitchen at the Salvation Army on Main St., and with the help of police and city street crews, delivered sandwiches to nearly 700 people, including 250 at Police Headquarters.

• • •

AND WHEN The Buffalo Evening News called to find out what the "Sally Ann" was doing, Capt. Geoffrey Banfield asked, "Can we send down some food for you"

And The News, like the rest of the community, opened its doors to pluck stranded motorists and bus passengers from the driving, 60mph blizzard that lashed the waterfront.

Nearly 200 were served coffee and soup.

"When we stumbled into The News building," said Mrs. Robert Sullivan of West Seneca, "our paper wouldn't throw us out."

In addition to the 200 or so waifs, some 500 News employes remained on the job throughout the night, many working to chronicle the storm.

• • •

NEWS NURSE June Soucise worked throughout the evening treating frostbite and tending three diabetics and arranged with Buffalo police to rush insulin to them if necessary.

Friendly, too, were the people at Tops Markets. They stayed open all night and sheltered stranded travelers.

Just as there were countless acts of corporate kindness, it was also the "Night of the Individual."

Take, for example, Mrs. Ruth Rusiniak, of 25 Center Ave., Cheektowaga. She saw the storm coming and went to her kitchen and whipped up enough soup, goulash and sandwiches to feed 120 persons who found shelter at the Bellevue Volunteer Fire Company.

Depew firemen took in 150 orphans of the storm and if that wasn't enough, they shared their dry clothing with them.

Members of the East Aurora Fire Company passed the hat and raised enough money to feed 50 people comfortably.

• • •

AND LONG after this storm is a memory, the people in Evans will remember Ruth Crawford, Judy Strade and Ken Dorner—all Red Cross nurses—who set up a first-aid station at First Congregational United Church of Christ and treated 10 people who were sick. Two of them were on their way home from the hospital.

On Grand Island, Erie County sheriff's deputies braved wind and driving snow to shuttle snowmobiles over the bridges to find insulin for those who were ill.

At the Connecticut St. Armory, the guardsmen who had been mobilized by the governor to help the city dig itself out, dug deeply into their own pockets to feed 100 persons who came in from the storm.

During the long night, the Red Cross popped up everywhere.

In Genesee County, volunteers looked after 170 persons at the Genesee County Community College and scores more at the Batavia Armory.

• • •

AND THEY came through with blankets and pillows for 300 who slept in Main Place Mall.

It was a night of big numbers . . . and hefty efforts.

There were 1600 housed at Bell Aerospace in Wheatfield, 1800 at Ford's Woodlawn Plant and 400 more at the Aud.

The Sabres organization saw to it that those in the Aud were given plenty of soup and hot coffee.

And there was also a welcome wee drop of whisky for those suffering from exposure.

City Hall sprung for soup and coffee. And the Post Office sent out trucks and found 400 who needed help.

Good people surfaced all night like cream in a bottle.

What, for example, can be said about the owners of four-wheel-drive cars who turned up at Buffalo precinct houses and chauffeured the police? One chased some burglary suspects in the Kensington-Bailey area.

• • •

THEN THERE were the 35 snowmobile owners who loaned their vehicles to the Sheriff's Department. One of them was used in Akron to rescue an elderly couple whose windows had been blown out of their home.

Sealtest rushed milk to six kids stranded at the Cold Spring Precinct and McDonald's saw to it that they had a Big Mac.

Heroic efforts? Precinct 16 police fed and housed 30 persons, gave oxygen to one and braved the elements to rush two expectant mothers to their homes.

School Supt. Eugene Reville threw open the doors of

(WNY Opens Doors, Continued on Page A-2, Column 1.)

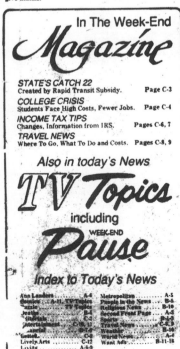

Braving Inferno, Winter's Fury, Firemen Save a Neighborhood

By DICK HAYNES

All off-duty Buffalo Firemen were mobilized and Civil Defense auxiliaries called up Friday evening as a runaway fire on Whitney Pl. threatened a whole West Side neighborhood.

Fire engine after fire engine became bogged down in snow or blocked behind abandoned cars and trucks on narrow streets.

The fire destroyed or damaged five houses on Whitney and three on Virginia St.

Firefighter John Niestopski, 47, of 9 Charlton Rd., Lancaster, suffered a leg injury and was reported in good condition in General Hospital.

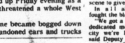

Picture on Picture Page

The first alarm was sounded at 7:53 PM, and 15 minutes later there was only one fire engine on the scene out of five dispatched. The others were stuck or blocked.

A division chief ordered the men to leave the apparatus and walk to the fire.

As the fire spread, firemen evacuated residents of a whole city block.

The second alarm was sounded at 8:18 PM and a third at 8:27 PM. The fire wasn't declared under control until 12:37 AM Saturday — 4½ hours after it began. But firemen were on the scene all night.

• • •

AFTER ALL firemen and auxiliaries had been ordered to report to the nearest firehouse, National Guard four-wheel drive vehicles were commandeered to ferry the men to the fire.

The Fire Department radio crackled with anxious messages:

"B-54, we've got four four-wheel-drive vehicles coming in from the armory. B-54, is that a whole city block gone there?"

"No, it's six 2½-stories and the back of another on another street, and it's still out of control," was an early [illegible].

There were a [illegible] messages like this:

"Roger, Engine 35, you're out of service with 30 cars and buses in front of you."

"Roger, Engine [illegible], you're out of service with 12 cars in front of you."

"B-56, get a four-wheel-drive out to Engine 32. We have 20 men we'll transport to the fire scene to give you manpower."

In all about 100 firemen fought the blaze with 25 lines.

"We got a rough fire. We got dedicated men. And we got a city we're lucky we saved," said Deputy Fire Commissioner Anthony Constantino.

• • •

COLD AIR held the smoke close to the ground. Walking on Whitney Pl. was like walking into a cloud, impossible to see anything and hard to keep equilibrium.

Knots of frightened and curious neighbors huddled on Virginia St., watching frosted firemen slosh through knee-deep ice water in the street.

Virginia St. looked like a hockey rink, tangled hose lines beneath the ice like a madman's version of red and blue lines.

Some firemen grumbled about the fire commissioner not mobilizing the department until 8:30 PM, after the near-disaster had struck. "He should have done it at noon," said one. "Then we would have had the men we needed right away."

Commissioner Constantino, unshaven and tired, set up a command station in the Spanish-American Alliance Club, 254 Virginia St.

Club members let firemen in and gave them coffee.

Commissioner Constantino embraced Ed Gonzalez, a club director. "We owe you a lot," he said.

"No," Mr. Gonzales replied. "We owe you, man. You saved our neighborhood."

• • •

RED CROSS Disaster Officer Anthony Corter said some of the evacuated families were being put up for the night in the basement of Holy Cross Church, Maryland and Seventh Sts., along with about 40 persons stranded by the storm.

Full names and addresses of the fire evacuees at the church were not available, but they included one family named Cruz with four children, another named Serono with six children, and a single woman.

A woman and one of the children suffered from frostbite, Mr. Corter said. All were given soup and mess gear.

The Fire Department said it hadn't determined the cause of the fire or a damage estimate.

Mr. Corter said that from talking with Spanish-speaking victims, he learned that the fire had started in the Serono flat at 162 Whitney

In The Week-End Magazine

Also in today's News **TV Topics** including WEEK-END **Pause**

Index to Today's News

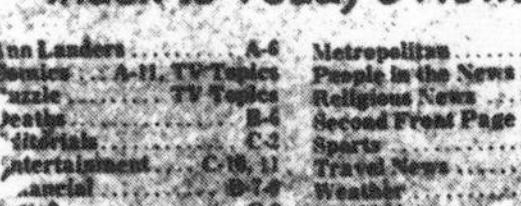

THE CINCINNATI ENQUIRER

A Combined Communications Newspaper

FINAL EDITION — SUNDAY, MAY 29, 1977 — PRICE 50¢

Sunday

Your Day

Partly cloudy today, high in the mid-80s, low in the mid-50s. Chance of rain 20% through Monday. The air pollution count that rose to the alert level of 219 Saturday is expected to be high again today. Details, weather map Page A-5. Art work can be seen at the grand opening of Lukeke Gallery, 11320 Grooms Road, from 12–5 p.m. No admission charge.

Smile

President Carter is determined to reduce American forces in South Korea, beginning with all officers who object to that policy.

Metro

Shock probation for convicts is examined on Page B-1.

High school valedictorians speak out on their achievements and challenges in a series beginning today. Page B-2.

Behind-The-News will appear in Tuesday's *Enquirer*.

"Beef" White is a street hustler and the Greater Cincinnatian. Page B-4.

Nation

Nine million Californians face possible mandatory electrical power blackouts this summer because of lack of water for operation of hydro-electric plants. Page A-5.

A once-vetoed bill holding homeowners and home purchasers harmless from Ohio's mechanic's lien law once they pay outstanding obligations is signed by Gov. James A. Rhodes. Page A-6.

Gov. Edmund Brown Jr., has vetoed a bill that would restore California's death penalty, fulfilling a vow he made five months ago. Page A-4.

World

Angolan troops search for rebels who kidnaped several government officials and fled the capital. Page A-10.

North Korean strongman Kim Il-sung still dreams of uniting the Korean peninsula under his Communist banner. But he speaks softly these days, trying to build an image as a man of reason. Page A-10.

At Home

Wooden houses? Remember? Here's a new, $179,000 lakefront home built almost all in wood. Page E-1.

Business

Auto air bag's developer worries lest Washington push it too hard. Page E-7.

In Our Opinion

President Carter's energy crisis may itself have run out of energy. Editorial, Page G-2.

The Enquirer urges approval of the Cincinnati school levy on June 14. Editorial, Page G-1.

Associate Editor Thomas Gephardt wonders if the Republican Party will ever be able to attract black voters. Page G-3.

Index

Eleven Sections
137TH YEAR. No. 50

120 Feared Dead, Scores Hurt As Beverly Hills Club Blazes

By NEENA PELEGRENNI
Enquirer Reporter

At least 120 persons were reported killed in a fire which ravaged and was still burning but under control two hours after it began in the Beverly Hills Supper Club Saturday night.

By 11:30 p.m., a physician, Dr. Mark Schwegman, said he counted 120 dead. At the same time reporters were able to count the bodies of at least 100 victims. Authorities wre covering the faces of the dead with sheets, clothing and any anything availabie.

A fireman said about 200 people were trapped in the Caberet Room of the Supper Club, and he feared most to be dead.

THE NIGHT club, on Alexandria Pike in Southgate, Ky., was described as an "inferno" and flames were reported at least 100 feet high from the intense blaze.

Bodies littered the hillside around the club. Others were reported jammed against a door leading outside.

Police were combing the bodies, many dressed in their best evening attire, for signs of life and looking in wallets for identification. A squad of six Catholic priests, on their hands and knees using flashlights, went from victim to victim administering the Last Rites.

PHYSICIANS ON the scene said many of those dead died of smoke inhalation. The morbid task of carrying out the bodies of the dead had to be halted shortly before 11:45 p.m. when fire engulfed the north portion of the supper club.

"It is the worst scene I have ever seen," said Wilder volunteer fireman Pat Tuemler, who pulled three bodies from the ruined supper club. "It is something you never want to see with your own eyes. People are charred all over in there."

SOME PATRONS told a grisly tale, reminiscent of Boston's Coconut Grove tragedy, of panic and persons being trampled as they fled the club.

Covington police reported as many as 150 patrons may have been trapped inside the burning building on Alexandria Pike in Southgate.

The fire broke out in the Zebra Room in the south end of the complex and quickly filled the club with smoke, Southgate Fire Chief Dick Reisenberg said. The Zebra Room had been cleared just moments before.

Deputy State Fire Marshal Tom Wald said the fire started under the floor in the Zebra room. Waitresses attempted to put it out with portable fire extinguishers but could not contain the blaze. Wald also said that a full team of fire and arson investigtors would be at the scene early Sunday morning.

Two hours after the initial blaze began, fire had also broken out at the main entrance of the building and was being fought by aerial fire towers.

BUSBOY WALTER Bailey instructed the 1200-capacity crowd gathered in the Caberet Room to see entertainer John Davidson to leave. Bailey grabbed the microphone from comedians on stage and in a quiet voice instructed everyone to leave. Bailey said it took him a full minute to convince the crowd there actually was a fire.

"I told everybody not to go out front because that's where the fire was, and I pointed to two directions where I could go," Bailey said.

A patron said those in the room were calm until the front exit was opened and the flames were visible. "They panicked and ran for a side exit. At least one woman was trampied," said Henry Freckman, 1305 Old State Raod, Cold Spring.

"THE DOORS suddenly opened and smoke was everywhere," said a patron in the club's Empire Room. "They just told us to run, stay calm, stay down below the smoke and get out as fast as you can.

"Suddenly the whole place was engulfed in flames. It was all black smoke. It all happened so fast. I heard a few small explosions, a few rumblings," said a woman who walked almost one mile to the next restaurant.

Eyewitnesses said the building's roof was engulfed in flames.

Police instructed Northern Kentucky's three major hospitals—St. Luke, Booth and the St. Elizabeth Medical Center—to be on standby to receive injured patrons from the fire scene and hospitals were implementing their emergency disaster plans to care for those injured.

THE FIRE broke out about 9 p.m.

Ambulances were trying to make shuttle runs between the supper club and hospitals, but were slowed by heavy traffic on U.S. 27 (Alexandria Pike).

Fire officials at the scene put out requests for aid from Cincinnati life squads.

—Enquirer (Gerry Wolter) Photo

Victims Of Beverly Hills Inferno

. . . doctors and life squad members look for signs of life and identification papers while blaze roars in background

Fire Toll Heavy Along Gourmet Strip

Most of the once glittering Gourmet Strip of Northern Kentucky night clubs has been charred by fires over the years.

The White Horse Tavern, which once stood at 1501 Dixie Hwy., Park Hills, burned to the ground January 26, 1972. No one was injured seriously in the blaze that routed about 75 persons.

The Lookout House, which once sat on the Dixie Highway near Kyles Ln. in Ft. Wright, is an empty field after an August 14, 1973, fire leveled the building. The club was closed for remodeling at the time of the fire.

BEVERLY HILLS Supper Club burned in a June 21, 1970, fire that caused $700,000 damage. The club was closed for renovation at the time of the fire.

The Town and Country Restaurant, 1622, Dixie Hwy., Park Hills, burned in a April 3, 1961, fire that started in an overloaded or shorted electrical circuit. Three firemen were injured fighting the fire. The restaurant was rebuilt.

The White Horse fire started in defective wiring and caused $300,000 damage. The blaze was so intense that employees who tried to check on the initial extent of it could not get close.

THE FIRE that gutted the Lookout House did $2.5 million damage. Arson investigators who probed the ruins said they found traces of a flammable liquid that spread the fire.

The 1970 Beverly Hills fire began at about 3 a.m. June 21, 1970, after workers had locked the doors about seven hours earlier. Seven firemen suffered minor injuries while fighting the blaze. Investigators never learned the cause of the fire.

The Town and County fire caused about $200,000 damage. Flames shot through the roof of the building as the first firemen arrived. An explosion minutes later knocked down a fireman and Carl Schmidt, then mayor of South Ft. Mitchell. Neither was injured seriously.

A fire at a Boston, Mass., night club, the Cocoanut Grove, November 28, 1942, killed 491 persons. Investigators said a busboy who lighted a match to change a light bulb inadvertantly set an imitation cocoanut tree ablaze. He was not charged. The fire was among the worst night club disasters in the nation.

TODAY Sunny, 90-95
TONIGHT Cloudy, 70-75
TOMORROW Sunny, 90-95
Details, page 2
Vol. 176, No. 203

NEW YORK POST

FRIDAY, JULY 15, 1977 25 CENTS

METRO
TODAY'S RACING

DAILY PAID CIRCULATION FOR JUNE 603,517

24 HOURS OF TERROR

- Several thousand looters and arsonists ran wild in parts of four boroughs during yesterday's blackout. It was the worst outbreak of rioting in the city's history and more than 3400 were arrested. Page 3.

- The blackout and the violence that went with it will cost uncounted millions of dollars. New York's disaster adds up to most expensive man-made one the nation has ever seen. Page 17.

- Inspectors fanned out through the city today in a massive sweep of stores and restaurants to guard against the sale of food spoiled after refrigerators and freezers were knocked out. Page 7.

- The blackout started because lightning struck three times — not in the same place, but close enough to trigger a crisis. It lasted 24 hours because of the enormous technical problems involved in restoring service. Pages 4 and 13.

- Con Edison is under heavy criticism on many levels as both the state and federal government begin investigations of why the second big blackout happened. Page 5.

- It was a time for heroes and well as villains. Some of the greatest benefactors were those involved in the life-and-death drama of the hospital emergency wards. Page 5.

8-page pullout picture section inside

BLACKOUT SPECIAL

1978

"To die in revolutionary suicide is to live forever."

What followed that statement from the Reverend Jim Jones, in Jonestown, Guyana, November 18, 1978, was incomprehensible: a mass murder-suicide of more than nine hundred members of the Peoples Temple.

It began after U.S. Representative Leo Ryan of California, investigating reports of abuse in Jonestown, was shot dead along with three newsmen and a Temple defector at an airstrip near the Temple settlement.

Within hours, Jones was urging his flock to kill themselves before they were killed by others.

Some drank freely from vats of fruit drink laced with cyanide. Medical aides squirted the poison into the mouths of squirming children.

Others were beaten and forcibly injected or gunned down. Jones died of a single gunshot wound by an unknown hand.

When the death throes ended, the bodies of 913 people were piled three deep in the muddy compound.

Stocks up 7.88
Page 65

San Francisco Examiner

114th Year No. 139
Monday, November 20, 1978
20¢

★★★★
Final edition
Complete stocks

JIM JONES IS REPORTED DEAD

Suicide-murders: 383 die

Examiner / Tim Reiterman, © 1978, San Francisco Examiner

Dead lie on Port Kaituma runway: From left, Rep. Leo Ryan, Don Harris, Greg Robinson, Patricia Parks and (rear) Robert Brown

82 children, his wife were among victims

By Jim Willse
Examiner City Editor

GEORGETOWN, Guyana — Peoples Temple leader Jim Jones and 382 of his followers died in a mass suicide-murder at the Jonestown mission, the Guyana government said today.

The bodies of Jones, his wife, and one of their children were tentatively identified today, the Guyana Ministry of Information said.

Former members of the temple were on the site of the 46-year-old pastor's jungle compound to make identifications. They reported finding the bodies of 82 children, 138 men and 163 women.

The causes of death of Jones and his immediate family were not disclosed.

Guyanese officials said seven former members accompanied Guyanese troops and national police to the remote compound. An estimated 600 members of the religious group from San Francisco were reported unaccounted for initially.

Today the State Department however said those numbers were calculated on an outdated census of the mission residents. An estimated 100 persons are now reported either

—See Page 18, Col. 1

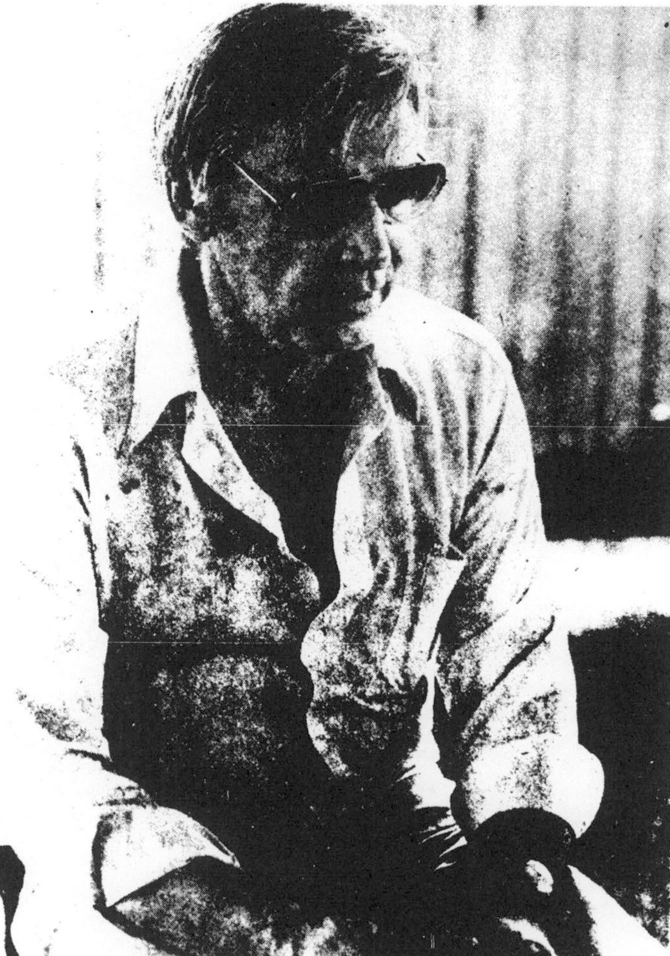

Examiner Greg Robinson, 1978, San Francisco Examiner

BLOOD FROM PREVIOUS ATTACK STAINED RYAN'S CLOTHES
Knife wielder tried to stab congressman at mission, but was disarmed

Last minutes in Jonestown

By Jim Willse
Examiner City Editor

GEORGETOWN, Guyana — "Mother, mother, mother!"

Screaming those words, the Rev. Jim Jones set in motion the wave of death that brought down the walls of Peoples Temple, two lawyers for the church said today.

"He was letting the people know he was about to join his mother," said Charles Garry.

"It was then that the automatic rifle fire started."

Garry, in an interview, and Mark Lane, at a press conference, described the ominous sequence of events that led to the deaths Saturday of temple members.

Lane suggested that not all the deaths may have been mass suicide by the temple's zealous followers.

"Judging by the automatic weapons, I think it may well have been the kind of suicide that occurred at My Lai," he said sarcastically.

Garry and Lane, who accompanied the delegation led by Rep. Leo Ryan to the temple's agricultural mission 150 miles northwest of here, escaped through the jungle when the carnage began.

After spending the night in the rain-soaked brush, they made their way to Port Kaituma six miles away.

The two returned to Georgetown early today, where they gave statements to police investigating the deaths.

The lawyers, who had been ardent supporters of Jones and his works, described the pressure-filled hours that preceded the deaths of Ryan and four other persons, including Examiner photographer Greg Robinson.

They said that despite a positive reaction by Ryan to the rural enclave, Jones and his key aides became increasingly disturbed by the presence of the congressman, journalists and "concerned relatives" of temple members.

"They had paranoia," Garry

—Turn to Page B, Col. 3

Examiner Greg Robinson 1978, San Francisco Examiner

THE REV. JIM JONES OF THE PEOPLES TEMPLE
Late reports from Guyana list him among many dead

1979

The worst fears of living near a nuclear plant: an accident.

It happened at the Three Mile Island plant near Middletown, Pennsylvania, in March 1979.

Evacuation plans were prepared for people living ten to twenty miles downwind of the plant, but it was not necessary to put them into effect.

There were no major casualties, no disaster.

The plant was shut down for years of repairs.

Sunday, November 4, 1979. Outside the U.S. Embassy in Tehran, Iran, mobs shouted denunciations of the United States and demanded, "Give us the Shah!" The Shah of Iran had been admitted to the United States to undergo surgery.

Armed mobs outside the embassy were not new. But on this day, the rioters seized the Americans inside and held them hostage. It was to be more than a year before negotiations attained their release.

At the White House in Washington, D.C., a peace treaty was formally signed by Egyptian President Anwar Sadat and Israeli Prime Minister Menachem Begin.

Erving paces Sixers win over Bulls – Page 1-C

SPORTS FINAL

The Philadelphia Inquirer

Vol. 300, No. 88 © 1979, The Philadelphia Inquirer Thursday, March 29, 1979 15 CENTS

Power Plant Leaks Radiation

Army will list Ft. Dix cuts today

Concedes impact will be devastating

By Aaron Epstein
Inquirer Washington Bureau

WASHINGTON — The Pentagon plans to announce today that it intends to halt the major function at Fort Dix — the basic training of Army recruits.

The decision was made despite a prediction by the Army's own researchers that the impact on the already economically distressed South Jersey communities around the bases would include a "drastic" increase in unemployment and a "significant" drain on the local tax base.

An internal Army study of Fort Dix, obtained yesterday by The Inquirer, says that the economic impact would be so devastating that "economic-recovery assistance, regardless of its forms, will likely be of long-term, probably permanent, duration."

The shutdown of basic training "could cause the elimination of 10,000 jobs in the private sector" and send the 9.9 percent unemployment rate in the vicinity of the base to 11.1 percent.

The study bore the date of February 1979, when the national unemployment average was 5.7 percent.

It has been known since last April that the Army was studying whether, in the interest of efficiency and economy, it should end basic training at Fort Dix or at Fort Jackson, S. C. In recent weeks, it became clear that Dix had lost.

Nevertheless, New Jersey's congressional delegation, which has headed off proposed Fort Dix cutbacks three times in this decade, remains hopeful that it can do so again.

But a staff aide to a leading southerner on the Senate Armed Services Committee said yesterday that the odds favored the Defense Department this time. He said that members of Congress from New Jersey and other northern supporters of Fort Dix have lost seats on congressional committees that control military budgets.

Fort Dix, a 62-year-old military base about 30 miles from Philadelphia and 17 miles from Trenton, is the largest employer in Burlington and Mercer counties, with the exception of the state government at Trenton, according to the Army study.

The study says that the planned elimination or transfer of more than 3,000 military and civilian jobs, plus the loss of 6,000 trainees (per train-

(See DIX on 6-A)

Philadelphia Inquirer / CHUCK ISAACS

Radiation leaked about 4 a.m. at Three Mile Island nuclear plant southeast of Harrisburg; public notification came three hours later

Mishap south of capital

By Thomas Ferrick Jr. and Susan Q. Stranahan
Inquirer Staff Writers

Radiation was released yesterday within 16-mile radius of the Three Mile Island nuclear power plant southeast of Harrisburg, after a valve broke about 4 a.m. in the cooling system of the reactor. The interior of the plant also was contaminated.

Officials at the plant, operated by Metropolitan Edison Co. of Reading, declared a general emergency about 7:45 a.m. at the site. It was the first time that a general emergency, which is one based on radiation levels, had ever been declared at a commercial nuclear reactor, according to the federal Nuclear Regulatory Commission. The leak was in the form of steam carrying radioactive iodine.

"This situation is more complex than the company first led us to believe," said Lt. Gov. William W. Scranton 3d at a news briefing in Harrisburg. "Metropolitan Edison has given you (the news media) and us (the state) conflicting information."

"There has been a release of radioactivity into the environment," Scranton said. "The magnitude of that release is still being determined, but there is no evidence yet that it has resulted in the presence of dangerous levels (of radiation).

"At this point, we believe there is still no danger to public health," he said.

The plant, on an island in the Susquehanna River, was closed shortly after the incident.

Radiation beamed through the four-foot-thick walls housing the reactor throughout most of the day, according to the Nuclear Regulatory Commission.

By last night, however, the reactor had been brought to a "safe condition" as a result of emergency cooling measures, federal officials said. Low levels of radiation still emanated from auxiliary buildings at the plant where radioactive waste water from bottom of the reactor was being stored temporarily, they said.

Radioactive steam was vented during the morning and early afternoon to try to relieve pressure in the reactor building, officials of the Pennsylvania Department of Environmental Resources (DER) said.

Federal officials said that intense heat, caused by the loss of circulating water, had apparently damaged

(See REACTOR on 8-A)

When the remote danger is at hand

By Joel N. Shurkin
Inquirer Science Writer

The radioactive iodine that leaked yesterday from the Three Mile Island nuclear power station near Harrisburg is one of the inevitable products of atomic fission, the nuclear process used to generate electricity.

It is fission that produces not only the heat to drive the turbines, but also potentially hazardous radioactive substances that, when everything goes right, are contained safely in a steel-and-concrete chamber. When something goes wrong, as happened at Three Mile Island, there is the possibility — usually considered remote — that radiation will leak out.

The remote happened yesterday.

According to a state official, the amount of radiation that escaped from Three Mile Island was quite small, about 5 to 15 millirems per hour. In the United States, the average exposure level each year is 100 to 120 millirems from a variety of sources, including the sun.

Scientists bitterly dispute what is a dangerous level of radiation. Some think that there is a threshold, and that any radiation that does not exceed that threshold does no harm. Other scientists believe that there is no such thing as a safe level.

In previous reactor incidents the radiation has always been contained in the plant. The accident at Three Mile Island appears to be the first in which the radiation got out.

As with about half the nuclear plants in the United States, Three Mile Island is a pressured-water reactor. The fuel used for the reaction, pellets of enriched uranium dioxide, is stacked in 12-foot rods in the reactor chamber.

How the system works

PRESSURIZER · STEAM GENERATOR · SECONDARY LOOP · TURBINE GENERATOR · CONDENSER · REACTOR · PRIMARY LOOP · FEEDWATER HEATER · CONDENSATE PUMP · COOLING WATER LOOP · COOLING TOWER

As the uranium gives off radiation, particles strike nearby uranium atoms, splitting more particles. One result of the atom splitting, called fission, is a great deal of heat radiation.

Coils of water, pressurized to 2,155 pounds per square inch to prevent boiling, pick up that heat and run it through the primary pipe system. That water, at about 600 degrees Fahrenheit, goes into a steam generator. The steam then goes through a secondary pipe system until it comes to a turbine connected to a generator. The steam turns the turbine at a speed of 1,800 revolutions per minute, generating about 20,000 volts of electricity.

It was the secondary system, carrying the steam, that failed at Three Mile Island.

(Finally, after the generators are

(See RADIATION on 8-A)

Callaghan loses vote; election due

By Ed Blanche
Associated Press

LONDON — The minority Labor government of Prime Minister James Callaghan was toppled last night by a single vote in the House of Commons, forcing national elections that could bring to Britain its first woman chief of government.

The vote was 311-310 on a censure motion, brought by Conservative Party leader Margaret Thatcher, that amounted to a vote of confidence in the government.

Disgruntled Labor Party members said that Callaghan's government was ousted from power because the members did not drag Sir Alfred Broughton, 72, from his hospital bed, where he is recuperating from a heart attack suffered a week ago.

Had Broughton been taken to the Commons by ambulance to cast his negative vote, Callaghan's government would have stood. The 311-311 tie would have been broken in Callaghan's favor by Labor Party member George Thomas, the speaker of the House who votes only in the case of a tie.

Callaghan's government in recent months has had difficulty coping with a number of strikes by the country's trade unions, which have protested Labor's attempts to control inflation by limiting wage increases. Callaghan is the first prime minister to

(See BRITAIN on 5-A)

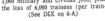

EMMETT KELLY, who made millions laugh as the circus clown, Weary Willie, died yesterday at the age of 80. Obituary, Page 4-D.

Weather & Index

CONSIDERABLE cloudiness, breezy and milder today and tomorrow. Highs today about 60. Lows tonight in the mid- to upper 40s. Highs tomorrow in the upper 60s to low 70s. Full weather report, Page 21-D.

Ira Einhorn charged with murder

By Dick Cooper
Inquirer Staff Writer

Ira Einhorn, a self-styled philosopher and poet, was charged with murder yesterday after the mummified body of a woman was found by police in a steamer trunk in the closet of Einhorn's Powelton Village apartment.

The body is believed to be that of Helen (Holly) Maddux, 31, who lived with Einhorn, 38, for several years before she disappeared in September 1977.

Police said the body was stuffed in the large trunk, wrapped in plastic, surrounded by Styrofoam packing material and covered with a newspaper dated about the time Miss Maddux was reported missing.

The Philadelphia medical examiner's office reported early last night that no positive identification had been made of the body. The cause of death was still under investigation.

Einhorn was in the second-floor rear apartment at 3411 Race St. when police raided it about 9 a.m. yesterday.

Police said Einhorn offered no resistance and seemed "nonchalant" as they searched his apartment and found the trunk containing the body.

After the grisly discovery, Einhorn was taken in handcuffs to the Police Administration Building at Eighth and Race Streets, where he was charged with murder about 2 p.m.

He was ordered held without bail by Municipal Court Judge Alan Silberstein, pending a hearing Wednesday in City Hall.

Police said Miss Maddux's parents hired a private detective to investigate her disappearance. For almost a year and a half, the investigator, J. R. Pearce of Glenside, Montgomery County, pursued leads.

About three months ago he went to Philadelphia homicide detectives and told them what he had found. Three weeks ago, a team of detectives was assigned to the case full-time and, working with Pearce, found new information that led to the raid yesterday morning.

Einhorn, a burly man with a full gray-flecked beard, had been questioned several times in the past about Miss Maddux's disappearance, police said.

He previously had denied knowing anything about her whereabouts and had refused to help investigators look for her, police said.

Yesterday afternoon, technicians from the crime laboratory used power saws to cut up the floorboards of the apartment and look for evidence.

The investigation into Miss Maddux's disappearance began in late 1977 after her parents, Mr. and Mrs.

(See SLAYING on 2-A)

MISSING PERSON

HELEN (HOLLY) MADDUX

AGE: 31 YEARS
DOB: 5/26/47
RACE: WHITE
HEIGHT: 5' 7"
WEIGHT: 112 POUNDS
HAIR: DARK BLONDE
COMPLEXION: FAIR
BUILD: SLENDER
SCARS: CIRCULAR SCAR 3" IN DIAMETER ON RIGHT SIDE OF RIB CAGE.

PP#: 495501
SS#: 454-80-3920

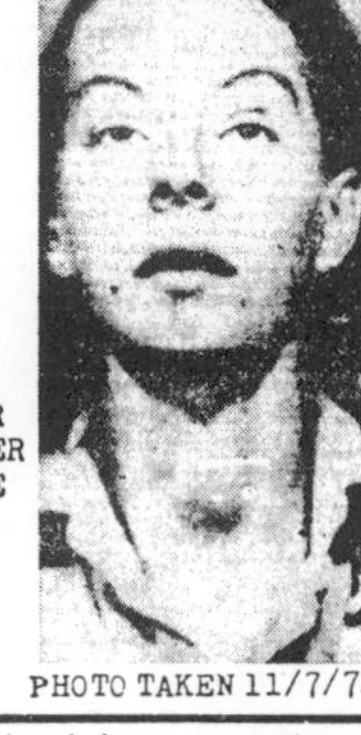

PHOTO TAKEN 11/7/74

Ira Einhorn (left) is charged with slaying Helen Maddux, shown in missing-person poster

1980

Mount St. Helens, a snow-capped 9,677-foot peak some 40 miles from Vancouver in southwest Washington state, had been threatening for months to blow its top.

At 8:32 A.M. on May 18, 1980, it did.

Two quick earthquakes shook the mountain and broke off a blister of ice and rock that had been bulging from its north slope. Suddenly, a wall of rock where the bulge had been blew out with a force of ten million tons of TNT—releasing energy pent up since its last eruption more than a hundred years before.

The eruption blew ash 13 miles in the air, dusted cities and farms in 4 states, and twisted the surrounding 150 square miles into a deathscape.

The flow of ash and rock and mud left fifty-seven people dead or missing.

Seattle Post-Intelligencer

THE VOICE OF THE NORTHWEST SINCE 1863

117TH YEAR, NUMBER 140 | P-I Phone Listings, Page A-3 | S | Monday, May 19, 1980 | COPYRIGHT 1980, SEATTLE POST-INTELLIGENCER, SEATTLE, WASHINGTON | 25 Cents

5 Killed as Volcano Blows — Ash Spreads to Montana

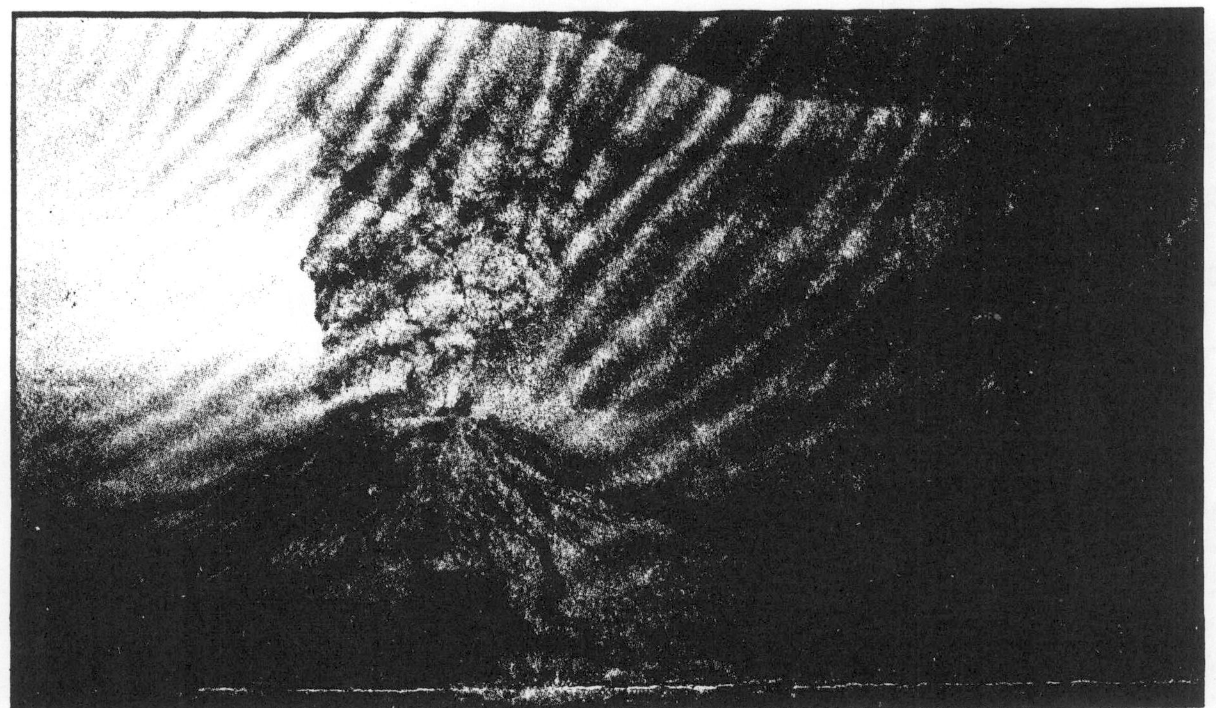

SMOKE AND ASH billow from Mount St. Helens and blow east, spreading through Idaho and into Montana. -P-I PHOTO BY GRANT HALLER

By Michael Sweeney

At least five persons were killed yesterday when a huge explosion tore off the top of Mount St. Helens and tossed up a towering wall of volcanic ash that darkened Eastern Washington, ignited scores of forest fires and set off flash floods that routed hundreds from their homes.

No lava was seen yesterday, but the five victims apparently were burned to death in their cars as they tried to flee a "pyroclastic flow" of red hot gas and ash that raced down the mountainside in the wake of the violent eruption.

Geologists who have been monitoring the volcano since it awoke March 27 after 123 years of dormancy, said yesterday's explosion spawned several pyroclastic flows, which are also known as "glowing clouds."

Military helicopter pilots who flew around the mountain yesterday afternoon said the five bodies were found in overturned cars near a Weyerhaeuser logging camp some 12 miles northwest of the peak.

None of the victims was identified last night, and authorities reported that only two of the bodies had been recovered.

Officials warned that more deaths were possible.

"These people were fried with the heat," said Air Force Reserve Capt. Robert J. Wead. "Trees and all the vegetation were laid out flat, singed, burned, steaming, sizzling — a terrible looking thing."

Wead and U.S. Forest Service spotter planes reported that Spirit Lake was, in effect, gone, and there was concern for the welfare of Harry Truman, the 83-year-old man who has refused to leave his lodge on Spirit Lake, and who has not been heard from.

Earlier in the day, Harry's lake had been reported bubbling and boiling from the heat generated by a "glowing cloud," and Forest Service officials who flew over the area said Harry's lodge appeared to have been buried in the mud.

Geologists reported last night that the explosion ripped more than 500 feet off the top of the 9,677-foot peak, which now reportedly measures a mere 9,100 feet.

"The devastation on the mountainside is incredible," said Air Force Reserve Lt. D. E. Schroeder. "Trees are knocked down, and animals are standing around in shock, covered with ash."

A State Patrol trooper who flew over the area said he saw dead elk "everywhere," and observed other animals walking around as though dazed.

The trooper also reported by radio that huge fir trees near Spirit Lake had been levelled by the force of a mudflow which reportedly covered sections of State Route 504 — the only highway to Spirit Lake — to a depth of 40 feet.

Twenty miles to the northeast, ash was reported three inches deep on the ground in the tiny logging town of Randle.

Across the Cascade Mountains in Yakima and Ellensburg, where falling

Back Page, Column 1

Blinding Ash Halts Traffic Across the State

By Lettie Gavin

At noon yesterday in Ephrata, it was so dark you couldn't see across the street. In Yakima, there was total darkness. In Ellensburg, the visibility was zero.

Mount St. Helens, erupting in its most violent blast yet, was spewing out tons of volcanic ash which blotted out the sun for hundreds of miles, closed highways and airports in Eastern Washington and drifted across Idaho and Montana, authorities said.

Eastern Washington took the brunt of the fallout from the eruption. The plume from the heaving volcano, rising like a huge cloud of smoke from a chimney stack, rose to more than 60,000 feet from the mountaintop and traveled on an east-northeast wind over Yakima, Ellensburg, Wenatchee, Ephrata, Pasco, Walla Walla, Omak and Spokane.

The National Weather Service reported that the plume of ash, as seen on satellite photos, was cone-shaped, with its southern base along the Washington-Oregon border and its northern leg straight across the state toward Spokane and points east.

Weather Service officials reported ash spreading as far as Great Falls, Mont., last night. Winds were expected to continue northeasterly for 24 hours, the Weather Service said.

In Wenatchee, the volcanic ash began to fall about 1 p.m. "It came right over the hill and was moving in pretty fast," said a spokesman for the sheriff's department. Residents were advised to remain at home, with windows closed, because of the poor visibility.

All county roads were closed in the Ellensburg area, 100 miles northeast of the mountain, about 2 p.m., and several cars were reported sliding into ditches because of the heavy dust and ash on the road.

Jan Tweedie, spokesman for the Kittitas County sheriff's department, said most of the department was being mobilized "until we catch up with this thing." She said the fallout was a half-inch deep in places, and that officers were using air filtration or surgical masks as they went about their duties.

"Every motel in the county is full," she said. Emergency housing was being arranged in Ellensburg and Cle Elum for stranded motorists.

"People can't go in either direction," said an Ellensburg motel manager late yesterday afternoon. "People are calling all over, looking for rooms and we're all full. It's still very dark here and there's all kinds of ash blowing around. It looks like gray snow."

All highways in and out of Yakima were closed. Interstate 90 was closed from Cle Elum, northwest of Ellensburg. The Blewett Pass highway linking Ellensburg and Wenatchee also was closed.

Yakima reported total darkness and very heavy ash fall, with up to a half-inch on the ground, about noon. "We are asking people to use common sense and stay off the roads, said Sgt. Larry Gamache of the sheriff's office.

He said there were reports of "zero visibility from all over the valley" and that traffic was "at a complete standstill. They're just not moving."

A Yakima motel operator reported that "the sky is black" and said people who had checked out earlier were returning because "they can't drive and they're covered with ashes."

Another Yakima innkeeper said there were "a lot of people stranded"

Page A-4, Column 1

Darkness at Noon as Mountain Goes Mad

By Laura Parker and Bill Prochnau
P-I Staff

EAGLES CLIFF, Skamania County — Suddenly, the sun was gone, the blue sky disappearing behind a riptide of boiling gray clouds.

Heat lightning danced in jagged bolts overhead. Trees swayed and the ground shook.

The daylight turned to darkness so quickly, Jess Baker of Battle Ground said, "The birds just went to sleep."

"God, it was quiet out there," said Bob Harju of Vancouver, Clark County.

Bob Brotmiller looked up at the boiling gray clouds churning out of Mount St. Helens and thought it looked like an atomic explosion. But there was no sound.

The three tree planters stood on a hillside about six miles across from the summit of Mount St. Helens when the volcano finally blew her lid.

Others were still closer.

Kathy Anderson and John Morris, who were directing a U.S. Forest Service replanting crew on the side of the mountain just four miles below the summit, described an awesome scene of flashing lightning bolts, a boiling cloud of volcanic ash that billowed out of St. Helens' crater so rapidly it turned day into night in a matter of seconds.

"I was afraid of being engulfed by gases and ash, it was spreading so fast," Morris said.

Anderson was in her truck the moment the mountain blew. Suddenly winds whipped around her in the dusk, the lightning-laced clouds moved down over her so quickly, "I figured any minute it was going to hit the top of the rig."

After recovering from the initial surprise, the group looked up at the mountain and, Anderson said, St. Helens' top was gone.

"The whole crater was two miles across and flat," she said.

Another dozen miles away, down in the little town of Cougar, Linda Elmire ran out of the country store her parents operate and looked up toward the mountain all of Cougar has been watching for almost two months.

"It was like one of those Biblical

Back Page, Column 1

15 Dead as Miami Rioting Rages On

MIAMI (UPI) — More than 1,100 National Guardsmen and hundreds of police could not control rioting, burning and looting for a second straight night yesterday in Miami's predominantly black "Liberty City" area. Police said the death toll in the first domestic riot of the 1980s had reached at least 15.

The rioting — compared by one official to the Watts riot in Los Angeles — began Saturday because an all-white jury in Tampa, Fla., acquitted four white former Dade County policemen in the beating death of Arthur McDuffie, a black insurance salesman, in Miami in December.

The Watts riot, in August 1965, left 34 people dead in the black section of the city and property damage was estimated at more than $40 million.

"We've almost given up trying to protect property," said Police Det. Randy Allen last night. "It's totally out of control. It's survival out there."

Flames from hundreds of raging fires cast an eerie glow over the city. Looting continued unchecked as mannequins — black and white — and other store debris littered the streets. Snipers took pot-shots out of nowhere at police and civilians and angry crowds of blacks roamed the streets at will.

Most of the riot victims were white, including two men who were yanked from a car and literally stomped to death. At one point yesterday

Page A-5, Column 1

IN TODAY'S P-I

TODAY'S CHUCKLE

You know why some women wear a girdle? To help them keep a stiff upper lip.

THE WEATHER

PARTIAL CLEARING after morning low clouds. Highs mid 60s; lows upper 40s. Winds northerly 5-15 mph. Chance of rain 20 percent by tonight. Table, Page D-3.

Rain Chances

Partly cloudy with a chance of showers. Highs in the upper 80s. Lows in the 70s. Winds east to southeast 10 to 15 m.p.h. (Details, Page 2A.)

SUNDAY'S TEMPERATURES

8 a.m. 79	2 p.m. 84	8 p.m. 82
10 a.m. 82	4 p.m. 85	10 p.m. 80
Noon 83	6 p.m. 85	Midnight 80

The Miami Herald

Monday, May 19, 1980 · Florida's Complete Newspaper · A Latin American Edition Is Published Daily · 58 Pages

Final Edition
20 cents
70th Year — No. 171

18 Die in City Under Siege; Fire, Looting Toll Is Heavy

By CARL HIAASEN
Herald Staff Writer

Bullets and firebombs ignited a Sunday of deadly racial violence in Dade County that pushed the death toll to 18 and sent a spasm of terror through merchants, motorists and community leaders — black and white.

Most of Sunday's dead were gunshot victims, reflecting a grim trend away from the rock-and-bottle episodes that opened Miami's worst-ever outbreak of racial violence Saturday night.

At least six policemen were injured — none critically — in sporadic shooting that punctuated the night. One was hit by a bullet and two others were injured by flying glass when they were caught in snipers' cross-fire from both sides of NW 135th Street at 30th Avenue.

Officials imposed a curfew from 8 p.m. Sunday to 6 a.m. today, ordered all public schools closed today and brought in more than 1,000 National Guardsmen in an effort to bring order to the county's turbulent streets.

"I don't want to be too optimistic, but I noticed a lull out there," Public Safety Director Bobby Jones said late Sunday night. "I only saw a few people on the street."

Two suspected looters were killed by police, a police lieutenant died of a heart attack, a black motorist was shot to death by police when he allegedly tried to run down officers, and a black teenager was shot fatally in the head by an unknown gunman.

Dozens of fires erupted at intersections, stores and businesses — many of them in areas where firemen could not go because of violence. Fifteen major fires raged out of control late Sunday, and snipers fired rifles at a rescue helicopter photographing the blazes.

"It's absolutely unreal. They're burning down the whole goddamn north end of town," said Miami fire inspector George Bilbery.

At least 270 persons have been injured since violence erupted Saturday night after the acquittals of four white ex-policemen charged in connection with the beating death of black insurance man Arthur McDuffie. In downtown Miami, numerous gunshot victims were admitted to Jackson Memorial Hospital's emergency room.

Andre Dawson, 14, was hit twice by gunfire from a passing truck or van as he walked near his home at 330 NW 84th Ter. late Sunday afternoon.

"Somebody just ran down the street and shot him in the head. Blew my baby's brains out. Oh, no. Why my baby?" sobbed Augustus Dawson, the boy's father. Andre's body lay in the street for more than an hour while an ambulance crew waited for a police es-

Turn to Page 17A Col. 1

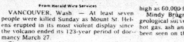

JOE OGLESBY

Blacks Can't Cure Travesty With Rioting

When Judge Lenore Nesbitt ordered the McDuffie trial moved to Tampa, she said she wanted to prevent a time bomb from going off in her courtroom.

That move now looms as a prime reason that Miami may now be experiencing the nation's worst race riot in years.

The move to Tampa may have been legally perfect, but I think it was a social travesty.

An all-white, all-male jury deliberated only 2½ hours to rid itself of a case that took more than a month to present.

A jury I once served on took two hours to decide a simple slip-and-fall case. Although only money was involved, we wanted to be damned sure we did it right.

It seems obvious now, with 20/20 hindsight vision, that a Miami jury might not have given such short shrift to so important a case. We have to live here; the Tampa jurors don't.

The tragedy of McDuffie's death now is compounded by more violence and more deaths. Violence breeding violence: a crowd gathers to signal their outrage — the whole community's outrage — at an unjust decision. Some hotheads want action. They talk tough, throw bricks and bottles, build up steam. The momentum builds, and pretty soon the situation is out of hand.

Looting and burning is a byproduct — perpetuated by hoodlums, thugs and punks looking for excuses to rip off people.

It must end.

There's no justification for riots. Death is permanent. The scars never heal. The emotional wounds forever warp minds. The real damage reaches far beyond the physical mess.

Yet, no one should be surprised. Not really. It has been building since the wrong-house raid on schoolteacher Nathaniel LaFleur's home. It was aggravated by the shooting death of Randy Heath by a Hialeah policeman, the sex molestation case involving an 11-year-old black girl and former Highway Patrol trooper

Turn to Page 16A Col. 5

— BRUCE GILBERT Miami Herald Staff

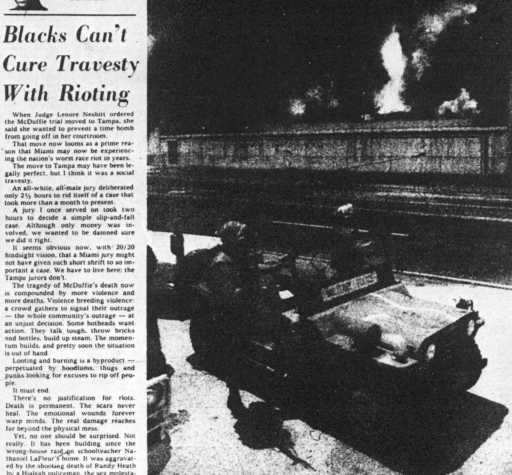

Guardsmen Take Position Across From Burning Norton Tire Co.
... black smoke from building on NW 27th Avenue and 54th Street filled city's sky

Random Acts Of Revenge: How It Began

By WILLIAM R. AMLONG
Herald Staff Writer

The first really bad incident was on NW 62nd Street. Miami's most deadly racial incident began for real then.

A driver trying to escape a rocks-and-bottle mob careered into an 11-year-old girl before hitting a house about 7 p.m. The crowd dragged him from the car and mauled him. A Cadillac ran over him again and again. Police seeking to rescue him and a passenger exchanged shots with black youths.

From there it spread throughout black neighborhoods for two days: random violence in search of specific vengeances following an all-white jury's acquittal of four Metro policemen accused in the beating death of Arthur McDuffie, a black insurance man.

Example: George Bravo and Carolyn Chiriboga were mopping the floor Saturday night in a Chicken Unlimited on NW 54th Street. Two black men came in. "That's for McDuffie," one said. Then they opened fire.

Rationale: "Let it be an eye for an eye and a tooth for a tooth," said Frank Williams, 22, one of about 30 black youths who pelted passing white drivers with rocks and bottles at NW 75th Street and 22nd Avenue as one of their number shot at the cars. "When we try it their way, look what they do to us."

Counterpoint: "I'm telling you they've got to get some kind of understanding that they're killing people

Turn to Page 18A Col. 1

Situation At a Glance

A FEDERAL GRAND JURY will review the evidence presented at the trial of four former Metro officers acquitted in the beating death of black insurance man Arthur McDuffie. The acquittal of the officers by a circuit-court jury sparked the violence in Dade County on Saturday and Sunday. **(Story, Page 16A.)**

EIGHTEEN PERSONS HAVE DIED as a result of the violence. In a televised address, Gov. Bob Graham pleaded for an end to "needless violence and rage." **(Text, Page 19A.)** Dade civic leaders proposed various solutions to stop the rioting. **(Story, Page 1B.)**

A DUSK-TO-DAWN CURFEW was imposed Sunday night in part of Coconut Grove and much of central and most of northern Dade.

DADE PUBLIC and parochial schools, and many private schools, will be closed today, as will Miami-Dade Community College. Metro Transit Agency bus service will resume at 6 a.m. today (though some delays are expected) except in areas affected by the curfew. **(Story, Page 1B.)**

A RUMOR CONTROL LINE is being manned by the Metro Civil Defense office. For information, call 596-8735, 596-8721 or 596-8722.

Complete Coverage, Pages 16A-19A, 24A and 1B-4B.

Monday Sampler

Oregon Frustrated Over Late Primary

For Oregon voters, the selection of presidential candidates has become a frustrating spectator sport. Because their primary falls late in the primary season, many believe that their opinion doesn't matter much anymore. **Page 12A.**

INDEX

7 Die as Mount St. Helens Erupts

From Herald Wire Services

VANCOUVER, Wash. — At least seven people were killed Sunday as Mount St. Helens erupted in its most violent display since the volcano ended its 123-year period of dormancy March 27.

The eruption, which began at 8:39 a.m. (11:39 a.m., Miami time), shot smoke and ash nine miles into the sky and produced a spectacular lightning storm that started numerous forest fires. Mudflows and floods destroyed bridges and forced evacuation of about 2,000 people.

Witnesses said the eruption blew out the bulging north side of the peak. A section of the mountain "just moved sideways and the whole thing went up," said Joe Sullivan, 32, of Toutle.

The volcano was erupting from both its crater and a vent on the northwest slope, said Worner Gerhard, geologist for the U.S. Geological Survey in Vancouver, Wash.

A geological survey observer who flew over the peak had not seen any lava, said survey geologist Joe Rosenbaum.

"The column [of ash] above the volcano is probably above 50,000 feet and may be as high as 60,000 feet," Rosenbaum said.

Mindy Brugman, a spokeswoman for the geological survey, said "pyroclastic flows" — hot gas, ash and fragmented material — had been seen on the mountain's north and west flanks.

"The devastation on the mountainside is incredible," said Air Force Reserve Lt. D.F. Schroeder. "Trees are knocked down, ani-

Turn to Page 10A Col. 1

Survival Is Brutal for Refugees As 14 of Their Number Drowned

By JANET FIX
And FITZ McADEN
Herald Staff Writers

Death came swiftly to the 14 Cuban refugees who drowned when the Olo Yumi capsized. Survival was brutal for the 38 who were saved.

For two hours, five-foot waves tossed them about as they clung to any debris that floated. Gasoline that seeped onto the water after the boat rolled over ate away at their skin.

One of the survivors, 14-year-old Ivis Guerrero, lost her entire family to the sea. She watched tearfully as her father, mother, grandmother and two sisters sank beneath the churning waves.

"My family is gone," Ivis said Sunday after a Marine helicopter airlifted her and the other survivors to Boca Chica Naval Air Station in Key West. Still stunned by the tragedy the day before, she could remember little.

"My family is gone," Ivis said softly. "I don't know what happened."

She walked off the helicopter alone and

Turn to Page 8A Col. 1

Sunny
Low in 60s, high in mid 80s. N winds 10 mph. Map, data 2A.

St. Petersburg Times

Florida's Best Newspaper

The Skyway disaster Page 8

VOL. 96 — NO. 288 76 PAGES * ST. PETERSBURG, FLORIDA, SATURDAY, MAY 10, 1980 · · · · · 20 CENTS A COPY

Freighter rams Skyway; span falls into sea; at least 30 die

By DEBORAH BLUM
St. Petersburg Times Staff Writer

At least 30 persons were killed Friday morning when a huge freighter slammed into the Sunshine Skyway bridge, toppling a 1,200-foot length of the bridge and several vehicles into Tampa Bay.

A Greyhound bus en route from Chicago to Miami — with a stop in St. Petersburg — and at least three cars and a pickup truck plummeted into the water after the 608-foot *Summit Venture* struck a support just south of the bridge's center span.

It was not known if anyone had boarded the bus in St. Petersburg.

By Friday afternoon, 18 bodies had been recovered — 11 females, including a baby, and seven males.

The bus carried a driver and 22 passengers. The driver was identified as Michael Curtin. The other victims were unidentified.

Coast Guard officials said late Friday that in addition to the 23 persons aboard the bus, there were four persons in a Toyota, one in a Lincoln Continental and two in an El Camino that plunged into the bay.

SO FAR, only one survivor is known. Wesley MacIntire, 56, of Gulfport, was admitted to St. Anthony's Hospital with a cut on the head and water in his lungs after his pickup truck dropped onto the freighter and bounced into the bay. MacIntire was picked up by crew members from the ship.

The Liberian-registered freighter was bound for Tampa to pick up a load of phosphate. It crashed into and damaged a support of the west main span and then struck and sheared off the support of the next span to the south at at 7:38 a.m. None of the 30 to 40 crew members was injured and the boat sustained only minor damage.

The St. Petersburg Times reached the *Summit Venture* on ship-to-shore radio in an attempt to talk to the pilot and the captain of the ship, but the person who answered simply said, "No comment!" before breaking the connection.

But the 26-year-old Skyway bridge was critically injured. Florida Department of Transportation (DOT) inspectors said repairing the shattered southbound span could take at least four years. They plan to reopen the parallel northbound span for two-way traffic sometime this weekend.

DOT BRIDGE inspection engineer Steven Plotkin said the concrete supports that hold up the 150-foot-tall Skyway superstructure are not designed to withstand such a crash.

"With a vessel like that, the pier (support) might as well have been a toothpick sitting there," Plotkin said. "It's like a toothpick being smashed by a sledgehammer. If the bridge was in perfect condition, it couldn't have held up under that kind of impact."

Building a bridge over a busy shipping channel always adds some risk, he added. This is the third time a ship has struck the Skyway this year. The other impacts, however, did only minor damage.

The DOT announced Friday that Hardaway Construction Co. of Columbus, Ga. will begin clearing debris out of the shipping channel today.

OFFICIALS are still unsure, however, how long the channel may be blocked. In January, when the Coast Guard buoy tender *Blackthorn* collided with an oil tanker just west of the bridge, a temporary channel was opened. Ships were sent around the scene of the collision, where the *Blackthorn* sank to the bottom and 23 crew members died. It took weeks to salvage the *Blackthorn*.

But Coast Guard Capt. Marshall E. Gilbert said shallow water in the area around the fallen bridge and the fact that other parts of the bridge hang close to the water make such an operation — a temporary channel — "unlikely" this time.

Two investigations into the accident have been scheduled. One will be conducted by the Coast Guard and the other by the National Transportation Safety Board.

Investigators said severe weather problems may have played a role in the disaster. At the time of the crash, winds were reported at 40 miles per hour, and a heavy curtain of fog and rain hung over the bridge.

Roadway from the Skyway lies across the bow of the *Summit Venture* near the sheared support of the bridge

St. Petersburg Times — ERIC MENCHER

inside

Death rode in on early morning storm

By DEBORAH BLUM and PAUL TASH
St. Petersburg Times Staff Writers

The ill wind and blinding rain of a blustery spring squall reached the Sunshine Skyway bridge Friday at the same moment a huge freighter did.

Drivers crept across the bridge's central span, going cautiously in a wet fog that clouded the water below and the steel structure above in thick white.

Then came the crash.

"I thought at first it was thunder," said Jay Hirsch, a paramedic with Florida Ambulance Service who was driving north on the bridge. "Then something hit the bridge so hard it knocked my car out of its lane. I kept going till I got across. When I looked back I saw it. My God, the bridge had gone down."

The 608-foot-long *Summit Venture*, a Liberian-registered freighter headed for Tampa to pick up a load of phosphate, slammed into and damaged one of the supports of the west main span, then sheared off a support just south of the center span at 7:38 a.m.

THE BOAT, longer than two football fields, rocked the bridge. It sheared off the support about 10 feet above the water line.

As the supports under the central span of the southbound lanes collapsed, the metal grid above began to twist away. Nearly 1,200 feet of metal and concrete roadway dropped into the gray-green waters of Tampa Bay.

At least three cars and a pickup truck fell with it. And then a Greyhound bus, bound south from Chicago with 22 passengers and a driver, went blindly into the bay 150 feet below.

Authorities say the final death count will be at least 30. Rescue workers had reports that a bus carrying migrant workers was "missing," but divers at the scene found no trace of a second bus.

A ST. PETERSBURG businessman driv-

See NARRATIVE, Page 13

Foreign, national front page news is on 3-A

He fell:

From the bridge, to the ship, to the sea

By RONALD BOYD
St. Petersburg Times Staff Writer

Wesley MacIntire drove head-first off the Sunshine Skyway bridge into the hands of a miracle.

"It was raining very, very hard. I almost decided not to go across the bridge, but I kept going. As I approached the high point of the bridge, the whole bridge started to sway. Then I could see the ship and the end of the bridge was breaking off. I couldn't stop. I just slid off, hit the ship and dropped into the water."

Wesley MacIntire's mini-pickup truck was now sinking to a resting spot under Tampa Bay.

"I remember opening the door and forcing my way out of the truck. I started swimming to the surface. I was swallowing a lot of water, but I finally made it to the surface. There was a piece of bridge girder there and I held onto that. I was vomiting a lot of water."

HE LOOKED above to the dangling span and saw headlights, some perilously close to the edge. Around him the waters were still. There were no screams for help, no evidence of the bus and cars that had just carried 30 persons to their deaths. Nearby the *Summit Venture*, bathed in rain and covered with debris, sat motionless.

See SURVIVOR, Page 10

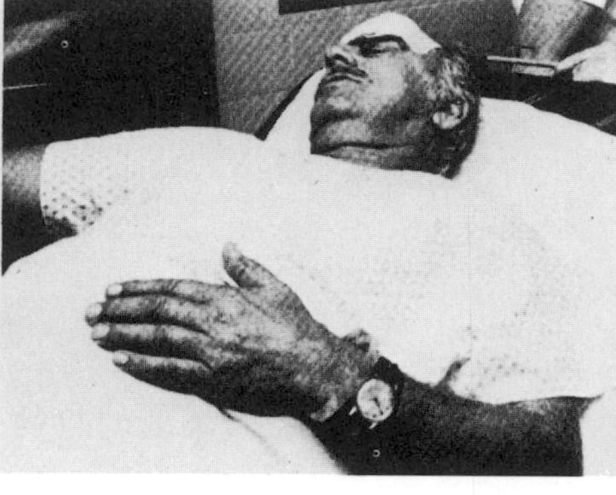

'I'm sore all over, that's for sure.'

— MacIntire is wheeled from emergency room at St. Anthony's Hospital.

St. Petersburg Times — ERIC MENCHER

1981

Barely an hour after the inauguration of President Ronald Reagan on January 20, 1980, the 52 hostages who had been held in Iran for 444 days were released.

Two months later, on March 30, gunshots were fired at President Reagan as he left a Washington hotel after a speech.

In surgery, a bullet was removed from the President's left lung and he recovered quickly.

Three others were hit by the gunfire, including presidential press secretary James Brady, who was partially paralyzed.

John Hinckley, Jr., was tried for the shooting and found not guilty by reason of insanity; he was committed to a government asylum.

A would-be assassin shot Pope John Paul II in St. Peter's Square at the Vatican. The pope was wounded, but recovered.

Police arrested Mehmet Ali Acga, who was later sentenced to life in prison.

On October 6, six Egyptian soldiers jumped from a truck during a military parade and fired automatic weapons and tossed grenades at the reviewing stand.

They killed President Anwar Sadat and five others. The assassins were later identified as Moslem fundamentalists.

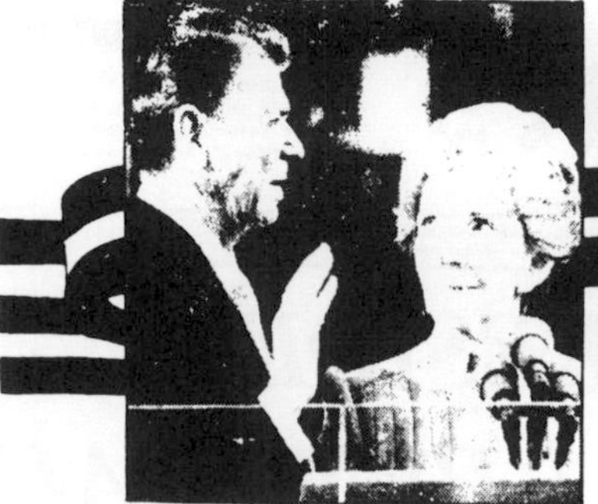

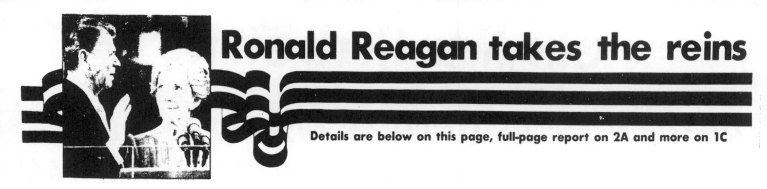

Ronald Reagan takes the reins

Details are below on this page, full-page report on 2A and more on 1C

Cloudy

Chance of precipitation
Details on Page 6A

Democrat and Chronicle

149TH YEAR   Published by Gannett Co., Inc., in Rochester, N.Y., Wednesday Morning, January 21, 1981   25 CENTS

Sunrise

Freedom: Day 1

Hostages land in Germany after joyous stop in Algiers; Carter greets them today

D&C Wire Services

WIESBADEN, West Germany — Smiling, exuberant and back in the hands of their nation, the 52 former American hostages from Iran came to the U.S. Air Force hospital here at dawn today on the last leg of their journey home.

The former captives received a tumultuous welcome from hundreds gathered on the grounds of the hospital at daylight, about 8 a.m. German time, 2 a.m. EST. Church bells rang through this town on the hills above the Rhine River as their police-escorted motorcade arrived.

Several hundred Americans and West Germans rushed down the street cheering as the two busloads of hostages arrived. Former Secretary of State Cyrus Vance rode in one of the buses.

Forty minutes earlier, the returning Americans received a similar welcome from a crowd of hundreds at the Rhein-Main airport 20 miles away. There, the former captives' 12½-hour, 4,550-mile journey from Tehran came to an end with their arrival from Algiers aboard two U.S. Air Force medevac aircraft.

"We've Got a Full Deck Now — 52," read one of the signs in the crowd. A huge cheer arose from hundreds of people gathered along the tarmac at the air base in frigid pre-dawn temperatures to greet the former captives as they arrived on two U.S. hospital planes from Algiers, where they were flown after release from Tehran.

Smiling and laughing, the ex-hostages followed one by one, some clean-shaven, others with the beards they grew in captivity.

One made a "V for Victory" sign at the television cameras, which carried the arrival in Algiers live to the United States.

Some of the hostages looked dazed but none appeared ill. All smiled or laughed as they embraced or shook hands with U.S. Deputy Secretary of State Warren Christopher and other officials in the receiving line. There were no tears.

They walked to a VIP lounge where waiters moved among them, serving soft drinks and Turkish coffee. The hostages, suddenly free, chatted and joked with Christopher.

"It's good to get out of Khomeini land," quipped one of the freed Americans.

Ex-hostage Barry Rosen, asked by a reporter what was the first thing he planned to do

Turn to FREEDOM, Page 4A

WELCOME
BACK TO
FREEDOM

One of the hostages shouts with joy as he leaves U.S. Air Force plane at Frankfurt, Germany. (AP)

inside

today

Scacchetti found guilty

Rochester City Court Judge Carl R. Scacchetti Jr. is found guilty in U.S. District Court of using his office to extort services and a gift.

He faces a maximum sentence of 20 years in prison, a $10,000 fine, or both, on his conviction on two counts of accepting free auto repairs and a 35mm camera worth $500. He was acquitted of one count of extorting a $262.10 check (1B).

Kodak earnings

Eastman Kodak Co.'s net earnings for 1980 are expected to be reduced by $130 million because of a change in accounting.

Kodak will restate its previously reported earnings for each of the first three quarters to reflect the change, a company official said (8D).

Murder-suicide

Greece police investigate what they are calling a murder-suicide involving a Greece couple in a Greenleaf Road Apartment last night (1B).

4 NEWS SECTIONS

● ● ● ●

Reagan starts work, freezes hiring

Nancy, Ronald Reagan leave Capitol after he took oath yesterday. (AP)

. . . his inaugural address emphasized need to limit the powers of the federal government.

D&C Wire Services

WASHINGTON — Ronald Wilson Reagan settled into the Oval Office yesterday to begin work on the "era of national renewal," he promised in his inaugural address.

One of his first acts was to make good on a promise by freezing federal hiring, minutes after his inauguration. The new president headed straight for the Oval office after watching the inaugural parade from the reviewing stand in front of the White House.

"I am more pleased than anything I can say," he told reporters. "As I say, it makes the whole day perfect now, the fact that all 52 hostages are on their way home, out of Iranian airspace."

As he made the rounds of his inaugural balls last night, Reagan announced to a ballroom of cheering supporters that "the prisoners of war" have landed in Algiers. Reagan made the announcement as he and his wife, Nancy, opened their evening of festivities on his first night as the nation's 40th president.

Reagan started to talk about the 52 freed hostages, but broke off and said, "I just won't call them hostages. They're prisoners of war."

"Incidentally," he added, "the Christmas tree lights have come on." The National Christmas Tree, which was dark through the holiday season in deference to the hostages, was lit earlier to herald their release.

In his inaugural address at noon yesterday, the new president made no reference to the hostages, emphasizing instead the need to limit the powers of the federal government, and to bring an end to unemployment and inflation.

He promised to begin immediately to deal with "an economic affliction of great proportions," and declared: "In this present crisis, government is not the solution to our problem: government is the problem."

Yesterday's ceremony — filled with patriotic music, the firing of cannon and the pealing of bells — marked the transfer of the presidency back to the Republicans after the four-year term of Jimmy Carter.

At the age of 69, Reagan is the oldest man to take the oath of office, and in five months he will become the oldest man to serve as president.

Carter, looking haggard after spending two largely sleepless nights trying to resolve the hostage crisis, flew to Plains, Ga., after the inaugural ceremony.

Reagan's briskly delivered speech, lasting 20 minutes, touched on themes from his campaign, particularly the invocation of the wisdom of "we, the people" — and its stern warning to "the enemies of freedom, those who are potential adversaries," that the United States stands ready to act "to preserve our national security."

"Those who say that we are in a time when there are no heroes, they just don't know where to look," Reagan said.

He spoke of "professionals, industrialists, shopkeepers, clerks, cabbies and truck drivers," and of "individuals and families who pay taxes to support the government and whose voluntary gifts support church, charity, culture, art and education."

Turn to REAGAN, Page 4A

more on the inauguration

"All the News That's Fit to Print"

The New York Times

LATE CITY EDITION

Weather: Partly sunny today; mostly cloudy and cold tonight and tomorrow. Temperature range: today 28-38; yesterday 36-43. Details on page D21.

VOL.CXXX . . . No. 44,835 | NEW YORK, WEDNESDAY, JANUARY 21, 1981 | 30 cents beyond 50-mile zone from New York City. Higher in air delivery cities. | 25 CENTS

REAGAN TAKES OATH AS 40TH PRESIDENT; PROMISES AN 'ERA OF NATIONAL RENEWAL'

MINUTES LATER, 52 U.S. HOSTAGES IN IRAN FLY TO FREEDOM AFTER 444-DAY ORDEAL

'ALIVE, WELL AND FREE'

Captives Taken to Algiers and Then Germany — Final Pact Complex

By BERNARD GWERTZMAN
Special to The New York Times

WASHINGTON, Wednesday, Jan. 21 — The 52 Americans who were held hostage by Iran for 444 days were flown to freedom yesterday. Jimmy Carter, a few hours after giving up the Presidency, said that everyone "was alive, was well and free."

The flight ended the national ordeal that had frustrated Mr. Carter for most of his last 14 months in office, and it allowed Ronald Reagan to begin his term free of the burdens of the Iran crisis.

The Americans were escorted out of Iran by Algerian diplomats, aboard an Algerian airliner, underscoring Algeria's role in achieving the accord that allowed the hostages to return home.

Transferred to U.S. Custody

The Algerian plane, carrying the former hostages, stopped first in Athens to refuel. It then landed in Algiers, where custody of the 52 Americans was formally transferred by the Algerians to the representative of the United States, former Deputy Secretary of State Warren M. Christopher. He had negotiated much of the agreement freeing them.

They then boarded two United States Air Force hospital planes and flew to Frankfurt, West Germany early this morning. They will stay at an American military hospital in nearby Weisbaden, where they will be visited by Mr. Carter, as President Reagan's representative, later today. They will stay in Wiesbaden for a week or less to "decompress," as one official described it.

The 52 Americans were freed as part of a complex agreement that was not completed until early yesterday morning, when the last snags holding up their release were removed by Mr. Carter and

Continued on Page A3, Column 5

Teheran Captors Call Out Insults As the 52 Leave

By JOHN KIFNER
Special to The New York Times

TEHERAN, Iran, Jan. 20 — The 52 American hostages began to roll down the runway to freedom today minutes as President Reagan was finishing his inaugural address.

As the Algerian 727 lifted off from Mehrabad Airport, ending 444 days of captivity for the Americans, they could see, most of them probably for the last time, a full moon picking out the sharp white peaks of the Elburz Mountains to the north. The time was 8:55 P.M., 12:25 P.M., New York time.

"God is great! Death to America!" cried the young Islamic militants who kept custody of the hostages to the last minute, hustling them to the stairs of the airplane.

They Soon Are 'Former Hostages'

The American diplomats, Marine guards and the other hostages stepped one at a time from a bus, whose windows were covered with checked curtains, into a clear cold night. As they touched the tarmac, two young militants, the hoods of their parkas up against the chill, took them just above the elbows and propelled them through the shouting crowd toward the Algerian plane with its red stylized bird emblazoned on the tail.

Looking dazed, some with long hair and beards that contrasted with the neat trims of their official days before the embassy takeover Nov. 4, 1979, they stumbled into the first-class section of the plane. Now they were what a bulletin on Pars, the state press agency, would describe later as "former hostages."

"They seem stunned, as if they cannot believe they are going free," Ahmad Azizi, the Government's director of hostage affairs, remarked to an Iranian state television crew covering the departure.

At 8:20, the doors were sealed, Pars reported, and the engines began to whine. A

Continued on Page A8, Column 1

United Press International

11:57 A.M.: Ronald Reagan being sworn in as 40th President by Chief Justice Warren E. Burger. Nancy Reagan held the Bible and Senator Mark O. Hatfield witnessed the ceremony.

FREEZE SET ON HIRING

Californian Stresses Need to Restrict Government and Buoy Economy

By STEVEN R. WEISMAN
Special to The New York Times

WASHINGTON, Jan. 20 — Ronald Wilson Reagan of California, promising "an era of national renewal," became the 40th President of the United States today as 52 Americans held hostage in Iran were heading toward freedom.

The hostages, whose 14 months of captivity had been a central focus of the Presidential contest last year, took off from Teheran in two Boeing 727 airplanes at 12:25 P.M., Eastern standard time, the very moment that Mr. Reagan was concluding his solemn Inaugural Address at the United States Capitol.

The new President's speech, however, made no reference at all to the long-awaited release of the hostages, emphasizing instead the need to limit the powers of the Federal Government, and to bring an end to unemployment and inflation.

'Government Is the Problem'

Promising to begin immediately to deal with "an economic affliction of great proportions," Mr. Reagan declared: "In this present crisis, government is not the solution to our problem; government is the problem." And in keeping with this statement, the President issued orders for a hiring "freeze" as his first official act. [Page B6.]

Wearing a charcoal gray club coat, striped trousers and dove gray vest and tie, Mr. Reagan took his oath of office at 11:57 A.M. in the first inaugural ceremony ever enacted on the western front of the United States Capitol. The site was chosen to stress the symbolism of Mr. Reagan's addressing his words to the West, the region that served as his base in his three Presidential campaigns in 1968, 1976 and 1980.

Oldest to Assume Presidency

The ceremony today, filled with patriotic music, the firing of cannons and the pealing of bells, marked the transfer of the Presidency back to the Republicans after the four-year term of Jimmy Carter, a Democrat, as well as the culmination of the remarkable career of a conservative former two-term Governor of California who had started out as a baseball announcer and motion picture star.

At the age of 69, Mr. Reagan also became the oldest man to assume the Presidency, and in five months he will become the oldest man to serve in the office.

Mr. Carter, looking haggard and worn after spending two largely sleepless nights trying to resolve the hostage crisis

Continued on Page B8, Column 2

Anxious Families and Towns Erupt Into Long-Postponed Celebrations

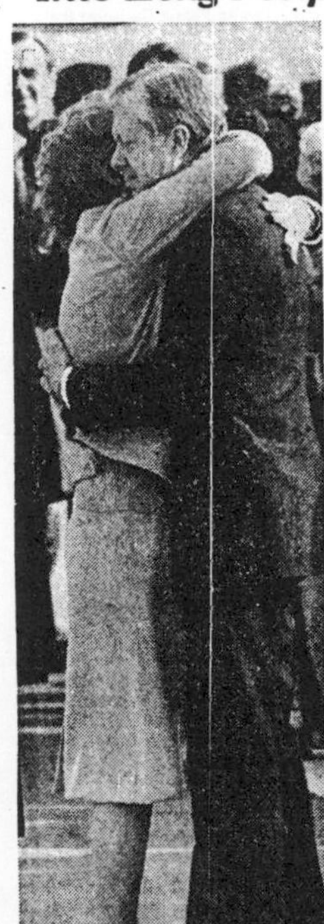

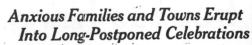

Black Star/John Troha for The New York Times

Anita Schaefer, wife of a hostage, embraced Mr. Carter at airport.

By JOSEPH B. TREASTER

Saying his final farewells at Andrews Air Force Base yesterday, Jimmy Carter spotted Anita Schaefer, the wife of one of the hostages, and exuberantly embraced her.

"Tom is in the air," Mr. Carter said, speaking of her husband, Col. Thomas E. Schaefer of the Air Force, who was the senior military officer at the United States Embassy in Teheran.

"Really, truly, Mr. President," she whispered.

"Really, truly — at long last," he said, "Tom is safe. I'll be with him tomorrow morning in Germany."

"Oh, thank God, Mr. President."

Then they both cried. And they embraced again.

The First Glimpse

As the hostages arrived in Algiers, relatives strained close to television screens for the first glimpse of their loved ones out of captivity in more than 14 months.

"There's Billy," cried Letezia Callegos, as her brother, Sgt. William Gallegos of the Marines, stepped down the ramp. His mother, Theresa, broke into deep sobs.

News that the plane carrying the hostages had taken off from Teheran came to Penelope Laingen, the wife of L. Bruce Laingen, the embassy's chargé d'affaires, as she sat in a reserved seat at the inauguration of President Reagan. A military policeman shouted the word for everyone to hear.

Some had gotten the word from radio and television broadcasts, and still others, like Marjorie Moore, the wife of Bert C. Moore, the administrative consul, received phone calls from the State Department.

Most of the homes of the hostages' families, torn by doubt, fear and anger for so long, exploded with joy. They cried

Continued on Page A5, Column 1

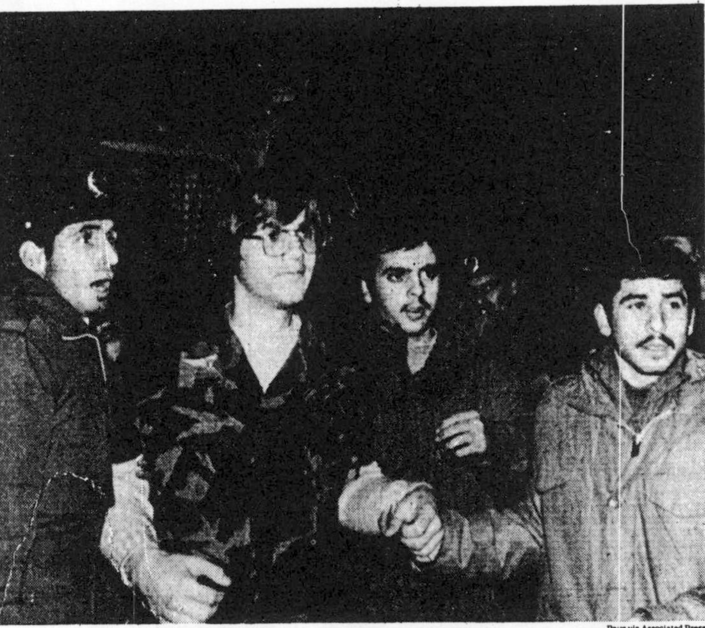

Pars via Associated Press

12:25 P.M.: Sgt. Joseph Subic Jr. propelled by militants to waiting plane at airport in Teheran

A Hopeful Prologue, a Pledge of Action

By HEDRICK SMITH
Special to The New York Times

News Analysis

WASHINGTON, Jan. 20 — For a President who has promised Americans a new beginning, an era of national renewal at home and restored strength and stature abroad, the release of the American hostages in Iran was exquisitely timed.

The extraordinary deadline diplomacy that put the 52 captured Americans into the air over Iran minutes after the howitzers thundered a new leader into office provided a graceful exit for Jimmy Carter, a hopeful prologue for Ronald Reagan and relief for a nation weary from 14 months of humiliation and seeming impotence.

Almost unavoidably the human drama in Iran overshadowed an Inaugural Address that was less an inspirational call to national greatness than a plain-spoken charter of Mr. Reagan's conservative creed, less a sermon than a stump speech, less a rallying cry than a ringing denunciation of overgrown government and a practical pledge to get down to the business of trimming it at once.

For all the new President's vaunted reputation as one of the nation's most polished political orators, his Inaugural Address offered surprisingly few rhetorical flourishes beyond the populist tribute to ordinary Americans that "those who say that we are in a time when there are no heroes, they just don't know where to look."

Although Mr. Reagan made no direct mention of the hostages, their release was on everyone's lips. Moments before Mr. Reagan took his oath of office, word that the hostages were about to be flown out of Iran swept through the crowd stretched out before the Capitol, and though that news was premature, it provided the perfect symbolic backdrop for

Continued on Page B7, Column 1

News Summary and Index, Page A2

More News And Pictures

The Inauguration

The Hostages

Summary and Index, Page A2

Weather

Today—Mostly sunny and pleasant, high 75-80, low tonight 48-54. Chance of rain is near zero today, 30 percent tonight. Wednesday — Showers and mild, high 72-76. Yesterday — 3 p.m. AQI: 25; temp. range: 67-60. Details on Page B2.

The Washington Post

FINAL

76 Pages — 4 Sections

Amusements	D10	Financial	C11
Classified	B 5	Metro	B 1
Comics	D13	Obituaries	B 4
Crossword	D15	Sports	C 1
Editorials	A20	Style	D 1
Fed. Diary	B 2	Television	D 8

104th Year ···· No. 116 · ©1981, Washington Post Co. TUESDAY, MARCH 31, 1981 Subscription Rates See Box on A2 20¢

Reagan Wounded by Assailant's Bullet; Prognosis Is 'Excellent'; 3 Others Shot

By David S. Broder
Washington Post Staff Writer

President Reagan survived an assassination attempt yesterday when a revolver-wielding gunman waiting among reporters and photographers on the sidewalk outside the Washington Hilton hotel fired a bullet into his chest.

The same assailant critically wounded White House press secretary James S. Brady and felled a Secret Service man and a Washington policeman.

In the 70th day of his presidency, Reagan underwent three hours of surgery at George Washington University Hospital to remove the bullet that entered under his left armpit, struck his seventh rib and burrowed three inches into his left lung.

On his way into surgery, the president gamely reassured friends: "Don't worry about me. I'll make it."

At 7:25 p.m., five hours after the shooting, the president was out of surgery and in stable condition. Dr. Dennis O'Leary told reporters the 70-year-old chief executive's "prognosis is excellent," adding that "at no time was he in serious danger." O'Leary said the president was "clear of head and should be able to make decisions by tomorrow." But he said Reagan may be in the hospital for two weeks and would not be "fully recovered" for perhaps three months.

Associated Press Photos

Secret Service agents shove President Reagan into his limousine after he was shot. At right, John W. Hinckley Jr., of Evergreen, Colo., was held in shooting.

The president's good spirits survived the traumatic day. At 8:50 p.m., according to White House aide Lyn Nofziger, with drainage tubes still in his throat, Reagan wrote a note to his doctors saying: "All in all, I'd rather be in Philadelphia." The line is a classic uttered by W.C. Fields when facing a lynching in "My Little Chickadee."

Vice President Bush, at a White House briefing held after his rushed return to the city, said he was encouraged by the medical reports and anticipates a "complete recovery" by the president.

"I can reassure this nation and a watching world that this government is functioning fully and effectively," Bush said.

Police subdued the suspected assailant on the scene. He was later identified as John Warnock Hinckley Jr., the 25-year-old son of a wealthy Evergreen, Colo., oil executive.

About midnight, Hinckley was formally charged in U.S. District Court here with the attempted assassination of a president and assault on a federal employe, the Secret Service agent. The suspect was being held without bond at an undisclosed location, and U.S. Magistrate Arthur L. Burnett, at the government's request, ordered that Hinckley undergo a psychiatric examination today and return for a preliminary hearing Thursday.

Sources said last night that the initial determination of the Justice Department was that the suspect had been acting alone.

Police said six shots were fired from a .22-caliber blue-steel revolver that Hinckley had purchased from Rocky's Pawn Shop in Dallas last Oct. 13.

A spokesman for the Hinckley family told reporters the suspect had been under psychiatric care, but offered no further details. A family spokesman in Colorado, attorney James Robinson, said the young man's family is "grieving and heartbroken by the tragedy. They love their son and will stick by him. Their hearts and prayers go out to the president and other victims of the shooting."

The Nashville Tennessean reported that a man of that name had been arrested at that city's airport last Oct. 9 with three guns in a suitcase. Two of the guns confiscated in Nashville were the same model .22-caliber revolvers used in the attempt on Reagan yesterday. President Carter had arrived in Nashville two hours before the arrest.

See PRESIDENT, A8, Col. 1

By Ron Edmonds — Associated Press

Secret Service agent Timothy J. McCarthy, foreground, Officer Thomas K. Delahanty, press secretary James S. Brady lie wounded.

Recently Under Psychiatric Care

Suspected Gunman: An Aimless Drifter

By Ron Shaffer and Neil Henry
Washington Post Staff Writers

John Warnock Hinckley Jr., charged in the attempted assassination of President Reagan, had been under psychiatric care and was arrested last October in Nashville carrying three handguns in his suitcase during a visit by then-President Carter.

His arrest in downtown Washington yesterday apparently followed several years of aimless drifting — years during which the 25-year-old son of a wealthy western oilman dropped in and out of college in Texas and traveled through Colorado and Los Angeles in search of a job.

Law enforcement officials said that Hinckley had been in Washington only one day before the assassination attempt, staying at the Park Central Hotel at 18th and G streets NW. He told an official last night that he had received medication for five months while under the care of a private psychiatrist in Colorado.

Snapshot pictures of Hinckley over the years show the dissolution of a young man from a healthy, clean-cut kid in suburban Dallas to a disheveled, glassy-eyed drifter looking for odd jobs near his parents' new home just outside the wealthy Denver suburb of Evergreen.

Lawyer James Robinson, a spokesman for the Hinckley family, said in Colorado that Hinckley had been under psychiatric care, but he refused to provide any other details last night.

Although the parents acknowledged their son's mental problems, news that he had been arrested for attempting to kill the president came as a shock.

"This is a joke, isn't it," said Hinckley's mother, Joanne, when a reporter informed her that her son was arrested in the shooting. She had been watching television reports of the assassination attempt and was not aware that her son was in Washington, she said. Then her voice began to crack, and she hung up the telephone.

See SUSPECT, A9, Col. 1

The Shooting

By Lou Cannon
Washington Post Staff Writer

It was a routine scene that Ronald Reagan as politician and president had played a thousand times.

Reagan had delivered his basic speech, appealing for support for his economic program and deploring the increase in violent crime which was "making neighborhood streets unsafe and families fearful in their homes."

He was leaving the Washington Hilton Hotel through a VIP side door onto T Street. His armored limousine stood waiting for him in a driveway about 12 feet away. Secret Service agents were all around him. It was 2:25 p.m. on a typically rainy spring day, and Reagan, dressed in a blue suit with a white handkerchief in his pocket, seemed happy to be president.

Outside the hotel more than 100 persons had gathered. Reagan, as he always does, paused and waved to the crowd. The crowd cheered. Nearby, the president's press secretary, James S. Brady, walked toward a staff car, not looking at the president. To Reagan's left, slightly more than 10 feet away in a roped-off area, members of the crowd mixed with reporters and television cameramen who were photographing the president's departure.

Michael Putzel of Associated Press, ready with the inevitable question, called out, "Mr. President."

Abruptly, the scene changed. Shots rang out, six of them in quick succession, with a slight pause between the second shot and the third. The shots appeared to come from the roped-off press area to the left of and below the president. To those close to the rope restraining the press, the shots sounded like firecrackers. A woman screamed. A Secret Service agent yelled, "Get back, get back." Other agents

See SCENE, A10, Col. 1

United Press International

Press secretary James S. Brady lies wounded on the sidewalk.

The Morbid Echo

By Haynes Johnson
Washington Post Staff Writer

Moments after the crackle of gunfire echoed off the stone wall outside the hotel, an eyewitness said, "I knew it was more than just firecrackers."

It was an unnecessary remark. Within minutes Americans everywhere knew it had happened again — another president shot, another political promise interrupted by violence.

Commentary

There was no way to escape this replaying of the old national horror. Over and over, hour after hour, in slow motion, in stop action, and in all the other modern techniques of electronic communications, television brought home the latest installment of a continuing American tragedy.

And once again it was all too familiar: the sudden pap-

See VIOLENCE, A12, Col. 3

Body of Black Child Found Near Atlanta

Authorities pulled the badly decomposed body of a black child from a river in a deserted area 16 miles from downtown Atlanta, another apparent victim of the elusive killer or killers who have murdered 21 black children there in less than two years.

Details on Page A5

Indonesian troops stormed an Indonesian jetliner in Bangkok, killing four of five hijackers and freeing more than 40 hostages. A soldier and the plane's pilot reportedly were wounded. Two American hostages were reported safe.

Details on Page A19

Poles Reach Accord; Union Suspends General Strike

By Brian Mooney
Reuter

WARSAW, March 30 — The independent Solidarity union movement suspended a potentially catastrophic general strike call today after marathon talks with the Communist government produced tentative agreement on major issues one hour before a union deadline was to expire.

The agreement seemed likely to relax, at least for the time being, the tensions building around the Polish crisis for the last several days as Moscow warned against "antisocialist" concessions to the labor leaders and U.S. officials warned against intervention by Warsaw Pact troops on extended maneuvers in and around Poland.

The tentative accord followed two days of intense negotiations among Poland's Communist leaders and between the union and the government. It appeared to result from compromise on both sides but still remained subject to ratification by Solidarity's National Consultative Commission, which was due to meet at union headquarters in Gdansk on Tuesday.

"I am 70 percent satisfied with the agreement," Solidarity leader Lech Walesa, a moderate who fought to steer his movement away from what could have been a fatal collision course with the authorities, told a nationally televised press conference.

"Tomorrow we go to work," said Andrzej Gwiazda, the second-ranking leader of Solidarity's 10 million members.

Walesa cautioned, however, that he can not guarantee that the union's decision-making executive body will accept the proposed accord. Solidarity, which staged a massive four-hour warning strike Friday that was unprecedented in Communist-ruled Poland, had called for an open-ended nationwide strike Tuesday if the government refused a series of demands.

At yesterday's Communist Party Central Committee meeting, the party leadership in the Politburo came under attack from the rank and file after it accused elements of Solidarity of launching a power struggle against the Communists. Faced with the challenge, three hard-liners offered to resign. But the Central Committee ended the stormy 18-hour debate with a vote of confidence for the leadership and a call on the union to exercise restraint and discipline.

Among the most significant developments to emerge from the meeting in reports today were a call for elec-

See WARSAW, A16, Col. 5

Workers' unity eases Poland's gravest crisis. *Page A16*

INSIDE

On Today's Editorial Page
'Stronger Than Danger'
Editorial And Cartoon
NATO's Best Bet
Editorial

ST. LOUIS POST-DISPATCH

FINAL
★ ★ ★
2:50 P.M. New York Stocks
Pages 2E and 5E

Vol. 103, No. 133 THURSDAY, MAY 14, 1981 N 20¢

Pope Alert, Is Visited By His Aides

Compiled From News Services

VATICAN CITY — Pope John Paul II was visited by two aides and a Polish nun today in the hospital room where he is recovering from bullet wounds inflicted Wednesday by a would-be assassin.

The nun led the group in prayer, officials said.

Dr. Alfredo Wiel Marina, an attending physician, said the pope appeared a little depressed but his temperature had returned to normal. "All tests conducted at 5 p.m. (10 a.m. St. Louis time) show results all within limits," he said. But he said, "the risk of infection is quite high because surgery was of an emergency nature."

The pope, who turns 61 Monday, was listed in "serious, guarded" condition, but doctors said he was making an excellent recovery. He remained under mild sedation and was being fed intravenously and was attached to a heart monitor.

His two secretaries, the Revs. John Magee and Stanislaw Dziwisz, and the nun, who was not identified, spent a few minutes in the ninth-floor hospital room, wearing surgical gowns, gloves and masks to protect against infection, said hospital spokesman Giulio Stella.

The chief Vatican spokesman, the Rev. Romeo Panciroli, said it was a miracle that the bullet that struck the pope in the intestinal area missed vital organs. "It just avoided the aorta, the urethra and the spine and hurt the intestine, something which is repairable," he told reporters.

An American, Ann Odre, one of two women hit by shots aimed at the pope, was in more serious condition than first believed, said Deacon Richard Siepka

See POPE, Page 11

Other Stories

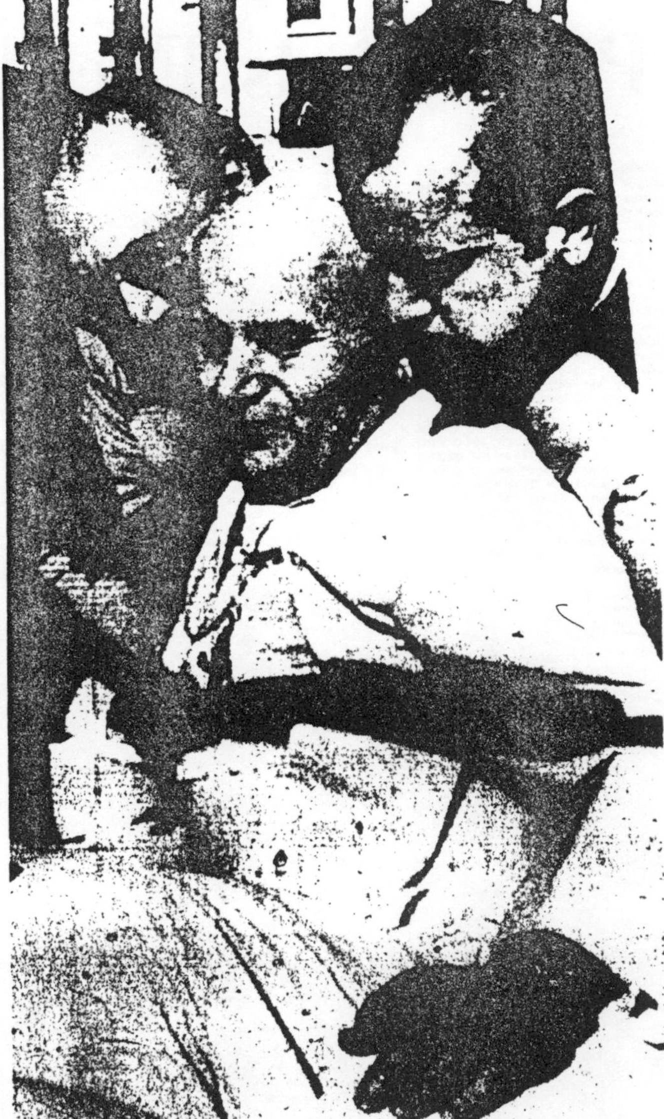

Pope John Paul II being assisted by aides seconds after he was wounded in St. Peter's Square by a gunman Wednesday. Blood from the pontiff's wounds covers his hand. The pope was rushed to a hospital, where he underwent more than five hours of surgery.

UPI

St. Louisans Present As Pope Is Shot

By Howard S. Goller
Of the Post-Dispatch Staff

Standing on a chair in St. Peter's Square, Angela Altadonna of St. Louis watched in horror as gunshots turned the roars of an adoring crowd into murmurs of disbelief and, finally, to silent prayer.

She and her husband, Anthony, were about 100 feet from Pope John Paul II when he was shot Wednesday by a would-be assassin. The Altadonnas had hoped to shake the hand of the pontiff when he passed.

The couple, on a tour of holy places in Europe, planned to leave Rome today, but without two of the 47 tour members. One is Ann Odre, 58, of Buffalo, N.Y., who was shot and wounded in the incident; the other is a Buffalo priest who is staying behind until Mrs. Odre can

See VISITORS, Page 11

Police Questioning Suspect In Assault

Compiled From News Services

ROME — A Turkish extremist who gunned down the pope he once labeled the "commander of the masked crusaders" for Western imperialism was questioned for a second day today by Italy's anti-terrorist police.

Mehmet Ali Agca, 23, was seized by the crowd in St. Peter's Square on Wednesday, seconds after a burst of gunfire seriously wounded Pope John Paul II and hit two American women bystanders.

Turkish police said Agca, whom they had ordered shot on sight, was a member of an extreme right-wing neo-Nazi group and had threatened to kill the pope during John Paul's visit to Turkey in November 1979.

Acga's background surfaced quickly after his capture at the Vatican.

"This same individual is currently being sought by Turkish authorities and by Interpol," Sukru Elekdag, Turkey's ambassador to the United States, said in Washington.

The Turkish Embassy said police had traced his recent movements to France, West Germany, Italy and Spain. "He is a well-known fugitive from Turkish justice — a terrorist who has been tried and convicted for the murder of a prominent Turkish journalist."

Acga's earlier threat against the pope came days after he escaped from an Istanbul prison where he was being held for trial in the slaying of the editor of Milliyet, the left-of-center Turkish newspaper that received his threats against the pope. His death sentence was approved by Parliament in absentia.

The dark-haired, clean-shaven young man faces the charge of the attempted assassination of a pope, police said today. The harshest punishment he could receive is life imprisonment.

The Turkish government said it had asked Italy to return the convicted terrorist "to settle the account in Turkey after he is convicted and has served his sentence in Italy."

After his escape from Turkish jails, Agca apparently went to West Germany, where more than 1.2 million Turks live as migrant laborers. His name was on a list of Turkish extremists prepared last year by a

See SUSPECT, Page 10

Americans Offer Prayers For Pope

Compiled From News Services

NEW YORK — Americans of all religions are decrying the growth of world violence and praying for the quick recovery of Pope John Paul II, the "gentle shepherd" of the Roman Catholic Church.

Catholic schoolchildren were led in prayer Wednesday; prayers were said in synagogues and special Masses were said in many communities for the pontiff, wounded in St. Peter's Square on Wednesday.

Priests and politicians expressed their dismay, as did Lutherans, Mormons, Jews, Methodists and other groups, both religious and secular.

President Ronald Reagan, who was wounded in an assassination attempt on March 30, sent a message to the pope saying: "All Americans join me in hopes and prayers for your speedy recovery from the injuries you have suffered in the attack. Our prayers are with you."

Vice President George Bush asked: "What's happening in the world? What kind of madness has been let loose?"

Sen. Edward M. Kennedy, D-Mass., who lost two brothers to assassins' bullets, said, "The greatest symbol of peace in the world has been struck down by this latest act of mindless violence."

Late Wednesday afternoon, Reagan administration officials and congressmen joined about 1,000 other people at St. Matthew's Cathedral, near the Capitol, to pray for the pope and to hear Archbishop James Hickey plead for an end to "a plague of terrorism and violence in our world."

Secretary of State Alexander M. Haig Jr., Labor Secretary Raymond Donovan, Richard V. Allen, who is Reagan's national security adviser, and House Speaker Thomas P. O'Neill Jr., D-Mass., prayed together in the front pew at the Mass, celebrated by Hickey, the archbishop of the Roman Catholic Diocese of Washington.

"It is with sorrow, with shock and with disbelief that we have received the news from Rome," Hickey said. He asked those present to "pray for the recovery of the holy father, that God restore him to health." He prayed that the "destructive weight of terrorism and violence be lifted from our world."

Outside the church, O'Neill said, "Two great world leaders within a period of six weeks; it's a sad commentary on the world."

First lady Nancy Reagan was

See NATION, Page 10

thursday

features

BIG WEEKEND FOR CONTRA CULTURE: Having fun is the only prerequisite for contra dancing (right). It's discussed on Page 2D of CALENDAR.

A PAIR OF STARS: John Archibald interviews two stars of the new movie "Take This Job and Shove It." One is Robert Hays, fresh from his triumph in the satirical "Airplane!" The other is Bigfoot, who happens to be a truck. Page 1G of Everyday

in today's
POST-DISPATCH
north
area news

Clearing, Cool

Official forecast for St. Louis and vicinity: Clearing and cool tonight, low in the upper 40s. Clear Friday, high in the low 70s. Fair Saturday, with thunderstorms likely Sunday and Monday. Mild temperatures are expected with highs in the mid-70s and lows in the 50s.

MONEY TALKS?

POST-DISPATCH WEATHERBIRD

inside

72 Pages

Reagan Reported Seeking Tax Cut Compromise

©1981, New York Times News Service

WASHINGTON — President Ronald Reagan, concerned by the unsettled condition of the financial markets, is prepared to accept less than the full amount of his proposed tax cut but wants congressional Democrats to make the first move toward compromise, a senior White House official said Wednesday.

But a White House spokesman today vigorously denied that the administration is prepared to compromise.

"This is no time for compromise — and that comes straight from the president," said acting White House press secretary Larry Speakes. "I know there has been no change" in the administration's position.

"In the weeks to come, we don't anticipate a change," Speakes said. But he added: "Our door is always open. We're ready to listen. I just know the president is not ready to compromise."

The report of a willingness to compromise came from an official who asked not to be identified.

He said in an interview that administration planners had become increasingly worried that the behavior of the markets would cause members of Congress to have second thoughts about voting for Reagan's programs.

He said that recent disarray in the markets had shown some Reagan aides that Wall Street was concerned that future tax cuts would widen the budget deficit. As a result, the administration is more willing to compromise on the size of the tax cut.

The administration is also taking steps to make additional spending cuts this year as a way of convincing the markets that Reagan is adamant about controlling deficits, he said. The decision to announce Social Security cutbacks this week, he said, was partly spurred by the need to deal with the financial markets.

In the same period that Reagan has won approval in the House and the Senate for his budget proposals, bond market prices have fallen to record lows, the Dow Jones industrial average has dropped substantially, and short-term interest rates have soared to near-record highs.

The cornerstone of Reagan's proposal has been a three-year, 10 percent annual cut in the personal tax rate, costing $44 billion in the first year alone. The main Democratic alternative has been advanced by Rep. Dan Rostenkowski of Illinois, chairman of the House Ways and Means Committee. It calls for a one-year, $28 billion tax cut.

The White House official said Rostenkowski's proposal was unacceptable in its current form. He said Reagan, in being prepared to compromise, might back off on the magnitude of his proposed cut but not on the concept of a multiyear cut in the marginal tax rate for individuals.

Nor would the president drop his insistence that the tax cut be geared toward increasing savings and

See TAXES, Page 9

Report Clears Prison System

By Terry Ganey
Post-Dispatch Jefferson City Bureau Chief

JEFFERSON CITY — A new report says there is no evidence of the use of excessive force within the state prison system but recommends the formation of an independent unit to investigate future allegations of brutality.

"To date, no evidence of excessive use of force has been found," said the report written by the staff of the Department of Social Services and made public today. "It should be noted, however, that our investigation, while extensive, has not had the benefit of trained and independent police investigators, with certain specific exceptions. Where police investigators have been used to interrogate, no positive evidence supporting allegations of excessive force or corruption has been obtained.

"Nevertheless, it is felt that in the

See PRISONS, Page 7

Bond Issue Is Approved For Toyota Dealership

By Jeff Gelles
Of the Post-Dispatch Staff

An $865,000 bond issue to finance the construction and equipping of a Hazelwood Toyota dealership was given initial approval today by the St. Louis County Industrial Development Authority.

The authority's 4-3 vote was taken without any public discussion. However, board members acknowledged the controversial nature of the proposal twice last month by choosing to delay the vote rather than taking it with less than the entire board present.

The bond issue was sought by Jim Lynch, owner of Jim Lynch Cadillac Inc., 9091 Dunn Road. Lynch, who has operated his Cadillac dealership since 1975, obtained a Toyota franchise in March 1980 to bolster the lagging sales of his American-made cars.

The greatest opposition to the proposal came from the United Auto Workers. In testimony to the board on Lynch's proposal, Jerry R. Tucker, international representative for Region 5 of the UAW, said industrial development bonds should be used to spur "the creation of jobs and industry" in the United States rather than to support industrial competitors of the United States.

But Lynch, after the board's

See BONDS, Page 10

Benefits Study May Be Urged

By Jon Sawyer
Post-Dispatch Washington Bureau

WASHINGTON — The six Democratic members of the House subcommittee on Social Security, including Rep. Richard A. Gephardt, D-St. Louis, plan to caution fellow party members not to jump too fast or too hard on President Ronald Reagan's proposal to shore up Social Security by cutting back future benefits.

"What the president has proposed is not new or radical and it should not be dismissed offhand simply because it was his proposal, not ours," Gephardt said in a letter that was drafted by his staff. The letter was expected to go out today over the signatures of Chairman J.J. Pickle, D-Texas, and the five other Democratic members on the subcommittee responsible for all Social

See BENEFITS, Page 8

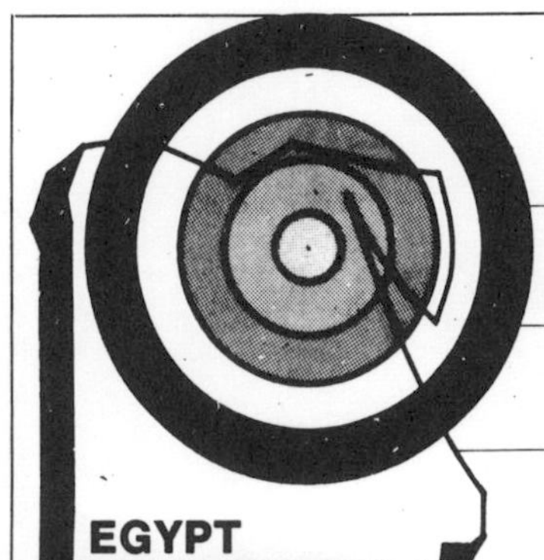

Mrs. Sadat Knew Husband's Life Was in Constant Danger **A3**

Metro **THE POST-STANDARD**

153RD YEAR VOL. 153 NO. 20 SYRACUSE, N.Y. WEDNESDAY, OCTOBER 7, 1981 25 CENTS

Showers Again
Variable clouds with a chance of showers are expected today and tomorrow. — **Full Report on Page A-5.**
High Today — 55
Low Tonight — 40

SADAT: World Loses 'Champion Of Peace'

Assassination Casts Pall of Uncertainty

Compiled

CAIRO, Egypt — Egyptian President Anwar Sadat was assassinated Tuesday by a group of rebel soldiers who broke away from a military parade and attacked his reviewing stand with Soviet-made AK47 automatic rifles and hand grenades.

Officials said five other dignitaries, including a Coptic Christian bishop and two foreigners, were killed and 38 were wounded, among them Egypt's defense minister and three American military observers.

Sadat, shot in the chest and shoulder, was rushed to Maadi armed forces hospital in a coma, his military uniform covered with blood. He died two hours later at 8:40 a.m. EDT after undergoing surgery and open heart massage, an official medical bulletin said. He was 62.

A doctor, his face streaming with tears, emerged from the operating room and broke the news to Sadat's wife Jihan with a Moslem saying, "Only God is immortal." Mrs. Sadat, who had watched the parade from a box just above the reviewing stand whre her husband was shot, collapsed in tears, witnesses said.

(Continued on Page A-4)

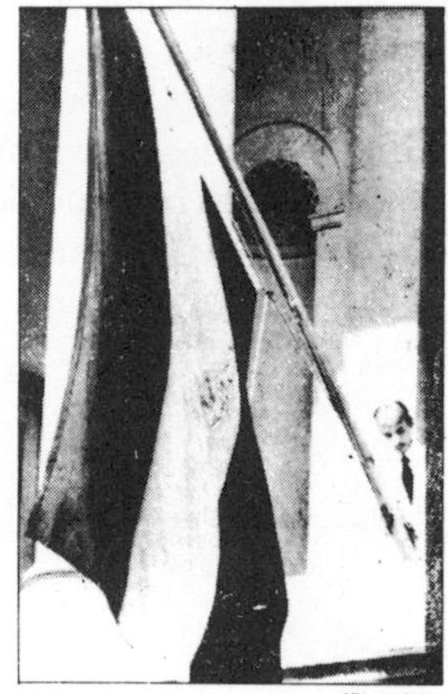

AP Laserphoto

An Egyptian Embassy employee in Washington solemnly lowers the Egyptian flag to half staff Tuesday after it was confirmed that President Sadat had died of assassins' bullets.

A Big Bang, Another . . . Pandemonium

By DAVID B. OTTAWAY
The Washington Post

CAIRO — It was toward the end of what had been a spectacular military parade, and nobody was paying much attention to the slow-moving shiny Russian trucks hauling behind them new South Korean artillery pieces on display for the first time.

Instead all eyes were turned upward toward the Mirage jets swooping only feet above the reviewing stand and leaving behind trails of bright red, blue and white smoke as they climbed up and over to make a colorful loop in the blue sky before flying away.

Suddenly one of the trucks came to an abrupt halt right in front of the reviewing stand where President Anwar Sadat and the entire Egyptian military and political hierarchy were seated Tuesday watching the parade marking Egypt's initial victory in 1973 over the Israelis along the Suez Canal.

I was wondering to myself whether there was another embarrassing breakdown in store, as already one motorcycle had conked out at the beginning of the parade just before passing the reviewing stand and the driver had had to push it along by hand.

(Continued on Page A-4)

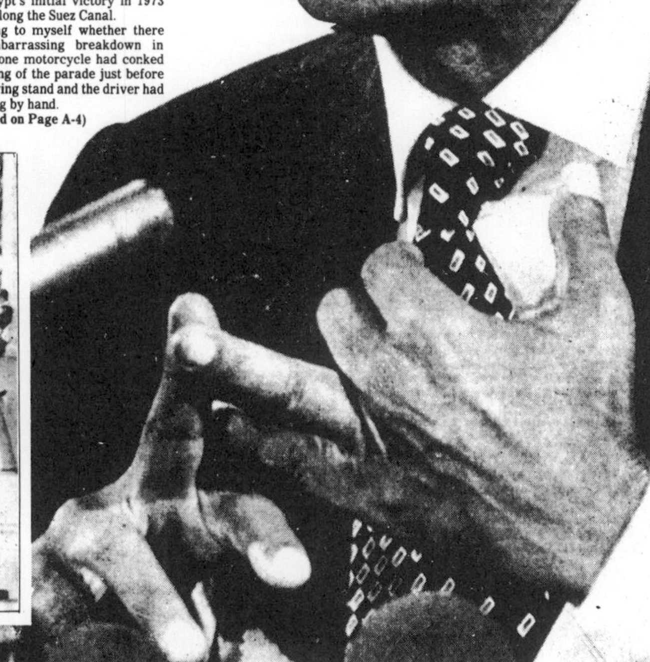

AP Laserphoto

Security men check around the doorway through which President Sadat was taken to a waiting helicopter after he was shot Tuesday in Cairo.

Inside

Lottery Winner: 518

Win-Four: 6327

1983

A Korean Air Lines jumbo jetliner carrying 269 civilians was shot down by a Soviet fighter pilot after the jet strayed into Soviet airspace en route from Anchorage, Alaska, to Seoul, Korea, on September 1.

The incident prompted a flood of international outrage and further chilled relations between the United States and the Soviet Union.

Electronic evidence showed that the Soviets had tracked the plane for two and a half hours and had made visual contact with it before firing at least two heat-seeking missiles. At least one missile found its target. Flight 007 plunged into the Sea of Japan.

The Soviets offered no apologies, accusing the United States of using a civilian aircraft for spying purposes.

The Brooklyn Bridge celebrated its one-hundredth birthday.

TODAY
Sunny, 70s
TONIGHT
Cloudy, 60s
TOMORROW
Chance of showers, 65-70
Details, Page 2

NEW YORK POST

METRO
SPORTS FINAL

TV listings: P. 79 WEDNESDAY, MAY 25, 1983 30 CENTS AMERICA'S FASTEST-GROWING NEWSPAPER

ABC AVERAGE SALES EXCEED **960,000**

THE LADY IS A CHAMP

★ IT was a night of a million stars — seen by throngs of New Yorkers as the sky exploded into a rainbow of bursting color.

★ A jam-packed crowd gaped in awe as night turned into day and New York toasted the proud lady who turned 100 years old yesterday.

★ Ten thousand firework shells made up the biggest collection of candles ever to appear on a birthday cake. Their designer James Grucci, who is aiming for a place in the Guinness Book of World Records, lived up to his promise that "New York has never seen anything like it" — and they probably won't ever again.

★ Happy Birthday grand lady, we all luv ya . . .

SOUVENIR COVERAGE OF THE DAY'S FABULOUS FESTIVITIES: **TURN TO PAGES 2, 3, 4, 39, 40, 41 & 42**

7 PAGES OF PHOTOS

"All the News That's Fit to Print"

The New York Times

Late Edition
Weather: Mostly sunny warm today, light northerly winds; mostly clear tonight. Sunny, warm, humid tomorrow. Temperatures: today 80-85, tonight 63-67; yesterday 73-77. Details, page C20.

VOL. CXXXII . . No. 45,788 NEW YORK, THURSDAY, SEPTEMBER 1, 1983 — 60 cents beyond 75 miles from New York City, except on Long Island. — 30 CENTS

Korean Jetliner With 269 Aboard Missing Near Soviet Pacific Island

May Have Been Forced to Land, but Its Loss Is Also Called Possible

By CLYDE HABERMAN
Special to The New York Times

TOKYO, Thursday, Sept. 1 — A South Korean airliner with 269 people aboard disappeared this morning near the Soviet island of Sakhalin, off the Pacific coast of Siberia, according to reports in Tokyo and Seoul.

Early reports said the plane, a Korean Air Lines Boeing 747 jetliner on a flight from New York to Seoul with a stop in Anchorage, had been forced down by Soviet Air Force planes and that all 240 passengers and 29 crew members were believed to be safe.

But an airline official in Seoul said this afternoon that an explosion might have occurred in midair.

Radar Said to Lose Plane

In addition, Japanese Air Force officials said they had tracked a plane flying near Sakhalin that suddenly disappeared from their radar screens. Just before that happened, the officials said, one or more other planes were observed flying close by. [South Korean officials said the plane was at 30,000 feet when it disappeared from radar, The Associated Press reported.

[According to a Reuters report from Moscow, the Soviet Union denied that a missing Korean Air Lines jumbo jet had been forced to land on Sakhalin. The news agency quoted a Japanese Embassy spokesman who said a Soviet Foreign Ministry official had told the embassy that the Korean plane was not on the island and that Soviet authorities had no other information about it.]

Little was clear, including why the plane, flight 007, might have been forced to land.

There was speculation that the airliner might have veered off course while flying near Sakhalin, whose southernmost tip is 25 miles from Japanese territory.

One of the passengers was said to be Representative Larry P. McDonald, Democrat of Georgia, who was flying to Seoul to attend a ceremony on the 30th anniversary of the signing of a mutual defense treaty between the United States and South Korea. In Washington, an aide to the Congressman said he was certain that Mr. McDonald was on the plane, The Associated Press reported.

Throughout the morning and into the afternoon, details of the plane's fate

Continued on Page D19, Column 1

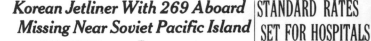

Associated Press

Representative Larry P. McDonald of Georgia was a passenger on the South Korean jetliner.

STANDARD RATES SET FOR HOSPITALS UNDER MEDICARE

New York and New Jersey Get Waivers, but Connecticut Must Comply on Oct. 1

By ROBERT PEAR
Special to The New York Times

WASHINGTON, Aug. 31 — The Reagan Administration announced today the first big step toward standard nationwide rates for hospitals treating elderly and disabled patients under the Medicare program.

Officials disclosed the basic standard rates that Medicare would pay for a hospital case in each of nine regions of the country, ranging from a high of $3,021 in urban areas of Illinois, Michigan and Ohio to a low of $2,142 in rural areas of Arkansas, Louisiana, Oklahoma and Texas.

Weighted Rates for Procedures

In calculating the Government's actual payment, the basic rate is multiplied by a factor intended to reflect the cost of different procedures. Coronary bypass surgery, for example, is given eight times the weight of a cataract procedure.

The new system, which uses predetermined rates for all patients with the same illness or injury, is known as prospective payment. It takes effect when a hospital begins its next fiscal year, on or after Oct. 1.

The system was designed to help the Government control Medicare spending for hospital inpatient services, which rose from $3 billion in 1967 to $38.5 billion this year.

New York, New Jersey, Maryland and Massachusetts have received waivers exempting them from the new Federal rules because they had their own cost-control systems using a different form of prospective payment for all hospital patients, including those covered by private insurance carriers. In Connecticut, general hospitals will be paid under the new system starting Oct. 1.

Announcement by Mrs. Heckler

There is much uncertainty about the effects of the new payment system, which was announced today by Margaret M. Heckler, the Secretary of Health and Human Services. Federal officials said it would not have a sudden or dramatic effect on Medicare patients. Hospital officials said the system would give them new incentives to control

Continued on Page B12, Column 3

Economic Index Shows Recovery Is Slowing a Bit

By PETER T. KILBORN
Special to The New York Times

WASHINGTON, Aug. 31 — A gauge the Government uses to predict the performance of the nation's economy suggests that the strong pace of recovery so far this year, which had begun to worry many economists, is slowing down, the Commerce Department reported today.

The department said its index of leading economic indicators rose three-tenths of 1 percent in July, the smallest of 11 consecutive monthly gains. But the Reagan Administration, and private economists as well, found more encouragement in the July figure than cause for concern.

The report cheered the stock market, lifting the Dow Jones industrial average 20.12 points, to 1,216.16, after days of desultory activity. [Page D1.]

"July's modest rise in the leading index is an early indication that the economic rebound of the second quarter will taper to a more sustainable pace," said Commerce Secretary Malcolm Baldrige. "Gains in the leading index in the range of one-half to one percent would be consistent with the

Continued on Page D13, Column 1

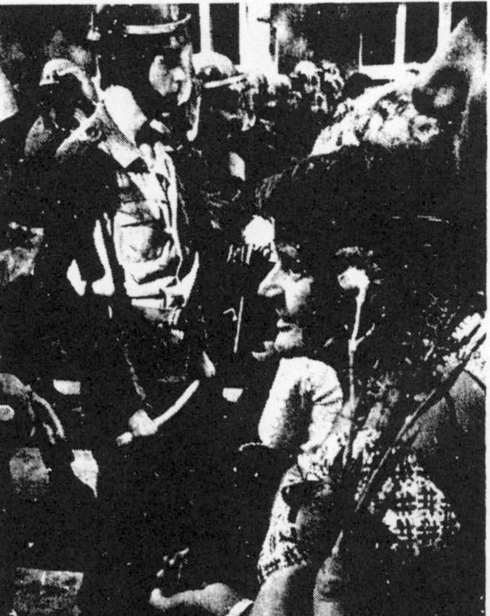

The New York Times / John Kifner

Policemen in Gdansk bar Poles from laying flowers at shipyard monument.

Thousands March in Polish Cities On the Founding Day of Solidarity

By JOHN KIFNER
Special to The New York Times

GDANSK, Poland, Aug. 31 — Tens of thousands of Poles demonstrated around the country today on the third anniversary of the accords that permitted the formation of the independent trade union Solidarity.

The biggest demonstration, according to reports arriving here, appeared to have taken place in the steel center of Nowa Huta, east of Cracow. A march attempted there by 10,000 people developed into street fighting between demonstrators and policemen who fired tear gas and used truncheons.

It was difficult to assess the effect of the rush-hour boycott of public transport that the underground had called as its main thrust. Gdansk streetcars, normally packed around 3 o'clock, had only a handful of riders. In other places the boycott seemed to have been less than total.

Fragmentary information from a variety of sources indicated that there had been some form of demonstration, including special church services, in at least eight cities, including Czestochowa, Lubin and Gdynia.

Here in Gdansk, thousands of flower-carrying Poles confronted policemen who had sealed off streets leading to a monument at the shipyard gate. The monument honors workers slain while protesting food price rises in 1970.

Lech Walesa, the Solidarity founder, was allowed through to lay a wreath. On his return, 3,000 people marched to a nearby church shouting, "No freedom without Solidarity!"

In the evening, there were brief clashes when a crowd of 5,000 left an evening mass chanting "Solidarity" and marched toward lines of riot police who were backed by water cannon.

The demonstrations here were on a smaller scale than a year ago, when crowds fought pitched battles with the police around the shipyard gate.

But the fact remained that Solidarity could still turn out supporters on the street after a year and a half of suppression.

For the Government, the protest was an indication that despite the announcement of the lifting of martial law, it had yet to win widespread allegiance.

The clashes in Nowa Huta, built in

Continued on Page A10, Column 1

The New York Times

Lech Walesa is allowed through.

KEY BEIRUT AREAS RETAKEN BY ARMY FROM MILITIA UNITS

TROOPS IN SHOW OF FORCE

6,000 Lebanese Soldiers Stage an Assault on Moslems — Marines Not Involved

By RICHARD BERNSTEIN
Special to The New York Times

BEIRUT, Lebanon, Aug. 31 — The Lebanese Army, engaging in a major show of force today, counterattacked the leftist Moslem militia units that had seized large parts of West Beirut.

The army sent about 6,000 troops in a combined armor and infantry assault that stretched across West Beirut. By the end of the day, it seemed to have gained control of most of the key parts of the city lost earlier to bands of Moslem gunmen.

"If the army wanted any piece of land, the army took it," a military source said. In the operation, "we had some vehicles destroyed and had some equipment and personnel captured," he said.

Curfew Imposed by Army

As the troops swept from east to west across the largely Moslem half of Beirut, small arms fire, rockets and artillery could be heard throughout the city. The Lebanese Army declared a 24-hour curfew early this morning and most of the streets were virtually deserted.

The Italian contingent in the multinational peacekeeping force reported this morning that 12 artillery rounds had landed in its compound, damaging vehicles and equipment. There were no casualties. None of the other members of the peacekeeping forces reported serious involvement in combat today.

In midafternoon the Commodore Hotel received direct hits by at least two shells during an attack that poured some 20 artillery rounds into the immediate vicinity. Most of the hotel's residents had taken shelter in a basement as the shelling appeared to get closer, and there were no injuries.

Streets Strewn With Rubble

Windows and some wall areas along the east side of the seven-story hotel were shattered and some sections of wall were caved in. The streets around were strewn with rubble; there were several burned-out cars and the nearby area was a morass of broken glass, paving stones and shell craters.

A tour by car through several parts of West Beirut showed the Lebanese Army in clear control of many areas that had been contested since fighting broke out between the militias, led by the Shiite Amal organization, and the army four days ago.

In the port area along the northern coast of Beirut, the army had set up numerous checkpoints today and placed armored personnel carriers and Saladin tanks at key crossings.

Green Line Is Quiet

The area, which suffered extensive damage during the civil war of 1975 and 1976 and is largely uninhabited, was a key battleground last night because of the proximity of the Holiday Inn, with its commanding view of both East and West Beirut.

A similar condition prevailed along the green line, the informal division between the Christian and Moslem sec-

Continued on Page A8, Column 1

Hospitals' Plans in City Called 'Unaffordable'

By RONALD SULLIVAN

Plans by New York City's private hospitals and medical centers to spend more than $4 billion on renovations and new technology should be drastically cut, the city's federally financed health planning agency advised Governor Cuomo yesterday.

The unit, the New York City Health Systems Agency, described the projected costs as "staggering by any standard" and "unaffordable." It warned that they would have to be borne by the taxpayers and that they would be damaging for the hospitals themselves, especially those in impoverished neighborhoods.

The state regulates all new construction in hospitals, private as well as public, on the ground that public funds, in the form of Federal and private insurance plans, pay for virtually all hospital construction. The New York State Department of Health is now seeking to extend that authority.

In February, the Governor imposed a freeze on major new hospital construction in an effort to halt what he regarded as a proliferation of unneeded and costly hospital expansion, especially in New York City. The freeze was intended to give local health-planning agencies enough time to submit recommendations for reducing construction and costs. The agencies were asked to submit their recommendations by Aug. 30.

More specific recommendations, such as exactly what each hospital should cut back or eliminate, are to be submitted Nov. 1.

In compliance with the Governor's request, the agency said hospital renovations in the city could be made for far less money. It said that major teaching hospitals in the city, particularly those on Manhattan's East Side, should help eliminate what it said were 1,300 excess beds.

In addition, the agency said, those hospitals should agree to merge expensive services rather than continue to compete with one another by offering both routine care and the latest medical technology to fewer and fewer patients.

Thus far, the agency said, such efforts "have been virtually nonexistent."

Meanwhile, the agency recom-

Continued on Page B14, Column 1

INSIDE

Astronauts Launch Satellite

The space shuttle astronauts launched a communications-weather satellite for India and talked by phone with President Reagan. Page A12.

Reagan Asks Federal Raise

President Reagan dropped his proposed pay freeze for 1.4 million white-collar Federal employees and urged a 3.5 percent raise. Page A18.

Associated Press

An honor guard carrying the coffin of Second Lieut. Donald G. Losey at Dover Air Force Base, Del. The bodies of Lieutenant Losey and Staff Sgt. Alexander M. Ortega were brought from Beirut, where they were killed Monday.

Marines Are Neither Combatants Nor Targets in Beirut, U.S. Insists

By BERNARD GWERTZMAN
Special to The New York Times

WASHINGTON, Aug. 31 — The Reagan Administration reiterated today that there was no reason to say the marines in Lebanon were the targets of Moslem militia units or that they were engaged in hostilities. It was the third such statement in as many days.

With pressure mounting on Capitol Hill for the Administration either to invoke that part of the War Powers Resolution that acknowledges that hostilities are imminent or to pull the troops out of Lebanon now that they have been fired upon, Secretary of State George P. Shultz said the situation could not yet be classified as hostilities involving the marines. Rather, he said, the marines were caught in the midst of widespread violence not necessarily directed at them.

Text of Shultz statement, page A8.

The distinction was important, State Department officials said, because a statement by the Administration that the marines are in combat or in hostilities would set off the mechanism by which Congress could force them to leave within 90 days.

On Monday, 2 marines were killed in Beirut by mortar fire and 14 others were wounded.

In Europe, the other countries that have contributed to the peacekeeping force in Lebanon accepted casualties among the French and American contingents with resignation. The French Defense Minister, Charles Hernu, said there was "no question" of withdrawing or reducing France's 2,000-member contingent. Britain and Italy also indicated they intended to keep their contingents in Lebanon. [Page A9.]

'Generalized Pattern of Violence'

At a news conference, Mr. Shultz said of the marines: "They are involved in a situation where there is violence, a generalized pattern of violence. They are defending themselves as they must and should."

Mr. Shultz, a World War II Marine combat officer in the Pacific, said there should be no doubt that if the marines are attacked "they will take care of themselves." But he added that

Continued on Page A8, Column 5

Special Edition

SYRACUSE'S MARINES: At least 1 wounded, 1 safe

Edward De Socio

Kevin Abrams

John Lux Jr.

Don Pontillo

David Condon

Richard Menkins

Bruce Herbig

Michael Episcopo

By Tom Schwendler
Staff Writer

The Marines were notifying three area families today their sons were wounded or killed in the Beirut bombing Sunday, the father of a Marine stationed there said early this afternoon.

James Condon, the father of Lance Cpl. David Condon who is in Lebanon, said he talked to the Marine headquarters near Hancock airport and was told an officer was notifying the families.

"He said he had three names of people in the area, and I guess at least one of them is dead," said Condon of 171 Clyde Ave.

■ WAITING, Page A5

SYRACUSE
HERALD-JOURNAL
VOL. 107, NO. 32,050
CITY EDITION

MONDAY, OCTOBER 24, 1983
25 cents

MASSACRE IN BEIRUT

Terrorists' twin bombings in Beirut horrify the world; Americans question U.S. role in Lebanon's tragedy

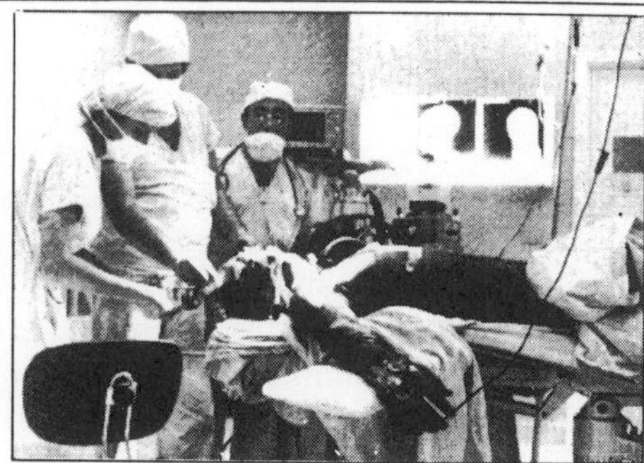
AP Laserphoto
A Marine in emergency surgery at a Beirut hospital.

A Marine, his leg deeply torn by the explosion at the headquarters building, is carried away by comrades.
AP Laserphoto

Stunned Marines regroup

Death toll may top 200, officials fear

BEIRUT, Lebanon (AP) — U.S. Marines reinforced security barriers, bulldozed smoldering rubble and awaited replacements today after a suicide terrorist bombing that killed 183 comrades under tons of concrete and wounded at least 75.

A second terrorist bombing seconds later killed 23 French soldiers, left 35 missing and wounded 15, the French Defense Ministry said. French President Francois Mitterrand made a surprise visit to Beirut and inspected the carnage but told reporters: "I have no declarations to make."

The Marines added sentries, set up more checkpoints and parked large trucks across all roads leading to their compound at Beirut's international airport, forcing all vehicles to halt for security shakedowns.

The Pentagon gave the American death toll as 183 from Sunday's blast, which occurred at 6:20 a.m. as most of the Marines slept. But U.S. Marine officials in Beirut said some Marines and Navy men might still be buried in the smoking wreckage of the command post. Tons of concrete covered at least two bunk areas and the basement.

■ BOMBING, Page A4

October 23, 1983 Day of Outrage

• Tragedy dramatizes lack of coherent Lebanon policy in Washington. **Editorial, A8.**

• Central New York congressman George Wortley cautions against a too-hasty reaction. **A6.**

• One local father learned Sunday night that his son, a Marine in Lebanon, was safe. **A5.**

• Six weeks ago, a Druse militia leader said: "It would not be difficult for us to kill 300 or 400 Marines in one night." **A6.**

Today's features

• **U.S. Marines** in Beirut reinforced security barriers and awaited replacements today after a terrorist bombing that killed at least 183 of their comrades.

• **French President Francois Mitterrand** arrived to inspect the pulverized building where a second bombing Sunday left at least 58 French soldiers dead and missing.

• **A hitherto unknown group** called the Islamic Revolutionary Movement claimed responsibility for the blasts.

• **Congress moved swiftly** to reopen the debate on why the U.S. peacekeepers are in Lebanon and how long they should stay.

• **President Reagan** grimly vowed that terrorists will not "drive us out" of Lebanon.

• **France and Italy** said their peacekeeping forces would remain in Beirut, but Britain said its troops will not stay indefinitely.

• **Israel's new prime minister,** Yitzhak Smahir, called the explosions "a despicable crime."

• **More than 300 Marines** gathered have left for Lebanon to replace those killed or wounded.

Marines must stay to keep peace: Reagan

By Helen Thomas
UPI White House Reporter

WASHINGTON — A day after at least 183 U.S. Marines died in a terrorist bombing in Beirut, President Reagan today defended the presence of U.S. Marines in the Lebanese peacekeeping force.

Reagan, in a statement televised nationwide, said peace is the reason the Marines are there and the reason they should stay.

"The reason they must stay there is quite clear. We have vital interests in Lebanon. We are part of a multinational peacekeeping force seeking the withdrawal of all foreign forces in Lebanon. By promoting peace in Lebanon we strengthen the forces of peace throughout the whole Middle East. This is a goal Republicans and Democrats share.

The president called the bombing the work of "viscious, cowardly, ruthless" enemies.

■ REAGAN, Page A4

1984

President Ronald Reagan won reelection in a landslide, carrying forty-nine of the fifty states in a record result.

It was the last day of October when India's Prime Minister Indira Gandhi walked out of her bungalow in her New Delhi compound.

Two members of her security guard, identified as Sikhs, shot her down. She died despite the efforts of a team of twelve doctors.

Mrs. Gandhi, daughter of Jawaharlal Nehru, India's first prime minister, had dominated her nation for fifteen of the previous eighteen years.

Within hours after the announcement of her death, India experienced its worst violence since partition in 1947. More than a thousand were killed in anti-Sikh riots.

Mrs. Gandhi's son, Rajiv Gandhi, succeeded her as prime minister.

A poisonous cloud of methyl-isocynate gas leaked from a Union Carbide pesticide plant on the outskirts of the city of Bhopal, India during the night of December 3.

The deadly leak became the greatest industrial accident in history, killing at least seventeen hundred people and sending thousands of others to hospitals.

Union Carbide later pledged $5 million for emergency relief.

New York Newsday
EDITION
THURSDAY, NOV. 1, 1984 ● 30 CENTS

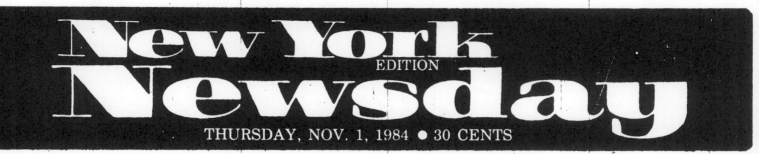

INDIRA GANDHI
1917-1984

The Assassination

- The Shooting
- The Violent Reaction
- Her Son Succeeds Her
- Her Life Story

1985

President Reagan journeyed to Europe for meetings with other world leaders. The trip, on the 40th anniversary of the end of World War II, included a controversial stop at a military cemetery in Germany, where some Nazi SS men had been buried.

A flash fire in the stands of a soccer stadium in Bradford, England, killed fifty-two people.

The space shuttle Challenger completed a flight of 2.9 million miles and 109 orbits of the Earth. The shuttle carried seven astronauts and twenty-six animals on the week-long journey and brought back a treasure of research data.

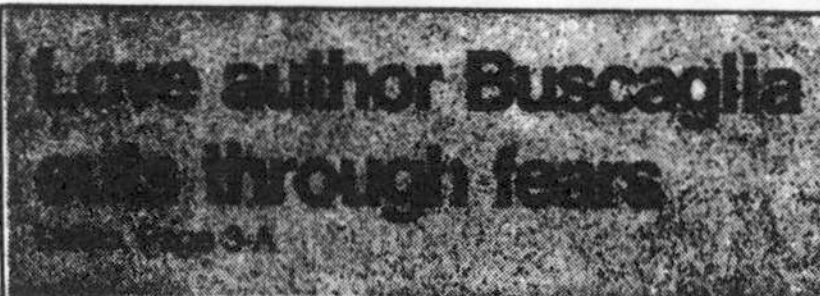

The boss:
How to work around quirks
Business, Page 1-B

Gold outshoots Gunslingers 35-9
SportsToday, Page 1-E

THE DENVER POST

May 6, 1985 | Voice of the Rocky Mountain Empire | Final Edition\25¢

3 down, 1 to go

The Denver Post / Damian Strohmeyer

The Nuggets' Mike Evans glides to the hoop as Calvin Natt (33) looks on. The Nuggets beat the Utah Jazz, 125-118, to take a 3-1 lead in the series. **Coverage begins on Page 1-E.**

Bitburg rites somber, brief

By The Associated Press

BITBURG, West Germany — President Reagan, making a determined gesture of reconciliation against a backdrop of protest, led an austere wreath-laying ceremony Sunday at the small military cemetery in Bitburg that holds gravestones of German war dead and SS troopers.

To mute the storm of protest arising from his homage at the graves of Nazis, Reagan spent an earlier hour at a concentration camp where 50,000 Jews and gentiles were put to death by Adolf Hitler's 12-year dictatorship.

"The horror cannot outlast the hope," the president said there — his message to those who accused him of ignoring the Nazi horrors.

Reagan, in one of the most controversial acts of his presidency, spent only eight minutes in silence at the Kolmeshohe Cemetery in Bitburg with West German Chancellor Helmut Kohl on a dank, gray day.

Neither spoke. Soldiers carried two wreaths of brightly colored flowers to the base of a slate tower. Close by two SS gravestones, the two leaders stood, tight-lipped, their hands on the flowers before them.

A bugler played "I Had a Comrade," the German equivalent of "Taps." Then both walked over to shake hands with a group of spectators, including German Army

Please see BITBURG on 9-A

INSIDE

Reuter

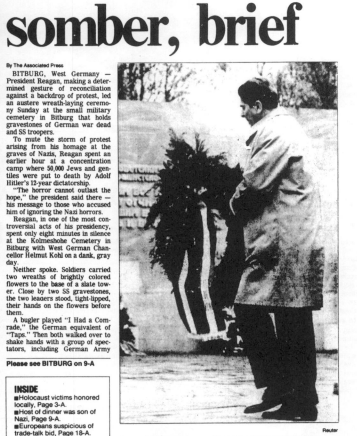

Reagan lays wreath at memorial obelisk at Bergen-Belsen camp.

Arapahoe 7th-fastest in growth

By Diana Griego
Denver Post Staff Writer

Arapahoe County is the seventh-fastest growing county in the nation, a report released Sunday shows.

The report, done by the New York-based Dun and Bradstreet Corp., estimated population changes between 1980 and 1984 for each of the nation's 3,123 counties with populations of 100,000 or more.

Both the nation's 25 fastest growing counties and the 25 counties suffering the largest population decreases were listed in the report.

Population in Arapahoe, the only Colorado county cited in the report, rose 28.4 percent during the four-year period. Topping the list was Fort Bend County in Texas at 45.8 percent.

Officials in Arapahoe County and Aurora — the county's largest city — were not surprised by the report.

"I'm not surprised at all," said Frank Mizner, Aurora's acting director of planning. "It's just a confirmation of everything we've heard before and what we're planning for."

Population in Aurora grew 39.2 percent between 1980 and 1984.

But Mizner said the city can handle the surge.

"We have ample water supplies and large expanses of easily developed land available. We're not re-

Please see COUNTY on 12-A

Park Towers condos sold for a song

Bruce Wilkinson
Denver Post Business Writer

The remaining 18 luxury condominium units in the posh 20-story Park Towers in Cheesman Park were sold Sunday — for a song.

Although Sunday's auction attracted about 1,000 people and brought in nearly $4.3 million, officials said most successful bidders got what amounted to 40 to 50 percent discounts on listed prices.

"We're disappointed," said Russell Keithly, president of Landex Properties Ltd.

Landex was formed by Aetna of Canada and the Cumberland Realty Co. of Vancouver, B.C., developers of Park Towers.

"It really didn't do as well as we hoped," Keithly said. "The people got terrific buys."

Charles Biederman, a principal in Robert Rouse & Associates, a competing auction company which has sold a number of Colorado properties, agreed there were "tremendous buys."

The widely advertised auction was conducted at the Marriott City Center Hotel by Sheldon F. Good &

Please see CONDOS on 12-A

Associated Press

Ethiopian famine victims believed ordered out of the Ibnet feeding camp received relief grain from the United States.

Famine donations fall short

Denver Post Wire Services

NAIROBI, Kenya — Donor nations have failed to make good on pledged food deliveries to famine-stricken Africa and only immediate action can avert a "major disaster" in the six hardest-hit countries, a U.N. report said Sunday.

A report issued by the U.N. Food and Agricultural Organization regional office in Nairobi said as of late April, international food pledges for 21 African countries facing severe shortages amounted to 6.3 million tons.

But the report said that only 2.7 million tons — or 42 percent — has been delivered. The 6.3 million tons in pledges still leave a continental shortfall of 700,000 tons, the report said.

Meantime in Ethiopia, Kurt Jansson, a U.N. assistant secre-

Please see FAMINE on 12-A

WEATHER

DENVER AREA: Mostly sunny, breezy and mild today, with a chance of an afternoon shower. High: 73-78; low: 49-54. Details on Page 12-C.

INDEX

Supercomputer wars/ Untapped resource costing state's early lead

By John Aloysius Farrell
Denver Post Medical/Science Writer

What Paris is to romance, what Motown is to soul, what L.A. is to sunsets, and what Philadelphia is to pretzels with mustard.

That is what Colorado could become to megaflops, gigaflops and nanoseconds.

We're talking supercomputers. Silicon monsters. The biggest, toughest, meanest number-munchers in the business.

Colorado State University in Fort Collins has one — one of just 142 in the world — the first ever to be ordered by an American university.

The state can use its supercomputer, say scientists at CSU, to stay out front in the race for high-tech jobs, money and prestige.

But that is not happening.

As other states proceed with ambition, no one in Colorado — not state government, not research scientists at its universities, not the business community — has taken the initiative to plot an aggressive and timely strategy to capitalize on this unique asset.

"The state is losing a focused, high-visibility opportunity to show the rest of the country it is serious about its plans to develop high-tech industry," says Gary Johnson, director of the Institute for Computational Studies at CSU.

"We're missing the opportunity to be at the forefront of supercomputing."

□□□

Its name is Cyber 205.

Tan and yellow with smoked-glass doors, it fills a fair-sized room in a nondescript building on a tree-lined block in Fort Collins, humming away and routinely analyzing, for example, millions of factors that will determine next week's weather.

It's an awesome machine, and its generation is transforming our world.

Chrysler, General Motors and Ford each owns one: They use their supercomputers to design fuel-efficient engines, aerodynamic cars and new safety features.

The National Security Agency and the CIA have supercomputers to crack secret codes and analyze the flood of data that arrive from a myriad of snoops and spys.

There would be no debate about President Reagan's "star wars" weapons system if supercomputers hadn't made it theoretically possible to try to target thousands of enemy missiles.

The Nuclear Regulatory Commission hopes to prevent another Three Mile Island accident by using a supercomputer to mimic the thousands of things that might go wrong at nuclear power plants.

And when makers of the motion

Please see CSU on 8-A

SANTA BARBARA NEWS-PRESS

The oldest daily newspaper in Southern California

130th Year—No. 348 | Three sections | C | Santa Barbara, Calif., Monday, May 6, 1985 | 44 Pages | 25 cents | Page A-1

17 missing in crash of U.S. craft

Military copter down off Japan coastline

TOKYO (AP) — A U.S. Marine helicopter plunged into the ocean today off the small Japanese island of Yakushima, and American military spokesmen said searchers found no trace of the 17 people aboard.

All the missing are believed to be Marines.

The CH-53D helicopter reported mechanical problems on a 195-mile return flight from Iwakuni, a Marine installation in southwest Japan, to the Marine base in Futemma, Okinawa, said Lt. Gary Shrout of the Yokosuka U.S. Navy Base, southwest of Tokyo.

Spots oil slick

The helicopter turned back toward Iwakuni, he said. Another CH-53D helicopter believed to be traveling the same route turned back a few minutes later and searched for the troubled chopper, but spotted only an oil slick, Shrout added.

Satoshi Imabayashi of the Maritime Safety Agency, Japan's coast guard, said the second helicopter sighted a man floating in the water with his face down and another clutching a fuel tank, but the second man soon disappeared into the waves.

The helicopter dropped a smoke candle to mark the spot and radioed the Maritime Self-Defense Force.

The helicopter crash is believed to have occurred at approximately 1 p.m. (9 p.m. PDT Sunday) about 15 miles south of the island of Yakushima, which is 80 miles south of Kyushu island, Trout said.

Search to continue

The chopper left Iwakuni, 431 miles southwest of Tokyo, at 10:05 a.m. for Okinawa, Japan's southernmost state.

Shrout said a Japanese coast guard vessel and a U.S. reconnaissance aircraft were continuing the search Tuesday.

AP Laserphoto

After laying a wreath at the Bitburg military cemetery, President Reagan and West German Chancellor Kohl, second and third from right, stand in silence. They are flanked by Gen. Matthew B. Ridgway, far right, and West German Gen. Johannes Steinhoff.

Reagan places wreath at Bitburg cemetery

By Terence Hunt
Associated Press

BITBURG, West Germany — President Reagan, making a determined gesture of reconciliation against a backdrop of protest, led an austere wreath-laying ceremony Sunday at the small military cemetery here that holds gravestones of German war dead and SS troopers.

To mute the storm of protest arising from his homage at the graves of Nazis, Reagan spent an earlier hour at a concentration camp where 50,000 Jews and gentiles were put to death by Adolf Hitler's 12-year dictatorship.

Thousands across U.S. protest visit A-24

"The horror cannot outlast the hope," the president said there — his message to those who accused him of ignoring the Nazi horrors.

Controversial act

Reagan, in one of the most controversial acts of his presidency, spent only eight minutes in silence at the Kolmeshohe Cemetery in Bitburg with West German Chancellor Helmut Kohl on a dank, gray day.

Neither spoke. Soldiers carried two wreaths of brightly colored flowers to the base of a slate tower. Close by two SS gravestones, the two leaders stood, tight-lipped, their hands on the flowers before them.

A bugler played, "I Had a Comrade," the German equivalent of "Taps." Then both walked over to shake hands with a group of specta-

See Page A-10, Col. 1

Shuttle back with wealth of knowledge

Sonic booms set off burglar alarms in L.A.

By Dennis Anderson
Associated Press

EDWARDS AIR FORCE BASE — Laden with scientific treasures from a week of orbital research, Challenger brought seven astronauts and 26 animals down safely in the California desert today — triggering sonic booms that set off burglar alarms as it descended.

The stubby-winged space shuttle touched down on the centerline of a dry lake bed runway at 9:11 a.m. PDT, completing a flight of 2.9 million miles and 109 orbits.

"Challenger, welcome home," called out Mission Control as commander Bob Overmyer brought the shuttle to a stop. "Nice job, Bob."

The ship's return touched off twin sonic booms over Los Angeles as it flew over the city and headed eastward to the desert. The booms rattled windows, setting off burglar alarms throughout the area. (The shuttle's route was not over Carpinteria as in past landings, therefore the booms were not heard in Santa Barbara today.)

Landing decision

Officials of the National Aeronautics and Space Administration decided on the California landing, on sand, rather than on the concrete runway of the Kennedy Space Center at Cape Canaveral, Fla., because of problems with the last shuttle landing there. Discovery experienced locked brakes and a burst tire when it landed at Kennedy on April 18, and NASA was concerned about landing the 107-ton Challenger, which weighed four tons more than Discovery, on concrete, pending resolution of the brake problem.

Tucked into the Spacelab 3 module in Challenger's cargo bay is enough research data to fill 50,000 volumes of 200 pages each, said Spacelab mission manager Joseph Cremin. There also are miles of film and more than 3 million frames of video data, some of which will be studied by scientists frame by

See Page A-11, Col. 1

Co-workers cheer return of scientist

By John Wilkens
News-Press Staff Writer

EDWARDS AIR FORCE BASE — Goleta scientist Lodewijk van den Berg couldn't see them as he dropped from the skies in space shuttle Challenger, but they were there: three busloads of co-workers and friends cheering his return to Earth.

"Lodewijk's coming home," beaming Jennie Beltran said.

She was one of 150 people who had gathered at EG&G on Robin Hill Road at 5 a.m. today to make the three-hour trek to this sprawling desert base near Lancaster.

They sat in bleachers on a small rise several miles away from the dry lake bed used as a runway, and although their view wasn't much, few complained.

"It's history," said Michael Martinez, an EG&G systems programmer.

The crowd gasped audibly and then applauded when back-to-back sonic booms thundered down at 9:06 a.m.

Shielding their eyes from the bright sun, they began searching the cloudless skies for any sign of the spaceship. When it was spotted minutes later, people began pointing and shouting. They cheered again

See Page A-11, Col. 1

News-Press photo by DOUG PENSINGER

Brooks Institute of Photography student Kathy Sarkissian, left, shows a flier and photograph of murder victim Kym Morgan to a shopper near the Mesa shopping center where Miss Morgan was last seen.

Mesa murder case

Police probe link to second woman

By Barney Brantingham
News-Press Staff Writer

Police today continued to search the mountainsides along East Camino Cielo for the missing torso of Kym Morgan, 24 — and also looked for a possible link with the November disappearance of a woman who lived only four miles from where the murder victim's head was found last week.

On Nov. 2, Penny Rae Schroff, 41, disappeared from a bar near the foot of San Marcos Pass Road. She later failed to appear for her son's wedding, for which she'd bought a present and a new dress.

Painted Cave resident

Mrs. Schroff, whose home is in the mountaintop community of Painted Cave, was last seen in Sniffy's, a bar at 4020 Calle Real.

About 40 persons, including Los Padres Search and Rescue team members, fruitlessly searched Sunday along East Camino Cielo for the missing torso, leg and arm of Miss Morgan. She had disappeared April 28 after telling friends she was going to meet a man who had answered her newspaper personal ad for a room to rent.

Suspect's description

Investigators also spent the weekend following up phone tips from people responding to a composite photo released Friday of a man seen talking to Miss Morgan in a Mesa parking lot shared by County Lumber and Santa Cruz Market the day she disappeared.

The man was described as 30 to 35, between 5 feet 4 and 5 feet 8 inches tall, with black hair, dark complexion, wearing two-inch ele-

See Page A-11, Col. 1

PG&E takes Diablo reactor on line for full operation

SAN LUIS OBISPO (AP) — The Diablo Canyon nuclear power plant's Unit 1 reactor was brought up to half power today and operators of the controversial plant said they expected it to achieve full commercial operation by Tuesday.

Engineers also prepared to load nuclear fuel rods into the plant's second reactor in preparation for low-power testing, possibly late next week, said PG&E spokesman Ron Weinberg.

The Unit 1 reactor reached 50 percent of full power early today, generating enough electricity for the Pacific Gas & Electric Co. power grid to supply 500,000 people.

"The goal now is just to stay up as long as possible and produce electricity," Weinberg said. At full capacity, Unit 1 generates 1.1 million kilowatts, or enough electricity to serve 1.1 million Northern and Central California residents.

The reactor reached 100 percent capacity several times during tests earlier this year. It was shut down March 28.

Inside the News-Press

Weather

Santa Barbara

Cloudy
Today's high to 2 p.m. 74
Tomorrow's high 72, low 55
(Details Page A-6)

Chubby alert!

A doctor has some advice for parents of chubby children: Turn off the television set. His research shows that heavy doses of TV make children fat. B-8

Beirut burns

Lebanon's President Amin Gemayel met the army's Higher Military Council in a crisis session today as Moslem-Christian fighting raged for the ninth day in Beirut. A-2

Death at the border

A gunfight near the U.S.-Mexico border, the latest in a string of violent episodes, has left a Mexican man dead and a U.S. Border Patrol agent wounded. A-4

Other features:

News-Press telephones

News: 966-3911
Circulation: 966-7171
Classified ads: 963-4391

News-Press photo by DOUG PENSINGER

Glad grad

Gerald Cullison II, a psychology major from San Diego, joined about 300 classmates in delivering a collective — albeit ungrammatical — sign of relief during commencement exercises Sunday at Westmont College.

The Globe and Mail

142nd YEAR. No. 42,252 METRO CANADA'S NATIONAL NEWSPAPER WEDNESDAY, MAY 8, 1985

Brief ceremony brought war to end 40 years ago

The writer of this report was in Reims as a correspondent of The New York Times on VE Day.

By DREW MIDDLETON
New York Times Service

NEW YORK — There was a brief ceremony in the industrial school at Reims, and then it was over.

General Walter Bedell Smith, chief of staff for General Dwight Eisenhower, the Supreme Allied Commander, presided. With him were General Carl Spaatz of the Air Force, General Frederick Morgan of the British army, Admiral Sir Harold Burrough of the Royal Navy, Air Marshal James Robb of the Royal Air Force, and France's General François Sevez. The Soviet Union was represented by Maj.-Gen. Ivan Susloparov and his interpreter, Colonel Ivan Zenkovitch.

General Alfred Jodl and Admiral Hans George von Friedeburg, the German representatives, were escorted in by two British officers. General Kenneth Strong, Gen. Eisenhower's head of intelligence, laid the surrender documents before them. Gen. Smith asked if they were prepared to sign. Gen. Jodl nodded. He and Admiral von Friedeburg signed, followed by Gen. Smith, Gen. Susloparov, and Gen. Sevez.

"I want to say a word," said Gen. Jodl, straight-backed and impassive. Switching to German, he went on: "With this signature the German people and the German armed forces are, for better or worse, delivered into the victor's hands. In this war, which has lasted more than five years, both have achieved and suffered more than perhaps any other people in the world. In this hour I can only express the hope that the victors will treat them with generosity."

The Germans marched out, and the Allied officers shook hands. A few minutes later, Gen. Eisenhower dictated a message to the Combined Chiefs of Staff: "The mission of this Allied force was fulfilled at 0241 local time, May 7, 1945." Hostilities ceased at one

END — Page 2

Prayers, parades in Berlin

By JOHN FRASER
Globe and Mail Correspondent

WEST BERLIN — In the divided city that rose from the ashes of Hitler's short-lived Thousand-Year Reich, they are commemorating the 40th anniversary of the end of the Second World War in wildly different ways.

West Berlin's main observances, held yesterday, were punctuated by prayers for forgiveness and reconciliation. In East Berlin, there was a mammoth youth rally in the evening at which tens of thousands of blue-shirted teenagers waved red flags. Today, battalions of Soviet and East German troops will parade through the city streets.

There could have been few more emotional moments, however, than those during an odd little ceremony at the former Plotzensee execution house in the bleak northwest section of the city. It was a ceremony observed by few people, and of the working press only two Canadian journalists from competing Toronto newspapers were present.

It was at Plotzensee that the high-profile enemies of the Nazi regime met their grisly deaths: by guillotine if they were lucky; by

TWO — Page 12

The Globe and Mail

THIS IS VICTORY

Germans in Prague Ignore Surrender; Continue to Fight

War Ends Officially At 9 A.M. Tuesday; Leaders Will Speak

Callups End; Can Volunteer For Pacific

May 8, 1945, headline brought news of Allied victory.

UPI

BELATED WELCOME HOME

When U.S. military forces pulled out of Vietnam 10 years ago, there were no parades for the returning fighting men. Yesterday, New York pulled out all the stops as 25,000 Vietnam vets marched down Broadway in a shower of tickertape.

Coalition rumors killed

Tories receive nod to form government

By DUNCAN McMONAGLE and SYLVIA STEAD

Grits gain a new lease on life Page 5

Ontario Premier Frank Miller was assured by the Lieutenant-Governor yesterday that he, and not an opposition coalition, will form the provincial Government this month.

John Black Aird's assurance to Mr. Miller and the Tories killed rumors that a Liberal and New Democratic Party coalition could recall the Legislature.

"I said that with 52 seats (four more than the Liberals), it was my intention to form a government and he accepted. He also accepted my intention to introduce my programs," Mr. Miller told reporters after meeting the Lieutenant-Governor on the Premier's first day back in Toronto.

The throne speech will be introduced some time after May 27, Mr. Miller said.

The Tories are prepared to negotiate with the province's opposition leaders on throne speech policies, but Mr. Miller warned that he will not necessarily adopt any of their

MILLER — Page 2

Davis-era Tories seen as saviors for Miller fortunes

By JOHN CRUICKSHANK

Premier Frank Miller is coming under intense pressure from within the battered Ontario Conservative Party to fire his closest advisers and replace them with veteran campaigners from former premier William Davis's era.

Two days after the May 2 election, which saw a charging Liberal Party drive the provincial Tories into a minority position with a loss of 20 seats, Mr. Miller met in Muskoka with Mr. Davis and Big Blue Machine members Norman Atkins, Hugh Segal, Thomas Scott and John Tory.

Although final decisions have not been made, Patrick Kinsella, the Tories' tough-talking campaign chairman, is expected to return to his consulting business in British Columbia and cease to have a role in Ontario politics. His place at the top of the ladder is likely to be taken by Mr. Atkins, Brian Mulroney's campaign boss in last year's federal election and a long-time adviser to Mr. Davis.

Michael Perik, Mr. Miller's principal secretary and protégé, is expected to leave and may be replaced by Mr. Tory, who served Mr. Davis as his principal secretary.

Conservative sources say that Mr. Tory and Ontario PC executive director Robert Harris hijacked Mr. Miller's election campaign in the final weeks before the vote, after it had started to go desperately wrong. With help from Mr. Segal, Mr. Atkins and Mr. Scott, the two men were able to save the party from humiliating defeat and a certain Liberal victory.

Tory veterans from the Davis days say the party only began to regain the support of its core vote after the campaign team unveiled, and began to promote, an 11-point election platform stressing social reform as well as Mr. Miller's economic program. Sources say that platform was conceived and writ-

DAVIS — Page 2

Your morning smile

Some people are so charitable they give until it hurts. Then again, some people have a low pain threshold.

4 on fast barred from entry to Canada

TOKYO (CP-Staff) — Four Afghan refugees, including a 5-year-old girl, are stranded stateless and on a hunger strike at Tokyo International Airport, after airline employees following a Canadian Government directive found they were carrying forged passports.

Khurshid Attai, 45, her daughters Rabila, 15, and Salma, 5, and nephew Shfi Faroze, 24, have been stranded at the airport since 5 p.m. Monday, when a CP Air ticket clerk told them they could not board a flight for Vancouver because their passports were not in order.

The passport check by airline ticket clerks followed a Canadian directive in early April for airlines to watch for illegal immigrants flying to Vancouver from Sri Lanka, Iran or Afghanistan on forged papers. The Immigration Department apparently had evidence that airlines were not checking passports and visitors' visas before allowing passengers onto flights.

Mrs. Attai, her children and nephew were the first to be detected at the airport since the Canadian order and now, because they have destroyed their forged passports, are left in legal limbo.

More than 30 hours after the four started their hunger strike, Mrs. Attai said: "I have decided it is better to be dead than not make my life in my ideal country, Canada."

In Ottawa yesterday, a Canadian official said the four would stand a better chance of getting into Canada by going to the Canadian Em-

PASSPORTS— Page 2

Fisheries officer says he took 'thousands' in foreign bribes

ST. JOHN'S (CP) — A former observer for the federal Fisheries Department says foreign fishermen frequently offer bribes to Canadian officials to overlook quota violations.

Speaking on the condition that he not be identified, he said he took thousands of dollars worth of bribes during a three-year period as a department observer off the Nova Scotia coast several years ago.

He said he was not surprised by recent allegations that the West Germans are taking more than their quota in cod.

He and other observers and fisheries officers were offered bribes by the Soviets, Japanese, Italians and others so their vessels could overfish without being reported, he said.

He once took a $1,000 bribe from an Italian captain who had doctored his logbooks to cover an extra 50 tonnes of squid, he said. In return for his oversight he also received a trip to New York, lodging and the services of two prostitutes.

One Christmas, he disembarked from a Japanese vessel with 15 bottles of whisky, two cartons of cigarets and 100 pounds each of tuna and swordfish, he said.

Observers preferred the Japanese, Italian and French boats, said another former observer.

Carl Goodwin, manager of Scotia-Fundy surveillance operations for the Fisheries Department, said he was aware of bribes being offered to some observers, but as far as he knows all were refused, reported and dealt with through diplomatic channels.

Cal Whelan, director of operations in the Newfoundland region, where the Germans do most of

WEST — Page 9

Mounties' recruitment policy criticized for bilingual drive

By PETER MOON

Women Mounties — Page M4

The RCMP is considering changes in its recruiting policy after complaints that its drive to make the force more bilingual has severely reduced the number of recruits from Western Canada.

In fiscal 1983-84, for example, 51 per cent of all RCMP recruits were from Quebec, where only 689 Mounties are stationed. By contrast, only 11 per cent of recruits came from the four western provinces, where 7,592 Mounties, more than half the force's regular police members, are employed.

Quebec pays nothing for the RCMP because the Mounties do only federal policing there. The four western provinces, which pay for the RCMP to provide provincial policing, have complained that in return for their payments the force should be taking a fair share of recruits from their residents.

"The provinces have expressed some concern, and I think quite legitimately," Assistant Commissioner Norman Inkster, the RCMP's director of personnel at headquarters in Ottawa, said in an interview. "We're sensitive to their needs."

To try to overcome the problem, he said, the RCMP is considering allotting recruiting figures to individual provinces.

Assistant Commissioner Inkster said he was aware that some Mounties, as well as some of the public,

MOUNTIES — Page 2

INSIDE

METRO

Ballet, opera want new hall

Toronto's premier ballet and opera companies want to build a $133-million hall and move out of the O'Keefe Centre, but local politicians are not keen on the idea. /M6

Quote of the day

"At this time in the afternoon of this particular Tuesday, no, I'm not prepared to say yes." External Affairs Minister **Joe Clark** makes a not-so-firm rejection of opposition demands that Ottawa encourage Canadian companies to fill the void left by the U.S. trade embargo against Nicaragua. /9

Gas companies fear price war

Cheap gasoline from Saudi Arabia and Europe could set off a long series of price wars at Canadian gas pumps after price deregulation takes effect June 1, some oil firms fear. /B1

Hydro picket limit is sought

Ontario Hydro will seek an injunction today to restrict picketing at three sites, including Nanticoke, where strikers damaged vehicles carrying managers into the plant yesterday. /M1

Mother's Day, Despite the Annual Hype, Can Nurture a More Lasting Recognition

By Walter H. Crockett Jr.
Of the Regional Staff

Breakfast in bed, dinner on the town, cards, candy, flowers and phone calls.

Today we take all the women who ever had children and mold their best qualities into something we call "Motherhood."

We put it on a pedestal, paint it with a broad brush, view it through rose-colored glasses, worship it publicly and rhapsodize about it in language usually reserved for pets and patriotism.

Tomorrow we haul it to the landfill.

Even one day of honor is better than no day at all, and it is better to be noticed just once than to be taken for granted all year round.

But can children and husbands find some more enduring, some more significant gift for their mothers and wives — something that will outlast the butter on the bedspread and the roses on the mantelpiece — something that will mean more to Mama than a handful of chocolates and a mouthful of platitudes?

Family counselors say yes, they can.

Recognition, communication, cooperation and affection are the larger gifts that mothers would like from their husbands and children, counselors say. But don't forget to clean up your room.

Undervalued

"In our society, much of a mother's job is undervalued because it's unpaid. It's treated as a given, as a right," said Judy Kasser, executive director of Jewish Family and Children's Services of Greater Boston.

Most mothers don't want to be paid for that work, she said. "They want recognition that what they're doing is appreciated. I think that husbands and fathers have to lead and not follow. They have to set the tone for the way the children respond to their mothers, for the appreciation, the recognition.

"A mother can't teach her children to appreciate her without being caught in the bind of looking like she's demanding and pulling something from them that they don't want to give," Mrs. Kasser said. "It's the father's selfless recognition and appreciation that sets the model for the children and will set a whole tone in the household."

The willingness to talk about things, to identify bad situations and work to improve them can be another lasting gift.

Turn to APPRECIATION Page 23A

All about mothers in NOW! Also, comments about Mother's Day on Page 2B and by Ann Landers in SUNDAY MORNING.

WEATHER: Mostly cloudy, High in the 70s
Details on Page 8A

SUNDAY TELEGRAM®

Final Edition

VOL. CI NO. 24

WORCESTER, MASS., SUNDAY, MAY 12, 1985

90 CENTS DELIVERED BY CARRIER

NINETY CENTS

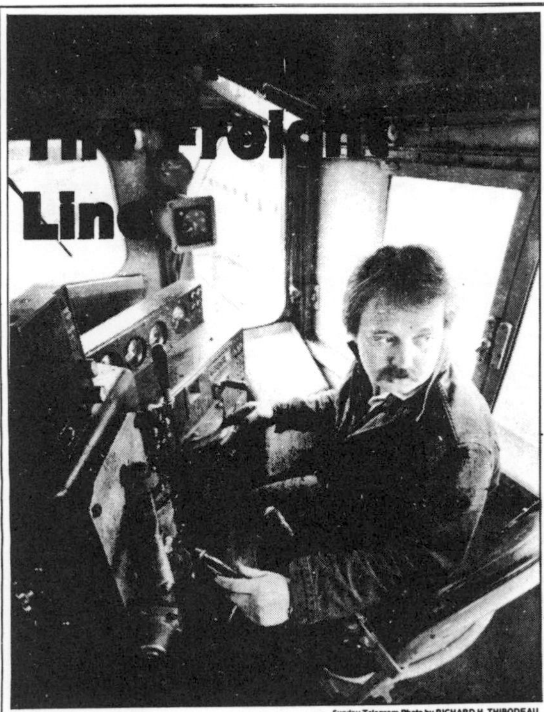

Sunday Telegram Photo by RICHARD H. THIBODEAU

Engineer Steve Buckless works the controls during freight trip to Gardner.

700 Tons at 27 MPH Far From a Joyride

By Russell B. Eames
Of the Telegram Staff

It's a different world. It's a world of back yards, junkyards and factories, abandoned cars and railroad ties littering the scenery along the tracks. Freight railroading.

The pickup, delivery, and shuffling of freight cars to get things from here to there in all kinds of weather is what freight railroading is all about.

Some days, like one cold, bitter and windy day last month, the run from Worcester to Gardner and back on a Providence and Worcester freight train can be a real a experience.

P&W, a subsidiary of Capital Properties Inc., has freight runs to Plainfield, Conn., to link up with Conrail; to Rhode Island, with the main yard at Central Falls to service that state; and to Gardner to link up with the Boston and Maine Railroad.

P&W did $12.1 million in freight business last year; this year it appears the company may do better. The freight volume is rising steadily, comparing monthly figures from last year, Vice President Ronald Chrzanowski said in a recent interview at the Southbridge Street offices.

Early Start

The daily run from Worcester to Gardner starts early in the morning with three crew members during the winter and spring months. That's expected to be cut back to two men in the summer, the crew members said.

Turn to 700 TONS Page 22A

150 Hurt at Stadium

41 Die in Fire

By Larry Thorson
Of The Associated Press

BRADFORD, England — A wind-driven fire raced through a wooden grandstand holding 3,500 fans at a soccer stadium in northern England yesterday, killing at least 41 people and injuring about 150, police said.

Millions of television viewers watched footage of the tragedy as flames and thick black smoke engulfed the main grandstand of Bradford's Valley Parade Ground within four minutes.

The soccer match was being filmed for regional broadcast Sunday, but scenes of the fire were shown on national television newscasts within minutes.

Viewers saw the soccer fans stampeding for exits and streaming onto the field in panic — some with their clothes and hair on fire.

John Domaille, assistant police chief of West Yorkshire, told a news conference that 40 were believed dead and "that figure could rise by an odd few." Police later

Turn to STADIUM Page 23A

AP Photo

Soccer fans flee stadium at Bradford City.

Sikh Violence Brings 700 Arrests

Bomb Toll Rising

By The Associated Press

NEW DELHI, India — A wave of bomb attacks blamed on Sikh terrorists killed 79 people in 24 hours on buses and trains, in parks and slums in northern India, leading to police raids on Sikh temples yesterday and more than 700 arrests.

It was one of the bloodiest 24-hour periods in India's 38 years of independence. Police said most of the victims were Hindus.

Sikh militants are seeking an independent homeland in the Punjab, or at the least more autonomy for the 13 million-member sect.

The victims were killed when bombs, most of them concealed in old transistor radios, exploded in New Delhi and in neighboring states of north India.

Authorities blamed Sikh terrorists. Police quoted witnesses in some cases as saying Sikhs had planted bomb-packed radios on buses, then escaped.

Turn to BOMBING Page 23A

May Heat Surprises

By Ted Bunker
Of the Telegram Staff

Sherlock Holmes shook the water from his shaggy black fur as Wendy Fink tried to prove to a doubtful stranger the black Labrador's name really was Sherlock Holmes. She showed the doubting Thomas the license tag.

"He's the reason we're here," Ms. Fink said, noting that people aren't allowed to swim in the pond at Elm Park. She said all she could want at that moment in the sunshine was a gin and tonic, and maybe a beach.

Turn to MAY Page 23A

Seclusion Is Over

Marva Can Plan Life Again

By Mark E. Ellis
Of the Regional Staff

WARREN — For Marva Bergeron, there is a future.

Most people take that for granted. They plan. They set goals. They contemplate where they will be in 10 or 20 years.

For Mrs. Bergeron and people like her, though, a future is something that seems almost inconceivable. It is something that, for years, they have little hope of ever having. When it is suddenly thrust upon them, it is a frightening prospect. How does a person begin to plan for life after spending more than 10 years contemplating death?

Mrs. Bergeron leads a quiet life in this rural community on the western edge of Worcester County. She and her family

Turn to MARVA Page 22A

Kenny Roberts on WCAT. ENTERTAINMENT.

Inside

This issue has 252 pages in 13 sections.

Megabucks

2 - 14 - 18 - 21 - 26 - 36

Details on Page 2A.

Real Estate Ads

Beginning today, classified real estate advertising will be in its own, separate grouping and may be found in the C (Sports) Section of the newspaper. The high volume of classified advertising has prompted us to make the move. We think the change will make it easier for readers to locate classified real estate advertising.

THE WASHINGTON POST reports that counterterrorists trained by the Central Intelligence Agency set off a bomb that killed 80 people near Beirut in March. Page 18C.

IF TELEPHONE RATE increases go unchecked, up to 6 million people may have to go without service, say two consumer groups. Phone companies reply: 'Baloney.' Page 17A.

POPE JOHN PAUL II arrives in the Netherlands for one of the most controversial trips of his seven-year papacy as Amsterdam protesters hang him in effigy. Page 5A.

POLICE IN NESSELWANG, West Germany, fire water cannons and tear gas yesterday at rioters protesting a reunion of former Nazi SS troops. Page 2A.

STILL A SUSPECT — Police Chief Theodore King of Pawtucket, R.I., indicates that Ralph Richard, whose wife has been charged in the death of their 4-month-old daughter, is still a suspect in the case. Page 15A.

Local people recall the Great Depression. SUNDAY MORNING.

SUNDAY

May 12, 1985
75 cents

OUR READERS SPEAK

'Why is it that nothing is heard about the approximately 50 million people butchered by the communists in Russia?'
– EDWARD T. OSTERGARD

Letters to the Editor/3B

ENTERTAINMENT

MORGAN FAIRCHILD

Her screen image as a scheming sexpot is a far cry from the real Morgan Fairchild who attends paleontology lectures, reads **Science Digest** and describes herself as 'just a nice kid from Texas.'

Story/1H

SPORTS

BI-DISTRICT CHAMPIONS

Moody 4
McAllen 2

Story/1F

LIVING

MOTHER'S DAY

Most of us love, admire and trust our mothers more than anyone else in the world. So why is it, asks staff writer Karen Brandon, we can't enjoy their visits?

Story/1G

Corpus Christi Caller-Times

ASSOCIATED PRESS

Fans, their clothes blazing, leap from grandstand to soccer field

Fire sweeps stadium

41 fans die, thousands stampede in Britain

The Associated Press

BRADFORD, England – A wind-driven fire raced through a wooden grandstand holding 3,500 fans at a soccer stadium in northern England Saturday, killing at least 41 people and injuring about 150, police said.

Millions of television viewers watched footage of the tragedy as flames and thick black smoke engulfed the main grandstand of Bradford's Valley Parade Ground within four minutes.

The soccer match was being filmed for regional broadcast Sunday, but scenes of the fire were shown on national television newscasts within minutes.

Viewers saw the soccer fans stampeding for exits and streaming onto the field in panic – some with their clothes and hair on fire.

John Domaille, assistant police chief of West Yorkshire, told a news conference, "We believe that there are 41 people who have lost their lives in this fire."

He said at least 149 people were being treated at three hospitals and he believed the number of injured would reach 200.

"At this moment I don't know what caused this fire . . . it could be arson," Domaille said. He did not elaborate.

Panic-stricken fans, some with their clothes ablaze, fled from the 77-year-old timber structure. Others in the stands tried to beat out the flames with their coats and jackets.

Witnesses said some fans perished in their seats. Others fled for gates at the rear of the grandstand but found them padlocked to keep out non-paying spectators.

Police tried to drag victims over the chest-high wall between the stand and the field. Domaille said about 30 policemen were injured, a half-dozen of them seriously.

The fire broke out at 3:25 p.m., shortly before halftime in Bradford City's English Third Division match against Lincoln City, and there had been no score.

The stadium, one of the oldest in England, was packed with 12,000 spectators for the end-of-season match, with some 3,500 fans in the main grandstand.

Please see Fire/10A

Quality of day care is varied

In Nueces, 4,000 in licensed centers

First of five parts, continuing in the Times

By Beth Arburn Davis
STAFF WRITER

One-year-old Glen, grinning and waddling the bandy-legged gait of a toddler, runs to the arms of Josie, one of two women who take care of him while his mother is at work. He is happy at Corpus Christi's YWCA Infant Center and only cries when the changing of his diaper prevents him from playing.

In other rooms at the center, some children play happily, some lay down and rest, giving in to morning drowsiness. In a hallway, a child hugs her mother tightly, tears rimming her eyes. She will stop crying the moment her mother is out of sight.

These scenes are played out daily across the city, across the nation, in increasing numbers.

After World War II, society assumed Rosie the Riveter would go back home to her kids and her kitchen. She didn't. She stayed on the job for a multitude of reasons, from economic need to personal satisfaction.

Women in the work force now number more than 65 percent, and an estimated 80 percent will have jobs by 1990. Most of these working women have children; 47 percent have babies under 12 months.

Please see Care/12A

KIMIKO FIEG/STAFF ARTIST

Man survives 140-foot jump from bridge

By A.J. Plunkett
STAFF WRITER

A 25-year-old Portland man shot two weeks ago by a Corpus Christi police officer yesterday survived a jump from the Harbor Bridge after another officer narrowly missed rescuing the man by a pants leg.

Arno Blaser Jr., 1201 N. Moore Ave. in Portland, jumped 140 feet from the bridge just before 4 p.m. yesterday, attracting a crowd of police as well as curious bystanders.

He is only the seventh person to survive a jump from the bridge since it opened in October 1959 and the second person to jump or fall from the bridge in the last week.

On Thursday, Nancy Pamela Jennings, 33, of Corpus Christi became the 17th person to die in a fall from the bridge in the last 26 years.

Police Capt. M.K. Burns said people on Corpus Christi Beach yesterday noticed a man standing on the east side of the bridge and notified police.

Police Sgt. Ralph Vasquez was crossing southbound over the bridge and spotted the man at the same time the call went out over the police radio, Burns said.

Vasquez turned around and went back up the bridge, then stopped to ask the man what he was doing. The man said he was on his way to Portland.

Vasquez offered the man a ride, but then "he put a leg over the rail and started to go over," Burns said.

"The officer grabbed for him and got part of his pants leg, but it wasn't enough," Burns said. "He hit and stayed up for awhile."

Two city Marina Patrol marshals, David Gonzalez and Gilbert Martinez, fished the man out of the water.

"We found him a little bit west of center from the bridge," Gonzalez said. "He was drifting into the inner harbor."

"He was keeping himself afloat," he said, but would ocassionally go under.

Gonzalez said he and Martinez had a difficult time reaching him until "he actually put his hand out."

The two hoisted Blaser aboard and took him to an AID Ambulance waiting on the south side of the harbor.

Ambulance attendants began treating him for possible back injuries, Burns said, then took him to Memorial Medical Center.

Last night, Blaser was in stable condition at MMC, said a nursing supervisor.

Only six others have jumped from the bridge and survived, according to *Caller-Times* news clippings. Seven workers fell during construction of the bridge and three survived.

On April 25, Blaser was arrested after being shot in the leg with a .357-magnum police service revolver during what police said was a scuffle with an officer.

Blaser and another man were caught after a high speed car chase involving police Sgt. Tim Revis and his partner, Isaac Valencia.

Please see Jumper/4A

A warm and windy day

Partly cloudy and windy. High today – mid-90s inland. Low tonight – mid-70s /**4A**.

INDEX

Boycotting shrimpers target 2 cities

San Antonio, El Paso are refused seafood as protest to bill proponents

By Felix Sanchez
STAFF WRITER

Some bay fishermen, aided by a number of seafood wholesalers, refuse to ship fresh seafood to San Antonio and El Paso in protest of a bill they believe may destroy their business.

The action apparently is designed to generate opposition to a bill that would place bay shrimping and oystering under the jurisdiction of the Texas Parks and Wildlife Commission.

FISH (Families Involved in Seafood Harvesting), a group of bay shrimpers and fishermen based in Seadrift, is organizing a boycott aimed at the two cities whose legislators support the bill.

Diane Wilson, a representative of FISH, said her group has received cooperation from wholesale fish and shrimp distributors in a number of cities along the Gulf Coast and throughout Texas, including Rockport, Aransas Pass and Corpus Christi.

The protest targets San Antonio and El Paso because of state senators there who voted in favor of the legislation earlier this month when it passed the Texas Senate.

'Maybe we're whistling in the dark but at least it's doing something.'
– Diane Wilson
FISH representative

Ms. Wilson said a boycott began shortly after the Senate vote on the bill.

"We're trying to cut off everything we can to those cities," she said. "Maybe we're whistling in the dark but at least it's doing something."

Meanwhile, a compromise version of the shrimping legislation was approved May 7 by the state House Environmental Committee. The newer version now contains several amendments backed by bay shrimpers.

Those amendments require that shrimp and management plans must be approved before the Parks and Wildlife Commision can adopt regulations on shrimping and oystering.

The new version came after protests by bay fishermen and shrimpers that it will drive them out of business and give deep-water Gulf of Mexico shrimpers an advantage in the highly competitive industry.

The new House bill also was amended by placing a six-year sunset provision to review the effects of the legislation in the future. The compromise was worked out with representatives of the bay and Gulf shrimpers.

John Gunther, owner of Bayside Express Seafoods in Corpus Christi, said he backs the continuing boycott.

"We won't service them with any fresh seafood at any time because it's their senator that caused this problem," Gunther said, saying that an El Paso area senator helped sponsor the original shrimping legislation.

Also supporting the boycott is Richard Keeton of the United Shrimping Association, an organization of 600 bay shrimpers, fishermen and oysterers.

As for the possibility of expanding the boycott to other cities, Ms. Wilson said it was not likely.

"It looks like now we have our hands full just with those two," she said.

Sullivan edges Andretti to win his 1st Indy 500/1F

Weather
Today
Thunderstorms 71/55
Tomorrow
Cloudy 69/51
Details on page 10F

The Detroit News

Michigan's largest newspaper. 112th Year No. 278.

Monday
May 27, 1985
20¢

Active members of the Michigan's 10th Infantry march to the Gordon grave site to place wreaths.

Civil War hero finally has his day

By James Kerwin
News Staff Writer

CROSWELL — Some 120 years after his last battle, Oliver J. Gordon finally was honored as a "hero" of the Civil War with the return of his "dog tag" lost on a parade field at the close of the war.

More than 100 people, some dressed in Civil War uniforms, gathered Saturday at his grave site in this rural community in Michigan's Thumb for a military ceremony that focused on Gordon's silver identification tag found in Virginia by a student of the Civil War.

The history enthusiast, retired Air Force Col. William McConnell, propped the glass-enclosed tag against the gravestone and presented duplicates to Gordon's relatives and the Michigan 10th Infantry Museum. Gordon served with the 10th Infantry, one of the units that participated in Sherman's March to the Sea.

THE GRAVE SITE itself had nearly been lost, having been put up for sale as a burial plot because

Please see **Cemetery/4A**

NEWS PHOTOS / DAVID C. COATES
David Rowley bows his head in silent tribute.

Death toll rises to 3,000 in storm off Bangladesh

DHAKA, Bangladesh — The death toll from a cyclone that sent tidal waves crashing into the islands of southeastern Bangladesh rose to at least 3,000, but officials and survivors said they fear that more than 15,000 may have perished.

There were reports of thousands of people missing from the storm that swept out of the Bay of Bengal Saturday, hitting the islands and the mainland as well. Army, navy and air force units were called out for relief operations.

Authorities said yesterday the 10-to-20-foot wall of water spawned by the winds of up to 200 mph washed away one island's population, causing havoc on other islands and the low-lying mainland.

Relief ministry officials estimate that at least 270,000 persons have been made homeless by the cyclone, the worst to hit the country since independence in 1971.

The Ganges River estuary hit by the storm is about 168 miles long, dotted with about 1,000 islands populated by 8.5 million people.

NEWS MAP

Officials said many of those who perished were among some 300,000 laborers who migrate to the coastal islands to help harvest rice every May.

By yesterday, 1,420 bodies have been recovered, rescue officials said. But many of the stricken areas remained inaccessible because of continuing foul weather and choppy seas.

OFFICIALS AT the Cyclone Control Room told of new reports of 1,000 dead at Sudharam in southern Noakhali district. There were many others reports of deaths by the hundreds.

Everybody who stayed on the tiny island of Urirchar was swept into the Bay of Bengal by waves 10 to 15 feet high, said officials at the control room.

The officials said some of the estimated 10,000 islanders on Urirchar were evacuated to the mainland before the hurricane hit, but at least 500 were reported missing so far.

No contact could be established with the island, 35 miles off the coast from Noakhali and near Sandwip island. But the officials, who cannot be identified under martial law regulations, told the Associated Press a plane that flew over the area reported the island raked clean by waves.

FOUR YEARS ago people who lost their land to erosion from rivers began settling on the four-mile square island. Many islanders lived on small boats.

Only one family of four has been reported rescued by search teams sent to the area.

"The devastation in the area is beyond description," said a stunned President Hussein Mohammed Ershad, who has ruled Bangladesh, an impoverished nation of some 90 million, since leading a bloodless military coup in 1982.

At Sudharam, tidal waves driven by winds around 200 mph washed inland Saturday, killing at least 1,000 people. Officials said yesterday that 500 bodies have been buried so far.

AT LEAST 400 fishermen drowned and scores were missing near the offshore island of Kutubdia when at least 25 fishing boats capsized in the storm.

The Bengali-language daily newspaper Ittefaq said that at least 4,000

Please see **Storm/4A**

25,000 in Beirut flee massacre

BEIRUT, Lebanon — As many as 25,000 Palestinians have fled their homes after a week of attacks on Beirut refugee camps by Shiite Muslim militiamen and Lebanese soldiers determined to prevent a resurgence of Palestinian power.

Unknown numbers of dead and wounded people were still thought to be trapped in the camps, still closed to the Red Cross, Palestinian sources said yesterday.

Beirut hospital sources said yesterday that 245 people had been killed and 1,000 wounded, not counting those who have yet to be evacuated from the camps, in the latest massacre over the past six days. The Red Cross said it could not confirm casualties because of the intense fighting which continued yesterday.

Shiite Muslims are battling Palestinian fighters for control of the southern Beirut area.

The militiamen and troops used machine guns and rocket grenades in continuing efforts to flush out Palestinian fighters at the Bourj al-Barajneh, Sabra and Chatilla Palestinian refugee camps, witnesses said.

AMAL MILITIAMEN battered the three besieged refugee camps with mortar and rocket fire yesterday but Palestinian fighters inside the camps vowed they "will not kneel."

Palestinian officials said that as many as 25,000 Palestinians had fled to Druse-controlled areas. They said those fleeing included Palestinians who left their homes outside the camps in fear after gunmen beat and abducted Palestinians in the center of west Beirut.

As President Amin Gemayel held

Please see **Lebanon/6A**

Soviets stay tough on 'Star Wars'

Washington Post News Service

MOSCOW — The Soviet Communist Party newspaper Pravda said today the Soviet Union would not agree to cuts in nuclear weapons as long as Washington continues its plans for a space-based defense system.

In a strongly worded editorial issued four days before the second round of arms negotiations opens in Geneva, the government paper accused the United States of jeopardizing an arms control agreement through its pursuit of the Strategic Defense Initiative (SDI). The editorial was one of Moscow's most forceful efforts to make abandonment of SDI the centerpiece of the Geneva negotiations.

"By refusing to stop its programs of developing attack space arms, the United States puts in question the very possibility of a limitation and the more so, a reduction of nuclear arsenals," said Pravda.

"The United States cannot count on any reduction whatsoever by the Soviet Union of its return-strike nuclear arms while Washington is furthering its program of measures to 'render impotent' Soviet nuclear arms."

Please see **Talks/4A**

STAR STRUCK

NEWS PHOTO / DAVID C. COATES
Madonna, the high priestess of pop, returns home for her first concert, a 13-song repertoire that lasts a little over an hour. See review 1D; Picture page 8B.

Poland's dilemma: Church vs. state

Poland

Spirit & sorrow
Last of two parts

By Jack Lessenberry
News Staff Writer

WARSAW — Every day, hundreds, sometimes thousands, of Poles quietly file by a flower-heaped grave in St. Stanislaw Kostka churchyard that symbolizes bitter new tensions between Poland's Catholic church and Communist government.

Crossing themselves, dabbing occasionally at their eyes, worshipers peer at the candles burning at the foot of the grave of Father Jerzy Popieluszko, a handsome young priest brutally murdered by government security men last fall.

Then their eyes turn to the nearby Solidarity banners — permitted nowhere else in the country — that openly defy the regime.

"SOLIDARNOSC, VERY good, yes — Solidarity! You know?" one man said inside the church, standing before a picture display of the priest's life. "Solidarity good, pope good."

Unique in the Soviet bloc, Poland has two major centers of power — the Roman Catholic Church and the Communist Party. One has the sup-

Please see **Church/6A**

Money

Providing for retirement is not the sole purpose of ESOPs, employe stock option plans./1C

Index

Circulation 222-2600 · Classified/977-7500

Scarface's secret

Does vault hold riches of Capone?

By Larry Green
Los Angeles Times

CHICAGO — A dank basement in the former headquarters of gangster Al Capone could turn out to be Chicago's equivalent of King Tut's tomb.

Workers rehabilitating the abandoned and debris-filled 10-story building have discovered a long, concrete "vault" believed to have been built by the late Prohibition-era gangster. They've also uncovered hidden stairways, including one leading to the building's basement near the vault.

"I feel like I'm on an archeological dig," said Patricia J. Porter, executive director of the Sunbow Foundation and current owner of the building south of the Loop business district.

Please see **Capone/6A**

PHOTO BY MARK ELIAS
Patricia Porter visits Capone's concrete vault.

China's newlyweds learn a lesson in lust

PEKING (Reuter) — Young men and women in China have been kept at such a distance from each other for so long and have faced such stern taboos that Peking social workers have begun offering public lectures for newlyweds.

About 30 couples recently gathered for twice-weekly meetings in a dingy hall to learn of the pleasure and hazards awaiting them in marriage.

"Ignorance of sex is an old cultural problem in China," said Tao Chunfang, a lecturer from a college for women officials, before her talk on how love develops in marriage. "For a long time it was never mentioned in public," Tao added.

Young urban couples face special problems because, after centuries of arranged marriages, they now choose their own partners.

Traditional Chinese attitudes do not equip young people for the exhilarations and disappointments of romantic love.

One young woman at the lecture put her problem simply.

"He says I know nothing about men," said Cui Wei, giving her tall fiance a playful shove. "He says I don't even know where the hair ends and the sideburns begin.

"In China, boys and girls keep very separate at school, they never learn anything about each other."

"We want a good and stable marriage, and we want to learn everything that can help us," said her partner, Fu Danting.

ACCORDING TO the timetable, they will hear experienced doctors,

Please see **China/6A**